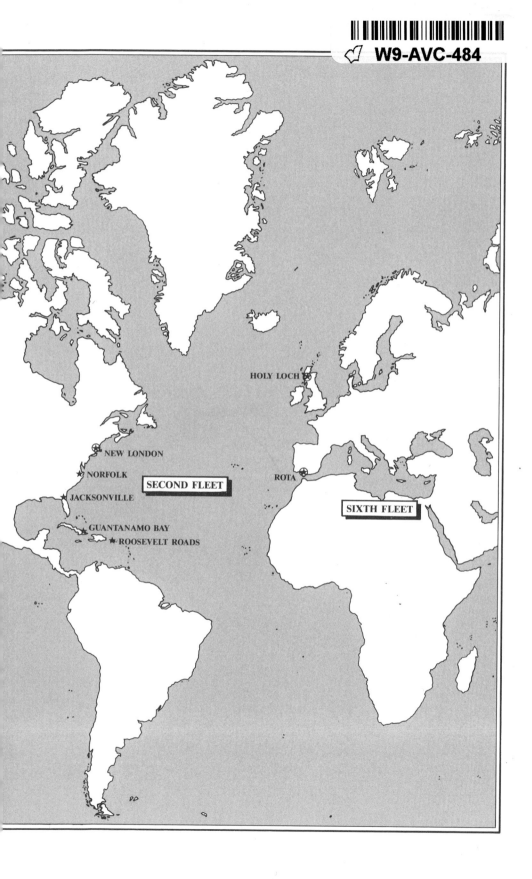

W9-AVC-484

HOLY LOCH

NEW LONDON

★ NORFOLK

JACKSONVILLE

SECOND FLEET

ROTA

SIXTH FLEET

GUANTANAMO BAY

★ ROOSEVELT ROADS

SHIELD

OF THE

REPUBLIC

SHIELD

— OF THE —

REPUBLIC

THE UNITED STATES NAVY
IN AN ERA OF COLD WAR AND VIOLENT PEACE

VOLUME I

1945–1962

MICHAEL T. ISENBERG

St. Martin's Press

New York

The Work Is for
My Love
Suzanne Hanson

This Volume Is Dedicated to the Men and Women of the
United States Navy

And in Particular

To These Three Old Salts:

Lieutenant Commander Tom Cutler, United States Navy (Retired)
Lieutenant Commander Noel Daigle, United States Navy (Retired)
Lieutenant Commander Don Sine, United States Navy (Retired)

SHIELD OF THE REPUBLIC
Copyright © 1993 by Michael T. Isenberg. All rights reserved. Printed
in the United States of America. No part of this book may be used or
reproduced in any manner whatsoever without written permission except
in the case of brief quotations embodied in critical articles or reviews.
For information, address St. Martin's Press, 175 Fifth Avenue,
New York, NY 10010.

Design by Michael Mendelsohn of MM Design 2000, Inc.

Library of Congress Cataloging-in-Publication Data

Isenberg, Michael T.
    Shield of the Republic / Michael T. Isenberg.
        p.   cm.
    ISBN 0-312-09911-8
    1. United States—History, Naval—20th century.   2. United States.
Navy—History—20th century.   I. Title.
E746.I8   1993
359'.00973—dc20   93-25723
                                                        CIP

First edition: November 1993
10 9 8 7 6 5 4 3 2 1

CONTENTS

PART THREE
TRIDENTS OF POSEIDON

PART FOUR
HANDS BEHIND THE SHIELD

PART FIVE
COLD WAR NAVY

ILLUSTRATIONS

(All illustrations courtesy United States Naval Institute)

Frontispiece illustrations:

Page 21: USS *North Carolina* (BB-55) being nudged to her berth in the mothball fleet. The drawdown in American naval power following World War II was drastic.

Page 167: Evacuation by sea: Beyond USS *Begor* (APD-127), the port of Hungnam blows sky-high, December 1950.

Page 285: A-bomb: Men of the USS *Saidor* (CVE-117) shield themselves against the flash from Test ABLE at Bikini Lagoon, 1 July 1946.

Page 431: The "Golden Thirteen" minus their warrant officer comrade, 1944. Ensign Dennis Nelson, who was to become a constant naval gadfly on racial matters, is far left, second row.

Page 569: Soviet SA-2 site at La Coloma, Cuba, on 10 November 1962, after the Soviet Union had agreed to withdraw its missiles from Cuba. Confirmation of these sites triggered the Navy's role in the Cuban Missile Crisis.

1. Navy storekeepers at Pearl Harbor listen to a Domei radio flash on 13 August 1945: World War II is over.
2. USS *Missouri* (BB-63), Tokyo Bay, 2 September 1945. All hands are on deck for the surrender ceremonies.
3. The Mahanian vision featured heavily armored, powerfully gunned battleships. This is USS *Indiana* (BB-1).
4. Alfred Thayer Mahan (1840–1914), c. 1905: The Navy's premier propagandist of seapower.
5. Admiral Ernest King, Chief of Naval Operations (1942–1945). Aware of the increased global responsibilities that would come to the Navy, King wanted as large a postwar fleet as possible.
6. James Forrestal, Secretary of the Navy, (1944–1947) and Fleet Admiral Chester Nimitz, soon to be Chief of Naval Operations (1945–1947), on Saipan, February 1945. At the time, the Navy's postwar plans were far from clear.
7. Harry Truman inspects an engine room aboard the USS *Augusta* (CA-31) en route to the Postdam Conference, July 1945. Truman liked sailors but, with the exception of Fleet Admiral William Leahy, had little regard for admirals.
8. The Swamp Fox: Representative Carl Vinson (D-Georgia), the Navy's congressional overseer.
9. Into mothballs: A sailor sprays a strippable film coating on a five-inch gun mount, November 1945.
10. A fraction of the mothball fleet: These destroyers and destroyer escorts are in San Diego, July 1950.

MAPS

ALL HANDS ON DECK, USS <u>MISSOURI</u> (BB-63)

─────── ☆ ───────

Night bells. Morning colors. Up the flagstaff snapped the banner that
had flown over the Capitol in Washington on 7 December 1941.
Beneath the Stars and Stripes, the big battleship rode smoothly to
her anchor under somber, overcast skies. All around her, on this morning
of mornings, almost 260 gray shapes speckled the calm waters of Tokyo
Bay—a minute sample of the victorious American fleet that had spanned
the Pacific Ocean to bring the Second World War home to Japan.

Still more ships, mostly older battlewagons and fast, modern aircraft
carriers, lurked just over the horizon, ready for any sudden move by an
enemy regarded as soundly defeated but still capable of treachery. "We were
loaded for bear," remembered the chief of staff of Battleship Division 1,
"just in case anybody pulled any kind of doublecross."

Even though the euphoria of triumph over a tenacious, sometimes fanatical enemy remained uppermost, suspicion remained. Only two weeks
before, in the wake of the two atomic bombs that had finally forced the
Japanese to sue for peace, Admiral William Halsey, the pugnacious commander of the Third Fleet, had warned his subordinates to be on the alert
for anything:

> THE NIP OFFICERS ARE STILL FIGHTING X THAT MEANS WE ARE STILL FACING
> AN ENEMY THAT HATES OUR CARRIERS LIKE THE DEVIL HATES HOLY WATER X
> UNTIL THE NIPS SURRENDER AND ARE DISARMED REPEAT DISARMED THEY ARE
> DANGEROUS AND NEED KILLING X. . . .

The next day one of Halsey's top carrier admirals, John ("Slew") McCain,
had reiterated the boss's order (in a message often misascribed to Halsey):
"All snoopers will be intercepted and shot down not vindictively but in a
friendly sort of way."

Still, the days since the immolation of Hiroshima and Nagasaki had shown, despite a few harebrained gestures by Japanese militarists, that the attackers of Pearl Harbor were beaten, exhausted, and ready to surrender. Even the limited value of *Tokko*, the special-attack suicide operations, had been squandered.

Accordingly, Halsey commanded all hands to splice the mainbrace in celebration; this order was meant only as a nod to tradition in a Navy that had been officially dry since 1914 and as an informal thank-you to those elements of the British fleet that had joined up in the Far East in the closing days of the war. But some of the admiral's own ships took him at his word. Aboard the destroyer *Twining* the wardroom liberated several bottles of "medicinal" whiskey, lit up their cigars, and carried on.[1]

Missouri lacked the happy-go-lucky informality of a destroyer. The mood aboard was serious and businesslike, but hardly overwrought. There had been no "sudden increase in chapel attendance or other religious reactions at war's end," most divine services drawing only about twenty people. Though her crew members were justly proud of their ship's starring role today, they just wanted to get home.

The practically new battlewagon was a showboat, especially picked by Secretary of the Navy James Forrestal and the commander in chief of the Pacific Fleet, Admiral Chester Nimitz, as the setting for the Japanese surrender. Reporters aboard cynically speculated that the home state of the new president, Harry Truman, might have had something to do with the choice. Almost everybody in *Missouri*'s crew had spent days preparing for the grand finale. Under the coordination of Bill Kitchell, Halsey's flag lieutenant, the light blond teakwood decks were holystoned to a dull gleam, the fancywork glowed cream white, and the brass fittings dazzled despite the massed clouds.

The Navy, as always, insisted on rehearsals. Hundreds of off-duty sailors were shanghaied as stand-ins while others dutifully marked areas on the deck where each VIP would be located. The honors appropriate to the dozens of dignitaries had to be learned, and ceremonial gestures were practiced till they became routine. General of the Army Douglas MacArthur would take the surrender in person, and he wanted the defeated Japanese emissaries to arrive on the battleship's veranda deck at 0900, on the second. The problem was that the delegation's leader, Foreign Minister Mamoru Shigemitsu, had lost a leg years before in China to an assassin's bomb. Undaunted, *Missouri*'s skipper, the popular S. S. ("Sunshine") Murray, had several sailors strap swab handles to their legs, mount the accommodation ladder, and limp across the quarterdeck. Murray doubled the average time (ninety seconds) to allow for Shigemitsu's age, added a minute, and scheduled accordingly.

There were numerous glitches: All the brass hats wanted a good view (impossible). MacArthur insisted that his general's flag be displayed aboard during the ceremony, against naval tradition and etiquette (Nimitz, the senior naval officer, graciously agreed that both his and the general's flags were to be broken at the forepeak at exactly the same height). The Japanese flags crudely painted on the bridge wings had to go (they were replaced by a kicking Missouri mule silhouetted against a picture of a five-inch-gun mount, surrounded by miniature Rising Sun emblems signifying every plane shot down by *Missouri*).

In the midst of the hubbub someone figured out that the battleship had no appropriate table over which to conduct the surrender ceremony. A hurry-up call produced a gallant reply from Admiral Sir Bruce Fraser, commander of the British Pacific Fleet. Sir Bruce offered an elegant mahogany piece that had gone through the Battle of Jutland back in 1916. Sweating sailors got the table aboard, manhandling their charge down ladders and through vertical hatches and finally stashing the antique in the executive officer's stateroom.

The rehearsals finally ground to a halt, none too soon for the whitehats impersonating the various admirals and generals. The play-acting had its moments, though. At one point a dungaree-clad seaman, "Admiral Nimitz," was simulating the pomp-filled arrival of the commander in chief, Pacific Fleet. As he stepped off the ladder onto the quarterdeck, the "admiral" took in the entire scene—a double row of eight sideboys, a ninety-member Marine honor guard, the officer of the deck, and Sunshine Murray himself—all rendering him a crisp salute. The seaman, in response, could only tip his dixie cup back and mutter, "Well, I'll be God-damned!"

Both victor and vanquished had a keen appreciation of the symbolic, and on this flat, dreary morning the spot on the open deck where the surrender was to take place was overlooked by a thirty-one-star American flag, mistakenly hung upside down and framed in reverse because the obverse had suffered decomposition from mildew. The musty old talisman had once flown over Commodore Matthew Perry's flagship *Mississippi* when "Old Bruin" first had steamed into the Bay of Yedo (as Tokyo Bay was then known) back in 1853.[2]

Since that time, less than a century before, Japan and the United States had each created modern, first-class navies while, until 1941, keeping an uneasy peace across the vast expanse of Pacific that separated them. There had been occasional gestures of amity, such as naval visits; this *Missouri* was not the first American battleship of that name to enter Tokyo Bay. In 1908, *BB-11* had entertained the Japanese navy while taking part in the famous round-the-world cruise of the Great White Fleet. Japanese and Americans, officers and midshipmen, had posed together for pictures, arms interlinked, under the shining twin barrels of the forward gun turret.

But that had been worlds ago, before Pearl Harbor, Tarawa, Saipan, Okinawa. Now Perry's accidentally inverted old flag beheld a scene of conquest. That *Missouri* should be the stage on which the surrender ritual was to be played out was, at the very least, ironic. She was barely eighteen months old, the last of the four *Iowa*-class battlewagons to be completed, and her combat exploits, such as they were, fell far short of those of many other ships in the bay that day. Before the war, battleships were thought by many to be the spine of naval warfare, technically designed to slug things out with their opposite numbers in the "line of battle." But *Missouri*, upon reaching the Pacific Theater, had found her role confined to anti-air warfare, shore bombardment, and running interference for the new stars of the fleet, the flattops.

Back in February she had shot down her first Japanese plane, off Iwo Jima. Two months later she sustained superficial damage from three separate kamikaze attacks. Until the very end of the war she guarded aircraft carriers, a distinctly secondary role. At last, with Japan prostrate before the Allies, its citizens drilling with wooden sticks, its cities in ashes, *Missouri* and other battleships steamed unmolested within sight of land, shelling steel mills and oil refineries on Hokkaido and industrial plants northeast of Tokyo.

—And that was all. Not a single Japanese warship had fallen to her massive sixteen-inch guns. Yet here she was, the prettiest belle at the ball, all decked out for her greatest moment, ready to welcome her panoply of visitors. Shortly after 0800, a ship's chaplain having offered up a prayer that everything would go well that day, Nimitz was bonged aboard (without goddamning himself), his flag broken smartly at the mainmast. Within the half hour came MacArthur, already designated by Truman as Supreme Commander for the Allied Powers, the man who would make Hirohito but a deputy emperor. SCAP, as usual, was not overly modest about his role: "Years of overseas duty had schooled me well in the lessons of the Orient and, what was probably more important, had taught the Far East that I was its friend."

Originally, Nimitz, with the Far East's Friend in mind, had ordered Navy Seabees back on Guam to trick up a landing craft to look like an Army version of an admiral's barge, replete with five stars on the bow and red and white seat covers. Much effort was expended transporting the "general's barge" to Tokyo Bay. Then MacArthur, mindful that he had twenty miles to travel from his quarters ashore in Yokohama to *Missouri*'s anchorage down the bay off Yokosuka, had refused to go in "that thing." "I want a destroyer," he announced, "and I want a new destroyer." A new destroyer he got, *Nicholas*. Once he was piped aboard *Missouri* and heartily welcomed by Halsey and his other old comrades in arms, all settled back to await the conquered.[3]

At the last minute, when the placemat-sized surrender documents arrived aboard, Sir Bruce's beautiful table was found to be too small. Calling four swabbies, Sunshine Murray sped to the wardroom and tried to snatch a table, only to find that the furniture was bolted to the deck. On to the mess decks, where the captain and his sailors confiscated a folding mess table: "You'll get it back," the skipper told his loudly protesting mess cooks. (They never did; the table ended up at the Naval Academy Museum.) Back again through the wardroom, where Murray nabbed a coffee-stained green baize tablecloth. In place, with the coffee spots hidden by an artistic arrangement of the surrender documents, "it didn't look too bad."

The table was ready, the galaxy of flag officers duly welcomed. The weight of stars aboard *Missouri* might well have sunk a lesser ship. Fleet admirals, admirals, and generals were front and center, of course, but so much brass had inundated the cruiser *San Diego*, designated as station ship alongside at Yokosuka, that her side boys got no rest; *San Diego* resignedly gave herself over to "Admiral's Day."

Allies great and small were now aboard "Mighty Mo" in abundance: soldiers, sailors, and airmen from Britain, Canada, Australia, New Zealand, China, France, the Netherlands, the Soviet Union. "The gangway looked like a subway entrance during the rush hour," remembered Nimitz's commander of submarines, Vice Admiral Charles Lockwood. The main deck was a complete Tower of Babel. Over one hundred high-ranking officers were on hand; a mere two stars carried no stroke at all.

While a privileged few mingled in the flag spaces with MacArthur and Nimitz, the rest waited on the main deck for the Japanese. The topside spaces of the battleship were jammed with sailors and reporters, blanketing the turrets, hanging onto the masts, wedged into ladders, and perched on railings. Among them was thirty-three-year-old Seaman First Class John Truman, from Independence, Missouri, the president's nephew.

One man who should have been there was missing. Taciturn Raymond Spruance, the blackshoe admiral who had directed a scratch force of American carriers to victory at Midway and had then obliterated most of Japanese naval aviation during the Battle of the Philippine Sea, remained aboard his flagship *New Jersey* (one of *Missouri*'s sisters) in Buckner Bay, Okinawa. MacArthur had invited him, but Nimitz wanted Spruance to plan for the pending occupation of Japan and wait in the wings to take command of the Pacific Fleet in case of a last-minute Japanese kamikaze effort against the assembled Allied leadership aboard *Missouri*.[4]

☆

But there was no kamikazes. Instead, a lone destroyer bearing a placard marked "B" (there were four shuttle destroyers, designated A through D), hove to about five hundred yards away. She was *Lansdowne* (DD-486), and she carried the Japanese surrender party. A member of Nimitz's staff who accompanied the group noted that "they sat quietly in the wardroom, seemed subdued, and talked little among themselves." *Lansdowne* had boarded her charges at 0700 and had taken a leisurely hour to steam down the bay. She idled for some minutes, until at last the Japanese were transferred by launch to *Missouri*.

There were eleven of them in all. In addition to the elderly Shigemitsu, they included the extremely reluctant General Toshijiro Umezu, who with his finely honed Japanese sense of ceremony knew well the humiliation he was about to face, and a young government bureaucrat, Toshikazu Kase. The remaining eight numbered two civilians, three army officers, and three navy officers. By 0842 they were all disembarked, and the destroyer obediently drew off to anchor in berth F-84 to "await their return from the surrender ceremonies."

As the Japanese boarded *Missouri* and were shown to their assigned places, all attention turned to the battlewagon's main deck and the pending arrival of MacArthur. No one noticed the insignificant little ship waiting patiently in F-84, a featureless attendant to a proudly bedecked queen. After all, *Lansdowne*, fully loaded, displaced only 2000 tons, a mere 3.5 percent of *Missouri's* 57,540 tons. Her main battery of four five-inch 38s were popguns compared to the nine triple-mounted, sixteen-inch 50s aboard the battleship. The destroyer's crew could have fit comfortably in a couple of *Missouri's* numerous berthing compartments.

Indeed, *Lansdowne* was little more than steel skin wrapped around four high-pressure water-tube boilers. One of the sixty-one-ship *Buchanan* class, she was bred to be a greyhound, her 36.5-knot maximum speed her hole card. But in actuality, like any other destroyer, she had gone through the war doing whatever she was asked to do, a jack-of-all-trades whose final assignment, here in Tokyo Bay, was in perfect consonance with the wide variety of roles she had been called on to perform.[5]

She had begun on the Panama Sea Frontier in the summer of 1942. There, in the approaches to the strategically crucial canal, she drew a strong sonar bead and laid four six-hundred-pound depth charges on the German submarine *U-153*, sinking the sub in 1500 fathoms with no survivors. Two months later *Lansdowne* found herself deep in the southwest Pacific, acting as escort for the carrier *Wasp*. On 15 September, as *Wasp* conducted combat air and antisubmarine patrols about one hundred miles from Guadalcanal, the Japanese submarine *I-19* slipped through the screen of *Lansdowne* and five other destroyers and launched four fish. Two of the warheads hit the carrier, forward starboard; a third passed harmlessly under *Lansdowne*.

Wasp was doomed. Within an hour, flaming aviation gas and exploding bombs made the carrier an inferno, and "abandon ship" was ordered. The survivors were picked up by the escorts, and *Lansdowne* drew the sad duty of delivering the coup de grace. She fired five torpedoes; all hit and three exploded, sending *Wasp* to her grave.

From then on, things got better. *Lansdowne* became part of Rear Admiral Willis Lee's Task Group 64, took distant part in the Battle of the Santa Cruz Islands, and humped around Guadalcanal for weeks, doing a bit of everything. She brought up ninety tons of ammunition for the island's embattled Marines, searched fruitlessly for a pesky Japanese submarine, and bombarded Japanese shore positions east of the Metapona River.

After rest and refit *Lansdowne* pasted Empress Augusta Bay, Bougain-ville, with shellfire; conducted a nighttime torpedo and gun attack against the Japanese naval fortress of Rabaul; and blasted a total of 193 rounds at a hapless Japanese cargo ship that chanced to stumble across her path, sinking the vessel in minutes. Then the destroyer took to guarding escort carriers, crow-hopping up the northern New Guinea coast. Wakde, Biak, Noemfoor, Sansapor, all passed in her wake. Finally, she took part in Spruance's triumph at Philippine Sea, shepherding big *Essex*-class carriers.

In short, the hard-working, tough little can had been to war, and her officers and men could take great satisfaction in her battle honors. ("The bombardment must have had a terrific effect on Jap morale and pride," one of them wrote of the Rabaul strike. "To have five destroyers steam into the very entrance of their stronghold, bombard them for an hour, and retire untouched could not fail to leave them considerably worried and chagrined.") But now she was just a bystander, watching from the wings as a ship with but a portion of her war record held the limelight.

Aboard *Missouri* the ceremony commenced. "I don't know what they're going to call this," whispered one correspondent overlooking the scene from the number two turret. "I hope it won't be the 'Missouri Compromise.' " A compromise this would not be; even though the emperor was to remain in place—a fact that some historians were to make much of—this *was* un-conditional surrender, and MacArthur, stepping forth in open-throated starched khakis, would accept the Japanese capitulation.

The general was the most consummate egoist in American military history, which was saying a lot (the section of his memoirs dealing with the Japanese surrender might as well have been entitled "Alone in Tokyo Bay"), but a considerable part of his public reputation had been justly earned, and this was his finest hour. Before him on the mess table, its scars carefully concealed by its cloth covering, lay two documents: the Allied surrender copy bound in green and the Japanese one in black, a ceremonial color in Japan. His hands trembling slightly, the Last Shogun stepped to the mi-crophone and began to read from a piece of paper, slowly, deliberately, using all the sonorous, mellifluous qualities of his magnificent voice:[6]

We are gathered here, representatives of the major warring powers, to conclude a solemn agreement whereby peace may be restored. The issues, involving divergent ideals and ideologies, have been determined on the battlefields of the world and hence are not for our discussion or debate. . . .

☆

The atmosphere was frigid as he spoke. Slew McCain, wrongly, thought the impassive mask worn by the Japanese delegation, its civilians in incongruous top hats and tails, its military men in ill-fitting, baggy uniforms, concealed a spirit of noncompliance and revenge. Halsey's chief of staff, Robert ("Mick") Carney, could muster no sympathy for the "despicable little bastards." But at least one of the defeated, Kase, was struck by MacArthur's eloquence and vision. As the words rolled on, the young diplomat saw the quarterdeck "transformed into an altar of peace."

> . . . nor is it for us here to meet, representing as we do a majority of the peoples of the earth, in a spirit of distrust, malice or hatred. But rather it is for us, both victor and vanquished, to rise to that higher dignity which alone benefits the sacred purposes we are about to serve, committing all of our peoples unreservedly to faithful compliance with the undertakings they are here formally to assume. . . .

"I had received no instructions as to what to say or what to do," the general later wrote. "I was on my own, standing on the quarterdeck with only God and my own conscience to guide me." Whatever was guiding him, his words were carrying clearly to the silent throng crowding the battleship from stem to stern. But his voice was not on radio (recordings would later be rushed to the communications ship *Ancon* to be flashed around the world). Most of the other ships in the bay could not directly follow what was going on.

One of these, quietly moored next to the dock at Yokosuka Naval Base in clear view of *Missouri*, was a squat, less-than-lovely destroyer tender, *Piedmont* (AD-17). Ships like her were a fixture wherever the fleet was provisioned, repaired, or outfitted. The first Allied landings in Japan proper had taken place less than a week before, and here sat the ungainly tender, parked alongside what her sailors already called "Piedmont Pier," going about her routine: servicing the forces ashore, repairing the broken-down light and power facilities of the sprawling naval base, feeding several hundred shore-based personnel, acting as a communications center for beach parties, and repairing the several destroyers and small craft lashed to her outboard side.[7]

Piedmont, at less than ten thousand tons, with a diesel-driven flank speed of eighteen knots and a sparse armament of five- and three-inch guns, could neither run with the hares nor hunt with the hounds. Nor was she supposed to. Her business lay in the backwaters of the war. The fictional Mr. Roberts, driven nearly out of his mind by the tedium aboard his supply ship, would have understood her well. She was one of thousands of vessels going by the somewhat demeaning title of "auxiliary," implying that these ships were somehow not in the mainstream of the war. The prewar logistics arm of the Pacific Fleet, called the Base Force Train, had numbered fifty-one ships; now Service Force Pacific totaled almost 3000 vessels of all kinds.

Auxiliaries like *Piedmont* did far more than simply repair ailing warships. They brought munitions, everything from flares through bombs to sixteen-inch shells. They carried refrigerated stores, dry stores, stores of everything imaginable. With them came the precious oil and aviation gasoline to slake the never-ending thirst of combatant ships and aircraft. There were floating drydocks, communications ships, tenders for anything that floated. Cargo ships, hospital ships, aircraft ferries. Minesweepers, net layers, personnel transports. Barracks ships, rescue vessels, tugboats—even ships to distill water.

Without the auxiliaries, the fleet could not steam, could not eat, could not be repaired, could not fight. Most importantly, these thousands of tacky, lumbering nonentities gave the fleet mobility, range, and endurance, without which the war could not have been carried across thousands of miles and two oceans. *Piedmont* and her sisters carried the fleet on their collective backs.

Generally, *Piedmont*'s war had been a dull one. Arriving in the Pacific in the summer of 1944, she had immediately taken her place in the harbor of Eniwetok with assorted repair ships, tenders, and drydocks. In September she shifted forward to gigantic Seeadler Harbor, off the north coast of New Guinea. As usual, the traffic over her decks was never-ending, a constant shuffle of supplies moving on and off, her shops hives of activity at any time of day or night. Early in 1945 she moved on to Ulithi, where she became part of the huge buildup for the Okinawa operaton. Her war was a regular round of supply emergencies, fouled-up requisitions, and insistent demands.

Sometimes her men, like Mr. Roberts, had trouble seeing exactly how they were contributing to winning the war. But they were, in spades. Even now, at peace in Tokyo Bay, they continued with their routine, as the famous voice rolled out across the decks of *Missouri*. The 2nd of September was a Sunday, a day of rest—yet *Piedmont*'s work went steadily on.

☆

. . . It is my earnest hope and indeed the hope of all mankind that from this solemn occasion a better world shall emerge out of the blood and carnage of the past—a world founded upon faith and understanding—a world dedicated to the dignity of man and the fulfillment of his most cherished wish—for freedom, tolerance, and justice. . . .

Henri Smith-Hutton, a member of Nimitiz's staff, was impressed by MacArthur's "firm, clear voice" and "statesman-like address." Smith-Hutton was also watching the faces of the Japanese delegation and thought he saw, among those who understood English, "a bit of surprise . . . it seemed to me as though they didn't expect such generous treatment."[8]

The general's words could not be heard aboard the submarine tender

Proteus, anchored about ten miles down the bay, nor did they reach her brood yoked alongside. Here, bunched together like so many slender dark-gray cigars, nested twelve weary submarine veterans of the Pacific war.

Among them were some very heavy hitters indeed. Here lay *Haddo*, whose seventh war patrol under the command of Nimitz's son, Chester junior, had sunk five Japanese ships; *Cavalla*, which ranked tenth in overall tonnage for a single war patrol, and which, with a six-torpedo salvo, had sunk the carrier *Shokaku*, veteran of the Pearl Harbor strike; and *Runner II*, whose skipper, Raymond Bass, had totted up eight war patrols and twelve Japanese ships. And here also, virtually identical to her mates in repose, rested the heaviest hitter of them all—*Archerfish* (SS-311).

Not much of her could be seen above the water, only the conning tower, a three-inch gun aft, and a few hatch covers and masts. She was less than fourteen feet wide, less than 1600 tons, a tiny mite to be braving the ocean depths. Her real power lay below, unseen, in her diesel engines, her tightly knit crew, and, above all, in her ten 21-inch torpedo tubes, six on the bow, four on the stern.

A member of the vast, 122-boat *Balao* class, *Archerfish*'s main business was sinking enemy shipping, whenever and wherever found. From time to time she also served as lifeguard for the crews of the B-29 Superfortresses engaged in leveling Japan, and this was the duty she had been conducting, in company with *Scabbardfish*, in November 1944. Released to conduct her regular antishipping patrols, she prowled the outer entrances to Tokyo Bay. Suddenly, on the evening of November 28, she gained an enormous radar pip at 24,700 yards.

The chase was on. For six hours *Archerfish* played cat and mouse on the surface with her quarry, slowly gaining and falling back while the contact zigzagged, unaware of her peril. Suddenly the target changed course and headed right for the submarine. *Archerfish* quickly pulled the plug, submerging and firing a bow spread. Four shots; a quick rudder order; two stern shots. *Archerfish* dove deeper and ran. Around her burst the depth charges from the maddened escorts. In the midst of the turmoil the sub's sonar operator thought he heard all six fish explode. Breaking-up noises came over the headphones.

Archerfish returned to Guam on 15 December, claiming to have sunk a *Hayatake-* (*Junyo-*) class carrier of twenty-eight thousand tons. The skeptics scoffed, maintaining that no Japanese carriers had been in those waters that evening. Not until after the war did the men of *Archerfish* learn that they had bagged the biggest ship ever sunk by a submarine, in fact, the largest warship built to that point. Her target had been the massive *Shinano*, converted to a carrier in secret and desperately sent to sea with a green, totally unprepared crew. Four of the submarine's torpedoes had hit; unable to conduct her own damage control, *Shinano* had gone down the following morning with her captain and five hundred men.[9]

One ship, fifty-nine thousand tons. *Archerfish* had emerged as the heavy-weight champion of the Pacific war. And, in her combatant role, she was only one of hundreds. The Navy had been preparing for unrestricted submarine warfare a full decade before Pearl Harbor, building its own submarines and working at the cutting edge of underwater technology. After a painfully slow start, the "silent service" had, in a few short months, carried the strategic battle to the very gates of Japan. Watching, reporting, attacking, the pigboats served as pickets, lifeguards (504 aviators rescued), transports, and intelligence collectors. Above all, the aggressive little boats *attacked*. Their prey was anything that floated and flew the Rising Sun.

Japan depended on her overseas possessions and conquests to survive as an industrial power, but American submarines systematically choked off her shipping lanes. For the entire war only 169 fleet boats operated in the Pacific. But they were enough; they cut the Japanese oil lifeline from the Netherlands East Indies, ravaged the imperial merchant marine, and, at the end of the war, routinely operated within the mine-filled Sea of Japan itself.

By the summer of 1945 the Japanese were being economically strangled, and the submarine was the major reason. Six out of every ten Japanese merchantmen sent to the bottom had been put there by the pigboats. Fifty-two of the doughty subs never returned from patrol; lost with them were 374 officers and over 3100 enlisted men.

Now *Archerfish* and her sisters were relaxing alongside *Proteus*, their war work over. Little attention was paid to the doings elsewhere in the bay. Indeed, many submariners were already ashore, boozily christening the new Submarine Officers Club, Yokosuka. *Archerfish*'s crew knew that at last, after seven war patrols, they were going home. The report of the day was a laconic one-liner: "In Tokyo Bay during surrender of Japanese forces aboard U.S.S. MISSOURI."

☆

. . . The terms and conditions upon which the surrender of the Japanese Imperial forces is here to be given and accepted are contained in the instruments of surrender now before you. . . .

Roland Smoot, a combat-seasoned destroyer flotilla commander, had clambered up on a gun turret for a better view. Straining to see, he spent most of the ceremony being elbowed by the press. To Smoot, the listening Japanese seemed "just as cold and officious as they could be. There was nothing friendly about that morning whatsoever."[10]

Nothing friendly. . . . The Japanese had so feared the American occupation's onslaught that the deputy prime minister had ordered the recall from the hinterland of every former prostitute, taxi dancer, and masseuse to volunteer for "sex amusement centers" to service the rapacious foreigners. About five thousand "volunteers" were considered necessary to administer to the unbridled lusts of the expected three hundred thousand occupiers. The fears went aglimmering; Halsey threatened dire punishment, and the incidents were few. Most Americans wanted no more than some sightseeing, picture taking, and a couple of glasses of beer.

Somewhere in Tokyo Bay that day—no one ever bothered to record where—rested a commissioned warship so anonymous that she even lacked a name. Along with *Lansdowne* she was officially part of Task Force 35, but among that imposing array, which included the battleship *South Dakota*, heavy and light cruisers, destroyers, destroyer escorts, and auxiliaries, she was the only one of her kind.

Landing Ship, Tank. A clanking name for an indescribably ugly creature. Yet concealed behind her hideous appearance (she looked like a dumpy building with a shopping cart—her well—plastered in front) was a one-word description: indispensable. So important were the LSTs that they had been given almost the number-one building priority in the United States, behind the fearsome aircraft carriers but before the urgently needed convoy escorts, before the submarines—before everything else. They soon became ubiquitous. Contracts had been let in every section of the country, and LSTs were routinely built miles from salt water—along the Ohio River, on the Great Lakes, and throughout the Mississippi Delta. In an amazingly short period of time, there were almost 1100 of them.

They were amphibians, designed both to cross oceans and to beach in shoal water. LSTs had ballast tanks just like submarines. Blowing ballast on beaching, they could discharge their cargo of men and matériel directly onto land over their bow ramp. Retracting the ramp, they could—with luck, strong engines, and a high tide—return to sea.

At 2100 tons, these diesel-powered, twin-screw ships wallowed ponderously in open water. No crew member ever forgot an ocean crossing on an LST (the vessel specialized in forty-degree rolls), and her temporary passengers always fervently wished that they were someplace else. Their skippers, for the most part, were practically rookies. "LST commanding officers," said one report, "are still short on seamanship and punch too many holes in the sides of ships they come alongside." During one operation, Iwo Jima, the hapless *LST-928* had managed to collide, in succession, with two other LSTs, one other landing ship, an attack transport, and two attack cargo ships.

Things got no better against the shore. Landing problems were both numerous and unexpected, and at night or in rough weather they simply multiplied. Men, overladen with combat gear, could step over the ramp into water above their heads; boat engines stalled; small craft drifted off; davit blocks jammed; tackle fouled. Cursing and the LST went hand-in-hand.

Yet they were badly needed, for they and their kind did what no other type of ship could do. They were part of a huge family of landing craft, many thousands strong by the end of the war. At Okinawa, more than 1200 landing craft had been used. Some steamed independently, and some were piggybacked on the decks of their larger sisters. Landing Ship, Dock (LSDs), Landing Craft, Tank (LCTs), Landing Craft, Infantry (LCIs), LCMs, LCVPs, LCAs—the list of acronyms was long and somewhat redundant, but all did the same thing: marry the sea with the land.

Across this bridge of amphibians, crewed at the end by 657,000 officers and men, the implements of victory rolled—into North Africa, Sicily, Italy; into France and the Low Countries; into the Solomons, New Guinea, the Philippines. In them Marines and soldiers stormed and took Tarawa, Kwajalein, Saipan, Peleliu, Iwo Jima, Okinawa. The LST was "slow, awkward, [and] wonderful," judged a man in a position to know, MacArthur's Seventh Fleet commander, Vice Admiral Dan Barbey. "Without them it is difficult to imagine how the war could have been successfully fought."

The amphibians were not built without strain. The chief of naval operations himself had championed their accelerated construction, but Ernie King, to put it mildly, lacked the soft touch. The sidetracking of other building programs in favor of the mandatory landing craft, in addition to creating inevitable problems with procurement, manufacturing facilities, and manpower, had produced endless bureaucratic snafus. By November 1942 the amphibians had slid from second to twelfth on the Navy Shipbuilding Precedence List. King and his staff had grossly miscalculated Allied requirements for amphibious assault vehicles, resulting in worldwide shortages and theater commanders screaming for more. By mid-1943 amphibious shipping had lost its former priority.[11]

Despite these brouhahas, some avoidable, some not, the ships got built, among them the nameless thing in Tokyo Bay. Like her myriad sisters she was doubtless crewed by Reservists. No self-respecting Naval Academy graduate wanted to be assigned to one. This particular LST, hull number 656, had labored away at her various tasks for over a year. In August 1944 she took part in Operation DRAGOON, the invasion of southern France, landing troops of the Army's 45th Division in the first and second waves. Four days later she did the same with French forces. The reserve lieutenant commanding concluded his operational report on a rare upbeat note: "During this entire period (15–25 August 1944) the ship, all machinery, gear and communications functioned satisfactorily."

During the worldwide redistribution of landing craft following the successful invasion of Europe, *LST-656* was shuffled to the Pacific. What operations she participated in there, if any, are unknown. Her young officers, as well as their almost equally inexperienced group commander, were not much for writing reports; battleships and carriers got first crack at the yeomen. The ship served, as always, as an obscure member of an obscure group, ferrying ashore what needed to be ferried ashore. Now she found herself in Tokyo Bay at the moment of triumph, unknown and unnoticed. And still indispensable.

☆

. . . As Supreme Commander of the Allied Powers, I announce it is my firm purpose, in the tradition of the countries I represent, to proceed in the discharge of my responsibilities with justice and tolerance while taking all necessary dispositions to insure that the terms of surrender are fully, promptly and faithfully complied with. . . .

In the second row of officers opposite the peace table stood John ("Jimmy") Thach, an outstanding naval aviator and tactician who had invented the famed "Thach weave." The flier was "very impressed" with the general's "professionally written, beautifully delivered address." Like Smith-Hutton and Smoot, Thach was looking right at the Japanese. "You could stand there and watch the expressions on their faces, and, inscrutable as they're supposed to be, it was apparent that they expected far worse treatment. . . ."

Ahead of Thach, in the front row amid a khaki-clad galaxy of naval stars—men like Bill Halsey, Charles Lockwood, Mick Carney, and Slew McCain—stood a big-eared, sharp-nosed vice admiral with golden wings pinned above his left shirt pocket. John ("Jack") Towers had first flown back in 1911. He was naval aviator number three, and he had relentlessly championed naval aviation for over three decades.

Anchored close by, in berth F-81, lay one of Jimmy Thach's and Jack Towers's own, the inelegantly named light carrier *Cowpens* (CVL-25). Unlike more slack ships, such as *Piedmont*, *Archerfish*, and *LST-656*, her proximity to the ceremony and her status as a heavy meant that today the carrier had to be shipshape. Accordingly, she had gone to flight deck parade at 0800, where Distinguished Flying Crosses, Purple Hearts, and commendations had been awarded to members of her squadrons and crew. *Cowpens* had a hookup with *Missouri*, and the carrier's men could hear MacArthur's words broadcast over the ship's public address system—"This final stroke in elimination of war in which we have participated since 7 December 1941," wrote her diarist.[12]

There were seven others like her, together called the *Independence* class. They were not supposed to have been carriers at all, but ten-thousand-ton cruisers of the *Cleveland* class. Pearl Harbor changed this thinking. Flight decks were slapped over the cruiser hulls; gear intended for a gun cruiser, such as ammunition hoists and barbettes, had to be removed; storage areas for highly flammable aviation gasoline were added. The flight deck made the ships extremely top-heavy, so blisters were added abeam to improve stability. Four square funnels dispersed stack gases on either side of the stern.

Thus, *Cowpens* was born a hybrid, and an extremely ugly one at that. She was also a makeshift. With a capacity of only forty planes, she could carry less than half the carrier wing of her big sisters of the *Essex* class. *Cowpens* had only two centerline elevators and one bow catapult, so her speed of launch and recovery was slower as well. She was cramped, crowded, and confined, a most uncomfortable ship.

Still, *CVL-25* could turn thirty-two knots and could carry out most of the missions of the *Essexes*, if on a reduced scale. From her commissioning and shakedown she had been in the thick of the Pacific war. She began in the fall of 1943 by training fledgling aviators in strikes against Wake and Marcus islands. Raids against Jaluit, Mili, and the Marshalls followed, keeping Japanese heads down before the assault on Tarawa. During that operation *Cowpens* provided air cover and interceptor defense.

Within a month she was hitting Kwajalein as part of Task Force 50, in the van as the growing host of Pacific Fleet carriers blasted through Micronesia. Early in 1944 she furnished the combat air patrol for a sweep around the Japanese bastion of Truk. By April she was off New Guinea, pounding airfields and defenses at Wakde, Samar, and Sarmi. In June she was up to her ears in the Marianas operation, in particular raiding and destroying important Japanese air assets on Iwo Jima and Chichi Jima. In the climactic Battle of the Philippine Sea, eight of her Grumman F6F Hellcats went against the opening Japanese raid from the first tallyho; every Hellcat returned home safely. The enemy kept coming, and *Cowpens* kept fighting. Twelve of her Hellcats, along with seven from *Essex* and eight from *Hornet*, opposed the fourth raid of the day and splashed thirty of forty-nine planes.

Then she rested, but only for a moment. By October *Cowpens* was part of the most powerful carrier arm ever put together, operating to the east of the Philippines. She served in the covering force for "Cripdiv 1," protecting the injured cruisers *Canberra* and *Houston*. The Japanese sent a flight of 107 aircraft against the slow-moving aggregation as the wounded ships crawled across the entrance to Luzon Strait, and in the ensuing melee, fighters from *Cowpens* and *Cabot* accounted for forty-one of the enemy. Within days *CVL-25* was in action again, striking the retreating Japanese Center Force, which had come within an ace of smashing the American landings at Leyte Gulf.

Following this battle, which virtually demolished the remnants of Japanese naval power, *Cowpens* went through her worst ordeal during the famous typhoon of 18 December 1944 (the storm that provided the basis for Herman Wouk's fictional *The Caine Mutiny*). She lost seven planes overboard and successfully fought a fire caused by one that had broken loose. Early in 1945 she struck Formosa, taking part in the aerial penetration of the inner ring of Japanese defenses. And she went on to take part in the first carrier strikes against the heart of Japan. She and her kind had become the heart of the "task force"—a variety of ships assembled under one command for a particular purpose.

Thus, the jury-rigged hybrid in F-81, obscene funnels on her rear end and all, had compiled one of the most distinguished battle records in the

Pacific. Her war birds had flown from the Gilberts through the Marianas to the Marshalls, over New Guinea and the Philippines, then on to Formosa and Honshu itself. Her crew basked in her well-earned honors, listening as the famous voice crackled over the PA. . . .

☆

. . . I now invite the representatives of the Emperor of Japan and the Japanese government and the Japanese Imperial General Headquarters to sign the instrument of surrender at the places indicated.[13]

At these words the cloud cover broke momentarily, and a ray of sunshine spotlighted *Missouri*. To the ship's senior chaplain, "It was so dramatic . . . as though all nature itself was smiling on what was happening there . . . it lit up the place. . . ."

The speech had taken less than five minutes. Shigemitsu haltingly moved toward the table, leaning on his cane. He took off his gloves and silk hat, sat down, dropped his cane, picked it up, fiddled with his hat and gloves, and shuffled the papers before him. Then he looked about for a pen. Halsey, exasperated, felt like slapping him, thinking "Sign, damn you! Sign!" "We all recognized the possibility of a Hari Kiri job," remembered Mick Carney maliciously, "and one news photographer had even provided himself with Kodachrome film, just in case."

Finally, an underling supplied a pen. Shigemitsu signed, followed by the crestfallen Umezu, who briskly signed standing up. Then MacArthur for the Allied powers, followed by Nimitz for the United States. Then a procession of Allied representatives, as the newsreel cameras whirred and the shutters clicked. As Nimitz was scrawling his signature, MacArthur put his arm around Halsey's shoulders and said, "Start 'em now!"

"Aye, aye, sir!" Halsey immediately gave an order. The spectators at the ceremony became aware of a low, full-throated drone coming from somewhere above the clouds, which had now closed in again. Those who had heard the sound before knew its source: B-29 engines. Fifty of the big bombers had been orbiting, waiting, and were now passing over in stately parade.

But above the drone rasped a higher pitched, buzzing, angry sound. Looking abeam to port, the men aboard *Missouri* could make out black specks on the horizon, first dozens, then hundreds, drawing closer, breaking into V-shaped echelons of threes and fives, diamonds and double diamonds. The black specks broadened, sprouted wings, bored steadily in toward the great battleship, their numbers climbing up to the four-thousand-foot ceiling.

On they came, the assembled might of American carrier air. Sweeping in at masthead height blazed a blue-winged cavalcade of 450 warplanes, their buzz escalating to a deafening roar. Some of the men at their controls were greenhorns, young men who had flown the routine, but still dangerous, strikes against the battered Japanese in the closing days of the war. But many more were veterans, combat-hardened aviators who had seen the Japanese navy checked at Coral Sea, turned back at Midway, and demolished at Philippine Sea and Leyte Gulf.

The planes they were flying had been summoned up by the fleet fighter director from the giant flattops of Task Force 38, lying just off-shore. They were a mixed bag, propeller-driven monoplanes all, part of a naval inventory of almost thirty thousand combat aircraft. Overhead flashed stubby, dependable Hellcat fighters, powerful in a climb, heavily armed (though not today), and with generous range; Curtiss SB2C Helldivers, unlovingly nicknamed "Big-Tailed Beasts," fast but brittle dive-bombers; Chance-Vought F4U Corsairs, their distinctive gull-wing shape clearly visible, more suitable for land-based action than for carrier operations.[14]

Here, in the minds of many of those watching, like Thach and Towers, was the future: naval air power—flexible, far-ranging, destructive—the spearhead of a naval revolution that had occurred within the forty-five months of the Pacific war. The men flying these aircraft saw themselves as an elite, the very best aviators in the world. In truth, they probably were.

As the observers looked on, the huge formation made a long, graceful curve and disappeared into the lowering mists draping Mount Fujiyama. To Mick Carney the scene "was breathtaking and made the spine tingle." Halsey, who had qualified as an aviator himself late in his career, glowed with pride, even though he still "would have liked to have kicked each Jap delegate in the face."

The signing over, the Japanese bowed stiffly and walked to the gangway. By 0933 they were back aboard *Lansdowne*, where the vengeful Halsey had ordered that they be denied amenities such as coffee and cigarettes (an order generously revoked by Nimitz). An hour later the destroyer discharged her cargo at the Custom House Pier in Yokohama. Meanwhile, MacArthur walked to another microphone and, this time through a live radio hookup, began to broadcast to the world. "Today, the guns are silent. A great tragedy has ended. A great victory has been won. . . ."

As the general had said at the conclusion of the signing ceremony: "These proceedings are now closed."

☆

So, the captains departed. MacArthur's and Nimitz's flags were hauled down, and once again Bill Halsey's flag flew above *Missouri*. The command duty officer aboard the cruiser *Saint Paul*, anchored in the berth next to the battleship, asked his skipper for permission to secure from the wartime anti-aircraft condition of readiness: "It seemed to me that the war was probably over." While mopping-up operations would continue for weeks, peacetime routine descended on the fleet like a curtain. Already Mighty Mo's postal clerks were busy hand-stamping the twenty thousand specially franked pieces of mail they would send out that day. "A ravaged world," optimistically wrote the Associated Press's man on the spot, "[is] now done with war."[15]

Missouri would ever after remain the transcendent symbol of Japanese capitulation. She had been, indeed, an important part of America's greatest military victory, but her appearance stage front, literally in the sunshine, may also be taken as only a minute index of the naval power of the United States, now, in September 1945, at its towering apogee. Despite their many differences in size, configuration, roles, and wartime records, *Missouri, Lansdowne, Piedmont, Archerfish, LST-656,* and *Cowpens* had more in common than the obvious fact that they were commissioned ships in the United States Navy. All of them had come into being *after* 7 December 1941.

Initially, they had been amateurs at the business of war, inexperienced vessels manned by mostly inexperienced crews. Nine of every ten sailors aboard them were Reservists. Only one out of every nine had worn a naval uniform prior to Pearl Harbor. Aboard *South Dakota,* some of the sailors hailing from the Appalachian outback had not even known how to use the telephone. They made mistakes at first, of course—plenty of them. But they learned. In an incredibly short time the ships and men became fighting units, the units task groups, the groups task forces, and the forces—fighting fleets.

The ships themselves were convincing testimony to American industrial muscle, flexed by the only economy on earth that became rich on the war. In a matter of months this muscle had created a saltwater behemoth. By war's end the United States owned half of the world supply of *all* shipping. Its navy numbered over 1200 combatant vessels. Among these were the carriers, almost 100 strong; 23 battleships; 73 cruisers; 733 destroyers and destroyer escorts; and 234 submarines. Aiding them were almost 1800 auxiliaries, 1200 patrol craft, over 600 mine craft, and a whopping 61,000 landing craft.

This seagoing titan of sixty-six thousand ships was crewed and supported by over four million men and women, 320,000 of them officers. Fifty thousand were aviators, flying everything from fighters to bombers to patrol planes to scouts—a grand total of seventy-five thosand aircraft. There were fifty thousand staff officers—doctors, lawyers, dentists, nurses, supply specialists, engineers, and chaplains. Eight thousand of these were women, just as women made up more than eighty thousand of the almost three-million-strong enlisted component.

The numbers were breathtaking, but what really counted was what this Navy *could do.* Ships like *Missouri* could establish a "naval presence," lob huge shells miles inland, put up a cloud of fleet-protecting ack-ack, or duel gun-to-gun with any opposing force. *Lansdowne* and her cruiser cousins could hunt submarines, escort convoys, and also pepper the sky with anti-air fire. *Piedmont* could support the fleet anywhere, making possible an irresistible mobile force moving at will over 70 percent of the surface of the globe—and at a top speed of thirty knots.

Archerfish could deny the use of the sea to the enemy, cutting his communications lines, sinking his supplies, drowning his troops—barring him from the means to wage war. Humble little *LST-656* and her family of thousands could project power onto dry land, whole armies propelled ashore at a point, place, and time of the Navy's choosing. And finally, *Cowpens* and her kind could raise a defensive umbrella over the fleet, hammer any threat within range offered by the enemy, and project deadly ordnance hundreds of miles inland.

This Navy gathered its own intelligence as well as used the resources of other combatant arms; could ferret out weak spots, plan accordingly, and strike swiftly; could feed, refuel, and rearm itself; could, almost offhandedly, build runways, hospitals, schools, golf courses, officers' clubs; could do its own medicine, dentistry, psychiatry. The Navy had its own laws—and even managed to pay for itself.

This Navy was tied together by radio communications on a worldwide scale; given the right circumstances, its elements could change their plans in minutes. The fleet had electronic eyes that could cut through clouds, see at night, and direct its fire control. Electronic ears helped its ships to hear underwater. Its destructive range had increased dramatically in but a few short months. The Navy could make war in three dimensions, over, under, and upon the surface of the ocean, controlling whatever area of sea desired. Here was a force that was fast, powerful, durable—the most dominant navy that had ever existed.

Such an oceangoing force could only have been dreamed about before 1941. Sir Bruce Fraser, in Tokyo Bay, commanded a fleet (Task Force 57) that would have made a respectable navy for many nations prior to Pearl Harbor. Fraser's command included five fleet carriers, two fast battleships, five cruisers, and eleven destroyers. Yet Task Force 57 was dwarfed at the surrender by Halsey's Third Fleet. And the Third Fleet, in turn, was only a fraction of the Navy, which, with its British and Canadian allies, had won the Battle of the Atlantic, made safe the Mediterranean, and successfully carried the war across ten thousand miles of Pacific Ocean to the Japanese homeland.

All of them, *Missouri*, *Lansdowne*, and the rest, and the men, too—Nimitz, Halsey, Slew McCain, Mick Carney, Sunshine Murray, Jimmy Thach, Jack Towers, Seaman John Truman—were part of the mightiest armada in history. Against this armada, the galley fleets of ancient Greece and Rome would have been instantly blown to kindling. The cannon-shooting sailing vessels of the original Spanish Armada and those of their doughty English opponents would have been the work of a few short minutes. The navy of Nelson, as strong, well-led, and masterful as its wooden-walled fortresses had been in their own time, nevertheless in all essentials remained akin to the sailing navies of three hundred years before; Nelson, for all his brilliance and fire, would have been helpless as well. The early steam and steel navies might have lived for hours rather than minutes, but despite their increasingly heavy armorplate and ever more powerful rifled guns, the navies of the Civil War, the Spanish-American War, and World War I were virtually defenseless against any threat from the skies or under the waves.

The American armada was, at the very least, a fourfold organization: a floating base, an air force, an army, and a fighting fleet, all in one. Almost all of the armada had been designed, built, manned, and launched within eighteen months of the Battle of Midway, "without question the greatest organizational feat of naval history." The ensuing engine of seapower transformed the vast reaches of the Pacific from a protective ally to a deadly enemy of the Japanese and made the Atlantic a broad highway leading toward the Allied conquest of Europe.

Indeed, in World War II "sea power reached the culmination of its influence on history." And no navy, in its own time, had ever been as supreme as was the United States Navy in 1945. The armada had fully realized its historic role as the "Shield of the Republic," with worldwide accomplishments that had been "indubitably superb." Yet for all their wartime record, the ships and the people were still but instruments of national policy, policy that often could be ill-informed, mistaken, or simply ignorant, and as an instrument of national policy its future roles would be judged.

For the moment the national policy was consensus. That consensus had been victory, and crushing, absolute victory had come. As MacArthur had pronounced, the proceedings aboard *Missouri* were now closed. In the new, uncertain world taking shape in the terrible shadow of atomic energy, what purposes the awesome collection of naval power within and beyond Tokyo Bay might serve remained to be seen.[16]

PART ONE

DECAY
—— OF THE ——
ARMADA

When I have won a victory I do not
repeat my tactics but respond to
circumstances in an infinite variety of ways.

—Sun Tzu, *The Art of War*

CHAPTER ONE

THE GHOST OF MAHAN

——————— ☆ ———————

I have not yet begun to fight! "Don't give up the ship!" "Damn the torpedoes! Full speed ahead!" The words echo down the years, gleaming sword points of the nation's naval heritage. Which hero said what, and in what circumstances, might be a little hazy, but the ringing phrases somehow embodied a particular and fulsomely self-congratulatory *tone* of American naval power—of what had been and what should be.

Americans traditionally spent little time thinking about the *uses* of a navy. Some would recall John Paul Jones, James Lawrence, and David Glasgow Farragut, maybe know the names of their ships at the time their famous words were uttered—*Bonhomme Richard* (1779), *Chesapeake* (1813), and *Hartford* (1864)—and even (perhaps) remember a bit of what these fighting sailors were doing while they were manufacturing such quotable quotes.

Still, for the people of the oceangoing world power that the United States had become by the twentieth century, the Navy simply *was*, a loyal instrument of national will to be exercised on demand. The modern service consistently ranked in the very top echelon as a source of pride and patriotic spirit, of course, but the fleet was usually out of sight, either clinging to its coastal ports or somewhere out there, over the horizon. Most folks, if queried about what their Navy did and exactly how its ships went about their business, would have been hard-pressed for an answer.

Certainly, some would have come up with the obvious: A navy was supposed to defend the homeland. To the cognoscenti, this partook of the "strategic defensive," an idea as old as navies themselves. The ancient Greeks, awaiting the onslaught of Xerxes and his Persian host, had sent envoys to Delphi to get the word. The priestess Aristonice did not disappoint:

> Though all else shall be taken within the bounds of Cecrops
> And the fastness of the holy mountain of Cithaeron,
> Yet Zeus the all-seeing grants to Athene's prayer
> That the wooden wall only shall not fall, but help you and your children.

At Salamis the wooden walls of the Athenian galleys held, and Greek civilization survived.

Seas and oceans could support the strategic defensive, but only if enemy forces could be prevented from using them to get at you. The Carthaginians learned this lesson against the Romans (to their everlasting grief), as did the medieval French agaist the marauding Vikings. The lesson was repeated over and over in naval history; the Germans had to be taught twice in the twentieth century. With a strong navy, surrounding water became a defensive moat, a fact that helped explain the centuries-long international success of the English, even battened as they were to an island no part of which lay more than seventy miles from salt water.

Shakespeare could see the outlines, even at the start of his country's rise to imperial greatness:

> England, hedged in with the main,
> That water-walled bulwark, still secure
> And confident from foreign purposes.

The water itself was a shield, behind which the island created first its sea-raiders and then its fleets, launching itself on the course of empire.

> This little world,
> This precious stone set in the silver sea,
> Which serves it in the office of a wall,
> Or as a moat defensive to a house
> Against the envy of less happier lands.

By the eighteenth century many Englishmen were positively euphoric about their imperial condition, and by then the Royal Navy obviously had had something to do with Britain's status. The fleet and trade, said Lord Haversham in the House of Lords, were well-nigh inseparable. "Both together are the wealth, strength, security and glory of Britain." This, the wooden-walled sailing navy of George Anson and Black Dick Howe, "hath ever been [England's] greatest defence and ornament; it is its ancient and natural strength,—the floating bulwark of our island."

Translated to America, the naval notion of the strategic defensive emphasized the idea of ocean moats (the Atlantic, after all, was somewhat broader than the English Channel and, as for the Pacific . . .) and, at least at first, downplayed the need for a powerful offensive navy. Before America's surge to empire in the late nineteenth century, the dominant way of thinking held that the nation's naval power had but two tasks: to protect the coasts and to harry the shipping of a hostile power. As late as the 1930s many in the United States firmly believed that nature itself had provided the firmest barriers of all. In naval terms this was the core of isolationism. President

Herbert Hoover made the point succinctly. "The first necessity of our government," he proclaimed on Navy Day (27 October), 1931, "is the maintenance of a navy so efficient and strong that, in conjunction with our army, no enemy may ever invade our country." To be doubly clear, he added: "Ours is a force of defense, not offense."[1]

Proclaiming a defensive posture begged the issue of exactly what was to be defended, and how. The course of modern American history had already, by 1931, made this issue deeply ambiguous. The fervent isolationist (an almost unknown breed after 7 December 1941) argued that the naval shield was meant only for the continental United States. But this argument did not sit very well with those American dependencies and interests in the Caribbean, not to mention the residents of the territories of Hawaii and Alaska. Beyond these lay the Western Hemisphere (of diplomatic and naval significance if only because of the symbolically important Monroe Doctrine), the Philippines, Europe, and China. Indeed, as one critic said, the naval shield could theoretically be extended to cover "every dollar invested by an American citizen on the wide surface of the earth."

The strategic defensive thus could, and did, have worldwide naval applications in the twentieth century. The idea was not to be confused with a naval policy of coastal defense. At least once in American history naval strategy had rested precisely on the defense of harbors and coasts, period. This, the notorious "gunboat policy" of Thomas Jefferson's administration, actually had much to offer. The policy was cheap. Such a posture avoided poking the American naval nose into the Napoleonic wars then raging in Europe, and, in keeping naval power close to shore, lessened the problems of manning and resupply. But in execution the policy was a disaster. The little gunboats provided no defense at all, and the British sailed with impunity up Chesapeake Bay and burned Washington as proof.

Nevertheless, coastal defense remained a premium concern for more than a century after the Navy's failure to defend the nation in the War of 1812. The first chief of naval operations, Admiral William Shepherd Benson, believed that the first responsibility of the Navy was coastal defense, and he was speaking almost two decades after spectacular American naval victories in the Spanish-American War had dropped dependencies in both the Caribbean and the Pacific into the country's lap.

But despite the claims of Hoover, Benson, and many others, even more Americans took great satisfaction in the ability of their modern steam-and-steel Navy to project power overseas, the essence of the "strategic offensive." Beginning with the victory over Spain, the Navy had gone on to take the strategic offensive in both world wars. Between conflicts its deployment patterns dispatched vessels far from their homeland, duplicating in many cases the deployments of the nineteenth-century sailing squadrons. Even before Pearl Harbor, American warships were routinely seen alongside in Naples, under the shadow of Sugarloaf in Rio de Janeiro, anchored off

Cavite in Manila Bay, and a thousand miles up the Yangtze River, deep inside China.

Just as the assertion of the strategic defensive left vague the question of what was to be defended, the strategic offensive held in abeyance the question of exactly how this was to be done. Wrapped up in this idea was an extremely fuzzy concept called "command of the sea." The wondrous words emphatically did not mean control of the ocean waters everywhere, all the time. Only Poseidon could do that. The root of the matter was the ability to use whatever part of the sea one chose while at the same time denying its use to whomever one wished—sometimes this was "the enemy." Command of the sea was thus, at best, a highly temporary claim, flexible, extremely adaptable, and sometimes pushed out of all proportion. (The Chinese in the 1920s may well have wondered what such "command" had to do with American gunboats chuffing up and down their rivers.)

For an insular power that aspired to use the oceans and seas for its own purposes, command of the sea seemed to be a strategic imperative. This was, after all, what Jones and Lawrence, in their ship-to-ship duels with the British, and Farragut, in his attack against the Confederate bastion of Mobile Bay, had been contesting. The notion had come to be the pivot of American naval thought, even though, as with the idea of the strategic defensive, its lineage extended back to the ancient Greeks. Themistocles, as he rallied the Athenians against the Persian menace, had put the matter bluntly: "He who commands the sea commands all."

The idea, ill-defined and inchoate but nonetheless powerful, was graven deeply into the battlements of modern American navalism.

☆

In 1945 a ghost walked these battlements, the shade of Alfred Thayer Mahan. Dead for over four decades when the surrender ceremony took place aboard *Missouri*, Mahan nevertheless remained a living intellectual legacy to those who made thinking about the uses of naval power their business.

Mahan had spent his life in the Navy, gaining distinction as a midshipman (second in a group of twenty in his 1859 Naval Academy class) but becoming a sailor who, at best, was uneasy at sea. He was an odd duck, the son of a distinguished military thinker at West Point, Dennis Hart Mahan, and a man whose goal was to think and write clearly about naval policy rather than to distinguish himself in battle—the dream of most of his contemporaries. Mahan smelled of the lamp in an age when a naval officer prided himself on marinating in brine and salt air.

The sobriquet "philosopher of seapower," which trailed Mahan down to the present day, was a gross overstatement. At his best he was a propagandist, a preacher, and a prophet. In the first two of these roles he did very well indeed. From his post at the new Naval War College in Newport, Rhode Island, and later from his retirement, his books and articles reached a worldwide audience and had a direct effect on men able to act on his ideas, chief among them his good friend Theodore Roosevelt. By the time of his death in 1914, Mahan had been eulogized as "the greatest writer America has yet produced," a man who had put "the United States on the path to imperial greatness."[2]

Like most thinkers who wrestle with a subject through a lifetime, Mahan changed his views somewhat as he watched his navy of sails and wood become one of steam and armor and as the naval powers of the world accelerated their developments in naval technology at a dizzying pace prior to World War I. Yet the outlines of his thought are clear.

For Mahan, dynamism rather than stasis was the human condition, and nations as well as people were its subjects. Struggle was thus inevitable (Mahan wrote in the heyday of that peculiar perversion of Darwin called social Darwinism), whether in the political, economic, or military spheres. Inside this world of flux, "principles" of seapower were to be discerned, just as his great model, the Swiss military theoretician Jomini, had done for land warfare in Napoleon's time.

Working away in his Newport study drafting lectures for the students at the Naval War College, the tall, ascetic officer drew his examples from history, most specifically the history of one country—England—and one institution—the Royal Navy in the age of sail. Mahan was an ardent Anglophile, and his theories told the British, in particular, precisely what they wanted to hear: they were great and their navy had made them that way.

As Mahan saw things, the imperative for commerce among seagoing powers gave birth to navies. "Commercial interests underlie and give rise to the creation of navies, and largely dictate their employment, in war as in peace." The economic competition for markets produced seapower. The flag, reversing the aphorism, followed trade. Oceangoing countries had no choice; they had to compete in trade to survive. To be "great," a nation must look outward, away from its shores.

His central concern, however, was not trade itself (late in life he backed off somewhat from his advocacy of trade in the creation of navies) but how to protect commercial enterprise and help trade prosper. Navies were therefore indispensable, all the more so because the inherent aggressiveness of men and nations rendered war practically inevitable. There was nothing new here; such ideas went back in American life at least to Alexander Hamilton. But Mahan was crystal clear about *naval*, as opposed to *commercial*, power. More than any other single factor, "the existence and proper use of organized sea power to ensure command of the sea has mightily influenced the course of human history." Seapower, in turn, involved geographic factors, financial and political aspects, and the composition of navies.

Closer to home, Mahan relentlessly plumped for a strong American navy. In the dawning age of American imperialism in which he wrote, his arguments for naval power seemed the merest common sense. The United

States, he smoothly asserted, was a "nation indisposed to aggression," but "others" were disposed "to thwart what we consider our reasonable policy." The only way the "others" could get at the United States was across the oceans, and as their force to do this must necessarily (in Mahan's time) be naval, so then the American force must be naval as well. The size of the other force was "the measure of our needed strength." There was no sub-stitute for naval preparedness, and in his demands to prepare for "anything that is likely to occur," Mahan came close to pleading for a garrison state.

The needed strength would come from America's industrial sinews. For Mahan the relationship between American industry and navalism was sym-biotic; the Navy defended the way to markets abroad, while business sup-ported a strong navy at home. He was far from alone in this line of thought. While Mahanian logic found an obviously responsive audience in coastal ports and burgeoning industrial centers, his ideas were heard far inland as well. A Kansas poet, writing in 1876 (at a time when the American Navy had reached rock bottom, ranked variously twelfth to nineteenth in the world, behind such renowned naval powers as Peru and Chile), put the case thus:

> Old Business is the monarch. He rules both
> The opulence of nations and their growth.
> He builds their cities and he paves their streets.
> He feeds their armies and equips their fleets.
> Kings are his puppets, and *his* arms alone
> Containes [*sic*] the muscle that can prop a
>   throne.[3]

With the possible exception of Benjamin Franklin and Mark Twain, no American author ever resonated in tune with the deeper concerns of his readers better than did Mahan. "Had Mahan written a quarter of a century earlier, his message would undoubtedly have fallen on barren soil, and a quarter of a century later he would have had little reason to write as he did." The man and his moment had met.

He was far from being the only prominent naval theorist of his time, but he unquestionably reached the widest audience, and his major concern was to indoctrinate his fellow citizens with the importance and significance of seapower for their country. "The advantages and disadvantages of the possession of sea power and its effects upon specific campaigns must always possess useful lessons."

☆

Mahan recognized that the Navy, as the prime instrument of seapower, was not the be-all and end-all of national purpose. "A navy is not an end, but a means," he declared. "He who wills the end—the policy—wills the means." Within these limits, however, he was clear about what the Navy was supposed to do. Ships might make port calls, survey land contours and sound ocean depths, conduct diplomacy, escort convoys, or clamp on blockades. All this was very well. But the main business of a navy was to *fight*. "To the ship of war . . . protection of the national shipping is the primary concern," and this protection, in a world of armed aggression, implied battle.

Mahan's disciples, such as Roosevelt, Admiral Benson, and hundreds of naval officers in the early years of the twentieth century, thus took to heart a basic Mahanian precept: the nation *must* build a powerful, balanced battle fleet capable of contesting and defeating any other fleet for command of the sea. The *nation*—as TR said, "the Navy is not an affair of the seacoast only." Roosevelt's successor, William Howard Taft, was succinct: "A Navy is for fighting, and if its management is not efficiently directed to that end, the people of this country have a right to complain."

This precept entered the histories and textbooks as doctrine, locked to the well-being of America and her people. "View it in whatever light we may," wrote one of Mahan's contemporaries, "the expense of maintaining a respectable and progressive navy is nothing more than a safe, economical and necessary insurance on the prosperity of the nation."

In Mahan's time a powerful fleet meant only one thing—battleships. His favorite historical examples were drawn from the sailing navies of the seventeenth and eighteenth centuries, and in examining those he had been most impressed by the vessels equipped and able to sail in line of battle, that is, those with enough guns and firepower to contest the seas with the best the enemy had to offer. This meant, at the very least, the seventy-four-gun British ship of the line, and the axiom extended upward to the mammoth 100s and 120s, such as *Victory*, the revered flagship of Horatio, Lord Nelson, at Trafalgar. The nineteenth-century naval technological revolution to steam and steel had changed the capabilities of the "battle ship," but not its role. As a specific type the battleship was the sine qua non of Mahanian doctrine.

Others had believed this before Mahan—he was far from an original thinker—but more were believers after him, to the extent that the battleship became the fundamental warship of the Navy in the early years of the twentieth century, its presumed capabilities the hinge on which all else turned: victory in battle, command of the sea, protection of trade routes and markets, and national prosperity.

In 1919, despite the advent of the submarine, the airplane, and anti-submarine warfare, the General Board of the Navy confidently asserted that the "battleship remains as heretofore the principle [*sic*] reliance of the sea power of a nation." Three years later, Assistant Secretary of the Navy Theodore Roosevelt, Jr., proclaimed that these vessels formed "the body of the Navy in the same way that the Infantry forms the body of the Army." If either body was defeated, the institution would fall. Curtis Wilbur, Calvin Coolidge's secretary of the Navy, told a House committee in 1924 that "modern naval engagements between first class powers, except in sporadic instances, will be fleet engagements"—and the battleship was queen of the fleet.[4]

Mahan believed that the Navy should have lots of battleships (because there was a lot of ocean to cover), although these need not be especially huge. Nor should they be armed with large-caliber guns only, like the *Dreadnoughts* the British began producing in 1906; mixed calibers were more suitable for different types of naval action. The irascible but brilliant Admiral Lord John ("Jackie") Fisher, champion of the *Dreadnought*, thought Mahan "passé" on this issue, but the American "was almost the Bible for the anti-dreadnought forces."

The rifled naval gun, then, was king. Mahan thought little of the offensive capabilities of the ram bow or the new torpedoes. His orderly, precise, controlled mind perceived that naval battles to come would be fought much as they had been under sail, with line of battle slugging against line of battle—orderly, precise, controlled.

The future of naval warfare, Mahan told his British admirers in 1894, lay "decidedly with the battleship," which was at its most effective when massed in the battle line. Not even the naval battles of the Russo-Japanese War of 1904–1905, in which mines and torpedoes had been used successfully by the victorious Japanese, shook him from his faith in the battleship and its mighty guns. He proclaimed that hoping to bring "an enemy to terms by commerce destruction alone, to be effected by a number of small cruisers, instead of obtaining control of the sea by preponderance of great fleets," was naive.

Submarines were developed, adopted, and did their deadly work at the hands of their young German *Unterseeboot* commanders in World War I; still, the battleship advocates remained true to Mahan. The airplane appeared—frail, underpowered, and lightly armed at first; the battleship advocates were unimpressed. A board headed by Admiral Edward Eberle reported in 1925 that "it cannot be said . . . that air attack has rendered the battleship obsolete."

After all, the battleship seemed so—so *useful*. In 1929 the national president of the Women's Auxiliary of the American Legion said her organization had no patience with those who clamored for friendships instead of battleships. "Battleships," she avowed, "make friendships sure." They were also showboats, terrific for admirals to ride when they visited foreign ports or paraded in naval reviews. The brass tended to be greatly attached to them. Indeed, one of Mahan's contemporaries, the pompous Arent Schuyler Crowinshield, asked to be relieved of his command of the European Squadron in 1903 when told that he could not retain his beloved flagship, the battlewagon *Illinois*, as part of a reconstituted all-cruiser squadron.

So Mahan's ideas survived, in theory as the justification for a strong navy and in practice as the heavily armored, heavily gunned battleship. Few battleship proponents cared to note that, before 1941, no American battleship had *ever* fought in the role in which Mahan envisioned: fleet versus fleet. The country's sailing Navy had been composed largely of frigates and had sortied either singly or in squadrons. An American "fleet" was a misnomer before the Civil War, and in that conflict Confederate naval inferiority ensured the lack of fleet action. Commodore George Dewey's much-celebrated triumph over the Spanish at Manila Bay in May of 1898 had been delivered by four cruisers, two gunboats, and a revenue cutter.

The victory at Santiago Bay two months later did involve the spanking new American battlewagons *Oregon, Iowa, Texas,* and *Indiana* against a Spanish force made up mostly of outgunned cruisers, yet this was hardly a fleet action but rather a galley-west stern chase with something of the verve of a fox hunt. Rear Admiral Hugh Rodman's five-ship Battleship Division 9, operating as Battle Squadron 6, had been assigned to European waters in World War I, but the Germans were lying low after Jutland, and no big-gun duels had developed.

Before World War II, then, although the submarine and the airplane were gaining their sometimes vociferous adherents and while the pace of American naval construction varied with the strength of isolationist sentiments, the length of congressional pursestrings, and the building limits of naval treaties, Mahan and like-minded naval theorists still held sway. Wargaming at the Naval War College, while including the new aircraft carriers, always concluded with a smashing fleet action among battleships (often called "BBs").

In 1939 the naval authority Captain William Puleston confidently declared that "today, in the American Navy, every officer who prepares for or discusses war, follows the methods and invokes the ideas of Mahan." And this meant BBs. Rear Admiral Ernest King, speaking in 1933 as chief of the Bureau of Aeronautics and nine years away from assuming his post as chief of naval operations, put the Mahanian case succinctly: "The backbone of the Navy today is the battleship. . . . It can stand up and take it and you have nothing else that can. . . ."[5]

☆

Alfred Thayer Mahan, said the authors of a highly regarded military history text written a decade after the end of World War II, was a "naval genius." He had initiated the fleet that had humbled Spain and convinced the world of America's great-power status. His naval theories were based on "sound, fundamental principles" that were as "valid in an age of air power as they were half a century ago."

—None of this was true. Mahan's influence within the Navy had been on the wane even before World War I. And if "genius" is the contribution of original, lasting thought, Mahan was far more the propagandist. As one historian somewhat snidely remarked, if Mahan "discovered nothing in particular he discovered it very well." Far from initiating any naval building program, Mahan had published his first important work, *The Influence of Sea Power upon History, 1660–1783*, in 1890—almost a full decade after the United States had begun to remake its decrepit fleet.

Most importantly, the results of World War II only continued and exacerbated a decades-long debate over the "validity" of Mahan's "principles;" some of these no longer seemed quite so ironclad. Mahan could not account for the rise of nonmaritime empires, such as those of Austro-Hungary, Russia, Germany, and the Ottomans. Even Britain's epic struggle against Napoleonic France, his great test case, involved many factors other than seapower.

Without doubt Mahan's writings had been an *inspiration* to generations of American naval thinkers. A small but steady flow of books, articles, and doctoral dissertations testified to this. What was at issue was his *influence*. Obviously, American naval skippers did not go into battle wondering what Mahan would have done. Mahan always was weaker at the tactical end of the scale and stronger as the strategic arena grew larger. Nor were senior officers especially adept at seeing any specific applications of Mahan's thought as they made naval policy. And anyway, to many of them Mahan had been too "political;" their tradition, they told themselves, lay at sea and not in Congress.

At least the appearance of paradox existed: a body of ideas widely accepted but rarely, in the historical sense, acted on. And even the ideas may have had their moment. "It is at least a question," wrote one authority in 1951, "whether the celebrated thesis of Alfred Thayer Mahan, however stimulating in its day, has not outlived its usefulness."

Basically, the Second World War had shown that "command of the sea" was an extremely nebulous idea and, in its Mahanian sense of ushering in total national victory, almost impossible to realize. Despite the huge scale of fleet engagements in the Pacific, for example, crushing American victories like Midway, Philippine Sea, and Leyte Gulf, triumph over Japan stemmed also from other sources—in particular, commerce-raiding submarines, amphibious assault, and air power. The new operative phrase was "power projection," which moved away from reliance on fleet engagements *only* to attacks against the shore and whatever lay beyond.

Diplomatic problems were also inherent in Mahan's ideas. His notion of American insularity implied a disavowal of involvement in Europe or the Far East in any permanent sense. Already, in 1945, the dominant American role in the infant United Nations pointed in the opposite direction. The direction was *outward*, into the world.

Operationally, Mahan had drummed away at the "principle" that the fleet must be kept concentrated and in American coastal ports, ready to sortie to the scene of action. The organization of the wartime operating Navy into "task forces," consisting of many types of ships with literally worldwide responsibilities, clearly obviated Mahan. In addition, the sheer size of the fleet in 1945 begged the question of its ability to "concentrate," as well as that of its capacity to maintain itself even if all of its ships ever got onto the same part of the ocean at the same time.[6]

Most importantly, Mahan and other naval theorists of his day had argued that *the primary business of navies was to fight other navies.* The fighting would be a showdown between massed "capital ships"—your best against the other guy's best. In Mahan's time this had meant an oceanic *High Noon* among heavily gunned, thickly armored battleship fleets. As Mahan had said, the capacity of the enemy fleet thus determined the capacity of yours. This was reductionism in terms of military analysis, a flaw also found in the method of Mahan's revered predecessor Jomini. Mahan tended to assume that mere counting—ships, guns, and so forth—was the essence of analysis.

In 1945, no other navy in existence had even remotely the power of the American Navy. True Mahanian doctrine would have called for a drastic scaledown in numbers of ships as of the end of the war, even if another suitable "enemy" could be found. Given the global scope of their missions as of 1945, naval officers had to oppose such a plan. "I hope you gentlemen will not take numbers as measuring the relative strength of navies," cautioned King, now a fleet admiral, in testimony before Congress. "I would like to emphasize that the strength of the Navy does not lie in the number of ships alone. . . ."

☆

Mahan's "capital ship," the battlewagon, had suffered greatly in prestige during the war. Part of the reason was pragmatic; Pearl Harbor had simply removed the bulk of the battle line, the Pacific Fleet battleships, from the board for the immediate future. Part was results, as aircraft carriers, for many the new "capital ships," had racked up an impressive series of victories against their Japanese counterparts. No longer were aircraft carriers merely the eyes of the battle line, the scouts; they had, in their own right, become a new "line of battle."

The battlewagons still had their defenders, and important ones. King himself made a spirited defense of their continuing usefulness in two reports to the secretary of the Navy, and Rear Admiral Forrest Sherman, already ticketed for higher responsibilities, said flatly in the summer of 1945 that "the battleship remains the most important type of fighting ship, not only because of its preponderance of fire power but in clearing areas for amphibious operations." Battleship theorists like Captain Miles Browning continued to work on battleship tactics as if the Mahanian heaven was still cloudless and the showboats would be around forever, because "the battleship is the heavyweight in any international stable of sea fighters."

The record suggested otherwise. During the rough half-century of American battleship design, seventy-three were projected, sixty-six laid down, and fifty-eight commissioned. From the first *Texas* and the famous *Maine*, the "second rates" commissioned in 1895, to the powerful *Iowa* class of World War II, they had progressed from coal to fuel oil, reciprocating engines to boilers, twelve-inch to sixteen-inch guns and seaman's eye to radar. In addition to the "old battleships" (OBBs), which provided all of the capital-ship victims at Pearl Harbor, ten new vessels of the type entered service during the war. Two *North Carolinas*, four *South Dakotas*, and four *Iowas* saw action. In addition, two of the badly designed *Alaska*-class battle cruisers were commissioned. Their combined combat record was good, but none of them participated in the Mahanian dream: surface action in the line of battle.[7]

The Americans were not alone in continuing battleship production. Germany, Italy, France, Japan, Great Britain, and the Soviet Union all had at least two more battleships building or projected as of 1940. Under the press of war, however, none of these countries could come close to the American rate of construction. Japan, for example, ordered over one million tons of warships under its Fourth Fleet Replenishment Program of 1940 and a million more after Pearl Harbor. Fewer than 20 percent were completed. By 1944 Americans were producing *thirty times* the Japanese tonnage, not to mention an endless cornucopia of other war matériel for themselves and their allies.

Japan, more than any other nation, clung to Mahanian doctrine. The best German battleships could do, bound as they were to a strategy of commerce raiding, was the *Götterdämmerung* of *Bismarck* in 1941. Italian battleships kept to their home ports after the disaster of Cape Matapan the same year. French capital ships, after being fired on by the British at Oran following the fall of France in 1940, were never a factor. The British used their battlewagons in the American mode, and the Soviet battleships remained on paper, the fleets they were intended to serve coastal forces at best. But the Japanese, despite their sinking of the British capital ships *Prince of Wales* and *Repulse* with land-based torpedo bombers off the coast of Malaya at the beginning of the war, still believed the battleship to be the "final arbiter."

Accordingly, the Japanese Combined Fleet was mesmerized by a single desire, to maneuver the opponent into a fleet-versus-fleet action. The hulking battlewagons *Yamato* and *Musashi*, the largest such warships ever built, were proof. *Kaisen yomurei*, the Japanese Regulations of Naval Warfare, which had been in use since the great victory over Russia, were the Japanese bible on the subject. "Battle is the sole means of victory," said the scripture. "Everything should satisfy what the battle demands."

The concept governed Admiral Isoroku Yamamoto's thought as his staff designed the plan that led to Midway and, two years later, still dominated Vice Admiral Jisaburo Ozawa's orders, which brought on the Battle of the Philippine Sea. Although both plans foresaw the use of aircraft carriers, both (along with the ambitious SHO-1 Plan, which led to Leyte Gulf) envisioned that, in the culminating moments, "the entire Japanese fleet would close on the enemy, destroying its fleet down to the last vessel."

The battleship and the concordant fantasy of the big-gun, blue-water armageddon did not save Japan. American air power kept the two giants at arm's length and slew the Japanese battlewagons before they could fight. *Musashi* was creamed by an aerial strike and sank in the Sibuyan Sea during the preliminaries to Leyte. *Yamato*, badly wounded by two bomb hits at the same time, survived only to be sunk during a suicidal sortie toward Okinawa in the last months of the war.[8]

Nor did the battleship, in its few surface engagements, materially advance the wartime cause of the United States. During the Allied invasion of North Africa in 1942 *Massachusetts* exchanged fire with the partially armed French battleship *Jean Bart*, which was inside the harbor at Casablanca. Three American shells exploded on their target, causing *Jean Bart* to flood by the stern.

Less than a week later, halfway around the world in the black night off Guadalcanal, *South Dakota* ("Big Bastard" to her crew) took numerous hits from a mixed Japanese force that included the battleship *Kirishima*. Heavily damaged and with numerous power failures, the Big Bastard remained afloat and survived to fight again. Her sister, *Washington*, engaged *Kirishima* with radar-directed fire for seven minutes, pulverizing the latter so badly that the Japanese were forced to scuttle her the following day.

In the close waters of Surigao Strait one October night in 1944, the spectral appearance of six OBBs (five of them had been sunk or seriously damaged at Pearl Harbor) marked the last stand of the battle line, the final major naval engagement in which air power, except in pursuit, played no part. But even here the sunken Japanese battleships *Fuso* and *Yamashiro* were also hit by destroyer torpedoes, and *Fuso* was sunk by torpedoes alone. "The last fight to the death between capital ships in which heavy guns were the main weapon on both sides" was the Arctic duel north of Norway in December 1943 between *Duke of York* and *Scharnhorst*, resulting in the sinking of the latter.

Accordingly the BB performance record, in terms of "command of the sea," indicated a vanishing breed. True, the two *North Carolinas* served with distinction, and *Washington*, in particular, probably had the best combat record of any new American battleship. *South Dakota*, with her Mark 4 radar, inaugurated the age of anti-air warfare in the waters off Guadalcanal, shooting down twenty-six enemy planes in a single day. She and the rest of her class proved to be tough and durable. The four *Iowas*, latecomers to the war, had an "undistinguished combat record," but still did their assigned tasks—shore bombardment and anti-aircraft defense—"superbly well."

This was not enough. The two *Alaska*-class battlecruisers that were built were failures, too weak to take the big hits and too slow to outrun an opponent. The five projected *Montana*-class battleships, intended as follow-ons to the *Iowas*, were never laid down. Mahan's capital ship seemed to be at the end of the line.

☆

The new capital ships, so said the experts, were the carriers. Their weapons were naval aircraft whose combat ranges of hundreds of miles dwarfed those of the naval gun. Although there were attempts to promote Mahan as a grand prophet whose principles were as applicable to the sky as to the sea, the conclusive American carrier victories in the Pacific, along with the crucial role of the escort carrier in the Battle of the Atlantic, suggested otherwise. There seemed to have been an abrupt departure from battleship-centered doctrine in these tactical and strategic victories, and relatively junior officers returning from the war zones to the Pentagon to help with postwar planning were eager to spread the message.[9]

The principal victims of the fleet carriers, the Japanese, never really caught on to the new decisiveness of air power at sea, and by the time they had an inkling, after the "Marianas Turkey Shoot" in June 1944, their naval clock was almost at midnight. Young gunnery officers aboard *Yamato* on her last journey, after heated argument, decided that BBs were doomed in an encounter with aircraft, a true but fatal prophecy for almost all of them. Japanese naval theorists had debated the question of battleships and carriers even before the war (as had the Americans), but the Japanese Navy's ruling circle had a "battleship superiority complex" that was not open to question until the clock was well past midnight.

The famous Admiral Yamamoto was a partial exception. He at least recognized the aircraft as far more than a variant of the scouting line, as a potent extension of naval cannon. In this sense the Pearl Harbor strike, usually thought of as some kind of vindication of naval air power, was in actuality a long-range shore bombardment. But Yamamoto was not quite the revolutionary many of his admirers believed he was. His plan for the Midway operation had as its goal the occupation of the island, along with luring out the Americans, who would then succumb to the pounding of seven *battleships*.

Things did not shake out that way. The decimation of the Japanese *carriers* picked the lock of the Japanese empire; without mobile, wide-ranging air power and highly experienced carrier pilots, the Japanese were forced back to the strategic defensive in the Pacific. By the end they were reduced to human torpedo attacks (the *kaiten*), which resulted in two minor sinkings in fifty-one tries, the far more deadly but equally futile kamikaze, and an ineffectual manned, rocket-powered missile, the *"Baka* (foolish) bomb," to be delivered from a mother aircraft.

None of these was naval air power per se, though all foreshadowed the coming of guided missiles. Naval air power, as a potential big punch, had been a source of debate in American naval circles for forty years. The tone had been set, ironically enough, by a nonnaval man, Glenn Curtiss, a pioneer aircraft designer and the first American, following the Wright brothers, to fly. After winning a prize for a daring flight between Albany and New York City, Curtiss had unburdened himself to reporters. "The battles of the future will be fought in the air," he predicted. "Encumbered as [battleships] are [with] their turrets and masts, they cannot launch air fighters, and without these to defend them, they would be blown apart." Thus the battle was joined—not with shells and bombs but with words—and the struggle raged for decades.[10]

Everyone, including Mahan, appreciated the *usefulness* of the airplane, but most people saw the new machines as eyes in the sky, offering differing perspectives of the scouting, or reconnaissance, carried out by cruisers and destroyers on the ocean surface. The scouting role remained primary, even after fleet games between the wars clearly indicated that airplanes could give surface vessels some nasty surprises.

Brigadier General Billy Mitchell's aerial destruction of the captured, modern German battleship *Ostfriesland* in a "test" in 1921 was a dramatic punctuation indicating these other possibilities. Naval illiterates, such as Senator William Borah of Idaho, immediately elevated the general's blanket claims for air power to the new dogma: "the battleship is practically obsolete." After he had sunk his battleship, Mitchell himself displayed the extremism and obstinacy that characterized both sides of the issue:

> Air forces with the type of aircraft now in existence or in development, acting from shore bases, can find and destroy all classes of seacraft under war conditions with a negligible loss to the aircraft. The problem of destruction of seacraft by [air] forces has been solved and is finished. . . . There are no conditions in which seacraft can operate efficiently in which aircraft cannot operate efficiently.

Army aviators, like the soon-to-be-court-martialed Mitchell, and a few young naval fliers, like Marc Mitscher, were seen as virtual heretics by their respective military churches. Army and Navy joined hands to protect orthodoxy. Enough that the airplane had proved itself in song and had joined the choir—aviators would not be allowed to conduct mass.

Mahan was indicted unfairly for his lack of consideration of the airplane (he died before the machine had proven its capabilities in combat), and, indeed, Mahanian doctrine found a new home with the carrier advocates. Admiral William Sims, who had commanded American naval forces in Europe during World War I, made no bones about his opinion: "The fast carrier is the capital ship of the future." Where naval orthodoxy saw aviation as, at best, an "adjunct" of naval power, and the Navy stubbornly relegated its growing squadrons of aircraft to secondary roles in its general doctrine for fleet operations, "neo-Mahanians" could argue that the master's gospel still held, only now armageddon would take shape as an all-carrier battle.

Amid all the word-flak, the United States went ahead to design and build a significant operational carrier arm in the interwar period. Air propagandists cried that naval aviation was being shortchanged in order to maintain a cohort of aging, obsolete battlewagons, but the figures showed strong budgetary commitment to the carriers, especially given the constraints of the depression economy. As a result, America entered World War II with the most balanced fleet in the world. There were now "carrier admirals" and "battleship admirals," but Mahan still seemed to hold; only the players had changed, or were about to, as a new naval generation battled within itself.

The submarine, however, was a different story. Mahan lived long enough to learn that three British armored cruisers had been sunk by a single U-boat at the beginning of World War I. Yet for him this particular technology (USS *Holland* had been commissioned in 1900, and his friend Teddy Roosevelt became the first president to dive in a submarine) was largely a defensive weapon.

Submarines might make an attempted blockade more difficult, but for Mahan they could be no more than commerce raiders, and he shunned commerce raiding as the strategy of last resort of the inferior naval power— the exact reverse of his theories. He could not imagine the submarine as the vanguard of a strategic offensive, nor could he, along with most naval officers for the next forty years, see how radically the little boats would alter the concept of "command of the seas." "In a world in which the fleet battleship was queen," said Mahan's leading biographer of the thought of his subject, "submarines were little more than interesting toys."[11]

In World War II the Germans and Americans proved what subs could do, underlining the lesson the former had begun during the previous war. The Japanese, on the other hand, completely misused their submarine arm, consigning most of their boats to coastal patrols, picket duty, resupply operations, and troop movements. The results, once the outer bastions of Japan's maritime defenses had been breached, led quickly to the potential starvation of the home islands.

Even given the American preponderance in industrial might, this was one of the greatest strategic miscalculations of the war. German submarines, used far more aggressively, numerously, and intelligently against Allied shipping, sank over 2500 merchant ships totaling over fourteen million tons. As in World War I, the U-boats came within a hair of driving the British to their knees. By contrast, Japanese subs sank only 171 vessels, less than one million tons of shipping.

Although the carrier stripped Mahanian theory of its beloved battleships, the flattop still allowed the decisive fleet engagement, even if the warriors were hundreds of miles apart. The submarine, however, stood

Mahan on his head. No longer, in 1945, did nonzealots know exactly what a "capital ship" *was*. Mahan could not be blamed for failing to predict nuclear power and its application to both surface and subsurface propulsion, nor could he have imagined his lineal descendants in the art of prophecy, who saw modern capital ships as only those with nuclear weapons aboard. But already, in the wake of Hiroshima and Nagasaki, the submarine had emerged as far more than a mere commerce raider. Mahan's "toys" now had the capacity to contend for "command of the sea."

☆

The ghost on the battlements was thus a paler shadow. Already in 1940 the historian Charles Beard, driven almost to distraction by the looming war on America's sea frontiers, had called Mahan a "veritable ignoramus." After 1945, amid the shattered debris of most of the world's navies, like would have difficulty meeting like; a battle fleet vying with its opposite number for command of the seas and the crown of "national greatness" would be difficult to imagine.

There was little argument, however, over the need for some kind of "big" navy. An isolationist American was now hard to find. The time when men like Beard could deride the "big navy boys" for their huge budget requests, diplomatic meddling, and political interference had gone, its passing marked by the shipboard pyres of Pearl Harbor.

"Will we need a navy to win?" earnestly asked a naval officer surveying the postwar years. His answer, unsurprisingly, was an unequivocal *yes:* "Even more than in the past, victory or defeat may come out of the sea." A navy remained necessary because now, more than ever, no industrial nation with complex needs for strategic raw materials was self-sufficient. The maintenance of national strength meant the necessity of international involvement— diplomacy, politics, and good deeds among nations aside. Seapower, although Mahan himself nowhere bothered to define the term, remained crucial to the life of the nation.[12]

In fairness, Mahan had never insisted that seapower was the sole, lasting essential in the life of nations. But extreme naval ideologues everywhere had quickly forgotten this caveat, and in 1945 American naval boosters rarely bothered to reason their way through their assertions about strong navies and the imperative need for them.

"Why should we maintain any navy after this war?" asked Secretary of the Navy James Forrestal three weeks after the Japanese surrender aboard *Missouri*. His answer: the United States, and its navy, should remain strong because "the outstanding lesson of the past quarter-century is that the means to wage war must be in the hands of those who hate war." At bottom, here was an uncritical recipe for a perpetual "big navy"—the Beardian nightmare come true.

Strength implied not only the ability but also the willingness to fight.

As Forrestal and other postwar naval backers well knew, this was an American seagoing legacy that long antedated Mahan, a deeply ingrained precept that was one of the foundation stones of the naval service. "The unvarying lesson," said Mahan, was that "only in offensive action can defensive security be found." The offensive in naval war, both strategic and tactical, was the function of the seagoing navy, the backbone of which was those vessels (his beloved battleships) "capable of taking and giving hard knocks."

There was nothing original here, either. As far back as John Paul Jones, who intended to take his ship in "harm's way," "true and lasting success in naval warfare" meant sinking or capturing ships, crippling or killing seamen. "This may be a rude—even a cruel—view," wrote Jones, "But I cannot help it." Jones, of course, was to his naval descendants the absolute paragon of the aggressive, fighting sailor. Generation after generation of naval officers was weaned on the *necessity* of both the strategic and tactical offensive. As an expert on naval tactics tersely pronounced: "The most important tactical maxim is—attack."

When James Lawrence was given command of *Chesapeake*, his secretary of the Navy wrote him, "It is impossible to conceive a naval service of a higher order in a national point of view than the destruction of the enemy's vessels. . . ." The urge, even the compulsion, to the offensive was far from a naval maxim only. The American Army, for example, enshrined the offensive as a "principle of war:" "Only offensive action achieves decisive results."[13]

As another secretary of the Navy affirmed in his annual report for 1905, "The business of the fleet is to fight." Such compulsion to action was a potent mixture of romanticism and hardheaded realism. The apotheosis was not an American at all, but Lord Nelson, from whom American naval supporters took at least as much as their British counterparts.

How could one improve on a man who, in his love of action, lost an eye and an arm while becoming a veritable mother (or father) lode of naval quotes: "If there is any work to do . . . *Nelson will be first*. Who can stop him?" Nelson had the great good luck to die in battle at the height of his greatest victory, Trafalgar ("No captain can do very wrong if he places his ship alongside that of an enemy"), and to British and Americans alike (Mahan burned incense to him) he became a naval god.

With Nelson, as with his numerous American admirers, the path to battle and victory was the way to the absolute summit. All must be risked for all to be gained. "We shall sail with the first breeze," Nelson wrote his mistress before one of his Mediterranean expeditions, "and be assured I will return either crowned with laurel, or coverd with cypress." He was serious about that—a subordinate made him a wooden coffin taken from part of the mainmast of *L'Orient*, the French flagship the admiral had conquered at the Battle of the Nile. Nelson kept the box braced upright against the bulkhead of his sea cabin, and inside its frame his remains lie today. Just before the Nile, he told his officers that within twenty-four hours "I shall have gained a peerage or Westminster Abbey." In the end he got the former, and as to the latter, he had to be satisfied with a crypt in Saint Paul's, next to Wellington.

Glorious the rewards of battle and victory! Perhaps only a spoilsport would note that Jones, who probably yelled his famous words to Captain Pearson of HMS *Serapis* near the beginning of their battle, had by its end a burning, sinking ship under him, with all but three of his cannons silenced. Had the British skipper not surrendered when he did, Jones would have been forced either into a dicey boarding operation or into fighting from underwater.

—Or would note that the rash and impetuous Lawrence *gave up the ship,* along with his life. The battle was over within fifteen minutes, because his ill-trained crew and unprepared officers were up against one of the Royal Navy's crack gunnery frigates, HMS *Shannon,* and one of its best captains, Philip Bowes Vere Broke.

—Or would note that, as Farragut's flagship *Hartford,* after the admiral's order (he did not say the words quite that way, but close enough), forged forward into Mobile Bay, her men could hear knocking noises against her copper bottom. These were caused by the cases of the Confederate "torpedoes" (actually mines) as they bumped and scraped past. Some of *Hartford*'s crew even heard the primers snapping. But none exploded. Farragut had hunted out, examined, and disarmed all the mines he could find before he ordered his ships into the bay.

Perhaps, then, luck was the handmaiden not of foolhardiness but of boldness mixed with prudence. No matter; naval engagements had an "absoluteness" to them, and men like Jones, Nelson, Lawrence, and Farragut staked everything they had on battle. The risk was the romance, and the results could shake the world.

Not every American agreed with this compulsion to the strategic and tactical offensive. George Washington, for one, did clearly see the need for a combat navy. ("Without a decisive naval force we can do nothing definitive," he wrote to Lafayette. "With it, every thing honorable and glorious.") But he could not perceive a naval strategy that extended overseas. Isolationists, anti-imperialists, and pacifists were also among those who, down the years, were only chilled by the blue-water tales of blood and thunder.[14]

—Not so Alfred Thayer Mahan. He blessed the romanticized idea of an aggressive, fighting navy with his scholarship. True, the further one got down into the weeds with him, the less useful he seemed. At the tactical level Mahan rapidly became a dinosaur. The primacy of the battleship, the advocacy of mass in the line of battle, the downplaying of the submarine and the airplane, and the central position of the decisive surface naval action all became easier targets as the years passed. As the dissertations, articles, and books continued to appear, any naval students worth their salt could cut their teeth on Mahan and prove him "mistaken" or "outmoded."

Mahan's notion that *the business of navies is to fight navies* was, however, something else again. Beyond this, his heritage lay in the larger issues. He had, after all, asked the big questions, dealing with what a navy was supposed to do and how that navy was supposed to accomplish its tasks. Not everyone agreed with his answers, not even in his own time.

But these questions were perennials, overshadowing all else concerning naval policy. They were always pertinent, even in the new naval world of 1945. And this was why, as American naval planners took up their task for the postwar years, the ghost still walked the battlements.

CHAPTER TWO

CRYSTAL BALL

☆

The United States Navy began to plan for its role in the postwar world at the height of its greatest conflict. In the middle of 1943—with the Allies past the end of the beginning, but with the beginning of the end nowhere in sight—Vice Admiral Frederick Horne, the vice chief of naval operations, asked for "suggestions concerning the size of the postwar Navy." Size, of course, directly influenced the missions a navy could perform, which in turn helped determine strategy, or at least should have.

Horne, like his boss, Admiral Ernest King, had won his aviator's wings relatively late in his career. He was a supremely efficient naval bureaucrat, in charge of a sprawling wartime empire of shipbuilding, logistics, and matériel. King, busy with a multifront war, gave him virtual carte blanche in running the chief's office. On top of this, with his likable personality, Horne managed to do much of the Navy's public relations work (King being particularly unsuited for this role).

Horne was also aggressive and ambitious, a "very smart, hard-working officer"—so much so that Ernie King more than once thought that his subordinate plotted behind his back with the civilian military secretaries to extend his power even more. (Horne, for his part, said that one of the things he could do on behalf of the Navy was keep King under control.) The vice chief's excursion into the future was thus in character.

Horne's call was answered by retired Admiral Claude Bloch, commander of the U.S. Fleet from 1937 to 1940 and now a member of the moribund General Board of the Navy, which had become an almost forgotten elephant's graveyard amid the upheaval of the war. Bloch responded with two very simple, sketchy proposals. First, for the maintenance of any respectably sized naval force at all, some form of compulsory military training would be needed. From this manpower pool, the Navy would induct from two hundred thousand to three hundred thousand men—less than 10 percent of its wartime force. Second, the Navy would have to maintain "peace and good order" in "certain areas" after the war, until a "world organization" could be created for the role.

Here was a beginning, but barely. Bloch envisioned a balanced fleet of carriers, battleships, cruisers, destroyers, submarines, and auxiliaries divided into task forces—three in the Atlantic and three in the Pacific. From these task forces would come smaller groups to patrol six "advance base areas:" the western Pacific, the central Pacific, the southern Pacific, the Caribbean, the southern Atlantic, and "European waters." Bloch's murky ideas were a combination of the classic Mahanian ideal of fleet concentration in home waters and the war-generated imperative of maintaining foreign stations.

As a "plan," Bloch's reply implied that the operational role of the postwar Navy would include almost worldwide naval patrol, with the possible exception of the Indian Ocean, then thought to be the exclusive preserve of the Royal Navy. The admiral stayed close to what he knew, which was ships and their capabilities. Tactically, he put the battleship on a par with the carrier, indicating his own love of the battlewagons and a lack of appreciation of the results of the Pacific carrier battles.

As strategy, however, Bloch's thinking was null. Something more had to be done. King acted quickly when Horne bumped Bloch's memorandum up to him. On 26 August 1943 the Navy Department established a Special Planning Section in the Office of the Chief of Naval Operations under the direction of another retired admiral, Harry Yarnell. Whereas Bloch was a Blackshoe, having spent most of his career with the surface navy, Yarnell was a Brownshoe, an "airedale." He was a former commander of the Asiatic Fleet, a career-long advocate of the fleet carrier, and so considerate a flag officer that he customarily and courteously repaid the official calls of his junior officers.

Yarnell set to work guided by the traditional naval view that "the enemy of a navy was a navy;" he was concerned only with other naval powers. Like Bloch, he saw the postwar Navy positioned in stations around the world, poised for trouble to start. Unlike Bloch, however, Yarnell offered the glimmerings of a strategy. He estimated the postwar naval capabilities of seven nations, excluding Russia as being a land power only, and judged the naval threat offered by each, which was none.

But Yarnell too was myopic; although he (accurately) foresaw no naval enemy in the near future, he could not imagine any postwar trouble *at all* that would require the use of naval strength. Surprisingly, he slighted the potential strategic roles of both aircraft and submarines. He did not forecast the advent of either nuclear weapons or nuclear propulsion, which was not unusual, given the cloak of secrecy veiling the Manhattan Project. But when Yarnell's planning document was distributed, on 22 September 1943, his work contained no inkling of the postwar emergence of the Soviet Union as at least a partial superpower (Russia, said Yarnell the next year, would be anxious to disband its army after the war); no hint of the coming erosion of the American public's support for a large postwar standing military; and no sense of the divisive interservice conflicts to come.[1]

As in all its wars, the Navy had entered World War II on a catch-as-catch-can basis. The naval goliath that helped crush the Axis powers had been fashioned on the basis of one crash program after another to deal with the specific enemies and situations of the war. The construction of landing ships was only one of many examples. That this triumphant naval force, in its almost overnight wartime composition, was suitable to postwar circumstances did not, however, follow automatically. Whereas strategists like Ernie King wrestled with the pressing, day-to-day problems of winning the war, planners like Horne, Bloch, and Yarnell, disassociated from the events out on the oceans, tended to be bound by the tunnel vision of the past.

By March 1945, with the Japanese home islands coming under round-the-clock aerial assault, King at last had the time to give serious attention to the shape of the postwar world. He found that the intermediate planning steps following Horne, Bloch, and Yarnell had been incremental and limited. In a letter to Secretary of the Navy Forrestal, the chief of naval operations clarified some issues that had remained muted or unspoken in the work of his three admirals.

By now naval leaders knew that the Navy would be in for the political fight of its life in order to maintain a substantial force after the war. The congressional purse was closing, as was typical after every American conflict. Yet Ernie King was a stubborn man, and what he had, he did not want to give up.

Whereas even Horne, master of bureaucratic intrigue, had admitted that the Navy would have to do away with some ships, King wanted to hang on to *all* of them, either steaming or in reserve. "Basic Post-War Plan Number One" advertised almost four thousand ships kept in active status. Whereas Bloch had envisioned a personnel strength of three hundred thousand at most, King wanted a *minimum* of fifty thousand officers and five hundred thousand enlisted, with about 70 percent of these afloat—roughly quintuple the fleet's prewar size. Like Yarnell, King saw the postwar Navy scattered around the world, but major elements, in his thinking, would be kept concentrated.

The strategic emphasis for King, as throughout the war, lay in the Pacific (his phrases were "the western part of the North and South Atlantic Oceans" and "the entire Pacific Ocean"). Few naval officers wanted their ships anywhere near Europe. This was the traditional stamping ground of the Royal Navy. Forrestal, a lifelong anti-Communist who was already warning against the Red Menace, had won few converts in his own shop. King and his fellow naval officers were content to let the Army develop a Europe-centered strategy.

In Forrestal's shop, King tried as best he could to keep the peace among his brethren over the issue of capital ships, because, in addition to the size and geographic parameters of the Navy, strategy would be driven by what its best ships could do. King assumed that the traditional surface ships would continue in their primary roles. Keeping everything meant *keeping everything*. Already, however, the carrier aviators and the submariners, who felt their respective platforms had earned the right to dominate the postwar fleet, were restless.

At the end of the war, then, precisely when the Navy's postwar plans should have been firmed up, guiding the ship into calm waters after a stormy passage, no such smooth transition was taking place. The grasp of strategic mission was feeble, the way ahead hazy at best, all hands were not bending to the same oar, and, from within, the boat was rocking.

☆

The Navy's foggy picture of the postwar world was conditioned not only by the vagaries of international geopolitics but also by its own bureaucratic turf wars and internal dissension. "It is no exaggeration to say that the [Navy] department was virtually as ill-prepared for peace in August, 1945, as it had been for war in December, 1941."[2]

The Navy's problems began at the top. Although the service continued to have many, and influential, friends at court, the friendship of the court itself had been lost. The new president, Harry Truman, not only lacked the empathy for things naval that his predecessor had continuously displayed, but in many cases he was hostile to both naval ideas and personalities. There was no consonance in naval planning between the Navy Department and the Oval Office. Now that victory was at hand, more than a few members of Congress were becoming outspokenly critical of naval budget requests. Among many politicians there was a growing impatience with the Navy's continuing inattention to what, for people like Forrestal, was clearly the new "enemy"—Russia.

All this made difficult the achievement of a coherent national strategy blending policy and naval capacity. And there were the comrades-in-arms, the Army and the Army Air Force. The former was already pushing, even before the war ended, for a proposal to "unify" the armed services in the name of efficiency. King, and everyone else who wore the blue and gold, said in effect that this unity would come over their dead bodies; they were convinced that unification would reduce the fleet to some kind of seagoing bellhop service.

Worse yet were those vocal upstarts, the Army pilots, in practice already members of a separate service. They wanted "independence," and more; most were convinced that strategic bombing had won the war and was far more "cost-effective," and that the atomic bomb (of which they currently were the sole mailmen) made them the possessors of the keys to the strategic kingdom. Accordingly, they were preaching the obsolescence of navies and the additional heresy that naval aviation should become part of a separate air force.

The politics, the Communist menace, and the interservice rivalries had all been around before Pearl Harbor, if played in a far more diminuendo key. The Navy's problems, however, were further complicated by two new factors. Demobilization would prove to be far more chaotic than Horne, Bloch, Yarnell, or King could have dreamed in their worst nightmares. The process, taking place helter-skelter over a span of months, would have a material impact on the ability of the Navy to do much that was consonant with any planning at all.

And there was *the bomb*. Nuclear power was the great unknown, the X factor, in the postwar equation. For now, the planners only dimly realized its revolutionary implications in both propulsion and weapons systems. At war's end they knew atomic power was just around the corner, but the shapes this genie would assume were vague at best, and is strategic implications more blurry still. No one doubted that the X factor would eventually play naval roles; exactly what these might be, nobody knew.

The planners—not only Horne, Bloch, Yarnell, and King, but also the several groups and committees that embellished their work—were planning in a vacuum. As they painstakingly listed their assumptions about the post-war world, all wore naval blinders. Their plans had little or no information gleaned from contemporary intelligence, political leadership, or foreign governments.

The Navy realized that the United States had become not simply a great world power but *the* world power, with fleets roaming the most remote seas and military bases in the farthest reaches of the globe. Vice Admiral Forrest Sherman, testifying before the Senate Committee on Naval Affairs in February 1946, said the Navy, with the other services, had to be maintained in such strength so that the penalties involved in going to war with the United States would be "severe, obvious, and certain."

But the naval service, like its civilian masters, could not perceive that this power was to become the instrument of idealistic politics—not the old imperial politics of grab, get, and hold, but the philosophical commitment to the exportation of "freedom" and "democracy." The "moral purity" of prewar isolationism was about to give way to the "moral self-justification" of American interventionism on a global scale. A major instrument of this intervention, acting in a role completely unimagined by the planners, would be the United States Navy.

Geographically, the Navy wore blinders as well. Ernie King was not the only naval officer for whom the Pacific Ocean was the center of American destiny. Practically no interest in Europe enlightened emerging naval views of postwar strategy. There was nothing new here; ever since the creation of the American empire half a century before, the Atlantic and Europe had always taken a back seat to the Pacific and Asia as a major concern of naval planning, the product of the presumed dominance of the friendly Royal Navy in its "proper sphere."

Some civilians, led by Forrestal, held a wider vision, centered on a flexible fleet committed to the needs of the nascent United Nations. The men in Navy blue, however, looked west. Presumably the British would carry on, and all would be as before. "Basic Demobilization Plan Number Two" saw things this way, that "Great Britain will cooperate in maintaining peace in certain sea areas of the world."[3]

Though King might want to retain the entire fleet, even he quickly realized that there would have to be major reductions. In this light, most of the planners assumed a postwar atmosphere of business as usual, just as before the war. America intended to make no military alliances, so there seemed to be no need for any kind of combined strategic thought, of the type featured by the Combined Chiefs of Staff during the war. Forrestal's vision of naval assistance to the United Nations was as a helping hand, not as part of a unified international force.

Accordingly, the Navy, and the rest of the American military as well, not only failed in its postwar planning function; *the Navy produced little or no "strategy" at all.* King and his naval planners were only partly to blame. American foreign policy objectives were far from clear as the war drew to a close, and any coherent military strategy under those conditions was almost impossible to develop.

Still, naval parochialism—the time-honored penchant for seeing the world through a filter exclusively colored blue and gold—had produced a series of partially uninformed and poorly considered ideas on postwar naval roles. This was not to be the last time such misjudgments would occur.

☆

Ideas certainly were not wanting. Indeed, the professional literature in the next few years was crammed with uninvited proposals about what to do with the naval instrument, made more urgent by the feeling that the instrument itself was being blunted both from outside and inside the military.

The oceans had not lost their strategic importance, and most of these homegrown theorists, regardless of their level of expertise, argued that the shrinking world produced by modern technology made seapower more important than ever. "Every other support of U.S. national strategy is second to sea power."

Seapower, all agreed, had a huge and crucial role to play. "The United States will not completely fulfill its great part unless it seeks the well being of men everywhere in every way, mentally, physically, and spiritually," passionately wrote one naval officer. "It will not fulfill its destiny of greatness at all if its purposes and efforts are not backed by strength, firm, resolute, positive, and powerful."

A big order. Seapower was to help people strive for ideological salvation, American-style; to promote world trade ("in bringing economic hope we bring light"); and to "prevent aggression wherever we can." Four possibilities lay ahead, according to one academic commentator. The Navy could disarm unilaterally, drifting into the shoal waters of benign neglect—a customary American postwar practice. The fleet could be limited diplomatically, by multilateral agreements, on the model of the interwar Washington treaties. Or the Navy could be used as an instrument of narrow imperialist gain. Of these first three options, however, none seemed rational or wise in the emerging climate of postwar internationalism. Therefore, the United States needed to use its Navy "in the interests of a community of nations."[4]

There seemed to be no way of avoiding a Navy of a peacetime size "previously unknown and uncontemplated." If anything, the peacetime Navy should be "too large rather than too small." Readiness was mandated by bitter memories of the Munich sellout and everything that had followed. "The Junkers and the Black Dragon are expecting the 'soft' democracies to forget again."

The Navy currently "stands in a category by itself," observed a naval enlisted man. As a basis for peace, the fleet must remain as a "war force, ready for the supreme test of battle." The battle, and the overall struggle, need not be one of annihilation, according to an admiral, but escalation was always possible, and the United States must therefore be ready. The country would never again be given the luxury of time to prepare.

America must, in other words, "forever look to the sea for its defense." This notion did not imply a new age of American militarism. There need be no threat to civil liberties here, nor any domestic problems with industrial concentration. Indeed, maintaining the nation's seapower would constitute a comparatively small drain on the rich and complex American industrial economy. Although the United States was now the sole remaining "insular" power in the world, the seas no longer formed protective moats. "We are utterly dependent upon sea transport" for certain vital materials—among them chrome, manganese, cobalt, tungsten, bauxite, and copper—without which the American industrial economy would not run and the country's strategic defense would be fundamentally impaired.

These analysts were realists, and unlike the early naval planners—Horne, Bloch, and Yarnell—they had the advantage of writing while the immediate postwar world was taking shape. They knew there was no hope for any form of absolute security in the modern age. But they also knew that seapower enabled the United States to place its attacking forces thousands of miles closer to an enemy homeland than the enemy could do with his forces in 1945. Control of the intervening seas was a must.

In short, the American Navy needed to be more powerful than the navy of any other power or *any other combination of powers.* Forrestal, a practical man who had every reason to be practical in his conduct of the secretaryship, had to be far less sweeping. He asked only for a navy tough enough to "overpower the strongest single enemy nation."[5]

Without much thought about the international implications of their demands, those who wrote on the uses of a postwar navy accepted the overwhelming preponderance of American naval power not only as a given but also as a *necessity*. Part of the reason was the obvious usefulness and flexibility of such power. Also, naval power was a potential mode of consensus between the older isolationism, which might want military power but fear foreign entanglements implicit in sending an army overseas, and the newer internationalism, which could help friends abroad while still using the Navy unilaterally.

The Navy needed to be prepared for anything and everything. As a "global policeman," wrote one officer in 1948, the fleet was a "perfect antidote" to the so-called "situational wars" in the world's ports, harbors, and coastal areas. With the addition of the carrier arm, "the combination is matchless for exerting the influence of law, order, and authority simply by its presence and the multiplicity of its powers to act."

To a man, the commentators all believed their country to be a naturally peaceful one. "Our national character is far from warlike," wrote one. To a man they also believed, as another said, that "the armed services must assume that the United States will sometime be involved in another war, no matter how much they, with the rest of the nation, wish to avoid it."

None of these men was chained to the actual necessities of naval planning, and as a result their dream sheets were long and inclusive. The postwar Navy should be huge, powerful, and global. The fleet should be able to dominate the seas, right up to and beyond the coastline of any conceivable enemy, and should be flexible, adaptable to any given situation, and effective all along the scale from small-unit tactics to grand strategy.

And they were in agreement on one more thing: no one, at least within the Navy, wanted to give up the armada.

☆

Everyone also believed that the postwar Navy would be only as good as its technology. The commentators not only uniformly praised the technological gains of the war just concluded, but also insisted on more. "Gadget war," of course, was not for everyone (witness Switzerland, whose best defensive "gadgets" were the towering, implacable Alps), but the Navy had learned to *need* its technology as junkies needed their fix.

At the time, no one thought much about any relationship between technology and strategy. Forrestal himself defined the Navy's mission as "control of the sea by whatever weapons . . . necessary." Yet already, well before the introduction of nuclear weaponry in the fleet, naval theorists were beginning to perceive their technology not only in terms of implements of destruction but also as a force to *deter* conflict. The latter tied technology irrevocably to strategic thought, but which determined which remained moot.[6]

Thus, implicit in the reluctance to surrender the armada was the notion that the Navy was not only a war machine heavily dependent on an ever-improving technology but also, in the increasingly uncertain and dangerous postwar climate, the peacekeeper at the gate. The fleet could not be content only with responding to "situational wars;" by steadily patrolling its beat, wars might be prevented. As a naval commander confidently said, "This country is peculiarly fitted for the role of world policeman."

The gloved fist of the fleet would make American policies "respected," according to the *Chicago Daily News*. The newborn United Nations would require naval power as well, not only because its members were linked by the oceans but also because any application of "sanctions" by the Security Council might well rest on maritime enterprises such as naval demonstrations or blockades. A few dreamers even envisioned elements of American naval power in some kind of ongoing international organization—a sort of multinational fleet—but the vast majority of naval theorists simply assumed that America's Navy was the nation's alone, its technology was national as well, and the country should use both as its leaders saw fit.

Forrestal argued that regardless of what weapons were developed, a strong Navy was still necessary. Practically all naval thinkers agreed. "Attacks upon us or attacks by us must cross on, over or under the sea," noted one. Even the looming shadow of the bomb could be taken in stride, for (most felt) the weapon was still just a bomb, still (for the time being) needed aircraft for its delivery, and (for the time being) was an American monopoly. Seapower was the imperative. Those who failed to heed the elements of seapower (read Germany and Japan) were doomed to defeat in war.

Yet even as the secretary of the Navy and his fellow advocates spoke of the enduring "lessons" of seapower, technology was beginning to drive strategic concepts, rather than vice versa. (Technology was not driving *strategy*—of the latter, as yet, there was little or none).

The prime example was that of the new saltwater queen, the aircraft carrier. Flattops were now proven quantities, and they were becoming, in their task force arrays, the new focus of postwar naval power. Planners were looking foremost at what these task forces *could do* and only secondarily at what *should be done with them*. Naval aviators were already claiming a "strategic" role for their aircraft and were lobbying for the introduction of the atomic bomb to the fleet. Aviation admirals were moving to the forefront; since 1942, 70 percent of those promoted to flag rank had been aviators, and many politicians were listening to them. Postwar Congresses, apparently, would look with favor only on those military forces that could deliver the knockout punch.[7]

Left in the lurch were other technologies and other strategic approaches. For example, the naval and Marine Corps amphibious assault mission was in danger of being completely cut adrift, and a future commandant of the Corps was forced to remind strategists of the importance of advanced bases, and of a force to take and hold onto them, even in the atomic age. "Ability to wage amphibious warfare must constitute an integral part of naval power," he observed. Air power alone was "so passive in the strategic sense as to be unacceptable as doctrine."

Indeed, ground forces of all kinds were hypersensitive to charges that modern weaponry had rendered them obsolescent. "A country cannot very well be occupied by bombs or battleships," groused one crusty ground veteran of the Italian campaign. "The final deciding factor in winning wars is the man with a weapon in his hand who overcomes the enemy and wrests his soil from him."

Then there were the submariners. None less than Admiral Spruance, himself a Blackshoe with experience commanding carrier task forces and fleets, was reported to have stated flatly that "the submarine beat Japan." The men who wore the dolphins took this as scripture. Submariners were a highly motivated, insular, and intensely clubby group—only seven Reserve officers received combat commands throughout the war—and they sought to move to the forefront as well.

Submariners, above all other naval officers, also saw themselves as the major claimants on the newest technological marvel, nuclear energy. To some, the bomb made surface ships simply sitting ducks, so many vulnerable targets. Only the submarine would be safe, running quietly underneath the waves on her new nuclear reactors. She would keep to the seas indefinitely, the "capital ship" of the atomic age.

The "strategic picture" for the postwar Navy, officially none too clear, was from the outside a crazy quilt of many voices, each pushing a special interest or technology. Aviators led the pack in this process, with submariners right behind. Marines and the poor dog soldiers ran a distant third and fourth. In addition, over everyone who offered opinions about the future roles of the Navy hung the specter of the possibility that technology, in whatever shape, would be all the more necessary because the sheer *size* of the armada was itself impermanent.

In the wake of the Japanese surrender, the Navy Department had proposed a peacetime establishment of 1079 ships and 667,000 men, figures that were seized on by Navy opponents and budget-conscious politicians, who proceeded to compare them unfavorably with the relatively minuscule prewar numbers. Forrestal estimated the initial cost of this peacetime Navy at $5 billion a year, an amount guaranteed to drive critics into a frenzy. "We . . . are being asked to support a naval establishment five times as great as we had when the world was shaking with the martial tread of dynamic, powerful, self-proclaimed enemies of the democracies," wrote one. "We are being asked to skim the cream off our standard of living. . . ."

Of course, said the critics, the Navy had done its job in spectacularly successful fashion during the war. In fact, the fleet had done *too well:* "The admirals worked themselves out of a job," said one observer. Already the powerful American battle fleets of 1945 seemed technologically obsolete.

Security might not lie in the creation of new forces of destruction at all, but rather in international "trust and brotherhood."[8]

And if technology alone could not provide that security, what then of a "strategy" of a big Navy increasingly dependent on technology?

☆

The postwar planners were working in a new naval world. Before, there had always been navies *against which to plan:* "the business of navies is to fight other navies." Out of such presumptions had come naval building races, naval disarmament conferences, and what Teddy Roosevelt had called a "spite navy"—"a navy built not to meet our own needs, but to spite someone else."

Now, the United States Navy reigned supreme. Before the war there had been a multiplicity of naval powers, with Britain, the United States, and Japan ranked at the top. Germany, Italy, France, and the Netherlands were in the second rank, with the Soviet Union trailing far behind. (Stalin probably killed more of his admirals than he sent to sea; he liquidated three of his four fleet commanders in his prewar purges.)

Now, the German *Kriegsmarine* was a memory, its surface ships paid off as early as 1943 in a desperate attempt to win the war with the submarine. Of 1170 U-boats sent forth, 968 never returned from patrol; eight of ten German submariners drowned in the Atlantic depths. All of Germany's remaining ships not scuttled at the end of the war were either distributed among the Allied navies or, in the case of the surviving U-boats, deliberately sunk in the Atlantic by the Royal Navy (Operation DEADLIGHT). Shattered Germany was left with a handful of tiny craft suitable at best for minesweeping.

Now, the well-engineered but poorly led Italian navy, which was to have been the overseer of Mussolini's *Mare Nostrum,* lay in ruins. In the words of one of its officers, it had been a "middleweight" against the British "heavyweight" in the Mediterranean. Addled *Supermarina* policy aside, the Italians had lost 269,000 tons of combat shipping by the time they switched sides in September 1943. Included were 112 surface ships and 65 submarines; almost 15 percent of their officers and men were killed. At the end the Italian navy was gutted, no longer even a regional power.[9]

Now, the navy of the third member of the Axis was simply obliterated. "This is, of course, the last time that the German and Japanese Navies are likely to be recorded in *Fighting Ships,*" the editors of *Jane's* solemnly declared in 1945. Outbuilt and overmatched after Midway, the Imperial Japanese Navy ultimately committed suicide. In the final analysis, its strategic errors notwithstanding, this navy could not bear the burdens of oceanic empire, especially one of such great expanse acquired so suddenly. By the end, the Japanese had lost eleven of fourteen battleships, twenty-one of twenty-five carriers, and thirty-nine of forty-four cruisers. In all the vast expanses of the Pacific, the United States Navy was sovereign.

France, like its enemy Italy, the possessor of a strong prewar regional navy, had scuttled most of its fleet at Toulon in 1942, following Hitler's order for the occupation of Vichy, France. What remained in 1945 was potentially powerful but mostly obsolete, including *Bearn*, the only French carrier. Out of an enormous prewar fleet, fourth in the world in 1939, only three light cruisers and three destroyers remained in good condition. Two hundred forty-nine warships had been lost, over eight thousand sailors with them. The French had big plans—they dreamed of three two-carrier task forces in the Mediterranean, Atlantic, and the colonies—but for the moment they had little more than ambition.

The residue of empire was also a problem for the Dutch. Their power in the East Indies had been erased in the Battle of the Java Sea in 1942. The Netherlands still belonged irrevocably to the sea, but the country could no longer produce a navy capable of defending colonies on the other side of the world. Indeed, its fleet was little more than a collection of a few destroyers and submarines. Like the French, the Dutch had plans for a postwar navy, but one that would be drastically scaled down, a "World War II US fleet in miniature."[10]

This left what was, in many ways the saddest story of all.

> . . . Maudlin stupid Mr Chips
> Owns several heavy battleships,

the detached expatriate poet W.H. Auden had written in 1940. Mr. Chips still owned his battleships, but the cost of maintaining them was helping to empty his already threadbare pocketbook.

The image of *Pax Britannica*, the century-long period of British naval predominance following Trafalgar, remained potent enough that the Admiralty could yet as of 1945 contemplate maintaining a massive global fleet. But economic reality dictated otherwise, and the Royal Navy was no longer the trump card British leaders had customarily played: "Britain alone cannot contain Europe in arms by virtue of its naval power."

Even without sensing the mighty tremors of anticolonialism that, within two decades, would completely sunder its empire, Britain quickly had to concede that the Royal Navy, for the first time in its history, could no longer protect British trade routes, and for the most basic of reasons: its people could no longer afford the price. The new Labour government was estimating a postwar navy of only one hundred thousand men.

Once, the fledgling American Navy had relied on Britain to police the sea-lanes of the world. In this sense the famous Monroe Doctrine, which was of no international standing whatsoever, had relied on British ships. Now the situation was reversed, and the irony was not lost on any British seaman. Americans were willing enough to extend the hand of naval friend-ship, even, as things turned out, to the point of peacetime alliance, but there was no doubt at all who was now the senior partner: the Union Jack no longer flew dominantly.

Initial American planning had assumed that the British would be able to return to their global naval role following the war, leaving to the Americans the Western Hemisphere and the Pacific. But within months of war's end the British were in dire economic straits at home and in the deepest political difficulty in many parts of the Empire, such as India and Malaya. If there was to be a global postwar fleet, its ships would not belong to the Royal Navy.

The relative naval decline of the British, which had antedated World War II, did not overly disturb professional Anglophobes, of whom there were many in the American naval establishment. Ernie King himself was not especially keen on the Royal Navy's butting in where its flag was not wanted, and in fact Sir Bruce Fraser's ships were permitted to operate in the Pacific during the final months of the war only after protracted nego-tiations. King stubbornly resisted British participation in what he considered to be an "American theater." "[King] seemed to regard [Pacific] opera-tions . . . as almost his own private war," said George Marshall. American naval supporters were eager for global hegemony, and most were not overly sorry to see the British naval decline not only continue but also accelerate.[11]

They should have been, because there was one more player. The words "Russia" and "navy" had historically been an unmatched pair. Despite the best efforts of Peter the Great and occasional sporadic attempts by suc-ceeding autocrats to create true blue-water fleets, the Russians had remained the classic example of a land power, their mass peasant armies and their practically infinite geography their best defenses. Their navy had suffered a terrific humiliation from the Japanese in 1905, and with the revolution and the Kronstadt Mutiny, the fleet came to be seen as politically unreliable as well.

Some Americans saw only politics here. If a country was Communist, if its feet were the least bit webbed, then its navy must *de facto* be aggressive, offensive, and a threat. The early warning signs seemed to be there in 1945, and alarmists ticked them off. Were we aware that eleven naval colleges existed in the USSR? that Soviet officials had expressed the hope that the Red Navy would soon be equal to those of the Western powers? that new ship designs were coming out of the yards in Leningrad? When Admiral Raymond Spruance took up his postwar duties as president of the Naval War College, he found the senior courses in naval strategy still centered on Japan. He immediately reoriented the entire syllabus toward Russia, a change that proved permanent.

All this was consonant with the historic *need* of the United States Navy for a suitable enemy against which to plan. But the postwar Soviet Union was in no position to deploy a global, or even a regional, navy. Its wartime losses, both in human casualties and in matériel, had been immense, on a scale little appreciated in the West. Its navy, as always, had acted as a coastal adjunct to land operations. What oceangoing ships the Soviets had were aging and technologically light-years behind those of the Western navies. Soviet strategy, conditioned by centuries of invasions from beyond Russian borders, remained defensive and almost entirely land-oriented. Leslie Groves, military head of the Manhattan Project and no friend of communism, admitted that "the historical record does not show a single instance when a move by Russia has been detrimental to the vital interests of our country."

In 1945 the Russians had the largest land army on earth. Anti-Communists saw this "horde" as the major menace, with Western Europe its goal. Even ardent American naval backers had trouble imagining the Soviet navy challenging the United States on blue water. True, Stalin had built the world's largest submarine fleet at the time of the German invasion in 1941, but his boats had not prevented the Wehrmacht from ransacking the western third of Russia. True, the Soviet dictator had plans for a substantial postwar navy, but in design this force was coastal and submarine-centered, which meant a strategy of commerce-raiding. This was not a navy to contest the high seas with anybody.

The Bear had not learned to swim—not yet.

☆

The American Navy, then, reigned supreme on the oceans of the world in 1945, but its crystal ball was clouded. The relative importance that the naval service gave the planning function could be measured by the men who initiated its postwar posture: a deskbound bureaucrat with irons in every fire and two superannuated admirals. Horne, Bloch, and Yarnell were all good naval officers, among the best in their profession, but they had no immediate experience of the new naval world taking shape during the war.

The planners tended to assume the status quo, with continuing American predominance ensured by technological fine-tuning. They, like their boss, Ernie King, did not see the effect that crumbling world empires and brushfire wars of national liberation would have on naval policy. Although the Axis naval menace had obviously been destroyed, the serious weaknesses of the Allied navies, relating mostly to their weakened or shattered economies, remained for the moment hidden.

For at least four years, from 1943 to 1947, the United States Navy tried fruitlessly to plan for a clearly defined role in the postwar world. The Navy knew itself to be powerful, dominant, and capable of wreaking terminal harm on any navy foolish enough to venture out against its ships and men.

But no such navy existed. "It is not easy to make a realistic estimate of what we will have to fight against in the next war," conceded one of King's planners. "However, we will do the best we can." The British, French, and Dutch were friends, albeit badly weakened ones; the Soviets, handcuffed by geography and their history, hewed to their traditional land-centered defensive strategy; the Italians were a cipher; and the *Kriegsmarine* and the Imperial Japanese Navy were with Davy Jones. All this made no difference; as Admiral Richard Edwards, one of King's planning team, insisted, the United States *must* have a balanced navy, including capital ships, whether or not any other power had capital ships or, indeed, any navy at all.

Not until 1949 would a leading American naval officer state the obvious: the naval world had changed, dramatically and irrevocably. Testifying before Congress, the commander in chief, Pacific, Admiral Arthur Radford (destined to relieve General Omar Bradley as chairman of the Joint Chiefs of Staff), urged that "the Navy today must be built not to meet an enemy navy. . . ."[12]

But the Navy *was* so built, with carrier task forces its fulcrum, and its planning problems were thereby multiplied. Part of these problems was but a reflection of American foreign policy in these years, which was crystallizing into anticommunism. (Anticommunism was difficult to give a naval dimension to, per se). Yet as a bipolar world emerged, centered on the Soviet Union and the United States, naval planners keyed their globalism and their instinctive strategic aggressiveness on the Russian "menace." The new "enemy," regardless of his naval capacity, would thus have an input into naval "plans."

So the American Navy, strong and for the moment omnipotent, positioned itself for the future. Its vision was narrow, constricted by its wartime experience. Of more immediate importance, its first postwar battles would be fought not on the high seas but in committees, congressional hearings, and cloakrooms. And these battles would be fought as the armada—the global policeman, the international arbiter—began, despite the best efforts of its leaders, to dissolve.

CHAPTER THREE

TOPSIDE I

———————— ☆ ————————

F ranklin Delano Roosevelt was one of the best friends the United States Navy ever had. Not that he was a tub-thumping naval booster in the tradition of his distant cousin Theodore; FDR was far too shrewd a politician for that. But his love of ships and the sea was ingrained, the heritage of a privileged youth spent sailing the rough waters off the Maine coast and straining at the oars on his grandfather's whaleboats.

Billy Mitchell, who *was* a tub-thumper himself on the subject of air power, once visited FDR in the White House and, as they talked, examined the presidential desk closely. "I have never seen a desk so cluttered with miniature ships and little things taken out of ships," he remembered. "Everything on the desk bore some relation to a ship." Mitchell got the message. "It depressed me," he sourly concluded.

He was far from alone in his mood. Many others were depressed, particularly those who tried to convince FDR that the world's primary colors were *not* blue and gold. But everything about the sea seemed to unleash his natural exuberance; at fifteen he had been given a copy of Mahan's *Influence of Seapower upon History*, and he had rapidly made the book dog-eared. When Woodrow Wilson's secretary of the Navy, the North Carolina newspaperman Josephus Daniels, asked FDR if he would like to come aboard as his assistant, Roosevelt did not hesitate. "How would I like it? How would I *like* it? I'd rather have that place than any other position in public life!"

This was not entirely romance and altruism, to be sure; after all, the assistant secretary's job had been cousin Theodore's springboard to the governorship in Albany and the White House. Still, FDR's love of the naval service began early and manifested itself in many ways, the best-known being the boat cloak in which he draped himself during the war years. As president he loved to speak to midshipmen at the Naval Academy, hopped rides aboard American warships whenever he could, and did his utmost to squeeze funds from Congress during the Depression years for a Navy he knew would have to get stronger, and fast. He even "fancied himself as some kind of naval strategist," said one admiral, who conceded that FDR did, eventually, become "a very well educated amateur."[1]

Roosevelt could not resist meddling. At one time or another he proposed the construction of "flying deck" cruisers, wooden antisubmarine patrol craft, and a flotilla of new ships designed in his sleep. He badgered subordinates about the location of channel buoys in the entrances to naval bases, reserved to himself the final approval of flag officer assignments, and directed the Navy Band to reduce the frills and flourishes in the playing of the national anthem. The Navy was part of him. In 1940 he told naval aviator Jack Towers that there was nothing to criticize about naval aviation. At the same time he virtually banned H. H. ("Hap") Arnold, head of the Army Air Corps, from the White House. At one wartime conference George Marshall, only half-jokingly, was forced to ask Roosevelt to "stop speaking of the Army as 'they' and the Navy as 'us.'"

To one and all he liked to reminisce about "when I was in the Navy," saying that he had known King, Nimitz, and Halsey when they were "on their way up." Indeed, as assistant secretary he offered to guide the destroyer *Flusser* between his summer island retreat at Campobello, New Brunswick, and the mainland. *Flusser*'s skipper, Lieutenant Halsey, had with great reluctance given FDR the conn, only to discover that the young patrician knew what he was doing when he was shiphandling.

Along the way Roosevelt made most senior naval officers, despite their innate conservatism, his ardent supporters. Kemp Tolley, then a junior officer, was certainly not one of these, but he conceded that FDR had the honeyed tongue when things came round to the Navy: "He could charm the birds out of the trees if he wanted to." FDR's wartime commander of submarines in the Pacific was typical of his naval generation. "The Navy will always have a great respect and reverence for Franklin D. Roosevelt, who pulled us out of the slough of despond in the early 30's, and got us into a condition of approximate readiness for World War II," declared Vice Admiral Charles Lockwood. "His farsightedness, in authorizing building programs and obtaining bases, undoubtedly shortened the war by many months and saved thousands of American lives."

Always, he wanted more Navy. He was, nonetheless, far from a rubber stamp for the brass. "The Admirals are really something to cope with— and I should know," he confided to one civilian adviser. "To change anything in the N-a-a-vy is like punching a feather bed. You punch it with your right hand and you punch it with your left until you are finally exhausted, and then you find the damn bed just as it was before you started punching."

But now he was gone, this consummate politician, a victim of war as surely as a combat soldier or sailor—felled by a cerebral hemorrhage at his Warm Springs vacation home on 12 April 1945. To the men hearing the news aboard the battleship *North Carolina*, "it was like losing a father." For the Navy his passing was a double shock; the fleet lost not only the commander in chief but also a friend.

☆

In his place in the Oval Office sat Harry Truman, former Army captain on the fields of France in 1918 and later colonel, 379th Field Artillery Regiment, Missouri National Guard. Not that his experience in World War I made Truman pro-Army or anti-Navy. In fact, he was intensely suspicious of authority, particularly the kind that wore stars. His distrust stemmed in part from the native parochialism of the small-town Missouri business community of which he had once been a member, and in part from a brand of midwestern populism that tended to reject the prestige of the uniform in favor of scrutinizing the man inside. "He had no respect for the services," asserted Admiral Charles Duncan. "In fact, he had a psychological bias against the regular services, officers in particular." This was an overstatement, but not by much.[2]

When Truman first came to the Senate in 1935, he was viewed as little more than a spear carrier for the corrupt Kansas City machine of Tom Pendergast. But he carved an independent path for himself, sturdily supported the New Deal, won the respect of colleagues on both sides of the aisle, and came to Roosevelt's attention when he chaired a special wartime watchdog committee overseeing military expenditures. The senator from Missouri proved a tireless worker, meticulous in his dealings with both business and the military, but he was appalled by the inevitable profiteering, waste, and inefficiency that accompanied the domestic industrial upheaval of the war.

Suddenly elevated to the vice presidency in January 1945, Truman was the outsider personified during FDR's last months. Not only did he not know where the bodies were buried (his ignorance of the Manhattan Project was only the most conspicuous example), he did not know the way to the cemetery. He had barely begun to get his feet on the ground when FDR died. Other than his work with the watchdog committee, which had been scrupulously fair, the Navy knew little about him.

But the signs were ominous. Harry Vaughan, a Truman crony from Missouri National Guard days, the new president's "military aide," and a man whose political views were characterized as "American Legion Baroque," was on record as saying that "during the Roosevelt Administration the White House was a Navy wardroom; we're going to fix all that." His master, in turn, put out the word via his staff that he did not want any Naval Academy officers on the presidential yacht.

Truman tended to view all military officers, and especially Navy officers, as little more than politicians in uniform, an attitude gained from his experience on Capitol Hill, where all he saw of the Navy was its admirals trying to wheedle more money out of Congress. He was convinced that "political cliques" ran both services; "this seems to be a fixation with him," observed James Forrestal. To this end, the president believed that all men who were to become officers should spend at least a year in the ranks before commissioning—another product of his populist roots. Matters were not helped when the presidential nephew, John, griped about the chow aboard *Missouri*. The president fired off a note to the Navy Department, a new supply commander was duly assigned (the old one failed to make captain), and the crew ate like lords—while the officers smoldered.[3]

Generals and admirals, Truman said, were "just like horses with blinders on. They can't see beyond the ends of their noses," primarily due to their narrow education at West Point and Annapolis. This attitude was only confirmed when his beloved only child, Margaret, was invited to swing the champagne bottle at *Missouri*'s christening. When she smashed her magnum against the bow, Mighty Mo refused to slide down the ways; as a result, Margaret and the admiral escorting her got a champagne bath. Two years later, as president, Truman wrote:

> Every admiral in nine hundred miles will want to be seen with the President. But they are going to be disappointed. I'll never forget what the admirals did to me and my sweet daughter at the launching of the *Missouri*.

"The navy as always," Truman believed, "is the greatest of propaganda machines." The admirals had attempted, along with the generals, to take over the economy during the war; he had seen them try their bureaucratic hustling before his committee, and he had not liked what he saw. Only William Leahy, the five-star naval adviser he had inherited from FDR, gained his trust, and even with Leahy he could not resist an occasional barb. "You know how those admirals are," he said when announcing a Florida fishing expedition with Leahy. "They get so they can't do anything without an aide, even bait a hook."

Harry Truman was far from doctrinaire. He could be argued with, persuaded, convinced. And he had the human touch. He liked to vacation at Key West. He chose the tacky naval base because the locale was secluded, he could stroll through the town wearing loud sport shirts, and its restaurants specialized in stone crab and key lime pie. He did not seem to mind the community's run-down look or its string of sleazy sailor bars, which occasionally spewed drunken brawlers into the streets.

And he could get along well with individual naval officers. Visiting *Missouri* on her homecoming to New York City, he was disappointed to learn that his rather obstreperous nephew had talked his way into an early discharge in Norfolk. He went on to inspect the crew and chatted with the men from his home state, specially grouped for his benefit, then clomped up to Sunshine Murray's cabin, where he had already arranged for an aide to deposit two bottles of bourbon in the skipper's safe. As the forewarned Murray dutifully made for the safe upon his leader's appearance, Truman doffed his hat and solemnly stated, "By virtue of the fact that I'm President of the United States and, as such, commander in chief of the Navy, I hereby declare that the captain's cabin of the USS *Missouri* is wet for one hour. . . . Where did you hide that whiskey?"

Woefully unprepared for the task of guiding America into the postwar years, Truman was nevertheless pragmatic and willing to learn. Still, his lack of contact with the working Navy and his inherent aversion to gold braid meant that a new day had dawned in the formerly rosy relations between the Navy Department and the White House. In the short term this meant that Truman and his secretary of the Navy were on a collision course.

☆

"Secrtary Knox died at 1.08 pm," Admiral Harry Yarnell informed his diary on 28 April 1944. "He was a fine man and a good Secretary with a great love for the Navy." Indeed; the old Bull Mooser had come into the Cabinet in July 1940 as part of FDR's attempt to build political bipartisanship on the road to war. Like his president he had worked himself to death in the war effort. A strong but adaptive leader, he had often given his brilliant subordinates their heads and then backed them to the hilt, along the way achieving the impossible: winning the respect and admiration of Ernie King.

Knox had been a tireless ambassador for the Navy Department, constantly visiting naval bases and ships around the world. He was a genius at public relations and an ardent proponent of the "management survey," ceaselessly trying to do things better. His leitmotiv had been cooperation and teamwork in the service of the war effort. "He understood the Navy, not only its problems, its achievements and its personnel, but its shortcomings," declared his chief of naval operations on the day of Knox's death. "He leaves us, secure in the knowledge that his energy and farsighted vision have been responsible, in great measure, [for the fact] that we are so far advanced on the road to victory."

Not all secretaries had possessed the skills and dedication of Frank Knox. There had been many low points, usually provided by incompetent political hacks such as Ulysses Grant's first selection, Adolph Borie, a white-whiskered Philadelphia merchant who knew nothing whatsoever about the Navy. Rutherford Hayes had appointed Richard Thompson of Indiana, whose only claim to fame was his nickname: "the Ancient Mariner of the Wabash." Men of this stamp would obviously not do in the midst of world war.

In Knox's stead FDR nominated his Dutchess County neighbor, James Vincent Forrestal. Born in 1892 in what was then Matteawan, New York, twenty miles south of the Roosevelt fief of Hyde Park, Forrestal was the youngest of the three sons of an Irish emigrant who had begun as a carpenter and gone on to establish a profitable business in contracting and construction. "Vince" Forrestal may have gained his drive and ambition from his father;

a compulsive workaholic and overachiever from an early age, he graduated from high school at sixteen. He then puttered around with local journalism for three years (his friends always felt his real calling was as a newspaperman), attended Dartmouth for a year, and ended up at Princeton, where he made his closest friend, the chairman of the *Daily Princetonian*, Ferdinand Eberstadt.

At Princeton, where he patiently bore the nickname of "Runt," Forrestal characteristically worked hard, established a reputation for generosity, ran with the right crowd and made the right fraternities, and himself became chairman of the *Princetonian*. His mates in the class of 1915 voted him "most likely to succeed" by a huge margin. But Runt was in a hurry and did not wait to graduate; although naturally shy, he was nonetheless enormously aggressive and ambitious, hypereager to make his way in the world. In 1916 he entered the prestigious banking house of William A. Read and Company (soon to become Dillon, Read and Company).

Forrestal was also patriotic. At the outbreak of war in 1917, he enlisted as a naval seaman and quickly transferred to the fledgling field of naval aviation. As a signal indicator of the lowly status of this branch of the service, he was dispatched to Canada to train with the Royal Flying Corps. He was given *three hours* of instruction, which included one (unscheduled) crash, and was designated Naval Aviator No. 154, returning proudly to the United States to receive his ensign's commission.

But he was not to fly against the Heinies. Instead, he spent the war months working for Admiral Benson in the chief of naval operations shop in Washington. He emerged at war's end as Lieutenant Junior Grade Forrestal and returned to the bond department at Dillon, Read.

There, in the interwar years, his career took off. He peddled bonds in the twenties boomtime; by 1923 he was a partner, by 1926 a vice president. He married a staffer at *Vogue* and, despite a cold and distant marriage, fathered two sons. His generosity (usually anonymous), fairness, charm, and sense of humor were all admired, as was his undoubted success. He read eclectically, went to the right social functions, and kept himself in physical trim. He had boxed at Princeton, but his most noticeable physical feature, a smashed-in pug nose, resulted from a sparring match in the mid-thirties at the Racquet Club.

In 1938, at the still-youthful age of forty-six, Forrestal succeeded Clarence Dillon as head of Dillon, Read. His intense ambition and fierce energy had brought him a long way in a short time. But in two years he resigned, driven now in a different direction, that of service to his country.

Forrestal, although he came from a Democratic background typical of most Irish-American families, was essentially nonpolitical. While his working environment was part of the "let's go down to the Trans-Lux and hiss Roosevelt" phenomenon, he himself had a liberal view of the Securities and

Exchange Commission and other financial reforms that FDR had foisted on Wall Street. Roosevelt knew about him and wanted him in the administration.

The day Frank Knox's appointment was announced, Congress created the post of under secretary of the Navy. Forrestal was duly nominated, and on 22 August 1940 he took over the new position as Knox's right-hand man on the civilian side. There were no precedents to guide him, other than the salty traditions of the service for which he had never lost his early affection. The intense flux of the war years further gave an open sesame to a man of his drive and energy. "His hobby was work," remembered an aide. "He was happiest when he was working, and he had no relaxation . . . no outlet . . . no way of releasing the tensions that he had."[4]

He seized his opportunity. Although no single individual could be credited with building the wartime Navy, Forrestal, more than anyone else, bought that Navy. He oversaw the vast inflation in ships and personnel, becoming the crucial human link between military demand and civilian production. He learned as he went, baking new pies and sticking his fingers in all of them, creating new legalities, new contractual arrangements, new forms of statistical management. Far from an orderly administrator, he nevertheless became the overseer of naval-related industrial production, the chief of procurement, an inventory manager, a programmer, and—necessarily— a prophet. Like Knox, he showed a flair for public relations.

Amid all the bureaucratic turmoil he, also like Knox, toured the world: London, to deal with Lend-Lease; the southwest Pacific, in the wake of Guadalcanal; Kwajalein, where he watched Spruance's battlewagons give the giant atoll the "Spruance haircut." In short, he made himself the only possible successor to Frank Knox; the widely respected pundit Arthur Krock wrote that his appointment was "the best thing for the Navy, for the war, and for the country." Forrestal was sworn in as secretary of the Navy on 19 May 1944—a well-prepared, confident, and altogether exceptional public servant (although he never admitted, then or later, that he was anything but an investment banker) with the total confidence of the president of the United States.

His new job did not change him one whit. At Iwo Jima he became the first secretary of the Navy to land under fire, at a time when control of that volcanic ash heap was still in doubt. While there, and witnessing the famous second unfurling of the Stars and Stripes atop Mount Suribachi, he remarked to crusty Marine General Holland ("Howlin' Mad") Smith, "Holland, the raising of that flag . . . means a Marine Corps for the next five hundred years"—a statement that Forrestal, and the Marines, would soon have occasion to ponder.

Forrestal quickly sensed the changing breezes that were blowing in with the administration. As a hardheaded businessman, he had no truck with pie-in-the-sky New Dealers, whom he called "intellectual muddlers," and he wanted nothing to do with the vestigial remnant that remained as Truman tried to get his "Fair Deal" off the ground. For his part Truman could get exasperated with his secretary of the Navy while conceding his undoubted managerial skills. "Jim wants to hedge—he always does," the president noted. "He's constantly sending me alibi memos, which I return with directions and the facts."

As an avowed naval supporter and internationalist, Forrestal rapidly tried to throw up dikes against the wave of economy and cost cutting coming from White House and Capitol Hill alike. Like most of his business associates he wore his anticommunism like a suit of armor, realizing sooner than his president and most members of Congress that Soviet and Red Chinese advances mandated the maintenance of a strong Navy and Marine Corps. He called for a study of Soviet philosophy, arguing that "we also laughed at Hitler."

Forrestal and King did not get along; the admiral was quick to make up his mind and would be infuriated when the secretary would "on-the-other-hand" the issues. Still, the two men shared the grim view that the world, far from being liberated from the sufferings of global strife, was entering a period of extreme tension, galvanized by ideological differences and Communist aggrandizement. Therefore, the Navy needed to backstop the United Nations; to keep itself superior to what, in Forrestal's mind, was the new "threat"—the Soviet fleet; to protect American interests abroad while carrying on its basic role of preventing an attack on the United States; and to support the other services in joint operations. When he was asked where America's Navy would float, Forrestal rejoined, "Wherever there is a sea."

Here was a view with wide support within the Navy. The new secretary had justly earned the respect and loyalty of the uniforms under him. Despite his own well-developed bureaucratic skills, he believed that neat organizational charts and precise wiring diagrams did not mean very much; only the men did. As one of his admirals noted in agreement: "Men and personalities are 90% of any organization."

And the secretary acted on this belief, choosing the men for the job at hand. Most of the desk-bound admirals in Washington were devoted to him, and his numerous trips to the fighting fronts, plus his obvious empathy with the men "out there," had given him new adherents, particularly among the aggressive younger flag officers. Traditionally, the Navy was not overly fond of powerful secretaries (for good reason, since a considerable share of these had been political hacks like Borie and Thompson, whose primary nautical experience had been in the bathtub), but Forrestal began his tour of duty with a strong following that, against storms raging both within and without the institution, would grow even stronger. This was particularly true on the air side, where Forrestal appointed aviators as vice chief of naval operations (DeWitt ["Duke"] Ramsey) and as deputies for air (Arthur Radford) and operations (Forrest Sherman). He also saw that Marc Mitscher got the new

Eighth Fleet and Jack Towers the postwar Pacific Fleet, while Aubrey ("Jake") Fitch became the first aviator superintendent of the Naval Academy.[5]

Forrestal would need all the help he could get, because the constant admirer in the old Navy boat cloak was gone, as was the press of war. On Capitol Hill more and more members of Congress were ready to go about business as usual. There, in the place where the old Navy had to be sustained and any new Navy had to be born, for nothing got done without congressional allies and congressional budgets, the Navy still retained many good friends.

Many good friends—and one great one.

☆

In his maiden speech on the floor of the House of Representatives in 1916, Carl Vinson, Democrat from Georgia, had not equivocated. National defense, he said, was a nonpartisan issue. "My country and its safety come before any party." For him, through a record fifty years of service in the lower chamber, this statement would be carved in stone.

He showed up in Washington in 1914, just after the young FDR had begun to learn the ropes as Josephus Daniels's assistant secretary. Vinson was born in 1883 in the rural backwater of Baldwin County, Georgia, and graduated from Mercer Law School. He began as a small-town lawyer in the old state capital, Milledgeville. Politics bit him; he first represented Georgia's Tenth District, then its Sixth, but in time he came to represent another constituency as well—the United States Navy.

Vinson profited from the congressional seniority system, an unimaginative and highly undemocratic series of rules and traditions that awarded even the most senile, should they live long enough, with key committee posts and chairmanships. (The South, because of its proclivity for returning members of Congress over and over, profited far more than any other section of the country from the seniority system.) But Vinson was far from senile; from the beginning he shrewdly marked his path within the House with special care. Where he was indistinguishable from most other moss-backed southerners on social and constitutional issues, Vinson, like many another young politician on the make, speedily found himself a special interest— national defense—and, within that, an abiding concern—the Navy.

In 1917, as the country began to gear up for war, Vinson was appointed to the House Naval Affairs Committee. There, as the uniformed Forrestal was doing at the other end of Pennsylvania Avenue, he began his military education, from the inside. During the war and the years of naval disarmament and treaty-making that followed, Vinson learned about ships, guns, and sailors. He followed developments in naval aviation with special care and was an apt pupil. In 1925 he became one of three congressional members of the nine-man Morrow Board, appointed by President Calvin Coolidge in response to the tempest created by Billy Mitchell's charges that the services were lethally mismanaging military aviation.

Vinson authored several of the board's recommendations, establishing the framework of development for both civil and military aviation. He supported the Navy's first important purchase of combat aircraft to arm the two big carriers, *Lexington* and *Saratoga*, fruits of the Washington Conference in 1921–1922. In 1930, having lived long enough, he became chairman of the House Naval Affairs Committee. And there, a small, wiry, balding man, glancing out at the world owlishly over his lowered horn-rimmed glasses, jovial when he wanted to be, arm-twisting when he had to, he did not "manage"—he *reigned*.

As the Depression deepened over the land, Vinson's concern with the deteriorating state of the Navy deepened as well. He sponsored bill after bill to beef up the fleet, all ground to pieces in the hopper of Herbert Hoover's trenchant philosophy of belt tightening. But with the coming of FDR, an old friend from World War I days, Vinson's luck (and the Navy's) began to change. At first the two of them bootlegged naval construction into reform programs such as the National Industrial Recovery Act. But then, beginning in 1934, came a series of laws, mostly generated by Vinson and known collectively as the Vinson-Trammell acts, after their little-known cosponsor and chairman of the Senate Naval Affairs Committee, Park Trammell of Florida.

Collectively, these acts revivified the Navy. Down the ways slid destroyers, destroyer leaders, submarines—over one hundred small ships for commerce raiding, antisubmarine warfare, and the scouting line. A carrier was included. The legislation provided, as well, for the replacement of obsolescent warships. Eventually, eight of the ten new battlewagons of World War II were products of Vinson-Trammell. Together, these achievements belonged more to Carl Vinson than to anyone else, "the masterwork of [his] early career."

By now, however, the "Swamp Fox" (a nickname bestowed for his skill in parliamentary maneuvering by some of his not-altogether-admiring colleagues) was just hitting his stride. New naval programs followed on an annual basis—1938, 1939, 1940—as Vinson, like his friend in the White House, became increasingly alarmed over international developments. At times the Georgian, with a secure seat and a steady feel for the political pulse of the House, was out ahead of FDR, who had to be concerned with powerful isolationist opposition on the question of naval legislation. In 1940, over the president's protest, the Swamp Fox pushed through a bill providing an additional 1.25 million tons of shipping—the nucleus of the two-ocean Navy of World War II. Vinson's vision was that of a fleet strong in both oceans, especially in carriers.

His pace quickened as war engulfed Europe and the Far East. Naval aviation strength was raised to ten thousand planes; sixteen thousand additional aviators were placed in the training pipeline; and twenty new naval air bases were established. All the bills in the world did not help the fleet of Pearl Harbor or in the Philippines, but when war came, Vinson had ensured that the Navy—his Navy—would not have to start from scratch. "I do not know where the country would have been after December 7, 1941," wrote Fleet Admiral Chester Nimitz, "if it had not had the ships and the know-how to build more ships fast, for which one Vinson bill after another was responsible." Admiral James ("Joe") Richardson, the fleet commander who was sacked by FDR for arguing against the fleet's forward deployment to Pearl Harbor on the eve of war, retained his admiration for the Swamp Fox. "He probably knows more about the Navy," remarked Richardson, "than any single officer in the Naval Service."

Of course, the political wheeling and dealing that Vinson had to do in the course of his parliamentary legerdemain was not without its cost. The saying went that if "one more military base or defense plant were built in Georgia, the state would sink under its own weight." The Swamp Fox began ensuring that the good 'ole boys back home got more than their share of the pie during the construction explosion of the war, a practice that would later be developed to a fine art by succeeding masters of the political-military nexus, men like Mendel Rivers of South Carolina and Richard Russell of Georgia. (The latter eventually became Vinson's alter ego as chairman of the Senate Armed Services Committee.)[6]

By war's end, one critic was saying bluntly that "Congressman Carl Vinson, a country lawyer from Georgia, runs the Navy." This was a gross overstatement, but Vinson's overwhelming power was not in doubt, nor was its constitutional basis. Article I, section 8, gave Congress the power to collect taxes for the common defense, and paragraph 13 of the same section enabled Congress to "provide and maintain a navy." More, paragraph 14 empowered the same body to establish rules for the government and regulation of both land and naval forces.

So there things stood. In Vinson's view Congress determined naval policy with each naval appropriation. He ran his committee with an iron hand; childless himself, he looked on committee members and supplicating admirals alike as his "boys," doling out rewards and punishments accordingly. They usually listened with great care and respect, because over the years the Swamp Fox had made himself a naval encyclopedia. (For one fuzzy-cheeked congressman who persisted in asking all the wrong questions at a hearing, he accurately and without notes reviewed the laws relating to naval tonnage going back to 1890.) When approached by a flag officer confident that his request had been approved by higher authority, meaning men in blue suits, Vinson was likely to say, "Don't take your shoes off before you get to the stream, admiral."

He was also capable, after blistering a witness uncertain of his facts with a *correct* recital of the same (he never went to a hearing unprepared), of ending a volley of questions with the benediction: "Gentlemen, it becomes very evident that this witness cannot testify adequately on the policy questions involved. Let us table the matter." His gaze seemed to be everywhere, looking out over those horn-rims; he watched the independent naval promotion boards like a hawk, and he was not above trying to influence the results.

In 1945, then, Carl Vinson was the Navy's bottom line. True, he was the fleet's bosom buddy, its premier civilian spokesman for naval air power in particular, but he was also the gatekeeper, the man who wrote the checks. He had never commanded at sea, served a day of military service, or trod foreign battlefields like Frank Knox or James Forrestal had. Indeed, he had been aboard a commissioned warship only a few times in his life.

His position, with all its official and subterranean permutations, made his power. Whatever the postwar Navy would be, whatever roles the fleet would be called on to assume, would have to pass through the appropriations process.—And here, on his own turf, he was a past master, "a legend in Congress who never got caught on a close vote without the necessary winning proxies in his pocket."[7]

Thus Vinson's fingerprints were all over House Concurrent Resolution 80: the "Composition of the Postwar Navy," on which hearings were held beginning 19 September 1945 by (naturally) Vinson's Naval Affairs Committee. Forrestal, King, Admiral Horne, all the bureau chiefs, and various planners all dutifully attended.

Inevitably, then, the Navy's future, whatever its shape, would have to pass muster under the eyes of the Swamp Fox.

☆

Of course, the gentleman from Georgia did *not* "run the Navy," although he certainly had quite a bit to do with that task. The day-to-day operations were in the hands of the men who wore gold braid, and at the summit of these, in September 1945, stood the formidable figure of Fleet Admiral Ernest Joseph King.

Ernie King came to the post of chief of naval operations by a long, tortuous route. His father was a stern, practical Scot who worked as a foreman in the railroad shops of Lorain, Ohio. He gave his son an ethic of hard work and common-sense learning, to the degree that the young man emerged as the valedictorian of his thirteen-member high school class.

In 1897, at the age of eighteen, King won an appointment to the Naval Academy after having his interest in the Navy piqued by an article in a boy's magazine. As he endured his education on the banks of the Severn, the Navy exploded onto the world stage with its victories over the Spanish at Manila Bay and Santiago Bay. The resulting acquisitions ensured that Midshipman King would have a future, with a fleet now playing a new role: imperial guardian.

During these heady years the boy from the lower-middle-class Ohio family became a man, and already key traits of his adulthood and naval career were pronounced. He proved to be exceptionally intelligent, particularly in mastering the nit-picking academic and military trivia served up to midshipmen of the day. An opportunist, he also indicated a remarkable shrewdness in furthering himself. (In the summer of 1898, he conned his way into orders for duty aboard the cruiser *San Francisco* and saw some action off Cuba.) He ended his Annapolis stint with the highest military rank in the brigade, graduating fourth in the Class of 1901.

King also indicated, early on, a furious impatience with lesser mortals and a flaming temper that could erupt in cannonade at any time. A good seaman during the droning routine of his early assignments and an officer who won the ready allegiance of his enlisted men, he still could not resist informing senior officers precisely how they were mistaken. Accordingly, he was twice placed in hack aboard the cruiser *Cincinnati* and was once suspended from duty (usually a career-killer) after a fracas with an admiral aboard the battleship *Alabama*.

Still, his merits were obvious, and he rose, at least in part through the time-honored naval tradition of cultivating senior officers, or "sea daddies." By 1915 he already had destroyer and torpedo flotilla commands under his belt. His most important sea daddy was Vice Admiral Henry Mayo, remembered in American naval history for his belligerent idiocy at the Tampico Crisis of 1914. In his personal dealings, however, Mayo was a quiet but demanding taskmaster; King became his chief of staff for the Atlantic Fleet during World War I.

In theory Mayo taught King the principle of allowing subordinates individual initiative. In practice, the younger officer's impatience and temper often canceled out this fine model of leadership. He left Mayo, however, having attained thorough seasoning in staff work and, although still a junior captain, with stars in his eyes.

To that end, King applied himself to a wide variety of naval tasks in the interwar years. He commanded a submarine flotilla and directed the salvage of the sunken *S-51* in the full glare of national publicity; shanghaied himself into an abbreviated flight course at Pensacola and got his wings at almost fifty years of age; and brilliantly commanded the new carrier *Lexington*. From there he ascended to flag rank (1933) and became chief of the Bureau of Aeronautics, where his scope for tactless, rude behavior widened to include congressional committees (Vinson versus King was always worth seeing) and other admirals.

Yet he prospered, because he was good, very good, and he had wider experience across the board with the operating Navy than practically anyone else in the fleet. He was "all-Navy" in a service that admired that quality above all others. As a vice admiral he commanded the carriers of the Battle Force and then, in 1937, ostentatiously threw his scrambled eggs in the ring to succeed Admiral Leahy as chief of naval operations.

But his time was not yet. He had made too many enemies, both within and without the service. His marriage, in 1905, had produced six daughters and a son (he was so competitive with his children that he pouted when he lost to them at Monopoly), but he had long since strayed off the reservation. His tall, slender figure and ascetic face, crowned by a slightly beaked nose, combined for a distinguished appearance. He liked beautiful women—lots of beautiful women—although the source of his magnetism mystified his brother officers, especially those who had felt the stings of his lash. "His appeal to women," said one, "was most unusual."

He also drank, in quantity and at times into a stupor. Many arguments would then erupt, with his sulphurous language peeling the paint off the bulkheads as he damned anyone whom he happened to have in his cross hairs at the time. This was not a combination—the womanizing and the boozing—to win friends and influence people. (What Ernie King thought of Dale Carnegie's then-current bestseller is not recorded.)

King had few close confidants among his peers—indeed, a fine question existed as to exactly who *was* his peer, and his junior officers detested him. One of these recalled that Ernie King was the only skipper he had ever heard curse his subordinates openly, and another shuddered to recollect that, as King paced the bridge of his ship, he could be "meaner than hell." Once, as commanding officer of *Lexington*, he had occasion to chew out the skipper of a destroyer underway alongside. When one of his own subordinates boldly suggested that perhaps King had been too harsh, he responded: "I don't care how good they are. Unless they get a kick in the ass every six weeks, they slack off."

Which is to say that FDR, and the Navy, were not yet ready for Ernie King's ass-kicking. The president instead chose the conciliatory, low-key Harold ("Betty") Stark, and King, thinking in disgust that his career had been derailed, hibernated among the members of the superannuated General Board. Stark and Frank Knox saved him, sending him to sea in December 1940 in command of the Atlantic Squadron. As the war clouds gathered, the idea became clearer that men of King's obvious talents could not be wasted. On 1 February 1941, when Roosevelt reconstituted the Atlantic Fleet, King was at the helm.

His slogan became "Do all that we can with what we have;" the Vinson-Trammell acts were pouring new ships into the fleet, and the Navy's schools were filling up, but time was the problem—never enough time. King worked himself and his men to a frazzle preparing for the war the admiral knew was looming. Indeed, several of his units were involved in shooting scrapes with the Germans well before Pearl Harbor; the destroyers *Greer, Kearny,* and *Reuben James* were all attacked with torpedoes, and the latter was sunk.

Pearl Harbor threw the Navy Department into disarray. In the words of one of King's staff officers, the place was like "an ant hill of which the top had been kicked off." When the dust settled, there was King at the top of the greasy pole, commander in chief of the U.S. Fleet. (The unfortunate resulting acronym, CINCUS, pronounced "sink-us," was quickly and mercifully changed to COMINCH.) "Lord, how I need him!" Knox wrote. King reportedly grumbled, "When they get in trouble they always call for us old sons of bitches."[8]

But the old son of a bitch was secretly pleased; he had reached his goal, and he went to work with a will. For several hectic months, as the Allies knew nothing but defeat on all fronts, COMINCH and the chief of naval operations worked in uneasy harness. But Betty Stark was not the man to direct a worldwide naval war, as he well knew. In March 1942, at his own suggestion, Stark vacated the office and moved to command American naval forces in Europe.

Now Ernie King stood alone, the singlemost powerful sailor in the history of the United States, in command not only of the American Navy but also of its vast bureaucratic apparatus. In 1942 he reached the mandatory retirement age of sixty-four, but FDR, who admired him greatly, would not do without him. After 1942 the president left all senior naval appointments to King.

The chief was aboard for the duration. He swore off hard liquor, chain-smoked furiously, and experimented with a bizarre array of uniforms, including sweaters, eccentric musty-gray suits, and natty breast-pocket handkerchiefs. (Nothing worked; when in the field, in particular, he always looked like he dressed from the bottom of the seabag.) He lived, almost like a monk, on the chief's yacht and went home only once a month, even though his wife lived in Washington. (The cynics said the workload alone was not responsible for this.)

And he *led*. Every element of the wartime Navy felt the stamp of Ernie King. He rewarded subordinates who took the ball and ran with it—Mayo had taught him that much—but he was death itself on the foul-ups and the malcontents. He had a hand in virtually every flag-rank officer selection and fine-tuned his choices for crucial operational commands with the touch of a virtuoso. Many aviators, like Jack Towers, became almost paranoid on the subject of King's influence with carrier commands.

On the other hand, Navymen believed that he "never excused a fault," a feeling with considerable truth. He was argumentative and vindictive, with the Army, the Army Air Force, the British, and every politician within range. "Admiral King is not going to expose my deficiencies," said the august George Marshall, "and I won't even admit that the Admiral has any." Although he and Marshall kept a wary, respectful distance, King characteristically responded by comparing the War Department to the alimentary canal: "You feed it at one end, and nothing comes out the other but crap." Most of the War Department was not as forgiving as Marshall. "One thing that might help win this war," Dwight Eisenhower confided to his diary, "is to get someone to shoot King." And Harry Yarnell confided to his: "King has made many enemies." Consistently and violently impatient, "he wanted it done yesterday." Precisely who was targeted for his shafts made no difference to King—his business was to win the Navy's war.

The *Navy's* war—that was the key. Never could he quite shed his salt-water parochialism, nor did he want to. Because of his abiding commitment to seapower, King skewed the "Germany first" strategy in the direction of the Pacific Theater. He willingly supplied the naval matériel for the assault on Fortress Europe, but Japan remained his number one priority. Always before him was the horrifying image of those bleeding American battleships at Pearl Harbor.

King demanded, and got, a redistribution of resources from the British and American Joint Chiefs that increased the mass of supplies being funneled to the Pacific. He displayed over and over the opportunism that had characterized his career, only now at the level of grand strategy. The shoestring Guadalcanal operation was his baby. He levered the Navy into the Gilberts, the Marshalls, the Marianas, and the island chains beyond. Both he and Nimitz persuaded Marshall to accept Army subordination to Navy command in Nimitz's area of the Pacific.

He was a disastrous military diplomat, and without Roosevelt's instincts for compromise on the grand scale and Marshall's workmanlike moderation, King's relish for confrontation and advocacy politics might have blown the Anglo-American alliance out of the water. He "had little humor in him" and could neither be joked with nor jollied along, not by the President, the Joint Chiefs, or anyone else. "I don't know whether anyone really got close to Admiral King," said a man who observed him often.[9]

That was all right by King; as he saw the war, walking the path to victory trampled human relationships. Winning was all. He was a fiery, dynamic war leader, a risk taker, one of the finest strategists the Navy ever produced, and when he ascended to the pinnacle with the rank of fleet admiral in December 1944, he gained a promotion justly earned.

In this sense he was made for war, this man constructed of barbed wire and razor blades, and with the death of his patrons Knox and Roosevelt and the coming of peace, he knew himself ill-suited to shepherd the Navy into the postwar years. He put his mark on successive revisions of the postwar plans, but his heart was not in his work. He was overaged and tired. Accordingly, he personally nominated Chester Nimitz as his successor, convinced Truman over Forrestal's objections, and left office in December 1945.

He was, as he called himself, in many ways a son of a bitch. But he was an *American* son of a bitch, and he had given what he had, which was considerable, to help win the war. To the extent that one man could make things so, the wartime fleet had belonged to Ernie King from the keels up. The Navy would miss him in the troubling times to come.

☆

Serving the president, the secretary of the Navy, and the chief of naval operations was the sprawling bureaucratic apparatus of the Department of the Navy, which had come a long way from its birth in 1798 when its first secretary, Benjamin Stoddert, could count his employees on the fingers of one hand. Naval bureaucrats, of course, were forever the bane of the seagoing naval officer. An exasperated Richard Morris, who led the first American squadron to the Mediterranean in 1803 to chastise the predatory Barbary pirates, set the tone for generations to come: "Gentlemen can in their closets plan expeditions at their ease, make winds and seas to suit their purpose, and extend or contract the limits of time and space; but the poor seaman struggling with a tempest on a lee shore must have something to eat." The "gentlemen in their closets" had to delegate adequate authority to their officer-run bureaus while retaining enough to ensure their own responsibility, an always difficult and sometimes impossible task.

And so things had gone, between the sailors at sea and the bureaucrats on the beach, for over a century and a half. The bureaucrats were necessary, and grew more and more essential as time passed, because the Navy was men *and matériel*. (The *Infantry Journal*, hardly an unbiased organ, had once groused that the only things military about the Navy were its Academy, the training stations, and the Marine Corps. The rest reeked with materialism and corruption, a mere "fighting industrial association.")

Matériel meant *things*, ships, hardware, and the like: how to order them, buy them, get them to the fleet, train sailors to use them without killing themselves—in short, an administrative jungle. In 1945 Forrestal was the biggest cat in the jungle, and he was not pleased by what he had seen.

The war had only exacerbated basic administrative problems that had long plagued the service, some connected with matériel and some not. Planning did not often coordinate with national policy, even when national policy was clear (which at the moment was not the case); civilian control within the department had naturally weakened during the war as the men on the fighting fronts tended to take the bit in their teeth and admirals like King and Horne carried out assaults on civilian bureaucratic turf like marauding Vikings; and the internal organizational operations of the department, despite Forrestal's best efforts as under secretary, remained decentralized and woefully inefficient. Naval officers were traditionally independent, instinctively resisting central control. The tradition encouraged both responsibility and innovation but also served as a justification for relentless bureaucratic infighting.

The central organizational problem lay with King himself. He wore two wartime hats: as commander in chief, United States Fleet, he reported directly to the president; as chief of naval operations, he was responsible to the secretary of the Navy. Indeed, he was the only formal point of contact between two hierarchies. This administrative hash, typical of FDR's way of doing things although historically of much longer duration, was compounded by King's attempts to directly control the department's bureaus, attempts analogous to a medieval "king" maneuvering against powerful barons. Finally, even Roosevelt could take the gaff no longer. In the summer of 1943 Frank Knox received a note: "Tell Ernie *once more:* no reorganizing of the Navy Dept. set-up during the war. Let's win it first. F.D.R."

Forrestal, like Knox, recognized that operating the fleet and initiating naval strategic planning rightfully belonged to men like Ernie King. But Forrestal, especially, became convinced, even before he headed the department, that civilian control needed to be definitive at all levels of the bureaucracy—a constitutional as well as a policy-oriented opinion. Forrestal and King continued to be polite enough with each other over this and other issues, but each knew a turf war was coming. King, like his deputy Horne an empire builder from way back, was blocked during the war from increasing his own administrative power only by Forrestal's determined opposition and FDR's intercession.

With peace, Forrestal, knowing King was leaving, moved quickly. The postwar Executive Order 9635, General Order 5, and Public Law 432 all increased the power of the chief of naval operations while clearly keeping the office subordinate to civilian leadership—compromises that satisfied both King and Forrestal. The latter's sense of rational management had been deeply offended by the enormous waste of the war months, and he created a civilian fiscal director (later the Office of the Comptroller) to ride herd on Navy finances. Next, he established the clumsily named Organization Top Policy Group, composed of the highest civilian and uniformed personnel in the department, to sort out conflicting civilian and military viewpoints. The initial focus of the group became postwar reorganization problems.

This group, a sort of standing committee, was not to be confused with the ad hoc joint civilian-military board chaired by Thomas Gates, which toiled through the weeks following the Japanese surrender to recommend structural changes within the department. With Forrestal cracking the whip, the Gates board rapidly reported. On 23 September 1945 the Navy Department entered the postwar era with General Order 223, which reorganized the shore establishment.

King's two hats became one, within the chief's office, and that officer became directly responsible to the president *through* the secretary of the Navy. There would now be, in effect, a three-tiered Navy: The civilian department, the shore establishment, and the operating forces.

Forrestal's tidying up of the lines of authority went further. The chief of naval operations was given five deputy chiefs, with functions roughly similar to those of the Army general staff: OP-01 (Personnel), OP-02 (Administration), OP-03 (Operations), OP-04 (Logistics), and OP-05 (Air). Deliberately, these deputies were not given the powers of the old bureau heads—their role was to handle the minor problems for the chief and free him to concentrate on major strategic and policy issues. Functional deputies, like Personnel, now worked alongside deputies for weapons, like Air; tension quickly developed between the two types of shops—and remained.

General Order 223 was Forrestal's initial bureaucrat stamp on the Navy and thus was heavily concerned with logistics. A new barony was created, the Office of Naval Matériel, to manage procurement. The secretary also gave the chief of naval operations control over strictly naval requirements ("consumer logistics") but left what he called "producer logistics" (many of the still-producing factory pipelines, for example) in civilian hands.

Out of General Order 223 emerged four potential centers of bureaucratic power: the secretary of the Navy, who would set policy with advice from the blue suits; the chief of naval operations, who would command the operating forces; the civilian department, which would handle the production end of the logistics tail; and the professional officers, who would administer everything on the operational end.[10]

—All very nice, except that the Navy's bureau system remained, scarred but unbowed. The bureaus had been in existence since 1842, when they were created as a "reform" to replace the ossified Board of Naval Commissioners. Originally there had been five, reporting directly to the secretary of the Navy: Yards and Docks; Construction, Equipment, and Repair; Provisions and Clothing (Supplies and Accounts after 1892); Ordnance and Hydrography; and Medicine and Surgery. In 1862 three more were added: Navigation (later the powerful Bureau of Naval Personnel); Equipment (hived off from Construction and Repair); and Steam Engineering.

Eventually, Equipment was abolished; Aeronautics was established in 1921; and in 1940 Construction and Repair was merged with Engineering to form the Bureau of Ships. Thus the "system" numbered anywhere from five to eight bureaus and, to any competent management specialist, was strangeness itself.

The bureaus became petty kingdoms, each carrying on its business independently of and unrelated to the others, each led through the decades by a rear admiral or a captain convinced of his "expertise" within his domain and having only the secretary as a final court of appeal. A good bureau head could play a secretary, especially an inexperienced or indifferent one, like a harp string. Indeed, one problem with the system lay with the secretaries themselves, most of them in office for a few years at best, and most of them complete landlubbers, ill-equipped to adequately judge the nautical merits, or lack thereof, concerning a host of proposals and questions emerging from bureaus usually at odds with one another.

Numerous boards and committees grappled ineffectually with the bureau system through the years, always running aground on the shoals outside the secretary's office. Naval line officers, those who had held command at sea or were preparing for the role, were convinced that bureau control should belong to the uniformed Navy, particularly after the creation of the post of chief of naval operations in 1915. Only in this way, they argued, could the fleet be properly outfitted, supplied, and kept in war-fighting trim. But successive secretaries were loath to give up "civilian" control, by which they meant control of the bureaus. A bureaucratic nightmare thus became an apparition cloaked in the shadows of the Constitution.

Consequently, with the advent of the chief's office, there had emerged after 1915 a bilateral organization of the Navy. The chief of naval operations, the military part, reported directly to the secretary. The bureaus, the "civil" part despite their many uniformed members, did the same. The secretary would adjudicate all differences.

Such a situation was calculated to drive any self-respecting chief of naval operations mad. Before World War II neither chiefs nor secretaries, coming at the problem from different angles, could rally sufficient congressional support for bureau reform. This hot potato was too much even for the efforts of the Swamp Fox. Thus, the basic problem still existed at the time of Pearl Harbor and had not done much to improve Ernie King's temper during the war—hence his spurned attempt to control the bureaus.

The war produced the pike to wedge out the key log in the logjam. In October 1941, as part of the gear-up for conflict, a Materials Division (OP-24) was created in the chief's office. The avalanche of war-related production simply buried OP-24, and in response a superagency, the Office of Procurement and Material (OP and M) was created on 30 January 1942 by simple secretarial fiat based on the president's wartime emergency powers. The superagency absorbed the hapless OP-24, and Forrestal, as under secretary, became its czar—OP and M was the base of his wartime power. The superagency supported and tried to adjudicate between the bureaus, not replace them. Still, its creation was a giant stride forward on the road to internal integration for the department. Forrestal remorselessly drove OP and M in analyzing the Navy's contribution to the joint war effort, distilling the fleet's operational requirements, and distributing the matériel produced by the bureaus.

During the war, practically unnoticed, the control of distribution of naval funds was given to the secretary through a ruling by the Navy's general counsel, thus chopping the legs from under the customary practice of treating each congressional bureau appropriation as earmarked exclusively for that bureau. OP and M was replaced in August 1945 by the Office of the Assistant Secretary for Material, but the superagency and the general counsel's ruling had indicated that, at last, the petty kingdoms were being brought under some sort of centralized control.

As 1945 drew to a close, then, Forrestal had most of his new administrative apparatus. For the moment the bureaus would be hobbled and the administrative pipelines given time to iron out and unclog. These reforms did not, of themselves, solve any planning problems, because most of the reforms dealt with the arcane world of budgeting, procurement, production, and distribution, not with the strategic *uses* to be made of matériel. Forrestal was proving enormously receptive to all kinds of suggestions concerning reform emanating from the Navy's combat leaders now returning stateside, but these men found a new bureaucracy, thanks to an energetic and willful secretary, already largely in place.

Now civilian officials rather than professional officers were assuming control of the procurement of the ships and weapons. The power of the purse ineluctably led to the power to set naval roles and missions. Men like Carl Vinson could start the money ball rolling, but the decisions about where the money stopped came to be centered, more and more, on the civilian rather than the military side of the Navy's own house. Constitutionally, this was all in good form, and, in 1945, this was what James Forrestal clearly wanted. For the naval profession, however, the trend augured by the Forrestal reforms would prove to be something else again.

Bureaucratic changes, of course, did not automatically ensure that things were done better. As Forrestal knew, humans made the difference. The secretary himself became exercised when he found that a man who only recently had been a seaman second class was in charge of making up the Navy's figures within the Bureau of the Budget. Forrestal made enough fuss to get Truman to agree to push "that type of person" out of the government service. But overall, the immediate postwar reforms, *in the hands of an able and strong secretary with plentiful naval experience*, were a much-needed improvement.

These were the "little problems," their partial resolution a welcome housecleaning after the hothouse atmosphere of the war years. The service, with Forrestal as secretary and King, then Nimitz, as chief of naval operations, had skilled and intelligent leadership, if at times these leaders were at odds. The Navy also had the crucial, if diminishing, support of many on Capitol Hill and, in Carl Vinson, had a champion beyond compare. Of utmost importance, the fleet had the universal approbation of a grateful nation.

But there were reefs ahead, threats (as some argued) to the very survival of the Navy. These would have to be navigated under a new president who was a question mark. The White House no longer constituted a "Navy wardroom." Many other pressing problems clamored for the time and attention of the unprepared man from Missouri, and the Navy obviously was not very high on his agenda.[11]

And, as all struggled to get their bearings in the unfamiliar postwar world—the untried chief executive, the consummate manager from Wall

Street, the wily congressman, the salty chiefs of naval operations, the un-named thousands in the naval bureaucracy—they had to confront the flood-tide of demobilization. They all expected some sort of drawdown, but no one was quite prepared for its gigantic dimensions.

For as uneasy peace settled over the land, the tremendous instrument of victory, the mighty armada, was rapidly eroding.

CHAPTER FOUR

DRAWDOWN

☆

T he armada had been built and manned to meet a national emergency. With Germany, Japan, and Italy flattened, not even the most optimistic Navyman expected the fleet to be maintained at anything near its wartime strength. In August 1943 Frank Knox got the inevitable demobilization process started with a letter to Ernie King establishing a "Special Planning Section," with Admiral Harry Yarnell as head. The section dabbled in postwar strategic plans, but its essence was to be "an agency charged with planning for post-war demobilization."

Yarnell, a courtly gentleman, spent some of his time on the demobilization project, but amid his Washington round of meetings and dinners the actual *process* of demobilization received relatively little of his attention. He was mainly concerned with publicity for naval aviation and public relations on behalf of his beloved service. Indeed, the Navy tried to stave off the inevitable as long as possible. In the final months of the war a building program began that was designed less to defeat already reeling Japan than to protect the Navy against predictable budget cuts. The pillars of the program were aircraft carriers, and three reached the fleet: *Midway* and *Franklin D. Roosevelt* in 1945, *Coral Sea* a year later.

The expected budget crunch came at war's end, within months after Yarnell's second retirement. After trying to hook in its various bureaus and agencies to Basic Demobilization Plan Number Two, the Navy Department at last came up with an annual figure for operating the postwar fleet: $6 billion. The catch was that Truman's Bureau of the Budget and several congressional leaders had already stated that the annual *total* military budget for the country would be about $5 billion. Some real dollar-slashing lay ahead, and to many in the Navy the budgetary knives were being applied "seemingly without reason."[1]

Harry Truman thought $6 billion was too much, and not only on fiscal grounds. He was deeply offended by Carl Vinson's House Concurrent Resolution 80, which in its statement concerning the size of the postwar Navy had, he felt, usurped executive functions. James Forrestal, for his part, believed that "we had our case very thoroughly in order." The secretary's essential goal was to maintain as much as possible of the fleet's V-J Day strength in combatant ships (almost 1300). He knew that the 3.4 million men and women in Navy blue would rapidly dwindle to a few hundred thousand, but he hoped that if a considerable number of ships could be kept in commission, the personnel would follow.

On the civilian side the Department of the Navy had made do with 68,000 employees in the prewar year of 1938; Knox's assistant secretary, Ralph Bard, had estimated a postwar size of 200,000—even as a guess, almost a tripling of the size of civilian support. In the upshot, the civilian strength of the department, in the manner of all bureaucracies, would level off at over 600,000 within five years of war's end. Either way, the 200,000 guess or the 600,000 eventual fact, the Navy felt that its civilian house would not stand cost cutting either.

Unfortunately for the Navy the nation was more than ready for peace and the concomitant reshuffling of budgetary priorities. Americans, heedless of the world around them, had demobilized quickly and chaotically after each of their wars. The difference this time lay in the growing necessity of internationalism rather than isolationism in foreign affairs and in the existence of the United Nations, which, if the new organization was not to repeat the sorry, impotent record of its predecessor, the League of Nations, had to have some recourse to armed strength in order to head off the threats of conflicts.

Declarations and treaties in abundance were in place in 1945, all affirming solid American stances on international issues—the somewhat vacuous Atlantic Charter of 1941 was an example. True to their past, however, Americans were, for the most part, notoriously unwilling to back up their fine words with adequate military strength. World War II had convinced many of them that any conflicts to come could be won on the cheap— cleanly, decisively, quickly—through the application of technology rather than the weight of sheer numbers. The Army would prove to be the major victim of this attitude, but the Navy suffered as well.[2]

And the Navy was vulnerable in another area, to charges of monetary waste. No other national organizations compared for bringing politicians out of the woodwork and provoking screams among the electorate. The "finger bowl episode" was trivial but typical. Long a standard on the Navy's supply list, the bowls were a residue of gentlemanly wardroom elegance in the serene days of empire. A routine reordering to replenish the war-depleted supply triggered an investigation that also uncovered the vital fact that the insignia on officer and crew silverware differed, thus duplicating costs. Such "scandals" were of twenty-four-hour duration, petty, and in part simple anti-Navy vindictiveness (what the dickens did those officers need finger bowls for, anyway?), but they played in Peoria—and Peoria had votes.

More seriously, because the Navy's strategic planning was in disarray, its leaders were extremely uncertain about the *specific* numbers of ships required for the postwar fleet. Dozens of vessels of all types were in the construction pipeline. King hoped to complete all ships "within one month of their launching date" on V-J Day, but he compounded the confusion by adding that "it is assumed that combatant ship contracts will not be cancelled on V-J Day."

King and Forrestal were doing their level best, trying any way they knew how to hang on to what they could, but no amount of planning could control what was coming. The tide of cost cutting was rising, but the fleet was not rising as well. Instead, its ships were being submerged.

☆

This was the initial wave that washed over Fleet Admiral Chester Nimitz when he assumed office as chief of naval operations. As with King, there had been few predictors of naval success in his background. Nimitz traced his origins to the medieval German knights who had conquered and settled Livonia, on the Baltic Sea. Most of the family became German tradesmen, although a few tried their luck with the merchant marine. Eventually, part of the clan emigrated to South Carolina, then on to Texas. There, shortly after his father, a hotel-keeper, died, Chester was born in the German enclave of Fredericksburg in 1885.

After attending Texas schools and clerking in a family hotel, young Nimitz met two West Pointers on their way to their first officer assignment. Impressed, he applied to the Military Academy, only to be told that there were no vacancies. His congressman suggested Annapolis, and in 1901, only a few months after King had departed, he became a "naval cadet." (The cadets, who had been "midshipmen" until 1870, became midshipmen again in 1902 at the behest of Theodore Roosevelt.)

Like King, the mild-mannered, likable Texan excelled. Ranked seventh in the 114-member class of 1905, he joined the battleship *Ohio* for his first tour. Aboard her he visited Japan in 1906 and met the famous Admiral Togo, conqueror of the ramshackle Russian fleet at Tsushima Strait. The Navy, in the wake of its smashing victories in the Spanish-American War, was exploding in size, and there were opportunities aplenty for aggressive, ambitious junior officers.

Nimitz, despite his amiable exterior, had the inner fire. He commanded in turn a gunboat, a naval base, and a destroyer, all before he left behind the single gold bar of an ensign. He almost left behind more than that. In 1908 he ran his destroyer, *Decatur*, hard aground in the Philippines. But as in the case of King, with his boozing and his sassing of senior officers, Nimitz was too good to toss away. He escaped his court-martial with a slight slap on the wrist, a letter of reprimand.

The expanding Navy offered many novel career patterns to officers of Nimitz's generation, and he chose submarines. He commanded several of the tiny craft, eventually leading the minuscule Atlantic Submarine Flotilla and lecturing on submarine tactics at the Naval War College. In 1913 he made a happy marriage and, unlike King, evolved a domestic pattern of stability and mutual support.

He went to Germany to study the technology of diesel engines, critical to operating the boats, and became an expert (although he lost part of a ring finger to the rotating gears in one of them). During World War I he emerged as the chief of staff to Captain Samuel Robison, an outstanding tactician and the commander of the Atlantic Fleet's Submarine Force. There, as King was doing at the same time under Admiral Mayo, Nimitz learned many of the tricks of the staff trade. Robison was a key sea daddy for him.

Nimitz stayed with the boats after the war. Interwoven with a tour as the exec of the battlewagon *South Carolina*, he did stints as the senior member of the Board of Submarine Design (by now he was regarded as one of the best engineering technicians in the fleet) and as the officer-in-charge of building the submarine base at Pearl Harbor. Back at the War College as a student, he war-gamed Pacific conflicts with Japan to such an extent that contemplation of that war became second nature to him.

His career was now rushing down the tracks as fast as possible, given the interwar doldrums, and the potentially disastrous destroyer grounding was ancient history. He served again with Robison while his sea daddy became, in succession, commander of the Battle Fleet and commander in chief, U.S. Fleet. Commands of a submarine division, a tender, and a heavy cruiser followed in rapid order. In 1938 he reached flag rank, his shock of hair snowy white by now, commanding first a cruiser and then a battleship division. He had had limited experience with carriers, but through his war-gaming and his habit of reflection he sensed their potential value, both as a strike arm and as the heart of the war-induced reorganization to come: the task force.

In 1939 FDR ordered him back to Washington as chief of the Bureau of Navigation. Here he tackled the task of finding and training competent men for the burgeoning fleet. Nimitz quickly expanded the class size at the Naval Academy, increased the number of Naval Reserve Officer Training Corps units, and introduced the V-7 program for accelerated training of officers. He made his mark—with Betty Stark, with Frank Knox, and with the president himself. On 16 December 1941, as the funeral pyres of Pearl Harbor were still smoldering, Knox summoned him to take command of the remnants of the Pacific Fleet.

He was the right man for the job, the kind of war leader the United States somehow manages to produce when needed most. His experience was broad, not so broad as King's, perhaps (whose was?), but he had been around. He knew the world of officer personnel like an open book, and he knew how to judge and select the people who could cut the mustard. His calm, exceptionally steady demeanor was a badly needed antidote to the subdued, chastened atmosphere he found in Hawaii.

Nimitz truly *cared* about his subordinates. He personally met at pierside each ship returning to Pearl from the war zone, from carriers to oceangoing tugs. "Every man in the Pacific Fleet thought that Admiral Nimitz had a personal interest in him," said one of his destroyer squadron commanders. He lacked King's flaming temper (". . . a lot more compassionate than Admiral King," reckoned a subordinate), although he could get mad enough when he had to, and at times he displayed a considerable streak of stubbornness, even with members of his own family. (When his son, Chester junior, tried to resign his commission before his twenty years for retirement eligibility were up, Nimitz, by now the chief, had no compunction about asking Forrestal to disapprove the request, which was done.)[3]

Probably his greatest accomplishment, after working successfully in harness with the other Pacific commander, the unmatched prima donna Douglas MacArthur, was his trust and confidence in the men who worked for him. His two major subordinates, taciturn, introspective Raymond Spruance and fiery Bill Halsey, were as unalike as night and day, yet under Nimitz's gentle handling they came to form the devastating one-two naval punch of the Pacific war.

Everyone seemingly had a say in Pacific strategy—FDR, King, the Joint Chiefs, the Combined Chiefs, the irrepressible and histrionic MacArthur—but Nimitz was the Navy's man on the spot, and he acted accordingly. He used his initially sparse number of carriers with boldness and daring, trusting in critical naval intelligence intercepts and making the decisions that led to the crucial stalemate at Coral Sea and the turn of the tide at Midway. He persuaded King to attack the Gilberts before the Marshalls and used his growing strength to strike directly at Kwajalein, the heart of the latter chain. The conquest of the Marianas followed. He diplomatically agreed with MacArthur about the value of invading Luzon (King wanted an immediate leap to Formosa, soon to be known as Taiwan), and he went on to take Iwo Jima and Okinawa while MacArthur overran the Philippines.

At the end, triumphant in the Navy's greatest conflict ever—the Pacific war—he viewed himself as the logical successor to King. So did King. But Forrestal had borne King's acerbity and brass-hatting long enough; he had not worked closely with Nimitz during the war and may have believed he would be getting just another, although slightly less disruptive, edition of Ernie King as chief of naval operations. Forrestal probably preferred Admiral Richard Edwards, King's deputy. To this end, on 6 October 1945 the secretary of the Navy urged Nimitz not to be the chief. The stubbornness surfaced, and Nimitz insisted. He well knew the post was the capstone of any naval line officer's career. King himself was not without resources; he advanced Nimitz's name in his letter of resignation to Truman, and he lobbied Vinson for support—which he got.

The upshot was that the president named Nimitz, but Forrestal exacted a price: the new chief would serve only one two-year term. Nimitz, mystified and offended, thus took office on a sour note. But soon his natural charm and ease of manner, plus his finely honed judgment skills, began to work their way with the compulsive, hard-driving secretary.

This was just as well, because in the midst of preparing strategies to deal with the emerging Cold War, organizing the peacetime naval force, and planning for any new ships and weapons that Congress saw fit to allow, Nimitz had to supervise the painful drawdown of the wartime Navy. As pressure from politicians, the folks back home, and Navymen themselves intensified, the new chief decreed that demobilization be carried out "swiftly."

☆

"Swiftly" hardly described the pace of the oncoming tidal wave. Truman was more accurate when, despite his far-from-pro-Navy viewpoint, he used the word *disintegration*. "It was no demobilization, it was a rout," mourned George Marshall. "We did not have enough to defend the air strip at Fairbanks." Makeshifts and shortcuts were the order of the day as constant reorganization became the norm and crisis management predominated. "Bring the boys home" blared the watchwords, as they had done after every American war. Forrestal and Nimitz, prodded ceaselessly by Congress and the press, were forced to respond as best they could.[4]

King's prescription for the drawdown had been rational and filled with common sense: "Complete demobilization of the Navy to its postwar strength will be accomplished by twelve months after surrender day, which is six months after assumed 'termination of the war' date." But the "postwar strength" was up in the air, kept aloft by the heat of executive, congressional, and military debate, and meanwhile the end-of-war euphoria sped the tidal wave inexorably onward. This was no rational drawdown; America was "pickling a Navy."

Truman tried to put the best light possible on the rapidly developing shambles. On 27 October 1945 he spoke in celebration of the twenty-fourth Navy Day to a throng of over one million gathered in New York's Central Park. "We are in the process of demobilizing our naval force," said the president. "We are laying up ships. We are breaking up aircraft squadrons. We are rolling up bases and releasing officers and men." But, he continued, "when our demobilization is all finished *as planned*, the United States will still be the greatest naval power on earth. . . ."

Forrestal disagreed. To him, the country "was going back to bed at a frightening rate, which is the best way I know to be sure of the coming of World War III." The secretary took to circulating among his friends copies of Kipling's famous poem "Tommy Atkins:"

For it's Tommy this, and Tommy that, an' "chuck him out, the brute!"
But it's "Saviour of 'is country," when the guns begin to shoot.[5]

Maybe, as the wartime commander of the Atlantic Fleet, Admiral Jonas Ingram, saw matters, the Navy was "too big for its own good" and needed to be pared into leaner, more fighting trim. But most of its sailors and many of its officers did not give a damn for this line of reasoning; they just wanted out, and fast.

Some of them had gotten restless even before V-J Day. The commander of submarines, Pacific, remembered that "requests from reserves for discharge came flocking into our offices until they looked like the fan mail department of a Hollywood star." Soldiers, sailors, and airmen alike started griping about the Navy's slowness in getting them home, and a few were not loath to talk to reporters eager for good end-of-war copy. Once the bitching hit the stateside press, the Navy started catching flak. A few sailors and others even organized protests, which did not do too much for the blood pressure of their admirals, leading some later analysts to assert that the biggest mouths belonged to those "whose backgrounds had a common pinkish hue." But such viewpoints were Cold War nonsense—these were men driven by nothing more than war-weariness and homesickness.

The Navy responded, heaving into action with practically all its available resources. Befitting its fondness for snazzy operational names, the service called the enormous task of moving millions of people thousands of miles to their homes and discharging most of them en route MAGIC CARPET. The day following V-J Day the Navy Department announced a point system for releasing over two million of its personnel within the next year and a half. What counted were the individual's age, time in service (particularly overseas), and dependency situation. Immediately, 327,000 were let go into civilian life, most of these already stateside. (Such preferential treatment did not do much to soothe the overseas protests.)

MAGIC CARPET needed carpets, and King was quickly forced to designate combat ships as troop transports. Public impatience, however, was not to be so easily shunted aside. Some exasperated citizens, not especially attuned to the economics of cost-effectiveness, proposed that the big B-29s be stripped and used as aerial buses. But the Navy bore the brunt of the pressure; when its leaders announced a plan to have many fleet units ceremonially visit selected ports as part of the same Navy Day festivities at which Truman spoke, a terrific uproar broke forth from those supposedly "marooned" in overseas pestholes.

Over three hundred transport vessels, most of them commissioned, were mustered. In addition, sixty-three carriers, seven battleships, and twenty-six cruisers became ferry boats. The Navy furnished 55 percent of the ships in MAGIC CARPET; merchantmen, contract shipping, and foreign bottoms did the rest. A few of the lucky veterans got home by air, like the returning vets in the Academy Award–winning film *The Best Years of Our Lives*. Most, though, came back the way they had gone over—by sea. By November 1945 more than three million men of all services had been returned from outside the borders of the continental United States, and still this was not fast enough.

Politicos screamed protests into the *Congressional Record;* the Senate Naval Committee held hearings, although to what end nobody quite seemed to know; and Senators Wayne Morse and E.V. Robertson threatened an immediate investigation of what Robertson called the "palpable inefficiency" in bringing the boys home. Several congressmen were not above intervening personally to get their favorites out of uniform early.[6]

There *was* inefficiency, in fact foul-ups on a level almost more than human (a member of the staff of commander of submarines Pacific said the whole thing "was a rat race, to be sure"), but there was also exceptional organization, good humor, and much happiness. The experience of the carrier *Wasp* (namesake of the ship to which *Lansdowne* had been forced to administer the final torpedoes back in 1943) was typical.

At first, *Wasp*'s officers and men were humiliated about their assignment to MAGIC CARPET—"from the scourge of Asiatic waters to a ferryboat in the Atlantic!" But they soon buckled down to work, carrying 1,200 repatriated Italian prisoners of war from Staten Island to Naples, there embarking 4,000 soldiers during a twenty-seven-hour turnaround. *Wasp*'s horde of passengers had little to do but sleep, eat, gamble (the card games and crapshoots were never-ending marathons), and anticipate. They dozed in temporary racks, five tiers high, fashioned out of spare piping. Frequently, they "hot-bunked;" some racks were never vacant. Heads were improvised along the sides of the hangar deck. Temporary steam tables kept the chow coming. Water from the flight deck dripped down through the number one elevator onto some of the sleepers.

Among the passengers were fourteen women—Red Cross workers, nurses, and medical aides—who had badgered the Naples officials incessantly until they got aboard. They were given the best quarters available, the cabins of the admiral and his chief of staff. The ship's *Hangar Deck Herald* reported that the ladies had been duly impressed by sleeping in the quarters that had formerly belonged to Admiral Slew McCain.

For women in uniform, the pattern was typical. All over the world, American females were cadging rides back home any way they could. When twelve nurses stuck on Manus asked for a lift, carrier commander Dan Gallery radioed back to their base commander: "Referring to your dispatch about the nurses. Can do, can do. Oh boy, oh boy!" Also typical was the comparative ease of *Wasp*'s journey. Eight days out of Naples—packed in like sardines, disheveled, but overjoyed—her passengers were in New York.

A brilliant combat record could not save a ship from MAGIC CARPET duty. *Enterprise*, with her twenty battle stars, seventy-one ships sunk, and 911 aircraft destroyed, was among the best. Yet "Big E" made two round trips between New York and Southampton in late 1945, her hangar deck full of tiers of piping and wire-spring bunks. After returning to Bayonne,

New Jersey, with a load of passengers from the Azores on 18 January 1946, she never went to sea again.

Merely getting to the States did not end the bottlenecks, of course. At the Washington end, Captain Wally Petersen and his group had worked out the point system (theoretically, the longer you were overseas, the sooner you got out), set up the release sites in coastal ports, and designed a human conveyor belt through which the men would be ushered out of uniform. But the Navy's pipeline was clogged somewhere, and so Vice Admiral Louis Denfeld, the chief of naval personnel, sent for his deputy, Bill Fechteler, and Fechteler in turn summoned an ace troubleshooter who was already drafting the great postwar naval educational plan that would bear his name—Rear Admiral James Holloway, Jr.

Fechteler told Holloway that demobilization in the Pacific, where the Navy had the greatest proportion of its people, was "completely chaotic." Holloway was commanded to bring order to the chaos. Armed with a hastily conjured title—assistant chief of naval personnel for demobilization (nothing got done without a title)—Holloway set forth, making whirlwind stops in Seattle, San Francisco, and San Diego. The problem, he found, was undermanning of the demobilization centers at the receiving end. The makeshift centers were simply swamped by the flood of humanity that the Navy was depositing on their neighboring docks.

Yeomen, disbursing clerks, anyone who could read a form, were pressed into service. The pace of processing began to pick up. Thanks to Forrestal's insistence, every man passing along the conveyor belt was given a new suit of blues; if this was not necessary, his blues would be cleaned and pressed for free.

The sailors were then herded, in groups, through some thirty cubicles, each one specializing in some bureaucratic intricacy of their lives. Each person had to be medically examined; pay and service records had to be closed out; certificates of discharge and satisfactory service had to be prepared. If the individual had less than seventy-five dollars on the books, he got his money in cash; if more, he received fifty in cash and the rest in a check. In the final booth each enlisted man, excluding chief petty officers, was offered a one-grade promotion if he would sign up in the inactive reserve. Many did.

At the end they gathered in a small auditorium, listened to the national anthem, and had a four-striper give them their discharges and a certificate of excellent conduct. Then they were out the door—but still not quite home.

Holloway also tackled the inland transportation problem. Most of the Pacific returnees, and the great bulk of those from the Atlantic, lived east of the Rockies. Railroad scheduling was a major headache. Holloway told a subordinate, Howard ("Red") Yeager, that Yeager now had a title of his very own, director of rail transportation for the Navy, and Yeager got cracking. He met with the president of the American Association of Railroads, and together they sorted things out, assembling the necessary rolling stock from scratch. "I think they reached as low as the Toonerville trolley," Holloway recalled.

The goal was to get the men home by Christmas, and most of them, thanks to Jimmy Holloway, Red Yeager, and the American railway system, got there in time. The heads in some of the southern railway cars froze up going over the Rockies, but no one seemed to mind. ·

Five months after V-J Day, more than 2.5 million of the 3.4 million servicemen in the Pacific were home, and the percentages were similar for the European Theater. In December 1945, naval releases amounted to almost fifteen thousand people *a day*.

MAGIC CARPET, despite its inevitable assembly-line snafus and miscalculations, had indeed worked miracles. All this was to the vast satisfaction of the American public, which saw its warriors come back far faster than they had gone over. Rear Admiral Malcolm Schoeffel, who was right in the middle of things as assistant chief of staff for plans, asked one enlisted man if the sailor was going back by MAGIC CARPET. "Well, Sir, it ain't my idea of no magic carpet," came the reply, "but I sure am glad to be on it."[7]

☆

Home was the sailor, home from the sea. But the ships, like *Wasp* and Big E, were "veterans" too, with their own campaign ribbons and battle stars proudly displayed on their bridge wings. Demobilization included them as well.

The successive demobilization plans, from tentative Number One on through Number Two, had ended up by calling for the following numbers of combatants to be retained on active service: twelve fleet carriers, ten escort carriers, four battleships, twenty-nine heavy and light cruisers, 126 destroyers, thirty destroyer escorts, and eighty submarines. Indeed, twenty-three carriers of all types were still in commission on 1 July 1946, although the total number of naval aircraft then available had shrunk from forty-one thousand to twenty-four thousand within the past year and kept plummeting.

Here still was the nucleus of a considerable naval force, but the torrential drain of manpower speedily rendered many of the ships practically inoperable. Captain Joe Worthington lost half the staff of his destroyer squadron and all but one of his doctors overnight. On the staff of the commander of Carrier Division 26, only the admiral and his operations officer were Regulars; the rest evaporated within weeks.

By the middle of 1946 Forrestal described the fleet as at a "dangerously low point of efficiency." A "very large number of vessels" could not go to sea because of lack of competent personnel to man them. "We couldn't have fought our way out of a paper bag," opined one veteran of Pacific amphibious warfare. When the leader of the amphibious forces (the ships of which the

Navy nicknamed "alligators" or simply "Gators"), Vice Admiral Dan Barbey, wanted to move his command ship *Catoctin* during maneuvers off Little Creek, he had to raid many other ships in the Norfolk area for hands, and even then *Catoctin* suffered a minor accident while underway. "Not a ship in the Navy is fit to go into action today," complained the *New York Herald Tribune*. "Too many chief petty officers, too many commissioned officers, and too many experienced seamen have been sent home." "The Navy just slid down the drafts," remembered a carrier division commander.

Even Nimitz could not keep his finger in the dike. Both he and Forrestal were sounding the alarm, but that was all they could do. In January 1946, *less than 150 days after the end of the war in the Pacific*, the chief of naval operations was forced to announce to the public that "your Navy has not the strength in ships and personnel to carry out a major military operation."

He was not crying wolf; the reality was sobering. The destroyer *Isbell*, a sadly typical case, operated at sea with a crew of 225—a good, solid number for her class of ship, except that 60 percent of them had never been to sea before. And many of the experienced men aboard her had only a few weeks or months left on their enlistments. There were three types of destroyer squadrons: one could operate, the second could eke out perhaps two days at sea by scraping up people from the waterfront, and the third could get only one of its ships underway per week by looting men from all the other ships in the squadron. Destroyer strength was thus, in practice, at least halved. Many ships struggled for enough bodies to man even one fireroom.

On the new carrier *Tarawa* there was only one barber aboard for the two-thousand-man crew, and he had to be shanghaied from the Norfolk Receiving Station just as he was about to depart on a twenty-day leave. (What this did to the quality of haircuts aboard was not recorded.) *Tarawa*'s handful of experienced electrician's mates had to sleep alongside their generators because there were not enough trained men to set up regular watches. There was one laundryman, ten cooks instead of twenty-four, and only a few experienced gunners. Aviation crews had to service three planes apiece rather than one.

The boats were no better off. The avalanche of requests to Submarines, Pacific soon produced a partially manned underwater force at best. Phil Beshany, a young officer just returned from overseas, was immediately hustled off to Galveston to take command of a submarine that even lacked a skipper. The submariners, among the most highly trained of the Navy's personnel, simply went home with the rest.[8]

These were not isolated examples; they were the norm. Officers throughout the fleet were griping constantly about the undermanning, and (a rarity) in writing. One aboard a carrier wrote that he was complaining only "because I feel that my professional career will be at stake should I be compelled to sail with my present division complement."

Time was needed for postwar boot training and officer programs to take up the slack, and meanwhile the Navy would just have to limp along. "Meanwhile," however, seemed a long time, and even seasoned professionals who had been through a drawdown before, on a lesser scale following World War I, got fed up. Jack Towers, who relieved Raymond Spruance in command of the Fifth Fleet, finally blew up over the impossible problem of keeping the required running count on the hundreds of naval landing craft scattered hither and yon across the Pacific and stopped counting. Many of the Gators, stripped and beached, rotted where they were.

☆

Rotting ships were not a navy. And the inability to man the fleet unavoidably led to the acceleration of ship demobilization. Ernie King, again with great precision, had envisioned a round number of one thousand ships in inactive status after the war. To this end, a major overhaul of preservation methods was needed.

The idea was to have an active fleet manned at about 70 percent of wartime complement; a reserve fleet rotated periodically with the active fleet and manned at about 30 percent of wartime; and an inactive fleet fully decommissioned. The last would be "mothballed," placed in a state of preservation sufficient to allow its elements to be reactivated in short order when necessary.

In 1940, when the ship activation teams had boarded the old flush-deck four-pipe destroyers of World War I vintage to prepare for FDR's destroyer-for-bases deal with England, they had found little but cracked deck plates, running rust, and frozen machinery. Almost none of the ships had been usable in their intended roles of convoy escorts. This time, the Navy wanted to get its mothballing right. A host of modern technological developments, such as plastic coatings, film preservatives, rubber seals, and dehumidification techniques, would ensure proper preservation.

King's 1000-ship figure rapidly went the way of most of the Navy's immediate postwar plans. Eventually 2600 ships were mothballed (Operation ZIPPER), theoretically composing the bench-warming second team. The goal was to keep them all in such a condition that they could be "ready for battle" within thirty days. This meant, in essence, a continuous fight against the elements. To forestall development of a rusting mass of useless hulks and mildewed equipment, Navymen went to war against a ship's natural enemies, which were legion: corrosion, verdigris, tarnish, mildew, salt air, electrolysis, harmful vapors, even sunlight.

The mothball fleet was to require relatively little servicing, be cheap to maintain, be kept in a twenty-year state of preservation, and be able to have its protective coatings and devices easily removed. The biggest change among the many from the earlier days was the umbilical cord attached to each of its members. This naval equivalent of an iron lung was an electrically operated, automatically controlled dehumidifer connected to the fire-main system. Dry air constantly circulated throughout every ship's bowels, even into otherwise airtight compartments. Thirty percent humidity was the ideal. The battleships each needed as many as six dehumidifiers to keep them dry.

The old and necessary custom of red-leading to prevent rust had not gone out of style, but now the thick, hard-caked grease that had frozen the gears of the venerable four-pipers was replaced by thin-film rust preventatives that were both adhesive and water-repellent. In an emergency the machinery could be operated with its preservative compound, because the compound would dissolve in the lubricating oil of the moving parts.

Guns, winches, capstans, torpedo tubes, and other movable topside gear on exposed weather decks were covered with strippable film packaging, tight-fitting rubbery stuff like a stretch girdle. This concoction was sprayed on and could be peeled off within minutes. The hulls above the waterline were coated with anticorrosive zinc chromate. Below, they received new protective paints, sprayed on hot and poisonous, to fight rust and the armies of seaborne microorganisms that loved to eat ships.

The first keepers of the mothball fleet were sailors specially trained in Philadelphia and San Diego in the arts of sealing and preserving ships. These men carefully stripped off the usable items, such as stores, radio gear, navigation instruments, and ammunition. Allowance lists, covering everything from bolts to surgical instruments, were double-checked. Careful instructions for unsealing each vessel were recorded.

After this, the sailors oversaw their charges to new homes—their "nests"—each ship berthed alongside others of her kind. One ship in each nest housed a small crew to conduct periodic inspections and do the paperwork for the silent members of her nest. Preservation, thus carried out, cost an estimated 1 percent of the amount required to build the ships in the first place.

Around the rim of the country, from New England to Puget Sound, they obediently moved, nudged along by sturdy little tugs, into their assigned berths—hundreds of ships, a graveyard fleet, suitably embalmed for the resurrection, "as peaceful as sleeping dragons." Within twenty-four months, reported the secretary of the Navy, their assigned berthing areas were filled to capacity, and they overflowed into valuable industrial space in naval shipyards.[9]

Wasp, after her MAGIC CARPET chores were over, dozed here; so, too, did Big E and other carrier veterans of the glory days when Marc Mitscher, Slew McCain, Arthur Radford and their like roamed the Pacific: *Essex, Bunker Hill, Hornet, Ticonderoga.* Into the nests nosed the ghostly battleships that had risen from the muck of Pearl Harbor to stand, one last time, in the line of battle at Surigao Strait: *West Virginia, California, Tennessee.* Surrounding them was an infinitude of naval power, in itself potentially the second strongest navy in the world (after the operational "first team"), cast aside now that its ships were deemed no longer "necessary:" cruisers, destroyers, baby carriers, submarines, transports, landing craft, minesweepers.

Like Barbarossa in his cave, they slept. Ideally, they would be summoned forth, in reborn youth, to fight other navies, as they had done in the past. But as they slept, the onward rush of naval technology passed them by.

For most, the resurrection was not to be. For them, the path led only one way—to the breakers.

☆

Parts of the remaining fleet had vastly differing destinies. Some went to foreign navies in the name of friendship and international peacekeeping. *Belleau Wood*, for example, became the French carrier *Bois de Belleau*. Many six-inch light cruisers were sent to South American navies, including *Phoenix*, lead ship of her class. She became Argentina's *General Belgrano* and was reserved for a special, tragic fate at the hands of the British nuclear submarine *Conqueror* during the Falklands War of 1982. Some were sold to foreign businessmen for scrap; this was the finale for the attack transport *Andromeda*, broken apart in Taiwan.

But mostly, over the months and years, the United States itself dismembered the armada. The cutting torches were at work almost at once, slicing into ships only a few years or even a few months old, and they kept on slicing. *South Dakota*, the beloved Big Bastard, was relentlessly carved apart in Kearny, New Jersey. Her sister *Washington*, whose huge guns had blazed forth against *Kirishima* off Guadalcanal, expired the same way. *Indiana* was torn asunder in Richmond, California; one of her anchors went to Fort Wayne, her mast and two forty-millimeter gun mounts were displayed alongside the football stadium at Indiana University, and 175 tons of her armor plating were stored underground in Salt Lake City to provide shielding for radioactive experiments. Big E slumbered alongside the south wall at Bayonne for more than a decade; finally, the torches and pneumatic hammers took her, too.

A few, like the reefer *Sirius*, resisted such indignities for as long as they could. During the process of being scrapped in Seattle, *Sirius* caught fire, rolled over on her side, and sank. She was raised, sank again, and finally had to be overcome while defiantly lying on her side.

From the remains came mountains of scrap metal, to be recycled into the products of the industrial age. Steel plating, turbines, propellers, valves, piping, boilers, turbine blades, reduction gears, uncounted miles of tubing, girders, rudders, diesel engines: in time they might emerge as automobiles, bridges, buildings—even, perhaps, as ships again—but the days when they had formed the pulsating heart of the armada were gone for good.

A few survived the massacre, in new incarnations. There was a small but flourishing business in war memorials. In carriers: *Intrepid* found a home in New York City, and *Yorktown* (descendant of the carrier lost at Midway) in Mount Pleasant, South Carolina. In battleships, much-prized by their home states: *Alabama* rested in Mobile, *Massachusetts* in Fall River, *North Carolina* in Wilmington, and the ancient *Texas* in Laporte. In cruisers: *Little Rock* incongruously ended up in Buffalo. In destroyers: *Cassin Young* went to Boston, *Joseph P. Kennedy* to Fall River, *Kidd* to Baton Rouge, *Laffey* to Mount Pleasant, and *The Sullivans* to Buffalo, while the destroyer escort *Stewart* found herself in Galveston. In submarines: *Balao*-class boats made their last voyage to Philadelphia, Honolulu, Hackensack, Fall River, San Francisco, Baltimore, even Muskogee, Oklahoma (*Batfish*). Members of the *Gato* class survived in Galveston, Mount Pleasant, Cleveland, Buffalo, Muskegon, and Manitowoc, Wisconsin (*Cobia*). *Requin*, from the *Tench* class, resided in Tampa. The small boys were not forgotten, either: Omaha, St. Louis, and Fort Worth each got a minesweeper, while Fall River received a creaky landing craft and two torpedo boats.

Others took on new roles. All four *Iowa*s would live on. No one knew quite what to do with them, but unlike the four *South Dakota*s and the two *North Carolina*s, they became neither memorials nor fodder for the torches. At times they were proposed as cruise-missile platforms or even Polaris missile ships. *New Jersey* would be reborn twice, in the sixties and again in the eighties, and eventually all four would steam again, as gun platforms and cruise-missile carriers. The escort carrier *Thetis Bay* became an auxiliary helicopter carrier and then the prototype amphibious assault ship (*LPH-6*). Several carriers became antisubmarine platforms, the cores of the postwar hunter-killer (HUK) groups. A few cruisers entered the modern age as anti-air warfare vessels equipped with new electronic suites and guided missiles. Future conflicts would draw forth a few more members of the mothball fleet, some in strange reincarnations.

And some, like the battle cruiser *Hawaii*, never found a home. She was 84 percent complete when construction was suspended in 1947, went into mothballs, and was slated for conversion to the world's first guided-missile cruiser. That never worked out. Next, she was scheduled to be a command ship. *That* never worked out. At last, having staved off the torches for the last time, she was towed to Baltimore to be dismantled.[10]

For a very few a special end was reserved—nuclear testing. The old battleships *New York* and *Pennsylvania* survived the atomic bomb tests at Bikini in 1946, only to succumb to conventional weapons. Not so the antiquated *Arkansas*, which was obliterated by an underwater nuclear burst at the same time, or *Saratoga*, shattered and consigned to oblivion at the bottom of Bikini Lagoon.

Like *Hawaii*, most members of the mothball fleet stayed away from the breakers for years, but the ending for almost all of them was inevitable. The summons would come with the words "stricken . . . stricken from Navy lists." And so, one by one, they went to the boneyard. Stripped at last even of their Navy designation, shepherded along by lowing civilian tugs, they made their last journey.

As the mothball fleet dwindled, so too did any potential effectiveness its ships might have had. Numbers alone did not tell the story; this was a fleet frozen in time, without any of the dynamism provided by racing naval technology. Some naval officers called the maintenance of these ghosts "a luxury we cannot afford." "A lot of bricks to make," dourly commented Rear Admiral Randall Jacobs, "but damn little straw to do it with."

In practice, the dreamed-of thirty-day reactivation process would prove to take months and even years. The mothball fleet was uniquely susceptible to personnel rifts, training foul-ups, labor strikes (some of its care devolved on civilian workers), and problems in repairing and renewing preservation equipment. These forlorn ships were easy victims of any whetted budget ax. Their total operating budget settled in at less than $14 million annually— far from enough to do the job adequately. By 1949 all scheduled quinquennial overhauls had been canceled. And the men who would man the mothball fleet, the Naval Reservists, were slumbering in almost the same degree of torpor as the ships themselves.

For noncombatants, cargo-carrying merchantmen mostly, there was the National Defense Reserve Fleet, created by the Ship Sales Act of 1946. By the end of the war, the United States was the owner and operator of the largest fleet of merchant ships the world had ever seen. At a cost of $13 billion, 6400 merchant ships had been built between 1937 and 1945; some had been sunk, most of these on the dangerous North Atlantic run, and many more bore the scars and hard usage of war. But when Japan surrendered, America held title to more than 5000 merchantmen.

Some of these immediately went to the breakers. Eventually, about 2000, many of them the classic workhorse "liberty ships," settled into the National Defense Reserve Fleet, divided into eight anchorages under the custody of the Maritime Commission. And there, like their warrior cousins, they simply atrophied.[11]

So the forgotten, landlocked remnants of the armada waited, most of them for the day of regeneration that never came, and the world moved on. Echoes of the past might ring from their steel bulkheads, but the men who had once given them life and purpose were gone.

They waited. Here and there a lonely anemometer might spin idly in a soft breeze. But over them no commissioning pennant streamed smartly from the masthead. The flag bags on their signal bridges, bridges that had once swarmed with activity, now stood empty. Sea gulls glided through their superstructures, staining every surface with their never-ending deposits and filling the air with their familiar wails.

Haze-gray paint blistered and flecked away from their metal skins. Aboard the heavies, with their wooden decks, grass grew between the planks. Inside, musty smells were everywhere, the odors of decay and death. Mess and wardroom tables stood bare, still bolted to the decks. The galleys were bleak, devoid of all but their basic fittings. Hydraulic oil slowly seeped from brittle engineroom and fireroom gaskets. In the firerooms themselves, where sweaty watchstanders had once stared incessantly at the vital boiler water level indicators, the glass was empty, cold to the touch. Sometimes, a power failure would occur on shore. Then, with their battle lanterns disconnected, every ship in the nest would become as dark as the inside of a coffin.

Slowly, despite the efforts of the keepers, time and weather did their work. The floating mausoleums decayed, their numbers ebbed, they became relics rather than warships. Given what they had done in life, their ending, to any sailor worth his salt, was almost intolerably sad.

☆

Beyond the ghostly world of the floating mausoleums, the drawdown proceeded with elemental force. Forrestal and Nimitz, despite their best efforts, were shoveling sand against the tide. The secretary had to defend his naval estimate of $5.1 billion for fiscal year 1947 with the fervor of a mother protecting her young; he got $4.1 billion. He pronounced demobilization complete as of 1 September 1946, but in fact the process, particularly regarding the ships, was still underway. As of 31 December of that year the Navy continued to be seriously understrength.

To be precise, the service on that date retained 319 major combatants, 724 lesser ships, and 1461 combat aircraft. Almost all were wretchedly undermanned; 491,663 Navy men and women remained in uniform, and the Marine Corps had shriveled to 108,798. About 25,000 raw recruits were coming in each month, but they were not enough. The most critical shortages, with shortfalls in the tens of thousands, were in the lowest enlisted ratings, seaman and fireman.

Of all these personnel, only about 10,000 were aviators, and many in this group were mere fledglings. Since V-J Day, the active fleet's combatant vessels had shrunk by 75 percent, other ships by 94 percent, its total aircraft by 64 percent. In personnel, the Navy now mustered a mere 14 percent of its size at war's end. Many shore billets, like that of the chief of navy salvage, were simply abolished. Others were carelessly lumped together under new (and misleading) names.

This was no mere drawdown—the dismantling of the armada was carnage.

Within a year the fleet's operating budget—the actual money the Navy Department pried loose from Congress—went from $16.8 billion to $5.6 billion, then leveled off at a little over $4 billion for the next three years, continuing at roughly one-third of the total military budget. In short, the painful monetary reductions were shared with the other services, and the

Army, in particular, got the short end of the stick. Still, the immediate future promised only more of the same. New construction was at a standstill, and no new ships whatsoever were built in 1947.[12]

But the Navy's missions did not go away with the coming of peace, and Chester Nimitz was expected to maintain a virtually worldwide naval presence. To do this, he had but a fraction of the once-awesome armada. The work of the drawdown had sliced away much of the excessive wartime fat, true enough, but with the fat had gone badly needed naval muscle. Real naval power had been irrevocably lost—to foreign navies, the decaying mothball fleet, the breakers, civilian life.

Thus, Nimitz and Forrestal had to contend with one basic problem: how to carry out global naval roles with a vastly reduced and largely untrained naval force while confronting another threat, this one, seemingly, to the very *independence* of their cherished service. For, as the drawdown went on its unstoppable way, the Navy found itself engaged on two more fronts, against a foe within the military gates and against a dread idea.

The enemy was independent air power, and all that implied. The idea was service unification.

CHAPTER FIVE

ENEMY

————— ☆ —————

The Navy prided itself on its role as shield of the republic, first line of defense, primary enforcer of the national will in foreign affairs. As naval leaders saw matters, their service, relative to the Army, had a much more active and positive role to play—"out there."

In addition, Navymen tended to be much more sensitive and querulous on the issue of civilian control. The Constitution was all very well but, as Rear Admiral Bradley Fiske had warned a generation before, "the naval defense of our country is our profession, not that of Congress." Such an attitude was bound to raise the hackles of Navy detractors; historian Charles Beard, for one, was quick to assert that civilian authorities were far from infallible but that their blunders were trivial compared to the "tragic havoc" wrought by a military that did not keep its place.

The Army was not quite so incensed by the Navy claim, for soldiers too had specific tasks to perform. In the interwar period, Army and Navy had cooperated relatively well on strategic planning through the Joint Board. The services seldom dueled politically, but on the other hand, neither went out of the way to help the other. Each was concerned, for its own reasons, about the "semiservice" of the other; if the Navy had its Marine Corps, pounding ahead in developing doctrines of amphibious assault, the Army had its Air Corps, nourishing ideas of strategic air power.

The Army and Navy were separate entities, distinct, Cabinet-level departments. In Congress, separate Military and Naval Affairs committees handled their authorizing legislation and prescribed such matters as promotion and recruiting. The two services operated from separate appropriations and, to all intents and purposes, were independent in the eyes of Capitol Hill.

World War II destroyed these separate political universes. The exigencies of global war forced joint command on the American military, both internally and, with the Combined Chiefs of Staff, externally as well. Army and Navy were placed in competition, to a far greater degree than ever before, for *everything:* budgetary funds, matériel, manpower, strategic roles, and the ear of the president. As a result, both services got smarter, craftier, and sneakier—more overtly *political*.

Thus, the old civilian-military tensions, although they never disappeared, were largely displaced by interservice rivalry well before the end of the war. "The services . . . undoubtedly found it easier and perhaps more virtuous to tangle with each other than to challenge civilian groups and arouse the hallowed shibboleths of civilian control," observed one scholar. The war was the first general conflict in which air power appeared as a major *strategic* factor; by V-J Day American Army airmen, though still not bureaucratically independent, were clearly a "third force" alongside the ground Army and the Navy. Where before there were two, now there were three.

Complicating matters still further was the fact that although the two elder services conducted plenty of joint operations (Normandy was the most conspicuous example), the new "air force" had to work almost constantly with both of its seniors in a wide variety of tactical and strategic roles. The friction at the top chafed daily, even though practice made the planning and execution of combined operations much more effective as the war went on.

Out in the field, however, members of the respective services tended to be bound together in the war effort, cooperating to get the best out of what they had. Vice Admiral Charles Lockwood, as he ran the submarine war against Japan, saw little but friendly group effort all across the Pacific. "It was not until the war was practically over," he recalled, "that we began hearing from the waffle tails and politicos, who had sat out the war in Washington, how badly the armed services got along together and how much we needed 'unification.' " Still, even Lockwood could be rubbed the wrong way, particularly when his submarines were bombed, as they occasionally were, by inexperienced Army Air Force pilots who could not tell one boat from another. Nor could AAF pilots hit much of anything when over water; their B-17s, in the words of one naval historian, "[missed] everything but the accolades at Midway."

Lockwood was typical of higher-echelon commanders who praised interservice cooperation; each element was part of a "splendid team." On the other hand, he angled for all the publicity he could get for his submarines, on the theory that otherwise, as the folks back home read the press releases, they "might gain the impression that the zoomies were winning this war singlehanded."[1]

Jealousy and intramural backbiting thus went on right alongside the "teamwork." And, when peace came, the teamwork went away.

☆

James Forrestal knew that service "unification" was coming. The process was desired by President Truman, with the memories of his Senate investigative experience fresh in his mind; by many in Congress, enamored of "efficiency" and cost cutting; and by the populace at large, although unification was hardly a major item of concern. To almost everyone, unification seemed a rational, businesslike thing to do.

Forrestal, despite his exceptional managerial background, was not so sure. In 1945 he delegated his Wall Street associate and old pal from Princeton days, Ferdinand Eberstadt, to "make an inquiry" into the subject. Eberstadt had served on the War Production Board and in other high government posts, and he knew his way through the bureaucratic maze as well as anyone.

There had been a previous "report" by a committee chaired by retired Admiral Joe Richardson, the man who, as commander of the U.S. Fleet, had unsuccessfully urged Roosevelt before the war to remove the ships from the trap of Pearl Harbor. The Richardson committee's report, delivered while the fighting was still going on, rested on a worldwide survey of military leaders. The report (to which Richardson himself characteristically filed a dissenting view) gave the impression that the weight of military opinion, both Army and Navy, overwhelmingly supported unification.

Indeed, most naval combat commanders surveyed by Richardson insisted that any postwar military organization must be tightly unified. Forrestal felt that the men in the field did not get the big picture; he hoped Eberstadt's reputation for objectivity would undercut the findings of the Richardson committee and still produce an argument which protected the Navy's interests without seeming to be simply resisting change.

Eberstadt admired the current British attempts at military centralization—"it does them credit"—and, using these efforts as a partial model, he came through for Forrestal. The Eberstadt report recommended an autonomous Air Force, which Forrestal regarded as inevitable anyway. There would be three "co-equal" services. The report called for a single secretary of defense to preside over all three services and a National Security Council to coordinate top-level policy-making on military and security matters.

All this was sugarcoating, the merest patina of unification. Eberstadt gave the secretary of defense virtually no *power*—no separate department, no meaningful authority over the separate services, and no way to deny each service direct access to either the president or Congress.

The Eberstadt report reflected classic Navy concerns. The service regarded itself as a fully integrated fighting machine. The Navy, after all, had its own warships, its own air force, its own supply forces and bases, and even (though the Marines would balk at this description) its own army, with *its* own aviation. Therefore—and Eberstadt had done nothing to modify this opinion—the Navy should continue to operate independently because the service was *already* a unified, self-contained force functioning under a single command.

Forrestal sold the Eberstadt report to the Senate. Late in 1945 the Naval Affairs Committee concluded that national security, "under present conditions," would *not* be improved by unifying the War and Navy departments. Ernie King, in his testimony, observed that "any step that is not good for the Navy is not good for the nation." As for unification, King told Forrestal: "Just say I am 'agin' it."

The committee, to Forrestal's and King's delight, even shied away from the idea of a secretary of defense, recommending in its best bureaucratic patois that War, Navy, and Air each be headed by a civilian secretary of Cabinet rank who would collectively "coordinate" their efforts. The Senate liked the idea of a National Security Council and a "Central Intelligence Agency," both civilian aspects of unification, but the solons plumped for the separate maintenance of both the Navy and Air Force arms.[2]

So, for the moment, Forrestal (an unabashed Mahanian) had kept the wolf from the door, to the extent that a newspaper could actually headline an article in November 1945 "Navy Advocates Unification." In fact, Forrestal had protected naval autonomy. Mahanian tradition remained alive. Here was high-stakes bureaucratic sleight of hand at its very best.

☆

The issue of universal military training (UMT) was a handmaiden of unification. This was the Army's baby; George Marshall and almost all of his generals supported the idea, and so did Truman. The plan was to ensure access, for all services, to a constant pool of trained personnel, in order to avoid the recurrent torture of gearing up civilians for military duty while lives were being needlessly lost.

The Navy was fond of UMT, too. Ernie King, dreaming perhaps, envisioned 118,000 trainees being siphoned annually through the boot camps. Chester Nimitz regarded UMT as "indispensable," arguing that the ever-increasing pace of technological development made trained people necessary. In December 1945 he signed off on a postwar Navy of 58,000 officers and 500,000 enlisted personnel, and he needed an assured supply of bodies. "I believe we have fought the last war," Nimitz wrote, "in which our homeland will be spared the violence of our enemies." Others beat the drum for economy, seeing UMT in the long run as a less expensive way to provide a trained reserve force.

Forrestal, with the agonies of the drawdown parading across his desk every day, wanted to pry loose all those eighteen-year-olds from the civilian sector. As early as 1944 he was sensitive to charges that this was the road to "any broad militarily dominated system of control." By 1948, he was convinced that the originally "lukewarm" Navy had now stepped into line behind the idea. However, Josephus Daniels, Wilson's secretary of the Navy, may have had a better feel for the national pulse on this issue. Daniels, a populist, had been convinced that UMT was "contrary to the basic philosophy of the Republic."[3]

Whether the old man was right or wrong (every public opinion poll concerning UMT between 1945 and 1949 showed between 63 percent and 73 percent of the public in favor), much smoke but little fire was generated by this debate between 1945 and 1948. In the end UMT was talked to death, expiring in congressional committee. In June 1948 the Selective Service Bill went to the president, having passed the Senate 78–10, and the nation, discarding UMT entirely, went to a peacetime draft that would last, with some changes, for twenty-five years.

In essence, universal military training died because of the historical, emotional antimilitarism of Americans and a claim that there was a method that did not need all those people, that could win wars on the cheap—a claim successively advanced by the Army Air Corps, the renamed Army Air Force, and, at last, by the United States Air Force.

☆

The Air Force. Its advent as a separate service was perhaps long overdue, but its independence flew on the wings of such gasconade that its very existence unsettled the Navy, to say the least. The air power advocates, like the Navy's battleship and carrier admirals, were divided within their own house, between concepts of strategic and tactical air power. But the "bomber generals" were senior, the "fighter generals" were very young, even by Air Force standards (which made them practically teenagers), and thus theories of "strategic bombing" fed the propaganda.

Nevertheless, all the Air Force officers, like those in the Army from which they had sprung, were used to a "passive" tradition of civilian control, in which their military chiefs, rather than an active secretary, such as Forrestal, actually ran the War Department. The fliers had youth, zeal, and ideas, and they were used to taking the bit in their teeth.

For the Navy the trumpets heralding independent air power were a war alert, breeding a deep suspicion that verged in some quarters on paranoia. The War Department quickly sensed this skittishness, but soothing words would not do. Robert Lovett, assistant secretary of war for air, a former naval aviator in World War I (holder of the Navy Cross) and a strong advocate of strategic bombing, had smoothly reassured a congressional committee that "the military organization in this country will find it necessary and desirable to maintain a highly specialized and efficient fleet air force as part of the Navy." This statement was too ambiguous and qualified by far, as were most aviation-related pronouncements issued by the War Department.

Navymen were convinced that there were two motives behind unification: an Air Force desire not only to steal naval aviation from the fleet but also to flat-out dominate the postwar military establishment. Jack Towers, the Navy's senior aviator, would accept unification only if naval aviation had adequate participation at the topmost level. Clearly, the Air Force brass did not want unification without autonomy, and Lovett, questioned closely on this point by Carl Vinson, conceded as much. And, to the horror of naval officers taught from plebe days to steer away from "politics" as they would from a typhoon track, the Air Force in 1945 began a massive public relations offensive aimed at promoting its independence and, increasingly in the eyes of the Navy, much more.[4]

Forrestal, with his personal ties to naval aviation and his pragmatic approach to administration, was deeply worried. In the fall of 1945 he launched his counterattack, using the "Secretary's Committee of Research on Reorganization" as his picket line. The resulting (and typically glitzy) acronym, SCOROR, was at least superior to its initial name—"Admiral Radford's Office."

Actually run for most of its life by Rear Admiral Thomas Robbins, Jr., a naval aviator, SCOROR lasted until July 1948. Its officers included, at one time or another, such hard chargers as Mick Carney, Forrest Sherman, and Captain Walter Karig, a reserve officer and influential author on naval subjects. From SCOROR emerged the game plans for the unification struggle and the order of battle for public relations counteroffensives against the Air Force.

SCOROR was the forerunner of OP-23, a shop—like all "OPs"—belonging to the chief of naval operations. OP-23, under the leadership of Captain Arleigh Burke, was to become famous (or notorious) in a different cause than unification. Through SCOROR, Forrestal employed his exceptionally keen sense of public relations to put the Navy's best foot (or fin) before the American people.

The secretary urged all naval officers to consider themselves at all times PR people for their service. (At the time about 750 officers were assigned to public relations tasks.) But Forrestal did not rest content with mere cheerleading. He used SCOROR, and other ad hoc units, to collect anti-Navy information; formulate the Navy's response to any "challenge;" create the Navy Department's "line" and get it out to key naval commands; brief all naval personnel scheduled for congressional or executive hearings; stroke corporate fat cats friendly to the Navy; and prepare speeches and articles for popular consumption.

SCOROR even conducted a search for a "Slogan for the Navy," which produced, among other candidates, the following: "The Navy is your frontier of freedom;" "The U.S. Navy, our country's frontier;" "The Navy licks them wherever they are—before they get here;" and, best of all, "Stop refutin' and start shootin'!"

Robbins, who had only two other officers and a secretary working full time for him, took the ball and ran. Under him SCOROR became the grandfather of modern naval public relations. He ransacked other department offices for the bodies needed to do specific jobs. SCOROR did research, drafted policy papers by the hundreds, rode herd on VIPs, and sent forth battalions of speechmakers. Captain Steve Jurika remembered speaking to audiences of anywhere from one thousand people to one monster rally (in Cleveland) of twenty thousand, all on the subject of unification. Robbins himself tirelessly toured naval bases to put forth the Navy's "official position." By the end, and to a considerable degree due to his own efforts, he could say, "I feel that the Navy emerged from the unification struggle in good shape."

☆

With SCOROR in the trenches, doggedly fighting the war of words, the battle over service unification was joined. Where the Army was concerned, naval officers willingly participated in joint studies, as long as the Navy saw no threats to its prerogatives or traditional missions. Examples included military policy in postwar Europe and universal military training.

There was tension between the two older services, to be sure. The Army, after all, was solidly behind unification. And there were those who felt that the Army coveted the Marine Corps, finding everything the gyrenes did, even amphibious warfare, to be redundant. General Alexander Archer Vandegrift, the Marine commandant, sent an urgent circular to his generals saying that the Corps was in for the fight of its life. "Our Navy friends rested too long on their laurels," Vandegrift wrote Holland Smith. "[Unification] is not the day when knighthood was in flower. . . . It's more like a street brawl than a tilting joust. . . ."

Roosevelt's venerable secretary of war, Henry Stimson, had professed to never quite understanding "the peculiar psychology of the Navy Department, which frequently seemed to retire from the realm of logic into a dim religious world in which Neptune was God, Mahan his prophet, and the United States Navy the only true Church." Stimson had a point: the Navy *was* parochial and more than a little mystic on its purpose in life, but this tolerant observation did not prevent the Army itself from mounting a slick public relations sally on its own behalf. (Robbins, after looking over a beautifully bound, neatly embossed, and well-written Army pamphlet, called the glossy product "one of the most insidiously dangerous studies I have yet seen.")[5]

Still, the upstart Air Force was the primary threat. The Joint Chiefs, in a magnificent understatement, had reported in April 1945 that "mutual lack of understanding between the several [service] components has not been eliminated." Since the summer of 1943, the same time the Navy had started preparing *its* postwar plans, Major General Lawrence Kuter, assistant chief of air staff for plans, had been doing the spadework for an autonomous postwar Air Force, to be based on the magical number of seventy groups. Truman, Marshall, Stimson's successor Robert Patterson, and Marshall's successor, Dwight Eisenhower, all supported the idea of air autonomy. (Eisenhower, a bit of a naïf in these matters, noted that "it appeared that all men wearing one color of uniform had one conviction while those wearing another color developed opinions to the exact contrary.")

In the spring of 1946 Nimitz, who "wore another color," sat down with Eisenhower and General Carl ("Tooey") Spaatz, commanding general of the Army Air Force, to try (again) to resolve conflicting service roles and missions. Spaatz, that March, had delivered an off-the-record diatribe to the Aviation Writers' Association, during which he seriously asked whether the country needed a navy at all. Nimitz, deeply concerned over the air power issue, would not get on board. Eisenhower, the mediator, could make no headway against this sort of stonewalling. Thus, the Joint Chiefs were themselves at odds over unification and gave little help to Truman.

The sticking point *was* air power, its proper strategic role and its "ownership." The air generals, in the wake of the aerial devastation of Germany and Japan, found themselves the sole, and possessive, owners of the atomic bomb. "Deterrence," a new strategic concept still in the early stages of formulation, was perceived as a "peculiar function" of the bomb and of strategic air power, not of the armed forces as a whole. In 1945 no one possessed the resources to attack the United States directly. Thus, to the air generals, deterrence was a blanket term covering not only the Sunday punch but also limited probes or challenges to American interests worldwide. In the Navy's view, this was a preposterous assertion that clearly poached on its own strategic turf.

Extremists outlined the new strategic world in clear-cut, crude terms: the atomic bomb had made seapower obsolete. More discerning air power advocates argued that in any case the "success" of strategic bombing had greatly reduced the value of the Navy and meant that air power had superseded seapower in importance across the board. In addition, naval targets held little appeal for theorists of strategic air power, who advocated destroying the enemy's "will to fight." In any event all that naval "presence" overseas ever did was meddle in diplomatic intricacies and exacerbate conflict. The Navy must thus be kept as small as possible to ensure peace, a sort of coastal police force.[6]

The basic evidence for these notions rested with the famous United States Strategic Bombing Survey, created in 1944 to study the results of strategic bombing in Europe and the Far East. The twelve-man civilian commission was aided by hundreds of interrogators and members of investigation teams. The charts, statistics, and first-person testimony were duly assembled, and the survey's report became public in November 1945, just as Forrestal was staving off the first wave of unification with the Eberstadt report.

The survey report's contents were debatable (strategic bombing most emphatically did *not* do what air power propagandists contended—break the will of the enemy to fight on), but the mass of data could be used to support practically any position. For example, the survey concluded that "Allied air power was decisive in the war in western Europe" but included both naval and tactical aviation in "air power." As to the Pacific, the air generals conveniently forgot the blood shed by the Marines and soldiers who had conquered the Marianas and Iwo Jima to give them the bases from which the giant Superforts flew against Japan. The generals also soon produced a snappy booklet entitled *Air Campaigns of the Pacific War*, using highly selective survey statistics and "proving" that the Air Force had dominated every phase of the war with Japan, especially after the advent of the B-29s.

For Forrestal, this was too much. He had tried friendly luncheons, backdoor interservice diplomacy, and compromise, so long as the Navy's essential roles were left undiminished. But men like Lovett and Patterson were hardheaded pros, too, and the secretary was tacking into a strong wind. He and his admirals saw the survey as inconclusive; if the report proved anything, then *naval* air power, with the exception of the bomb in its strategic role, was fully as important as anything the "pilots" had to offer. (Those who drove Air Force planes were "pilots;" the Navymen, with pride, spoke of themselves as "aviators.")

Now came bureaucratic war to the death. The enemy was *not* the autonomous Air Force—that had been conceded—but the strategic claims of independent air power. Both sides came out swinging. On behalf of the Air Force a novelist and former Navy Seabee, William Bradford Huie, became far and away the best-known popularizer of the effulgent claims of air power. Huie, in his "case against the admirals," ran off every count he could think of: the Navy was obstructionist, stubborn, and medieval in its conception of the brave new world of strategic air power; its practices were "outmoded, wasteful, and inefficient;" and its leaders deliberately sabotaged the war effort through unnecessary duplication and needless service rivalry.

Huie did not blame naval officers for the Chicago Fire, but practically every other naval "failing" was on parade, for these were *personal* as well as institutional faults. "The Navy's rigid caste system, with its lavish officers quarters and clubs and the cynical abuses of power by regular Navy officers, did more than any other aspect of the war to engender bitterness and disillusionment among our civilian service men." (Somebody must have really gotten to Huie during his Seabee days.) Air power would set things aright. "The admirals are cringing from the handwriting on the wall," trying to escape "*inferior command position.*" Vice Admiral Fitzhugh Lee surely spoke for all his contemporaries when he called Huie's major opus "a scurrilous book."

All this would have been ludicrous, except that in terms of his ability to reach a wide readership Huie was, by a large margin, the Air Force's most influential flack in the war of words. The Navy had no one to match him (though Robbins certainly gave his best shot). Huie's attacks made the pages of the *American Mercury* and *Nation's Business*, and, most importantly, were reproduced in the bible of middle-class mores, the *Reader's Digest*. From him readers found out about the "backwardness of the Navy brass" ("Should they be allowed to continue in their ancient ways of running things?") and how that same brass "imperils our defense" ("The admirals are showing their usual contempt for the hopes of the American people").[7]

Huie was a loudmouth on the fringe and an ill-informed scandalmonger to boot. His ill-tempered fusillades embarrassed almost as many Air Force officers as they angered Navy officers. But naval supporters tended to take him and others of his ilk at their insulting word, and here, on the furthest reaches of rational discourse rather than on the more solid, conciliatory central ground of reasonable compromise, the battle was joined.

☆

On the surface, Forrestal's battle plan *was* rational. The secretary decreed that naval aviation, the arm whose independent existence was most threatened by the air power gospel, was part of the fort that must be held at all costs. With SCOROR in the van, the public was assured that the heart of the postwar Navy was its air power, tied to invincible carriers. "DCNO (Air) should again take unto itself the job of glamorizing Naval Aviation including, of course, the Fleet Air Wings," Robbins advised Arthur Radford. "What . . . is needed is a Hollywood press agent . . . to think up stunts and ideas and *feed* this stuff into PubInfo."

The nation's air strength was *significantly shared* by the Navy and did not belong to the Air Force alone. The significance lay, not in the possession of the bomb, for this the Navy could not as yet claim, but in certain geographic situations (the Pacific war was a case in point) where carrier air was the only way to get at the enemy.

As a result, Forrestal's ploy "assured the success of the naval aviators' bid for the dominant position in the postwar Navy," said one naval analyst. Unfortunately, this development came not from any reasoned strategic calculation but as a direct result of tawdry interservice squabbling and the Navy's deep-seated concern that its interests be at the table when the strategic menu was served. The gambit also marked a subtle shift away from the old Mahanian dictum that the business of navies was to fight navies and in the direction of projecting naval power, through its air arm, directly against land forces.

The days had passed when naval air had been seen, even by the most salty Blackshoes, as only some kind of fleet appendage. "The airplane has a definite function in the gunnery organization of every ship," old Admiral Yates Stirling had pontificated before the war. "Airplanes will be the eyes of the fleet." His compatriot, Admiral Clark Woodward, agreed: "The air arm is a very efficient adjunct, but it is only an adjunct and can be nothing else. Airships can never win a war; they can never win a battle." And Admiral William Leahy, as chief of naval operations, had informed Congress that the battleship was "the best of all modern weapons."

Here was the "gun club," composed of the believers in the big naval gun, in full bloom. The gunclubbers had been forced to beat a retreat during the war, but some of them were still around, and even the retirees could still get vocal. If the gunclubbers had to have air power jammed down their throats and see their beloved battlewagons relegated to the last pew, they would still swallow the airplane as the *Navy*'s strike arm. They would take their stand, if reluctantly, alongside their flying comrades.

Thus, in this view, whether or not the Air Force gained its independence, its *strategic planning* should not only be integrated with that of the Navy but the Navy should also by rights be the "senior partner." Navymen sneered at the prospect of land-based planes, flown by "pilots," operating over open water, and indeed the lack of over-water success in both scouting and bombing by big Army aircraft during the war had been conspicuous, the Midway episode being the most pertinent example. "Command of the sea," sneered one of the Navy supporters, "belongs to him who goes down to the sea."[8]

As the war of words heated up at the lower levels, Truman and Forrestal were airing their own differences. In April 1946, following the failure of Nimitz, Eisenhower, and Spaatz to get on the same page, the exasperated president finally exploded, fuming that naval officers should refrain from expressing opposition to the Army's unification package, based largely on the plan of General J. Lawton ("Lightning Joe") Collins. The press, also choosing up sides, with each pundit a self-pronounced strategic expert with his own idea of effective unification, commented at tiresome length on this "muzzling" of the Navy.

Truman, persuaded largely by the one man in Washington for whom he had overriding respect, George Marshall, had indeed bought the key idea behind unification, that of a single Cabinet-level Department of Defense. To the president, much of the Navy's resistance was "political;" he believed that the Navy Department was simply trying to cling to Cabinet status. He was not mistaken.

Forrestal, his in-house Eberstadt report, and the Navy itself did not see things that way, and the Navy to a man opposed the merger concept implicit in the Collins plan. At first the secretary ordered his officers to hunker down and shut up, but then Rear Admiral Aaron ("Tip") Merrill, a seasoned combat commander, unleashed his guns at a public dinner, Truman threatened disciplinary action, and Forrestal issued a ukase declaring that no more words would be forthcoming other than in congressional testimony (where SCOROR's smoothies would have a chance to pave the way).

Much of the public was beginning to see the Navy as a roaring naysayer—"opposed" to this, "opposed" to that—but thanks to Carl Vinson and other stalwarts on the Hill, Forrestal knew that no unification bill would be passed without the Navy's stamp of approval. Forrestal could thus afford to stand as a proponent of reason and compromise, and he did. "The Navy has no real grounds for fear," said one commentator. "It has the brains, the technical capacities, the knowledge of war, and the esprit de corps to take care of itself in any kind of administrative setup."

True enough, but there was still the president to convince. Harry Truman's instinctive populism, paradoxically, came to the Navy's rescue. The Collins plan featured a single military chief of staff, and Truman soon came to share the widely held congressional opinion that such a figure might become that dreaded antidemocratic demon, the "man on horseback." Secretary of War Patterson followed the lead, and the logjam began to break. Forrestal still opposed the idea of a single Department of Defense and even threatened resignation over the "mass play–steam roller tactics of the Army."

Nevertheless, Truman and Forrestal were not fundamentally opposed. Forrestal had backed the president on universal military training and the extension of the draft. In June 1946 the two exchanged a series of letters, the upshot of which was that Forrestal, with feet dragging, conceded the single secretary of defense. In return, Truman promised that the Navy would keep most of its land-based aviation (a victory over the Air Force), retain its integrity as a department (a victory over the Army and the Collins plan), and retain a good deal of "autonomy" (an open sesame for strategic planning).

Forrestal was in a mood to be pleased. Writing to retired Marine General Thomas Holcomb, the secretary confessed, "To be fair to [Truman], he has exhibited a most extraordinary degree of patience and tolerance and understanding, in addition to which he has acquired a good deal more fundamental knowledge of the Navy. . . . If it had been anyone but Mr. Truman I think I would have been fired long ago."[9]

Slowly, the details were worked out. The main architects were Forrestal; two of his admirals, stubborn Arthur Radford and the more conciliatory Forrest Sherman; Lovett; W. Stuart Symington, the new assistant secretary of the Army; Eberstadt; General Lauris Norstad (another moderate); and former assistant secretary of war John McCloy. Sherman and Norstad worked intensively for months, and in January 1947 their last draft, looking very much like the Eberstadt report, was reproduced.

On the surface, then, the Navy had won.

☆

Below the surface, though, everyone—including the American people— had lost. Naval heroes from the war years had stooped to enter the fray and emerged with muddied shoes, both black and brown. For example, Fleet Admiral William Halsey had told Forrestal that he favored "the establishment of a single department of the armed forces if such establishment does not weaken the position of the U.S. Navy in the scheme of things." For Halsey and his brother officers the caveat was everything; when the "scheme of things" evolved such monstrosities as doctrines of strategic air power and the Collins plan, Bill Halsey and practically every other naval officer got cold feet, and they got vocal.

In Congress, where the Swamp Fox held the Navy's banner aloft as always, there was also verbal swordplay. Vinson told Truman as early as 1945 not to bother producing a unification bill based on the Collins plan, because "it would not pass either this winter, next winter, or the winter after." For the benefit of his colleagues the Swamp Fox conjured up a series of nightmares—German and Japanese militarism, the Kaiser, Hitler, Tojo— all somehow wrapped up in an insidious scheme of military power politics designed to "sink the Navy." Other congressmen, such as Ohio Republican John Vorys, fought back, charging that Vinson and the admirals did not truly reflect the views of the average guys in the fleet: "From Washington to Okinawa the Navy underlings are for amalgamation to save lives and money and time in buying and training and operations."[10]

But men like Vinson and the admirals got the ink, they felt threatened, and they were mad. The gold braid, most of them, quickly joined their Air Force opposite numbers in the gutter. They indulged in character assassination; Robbins, the head of SCOROR, sarcastically said that as a speaker Tooey Spaatz was "one of the ablest assistants the Navy can boast." They ordered their officers to spy on the other services; in one instance an alert marine lieutenant colonel asked two Army Air Force captains exactly who had been tasked with deciding how to equip planes for search missions in the AAF's "Directive to the Strategic Air Forces." The two captains cooperatively let their directive be copied in return for crumbs of information from the Navy Department concerning *its* search missions.

Filching internal documents from sister services became a mini-industry in the Pentagon. Unauthorized tape recordings were made by all sides. Robbins, responding to a rash of popular public air shows sponsored by the AAF, suggested that someone from the Navy attend and report on audiences, planes, and "type of propaganda." Naval aviator Jimmy Thach was convinced that the head of the public relations office at each key Air Force base was a "recent graduate of the psychological warfare school."

Forrestal, with Tip Merrill's salvos fresh in his memory, tried to control the backbiting, but his bureaucratic moderation had little effect on his subordinates. The Army (including its pilots) and the Navy faced each other across a century-and-a-half-old divide, defined by differing concepts of organization, administration, and operations. Never had American military policy been truly integrated. The rise of air power had simply kindled long-smoldering service discords to a flame, fanned by the war of words. "This nation," pronounced one naval supporter, should avoid the idea of a single military boss and the "single military concept [read: strategic air power] as it would avoid the plague."

Verbal overkill produced the inevitable—public demeaning of each other's service. A prime instance came when the good citizens of Norfolk,

Virginia, in the name of interservice harmony, sponsored a golf match for flag officers of the Army and Navy, to be followed by a stag dinner. At the dinner, AAF Brigadier General Frank Armstrong, Jr., rose after a few drinks to say, among other things, that the B-29s had won the war against Japan, although "I will say the Navy supplied us;" that the Air Force was here to stay, even in the Navy town of Norfolk; and that

> We are going to take over Navy shore-based aviation. We'll leave you a couple of carriers. They will soon be obsolete, if they are not already. But we don't propose to continue asking permission to cross the Mississippi River.

Armstrong, who probably was not familiar with Dale Carnegie, concluded by observing that "the Marine Corps is a small bitched up Army talking Navy lingo. We will put them in the Army and make real soldiers out of them."[11]

Within the week these remarks, assiduously collected by the admirals in attendance, were lying on the desk of Chester Nimitz, chief of naval operations. Even drunken patter had become part of the everyday workload. A sign posed in a Navy officers' club declared: "No drinks served to lieutenant colonels of the Air Force under 21 years of age who are not accompanied by their parents." In such an atmosphere—in which personal gossip ran rampant, service-oriented slurs were the coin of common discourse, and institutional customs and traditions built up through the years became barricades—the achievements of men like Forrestal, Sherman, and Norstad seemed remarkable indeed.

The most amazing aspect of "unification" was its achievement at all.

☆

But only in part. The National Security Act of 1947 was an omnibus compromise, and as such the law pleased almost no one—with the possible exception of Harry Truman, who may have thought that he had put interservice bickering behind him once and for all.

The president signed Public Law 253 on 26 July 1947 and thus opened the modern era of military management (and mismanagement). The act created the National Military Establishment, comprising the executive departments of the Army, Navy, and Air Force. A secretary of defense was given the "power" to exercise "general direction" over these departments; this waffling prose was there at the Navy's insistence. The new Air Force "shall include aviation forces both combat and service not otherwise assigned"—another Navy victory. The act also established the National Security Council and the National Security Resources Board and gave statutory basis to and redefined the functions of the Joint Chiefs of Staff, the Central Intelligence Agency (Ernie King loathed the whole idea of a CIA), the Research and Development Board, and the Munitions Board.

This was not true "unification." The Army had supported strong central control because its leaders believed they would otherwise lose in congressional budget competition with the other, more "glamorous," services. Eisenhower, with his extensive experience with "triphibious" warfare in Europe, even advocated a single service with a single uniform and a single service academy (this did not go down well on the banks of the Severn). The Air Force, riding its strategic air power hobbyhorse and secure in its unilateral possession of the bomb, was confident that its will would be fiat within any unified command. Only the Navy held out, fearing subordination to landlubbers and the loss of naval aviation to the "pilots" (whose spiffy new sky-blue uniforms were soon to be derided as suspiciously akin to those worn by Greyhound bus drivers).

Truman wanted Patterson as his first secretary of defense, but that staunch supporter of centralization saw the handwriting on the wall and refused the post. Ironically, Forrestal, the next choice, accepted—"ironic" because, in his new position, he found that he and his men had done their work too well, and that he had little authority at all. And anyway, there was no such thing as a "Department of Defense" for him to manage. The service secretaries, although not of Cabinet rank like Forrestal, were authorized to make end runs around him and go directly to the president. All the service secretaries also sat on the National Security Council, providing a babble of competing claims. There was no head of the Joint Chiefs—yet another committee had been formed. True, the Joint Chiefs reported directly to Forrestal, not the president, but they did not do so with a combined voice.

In short, no rational military policy could come from this scheme. The Navy saw unification as coordination of effort, voluntary cooperation among the services up and down the line, with the "national interest" as the guide. The other services saw unification as synonymous with centralization of authority, although they clearly differed over who should be in the driver's seat and exactly what road map of military policy he should be using.

No one and *no single group* spoke for the American military. Not the Joint Chiefs, who quickly fell to guarding the historic prerogatives of their respective services like so many German shepherds. Not the National Security Council, which had no mechanism to weigh the value of diametrically opposed ideas. Not the service secretaries, operating in quasi-independence and naturally loath to see their direct path to the president blocked. And certainly not Forrestal himself, restless but imprisoned in the vague fetters of the act he had done so much to create.

The unintended result of the National Security Act of 1947 was that, in actuality, only the president himself could resolve conflict over national military policy. Moreover, the deliberate fuzziness of the act defeated its purpose, which was to provide the president with the best *advice* possible on national military and security policy.[12]

The Navy could live with the act; the unwieldy hybrid was mostly of its own creation, and its seadogs retained their prized "autonomy." For years they would continue to call the idea of *real* unification the "perennial fallacy." From the viewpoint of coherent national policy, however, the act was a disaster, and Forrestal, working his customary sixteen hours a day in his new post and exhausting relays of stenographers with his machine-gun dictation, was quick to see its dimensions.

When he was piped over the side of the USS CONCRETE (as the Navy Department was called) to become secretary of defense, Forrestal became the supervisor of a federation of seven officials—the three service secretaries and the four Joint Chiefs. The fourth was designated by the act as "Chief of Staff to the President," Fleet Admiral Leahy's position. But Leahy was equipped neither by personality nor by the act to force the Chiefs and their services into some kind of unified policy. The first secretary of defense, in effect, could neither *plan* nor *lead*.

Blood could not be squeezed from a turnip, and any kind of reasoned, coherent national military policy could not be produced by the National Security Act of 1947.

☆

Forrestal was not a man to rest his oars, and he characteristically set about repairing an intolerable situation. In March 1948 at Key West, and again in August at Newport, he and Leahy secluded the three uniformed service Chiefs (Omar Bradley for the Army, Louis Denfeld for the Navy, and Tooey Spaatz for the Air Force) and tried to halt the departmental infighting over missions. By now Forrestal had some international cards to play: the Soviets had created an Eastern "bloc" in Europe and were a clear threat; Czechoslovakia had "fallen" to communism early that year under suspicious and brutal circumstances; and a bit later the Russian blockade of Berlin had begun. Three billion more dollars were therefore available in the military budget.

At Key West the secretary of defense ordered the Joint Chiefs to agree on "who will do what with what." The idea was to smooth out the appropriations process, which drove both weapons procurement and national strategy, by mutual consent, establishing clear-cut goals and missions for each service. Strategic air warfare was assigned as a primary function to the Air Force. The Navy received as a primary function "the conduct of air operations necessary for the accomplishment of objectives in a naval campaign." The Navy would participate in any overall air effort "as directed by the Joint Chiefs of Staff." But this was too fuzzy for the Air Force; the USAF insisted on sole possession of the strategic role, the Navy balked accordingly, and Forrestal was back to square one.

There was something on paper, signed 21 April 1948, called the "Agreement on Service Roles and Missions," but this counted for little, given the strategic impasse. In addition, the agreement permitted the Joint Chiefs to appoint one of their members as a commander of a designated "unified command" in any strategic area outside the United States, thus creating a military chain of command bound to short-circuit civilian control.

Forrestal chafed under all these bonds, and indeed the "National Military Establishment" was having more than its share of teething problems. No one in Forrestal's modest suite of offices facing the Mall (he had only sixty people at first) dared use the resulting acronym—NME—although ENEMY was as good as any other single word to describe the bitterness and hostility generated by unification. The emotion masked the small successes, such as the merger of some Navy and all USAF strategic airlift resources on 1 June 1948 to form the Military Air Transport Service (MATS).

Beyond the Mall few Americans had the slightest idea what ENEMY was supposed to do. A youngster from Ohio plaintively wrote that her teacher had assigned her to write about "National Defense" but that she had been unable to find any information in textbooks, almanacs, encyclopedias, or other reference books. Others, trying to help out, sent in intricate plans for flying submarines or designer sketches for chic new military uniforms. A farmer said he had read about how atomic bombs could make vegetation grow better; he requested that one be dropped on his farm ("well, not on *his* farm, but nearby").[13]

"Unification" had to be done again—in fact, military "reorganization" would become a staple of the postwar years—and the first try came with Truman's move to amend the National Security Act of 1947. The president, spurred on by Forrestal, submitted his request to Congress in March 1949, the same month that Forrestal, driven into deep depression through strain and overwork, resigned.

On 10 August 1949 the result emerged: amendments to the 1947 act. The three services had their status as executive agencies stripped from them and were downgraded to military "departments." Their secretaries no longer sat on the National Security Council. The Office of Secretary of Defense, within a Department of Defense, was created (ENEMY went by the boards). The Cabinet-level secretary got one deputy and three assistants, in addition to increased power over the military budget. He was to have "all administrative authority." Civilian control over service-originated plans, programs, and policies was thus strengthened.

The Joint Chiefs did retain some significant control over service command functions, and they received a nonvoting chairman. But the central problem, of whether they were to command or only to advise and plan, was not faced squarely. The problem remained, a conceptual gray area certain to produce tension, misunderstanding, and more infighting.

The color gray extended to the military departments themselves, which in effect became halfway houses between Forrestal's early idea of departmental "coordination" and the Army's single-department concept. The three service departments, now of sub-Cabinet rank, remained nominally independent as services yet administratively controlled by the secretary of defense; thus they "floated in ambiguity." In-house, at the Navy Department, the Navy Act of 1948 had given both civilian secretaries and admirals more power at the expense of the bureaus. The General Board, by now vestigial, at last voted to abolish itself in 1951.

But this in-house power worked against unification, particularly in the military area. Patterson had wanted a single, supreme chief of staff presiding over his own general staff for all three armed forces (the German model), a true "joint" command, and this did not happen either.

☆

By 1949, then, the Navy had fought the unification battle. The outcome was not to be measured in words like "victory" and "defeat" but in trends and portents.

Civilian control over the Navy's operations, from the budgetary process to the fleet at sea, had undoubtedly been increased. The Navy's cherished insularity from the other services, while still there, was no longer as impervious to outside forces. In general, however, the Navy had maintained its distinctive integrity against what its leaders regarded, with considerable worry approaching hysteria, as a hostile takeover, both in the strategic and in the bureaucratic sense. Navy air was still *navy* air, and the Marines (by the skin of their teeth, many felt) were still *Marines.*

The cost of unification, however, was heavy, and the battlefield was littered with wounded. For the carnage, most of which could have been avoided, there was plenty of blame to go around. The Army deserved the least censure; its soldiers were, perhaps undeservedly, lowest on the strategic totem pole in the postwar world, and they were well aware of their position. Army leaders, for self-protection, thus strongly supported unification. Apart from this, they usually maddened Navymen only insofar as they sniped at the continued usefulness of the Marine Corps or supported some silliness sponsored by their pilots.

The Air Force, however, possessed all the increasing power, impatience, and brashness of adolescence. These traits were, at bottom, what drove the Navy to the verge of paranoia. As a result all the services, but the Navy and Air Force in particular, descended rapidly—far too rapidly—into a gutter world characterized by spying, character assassination, and halftruths. In the process the true goal of unification, the strengthening of *national* defense, got lost. The ENEMY, as matters developed, was in one's own backyard, not over the hill in the next town.

In this tendency to lose sight of national goals in the conduct of interservice rivalries the Navy bore a full measure of responsibility. Forrestal's comparative moderation (though he could stall and delay with the best of them), and his bureaucratic change-of-front as secretary of defense, were not matched by conciliatory gestures on the part of his admirals. Driven by the not entirely unreasonable fear that they were about to lose their much-esteemed and time-honored strategic role as the country's first line of defense, the men in Navy blue and gold, with a few exceptions such as Forrest Sherman, responded in a blatantly parochial manner that fully matched that of the Air Force and only exacerbated the problem.

The result, from the standpoint of national defense, was disaster. "Unification," or "reorganization," was at best partial and remained to be done again (and again). The argument commonly advanced, that this war was the price a democracy, with its contending interest groups, must pay for compromise, was only a partial explanation.

For almost four years after V-J Day the national strategic focus was unclear. The *outside* "enemy" was clearly emerging as the USSR, but the exact shape of the national strategy to be derived from that fact was a matter of the most intense debate, wrapped within the question of unification. For this lack of focus all the services, their civilian heads, and the president himself were to blame. The result of the debate was more ambiguous compromise, but this was not necessarily inevitable. Much of the ambiguity might have been prevented by less service parochialism and more attention to the needs of the nation.

Rear Admiral Raymond Tarbuck had the unique distinction of being the only naval flag officer to serve with the Army, the Army Air Corps, and the Marines during his career. His comment thus had special relevance. To Tarbuck, the interservice brouhaha that resulted in the National Security Act of 1947 "was not unification—it was schism."[14]

The poisonous atmosphere produced by unification would seep down the years. Of course, members of the respective services would often work smoothly and effectively together. But the poison produced running sores that would not heal. Their cancerous presence would be apparent in annual battles over the military budget, in strategic planning, in demeaning arguments over credit and awards, and, most importantly, in joint operations.

Still, unification did not *fail*. By 1949 there was, after all, a single Department of Defense, a civilian secretary with significant (though far from omnipotent) power, and Joint Chiefs of Staff with *some* clear missions. A national military policy was eventually to emerge. But neither did unification *succeed*. Decades of service independence, unique missions, and the intangible but mighty weight of tradition could not be swept away so easily.

—For this lack of success, for the partial nature of unification, and for the actual shape unification took (for good or ill)—the United States Navy was most responsible.

CHAPTER SIX

NAVAL GLOBALISM
ON A SHOESTRING

────────── ☆ ──────────

A t sea, the only limits to the Navy's power came not from any "enemy" but from the ability to sustain its far-flung operations. "[The Navy's] size," observed Rear Admiral William ("Deak") Parsons in 1947, "is dictated more by the vastness of the oceans over which control would be exercised than the strength of possible animate adversaries."

But this problem, in itself, rapidly became daunting after the war's end. While the conflict was raging, the overseas fleet had been nourished by over twelve thousand seaborne shipments *a day* from the ports of the United States. Out of the endless American cornucopia had poured oil from Texas, flour from Minneapolis, clothing from Brooklyn, and lumber from Oregon; peaches, eggs, and beer; landing craft, generators, engines, and ammunition; canvas, paint, and carbon paper.

No fewer than eight separate Navy transportation units (with arcane titles such as "CNO-OP-05P–Tanker Control") had handled this flood. The foul-ups were many and monumental, but with amazing regularity the material got to its intended destination. In knitting the worldwide Navy together and keeping the fleet afloat and fighting, the supplies and their transport made victory possible.

Much of the transportation load had been borne by a merchant fleet run by 130 shipping companies, acting as agents of the government. But like their warrior cousins, the merchant ships practically evaporated with the coming of peace. The Merchant Ship Sales Act of 1946 provided for the sale abroad of many of these vessels at bargain-basement prices; over 1100 passed into foreign hands. Through this maritime version of the Marshall Plan of the following year, such countries as Great Britain, Norway, France, Denmark, and Italy were able to either equal their prewar merchant tonnage or come close. Even so, by the end of 1949 American operators still owned over 1100 oceangoing vessels, with an aggregate tonnage 43 percent greater than the 1939 U.S. merchant fleet.

—But as far as the Navy was concerned, this was surface gloss. In fact, the number of merchant ships *consigned to naval support* rapidly dwindled as the ships themselves rotted in the reserve fleet, passed into private hands, or were torn apart. When Congress decreed that 50 percent of the commodities consigned for the European Recovery Program be transported abroad in American bottoms, the lawmakers found that labor costs alone had already made the American merchant marine noncompetitive on the international market.

The problem, unfortunately, had no real solution, short of socializing the merchant marine or constructing an enormous fleet of commissioned auxiliaries for the Navy. A partial answer lay with the Military Sea Transportation Service, established on 1 October 1949. This agency was to provide oceanic transport for the Department of Defense and was controlled by the Navy. It operated about 220 ships on its own and chartered 200 others from the private sector. But only twenty-six of its ships were commissioned naval vessels.[1]

Thus the Navy, with worldwide tasks to perform, entered the postwar years with the bulk of its wartime fleet laid up, given away, or scrapped. Most of its officers and sailors were back on the beach. And the very lifeblood of its overseas existence, its transportation support, was severely weakened and, in an emergency, undependable.

And naval tasks *were* global. In addition to operations decreed by geopolitical strategy, there were the time-honored naval roles of experiment and exploration. In the winter of 1946, for example, there was the new carrier *Midway*, in the midst of the ice-flecked waters of the Labrador Sea, testing the feasibility of carrier operations in the Arctic (Operation FROSTBITE). At the other end of the earth, a few months later, Rear Admiral Richard Cruzen took Task Force 68 (4700 men aboard twelve ships and a submarine) to Antarctica for exploration and to stake American claims in case territorial negotiations took place (Operation HIGHJUMP). Each of Cruzen's ships steamed an average of eighteen thousand nautical miles. To support HIGHJUMP, the thirteen-vessel task force loaded out from both the East and West coasts with enough supplies to sustain eight months of polar operations.

The public expected such activities from its Navy, and the Navy had to keep stretching, training, testing. But the continuous support that was required—the mountains of supplies, the shipping, the need for friendly bases—was in its enormous scale unlike anything the prewar peacetime Navy had known.

For this was indeed a new world, and the Navy's role, apparently, would run from corner to corner.

☆

Without doubt the Navy *wanted* this role: "Can do!" Its strategy, in embryonic form, insisted on maintaining a variety of capabilities rather than, as in the Air Force mode, prescribing for a specific kind of war. "Flexibility" was the watchword—the Navy would be flexible enough to deal with "isolated danger spots" as well as to meet the requirements of theater or global war.

To the Air Force such a program was wishy-washy—"a little bit of everything"—and was no "mission," peacetime or otherwise. The problem of definitions was not overly important (Forrestal once commented that the peacetime mission of the armed services was to destroy the secretary of defense), but the problem of worldwide *focus* certainly was. The argument was over where the Navy's comparatively scant resources should be directed, and in what proportion.

In the Western Hemisphere the Caribbean remained, as its waters had been since the turn of the century, a pond dominated by American naval exercises. Cuba, Puerto Rico, Panama—all were a settled part of naval routine. Naval interest in Latin America, with the towering but largely empty symbolism of the Monroe Doctrine and hemispheric politics in support, might have been expected to be intense, but such was not the case. After all, Buenos Aires was almost twice as distant from New York as was London.

World War II caused almost all the navies of the region to fall into the American orbit; by 1945 "Latin American naval policy was almost completely shaped by the United States." *Yanqui* influence was everywhere, with naval missions in every major Latin American nation except Juan Perón's Argentina. Brazil, in particular, had close naval ties with the United States, stemming from wartime basing policies. But Washington, particularly after the Rio Treaty was signed in 1947, tended to take its south-of-the-border allies for granted.

Before the war, the United States had shared its naval influence in Latin America with the British, and Germany, Italy, and France had also made their presence felt. But now the *yanquis*, with their surplus warships, manufactured export goods, and increasingly greedy markets for the raw materials of the region, were unrivaled. Forrestal, told by Admiral Richard Edwards that "the Army was in pell-mell haste to equip all the South American countries with armaments" on the grounds of hemispheric reciprocal defense, was not so sure that this was the best policy.

Yet the deals for surplus arms ground on. In cruisers alone, for example, Argentina received *Phoenix* and *Boise;* Brazil, *Philadelphia* and *St. Louis;* and Chile, *Brooklyn* and *Nashville.* American naval concern, however, looked past Latin America to the world beyond the hemisphere. Not for fifteen years, until communism was injected into the area, would the Navy (and the United States) move Latin American affairs to the front burner.[2]

☆

The enormous reaches of the Pacific Ocean were a different story. "The Pacific is our natural property," Henry Adams had written, and after World

War II few Americans would have gainsaid him. American officers like Vice Admiral Charles ("Savvy") Cooke, Jr., the immediate postwar commander of the Seventh Fleet, felt the United States needed a "fleet in being" in the western Pacific, which meant not just surface and air power but a trained amphibious assault force. This opinion was understandable; the Navy's most glowing image of itself was that of its final triumphant year of war in the Pacific: of fast carrier task forces sweeping through Japan's island bastions at will, of bloody but ultimately victorious amphibious assaults against a fanatical, determined enemy, and of the silent, deadly submarines wreaking havoc on Japan's overseas lifelines. "To Be Specific, It's Our Pacific," as the title of one Tin Pan Alley jingle ran.

By contrast, the chill waters of the northern Atlantic, though strategically critical, had offered only the relative drudgery of convoy duty, antisubmarine warfare, and shore bombardment. Besides, the Atlantic had had to be shared with the British and Canadian navies. In the Pacific, although the Americans had at first pleaded for British help, by August 1944 American opinion (chiefly Ernie King's) was solidly against the Royal Navy's entering either MacArthur's or Nimitz's theaters. Over King's vehement protest, FDR and Churchill had things otherwise, and in November 1944 the new British Pacific Fleet, eventually consisting of two modern battleships, three fleet carriers, five heavy cruisers, and assorted auxiliaries, was formed under Admiral Sir Bruce Fraser. This aggregation operated as a task force under overall American command until the surrender of Japan.

King's reasoning was emotional and crude but was clearly representative of that of the great majority of his countrymen. War veteran Dean Rusk, a future secretary of state, remembered that he "personally wanted the United States to control every wave in the Pacific." Concerning the Pacific, King said in April 1945, "these atolls, these island harbors will have been paid for by the sacrifice of American blood." Thus, the Pacific islands of right should remain under American control. This was Bill Leahy's opinion as well, and also that of every other naval leader.

The United Nations charter dealt with the issue in its Article XII, concerning the International Trusteeship System. The only "strategic trust territory" authorized, in a document that looked for "progressive development towards independence" for all the world's colonial peoples, was that covered by the former Japanese mandates in the Pacific. But of the eleven "trust territories" authorized, including Micronesia, all—which were once the charges of Britain, France, Italy, Belgium, New Zealand, and Australia—would become independent by 1975.

—All except Micronesia. And in this exception the United States Navy was deeply involved. In February 1943, months before the island assaults began in the central Pacific with Tarawa in the Gilberts, the General Board, under the direction of Admiral Thomas Hart, former commander of the

Asiatic Fleet, began to study the problem. These professional naval officers deeply distrusted any international organization as an instrument of collective security; they had spent much of their careers watching the dismal failures of the League of Nations. They saw good reasons—stability, for example—for the continued existence of the British Empire but also foresaw the continued need for American naval strength.

The board found that the Navy's postwar defensive requirements would of necessity be worldwide. In the Pacific the shield would need to cover Clipperton and the Galapagos Islands to the east; the Marquesas, Samoa, the New Hebrides, and the Solomons to the southwest; the Marshalls, the Gilberts, the Ellices, and the Bonins; Wake, Truk, and Formosa; and the Aleutians. After all, pronounced the board, many of these areas were being won by *American* "effort, blood, and treasure."

There were three reports by the General Board in all, each sounding the same themes. By the time these reached Roosevelt's desk, in June 1943, they formed a "blueprint for transforming most of the Pacific into an American lake." FDR was cautious, but he recognized the need for postwar bases (no more agonizing island-by-island assaults across the Pacific) and accordingly directed Rear Admiral Richard Byrd, the Antarctic explorer, to make an on-the-spot inspection of possible base sites.

The Byrd Mission checked out a total of 130 islands. In a "Dear Franklin" letter the admiral was blunt, recommending that "after this war the sovereignty of no island in the Pacific be changed without full agreement from the United States." In November 1943 the Joint Chiefs of Staff weighed in with a postwar basing plan that girdled the world with prospective American bases. In the Pacific the outermost American defense line would run from Attu in the Aleutians through Paramishiru, the Bonins, the Philippines, New Britain, the Solomons, Suva, Samoa, Tahiti, and the Marquesas, curling back eastward in a giant arc to Clipperton and the Galapagos Islands. The area encompassed was virtually the entire Pacific Ocean.

If any of the war's Pacific battlefields needed to be placed *permanently* inside the American defense system, they were the islands of Micronesia. The Joint Chiefs believed that nothing less than absolute sovereignty there was suitable. This was the Navy's official view as well. Captain H. L. Pence, officer-in-charge of the Occupied Areas Section of the Navy Department, argued that peace could be maintained only by ringing Japan with military bases, most of which would have to be in Micronesia. Pence, a consummate racist, boiled the Pacific war down to a question of racial survival: "White civilization was at stake. . . . [W]ar was inevitable and a good thing. When one nation [Japan] became an international bandit it should be eliminated." To Pence, "every step should be taken to assure the absolute dominance of the position of white rule in the Pacific."

Pence was a bigoted extremist, but his strategic views, regardless of their source, were not out of whack with those of the General Board and the Joint Chiefs. FDR, the seasoned politician, would never buy such a rationale, at least publicly. He was concerned with civil control, economic aid, and education for the natives. An American trusteeship for Micronesia, in his words, "does not necessarily involve a decision on permanent sovereignty." The Joint Chiefs, however, from their more narrow perspective, noted that, regarding the continuation of British military power in the region, a "substantial change has taken place." Only the Russians and the Americans would emerge as prime military powers from this war, and the Pacific belonged to those who could garrison and hold its islands.

Roosevelt, however, did not see matters that way. In November 1944, as Sir Bruce Fraser geared up his fleet to join the Pacific war, the president told his advisers that, as far as he could tell, all a permanent American takeover of any of the Pacific islands would do "would be to provide jobs as governors of insignificant islands for inefficient Army and Navy officers or members of the civilian career service." FDR wanted the Pacific islands fortified and capable of defense (the shadow of Pearl Harbor loomed over him as well) but also placed on a path to independence. In March 1945, shortly before his death, he was still saying "that neither the Army nor the Navy had any business administering the civilian government of territories; that they had no competence to do this."[3]

But now FDR was gone, and the question of the Pacific would not be resolved along his lines. When a bill was introduced in Congress pertaining to the postwar government of the Pacific islands, Forrestal sarcastically suggested that Secretary of the Interior Harold Ickes (a strident foe of military governorship) be made king of Polynesia, Micronesia, and the entire Pacific Ocean Area. Forrestal's canon was that "the United States is to have the major responsibility for the Pacific Ocean security."

Chester Nimitz agreed, because "the ultimate security of the U.S. depends in major part on our ability to control the Pacific Ocean . . . these islands are part of the complex essential to that control and . . . the concept of trusteeship is inapplicable here because these islands do not represent any colonial problem nor is there economic advantage accruing to the U.S. through their ownership. . . ." The one "colonial problem," the Philippines, gained its independence (as promised) in 1946; besides, the grateful Filipinos, in May 1945, had already signed an agreement giving the United States all the military and naval bases desired. The Philippines Rehabilitation Act of 1946 provided for $520 million in aid and transferred $100 million in surplus property to the new Filipino government. The great naval installation at Subic Bay, on the west coast of Luzon, was being beefed up for the ships of the Seventh Fleet.

And so the power vacuum would be filled. As the islands were captured, Navy personnel remained, first as conquerors, then as administrators, governors, educators, builders, health specialists, and scientific experimenters. These roles were not new; the Navy had governed Guam and American Samoa since the end of the Spanish-American War but with a decidedly heavy hand and decidedly mixed results. Now the service was being given control of about 1500 islands, atolls, and reefs, in total area about the size of Rhode Island.

In October 1945 Truman appointed a committee composed of the secretaries of war, Navy, state, and interior to make recommendations about the problem. Not surprisingly, Forrestal's views prevailed. The decision was to let the process of conquest-produced administration go forward, in effect leaving the Navy in control and creating a comprehensive basing system in both the Pacific and Atlantic oceans. Ickes was livid; he felt (correctly) that he had been the victim of a bureaucratic end run. To him, the Navy was establishing a "tyranny" in the islands, in defiance not only of Roosevelt's wishes but also of sacred American constitutional precepts. According to Ickes's information, one naval officer had described the natives in his care as follows:

> These gooks are the dumbest, most worthless, lazy, filthy, no-good, no-account people I have ever seen. They lie, cheat, steal and have no morals. They smile and wave at you, but they would cut your throat in a second if they weren't afraid of American planes.

Without doubt the Navy's activities among the Pacific islanders were underlain with racism, both benign and viciously oppressive. But the driving force that led the Navy to stay, to build its bases, officers' clubs, roads, hospitals, and schools, was strategic. The United States was never to *fortify* the islands of Micronesia in a strategic sense, as the Japanese had done after World War I. But the American *presence*, particularly in military guise, became well-nigh universal.

These islands had been fought for, paid for in blood. King had a handle on what had happened—the Pacific was payback for Pearl Harbor. The natives counted for little, national defense was everything. In 1947 the United Nations granted the United States military control over a huge stretch of the Pacific. FDR was dead, Sir Bruce Fraser and his fleet had gone home, and the vast western ocean was now the biggest American lake.

☆

Concerning Japan, the opinionated Captain Pence not only supported an iron cordon of American bases around the Japanese home islands, he wanted the Japanese destroyed, believing that the United States had been too kindly disposed toward them. The Pacific, said Pence, was "our lake," and the Japanese were in the Pacific.[4]

Again, Pence was on the extreme edge. Instead of grinding the Japanese to powder under his victor's heel, Douglas MacArthur was engaged in some of the finest work of his long, storied career, recasting a feudal society, remolding a national economy, and inaugurating a democratic political system. The Navy was deeply involved in the Japanese occupation—which would last for six years—primarily because of its interest in overseas bases. The premium base was Yokosuka, the gateway to Tokyo Bay. By 1950 *Pravda* was announcing that "the American imperialists have settled down in Japan and have no desire to leave it."

Pravda was right. The Fifth Fleet, the naval element of the occupation forces, had indeed settled in. (The Seventh Fleet was operating on the edges of the Chinese maelstrom, moving American and Nationalist troops here and there, while the Third Fleet had been downgraded to MAGIC CARPET duty.) Rear Admiral Benton Decker, one of the postwar base commanders at Yokosuka, eventually gave out that the United States would require the base permanently. As the lines of the Cold War solidified, the use of excellent island bases overseeing the east coast of the Soviet Union and, eventually, Communist China became too good an opportunity for naval policymakers to pass up.

The Navy had also played a major if largely forgotten role in Japanese repatriation after the war. Surrender had found surviving Japanese forces, many of them near starvation, scattered in a huge arc throughout East Asia and the southwestern Pacific. In the two years after V-J Day the Navy, using any shipping its people could get their hands on, repatriated over four million Japanese back to their homeland. Over one hundred of these vessels were crewed by the Japanese themselves.

In addition, one million Chinese and Koreans, most of whom had been shanghaied to Japan to do war work, were carried back to their countries. Vice Admiral Robert Griffin, commander of naval forces in the Far East, had to scrape past the bottom of the barrel to accomplish this job. Naval planners had figured on the support needs of the Seventh Fleet and on the costs of the occupation of Japan, not on some seemingly perpetual ferryboat operation—but finally, by 1947, the thing was done.

Further, the Navy had to sweep over ten thousand American mines sown in Japanese coastal waters by B-29s and submarines; over fifty-five thousand Japanese mines had to be taken up or destroyed as well. The Naval Analysis Division of the Strategic Bombing Survey showed up, to sift through the rubble of war. There were technical missions, communications units, hydrographic experts, Marines, and Seabees with their endless bulldozing. Sailors trudged up Mount Fujiyama in their skivvy shirts, confused geishas with prostitutes, and tried to outbargain impoverished Japanese merchants. This American invasion clearly would last longer than the first one, that of "Old Bruin" Perry back in the 1850s.

With all the stir, the bases were what really counted. Despite the general roll-up of most wartime bases, the Marianas remained crucial in the Pacific, and Yokosuka likewise in Japan. The first American commander at Yokosuka (which had been lightly bombed during the war) had little empathy for the natives. A sign outside his office proclaimed: "Remember, these are the bastards that raped Nanking!" But the usefulness of "Yoko" and other bases, such as Sasebo, quickly surfaced. Mick Carney, serving a postwar tour as deputy chief of naval operations for logistics, argued that the United States should retain its air and naval power in Japan "as long as our national interests require."

Benny Decker, coming to Yoko in April 1946, soon made his policy clear: the United States was going to clean up the base and the city with an eye to an American naval presence lasting "anywhere from ten to fifty years." Griffin, his boss, tried to dampen such statements, but Decker had MacArthur's ear and those of the movers and shakers back in the Pentagon as well. Decker's basic notion, increasingly held by many Americans, was of a peace treaty (eventually signed in 1951) by which the United States would guarantee Japanese internal and external security. In return, Tokyo would provide necessary basing privileges, accept American advisers, and in this way become a bastion of anticommunism in the Far East.

The first East Asian war plans developed by the Joint Chiefs of Staff, in April 1947, had as a foundation the concept of "holding Japan." The diplomats wanted Tokyo to be friendly, politically stable, economically sound, and militarily dependent on Washington. But this did not necessarily include basing privileges. Thus, the battle was joined, at the highest levels.

The struggle was resolved not only by the deepening Cold War but also by dollars. Three years after V-J Day, American demobilization was complete; national military expenditures had fallen from 82 percent of total expenditures in 1945 to 36 percent. The naval budget had dwindled to one-seventh of its 1945 total. Truman was promising still more austerity. Under these conditions Yokosuka and its sister Japanese bases were simply too good to give up. They were meteorologically superior to those on Okinawa (which seemingly got in the way of every typhoon track in the western Pacific), they were already operating (and with incredibly low local labor costs), and they were strategically well placed.

In fiscal year 1949 Yoko provided $1 million more in services than its operating cost; replacing Yoko with a comparable base elsewhere in the area would carry an estimated price tag in excess of $600 million. In fact, Yoko blossomed: the base harbored quarters, machine shops, drydocks, huge cranes, and a completely equipped naval hospital. Yoko raised poultry, grew mushrooms, provided yachting expeditions, and offered roller-skating and bowling. Booze was duty-free; a bottle of gin cost sixty cents, and a bottle of good aged whiskey a dollar and a half. Women could be had for pennies, and a live-in "maid" cost a few dollars a month. The phrase "liberty port" hardly did Yoko justice. Life was soft there, and getting softer.

The Joint Chiefs and Louis Johnson, Forrestal's replacement as secretary of defense, needed no further convincing. Strategic needs and pocketbook exigencies won the day. Benny Decker may have preached the loudest, but he had most of his senior officers solidly behind him in the choir. The Navy *needed* Japan. Naval desires in this regard became national policy even before the Korean War confirmed the military usefulness of the Japanese bases. The Seventh Fleet, which had begun as MacArthur's amphibious assault force in the waters around New Guinea, would stay in the western Pacific after the Fifth Fleet was disestablished.

The policy emerged in the spring of 1949. Japan now had a new constitution and a popularly elected government. The major war-crimes trials, more than unfair and potentially divisive, were history. MacArthur was relaxing the leading strings of the occupation. In this atmosphere Truman sponsored NSC 13/3, the National Security Council's policy paper terminating all restrictions on Japan's use of former war industries for nonmilitary production. NSC 13/3 also was a preview of a "friendly partnership" with the Japanese, not only calling for retention of bases on Okinawa but also cautiously anticipating *permanent* American bases in Japan—most notably, Yoko.

The Navy, generally, was a good neighbor in Yoko and the other bases, so good that the government of Prime Minister Shigeru Yoshida welcomed its continued presence, even after the peace treaty was signed in September 1951. American paychecks counted for a lot, of course, but Decker and other base commanders took great care not to offend local customs. When Decker finally left Yoko, in June 1950, he received bushels of commendatory letters from the Japanese, who placed a bust of the admiral in the city's Seaside Park. Relations were "very cordial," remembered another American flag officer.[5]

Yoshida may have hoped that his American visitors would be only temporary houseguests. But his country's new constitution renounced war as an instrument of national policy and prohibited any military force whatsoever except for policing functions. With this unique document the Japanese metaphorically bared their chests to their conqueror and the world. And the world was an unfriendly place. "We are being gradually pushed out of Asia by the Communists!" screamed one American naval commentator. "The sole remaining base which is available to us in that area is Japan. To lose Japan might well mean disaster."

The Navy did not lose Japan. The Seventh Fleet helped smash the Empire and then, a welcome guest at most times, an exceedingly unwelcome one at certain moments, its ships and men stayed on.

☆

The historic naval relationship with China had been much more complex. From the earliest American trade with the Chinese in the 1780s, the mysterious Celestial Kingdom had held a fascinating allure for many Americans, the Navy included. There were all those people to be Christianized; all those markets to be crammed with American trade goods; the incredibly cheap labor.

For the Navy, China's deeply indented coastline and great rivers had meant seaports and strategic advantage, though these had to be shared with other powers. The famous Open Door policy of the turn of the century had been far more economic than naval, but with Japan as a potential enemy in the region, the Navy had begun to count on China. The tiny Asiatic Squadron had routinely used Chinese ports and even operated regularly hundreds of miles up the country's rivers.

This China—the China of happy Christians, contented consumers, friendly and potentially democratic allies—had been an illusion, one of the most compelling of the twentieth century. In fact, for most of the first half of the century there had been no "China;" rather, the word described a land mass ceaselessly mangled by contending warlords, a primitive economic system that existed at a fragmented, localized level, and a society of hundreds of millions that was both misruled and oppressed.

China had been at war for years before Pearl Harbor. Even as FDR had sought to make China one of the "Big Four" Allies during the war, the Chinese had been deeply, bloodily divided among themselves. The question of whom the Nationalist leader, Chiang Kai-shek, regarded as his primary enemy, the Japanese or the Chinese Communists, was at best a toss-up. But many American naval officers stationed in China became admirers of Chiang and warm adherents to the Nationalist cause. The few admirals who raised obvious questions about Chiang's cliquish leadership and his abysmal, corruption-riddled military organization were roundly criticized. So was anyone else. "[Truman] is all right—he's behind Chiang," said Bill Leahy. "But those pinkies in the State Department can't be trusted."

Chief among Chiang's American fans was Savvy Cooke. (After he retired from the Navy, Cooke even worked for the Nationalists for a time.) Cooke was typical of those Navymen who insisted that the United States should not prematurely leave China at war's end, because there was an internal Communist threat to be quelled. There was also a strategic angle. The Navy had looked on the Chinese coastline as providing bases from which to blockade Japan—Ernie King had gone so far as to insist that a major objective of the drive across the Pacific had been the establishment of a naval base at or near Amoy—and many officers wished to keep this coastline open.

After V-J Day the Navy did stay, at times directly aiding the Nationalist cause. Chiang's forces were advised, until 1948, by the 1400-man-strong Naval Advisory Group; in the two years after the war 131 American naval vessels valued at $140 million were transferred to China; and $17.7 million of naval ordnance went to the Nationalists. More than fifty thousand Marines were put ashore at Tientsin and Tsingtao in the fall of 1945. American naval vessels ferried Chiang's troops, five armies of them, north to fight the Communists in Manchuria. The commander of the VII Amphibious Corps reported the landing of the Chinese 89th Division near Shanghaikwan, observing that the Chinese were "well disciplined. Docile. Very young. No contagious diseases. Apparently first experience with plumbing and initially mistook urinals for wash basins and dark corners for heads. Many seasick. Troops have left but odors linger." Even so, recalled the officer, "the thing we actually did the most was run the mail."[6]

Such operations were not the acts of a neutral, and in fact the United States was far from neutral in the Chinese civil war. America backed the anti-Communist horse, for ideological as well as deeply historical reasons. Navy intelligence teams operating out of Mukden, for example, routinely gathered information on Communist operations. But Chiang presided over a hollow shell, and his base in the countryside rapidly eroded.

Death and decay were everywhere. The cruiser *Los Angeles*, moored off Shanghai ("a real riproaring Oriental liberty town"), became accustomed to treating exotic strains of venereal disease and having her sailors carved up by knife fights in Blood Alley, but her men never became used to the daily spectacle of a small tugboat chuffing downriver, always towing two or three Chinese bodies. The tug would tie the bodies to a buoy next to the cruiser, where the Americans could see the naked corpses spread-eagled in the water until late in the day, when another tug would collect them and tow them away.

By 1948 a force of American ships under Vice Admiral Oscar Badger found itself bottled up in Tsingtao, the old German colony. The Navy ostensibly had the mission of showing the flag and helping China in its "postwar recovery." But there was no recovery; in fact, Tsingtao was jammed with three hundred thousand refugees, most of whom had no shelter whatsoever. People were starving in the gutters, ignored by passersby. Inflation in the seaports was out of sight; beggars in Tsingtao were hesitant before accepting anything less than a Nationalist $10,000 bill. (One naval officer paid thirty-three million Chinese dollars for a mediocre meal in Shanghai.)

Badger, a hard-working, bushy-browed dynamo, was in an impossible position. He spent his time conferring with Chiang or the generalissimo's lackeys, lecturing VIP guests on the importance of China, or simply pacing his cabin on board his flagship, *Estes*, in frustration. When a reporter asked him if he would fight to save Tsingtao, Badger exploded: "I'm fed up with war. If people had any sense, the atom bomb would have ended war!" The admiral saw his mission as one of "[stabilizing] the China situation." How the Navy was to do this, he did not say.

As the Nationalist cause went down the drain, many in the Navy got angrier at the prospect of "losing" China. Chiang, that "tough, sincere patriot," deserved, in this view, the fullest American backing in his noble campaign against the "worldwide" menace of communism. And there was not simply the specter of ideological defeat; there were the resources: the Manchurian ore and coal, the labor, the ports, the people. China became an intensely emotional issue for Americans in 1948 and 1949, not least to many Navymen who fondly remembered their palmy days as part of the prewar Asiatic Squadron.

—Their concern availed little. The Nationalists tried to close Communist-held ports to overseas arms supplies, a futile gesture when the great strength of Mao Tse-tung's armies lay in the countryside. In the end Chiang's organization, rotten and defeatist, crumbled away, its remnants and their leader eventually fleeing to Taiwan (where Chiang continued to receive strong American support, even though the Joint Chiefs declared that they did not have the forces available to defend the island, given reduced military budgets and global obligations). "Communism is on the march not only in China but throughout East and South East Asia," one naval observer solemnly intoned.

The Navy took part in the last dismal moments of Nationalist China, evacuating foreign nationals from surrounded seaports like Tsingtao, Shanghai, and the famed resort city of Chefoo. In the latter port the destroyer *Higbee* took on five stretcher cases (four nuns and a priest), seventy-six more members of religious orders, and an Armenian merchant whose sole possession was a full case of scotch. But humanitarian missions such as these were all the Navy could do; the Communists were a land power with no navy whatsoever, and Mahanian precepts would not work off the China coast.[7]

By the end of 1949 all the ports were gone, and American bluejackets had seen their last of China. There was no longer a "China card" to play in Far Eastern naval diplomacy. When vessels like *Higbee* turned their sterns to the Chinese coast, no one could know that more than three decades would pass before American warships would again heave to in the harbors of mainland China.

☆

As vital as the Pacific region seemed to be to American interests, and despite the "fall" of China to the Communists, the dagger of hostility to the United States, as policymakers saw matters, pointed toward Europe and the Atlantic. Forrestal's major contribution to postwar naval planning had been to identify the Soviet Union, despite its decided lack of blue-water naval power, as the nation's most probable enemy. To him the Stalin regime was a totalitarian dictatorship on a par with Hitler's. Although Truman and his diplomatic aides at first hoped for postwar Allied harmony, Forrestal and his naval planners from the beginning assumed the opposite.

The result was a shift in naval strategic focus, both from the Pacific to the Atlantic and from oceanic conflict on the Mahanian model to naval operations against the shores. The shift took years to accomplish, was not readily apparent at first, and certainly did not silence those who saw the Pacific as the key to national defense. As certainly, the Navy lacked a clearly defined global strategic concept at the end of the war, and the service was obviously groping for some way to align its awesome naval predominance— in carriers, amphibious assault techniques, and oceangoing submarines— with the obvious lack of any blue-water threat.

The Joint Chiefs, in October 1945, had produced a planning paper (JCS 1518) entitled "Strategic Concept and Plan for the Employment of United States Armed Forces," which identified the USSR as a major antagonist and Great Britain as a probable ally. At King's insistence the Navy was wedded to the importance of forward offensive operations in the postwar world. The problem was how to integrate the strategic proposition with operational details.

In April 1946 the planners for the Joint Chiefs, fully aware of the continued might of the Soviet army, estimated that in a major war pitting the Soviets against the British and the Americans, the USSR would overrun most of western continental Europe, European Turkey, Iran, Iraq, the Suez Canal (possibly), Korea, Manchuria, and northern China. This assessment, based on inflated guesses about the postwar strength and capabilities of the Red Army, was far too gloomy but nevertheless bad news for the U.S. Navy, because very few of these areas could be directly influenced by naval power. By necessity, then, the Navy began to plan for operations in the Mediter-ranean and other regions on the edges of Europe. This planning was a reversal of the American strategic posture toward Europe during World War II and an adoption of Churchill's much-maligned (by Americans) peripheral strategy.

Early on, the Truman administration demonstrated little concern with either the Med or the Middle East. These were traditional British areas of naval concern, part of the famed "lifeline of Empire." The American army, especially General Marshall, concentrated on northwestern Europe and a potential replay of the Normandy triumph. American naval officers, during these months, still tended to hew toward the Pacific arena. But as the Soviets steadily established their hegemony in Eastern Europe and British economic weakness became increasingly apparent, what had once been seen solely as a preserve of the Royal Navy drifted into the foreground of naval planning.[8]

One measure of the drift came with experiments like FROSTBITE, looking to Arctic operations as a way to get at the Soviet Union. Another was a renewed emphasis on antisubmarine warfare, because if the Soviet navy had a strong suit, their hundreds of diesel-powered submarines held that potential. The Red Army had captured most of the U-boat production and assembly sites in eastern Germany and had received many German submarines as reparations, including the long-range, state-of-the-art Type XXIs.

At the prompting of Forrest Sherman, then head of the Strategic Plans Division (OP-30), Navy planners targeted not only Russian subs but also airfields, depots, factories, shipyards, and bases. Aerial bombardment and offensive mining were seen as tactics to prevent the boats from even getting to sea. Carrier operations were envisioned for the North Sea, the Med, the Barents Sea, and the Sea of Japan. American submarines would act as sub killers.

Naval Strategic Planning Study 3 (March 1947) expressed confidence in the ability of the Navy's primary offensive arm, the carriers, to operate against the Russian coastline, even in the face of numerically preponderant Soviet land-based aviation:

> Carrier air power, operating from the highly mobile, self-defending, and self-sustaining bases embodied in the carrier attack force, is the only weapon in the possession of the U.S. which can deliver early and effective attacks against Russian air power and selective shore objectives in the initial stages of a Russo-American conflict.

Such a proposal enraged the planners' opposite numbers in the Air Force, who saw themselves as the sole custodians of strategic bombing and figured that the Navy, as usual, was poaching on their strategic turf.

Therefore, as the bureaucratic wars ground on and NSPS 3 remained as written (with the Navy seeking a nuclear strategic role by maneuvering for a large carrier suitable for aircraft big enough to lug an atomic bomb), the Navy's attention centered more and more on the periphery, particularly the Med and the oil-rich Persian Gulf. Sherman and his men had relegated the Pacific, as a strategic focus, to a secondary status. Combat-proven Pacific combat teams, such as Marc Mitscher and his chief of staff, Arleigh Burke, were reassigned to the Atlantic. All three of the new *Midway*-class carriers, the best the Navy had, would remain there as well, even through the Korean conflict.

All the internal turmoil was lost to the public; this initial "maritime strategy," unlike its 1980s successor, was formulated and achieved within the Pentagon, by blue-suiters, with the absolute minimum of attendant publicity. The weapons balance was in the Atlantic; the interest was in the Mediterranean; and the planning was largely devoted to how to get at the Soviets from the European end. Tactically, Sherman played down the Soviet surface fleet (about seven or eight hundred assorted vessels, a good share either coastal or riverine) as of "low combat value." The basic problem lay with the Red submarines; once these were disposed of, the continent of Europe could be breached again, just as its defenses had been in World War II.

Despite Chester Nimitz's experience as the wartime naval leader in the Pacific, the new strategy belonged to the chief of naval operations as well. Sherman was Nimitz's valued exec—he had served him as head planner in the Pacific from late 1943 to the end of the war—and the two men trusted each other implicitly. (Nimitz had asked Sherman to stand behind him at the Japanese surrender aboard *Missouri*.) Both Nimitz and Sherman were centrists, striving for a balanced postwar fleet. Some aviators, led by Arthur Radford, saw the carrier as the *only* answer to Soviet seapower, but Nimitz and Sherman, both expecting the big carrier and the atomic bomb for the Navy, held the line against putting all their eggs into one basket. By the time Sherman left Washington early in 1948 for a seagoing command in the Med, the Navy's strategic revolution, featuring a balance of forces targeted against the European periphery, had been accomplished.[9]

Along the way had come the sad recognition of the relative decline of the Royal Navy, a nice historical turn of the cards. (An English naval publication, back in 1876, had cruelly and correctly observed that there "never was such a hapless, broken-down, tattered, forlorn apology for a navy as that possessed by the United States.") The Joint Chiefs, as early as July 1944, had been brutally clear on the new arrangement: "Both in the absolute and relative sense . . . the British Empire will emerge from the war having lost ground both economically and militarily." Further: "The relative strength and geographic positions of [the United States and the Soviet Union] preclude the military defeat of one . . . by the other, even if that power were allied with the British Empire."

Clement Attlee, the new British prime minister, was convinced that his empire could no longer take care of itself: "The conditions which made it possible to defend a string of possessions scattered over five continents by means of a fleet based on island fortresses have gone." The Royal Navy had suffered grievous wartime losses: 1525 warships, totaling almost one million tons, and over fifty thousand men. The British were bankrupt, with overseas debts fifteen times their reserves of gold and foreign currency. Their export trade was one-third the level of that in 1939, and their visible exports could finance only 10 percent of their overseas requirements. Their industrial machinery, particularly in shipbuilding, was woefully outdated. Attlee was predicting "economic disaster" if defense expenditure was not deeply pared and manpower redeployed to civilian life. "Our sea power is not supreme," admitted the South African tower of empire, Jan Smuts. "Our former unique sea power is no longer the sure shield." Attlee, despite his pessimism, remained confident: "In present circumstances [it is not necessary] to have a large fleet ready for action as there [is] no one to fight."

The Royal Navy was hardly impotent; the British fleet was still, in the late 1940s, far and away the second strongest naval power in the world, but relative to even the American Navy after drawdown, its capabilities had diminished appreciably. In 1945 the British had almost 900 major warships and 866,000 men and women in naval uniform. There were about 3000 minor vessels and nearly 5500 landing craft. But the British had badly overstrained themselves in war, and the budgetary ax was relentless. Despite an extraordinary mobilization of their domestic resources, their industrial plant was badly worn down; their gold and dollar revenues, once as solid as Nelson's Column, were vanishing; and their export trade, increasingly dependent on American largesse, was withering. Lord Keynes called the situation a "financial Dunkirk," which had only the worst implications for the Royal Navy.

The British were being forced to make much harder decisions in naval policy than the Americans, cutting down to the bone at first and then, to the dismay of their sea dogs, right on through. By 1947 their ability to defend even the precious Atlantic sealanes was in doubt. In a European war these sealanes would be crucial, and not only for Europe. "The Atlantic Ocean," in the words of one naval authority, "and no other sea or land area is basic to our ability to wage war anywhere on earth." The Atlantic, not the Pacific, had become the "Sea of Decision."

—Such was the measure of the strategic shift.

☆

American sailors were no strangers to the Mediterranean. The United States had adopted a peacetime policy of dispersing its warships to distant cruising stations as early as 1801, when the minuscule Mediterranean Squadron first poked its nose inside the Strait of Gibraltar to keep an eye on the predatory Barbary pirates. This force usually stayed small and sometimes vanished from the Med altogether, but by the Civil War a naval presence there had become a permanent fixture in American policy.

Stationing warships so far from home, in areas where they could easily get into trouble, made the squadron a favorite target of congressmen intent on shrinking naval expenditures. "The Mediterranean Ocean! A fleet there!" cried Fernando Wood. "How absurd!" Samuel S. ("Sunset") Cox charged in 1870 that naval officers assigned to the Med did little but hobnob with broken-down dukes and saunter into operas. "Our people can rest assured that their European Squadron [as the ships of the operagoers had been renamed] is naught else but a picnic for which they must pay the bills."[10]

There was plenty of this sort of thing, of course—the varied pleasures of ports like Villefranche and Port Mahon were hard to pass up—but the distinguishing aspect of peacetime American naval policy in the Mediterranean was that there seldom was one. The Navy, moving solemnly from place to place and showing the flag, was essentially a reactive force, responding to a crisis or to the needs of American citizens in the area. With V-E Day little changed. When Vice Admiral Bernhard Bieri relieved Rear

Admiral Jules James as commander, U.S. Naval Forces Mediterranean, at the end of the war, he "never did receive from anyone a statement of our policy in connection with any government in the Mediterranean, or bordering the Mediterranean."

Bieri's command had been created in February 1946 from the wartime "United States Naval Forces Northwest African Waters." At that time, throughout the entire sea, only one cruiser and two destroyers were showing the American flag. Within a month, however, things began to change. The pretext was the return of the remains of the deceased Turkish ambassador to the United States, Mehmet Munir Ertegün, to his native land. The catalyst, however, was the Soviet Union: its troops were still occupying northern Iran, there were military movements close to the Turkish border with Russia, and Soviet diplomats were campaigning for the withdrawal of British forces from Greece.

Missouri was assigned the task of carrying the ambassador home. President Truman liked the idea, which had probably been generated by the fertile mind of Admiral Richmond Kelly Turner. Forrestal wanted to make a naval parade, assigning the carriers *Franklin D. Roosevelt* and *Midway*, as well as a horde of cruisers and destroyers, to accompany the battleship (not even Nelson had had that kind of send-off). The State Department squelched this request, however, and *Missouri* made her way through the Med accompanied only by the cruiser *Providence* and the destroyer *Power*.

The Turks gave the Americans an extraordinarily warm welcome. So did the Greeks, in April, when *Missouri* anchored off Piraeus, the seaport of Athens. This was enough for Forrestal. He quickly began, with the State Department's consent, to dispatch small numbers of cruisers—no task forces—to the Med to show the flag in as many places as possible. By the end of June, Bieri's flagship, the cruiser *Fargo*, was visiting Trieste in response to Marshal Tito's Yugoslavian claims to Venezia Giulia.

And in August came the 45,000-ton *FDR*—the first peacetime appearance of American naval air power inside Gibraltar. Her arrival created a far greater stir than *Missouri*'s visit; the latter could be written off in the language of international courtesy, but *FDR* was there to train and be a *presence*. As the multisided Greek civil war thrashed on, the carrier, along with the cruiser *Little Rock* and five destroyers, visited that troubled country. The Soviets duly recalled their ambassador to Greece. (So what? asked Bill Halsey. "It is nobody's damned business where we go. We can go anywhere we please.")

Clearly the eastern Mediterranean, with Greece and Turkey as the initial focal points, was emerging as the first naval focus of the Cold War. Russia had made territorial demands on the Turks, and Stalin was supplying weapons to twenty thousand guerrillas in Greece. Here, and through the vital Bosporus into the Black Sea, American sea and air power could be brought within reach of much of the economic strength of the USSR. Already the naval aspects of "containment," a mostly economic policy suggested by the diplomat George Kennan in 1947 and embedded in $400 million of economic aid to Greece and Turkey (the first act of the Truman Doctrine), were taking shape.

Forrestal responded to questions about why Admiral H. Kent Hewitt's Twelfth Fleet was being kept in the eastern Atlantic and Bieri's Mediterranean force was being steadily augmented. To support the Allies in their occupation of Europe, he said—but because this process could not last forever (as then was thought), the secretary added that while the United States was seeking no naval bases in the Med, the Navy would stay "to protect United States interests and support United States policies in the area."

Within the span of one year, 1946, Forrestal's insistence on an American Mediterranean force had brought results. Checking communism and trying to compel the Kremlin to participate in a general settlement of those world problems left so painfully unfinished at Potsdam had been the excuse; Forrestal was also concerned that the Med remain a "free highway" for the critical industrial materials increasingly needed by the United States. The end result was a powerful American naval force, called the Sixth Task Fleet in 1948 and the Sixth Fleet after 1950, cruising the sea from end to end—a fact of international life.

The Med was central to the new naval policy. Indeed, when Nimitz ordered Mitscher in January 1946 to form a staff for the new Eighth Fleet, ostensibly to operate in the Atlantic, the real reason was to prepare a trained force to deploy to the Mediterranean in case of crisis. Mitscher told Burke that they had three months to get combat-ready.

Sherman's was the guiding hand here; he, like Truman, had proposed the *Missouri* cruise. But the strategic voice also belonged to Forrestal. For the first time in the postwar period, naval operations had been linked with foreign policy in a specific area of the globe.

After a century and a half of careful abstention from peacetime involvement in the affairs of Europe, American naval forces were steaming within months of the end of the war off the continent's rim, ready to intervene if so ordered. This action, the work of Forrestal, Nimitz, Sherman, and their naval planners, took place well before assistance was given to Greece and Turkey, before the Berlin airlift, and before the formation of the North Atlantic Treaty Organization. In this case, where the gray ships steamed, national policy soon followed. "It is my hope," Forrestal wrote Bieri, "that the American policy will be to have units of the American Navy sail in any waters in any part of the globe. I am anxious to get this established as a common practice so that the movements of our ships *anywhere* will not be a matter for excitement or speculation."[11]

Certainly the Navy began to materialize in practically every corner of the Mediterranean. Elements of Rear Admiral John Cassady's Carrier Division 1 spent August and September 1946 in Lisbon, Naples, Piraeus,

Salonika, and off Trieste in the Adriatic. Nor was the African coast neglected. Bône, Philippeville, Bougie, Algiers, Tangier, and Casablanca all received American sailors. Moscow cried "gangster of diplomacy," but this only proved to Forrestal that the new policy had struck a nerve. In one year, February 1946 to February 1947, American sailors visited more than forty Mediterranean ports. Their ships included two aircraft carriers, *Missouri*, seven cruisers, eighteen destroyers, and four auxiliaries. A policy of rotation back to the United States was quickly set up, and American naval activity in the Med became a going concern.

The great enclosed sea would never leave the forefront of American naval planning. The Near East would become more, rather than less, important in policy-making. With the new Russian frontier on the Elbe River, the ability to counterpunch through the Mediterranean assumed increasing importance. Greece eventually subdued her Communist partisans, and Iran and Turkey became American clients in the Cold War. All three needed to be kept, if not "safe for democracy," at least "safe for the West," and naval power was a key ingredient.

For the moment America's naval role in the region was benign. In May 1947, during the week the momentous Truman Doctrine was approved by Congress (food and supplies began moving to Greece and Turkey immediately), American sailors held swim call in Suda Bay, Crete; hosted the Greek royal family in Piraeus; and clambered off the carrier *Leyte* into the streets of Istanbul. Back home all this made good copy. *Life* beamed that "the U.S. Navy had not been so popular since Stephen Decatur in the historic *Intrepid* beat the Tripoli pirates in 1804."

Some went beyond the call of duty. Rear Admiral George Dyer was photographed, replete in beribboned blues, riding muleback up a narrow, dusty cobblestoned road to visit a Cretan monastery. Others went outside the call, doing their diplomatic work by discovering Greek ouzo, a perfectly lethal drink which rendered entire liberty sections absolutely useless for the next twenty-four hours.

Great Britain, the former dominant power in the Mediterranean, found the Americans regrettable but necessary. Regrettable because the Royal Navy was watching its former world-girdling power drain away. But all too obviously necessary because the Labour government and its military had been forced to return to the old prewar "ten-year rule" in 1946: plan as if there would be no war for ten years. Of Britain's whopping balance-of-payments deficit of six hundred million pounds in 1947, one-third was due to military expenditure in Europe and overseas. The disastrous 1946–1947 winter gave the British no choice. They had to prune their overseas commitments.

—Prune they did. The British bailed out of the Indian subcontinent in indecent haste, leaving disorder, riot, and hundreds of thousands dead.

With the home country increasingly dependent on the flow of Middle Eastern oil, a single British frigate was left to control the Persian Gulf. Departure
from Burma and Ceylon quickly followed. Within a period of six months,
over half a billion people left the British Empire. Aside from Malaya and
Hong Kong the British in the Far East were gone. So were the Dutch, who
pulled out of the East Indies in 1948. Only France was left—a second-rate
naval power struggling with a hopeless colonial war in Indochina. And the
United States.

But Britain's deep-seated economic woes could not be lessened only by
amputating the furthest limbs of its empire. In 1946 Attlee had even suggested a complete withdrawal from the traditional British zone of influence
in the Near East. This move was stifled by the Ministry of Defence and
the Foreign Office, but the sore of the endless Arab-Jewish conflict in Palestine gave the government no rest. By 1948 the British were gone from the
eastern Mediterranean north of Suez, although their total force in the sea
remained considerable: one carrier, four cruisers, eleven destroyers, nine
frigates, and two submarines.

Attlee's government also had been forced to cut off aid to Greece and
Turkey, which had prompted the steps that led to the Truman Doctrine.
Many Americans did not like the idea of shouldering Britain's "imperial
burden," but Truman couched the notion in ideological rather than imperial
language. The Navy thereby became an instrument to "support free peoples
who are resisting attempted subjugation by armed minorities or outside
aggression"—not simply an instrument of national policy and power, but
of *ideas*.[12]

Much of this mission was a bit hazy to the men on the spot. "It was a
lot of conjecture," said the commander of Carrier Division 6. "You always
wondered what was going to go on in the Middle East." One reporter told
a naval aviator he had come to the Med to discover what the Navy was
doing. "If you find out, let me know," replied the airedale.

Because Forrestal rotated the three Atlantic task forces into the area,
sailors were given little idea of *permanence*. Visits to the Med became a medley
of training exercises and a flurry of port calls, then back past the Rock and
home. There was no fixed basing policy—the tenders took care of minor
repairs—and Med duty became a perpetual, and usually sunny, cruise. A
few chest thumpers began to call the Mediterranean an "American lake,"
but (unlike their vacating of the Pacific) the British, weakened as they were,
still maintained a fleet presence, one with permanent bases at Gibraltar,
Malta, and Cyprus.

Most American sailors devoured the liberty, savored the experiences,
and were glad to go home. A few, like aviator Robert Brewer, had a stronger
sense of the Med, "mother sea of a hundred empires and of a thousand
kings." Such romanticism, however, had no place in the reckonings of salty

veterans like Chief Boatswain's Mate James Kenneth Buchanan, of *Midway*. During the war everyone had been a fighter, groused the chief. Now, sailors' business was *diplomacy*, and they were supposed to be "friendly."

To many veterans, this was an unwelcome turnaround, not at all what a navy was supposed to do. People were expected to be on their best behavior during liberty—again a departure from tradition (albeit a tradition that was more honored in the breach than in the observance). The Navy apparently expected its off-duty sailors to play baseball, frequent cafés, and go to museums. Shore patrols were everywhere, usually one petty officer to every twenty men (an unusually high ratio of armbands), to the point at which one disgruntled whitehat in Taranto, the Italian naval base, grumbled, "I wouldn't mind coming back here sometime without the Navy nursemaids."

By the early 1950s some analysts were calling the Mediterranean, in its turn, "the sea of decision." With the perceived descending of the Iron Curtain, the Med seemed to be a place "where the balance of power is tested and where gains or losses are gauged." Certainly the American Navy saw things that way. The fleet was generally welcomed throughout the ports of the region—and not simply for the boost its sailors gave local economies. One Greek political leader called the Sixth Fleet's ships "gray diplomats."

They needed to be, for the Med—with its wide variety of political traditions, religions, social customs, and ethnic differences—would seldom be serene.

☆

By strategic definition the Army and the Air Force were the major players in any scenario involving continental Europe, although the Navy had a role to play there as well. Even during the famous Berlin airlift (1948–1949), two Navy transport squadrons, VR-8 from Honolulu and VR-6 from Guam, with eight hundred personnel, flew more than ten hours per day in the difficult winter weather blanketing Berlin, helping carry the supplies into Tempelhof Airport that kept the city going. In Washington the Berlin problem was a hectic round of crisis management, but the Navy and Air Force made the actual resupply operations a matter of routine.[13]

Berlin was a symbol of a larger problem: possible war on the central European plain, this time against the powerful Red Army. (In March 1948 Louis Denfeld, the chief of naval operations, believed war was coming over a crisis in Czechoslovakia.) The Truman Doctrine was followed by the Marshall Plan of economic aid for Europe. "Hungry men make Communists," pronounced one diplomat. "Fed men do not."

From these ingredients—fear of Soviet aggression, economic support for Europe, and the somewhat ambiguous idea of "containment"—eventually came the North Atlantic Treaty Organization, established on 4 April 1949. NATO was initially more a psychological ploy, to give Europeans the "will to resist," rather than a device to halt a Soviet offensive—which was not then anticipated. The heartland of the Atlantic alliance originally lay in France, Belgium, Luxembourg, the Netherlands, and Great Britain. But the driving engine, the indispensable power source, was the United States. Indeed, the British were assuming American support in any general European war, right from the start. In this, the first peacetime alliance in its history, the United States not only broke with a diplomatic tradition dating back to Washington but also eventually gave its seapower a potentially crucial theater wartime role. American foreign policy was in the process of becoming militarized.

The Navy came to have several well-defined tasks under NATO. Even in 1946, with nine of the Navy's fifteen carriers and three of its four battleships assigned to the Atlantic, the Pacific had become a secondary theater. NATO fed directly into the new strategic concerns. The crucial strategic imperative was oceanic supply and reinforcement from new world to old, on the model of the two world wars. Naval duties thus included merchant convoy, antisubmarine warfare, amphibious assault, and carrier offensive against the rim of Europe. Reinforcements would take time; at the initial Brussels meeting of the NATO military planning group, the U.S. representative told his European counterparts not to expect much American help until the later stages of a war. Therefore, the Navy argued for a strategy designed to hold the line in Europe as far east as possible.

The fleet began to see itself as a critical part of the "sword of NATO." Admiral Richard ("Close In") Conolly became the overall commander of the theater, with a separate British naval commander and an American task force commander. The Med, in the broad picture, became NATO's "southern" flank. The Royal Navy was less than enthusiastic about Americans being in overall authority in *both* the Atlantic and the Mediterranean, and disputes over NATO's command structure grumbled on into the 1950s.

In its early years the alliance was more a political sounding board than a refined series of military calculations. Its military strength was at first little more than embryonic, but its strategic intent was clear. In addition to the use of nuclear weapons (felt to be necessary to counteract the expected Soviet troop advantage), NATO's planners were committed to building up large continental armed forces. In effect, this idea tied the Atlantic naval powers of World War II—Canada, Great Britain, and the United States— to *permanent* military obligations directed at the European continent. Here was a true sea change in American naval strategy.

Within ten years the combined strength of the NATO navies, excluding that of the United States, grew to over 340,000 officers and men. Yet everyone understood that the Americans were providing the indispensable naval support of the alliance. Their technology and economic resources ensured that. As joint exercises began to be held and various command slots parceled out,

Americans found themselves stretched oceanically once again. But this time, unlike their situation in the Pacific, they were committed *by treaty* to a transoceanic strategy.

Vice Admiral Jerauld Wright, one of the first naval diplomats assigned to NATO, found a growing bureaucratic hive of commands, regional planning groups, and military committees. He was a bit chary of matching an alliance against a single totalitarian state ("we are comparing democratic moral righteousness with totalitarian physical force") and hoped that national selfishness would not doom this attempt at continental defense. NATO strategy meant teamwork, said Mick Carney as he became chief of naval operations in 1953. How this teamwork would be accomplished he did not say, but "without adequate control of the sea, and without the ability to deny its sinister use to the enemy, NATO will perish."

—Whereas the Navy would be alone in the Pacific, then, the Atlantic, after 1949, meant international partnership. And this idea cut squarely across the grain of American naval tradition and practice.

☆

By 1950, a scant five years after V-J Day, only the polar regions, the south Atlantic, and the Indian Ocean, of all the major waters of the earth, were not a part of the American naval strategy (and all would eventually be encompassed). Although the prewar Navy had *operated* globally—friendship visits, reactions to crises, round-the-world cruises—the fleet had never defined itself through a worldwide peacetime strategy.

Now such a strategy had emerged, supported by the flow of American dollars overseas. Four days after the Senate approved the NATO Treaty, Truman sent the unprecedented peacetime military assistance program to the Hill. Senator Tom Connally called the bill the most difficult foreign policy legislation to enact since the battle over Lend-Lease in 1941.

But the act became law. The Mutual Defense Assistance Program granted $1.4 billion in continuing military aid to Greece, Turkey, Iran, the Philippines, and even Korea (whose presence inside the American defensive shield was uncertain by the end of 1949). Almost $1.2 billion of this was ticketed for NATO members. By 1952, 80 percent of American assistance to western Europe consisted of military items.

Initially, the impact was mostly psychological, and the business of getting the supplies moving was a ponderous one. At the beginning of 1950 NATO had only twelve divisions (randomly deployed against an estimated twenty-five well-trained, well-equipped Soviet divisions), four hundred planes, and a handful of naval vessels. Americans generally supported this aid—a 1945 poll had indicated that they preferred to keep up spending on the armed forces even at the cost of unbalancing the budget, and anti-Communist sentiment had kept this attitude alive—and the public generally seemed more willing to pay for larger military forces, both at home and abroad, than were members of either political party in Congress. In fact, by a margin of almost three to one, Americans favored armed strength over the Marshall Plan as the best way to avoid war.

American seapower was a direct beneficiary of this attitude. Even in its relatively weakened postwar state, the fleet did not retract to the Western Hemisphere, and indeed that region was very low on its list of naval priorities. Instead, impelled by partially faulty but nevertheless real perceptions of Communist purpose, by the clear decline in British naval sovereignty, and by its own tradition of aggressiveness and can-do behavior, the Navy stayed on. American warships, on any given day in the late forties, could be seen plying the Atlantic, visiting any of dozens of Mediterranean seaports, nestling alongside a pier in Hong Kong, operating in the South China Sea, cruising the vastness of the Pacific. Truman signed eighteen military executive agreements during his tenure, and most of these benefited the Navy.

A global Navy—but with a not-quite-global pocketbook. From retirement, Admiral Jack Towers cautioned that "it is reasonable to have policemen around when mob violence threatens." Drawdown meant that the naval policemen, as powerful as they were, would be stretched thin given the enormous scale of their worldwide mission. By the middle of 1949 only two cruisers, one destroyer squadron, and one small amphibious assault group were in the western Pacific. The occupation of Japan and Korea was supported by a cruiser and four destroyers. A carrier, four cruisers, and one or two destroyer squadrons rotated through the Mediterranean. Only one carrier (the announced centerpiece of the new strategy) was thus deployed forward.[14]

—And that was all. The Navy would plan, train, and sketch in its technological future, but the fleet could not cover all its strategic bets at the same time. Because its role in the overall American strategic picture was still unclear, the Navy was presenting itself as a sort of utility infielder of strategic purpose, showing up at the critical point at the critical moment. Whether the service could make good on this claim, with the forces available, remained to be seen.

For the moment, around the world, the fleet operated on a relative shoestring, with a true worldwide strategic role seemingly denied by the Air Force and its atomic bomb. Here was a question that burned through the American military establishment like a fire arrow, and, in 1949, finally erupted in conflagration.

CHAPTER SEVEN

REBELLION IN GOLD BRAID

─────── ☆ ───────

I n the early morning hours of 22 May 1949 James Vincent Forrestal, forty-eighth secretary of the Navy and first secretary of defense, sat reading from a poetry anthology in his room on the sixteenth floor of the Naval Hospital at Bethesda, Maryland. The giant medical complex had been his home since 2 April, when psychiatrists determined that his depression had become so severe that hospitalization was necessary.

Forrestal, the overachiever, had always been wound tight; the strains of running the Defense Department had only made him more weary, more nervous. Upon taking the post he had joked that by the end of the year he would need the combined attention of Bishop Fulton Sheen and the entire psychiatric profession.

Now the joke had turned sour. His marriage, always distant, was gone in all but name; his wife was a bedridden alcoholic. Early in January, Harry Truman's advisers had noticed that the secretary's unconscious habit of scratching the crown of his head had become so obsessive that a patch of raw flesh was beginning to appear. The inner torment was clearly getting to him; at times he would irritably complain that he hated his job. He expressed fears that Zionist, Communist, and FBI agents were after him.

Truman could not help but be alarmed. By the end of January he and Forrestal had agreed that the secretary should resign. But the prospect of laying his burden down did not lift the weight of depression from Forrestal; instead, he got worse. On 28 March he left office. Friends hoped a vacation at Robert Lovett's estate on Hobe Sound, Florida, would help, but Forrestal, within hours of his arrival, was off the deep end. Bethesda was the logical choice.

There, he seemed to respond well to treatment. Truman and other visitors noticed that he seemed to be returning to his old self. The dark moods were still there, but they were less frequent and less severe. By the middle of May his physicians had relaxed some of the restraints placed on his movements around the hospital; they were looking forward to his release in about a month.

Methodical and precise as usual, Forrestal was copying on that May night as he read. The words were from a translation of Sophocles, the powerful, somber "Chorus from Ajax:"

> Fair Salamis, the billows' roar
>> Wanders around thee yet,
> And sailors gaze upon thy shore
>> Firm in the Ocean set.
> Thy son is in a foreign clime
>> Where Ida feeds her countless flocks,
>> Far from thy dear, remembered rocks,
> Worn by the waste of time—
> Comfortless, nameless, hopeless save
> In the dark prospect of the yawning grave. . . .

—He copied a few more lines, laid the sheets neatly in the back of the book, and turned the book open to Sophocles. Sometime around 0300, he left his room and went down the corridor to a small kitchen that he had been encouraged to use. The kitchen had a window, unscreened.

No one else was about. Forrestal opened the window—and went through.

☆

The demons that pursued him, whatever they were, had brought down a great champion of the Navy. Part of his depression had doubtless been caused by his growing inability to deal with the situation into which his beloved service was rapidly careening; his suicidal plunge was a tragic accompaniment to yet another naval struggle. At least the man was spared most of the sorry spectacle that was taking place even as he ended his life.

Forrestal had been replaced as secretary of the Navy by John Lawrence Sullivan, his under secretary, whom Forrestal had recommended to Truman. Sullivan was a New Hampshire Irishman, lumpy-faced and red-haired, with a stubborn set to his jaw. He had been raised in an atmosphere of law and politics by his lawyer father.

In the year of his pugilistic namesake's death, 1918, Sullivan left Dartmouth for a three-month stint in the Naval Reserve. He eventually graduated from Dartmouth in 1921, went through Harvard Law, and began to practice in his home state. Despite Roosevelt's overwhelming national popularity during the Depression years, FDR's lengthy coattails did not extend to the New Hampshire mountains, where the rock-ribbed citizenry rejected the Democratic Sullivan's two runs for the governor's chair, in 1934 and 1938.

He showed up in Washington in 1939 as an assistant to the commissioner of internal revenue. From there Sullivan became an assistant secretary of the treasury. At war's end he set out to practice law in Washington but was quickly drawn into the Truman administration as assistant secretary of the Navy for air. His qualifications were that he was a "deserving Democrat" and very much a bureaucratic man-about-town. He was also a good socializer and a topflight golfer, a former New Hampshire amateur champion who often packed his clubs along on naval inspection trips, cudgeling reluctant admirals onto the links with him (where they were invariably creamed).

But unlike Forrestal, Sullivan did not have the Navy in his bones. To gain experience he traveled—chiefly to the western Pacific, where he was much impressed with carrier operations. In mid-1946 he became under secretary, replacing Artemus Gates, and in this position he helped Forrestal try to iron out the bureaucratic wrinkles in the National Military Establishment. Sullivan developed into a strong centrist, like Chester Nimitz and Forrest Sherman, admitting the importance of the carrier but opposing any strategy that relied upon a single weapon and delivery system.

Naval officers were of two minds about him. Some extremists felt that he was a well-meaning plugger but little more. Most admirals, while generally keeping their distance, found him open and forthright. "The difference between talking . . . with Forrestal and Sullivan was like day and night," said Robert Dennison, Truman's naval aide and a future four-star admiral. "Sullivan would tell you what he thought and you never knew what Forrestal thought. . . ."

The new secretary and his chief of naval operations seemed to get along well enough, but Sullivan enjoyed Nimitz's counsel for only three months. In December 1947, true to his bargain with Forrestal, the fleet admiral stepped down. Sullivan, in a non-Cabinet position, had no role in picking the new chief.

But Forrestal did. When Truman asked for his advice, Forrestal replied that there were three top candidates: Duke Ramsey, William ("Spike") Blandy, and Louis Denfeld. Forrestal, although concerned about Denfeld's "political activity," told the president that Truman "would find Denfeld the easiest of the lot to work with."[1]

—*The easiest of the lot.* Forrestal's judgment was on target; Louie Denfeld was kind and genial, an old-school gentleman. Born in Massachusetts, he had been reared in Minnesota, from where he received his Annapolis appointment. After graduating in 1912, he served on destroyers during World War I. From there he began a career in naval personnel work, where he proved to be a paper-pusher with few peers. His interwar sea tours included command of a submarine and a destroyer squadron. His key sea daddy was none other than William Leahy, then chief of naval operations, who brought Denfeld on board as his aide.

Denfeld spent most of World War II behind a desk, as assistant to the chief of the Bureau of Personnel. He finally got to command a battleship division in the Okinawa campaign and then became chief of the Bureau of Personnel, where he had to cope with the avalanche of personnel problems during the drawdown. He moved to command of the Pacific Fleet in February 1947.

His path to the top had been, like his personality, smooth and sure, but he bore the stigma of the paper shuffler amid an arena of warriors. Denfeld's jowly, full-lipped face and horn-rimmed glasses did little to dispel the image. He had been on Nimitz's own list of possible successors, too, but well down, behind Ramsey, Blandy, Close In Conolly (the nickname came from his penchant for putting the muzzles of his ships' guns smack up against the enemy shoreline), and Savvy Cooke. Ernie King, in retirement, plumped for Cooke, but the decisive voice was that of Leahy, Truman's naval adviser and practically the only naval officer the president trusted—and Leahy supported his former aide.

Denfeld was thus a compromise candidate. Spike Blandy was the general choice of the surface line, Ramsey of the aviators. Because of the debatable nature of the choice, Truman offered only a two-year term. Denfeld, who wore the submariner's dolphins, brought aviator Arthur Radford on board as his vice chief.

The new chief was a man of high moral principles, but he lacked something as an inspiring leader. Admiral Charles Griffin, who worked for both Sherman and Denfeld, admitted that the latter was "a very fine man." But "he would be the first to admit that he was not one of the most brilliant CNOs we ever had. He was no Forrest Sherman."

Nor was he Ramsey, Spike Blandy, Close In Conolly, or Savvy Cooke. Denfeld, in a time of intense upheaval for the Navy, quickly proved Griffin's point. He disliked joint responsibilities—he had had little experience working with the other services, and the interservice paper flow too often did not go his way—and kept somewhat aloof from the unification struggle and the infighting of the rest of the Joint Chiefs. Instead, Radford, Sherman, and Mick Carney, then deputy chief of naval operations for logistics (OP-04), became the Navy's point men. Carney, never one to mince words, described things this way:

> We . . . were doing all the work on the JCS, one or the other of us. Questions would come up on technical questions, where Raddy and I had lived through it and knew what the hell we were talking about . . . and Louie, he wouldn't know his ass from third base about it.

In this crowd of piranhas Denfeld was seen, relatively speaking, as a weakling goldfish, a classic "desk admiral." ("Not . . . a very strong man," said military commentator and Naval Academy graduate Hanson Baldwin, who knew him well.) Radford's role accordingly blossomed; he, not Denfeld, became the Navy's spokesman on questions of strategy and unification. Radford, the highly intelligent and blunt aviator, also pushed the issue of naval strategic air power to the limit, with very little check from his superior.[2]

Denfeld, as things developed, was holding the leading reins very loosely—if he had quite grasped them at all.

☆

Both Sullivan and Denfeld, driven in part by the insistence of aviators like Radford, supported Project 6A, a "supercarrier," which appeared in the Navy's shipbuilding program for fiscal year 1949. The idea, originally approved by the since-deceased Marc Mitscher, had been around as far back as 1945. Project 6A's budget, $6 million, was minuscule, intended for start-up only, but the Navy knew that in the budget world a foot in the door was a necessary prelude to open sesame. Radford's promoting and the loud insistence of Rear Admiral Daniel Gallery, director of the Navy's new guided missile program, had done their work: Denfeld, in particular, became convinced that the Navy needed a supercarrier.

The issue was mostly one of atomic strategy. Gallery had warned Denfeld that the Air Force was bent on producing heavy atomic weapons that only its land-based bombers could deliver. Lighter "tactical" bombs, which could be carried by smaller naval attack aircraft, would be opposed. What seemed, then, to be a debate over the proper technology for atomic delivery systems was in fact viewed by both services as a fundamental debate over the direction of national strategy.

—And there was a complicating factor. Throughout the winter of 1947–1948 Forrestal had been unable to get the Joint Chiefs to arrive at real unanimity concerning service roles and missions. In the Navy's view, what was taking shape was an unholy Army-USAF alliance, with the Air Force supporting the Army's demand that the Marine Corps be reduced (because of role redundancy, argued some of the Army brass). In return the Army would support the large, land-based atomic bomber as the nation's number one strategic punch. "The Army–Air Force party line is that the Unification Act is wrong and needed to be amended," Denfeld told Sullivan. "The attack is on the Marine Corps and the role of naval air." Even the normally levelheaded George Marshall was heard to remark, "I am going to see that the Marines never win another war."

At the Key West Conference, with Forrestal's aid, Denfeld got agreement to proceed with 6A and with the Navy's own atomic weapons program. But the Joint Chiefs continued to wrangle over their respective slices of the shrinking budgetary pie. Forrestal, exasperated, finally decided to carve the pie equally into thirds, which was fine with the Army. But the Air Force was adamant about expanding the number of its air groups, from fifty-five to seventy. Here Denfeld balked, and some USAF generals retorted that there was no longer a need for a large American Navy. The Soviets were naval midgets, and besides, naval aviation should, by right, be absorbed into the Air Force.

This was an old debate, extending back more than thirty years, but the Marine Corps issue and the compelling question of national strategy added the mustard. As the war of words escalated, Denfeld and Sullivan gave 6A priority over several other shipbuilding projects. Sullivan decided to cancel the completion of thirteen ships, shifting the freed funds to the supercarrier. Both Sullivan and Denfeld were simply trying to get *one* supercarrier (to be called *United States*), but the voluble Radford and other aviators were pressing for *four*, and they had the support not only of Vice Admiral Earle Mills, chief of the Bureau of Ships, but also of the key player on the Hill, Carl Vinson himself.

Throughout 1948 Forrestal, Sullivan, and Denfeld defended the supercarrier against all comers. Truman, the populist, asked for a vote by the Joint Chiefs on the idea; the response came back 3–1 (Leahy, Denfeld, and Omar Bradley) for 6A, with only General Hoyt Vandenberg, the Air Force chief of staff, in opposition. Denfeld then proposed that the supercarrier "be equipped to bomb strategic targets within an area of naval operations"— a euphemism for tactical nuclear weapons. Finally, in August 1948, a contract was let for construction of *United States*.

The contract did not end the backbiting and sniping; in fact, the cascade of accusations, from all sides, increased. The Pentagon was sliding into anarchy. All this did nothing to improve Forrestal's deteriorating mental condition. Not only did he feel himself entwined in an ongoing administrative nightmare within the Department of Defense, but he could not, despite his ukase forbidding unauthorized public discussion of controversial subjects by the service secretaries, the Chiefs, or their assistants, even control his own people. Forrestal told Dwight Eisenhower that among all his admirals he felt he could trust only Sherman, Blandy, and possibly Conolly.[3]

The secretary's major problem lay with his favorites, the naval aviators. They were volleying back everything the Air Force served, and they were difficult for Forrestal to control—particularly since he (as well as they) saw naval aviation as the Navy's future.

Navy fliers had always been naval officers first and aviators second, unlike their opposite numbers in the Army, who had been agitating for an independent Air Force since the days of Billy Mitchell. "For twenty-five years," Mitscher told Forrestal, "Naval Air had been trying to protect itself both within the Navy and outside the Navy." Before the war, naval aviation had gotten as high as 10 percent of the naval budget only once, in 1938. In 1940, only 16 percent of the Navy's officers were in aviation. But the war had vindicated the aircraft carrier as against the battleship. Basic Post-War Plan Number One, for example, allotted 42 percent of the naval budget for aviation. And aviation admirals, like Slew McCain, Aubrey Fitch, and Lynde McCormick, had called for even more.

Forrestal himself, along with Artemus Gates (a pioneer naval aviator in World War I, decorated for combat heroism), bought this pitch. Aviation stock within the Navy, which had risen dramatically during the war, thus continued to soar. At the time of Pearl Harbor only two jobs in the entire Navy had been reserved for aviator admirals as a matter of policy. Only ten of the Navy's eighty-four flag-rank officers were aviators. But the fliers increased their numbers at this level by a factor of six during the war, while nonaviators were only doubling. By 1949 four out of every ten line officers were aviators, and fully one-third of the Navy's top billets belonged to aviation.

—And their power was growing even beyond the numbers. Men like Mitscher and Sherman had Forrestal's ear; Fitch received the prestigious post of superintendent of the Naval Academy, the first aviator to get the job; and his commandant of midshipmen was another distinguished Pacific naval aviator, Captain Stuart Ingersoll.

Forrestal liked the future-mindedness of the aviators, as opposed to what he saw as the crustiness and stubbornness of the Old Guard; he liked their accent on technology, on research and development, on getting things done. He tagged Radford for both postwar planning and the unification battle, Tom Robbins for SCOROR, and young aviation captains like Edmund Taylor, William Smedberg, and Charles Buchanan (all future admirals) for positions of greater authority. Vinson helped, by pushing a bill retiring forty-three flag officers (through the simple expedient of lowering the statutory retirement age from sixty-four to sixty-two). In the first major postwar flag selection, fourteen out of the eighteen new slots went to aviators.

Forrestal summed up: "The actual fact is that the Navy is becoming an air navy. . . . The leading commands of the Navy will in time be occupied by men who deal with air in one form or another." "To say which of the three services is most important in warfare," reasoned Savvy Cooke, "is like trying to determine which is the most important leg of a three-legged stool." But of Cooke's four "general types of military operations"—sea control, friendly land control, enemy land control, and amphibious operations—two clearly belonged to the Navy. And to its aviators.

☆

Forrestal did not oppose a land-based force of strategic bombers. As secretary of defense he began to see this as a hole card in any military confrontation in central Europe. But the Navy's *tactical* air arm was nonnegotiable, and as to strategy, "for some time to come, control of the land, sea and air will be interdependent, and . . . no one instrument will suffice for all these purposes."

Forrestal and most of his admirals saw this position as one of reasoned moderation; to the secretary, the Air Force lacked "wise and experienced leadership in the upper ranks." He told Vandenberg that the Navy believed the USAF wanted to control *all* naval aviation, sweetening the medicine by supporting *only* one supercarrier for test and evaluation of a long-range bombing plane. Naval air sought to be the Air Force's strategic *helper*, not its opponent.[4]

To the powers-that-be in the Air Force, this was so much prop wash. Feisty young generals like Curtis LeMay, convinced that Germany and Japan had been obliterated by strategic air power, argued that the heavy manned bomber had greater range and payload, was more flexible, and could place its sticks more accurately than anything the Navy had. And not only was the big bomber the atomic punch; the Air Force was saying that bombers could be jacks-of-all-trades in conventional war as well.

Once again, the classic Air Force overstatements, the overweening claims to strategic superiority (which were *not* the views of the more moderate USAF officers), were what got the Navy's attention. These overstatements were drawn from extremists such as Billy Mitchell, who was seen as a martyr by the young air generals, and Alexander De Seversky.

What really irked the Navy brass was the assertion that ships could do nothing against what De Seversky called the "locust swarms of giant airplanes." "Saw Disney's 'Victory through Air Power' [taken from De Seversky]," Harry Yarnell told his diary. "Clever propaganda for an independent air force." Ships, on the other hand, could not attack airplanes; a land-based squadron of huge bombers could sink 250 battleships; nothing sent to sea could withstand the lethal hailstorm from the air. The solution was an aviation arm "thoroughly cured of inherited naval obsessions."[5]

Only air power could have won World War II. The big bomber was the "key to modern strategy." Thus, navies, even during the war, were at best "supernumeraries," and besides, the American admirals had killed their best salesmen—the Japanese. The time was fast approaching when even the word "seapower" would lose all real meaning.

De Seversky listed several "principles" of air power—control of the air, striking radius, and the like, including, as a fundamental point, the observation that "navies have lost their function of strategic offensive." "Air power is this nation's first line of defense," General George Kenney told the Senate Committee on Military Affairs in November 1945. "Only in air power can we find a weapon formidable enough to maintain peace." Jimmy Doolittle, the Air Force's predominant public hero, agreed, and told the same group that the USAF deserved most of the credit for winning the war in the Pacific.

Particularly infuriating was the oft-repeated assumption that all this was so *obvious*, that only mossbacked fossils in admirals' uniforms could possibly fail to read the handwriting on the wall. "Navies are no longer lords of the seas . . . [they] are already finished." "We can't deter Russian aggression with Navy weapons." Doolittle announced that once the long-range heavy bombers were on line, "we will not need carriers."

The Navy should not be abolished. Its ships would still have ancillary roles in blockade and escort duty, as well as in conducting limited aviation outside the range of land-based aircraft (then around seven hundred miles). But to "those of us who have grasped the meaning of genuine air power," the Navy as a *strategic* force was as extinct as the dinosaur; "every American—man, woman, and child—must be an airman in his heart." To his credit De Seversky recognized that air power was futile against an economically underdeveloped area. But this critical caveat was lost in the uproar.[6]

The Air Force position, as of 1948, centered on its budgetary claims for seventy groups, built around the new (and, to the Navy, grotesque) B-36 bomber. Even Vinson admitted that the money had to be spent to "get our Air Force prepared to keep our only possible enemy from our shores." All right, responded one naval officer: "self-criticism and self-cleansing are good for the soul." But enough was enough, and again the voices of moderation, on all sides, were being drowned in the cacaphony surrounding the question of which service was to bear the nation's strategic lance. Suggestions of cooperation were not being heard.

☆

A "budgetary crisis" was the excuse. Military expenditures for fiscal year 1948 were $10.9 billion, and for the following year $1 billion more. Truman, with his surprising election triumph of 1948 in his pocket, was determined to keep military costs down. He understood the significance of programs like the Marshall Plan in undergirding America's international leadership in peacetime. But he was much less clear about what the new global requirements meant when translated into the economics of the military infrastructure needed to support them.

Truman requested "only" $14.2 billion for fiscal year 1950 (in the wake of the Czechoslovakian and Berlin crises). The Joint Chiefs considered this about half of what they needed. The military's share of the pie seemed to be (relatively) shrinking, which gave a sense of urgency to all that followed: a fight for bigger slices of the pie, a resulting completion of one's very own weapons system (B-36 or supercarrier), and strategic supremacy for the victorious service.[7]

As they girded for battle, naval officers lashed back at the air-power extremists. Strategic bombing was *not* the all-purpose form of military power claimed by the Air Force; both naval and ground forces were needed to support and complement land-based air; and for certain kinds of military operations, *including* strategic bombing, carrier forces could be far more effective than land-based bombers. Radford led the charge, particularly concerning the last point, but he was far from alone. Air admirals like Ralph Ofstie were quick to argue that big bombers did not "pull their weight" in the specific postwar strategic situation; the bulk of current funding for strategic air should be funneled into tactical air (read: naval aviation).

Time for General Quarters. Things were getting out of hand. The irrepressible Dan Gallery wrote a memo (leaked to a syndicated columnist by someone else) arguing that "the time is right now for the Navy to start an aggressive campaign aimed at proving that the Navy can deliver the Atom Bomb more effectively than the Air Forces [*sic*] can." Sullivan and Denfeld quickly denied that Gallery's outburst represented their views, reprimanded him, and disavowed the memo. Gallery himself was propelled out of town for a couple of weeks to cool his heels on an "inspection trip." His proposal earned a counterblast from Tooey Spaatz to the effect that he, Spaatz, would personally block any attempt by the Department of Defense to split the strategic bombing role with the Navy.[8]

The fat was in the fire, and no clear command guidance was forthcoming, from either civilians or military men. The Truman administration seemed to view only the fiscal bottom line, and, in the words of Vice Admiral Howard Orem, "the Supreme Court deliberates, the Congress legislates, the Joint Chiefs of Staff just bicker."

Still, the keel of *United States* had been laid. Designed to the specifications of Mitscher and Gallery, she would displace sixty-five thousand tons (two and a half times the displacement of the wartime *Essex* class), handle one hundred thousand pounds of aircraft and related equipment, mount four powerful catapults, and carry an air wing of eighty fighters and eighteen bombers. Estimates of her eventual cost ran from $189 million to $500 million, a huge chunk of Truman's budget, and for only a single platform.

CVA-58 would be "a flattop that is really a flattop." Her island structure would be shorn away, leaving only her gigantic flight deck, almost one-fifth of a mile long. From this vast runway the Navy hoped to launch planes of any shape and size (including atomic bombers) for the next few decades. Rear Admiral John Cassady, now assistant chief of naval operations for air, dreamed of one-hundred-thousand-pound jet bombers screaming off this deck and lugging atom bombs one thousand miles inland.

And despite Forrestal's disclaimer, many among the Navy brass, and not only the air admirals, hoped that *United States* would be but the first of a host of supercarriers. These vessels would cement the Navy's nuclear role and strategic position, once and for all.[9]

☆

Into this potent witches' brew of strategic argument, interservice squabbling, and personal rancor now came the final ingredient: Truman's replacement for Forrestal as secretary of defense. Harry Truman had many strengths as president: he was honest, hardworking, and generally no-nonsense, with an increasingly firm idea of both the possibilities and limitations of presidential power. But among his weaknesses was a penchant for rewarding friends and wheelhorses for the Democratic party; the president was a down-the-line party man, and he liked loyalties. Few had been more loyal than Louis Johnson of West Virginia.

Johnson was a bear of a man, six feet two inches and 250 pounds, a self-made millionaire who was not at all hesitant in boasting about his achievements. Seven years younger than Truman, he had begun as a lawyer but also had longtime ties with the military. He had served with the American Expeditionary Forces in France during World War I and, like Truman, had stayed with the uniform—in Johnson's case the Army Reserve, where he eventually emerged as a bird colonel.

But always he was the politico, serving a term in 1932 as national commander of the American Legion. As the country drifted toward conflict in the late thirties, FDR had repaid some political debts by appointing him assistant secretary of war. There he stayed for three years (1937–1940), helping to spur construction of the B-17 bomber.

Once inside the federal bureaucracy, however, Johnson proved to be such a relentless conniver and self-server that even FDR, who could tolerate almost anyone if he could keep him at arm's length, was forced to remove him from the post. He spent the war years as Roosevelt's "personal emissary" to India and in a variety of equally meaningless odd jobs.

But Johnson's unbending ambition remained unchecked, and he was a Democrat. When Truman could find no one to handle his campaign finances in 1948 (Governor Thomas Dewey of New York was way ahead in all the polls, and Truman was being written off by the "experts" as a lost cause), Johnson stepped forward. He probably gave $250,000 of his own money to the campaign, wheedled over $2 million more from reluctant donors, and financed Truman's unforgettable whistle-stop victory.

Thus he rose to the top of the president's IOU list, and Truman came through. Louis Johnson, who by now was seeing himself as presidential timber, the obvious successor to Harry Truman in 1952, became the second secretary of defense on 28 March 1949. His only claim to the position, other than Truman's debt to him, was his military background, but in truth he had about the same degree of military expertise as Truman's other military crony, Harry Vaughan, which was to say, little or none.

Johnson fancied himself a man of action (he was all too obviously no thinker), and he saw his central tasks as those of bashing Pentagon heads together, getting everyone under a tight budget lid, and making "unification" really work. He began by evicting Army officials from the largest office in the Pentagon, appropriating John Pershing's desk, and barking commands at any generals and admirals within earshot.

None of the men in uniform were fooled. No less an observer than Omar Bradley wrote that Johnson knew very little about strategy or weapons systems. Others were even less charitable. "He was an idiot," one naval officer recalled, "a perfect idiot."

The new secretary of defense was arrogant, a bully and a braggart, and because of his earlier connection with the B-17 program he perceived himself an expert on strategic air power. These traits, coupled with his desire to impose a maximum military budget of $12.3 billion (he cast himself as a fiscal savior as well), led quickly to his first major move.

Within days of taking office, and without so much as a word to either Sullivan or Denfeld, he canceled construction of *United States*. "The Navy has built its last big carrier," he told some associates, and to some others he revealed that he would leave the Navy with one carrier only, "for the old admirals to ride around on."

Shortly afterward, he announced to a group of reporters that Marine aviation would be transferred to the Air Force. As a footnote Secretary of the Army Kenneth Royall informed a Senate panel that the entire Marine Corps should become part of the Army. Johnson followed up by issuing "Consolidation Directive No. 1," centralizing clearance procedures on all public statements, which was speedily and correctly recognized as a "gag order" by his military subordinates.

Carl Vinson, now chairman of the inclusive successor to the House Naval Affairs Committee, the Armed Services Committee, was alarmed and laid down the law. In late April he summoned Johnson to his office and told the secretary that such pronunciations, by Johnson or any of his subordinates, had damn well better be cleared with Congress first. Vinson forced the momentarily chastened secretary into writing a letter saying that his department would in the future follow this procedure.[10]

☆

Vinson's damage control came too late; the flooding could not be stopped. Sullivan, a man who, according to his naval aide, "had something of an Irish temper," knew he had been blindsided; he promptly resigned. Actually, Sullivan had submitted a routine resignation letter to Johnson upon the latter's assumption of office. Now Johnson interpreted the letter to suit himself, saying that "Sullivan has joined the aircraft carrier issue on personal grounds, and I believe that he . . . will soon regret his action. . . ." Truman, appalled by Johnson's behavior, said he did not blame Sullivan for quitting. Still, the president did nothing to intervene.

Johnson thereupon crashed a quiet naval farewell ceremony for Sullivan, barging through the proceedings and enraging the admirals present, who "looked daggers at him." (One of them later characterized the defense secretary as a "criminal.") "You can't do that!" Sullivan's senior aide recalled. "When Al Capone kills them in Chicago, he sends them flowers, but he doesn't go to their funeral."

They all saw Johnson as little more than a shill for the Air Force. And both Johnson and the USAF required their meed of correction. Captain Arleigh Burke, who had his impish moments, sent Mick Carney a memo on "Important Unification Matters:"

1. It has been forcibly brought to our attention by a naval aviator that there are no prayers in the Army and Navy Prayer Book for the Air Force. It is remarkable that there should be an attempt to consolidate the Chaplains Corps [a dig at how far Johnson's ideas on "unification" were going] before preliminary steps have been taken to keep the Air Force from going to hell.
2. It has been suggested that one of the following alternatives be adopted:
    (a) That a prayer be devised for the Armed Forces and that individual unilateral prayers for individual services be prohibited, or
    (b) That a prayer be devised for the Air Force and inserted in the proper place.
3. Of the two alternatives, this office prefers number one due to economical reasons. A simple prayer may suffice for all three services and save the time and efforts of individual action.
4. This memorandum is addressed to you in view of your paradisiacal proclivities and because the Air Force may be in need of their proportionate share of rectitude.

Johnson handpicked Sullivan's replacement, and the result was, for the Navy, disastrous. His choice was Francis Matthews, an Omaha attorney and a prominent layman in the Roman Catholic church. Matthews had done wartime work for the United Services Organization, which had brought him to the attention of Washington officialdom. Truman had appointed him to the President's Commission on Civil Rights, and in 1948 he had helped deliver Nebraska for the president. His naval (and military) experience was nil.

From his swearing-in ceremony on 25 May, Matthews quickly earned his Pentagon nickname: "Rowboat." He admitted, in a speech to the Naval Academy Class of 1949, that he had had "little prior training or preparation" to guide him (actually, he had had none), but he said he expected to learn quickly.

As far as the Navy was concerned, its new service secretary was a cipher, about as far from Forrestal's hardheadedness, bureaucratic savvy, and strategic wisdom as the Washington Senators were from first place in the American League. Worse, he was Johnson's man, a total loyalist (more like a servile toady, as the Navy saw him). At a time when the Navy needed all the bureaucratic leverage possible, the service found itself on the hit list of the secretary of defense and without any protection whatsoever from its top civilian.[11]

As a result the Navy's case amid the growing turmoil was carried to the public by Radford and more junior officers, such as Burke (who had been urgently summoned from command of the light cruiser *Huntington*) and Commander Thomas Davies. These men were kept busy mustering the Navy's "facts" in Denfeld's Office of Organization and Policy Research (OP-23)—Burke had picked the number from a blank spot on the office code list. OP-23 was the Navy's propaganda mill. Compared with the Air Force propaganda blitz, Burke and his spartan band of twelve officers ran a shoestring operation, but OP-23's activities were enough to draw cries of foul play from the opposition and draw the attention of even the Oval Office.

Amid the increasing flak that OP-23 was taking from the Air Force, Burke fielded voluntary suggestions from various overworked admirals and tried to put together a coherent PR package, but events were rapidly moving beyond his, or anyone else's, control. "Don't get discouraged and keep up the good work," Radford told him. "Looks to me as though the showdown we've wanted will come this summer. It's up to Mr. Vinson."

In May, Cedric Worth, a civilian administrative assistant to Under Secretary Dan Kimball, wrote an anonymous (and rapidly public) letter charging political chicanery and corruption in the B-36 program ("gross and vicious lies against men of high repute," huffed *Air Force Magazine*). The charges and countercharges flew all summer, and Vinson had little choice but to bring forward a special investigation under the control of his committee.

The first hearings, held in August, found that Worth's claims were full of holes. Johnson appeared, sounding the tocsin for further spending reductions on the order of a billion dollars, with the Navy targeted as the prime sacrificial victim. The number of heavy carriers was to be cut from eight to six and light carriers, from eleven to eight; naval aviation was to be reduced by one-third, its number of planes cut in half; seventy thousand Navymen would be discharged; the Marines would lose half their aviation strength. Active and retired naval officers were firing salvos all over the place, and the press had a field day.[12]

One of these officers was forty-seven-year-old Captain John Crommelin, fiery and emotional, an outstanding combat aviator, and holder of the Purple Heart—he had been blown off a carrier deck during the Pacific war and seriously wounded. He was a former skipper of the carrier *Saipan*. In the summer of 1949 he had just completed a course at the National War College, was assigned to work for the Joint Chiefs, and was clearly in line for higher duty. He was a zealot for naval air power, one of five brothers—the "fabulous Crommelins"—who were all Naval Academy graduates, four of them aviators, two of them dead in combat in the Pacific.

Navy blue ran in Crommelin's veins, and right now his blood was boiling. On 11 September 1949 he went public with a statement to the effect that the Navy's combat strength was being whittled away by the Pentagon and that naval morale was being damaged beyond repair.

> I believe in long-range heavy bombers and I want the United States to have the strongest Air Force in the world, but I also believe that a strong,

progressive Navy equipped with the great offensive power of carrier and Marine Corps aviation is essential to the success of any bombing program which the United States may be forced to conduct.

I do not believe in the General Staff concept [which Crommelin and many other naval officers regarded as a particularly odious offshoot of the unification battle]. I know that salt water and politics do not mix.

Behind the scenes, many among the Navy brass were rooting for Crommelin, who was clearly ready to fall on his sword and was revealing more than a tinge of the martyr in his makeup. Burke was typical:

I advised John [Crommelin] against starting his blast because I thought his timing was poor, and I also thought that some of the things that he was trying to prove were not actually true. Above all, I thought that he would do harm to the Navy's cause. Now I am not so sure but what he is right. In any case, it is a fight for the existence of the United States. [Burke probably meant the country here, rather than the carrier.]

On 15 September, Crommelin was assigned by his naval seniors to the post of deputy chief of naval personnel, a slot traditionally held by a rear admiral; clearly, he was in line for flag rank. Matthews, within seven hours, reversed his admirals and limited Crommelin to a captain's billet in the office of the deputy chief of naval operations. Truman, by now more than weary of the whole thing, supported Matthews.

Crommelin was not finished. Not content with a statement of his own (he was, after all, not of flag rank), he sneaked copies of internal Navy Department correspondence, to which he had right of access, bearing on the B-36–versus–supercarrier issue and leaked them to the press on 3 October. Among these was a letter from Vice Admiral Gerald Bogan, commander of the First Fleet.

Bogan moaned about the future of national security if national military policy was not drastically changed, about the pending deep cuts in naval aviation, and about the wrongheadedness of beefing up the strategic bomber force. Both Radford and Denfeld, in their forwarding endorsements, conceded that Bogan's views were shared by a large number of naval officers. Denfeld added that "naval officers . . . are concerned that a Navy stripped of its offensive power means a nation stripped of its offensive power."

All this breast-beating was supposed to be "private." Crommelin's move of the correspondence into the public arena quickly earned him a suspension from duty by Radford's replacement as vice chief of naval operations, Vice Admiral John Dale Price. Congress reacted as if goosed with a belaying pin; its hearings concerning the matter were hastily reopened on 5 October 1949.

There then ensued a media circus. (Close In Conolly called the whole thing an "animal act.") On parade were Johnson; Bradley; J. Lawton Collins, the Army chief of staff; Vandenberg; General Clifton Cates, commandant of the Marine Corps; civilian secretaries; and a galaxy of lesser lights. All the vitriol that had been pent up since the unification struggle came spewing out, and this time there was no Forrestal, or anyone else, to shut off the flow.

Ostensibly, all the witnesses were there to give their reasoned views on unification and national strategy. In actuality, the hearings rapidly degenerated into a bitching forum in which senior officers vented their spleen against sister services.

Vandenberg argued that the Navy's primary role was now one of antisubmarine warfare; the carrier was not a strategic weapon. Bradley, who called the Marines a bunch of "fancy Dans," predicted an end to future amphibious operations, a surprising judgment by a superb officer who had played a key role in the Normandy operation. In the process he also managed to disparage Denfeld's war record. Cates countered by saying, in effect, that any prophecy concerning the end of amphibious assault was hogwash (he would be vindicated—in spades—within the year) but that amphibious warfare would have to go by the boards anyway if the budget cutting continued.

Radford carried the ball for the Navy (actually, more for naval aviation) with both force and skill. He parried most of the Air Force claims to strategic monopoly. The whole USAF concept of strategic bombing was "childish;" the ideas of the air generals meant the "mass killing of civilians;" the B-36 was a "billion-dollar blunder."

Ernie King and Chester Nimitz were part of the lineup; so too were men of the stature of Raymond Spruance, Thomas Kincaid, and dozens of other admirals and Marine generals. Spike Blandy said that Johnson's budget cuts would render the Navy inadequate as a fighting force. Burke, a surface line officer, testified frankly that the United States was a maritime nation and would always need to "command the sea." And Captain Frederick Trapnell, chief test pilot at the Naval Air Experimental Station at Patuxent River, Maryland, rubbed salt in the wounds by contending that the new Navy jet fighters could easily take out the B-36.

Denfeld, however, was the Navy's crucial witness by virtue of his office. ("Denfeld hasn't been disloyal—yet," Johnson reportedly said.) All summer he had tried to keep an even keel as the controversy swirled about him (the press, noting his moderation and his polished manner, had christened him "Uncle Louie"), and he had finally decided that the prerogatives of the Navy, not simply the claims of the air admirals, were at stake and had to be defended. Accordingly, Denfeld charged that unification was not being implemented as Congress had intended, that the notion did not mean that the Army and Air Force (by 2–1 votes by the Joint Chiefs) should control the Navy's future.

To the Navy's discredit, however, Denfeld clearly distorted the strategic position of the Joint Chiefs of Staff, arguing that the American military was now committed to the *sole* strategy of an "atomic blitz" by the new B-36s. He knew better; the NATO defense of Europe was predicated on a stand against the USSR by conventional forces on the banks of the Rhine. Atomic weapons were a critical part of this strategy, but only a part. Denfeld had signed off on this strategy, and he had approved, as a member of the Joint Chiefs, the purchase of additional B-36s. In addition Denfeld's testimony, and that of some of the other admirals, bore more than a tinge of hypocrisy, because their ulterior motives included not merely the salvaging of naval strategic roles but the refunding of the supercarrier as well. The Navy had a "hidden agenda."

Behind Denfeld's words also lay a considerable distaste for military amateurism, common to men in uniform. Denfeld saw Johnson and Matthews as little more than political hacks—in this he was decidedly correct—and, therefore, doubly dangerous to the Navy's position. Here he was decidedly wrong, as this objection ran squarely up against imperatives in the Constitution concerning civilian control of the military.[13]

Matthews, completely in Johnson's leading-strings, was not really concerned with the Navy's combat capability; he knew little about the subject anyway. He saw his role as one of budget shrinking, because that was what his president and his secretary of defense wanted, and Denfeld's testimony in this light was disloyal and subversive; the chief of naval operations would have to walk the plank.

Matthews offered Denfeld a lesser post; Denfeld refused. Then the secretary asked for Denfeld's resignation; Uncle Louie sent in a letter of retirement instead. Matthews complained to Nimitz that Denfeld had kept his civilian leadership in the dark on matters such as naval developments and unification, as well as having failed to maintain a "harmonious relationship" with his superiors. This was true, although Denfeld obviously felt that the Navy's position could never be illuminated by such dim bulbs as Johnson and Matthews.

The Navy had had its chance. In fact, on 26 September, just before Crommelin blew the lid off and caused the second hearing, the carrier *Midway* hosted some top brass—Johnson, the three service secretaries, and Bradley—and put on an aerial dog-and-pony show. Afterward, Commander John Hayward strapped Johnson, Secretary of the Air Force Stuart Symington (despised as a complete liar by many admirals), and Bradley into one of his P-2Vs for a flight back to the mainland. One carefully planned crash and everything would have been over.

☆

—But everything was not over. The ripples from this particular bureaucratic bloodbath would prove to be wide and lasting. The report of the congressional committee, *Unification and Strategy*, was vintage Vinson, emphasizing the budgetary authority and responsibility that lay with Congress, pleading for greater cooperation within the Defense Department, and conceding that military expertise had its place—within its own "spheres of competence."[14]

Congress, including Vinson, now supported the Army–Air Force position on weapons systems, at least on the surface. The B-36 got a clean bill of health. But the big bomber would never live up to expectations and would shortly be overtaken by the intermediate-range, jet-powered B-47 and then by the spectacularly successful B-52, which eventually would become the longest-lived aviation weapons platform in the American armory. Nor would the seventy groups fly, at least at the time—Truman recommended forty-eight. ("The boys who fly . . . evidently think that the whole National Defense Budget should be placed in the 'air'," said the president, "and I put air in quotation marks because that is exactly where it would be.")

United States was dead. But the Navy, within a few years, would get its supercarrier (appropriately named *Forrestal*) and, in time, three more of the same, stepping-stones on the way to the real strategic role that would emerge with Polaris. The Marines, holding on by their fingernails, would survive and, within months, actually begin to prosper.

The congressional hearings, however, did nothing to resolve the strategic debate over *means;* the B-36 was temporarily vindicated, but the case for carrier-borne aviation did not vanish. These arguments would churn ever onward. Additionally, even though Vinson and his committee optimistically included the word *unification* in their report, the hearings accomplished almost nothing in that direction. The secretary of defense received some control over supplies, but there was no forthcoming streamlining in either weapons design or weapons production. Most importantly, the combined questions of strategic delivery systems and of their ownership remained clouded.

The arena was littered with bodies in Navy blue. Chief among these was Denfeld, seen by some as simply an "oleaginous timeserver" who had been the worst kind of choice as chief of naval operations: a compromise. Many argued that his dallying with Republican politicos was a tactical mistake sure to offend Truman, that prince of partisan politicians.

Denfeld's supporters praised his unassuming informality, calm objectivity (or the appearance thereof), and (in some situations) his quiet persuasiveness. Rowboat Matthews, in a rare difference of opinion with Johnson, had even asked before the hearings that Denfeld be reappointed to a two-year term, and on 10 August Truman had announced that Uncle Louie would be reappointed in December, at the end of his first term.

But Denfeld was not seen as a martyr by everyone, even within his own church. Many naval aviators saw him as a reluctant convert, even a backslider. Not even his deathbed conversion to Radford's position, made clear at the second hearing, helped him here. All that Denfeld's change of heart in the direction of naval aviation (which was predicated more on the needs of the entire Navy than on pacifying the aviators) had earned him was the conviction, on Matthews's part, of a double cross.

Matthews had thought of Denfeld as a moderate; he was. Denfeld regarded himself as a sacrificial lamb; he was. But in truth he had been placed in an impossible position, the classic dilemma of the moderate: in his case attempting to be loyal both to the concept of unification and to his own service. In the end these mills ground him exceedingly fine.

Uncle Louie did not go without honor. The Brigade of Midshipmen doffed their hats to him at the Army-Navy game, chanting, "We want Denfeld!" Bill Halsey declared his abiding pride in the departing chief. The press, although divided, made much of his courtliness and kindly behavior.

Denfeld had never been the puppet his critics said he was, but neither had he been a popular figure in his own service, at least until after he had been fired. Then, dozens of officers lined up to shake his hand, and a delegation of 250 enlisted men also trooped into his office. Their spokesman, a chief petty officer, asked: "If they can do this to a man like you, what is to happen to us?" Denfeld shot back: "No service and no individual will stop the Navy."[15]

Still, he was gone, jettisoned over the side. He had been "the wrong man, in the wrong place, at the wrong time." He salved his ego somewhat by going public with his side of the story, "Why I Was Fired." He told his readers that he had been a "victim," the "first target"—"Never in my 41 years in the Navy have I seen even the most culpable seaman given the disdainful treatment I received." He seemed angrier at the *manner* of his dismissal (he got the word from John Dale Price, who had heard the news over the radio) than at the act itself. But Uncle Louie, in the end, remained a convert: "The modern Navy is a carrier Navy."

Off the plank with him went Gerry Bogan, forced into early retirement; Spike Blandy, commander of the Atlantic Fleet and once within a hairsbreadth of the top position, opting for early retirement as well; and John Crommelin, who would have been in the zone for rear admiral that year and who was threatened with a court-martial, furloughed, and forced into early retirement, returning to his home in Alabama. Radford's star, for the short term, fell also; he had been bounced from Washington as early as May to command the Pacific Fleet.

As for the obnoxious Burke and his crowd, Matthews sicced the Navy's inspector general on OP-23. For three days the men of OP-23 were kept under virtual house arrest while a team of investigators and Marine guards ransacked their files. Burke cheekily requested that he be charged with some offense so that he could "enjoy the rights of a criminal." Matthews later apologized, but the headsman's ax was clearly hanging over OP-23.

For his part, Rear Admiral Dan Gallery would never become a vice admiral. But that hardly muzzled the man who was no stranger to the press and who had gotten a lot of mileage out of his wartime capture of *U-505*.

"Don't Let Them Cripple the Navy!" he pleaded with the readers of the *Saturday Evening Post*, following up with another broadside in *Collier's*.

"I am heartily in favor of a powerful air force," wrote Gallery. But "a certain amount of duplication can be a very good thing. Even Mother Nature is guilty of duplication when she provides us with two hands." And the Navy was being ravaged, "the only service which is feeling the heel of thought control." This was too much for Matthews, who called Gallery's charges "inflammatory . . . inaccurate . . . contemptuous . . . and disrespectful." Gallery, who expected a court-martial, got a letter of admonition.[16]

On 31 October, Truman, putative head of "thought control," asked Nimitz to return as chief of naval operations. Nimitz, perhaps still smarting from Forrestal's offer of the two-year term, refused. The president then asked for a recommendation; either Forrest Sherman or Close In Conolly, replied the fleet admiral. "And of the two, which would you recommend?" queried Truman. "Sherman is younger," said Nimitz, "and even less involved in politics."

—And so the change came to pass. Forrest Sherman was summoned from command of the Sixth Fleet to take the helm. Nimitz's old protégé would have to pick up the pieces.

☆

The press dubbed the affair "the revolt of the admirals," a moniker that has stuck. But there was no "revolt," in the sense of one faction seizing power from another, nor did the affair involve all "admirals" only. Many admirals, like Sherman and Conolly, stayed moderate or were uninvolved. And many of the key players, men like Crommelin, Burke, and Trapnell, were not of flag rank.

What had ensued was a rebellion in gold braid, highly emotional, at times conflicting, and laden with deeply felt convictions concerning naval prerogatives and strategic roles. Nor was this a rebellion that, failing to sweep all before, nevertheless had the support of the entire service. Reporters found that many officers and men, such as those aboard Conolly's flagship, the cruiser *Columbus*, viewed the whole thing as little more than a tempest in a Pentagon teapot. Despite the foreboding claims of men like Denfeld, Bogan, and Crommelin, morale seemed to be high in both the Atlantic and Pacific fleets.

Still, the Navy had been hurt, and hurt badly. For the moment the supercarrier idea, like *United States* herself, lay lifeless. The Navy had been forced to gut its other building programs to build *United States* and now had nothing to show for its sacrifices.

And more: James Forrestal, generally pro-Navy to the core and wise in the ways of Washington, was in his grave. Louis Johnson, who had presented himself at the hearings as a budget pruner acting on the public behalf against the self-serving claims of the services (and the nasty Navy in particular), was at his summit. John Sullivan, who although not regarded with great fondness by most of his admirals had nevertheless begun to master the intricacies of his position and had come around to support the big carrier, was gone.

The Navy was left with Rowboat Matthews, a man of such cartoonish demeanor that he once sent part of the nation's secret war plans to the cleaners in his jacket pocket. "Work is my hobby," revealed Rowboat, "and right now my hobby is the Navy Department."

The rebellion was "one of the sorriest spectacles in American military history." All sides were culpable: the Air Force, for its brashness born of adolescence and its almost hysterical propaganda blitz in favor of an uncertain strategic platform, the B-36; the Army, with its blinders vision regarding Marine duplication of its functions, in particular the highly complex mission of amphibious assault; Louis Johnson, whose bull-in-the-china-shop approach practically guaranteed a smashup; and the Navy, which throughout was deeply divided, poorly led, and all too clearly not in control of its own house. The hidden agenda regarding the supercarrier was clearly recognized by the Army and Air Force, which also played to Johnson's not inconsiderable prejudices with great skill. Worst of all, when the smoke of battle had cleared, the real issue remained unresolved: how to determine appropriate roles for the executive, Congress, and the services in the conduct of national strategy and national defense.[17]

Finally, blame rested with the man who had proudly declared that the buck stopped with him. Defense, after all, was firmly within the executive branch. By not stepping in early and decisively, Harry Truman allowed a simmering kettle to come to a boil. By choosing Johnson to succeed Forrestal, he provided (on the worst sort of grounds, the narrowly political) the match which touched off the firestorm. By keeping his attention *only* on the fiscal bottom line, he helped turn a comparatively normal budgetary debate into a disgraceful interservice brawl.

—This particular buck passed the president by.

STERN WATCH I

———— ☆ ————

T o most men," wrote Coleridge, "experience is like the stern lights of
a ship, which illumine only the track it has passed." The Navy's track
through the immediate postwar period had been a rough, choppy
passage, and as with a ship moving at high speed, the turmoil in its wake
took some time to subside.[1]

As thoroughly prepared as the Navy tried to be for peacetime, the
service rapidly found events moving beyond its control. The end-of-war
euphoria and the pell-mell rush to get the boys home was expected, but
what had been planned as an orderly flow of discharges and decommis-
sionings instantly became a cascading flood. As sailors and ships departed,
the Navy's ability to sustain any kind of reasonable overseas presence dwindled to the point at which, for about two years following V-J Day, any
serious overseas crisis would have found the fleet unable to respond.

This was an international posture unbefitting the only economic victor
of the war. "We are the giant of the economic world," noted Harry Truman.
With only 6 percent of the world's area and 7 percent of its population, the
United States had 46 percent of the world's electric power, 48 percent of
its radios, 54 percent of its telephones, and 92 percent of its modern bathtubs.
In 1947, America controlled 50 percent of the world's known oil reserves,
was the world's largest producer of coal and steel, and had eight times the
combined automobile production of England, France, and West Germany.
(By 1951, American automakers were building seven million cars a year,
compared to the Russian annual output of sixty-five thousand.) In 1948 the
United States produced over 40 percent of the world's goods and services
and almost one-half the world's industrial output.

The Navy—and the nation—were lucky. In the midst of such prosperity, no emergency calling for the application of naval power developed.
Painfully, the service began to adjust itself to the unprecedented combination
of shrunken budgets and global demands. But the fleet was stretched thin,
very thin. If the Navy was to be the worldwide cop on the beat (and, in
truth, Navymen eagerly seized upon this role), the people making its decisions soon found that their ships could not be everywhere at once, could

163

not respond rapidly in certain areas, and could provide but a minimal presence in increasingly important sectors, like the western Pacific.

World War II had vindicated the United States Navy, in its own eyes and in the eyes of the public. Never had the gospel of seapower, regardless of its several churches, shone forth so brightly. *All* had been vindicated: the Navy's ability to project power, over seas and onto land; its planning, leadership, and organization; and its technology, particularly the big aircraft carrier.

Above all, its fighting spirit had been both proven and confirmed, on a scale unmatched in all its storied past. The Navy emerged, covered with laurels (or, more appropriately, seaweed), its public reputation at a higher level than at any time in its history, not excluding the hyperromanticized era of the Barbary Wars.

All this triumph made life doubly hard for the Navy, as conservative and tradition-bound a major institution as any to be found in America, especially in changing its ways. The fleet entered the postwar years wedded irrevocably to the doctrines of the strategic and tactical offensive: attack! Carry the battle to the enemy! Unfortunately, as many critics noted at the time, the enemy had been eradicated—at least any enemy, like Germany and especially Japan, that seapower could get at directly.

That the Soviet Union was the new peacetime candidate for the enemy's role was readily agreed upon, and naval strategy was accordingly refocused, but planning took a while to catch up with the deepening hostilities of ideological warfare. Naval officers like Bill Leahy loathed communism (FDR once told Leahy that politically the admiral belonged in the Middle Ages), and this hatred often pushed aside reasoned assessment. As the Russians took their place as the new naval menace, American planners found that making them fit the prewar roles filled satisfactorily by the Germans and so nicely by the Japanese was difficult. First, the USSR was a classic land power, and although its routes to blue water passed through a variety of narrow choke points, the Russians had proven that they could wage continental war ad infinitum, using their own immeasurable human and natural resources.

Second, the Russians had no blue-water navy to speak of, and their national strategy, always, was conditioned to the land battle. In any Mahanian sense they could not be engaged. The American Navy struggled for years (and would continue to struggle) to fit its offensive-mindedness, its carrier task forces, and its fond wish for oceanic battle into planning scenarios that could be immediately and strategically useful against the Soviet Union.

This struggle was made the more imperative by the rise of the Air Force to strategic prominence. Regardless of the merits of either side of the strategic debate between Navy and USAF, naval leaders were not about to step aside for any strategic concept that seemed to shoulder them from center stage into the wings. The unsettled wake left through these years was made more turbulent yet by arguments over unification and strategic weapons systems.

The Navy got most of its way in the initial unification face-off; nobody won during the rebellion in gold braid. Clearly, the *quality* of naval leadership was in temporary decline. From James Forrestal to John Sullivan to Francis Matthews was a steep and calamitous plunge, and unfortunately for the Navy, its first postwar secretary was to prove its best. On the uniformed side, Ernie King and Chester Nimitz were, by any measure, head and shoulders over Louis Denfeld.

Even so, top-drawer leadership throughout would not have spared the Navy its immediate postwar problems. The best of leaders—and Forrestal, King, and Nimitz were certainly among these—could not have coped with the rock-and-a-hard-place problem of worldwide naval demands versus budgetary constraints, the impassioned pleas to bring the boys home and "return to normal," or the continued blustering of air-power extremists.

The Navy quickly found itself an instrument of the developing Cold War, which fit in nicely with the virulently anti-Communist stance of its leaders but which meant that the fleet would take its place as a spear-carrier for relatively benign American imperialism in the emerging bipolar postwar world. The anthropologist Ruth Benedict, who had done war work for the Office of War Information, had seen this problem coming:

> With every occupied country the United States assists in freeing from Axis domination, with every Asiatic country where we operate in cooperation with the existing culture, the need for intelligent understanding of that country and its ways of life will be crucial. . . . The danger—and it would be fatal to world peace—is that in our ignorance of their cultural values we shall meet in head-on collision and incontinently fall back on the old pattern of imposing our own values by force.[2]

—Here was prophecy pertinent for the future. Everywhere the Navy went—and its ships were going practically everywhere—the fleet was a signal of *American* wishes, desires, and demands—an ideological as well as a military force.

And so the waters roiled on. "Though we had peace, yet 'twill be a great while e'er things be settled," the skeptical poet John Selden (who wrote during the upheaval of the English Civil War) had intoned. "Though the Wind lie, yet after a Storm the Sea will work a great while."[3]

—*The Sea will work a great while*. And as the Sea worked, the question remained whether the all-conquering armada could rise once again to a challenge from abroad.

The challenge would come, as such things usually do, from a quarter largely unexpected. And half a world away.

PART TWO

FLASHPOINT: KOREA

Appear at places to which he must hasten;
move swiftly where he does not expect you.

—Sun-tzu, *The Art of War*

CHAPTER EIGHT

COME-AS-YOU-ARE WAR

—————— ☆ ——————

On 25 June 1950 the North Korean army surged across the 38th parallel into South Korea and began propelling the Republic of Korea's army (the ROKs) and a few scratch American forces down the peninsula. The sudden offensive, while not a complete shock to Washington, was nevertheless unexpected and found the United States Navy in a peacetime condition. "We were caught in a very weakened state," remembered Jimmy Thach.

The Navy was no stranger to the shores of Korea. As far back as 1867, Commander Robert Shufeldt had taken *Wachusett* there to investigate the fate of the American merchantman *General Sherman*. Shufeldt discovered that the ship had been set ablaze by xenophobic Koreans—every man aboard her had been drowned, clubbed to death, incinerated, or beheaded.

As a metaphor, the rather decisive end of *General Sherman* was perhaps an accurate indicator of things to come. Rear Admiral John Rodgers led a motley, decrepit group of ships against some forts on Kangwha Island in 1871, bombarding and blasting away against Koreans armed with feudal weapons, all in the name of gaining a shipwreck convention and trade treaty. He failed.

Eventually diplomacy had its way. Shufeldt negotiated a commercial treaty in 1882 (the last such activity by a serving naval officer). But relations with Korea, a land remote and misunderstood—when the country was not completely forgotten—were always on the back burner in Washington.

Korea was called the Hermit Kingdom with reason, but the modern world crowded in, finding the country seldom strong enough to act independently in foreign affairs. Geography wedded the peninsula to China, but the growing might of Imperial Japan brought Korea under the Rising Sun in 1910. There the Hermit Kingdom stayed, restless but helpless under Tokyo's control—the "Ireland of the Far East."

As the Pacific war rushed to its atomic climax, Korea inevitably became part of the spoils. The best bet to "unify" Korea and keep the country safely

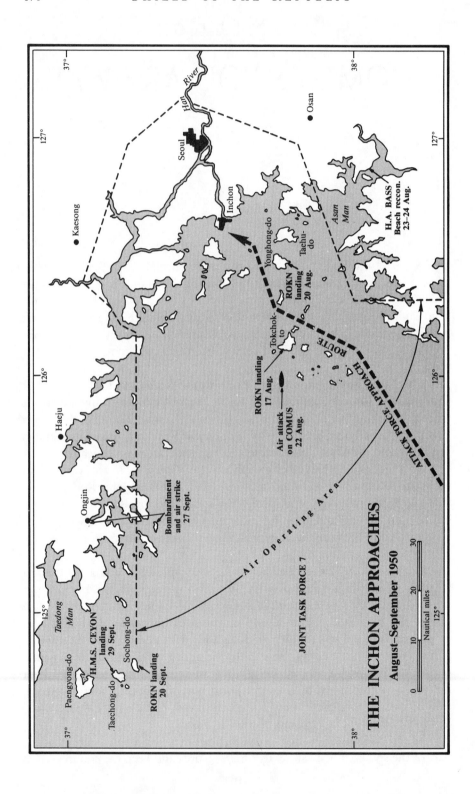

THE INCHON APPROACHES
August–September 1950

in the forming American orbit seemed to be an elderly conservative nationalist named Syngman Rhee. Holder of a Princeton doctorate, Rhee had lived in the United States for most of the thirty years before 1945. He wanted a Korea that would both repudiate Japanese hegemony and serve as a Far Eastern bastion against communism.

These goals were fine with American leadership, but Rhee himself, in the Navy's view, was not the man to achieve them. A report compiled for the Navy Department called him and his leading Korean supporters "frustrated and unemployed men." Indeed, the department considered Korea bereft of leadership of any kind, fearing that the country could fall into the kind of dangerous power vacuum that had ushered in Soviet dominance in Poland and the Balkans as the war in Europe ended.

Apart from the quality of leadership in any emerging, self-governing Korea was the question of the strategic value of the place. By V-J Day, State Department hard-liners were already arguing that Soviet occupation of Korea (a real possibility, since Stalin, in this instance true to his word at Yalta, had entered the war against Japan exactly when he said he would—three months after V-E Day) would threaten American interests in the Far East. The Pentagon, however, was convinced that Korea would have no strategic value in case of a general world conflict. American forces could be better used elsewhere.

To forestall a power vacuum, the United States occupied Korea with two divisions, totaling about 45,000 men, lifted there by the Seventh Fleet in early September 1945. The War Department, which was footing the bill, conceded the *political* value of Korea in keeping the Soviets at bay in Asia but believed that there were more important fish to fry in Europe.

The dividing line between the Americans and the Russians, who duly occupied the north, was almost casually chosen at the 38th parallel. As the line hardened into a boundary with international connotations, the cavalier manner of its choice could easily be seen as a mistake. Commodore Ruthven Libby, who as senior naval member of the Joint War Plans Committee had a hand in drawing the line, was sure a mistake had been made:

> Nobody stopped to think that all the brains and energy, and all the power plants and everything in Korea was [*sic*] north of the 38th parallel and that south of it was just rice paddies and peasants. . . . All the zing was really north of the 38th parallel.[1]

In any event, America threw its entire support behind Rhee, a querulous old man who had forgotten nothing about his own oppression by the Japanese but had remembered little about the conduct of democracy in his second homeland. The policymakers at State obviously hoped he had some anti-Communist zing of his own.

To the north, the Soviet Union, true to its Eastern European form, had created a Communist Provisional People's Committee, headed by a mysterious, paranoid figure named Kim Il-sung. The State Department, sensing more than an echo of Poland, divided Germany, and the Balkans, presented a resolution to the United Nations that called for the United States and the USSR to hold elections in their respective zones by the end of March 1948. In August, American occupation forces transferred internal political authority to Rhee's government. Visiting Seoul, Douglas MacArthur proclaimed that the barrier of the 38th parallel "must be torn down." If South Korea were attacked, he further announced, he would "defend it as I would California."

The Cold War had reached the deep-freeze stage; a Korea unified through peaceful, democratic elections sponsored by the United Nations was never in the cards. South Korean internal politics were severely polarized; Kim had agents inserted to do their usual work, but there was plenty of home-grown opposition. Rhee, however, had the backing of not only the Americans but also the fervidly anti-Communist South Korean right; he was a consummate law-and-order man (with the accent on order); and he was the only major political leader in the south to favor a separate (South Korean) government.

By December 1948 the United States was "rigidly committed" to Rhee and to the establishment of an anti-Communist government for South Korea. As proof, when most of the American soldiers went home, a token force of "advisers" to the ROKs remained. On the other hand, MacArthur told a congressional delegation that "South Korea is in no danger of being overrun by North Korea."

Rhee's leadership had the smallest measure of the liberalism of Woodrow Wilson, who had been president of Princeton when Rhee had studied there. His style, which was autocratic and authoritarian, did little to cure the marked instability of South Korean politics; the old man quickly clamped down with a program of repression that included martial law. Nor was he hesitant to call for American military aid. For example, on the island of Cheju, off the south coast, guerrilla units from the *South* Korean political left burned villages and killed a number of rightists and police officers. An American destroyer had to be stationed between the island and the mainland to prevent guerrilla infiltration.

Seoul, on the banks of the Han River, was far from being the capital of an idyllic democracy.

☆

Korea's location was its primal curse. A thumb pointing downward from Southeast Asia, the country had been the hinge of Sino-Japanese conflict. When Chiang Kai-shek lost the Mandate of Heaven and fled to Taiwan, any Communist threat to the Nationalist-ruled island almost axiomatically involved Korea. The Soviet Union, while withdrawing most of its troops from

North Korea, was not above keeping "advisers" there, as the Americans did in the south. In addition, Stalin maintained an intense ideological interest in Kim's progress and, while the aging despot in the Kremlin almost certainly did not plan the North Korean attack, he met with Kim in Moscow and, by failing to negate the idea, gave the offensive his blessing.

In short, the Koreans once again were living up to their own description of themselves, shrimps crushed in the battle of whales. The Hermit Kingdom had become a magnet for Cold War tensions. On 26 January 1950, the Rhee government signed a military assistance agreement with the United States; there followed a visit to South Korean military installations by the Joint Chiefs, including Forrest Sherman, the new chief of naval operations. The Chiefs found precious few installations, particularly any in working order. If American power was to help Korea, such forces would have to come from outside the peninsula.

—Which mostly meant Japan. When the Chiefs got there, Benny Decker informed them that Yokosuka was the only American base west of Hawaii capable of repairing major warships during a conflict (Subic Bay was not yet fully geared up). Decker wanted another $6 million to keep developing his pride and joy. Sherman agreed and warned that any reduction in American forces in Japan would invite Communist meddling.

Life was still soft in Yoko. MacArthur, surrounded by a group of military sycophants described by George Marshall as a "court befitting an oriental satrap," had become celebrated, a bit too fulsomely, as the founder of post-war democratic Japan, but these accomplishments were not reflected in any accompanying military might.

Not only did Yoko serve as Seventh Fleet headquarters; the port was the pleasure capital of the Far East. Yoko proper contained about 5000 prostitutes and 1500 whorehouses, the latter replete with tea service, *hotse* baths, and the tender ministrations of geishas. For those not in the mood (or exhausted), there was nearby Sarushima (Monkey Island), an Oriental Las Vegas, forerunner of Seoul's notorious Walker Hill. Sailors assigned to Yoko did not resist overmuch; they even had their own song:

> Beer *beree naisu* and girls all around,
> Up on the hill where the "cherries" bloom
> I'm gonna make us a home sweet home.
> > Baby, what you do to me!

> A long time ago this town was full of fight,
> But now we've pretty rainbows to light up the night,
> Classy taxicabs to go scooting all about,
> And kisses in the rain when the moon comes out.
> > Baby, what you do to me!

Up on the mountain I look down at the sea—
Ships going, ships coming, and one ship of love for me.
Rocking gently on the waves, rocking to and fro,
Oh I want to get on board, to get on board and go!
    Baby, what you do to me!

Sailors in Yoko had things easy, too easy, but they still got to sea, still exercised when their skimpy budget allowed. The Seventh Fleet's operational focus, in early 1950, was increasingly on Taiwan, not Korea. Leading Republican politicos, not all of them part of the shrilly hysterical China lobby, wanted more aid for Chiang's government-in-exile, looking toward the day when the China that had been "lost" would be recovered. Senators William Knowland and Robert Taft publicly urged that the Navy be used *directly* to defend Taiwan. To tamp down this brushfire, Harry Truman issued a press statement on 5 January to the effect that Taiwan was clearly Chinese territory; there would be no further involvement in the Chinese civil war, nor would military advice or assistance be furnished the Nationalists.

A week later Secretary of State Dean Acheson, debonair, donnish, and the bête noir of the China lobby, spoke at the National Press Club. His remarks covered too much ground in too little time. Acheson was frank to admit that Chiang and his minions had failed on the mainland because of their own corruption and ineptitude. The Soviet Union, he said, far from being the ally of the new holders of the Mandate of Heaven, the Chinese Reds, represented Communist imperialism and was Mao Tse-tung's enemy.

Then the secretary turned to military policy. He defined the American shield in the Pacific: its rim started in the Aleutians, ran through Japan to the Ryukyus, and ended in the Philippines. This definition reflected a National Security Council assessment (NSC 48/2) and agreed with MacArthur's ideas. Acheson mentioned neither Taiwan nor South Korea; his implication was that neither area was considered vital in Washington. He concluded with a vague reference to the as-yet-untried United Nations as the ultimate peacekeeper for such areas.

Only a military assistance agreement, and that of a minimal nature, bound the United States and South Korea. Both Truman's and Acheson's remarks could easily be read as follows: in case of trouble involving either Taiwan or South Korea, the United States would be unwilling to act. In May 1950, Tom Connally, chairman of the Senate Foreign Relations Committee, said the Soviet Union could seize South Korea without resulting American intervention; the peninsula was not "very greatly important."[2]

☆

The blue water connecting Japan, Taiwan, and South Korea, if that stretch of troubled sea belonged to anyone, belonged to the Seventh Fleet, even diminished as the fleet was. There simply were no other contenders.

Mao was a continentalist; he had won China on the strength of guerrilla forces that had become enormous land armies. He and his men knew little about seapower and cared less. His navy was seen as an expendable entity with the sole purpose of defending China's coastal zone. In 1950 this mélange consisted of a "junk assault force" manned by soldiers and ignored by *Jane's*. The naval remnants that Chiang took with him to Taiwan, mostly American castoffs, could easily dominate the central and southeastern coasts of mainland China and were, in fact, already harassing Communist coastal shipping.

The Soviet Union, for its approximately two weeks of war against Japan, had gained the Kurile Islands, southern Sakhalin, and (temporarily) the northern half of Korea. The Sea of Okhotsk, shallow and island-locked, had become a Red lake. But Russia's northern bases in the "Sea of O" were icebound much of the year; its outlets to the Sea of Japan—the Tsugaru, Tsushima, and Soya straits—were controlled by the Seventh Fleet. Ports south of Vladivostok were checked by American bases in Okinawa and the Philippines. Only Vladivostok was a dependable base for the Soviet Pacific Fleet, and this aggregation of ships was a poor sister to the Baltic, Black Sea, and Northern fleets.

As for the two Koreas, like Mao's "navy" each had such infinitesimal seapower that neither was deemed worthy of inclusion in *Jane's*. South Korea's navy, created from scratch in 1948, had about five thousand men. (Sunshine Murray, after an inspection tour, said the country needed a coast guard more than a navy.) Its principal base, at Chinhae on the south coast, was home to a checkered assortment of tiny, formerly American, motor minesweepers, as well as to a few other minesweepers and picket boats left by the Japanese. Morale had been low, but by 1950 the South Korean sailors had themselves subscribed to buy one of four brand-new 173-foot patrol craft. Still, with this puny force South Korea could not even defend its own coast.

Kim's "navy" was in even worse shape. His seapower consisted of about forty-five small craft, including a few sixty-foot aluminum-hulled Russian torpedo boats. The Soviets administered a small training program for North Korean "sailors" at Najin, in the northeast, and also enjoyed the use of base facilities there and at Chongjin and Unggi.

The North Koreans, other than a few coastal infiltration operations, were not coming south by sea. They could not. Neither could Mao, or Stalin. Thus the Seventh Fleet, part of a navy built for engagement on salt water, literally *had no naval power to fight in the Far East*.

If Truman's and Acheson's remarks defined American policy toward Korea and Taiwan, all this was academic. But American policy was, at best, clouded and confused. In the spring of 1950 the National Security Council had produced yet another top-secret document, the soon-to-be-famous NSC 68, which sounded the Cold War alarm and heralded the end of Truman's $13 billion military budgets.

James Forrestal and the Joint Chiefs had pounded the table for years over the fact that American military spending fell far short of the country's growing burden of overseas commitments. NSC 68 said this clearly: "It is imperative that this trend be reversed by a much more rapid and concerted build-up of the actual strength of both the United States and . . . the free world." In conclusion, "the cold war is in fact a real war in which the survival of the free world is at stake."[3]

—A "real war." In the Far East, the umbrella of NSC 68 clearly sheltered Japan, where the sailors based at Yoko carelessly frolicked on amid its peacetime gaudiness. Its shade protected docile Okinawa and extended to the Philippines, where the United States had received a ninety-nine-year lease on twenty-three military bases, including the huge and still growing naval complex at Subic Bay. Whether its coverage extended, in June 1950, to Taiwan and South Korea was a moot point. Certainly, however, the American *global* effort to "contain" Communist expansion had been formulated *before* the North Korean attack.

And those men streaming south across the 38th parallel were *Communists*. The invasion, proclaimed Rowboat Matthews, still in place as secretary of the Navy, "added another chapter to the communist bid for world domination." Rowboat was clear about what this meant, and he doubtless spoke for millions of his countrymen: "The communists want to take over our country because it stands for freedom and decency and opportunity—which are contrary to their system of dictated life."

So ideology counted above all—above the rather careless remarks of the president and his secretary of state and above the lack of any binding international agreement. NSC 68 was the truer blueprint, and America would go to war in Korea against communism.

☆

Forrest Sherman had ordered a series of Korean port visits for the Seventh Fleet during the spring, as tensions heated up along the border. On 5 April the *Essex*-class carrier *Boxer* showed up off the west coast port of Inchon, deploying its gunmetal-blue Corsairs, Skyraiders, and Panther jets over the city in a show of strength. "You are our friends," an enthusiastic Rhee told the sailors. "Come again, come often, and stay longer."

Now they would *have* to come again. In a matter of days the North Koreans took Inchon, overran Seoul, crossed the Han, and drove south down the peninsula toward the port city of Pusan. Kim's combat army was ninety thousand strong, with about two hundred Russian-made T-34 tanks, two thousand guns, and an air force of about 210 Russian aircraft. Along the way they gobbled up South Korean airfields, denying them not only to Rhee's pygmy air force (sixteen aircraft, thirteen of which were observation planes) but to the USAF as well. The northerners "had that fanatical purpose of Communists," according to one naval officer, whereas "the South Korean . . . he's a peace-loving man and he didn't like to fight."[4]

The shock waves rocked Washington. On Sunday afternoon, 25 June, the United Nations Security Council (the Soviet Union, foolishly, had boycotted the meetings at the time of the crisis) approved an American-sponsored resolution calling for an end to the fighting and the withdrawal of the North Koreans to north of the 38th parallel. The same evening, Truman, having returned to the capital from a vacation in Missouri, ordered American air and naval forces to prevent the North Koreans from interfering with the evacuation of American dependents from the Seoul-Inchon area. The planes were to operate south of the 38th parallel *only*—a hint of the political restrictions to come.

In Korea everything was falling apart. The dusty roads leading south were choked with fleeing refugees and panicky remnants of shattered army units. North Korean armor—the dread T-34s—rammed far ahead, shooting up most of what little resistance there was. The sixty-five thousand ROKs had no tanks and only ninety short-range field guns; they were folding fast.

Within three days of the attack, Truman ordered elements of the Seventh Fleet to the Formosa Strait, as much to keep Chiang away from Mao as vice versa. So commenced the Formosa Strait patrol ("something of a bluff," remembered Dean Rusk). Thousands of Chinese junks cruised the mainland coast within easy range of Taiwan. To find out what would sink a junk, the Navy towed one out to sea and riddled its hull with gunfire, only to rediscover an axiom from the days of sail: wood floated.

Chiang, at first, registered gratitude; he admired the Navy, he said, "particularly because they always willing come to help of friends in need [*sic*]." The Red Chinese, in the person of foreign minister Chou Enlai, called the naval patrol "armed aggression against the territory of China." From these differing viewpoints came the notion, pushed forward primarily by the more demented sectors of the anti-Communist right, that the Seventh Fleet was somehow "shielding" Communist China, keeping the Nationalists and their Supremo from "unleashing" their righteous vengeance. The issue would not die.

Douglas MacArthur was the obvious choice for overall command of all forces in the theater—naval, ground, and air. Unfortunately, where Truman and the Joint Chiefs wished to rein in Chiang ("the Seventh Fleet will see that [Chiang will] . . . cease all air and sea operations against the mainland," said the president), MacArthur, weaned in a school of conflict in which the imperative of victory precluded compromise, wanted to use any force available—and that included the Nationalists—against *communism*. For Mac-

Arthur, militarily honored beyond any other man in American history, this was the grand finale, the ultimate world struggle, a war between darkness and light: the Apocalypse. He responded like an old firehorse bolting from the barn.

Initially, Washington was fully behind its Man in the Far East. Air support for dependent evacuation was supplied instantly; elements of the Seventh Fleet sortied north from Subic; shipments of ammunition and military hardware to the South Koreans under the Mutual Defense Assistance Program were sped up. At first, the Washington planners believed that air power and seapower would be enough, and MacArthur was cautioned to use American ground forces only to provide essential communications and services.

Nothing helped. The North Koreans were moving south like lemmings, headed for Pusan and the sea. MacArthur, five days after the attack, was forced to recommend the use of American ground combat forces. The key day was 30 June. Truman met with Acheson, Louis Johnson, the Joint Chiefs, and congressional leaders. The president and his men meant to "hold on" to Korea. Therefore, "certain supporting ground units" would be committed to action (these soon became the Eighth Army), and MacArthur was authorized, under conditions of "military necessity," to bomb north of the 38th parallel.

A naval blockade of North Korea, supported by Sherman with some apprehension ("I was fully aware of the hazards involved in fighting Asiatics on the Asiatic mainland"), was proclaimed. Sherman wanted allied help; without this, in George Marshall's words, the blockade would "leak like a sieve." Furthermore, Red China could still get supplies over its long land border with the Soviet Union, and any great disruption of Mao's economy, through the blockade process alone, was bound to be a long-term proposition. The idea was not new; Truman, enraged over the house arrest of an American diplomat in Mukden the year before, had proposed a naval blockade of north China.

—But there were not enough ships.[5]

☆

For Korea, the Navy had to "come as you are." Unfortunately, the naval cupboard in the Far East was practically bare. Only about a third of the Navy's active strength was in the Pacific—the result of the strategic shift—and of that, only one-fifth was in the Far East. On 1 January 1947, seven theater commands had been established, with commander in chief, Pacific (CINCPAC), as one of them. CINCPAC was double-hatted; as CINCPAC, both the Army and the Air Force in the Pacific reported to him. As commander of the Pacific Fleet, he reported to himself (the two hats would not be split until 1958). CINCPACFLT—in 1950, Arthur Radford—commanded all naval forces in the Pacific, including Seventh Fleet. MacArthur had the Far East Command—all American forces in Japan, Okinawa, Korea, the Bonins, and the Philippines. MacArthur's navy, Naval Forces Far East, thus contained about 7 percent of American naval power, and its marching orders mentioned only logistic support for the small American mission in Korea.

Its commander was Vice Admiral C. (for Charles) Turner Joy. A mediocre middle (eighty-fourth out of 177) in his Academy class of 1916, Joy had made a career as a gunman; he had been involved mostly with cruisers and battleships, specializing in ordnance. He had commanded the light cruiser *Louisville* during the fighting around the Rennell Islands in the South Pacific, and as a flag officer he had taken Cruiser Division 6 from the Marianas to Okinawa. He had been in charge of MacArthur's navy since August 1949.

Joy had a bit of punch in Task Force 96, Naval Forces Japan. This outfit's most powerful unit was its flagship, the light cruiser *Juneau*, a weird concatenation of sixteen five-inch dual-purpose guns that was named after the light anti-aircraft cruiser sunk in 1942 by a Japanese submarine following the Naval Battle of Guadalcanal. At six thousand tons and a flank speed of thirty-three knots, *Juneau* was more a heavyweight destroyer than a big-gun cruiser, designed for antiair warfare. In support she had a division of four *Sumner*-class destroyers (more five-inch guns), a group of minesweepers, a single diesel submarine (*Remora*), and, because Joy reported to MacArthur and MacArthur still wore his hat as Supreme Commander Allied Powers, the token presence of an Australian patrol gunboat, *Shoalhaven*.

Turner Joy also had Task Force 90, the Amphibious Force, Far East, commanded by Rear Admiral James Doyle aboard his flagship, *Mount McKinley*. Jimmy Doyle, who graduated from the Academy three years after Joy, had begun in destroyers. He was a studious, reflective sort, and found time to get a law degree from George Washington in 1929. He had become an amphibious specialist the hard way, learning the trade in the dangerous waters around Guadalcanal. Doyle went on to do graduate work in a tough school: he had been Richmond Kelly Turner's operations officer during the Central Pacific landings.

But the awesome amphibious might he had become used to in the Pacific was gone. The Navy's 610 amphibious ships of 1945 had become ninety-one. Nor were the Gators a high service priority. There were thirty-eight line officers of flag rank in 1950, and the chief of naval operations had only a captain to report to him about amphibious warfare. Jimmy Doyle was one of the top-notch Gator specialists in the Navy, and he had exactly one attack transport, one attack cargo ship, one LST, and one fleet tug working for him. At the moment, this made little difference; there were precious few troops to lift.

Joy's staff was skeletal, 28 officers and 160 enlisted; he had no air or weather specialists, depending on Guam for those. No mine warfare experts were aboard. The operations plans, such as they were, concentrated on war with the Soviet Union, featuring passive defense and evacuation procedures. There was no logistics command (even though the staff was charged with supporting those advisers in Korea), no torpedo shop, no electronics repair. An ordnance facility existed, stocked with a mere three thousand tons of ammunition; so too did a naval hospital—with a capacity of one hundred beds. Naval Air Facility Yokosuka had two or three flying boats; the total strength of land-based naval air in Japan was one target tow plane for anti-aircraft gunnery training.

In short, Naval Forces Far East could not conduct war on any but the most minute scale. But the Seventh Fleet could. The Fleet was commanded by Vice Admiral Arthur Struble, a Blackshoe like Turner Joy. Struble had been the exec of *Arizona*, lucky enough to be relieved just before Pearl Harbor. They called him "Rip" for a reason; he could flare out at subordinate or superior alike and in fact had never gotten along with his boss in the Pacific, Dan Barbey. Still, working for Uncle Dan in the host of amphibious landings that made up the conquest of the Philippines, Struble, like Doyle, learned the ways of the Gator Navy.

After the war he rose to become Louie Denfeld's deputy for plans and policy, where he had been the Navy's premier spokesman at the Joint Chiefs' meetings. As Seventh Fleet, Rip Struble reported to Arthur Radford back in Pearl Harbor.

Seventh Fleet had the only attack carrier in the western Pacific, *Valley Forge* (*Boxer* had been rotated back to the States in May). "Happy Valley" was an improved postwar *Essex*-class, completed in 1946. She operated Carrier Air Group 5, eighty-six planes, the first group in the Navy to routinely fly the new jet aircraft. There were two jet fighter squadrons (thirty Grumman F9F-2 Panthers), two piston-engine fighter squadrons (Vought F4U-4Bs, the famous gull-winged Corsairs), and one piston-engine attack squadron (Douglas AD-4 Skyraiders).

Valley Forge could conduct night missions, radar search missions, and photographic missions—but there was only one of her. She was even more critical because the few USAF planes based in Japan were short-legged, especially the fuel-gobbling jets, and therefore could spend little time over Korean targets.

The carrier was the heart of Task Force 77, which included one cruiser (eight-inch *Rochester*) and a screening group of eight destroyers. In addition, Struble owned four fleet submarines (including *Remora*, on loan to Turner Joy) and a submarine rescue vessel. He had all the patrol planes in the western Pacific, centralized on Guam under Fleet Air Wing 1, featuring P4Y-2 Privateers and PBM-5 Mariners and supported by the seaplane tender *Suisun*. For logistic support, he had a destroyer tender, an oiler, a refrigerator ship, and a fleet tug.

Rip Struble was senior to Turner Joy; the latter, working directly for MacArthur, the theater commander, had no aviation section on his staff and no direct control of either the carrier strike force or the patrol squadrons. The Navy's principal base facilities, at Yoko, Guam, and Subic Bay, were at considerable distances from Korea.

In sum, here was a rather dismal catalog. The fleet was ill-prepared. But, prepared or not, the battle flags were flying. Turner Joy, Rip Struble, Jimmy Doyle, and their men were going to war.

☆

Korea is a peninsula; this simple geographic fact dictated most of the naval possibilities of the war. As Kim's army, three infantry divisions with armor and air support, rolled south, eventually bottling up South Korean and American forces around the port of Pusan, its supply lines got longer, its resupply problems multiplied, and its flanks—its vulnerable seaward flanks—were left hanging in the air, totally indefensible.

At first the North Koreans had enough amphibious "lift"—a few junks and rickety steamers—to put troops ashore in the south. The South Koreans went after these infiltrators, and on 25 June, right at the outset, one of their small patrol craft sank a thousand-ton steamer northeast of Pusan, drowning most of the six hundred soldiers aboard (the largest "surface engagement" of the war). The suddenness of the onslaught, however, made evacuation the first emergency priority, and along both coasts destroyers covered the flight southward as best they could, as *Mansfield* and *De Haven* did off Inchon.

Pusan had become a miniature version of Normandy, a beachhead, and ammo from Japan began to be funneled there to support the embattled soldiers. On 25 June, back in Washington, Sherman wanted to get Struble out of the Philippines and headed north. The next day Turner Joy, speaking in MacArthur's name, got the Seventh Fleet going toward the Formosa Strait. On the 27th, leaning on MacArthur's five stars, he got operational control of Struble. *Juneau* and her destroyers were ordered to patrol the Korean coast, oppose hostile landings, cover evacuations, and provide on-call fire support. *Juneau*, as might be expected in her rapid transition from peace to war, got trigger-happy; her first victim was a South Korean motor launch, blown to bits by mistake.

At midnight on the 29th the five-inch cruiser finally got down to business, conducting the first shore bombardment of the war, against Mukho. Still the North Koreans swarmed southward, moving inland whenever they could to get out of range of the naval guns.

All the naval power immediately available was rapidly assembling. Truman, wisely, had made this a "United Nations" war, although the phrase "police action," which he had carelessly used at a reporter's prompting at a press conference, would haunt him for the rest of his term. Accordingly,

British Commonealth units, already in the Far East under the command of Rear Admiral Sir William Andrewes, began to show up. Australia, New Zealand, and Canada prepared to send warships.

Sir William was far from toothless; he had *Triumph*, a thirteen-thousand-ton light carrier with forty aircraft; *Belfast* and *Jamaica*, six-inch light cruisers; and three destroyers and four fighters, including little *Shoalhaven*. Joy took Andrewes under his umbrella, modifying his own Operation Order 5-50 to limit the Commonwealth ships to Korean operations only. Taiwan (where Struble's Corsairs and Skyraiders were scanning the strait) would remain a purely American affair.

Turner Joy, even with Commonwealth support, was stretched to the limit. His staff would eventually expand to 1200 by November, but in the meantime he had to guard Taiwan, support Rhee's government (which was fleeing south in complete disarray), blockade North Korea, evacuate American citizens, and be ready for more of the unexpected. His Plans Section went port and starboard—twelve hours on, twelve hours off. The ops officer moved a cot into his office. The communications people saw their encrypted traffic, always a headache, multiply by a factor of fifteen within days. Through them Joy had to maneuver not only his own Naval Forces Japan but also Struble's Seventh Fleet, Andrewes's Commonwealth ships, and Doyle's Gators, the latter valuable for their lift capacity alone.

Yoko stirred from its torpor, but the place had to have help. The Japanese port of Sasebo was five hundred miles closer to Pusan than Yoko was; Sasebo expanded apace. Joy hustled ships into the blockade line as quickly as they could load their magazines and get up steam. He scraped shipping from Japanese and American civilian contract sources to provide lift. The Navy began to learn the myriad horrors of supplying a sudden, faraway war.

All of this—the building of stockpiles, the creation of a logistics chain, and the getting of vessels to the fighting zone—took time, and meanwhile the Pusan perimeter shriveled, eventually settling into a small square running from just outside Musan (west of Pusan) north to Taegu and then over to an area near Pohang on the east coast. The most obvious use of seapower was to strike the enemy's flanks, relieving the pressure on the beleaguered soldiers inside the perimeter. If the defenders went under, Korea would fall—and getting back onto the peninsula would be a different military proposition entirely.

Seapower's greatest asset was its mobility, and in early July Rip Struble got going. He took Task Force 77 (*Triumph*, with its Fireflies and Seafires, had joined up) around the peninsula into the Yellow Sea to go after targets around the North Korean capitol of Pyongyang.

0600, 3 July: For the first time since World War II, an American carrier deck hummed with combat activity. First up from Happy Valley were the rocket-firing Corsairs, followed by the workhorse Skyraiders, each loaded with two five-hundred-pound bombs and six one-hundred-pounders. Last off were the screaming Panthers, flying into battle for the first time. The swift jets overtook the props on the way; the first Panther sweep over the surprised North Koreans took out three parked planes. The jets swept in again, igniting hangars, revetments, and ammo dumps. The Skyraiders and Corsairs dove in after, scoring a direct explosion on a fuel storage farm. No enemy hits were reported.

The aviators went back in the afternoon and again the next day. Rockets and bombs took out a railroad roundhouse, a station house, tracks, and repair sheds; fifteen locomotives were destroyed; countless boxcars were set ablaze. All the fliers returned safely to Happy Valley, although a few of their planes were so shot up as to be unusable.

The Pyongyang strike was a carrier classic, seapower applied in the role of land interdiction. *Valley Forge*'s eagles went on to destroy at least thirty-eight North Korean aircraft during July, a prime factor in ensuring that the North Korean air force (which featured thirty-three obsolete YAK fighters and twenty-one equally antiquated Ilyushin attack bombers) never played a pivotal role in the struggle for the perimeter.[6]

Another attempt to reduce the pressure on the soldiers came at Pohang, sixty-five miles above Pusan. Jimmy Doyle's Gators were eager to find a way to get at the North Koreans from the flanks, and at first they had planned to place two regimental combat teams on the west coast. The speed of the North Korean advance doomed that idea. On orders from Joy, Doyle's group worked at a tremendous pace. Normal amphibious planning took weeks or months (in the case of Normandy, years). Operation BLUE-HEARTS chose Pohang as its target on 10 July; Doyle's ships got up steam four days later; the 1st Cavalry hit Pohang on the morning of 18 July. The city was still in friendly hands ("no enemy ground or air attacks materialized," recorded Doyle's diarist), and the 1st Cav rapidly took its place on the right edge of the shrinking perimeter.

Pohang was a scratch operation, and the fact that the city was soon temporarily lost to the North Koreans could not detract from Doyle's demonstration of what amphibious lift could do on short notice, just as the men of *Triumph* and *Valley Forge* had done for carrier air over Pyongyang. Yet Pohang also highlighted several problems that were to become running naval sores during the conflict. Adequate intelligence was always in short supply, even in this case, when the port was not held by the enemy. Shipping was inadequate, and many of the bottoms available were not directly configured for amphibious assault. (Some of the troops arrived in ships crewed by "enemy aliens"—Japanese.)

Most importantly, Pohang, or any other strictly naval operation, was not the quick saber stroke that would end the war. The foot soldier, as he usually did, would determine the outcome. Because the Pohang landing was unopposed, observers had difficulty seeing the potential effectiveness of seapower; the 1st Cav had boarded trains to take them to the front, and some of the twenty-six correspondents embarked on *Mount McKinley* seemed disappointed that they had not been treated to a Tarawa-style bloodbath. Doyle's public relations officer reported, somewhat disconsolately, that "the fact that the landing was unopposed detracted a great deal from its news value."

☆

Taken together, these three factors—*Juneau*'s shore bombardment, the sallies from *Triumph* and *Valley Forge* into the skies over North Korea, and Jimmy Doyle's unopposed landing at Pohang—outlined much of the naval effort in Korea. All depended on local command of the sea. While much of the fighting (and most of the dying) was being done by the men on the ground, the Navy sought to hedge in the Korean peninsula with its multiplicity of firepower.

Pusan was the immediate problem. The North Koreans had armor and still, despite the carrier raids, were able to put up a few aircraft; the South Koreans had neither. The leaders of Kim's peasant levies were combat-tested veterans, blooded in the Chinese civil war; a few, fighting in Soviet uniforms, had even survived the cauldron at Stalingrad. But Kim, like Rhee, had only the most slender industrial base. The North Koreans depended on European Russia for resupplies (Stalin could not resist dabbling in this war), and the capacity of the Trans-Siberian Railroad was only some seventeen thousand tons per day, less than what Pusan was handling even in early July and far less than what the American giant, once aroused, could shovel across the Pacific.

Thus, Korea in its early stages was a race between the North Koreans hammering against Pusan and the UN efforts (largely American) to sustain the beachhead. From the 38th parallel to Pusan, as the crow flew, was 225 miles; from San Francisco, the area of the greatest American munitions stockpiles, to Pusan by great circle was around 5000 miles. These distances became the early logistics parameters of the war.

Across the Pacific, every available ship was snatched up for duty. By mid-July all the Army forces in the Far East were committed or scheduled for commitment (except for the 7th Division, held back to garrison Japan), and they had to be hauled to Korea—most of them by sea. Ammunition requirements went from zero to 77,000 tons in the month of August. Yoko's ammo stock of three thousand tons evaporated overnight. The Military Sea Transportation Service, hijacking crews from every seaport possible, alone moved 312,000 tons of supplies and thirty thousand passengers in July.

And the warships and warplanes gathered. *Boxer*, waiting to enter a West Coast navy yard for repairs, was immediately turned around to ferry 150 USAF F-51s; *Philippine Sea*, another carrier, was scheduled for deployment in October; she was sent hotfooting west. Patrol Squadron 6 moved forward from Barber's Point. The escort carriers *Sicily* and *Badoeng Strait*, postwar

CVE-105 types, steamed west with their escorts. Bigger guns were needed, too; *Juneau* and her cans were not enough. There was no active battleship in the Pacific Fleet, so the eight-inch cruisers would have to do for the moment. *Helena* and *Toledo*, *Baltimore*-class eight-inchers, headed toward Korea.

Success on the peninsula would rest, at bottom, on American bottoms, lift capacity, the ability to get men and supplies to the fighting. Fleet logistics became an emergency exercise in hand-to-mouth living. The Pacific Fleet had decommissioned its last hospital ship and its last fleet stores issue ship. (The lone remaining dock landing ship had avoided this fate only by being scheduled for Operation GREENHOUSE, the atomic testing series then taking place at Eniwetok.) To lift ammunition, the commander, Service Force Pacific Fleet, had only one ammunition ship, *Mount Katmai*.

On 10 July Service Squadron 3 was established at Buckner Bay, Okinawa. The giant was beginning to stir, and across the Pacific, Service Force units vectored toward Korean waters: destroyer tenders, reefers, tankers, repair ships, cargo ships, fleet tugs. They would be the seagoing matériel base by which South Korea would be held.[7]

A peninsula meant amphibious war, and amphibious war meant Marines. Jimmy Doyle had a small lift ready for them; he needed more. Korea was made for the Corps. Help was needed *fast*, and the Leathernecks lived with their bags packed. Every man in their ground elements was trained to handle a rifle. All their aviators had infantry training, and the members of their ground-air team, small but intensely professional, had been honed on the island assaults of the Pacific war and were, quite simply, the best in the world at what they did—close air support. In addition, marine aviators were all carrier-qualified, and their squadrons could operate from the flattops mustering off the Korean shore.

The Marines, styled the "1st Provisional Marine Brigade," came from the West Coast, Pendleton and El Toro, and they brought their own amphibious lift with them: attack transports, cargo ships, dock landing ships. All of them were underway, steaming west, by 14 July, the vanguard of thousands to come. On the 10th, MacArthur had asked the Joint Chiefs for the entire 1st Marine Division. Many naval leaders, like Sherman, feared the specter of a ground war in Asia, but MacArthur was on the spot, a crisis was upon them all, and SCAP got what he wanted.

In the air the story was the same: take what was available, saddle up, and go. The buildup meant increased cargo capacity, fuel storage, and spare parts inventories. Along the way west, aviation facilities had to be beefed up: Oahu, Midway, Johnston, Kwajalein, Guam.

The Air Force, of course, wanted to get right to work leveling North Korean cities. Major General Emmett ("Rosey") O'Donnell, head of Bomber Command, said he was ready to start "burning five major cities in North Korea to the ground, and to destroy completely every one of about 18 major strategic targets." The shibboleth was alive: bomb them into submission, win on the cheap. But Truman vetoed the idea, not only because heavy strategic bombing would embody a dramatic and politically unacceptable escalation of the "police action," but also because what, exactly, the industrially primitive North Korean economy offered by way of "strategic targets" was not altogether clear.

The immediate problem was not North Korean industry, what little there was, but that North Korean army butting up against the Pusan perimeter, along with its extended, vulnerable supply lines. Here was the naval focus, and as July ground on, everything gravitated toward the peninsula: fighting ships, planes, and their necessary auxiliaries; sailors, soldiers, Marines; food, fuel, ammunition. Daily, the vast expanse of the Pacific was shrinking.

—But so, too, was the Pusan perimeter.

☆

Korea extends over six hundred miles, from the forbidding wastes of Manchuria to the relatively mild climate of Pusan, roughly the latitudes between central Oregon and Los Angeles. But the peninsula is almost never more than two hundred miles wide; only in a small strip along the northern border is any part of North Korea more than one hundred miles from salt water. Almost all of Korea lay open to carrier warplanes and naval guns.

This was a recipe for naval interdiction; the climate, however, was not. Weather in Korea was seldom "right;" the Hermit Kingdom is a land of climatological extremes. The mountainous north, where the winter gales blast down from Siberia, is most decidedly not central Oregon; the mean January temperature there (without the wind) is fifteen degrees Fahrenheit. Cotton can be grown in southern Korea, but the summers are hellishly hot, with debilitating humidity thrown in for good measure. Summer is also the typhoon season, and the peninsula is occasionally drubbed by one of the fierce storms that form over the Marianas and veer erratically across the western Pacific.

The land itself is fragmented into the knobby, isolated north; a strip pressed against the east coast by a mountain spine; and, to the west and south, a broken piedmont subdivided by a series of river basins. The ragged coastline measures some 5400 miles. On the east, the hundred-fathom curve runs close to shore (except off Wonsan and Hungnam)—good news for shore bombardment ships. In the south and west, however, countless coastal islands, deeply indented bays, and miles of shallows and mud flats tended to impede rather than foster seaborne operations.

These were the naval facts of life in Korea. In mid-July, as Task Force 77 withdrew to Okinawa to replenish, the Navy concentrated on shore bombardment along the east coast, resupplying Pusan, and planning some kind of counteroffensive.

☆

More problems were beginning to surface, beyond those noticed at Pohang. The most grating of these concerned the air picture. The use of carrier air beyond the beach meant coordination with the Fifth Air Force, under command of Lieutenant General George Stratemeyer. The current roles and missions statement, dating back to the painful days of the Key West Conference, made interdiction of enemy land forces and communications an exclusive USAF function. The Navy could participate, but only after walking through a bureaucratic maze.

The Pyongyang strike had been an end run around the maze. Stratemeyer wanted his air picture tidied up. He duly asked MacArthur for operational control of all naval aircraft in the theater. Here was the first wartime assault on the integrity of naval air, fully expected in the wake of the 1949 rebellion. Stratemeyer's ploy failed; instead, he got "coordination control," which was practically meaningless.

Many problems were also developing at the tactical level, and their solutions, if any, were being delayed by the overriding concern for Pusan. Stratemeyer's failure, however, meant that the Navy in Korea would run its own air show.

—Which was fine by Rip Struble. He left Okinawa topped off and headed for the North Korean coast. On the 18th and 19th of July, Happy Valley's aviators hit railroads, industrial plants, and airfields from Pyonggang (not to be confused with Pyongyang) and Wonsan north through Hungnam and Hamhung—the first naval air strike in the east. At Wonsan, a dreary railroad and manufacturing city of 150,000 at the head of the Korean Gulf, Skyraiders blew up a large oil refinery that burned for days, its towering plumes of smoke easily visible offshore to the men of Task Force 77.

Close air support, which was completely catch-as-catch-can, was not going so well, primarily due to target-spotting difficulties and communications foul-ups. Jimmy Doyle, who had seen the problem firsthand at the Pohang landing, was aghast at the state of Army and Air Force control of tactical air. Neither service was prepared for the timing and precision required for close air support. The Army had concentrated its limited training budget on ground operations, while the USAF, true to its heritage, had been mesmerized by what its leaders believed to be the rewards of strategic air.

Not that the Air Force ignored tactical air; in fact, the Ninth Air Force in Europe had done excellent close support work. But neither the Air Force nor the Army spent much time thinking about the problem, and neither gave control of aircraft to frontline units. As a result, particularly along the Pusan perimeter, "everything was a mess," observed Jimmy Thach. Naval aviators, unable to get any kind of coherent direction from the ground, simply had to "turn to interdiction on their own or dump their ammunition."

Naval aviation during July was limited by these control problems, and strikes in the north, while materially hurting the North Koreans, did nothing to directly relieve the perimeter. The cost, however, was slight, especially compared with the pounding that the ground troops were taking daily around Pusan: six aircraft, one flier. The Navy flew 716 combat and 431 patrol sorties during the month, most of them from Happy Valley. The aviators claimed twenty-six enemy aircraft destroyed (thirteen probables), and numerous tanks, locomotives, power stations, and bridges—victims of everything from thousand-pound bombs to Tiny Tim rockets.[8]

Turner Joy's ships had been working both sides of the peninsula during the month. While his patrol planes prowled the seaward flanks, the gunnery units escorted the steadily increasing flow of incoming shipping, supplied on-call fire against enemy positions, and tried to interdict North Korean resupply efforts whenever they could.

Joy now had Struble, Doyle, Service Squadron 3, the patrol squadrons, the Formosa patrol, and even the flyspeck South Korean navy under his wing—the lines of authority were being ironed out. (Commander Mike Luosey, stateside, found himself designated "deputy commander, Naval Forces Far East" and was bundled onto the first plane for Korea. Once there, with one lieutenant and five enlisted men, he assumed operational control of the entire South Korean navy.)

The Marines arrived on 2 August. By the evening of the next day, they were deployed on the perimeter.

☆

On through the sticky heat of August and into September, as the naval reinforcements coursed westward, the perimeter held. Joy was convinced, with reason, that naval support had made this possible. The gunfire call missions, the air strikes, the hustling of the Marines into the perimeter, the bridge of ships bringing personnel and munitions—all were indispensable. MacArthur was equally adamant: "In Korea I knew that if our meager forces were impelled to fall back to Pusan proper [they almost were], the Navy could hold open our lines of supply, and under its guns we could hold a beachhead indefinitely."

Maybe so, but as the Duke of Wellington said in another context, " 'Twas a damn close run thing." The only important advantages for the UN forces, for the moment, were at sea and in the air. As planning for a counterstroke went forward, these advantages were critical—and they were used.

Inchon was bombarded by gunships and pasted from the air. The newly arrived *Toledo* and her destroyers ranged the east coast, blasting troop and supply concentrations by day and illuminating by star shell at night. Cruising with impunity some seven thousand yards offshore, sending her spotters to the beach by whaleboat, *Toledo* helped keep the battle line stable. All along the coast, American warships were clamped as tightly as they could get, only occasionally receiving return fire.

The carriers now had close air support as their number one priority, followed by aerial interdiction south of the 38th parallel and then strategic targets (shared with Bomber Command) to the north. But Jimmy Thach was right: the close air support mission was a hash from the get-go. Aircraft from all services were constantly mishandled in the tight quarters over the front lines. The controllers were too few and poorly trained in the bargain. Communications circuits were a free-for-all. In times of crisis (which was practically every day around the perimeter) the air picture was in shreds.

Rip Struble fought to get out of these constraints, and he succeeded. By mid-August the primacy of close air support was a dead letter. Even before then Struble had broken loose, making Task Force 77 what the Navy wanted, an independent striking force. He steamed into the Yellow Sea again, with *Valley Forge* and the recently arrived *Philippine Sea*, to hit the area just south of the parallel. The realities of the "civil war" they had become part of were brought home to the sailors of Task Force 77 when, seventy miles off Mokpo, they passed through waters containing dozens of floating bodies, tied together in bundles, hands lashed behind their backs.[9]

Also in August, Turner Joy sought to create havoc behind the North Korean lines by landing raiding parties. The enemy's main lines of communication to the Soviet maritime provinces, road and rail, were pressed against the sea on the mountainous east coast. *Juneau* had landed a small group of demolition specialists there in the first days of the war, and several destroyer-type ships followed up. British and American commandos went after bridges and tunnels, in particular.

Joy was laying on carrier strikes in the east as well, but in the midst of this interdiction, ships had to be diverted to lift troops out of Pohang, where the eastern edge of the perimeter was collapsing. Mike Luosey rustled up some LSTs at Pusan and, aided by the destroyer *Wiltsie*, evacuated about seven thousand people, almost six thousand of them ROKs—a nifty amphibious operation in reverse, another demonstration of the scratch flexibility of seapower, and, unfortunately, a harbinger of things to come.

Luosey's peewee navy was also busy all along the coast; American carrier air and the gunships had forced the North Koreans to try coastal resupply once again. During the week of 13 August the South Korean navy fought five engagements in an arc between Kunsan and the southwestern tip of the peninsula. The highlight occurred when one of Luosey's midgets, *YMS 503*, ran across forty-five small craft and shot them up, sinking fifteen and capturing the rest.

☆

By the end of August the strategic picture in Korea was extraordinary. Of pertinence was the question of who was encircling whom. While the North

Koreans probed the perimeter, looking for soft spots, their own flanks, communications, and supply lines were under continuous attack from sea and sky alike. They were traveling by night, using handcarts, horses, oxen—anything to get themselves and their equipment safely to the front.

But the Fifth Air Force and the Navy, despite their close support problems, were taking a fearful toll. When the terror from the sky was added to what the Eighth Army and the ROKs were doing on the ground, the carnage in the North Korean ranks was terrific. (They could handle most of what was thrown at them, some North Korean prisoners said—all but the terrible pounding from "the blue planes.")

By 1 August the Pentagon was estimating North Korea's losses at 37,500. (Kim had probably lost over 50,000 by that time.) His feared T-34 tanks had dwindled from 150 to 40-odd, many of them victims of the blue planes. By 4 August the Eighth Army alone, sustained from the sea, had front-line forces of 92,000, compared with the North Korean total of 70,000.

Pusan, despite the pressure around its edges, was booming. Daily, seapower brought the men and their implements of war. Kim knew he must win quickly or not win at all. Late on the night of 31 August the North Koreans launched a feverish assault against the perimeter. The soldiers and Marines met the attack with the help of Happy Valley and *Philippine Sea.*

Rip Struble had left Task Force 77 to take part in planning; the carriers now belonged to Rear Admiral Edward Ewen. As if to demonstrate even more firmly the flexibility of carrier air, Eddie Ewen disengaged in the middle of the fighting around the perimeter and moved up into the Yellow Sea to soften the region north of Inchon again. On this operation, Lieutenant Junior Grade Richard Downs jumped a twin-engine bomber with red star markings and shot his target down; the body of a Russian aviator was fished from the sea. Here was one of the first indications—there were to be many—that the North Koreans were not acting alone.

Through the first week of September savage combat raged all along the perimeter, but the ROKs, Marines, and Eighth Army stood fast. By the second week the results were obvious. The perimeter, thanks to the ground troops and the mobility of naval firepower and resupply, would hold.[10]

The ferocity of the enemy offensive had redoubled the pace of work on a plan to drive the North Koreans not only from the south but also out of the war. The plan rested on seapower, on its flexibility, adaptability, and, above all, its capacity for *surprise.*

The surprise was scheduled far up the west coast: Inchon.

CHAPTER NINE

ROAD PAST WOLMI-DO

☆

Inchon, according to one Marine officer, was "about the same size and general attractiveness as Jersey City." This was perhaps too flattering an assessment, but even so, the Navy was not interested in tourism. Inchon lies eighteen miles west of the ancient capital of Seoul and serves as its seaport. A railroad connects the two. For naval purposes, the city has played Piraeus to Seoul's Athens.

In the summer of 1950, the flexibility and the total dominance of UN seapower made any point on the peninsula a potential target for an amphibious strike. The east coast, however, features those craggy mountain spines; the rare flat areas allow fewer towns, road nets, or rail lines. Exploitation of the interior would be much tougher from the east.

The west coast is more inhabited and alluvial. Any landing there would be more likely to interdict North Korean supply lines. Three possibilities existed, in order from north to south: Pyongyang, Inchon, and Kunsan. The first was too far behind the lines, and in Manchuria's backyard. Kunsan, to the south, had the best physical and geographical aspects, but to Douglas MacArthur, this choice was too close to the Pusan perimeter. "The amphibious landing is the most powerful tool we have," he told his naval planners. "To employ it properly we must strike hard and deeply in enemy territory." (Dwight Eisenhower, back in February, had declared that "an amphibious landing is not a particularly difficult thing.")[1]

Planning for a Gator assault on Inchon had gone forward even as the North Koreans were being bloodily checked on the perimeter and the ROKs and Eighth Army were steadily building up around Pusan. MacArthur later claimed that he had been struck by the Inchon idea as early as 29 June, while he was witnessing the collapse of ROK resistance just south of Seoul.

Although the implementation was clearly his, the original notion did *not* belong to MacArthur. An amphibious end run was a tactic obvious to anyone with a shred of naval sense, and in fact the Pentagon had approved a plan (SL-17) a week before the North Korean attack that envisioned a retreat to Pusan, followed by an amphibious assault through Inchon. MacArthur and his staff worked from SL-17. The basic plan, CINCFE 100-B, was ready on 12 August.

On the 23rd and 24th of August the big guns gathered to discuss Operation CHROMITE at MacArthur's headquarters in Tokyo. Turner Joy and Jimmy Doyle were on hand, but they were outnumbered by the visiting firemen. Forrest Sherman and Lightning Joe Collins, the Army chief of staff, had come from Washington. Arthur Radford had flown out from Pearl Harbor, bringing Lieutenant General Lem Shepherd, commander of Fleet Marine Force Pacific, with him.

The group quickly got down to brass tacks over Inchon. MacArthur saw the Navy and its amphibious capabilities as his hole card. He had used Dan Barbey's Gators with great success along the New Guinea coast and throughout the Philippines, he knew what the amphibians could do, and he saw Inchon as the masterstroke that could end the war.

To the admirals, the men who had the responsibility to get him there, the place was an amphibious chamber of horrors. The western shoreline of Korea is washed by herculean tides that average twenty-nine feet and peak at thirty-six; only the Bay of Fundy has a greater tidal bore. The city's harbor lies pocketed by numerous small islands through which the Yellow Sea heaves periodically, leaving gooey mud banks that extend hundreds of yards to seaward. In the midst of this unappetizing seascape lies Flying Fish Channel, a twisting, dead-end sea-lane, narrow and shallow—even in the best of conditions a navigator's nightmare.

Tidal currents in the approach channels rarely drop below three knots, and in Flying Fish Channel they sometimes reach seven or eight knots, close to the top speed of some landing craft. The Salee River, which flows sluggishly past Inchon to the sea, is a nautical straitjacket with no room for maneuvering. One sunken or disabled vessel there could clot the entire operation.

Any or all of the offshore islands could be used as points of attack on an amphibious force, and one of these in particular, Wolmi Island (Wolmi-do), blocked a direct approach to the city. The North Koreans had destroyed the navigation lights in Flying Fish Channel, which made little difference—there were no reliable charts of the area.[2]

And Inchon was a *city* of 250,000 people, protected by seawalls. Its buildings, streets, and alleys were open invitations to the grim prospect of house-to-house fighting. There were no suitable landing *beaches*, as had been available in virtually every instance in World War II. The one contrary example, the catastrophic British-Canadian raid on the French port of Dieppe in 1942, inspired confidence in no one.

Turner Joy did not like this one bit. Thrashing about for an alternative, he sent the fast transport *Horace A. Bass*, covered by *Badoeng Strait*, into the Yellow Sea, where her raider and underwater demolition groups did night reconnaissance of possible beaches to the north and south of Kunsan. Sherman and Collins both favored Kunsan. Lem Shepherd wanted Asan Man, thirty-eight miles below Inchon.

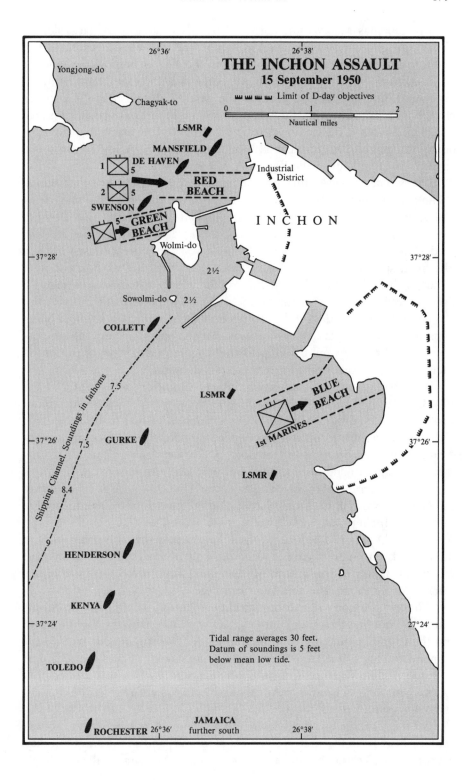

THE INCHON ASSAULT
15 September 1950

Limit of D-day objectives

Nautical miles

Yongjong-do

Chagyak-to

LSMR

MANSFIELD

DE HAVEN

1 | 5

RED BEACH

Industrial District

2 | 5

SWENSON

GREEN BEACH

3 | 5

I N C H O N

Wolmi-do

2½

Sowolmi-do 2½

COLLETT

Shipping Channel Soundings in fathoms

7.5

LSMR

BLUE BEACH

7.5

GURKE

1st MARINES

8.4

LSMR

9

HENDERSON

KENYA

Tidal range averages 30 feet.
Datum of soundings is 5 feet
below mean low tide.

TOLEDO

JAMAICA
ROCHESTER 26°36′ further south   26°38′

But Douglas MacArthur, bolstered by SL-17 and his remarkable, visionary imagination, was clamped to Inchon and to the road beyond—past Seoul to the 38th parallel, to the creation of a line of firepower extending coast to coast across the peninsula. Air Force B-29s were obliterating many urban and industrial targets north of the parallel, diminishing the enemy's chances of reinforcement. MacArthur's vision was that of a classic hammer-and-anvil strategy, the hammer to be provided by the amphibious assault of the Marines and Major General Ned Almond's U.S. Army X Corps, the anvil by the breakout of the Eighth Army and the ROKs.

For two days MacArthur did not argue with his fellow brass, he *orated*. ("The prestige of the Western World hangs in the balance.") No one, eventually, opposed him. Forrest Sherman, who had been a fresh-minted ensign the year MacArthur put on the stars of a brigadier general, came around; he declared that MacArthur's was "a great voice in a great cause." (When Sherman, speaking of Flying Fish Channel, said that he "wouldn't hesitate to take a ship up there," MacArthur exclaimed: "Spoken like a Farragut!") Jimmy Doyle, as steady as they came, "a most imperturbable individual," was nevertheless horrified at the prospects of Inchon; the best he could bring himself to say about CHROMITE was that the operation was "not impossible." Rip Struble would command the seagoing part, in an operation he later (after its success) called a "courageous decision."

The various staffs redoubled their efforts, tuning and retuning CINCFE 100-B. CHROMITE was scheduled for 15 September, timed for maximum spring tides. Hydrographic and oceanographic data had to be generated. Tidal and current information was needed desperately. Figures on sea conditions, water temperature and transparency, underwater contours, and bottom sediments needed to be ginned up, practically from scratch.

Major General Oliver Smith's 1st Marine Division, with attached Army and South Korean units, would have a D-day strength of 25,000; they were to capture Inchon and move twelve miles inland to take Seoul's Kimpo Airfield on D plus 2. The area involved was roughly that of Saipan—where there had been no great cities and no difficult hydrographic problems and where the flanks of the assaulting force had been protected by the vast reaches of the Pacific and the American fleet.

Almond's X Corps, reinforced to almost 70,000, would drive on Seoul, taking and holding the capital until contact was made with the Eighth Army and the ROKs coming up from the south. "All this amphibious stuff," said Almond, taking a leaf from Eisenhower's notebook, "is just a mechanical operation." The distance from the perimeter to Inchon was around 140 miles, more than twice that at Anzio beachhead, where a similar linkup had taken *four months*.

All these problems were known and discounted by MacArthur; he was banking heavily on the strategic element of *surprise*, and on the Navy's ability to get the troops through the chamber of horrors. The rise and fall of Inchon's tides meant that the time of attack was limited to two short periods each day. The corkscrew entrance channels extended *thirty-four miles* to seaward. Thus, vessels of low power and poor maneuverability—amphibious assault craft—would have to attack in daylight, and they would be unable to retire seaward at night. Indeed, at certain times they would be high and not-so-dry on the mud flats, just as if they had been plunked down there by some giant's hand.

Inchon's navigational hazards and tidal silting had limited its cargo-handling capacity to about 10,000 tons a day, less than half that of Pusan. There were almost no piers; the port had only five berths in its tidal basin (Pusan had thirty). Only about fifty ships could rest in Inchon's outer anchorage, and lighterage was an exceptionally inefficient way to move cargo inland.

And then there was the problem of the assault itself. Only two marginally adequate landing points existed: Red Beach, on the western shore, and Blue Beach, in the southeastern section of Inchon—and "beach" was for both a courtesy name only. The two spots were four miles apart, at opposite ends of the city. They were lined with piers and seawalls and would have to be taken with scaling ladders, which limited tactical mass. Each beach could be enfiladed by the North Koreans, if they were alert enough and knew what they were doing.

Finally, there was Wolmi-do, the cork in Inchon's bottleneck. A causeway connected the waterfront to the island, which with its little satellite, Sowolmi-do, dominated and divided Inchon's outer anchorage. Wolmi-do, with its 350-foot hill and its unknown defensive strength, had to be taken.

Inchon was "not impossible," Jimmy Doyle had said. Impossible or not, Douglas MacArthur had spoken. ("If MacArthur had gone on stage," avowed Doyle, "you never would have heard of John Barrymore.")[3]

From 24 August onward, CHROMITE was on.

☆

In early September, as the North Koreans pounded against the perimeter, the Joint Chiefs got cold feet over Inchon. Sherman, out from under MacArthur's shadow in Tokyo, may still have been speaking like Farragut, but he was having second thoughts. All the Chiefs resumed a tactful campaign to get MacArthur to either delay CHROMITE or switch to Kunsan. MacArthur was not used to second-guessing; mortals did not question decisions from Olympus. He responded that there was "no question" about Inchon and that the chances of success were "excellent." On 8 September the Joint Chiefs met with Harry Truman for a last look-see. Inchon got its final green light.

By then the gathering of forces for what MacArthur called his "Han River dream" was well underway. Turner Joy and Almond got into a shouting match over details, and there were snags aplenty—mostly over logistics and combat loading—which was understandable given the quickstep at which everyone was working. But CHROMITE moved ahead.

Army personnel who had served in Inchon before the war were tracked down and grilled. Photo reconnaissance missions were laid on. And, on 1 September, Lieutenant Eugene Clark, with two interpreters, some small arms, and a radio, was put ashore on the tiny island of Yonghung-do, fifteen miles below Inchon, with orders to snoop around and report.

Clark, a mustang, was right out of *Terry and the Pirates*, a former chief yeoman who had sailored through the Pacific war. After V-J Day he had become an officer and had commanded two ships, including an LST that had bucketed up and down the China coast. He had been moldering away on MacArthur's staff when the North Koreans invaded.

Once established on Yonghung-do, Clark commandeered the only motorized sampan available, organized gangs of teenage boys into coast-watchers, and set up two machine guns facing the nearby enemy-held island of Taebu. For two weeks Clark roosted, fighting outlandish sampan battles with puzzled North Koreans and capturing an occasional infiltrator from Taebu-do. Nightly, a naval version of Fagin, he sent his eager teenagers into Inchon, instructing them to judge the size of the mudflats, measure the heights of the seawalls, count the defending troops, and chart gun positions and observation posts. One moonless night he himself rowed into the harbor and wallowed about on the mudflats, proving that neither Marines nor their tanks could negotiate the morass.

During his nocturnal prowls, the ex-chief captured about thirty small vessels, some of them carrying policemen or soldiers—who talked. As Clark radioed back his discoveries, the gaps about Inchon began to be filled in. (He would win a Navy Cross for his adventures.)

Meanwhile, Rip Struble created Joint Task Force 7, the hammer that would strike Inchon. The force included three carrier units, for any self-respecting amphibious assault brought along its own air. One of these was *Triumph;* the second was made up of the escort carriers *Sicily* and *Badoeng Strait,* under command of Rear Admiral Richard Ruble. The third had the fast carriers and belonged to Rear Admiral Eddie Ewen.

Ewen had been an all-American end at the Academy, the only man to captain Navy's football team twice. All Hanson Baldwin could remember about his own plebe year (1920) was that he and his hapless classmates had been forced to provide practice-field fodder for human cannonballs like Ewen. After graduation, Ewen went naval air, and during World War II he skippered the light carrier *Independence* in the Pacific.

There he won the Navy Cross and became an early expert in the demanding regimen of night carrier operations. A "superb leader," avid golfer, and hard charger ("I'm easily satisfied—with the best of everything," he would say), he was Sherman's personal choice to run Task Force 77. Ewen had been hustled to Korea because of his dynamic aviation experience, and he came looking for the action. His planes, along with those of Ruble and the British, worked over the west coast for the first two weeks in September, concentrating on Inchon.

Jimmy Doyle led Task Force 90, the attack force. He had five cruisers and twelve destroyers for shore bombardment, and most of these would home in on Wolmi-do just before the landing. Throughout the operation, shorebom and close carrier air support would continue. No USAF planes were to operate in the objective area until D minus 3, unless Rip Struble wanted them—and because of the continuing communications snafus, he did not.

Altogether, Task Force 90 numbered 180 ships, including units from the Royal Navy, New Zealand, and France. Mike Luosey rustled up a few South Korean patrol craft and minesweepers. Forty-seven LSTs, over half of them manned by Japanese, would provide the bulk of the landing force. In addition, over twenty auxiliaries were available, and the skies would be filled with naval patrol and reconnaissance aircraft.

The tormenting snags would have daunted a less egocentric commander than MacArthur. His training in the English language had been curiously deficient: he was familiar only with the first person singular, and his account of Inchon would read the same way. But the admirals were continuously bedeviled. There was no time for joint training, and—what really bothered amphibious specialists like Doyle—no time for rehearsal. The logistics snarls were on a heroic scale. There was no time for feedback from subordinates. All Eddie Ewen got as instructions on how to employ his carrier air was a forty-minute briefing.

MacArthur, characteristically above the clouds, was unfazed. He intended to hit Inchon from the sea with everything he had, and on time. Joint Task Force 7 mushroomed to 230 ships; except for a few gunships held back to support the flanks of the perimeter, Struble had every combatant unit available in the Far East. X Corps alone needed 120 ships for lift, while the remaining vessels were assigned tasks of gunfire, air support, minesweeping, screening, and other duties.

Fortune was favoring the bold. Kim Il-sung had allowed almost all his assault troops to batten fast against the perimeter. They possessed no real flexibility of movement, and they could not readily redeploy to meet a threat in their rear. Almost like frantic bugs against a summer screen, they continued to hurl themselves against the perimeter, even though evidence that the UN forces were concentrating on Inchon mounted steadily in early September. The Red Chinese, increasingly nervous about war moving onto their northeastern doorstep, shifted some of their troops northward, but they provided no reinforcements to the North Koreans. No enemy vessels of any kind showed up to contest the seas, and in the air Ewen's and Ruble's planes roamed almost at will.

But, for the first time, an opponent arrived that was to harrow the Navy throughout Korea: mines. As early as 10 July, Soviet-made mines were rolling south down the east coast railway from Vladivostok. Mine schools were established at Wonsan and Chinnampo. Four thousand of the weapons reached the south, and behind these Wonsan and Chinnampo were quickly mined. Some Russian naval officers got to Inchon before Ewen's aviators knocked the connecting bridge down, and the port, along with Kunsan and Mokpo, was sown with a few more devices.

Even so, the North Koreans remained amazingly blind to the adaptability of seapower. Only two thousand troops were stationed in the vicinity of Inchon, and against them MacArthur was throwing seventy thousand assault troops, stripping Japan bare of American ground forces to do so.

On 12 September the general boarded *Mount McKinley* at Sasebo. Typhoon Kezia blasted the assault force the first day out, then veered away. The storm left everyone a bit unsettled. MacArthur was as conscious of his gamble as anyone. "If I failed," he wrote in his constricted brand of English, "the dreadful results would rest on judgment day against my soul."[4]

☆

Mount McKinley plowed on, "the most flag-ridden flagship in the history of the U.S. Navy." Aboard were twelve admirals and generals, countless colonels and naval captains, and innumerable correspondents and photographers—MacArthur wanted the press on hand. Only eagles and above rated a rack; junior officers could not even commandeer a cot. Even before she sallied forth from Sasebo, Eddie Ewen's fliers began pounding Inchon for real. Starting on 10 September, the city and Wolmi-do were struck during daylight for four successive days. Corsairs and Skyraiders streaked in from the sea continuously, blasting the city and the little island from end to end.

Gene Clark had radioed back plenty of information on Inchon and Wolmi-do, and Marine air, primed with incendiaries, had burned away much of the top cover on the island. Three hundred defenders were still there, burrowed into trenches and caves.

At 0700 on 13 September Rear Admiral John Higgins's Gunfire Support Group of five destroyers headed in column up Flying Fish Channel on the floodtide, *Mansfield* in the van. Behind them steamed the cruisers, while overhead orbited combat air patrols from Task Force 77. Shortly after ten, the cans entered Inchon's outer harbor.

Floating mines were spotted; no minesweepers were immediately available, and *Henderson*, the tail-end destroyer, was detached to try to take care of them. She found only about two dozen, all obsolescent contact types, not the tougher, more sophisticated influence mines.

Around noon Ewen's planes began to work over their targets again, Skyraiders packing the heavier ordnance. As the explosions pocked the city, the destroyers boldly took their assigned bombardment positions inside the harbor, some within a thousand yards of Wolmi-do. Anchored at short stay, their bullnoses swung south, into the flood current. The five-inch batteries swiveled to port. No sign of life on Wolmi-do.

Shortly after 1300 the five cans opened up, and for a few minutes they had everything their own way. Then the North Koreans responded with their batteries of Russian-made 76-mm fieldpieces. *Swenson, Collett,* and *Gurke,* the three ships closest to the island, all took hits; *Collett* had to switch to local fire control. *Gurke* was struck by three shells, and a near miss killed an officer on *Swenson.*

After firing about a thousand rounds, the destroyers weighed anchor and headed back to sea. Then the cruisers came on, six- and eight-inch guns blasting away (with time out for another air strike) until almost 1700. Behind them, the shorebom ships left Wolmi-do smoking, with a number of the enemy entombed in their caves. The entire bombardment, while necessary, had alerted every North Korean between the Yalu River and the perimeter to what was coming.

The next day saw more of the same. Wolmi-do and the entire Inchon area were pasted from sea and sky. No ships were hit this time, and counterfire was sporadic and ineffective. Looking over the damage reports on *Mount McKinley,* the man in charge was encouraged. The island was a shambles, with about one-third of its defenders already dead. Radio Hill, as the Americans called the island's heights, had been scorched bald; Jimmy Thach's *Sicily* aviators had drenched Wolmi's western half with ninety-five thousand pounds of napalm.

Wolmi-do was ready for the Marines.

Darkness, the morning of 15 September: in they came once again, this time to land, coasting along on the flooding tide. As the Gators and their gunnery support moved upchannel at darken ship, the light at the mouth of Inchon Harbor suddenly snapped on. Gene Clark, buccaneering to the end, had snuck onto tiny Palmi-do and, for his grand finale, lit up the navigation beacon. (MacArthur, uninformed about Clark's derring-do, thought that the lit beacon indicated North Korean carelessness.)

Offshore, in the predawn gloom, Ewen's carrier decks were jam-packed with men and planes. The first of the day's swarm of barrier patrols, combat air patrols, and deep support strikes was launched. Dick Ruble's escort carriers fired off ten Corsairs, targeted for Wolmi-do. At 0528 the show began, as the first airborne strike group reported in to the Air Direction Center aboard *Mount McKinley.*

At 0540 Captain Norman Sears and his Gators signaled "Land the landing force—away all boats!" Twenty minutes later, as the squat landing craft wheeled into their characteristic circling patterns, the destroyers and cruisers opened up again, creaming every target in sight: Wolmi-do; Sowolmi-do, its satellite; the outer reaches of Inchon; and, particularly, the landing area of Blue Beach. High overhead, the Corsair leader rolled over and started down.

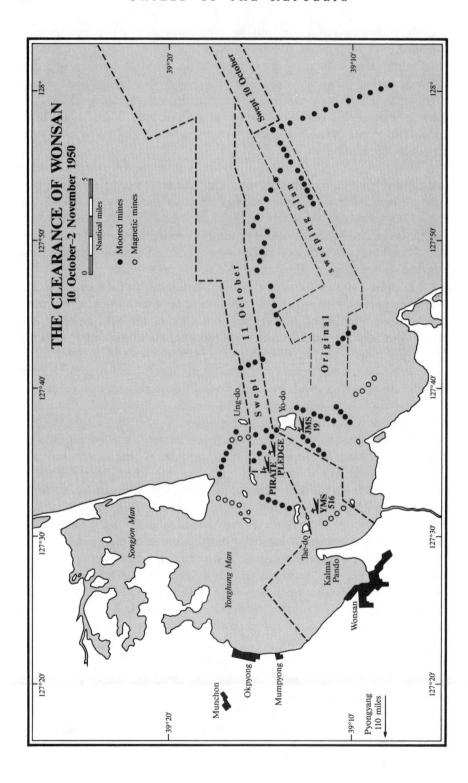

THE CLEARANCE OF WONSAN
10 October–2 November 1950

Wolmi-do shuddered and heaved in agony, partially hidden under a pall of smoke. To the chorus of exploding shells and bombs was added the whooshing roar of rocket fire from three specially configured rocket ships (LSMRs), each of them carrying one thousand five-inch spin-stabilized rockets. The LSMRs churned clear just before 0630; then the gunships broke off to allow final strafing runs by the unopposed Corsairs.

L hour, 0630: The first wave hit Wolmi-do, carrying the 3rd Battalion Landing Team, 5th Marines. Supplies and tanks followed in quick order. Within thirty minutes the Leathernecks had overrun the northern half of the island. Rip Struble was just going over the side into a small boat to look things over when he received a message. "The Navy and the Marines have never shown more brightly than this morning. MacArthur."

Daylight, now—warm and pleasant, with an overcast cloud cover. A little after 0800 the Marines took Radio Hill. MacArthur was watching from *Mount McKinley*'s bridge. When he saw the inevitable American flag that Marines always seemed to carry in their backpacks fluttering gaily from the heights, his face lit up like a neon sign. "That's it," he said. "Let's go down and have a cup of coffee."

By noon Sowolmi-do had fallen, after an assault over its narrow causeway and an air strike from the constantly orbiting Corsairs. Total Marine casualties were seventeen wounded; 108 North Koreans had been killed and 136 captured. By noon, also, the tide had receded and the sun had come out. The amphibians lay like nesting turtles, no longer cradled by the sea. Across the emerging mud flats the Marines and sailors gazed upon the silent, burning city and its invisible garrison. They pondered the seven-hundred-yard strip of pavement extending eastward, to Red Beach.[5]

The lock to Inchon had been picked.

☆

As the afternoon wore on, the unpredictable Korean weather changed; rain squalls and low clouds, combined with the smoke rising over the city, darkened the sky by the minute. In the gathering gloom hastily summoned minesweepers sniffed through the intended anchorage areas in the outer harbor. Aerial observation planes lazily circled overhead, their vision increasingly blurred by the clouds and mist. At ninety-minute intervals Corsair strikes roared in, dropping napalm and five-hundred-pound bombs. The Skyraiders also pounded away, with bomb loads up to thousand-pounders.

The big-gun cruisers *Toledo* and *Rochester*, along with their British sisters, the light cruisers *Kenya* and *Jamaica*, leisurely worked over Red Beach, Blue Beach, and the Inchon waterfront. Every effort had been made to limit the targeting to military areas, but the bombs and shells could not distinguish between soldier and civilian, and the carnage extending inland from the seawalls was terrific.

Slowly the waters rose again—the afternoon tide. By 1300 the transports and landing craft were standing in. Down the nets went the assault troops, while overhead, planes from Ewen's fast carriers, now augmented by *Boxer*'s air wing, softened up the landing areas for the last time. By 1700, amid the weather-and-man-made dusk, over five hundred landing craft were chugging toward their assigned beaches.

A final cacaphony of bombs and shells was overscored by the pipe organs aboard the rocket ships. (The Marines heading shoreward were both impressed and alarmed by the rocket contrails zipping just over their heads.) At 1725 the ramps plopped down, and two regimental combat teams hit Inchon.

At Red Beach two battalions met only scattered automatic weapons and mortar fire. Their worst enemy was in their rear; some skittish LST sailors cut loose, killing one man and wounding twenty-three others. Angry Leathernecks lobbed a few rounds back at the LSTs, scaring the bluejackets away from their guns. Within an hour the Marines were working their way into Inchon toward high ground, and tanks and troops from Wolmi-do charged down the strip of causeway to join in.

Blue Beach was tougher. There the mortar fire was considerable, destroying one tracked landing vehicle with a direct hit. The rocket ships and *Gurke* quickly silenced the mortar squads, however. Up and over the seawall went the Marines, hurling grenades ahead of them, the men condensed into columns by the scaling ladders. Smoke, rain, and sunset scattered some of the assault forces, but here too, the Marines quickly disappeared from the beach into the darkening city. Rip Struble, with Almond and Shepherd aboard, arrived alongside the Blue Beach seawall during the attack. A Marine ready to blow a hole in the seawall to allow tracked vehicles ashore yelled, "Lay off, you stupid bastards!" The barge coxswain yelled back, "This is Admiral Struble's barge." "I don't give a shit whose barge it is," came the response. "Get it clear before I blow the seawall!" The barge retreated.

The Marines retained their air support for about an hour, and the destroyers and cruisers kept up their call fire; each battalion had a can in direct support. Night illumination, this first evening, did not work; the harbor's configuration was not right, and the destroyers were too close for their star shells to fuze properly. Still, the Marines pressed on, house to house and block to block. By midnight the landing force had reached its initial phase lines.

Through Red Beach streamed the logistic buildup, on time. The First Marines rapidly attained their initial objective, the high ground north of Blue Beach that commanded the road to Seoul. D day's price was 174 casualties, including 21 dead and 1 missing. The Navy lost only two men, both seamen, and one of these, as sailors sometimes were wont to do, fell through a hatch and died of head injuries.

The cost was light, certainly compared with the carnage on some of the beaches of the Pacific. The reason went beyond MacArthur's strategic surprise, despite days of clear-cut warning in the form of carrier strikes and shore bombardment. The North Koreans had stocked Inchon only with those two thousand men of their 226th Marine Regiment, and they were grass-green. This outfit had also been thinned out to cover a small South Korean landing on Yonghung-do (where Gene Clark had gone to work two weeks before). And the smashing blow from the sea had left them incapable of serious resistance, even from within a city protected by tides, mud flats, islands, and seawalls.

Further, the communications hitches that had plagued earlier joint operations were, for the moment, blissfully absent. "My kids just wander around," Ewen had fumed earlier, "their racks loaded with bombs and rockets and no place to put them." At Inchon the kids did not wander around; Marine and Navy spotters laid on accurate coordinates, and the hail of bombs and shells produced dazed or dead North Koreans—as well as some South Korean civilians.

Late that first afternoon MacArthur toured the harbor on Struble's barge, which had survived its threat from Marine explosives. "Our losses are light," he cabled Washington. "The command distinguished itself. The whole operation is proceeding on schedule." Earlier, he had promised Almond that everyone would "be home by Christmas." Arleigh Burke, now a rear admiral and Turner Joy's deputy chief of staff, applauded: "This operation really shows the greatness of that man."[6]

☆

The schedule inevitably slipped a bit behind, but not by much. The supplies poured in; despite the geographic and hydrographic problems, all first-echelon shipping had been emptied by D plus 4. Three days later, 54,000 people, 6600 vehicles, and over 25,000 tons of cargo were ashore. But the North Koreans were beginning to react.

On D plus 2 they counterattacked as best they could, but the Marines, supported by *Sicily*'s Corsairs, pushed them steadily eastward along the highway to Seoul. Kimpo Airfield was captured. By 21 September the Fifth Marines were within a mile of the capital, and the Han River dream was becoming reality. The North Koreans were bringing some artillery into play, though, and time had to be taken to deal with this.

In the air, the only counterattack the North Koreans had been able to muster came on D plus 2, when two of their ancient YAKs found *Rochester* and *Jamaica* anchored fast in their fire-support positions south of Wolmi-do. A single hundred-pound bomb bounced off *Rochester*'s aircraft crane and failed to explode. There were seven near misses, and one man aboard *Jamaica* was killed by strafing. The British, in turn, splashed one of the YAKs.

—And that was the sum of the North Korean air defense over Inchon. Within days of the landing, the North Koreans around the perimeter found their supply spigot, which had never run at full flow because of the interdiction campaign, practically cut off. The hammer was descending, and those on the anvil knew they were in the way. Men who should have been shepherding resupply operations had to be rushed pell-mell into the Inchon-Seoul corridor, where the soldiers and Marines kept shouldering persistently inland.

The Eighth Army and the ROKs were poised to break out from the perimeter. Even as the Marines were sweeping over Inchon's seawalls, the Navy aimed a diversionary bombardment at Samchok to help pave the way. Among the shooters was the only active vessel of her class in the fleet; five weeks before she had been dozing peacefully in New York with her summertime load of midshipmen. Now *Missouri* had returned to WestPac. Once again an American battlewagon was on the gunline, belching forth fifty-two rounds of high-capacity sixteen-inch shells and taking out a railroad bridge.

North of the parallel the few remaining naval units on the east coast also got busy. The submarines *Segundo* and *Perch* landed demolition teams. Gunfire interdiction picked up. But the mines were in far greater abundance there than in the west. On 26 September the destroyer *Brush* was mangled by a mine off Tanchon; thirteen crewmen were killed and thirty-four wounded. Two days later a ROK minesweeper lost twenty-six to a mine off Yongdok. And within two more days *Mansfield*, which had come around from Inchon, was nosing her way into Changjon to rescue a downed Air Force pilot when her bow was blown off in an explosion that injured twenty-eight of her crew.

The worst came on 1 October, near Yongdok, where the tiny motor minesweeper *Magpie*, just arrived from Guam, was resolutely sweeping the outer reaches. Suddenly she tripped a mine and instantly disintegrated; twenty-one of her thirty-three-man crew were lost with her.

The mines had their effect—they made this last week in September the costliest of the war for UN naval forces in terms of casualties—and the east coast gunships were warned not to cross the hundred-fathom line. Even *Perch*, specially configured for commando infiltration, was limited to a single raid, and that from beyond fifty fathoms.[7]

Aided by the Inchon landing and by these dents on the peninsula's periphery, the Eighth Army and the ROKs breached the weakened perimeter and sped north, USAF tactical air hounding the fleeing North Koreans all the way. Kim's men retreated even faster than they had advanced; Seoul was recaptured on 28 September (the battered city would change hands two more times during the war), and the following day there was Douglas MacArthur, symbolically delivering the capital back to Syngman Rhee.

By early October the enemy had either surrendered by the thousands or been chased back across the parallel. The hammer did not fall completely; no senior North Korean officers were captured, and thousands more of Kim's soldiers escaped up the narrowing gap along the east coast. But South Korea had been "liberated," and the original aims of the United Nations had been met—*within one hundred days of the North Korean invasion.*

The campaign probably should have ended there . . . *should* have.

☆

Back in August, when Forrest Sherman and Lightning Joe Collins had come out to talk about Inchon, MacArthur's goal had been to destroy Kim's army. Everyone agreed that the pursuit of this aim should not be constrained by the 38th parallel. But now the giddy euphoria of dramatic, decisive victory and the opportunity to slay the ideological demon in his lair produced the key strategic decision of the war. The fox was up, the hounds were baying, and the chase was on.

In mid-September the Joint Chiefs gave MacArthur the view halloo, granting him permission to plan for operations in North Korea. On the day before Seoul was retaken, the general was authorized to go north to "complete the destruction of the armed forces of the aggressor." No one gave much thought to the Soviets or the Red Chinese. The scent of the kill was in the air. UN forces were pointed north, Eighth Army on the left, X Corps, Marines, and ROKs on the right. Inchon had paved the way. Later, Collins would say that, following the triumphant landing, MacArthur had marched "like a Greek hero of old to an unkind and inexorable fate."

The Eighth Army targeted Pyongyang, the North Korean capital. X Corps would be reembarked at Inchon, steam around the peninsula, and, around 20 October, assault Wonsan, 115 miles northeast of Seoul (Operation TAILBOARD). There had been some abortive planning for an amphibious landing at Kunsan, after all, but the breathless pace of the UN offensive made the operation unnecessary. Almost all of South Korea had been cleared *in two weeks.*

MacArthur and his sycophantic staff had been drugged by the opiate of Inchon. Flaunting their overwhelming seapower, they were now ready to use the amphibious weapon at will. In Washington, the Truman administration was planning to occupy the entire peninsula and unify Korea to its Chinese and Soviet borders. While Omar Bradley, the chairman of the Joint Chiefs, went along with this idea, he was increasingly cynical about the amphibious weapon and MacArthur's intended use of the Gators:

> There was an aura of glamor about an amphibious landing. A sudden bold and decisive strike in the enemy's rear made big headlines and generated editorials about "military genius" at work. In the first act, MacArthur had overridden staff objections and pulled it off at Inchon, bringing down the curtain amid thunderous applause. A second-act curtain would generate even more headlines, editorials and applause.

The second act was to be Wonsan. But the mines that had hit *Brush*, *Mansfield*, *Magpie*, and the South Koreans had made everyone cautious. Wonsan would have to be swept well in advance of the assault. Struble moved Joint Task Force 7 around to the east coast and waited for his minesweepers, under the command of Captain Richard Spofford (one of the few naval officers with career mine experience), to do their stuff.

Wonsan was a real prize. Depsite having been worked over by the Fifth Air Force and the Navy during the summer, the city's docks remained practically undamaged. Protected by a breakwater, they featured a nine-hundred-foot concrete wharf, sheds, cranes, and rail sidings. Wonsan had both rail and road connections up and down the east coast, and there was also a fine airfield.

Along that coast the ROKs were racing toward the city, driving the disintegrating North Korean People's Army before them. Crossing the parallel on 1 October, they were within a week only a few miles short of Wonsan. By this time Struble's ships were assembling anew—the most powerful naval show of force yet. The carrier *Leyte* was on line now, along with the veterans *Valley Forge* and *Philippine Sea*. *Missouri* showed up as well, bringing with her numerous cruisers and destroyers. In addition, the USAF and naval air owned the skies over much of the north. With the pending collapse of Kim's army, the prospects for ending the war—on UN terms—had never been better.

On 14 October, after docking in Yokosuka to have her propeller repaired, *Boxer* reported in. For the first time since 1945, four *Essex*-class carriers were operating in unison, under Eddie Ewen's baton. The admiral celebrated on the following day by sending out 392 sorties to aid the ground troops and harry the North Koreans scrambling through the hills.[8]

Meanwhile, the speed of the ROK advance led to debates over how best to take Wonsan—by sea or by land. Most of the Army brass wanted to go by sea; the heavy logistics load on Inchon would be lessened, X Corps would be positioned to strategically envelop the fleeing enemy, and sealift was the cheaper way to go. The Navy, however, was reluctant. Turner Joy argued that X Corps, its way cleared by the ROKs, could get to Wonsan overland much quicker. If everything the Navy had was staged off Wonsan, the support and resupply of other operating areas along the peninsula—particularly of the Eighth Army in the west—would be inhibited. Finally, Joy was getting ominous information that Wonsan had been far more heavily mined than Inchon.

MacArthur listened, but the Navy's caution did not remove his amphibious bug. He considered alternative sites for an amphibious operation, like Hungnam and Iwon, but he eventually chose Wonsan. The UN forces would come at the city from both land and sea, in the latter case hewing to the 20 October timetable.

Even as the "rambling ROKs" were eating up the ground on the way to Wonsan, averaging fourteen miles a day, Joy reluctantly gave Struble the amphibious go-ahead. Arleigh Burke insisted that the whole thing was "unnecessary." The Joint Chiefs had been shocked; "To me it didn't make sense," Bradley later wrote. But after Inchon no one was questioning MacArthur's judgment. Truman's civilians gave a warm endorsement, and the Chiefs, including Bradley, added their approval.

Beginning 10 October, reports began to come in from the minesweepers probing the edges of Wonsan Harbor: there was more mine interference than expected.

☆

Again, the mines. By 1950 mine technology was available in bewildering variety, a supermarket of hidden destruction. The things could be set adrift, be moored, or be sown to lie in ambush on the bottom. They could be rolled over the gunwales of surface craft, ejected through submarine torpedo tubes, or parachuted from airplanes. They could be engineered to explode on contact (the classic horned mine of the cartoonists), through "influence" (magnetic, acoustic, or changes in water pressure), or by control from shore, usually electrically.

The United States Navy had had an exceptionally uneven relationship with these "weapons that wait," both offensively (minelaying) and defensively (sweeping and disarming). Mines were sown and then left to do their work; sailors and aviators did not usually have the satisfaction of seeing their prey buy the farm. Then there was the notion that mine usage was unethical, even in war: they could blow up any target that came along, even a civilian passenger liner full of innocents. The man who had damned the torpedoes (mines) at Mobile Bay, David Glasgow Farragut, maintained that he had "never considered [the use of mines] worthy of a chivalrous nation. . . ." The Navy was historically inattentive to mines, mining, and mine countermeasures, regarding the specialty as "unpleasant work for a naval man, an occupation like that of rat-catching."

Still, mines held a definite allure. They were, as naval weapons systems went, dirt cheap, and they could be quickly developed and deployed. A single mine could cause enormous losses, with no possible response from the victim. As a result, mines were obvious weapons of choice for the weaker sea powers. During the Revolutionary War, David Bushnell had tried to use them against the British in the Delaware River (the mock-hilarious "Battle of the Kegs"); the Confederacy enjoyed some success with them in the Civil War; Japan used them with great effect against Russia; and Germany sowed state-of-the-art mines from aircraft in World War II.

The weapons, however, were double-edged. Once a mine was used, its secrets were potentially the enemy's as well, as the Germans sowing those air-dropped mines found out to their distress. A powerful navy could injure itself by sowing novel and effective mines. For all these reasons, America's serious work with mines, which dated from the 1880s, had been extremely spotty.

The Bureau of Ordnance began to manufacture its own mines around 1915, using a simple spherical steel case and a TNT charge. Concurrently, a full-time "mining officer" became part of the bureau's staff. Three years earlier the first "minelayer," *San Francisco*, had been supplied with a "war allowance" of mines. But no effective mine program was developed in the United States before 1917.

World War I brought crash mine programs, and Americans participated fully in sowing (and later sweeping) the great North Sea barrage. But with peace came more desuetude. Administrative bickering and lack of interest were rife; responsibility for mine development was divided between the Naval Ordnance Laboratory and the Naval Gun Factory; and few Navymen wanted to be ratcatchers.

No one bureau owned the mines. The Bureau of Ordnance supplied the fleet with weapons, the Bureau of Ships provided ships, the Bureau of Aeronautics produced planes, and the Bureau of Personnel trained the people. All these, and more, were potentially concerned with mine warfare, but not one of them had the authority to direct that mining, or mine removal, be undertaken.

Mine specialists, the few that existed, were in career dead ends. The Navy brass was interested in the big stuff: battleships, carriers, cruisers. No experimental mine equipment was bought, and at one time the budget for connected work on depth charges was $25 a month. One urgent job required a small DC motor, which could be purchased on the open market for $15 to $20. The laboratory was forced to obtain *two* purchase orders, each for less than $10, for the motor frame and armature; the supplier was told that the lab would accept the two parts assembled.[9]

This nickel-and-diming vanished with World War II, and eventually thousands of top-notch mines were sown, mostly in the home waters of Japan and mostly by specially configured B-29s. But V-J Day brought the same old story. During the war, the Navy's Pacific minesweepers had numbered well over five hundred; by 1950, the minesweeping force in the Far East consisted of four 180-foot steel-hulled vessels (three of these in caretaker status) and six wooden auxiliary minesweepers. Fully 99 percent of the Navy's mine personnel in wartime had been Reservists; by 1950 practically every sailor in this specially trained and highly technical reservoir of manpower was gone.

Mine warfare was not merely on the back burner—the specialty had fallen off the stove. All minelayers in the Pacific (as distinguished from the sweeps) were in mothballs. All mine locator ships, the mineman's Seeing Eye dogs, had been scrapped, except for three survivors in the Atlantic. There were no active minesweeper tenders. In 1947 Chester Nimitz had been forced to dissolve the mine warfare command in the Pacific. Only three officers in the entire Pacific Fleet (Spofford was one of them) had any kind of operating experience with mines. The mineman rating itself had escaped being abolished in 1948 by the narrowest of margins.

Training in mine warfare, by 1950, was at a standstill. Destroyer-type minesweepers (the war-bred hybrid shortly to be made famous by the fictional USS *Caine*) were mostly used in antisubmarine warfare. The general attitude throughout the Navy was that any competent line officer could gear up for mine warfare when the need arose. Little was required in the way of research, training, or experience.

Naval vessels no longer had paravanes installed as protection against the classic moored contact mine. Facilities for degaussing (a technique for rendering metallic ships' hulls less susceptible to magnetic mines) were cut drastically. Destroyer sonars, which could have been modified into acoustic patterns capable of detecting moored mines, were left unmodified. No realistic drill mines existed for training.

—And Wonsan lay dead ahead.

☆

The Russians and North Koreans had been busy within the harbor. Not that their mines were state-of-the-art; many dated back to 1904 and the Russo-Japanese War. Not that their minelaying techniques were sophisticated; almost all the weapons were simply rolled over the sides of sampans or junks, "very much like . . . [in] the time of Christ," one American naval officer said. But where Inchon had featured, at most, only a few dozen easily detectable mines, the enemy sowed Wonsan Harbor with over three thousand moored and magnetic-influence mines, packed into an area of four hundred square miles. Only about two hundred of these were sown in the approach channels. The rest were scattered about the harbor, their assembly and placement supervised by Russians.

Even as the Navy began edging into the field, on 10 October, the ROKs had already secured the city. The mine-removal problem continued to be a most dangerous game, one without much enemy opposition but under the stupidly continuing pressure (now needless) of MacArthur's 20 October deadline. Three fleet minesweepers began pecking away, their inexperienced skippers periodically reporting with astonishment as the field grew and grew. The big sweeps, however, could not handle the shallow water, where many of the magnetic mines were located. Smaller, wooden-hulled sweeps were quickly hustled over from Japan, and in the interim, with X Corps's "invasion date" drawing closer, Eddie Ewen was ordered to "countermine," using thirty-nine bombers to drop thousand-pound bombs into the fields, hoping to set off a chain reaction of harmless explosions. The tactic had not worked against Axis mines—and did not work at Wonsan.[10]

The geysers from the countermining had barely subsided on the morning of 12 October when three of the hastily summoned wooden-hulled sweeps—

Pirate, *Pledge*, and *Incredible*—stood smartly in, echeloned to port in standard sweep formation. The three rotated the point on a daily basis; today was *Pirate*'s turn. They were smart, but unready. The three mites had no paravanes, no small boats had been sent in ahead to scout the water, and their eye in the sky, one of the new-fangled helicopters, could talk to them only through their escort, the destroyer-minesweeper *Endicott*.

At 1112 they entered unswept waters, streaming three hundred fathoms of sweep wire with cable cutters attached. As they swept left around the hilly island of Yo-do, located squarely in the harbor mouth, they had already cut the cables of many mines—a forest of unexpected mines—and these were bobbing to the surface in their wakes. At high noon the helo alertly reported three more lines ahead; *Pirate*'s sound gear began pinging off underwater contacts.

Nine minutes later *Pirate* stumbled into a mine and blew up; she capsized and sank within four minutes. *Pledge* halted, lowered her whaleboat to help the survivors, and cut loose her gear. Previously unobserved enemy batteries on Sin-do, an island farther inshore, suddenly opened up, and the little sweep desperately struggled to conduct a gunnery duel while at a standstill and smack in the middle of a minefield.

Endicott tried to help with her own guns as *Pledge* frantically hauled injured, waterlogged men aboard. With her whaleboat again fast, *Pledge* cranked her engines and hove to port, trying to head for cleared waters. She veered out of the swept lane, and another mine was waiting. When she went down, the total American losses for an hour's work in Wonsan Harbor were thirteen dead or missing and seventy-nine wounded.

Horrified, the Navy recoiled. A practically nonexistent naval force had bloodied its nose. Rear Admiral Allan ("Hoke") Smith commanded the transport escorts waiting out at sea. He was a tough, seasoned officer, a former skipper of the Big Bastard—*South Dakota*—and the man who had been in charge of refloating *Missouri* after the showboat had embarrassingly gone aground off Norfolk back in January. Smith declared that, at Wonsan, "control of the seas" had been lost.

Mine disposal was eventually accomplished by strafing (which would not have worked with more modern mines), by underwater demolition teams from the high-speed transport *Diachenko*, and by sweeps, including those of the embryonic Japanese Maritime Safety Agency. In the process a ROK minesweeper disintegrated while passing near an influence mine. Only on 26 October, almost a week after the target date, was the channel declared clear for the attack force.

By that time, of course, the ROKs had rambled through Wonsan and were headed north. The landing was correspondingly scaled down, with only the Marines being put ashore. For them, high time. Rip Struble's ships had steamed up and down the coast as the mine removal cautiously proceeded. Even Bob Hope's USO show arrived in Wonsan to entertain Amer-

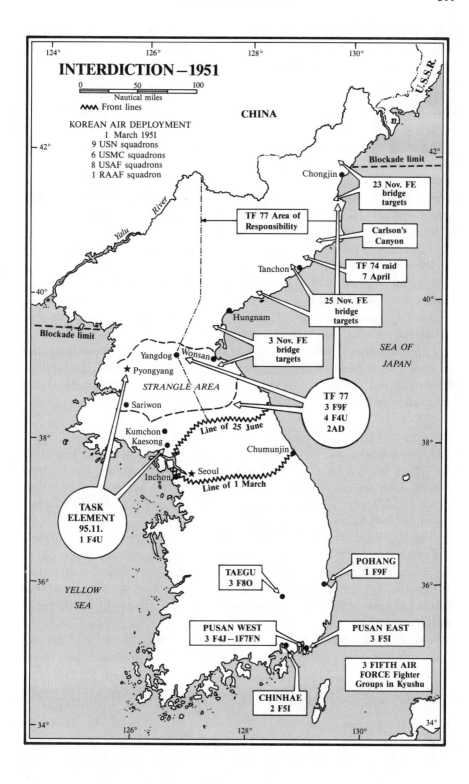

INTERDICTION — 1951

0   50   100
Nautical miles
ΛΛΛ Front lines

KOREAN AIR DEPLOYMENT
1 March 1951
9 USN squadrons
6 USMC squadrons
8 USAF squadrons
1 RAAF squadron

CHINA

U.S.S.R.

Blockade limit

Chongjin

23 Nov. FE bridge targets

TF 77 Area of Responsibility

Carlson's Canyon

Tanchon

TF 74 raid 7 April

25 Nov. FE bridge targets

Hungnam

3 Nov. FE bridge targets

Yalu River

Blockade limit

Yangdog   Wonsan

★ Pyongyang

STRANGLE AREA

● Sariwon

SEA OF JAPAN

TF 77
3 F9F
4 F4U
2AD

Kumchon ●
Kaesong ●

Line of 25 June

Chumunjin

TASK ELEMENT 95.11.
1 F4U

Inchon   ★ Seoul

Line of 1 March

POHANG
1 F9F

TAEGU
3 F8O

YELLOW SEA

PUSAN WEST
3 F4J — 1F7FN

PUSAN EAST
3 F5I

3 FIFTH AIR FORCE Fighter Groups in Kyushu

CHINHAE
2 F5I

icans already there, while the Leathernecks trapped aboard the rolling transports fought boredom, seasickness, and an epidemic of dysentery, all the while cursing "Operation Yo-Yo." One ship reported 750 Marines on the binnacle list.

At last, on 26 October, around thirty thousand men, led by Chesty Puller's 1st Marines, landed at Wonsan, "as anti-climactic a landing as Marines ever made." Three days later, the Army's 7th Division landed farther up the coast at Iwon, also unopposed—about thirty thousand more men. They found the ROKs had been there, too.[11]

On the other side of the peninsula, Chinnampo, a port that was to Pyongyang as Inchon was to Seoul, was opened as well. Here were the same Inchon-like problems of tidal currents, small islands, and mud flats. But the tremendous ebbs of the Yellow Sea exposed most of Chinnampo's mines at low water; on 3 November a South Korean minesweeper made safe passage into the port.

No lives were lost and no ships damaged at Chinnampo. Only five mines were cut by sweeps; the rest, eighty in all, were credited to patrol planes, underwater demolition teams, and weather. Wonsan had taught the Navy a bitter lesson. Once again, mine warfare went back on the stove.

"The Russians apparently have everything we have and everything the Germans had in mining techniques," Hoke Smith summed up. "The United States must put minesweeping on the same priority level as antisubmarine and carrier warfare."

☆

Most of this advice was lost in the intoxication of the push north. The UN forces were headed for the Yalu River, as fast as they could—the Eighth Army still on the left, the ROKs, the Marines, and X Corps still on the right—divided now by the forbidding central spine of Korea's mountains. Home by Christmas.

The Red Chinese threat was virtually ignored. There had been diplomatic warnings, sent mostly through neutral India, but these had been regarded as suspect. MacArthur, at the controversial Wake Island conference with Truman on 15 October, had promised a terrific slaughter if Mao entered the war. The general's own intelligence officers were writing off the warning signals.

This was the way war should be, chasing a now-tattered, defeated enemy to his ultimate, humiliating surrender. The road past Wolmi-do had been cracked wide open. For the moment, as the crisp autumn air of North Korea began to give way to wintry Siberian blasts, Douglas MacArthur's reputation was, one final time, at a giddy peak. That reputation rested on the masterstroke at Inchon, and while MacArthur had not conceived of the operation per se, he had given CHROMITE the go-ahead. So the bulk of the credit was his, although the naval officers deserved some too. They had done their jobs, explaining the difficulties, and then had gotten on board and brilliantly pulled off a hurried, complex, and potentially dicey amphibious assault.

Only a year had passed since Omar Bradley, with all the weight of the five stars gleaming on his shoulders, had spoken to the House Armed Services Committee, predicting that "large-scale amphibious operations will never occur again." Louis Johnson, not to be outdone, had told Close In Conolly, "There's no reason for having a Navy and Marine Corps. . . . Amphibious operations are a thing of the past . . . and the Air Force can do anything the Navy can do nowadays. . . ."

Inchon was the vindication of amphibious assault. CHROMITE was never the supremely hazardous gamble that later emerged in MacArthur's hyperactive imagination (5000 to 1, he said). But the operation was gamble enough, succeeding, despite the admittedly dangerous obstacles, because the Navy and the Marines had an amphibious track record and knew what they were doing. True, the North Koreans were woefully unprepared for an attack from their seaward flanks. Yet that was *precisely what an amphibious assault was ideally designed to do:* hit the enemy where he was weakest and least suspecting.

Inchon took place exactly eighty-two days after the North Koreans breached the 38th parallel. The landing's dazzling success, however, obliterated in the public mind the later struggle at Wonsan. A price had to be paid for MacArthur's fixation with amphibious assault (which should always be an *option*, seldom a *necessity*)—and at Wonsan the Navy paid. At Struble's insistence, Joy and MacArthur had, eventually, delayed the Wonsan landing. But the hurry-up in the meanwhile had been at least partially responsible for the loss of *Pirate* and *Pledge*.

"Let's admit it," Forrest Sherman said of Wonsan. "They caught us with our pants down." The mines of Wonsan, had the landings been opposed to any degree, could have brought disaster. Hoke Smith, momentarily panicked as he may have been, had been right: a vastly inferior naval power, with simple weapons crudely deployed, had caused the Americans to temporarily lose control of what they wanted to do at sea. Rip Struble urged that mine warfare be "pressed vigorously."

These memories, to the troops on land, were forgotten or unknown. On they went, past Wonsan, through Iwon, on to Hungnam. Behind the lines Secretary of the Navy Francis Matthews showed up at Wonsan and indicated he had lost none of his touch by telling Jimmy Doyle and the crew of *Mount McKinley* that this was the first visit he had paid to any ship of the United States Navy. Rowboat had been in office for a year and a half.

While the armies moved north almost at will, the UN naval forces were cruising undisturbed along both coasts. As sweeping got better and ports were opened, the logistics load eased. In Yoko, Turner Joy began to study questions of postwar redeployment. Late in October, out of aviation munitions and almost out of targets, Eddie Ewen's fast carriers retired to Yoko and Sasebo. "At this time," said Ewen, "it became definitely apparent that the remaining Korean territory held by the enemy forces was so small that there was not enough physical space for all the effective aircraft available."

On 1 November Struble dissolved Joint Task Force 7 and steamed back to Sasebo. With the coming of November the total American naval population in Korean waters, which had reached 79,000 in mid-October (from a mere 11,000 in June) was at 75,000 and on the way down. Off the coast, winter now gripped the Sea of Japan. Surely the campaign, so desperately begun around Pusan, so dramatically supercharged at Inchon, was over.

Late in October, as UN forces reached the Yalu in some sectors, a few Chinese prisoners were taken. They talked freely, named their units, and said they had recently moved across into North Korea. There were rumors of massing planes and men just across the river in Manchuria.[12]

—The warning signals, like the diplomatic gestures before, went unheeded.

CHAPTER TEN

STALEMATE

———— ☆ ————

Douglas MacArthur's plan for breaching the 38th parallel had assumed that North Korea had little resistance left (true enough) and that neither the Soviet Union nor Red China would enter the war as a result. The latter premise was not universally accepted, and among the doubters was the chief of naval operations. "[MacArthur] seems very disdainful of our concern over a major conflict with the Chinese," Forrest Sherman ruminated. Some others were not; Arleigh Burke, on Turner Joy's staff in Tokyo, began to stash one out of every five transports that arrived from the West Coast. Within weeks he had some ninety ships for emergency lift.

Mao Tse-tung did not have a top-notch military force, not by a long shot. His men had only recently emerged from their long-held guerrilla tactics into traditional army formations, and they were notoriously deficient in modern aircraft, tanks, and heavy artillery, despite the harvest of American-supplied Nationalist matériel that had fallen to them during the just-concluded civil war. Their logistics were primitive, their communications worse.[1]

—But there were a lot of them. Both MacArthur and the Joint Chiefs, using Western logic, believed that Peking would commit no more than token troops along the North Korean border and that the Chinese leaders would believe that UN forces would stop exactly where they had said they would— at the Yalu River. Both Tokyo and Washington estimated that only about twenty thousand men would be involved in such a demonstration, placed there to reassure the Communist world more than anything else.

In fact, the Red Chinese had massed over 250,000 soldiers, with more on the way, and they meant to fight; their calculus was of a different order than that of the Americans. By 1 November, moving mostly at night, tens of thousands had already crossed the Yalu and had gone to ground amid the bare steeps of North Korea. As skirmishing in the frost-girdled mountains mushroomed into a full-fledged enemy assault, MacArthur radiated confidence. He boasted that his aerial offensive had turned part of Korea into a desert, and he expected his air superiority to do the same to any Chinese foolish enough to come south.

They already *were* south, and on 25 November they unleashed a massive counterattack all along the line, featuring almost 300,000 of their own troops and about 65,000 North Koreans. Within a week the reeling UN command had taken 11,000 casualties. American goals began to shift dramatically, from the "unification" of Korea to the possible negotiation of an armistice line somewhere near the 38th parallel.

The attackers were not especially skilled, and much of their military technology was vintage. Americans used words and phrases like "hordes" and "human waves" to describe and explain away their success. But MacArthur's overconfidence and his badly flawed troop dispositions were critical to the UN collapse. Morale shattered in many frontline units, and once again Communist forces began to surge south.

For the Navy, the problem quickly became that of supporting a retreat. (Turner Joy came up with the slogan "assault in reverse.") Naval air could help, but the pell-mell abandonment of forward bases brought the problem of range to the forefront, and the deepening winter weather presented a huge obstacle. Also, there was the darkening specter of enforced evacuation from the peninsula; the Joint Chiefs were beginning to have nightmares of another Dunkirk.

In the west, the Eighth Army was being overwhelmed, and the recently opened port of Chinnampo was threatened. The port was evacuated, with great skill, between 4 and 6 December, but such necessary measures only hastened the collapse. The Chinese rolled through Pyongyang and on to the 38th parallel.[2]

Everyone was badly rattled. Back in Washington, Harry Truman was asked at a press conference whether atomic weapons would be used in Korea. He responded that the United States would use "every weapon we have," that as far as the bomb was concerned, there had "always been active consideration of its use," and that the military commander in the field [MacArthur] would decide whether to employ such weapons. The final assertion was simply a misstatement, which did nothing to calm America's allies, and if Truman meant his words as a warning to the Chinese, they served as nothing of the sort.

In the east, the Marines, the ROKs, and X Corps were battling both the Chinese and the cold. In late November a number of units found themselves surrounded at the Chosin Reservoir, fifty miles north of the port of Hungnam at an altitude of 3400 feet. Snow was starting to blanket the plateau on which the reservoir stood. Canteens began to freeze, then burst. With December, temperatures nosedived to twenty-five below zero. There were twenty-five thousand exhausted men up there on the plateau, connected to Hungnam only by a single twisting, narrow road that could not take heavy traffic. Against them were committed eight Chinese divisions totaling about sixty thousand troops.

Eddie Ewen's Task Force 77 was back on line after hurriedly replenishing in Japan, and Ewen sent thirty-nine sorties over the reservoir on 30 November. But weather fouled the operations, and under the 100 percent cloud cover the defenders were taking heavy losses. The next day they began to pull out, heading down that narrow defile through the Toktong Pass, Hagaru, and Kotori—heading for Hungnam, the sea, and safety. For the Marines the march became Anabasis, an epic "advance to the rear" that rightfully took its place among the legends of the Corps. Fighting brilliant small-unit actions all the way, they were covered as they moved by Ewen's aviators.

After 2 December all of Task Force 77's aircraft were devoted to guarding the march. They strafed and bombed Chinese positions in the hills, provided fighter cover to transports flying precious supplies into Hagaru, and circled over the strung-out column to warn of enemy positions ahead or on the flanks. The sorties catapulted daily into the wintry air—against the reservoir, against the village of Yudam-ni to the west, against the road linking the Toktong Pass and Hagaru. On one day, 3 December, the air controllers handled 359 planes, most of them belonging to Ewen.

Everything the Americans had was thrown into the corridor; Rip Struble had been forced to cancel attacks on the Yalu River bridges. On 5 December the carrier *Princeton* arrived, catapults cocked. The result was a record 248 sorties from Task Force 77. The workhorse, once again, was the Skyraider, a carrier-borne Percheron whose weapons load was greater than that of the classic B-17. The Marines did not yet have jets in Korea, and the nearest Air Force jet squadrons were two hundred miles away, at Kimpo Airfield. Thus, Ewen's Panthers provided the hovering combat air patrol, keeping their eyes peeled across the Yalu for the MiG concentrations reported there.

On 7 December Ewen's three fast carriers (*Princeton*, *Philippine Sea*, and *Leyte*) and *Badoeng Strait* were joined by the latter's sister, *Sicily*. Bad weather could not prevent 216 sorties. Below the hard-working aviators, the Marines and other UN forces were freezing, taking casualties, and providing constant targets for the enemy swarming in the hills around them—but they kept fighting, and moving.[3]

After a week of desperate combat, the Marines, the ROKs, and X Corps reached Hungnam. There they found Task Force 90, waiting with an evacuation strength of twenty-eight ships. Getting that many together had been "hard work," Jimmy Doyle laconically remarked—he had Burke to thank for many of the ships he did have.

The Chinese had taken terrific casualties from both ground and air, and they chose not to press the evacuation process. A contributing factor lay with Ewen's naval and Marine aviators, twenty-two squadrons' worth (a few flying from land bases), whose four hundred planes saturated the shrinking perimeter around the port. Offshore stood *Missouri*, *Saint Paul*, *Rochester*, and seven destroyers, snow on their decks and ice crusting their forecastles, pumping out a total of twenty-two thousand shells either on call or at random.

The Marines embarked first, then the ROKs, finally the Army. The last ground troops were out of Hungnam by 21 December. The Navy had, in effect, carried out an amphibious assault in reverse. From Hungnam were sealifted 105,000 troops, 17,500 vehicles, 350,000 measurement tons of cargo, and 98,000 Korean refugees—a major city embarked for sea. From Wonsan 3800 troops, 1146 vehicles, 10,000 tons of cargo, and 7000 refugees had also been lifted out.

Sadly, thousands of Korean civilians were left behind, at the mercy of the enemy. The whole thing had the combined air of organization and slapdash, but the timing was immaculate. "Inconsistency and variation were the norm," Doyle remembered; "ingenuity and experience got things done."

Behind its retreating sterns, the Navy left four hundred tons of frozen dynamite (too dangerous to move), five hundred 1000-pound bombs, and two hundred drums of gasoline. Demolition teams got to work, and as the last ship cleared the harbor Jimmy Doyle gave the order. Hungnam and its waterfront went up in a titanic fireworks display.

Overhead circled a lone Corsair off *Princeton*, flown by Lieutenant R.B. Mack. From fifteen thousand feet he watched the last LSTs loading and lumbering off, the gathering fires around the docks, and the final cataclysmic explosion: "The ships below formed up single file, nose-and-tail like circus elephants, and headed seaward and then south to Pusan." A few delivered Parthian shots at the Chinese drifting down from the hills.

As he headed for home plate, Mack called up his air controller aboard *Mount McKinley*. "Merry Christmas," they said to each other.
—Christmas Eve in Korea.

☆

The magnificence of the pullout from Hungnam and the other northern ports could not hide the obvious: defeat and retreat all along the line. On 4 January Seoul was abandoned, and now there was an Inchon-in-reverse. During December 32,000 troops were taken back out through tortuous Flying Fish Channel. As with Hungnam, the port's facilities were blown up, but only after 130,000 people, half of them military, had been sealifted to safety.[4]

As the front collapsed back upon the Han River, the war became even more of a land struggle. The Navy, which had performed well on the periphery, now faced anew the problem of how to integrate its overwhelming seapower into a land campaign, there being no corresponding naval force to go after.

As the battle lines stabilized during January and February, Jimmy Doyle performed his last mission with Task Force 90, transporting refugees and prisoners to the islands of Koje and Cheju off the south coast. Then, in the game of round-robin continuously played by American flag officers, he was

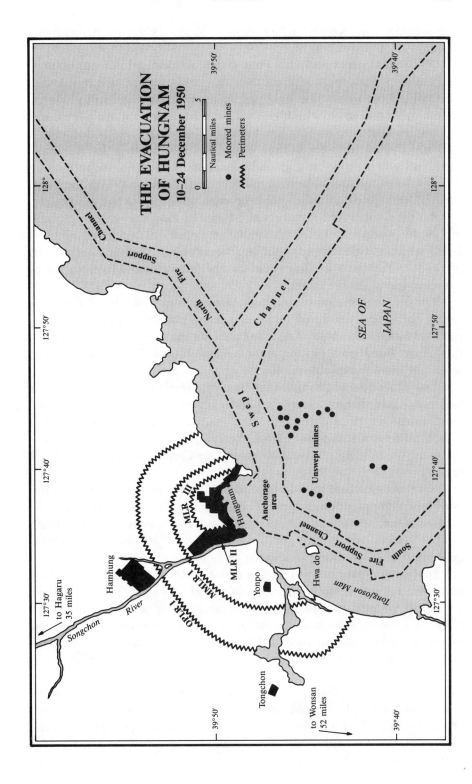

THE EVACUATION
OF HUNGNAM
10–24 December 1950

Nautical miles

● Moored mines
ᴡᴡᴡ Perimeters

gone—named the commander of Arthur Radford's Pacific Amphibious Force.

While the transports plied down the coasts, relocating hundreds of thousands, the minesweepers kept up their dangerous harbor clearance work, even behind the lines. The small ships endured short hours of daylight, bone-numbing weather (with high winds and freezing spray the norm), and the omnipresent danger of mines. Fifteen sweeps were now available, and they had the support of a mother vessel, the dock landing ship *Comstock*. Patrol planes, helicopters, and underwater demolition teams were being dovetailed into both minehunting and disposal. Early in 1951 Mine Force Pacific Fleet was reestablished, and the sweeps once again had a home.

But the peril never left them. On 2 February *Partridge*, sweeping a mile off Sokcho, just north of the 38th parallel, exploded and sank in ten minutes, losing ten men. Still, the spotlight now being cast on their specialty began to produce results. *Partridge* would be the last of four American minesweepers lost to enemy mines.

The carriers were mustering, too. *Leyte* left, but *Valley Forge*, *Philippine Sea*, and *Princeton* remained in Korean waters, and *Boxer* returned after overhaul in San Francisco. And more were on the way, from the mothball fleet: *Essex*, *Bon Homme Richard*, *Antietam*. By autumn Radford would have seven fast carriers available for Korea.

Task Force 77 had flown in support of the battle line in January, doing long-range interdiction, emergency close support, cover for landings and evacuations—anything that was needed. As the ground situation solidified in late winter under the new Eighth Army commander, General Matthew Ridgway, the problems of close air support and aerial interdiction surfaced once again.

Naval aviation (and the Marines) liked close support more than did the Air Force. The predilection was reflected in training and doctrine, in tendencies in aircraft design that gave naval aviators heavier loads and more time on station, and in seaborne dive-bombing techniques derived from a generation of experience with moving ships as targets.

Joint communications were still a major problem, but the Army-Navy nets were becoming increasingly reliable, and coordination of carrier air with Fifth Air Force had also improved. The carrier air groups had particular advantages not only when they handled their own communications but also in interdiction, which in early 1951 primarily meant destroying rail and highway bridges. The standard Air Force fighter-bomber, the F-80 Shooting Star jet, lacked sufficient range and lift to operate north of the Pyongyang-Hungnam axis, even when modified with tip tanks. If the F-80 flew from Japan, the slender plane could rarely tote more than two rockets and a tank of napalm. The F-51 Mustang was prop-driven, and despite its sturdy lift and endurance was vulnerable to the increasing threat of the MiG jets up north.

The Air Force, true to its heritage, preferred strategic bombing. The B-26 and the B-29 were doing their stuff in the skies over the north, but both were unsuited to small targets, front-line interdiction, and on-call close support. The B-26, in addition, was limited by altitude and was vulnerable to anti-aircraft fire, and the B-29 needed a convoy of escorts to fend off enemy fighters. These horizontal bombers were less flexible than the carrier planes in both approach routes and attack tactics. Among the carrier aircraft, the Skyraider's payload and accuracy were making its aviators bridge-busters par excellence.

Turner Joy and Rip Struble wanted naval air kept in close support of the congealing battlefront. The USAF wanted the carriers to use their mobility for deep interdiction, to inhibit any renewed Chinese offensive. The long-term result was that the Navy would do both.

Korea had become a huge naval beachhead; the retreat from North Korea had forced redeployment of most land-based air back to Japan. In a normal amphibious scenario, the peninsula was again at the stage that preceded the introduction of garrison air. The Fifth Air Force accordingly had to momentarily abandon its interdiction function, and as Task Force 77 began an extended stint off the northeast coast on 26 February, the role became the Navy's by default.

Along that coast the surface fleet still steamed, now carrying out siege operations. Recently evacuated Wonsan, for example, found itself under naval bombardment every single day in March. All its important harbor islands remained occupied by UN forces, and among these were some spotters. The shorebom ships broke the record for continuous naval shelling set at Vicksburg almost a century before.

Underneath the whistling rounds the sweeps crept in and out, playing their deadly game; of the twenty-eight mines swept along the coast during March, twenty were at Wonsan. The Soviets kept up their rail-borne attempts at mine resupply, and the light cruiser *Manchester* managed to detonate a boxcar full.

The enemy's transportation nets became prime targets of a coordinated air-sea interdiction campaign. There were two chances of his using the sea for resupply: exceptionally slim and none. His logistics thus depended on two principal land nets: the western road and rail complex, in which lines from the lower Yalu joined just north of Pyongyang, and the eastern grid, where routes from Hoeryong and Hyesanjin met at Kilchu and continued down the coast to join the transpeninsular line below Hungnam. The former, less distant from the remaining southern UN bases, became the targets of the Air Force's Bomber Command. The latter belonged to the Navy.

Interdiction was tough. Naval aviators were not going against a modern economy stippled with prominent industrial concentrations. Most enemy troops subsisted on a supply basis of ten pounds per man per day (the Eighth Army's corresponding figure was sixty pounds, the Fifth Air Force's sixty-four). Even when road and rail net tonnage was cut way down—to between five hundred and a thousand *total* tons per day—enough was still getting through, and the enemy foraged as well as fought. Besides, he was not confined to his roads and his rails. He moved at night, through the hills, using his manpower as beasts of burden—a tactic as old as war itself.

He was hard to spot and hard to hit, and even his points of concentration, the critical bridges, were extraordinarily difficult to knock down. Modern reinforced concrete bridges, the Navy soon discovered, required the main battery hitting power of a heavy cruiser or a battlewagon or a Skyraider's full load. As experience piled up during the early months of 1951, Seventh Fleet found out that about sixty rounds of sixteen-inch gunfire or twelve to sixteen Skyraider sorties meant one bridge destroyed. Two a day was the average capability, and the results did much to mess up the enemy logistics. But trucks could be detoured, and those human packhorses still kept moving south.

To Task Force 77, now commanded by Rear Admiral Ralph Ofstie, rendering a bridge "inoperable" meant destroying at least one of its spans. When the carriers left the line on 4 April to replenish, after thirty-eight straight days of aerial interdiction, their aviators claimed fifty-four rail and thirty-seven highway bridges; tracks had been ruptured in over two hundred places. The east coast rail system, which had carried two-thirds of the enemy's traffic in February, had been reduced to half that amount.

By now, over half a year after Kim Il-sung's invasion, the reshuffling of men and ships to Korea had become routine. Doyle was gone, Ewen was gone, and Struble's turn came on 25 March, when he relinquished Seventh Fleet to Vice Admiral Harold Martin. Martin's essential problem was to match the technological sophistication and seagoing dominance at his command with the enemy's primitivism—and this was no easy task.[5]

Early April: Ridgway had stabilized the land battle and had launched a deliberate strategy of simply killing the enemy, trying to force him to treat for an armistice. The interdiction campaigns were underway. The Eighth Army and the ROKs, operating in the midst of an oratorical parade of bloody operational tags (THUNDERBOLT, KILLER, RIPPER) and supported by naval planes and gunfire, reached an operational line ("Wyoming") that again took them across the 38th parallel by 22 April. The Navy helped by staging two amphibious feints—one for each coast—to support THUNDERBOLT, and another, off Chinnampo, to help RIPPER.

Land combat was no longer a war of movement but of deliberate, calculating attrition. Stalemate.

☆

By America's reckoning, in a stalemated war the side with the most guns and butter would win. This had been the recipe in the Civil War and both world wars. The result simply could not be otherwise, and accordingly the giant's economy and dormant military muscle began to stir, moving beyond the crisis mechanisms that had saved South Korea to the routine of logistical reinforcement.

Almost everything came by sea, including six of every seven people. Every soldier and Marine landed in Korea was accompanied by five tons of equipment. Over sixty pounds of supplies per day were needed to keep each one of them there. Fifty-four million tons of dry cargo and twenty-two million tons of petroleum products were delivered by ship. For every ton of freight that crossed the Pacific by air, 270 tons moved by sea. "We could not have existed in Korea without the Navy," said General James Van Fleet, who took over the Eighth Army from Ridgway.[6]

The Military Sea Transportation Service bore the brunt of this ferry work—forty-one million tons of cargo and seventeen million tons of petroleum products. The sealift carried fuel trailers, Air Force jets, 105-mm howitzers; spare parts for everything from helicopters to radios; and over two million personnel in a single year, enough to repopulate the two Dakotas and have enough left over to refill Seattle. By the middle of 1951 the MSTS had increased its lift to 445 ships, the predominant portion ticketed for Korea. During the war its costs averaged about $600 million a year. Over two hundred other vessels were taken up from commercial charter.

About 9700 naval personnel helped crew these ships, alongside 14,000 civilians. The vast movement of men and supplies generated new thinking about cargo handling, docking, fuel conservation, and off-loading. The "roll-on, roll-off" idea began with Korea. By war's end more than 90 percent of all personnel and matériel entering the peninsula had been brought by the Military Sea Transportation Service.

And there were the fighting ships. For mothballing the two thousand vessels in the Reserve Fleet, American taxpayers had shelled out $213 million between 1946 and 1951. ("The cheapest insurance policy in history," bragged a Navy spokesman.) Now some of these ships were summoned forth from their sleep, according to need. Their activation time averaged thirty days, whether they were LSTs or carriers. By April 1951, 381 activations had taken place: 13 carriers, 2 battleships (*New Jersey* and *Wisconsin*), 2 heavy cruisers, 77 destroyers and destroyer escorts, 13 submarines, 31 of the critical minesweepers, 7 patrol vessels, and 236 amphibious and auxiliary types.

Many of the landing craft that squatted forlornly in the mud flats off Inchon had come from a mothball base in Texas. By 1951 gun-line and carrier stations alike featured formerly mothballed vessels. The hibernating ships were awakened from their berths in Philadelphia, Portsmouth, Charleston, and New London, hastily supplied with crews, and sent west. Naturally, things were a little shaky. Aboard the escort carrier *Bairoko* the crew was so green that only her skipper, William ("Red") Raborn, was qualified to stand an underway deck watch. Many recalled Reservists were experiencing their first time at sea. Some of the *Fletcher*-class destroyers had neither the desired firepower nor useful fire control systems; they went anyway.

About a year passed between the moment the chief of naval operations willed a mothballed ship into service and the time she fired her first shot in anger. Her grease would be scraped off, and she would haltingly move through her shipyard and performance trials, be married with her usually inept crew, and be given spare parts and provisions. She was checked and double-checked: at Guantanamo Bay, San Diego, Pearl Harbor, or Yokosuka if necessary. Nevertheless, her workup would often be careless and slovenly, and many ships were not fully up to speed even by the time they first saw the Korean coast. Hence, for some the war offered dangerous on-the-job training.

Despite all this, mothballing proved itself in Korea. The total cost of reactivation, including electronic updating, was $120 million through April 1951—about 2.5 percent of replacement cost. Fleet carrier strength escalated from eleven to seventeen, and battleships from one to three. Cruisers, destroyers, submarines, and Gators—all swelled in numbers. Early in 1951 the politicians approved $2 billion worth of naval construction, including a fifty-seven-thousand-ton carrier that the Navy swore was not merely a replay of *United States* (the vessel would become *Forrestal*). "The Navy," observed Sherman, "is in pretty fair shape." "Congress apparently has to be scared by a reality," grumbled another admiral.

The fleet's manpower was in pretty fair shape, too. Unlike the other services, the Navy could treat its Reservists as a single pool to be drawn on at discretion. Reservists made possible the cranking up of the mothball fleet. Of 230,000 officers and enlisted added to the rolls during the first eight months of Korea, half were Reservists, and of these, 70 percent were at sea, doing their jobs, by March 1951. Overall, naval manpower increased by 60 percent, and the number of combatant ships went up by 50 percent.[7]

In the air the story was the same, only more so. Old aviators learned new tricks. Some had to transition from propeller-driven fighters like the Corsair to the newer Panther jets. By November 1951 fully 75 percent of all Navy sorties over Korea were being flown by Reservists.

VA-702, a Reserve attack squadron from Dallas, was typical. Called up on 20 July 1950, its aviators checked out their Skyraiders at Whidbey Island a week later and were piled immediately into refresher training. There was much to learn and relearn: navigation, night flying, instruments, tactics, gunnery, bombing, electronics, rocketing, mining, close air support. By March 1951 the "Texas Squadron" was flying strikes off *Boxer*.

The Seabees were back in business also; the members of these indispensable naval construction battalions had dwindled from the quarter million of their glory days in the Pacific war to a mere six thousand by 1950. By the end of 1951 the Seabee Reservists alone numbered seventy-five thousand, many of them in Korea. They included every construction specialty known:

builders, drivers, surveyors, electricians, mechanics, steelworkers, utilities specialists. All staged at Port Hueneme, California, on their way west, and once on the peninsula they were soon busy working their usual miracles from scratch.

By the spring of 1951 the resupply and remanning in Korea had, for the Navy, become routine. The hundreds of cargo ships, the dozens of reborn fighting ships, and the hundreds of thousands of Reservists and new enlistees—were almost all marked for contribution to the war effort.

Exactly how this contribution was to be made, though, in a war of stalemate, remained to be seen.

☆

As the Eighth Army and the ROKs checked a new enemy offensive, Task Force 77 went back to work on interdiction and close air support. During April and May 1951 carrier aviators (somewhat overenthusiastically, as was common with the breed) claimed twenty-one thousand enemy killed. The communications snags were still there, though; controllers were being swamped, and much ordnance was being dumped for lack of a target. Processing delays from request to receipt of aircraft were averaging an unacceptable ninety-five minutes.

Along the east coast, the gunships were busy, too. The recently arrived heavy cruiser *Los Angeles* and the demothballed *New Jersey* were firing rounds till paint flaked off their gun barrels; at one point the crew of *Los Angeles* was taking on ammunition from a cargo ship on one side, wrestling the shells across her deck, and unloading them through her muzzles on the other.

Vehicles, armored columns, supply dumps, men—anything that moved or could be spotted were potential targets, from either air or sea. But the enemy kept moving, forced onto secondary roads or into the hills. This was Operation STRANGLE, but not enough strangling was going on; total north-south enemy vehicle sightings remained about the same into the summer.

And the enemy was fighting back. His anti-aircraft fire was becoming more accurate, more deadly. From April through June, Task Force 77 lost three Panthers, eight Skyraiders, and nineteen Corsairs. On 18 May the carriers suffered their worst single day of the war, when six planes failed to return.

The enemy's coastal batteries were multiplying, too, and not merely around besieged ports like Wonsan. Ships were being hit. On 14 June the destroyer-minesweeper *Thompson*, having closed to 40-mm range off Songjin, got surprised when her targets suddenly wheeled out four guns, opened fire, and scored thirteen hits before she could get clear. One round decapitated the chief quartermaster, and as *Thompson* fled to the open sea her bridge was "literally spattered over every square inch" with blood and brains.

Mines were an omnipresent menace. Sweeping was becoming more and more effective, but drifting mines were now a greater threat than anchored or strewn fields. The Russian-made moored mines were fused to remain armed after snapping their tethers. Many had been deliberately launched as drifters, to take advantage of prevailing southerly currents off the east coast. Reports of floating mines began to come into Turner Joy's shop from the South China Sea, the Sea of Japan, even the north Pacific. In June the destroyer *Walke*, steaming along in a carrier screen sixty miles offshore, hit a floater that exploded on her port side aft, killing twenty-five. By the fall of 1951 more than three hundred mines, many of them still armed, had washed up on Japanese shores.[8]

When truce talks at last began, in mid-1951, the interdiction program continued. The Fifth Air Force kept pounding its westernmost targets, and Task Force 77 kept launching strikes in the east. The air strikes and the shore bombardment were placing real stress on the enemy—his Department of Military Highway Administration, charged with road repair, had grown to some twenty thousand men.

But his soldiers were still getting the supplies they needed. The North Koreans and Chinese were proving to be diligent, determined, disciplined, and persistent fighters. They were better fed now, had more tanks, and were getting more ammunition. They fired off eight thousand artillery rounds in July 1951 and forty-three thousand during November. The enemy now had five hundred heavy anti-aircraft pieces and two thousand automatic AA weapons. He was not exactly prospering as negotiations ground on, but interdiction was not driving him to his knees, either.

Despite the enemy's increasing material strength, the battle line generally crept northward as the negotiators fenced, first at Kaesong, then at Panmunjom. The UN group was led by Turner Joy. UN forces maintained command of the air over most of North Korea, and the Navy and its allies controlled the coasts. Shore bombardment at places like Wonsan, Songjin, and the Han River estuary took place daily.

Korea was under naval blockade.

☆

The blockade had been proclaimed almost immediately, back on 4 July 1950. Both the Soviet Union and Red China were quick in their denunciations, and Joy had to ask Sherman if Soviet or Chinese merchantmen were to be barred from North Korean ports. The answer was that *all* warships, excluding North Korea's, would be allowed to enter; all other ships of any nationality were barred.

By mid-1951, as the truce talks began, the blockade had become very tight and very tough. The blockaders were doing some unique things, such as patrolling for and chasing trucks and trains. There was no active surface naval opposition, no submarine opposition, and practically no enemy air.

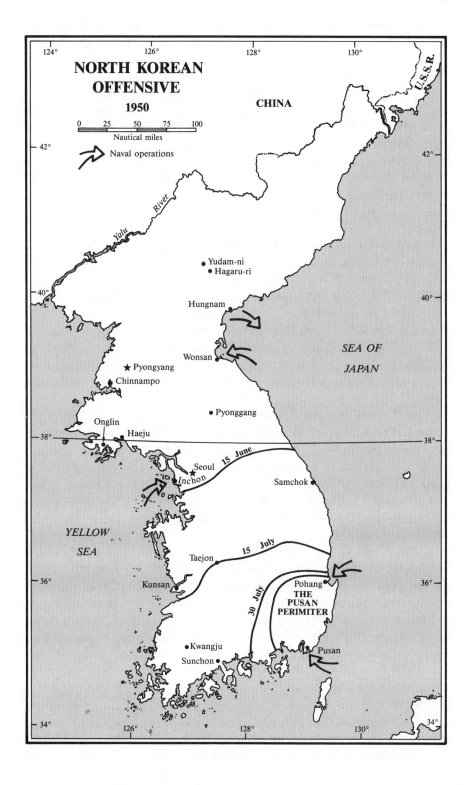

NORTH KOREAN OFFENSIVE 1950

0 25 50 75 100
Nautical miles

Naval operations

CHINA

U.S.S.R.

Yalu River

• Yudam-ni
• Hagaru-ri

Hungnam

Wonsan

SEA OF JAPAN

★ Pyongyang
Chinnampo

• Pyonggang

Onglin
Haeju

Seoul
Inchon

15 June

Samchok •

YELLOW SEA

Taejon
15 July

Kunsan •

30 July

Pohang
THE PUSAN PERIMITER

Pusan

• Kwangju
Sunchon •

UN naval forces had complete control of the entire five-hundred-odd miles of North Korean coastline, with the occasional exception of the dreaded mines.

But blockading was tough on the blockaders as well. Korea's distinctive geography, hydrography, and climate were always in the way. The blockade was imposed thousands of miles from the American mainland, and ultimately the ships had to be sustained from that distance. Even the bountiful American garrison back home could never spare as many vessels for blockade duty as were needed. And, under international law, the requirement for an "effective" blockade held that every portion of a blockaded coast had to be under surveillance at least once every twenty-four hours *by ship* (not by air)—a demand that made not a few naval crews busier than a scattered antpile.

The heavyweights—the battlewagons and the eight-inch cruisers—would be called in for specific jobs, but the real burden of blockade was carried by the small boys: minesweepers, frigates, destroyer escorts, and destroyers. Their war was remote, often bitter, dreary, and dangerous. They were seldom alone, though—other ships were usually in the vicinity—and along the way UN vessels learned to communicate and operate with one another. New Zealand destroyers took oil from American tankers; the single Thai frigate was issued American foul-weather gear; a sudden appeal from shore produced the mandatory olive oil with which to bake bread for Turkish troops.

The "United Nations Blockading and Escort Force" (Task Force 95) operated all over the place. According to Sherman, "There [were] only about half a dozen naval officer's jobs out there where the officer is actually participating in the war," and operating Task Force 95 was certainly one of them. The Task Force *was* the blockade, and the blockade was one of four ways the enemy's exposed coastline could be exploited. (The others were battering him with naval gunfire, landing raiding parties, and besieging his ports.)

As the months passed and the negotiators at Panmunjom mostly talked past each other, the blockading inexorably did its work. Three of the enemy's five main lines of supply were first harried, then clogged, and finally blocked: the deep-water shipping along the east coast; the shallow-water coastal shipping in the west; and the deep-water shipping routes from China and Manchuria into North Korea. He was denied the use of the sea for military movements, resupply, even fishing. The blockade became virtually 100 percent effective, with only the smallest trickle of coastal, nocturnal traffic getting through.

The siege of the ports of Wonsan, Songjin, and Hungnam was continuous. The Navy was clamping on its first blockade since the Civil War, and especially with the tremendous advantage bestowed by the lack of air or naval opposition, the process was working splendidly.

One measure of the hurt came in September 1951, when the North Korean minister of national defense and a deputy commander of the Chinese army met with the chief of the Soviet military advisory group in the Chinese border city of Antung. The demands were that the USSR rush fresh supplies to Korea and that Stalin's navy be used to counter the Americans. The Soviets refused. There would be some continued Soviet resupply (by no means as much as Stalin could afford, however), but as to challenging the United States Navy at sea—*nyet*.[9]

Another measure came later that winter when the destroyer *Douglas H. Fox* took some North Korean prisoners. The captives gave valuable information about their minelaying activities. They also said that their own navy was a token force, had no duties to perform, and had transferred almost all its sailors to the army. None of the North Koreans knew of the existence of a single North Korean naval craft.

The blockade did not extend to Chinese ports. That was diplomatically risky, the allies would not go along, and besides, there was simply not enough Navy to undertake that gargantuan task. A possible alternative, using Chiang's Nationalist forces on Taiwan not only for land fighting but also for blockade duty, was the hottest of political hot potatoes. Among the leading American policymakers, both military and civil, only MacArthur wanted to pick up this potato—and that was not support enough.

So the blockade kept on, day after day, week after week, and the gunships kept shooting. They had helicopters now for spotting (*Helena* used the first one, in August 1950), but not every ship had them, and the destroyers, which expended about 90 percent of the bombardment ammo, rarely got a whirlybird to help them. Also, as every helicopter jock knew, the things did not naturally want to fly. They were very vulnerable to enemy fire, even of the popgun variety. In Wonsan harbor, for example, using them for spotting became so dicey that they were mostly reserved for minehunting or search and rescue.

Spotting planes were used occasionally, but there was the same problem of risk and, also, of communications, since some of the spotters were Army or USAF. Enemy anti-aircraft drove both props and jets (whose higher speeds and fuel-gulping propensities at lower altitudes made them marginal spotters anyway) to heights where their vision was borderline at best. There was never enough reliable spotting, but the Navy got better at the specialty, so did the other services, and ships' guns got more accurate as well.

The fire from the battlewagons was usually one barrel at a time, unlike the thunderous nine-gun salvos of World War II, which could set a fifty-thousand-ton ship sideways in the water. Villages and residential areas were off-limits, and the sixteen-inch batteries, in particular, were most carefully controlled.

By the time a single five-inch shell reached station off Korea, the cost of its arrival amounted to about $200. "Unless it did that much damage," said Rear Admiral John Gingrich, one of the serial commanders of Task Force 95, "we were hurting ourselves more than the enemy." Naval gunfire had to be target-tailored, the heavies against bridges and railway tracks and the small boys against enemy troop concentrations and repair parties. The tactics became so detailed that some ships specialized in firing specially fused shells *over* targets at the hills and embankments beyond, hoping to cause earth-slides that would block resupply arteries.[10]

The gunships also fired in support of the occasional UN offensives in this curious, dangerous conflict of stalemate and position. Even the ancient destroyer tender *Dixie* got into the act, setting a record of sorts by expending 204 rounds from her feeble five-inch guns against the beaches at Kosong. But most of the action came in the form of deliberate missions of interdiction. Operation COBRA, late in the war, featured *Missouri*, in plain sight of the "Communist coast" above the 40th parallel, blasting away at a railway tunnel on the beach, a scant 1500 yards away. This particular tunnel had been battered before, repaired before (usually within four days), destroyed before, and rebuilt before. Above the tunnel two helicopters hovered, reporting the results of each shell explosion from their grandstand seats. The whole scene had the unmistakable aura of the operating room. Mighty Mo was also protected by her destroyers and by an unseen screen of Task Force 77's fighters, operating over targets farther north, watching for wandering MiGs. On this operation one of the helos went down. Its three-man crew perished, either from enemy gunfire, crashing into the water, or exposure to the frigid sea, where the life expectancy in winter weather was one minute.

The tunnel collapsed. And every man on the operation knew that he would probably be back again.

Missouri and her two *Iowa*-class sisters, *New Jersey* and *Wisconsin*, endured this routine for two years, as did the cruisers and numerous small boys. On a single mission hundreds of projectiles could be hurled at North Korean targets (each sixteen-inch shell weighed over a ton), to the point where ship's caulking would burst from its seams and deck planking warp loose. "New records are being established every week," said the Navy proudly.

To what end was another question. Some American rounds pulverized not only civilians but also friendly forces; a cruiser shelling the island of Yo-do off North Korea's east coast inadvertently killed several intelligence agents stationed there. A few skippers would not accept call-fire requests from non-Navy spotters; in one case Navy reluctance to shoot had to be resolved by the commander of the Pacific Fleet himself, who happened to be steaming by aboard *New Jersey*. Operations could be, and were, stopped and started when new commanding officers rotated into position or when there were on-board glitches with the guns or fire control systems. And each captain had his own, sometimes highly individualized, shore bombardment techniques.

On top of this, the Navy could hurt itself, through carelessness, thoughtlessness, or the luck of the draw. On 21 April 1952 the eight-inch cruiser *Saint Paul* was plastering shore installations in Kojo, banging away throughout the day in a process that was by now well-rehearsed. Suddenly, at around 1600, a tremendous blast from turret one rattled the cruiser from stem to stern, making her lurch like a hooked marlin. Amid swirling, poisonous fumes, damage control teams pulled thirty bodies from the steel-ringed gun room, upper powder-handling station, and shell deck. All had died from suffocation.

A gunpowder fire of unknown origin had caused the Navy's greatest single loss of life in Korea.[11]

☆

Closer to shore, inside the hundred-fathom line and beneath the overarching fire of the gunships, the Navy's work went on as well. An increasing number of minesweepers busily ferreted through harbors and estuaries, doubly alert after the disaster at Wonsan. Most of them now had small craft or tugs as escorts and carried some kind of locator equipment. Helos, when available, were used effectively.

The sweeping, although conducted with mounting success, could not erase the embarrassment of Wonsan, where the world's most powerful navy, consummately prepared for triumph at sea, had been compelled to shut down operations and steam out into the Sea of Japan for a week, forced there by weapons dating back to 1904. Nor could the hardworking sweeps ever completely guarantee safety.

Mines struck suddenly, even when crews knew mines were around and when crews were at peak alert. The destroyers *Walke* and *Smalley* were hit off Hungnam, and thirty-five men were killed. In October 1952 the fleet ocean tug *Sarsi*, patrolling off the same hot spot, was sunk by a drifting mine, losing four men. *Sarsi* was the last of five American ships to go down from mine damage.

Theories abounded as to how best to confront the mines. One that went the rounds held that a ship making ten or more knots out on blue water was safe, because the bow waves would push a floating mine aside. The destroyer *Barton* unwillingly disproved this idea. Part of a task force steaming at fifteen knots ninety miles off Wonsan in September 1952 after dark, *Barton* ran into a mine that fractured her shell plating from keel to main deck, gutted the forward fireroom (all five engineers there were lost), and ripped open to the sea a gash forty feet long. She was lucky to survive.

Such tragedies reflected the simple truth: there was no quick fix in mine warfare—only patient, careful sweeping and constant, intense vigilance at sea. By the end, over a thousand mines would be swept from the edges of Korea. And the sweeps also went after fishermen entering blockaded waters (the "flycatcher patrol," such as the one *Sarsi* had been conducting when she ran afoul the mine); gathered mine intelligence; trained ROK minesweeping teams; and, always, studied their newly fashionable specialty. They even fired their single three-inch popguns at anything they thought deserving.

Far from glamorous duty, this, but minemen proudly displayed their motto: "Where the fleet goes, *we've been!*" They learned to spot magnetic mines and render them harmless; to respond quickly to emergency appeals from this or that port area; to use extreme caution around the lethal combination of magnetic, acoustic, and pressure mines, most of them lying silently on the bottom; and to go over a single area with their combs of cables and paravanes again and again ("check sweeps") until they were absolutely sure the zone was clear.

At times they operated alone, sometimes in line-of-bearing formations. A "shoestring navy," they came under enemy fire often and kept on working. Some of their crews became adept at rifle fire, drilling the occasional floater in hopes of a harmless detonation. Most of them were Reservists. "Some of 'em have never seen a minesweeper before," said Lieutenant Commander Wells Bill, operations officer of Mine Squadron 3, "but they get indoctrinated in a hurry."

Only 2 percent of Navymen off Korea rode the sweeps. When the end came, they accounted for 20 percent of the Navy dead.[12]

Even closer to shore lay the realm of the frogmen—the underwater demolition teams. Born in the early days of World War II to sneak ashore on potential landing beaches, the highly trained teams relied on stealth and surprise. Usually landed from submarines or high-speed transports like *Diachenko*, they boated or swam ashore, their only armor rubber suits, their only weapons sheath knives and small arms. Their main business was gathering intelligence, but they also destroyed fishing nets (fish were a staple of the North Korean diet, and the harvest was a million tons a year in peacetime), tangled with shore gun emplacements, blew up railroad tracks, and even had a go at trains and truck convoys.

They usually worked at night and, if they were lucky, got back to their mother vessel at dawn. Among the toughest men the Navy had, they were trained to be quick and self-reliant. The information they brought back not only meant improved targeting—their night work also saved American lives.

And finally, on the shore itself, landing raiding parties was a primary part of the interdiction function. These missions were usually conducted in the utmost secrecy by specially configured submarines. Subs had done this before—Makin and the Japanese homeland were two examples—but most of the Navy brass had considered the technique a sideshow. Not now, though, with intelligence information at a premium and interdiction the major seaborne strategy. One submarine officer "begged to be allowed to go to Tokyo and perhaps explore and find somebody who would be acceptable [*sic*] for using a submarine for anything." And "anything" was what came down.

Perch found herself outfitted with a huge, bulbous projection on her afterdeck (to house the motor skimmer for her commandos), and in September 1950 she landed a team of sixty-seven Royal Marines from the 41 Independent Commando Unit near Wonsan. *Perch* surfaced quietly at dusk, launched her raiders, and disappeared. Once ashore, the commandos took small-arms fire, sapped a railroad tunnel, got back in their launch, and returned to mother—minus one man. As *Perch* headed back across the Sea of Japan, she got a report from the destroyer *Maddox*, lurking offshore. *Maddox* had heard a muffled explosion; an unsuspecting engineer had taken his train into the tunnel and tripped the pressure detonator left under the tracks.

Not all such missions produced such gratifying results. But with no real enemy shipping to target, boats such as *Perch*, *Pickerel*, and *Catfish* were out and about, snooping the Formosa Strait, scanning the China coast, or monitoring Chinese traffic. The submariners were the same rollicking breed that had made life miserable for the Japanese. *Perch*'s skipper, a wild-eyed redhead named Bob Quinn, drank his way through Japanese hot baths and had enough left over to fine-tune raids like that with 41 Commando.

The boats provided intelligence for Gator ops, photographed selected objectives ashore, and landed raiders and patrolling parties. They were at Inchon, but most of their work, due to the hydrography, came off the east coast. They too developed into key players in the interdiction game, doing what they could with what they had.

Life at sea, for all elements of the Navy, developed into a certain routine in the stalemated war. "No comment" and "nothing to report" were standard entries in the war diaries and action reports. "We had learned to live with an unsatisfactory situation and still do a good job," remembered the skipper of the *Sumner*-class destroyer *De Haven*— "no matter how dull it was." The enemy got into routine, too: night-heckling aviators reported that drivers in truck convoys sometimes did not even bother to douse their lights when under attack.

When compared with the life their compatriots were living in the trenches and dugouts of Korea, sailors' duty gave them little to complain about. At sea there were no fleas, flies, or lice, no bunker life. There was little to be feared from enemy aircraft, submarines, or surface craft. But their existence was still irritating, uncomfortable, and unpleasant. At general quarters ships would button up, and the hot Korean summers turned the lower decks into a stifling steambath. Sound sleep was next to impossible; irregular gunfire would jar loose the glass wool insulation from the overheads, and few men could rest easy under the noise and the shower of glass fiber flakes. Winters brought the biting Siberian winds, sullen, rolling seas, and subzero temperatures. Underway refueling and replenishment often had to take place on a downwind course, regardless of the tactical situation. Ships' superstructures were frozen beneath tons of ice, sealing depth charges in their racks and locking gun mounts in azimuth.

—And the endless sieges went on: Wonsan, Hungnam, Songjin. At Wonsan the men aboard the ships could hear the enemy ashore scrambling about after dark, taking rails out of caves and laying tracks. The trains ran at night, and at about 0400 the tracks would be taken up and put back in the caves. Every once in a while, among the tens of thousands of shipboard rounds hurled off into the darkness, one would hit some munitions, bringing a welcome explosion. And the next night, the trains would run again.

The on-scene commander there bore the bitterly honorific title "Mayor of Wonsan," a mocking reflection of what the war had become. Warships patrolled their sectors, day after day after day. Minesweepers sifted through areas until each drop of water seemed to have a personality. Men were dying—157 sailors by the middle of 1951—but tedium had settled in, blanketing a war that now was not to be "won," but negotiated.[13]

Which meant that Korea had become *political* in the most meaningful sense and that the fundamental decisions affecting the course of the war— on land, on the gunline, against the shore, or out where the carriers roamed—would be made in Washington.

CHAPTER ELEVEN

TOPSIDE II

——— ☆ ———

H arry Truman could have done without Korea. By mid-1950 Red-baiting hysteria in the United States was in full swing, spearheaded by the smear tactics of Senator Joseph McCarthy of Wisconsin. The State Department was conducting more in-house investigations than diplomacy. A form of national paranoia concerning "communism" was settling in again—there had been an earlier Red scare after World War I.

To add to the president's troubles, the economy still had not shaken down completely from the Second World War. Domestically, there was much to command Truman's attention, what with big industry dissatisfied, wage and price controls looming again, and witchhunts for pinkos and comsymps of every shade. And Korea would not go away.

Until December 1950 Douglas MacArthur's rosy vision of the Korean situation seemed to Washington to be the correct one, and Korea only one among many pressing international problems. But as UN forces reeled before the Red Chinese onslaught, the pressures on Truman began to mount. Nobody wanted to cut and run; the question was how much American power should be committed to the remote peninsula, and to what end.

As the ground war became positional and neither side made more than local, limited efforts to change the conflict's shape, Korea became Truman's major headache. By mid-June 1951, with the front stabilized along a general line from Munsan to Kosong, the United States had chosen the route of truce talks. America's dominant firepower and mobility, as well as the flexibility and quick-strike capacity of the Navy, were no longer to be used—except in the narrowest and most restricted sense.

Actual armistice discussions began on 8 July. Matthew Ridgway, now in command, wanted a negotiator "who can sit for six hours and neither blink nor think of taking a pee." With Turner Joy as chief of the UN delegation, he had his man. Arleigh Burke was the Navy's representative. The Communists shortly drove Joy half mad with their bickering and obtuse behavior. The admiral said, as an analogy, that Americans arranging a baseball game might debate the place the game was to be played, the starting time, and the umpires. The Communist agenda, on the other hand, would decide that the game would be played in Shanghai, at night, with Chinese as umpires. (At some meetings, one of the Chinese would refer to Joy as the "Senior Delegate . . . whose name I have forgotten.") Joy eventually riposted that the Communists would "grow old sitting at the table" before there were any more UN concessions. He would later write a splenetic book (*How Communists Negotiate*) about his experiences—which may have hastened his early death in 1956.

As the talks droned on, the Navy kept up its shore bombardment, coastal interdiction, air strikes, and minesweeping. But none of these tasks were dedicated now to *victory*. Harry Truman was trying to negotiate a truce while continuing to fight for advantage, and the United States had not done this since the far different circumstances of the War of 1812. Americans conditioned by two triumphant world wars were increasingly impatient with the inconclusive results and the mounting casualty lists.

Truman, never long on temper anyway, had his dander up months before the talks began, and the main reason was MacArthur. The two men simply were not made for each other (the argument could be made that the Jovian general was not made for anybody), and by the beginning of 1951 most of the key people in Washington had realized that the Last Shogun had completely misread both the strategic and tactical situations in Korea.

Naturally, MacArthur did not agree. Political policy was to blame for the disasters of the Chinese offensive, said he. Chiang's Nationalists should be thrown into the breach. The war should be escalated and fought to the finish. Now.

The president was not about to take these recommendations, and neither were most of his advisers. For one thing, the UN allies favored a negotiated settlement; all had far weaker economies than the United States, and all had bigger fish to fry at home. For another, whichever way he turned on the Korean issue, Truman would enrage a significant body of the electorate. The war on the peninsula had become part of the Red-baiting climate.

The strain showed. The president grew more snappish, more stubbornly determined than ever to reach a "reasonable" settlement that guaranteed an independent South Korea and protected its future. Truman had always had a tendency to say exactly what he thought. Back in September 1950, around the time of Inchon, his long and rather petty distrust of the Marines and Navy admirals had surfaced, in response to a letter from a congressman proposing that the Corps be enlarged. "For your information, the Marine Corps is the Navy's police force and as long as I am President that is what it will remain," Truman fired back. "They have a propaganda machine that is almost equal to Stalin's."

The congressman naturally released the letter to the press. That crack (which was probably not that far from the truth) brought Truman the antipathy of Marines worldwide and forced a public apology to General Clifton Cates, commandant of the Marine Corps. A later dig about publicity-seeking Leathernecks brought him a public rebuke from a group of wounded Marines in Yokosuka. And the press would not let up on him over Korea.

Truman was the first American leader to try to fight a limited war, and he was having a stormy time. Washington seethed with political quarreling and internecine factional struggle; agriculture, business, labor, and consumer organizations were all grappling for interest-group shares in the postwar economy. In the midst of a conflict growing more unpopular by the day, Truman was being forced back in the direction of politically suicidal controls over wages, prices, rents, production, and credit.

The president's penchant for cronyism was coming home to roost; influence peddlers were all over the place. There was no great graft, but the pattern was clear, at least to the administration's critics. And to make his job even harder, Truman had already announced that he would not run again in 1952.

By early 1951, well before the truce talks began, mail was already pouring into Congress by the bushel, constituents asking why their sons had to stay in Korea. The president's popularity, measured by the newfangled (and widely believed) public opinion polls, was in free-fall. Truman and MacArthur, as the administration sought to place a political hammerlock on Korean strategy and tactics, were headed for a showdown.[1]

On top of all this, two of Truman's top civilians in the Defense Department had proved to be disasters.

☆

The Pentagon, by virtue of its corporate mentality, could never be comfortable with a war of stalemate and attrition. Military men were obviously concerned for the operational safety of their forces. They were also well aware of Truman's domestic problems, specifically those stemming from the budget and public opinion. And they were beginning to learn that their roles now included explaining to the politicians the *limitations* inherent in the military aspects of the country's foreign policy.

Admirals and generals worried about the safety of UN forces if they could not attack enemy "sanctuaries" in North Korea or Manchuria. They worried that a war of attrition near the 38th parallel would weaken the ability to defend Japan, the linchpin of America's Far Eastern policy. And they worried that an extended campaign of attrition would turn an already war-weary and confused public even more against the conflict.

The Pentagon civilian in charge at the outset, Secretary of Defense Louis Johnson, quickly became an impossible burden for Truman. David Lilienthal, chairman of the Atomic Energy Commission, had correctly predicted that Johnson's appointment would produce a "terrible strain for democracy." Moreover, Lilienthal (and many others) detested the "overfed, cigar-chewing, red faced" Johnson cronies, the kind of "vultures" seen "hanging around the courthouse." Johnson himself could not stop his crass bureaucratic jockeying for position and deeply resented the president's close working relationship with and deep esteem for Secretary of State Dean Acheson. Ham-handed public relations had become the norm for him. He was "well on his way to a new world record for enraging people."

His theatrics over trimming the military budget did not help in certain quarters (namely, those parts of the Pentagon where people wore uniforms) when Korea came along. To be sure, the budgetary slicing was Truman's policy, but Johnson had wielded the knives with relish, "more Catholic than the pope in doing it"—and he had carved away with maximum noise and minimum tact. Above all, he wanted the largest slice of the influence pie for himself. "Louis is ambitious," FDR's secretary of war, Harry Woodring, had once observed. "With him it's sort of like being oversexed."

By early September 1950, as MacArthur was staging for Operation CHROMITE, Truman had had enough: he told Johnson that he would have to resign. As of 12 September, there was still no letter of resignation forthcoming. Truman, who had already talked to George Marshall about coming out of retirement to head the Defense Department and had won Marshall's assent, wanted Johnson to recommend Marshall as his successor. Following a Cabinet meeting that day, Johnson trailed Truman into the Oval Office and begged not to be fired. Then he handed Truman the resignation letter drafted by the presidential staff—unsigned. "Louis, you haven't signed this," Truman said in his flat, nasal Missouri drawl. "Sign it." Like most bullies, Johnson broke down at this ultimate confrontation. Weeping, he knew that his fevered dreams of national political leadership were at an end. "You are ruining me," he cried—but he signed.

Congress had to pass special legislation to accommodate Marshall; a military man, by law, could not serve as secretary of defense until he had been away from active duty for ten years. Only the right-wing lunatics opposed the nomination. Senator William Jenner of Indiana gained an immortality of sorts by charging that Marshall "is not only willing, he is eager to play the role of a front man for traitors."

George Catlett Marshall was aging and tired, a man richly deserving of his honors, the thanks of the nation, and a rest justly earned. But his métier was *service*, and although both he and the president knew that his tenure would be a stopgap (he promised Truman one year), he came to serve once more, a man who could not be cowed, dictated to, or pushed around—not even by Douglas MacArthur.[2]

Francis Matthews, on the other hand, was rudderless; with the axing of Johnson, the secretary of the Navy had lost his sponsor. Until Korea, he had marched obediently to his boss's drum, curtailing naval functions right and left. Now he had to reverse course and direct an around-the-clock naval expansion. Out of mothballs came the ships; $446 million was suddenly available for naval aviation; Truman signed Representative Carl Vinson's bill for creating an "atomic navy;" and Matthews disclosed that work on guided missiles aboard the converted seaplane tender *Norton Sound* had passed beyond the experimental stage.

Rowboat, plowing along as best he could in a crisis atmosphere for which he was completely ill-suited, reversed course too well. He found a new rudder, anticommunism, and with this credo he steered directly onto the shoals. He never quite grasped the notion of limited war, nor did he get in line with Truman's desire to negotiate the allies out of Korea.

The climax began even before Johnson's firing, during an address at a celebration marking the sesquicentennial of the Boston Naval Shipyard. There, Rowboat got carried away about Korea, the Communist menace, and rearmament and declared that Washington should take the gloves off and consider "instituting . . . a war of aggression for peace." This was too much; Truman ordered such talk stopped, and Matthews's days on board were numbered.

Dean Acheson had felt that Louis Johnson, with whom he had worked closely on such matters as the drafting of NSC 68, was mentally ill. (Several years later Johnson underwent an operation for a brain malady that proved fatal.) Matthews had no such excuse. He was trying, paddling hard in heavy surf, but he was in way beyond his depth.

Robert Lovett was brought in as Marshall's deputy, clearly in the line of succession to be secretary of defense. Matthews now had no friends in court, no allies among the admirals. The aviators, in particular, were eager to shove him over the side in favor of his under secretary, Dan Kimball. With Truman's declaration of a national emergency on 16 December 1950, Matthews got new powers: he could recall retirees to active duty; authorize contracts without calling for bids; and disregard statutory limits on numbers of flag officers.

—But he had the trust of no one who counted, and as the months passed into 1951 he became even more of a nonentity. The only problem he presented was how to ditch him with dignity. The traditional solution, a lower-grade ambassadorship, was finally found in June, when the Roman Catholic layman was assigned to the embassy in Dublin (he had only fifteen months to live). Kimball was named his successor.

Dan Kimball was from St. Louis. He had won his wings during World War I as a hell-for-leather Army air cadet, training in the same class as another free spirit, Jimmy Doolittle. In 1920 he went to work for the General Tire Company, where he stayed for twenty-nine years. He evolved into a crack manager and industrial innovator; during World War II he headed the development program for jet-assisted-takeoff devices at General Tire's manufacturing subsidiary, the Aerojet Engineering Corporation.

In 1949 John Sullivan brought Kimball to Washington as assistant secretary for air. He almost resigned with Sullivan in the flail over *United States*, but Johnson persuaded him to remain. When Matthews replaced Sullivan, Kimball moved up to under secretary. He was a moderate, a conciliator; he got along with almost everyone, a rather novel attribute in the highly charged Pentagon atmosphere of 1949–1950.

Kimball created intimate working relationships within the Navy Department and made part of his business personally meeting and getting to know many of his counterparts in other agencies. This process was smoothed by Kimball's bonhomie: he was a club-car American, a backslapper, jokester, friendly drinker, and teller of tales. For these reasons some naval officers, such as the occasionally acerbic submariner Slade Cutter, saw him as "just a political hack." If he was, he still had undoubted organizational skills and carried bigger caliber than the unmourned Rowboat.

The new secretary's fundamental tasks were to support the Navy in Korea, strengthen the fleet to meet problems elsewhere in the world, and do all this without fundamentally dislocating the national economy or adding more weight to the presidential burden. These chores he attacked with considerable energy and success. Now, with Marshall and Kimball in place, Truman could rest easier about his naval flanks.[3]

Unfortunately, among Kimball's first duties was a sad one: he had to recommend a successor for a great chief of naval operations.

☆

"Ask Forrest" had been the word around Chester Nimitz's Pacific Fleet headquarters during World War II whenever a difficult problem had come up. Find Nimitz's deputy—"ask Forrest."

That was the way things had always gone for Forrest Percival Sherman: he *knew*. Somehow, his life shook out as if he had *known* from the beginning. His roots gripped deeply in his New England heritage; his mother was a descendant of John and Priscilla Alden. Forrest was born in Merrimack, New Hampshire, in 1896, one of six children. His dad, a salesman of school textbooks, soon moved the family to Melrose, Massachusetts, where the boy grew up in a world of books and constant reading.

In 1904 he was taken for a visit aboard the spanking new battleship *Kentucky*. Fascinated by her gleaming brightworks, her big guns, her seemingly irresistible *power*, he was from that point in thrall to the idea of a naval career.

He became familiar with the sea. Model shipbuilding was a much-loved hobby. He went sailing in Buzzard's Bay with his grandfather, a retired New Bedford whaling skipper. One day, far out in the bay, the old man died of a heart attack. Twelve-year-old Forrest, unrattled, calmly placed his grandfather's body in the bilges, lowered the catboat's ensign to half-mast, and sailed safely home.

Even as a teenager Sherman's consuming ambition, tireless energy, and exceptional skills were obvious, all bending toward the Navy. In 1914 he entered the Naval Academy, following two precocious years at the Massachusetts Institute of Technology. His fellow mids regarded him as cold and aloof, but everyone recognized his unusual promise. He not only tackled problems, he *mined* them, turned them inside out, mastered every detail. "You can't make good marks if you're popular," he told his sister—and Forrest Sherman made good marks. Both his astounding intellect and his impeccable manners set him apart. He preferred horsemanship and fencing to the sweatier athletic pursuits.

"He wasn't really cocky," remembered his roommate, "he just wasn't uncertain." Sherman was a walking encyclopedia of naval history; during the dining-hall come-arounds from the upperclassmen he always had the answers. They finally ordered him under the table, where he patiently sat, without his dinner, quietly enduring his hazing. On frosty nights he was shoved under a cold shower, his bedding tossed in after him.

Sherman stood the gaff and came back for more. The Academy stressed rote recital in place of actual thinking, and the youth from Massachusetts could do both. His instructors would respond to a difficult question in class by having him stand up and reel off the answer, invariably correct. These stunts should have marked him like Cain, but he was simply too good, too talented, and he kept right on going.

A six-footer with ruddy complexion and regular, handsome features, "Fuzz" Sherman (the nickname, taken from his initials, F.S., would not, unlike most other Academy monikers, take hold) was ticketed early for ultimate success. "Above all, Sherman knows his job," said his *Lucky Bag* (the Academy yearbook). "When he is given a thing to do he finds out all there is to be found out about it and the job is well done." He led his class in ordnance and gunnery. When the Class of 1918 was graduated a year early due to America's entry into World War I, there was Fuzz Sherman, second out of 199.

Off he went, to the gunboat *Nashville*, escorting convoys and patrolling for submarines in the Mediterranean. Then to the destroyer *Murray*, in the Atlantic. He came to the attention of Rear Admiral Newton McCully, Jr., who commanded the postwar Control Force of escort ships in that ocean and who took him on in 1921 as his flag lieutenant—an exceptionally responsible billet for one so young.

Meanwhile, Sherman had seen the future: not gunboats and destroyers, but naval air. In December 1922 he won his wings, and his career took off. He made himself into a skilled aviator, so good that he was invited back to Pensacola in 1924 as a flight instructor. Along the way he married (1923) and contributed several essays on education to the *Proceedings* of the Naval Institute. He always liked the intellectual side of his career, and in 1930 he came back to the Academy for a two-year tour teaching flight tactics. Forrest Sherman was on the road up.

The obvious seagoing choices for him lay aboard the big carriers, the two thirty-three-thousand-ton battle cruiser hulls that the Washington Disarmament Conference had allowed the United States to convert to the largest flattops in the world. He was part of *Lexington*'s precommissioning detail in 1927 and then reported to his squadron aboard *Saratoga,* where he commanded Scouting 2 and the famous Fighting 1. He won a Navy E—personally—for dive-bombing and fighter gunnery in 1932. Then he served as flag secretary to the fleet's carrier commander, the demanding Rear Admiral Joseph Mason ("Bull") Reeves—the nickname was no mistake—and to Reeves's relief, courtly Harry Yarnell.

A tour heading the aviation ordnance section of the Bureau of Aeronautics followed, and in 1936 Sherman returned to the carrier fleet as navigator of tiny *Ranger.* By now a commander with a solid reputation for staff work, he served Claude Bloch as aviation officer during the admiral's successive tours as commander of the Battle Force and of the U.S. Fleet. He continued to read constantly—mostly economics and world politics (he liked the big issues)—and the scholarly articles kept coming.

Reeves, Yarnell, and Bloch all praised him to the skies—as a bright, alert master of detail—the man who *got things done.* Admiral Harold Stark, the chief of naval operations, brought him into his War Plans Division, where Sherman's tact and moderating skills impressed everyone, especially during his concurrent service on the Canadian–United States Joint Board of Defense. His immediate boss, the irascible Richmond Kelly Turner, was an impossible man to please. And Turner, who labeled his assistant the "box of brains," said, "He was a greased-lightning operator . . . always had a plan—never left anything to chance."[4]

With Pearl Harbor, Sherman was assigned to the Joint War Plans Committee, where he got his first taste of wartime joint operations. Upped to captain, he immediately angled for a slot where the action was: carrier command. In May 1942, as the Japanese were still running wild across the Pacific, he took charge of *Wasp.* Characteristically, he immediately began to work out a flight plan for his air group, one that became a model for all American carriers.

Wasp covered the Guadalcanal landings and, under Sherman, developed into a taut, efficient, happy ship. But her time was short. On 15 September, three hundred miles southeast of Guadalcanal, a Japanese submarine hit her with three torpedoes. Amid an inferno of smoke and exploding ammunition, her skipper maneuvered his dying carrier so the flames blew away from her hull, backed her stern clear of the flaming, gasoline-streaked water, and finally, reluctantly, gave the order to abandon ship.

He was the last man off, burned and badly shaken up by depth-charge concussions once he was in the water. He lost 193 men, but his actions had helped save 2054—and he had won the Navy Cross.

No captain liked to lose his ship, and this was a failure that Sherman, ever the self-censorious perfectionist, felt could have crushed his career. He was rescued by Admiral Jack Towers, the commander of Nimitz's air arm, who needed a chief of staff. In that billet Sherman's diplomacy was decisive in moderating differences between Nimitz and Towers, who was acutely sensitive about slights to naval aviation, imagined and real, and who was a thorny cuss in the best of times. As the fleet shifted from the strategic defensive to the offensive, Sherman navigated a desk in Pearl Harbor, co-ordinating the deployment of the rapidly swelling numbers of naval aircraft throughout the Pacific.

In November 1943, acting on Towers's advice, Nimitz transferred Sherman to his own staff as assistant for plans, with the rank of rear admiral. In March 1944 he became deputy chief of staff for plans and head of the fleet's war plans division. The two men—the soft-spoken Texan running the Pacific war and his omniscient, pragmatic assistant—developed into a perfect team. "Forrest Sherman . . . really directed the war in the Pacific," said another member of Nimitz's staff, G. Willing ("Wing") Pepper.

Sherman, in fact, was Nimitz's alter ego. Often, the two would disappear together into the fleet's map room, and there, surrounded by plots showing the far-flung American naval units at work, they would talk, think, pore over the charts and bounce ideas off each other. Sherman "had ideas just bubbling out . . . very sound," observed a subordinate. "Sherman never hesitated when things looked worse," his chief remarked. "He's a realist without being a pessimist." He often represented his boss at Washington briefings, where Ernie King, a man of little patience and less politeness, gave him a better hearing than most. Sherman also contributed materially to Pacific grand strategy, recommending the bypassing of key Japanese strongholds like Maloelap and Wotje.

He was the nonpareil problem solver—"ask Forrest." He became Nimitz's man even as he honed his razor-edged ambition; as a result he got into argument after argument with Jack Towers, unafraid to contradict a legend in naval aviation. And at war's end, aboard *Missouri* in Tokyo Bay, Nimitz summoned him, along with Bill Halsey, to stand at his side to accept the Japanese surrender.[5]

With his considerable staff experience, Sherman was soon up to his neck in the troubles of the postwar Navy. Nimitz got him promoted to vice admiral and another desk, deputy chief of naval operations for operations (OP-03). There, he became deeply involved in national military policies and interservice politics. Sherman believed that the Air Force and Navy should share the strategic bombing role. His talks with a Truman adviser, Clark Clifford, and with Major General Lauris Norstad of the Army Air Force led directly to the National Security Act of 1947.

He was always the diplomat—suave, charming, cooperative, and conciliatory. He was not a bitter-ender on naval air power, like Arthur Radford, John Crommelin, and others, but instead bore steadily from within, fostering the development of a naval atomic capability with the new AJ-1 Savage bomber. Such maneuverings did nothing to improve his popularity among his fellow flag officers—most felt he was too much the politico, too much the compromiser—but he was still the Fuzz Sherman of his Academy days, setting his sights and calmly, ceaselessly moving to achieve his institutional and personal goals.

Sherman was remarkably uninterested in personal popularity, although he had been popular enough aboard *Wasp*, his only at-sea command. He sailored on with integrity, intelligence, and loyalty, and he survived the heavy seas that washed overboard men like Louie Denfeld, Gerry Bogan, and Spike Blandy. In 1946 he drafted the first postwar plan to envision a superpower conflict between the United States and the Soviet Union. He contributed to the Truman Doctrine and to plans for aid to Turkey and Greece the next year.

Denfeld sent him to the Med in 1947, and there, in command of what would become the Sixth Fleet, he was all over the place. Under him, the fleet exercised in monthly tactical problems. He drew up strict rules for comportment ashore and, for the most part, they were followed. As the Greek civil war flared, his units supported the royalist regime in Athens against a Communist-led insurrection; they helped stiffen Turkish resolve against continuous, historic Soviet pressure; and his ships hopscotched up and down the Tyrrhenian and Adriatic coasts to convince the Italians that the United States was fully ready and able to defend Europe's southern flank.

Thus Sherman was remote from Washington when the rebellion in gold braid erupted. He was far from a political innocent; his fingerprints were all over the unification formula, and he knew that many of his brother officers resented him for that. He also knew that political tar babies like the rebellion could soil an ambitious officer beyond recovery. Still, he could not resist flying back to Washington, wanting to testify at the October hearings. Johnson and Matthews, however, talked him out of appearing.

Back with his command, he walked on eggs. When Representative W. Sterling Cole, the ranking Republican on Vinson's committee, sent an open telegram to every admiral asking for views on Denfeld's testimony, Sherman replied that he agreed with some parts, disagreed with others, and was not in the know about much of what had gone on. He supported Denfeld and the rest when they called for naval preparedness.

This was not exactly "damn the torpedoes" behavior, but his tact produced results. Johnson proposed him to Truman as Denfeld's relief. Truman wanted Nimitz, and when the fleet admiral declined, the choice came down to Sherman or Close In Conolly. Conolly had played a bit of politics during the unification dispute, and Truman was tired of being burned in that particular area.

So on 2 November 1949, three days after his fifty-third birthday, smuggled into Washington incognito in civvies, the box of brains became chief of naval operations. He was the youngest chief ever appointed, the first career aviator to hold the post. Forrest Sherman had arrived.

☆

He faced a hostile officer corps. Many of the senior officers had laid their careers on the line to resist what they saw as service integration, and they viewed him as a naval version of the Artful Dodger, too polished and too slick by half. ("Forrest had always tried to put a banana peel under both of us," said Mick Carney, speaking of himself and Radford.) As Sherman was sworn in, there was a stony silence among his uniformed audience; many of the admirals pointedly went down to applaud Denfeld as he left the Pengaton.

Even some of his own, the naval aviators, held him in disdain. A crack he had made in the Sixth Fleet about its greatest single deficiency being carrier captains had made the rounds. Others were repelled by his aloofness, his cold, calculating style. Clifton Cates, who later warmed a bit to him, thought he was thumbs-down on the Marines.

The new chief read these attitudes with sadness. "I have always set my sights high," he told Towers, but "the developments which preceded my assignment were not to my liking and the assignment at this time was not of my seeking" (which was true).

Nevertheless, he was the man in charge, and he began to get down to business. He soothed Johnson and Matthews to prevent any further beheadings of obstreperous admirals. He returned Crommelin to duty, but when that firebrand refused to shut up, Sherman got him a tombstone promotion to rear admiral to pave his way into retirement. As for Arleigh Burke, both Johnson and Matthews wanted a public execution, and both refused to endorse his selection for flag rank. Burke was as popular within the Navy as Sherman was not; the chief appealed directly to Truman, and Burke was saved, soon to be vectored to Korea to work with Turner Joy.

Sherman seemed to be moving on every front at once, "always about three years ahead of the others." Ties with Vinson, who had begun to wander off the naval reservation in the direction of the Air Force during the rebellion, were reestablished. Sherman took to working the cloakrooms like a ward heeler, cultivating pivotal senators like Virginia's Harry Byrd; Norfolk's shipbuilding and repair facilities flourished. He resurrected the custom of uniformed naval personnel in Washington. ("The uniform carries considerable prestige on Capitol Hill.") He saved *Missouri* from mothballs by the simple expedient of making her a training ship for the Naval Academy, and when her big guns were needed off Korea, she was there. He wheedled $78 million from a pinchpenny Congress for an expended antisubmarine warfare program, and he struggled to beef up the Pacific Fleet, which had been cut beyond the bone.

Within six months of taking office, Sherman had begun to steer the Navy out of the slough of despond. While loyal to the unification concept (he, after all, had been one of its few naval champions), he relentlessly

pushed the Navy's causes whenever he could. He disbanded OP-23—
Burke's outfit had become much too controversial, a lightning rod for Navy
opponents—but he rescued Burke. Naval public relations did not disappear;
instead, under Sherman the service began to evolve a glossy polish and
approbative public image that came to rely on the most advanced Madison
Avenue techniques. He chose Lynde McCormick, a submariner, as his vice
chief, a clear signal that the Blackshoes no longer dominated the fleet.[6]

He locked the Navy into place in national strategy, projecting an early
offensive against Soviet shipping, naval and air forces, bases, and installations, along with blockading and mining (JCS 1844/46). He tried to prepare
the service for over-the-pole Arctic operations. After examining the plan to
reinforce Europe (OFFTACKLE), Sherman went about strengthening the
Mediterranean flank. As for the Pacific, only his personal intervention made
sure that Rip Struble had at least one carrier task force when the need arose.

And more: Sherman sneaked a portion of the budget increase in the
spring of 1950 into the development of a nuclear submarine (which would
become *Nautilus*). On 25 April, at his request, Congress authorized construction of the supercarrier Johnson had canceled only a year before. Meanwhile, the chief traveled. He personally inspected all his major commands,
asked probing questions of admirals, seamen, and everyone in between, and
expected and got written follow-ups from his discussants. Like Scarlett
O'Hara, he was fond of saying "tomorrow is another day" if he caught his
foot in a bight; that simply meant another tack was needed. He brought in
new, younger blood to replace the superannuated commanders of World
War II, men like himself, eager to shape the future. Always he worked
incredibly long hours, twenty a day at times—driving, driving, driving.

Omar Bradley became an admirer, calling Sherman "one of the most
impressive military officers I ever met . . . urbane, intellectual, diplomatic
and smart as a whip." Of all the Navy's admirals, Sherman probably most
deserved Bradley's "Fancy Dan" tag—a false rumor went around that he
was given to formally dining with his wife each evening—but he made his
savoir faire work for him, and for the Navy. Marc Mitscher had considered
him "too damn brilliant," and Captain Everett ("Swede") Hazlett, who
corresponded regularly with his Kansas childhood buddy Dwight Eisenhower, called Sherman "sarcastic, a bit of a snob, and hard to know." Close
In Conolly, his formidable rival, portrayed him as a "compromiser and
temporizer."

All of this, in perspective, was true enough, but he was the man the
Navy needed. In the months before Korea, in his quiet, steady, yet hyperkinetic way, he delivered a bravura performance. None less than Arthur
Radford told Sherman that the chief "was about the only man who could
handle the job at that time," and Raddy, like his pal Mick Carney, was not
one to curry favor or deliver the easy pat on the back.[7]

—Simply bravura.

☆

Then came Korea. Forrest Sherman, moving from strength now, oversaw the renaissance of the Navy and Marine Corps. He stressed the central role of the carrier task force, sent Eddie Ewen forth to take charge of Task Force 77, made sure Radford, out in Pearl Harbor, got the quickest possible reinforcement of flattops. His goal amid the crisis was a truly balanced fleet: not only the carriers but also antisubmarine vessels, missile ships, and submarines. He jollied Congress into increasing the Navy's manpower and got Truman's authorization, in July 1951, for a major shipbuilding and modernization program. He worked hand-in-glove with both Marshall and Bradley, and both came to respect him deeply.

Frank and articulate as always, he was no less the smoothie when he had to be. ("Since I joined the Joint Chiefs of Staff I have been gratified at the spirit of co-operation that I have received and the willingness and obvious intention of the members to meet the Navy more than half way.") But where Korea was concerned, he was a hard-line, anti-Communist hawk.

On 24 August 1950 he and Lightning Joe Collins conferred with MacArthur in Tokyo about Inchon and paid a quick visit to the peninsula. The problems surrounding the landing worried him, but he got on board and applauded the general's success. After some initial unease, Sherman always felt that the decision to intervene in Korea had been "sound," and he quickly suggested the idea of a naval blockade to Truman. In fact, he liked the blockade idea so well that he was soon calling for a blockade of Red China, the lifting of restraints on Chiang Kai-shek, intermittent aerial reconnaissance of Manchuria and the Chinese coast, and "logistical support" for anti-Communist guerrillas operating on the Chinese mainland—all MacArthur ideas. Truman had to rein him in.[8]

And he responded, because he was no Douglas MacArthur. The general wanted the Seventh Fleet, deeply committed around Korea, to cruise off the Chinese coast in a "show of force," and Sherman knew (as he should have known concerning the blockade idea) that he did not have the men and guns for the job—not while supporting Korea at the same time.

He followed MacArthur's line for a time because he believed in victory in Korea and because he knew the Navy had a role to play. He worried over the naval support as his ships, during the push north, came dangerously close to Vladivostok. But he never, like MacArthur, saw some kind of anti-Communist Armageddon taking place on the peninsula. (In fact, his focus remained Europe-centered.) From the strategic viewpoint, Sherman did not like Korea one bit. At last, after MacArthur had disobeyed presidential orders for the final time by unilaterally offering to confer with the enemy, Bradley assembled the Joint Chiefs on 8 April 1951.

The chairman paraded them before Marshall, and the sorry record of MacArthur's repeated acts of insubordination was reviewed. All of them, including Sherman, said that from a military viewpoint the general should be relieved. MacArthur was all-too-obviously not in harness with the official policy of limiting the war in Korea; he had violated a Truman directive that all officials obtain clearance of public statements on military or foreign policy, not once but continually; and he had not submitted, as constitutionally mandated, to civilian control. In fact, Douglas MacArthur had for almost a year waged war in Korea largely on his own hook, not only out on a limb but off the limb, suspended there by his early successes, his towering reputation, and his overpowering personality.

And now the end had come. Marshall, Bradley, and the Joint Chiefs— all were influential, although not the only, voices leading to Truman's decision. The relief of MacArthur by Matthew Ridgway was messy—in fact a public-relations disaster for the administration—but the thing had to be done, and Sherman played his part. He probably would have signed on to the mock schedule prepared by Truman's staff for the general's homecoming:

1230	Wades ashore from snorkel submarine
1231	Navy band plays "Sparrow in the Treetop" and "I'll Be Glad When You're Dead You Rascal You"
1240	Parade to the Capitol with General MacArthur riding an elephant
1247	Beheading of General Vaughan at the rotunda
1300	General MacArthur addresses members of Congress
1330–1349	Applause for General MacArthur
1350	Burning of the Constitution
1355	Lynching of Secretary Acheson
1400	21-atomic-bomb salute
1430	Nude DARs leap from Washington Monument
1500	Basket lunch, Monument Grounds

Douglas MacArthur did indeed ride the elephant, making speeches before carefully selected (and increasingly bored) conservative Republican audiences in the 1952 campaign and serving mostly the Taft wing of the GOP. But he faded away quickly, more quickly, certainly, than he would have thought possible after his memorable departure oration before a joint session of Congress.

—And Korea remained, a gnawing, major problem, by no means one of only MacArthur's making but one concerning which all American military leaders, no matter how reluctantly, now conceded would be fought with limited means, toward limited goals.

☆

Korea, however, was *not* Sherman's major concern. He fully accepted the policy of Communist containment, but on a *worldwide* basis. This meant deploying the fleet forward and increasing naval aid to the allies. Specifically, the policy meant more support of the European theater and beefing up the North Atlantic Treaty Organization. In this regard, the British had to be ushered as gently as possible into their new role as a subordinate seapower, and strategically significant fascist Spain, positioned at the crucial corner where the Atlantic became the Mediterranean, had to be neutralized or won over.

The Soviet navy bothered Sherman, but not overmuch. He told Bernard Baruch that Soviet naval policy made him yearn for a stronger Pacific Fleet, but "I still feel that Germany is the more critical spot, even though not so much a naval problem." The European Theater, then, was primary for Sherman, as for all of Truman's top planners, although the Navy would clearly play a subordinate role there.[9]

Assuaging the British was a problem. At the time of Pearl Harbor, Great Britain had mounted a navy of 363 combat ships and 300,000 men, and the Americans had 339 combatants and 353,000 men—the two fleets were at rough parity. The war exhausted Britain but gave new strength to the United States. Ten years after Pearl, the bell had tolled: Korea and anticommunism had swollen America's Navy from its immediate postwar doldrums to 958 combatants and 705,000 men. Britain, even though remobilized to a certain extent for Korea, was on an economic shoestring. The Royal Navy had only 175 combatants and 150,000 men—a fifth of the American strength.

In one area alone, weapons development, Sherman was spending $500 million in the single year 1951, about as much as the entire annual budget of the British admirals. The Americans were expending at approximately *twelve times* the British rate for building future naval strength. And the gap was widening.

Their growing inferiority made the British doubly sensitive to issues such as command questions in NATO and the Mediterranean. Reluctantly, they accepted the fact that the supreme naval command in NATO would go to an American admiral. (The acronym SACLANT—Supreme Allied Commander Atlantic—came later, and would be another hat worn by the commander in chief, Atlantic Fleet.) After some bitter negotiation, the ocean was chopped into portions, with the eastern Atlantic the bailiwick of the boss of the British Home Fleet, a British admiral as his deputy, and a separate command for the English Channel, also held by the British.

In the Mediterranean the Americans wanted Sixth Fleet's carriers and Gators firmly in support of the imagined land battle on NATO's southern flank. As in British home waters, history weighed heavily with the Royal Navy here; its admirals were set on maintaining their seagoing communications under their own command throughout the entire stretch of sea. Eventually this clash of concepts led to wrangling between the American-led Southern European Command (CINCSOUTH) in Naples and the British command on Malta. Mick Carney was running the show in Naples, and his feisty personality did little to improve matters.

Finally, in December 1952, the quarrel was resolved in an uneasy compromise. A new NATO headquarters became operational on Malta, with the British fleet commander serving as NATO commander for the Mediterranean, responsible to the Supreme Allied Commander Europe for all naval operations *except* those of the Sixth Fleet. This was hardly a unified command, but the best that could be stapled together under the circumstances.

Then there was that Spanish corner. The Americans wanted a major naval command set up in Lisbon under one of their own. The British, who already had a flag officer just down the road in Gibraltar, claimed a predominant interest in shipping in the area and vehemently disagreed. The patchwork here involved a small integrated staff at Gibraltar and a new command (IBERLANT) delegated to the British Eastern Atlantic commander. The actual creation of the command on the model the Americans wanted did not come until the midsixties.

In the meantime, the Americans worked Francisco Franco's dictatorship for naval advantage. After two years of bargaining, a ten-year treaty of economic assistance and military cooperation was signed. (Spain was not a member of NATO and would not join for over two decades.) The Strategic Air Command began building three major air bases, and the large American naval base at Rota started to take shape.

By 1965 the United States had provided $1.8 billion in military and economic aid to Franco—the price of the Spanish corner. Much of the expense of modernizing the dictator's military was borne by America; for example, Spain ranked sixth in the world in gross tonnage by the midsixties, ahead of the United States.

When the stack gas had settled, the British, in spite of their clear naval inferiority, had done quite well for themselves. Four NATO commands were theirs: Eastern Atlantic, Allied Forces North, Mediterranean, and Channel. The Americans conceded these not only because of the rich history of the Royal Navy in these waters but also because the British were doing the most, by far, to support UN-U.S. naval operations in Korea.

Triumph, Jamaica, Belfast, and several small boys had gone to war immediately. *Jamaica* and *Black Swan,* along with *Juneau,* fought the only real surface action of the war, against some North Korean torpedo boats off Chumunjin on 2 July 1950. On the next day *Triumph* was at *Valley Forge*'s side for the first carrier strike of the war. The day following, when Truman announced the naval blockade, the Royal Navy began its main naval task of the conflict, clamping on ships up and down Korea's west coast. The British were deeply involved with Inchon—*Triumph*'s Seafire fighters and even her ancient Firefly spotter aircraft made material contributions—and fought the mine menace off Chinnampo alongside the Americans.

By the end, thirty-two Royal Navy warships had seen service around Korea. Largely resupplied by the Americans, they collectively steamed over two million miles and consumed over half a million tons of fuel. More than twenty thousand carrier sorties were flown by British aviators, and seventeen thousand naval and Royal Marine personnel did time in the theater. Korea was a major British naval war, although only twenty-five officers and seventeen ratings lost their lives.[10]

So the British got their European naval commands, but there was no question of who actually owned the Med in terms of naval power. Under the overall direction of Mick Carney in Naples, Sixth Fleet ruled the inland sea. In spite of Korea, the fleet's strength doubled in 1951 due to concerns of the Truman administration that Korea was only a sideshow and that the critical area for Communist expansion remained Europe.

The fleet's popular commander, Vice Admiral Matt Gardner, had a face bashed in port and starboard, a souvenir from his salad days in naval aviation, when he had been one of the three "Flying Fish" who had perfected upside-down flight (a nice trick in open cockpits). Under Gardner, who had commanded *Enterprise* in World War II, the fleet continued the Sherman-induced exercises and restlessly roamed: the Riviera, Capri, Malta, Greece, Crete.

Liberty was the best. "The Sixth Fleet works hard. It also plays hard, but it plays clean," enthused one obviously underinformed journalist. "Officers and men of today's fleet have no time for the tawdry charms of Neopolitan tarts, and business was never worse for the pimps who muster daily on the quayside at Naples, wearing baffled looks." A real gilding of the lily, perhaps, but Sherman's and Gardner's discipline and diplomatic caution were undoubtedly paying friendship dividends.

As for Carney, he worked like a stevedore. He tromped around on Italian army exercises high in the Alps, clad in furs and shod in combat boots; toured liberty ports in civvies, striking up conversations with unsuspecting sailors on shore leave; and supported international unification of naval operations to anyone who would listen. "The Americans have put the *carne* [meat] into defense," punned the Italians.

The Med was lotusland: sun-drenched beaches featuring the newest in atomic-age feminine swimwear, the "bikini;" submarine fishing; wine drinking from leather flasks; and an occasional sailor reeling about a Spanish bull ring in a drunken *baile de toros*. But there was serious business, too: continuous drills, underway replenishment exercises, gun shoots at air-towed sleeves, carrier training against both sea and shore targets. Amphibious landings became routine—in Sardinia, Crete, and Sicily's Augusta Bay.

Overhead, carrier aviators off *Coral Sea* and *Oriskany* grew familiar with every detail of the Mediterranean coastline. At one stage they flew 950 practice sorties in four days. Dan Gallery was there, exiled from the Washington hothouse to a role in which he reveled, CarDiv commander, and he hawkeyed his flight decks just as he had done in the days when he had been a fresh young hotshot aboard *Langley*. Western Med, eastern Med; Pisa, Port Lyautey, Cyprus; Albania, the Hellespont, the plains of Troy—American Skyraiders, Corsairs, Banshees, and Panthers ranged the skies.

The strategic concept was to use seapower to get at land power, and to this end Sixth Fleet drilled and drilled. The fleet was over forty warships now, fifteen thousand sailors and Marines, all on a Korea-induced condition of readiness. The three *Midway*-class carriers deployed to the Med, not the western Pacific. Gardner's ships were still "gray diplomats," still welcomed almost everywhere along the coasts—and not simply for the sailors' paydays. His men were watching one thousand miles of Russia's extended southern flank, and they did everything with no fixed bases. They depended on their auxiliaries and the Atlantic lifelines, stretching back to Portsmouth, Boston, Newport, Brooklyn, Norfolk, and Charleston. Their ships rotated about every six months.

Not everyone wanted them there; some critics saw a danger in leaving so many precious naval eggs locked in the Mediterranean basket, where no point was more than two hundred miles from the beach and where they theoretically could fall under the cloud of Soviet land-based air. But Matt Gardner was confident in the interception abilities of his F9F Panthers, and so was the Navy. His fleet was modern—none of its capital ships had fought in World War II—and his gray diplomats were in the Med to stay.

And there they roamed, from Gibraltar in the west to Beirut in the east, 2330 miles of sea, suspended between Europe and Africa like Mohammed's coffin. On watch.

☆

Korea was not all there was to the Far East, either. The Navy was supporting the struggle by the French to hang on to the shreds of their colonial power in Vietnam, by sending surplus ships, lifting refugees, and hauling supplies. There was a Communist-led rebellion in the Philippines that heightened concern over American bases there. Taiwan was a constant worry.

The standard analysis was that the Navy was out there on the "fringe," tying together "free" nations in their battle to resist communism. Japan, however, was a special case. Japanese problems did not relate to any Communist threat but to the inability of the recent enemy to defend itself. Turner Joy deputized Arleigh Burke, among other chores, to revitalize the Japanese navy. From his room in Tokyo's Imperial Hotel, Burke began to talk with his former foes.

Japan had begun to prosper, in part from the Korean War, but its sea approaches and coastal waters were an open book. The country was helpless against any outside threat, and this meant an even greater stretch for the American Navy. Japan's only combatants, in 1951, were minesweepers and small craft, a pitiful remnant of the once-mighty Imperial Japanese Navy that had, for a glorious moment, dominated half the Pacific. These shards were manned by enlisted men and controlled by a civilian, and all were busily engaged in one housekeeping task: removing the thousands of mines planted in home waters by the B-29s.

Burke thought for a while. At Vladivostok and other Siberian ports were some beaten-up frigates that the United States had Lend-Leased to the Soviets. The USSR had now decided to give them back, and Burke latched on to them for cannibalization into a couple of fairly good frigates. From somewhere he grabbed an airplane to spot floating mines, got permission for the Japanese to increase the size and speed of their antismuggling patrols, and helped them gain the authority to actually load their ships' guns.

The State Department, on finding out what was going on, threw a fit and ordered a halt, but by that time the embryonic Japanese naval rebirth, thanks to Burke's artificial respiration, was underway. When the final peace treaty between the two nations was signed in September 1951, Japan's right to self-defense was explicitly recognized, and a miniature Japanese navy, the Maritime Self-Defense Force, came into existence, in its ranks many former Imperial Navy officers who had previously been purged. They acknowledged Burke as their "mighty benefactor," and at least one small albatross had been removed from the American Navy's neck.[11]

Beyond Japan and the immediate naval problems of Vietnam, the Philippines, and Taiwan, all of Asia remained of critical concern. The area was considered less vital to American interests than Europe, but in the feverish anti-Communist climate everything seemed at stake, everything counted. The old dream of infinite markets for American products lingered, but this had been largely overtaken by fears that Asia's sprawling littoral, with its hundreds of millions of impoverished, poorly governed people, was wide open to Communist appeals. Thus, the naval role there was potentially huge, although, as one commentator put the matter, "Rarely in history has the trident been grasped with less enthusiasm."

But grasped the trident was. The American response in Korea, in the minds of many naval backers, should serve as a warning to any aggressors both within the region and beyond. The truth, said Rip Struble, was that "our control of the sea enables us to concentrate our military power at points on the perimeter of the European-Asiatic continent more quickly, more easily, and more economically than can any aggressor who does not have sea power."

"The borders of our own security have necessarily become those of the free world," wrote a naval analyst, "and we are at last preparing to defend them."

☆

These "borders of the free world" outlined Forrest Sherman's naval domain, and during one of his ceaseless border checkups in July 1951 he found himself, along with his wife, Dolores, in Europe. He had begun to suffer from insomnia and was increasingly prone to periods of intense fatigue. Still, though he had chronic low blood pressure, he had breezed through his annual physical the previous October, even retaining clearance to fly.

He talked with Franco in Spain, doing spadework for the American bases. There was a whirlwind of receptions. He met with the NATO commander, Dwight Eisenhower, in Paris, got the support of the French naval staff for a basing plan, and battled with the British over NATO command arrangements. Then he was off to Naples, for a round of conferences with Mick Carney.

In Naples he and his wife attended the opera. The next morning, 22 July, he suffered a mild heart attack, followed shortly by two massive coronary seizures, the second fatal. That very day his remains were piped over the side of Carney's flagship, *Mount Olympus*, and five days later he was laid to rest in Arlington.

Forrest Sherman was fifty-four years old. He had, quite literally, worked himself to death.[12]

In his stead came Admiral William Fechteler, commander of the Atlantic Fleet. Bill Fechteler's father, Gustav, had been a four-star admiral, too; the Naval Academy was the son's destiny. Born the same year as Sherman, 1896, he had entered two years earlier, in 1912. There he proved quiet, popular, and bright, graduating eighteenth out of 177 in the Class of 1916.

He went with the battleships (*Pennsylvania* was his first) and developed an affection for the big guns that characterized his entire career. His duties rotated among the battlewagons, shore tours at the Naval Academy and the Navy Department, and the Asiatic Fleet. He was ambitious enough and wanted to get ahead, but he lacked the whetted edge to his drive that cleared the way through the ranks for peers like Sherman, Radford, and Carney. Subordinates found him humane, salty, likable—a sailors' officer. From some port of call he sported a tattoo on his arm, rare for an Academy grad and rarer still for a future flag officer.

Pearl Harbor found him a captain, the staff operations officer for the Pacific Battle Fleet's destroyers. During the war he commanded *Indiana* and earned flag rank, becoming head of Amphibious Group 8 in Dan Barbey's Seventh Fleet. In the postwar years he ran a desk at the Bureau of Naval Personnel and commanded the Atlantic Fleet's battleships and cruisers. Politically unambitious, he steered clear of the rebellion in gold braid. The assignment to command the Atlantic Fleet brought his fourth star and, he believed, the end of his career.

Radford, Carney, McCormick, Conolly, and Vice Admiral Donald

("Wu") Duncan were all possibilities for the chief's slot. Each of them was run past Harry Truman for a look-see and a brief chat. By a process of attrition, the choice came down to Bill Fechteler. Radford wanted to stay in place with the Pacific command while Korea lasted; Carney was deeply embroiled in the shakedown of the NATO command structure and the organization's other teething problems; McCormick loudly proclaimed that he wanted a fleet command; Truman had already passed over Conolly in favor of Sherman; Duncan was too inexperienced. Dan Kimball wanted Fechteler, with whom he had already worked harmoniously and who had Carl Vinson's support.

Fechteler knew he was, at best, a caretaker chief of naval operations. Warm and informal, he was temperamentally ill-suited to big ideas, initiative, and sudden changes of course. The other Joint Chiefs, perhaps too unkindly, came to consider him their weak link. His overriding desire was to keep the keel angle established by Sherman, and this he strove to do. Of his two-year tour in office he would declare, "I don't know that I could say that I contributed anything of great significance to this thing ever."

But he kept his balance. Under his custodianship, for example, the Navy, worried as usual about its public image, delayed cooperating with Stanley Kramer's film production of *The Caine Mutiny* for two years. Finally, the whole flap landed on Fechteler's desk. "This guy Queeg is a screwball," he said. "But what the hell. I've known lots of screwballs in the Navy in my time. I don't see where it's going to do any harm." And Kramer got his Navy cooperation.

Modest, self-effacing, relatively colorless, Bill Fechteler in his heart remained aboard his beloved battleships. His time in command of *Indiana* provided his grandest memories of naval service.

Truman made one more change that August. True to his word, George Marshall stayed one year as secretary of defense. He made no earthshaking changes, but he had stood fast against the muddy flood of anti-Communist vitriol whose initiators had attempted to stain even his unparalleled record, and he, too, had recommended firing MacArthur—probably his greatest service to an embattled president. With his resignation, a giant left the Pentagon.

His deputy, Robert Lovett, had seemingly assisted everyone in Washington, particularly Henry Stimson, as assistant secretary of war, and Marshall, previously, as under secretary of state. Lovett knew where the bodies were buried; although born in Huntsville, Texas, in 1895, he was the ultimate Washington insider, a Harvard-trained banker and a classic member of the Europe-centered "eastern establishment." (Such an establishment actually existed, not as a tightly controlled club but as an aristocracy of policymakers open to merit.) He was a whiz as a bureaucratic problem solver, a supreme detail man. "I don't want a briefing," he would say. "I just want the facts."

Featuring a wit at once dry and wry, Lovett rapidly established firmer control over the Pentagon's endless bureaucracy than any previous secretary, Forrestal included. He was good at thinking ahead, to the military shape of things to come. When the brass had wanted more battleships in World War II, Lovett, the old naval aviator (Number 66, 1st Yale Unit, and a wing commander in 1918), pressed for bombers. Now, with the USAF begging for more big bomber wings, he urged missiles. He was an investment banker by trade, and as far as the Navy was concerned, his assignment of the fleet's future was clear: carriers and nuclear submarines.

By August 1951, then, Truman's new naval team was aboard. The strategic design still emphasized a focus on Europe and the Mediterranean. But, sideshow or not, that war in Korea still ground on, the casualties piled up, and the stalemate was gridlocked into a pattern of eternal, arid denunciations by both sides at Panmunjom.[13]

Negotiate while fighting, but fight for negotiating advantage. For the Navy, seeking maximum effectiveness at minimum cost, the major element of its emerging role in the stalemated conflict was becoming clearer by the day.

—Air war.

CHAPTER TWELVE

KITCHEN SINK

———— ☆ ————

D ay after weary day, watch upon tedious watch, the war dragged on. Steaming summer heat gave way to autumn coolness, then all too quickly to frigid, biting winter, and on to the thaws and rainy muck of spring. Warships and their crews were deployed to the Korean coast, toiled through their allotted times, and went away—some to return again, and again.

The crews had to be trained and retrained. Readiness had to be maintained, doubly so in a war of stalemate and position. Day after day the gunships pounded the coasts, aircraft ranged up to the Yalu, support units patiently kept up resupplying the UN forces. There were attempts to conserve lives and machines. For the aviators, pullout altitudes were raised, and passes over a target were limited; for the gunships, the Seventh Fleet commander soon restricted unobserved gunfire and reduced speeds.

—To little avail. Despite the military stagnation, overload on the communications circuits piled up. The traffic in 1952 was 50 percent higher than that of late 1950, a time when large operations had been afoot. By May 1952 the bomb tonnage dropped on Korea by the Navy and Marines *alone* had already equaled their total for the entire Pacific War.

The naval sieges continued. Off Wonsan, the honorary naval "mayor" would ceremoniously pass on the gilt key to the city to his relief. Here, in addition to the heavy and continuous shore bombardment from cruisers, destroyers, and an occasional sight-seeing battlewagon with a flag aboard, other ships were maintained on station: four or five minesweepers, their tender and a tug, a few extra destroyers. And Wonsan was not unique.

Interdiction continued. The Air Force came to regret its savagely named Operation STRANGLE, which indeed smashed rails, shot up trains, knocked down bridges, and harassed truck columns but "strangled" nothing. The supplies somehow kept coming. The enemy bypassed or repaired the wreckage, moved at night, used himself as a pack animal, and hid out during the day.

Close air support continued. The "blue planes" were still the most feared American weapon; they worked in tight, very tight, and their accuracy was generally superb. The North Koreans made no effort to contest UN control of the air, and their refusal to go after the carriers offshore, along with the extremely limited responses of the Chinese and Russian pilots who came later, meant that the flattops became maneuverable islands right off the peninsula's coasts, their aircraft operating directly over the front lines.

—A "rather luxurious condition," to be sure. The problem was to translate the novel situation into combat and diplomatic effect.

☆

In early November 1950, as the Chinese counterattackers poured down from the North Korean hills, Task Force 77 was ordered to participate in the campaign to isolate the battlefield. The Navy was given two tasks: to perform armed reconnaissance and to destroy the six major Yalu River bridges of the seventeen that linked Manchuria and North Korea. Thus began more than two years of effort by naval aviators from the fleet carriers to choke off the enemy's supply lines. They by no means worked alone; other UN air arms— the escort carriers of the blockade force, the Fifth Air Force, and the 1st Marine Air Wing—all took part in this basic strategic mission.

The primary assignment of all this land- and sea-based air power was, in effect, to sever the Korean peninsula at the Yalu and Tuman rivers, float the entire southward land mass away from the Asiatic mainland, and leave the newly cut-off enemy forces to be attacked at will from air and sea. In theory, the overwhelming UN aerial advantage would win the war, the dream of air-power theorists since the 1920s.

Task Force 77 could usually operate about 150 aircraft a day and on average lost about one operating day out of four due to weather or other conditions. Against this capacity, the enemy was running hundreds of trains and thousands of trucks through an area about the size of Minnesota, energetically and ingeniously moving his supplies when he could, camouflaging them when he could not.[1]

Moreover, part of the enemy's defenses could hide, north of the Yalu in Manchuria, safe from aerial attack. His anti-aircraft units, MiG interceptors, supply dumps, and troop concentrations were, by American and UN fiat, given "sanctuary" across the border. Harry Truman had forbidden any bombing of Manchurian objectives after a foray against the port of Rashin, which was perilously close to the Russian port of Vladivostock. Some critics, like George Kennan, called bombing missions like this "frivolous and dangerous;" the Bear might be driven to anger by such tickling.

To men like Kennan, far away from the combat and with worldwide perspectives, the continuous insistence by American military men that they be allowed to strike the enemy in his havens was a recipe for disaster. "There was never the slightest doubt in my mind, and I fail to see how anyone could have entertained any," Kennan wrote with his customary self-deprecatory assuredness, "that the demand for permission to bomb beyond the Yalu was equivalent to a demand for expansion of the Korean War into a full-fledged war with both the Soviet Union and China."

Therefore, naval aviators and all other aerial forces operated on a leash, the bureaucratic nomenclature of which hardened into something to become all too familiar to fighting men in the postwar era: "rules of engagement." Few in uniform, particularly veterans of the no-punches-pulled flying of World War II, could accept such logic. Vice Admiral Wu Duncan, vice chief of naval operations, was asked if the Navy could direct its carrier air into "enemy-controlled air space and recover it without unacceptable losses." "Moving in and wresting control of the air from the enemy is included in our plans," Duncan sourly responded. "We expect to achieve it in the areas in which we operate."

—"Are allowed to operate" might have been the more appropriate phrasing. Every naval aviator, beginning with the deputy chief for air, Vice Admiral John Howard Cassady, believed that the aviation program in Korea was "fundamentally sound," as far as things went. The fliers were skilled, and they got even better with experience; their training was thorough, much more so than that of their opponents; the doctrine, with minor glitches, seemed effective. There were "plenty" of targets to shoot at in Korea, said Cassady, "and profitable ones." He was fond of citing statistics: 934 separate railway cuts in December 1951, 4694 cuts in the first year of interdiction. "The enemy has taken terrific punishment—he couldn't continue to absorb it indefinitely." As for the enemy's use of oxcarts, human beasts of burden, the shroud of night, however, "he's done a remarkable job."[2]

But the bulk of the industrial sources of the enemy's military strength was not in North Korea and thus immune from air attack. Officially, naval aviation leaders like Duncan and Cassady played the game, doing the best they could while unofficially straining at the leash. They argued that the naval needs of NATO, the creation of smaller atomic weapons (thus enabling the bomb to go to sea), and the Korean situation had reemphasized the need for carrier air; that carrier mobility was critical in Korea; and that, perforce, the Navy should have a greater share of the military budget.

They were proud of their hardware. In the Douglas AD-1 Skyraider the Navy had, pound for pound, perhaps the best airplane in the world for day-in, day-out bombing and rocketing. The Chance-Vought F4U Corsair was still among the fastest piston-engined planes in existence. The first generation of carrier jets, the Grumman F9F Panther and the McDonnell F2H Banshee, had twice the range and twice the endurance of the short-legged MiG-15, a defensive interceptor.

But the MiG had to operate only in its own airspace, in a defensive mode. Even Cassady had to concede that the MiG, over its own turf, flew and climbed faster than either the Panther or the Banshee. The F3H Demon and the F9F-6 Cougar were in the pipeline but were months, even years, away. Observed one critic, "The U.S. Navy has the world's best piston engine air force in a jet engine age."

This characterization was a bit unfair, but the critique persisted, as did the Air Force's position on strategic air power, which had not gone away but instead had emerged with renewed strength during Korea. The "zoomies" argued that carrier air warfare was exorbitantly expensive. They estimated that the cost of creation of a four-carrier task group with its surface support, such as occasionally operated off Korea, ran to about $2.5 billion— about 20 percent of the Defense Department's entire pre-Korean budget. A B-50 group could deliver about fifteen times the bomb tonnage in a given period of time. Carriers were inefficient: half the carrier task group's planes had to be kept overhead or on deck, ready to defend the ships themselves. Carrier striking power was short-lived: a task group could launch and recover for only about three days before withdrawing to replenish and refuel. Carriers were vulnerable to weather that land-based air could fly through or over. Carriers could be had by land-based air; they were easy targets for submarines and mines.

All these arguments had some measure of truth, if in descending degrees of credibility. In response, Bill Fechteler ordered his admirals to keep their mouths shut, letting carrier air and its undoubtedly important mobility and accuracy do their talking for them. The Navy's brass, even the impulsive Arthur Radford in Pearl Harbor, adopted a position of "martyred silence" in the one-sided debate. Fechteler did most of the talking, and his remarks were characteristically sotto voce:

> This country needs a strong Air Force, but it needs a strong Army and Navy too. The Navy needs its aircraft just as the nation needs a reliable flow of many raw materials from overseas. . . . The purpose of a Navy is simply to move a lot of power over the surface of the earth to the place where needed in order for us to be able to come and go on the sea.

Besides, there were other components of naval air power at issue than the planes that flew from the high-visibility carriers. The patrol squadrons, neither glamorous nor newsworthy but necessary and valuable, were in the air constantly. They snooped for enemy shipping, fishing, or mining activities, kept a weather eye cocked for the occasional typhoon, watched over Taiwan and its troublous approaches, and acted as a dependable aerial component of the Korean blockade.

These squadrons, made up mostly of Martin PBM Mariner seaplanes and Convair P4Y-2 Privateers, usually spent long hours in the air, interspersed with occasional relief like providing flare illumination for Marine night intruder pilots. But they also carried men and supplies and, although the enemy submarine threat was nil, their aviators kept their antisubmarine warfare skills finely honed. The big, clumsy aircraft were beginning to pack electronic gear to monitor enemy communications and radar frequencies, continuing to develop the doctrine of electronic warfare begun in World War II.

Helicopters, a freaky new toy at the end of that war, were now coming into their own. The whirlybirds, at first primarily four-seat Sikorsky HO3S-1s, quickly showed their worth in air-sea rescue. Carriers learned to rely on their hovering "angels," which supplemented the traditional plane-guard destroyer and provided the generally quicker response time that could mean the difference between life and death for a downed aircrew. By 1952 the helos were lancing deep into enemy-held territory on rescue and intelligence missions. They transported troops and even artillery (slung underneath), spotted for naval gunfire, and evacuated the wounded.

The helicopter grew from infancy to maturity in Korea. By war's end, using Sikorsky HRS-1s operating off *Sicily*, the Navy had even begun to perfect the technique of shipborne helicopter assault, which was to lead to the "vertical envelopment" doctrine of later years. Gas turbine propulsion made the ungainly birds more dependable, longer-legged, and more powerful. The helo's versatility in combat meant that, in an amazingly short time, the former toy had earned its place.[3]

Thus, naval air power in Korea was rich in resources, varied, multidimensional. Whether this multiplicity of uses could translate into peace on the terms sought by the Americans and the United Nations was, however, quite another question.

☆

Around the clock the carriers worked, steaming from carefully plotted coordinate to coordinate across the cobalt waters of the Sea of Japan. Flight decks were a turmoil of activity, men in multicolored jerseys scurrying to perform their special roles for launch and recovery. Amid the tumult waited the "hot papa," swathed in his cumbersome suit of white asbestos, ready to dash into the flames in case of a bad crack-up.

After returning planes had moved into their standard racetrack formation to port for retrieval, the landing signals officer, waving two orange paddles, guided them in from his screened perch astern on the flight deck; aviators ignored him at their peril. As each plane snagged an arresting wire with its extended tailhook, a green-jerseyed sailor raced forward, freed the hook, and quickly ducked aside as the plane made its way to its assigned parking zone forward, wings folding. Blue-jerseyed plane pushers meanwhile sweated to get their aircraft into catapult position for launch. High above, on the after end of the carrier's island in primary flight, the stern-eyed "CAG" (air group commander) and his staff oversaw everything.

Day and night, around the clock. In the darkness the catapult officer's paddles became glowing red wands, swooping down to set off the hydraulic slingshot, launching its cargo into the sky with the roar of an express train. Occasionally a plane clawed frantically at the air, stalled, and nosedived off the bow, exploding in a jagged sheet of white fire. Amazingly, with the destroyers and the angels moving in rapidly to assist, only a few aviators lost their lives in these crashes.

Sometimes the weather, either a howling typhoon or a winter sleet storm, stopped the flattops. But not often. The launches and recoveries went on. The aviators flew against the coast over deadly seas and into the face of increasingly heavy gunfire, delivered their ordnance, and returned over the oily dark ocean to land on their heaving postage stamp of a carrier deck. To one observer, James Michener, these men were cut from the same cloth as Roland or Prince Hal, "engaged in a profession in which men must expect to die." Although some of them may indeed have "live[d] for danger," as Michener overheatedly wrote, all of them were frightened to a certain degree by what they were being asked to do. Their caustic sense of humor helped, but what they all shared was determination, integrity, self-discipline far beyond the ordinary, and a sense of duty that, under the conditions in which that duty was carried out, became courage.

—And they kept coming back. One squadron leader, Paul Gray, was shot down five times, on three occasions ending up in the freezing sea. Some bailed out over water or crashed on land behind enemy lines, spending hours or days evading enemy soldiers, hoping for rescue. And some had to take to rafts, praying for a lifesaving destroyer or helicopter.

The pace of operations seldom let up. The early days, when *Valley Forge* had been forced to operate alone, gave way to three- and four-carrier formations, with two or more hot decks always working. Much of the time the flattops operated within fifteen minutes' flight of the front lines. This was both good and bad news for their aviators, because daily multiple sorties fatigued both mind and body, leading to carelessness in the air.

Still they flew—on the edges of summer and autumn typhoons, amid winter gusts of arctic air that could heel a plane on its side, into Korea's typically hyperactive springtime polar front. Practically all their strikes were "weather-sensitive" to some degree, and each carrier was eventually assigned an aerological staff to sort things out. The battlewagons got them also, to support the decisions of the fleet commander.[4]

As the sorties accumulated, so did the data. Carrier-based jet aircraft proved their worth. *Essex* was the first carrier sent to Korea with the new, heavy catapults needed to fire off a fully loaded jet, and with this advantage her VF-172, flying Banshees, could participate completely in attack missions. The adaptability of naval air power, always obvious to its proponents, became more evident to all concerned. Banshee aviators boasted that there was no enemy target they could not hit within twenty-five minutes of launch from eighty miles at sea. The jets were too fast for much of the enemy anti-aircraft, and both Banshees and Panthers proved to be gratifyingly rugged and durable. Their maintenance teams had an easier time, too, compared with those working on the more temperamental Skyraiders and Corsairs.

"The jet [has been turned] from a defensive to an offensive weapon of naval airpower," asserted Rear Admiral John Perry, one of Task Force 77's commanders. Unfortunately, neither Perry nor any other carrier task group commander was around long enough to see much of this or any other development. The Navy's policy of command rotation, which became absolutely frenetic in wartime to ensure that as many flag officers as possible got a piece of the action, meant that Task Force 77 went through a revolving door of leadership—too many leaders by far. Thirteen rear admirals served as commander during the Korean conflict. Because of replenishment and ship rotation, the command of the task force changed roughly every two weeks; over the length of the war, roughly three years, there were *fifty-six changes of command*.

No matter; aviators flew under whoever was in charge, joined now by the Naval Air Reservists (eventually numbering thirteen squadrons). Most of these, scant months before, had lived placidly in the vicinity of their reserve squadrons, around Kansas City, Chicago, Memphis, Dallas. They were farmers, lawyers, merchants—a cross section of middle-class American life. But they had kept reasonably sharp through the twenty-one naval air stations and seven Naval Air Reserve training units. There were thirty-five thousand of them—aviators, aircrewmen, ground teams—and many of them were in the skies over Korea by mid-1951.

Typical perhaps was VF-884, a fighter squadron from the Kansas City area. The "Bitter Birds," one of the first Reserve squadrons in action, flew for seven months off *Boxer*. By November 1951 they were back home, mustered out, minus three of their number who never came back. Or Attack Squadron 702, out of Dallas. They flew off *Boxer*, too, alongside the Bitter Birds. Most of them wanted to be civilians again, and fast, but in the meantime they put their Skyraiders into the air every day, right along with the Regulars. By the time their tour was up, every one of VA-702's aviators had logged, in terms of distance flown, once around the world at the equator.[5]

And so they kept on flying, all of them, Regulars and Reservists alike. Their carriers roved at will, at times almost running aground to plant a squadron right on top of the enemy. (Jimmy Thach, skippering *Sicily*, once anchored so near the beach that his bridge came under small-arms fire from the shore.) The planes often flew at lawnmower altitudes, strafing, rocketing, simply trying to scare hell out of the enemy's peasant levies.

Launch, strike, and recover. Day after day after day.

☆

As always during wartime, technology leapfrogged ahead. The early jets, underpowered and lacking lift augmentation, were unforgiving, intolerant birds. One jet squadron, in the first month of the war, registered fifteen crashes in three weeks. Despite their courage and cockiness, even the best aviators got edgy over the jets' fuel-gobbling habits and rigid performance parameters. Some disasters were incredible; one Panther came in too high while landing, missed every arresting wire, plunged through all the crash barriers, wiped out two more Panthers, and started a fire that damaged several other planes before finally plunging over the side.

A Task Force 77 staff officer, Gerald Miller (who eventually rose to vice admiral), witnessed such a flight-deck maelstrom. "I can still remember the admiral walking over to the opposite side of the bridge," he recalled, "putting his head down on his hands, and shaking. It was so bad he couldn't even get mad. It was a horrible mess." The straight-deck carrier left little margin for error.

Eventually these lethal lessons would strike home. The angled deck would replace the treacherous straight deck, providing a landing area away from parked planes. The era of spectacular barrier leaps and jet tangles forward of the bridge would fade into bad memory. The more powerful steam catapult would replace the hydraulic version, and the automated mirror landing system would retire the landing signals officer with his orange paddles and his screams of outrage. In-flight refueling would largely eliminate the life-or-death pressures of getting back on deck with the remnants of the fuel one had departed with.

In the meantime, mangled jets and dead aviators led to stopgaps. Development of the angled deck, a British innovation, was speeded up. The Navy introduced a nylon tape–and–cable barricade to snare runaway aircraft more effectively. The older Davis barriers went the way of all outmoded technology. Flight deck firefighting teams became supremely efficient. Only one major fire, aboard *Boxer*, plagued Task Force 77 in all its time off Korea. (The carrier suffered nine dead, thirty injured, and eighteen aircraft damaged or destroyed.)[6]

The weaponry got better. The ordnance still did not always hit what was aimed at—one series of jet sorties claimed sixteen large buildings, a coal dump, and eighty sheep—but as both aviators and planes improved, so did their accuracy. The Navy began the war with the high-velocity aerial rocket (HVAR), a solid-fuel, fin-guided projectile with a five-inch explosive warhead. HVAR and its larger, less precise cousin, Tiny Tim, proved ineffectual against the sloping armor of the Russian-made T-34 tanks, and they were soon supplemented by the more powerful, if equally inaccurate, antitank aerial rocket (ATAR).

Napalm was a useful (if indiscriminate and horrifying) weapon, carried in bomb form by both Skyraiders and Corsairs and toggled off from as low as two hundred feet in modified drop tanks. This weapon was fiendishly inaccurate as well, but that was part of the idea; a single drop created a fireball up to 275 feet long and nearly 100 feet wide, incinerating anything in its path. Aviators used the thickened mixture of jellied gasoline against every possible target: tanks, trains, trucks, troops, airfields, railroad fixtures, harbors.

Rockets and fragmentation bombs proved deadly against troops, light vehicles, and emplacements. Twenty-millimeter cannon were used in straf- ing runs and were also handy in the rare instances of aerial dogfighting. The slower, propeller-driven aircraft, particularly the husky Skyraider, were better suited for ground support, but their survivability was a problem. Low and slow meant better accuracy but also made a better target. The Skyraider eventually received additional armor sheeting on its underside (making the plane even slower, but with a more confident occupant). For its part, the Corsair had a badly placed oil cooler, inviting small-arms and shrapnel damage.

The Navy began the war with 9422 combat aircraft; eventually, after attrition, the service ended with 8818. But the carriers multiplied: in 1950 there were fifteen in commission, and by 1953 thirty-four (one-third of the World War II peak). The number of aviators also doubled. Their planes improved marginally, but the real answers were still in the testing stage and on the drawing boards.

The straight wings of the Panthers and Banshees led to fuel wastage; despite their undisputed effectiveness, their stay time was accordingly brief. The Navy had the swept-wing McDonnell F3H-1 Demon under develop- ment, but this aircraft was already bedeviled by the propulsion problems that would eventually cripple the entire program.

Three fine planes would eventually emerge, drawing on the lessons of the Korean experience—one of them almost in time to see combat. This was the swept-wing version of the Panther, the F9F-6, -7, and -8 Cougar family. The North American F-86, used by the Air Force and lauded for its exploits against the MiGs, was navalized as the FJ-2, -3, and -4 Fury. And in 1953 the Bureau of Aeronautics authorized development of the Vought F8U-1 Crusader, a supersonic fighter destined for long and effective life.

In the meantime, the Navy had to rely on the superior training and skills of its aviators and slightly more powerful versions of Skyraiders and Panthers. At the beginning, sorties took place at a jet-to-prop ratio of 1:2. By the end, the ratio was 4:3. Although the carrier Navy would not become all-jet until the last Skyraider retired from the fleet in 1968, by 1953 some air groups were already operating three jet squadrons and only one prop squadron. The first bomb-loaded jet strike left a carrier on 1 April 1951, and from that point on the path into the future was clear.

The use of jets, especially as ground-attack aircraft, forced changes in doctrine, primarily because of the higher speed. The Banshee, in particular, developed into a superb fighter-bomber for bridge and rail strikes. Its rugged build, ease of maintenance, and resistance to flak damage made the doctrinal changes worthwhile. Cutting a rail line no more than sixty inches wide while zipping by at four hundred knots was no easy task; VF-172, flying Banshees toting 250-pound bombs or HVARs and ATARs, claimed 35 percent effectiveness at the business.

Still, there was no constant, unvarying doctrine. Everyone had his own special recipe for bomb loading, glide bombing, toss bombing, bomb fusing. Everyone knew the *best* way to use Tiny Tims, variable time fuses, HVARs, ATARs, 20-mm, 50-caliber machine guns. In ready rooms throughout Task Force 77 the arguments raged, and when the moment came, many aviators simply went ahead and did things their way. An exasperated Eddie Ewen was moved to comment:

> It can be said without exaggeration that the number of views regarding the proper ordnance and best method of delivery on any given target exceeds the units of ordnance to be delivered on the target multiplied by the number of aviators assigned to the attack.

Technology went beyond the planes and their ordnance; in the modern age the Mark I, Mod 0 eyeball was still useful but not nearly enough, not when two jets could close at a thousand miles an hour. Fleet air defense was revolutionized. The new SPS-6B radar could detect a single B-29 operating at twenty thousand feet as far as 180 miles away. The radar had a 75 percent chance of detecting a single jet before it got within 35 miles. Communication between the orbiting combat air patrol and the carrier's combat information center (CIC)—the fleet's brain—improved markedly. Perfection was impossible—in 1951 a pair of MiGs completely evaded detection and boldly overflew Seoul before leisurely heading north again—but the aerial defensive curtain around the flattops drew ever tighter.

Airborne identification, friend or foe (IFF), was initially unreliable, not least because aviators were exceptionally careless in using the gadget. The old Mark III led to false alarms when friendly aircraft displayed the wrong codes (which happened too often for comfort). There were several tense moments in task force CICs until incoming "bogeys" were sorted out. The new Mark X was more secure and helped calm carrier commanders a bit.[7]

All of this—the platforms, ordnance, electronics—helped make the Navy practically invulnerable to the enemy. At sea.

☆

But the aviators went to work over land, and the process began with close air support. Friendly troops on the ground constantly pleaded for planes, immediately, and the strategically minded Air Force was mostly uninterested. Naval and Marine aviators, on the other hand, were specially trained for the role, used to taking a look from very low altitude.

Forward air controllers, especially if they were Marines, were often aviators themselves, and they could deliver blistering criticism if the planes were late, came in too high, too fast, or too slow, or simply missed their targets. Both USAF and Navy systems of close air support had merits as well as weaknesses, but as with ordnance, everyone, particularly the controllers, had an opinion.

The Army Air Corps had developed a family of light but heavily armed attack aircraft, culminating in the A-26 Invader (which, as the redesignated B-26, soldiered through Korea and beyond). Anglo-American fighter-bombers and troops, using light spotter aircraft as well as ground control teams, had worked together effectively in northern Europe and Italy. Meanwhile, building on Marine experience in Central America, the Navy had evolved its own system, beginning with the bloodbath at Tarawa in 1943.

The independent Air Force favored a rigid, tightly structured approach to close air support. The zoomies believed the system should function as an adjunct to, not a substitute for, an Army division's artillery. As a result, the USAF conceived of "close" air support as seldom closer than one thousand yards in front of friendly troops. Artillery would take care of the interstices, with less danger of hitting one's own.

The Navy and Marines trained to support amphibious assault and the move inland. For them, close air support was a substitute for artillery, the heavy pieces of which usually could not be brought into play during the early stages of a landing. Highly trained ANGLICO (Air-Naval Gunfire Liaison Company) personnel would radio strike requests either through the Marine brigade net to shipboard, if a beachhead had been established, or to the carrier directly.

With the Navy-Marine system, the danger to friendly troops from their own aerial ordnance clearly escalated. On the other hand, when a ground commander was directly engaged with the enemy, ordnance delivered half a mile or more to the rear of the battle line would not help much.

When he asked for USAF support around Seoul in the spring of 1951, Matthew Ridgway found that the pilots had little heart for really close-in support missions. They were not trained for the role, and their superiors adamantly insisted that the Eighth Army could be supported better by deep interdiction raids on enemy communications and supply lines. The Navy, in response to Ridgway's plea, ginned up both *Sicily* and *Badoeng Strait*, with their attached Marine squadrons, plus a Marine land-based jet squadron—all of which provided close air support and bombardment for the Eighth Army until Seoul was relieved.

Most of the people who needed the support, the doggies, saw the problem the Navy's way. One Army officer damned the Air Force's ideas of close air support as follows:

If you want it, you can't get it. If you can get it, it can't find you. If it can find you, it can't identify the target. If it can identify the target, it can't hit it. But if it does hit the target, it doesn't do a great deal of damage anyway.

At one time, in early 1951, naval and Marine aviators were flying as many as five hundred or more close support missions a day. The people ordering these strikes, the men on the ground, opted for the Navy system for the simplest of reasons: closer was better. At Chosin Reservoir, on-call Navy-Marine air power destroyed seven Chinese divisions, enabled the crucial evacuation at Hungnam to take place, and partially offset the calamitous collapse of the Eighth Army to the west. Navy planes eventually unscrambled enough frequencies so that on-call strike missions, while never losing their risk or the quality of the unexpected, in the last two years of the war took on some of the patina of the routine.[8]

In air-to-air combat, things were never routine. On occasion the MiGs would venture south of the Yalu, and then the Navy jets displayed their dogfighting capacities. The Panther was able not only to protect bombers but also to take out attacking MiG-15s. One naval officer estimated that the Panther had a 3:1 kill ratio over the MiG in combat.

The larger air picture was somewhat gloomier. Enemy anti-aircraft fire became far more voluminous and accurate, particularly around the obvious targets, and the MiGs were far from pushovers, particularly when flown by experienced Chinese or Russian pilots. (The 3:1 Panther ratio was hotly debated.) Half of the 1400 Chinese planes were estimated to be MiG-15s, and Air Force chief of staff Hoyt Vandenberg had to admit that this aircraft could outperform the F-86 in many respects.

During Operation STRANGLE, attacking UN planes were harried by MiG interceptors, lit up by radar-directed searchlights, and tracked by deadly flak artillery that struck as high as thirty thousand feet. In January 1951, the worst month of the overall air war for the UN, forty-four planes were reported down from flak alone. By the month's end more than six hundred American aircraft had been lost since the war's inception, either through aerial combat or, far more frequently, from ground fire. The loss of enemy planes, which usually scooted north to sanctuary when under pressure, was estimated at half that total. Enemy aircraft rarely came out in strength beyond "MiG Alley" in northwestern Korea and generally operated over a supporting safety net of anti-aircraft artillery.

By April 1951 the best estimates credited the Chinese with 1250 planes tucked into Manchuria, of which about 800 were Soviet-built jets. Vandenberg believed that the United Nations was close to losing air supremacy over the north; the big B-29s were particularly vulnerable. The chunky MiG-15 was specifically designed to take on the Superfortress and, left to its own devices, did very well indeed at this task. As a result, many Navy missions necessarily encompassed escort and interceptor roles rather than strike roles.

But the anti-aircraft fire was the toughest opponent. By mid-1951 the enemy was routinely using early-warning and gun-laying radars, gleaned from every source possible: the Soviet Union, Great Britain, Japan, the United States, and even some of the spoils from Nazi Germany. The Strategic Air Command, out of necessity, began ferret electronic reconnaissance, snooping for enemy electronic emissions, in August. Task Force 77, for its part, reconfigured some Skyraiders into electronic countermeasures (ECM) detachments, and naval patrol squadrons maintained their own electronic ferrets off the Korean, Russian, and Chinese coasts. By the summer of 1952 electronic sniffing indicated 109 enemy radars in North Korea, some of them as close as four miles to the stabilized front lines. Eventually, this troublesome wizard war would produce the Navy's first electronic reconnaissance and countermeasures squadron, VQ-1, commissioned at Iwakuni, Japan, in mid-1955.

In the interim, however, radar-guided ground flak did considerable damage. The Navy and Marines lost 384 tactical aircraft to anti-aircraft fire from mid-1951 through the armistice. Of these, the slower props were by far the more vincible; 193 Corsairs and 102 Skyraiders were among the victims.

With all these problems, and because aerial interception was not among its primary roles, the Navy made only one ace during the Korean War. He was Lieutenant Guy Bordelon, flying a Corsair on detachment from *Princeton*. And, indicative of the nature of the air war, Bordelon's five victims, downed near the end of the conflict, were all "Bedcheck Charlies," whose sole purpose was to drone overhead, engines deliberately out of synch, and keep UN troops awake, occasionally lobbing down one or two small bombs. These were pokey, obsolete Russian-made Lavochkin fighters, YAK-18s, or even biplanes (last used for crop-dusting in Iran). The romantic, daring duels in MiG Alley, much hyped in press and film, did take place (mostly involving USAF planes in the west), but for the Navy they were atypical.[9]

☆

Far more typical were the strike missions, the interdictive raids against whatever helped the enemy wage war. Task Force 77 got into bridge busting in November 1950, in response to the Chinese onslaught, as *Valley Forge* and *Philippine Sea* hit the Yalu River bridges.

Traditional doctrine called for attacking aircraft to "walk" their bomb sticks down the line of a bridge at a slightly offset angle, to ensure that at least one bomb struck paydirt. Bridges were rugged targets; their wooden flooring could easily be replaced, and their most vulnerable points—trusses, supports, and abutments—were hard to hit. In the case of the Yalu missions, furthermore, Manchurian airspace was inviolable by political fiat. Thus, the bridge busters had to attack from a perpendicular angle, and their rules of engagement forbade flak-suppression flights from taking out anti-aircraft installations on the Manchurian side. The combat air patrols could not tangle with enemy fighters over Manchurian territory, nor could they engage in "hot pursuit" into the sanctuary.

The planes of Task Force 77, which was steaming in the Sea of Japan, had to cover the 225 miles to the bridges; dodge the fire of the flak emplacements; fight off MiG interceptors (the Panthers claimed three on these first strikes, against none lost); try to take out the bridges with 1000- or 2000-pound bombs in the most difficult way possible, from the side; and get back to home plate safely. Such self-imposed restrictions hedged in the naval role, particularly in the far north, for the remainder of the conflict.

From these first strikes—some of the bridges remained standing, and the Chinese kept streaming across the frozen Yalu anyway—the emphasis of naval aviation shifted from battlefield support to interdiction. Except in emergencies, naval close air support increasingly came from Marine squadrons ashore or the escort carriers.

Interdiction was a costly proposition. Vice Admiral Ralph Ofstie, another Task Force 77 commander, estimated the price tag on these missions: $18,000 for one rail cut, $55,000 for one bridge down. The explosives bill for one cubic yard of earth detonated was about $100, in Ofstie's words, "a pretty expensive dirt moving operation." More to the point, the North Koreans speedily developed highly capable repair teams, dragooned from any source of manpower available. And their increasingly effective anti-aircraft defenses, placed where they would do the most damage, around the obvious targets, took a high toll of attacking aircraft. "I am beginning to wonder," said Ofstie, by then deputy chief of naval operations for air, "about the value returned for the present sustained attacks in carrying on the interdiction program in Korea."

Ofstie was too hesitant by far. In fact, the battlefield was *not* being interdicted. Naval air power quickly battered North Korea's eastern bridges and rail nets; the enemy simply shifted most of his load to his western networks. There, the Fifth Air Force lacked aircraft that could hit bridges dependably with two-thousand-pound bombs, and the Skyraider, which could, was more and more a sitting duck for anti-aircraft fire. The enemy increasingly shifted to truck transport—more flexible, harder to spot, and harder to hit. His truck count jumped from 7300 in January 1951 to 54,000 in May. Almost everything traveled at night, and repair efforts were matching the pace of destruction.

The interdiction effort—costly, vigorous, exceptionally dangerous—was probably doomed to fail, short of the use of tactical nuclear weapons on enemy massing and choke points. The sanctuary in Manchuria meant that naval, and UN, air power was fated always to strike at the tentacles rather than the head of the enemy's operations—and the tentacles always grew back.

Without doubt, interdiction gave the enemy a terrific resupply burden and caused him widespread damage and loss. But nothing changed on the fighting front, and whenever the enemy chose to attack, usually in simple spoiling operations, he seemed to attack with ample logistic strength. Captured prisoners indicated that they had plenty of food, clothing, medical supplies, and ammunition for their small arms. In the last six months of 1951, UN forces received about 200,000 rounds of artillery and mortar fire per month from the other side; the average per month in 1952 was around 350,000 rounds.

In short, the theory was not working. Air power was not winning the war or even making the enemy more amenable to settle at the truce table. Even given the necessary political constraints on the use of the atomic bomb, more pertinent reasons existed for this slap in the face to air power propagandists. The enemy, even with his fourth-rate economy (or, more probably, *because* of his fourth-rate economy), showed an amazing ability to absorb punishment and carry on. The fountainheads of his supply lines were as secure as Fort Knox. Weather and the carapace of night often protected his movements. The stalemated war meant that his rate of expenditure of everything—ammo, clothing, food, the lot—was less than would otherwise have been the case in a war of movement, and thus he needed proportionately less resupply. Finally, and of critical importance, his supply network was exceptionally primitive, which made for easier shifting of routes, easier repair, and easier replacement.

Unsurprisingly, the morale of naval aviators, flying day after day and seeing few results from their hazardous work, was problematic. Commander Marsh Beebe, head of *Essex*'s Air Group 5, said one of his toughest jobs was to keep up the morale of his men. In four months, August through November 1951, Beebe's aircraft were struck 318 times, resulting in the loss of eleven aviators and twenty-seven planes.

> A pilot would go out one day, do a first-rate bombing job on a bridge or leave several craters in a railbed, and come back the next day and find that all the damage had been repaired overnight. It was hard for him to see how his efforts were having any effect on the course of the fighting. . . . The war in Korea demanded more competence, courage, and skill from the naval aviator than did World War II. The flying hours were longer, the days on the firing line more, the antiaircraft hazards greater, the weather worse. . . . The public appreciation and understanding of the pilot's work was [*sic*] less. . . .

Marsh Beebe was a man in a position to know. And things got no better, to the point where one night-heckler aviator gave vent to his frustration in doggerel:

It weren't no fun in 51
Tried and True in 52
Still out to sea in 53
Don't want no more in 54
Still alive in 55
Amidst the blitz in 56
Almost to heaven in 57
No homecoming date in 58
Remain on the line in 59
Pack up your ditty in 1960
To hell with this poem
We want to come home.[10]

☆

But they were *not* coming home, not so long as the negotiators waffled on at Panmunjom. Day after remorseless day the targeting information came in, the attack routes were diagramed, the briefings were held in the ready rooms, the missions flew.

The classic came early on, in March 1951. Flying back to *Princeton* after a strike on Kilchu, in northeastern North Korea, Lieutenant Commander Clement Craig spied a railroad bridge thrown across a valley eight miles southwest of the town: a single-track, six-span structure 650 feet long and 60 feet high. Tunnels abutted both sides; such a target, he thought, would be difficult to bypass, difficult to repair.

Craig got word to his skipper, Lieutenant Commander Harold Carlson, and that very afternoon, 2 March, VA-195 struck the bridge and damaged the southern approach. The next day Carlson led his Skyraiders on a second strike, dropping one span, damaging a second, and shifting two more out of line. Ralph Ofstie, at the time commanding Task Force 77, christened the chasm "Carlson's Canyon." On 7 March a third attack dropped the northernmost of the shifted spans.

One bridge, three strikes: enemy troops moved to repair the damage like so many worker bees, vehicles piled up, and supplies lay in mountains, unable to move. On 15 March a fourth strike knocked down some wooden replacement spans, dropped another span at the southern end, and damaged the northern approach. Large piles of wooden ties grew in the gully, preparatory to more reconstruction. B-29s twice seeded the valley floor with long-delay bombs. The piles kept growing. By 30 March cribbing of the four central spans and the northern approach had been completed, transverse members had been installed, and only rails were lacking.

By now Carlson's Canyon had taken on a life of its own, a hydra-headed mutant seemingly impervious to attack. Ofstie sent off strikes five and six on 2 April, blowing the whole works and leaving only the concrete piers.

—And still the mutant lived. A labor force was put to work building a four-mile, serpentine road bypass requiring eight new bridges of its own, but all of them short, low, next to impossible to hit, even easier to repair than the original span.

Six strikes, and still the supplies kept moving. Task Force 77, in despair, turned to new targets.

In microcosm, what happened in Carlson's Canyon spoke volumes about the air war in Korea: the courage and initiative of both sides and the futility experienced by naval aviators. When James Michener, working as a journalist, visited *Essex* and talked with Marsh Beebe and his men, he heard the story of Carlson and his VA-195 and took the measure of the aviators of *Essex*.

In the author's imagination the carrier herself became the fictional *Savo;* Beebe, the stocky and aggressive "CAG;" the landing signals officer, "Beer Barrel." The admiral and the helicopter rescue pilots were modeled as well. Coupled with the reluctant Reservist, Harry Brubaker, the epic of Carlson's Canyon became the best naval fiction to emerge from the Korean War: *The Bridges at Toko-ri.*

Going after the enemy's industrial facilities, such as they were, seemed a better bet than such exercises in futility as attacking the span near Kilchu. In mid-1952 the Navy began to strike at North Korea's electrical power network and remaining industry. Without doubt the new tack resulted from the indecisiveness of the interdiction campaign, but the negative results to that point at Panmunjom played a role, as did the strategic idea that preventing the enemy from increasing his capacity to wage an offensive would lead him to seek a negotiated settlement.

A previous and bizarre example of the latter type of thinking had concerned the Hwachon Reservoir, which lay athwart the Pukhan River. The reservoir's dam had been hit before, but in April 1951 the Eighth Army wanted the structure destroyed so the enemy could not close its sluice gates, dry up the river below, and send his troops across the dry riverbed, thus eliminating the need for bridging. The Navy got the order. *Princeton* sent out six dive-bombers, each equipped with a two-thousand-pound bomb. They punched a hole in the dam itself but missed the sluice gates.

The next day, desperation bred innovation. Eight of the bombers were fitted with torpedoes. No naval aircraft had been called on, ever, to torpedo a dam. But *Princeton*'s airmen went at the job like a training mission; six of their torpedoes ran true, the center sluice gate was smashed, and the Hwachon Dam vanished as a worry for the rest of the war.[11]

Now the emphasis was on the sources of the hydroelectric power produced by such dams. North Korea had four major hydroelectric generating facilities, three of which supplied the east coast power grid. The fourth, Suiho, located on the Yalu, was the fourth-largest power generating station in the world. Its four hundred thousand kilowatts fed not only western North Korea but also much of Manchuria.

By June 1952 Suiho's moment had come; the Truman administration, bedeviled during an election year by a hundred little crises at home and the endless Korean conflict abroad, decided to up the ante. The Air Force and the Navy threw in practically everything they had, on the Navy's part, the combined strike groups of four carriers: *Boxer, Bon Homme Richard, Philippine Sea,* and *Princeton.* For the first time since the Yalu River strikes back in November 1950, Task Force 77 launched a trans-Korea assault into the heart of MiG Alley.

No MiG rose to the challenge. The Panthers acted as flak suppressors while the Skyraiders barreled in, each one toting two 1000-pound bombs and one 2000-pounder. In a little over two minutes, eighty-five tons of bombs rained down on the target. Bright flames billowed from Suiho's powerhouse. The escaping aviators left only choking dust and monuments of rubble. The giant hydroelectric complex was out of the war. "Just a fine operation," commented Paul Stroop, *Princeton's* skipper.

By the end of the bombing campaign against its generating plants, North Korea was, electrically speaking, virtually powerless. Ninety percent of its generating capacity lay in ruins. Indeed, all of North Korea was blacked out for two weeks. This kind of aerial assault, unlike the interdiction campaign, seriously damaged the enemy's potential to wage war. "You either accept our fair and just proposal [at Panmunjom]," a satisfied Harry Truman wrote of the enemy in his diary, "or you will be completely destroyed."

☆

Venting presidential spleen into a diary was one thing; bringing this hideously unsatisfactory war to a satisfactory conclusion was quite another. As time passed, some technological tinkering went on in the search for something, anything, that would pry open the lid on progress at the talks. Some experiments were run with obsolete war-surplus F6F Hellcat drones, which were packed with explosives and, guided by Douglas AD-2s fitted with television receivers, sent off in an inquiring frame of mind to look for targets. Restlessly, the admirals tinkered with mission planning too, seeking some other aerial magic now that sites like the Hwachon Dam and Suiho had been laid waste, and still the enemy fought on.

One gambit was the so-called "Cherokee Strike," the brainchild of outspoken Vice Admiral Joseph ("Jocko") Clark, commander of the Seventh Fleet and a man proud of his Indian heritage. Jocko looked on the vacuum left by the easing off of interdiction and the elimination of industrial targets and abhorred. Beginning in October 1952, he cranked up Task Force 77 against concentrations of supplies, artillery, and troops behind enemy lines.

Through January, and after glitches with both the Army and Air Force had been worked out, the Cherokee Strikes absorbed more than one-third of the Seventh Fleet air effort. "For want of something better to do the carrier air groups were hauling explosives in and dumping them in the general neighborhood of the front." In a way, this was the Navy's response to its leash—targeting policy, engagement restrictions, weapons selection—a response that, in substituting sheer volume of ordnance for accuracy or anything else, came close to a declaration of strategic bankruptcy.[12]

Naval aviators were, however, at least avoiding a particular routine, a habit that earlier in the war had cost them dearly, and whatever else they accomplished, the Cherokee Strikes cheered up the UN frontline troops markedly (although some of the bombs inevitably fell inside friendly lines.) While interdiction continued to the very end, the effort dwindled appreciably. Bridge and rail-busting strikes were used only to keep the enemy's repair parties tied down and his anti-aircraft units dispersed. In the final year of the war, in addition to the Cherokee Strikes, everything from the hydroelectric plants on the Yalu to zinc mills were attacked—more than forty times.

Navy fighters continued to scrap with MiGs, generally coming out on top. These results stemmed not so much from the superiority of their aircraft as from the training and skills of their aviators. In the hands of a good pilot, the MiG could beat the Panther—but the box score went the other way. The primary function of the fighter, air-to-air combat, was largely subordinated to flak suppression, bombing, and rocketing. But the men who flew the fighters lived for air-to-air, and occasionally they got their wish.

With the drift and frustration symbolized by the Cherokee Strikes came a psychological ploy, a fake amphibious landing. In mid-October 1952 naval planners directed a feint at a twenty-five-mile-long belt of shore around the insignificant coastal community of Kojo, just south of Wonsan. The purpose was again to tighten the screws on enemy negotiators. To be successful, the feint would involve not only the massing of amphibious forces but also a massive display of carrier air power against shore targets. The planners hoped these activities would serve as a magnet to draw the enemy to the "landing area," where his troop concentrations could be hammered.

Unfortunately, the knowledge that the whole thing was a fake was kept at the highest flag level. Everyone else, unwittingly, worked like beavers, trying to ensure another Inchon. On D minus 3, Task Force 77 flew 667 sorties against targets around Kojo. Brisk anti-aircraft fire downed five carrier aircraft. Weather snarled the amphibious force. Nothing happened.

The carrier commanders, who had also been left in the dark, and their aviators were furious when they found the entire routine had been a ruse, and an unsuccessful one at that: the enemy did not bite. The top echelon began to refer to the useless operation as "training," but this scarcely placated the men who had flown the planes or ridden the Gators. The "Kojo Feint" had cruelly, recklessly, and needlessly cost American lives—the "largest-scale fraud in military history."[13]

The Cherokee Strikes and the Kojo Feint were ample indicators that naval air power, and UN air power in general, had almost reached the end of its rope. When conventional air power saturated targets, when an entire country was left without electricity, and still the desired results were not produced, only one air alternative presented itself.

Task Force 77 had never had armed nuclear weapons, even though plans existed for their use. Back in the summer of 1950, nuclear-capable B-29s had been deployed to the United Kingdom and Guam, but the fissionable cores of their bombs had been left Stateside, under control of the Atomic Energy Commission. Truman, in December 1950, had authorized unassembled bomb components to be stored aboard a carrier in the Far East. Armed nukes, however, had never come near Korea. Now, toward the end, in mid-July 1953, Jocko Clark pleaded for the weapons to be placed aboard his carriers as a "precautionary measure." This was done.

But orders from on high to deliver the bomb never came. And so the airmen were left with increasingly dangerous and increasingly meaningless missions, not to "win" but to "get an armistice." The bitter irony did not go unnoticed by men who were trained to go all-out for victory.

While celebrating leave in Yokosuka, a group of Paul Stroop's aviators off *Princeton* got to grousing about their situation, finally deciding after a few drinks that they had thrown everything against the enemy but the kitchen sink. The light bulb went on, and a kitchen sink was duly liberated from some sailor dive in Yoko, going to sea with the carrier.

Princeton's initial target, once she got back on line, turned out to be Pyongyang. The sink was hauled up on deck and bolted to a bomb. (Eventually, *Princeton* would receive an award from a plumber's union in Alameda, California, for her creative ordnance package.) Stroop posed proudly alongside for a picture.

—That day, the kitchen sink whistled down on Pyongyang.

☆

—Not even the kitchen sink worked. The war, like some crazy perpetual-motion machine, simply cranked on, even accelerating as the summer of 1953 drew near. The truce talks finally moved off dead center, and both sides maneuvered for yards of Korean earth as if they contained precious gems, trying to gain an advantage before the signing.

Dwight Eisenhower, the new president, was committed to ending the Korean War, and his administration was not above saber-rattling to accomplish that task. On 19 May the Joint Chiefs recommended naval and air operations "directly against China and Manchuria," including the use of nuclear weapons if necessary. These recommendations were approved by the National Security Council the next day. Publicly, Eisenhower announced that Seventh Fleet would no longer stand between Formosa and mainland China. Nationalist guerillas, guided by the Central Intelligence Agency, launched more than 200 raids against Mao's coastline during the first five months of 1953.

THE BIKINI TESTS
1946

DD Destroyer **SS** Submarine **APA** Attack Transport **LST** Landing Ship Tank **LCI** Landing Craft Infantry
LCI (L) Landing Craft Infantry Light **LCT** Landing Craft Tank **ARDC** Floating Drydock **B** Barge

Eniwetok Atoll
Bikini Atoll
Utirik Atoll
Kwajalein Atoll
MARSHALL ISLANDS

Target Array for Test Baker

Target Array for Test Able

Off Korea, naval efforts in support of the battle line increased. Gunships like *New Jersey*, *Manchester*, and *Saint Paul* were doing the same thing with Task Force 95 that their sisters had done back in 1950. The naval aviators were also supporting the battle line, just as *Valley Forge* and *Triumph* had done three years before. Task Force 77, with its mother-hen auxiliaries, simply planted itself near the eastern end of the 38th parallel and flew its strikes. The number of sorties rose steadily, from 4343 in May to 6423 in July. Aircraft ordnance tonnage almost doubled during the same period.

Maintenance suffered, gear broke down, electronic equipment balked, and exhausted sailors grabbed catnaps whenever they could. *Lake Champlain* broke both her catapults; *Princeton* and *Philippine Sea* suffered shaft vibrations. *Boxer* had to be kept on line longer than expected, and as a result she set a fleet record on 23 July with her 61,000th landing. Things happened so fast that strike results were usually unavailable or wildly inaccurate. Support of the Eighth Army, in these final, hectic throes, became an enormous trucking operation in which "statistics of sorties flown and ordnance dropped acted to conceal the central question of whether the drops hit anything worthwhile."

Almost miraculously, the end finally came, perhaps sped up by Eisenhower's tougher public line and a behind-the-scenes threat to use nuclear force. On the morning of 27 July the armistice was signed, to take effect that evening. Task Force 77 spent the final day striking airfields in the north. Off Wonsan, the cruisers *Bremerton* and *Saint Paul* kept shelling away. The amphibious ships readied themselves for the repatriation of prisoners, the volatile issue that had stalled the talks for months.

At 2200 the "mayor" ordered the American ships in Wonsan Harbor to turn on their lights—three years, one month, and two days after the North Korean People's Army had breached the 38th parallel. The Korean War was over, with the borders of North and South approximately the same—*status quo ante bellum*.

Air power, including naval air power, had not on its own defeated North Korea and its allies. The Navy's floating airfields, operating with impunity from the seas around the peninsula, had indeed played a critical part in preventing the North from overrunning the South. But UN airmen, short of expanding the war or fundamentally changing its shape, could not effectively work their will on the enemy. Interdiction might have proven decisive, but only if the Manchurian sanctuary could have been attacked— and political constraints never permitted this stratagem. For naval aviators and their Air Force and Marine counterparts, the "sanctuary" idea remained an open sore.

Naval air power succeeded in Korea within carefully defined limits. In the defense of the Pusan perimeter, sorties of the blue planes from offshore probably tipped the scales; the aviators blanketed Inchon, helping the landing succeed; they provided the shelter beneath which the battered Marines and soldiers retreated from the Yalu to Hungnam; they helped stabilize the front and carry the war north again. Above all, and despite the morale-sapping restrictions on their operations, the close air support, interdiction, and bombing raids from the flattops undoubtedly played a central role in driving the enemy to the truce table, keeping him there, and, eventually, producing an uneasy peace.

During the war the aircraft carrier, having no opposite number to fight, became a source of mobile air power in an environment where land-based air was nonexistent or inefficient. Electronic warfare came into its own. In 1953 the Navy even put a modified Combat Information Center into the air, a restructured PB-1W Flying Fortress that, in its airborne early-warning function, became the grandfather of the sophisticated Grumman E-2C Hawkeye. Fleet air defense improved by leaps and bounds. Communications at every level, although a long way from perfection, became far more reliable and effective, especially when the chips were down—in combat.[14]

The memories were there, and the results too: Carlson's Canyon; the unique strike against the Hwachon Dam; a specially targeted air assault on top enemy leaders gathered at Kapsan in October 1951, which killed five hundred of them; the Suiho raids; tussles with MiG interceptors high over the Yalu. But the dreary round of repetitive missions was the real story, the risk without the ultimate reward of conclusive victory. Life-threatening situations themselves became routine. Paul Gray, the skipper of VF-54, was downed so often that his ready room aboard *Essex* posted a sign: "Use caution when ditching damaged airplanes in Wonsan Harbor. Don't hit CDR Gray." (Gray received three Distinguished Flying Crosses for his Korean adventures.)

The blue planes did everything they were allowed to do, and more: fighter cover, light bombing, interdiction, flak suppression, close air support, night attack, combat air patrol, early warning, antisubmarine work, night heckling, aerial reconnaissance, air-sea rescue. They made mistakes—at times a flight of Skyraiders would zero in on an ox-cart, or a screaming section of Panthers would take off after a bicycle—but they never stopped. They persevered, and if they did not prevail, they made a difference.

Korea was a small affair compared to the upheaval of world war, even though, as Rip Struble said, the conflict was "a major war confined to a small area." The Navy, which never operated more than four fleet carriers together off the Korean coast, flew 276,000 combat sorties—only 7000 short of its World War II *total*—and dropped 177,000 tons of bombs—74,000 tons *more* than the total load dropped by the Navy in all theaters of the world war. This despite a critical shortage of naval aviators in the junior ranks and a breathtaking, battering operational pace.

The material cost, for the Navy and Marines, was 1248 aircraft, more than 1 per day for the duration of the war. Somewhat fewer than half (564) were lost to enemy action, with the doughty but vulnerable Corsairs (302) and the plodding Skyraiders (124) leading the list. A typical fighter airplane cost about $250,000, compared with the World War II price tag of $60,000, so these losses were far from insignificant. More important were the people: on average, a carrier air group sent to Korea would lose 10 percent of its highly trained aircrew to either combat or operational losses before deployment was over. Not everyone led the charmed life of Paul Gray.

If the carrier's power projection ashore made a difference, much of this impact was hidden in the sealed records of North Korea and Red China. For naval aviators the intense frustration remained, a haunting legacy of an "unwinnable war." Almost paradoxically, a primitive economy, although not immune to air attack, had kept on ticking, kept on making war. Targeting restrictions, however pertinent and correct they may have been, hogtied aerial potential and worked against strategic goals. Only duty, and the attendant willingness to take the risk, came to matter.

When *Bremerton* and her two destroyers, *Wiltsie* and *Porter*, fired their final salvos against Wonsan targets at 2159 on 27 July 1953, the best thing that the Navy could say about the Korean War was that, at long last, the dismal conflict was over.[15]

STERN WATCH II

──────── ☆ ────────

I n Korea, wrote one observer, "The Navy sees itself on a treadmill, fighting a war that may never end." But the end did come, and the treadmill finally ground to a halt. With the cessation of stalemated fighting came also a new realization of the Navy's roles in the postwar world.

The relentless treadmill had taken a fearful toll on the war's exhausted participants. Korea was left a charnel house; fresh graves dotted the peninsula from end to end. North Korean and Chinese losses were estimated at 1.5 million killed and wounded. About 1 million Korean civilians on both sides of the 38th parallel were casualties. Overall American losses included 33,000 dead and 100,000 wounded. Other UN forces suffered around 3000 dead and 15,000 wounded. As for the South Korean troops, their butcher's bill for resisting invasion appeared to be about 400,000 killed and as many more wounded or missing.

—At least two million were dead and three million more wounded, in a war that had never been declared. About one-third of the population of the two Koreas was either dead, wounded, or displaced (the modern euphemism for having one's abode blasted down around one's ears). Agricultural production was down by a third; millions wandered the roads, seeking food and shelter; most of the North's factories and industries had been leveled. Seoul was the most battle-scarred city in the world.[1]

Such was "limited" war. By November 1952 the United States was taking casualties at the rate of a thousand a week. More bombs were dropped on Korea than America had delivered in all theaters during the first two years of World War II. The Eighth Army used about the same weight of artillery and mortar shells as was fired in all of Europe from D day to V-E Day.

Not that the use of force by Americans in the postwar era was new. Already by 1947 the United States had used limited military force, or threatened its use, sixteen times. Force was ingrained as an instrument of national policy well before Korea. But the *scale* was completely unexpected and shocking.

The response to limited war was predictable: the world became even more of an armed camp. From 1950 to 1953 the annual military expenditures of the United States better than tripled, from $14.5 billion to $49.6 billion, a level that would be roughly maintained through the fifties and would then increase. The USSR's outlays went up by two-thirds, to $25.5 billion. Among the lesser economies, British costs doubled, and French spending rose by 250 percent (mostly for Vietnam).[2]

Personnel wearing American uniforms doubled, to almost three million. The number of Air Force wings rose from 48 to 108. And the Navy increased its commissioned ships from 671 to over 1100. The Korean War, although not the complete cause of this hardened military posture, also accelerated the development of an American garrison state and its accompanying siege mentality.[3]

In this trend the Navy had a major part. Korea was shaped, initially, not by the heavy bomber and its atomic weapon or by the scratch troops thrown into the breach at Pusan but by the naval response of carrier interdiction, resupply, and amphibious assault. In fact, Korea was a classic exercise in the predominance of seapower. Everything rested on oceanic command and communication, because only thus could effective numbers of fighting men be transported, resupplied, and kept fighting. In the western Pacific, American naval strength mushroomed in the first four months of the war from 86 to 274 ships; in the first year, naval personnel there increased more than sevenfold.

Admittedly, the Navy's initial reluctance to use its amphibious power meant that, in the war of movement that defined the first few months of the conflict, the service "sailed somewhat reluctantly to glory." But sail the Navy did, and even when the front stabilized, the nature of the peninsular war meant the supporting naval action was still of prime importance. There were other UN navies there—the British, of course, and also French, Dutch, Colombian, and Thai units—but the burden was squarely on America's seapower.

There were problems aplenty: electronic malfunctions; maintenance breakdowns; enough communications hitches to tax the patience of a saint (no naval saints emerged from Korea); operating limitations on both ships and planes; squabbles over proper coordination of the air assault; the infernal weather; and above all, the damnable mines. None of these, nor the countless other nagging vexations, was ever fully surmounted, but in the final analysis, they did not have to be.

Without naval opposition, American seapower was the logistical breath of life to the UN effort. Logistics movement in the western Pacific took place on a World War II scale. Fleet expansion occurred in everything from attack carriers to liberty boats, and most of the additions ended up off Korea. The Pacific Fleet expanded its number of ships by 50 percent, and, indicative of American estimates of "Communist" pressures worldwide, the Navy's Atlantic and Mediterranean presence was beefed up as well.

The cost to the Navy for all this activity was, when compared with the overall price paid by American forces, decidedly minimal. Indeed, the service's largest single tragedy during the war occurred not in the Pacific but the Atlantic. In April 1952, while in the midst of night flight operations, the destroyer-minesweeper *Hobson* veered in front of *Wasp* and was sent to the bottom, with a loss of 175 lives.

In Korea, 279 Navymen (including aviators) were killed in action, 23 died of wounds, and 156 were missing—a total of 458—and 1,576 more were wounded. The Navy's share of American dead was 1.4 percent, of wounded 1.6 percent. Five ships were lost—the four minesweepers and the tug—all to mines. Eighty-seven more were damaged: four from mines and the rest from shore batteries, a gauge of the blockade's close quarters.[4]

On paper these statistics downplayed the Navy's contribution to an almost farcical degree. In reality, "the continuing importance of sea power emerge[d] as the most significant lesson to be learned from the Korean War." The United States Navy not only helped hold the line on "Communist" expansion but did so thousands of miles from home, on the very edge of the enemy's landmass. The fleet emerged as the fundamental military instrument of "containment," which, whatever the form that idea had previously taken, now clearly had a military dimension. "As a defensive doctrine containment has more than proved itself," reflected one naval analyst. "It certainly must be continued."

Some saw the failure to "win" in Korea as the "sentinel mistake" of the war. But such attitudes obscured the larger significance of the naval effort. "The Korean War . . . has been a war to prevent a larger war by serving notice on a ruthless enemy that he can go so far and no farther," said Turner Joy. "There is no quick, easy, cheap way to win a war . . . but for the Navy the war in Korea would [have] come to a sudden halt."

Joy's sermon had a greater purpose than mere boosterism. "There is nothing inevitable about our own survival," he preached. "History is littered with the graves of civilization that assumed all is well." The guards must be posted at the gates; their vigil must be constant. Anything less courted national suicide.

In Korea the guards had done their assigned work, and in the aura cast by the light from this "limited" conflict, some could see "victory." If political considerations in the postwar world required limited objectives, and if the formulation of military strategy now rested mostly with civilian policymakers, still the invulnerability of American naval force made the Navy a mandatory tool for reaching those objectives, shaping those strategies.[5]

Simply put, Korea "globalized" the Cold War and made the United States Navy a seemingly necessary instrument in this globalization. Back in 1796, as George Washington delivered his warning against "entangling alliances" to his countrymen, Congressman Theodore Sedgwick of Massachusetts had rashly predicted that by 1953 America (which had, in 1796, no frigates, no Navy Department, and but an honor guard of officers and sailors) "will doubtless be found to possess naval strength equal to that possessed by any other power whatsoever." There were few such dreamers in those early days: another had been the ferociously tempered congressman Matthew Lyon, who imagined the time when "this nation is destined . . . to wrest the trident from the very hand that now holds it." Now, Sedgwick's and Lyon's dreams were reality.

World War II brought them to fruition, and the "entangling alliances" had come to pass. Korea was the exclamation mark. The United States far and away outclassed everyone else at sea. Its Army could be opposed (and, as in Korea, by great numbers). Its Air Force had the bomb, but the thing seemed too frightening, too counterproductive to use; besides, the big bombers needed land bases. But the Navy—the Navy could rove the oceans at will, uncontested—global.[6]

In 1953 almost no Americans perceived in this naval hegemony any but the most benign intentions. No imperialism, no exploitation, no arrogance— only a critical means through which America could work its will in world affairs. This comforting notion of *Pax Americana*, while including many benevolent facets, in the last analysis floated on the keels of Navy warships. If there was to be an "American Century" (the phrase was that of publishing magnate Henry Luce), the Navy would play a considerable part.

There seemed little more to ideas like these than "enlightened self-interest," in opposition to the crystal-clear wickedness of international communism, a communism that few people troubled to distinguish from incipient nationalism. There was, just as in World War II, an *enemy*—to be identified, singled out, opposed, conquered.

Hence the Navy steamed away from Korea as a secular vicar of international power and order, on American terms. The service was central to the developing, and dangerous, "illusion of American omnipotence," the conviction that every American objective could be reached; that the application of power, no matter how reluctantly applied, would produce the desired results; and that military solutions, if "limited," would nevertheless work better than necessarily unsatisfactory diplomatic ones.

The success, or failure, of the American-led UN intervention in Korea would long be debated. For the Navy, what was beyond debate was its renewed stature, indeed its *necessity* in the postwar world. The Korean flashpoint produced a Navy for a new kind of battle. The carriers, Gators, auxiliaries—all of them had become central to a garrison state of war, cold war.[7]

And if a cold war suddenly became hot, the Navy, the front line of defense, must be ready, shield high. Perpetual preparedness seemed the only possible conclusion. As a result, across America, the naval workshops stepped up their pace, as the armorers went about fashioning the tridents of Poseidon.

PART THREE

TRIDENTS

— OF —

POSEIDON

Therefore when those experienced in war
move they make no mistakes; when they act,
their resources are limitless.

—Sun-tzu, *The Art of War*

CHAPTER THIRTEEN

TECHNO-EMPIRE

☆

To the ancient Greeks, the god Poseidon initially had nothing to do with the sea. He built no ships, fought no naval battles. Poseidon's realm was ashore; his mastery lay in the arts of horsemanship. Originally he was neither a god of war nor a cult figure, but a rather insignificant deity.

Somehow this harmless equine god left dry land behind. By the fifth century B.C., Poseidon was depicted either gliding along the waves accompanied by sea nymphs or, when alone, brandishing a trident or thunderbolt, perhaps representing two contrasting moods of the sea. During the great age of Athenian naval dominance in the Aegean, he appeared neither armed nor threatening. The Athenians pictured him as encouched or enthroned; he held his rather ornate trident as a three-pronged scepter.

War changed Poseidon. As Athenian maritime dominance gave way to a time of competing Mediterranean navies, he rose up and stood, sometimes posing with one foot on a chariot. Dolphins rather than sea nymphs became his blue-water consorts. And the trident no longer served as his regal scepter. Now the fancy filigree work around the shaft and points had vanished, leaving only the barbs—stark, purposeful, menacing.

The trident had become a weapon.

☆

The Greeks used reason to try to understand and assimilate eternal verities, creating goals toward which people might aspire. To them, reason could never connote the *means* toward these goals. They believed that all crafts had been invented in heaven and taught to humans by the gods. (Greek mythology was replete with stories of automatons displayed in temples as part of a god's presence.) The Greek word *techne* did not mean rational science, as understood over two millennia later, but rather bore a heavy freight of theology, mysticism, and magic.

Over the centuries the irrational faded but slowly, never to vanish entirely. To laymen in particular—and this included practically everyone—technologies retained their aura of mystery, of the impenetrable. People who seemed to create or master technologies were usually held in high honor and specially paid (like early naval gunner's mates) or were feared and condemned.[1]

Technology and war, always interrelated, maintained a rather even developmental pace until about the middle of the nineteenth century. Military technology changed so slowly that both sides in a war generally had similar equipment—"symmetry." Nelson's navy, in all essentials, was akin to that of Elizabeth I two centuries before, and to that of his French and Spanish opponents at Trafalgar.

The industrial revolution and the machine age accelerated technological development manyfold. Competing nation-states meant competing national technologies, and arms races a century ago tended to be competitions in *quantity* of troops, guns, or capital ships. But with the mass wars of the twentieth century, the distinction between the military specialist with his arcane technological skill (that naval gunner's mate, for example) and the civilian, theoretically untouched by all these advancing species of weaponry, began to erode.

Ideologies once more began to clash, only now they featured military technologies of the most devastating kind. These weapons brought every civilian within reach, not of a carefully circumscribed battlefield around the rim of which a noncombatant *might* get hurt, but of an indiscriminate slaughterhouse. The weapons could not distinguish uniform from suit, man from woman, adult from child.

Twentieth-century technologies also developed a startling tendency to feed off themselves. Not in the sense that they operated independently of people, of course; humans created technologies, and they alone were responsible for them. Rather technologies in a century of intense national and ideological rivalry, of total war, were boosted along by pride, fear, patriotism, and the seeming imperative of military "readiness."

To be *ready* meant that one's military technology had to be in place when the balloon went up, because the "threat" was omnipresent; there would be no time for development once the shooting started. Thus, peace was a time to prepare, and preparation unavoidably meant technological development. Terms like peace, war, and security no longer had the clear, finite dimensions that at one time seemed to define them. And the accompanying depersonalization of combat (the Athenian sailors had boarded or rammed their victims and met their enemies face-to-face; battleships could duel at twenty miles) brought something else: more and more, men in war or preparing for war existed to serve machines, rather than vice versa. In this much narrower sense, modern technology could be said to have a mind of its own.

As technology became ever more involved and complex, its mystery deepened even as machines became an unavoidable and indispensable part of everyday life. Only highly educated specialists, some of these with the political savvy of a gerbil, seemed to understand how the machines, particularly the weapons, *worked*. Americans, in particular, loved their gadgetry, not least their military toys, and the more sophisticated technology had little or no connection with national policy yet was expected to be on call as a possible solution to national problems. "We don't know what we want," drawled Will Rogers, "but we are ready to bite somebody to get it."

In the international arena, applied technology was *power*, and power was seen as a guaranteed way of getting things done. That this attitude was fundamentally careless and dangerous was scarcely glimpsed in 1945. "Americans are childish in many ways and about as subtle as a Wimpy burger," observed the cultural critic Tom Wolfe. "But in the long run it doesn't make any difference. They just turn on the power." On a more brutal level, according to the journalist Hunter Thompson, America after its total war triumphs had become "just a nation of two hundred million used car salesmen with all the money we need to buy guns and no qualms about killing anybody else in the world who tries to make us uncomfortable."

Technology had become . . . *convenient*. And more: Once, war had been waged by men using machines. Now, war was increasingly a contest among machines that were operated and maintained by men. Strategies therefore tended to be bound by the capabilities of the machines. The older technological mind-set sought to shape the present in accordance with a vision of the future. The newer mind-set based the future on present technology, and thus the machines served as blinders to possibility.

Major modern weapons systems came to be designed to fight not men but other machines. If "symmetry" in weapons systems existed, the technologies might fight to a decisive end: American versus Japanese carriers in the Pacific. But if "asymmetry" existed, the end could be decidedly obscure and unclear, and the pertinent uses of technology could become unclear as well (as naval aviators found out in Korea).

Such tendencies were not *national*, although the technologies, because of their complexities and expense, were mostly creations of the modern nation-state; they belonged to the nature of technology itself. The German army in World War I found that "optimal use of weapons alone shaped command and deployment." Indeed, the arts of operational planning and strategy frequently deteriorated into a mere problem of managing armaments. The "strategist" was too often an organizer of weapons or, to use a popular professional model from the World War I era, an engineer.

Because the weapons were ever more destructive, strategies for their use widened. Once strategic thinking had implied a sort of operational calculus of efficiency, limiting and concentrating the war effort. Now, "strategists" offered rationales for escalating force and the threat of force. Any limits to such thinking became increasingly difficult to discern. In fact, battalions of "pocket strategists" issued forth with obiter dicta, the common denominator of which seemed to be that they had sacrificed the art of thinking about war in favor of parading their knowledge of its implements.[2]

Only the shortest of steps remained to link national strategies directly to weapons and their capacities, and by 1945 this step had been taken. For the United States, the only major power to emerge from the war economically strong, the seeming imperative to continue to develop arms went almost unquestioned. "Our national existence," asserted two military historians, "may depend upon the ability of Americans—civilian and military alike— to develop, *without limitation or inhibition upon the free flight of imagination*, new tactics and techniques and weapons, to be applied in cold war or in hot in accordance with the proven principles of the military art."

Many people simply shrugged off the implications. Modern technology bestowed so many gifts—the refrigerator, the television set, the ubiquitous automobile—and besides, the urge to indulge in "the free flight of imagination" was too strong to be resisted. There was, claimed one analyst, such a thing as a "technological imperative—when technology beckons, men are helpless." Maybe, but people made technology, not vice versa, and to credit *techne*, with all its mysteries, with a mind of its own was to surrender the better part of the human spirit.

☆

Navies were historically highly conservative in their technologies. Ships were expensive and, once sunk, did not come back. Despite the noble tradition of fighting admirals risking everything with their fleets, the record suggested precisely the opposite. Nelson was worshiped because he was Nelson, not because he took substantial risks.

Certainly the *size* of twentieth-century navies expanded. So did the reach of their weapons systems. But even though the battleship gave way to the carrier (which was really only a device for launching munitions farther and with hopefully greater accuracy), and even though the submarine emerged as an independent strategic force of its own, the fundamentals of warfare at sea remained the same: the projection of power from a floating platform.

Various systems came and went—guns, rockets, propeller-driven airplanes. Whichever technologies were in current favor tended to condition naval capacities and, thus, naval strategies. If a technology was almost never top-drawer and yet stayed around (the sea mine was the classic case), the weapon usually emerged embarrassingly often, as mines did off Wonsan in Korea, to mess things up.

Ship technologies were still quite conservative in the postwar era, the aircraft carrier being the most prominent case in point. But now, beyond the platforms, the hot technologies were what counted. "With the developments in weapons and equipment that have taken place since World War II," James Forrestal reported in 1948, "it is apparent that radical revisions of combat tactics and concepts are necessary, and the Navy is preparing itself in accordance with these developments."

"*Ex scientia tridens*" reads the motto of the United States Naval Academy: "From knowledge, sea power." Lest this be thought of a piece with any old military academy motto, consider West Point's "Duty, honor, country," or the Air Force Academy's "Man's flight through life is sustained by the power of his knowledge." Only the Navy directly relates the acquisition of knowledge to military force.

"Knowledge," in the Navy way of things, most often meant the mastery of technology, the unraveling of mysteries directly relating to the nautical enterprise and naval power. As a result, the sheer pace of technological change mandated continuous learning and relearning. No sooner was one technology in place, doing its work, than "experts" (the ones who had unraveled the mysteries) decreed its obsolescence.[3]

Sometimes a technology was through even sooner. A prime example was the Navy's powerful radio telescope, to be located at Sugar Grove, West Virginia. This eye-to-the-sky was designed to be exquisitely state-of-the-art—six hundred feet in diameter, thirty-three thousand tons, its electronics sensitive enough to probe thirty-eight billion light-years into space. Almost $100 million had been spent or obligated for Sugar Grove before Secretary of Defense Robert McNamara called a halt in 1962, citing "major advances in science and technology." The millions were gone, and Sugar Grove never looked at the heavens.

The Navy periodically tried to get a handle on this waste. There was an attempt to create a "Naval Technical Corps" in 1959 to provide a home for engineers, ordnance specialists, aeronautical experts, communicators, hydrographers, and other delvers into the mysteries. This effort died a lingering death amid the bureaucratic wars of the Pentagon, and naval attempts at technological efficiency, particularly on the budgetary end, were most often hit-or-miss, program by program. Moreover, the research and development that supported technological change tended to occur in the Navy in a piece-by-piece, incremental fashion. Existing technologies were tinkered with, "improved," not only because they were considered too expensive to completely replace but also because the Navy's technological conservatism wedded the decision makers to beloved weapons systems—first the battleship and then the carrier.

Research and development not only persistently hurtled forward in the postwar years; its processes expanded with incredible speed. The sleepiness that had characterized the interwar period was gone for good. In 1959, as a sample, the Navy was developing an all-weather low-altitude attack aircraft (A2F); an internal-combustion catapult power-plant for the nuclear-powered carrier *Enterprise*; a close-support artillery weapon for the Marines; the Navy Tactical Data System; an assault landing craft (LCA); guided missiles of various families—Eagle, Sidewinder, Sparrow, Bullpup, Corvus, Talos, Po-

laris; earth satellite navigation systems, communications systems, relay systems, electronic reconnaissance systems, and weather, surveying, and
interception systems (the list was virtually endless); sonar; torpedoes; drone
helicopters; and even mines.

Any single one of these would have practically exhausted the comparatively meager resources of the prewar Navy. And the weapons and associated systems were far from the whole story. The Navy launched high-
altitude balloons to scrutinize the upper atmosphere; pioneered in a new
branch of chemistry (perfluorobenzenes), an upside-down world where materials resisted change at high temperatures; plumbed the ocean depths with
the bathyscaphe *Trieste*; used computers, game theory, and automatic data
processing to help shuffle numbers ever faster; photographed the sun; used
ultrasonic waves for special types of brain surgery; developed higher-quality
steel for submarine hulls; inaugurated a Space Surveillance System; carried
out experiments involving elasticity in structural mechanics; and developed
solid-state physics to a high art, helping to create such revolutionary devices
as transistors.

"A comprehensive research program is being prosecuted," noted Secretary of the Navy William Franke. He was not kidding. At any given
moment the Navy had minds working at every link in the R and D chain,
from dreamy concepts to watch-on-watch fleet operations. Everything was
fair game; when Navy researchers suspected that the hydrodynamic drag
of fish, whales, and porpoises was considerably less than that of rigid bodies
of the same shape and size, marine life played its part in the redesigning of
naval weapons and underwater craft. And the research was rewarded; in
1960 no fewer than thirty scientists directly associated with Navy programs
were honored for their work.[4]

The R and D people were geared to an accelerated pace of technological
innovation that never stopped. Using a botanical analogy, one critic saw
previous technology as a fruit-bearing tree, in which change had taken place
only by genetic accident—very slowly. But then innovation "came to re-
semble a potted plant. It has not been allowed to develop naturally, but is
deliberately manipulated to answer the grower's needs." Further, since invention was *demanded* rather than *spontaneous*, the resulting technological
systems were necessarily incomplete all the time; they were never "finished."
Thus the modern term "advanced"—to describe a technology which is not
yet working, might never work, and perhaps should not have worked in the
first place—the creeping incrementalism of up-to-the-minute R and D.

Still the pace quickened, under the press of nationalism, Cold War,
greed, even simple curiosity. In one sense the Navy *was* technology, could
not exist apart from technology. The service, as all navies always had,
depended on the researchers, the scientists, the thinkers, the men who knew
the mysteries—just like those Athenian shipwrights.

In the post-1945 period, the men who knew the mysteries were more important than ever. The time of the weaponeers, never far off, had come round again:

> Now thrive the armourers, and honour's thought
> Reigns solely in the breast of every man.
> They sell the pasture now to buy the horse,
> Following the mirror of all Christian kings . . .
> For now sits Expectation in the air. . . .

☆

Naval leaders in the early twentieth century had been somewhat less than dynamic regarding the military potential of scientific research; only the coming of the Great War moved them off dead center. A civilian had to get their attention; none other than Thomas Edison initiated contact with Secretary of the Navy Josephus Daniels concerning scientific research to aid the Navy. In 1915 the secretary wrote the Wizard of Menlo Park about the possibility of creating "machinery and facilities for utilizing the natural inventive genius of America to meet the new conditions of warfare. . . . "

The result was the Naval Consulting Board, a collection of business executives, engineers, and inventors. The board proposed a "special naval laboratory" and actually saw money allocated, but when America went to war, the idea got lost. (Its members spent most of 1917 and 1918 fruitlessly screening public suggestions for anything of military value.) But the board set the pattern: military and naval R and D in the United States would be a combination of government and private enterprise; the profit motive would never be absent.

Efficiency, although not foreign to government operations such as Navy yards, did not rank high on the value scale, and the Navy beyond all other national institutions was usually top-heavy with traditionalism and inertia. Indeed, Franklin Delano Roosevelt, as Daniels's assistant, banned "Taylorism"—a work-related series of efficiency mechanisms for human beings—from all the yards, a restriction that remained in force until 1949.

There were other barriers. Before World War II questions of profit as well as efficiency made effective cooperation between government and private enterprise uneasy. Above all, funds were hard to come by, even after Representative Carl Vinson had helped open the purse a bit during the Depression. Government bureaus themselves did relatively little research, and the largest appropriations customarily went to agriculture (there was *always* a "farm problem"), not to industry.

As late as 1937 only 2 percent of federal government expenditures were going for research, as compared to 4 percent in some industries and as high as 25 percent in some universities. Although the Great War had led to an increased military sponsorship of research in the private sector, peace closed the pocketbook. The major research agency to emerge from the war, the

National Research Council, relied mostly on private funds for its operations.

World War II changed all that. The partnership between government and private enterprise so haltingly begun by Edison and Daniels became not only a going concern but a healthy giant. Scientists of every persuasion provided the wherewithal for what Winston Churchill dubbed the "wizard war"—conflict in which brainpower was more important than bullets.

For the Navy, the results of the wizard war were astonishingly dramatic and could be seen on every front: in the frigid North Atlantic, where Allied hunter-killer groups stalked the deadly wolfpacks; over the beaches of North Africa, Sicily, Italy, Normandy, and the Pacific; and against the terrifying kamikaze off Okinawa. In World War II the wizards not only made a difference—they made themselves essential and irreplaceable. The fleet could not do without them.

The Navy's Demobilization Plan Number Two emphasized not only research but also the necessity of maintaining a technological lead. Here was a quiet but striking sea change. The Navy had always been interested in R and D, but except in wartime this interest was usually expressed at an exceptionally low level. (Teddy Roosevelt's presidency was an exception.) Both funding and trained personnel were scarce, and the service's conservatism bred both caution and inflexibility. In 1940 about 1 percent of total naval expenditures went into research.

Then came World War II and the Cold War. By the mid-fifties the research figure was 6 percent. The dollar increase went from less than $9 million in 1940 to $526 million in 1954—both years of "peace." By 1959 a three-star admiral was in charge of the Navy's research program.

Part of Plan Number Two even suggested that the inception and outcome of the next war would be *determined* by technological advance. "It must be assumed that the next war will descend upon this country abruptly," predicted the planners, "and will be prosecuted by enemies equipped with revolutionary new weapons developed through great scientific research effort. The Navy therefore needs a research program in the years of peace far larger than heretofore."[5]

By 1953 such programs were annually producing almost $7 billion worth of ships, planes, munitions, and other naval material. About 20 percent of the dollar value of the Navy's prime contracts went to small businesses, but an increasing amount of R and D money filled the coffers of single-source major suppliers. *Everything* was "developed," from high-performance jet aircraft to "itchless" underwear. (This last item, which took more than four years of "research," was "of more than casual interest to the wearer," said the secretary of the Navy).

Technology was king. Technical books and training manuals of all kinds poured from naval presses: atomic energy, nuclear physics, servomechanisms, guided missiles, radio, electronics, radar, fluid dynamics, metallurgy. What a sailor did not know, more than ever before, could hurt or kill him.

Technology demanded learning, and of a certain kind. As one whitehat remarked, "This is a new, new Navy."

—Indeed, and a Navy so dependent on technology and technological change that the service, willingly or not, had become an enormous realm of technology, a "techno-empire."

☆

The empire was defined technically and pragmatically, rather than intellectually. Abstruse meanderings amid theoretical outposts were usually not encouraged. The Navy historically had a rather poor relationship with the social sciences anyway. Whereas both the Army and Air Force routinely invited prominent social scientists to lecture at their war colleges and other advanced schools and set their fast-track officers to studying for graduate degrees in the social sciences, the Navy did neither. In 1959 only six naval officers were on full-time assignment as graduate students in social sciences at civilian universities.

The Navy felt its technology to be of dominant importance. In 1946 the service negotiated agreements with more than forty-five schools and industrial firms—the likes of Columbia, Harvard, Johns Hopkins, MIT, General Electric, Firestone, and Sperry Gyroscope—for studies in several dozen fields. No social science here; the Navy wanted developments in electronics, nuclear physics, chemistry, metallurgy, and guided missiles—anything that could help its vessels keep the sea and fight.

Forrestal was behind these moves. The top officers in charge, Rear Admirals Harold Bowen, a crusty curmudgeon who had pioneered in high-temperature, high-pressure steam engineering, and Luis De Florez, a hyperkinetic Reservist and MIT-trained inventive genius who designed innovative systems in petroleum engineering and, with the Navy, invented numerous training devices such as aviation simulators—both these men believed that research was the foundation of a modern industrial nation. Bowen commented that "the fruits of the government-supported research program of World War II are being given to civilian institutions." The Navy and American industrial progress would go forward, hand-in-hand.

The Navy, civilian schools, and private enterprise had worked in harness before. But the postwar years saw something new, not only in the scale of the interrelationship but also in the rise of the "defense intellectual," who gravitated among ivory towers, business conference rooms, and "think tanks" that operated off increasingly lucrative government contracts. Many of these people were "operations analysts," a breed that had won its spurs in World War II by doing valuable work on convoy escort problems in the North Atlantic.

The operations analysts formulated models, derived theories (they loved theories), verified ideas, made conclusions. They went up the gangways themselves and studied everything from flight-deck procedures to the movement of chow lines. Among them were mathematicians, physicists, economists, and even a stray sociologist or two. By the early sixties the Navy had banded two hundred of them together in the Operations Evaluation Group, which contracted for specific project work. Unlike the better-known RAND Corporation of Santa Monica, California, which emphasized strategic thinking for the Air Force, the Navy's group did a bit of everything, from the keel plates up. Most of its work was valuable, and some, in the tradition of the itchless underwear, was a bit silly, but its analysts had the ear of Navy brass, their numbers and equations took on a life of their own, and they prospered.

American scientists were placed in a master file of specialties: engineers of all kinds, geologists, geophysicists, computer experts, the lot. Questionnaires went out to fifty thousand scientists—a fathomless pool of technical expertise, to be tapped on demand. Naval research had become big business.[6]

The techno-empire had no single head and had many hearts. The strongest pulse beat in the Office of Naval Research (ONR). The office was born (by Public Law 588) on 1 August 1946, authorized to support the basic research of university scientists as well as to lead the Navy's in-house research program. The two temporary wartime bodies charged with these functions, the Office of Scientific Research and Development and the National Defense Research Committee, disappeared with the coming of peace, and something new was needed to carry on naval R and D.

Captain Robert Conrad, an engineering officer who was fated to die prematurely of leukemia in 1949, was one of the principal architects of ONR, and so was Bowen, who became its first commander. The latter received unused wartime funds from an approbative Forrestal to jump-start the new agency, and Conrad romanced university scientists to participate.

The civilians were suspicious; they feared that federal support of their work would mean federal, or military, control. Many of them loathed directed research and wanted to go where their minds and interests led them. Some, who had had their fill of the wartime "military mind" and its peculiar ways of doing things, simply wanted to be let alone in their civilian pursuits.

But Conrad kept pitching. He was a convincing speechifier, and he managed to work out a contractual system remarkably free of bureaucratic red tape. Further, ONR was subdivided into disciplinary branch units, each of which was encouraged to retain informal ties with corresponding university departments. The branch units, run by civilian scientists, had considerable autonomy and, as the future would show, could at times run off the reins altogether. Finally, Conrad argued that the Navy would really listen to civilian judgments, particularly on contract proposals. There, scientific acumen was at a premium, as proposals for basic research were not submitted on a bid basis.

These were honeyed words, but ones with real sugar, and the scientists came, supped, and stayed. As a result, naval research became a robust concern within months of V-J Day. ONR settled into "T-3," a drab-gray wartime "temporary" building on Constitution Avenue that was its home for eighteen years, until the scientists moved to Main Navy.

The brains produced. Out of ONR's shops, study groups, and sponsorships flowed ideas that literally changed the world, among others the initial concept of a submarine-launched ballistic missile (Polaris), the electronically suspended gyroscope, masers and lasers, electronic navigation, long-range sonar, and oceanography and deep ocean exploration.

The office did all this with a rear admiral in charge and with about a hundred scientists on its headquarters staff; in twenty years the personnel roster grew by less than one-third. But the budget swelled. Bowen got $43.8 million for fiscal 1947; two decades later the amount had tripled. Roughly half went to "R" and half to "D," each half *very* loosely conceived.

The early occupants of T-3 generated "a little of the atmosphere of early Christians spreading a new gospel of the partnership of science and government." In one sense their evangelism succeeded too well, because by the mid-sixties the Navy had to compete for technological expertise not only with the civilian sector but also with no fewer than eight federal agencies, each of which was by then deeply involved with supporting academic research. And by then ONR was so understaffed that the agency had to "tread water awfully fast to keep its head up."

But most of the actual work was being farmed out from T-3, to the extent that by 1948 "virtually every outstanding scientific laboratory in the country, whether it be part of a big industrial plant or part of a university's science department, is working on some phase of the research program of ONR." This "tremendous scientific effort" was "in the interests of the Navy and the national security."

Even before Korea the office had become, in an amazingly short time, the principal supporter of fundamental research by American scientists. ONR directly employed more than one thousand of them, ran three naval laboratories and six branch offices, and sponsored a huge university program, with over 1100 projects at more than two hundred institutions. By itself, T-3 accounted for almost 40 percent of the national government's total expenditure on pure science.

The early frostiness of the academics melted under the benevolent sunlight cast by government money and by a surprising lack of constraints on their work. By 1949 T-3 was receiving four times as many applicants for projects as ONR had money to support. In addition to the maximum freedom bestowed on the contracting scientists, the Navy pushed hard for an exemplary working relationship between uniform and gown—and generally succeeded, so long as the subject was technological and could be perceived, in even the most remote way, as having naval benefits. To smooth the process, there were about a dozen "advisory panels," a "naval research advisory committee," and, of greatest importance, a crucial network of personal contacts radiating outward from T-3 to campuses and businesses all over the nation.

Bowen could be stubborn as a seawall when he got his hackles up (as he had done when trying to get his new steam-engineering concepts introduced), and he was adamant about the value of "basic" research—which meant the researcher did not know exactly where he was going, but he would like to try to get there. This attitude could not help but attract scientists. Many who might have drawn the line on being directly involved with weapons systems (many did not, and took to weaponeering like ducks to water) worked in perfect contentment on low-temperature physics, cosmic rays, dwarf stars, economic mathematical structures, or nerve biochemistry. Scientists were encouraged to "dream freely," in hopes that their dreams might metamorphose into military reality. The Navy even supplied the money to facilitate an entomologist's study of the army ant.

But the blue uniforms were never completely out of the loop. Even much of the basic research had *naval purpose*, even if that purpose was a bit hard to glimpse, particularly as seen through congressional spectacles. There was, for example, a psychological study of eighteen captains who had distinguished themselves in combat, to the end of determining what qualities made up outstanding naval leaders; the construction of a "high-speed electronic calculating machine," expected to multiply 40,000 ten-digit numbers per second; studies in statistical probability theory; and improvements in medical technology.

Once the scientists got the gist of the commitment of Bowen and ONR, they proposed most of the projects themselves. In this dawning age of grantsmanship, many highbrows rapidly developed a lowbrow nose for where the money was. ONR selected only "projects which it consider[ed] pertinent to its own plans," but this pertinency proved practically as broad as scientific endeavor itself. Still, clever scientists who did not trouble overmuch about the ethical problems of war and its associated weaponry could easily dovetail their research interests with arcane matters such as the aerodynamics of supersonic jets, new fuels for rocket motors, aviator safety, computer application to engine assemblies, or the examination of rare metals. Indeed, the scope of such problems was quite literally infinite and, therefore, so was the Navy's grasp—limited only by dollars and the human imagination.

Above all disciplines, however, the Navy favored physics and applied physics, for obvious reasons. Here was the unseen universe of atomic energy, the wonders of solid-state physics, optics, heat, electricity, magnetism. Low-temperature physics attracted a healthy interest, as did experiments in superconductivity and thermal fluctuations. Anything with even the most remote application to naval ordnance held possibilities. "There is scarcely an area of pure research," said one naval physicist, "for which a need does not exist in the formidable technical enterprise that is the Navy." By 1953 the Physics Branch had contracts out with over five hundred physicists in academia, industry, and government; more than half of these people were equipped with doctorates.

The Navy used its physicists, and all its scientists, not only as researchers but also as administrators. Much of the time the service's contracting policy was in the hands of civilians, not admirals. Thus the empire, from the very beginning, was beyond the control of any one person, particularly a man in uniform, but such was the power of the technological mind-set, and the fervent belief that technological progress ensured the welfare of the nation, that the contracting process went its way largely uncontested, even by most of the members of Congress who voted the funds.

Eventually, of course, there were checks. After a decade of full-blast funding, even the Navy brass became concerned over rising costs, the increasing complexity of naval technological systems, and the chastening realization that *everything* could not be developed at once, or was even worth "developing." There were limits, after all, in the physical world, and in many areas of speed, weight, and power the Navy was pressing the outer edges of the envelope.[7]

When the slowdown came, however, the techno-empire was in place, functioning smoothly, and essential.

☆

The empire was vast. The working cornerstone was the Naval Research Laboratory (NRL) in Washington, which ran programs in three major fields: electronics, materials, and nucleonics. The lab consisted, in 1960, of about 1200 scientists housed in eighty-four buildings clustered along the Potomac. Its lineage went back to 1920, when twenty handpicked civilian scientists had arrived.

The lab's record was exceptional. Its list of developments and inventions read like a barometer of modern applied science: shortwave radio, radar, sonar, electronic countermeasures against radio-controlled bombs, sonobuoys, fluorescent dyes for downed aviators, X-ray machines for ship's hulls. By 1960 NRL was working on five hundred projects, not only scouting the depths of the sea but also pushing out into space.

Its mission, originally defined as increasing "the safety, reliability, and efficiency of the fleet by the application of scientific and laboratory experimentation to naval problems," had broadened, like ONR's role, to take in virtually every nook and cranny that could be called "scientific." NRL's equipment was cutting-edge, including some pieces of apparatus and facilities that did not exist elsewhere in the form required for Navy work, such as betatrons, electron microscopes, and an altitude chamber. In its time, the lab had operated under the secretary of the Navy, as part of the old

Bureau of Engineering, and, during the war, as a field activity of the Bureau of Ships. Now, taken under the sheltering wing of ONR, NRL hit full stride.

Some of its creations were shrouded in secrecy, particularly those having to do with atomic energy. (The lab had initiated a liquid thermal diffusion process for separating uranium 235 from uranium 238.) But most of its work, like "window" (chaff) for cluttering enemy radar screens, got to the fleet as quickly as possible.

Many projects were farmed out. The Navy adopted a formal small-business policy in 1951, and many admirals urged their prime contractors to subcontract on the widest scale possible. But modern R and D, as the lab amply demonstrated, took expensive equipment and large numbers of highly skilled scientists and technicians. The small contractor, in spite of the policy, was being continuously pushed toward the margin as the techno-empire became increasingly dependent on large companies (which only got bigger) and single-source suppliers.

But most of the really critical developments remained in-house. A conspicuous example, in 1959, was the dream of a controlled fusion reaction: one small bucket of water yielding enough heavy hydrogen to make the fuel equivalent of three hundred gallons of gasoline. NRL's physicists created a magnetic mirror arrangement whereby deuterium gas flowed into a tube and was ionized. Four million amperes of electricity created a "magnetic shock" in the tube. The resulting plasma gas was pinched to the center of the tube and superheated to twenty million degrees centigrade, forcing deuterons to collide and fuse. These were signs that the temperature was high enough to overcome the powerful natural electrical forces that kept each atomic nucleus apart, causing the nuclei to come together with a corresponding release of tremendous energy.

Such experiments, announced as "peaceful," nevertheless had obvious military applications. Moreover, they were state-of-the-art, clearly beyond the reach of all but the most sophisticated scientific laboratories. The Navy did not "bottle fusion," as the press described the experiment, but the dream was alive, and work went on.[8]

NRL was only one of a chain of in-house labs, many of them geared to special missions. Despite occasional congressional complaints that the empire had become too large, too complex, and too expensive, the money was usually there, because the miracles emerged regularly, and the Navy was far from reluctant in giving them ample publicity. Most of the new weapons and equipment were products of a competitive bidding process of sorts, but the sky-high expense meant that fewer and fewer players could afford the game.

In White Oak, Maryland, stood the Naval Ordnance Laboratory (NOL), like ONR born in 1946. Before World War II naval ordnance specialists had limited themselves largely to mines and the big guns. Their home was the antiquated Naval Gun Factory, which by the end of the war was literally bulging at the seams. Now, NOL ran a giant wind tunnel, a 130-ton hollow cylinder fifty-two feet in diameter; cranked up the largest mobile X-ray generator in the world, a weird structure of bells, buzzers, and flashing lights surrounded by thirty-six-inch-thick concrete walls; tested ingenious mine configurations; and conducted devilish shock tests on anything that moved on, over, or beneath the sea.

Above all, the ordnance lab designed and tested *weapons*, of startling variety and lethality. Guns, mines, and missiles were only a start. There were aeroballistics studies, explosives testing, shock waves pounding on nose cones, X-ray diffractions to determine the precise atomic structure of materials, and underwater acoustics research. From 1955 to 1965, NOL completed 125 weapons systems or ordnance devices and released them into production.

Of course, White Oak, in the suburbs of the nation's capital, was not exactly the place for testing explosives (although a counterargument could certainly be made). The explosions took place in the desert wastes of southern California, at the Naval Ordnance Test Station in China Lake. The Navy moved to the Mojave Desert in 1943, originally building and testing rockets designed by Cal Tech scientists. But the 1712 square miles of this isolated, barren wilderness were too good to limit to rockets. Within a few years anything remotely connected with naval weapons passed through China Lake: air warfare systems; antisubmarine warfare systems; warheads; fuses; guidance, propulsion, and fire control systems; even parachutes.

Unlike other Navy labs, China Lake (renamed the Naval Weapons Center in 1967) operated in partnership with private industry. Its optical component technology center, for example, was used by industrial and university scientists alike. Probably the most famous tests at China Lake involved the new air-to-air and air-to-ground missiles, including the famed Sidewinder and the radiation-seeking Shrike. The Sidewinder was developed by William McLean while he was tinkering around in his garage. By the mid-sixties McLean, as the civilian technical director at China Lake, was the R and D boss of an empire within an empire. China Lake had become the largest military laboratory in the Western world. McLean, a folksy, down-to-earth sort, was typical of his scientific breed in his approach to weaponry. "You don't start with a military requirement," he said. "You start with the new equipment and develop the tactics to match its characteristics." Technology ruled.[9]

Everywhere in the techno-empire, the "new equipment" sprang from human minds, went through its tests and teething problems, and eventually (for the most part) got to the fleet. In Dahlgren, Virginia, the Weapons Laboratory (which dated back to 1872) tested naval guns, duplicated air blast effects of nuclear weapons, used electron microscopes to examine the metal pores of barrels, and computed ballistics tables. Every naval gun, from the old 40-mm to the sixteen-inchers, passed through Dahlgren. In the modern era the Weps Lab broadened its span to include atomic weapons, missiles, drones, and electromagnetic radiation (which could play dreadful tricks with ordnance).

In Philadelphia lay the Naval Air Engineering Center (105 buildings on 707 acres), where design data were gathered for future aircraft carriers, the structural integrity of airframes was tested, and aircraft engines designed and evaluated. Everything surrounding the queen of the modern fleet, the flattop, was grist for the center's mills. Just to the north, in Bucks County, was the Naval Air Development Center, which translated prototypes into operational configurations. Known throughout the Navy as "Johnsville" since its establishment in 1949, this center delved deeply into the esoteric world of communications data links, instrumentation, and avionics systems. Anything the Navy flew was shaped by Johnsville.

—And when the things flew, they usually flew first at the Naval Air Test Center, in Patuxent River, Maryland. "Pax River" gave the Navy's stamp of approval to operational aircraft. By the late sixties more than two hundred models of aircraft proposed for use by naval or Marine aviators had been wrung out at Pax River. Here was the home of the Navy's flying elite, the test pilots, and their school, and here aircraft were tortured through every conceivable maneuver to see if they could stand the strain and tempo of fleet operations.

Pax River, while the largest, was only one of twelve test bases for naval aircraft, and naval aviation was in the forefront of budget expenditure. By 1969, a state-of-the-art naval aircraft system could run to more than $30 million a copy, once the incredibly intricate avionics were factored in.

But the dollars flowed everywhere within the empire: to the David Taylor Model Basin in Annapolis, where hulls and ship configurations were tested; to New London, Connecticut, and the Submarine School; to the Naval Electronics Laboratory in San Diego; to the rapidly growing missile kingdom in Point Mugu, California; to laboratories specializing in mine defense, gas turbines, training devices, radiology, boilers, even personnel research. And even overseas: ONR had maintained a branch office in London since 1946.

—The dollars pumped continuous life throughout the system, and the techno-empire thrived.

☆

The Navy, of course, trumpeted its technological triumphs to the public. These were almost always presented in the familiar parameters of speed, distance, and power. The weapons were faster, went farther, were more accurate, packed far more explosive force. But these developments were only continuations of processes that had begun when man had first picked up a stone to bash in his enemy's skull.

The real changes were occurring almost unnoticed by those outside the empire. To begin with, the Navy was undergoing an all-pervasive electronic revolution. Ship propulsion systems were becoming automated; fire control systems began to stabilize themselves and become instantaneously self-correcting; projectiles carried their own guidance brains. The electronic senses, particularly radar and sonar, vastly multiplied the capacity of sailors to see through fog, clouds, and water. Electronic guidance systems even began to fly airplanes, to the horror of generations of seat-of-the-pants aviators.

The new electronic systems were complex beyond anything the Navy had ever seen. They demanded a new priesthood of technicians, programmers, and "specialists," all of whom spoke mysterious languages and without whom the damned things would not work. Civilian "technical representatives" became a routine part of ship's components. Training schools in the mysteries expanded and broadened, to the point where many enlisted men and officers spent a year or more in the classroom before they even saw salt water.

The search for improved accuracy, the imperative demand for more range and speed, the need not only to "keep up" but to "stay ahead"—all drove the electronic revolution. Aircraft tended more and more toward being automated missiles with a human being aboard as a passenger—the "spam in a can" of the coming astronaut age. Submarines increasingly became enormous underwater sound-detection machines. Surface ships ballooned in size. (The *Spruance*-classs destroyer had the displacement of a World War II light cruiser, and more than three *Essex*-class carriers were needed to displace the amount of the new nuclear carrier *Enterprise*.) Their number of automated systems followed suit. A sailing ship had been *labor-intensive*—the famed fighting frigates of the War of 1812 had swarmed with crews of four hundred or more—but the modern naval vessel was *technology-intensive*, with system piled upon complex system. The manpower was there not so much to *operate* as to *tend*.

Traditionalists feared that a "robot navy" was in the works, but in fact the power of decision never left the human mind. What had changed with the electronic revolution was the staggering amount of information the machines gathered, processed, and displayed. Human beings were left with the problem of whether to trust what emerged. They wanted the increased reliability brought by the revolution, but they also wanted to keep the flexibility of making decisions for themselves.

The revolution, furthermore, was continual, simply because systems produced countersystems in an electronic dialectic. For example, electronic countermeasures, so central to Churchill's wizard war, rapidly spawned electronic counter-countermeasures, ECCM, in which thousands of Navymen happily spent a career.

The revolution also brought a profound change in warships. The old armored leviathans, giant tortoises designed for slugging combat on the ocean's surface, seemed to be in their last throes during World War II. Now came the expectation of combat at great ranges, far behond those of human eyes and ears. The naval gun went into a long twilight of demise as the primary armament. Warships took off their carapaces and became loaded with standoff anti-aircraft and antisubmarine weapons. Electronic equipment came abroad in bewildering array, enabling the vessels to see at distances of over one hundred miles.

But the ships themselves were increasingly fragile, for there was no free lunch in naval architecture: everywhere something was added, something else was lost. When missiles and their associated electronic systems came aboard, the traditional passive defense of armor plate, protected decks, and sturdy construction departed. Naval warfare, clearly, was expected to occur at ever-increasing ranges and speeds, and of all the systems aboard modern warships, those relying on electronics were supreme.[10]

Electronics permeated the ether. Naval radio covered almost the entire frequency spectrum, from very high-powered, low-frequency stations (below twenty kilocycles) through the various bands used for radiotelegraphy, radioteletype, radiotelephones, and television. The bands extended into the microwave region for radar and other communications, into the infrared zone, and even into the radioactive band of the electromagnetic spectrum, where frequencies were as high as one hundred trillion megacycles or more—a fantasyland where electromagnetic waves were also known as rays or particles.

The Navy was one of the greatest communicators anywhere. Although the Bureau of Ships had the dominant electronics organization, every part of the techno-empire worked with and depended on communications electronics. Radar was now part of every vessel, even the tiny patrol craft, which sprouted "radome" bulbs on their masts. A World War II submarine carried about five hundred electronic tubes. Now this number increased to the point at which a ship's building plans had to be enlarged to contain the banks of sensors. The transistor, devised in 1947 by AT&T's Bell Laboratories and patented in 1950, proved, with the integrated circuit, to be the answer—the basis of all solid-state technology. But the micronic revolution within a revolution—transistors and microchips replacing the bulky, heat-producing tubes—was not quite yet accomplished in the fifties. And radio linked every element within the Navy to every other element, a worldwide web of communication.

Long-range navigation (loran) made location at sea, based on electronic lines-of-bearing, far more reliable. Radar reached out farther and farther. Sonar began to sniff passively at ranges thought impossible only a decade before. Aircraft carriers and other heavies became equipped with high-frequency direction finders. Guided missiles, such as the Loon, were completely dependent on their electronics systems.

In fact, electronics tranformed the Navy. The Electronics Program, inaugurated in the Naval Reserve in 1946, included one-third of all personnel in organized Reserve units, and this merely reflected the accent on the active side. Many ratings were electronics-centered—radioman, radarman, sonarman, fire control technician—and others, such as electrician's mate and interior communications technician, worked routinely with electronics. Still others had to learn to cope in the new world, like the classic rating of quartermaster, which had to master the intricacies of loran.

There were three roughly defined electronics fields: communications (radiomen), combat information center (radarmen), and antisubmarine warfare (sonarmen). But the specialties and subspecialties multiplied like protozoans, until seemingly almost everything, in one way or another, was connected with electronics.

By 1960, for example, the Navy had made the moon a communications satellite, bouncing radio signals off the lunar surface. A "moon relay circuit" was in place between Washington and Pearl Harbor. Radars were carried, even in transport aircraft, not only for navigation but also for ground mapping and collision avoidance. Air tracking became automated; experiments were conducted into automatic control of aircraft while landing. High-temperature electrical cables, insulated above the melting point of tin, made electronic circuits and electrical connections ever more dependable. High-frequency radar now looked beyond one thousand miles, bouncing its signals off the ionosphere. (Microwaves and ultrahigh frequencies normally used for radar were limited to line-of-sight ranges, unless the atmospherics were unusually freaky.)

In San Diego, out on Point Loma, the Naval Electronics Laboratory of over a thousand people stocked ten thousand parts, and the parts themselves were elements of the revolution. They got steadily smaller, more durable, and more reliable. The Navy was a leader in electronics miniaturization, with obvious benefits for shipboard operation. By the sixties the brains at the Naval Ordnance Lab had even created an electronic device as simple and almost as small as a nerve fiber, bypassing the then-novel transistors and also resistors, capacitors, and inductors. The device, called a "neuristor," could propagate signals along its length without any attenuation.[11]

By no means did all the miracles apply only to naval purposes. The Naval Observatory in Washington, founded back in 1842, continued its roles of examining the universe and providing standard timing, accurate to one one-thousandth of a second, for a nation that relentlessly scheduled itself. Its astronomical research program was run in the clear air of Flagstaff, Arizona. The observatory provided the Nautical and Air Almanacs, indispensable for getting around on, under, or over the seas. And its obsession with time came to include quartz crystals, then cesium clocks, which helped pinpoint the positions of artificial satellites as they streaked around the planet.

The Naval Research Lab mounted a huge chafing dish on the roof of its three-story headquarters to search for "galactic radiations," radio signals given off by the sun and stars. Its eighty-five-foot-diameter radio telescope on the Potomac worked at incredibly short wavelengths, studying the radiations of Venus, Mars, and Jupiter. Out in Flagstaff, the observatory's forty-inch Richey-Chretien reflector electronically tracked stars from its 7600-foot elevation, and the same stars had their ascensions and declinations measured by the observatory's Transit Circle Divisions.

High in the Arctic, the icebreaker *Eastwind* hunted for cosmic rays, speeding galactic streams of atomic particles that constantly bombarded the atmosphere. Huge plastic balloons hovered fourteen miles above the earth, listening, measuring. Big Viking and Aerobee rockets were fired aloft, laden with counting, tracking, and telemetry equipment.

All of this was basic, useful research, but most of the basics had applications for the Navy. Those cesium clocks, for example, in due course flashed their atomic-generated time signals to commanders of Polaris submarines, and those satellites, many of them, were not simply circling the earth—they were spying.

☆

The electronic revolution, in the 1950s, coalesced into the fundamental symbol of the modern age—the computer. The Navy had done experiments with calculating machines at Harvard during World War II, but little or none of this had reached the fleet.

"The Office of Naval Research," the secretary of the Navy revealed in 1950, "has developed large, high-speed digital computing machines." An epoch began. The Special Devices Center created the supersecret Project Typhoon, which was in actuality a huge mechanical brain, a new type of electronic multiplier that was a hybrid analog-digital apparatus. Typhoon, once unveiled, proved capable of solving a simulated air-defense problem in which a high-speed bomber was successfully attacked by a radar-controlled, rocket-propelled, supersonic guided missile.

The computer came on board to stay. By 1954 the IBM Corporation had developed a superspeed electronic brain for the Navy, dubbed NORC (Naval Ordnance Research Calculator). NORC, which found a home at Dahlgren, quickly went to work on complex aircraft, missile, and engine design problems. IBM went on to establish a most profitable relationship with the Navy, providing ever-more-capable computers and pioneering in thin-film electronic circuitry, which saved even more shipboard space. By the early sixties computers were routine ashore; the Atlantic Fleet Computer Programming Center was set up at Dam Neck, Virginia, in 1963.

Thin-film microcircuity and semiconductors spearheaded the micronics revolution, along with the well-known transistor. Size and weight reductions of 60 percent to 90 percent were reported for various systems. By 1962 most Navy computers contained around five thousand microcircuit elements, and the miniaturization process was, if anything, proceeding at a greater tempo than the expansion of the widely publicized parameters of speed, distance, and power.[12]

The early electronic brains had been built with vacuum tubes, and the thousands of filaments cooked out a tremendous amount of heat. The resulting requirements, for huge power supplies and tool-shed-sized air-conditioning equipment, made the cumbersome gadgets distinctly marginal for shipboard use. Moreover, these first models were digital, performing simple arithmetic in step-by-step processes.

The Navy accordingly concentrated on analog computers like the Mark 1A. But the development of the transistor and the magnetic core memory made possible seagoing computers of exceptional speed and reliability. These follow-on digital computers were soon spitting out shiploads of information—figuring weapons needs, ordering spare parts and supplies, controlling air intercepts, displaying tactical data, printing pay lists, and maintaining personnel records.

Along with the machines came new skills and ratings, like the data processor. Shipboard language, always a babble of tongues to lubbers, became larded with words and phrases like *bit*, *Boolean algebra*, *logic circuits*, *binary-to-decimal conversion*, *bistable element*, and *access time*. The shipboard brains were stupendously fast, and they were also stupendously stupid. They had to be told exactly what to do, and in the correct sequence—which meant that they had to be babied by specialists far removed from the traditional sailor's skills exemplified by boatswain's mates and signalmen.

Computers rapidly married other computers, merging into operational systems, and in this first generation of naval computing the greatest success in this regard was undoubtedly the Navy Tactical Data System (NTDS). NTDS was, in effect, an electronic brain ("binary digital data system") for an entire assemblage of ships, not a simple electronic show-and-tell for a single ship (as Combat Information Centers had been). NTDS covered the whole sensor picture, but the system emphasized the air side and was primarily designed for fleet air defense, allowing the commander a firmer means of centralized control than ever before. Additionally, NTDS integrated weapons systems into search, acquisition, and tracking systems. Computers talked to computers, displaying their information on NTDS-equipped ships throughout the formation. By 1962 the first NTDS-equipped ships—the carrier *Oriskany* and the destroyers *King* and *Mahan*—were operating at sea.

Many officers worried that the machines were usurping human command and control; the machines' keepers soothingly noted that all the gadgets did was to acquire, disseminate, and resolve information. The truth lay somewhere between; no person could calculate with the speed of the gadgets, and none of the gadgets could *think*. The problem for the modern commander was to *understand* NTDS, and all his electronic systems—both their capabilities and their limitations. No officer could at once be an expert in computers, radar, sonar, countermeasures, communications, weapons, and so on. At some point, the man in control had to trust his machines.

The best face that could be put on the revolution went this way, as regarded NTDS:

> The real significance of NTDS is that it makes a truly coherent weapon system of those assemblies of separate subsystems we have called ships. By replacing man as the integrating element of the weapon system, the machine takes over the tasks for which it is best suited and thereby frees man of the necessity to fragment his effort and attention in order to reduce the problem to manageable increments.

—Such doublespeak may have been the language of the future but hardly resolved the "problem" of those who served aboard "those assemblies of separate subsystems we have called ships." "In the process of this electrification and electronification of the Navy," said one admiral, "we have reduced greatly the size of our computers. We have, I'm afraid, also increased significantly our reliability problem, our maintenance problem, . . . [and] our cost."

The electronic revolution was, in many respects, outpacing the ability of Navymen to deal with its products.

☆

There had been a day, not too remote in time, when the commanding officer of a naval warship was truly king in his floating world, the "dear old days," said Robley ("Fighting Bob") Evans, "before steam and modern guns took all the poetry out of our profession." The skipper dispensed rough-and-ready justice, unsheathed his guns according to his own judgment, and conducted diplomacy as he saw fit. But the coming of the underwater cable telegraph (Washington was connected permanently with London in 1867) was the harbinger of the end of his operational independence.

Once, when a captain hoisted anchor for a cruise, he escaped from the control of the Navy Department. To be sure, he sailed under general orders, but squadron commodores and their skippers operated on the loosest of tethers, glorying in their responsibilities. Wherever their wooden walls cut water, *they* were "America." But the telegraph, and then the wireless, tightened the tether. Sailors became cautious; a mistake could become known to the powers-that-be in minutes rather than months.

"The cable spoiled the old Asiatic system," fumed Rear Admiral Caspar Goodrich, one of the old guard. "Before it was laid, one was really somebody out there, but afterwards one simply became a damned errand boy at the end of a telegraph wire." In the 1850s over one-quarter of American diplomatic activities abroad were conducted by naval officers; by the 1880s only

7 percent were so conducted. In 1916, as a result of Admiral Henry Mayo's heavy-handed conduct at Tampico, Mexico, a few years before, Secretary of the Navy Josephus Daniels inserted the following in Article 1648 of Navy Regulations:

> Due to the ease with which the Navy Department can be communicated with from all parts of the world, no commander in chief, division commander, or commanding officer shall issue an ultimatum to the representative of any foreign Government, or demand the performance of any service from any such representative that must be executed within a limited time, without first communicating with the Navy Department, except in extreme cases where such action is necessary to save life.

This was the first step—the end of *naval* diplomacy. More and more firmly, the bonds between ship and shore tightened. As late as the Spanish-American War, ships sent news ashore by carrier pigeon. But on 2 November 1899 Guglielmo Marconi transmitted the first official radio message sent from an American naval ship, and from that point onward the "damned errand boys" were on very short tethers indeed. By the 1920s Rear Admiral Harry Knapp was explaining that

> the ease of modern communications make[s] the most resolute and self-confident man think twice before adopting a course of action that he would adopt without hesitation if so situated that weeks or months would be necessary for consultation with the home government; while the irresolute or self-distrustful man, or one who fears to take responsibility, has under modern conditions a ready reason for doing nothing until he had been told what to do.

The traditional assumption was that naval subordinates at sea operated constantly under a senior's eye—and that senior wore a naval uniform. But developments in naval communication in the twentieth century seriously eroded this relationship, bringing, again almost unnoticed by the public at large, another revolution within the techno-empire.

By the 1950s naval communications was part of a vast network of ship-to-shore and air-to-ground circuits that tapped into the nets of other services, government nets, the International Telegraph Union, and civilian and military electronic organizations beyond counting. As with weaponry, increased traffic loads meant more and more automation; the manual code wave circuit (the Navy's analogy to the civilian telegraph) went the way of the horse and buggy. Like those artifacts, CW was still around, taught to every radioman striker (CW was reliable, but very slow). However, radioteletypes, multiplexers, and ultrahigh-frequency (UHF) circuits had taken over.

The Naval Communications Service was the nervous system of the

Navy. Its stations were positioned around the globe. The most powerful transmitter in the world, over one million watts, went on line in the early fifties, its transmitting antenna extended between two western mountain peaks, providing effective all-weather communications with the entire Pacific basin. By January 1952, the volume of traffic on all Navy circuits approximated the peak load of World War II, and kept growing.

Thus were the fleet and the techno-empire knit together. Signalmen with their flaghoists, semaphore, flashing light, and rapid hand wigwags were far from obsolete; visual communication was still the most secure way of doing things, because anything launched into the electromagnetic spectrum could be picked off by anyone with a correctly tuned receiver. But the ability to communicate instantaneously with all that seapower, to control all those weapons, to move fleets at will across vast expanses of ocean, was enormously seductive. [13]

The real revolutions, then, were only partially the work of the armorers. Out there at sea, by the 1950s, was by far the most powerful navy in the world, and its ships could be headed at a moment's notice for any location. The *power* to do this, to maneuver tens of thousands of men aboard millions of tons of haze-gray, was increasingly centralized. The naval world, then, was shrinking with extreme rapidity, even as the tridents of Poseidon were increasing apace in range, accuracy, and lethality.

—Particularly the atomic bomb.

CHAPTER FOURTEEN

A-BOMB

———— ☆ ————

Modern technological weapons, observes Montesquieu in his *Persian Letters*, mean that there is no longer "upon the earth a refuge from injustice and violence." He was writing in 1721, in an era of relatively limited, comparatively polite warfare. What the baron might have thought of nuclear weapons surpasses imagination.

Initially the Navy, which had never been especially interested in Montesquieu, was not markedly interested in atomic energy either. When, in 1939, the émigré scientists Enrico Fermi and Leo Szilard began a crash effort to alert the Roosevelt administration to the potential horror of a German-made atomic bomb, their lobbying resulted in a meeting with Rear Admiral Stanford Hooper, the director of technical operations for the Navy. Hooper himself knew nothing of nuclear physics; he had been the first "fleet wireless officer," back in 1912, and was a lifelong communications specialist.

Fermi did the presenting, at the Navy Department on Constitution Avenue. When the desk officer went in to announce the physicist to the admiral, Fermi overheard the man say, "There's a wop outside." (The Nobel Prize apparently cut no bow wave in Hooper's shop.) In a ramshackle old room, Fermi appeared before an audience composed of Hooper, other naval officers, Army ordnance specialists, and two civilian scientists from the Naval Research Lab.

One of the civilians, Ross Gunn, had earlier watched a fission demonstration; his specialty was submarine propulsion, and he wanted to hear more about an energy source that burned no oxygen. Most of the people in the room, however, were infants in the strange playground of neutron physics. Fermi talked for an hour, emphasizing the possiblity of a "chain reaction" and mentioning in passing the problem of assembling a sufficiently large mass of uranium to capture and "use" secondary neutrons before they escaped.

A naval officer taking notes perked up. He asked about the size of the mass of uranium—perhaps the stuff might fit into a gun breech. Fermi riposted: the mass might turn out to be the size of a small star, he said.

—But he knew otherwise.

The Navy found the concept of neutrons diffusing through a tank of water, with some hypothetical chain reaction releasing enormous quantities of energy, entirely too much at sea. Fermi and Szilard were able to wangle only a measly $1500 grant from the Naval Research Laboratory for fission research.

When war came, and the Manhattan Project kicked in, the Navy was on the outside. Although a few scientists like Gunn retained their interest in atomic propulsion for submarines, the real action lay with Major General Leslie Groves of the Army and the development of the atomic bomb. Even before Groves took charge of Manhattan in September 1942, FDR had specifically instructed his scientific adviser, Vannevar Bush, to exclude the Navy from the development of the bomb. Bush, with slight disobedience, encouraged funding of NRL's work in this area, and Groves followed the lab's experiments, but the information flow on atomic research generally went from Navy to Army, not vice versa.[1]

Ross Gunn was not interested in bombs; within three days of the Fermi meeting he prepared a memo outlining a project for a nuclear reactor for submarine propulsion. The note-taking officer, Captain Garrett Schuyler, was an ordnance specialist, the first engineering-duty-only ordnance officer in the Navy and an extremely conservative individual, rarely open to new ideas. Yet Schuyler produced an exceptionally clear summary of Fermi's remarks and, like Gunn, immediately recognized the importance and naval possibilities of atomic fission.

But Gunn and Schuyler were not the Navy. With a war on, and with the Army in clear and (because of Groves) domineering charge of the Manhattan Project, naval leaders were far too busy to give much attention to atomic research. When Fleet Admiral William Leahy found out what the Manhattan Project was about, he snorted, "The bomb will never go off, and I speak as an expert on explosives."

Leahy *was* an expert on explosives, but the mysteries of atomic fission were as foreign to his naval generation as the far side of the moon. Moreover, many Navymen were horrified at the indiscriminate destruction the bomb implied. Like Leahy, they later insisted that the air and sea blockades, if left to do their work, would have brought down Japan with much less loss of life. After Hiroshima and Nagasaki, Leahy wrote:

> Being the first to use [the bomb], we had adopted an ethical standard common to the barbarians of the Dark Ages. . . . There is a practical certainty that potential enemies will have it in the future and that the atomic bomb will sometime be used against us. . . . Employment of the atomic bomb in war will take us back in cruelty towards noncombatants to the days of Genghis Khan. . . . These new and terrible instruments of civilized warfare represent a modern type of barbarism not worthy of Christian man.[2]

There were many in the Navy who agreed with Leahy, but practicality was never far from the surface. James Forrestal, the archetypal Cold Warrior, flatly asserted that the bomb and the brains behind the weapon were "the property of the American people." He argued that the United States should not try to buy the understanding of the Soviet Union by sharing atomic secrets. Appeasement had not worked against Hitler; atomic appeasement would certainly not work against Stalin.

Ernie King, like Leahy, thought the cost of invading Japan would be too heavy in American lives. Seapower, by way of blockade, and conventional air power could force Japanese surrender. And, also like Leahy, King was completely in the dark about the Manhattan Project. The chief of naval operations did not like to ask questions or show ignorance of any kind; if he heard an unfamiliar word, he would reluctantly turn to a handy reference book. Once, talking with Groves, King was completely frustrated; his dictionary had no definition for "nuclear fission."

King was also slow to grasp any naval role for the atomic bomb. On 14 August 1945 he forwarded to Forrestal his "Recommended Policies on Ordnance for the Post-War Navy." These policies classified naval ordnance into four categories, but none of the categories included nuclear ordnance—this a week *after* Hiroshima and Nagasaki. And the topside leadership, mostly, was equally slow. As late as 1948 one admiral was dining off potentially radioactive silverware in his flag mess (the setting had been recovered from *Nevada*, sunk during the Bikini tests) and announcing no harmful effects.[3]

☆

In the entire Navy, there was only one man really close to the development of the atomic bomb. William ("Deak") Parsons, after graduating from the Naval Academy in 1922, had made a career in naval ordnance. Even before Pearl Harbor he had become "without doubt the premier ordnance expert of the modern Navy," according to one admiring admiral, Frederick Ashworth; "a ball of fire," said another.

Before the war, Parsons worked with the fourteen-inch main batteries of the old battleships to solve their chronic fall-of-shot dispersion problem. He saw early on the benefits of the Naval Research Lab's high-frequency-radiation experiments, which gave great promise for a far-ranging capability to detect both air and surface targets. After Pearl Harbor, Parsons, now a balding captain, was deeply involved in one of the crucial ordnance developments of the war, the anti-aircraft proximity fuse. By then he had a reputation, not only as an ordnance brain but also as a gentle, kindly man, the "first true scientist in uniform."

King shipped Parsons off to the Pacific to teach the use of the new fuse (which was to prove its worth multifold, especially against the fearsome kamikaze). Parsons asked for a one-way ticket; naval spurs were being won in the waters to the west, and he wanted his. But he was far too good at what he did. Early in 1943 he was ordered to Los Alamos as J. Robert Oppenheimer's deputy, and there, on the high plateau of the New Mexican desert, Deak Parsons became the weaponeer on the atomic bomb.

Through his association with Oppenheimer and the other magnificent minds at Los Alamos, Parsons earned the equivalent of a doctorate in nuclear physics. He was talented enough to work with John von Neumann, the theoretical mathematical genius and a leading godfather of the computer, on the problem of establishing the critical mass for the plutonium weapon. They came up with a system of high-explosive lenses, spherically shaped, that focused a shock wave of conventional explosives detonation into the "implosion" that produced the needed critical mass. This was the device used for the first test, at Alamagordo on 16 July 1945, and for Fat Man, the plutonium weapon dropped on Nagasaki on 9 August.

But Parsons's real baby was the uranium weapon, Little Boy. He designed the casing and the tail of the bomb. Transferred to Tinian in the Marianas to await the word to go, Parsons feared that a mechanical problem aboard the designated B-29, *Enola Gay*, could cause a disastrous aborting of the mission, creating a fire on the runway. Then, possibly, the powder charge for Little Boy's gun-type trigger could cook off, producing a low-order nuclear detonation. There could then be massive radioactive contamination of the entire north end of the island, and the strategically important runways could be out of commission indefinitely.

Little Boy would have to be armed in midair. When *Enola Gay* lumbered off Tinian's runway at 0245 on 6 August 1945, Deak Parsons rode aboard. His baby, a huge cylindrical shape with big, boxlike fins, lay slung by itself in the specially configured bomb bay. Little Boy contained two cans filled with 137.3 pounds of U-235; his total weight was 9700 pounds. Four antennas bristled from his tail. His tungsten-steel nose glistened, and on his gray flanks were scrawled obscene greetings to Emperor Hirohito.

As the B-29 and its escorts droned steadily northeastward, clawing for altitude, Parsons went to work in the bomb bay, first straddling Little Boy, then lying on his back, then wriggling around on his belly. Consulting an eleven-point checklist, he tested the critical barometric switches, checked and closed the bomb's complex circuits. He sent current racing through Little Boy's test leads, watching for the safety signals of the green monitor lights. Finally, he inserted the gunpowder and detonator behind the fissionable "bullet" of uranium 235. Inside the bomb's casing, the two cans of uranium were separated by less than five feet of hollow shaft.

Just before 0730, with *Enola Gay* over thirty thousand feet and at drop altitude, Parsons had his assistant, Lieutenant Morris Jepson, cut the umbilical cord linking Little Boy to the plane: the bomb became "final." As *Enola Gay* homed in on Hiroshima, the target city, Parsons threw the switch that put the bomb on its own battery power. Four minutes, three, two . . .

At 0815 Little Boy fell free, tail ticking. Inside him were four clocks, four barometric switches, and four radar rigs to measure his fall. After fifteen seconds, Little Boy began to listen for the faint echoes of his radar signals bouncing back off the earth. He was counting the echoes—ten, twelve, fourteen . . .

On the nineteenth echo, when Little Boy was between 1500 and 800 feet above the city, the pulse ignited the powder charge, which sent one uranium mass bulleting through the hollow shaft into the other. Nuclear fission.[4]

—And Hiroshima was incinerated in atomic fire.

☆

Members of Congress, at least since the turn of the century, had always liked the idea of strategic concepts that did not greatly risk ground forces and promised overwhelming defeat of an enemy far from American shores. Before Little Boy plummeted down on the unsuspecting Japanese, the Navy had been the primary service for fulfilling these concepts, as defective as they might have been.

Now came the atomic bomb, and the emergent Air Force owned the weapon and its delivery system. Clearly, the Navy had to come to terms with this dramatic new technology, and fast. Within a month after Hiroshima, Forrestal decided to create a new staff division at the highest level, charged with the extremely broad responsibility of developing naval applications of nuclear energy, as well as of missiles and other weapons.

By October 1945 the Office of Special Weapons (OP-06) was on-line. Forrestal picked the kinetic, aloof Spike Blandy (still years away from his embroilment in the rebellion in gold braid) to head the shop. Born in New York City in 1890, Blandy had been appointed to the Naval Academy from Delaware. At Annapolis, he had excelled in mathematics and gunnery, graduating first in the Class of 1913. He became an ardent gunclubber; by 1924 he was chief of the gun section in BuOrd. He became a master with the guns, and his knowledge of gun design and manufacture was unparalleled. In February 1941, after command of the destroyer *Simpson*, Destroyer Division 10, and the former battleship *Utah* (reclassified as a target ship), he became the youngest line admiral in the Navy.

Blandy had trodden a rocky road during the war as chief of naval ordnance, his major headache being the scandalous torpedo situation (American torpedoes had the lousy habit of not detonating when they squarely hit their targets), but he was greatly respected and obviously ticketed for higher things: OP-06 brought him his third star. As a bonus, he was an ordnance specialist without peer, and he had capped his wartime service by commanding all bombardment and demolition activites before the invasion of Okinawa.

Deak Parsons, promoted briefly to commodore and then to rear admiral, became his assistant. He was uncontrite about his role aboard *Enola Gay*.

"I knew the Japs were in for it," he said, "but I felt no particular emotion about it." Parsons immediately began shipping junior officers out to the Sandia base in Albuquerque to learn bomb assembly techniques. Two other up-and-comers, Commander Frederick Ashworth (who had been on the Nagasaki mission) and Commander Horacio Rivero, completed the original four-officer staff. As an indicator of how many men in the Navy knew anything at all about atomic energy, in April 1946 Blandy's entire outfit numbered only thirteen officers.

OP-06 began by sketching out tests using atomic bombs against naval vessels. Ernie King, finally awake to the strategic implications of the new weapon, revealed the tentative details of the plans in late October 1945, and the Air Force immediately began to agitate for a piece of the action. The controversy over which service should conduct these tests, or whether they should even be conducted at all, played its part in the unification struggle that was coming to a boil. Memories of Billy Mitchell's bombing of the *Ostfriesland* in 1921, the results of which had divided air power and seapower theorists ever since, bubbled up as well.

Early in 1946, Harry Truman decreed not only that the Air Force would be allowed to participate in the tests but also that the other armed services and a group of civilian scientists were to be included. Blandy obediently set up Joint Task Force 1 under his own command to conduct the tests, subject to the overall supervision of the Joint Chiefs and Groves. In short, the Navy had lost control of its own project.

Blandy named this joint effort Operation CROSSROADS, because, he said, warfare had come to an historical turning point due to the atomic bomb. OP-06 had to assemble a joint task force numbering around 230 ships, 150 planes, and 42,000 men, choose a test site, and develop procedures for carrying out and recording the tests. Parsons, Ashworth, and Rivero were earning their pay. Not the least of Blandy's problems was to try to dispel public concerns, while dealing with the hyperinquisitive press. One senator (Democrat Brien McMahon of Connecticut) expressed his alarm that an atomic explosion beneath the surface might set off a chain reaction of atoms in the water and blow up the entire ocean.

OP-06 wisely dealt directly with the press, at least in the preliminaries. CROSSROADS had as its main purpose measuring the effect of nuclear explosions on ships. The tests were *not* to see how many ships could be sunk with one bomb; were *not* some kind of Army Air Force versus Navy contest (these overtones never went away, though); and were *not* rigged to show the Navy as far from obsolete in the atomic age. The Navy hoped to get information affecting changes in ship design, tactical formations at sea, anchoring distances in port, and the overall strategic disposition of ships. The operation was *not* to test the atomic bomb. Air Force supporters, fully ensnarled in the unification controversy, screamed that the deck was stacked in favor of seapower.

Secondarily, CROSSROADS was intended to help measure explosive effects on aircraft and other military equipment; aid in learning more about the effects of nuclear blasts (almost nothing was known, for example, about the long-lasting effects of radiation); and produce volumes of specific scientific data. Blandy tried to lower the temperature of interservice squabbles a bit by insisting that CROSSROADS was a joint military and scientific venture. At least six officers, including one admiral, were fired when they kept on plugging for naval control.

The test site was selected: Bikini Atoll in the Marshall Islands. Bikini was part of the spoils of the Pacific war, controlled by the United States. The atoll featured a big, protected anchorage; languid weather patterns with predictable winds up to sixty thousand feet; and water currents leading away from shores and shipping lanes. "We located the one spot on earth that hadn't been touched by war," cracked Bob Hope, "and blew it to hell."

Unfortunately, the place had previous residents. Bikini's 162 inhabitants were summarily relocated; no one asked them their opinion—they simply happened to live in an American lake and were in the way. There was concern that the explosions would kill large amounts of marine life, whale and tuna in particular. The Navy got the Fish and Wildlife Service of the Interior Department (whose expertise on nuclear effects was questionable) to declare that the fishing industry had nothing to worry about.

The bombs to be used in the test were plutonium implosion weapons, like Fat Man. Their yield was about twenty-three kilotons. There would be an air drop (Test ABLE) and a subsurface explosion (Test BAKER).

In the spring of 1946 the intended victims began to assemble in a corner of Bikini's ten-by-twenty-mile lagoon. The old battlewagons *Arkansas, New York, Nevada,* and *Pennsylvania* (once the flagship of the U.S. Fleet) were tethered in place, joined by the historic carrier *Saratoga* (whose twin, *Lexington,* had perished at Coral Sea) and the light carrier *Independence.* They were far from alone; around them, staked to the lagoon floor like so many sacrificial goats, were the heavy cruisers *Salt Lake City* and *Pensacola,* destroyers, submarines (some submerged, some on the surface), transports, cargo ships, and landing ships. There were even concrete barges and a concrete drydock.

The ships were arranged in rough X patterns for both ABLE and BAKER. A Japanese battleship, the ancient *Nagato,* and the light cruiser *Sakawa* (commissioned in 1944 but never operational) were added, as was the German heavy cruiser *Prinz Eugen.* Finally came the refitted assault transport *Burleson,* carrying 204 real goats, 200 pigs, 5000 rats, 200 mice, and 60 guinea pigs. As usual, when humans "tested," other creatures would be exposed to suffering. Already the National Cancer Institute was worried about possible genetic defects from radiation, and *Burleson* also carried insects that could be genetically examined.[5]

Nevada was at the center of the X, the bull's-eye ship for ABLE. For her final agony (she had been the only battleship in Pearl Harbor to get underway on 7 December 1941), *Nevada* was painted a garish red, with her decks and turret tops white, like some tawdry old tart on her last assignation. She and her sisters were loaded with fuel and ammunition, so secondary damage could be judged, but they were phantom ships, with no hands primed for damage control. Forty people had volunteered by letter to remain aboard the vessels (including a lifer at San Quentin), but the Navy had refused them all.

The target ships were collectively valued at $400 million, leading some members of Congress to ask why that much money should be sent to the bottom of the Pacific. Blandy correctly pointed out that salvage value was about 1 percent of book value and that the Navy was getting a bargain. A few critics saw the Bikini tests as a crude flexing of America's nuclear muscle at a time when international control of atomic energy was still under serious discussion. At the request of Secretary of State James Byrnes, the tests were postponed until July—but not canceled. On the eve of the first test, Forrestal, Chester Nimitz, and Dwight Eisenhower all went on radio to emphasize to the American people the urgent need for the explosions.[6]

☆

At 0540 on 1 July, a modified B-29 named *Dave's Dream*, a foot-high picture of Rita Hayworth painted on its fuselage, lifted off from Kwajalein for Test ABLE, a plutonium weapon aboard. At the site, numerous observers were waiting: scientists, a presidential commission, representatives from the Joint Chiefs, United Nations personnel from eleven countries, even reporters from the Soviet Union.

Dave's Dream was only seconds off schedule, dropping its bomb from over thirty thousand feet. Just before 0900 the twenty-three-kiloton weapon detonated, producing the now-familiar giant white mushroom cloud. The blast was off-target, however, between one and two nautical miles to the west of *Nevada*. Along that radial of the X, a destroyer and two transports sank, another can capsized, and *Sakawa* was so badly holed she sank the following day. *Independence* and the submarine *Skate*, both within half a mile of the explosion point, were badly damaged.

Every target vessel within 500 yards (one-quarter of a nautical mile) from surface zero was sunk or seriously damaged. Ships beyond 750 yards *seemed* to have little induced radioactivity or contamination. Of the living creatures aboard, 35 percent were killed; the press reported, with preposterous accuracy, that 10 percent died from the air blast, 15 percent from radioactivity, and 10 percent "during later study."

Because the bomb missed its target, no capital ship was really close to the point of detonation. ABLE, in this important respect, was thus inconclusive. Still, the test led to the sort of doggerel the Navy could dredge up at a moment's notice:

The bomb has burst,
It's done its worst,
Our Navy's still afloat.
The Admirals grin like
Cheshire cats,
But what's happened to
The goats?

For BAKER, on 25 July, the ships were rearranged. The underwater blast would take place ninety feet directly under a hapless target ship, *LSM-60*. Again the radials branched out in an X-pattern, although this time the bomb would by definition be on (or under) target. *Arkansas* and *Saratoga* were positioned to receive maximum damage. The livestock for BAKER included twenty pigs and two hundred white rats.

At 0835 BAKER blew. Visually, this first underwater blast in history was spectacular. Observers watching from a plane fifteen miles away thought the whole floor of Bikini's lagoon had simply been flung into the sky. BAKER produced two shock waves: one above water, which appeared as an enormous column of water and air, and an underwater one, radiating out at a rate of one mile per second.

LSM-60 vaporized. *Arkansas* went down almost at once, after her twenty-six-thousand-ton bulk had been lifted bodily out of the water by the force of the blast. Sara lasted only a matter of hours. Six other ships were sunk. The sailors nicknamed Bikini "Nothing Atoll," and the island quickly entered the language to describe a skimpy bathing suit.

But the destruction was not the real story. Because of its underwater nature, BAKER produced an exceptionally dirty explosion. Unlike ABLE, whose radioactive dust and ash had been dispersed aloft by winds, BAKER sent tons of radioactive water cascading down on the surface ships; all twenty pigs died from drinking the stuff. Human casualties from BAKER would have been terrific. The Joint Chiefs' representatives calculated that people close to the blast, even if protected from the shock, would have been dead in days or weeks.

Four days after BAKER, Bikini Lagoon was saturated with radiation, still unsafe for inspection parties. More than 90 percent of the target vessels, even to the ends of the radials, had been contaminated. Radioactivity on this scale had not been expected (American scientists had not gotten to Hiroshima and Nagasaki until weeks after those explosions, and those had been air bursts), and not until ten days after the underwater blast were all the target ships reboarded.

To the public at large, however, the two explosions (a planned third was canceled) were big bangs that had left lots of ships still afloat. One newspaperman flippantly declared that "the next war's not going to be so bad after all." ABLE received the wider press coverage, and the harrowing

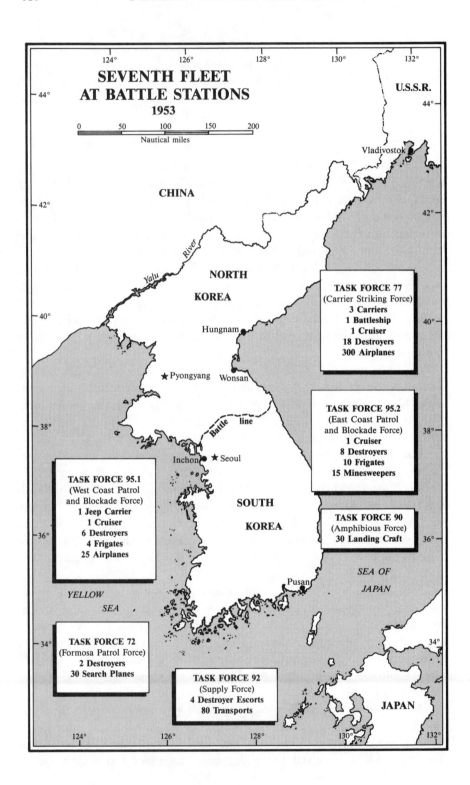

SEVENTH FLEET AT BATTLE STATIONS 1953

0   50   100   150   200
Nautical miles

U.S.S.R.

CHINA

NORTH KOREA

Yalu River

Vladivostok

★ Pyongyang

Hungnam

Wonsan

Battle line

Inchon   ★ Seoul

SOUTH KOREA

Pusan

YELLOW SEA

SEA OF JAPAN

JAPAN

TASK FORCE 77
(Carrier Striking Force)
3 Carriers
1 Battleship
1 Cruiser
18 Destroyers
300 Airplanes

TASK FORCE 95.2
(East Coast Patrol
and Blockade Force)
1 Cruiser
8 Destroyers
10 Frigates
15 Minesweepers

TASK FORCE 90
(Amphibious Force)
30 Landing Craft

TASK FORCE 95.1
(West Coast Patrol
and Blockade Force)
1 Jeep Carrier
1 Cruiser
6 Destroyers
4 Frigates
25 Airplanes

TASK FORCE 72
(Formosa Patrol Force)
2 Destroyers
30 Search Planes

TASK FORCE 92
(Supply Force)
4 Destroyer Escorts
80 Transports

radioactive aftermath of BAKER got relatively little play—nobody cared about a bunch of dead pigs. William Laurence of the *New York Times*, who had written on the bomb from the time press coverage was allowed, said that the average American "had expected one bomb to sink the entire Bikini fleet, kill all the animals aboard, make a hole in the bottom of the ocean, and create tidal waves that would be felt for thousands of miles." Because nothing of the sort happened, many Americans carried onward from Bikini the illusion that the bomb was just another weapon, not a quantum leap in ordnance. The bomb was extraordinary, yes, but scarcely earthshaking. After all, dozens of ships were still afloat.

For the Navy, however, the tests were exceptionally important. Ships would have to undergo some design changes to decrease the vulnerability of their superstructures. ABLE, in particular, had mangled topsides beyond recognition. Gaskets, seals, and fittings had to be reexamined. Water washdown systems became mandatory. Ventilation systems had to be screened and filtered. In short, the Navy began to learn to button up, to a far greater degree than even the traditional Condition I—General Quarters.

Beyond Bikini, the idea of mutually acceptable international controls on atomic energy, never very strongly held within the Truman administration, was strangled by the emerging Cold War. The legacy of Bikini, somewhat ambiguous to the public, remained strictly military and acceptable to many of those in the Navy. Deak Parsons was always wary of the "articulate scientific propagandists" and the "wild 'liberal' crowd" who were "crackpots who periodically predict the end of the world." Ralph Lapp, of the Office of Naval Research, would eventually produce (in 1949) a book entitled *Must We Hide?*, in which he compared the risks of radiation to the risks of automobile travel. And the Catholic chaplain at the Naval Academy, Francis Murphy, insisted that the development and use of the atomic bomb was "in accordance with the divine plan." Following the tests, Spike Blandy put the case this way:

> I believe that if there is atomic warfare in the future, naval war will not be exempt from it. . . . Unless some plan which is at the same time practical, reliable, and acceptable to all nations, is devised for outlawing the atomic bomb, there will be atomic warfare. . . . But as a result of Operation Crossroads, the United States will at least be better prepared for such warfare than any other nation on earth.

—In November 1946, Blandy and his wife (wearing a hat of disconcertingly mushroom-shaped flowers) smilingly cut an angel-food cake in the shape of an atomic-bomb cloud at a Washington party.[7]

☆

CROSSROADS was much more than an atomic test. As the men in OP-06 assessed the results, the fleet had been hit by atomic bombs and had "survived." Thus, the Navy was still viable in the atomic era. The natives of Bikini were conveniently forgotten (moved to Rongerik Island, they were never returned to their atoll), and some of the personnel who entered the contaminated zones after the blasts may have suffered the effects of residual radiation years afterward. Almost nothing was known about radiation effects on humans in 1946; some naval commanders at Bikini had even allowed their men to sleep in their shorts on the decks of contaminated ships. The federal government (and the Navy) began, with Bikini, a series of all-too-comforting announcements that every precaution had been taken, that atomic testing was "safe."[8]

The Navy knew better. Two days after BAKER, Joint Task Force 1 had, under a continuing cloak of top secrecy, selected samples of radioactive equipment for special decontamination tests. Initially, the equipment was blasted with grit from various materials: ground corncobs, ground coconut shells, ground coffee, rice hulls, barley. Nothing short of sandblasting seemed capable of removing all of the radioactivity. Simply painting over the radioactive surface (painting any part of a ship was the traditional Navy way) did not help, because gamma radiation remained. Salvors, in peril of radioactivity themselves, tried high-pressure water and chemical foam, with mixed results.

Detergents were tested: soap powders, lye, volatile naphtha. Acetic, hydrochloric, and sulfuric acids were tried. Absorbants like flour, corn-starch, and activated charcoal were spread. Nitric acid proved able to de-contaminate brass surfaces, but the ships were not made of brass. Most reagents reduced the amount of radioactivity only if they actually removed paint or surface corrosion.

And people moved about amid all this. The crew of *Skate*, for example, was allowed to reboard their boat with a minimum of precautions, even bringing food aboard. As *Skate*'s exec remarked, "The age of innocence ended several days later," when instruments started to reveal the danger. By 31 July Blandy began to issue stricter safety guidelines.

Part of the contamination was being produced by plutonium, which, if ingested, was a serious health hazard. Moreover, plutonium emitted alpha particles, and Joint Task Force 1 had no monitors capable of detecting them—an inexcusable lack of judgment. As the problems multiplied, the effort to decontaminate vessels still in Bikini Lagoon was halted on 10 August. Target ships were towed to Kwajalein to be cleansed.

On 27 August Nimitz hurriedly issued a radiological safety program for the Navy. The Bureau of Medicine and Surgery was directed to establish safety tolerances and regulations. (Practically no naval physicians were familiar with atomic energy.) BuMed was to determine the physiological effects of atomic radiation, develop needed technology for diagnosis, and devise treatment methods. The Bureau of Ships began a crash program to provide shipboard instrumentation, such as Geiger counters and radioactivity badges, to monitor fallout levels.

Three days later Nimitz directed that all ships found to be "radiologically unsafe" were to be sunk in deep water. Meanwhile, a special disposal unit worked until November to remove the contaminated ammunition aboard the target vessels. Some of the victims remained at Kwajalein; several were towed to Pearl Harbor, Puget Sound, and San Francisco for additional inspection.

Eventually, Joint Task Force 1's radiological safety adviser, worried about alpha-particle emitters, decreed that all the observer ships that had spent an accumulated ten days or more at Bikini after BAKER were to avoid dry-docking until further notice. Also, they were not to expose saltwater surfaces that had received the contaminated sheets of sea, allow personnel to breathe fumes resulting from welding or cutting, or let them inhale dust originating from surfaces contaminated by salt water.

In short, BAKER created an abysmal mess, one that was doubly dangerous because no one could be certain how to deal with the unexpected radiation levels. By the beginning of 1947, 80 of the 159 nontarget ships that had been in the vicinity of the blast had been granted final radiological clearance. The lesson: even if ships stayed afloat in the area of a nuclear burst, the resulting radioactivity could cut the power of a fleet at least in half for months.

All the decontamination was top secret. Some scientists believed, falsely, that the radioactive contamination might provide a source of plutonium for future explosive devices. Also, the "efficiency" of the plutonium bombs had to be determined by analyzing the radioactive debris from the target ships. Clearly, the Navy had to institutionalize its study of radioactivity.

On 18 November, the temporary facilities that had greeted some of the Bikini targets in San Francisco became the Navy's Radiation Laboratory (changed to the Naval Radiological Defense Laboratory in 1948). This lab, which lasted until 1969, became the Navy's primary source of information on the effects of nuclear weapons.

All of the nontarget ships from CROSSROADS, inspected under the imprimatur of the new lab, eventually received final clearance. Every target ship was eventually sunk; the last to go was *Independence*, Eddie Ewen's old command in the South Pacific. She stayed in San Francisco until 1951, providing a treasure chest of knowledge about ship contamination. Then, unceremoniously, she was deep-sixed.[9]

☆

America's nuclear strategic planning was as hazy and ambiguous as the results of CROSSROADS. The Atomic Energy Act of 1946 made nuclear weapons a separate part of the national arsenal: the president was given sole authority concerning their use. The obsessive secrecy surrounding the CROSSROADS cleanup was typical of the entire atomic weapons program, to the extent that Truman himself was not officially advised of the size of the nation's nuclear stockpile until the spring of 1947 (although Eisenhower, the Army chief of staff, got information from Groves and apparently briefed the president informally in September 1946).

This ignorance extended to the Navy. As late as February 1947 Forrestal thought his chief of naval operations knew the size of the stockpile, while Nimitz thought Forrestal knew. Neither did, and if they had, disbelief would have followed.

From 1945 to 1949, later to be seen as years of American "nuclear monopoly," there were exceptionally few atomic weapons in the cupboard. At the end of 1945 only *two* existed. When David Lilienthal took over as chairman of the Atomic Energy Commission in January 1947, he inspected his facilities and found exactly one bomb, with no personnel on hand to build more. By July 1947 there were thirteen bombs, a year later, fifty. None of these weapons was in assembled form. All were Mark 3 plutonium implosion bombs, like Fat Man. They were exceptionally inefficient in their use of fissionable material (lots of radioactive waste, as with BAKER; each weighed over ten thousand pounds fully assembled; and to assemble each one took thirty-nine men more than two days.

The Air Force owned them. The weapons could be loaded only by installing a special hoist in a pit twelve by fourteen feet and eight feet deep, trundling the bomb into the pit, rolling a specially modified B-29 over the pit, and heaving the assemblage into the bomb bay. In 1948 the Strategic Air Command, then one year old, had only about thirty B-29s that could do this, all of them part of the Hiroshima-Nagaski outfit, the 509th Bomb Group, based in Roswell, New Mexico.

In short, the public's notion during the era of monopoly that any threatening situation would immediately produce swarms of atomic bombers zeroing in on the Soviet Union was farfetched in the extreme. Still, the bombs *existed*, and a place had to be found for them in national strategy.

Harry Truman saw the bomb as an apocalyptic terror weapon, and like every president since, he recoiled from even the thought of its use—even though, when the time had come to decide on Hiroshima and Nagasaki, he had had no second thoughts. (He would go to his grave believing that he had in those cases done the right thing, that countless American lives had been saved thereby.) He focused exclusively on establishing civilian control over America's nuclear resources and seeking international control of atomic energy in the United Nations.

In the first instance he succeeded, in the second he failed. The Atomic Energy Commission gave him civilian control, despite military demands to the contrary. Although UN control remained the only official American policy into the summer of 1948, this foundered on American posturing in the General Assembly and on Soviet intransigence.

Meanwhile, the military (meaning mostly the Air Force) proceeded with its atomic targeting plans. The first target list was produced in the summer of 1947 and incorporated into Plan BROILER in the fall. The Joint Chiefs' FROLIC and HALFMOON followed, each placing heavy emphasis on an atomic air offensive. Although Truman ordered an alternative conventional plan prepared, the Berlin crisis in 1948 led Forrestal, by then secretary of defense, back toward atomic planning.

On 16 September 1948, NSC 30 appeared, the sole general statement by the National Security Council on atomic warfare policy to win presidential approval until 1959. This document concluded that the military, in case of hostilities, "must be ready to utilize promptly and effectively all appropriate means available, including atomic weapons." But the president retained the power to decide on their use.

And that was that. NSC 30 did not consider what conditions might justify the use of the bomb, what objectives could be obtained through its use, or, incredibly, even what targets might be suitable. Late in 1948, some of these questions were addressed in NSC 20/4, prepared by the State Department at Forrestal's insistence. In exceptionally general terms, NSC 20/4 said that America's goal in a war with the Soviet Union would be to reduce or eliminate Soviet, or "Bolshevik," control both inside and outside that country. The paper foresaw no need to occupy the USSR (as if this could be done, short of relocating the entire American population) and established no "predetermined requirement for unconditional surrender." This ethereal guidance was all the military got under Truman, and the language prefaced all American war plans through 1954.

Thus the National Security Council—which, if any agency did, had as part of its business to advise on the use of the bomb—offered no guidelines whatsoever on when and how the weapon might be used. The decision and moral responsibility were left with the man in the White House, imposing the most crushing burden of the modern presidency. Planning continued, but no one then foresaw how the numbers of prospective Soviet targets would mushroom, how both atomic weapons and their delivery systems would grow increasingly sophisticated and complex, and how, with the Soviets' development of their own bomb in 1949, operational planning would become increasingly rigid. This meant that each successive president would find narrower and narrower choices available in a nuclear confrontation and less and less time in which to make these choices.

Slowly, the nuclear stockpile grew, and so did the size of the Air Force's contemplated strategic offensive. BROILER called for 34 bombs to hit twenty-four Russian cities; HARROW, which supported FROLIC and

HALFMOON, envisioned 50 bombs hitting 20 cities. TROJAN, approved in December 1948 during the Berlin crisis, called for 133 bombs and seventy cities.

But even the Air Force began to have doubts about what all this devastation could produce. Lieutenant General Hubert Harmon, chairing an ad hoc committee to examine TROJAN, reported to the Joint Chiefs in May 1949 that even if all 133 bombs detonated precisely, this urban evisceration of the Soviet Union would not, by itself, "bring about capitulation, destroy the roots of Communism, or critically weaken the power of Soviet leadership to dominate the people." Industrial capacity would be reduced, troop mobility would be impaired, but follow-up attacks would be needed.

The Harmon report led directly to an expansion in the rate of production of atomic weapons and to the direct involvement of the Strategic Air Command in the defense of Western Europe through NATO. For the Navy, the report was manna from heaven. Here was an Air Force three-star saying that an aerial strategic atomic offensive could not do everything. Naval critics of the USAF's atomic strategy, already heated up by the unification struggle and coming to a second boil over the B-36 versus supercarrier issue, objected adamantly to the atomic offensive as the central, and seemingly *sole*, national strategy. Many, like Arthur Radford, doubted the efficacy of attacking urban areas in the first place. Others, like Ralph Ofstie, thought that such plans were "morally wrong." (Some cynics argued that the Navy found "immoral" any weapon its ships and planes could not use.)

The core of the problem was not moral but technical. As of 1950 the weapons were too crude, their delivery systems too imprecise, to consider tactical nuclear targeting. OFFTACKLE, in October 1949, called for 220 bombs to hit 104 cities, with a reattack reserve of 72 weapons—which meant every weapon then in the arsenal, and more. The numbers were bigger, but the objective was still to disrupt the Soviet will to wage war, the old (and discredited) dream of air power theorists.

The first postwar strategic concept from the Joint Chiefs, impregnated with the bitter memories of Pearl Harbor, had held that the United States must be ready "to strike the first blow if necessary . . . when it becomes evident that the forces of aggression are being arrayed against us." After Bikini, the Joint Chiefs recommended that "acts of aggression" include the readying of atomic weapons against the United States. How this "readying" was to be ascertained was left unclear. Congress, said the chiefs, should authorize the president, after consulting his Cabinet, to order atomic retaliation.

This proposal, a knee-jerk reflex triggering an automatic atomic exhange, was never accepted but was kicked around until the first weeks of the Korean War, when the Joint Chiefs, at Forrest Sherman's suggestion, stopped pressing because of the clear constitutional problems involved. Also, as Nimitz had already noted, Americans would not support automatic punishment of nations for acts that did not directly concern the United States—and "acts of aggression" was about as foggy a notion as international relations had to offer.[10]

Forrestal had seen America's exclusive possession of the atomic bomb as one of the "outstanding military facts in the world." Because of this monopoly, the United States could assume certain risks—military risks— to try to restore world trade, reshape the balance of power (so long as this clearly favored American interests, of course), and do away with some of the conditions that bred war. "The years before any possible power can achieve the capability effectively to attack us with weapons of mass destruction," he wrote, "are our years of opportunity."[11]

☆

They were certainly the Navy's years of strategic opportunity. The service— at least John Sullivan, when he became its secretary—was willing to concede the responsibility for aerial strategic warfare to the Air Force, but what was not conceded was the junior service's claim to atomic exclusivity. Nimitz himself set the tone:

> The atomic bomb is undoubtedly the most potent offensive missile yet developed. The United States Navy will utilize that weapon, and will utilize any other more powerful instrument that the mind of man devises, just as it utilized gunpowder, armor-piercing shells, submarines, and airplanes to make America powerful on the sea.

But Nimitz, believing that the bomb might be outlawed or considered too horrible to employ, came to oppose the inclusion of atomic strategy in the nation's war plans. Not so some of his junior admirals. Dan Gallery, opinionated as ever, declared that strategic bombing, targeted at enemy political and industrial centers, would decide the next war. He wanted to develop carrier-based nuclear bombers and get to proving that the Navy could deliver the bomb better than the Air Force. Ralph Ofstie was of the same mind.

But Gallery, Ofstie, Radford, and others soon saw that this ball bowled in the Air Force's alley. No carrier plane, no matter how hoss-tough, could lug the payload of a B-29, much less that of a B-36. Therefore, air admirals like Ofstie began to stress the indiscriminate, terrifying nature of atomic targeting. They were a generation younger than Leahy (who had graduated from the Naval Academy in the year William McKinley took the presidential oath of office, 1897), and whereas Leahy's argument rested strictly on moral precepts learned as a young man in the late Victorian era, precepts he saw as ends in themselves, the younger men were using moral issues to spearhead a specific program: naval possession of the atomic bomb, leading to an appropriate naval share in national nuclear strategy.

By no means were all of the claims of naval air enthusiasts so much hot air. Their concerns over the ability of long-range strategic bombers to penetrate modern anti-aircraft defenses were well-founded. The big bombers had to fly from fixed bases, which could themselves be immobilized. They needed fighter protection, which long ranges might preclude. But the biggest goad behind their attack was the fear that should strategic nuclear bombing become the heart of national military strategy, the Navy (which had no strategic bombers) would be relegated to a permanent back seat, the Shield of the Republic no longer.[12]

With the B-36 coming on-line and the plane that would become the B-52 already on the drawing boards, the Navy saw the Air Force in perpetual control of the bomb. Moreover, the president's Air Policy Commission, chaired by a Philadelphia lawyer and former assistant secretary of state, Thomas Finletter, had concluded in the summer of 1947 that the United States should have a nuclear deterrent strategy based primarily on the atomic bomb delivered by the long-range bomber. The Finletter report also specifically emphasized the deterrent value of the weapons when targeted on enemy cities rather than military installations.

General Quarters. Naval cannonades filled the pages of the U.S. Naval Institute *Proceedings*. Let the Army and Air Force stay in business, by all means, but "depend during the coming decade upon the world's greatest navy with emphasis on air carriers and submarines provided with essential bases." Naval, as opposed to national, war plans should develop ships and aircraft to meet an enemy offensive, launch an invasion, and make a naval atomic attack. "The atomic bomb is not a prelude to a diminishing role for [the naval] arm of the nation's defense."[13]

The atomic bomb could not transport cargo or move men and munitions. Its potential against a dispersed task force, as Bikini seemed to prove, was marginal, and besides, the task force's lethal fighter-interceptors would make hash of approaching enemy bombers. An efficient "atomic navy" should be created, capable not only of delivering nuclear weapons but also operating on nuclear propulsion. The effects of atomic radiation had been grossly overstated; the bomb was a weapon, like any other, and should take its proper place in the national arsenal.

Moreover, exclusive reliance on the bomb was compared to placing a howitzer in the kitchen; counting on only a single, pulverizing weapon would destroy the roaches, all right, but also blow away the house along with them. Exclusive dependence on atomic weapons would jeopardize national security. "The strategy of victory through the sole agent of mass atomic destruction," reasoned one naval officer, "is not only morally untenable, but has dubious chances of success politically and militarily."[14]

The Navyman who had been there from the first gave his opinion, too. Deak Parsons (who would die tragically before his time, of a heart attack in 1953) stood behind the value gained from the Bikini tests. Most of his comments following those tests and his previous ride aboard *Enola Gay* were devoted to the engineering and scientific aspects of the bomb, but even he stood in awe of the tremendous power he had helped to unleash. "After all, an atomic bomb is hardly a subtle phenomenon!" he exclaimed. But Parsons was Navy before he was an atomic weaponeer, and he cautiously came to conclude that "at least for the coming generation, use of the sea and therefore control of the sea will continue to be decisive."

In general, the Navy contended that the atomic bomb, in sole custody of the Air Force and tailored to the strategic design of air power, was not only immoral but also strategically ineffective. Some of the logic was less than compelling, and a few naval officers got carried away. One commander told Congress that if you stood at one end of Washington's National Airport, wearing nothing more than the clothes on your back, and an atomic bomb exploded at the other end, you would be all right.[15]

☆

The Berlin crisis unnerved American policymakers. Harry Truman ordered a crash program to build more atomic bombs. The production line was revved up to the point at which the weapons were being built at the rate of nearly one per day. By 1953, when Eisenhower entered the Oval Office, the atomic arsenal had grown to around 1600 weapons, most of them "small," in the twenty- to fifty-kiloton range. (In 1953 the Soviets still had no nuclear weapons *deployed* operationally.)

This renewed emphasis on atomic weaponry was not lost on the Navy. The three 45,000-ton *Midway*-class carriers were big enough to handle the larger atomic-delivery aircraft, but the problem was the plane itself. In its haste to get into the growing atomic supermarket, the Navy proceeded at two levels: developing its own nuclear-capable plane and modifying an existing aircraft to haul nuclear ordnance.

The stubby North American AJ Savage was already in the design stage in 1946, with a capability of six tons of bombs at two thousand miles, but the plane was not scheduled for fleet delivery until late 1949. *United States,* the supercarrier whose big decks would have been home to the Savage, was history, courtesy of Louis Johnson's cancellation.

Makeshift was the order of the day. As early as 1947 the Navy had inaugurated Project 27A, which strengthened the flight decks and catapults of nine *Essex*-class carriers and upgraded them to launch and recover aircraft weighing up to forty thousand pounds. Six of the carriers were retrofitted with magazines and hoists capable of storing atomic bombs. But there was still no aircraft that could carry the weapons.

The stopgap plane came from an unlikely place. At the end of World War II, no *carrier-based* aircraft could carry a payload of more than two thousand pounds. The big, land-based P2V Neptune, which entered service in the summer of 1946, could. And the P2V had a champion.

In the spring of 1947, Commander John ("Chick") Hayward went to Forrest Sherman, then deputy chief of naval operations for plans, with an idea. Chick Hayward was a former test pilot and "damn fine leader," a combat aviator who had skippered Bombing 106 in the Pacific. He was also a bit on the quirky side. Once, after Sherman had become chief of naval operations, Hayward flew his boss from Albuquerque to San Diego in a Savage. The aircraft was a strange hybrid, two props and a jet in the rear, and Sherman, the old biplane jockey, was not completely familiar with how the thing worked. He took the controls, at which point Hayward surreptitiously cut the propellers. And there Sherman was, flying along with two idled props, wondering what could be keeping him in the air—at least that was how Hayward told the story.

Hayward asked Sherman, in that spring of 1947, to lend him several of the Neptunes; if he could get them, he promised, he would find some way to fly them off carriers. Sherman knew that Hayward was a man who could make end runs around problems. Both men realized what was at stake, and Chick Hayward got his planes.

The P2V was a horse. In September 1946 a modified P2V-1, the famous "Truculent Turtle," had taken off at eighty-five-thousand pounds from Perth, Australia, and flown nonstop for over fifty-five hours without refueling, eventually settling down in Columbus, Ohio. Hayward sought to modify the plane for nuclear delivery.

Tests quickly showed that landing the cumbersome, wide-winged Neptune aboard a modified *Essex* or a *Midway* would be a grim prospect indeed, a real crapshoot. Hayward recommended that in the event of war the planes drop their loads from high altitudes at high speeds and then attempt to reach friendly land bases. If none was available, the aviators were to ditch near friendly forces, where the P2V's empty bomb bays and fuel tanks would give temporary flotation (provided, of course, that the aircraft did not smash to pieces on ditching). If this was not haphazard enough, the Neptunes had only a pair of 20-mm cannons in the tail turret with which to defend themselves, and there was no midair refueling capability. In addition, the Navy had no long-range fighters to provide cover.

Still, Hayward forged ahead, concentrating on getting the Neptune, with its bomb load, *off* the carrier. He stripped two P2Vs of surplus equipment, installed tail hooks, and inserted extra fuel tanks in the nose and waist. To maximize range, the planes were pruned of their radomes, antennas, turrets, astro hatches, and tail skids. A "hydro flap" was added to each plane to facilitate ditching—hardly a confidence-builder for the aviators. The bomb bays were reconfigured to provide the shackles, sway braces, and electrical connections necessary to roughly duplicate the bomb bay of *Enola Gay*. The planes also got reconfigured APA-5 radars for high-altitude bombing.

Hayward figured that with jet-assisted takeoff (JATO) the remodeled

Neptunes could get off a *Midway*-class deck with a few feet to spare between the starboard wingtip and the island. At least, that was what the measurements showed. On 28 April 1948, flying off *Coral Sea*, Commander Tom Davies, who had flown the Truculent Turtle, proved the case. His Neptune, never meant to fly off carrier decks, scraped by the island and lumbered aloft, assisted by a boost from the detachable JATO bottles. For Chick Hayward, this was the "go" signal.

Twelve Neptunes were redesignated as P2V-3Cs and plunged into a full round of training flights. In September 1948 Composite Squadron 5 (VC-5) was placed in commission at Moffett Naval Air Station, south of San Francisco, with Hayward as its skipper. The AJ-1s began to come into service a year later. In January 1950 VC-6 was born, shortly to move to Pax River. Both squadrons flew a mix of Neptunes and Savages. They could carry the Mark 4, a twenty-kiloton descendant of Fat Man manufactured at Los Alamos, as well as Little Boys.

By February 1950, jury-rigging all the way, the Navy had the atomic bomb at sea, with a rudimentary attack capability for carriers. Sherman, as chief of naval operations, had persuaded the Atomic Energy Commission to put several Little Boys in reserve especially for the two composite squadrons. The Neptunes were about as adaptable for carriers as DC-6 commercial airliners, but there they were (even Sherman admitted that this was a primitive way to solve the problem), along with the Savages, the Navy's atomic delivery "system."[16]

Now the Navy was in the nuclear strategy game, if not exactly on the ground floor at least in the basement. And the tune accordingly changed, from one of criticism of Air Force doctrine to one of "partnership." Admiral Lynde McCormick, as acting chief of naval operations following Sherman's sudden death, explained the Navy's new outlook this way:

> It is in our interest to convince the world at large that the use of atomic weapons is no less humane than the employment of an equivalent weight of so-called conventional weapons. The destruction of certain targets is essential to the successful completion of a war with the U.S.S.R. The pros and cons of the means to accomplish their destruction is purely academic.

—*Purely academic.* In September 1949 an analysis of rainfall from the Aleutians (Operation RAINBARREL) was passed on to the nuclear specialists in OP-06. Some samples contained cesium; no American nuclear burst was responsible. The rain clouds had drifted east, laden with radioactivity, from Siberia.[17]

Now there were two members of the nuclear club.

☆

The nuclear arms race began in earnest. In early 1950, as VC-5 and VC-6 were winding up to go to sea, Truman, advised by his specialists that the Russians, now in possession of the atomic bomb, could go ahead to create an atomic "trigger" for a fusion weapon, reluctantly launched a program to develop the "super," or hydrogen, bomb. "The bomb will be constructed because we dare not afford not to build it," unelegantly editorialized the *Washington Post*. "It would be shirking of responsibility to leave the American people one fine day to face a stand-and-deliver ultimatum from a Soviet Union armed with the H-bomb."

By 1952, in the midst of the seemingly interminable Korean War, the nuclear theoretician Edward Teller (who had been urging development of the super since 1946) and the mathematician Stanislaw Ulam had found a way to generate sufficient heat and pressure to keep a fusion reaction going. The first test of the device took place on 1 November 1952 on Elugelab, in the Marshalls. The test, called MIKE, yielded ten megatons, roughly one thousand times the energy released by Little Boy over Hiroshima less than seven years before. Elugelab, an island one mile in diameter, disappeared.

Two years later the Navy was conducting hydrogen bomb tests on Eniwetok (BRAVO, part of the CASTLE series), a replay of CROSS-ROADS at a far more destructive level. By now tests of saltwater washdown systems aboard the destroyer *Dortch* and light cruiser *Worcester* had indicated that topside radiation could be cut down to a fraction of its original strength. *Worcester* also had to undergo the humiliation of being bathed in a mist of acid fuchsin, a red dye, temporarily leaving the cruiser so mottled that one of her consorts signaled, "Sail on, o ship of fuchsia!"

CASTLE comprised five detonations, and the Navy participated in all of them. The Eniwetok tests were a radiological disaster for several unsuspecting Japanese fishermen, one of whom died, and 236 islanders in the path of the fallout were hospitalized. But the Navy was satisfied that its ships, even under an awesome cloud of hydrogen-bomb debris, could survive if they were properly buttoned up.

The hydrogen bomb gave a boost to naval claims for a share in national nuclear stategy. The super made USAF airfields even more vulnerable, and now even some naval detractors began to see virtue in mobile, seagoing air power that could deliver nuclear ordnance from unexpected directions and locations. James Smith, Jr., the Navy's assistant secretary for air, envisioned the future carrier striking force as

> . . . a handful of large ships able to maintain high speeds in all conditions—say three large carriers, seven cruisers, and two high-speed supply ships per task force. . . . This force will be spread out over an ocean area the size of the state of Maine. It will be so widely dispersed that no single weapon of any size we can now visualize can seriously damage more than one ship.

By 1956 the Navy's new supercarriers and reconfigured older carriers had the capacity to deliver the hydrogen bomb. The twin-engine, jet-propelled A3D Skywarrior, cousin of the USAF's B-66, was coming on line, with a combat radius of a thousand miles and a bomb bay configured for the super. The slower, smaller Savage was still around, although the Neptune had gone back to its original work as a sub-hunter and reconnaissance aircraft. Even jet fighters like the Fury and Banshee could be configured to tote smaller atomic weapons, which were now being "miniaturized" at a fearful pace. The Mark 5 entered service in 1952, a 3600-pound nuclear device; the first generation of weapons had weighed three times as much.

These planes provided no substitute for the truly heavy payloads that could be packed by the land-based B-52s, but their flexibility and mobility of operation gave the Navy a lasting role in nuclear strategy.[18]

☆

The Navy had participated in a strategic revolution without parallel in the history of weapons and warfare. Before 1945, the "Year Zero," men and governments prepared for war in order to be able to fight if and when war came. Now, the atomic and hydrogen bombs had produced a seemingly necessary strategy of nuclear deterrence: remaining able to fight, using weapons of fiendishly horrible proportions, *in order not to fight*. If full-scale war were to occur in the modern age, strategy had already failed.

Nuclear weaponry created such absolute, pulverizing destruction that limited victories or defeats, the only kind of war Baron Montesquieu ever knew, now seemed impossible once the bombs were unleashed. (A healthy closet industry, headed by Herman Kahn, argued the opposite case but gained few adherents.) Pre-1945 "front lines" no longer made sense on a nuclear battlefield. Therefore, unless the purpose was to incinerate millions, make large portions of the planet uninhabitable, and leave radioactive damage to poison countless future generations, nuclear weapons were practically *useless* in waging war. American (and Soviet) nuclear strategy therefore rapidly centered on *possessing* and *threatening*, rather than *using*, and both countries endlessly proclaimed that their ever-expanding nuclear arsenals were "defensive" only.

Led by the Air Force, many military men (and politicians) placed increased faith in nuclear deterrence in the ten years following V-J Day. But no one knew how many bombs were enough to "deter," and in addition, after CROSSROADS only the three blasts in the SANDSTONE series (April and May 1948) were conducted until 1951 (and some even suggested canceling the latter in case the then scarce bombs were needed for the Berlin crisis). Threat, not use: as late as the early fifties no American strategic bomber ever carried a bomb armed with a fissionable primer.

Thus, everything depended on the enemy's willingness to *believe* the nuclear threat and to reason within the same rational matrix as that used by American policymakers. Forrestal, for one, had deep doubts that the weapons would be decisive, even if they were used. Truman was willing to use them, but only in the most dire emergency. As one commentator observed, as early as 1946, "unless the Russians were fool-hardy enough to force us . . . to use the bomb in defense of other countries or of interests we deemed vital, it would seem as if our sole possession of the atomic weapon was not going to be of much service to us or the world."[19]

The very concept of nuclear strategy was delicate and unpredictable in the extreme, to the point that careless remarks could rattle tempers and produce quick responses. When Secretary of the Navy Francis Matthews spoke at the Boston Naval Shipyard in August 1950, after the Korean War had broken out, he proclaimed that in the name of a peaceful world the United States should be ready to pay "even the price of instituting a war to compel cooperation for peace." Americans must be "aggressors for peace."

—This was vintage foot-in-the-mouth Rowboat; unfortunately, he was speaking in the midst of a nasty war and following the emergence of a bipolar nuclear world. Truman's top civilian and military leaders roundly denounced Matthews, and shortly he was gone. But the implications were clear: the mere existence of the weapons made everyone twitchy, and no one quite knew how to integrate them into national strategy.

The Navy, particularly its aviators, certainly tried. Whereas the Air Force continued to use the yardstick of bomb tonnage dropped as the prime measure of bombing capability, the Navy held to the ideas of bombs delivered on target and the attainment of strategic and tactical objectives. There were thus, even at this macro level, decided differences in how to assess strategic objectives. Nonetheless, the Navy clearly had to give strategic ground to the big bombers. Naval aviators *never* saw themselves as usurping the USAF's strategic role; rather, carrier aviation would be complementary to the targeting of the Strategic Air Command.

In this view, the Atomic Age had not materially altered Mahan's concepts of seapower. Technology had changed, and tactics would have to change, but the essential strategic underpinnings of Mahanian doctrine were sound—with the not-so-minor caveat that there seemed to be no other *navies* around to fight. Some of the "analysis" was downright harebrained ("There will be no radiation hazard after air bursts," wrote one "authority"), but Navymen everywhere tended to see nuclear weapons as basically an enhancement of naval, and therefore American, power.[20]

The Navy emphasized precision, selective targeting, flexibility, and surprise as its contributions to nuclear strategy. "Naval atomic warfare should be militarily sound, effective, morally right, and helpful to postwar security," concluded one naval officer. *But*: "There should be no hesitation or reluctance, for either moral or historical reasons, for naval preparedness to participate in a global atomic war." As a statement of ambiguity and strategic confusion, this could hardly be bettered.

Nevertheless, the weapons were there, and in rapidly increasing numbers; the Navy now had them and could deliver them, and the "debates" over them were largely circumscribed by technological and tactical factors. The nukes were now a *given*.

With the Neptunes and Savages at sea, the Navy had become "air-atomic," and most of the service's nuclear strategic thinking went into sustaining the carrier-based bombers and making them a credible deterrent. There were other aspects to the Navy's involvement with nuclear weapons, of course. The Naval Radiological Defense Laboratory, for example, did studies aplenty on radiation hazards, announced that there were three classes of fallout shelters, and figured that the cost of bomb shelters for everyone in the United States would be $20 billion. But all this was ancillary, the dark, forbidding side of "the facts of life in the atomic age." No one was reading Montesquieu.[21]

—What counted were the weapons. And the weapons drove strategy.

CHAPTER FIFTEEN

FLATTOP

———— ☆ ————

There was one undisputed queen of the postwar Navy. As one spokesman observed, with only slight exaggeration, "the fleet in the postwar context is aircraft carriers." Ernie King, in a report summarizing naval triumphs during the war, praised the carrier as both an "integral and primary" component of the fleet. The flattop, in short, had arrived. Around her swirled the strongest currents of naval strategy, and in any major crisis she was deemed irreplaceable. The crucial strategic issue, how the Navy could come to grips with the land power of the Soviet Union, featured the carrier heavily, even though that country, with its vast and productive hinterland, was immune to naval blockade.

Two major naval roles had evolved by the early 1950s. Sea control, particularly in its NATO guise—aligned against Soviet submarine and land-based-bomber forces—was always at the forefront. And the projection of naval force onto land, although much more difficult to fit into an anti-Soviet scenario, was generally apropos to the crisis environment of the Cold War. In either of these roles, sea control or power projection, the flattop was the centerpiece of naval strategic thought.

In November 1947 the Navy's General Board, in decay but still planning away, produced, with the concurrence of the chief of naval operations and the Atlantic and Pacific fleet commanders, an unofficial planning document of forces needed to fight a war eight years down the road—in 1955. The plan, CHARIOTEER, keyed on four fast carrier task forces, supported by three logistics groups. Each of the task forces would have a *United States*-class vessel at its heart, supported by one *Midway* and two *Essex* 27A conversions. Each logistics force itself would contain two escort carriers and one fleet carrier. Thus, the first naval view of the postwar world from a flattop's island envisioned twenty-five flight decks, spearheaded by the four supercarriers.

Technology was supreme, and the quintessential naval technology was the flattop. "Technology itself may be today's primary air power theorist," commented one scholar. "Invention may, for the moment, be the mother of application." Amid the explosion of naval development—the ships, the electronics, the airframes, and the rest—the carrier, so central to naval strategy, also loomed as the veritable backbone of raw American power abroad.[1]

But even its impressive technology had limits. By 1945 the *Essex*-class carrier, only a few years old, was already bursting at her seams. Aircraft grew substantially heavier, arrested landings were more and more mandatory, and the bigger airframes required a catapult to sling them into the sky. The theoretical limits of both arresting gear and catapults defined aircraft design for the likes of the Hellcat and the Corsair.

The temptation to break these limits was based not only on technology, however. A carrier was the most expensive single piece of military hardware anywhere, by a huge measure—expensive to build and expensive to keep operating. No nation, not even the United States, could support many of them. The General Board's twenty-five-carrier estimate of 1947 was less than a quarter of the massive wartime carrier fleet of only two years before. To build carriers meant to make highly expensive choices, which automatically made carriers politically contentious issues; the cancellation of *United States* in 1949 was merely the example that proved the rule. Therefore, the notion grew of a *multipurpose* flattop, one very large basket into which as many mission eggs as possible could be packed.

Seventh Fleet carriers like *Valley Forge* and *Boxer* were among the first combat units to respond to the war in Korea, thus vindicating naval claims about the value of mobile, flexible carrier striking forces. Even Louis Johnson, a year after he had scuttled *United States*, was moved to tell Forrest Sherman that "I will give you another carrier when you want it." Sherman, of course, did not want just any old "new carrier;" he wanted a supercarrier—*United States* redivivus—and he succeeded.

By the end of the Korean War, the active fleet had grown from seven to twelve attack carriers and from eight to fifteen light and escort carriers. And Korea proved something else: that fast-carrier task forces lent themselves to rapid intervention—"crisis intervention"—in local conflicts, and thus seemed ideally suited to patrolling the oceanic block as local or regional policemen. Theorists would be forever predicting the decline of the flattop, just has they had done for the battleship, but the former would persist (as indeed would the latter, in new roles) because carriers *were* so flexible, so multidimensional—so *useful*.[2]

The carrier, as with the battleship previously, was now placed at the summit of a heirarchy of ships, a hierarchy that was "the central premise of military naval architecture until the middle of the twentieth century." Bigger was better (Secretary of the Navy John Lehman would be reciting this litany in the 1980s), and like must fight like. The Navy finessed the latter point—only the British, among all other maritime nations in the 1950s, possessed a carrier force that could possibly take the seas against the Americans, and they, staunchest of allies, did not count—in favor of the versatility offered by the "can-do" flattop.

☆

—Carrier designers responded. Round-the-clock operations, pioneered by Eddie Ewen's *Independence* in the Pacific war, were already the norm. But the heavier, more capable new aircraft needed help, both day and night.

The only method of taking off from or landing on a World War II aircraft carrier was right down the centerline of her flight deck. And the flight deck was seldom clear. Its after two-fifths was the touchdown area, a maze of arresting wires. The next fifth featured the barricades, a last-ditch tangle of steel wires and nylon rope to halt aircraft that did not snag the arresting gear. The forward end of the flight deck was the parking area, where planes were serviced or snugged in chocks waiting to be struck below to the hangar deck, via centerline elevators.

This clutter was incredibly dangerous. Unused but still-armed rockets and bombs could be jarred loose on landing and streak across the flight deck; wing and nose guns could be inadvertently triggered when the wheels touched down, converting the deck into a shooting gallery; poor landings or hook bounces could propel or vault a plane through or over the barriers into the crowded parking area. All in all, "it was pretty bad," remembered Vice Admiral Gerald Miller. A too-common example, from *Antietam* off the Korean coast:

> 2/29/52—Air operations. Flew 77 sorties. At 1000I an F9F accidentally fired one 20 mm round upon landing. Cause of accident not yet determined. The projectile hit Greenway, A.L., AB3, 211 48 37, USN, critically wounding him in the abdomen.

The new jets, like the F9F, made everything worse. Barrier crashes escalated exponentially; the conventional wire barrier had a disconcerting tendency to ride up the smooth nose of the low-slung, tricycled-landing-gear jets, with the fair chance of smashing the cockpit Plexiglas and decapitating the man within. The new nylon Davis barriers helped, but the speeds and weights involved still multiplied the peril.

A carrier flight deck was one of the most potentially deadly places anywhere. The strain was tremendous and, during flight operations, constant. "Without any question," said Admiral Charles Griffin, "the incidence of emotional fatigue is much higher on the attack carrier than perhaps on any other single type of navy ship."

A partial solution came with the angled deck, pioneered by the British. This deck, flush with the centerline deck but offset some eight degrees to port, offered an open area for takeoffs and landings, leaving the forward edge of the straight deck still reserved for parking, arming, and launching aircraft. With the extra landing area, longer runouts of arresting wires were possible, resulting in lower arresting stresses on both flight deck and aircraft.

Planes missing the wires on one pass were not in danger of piling up forward but could go around the racetrack for another attempt. "Power-on landings" produced lower aircraft sink speeds, thus reducing stress and shock when the wheels plumped down, and provided an emergency reserve to pull away at the last moment.

Wasp was used in 1952 to develop approach techniques and power-on landings. A simulated canted deck for further tests was painted on *Midway* the same year. That fall, *Antietam*, back from Korea, was modified in the New York Naval Shipyard. Her landing area was increased 20 percent, to about 75 feet by 525 feet. When she put to sea for tests, a substantial improvement in flight deck safety was immediately noticeable. During her first six months of angle-deck operation, *Antietam* registered over four thousand landings, both day and night, without a single barrier or deck crash.

A second partial solution was the steam catapult. When Eugene Ely landed his rickety kite aboard *Pennsylvania* back in 1911, his arresting gear was a parallel series of ropes extended at three-foot intervals between sandbags. Catapults did not even have that primitive history. *Langley*, the converted collier that became the nation's first carrier—the revered "Old Covered Wagon"—had none. Biplanes, aided by the carrier turning into the wind and kicking up what little speed she could to get some breeze across the bow, simply gunned their way down the flight deck and tried to take off. By the 1930s designers had experimented with flywheel catapults, gunpowder catapults, and catapult guns, all developed to get an airplane weighing over five thousand pounds up to forty-five miles an hour in a run of less than forty feet—at which point, they hoped, the thing would want to fly.

By World War II the newer carriers were equipped with flush-deck, hydraulic cats, but the armor, armament, and heavier combat loads of their aircraft meant longer takeoff runs. Cat shots became increasingly necessary—by 1945 the fleet carriers were conducting catapult launches 40 percent of the time; the light carriers, 70 percent; and the tiny jeep escorts, constantly. The jeeps were the first carriers to use cats as normal procedure rather than as an emergency measure.

Catapults saved deck space, made launches of heavier airframes possible, and eased the perils of night operations. But as with the straight deck, the advent of jet aircraft changed the catapult picture. Jets had low initial thrust and needed a high speed for takeoff, a reflection of the incessant need of their engines to suck in air at increased velocities. During Korea the H8, a slotted-cylinder hydraulic catapult, was the workhorse of the flattops. But by then the evidence was clear that detonated or hydraulic cats were unsatisfactory and unsafe for the heavier, more demanding jets.

The British, again, had an answer: the steam catapult. In April 1952 the Navy made arrangements for the manufacturing rights to a British-designed steam cat. As modified, the American version consisted of two long, slotted cylinders running side by side directly under the flight deck. Steam admitted through a launching valve propelled a piston down each cylinder, connected by a crosspiece. At the midpoint of the piston-connecting crosspiece was the launching hook, which extended up through a slot in the flight deck and attached to the aircraft towing bridle.

On 9 February 1954, a fifteen-ton metal mass was blasted down the flight deck of *Hancock*, moored in Puget Sound, and the steam catapult was on its way to the fleet. Just in time, for the hydraulic cats had developed a lethal history of "dieseling" during retraction, like a high-compression engine after shutting off the ignition with fuel octane too low. When dieseling happened, internal pressures in the catapult system could rise to over five thousand pounds per square inch. *Leyte*, an *Essex*-class carrier just returned from Korea, suffered such an accident, losing thirty-three men. But *Bennington*, another *Essex*-class, provided the literal death knell of the hydraulic cat.

In May 1954 she was steaming off Quonset Point, Rhode Island. In the middle of air ops on the morning watch, the port catapult's one-inch-diameter relief plug blew under the pressure of dieseling. A vaporized stream of hydraulic fluid sprayed into the air circulation system, throughout forward officers' country, and as deep as Main Damage Control on the fifth deck. Several men, led by a chief warrant, remained on duty there until they perished of asphyxiation. Thirty-three stewards in officers' country on the third deck struggled to open secured wardroom doors, but in the wrong direction. They died to a man.

Some of the spray flashed into ignition, and there were fires. The carnage was terrific. Three hundred injured men, most of them burned, accumulated on the flight deck. The final toll of dead was 104, and the state of Rhode Island declared a morticians' emergency.[3]

Bennington, like so many other flattops before her, had become prey to the exacting demands of carrier operations.

☆

Such disasters, tragic as they were, could not deter naval aviators, who at midcentury were flying high. One of their own, Forrest Sherman, was chief of naval operations, and their specialty was moving ahead in great strides. Jet aircraft, operating at all hours, became staples aboard carriers; by 1951 both Sixth and Seventh Fleet carriers included at least one jet squadron. Twin-engine and multiengine aircraft, like the Neptunes, were flying off the flattops; all-weather flight was a reality; the "observation planes" that had once been slung off battleships and cruisers were now history, and carriers brought along their own eyes in the sky; helicopters were no longer novelties on the flight deck.

Technically, not only the jet but also the compound aircraft engine—a combination of reciprocating and turbine types—had arrived. The turbo-

Navy storekeepers at Pearl Harbor listen to a Domei radio flash on 13 August 1945: World War II is over.

USS *Missouri* (BB-63), Tokyo Bay, 2 September 1945. All hands are on deck for the surrender ceremonies.

The Mahanian vision featured heavily armored, powerfully gunned battleships. This is USS *Indiana* (BB-1).

Alfred Thayer Mahan (1840-1914), c. 1905: The Navy's premier propagandist of seapower.

Admiral Ernest King, Chief of Naval Operations (1942-1945). Aware of the increased global responsibilities that would come to the Navy, King wanted as large a postwar fleet as possible.

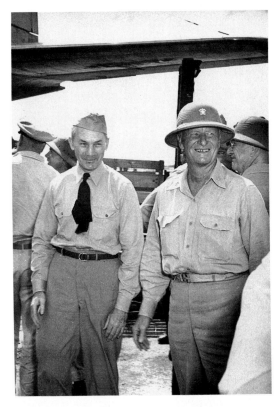

James Forrestal, Secretary of the Navy (1944-1947) and Fleet Admiral Chester Nimitz, soon to be Chief of Naval Operations (1945-1947), on Saipan, February 1945.

Harry Truman inspects an engine room aboard USS *Augusta* (CA-31) en route to the Potsdam Conference, July 1945.

The Swamp Fox: Representative Carl Vinson (D-Georgia), the Navy's congressional overseer.

Into mothballs: A sailor sprays a strippable film coating on a
five-inch gun mount, November 1945.

A fraction of the mothball fleet: These destroyers and destroyer escorts are
in San Diego, July 1950.

Vice Admiral Forrest Sherman welcomes Secretary of State George
Marshall aboard his Sixth Fleet flagship, USS *Albany* (CA-123),
17 October 1948.

The Key West Conference, March 1948: Unhappiness over interservice squabbling is reflected on several faces. Front row, left to right, are Admiral Louis Denfeld, Chief of Naval Operations (1947-1949), Fleet Admiral William Leahy, James Forrestal, Secretary of Defense (1947-1949), Air Force General Carl Spaatz, and Army General Omar Bradley.

Admiral Charles ("Savvy") Cooke,
typical of many American naval
leaders who supported the doomed
Nationalist Chinese cause.

Into the peacetime Mediterranean: USS *Missouri* (BB-63) anchored off
Istanbul, April 1946. On her port bow is *Power* (DD-839), on her port
quarter the Turkish battlecruiser *Yavuz* (the former German *Goeben*).

The supercarrier that never was: A seakeeping model of USS *United States* (CV-58). The cancellation of her construction triggered the rebellion in gold braid.

John Sullivan, Secretary of the Navy (1947-1949), who resigned following cancellation of *United States*, flanked by two antagonists: Secretary of the Army Kenneth Royal (left), and Secretary of the Air Force Stuart Symington (right), February 1948.

Carrier Air Group 5 off *Valley Forge* (CV-45) strikes Inchon, July 1950.
The view is east, over Suwolmi-Do.

A taste of Korean weather: The flight deck crew of USS *Badoeng Strait*
(CVE-116) gets to work, November 1950.

Airman William Lawton pulls through the prop to prime the engine on a F4U Corsair fighter aboard USS *Philippine Sea* (CV-47) in a snowstorm off Korea, November 1950.

The mudflats at Inchon: LSTs and LCMs high and dry, unloading cargo, 16 September 1950.

Navy minesweepers under fire off Wonsan, November 1950.

Louis Johnson, Secretary of Defense (1949-1950) was very much at home in his Pentagon office until fired by Harry Truman.

Francis Matthews, the widely despised Secretary of the Navy (1949-1951), aboard USS *Franklin D. Roosevelt* (CV-42) in 1949.

Carlson's Canyon after several Navy attacks, 30 March 1951.
Enemy traffic still moved across the valley.

Torpedo hits by Navy Skyraiders on the Hwachon Reservoir, 4 May 1951.

The techno-empire grows as James Forrestal adds mortar to the cornerstone of the Naval Ordnance Laboratory, White Oak, Silver Spring, Maryland, on 15 August 1946.

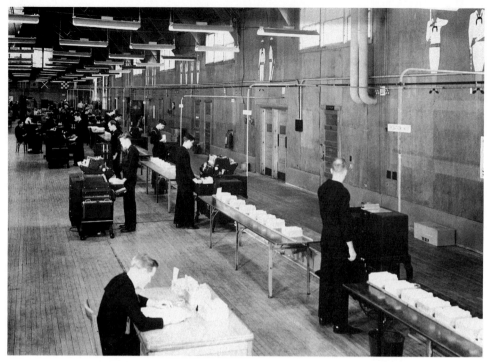

Sailors doing sorting based on IBM machinery, 1947. Electronics irrevocably altered the postwar Navy.

Test BAKER at Bikini Lagoon, 25 July 1946.

props were on display, in platforms like the Douglas AD-2 Skyshark and the Convair XP5Y patrol plane. The turboprops, gas turbine engines driving conventional propellers, were less than half the weight of conventional reciprocating engines yet could put out almost twice the horsepower. Chick Hayward's Neptunes, lugging combat loads, were routinely taking off from carriers.

The carriers steamed, with their attendant escorts, in far-flung formations, looking from the air like a few specks of pepper on a desk blotter. Flying from shore, all-weather planes like the potbellied flying radar stations of VC-12, based at Quonset Point, sent out probing electronic fingers that extended far beyond the perimeter of the task force, groping for anything on, or above, or beneath the surface that might menace the heavy and her flock. At sea, the AF Guardian (which, fully loaded, weighed more than a DC-3), the Skyraider, and the Skyshark ranged out from home plate, scopes aglow within their sealed cockpits.

By 1954 70 percent of the planes in the Navy's sixteen carrier air groups were jet-powered. In all, almost fifteen thousand aircraft were in the inventory, 60 percent of them operated, from land and sea, by active-duty aviators. Among the planes were lightning bolts like the Douglas F4D Skyray, a fighter that set a world's speed record of 752.9 miles per hour; the McDonnell F3H-1N Demon, a trouble-plagued all-weather fighter-bomber; the Grumman S2F Tracker, a twin-prop destined for a long life as an antisubmarine platform; and the Chance-Vought F7U-3 Cutlass, another plane bedeviled by engine production difficulties.

Mick Carney, as chief of naval operations, took a look at this array and remarked, "Additional responsibilities may be expected to increase with the Navy's ever-increasing range of tactical influence." With the carrier and her brood, technology drove strategy more powerfully than ever.[4]

The Navy was in love with its carriers. By 1957 the service had settled on the number of fifteen attack carriers—two of them constantly in the Mediterranean, four in the Pacific—as its magic number. This number would be carved in granite for thirty years, a perpetual "necessary" standard.

Naval supporters proclaimed the carrier did not depend on property gained by diplomatic deals (a jab at the Air Force and its growing string of overseas bases); that the ship was mobile, elusive, diversified, and constantly ready; and that the enemy was forced to dilute his defenses and scatter his detection forces to deal with her. "It is the unanimous opinion of all high-ranking Navy and Marine officers that Naval and Marine Corps aviation are the spearheads of these two Services," intoned the president of the Navy League. "Naval aviation must progress and expand at a rate commensurate with the development of Soviet Navy and Soviet Air Power." Carrier air had proved itself in Korea, said Admiral Arthur Radford. "The performance of carrier forces was the highlight of Naval combat operations."

Such power and potential could not be allowed to wither away. Already the nuclear-powered carrier was hull-down over the horizon, and the existing carriers were proven studs: in all of World War II the United States lost eleven of them in action, about 10 percent of the country's total number of flattops. Six of these were escorts, with tissue-thin merchant hulls; four were older prewar ships, including *Lexington* and *Hornet*; and one was a light carrier. Not a single *Essex*-class ship was sunk, and those that were damaged spent less than 10 percent of their service time under repair.

—All in all, she was the queen of the fleet. No wonder Sherman, addressing the graduating midshipmen at the Naval Academy shortly before his untimely death, could say: "It is my earnest conviction that the future of Naval Aviation has never been so challenging, so vital, or so bright."[5]

☆

The naval aviators waited for the supercarrier and, in the meantime, the *Essexes* and *Midways* carried the load. Nine *Essexes* received conversions (Projects 27A and 27C), which beefed up their landing decks, strengthened their elevators, and enabled them to support atomic bombers. Renamed the *Oriskany* class, these reworked ships were also scheduled for angled decks; the mangled *Bennington*, which had to go into the yards anyway, was the first to get hers. Six more *Essexes*, renamed the *Hancock* class, got a more extensive facelift, including steam catapults. All these thirty-three-thousand-ton conversions, more heavily armored now, could operate the Savage and launch, but not recover, the Neptune. Their future, however, lay mostly in antisubmarine warfare.

The three forty-five-thousand-ton *Midways*—the lead ship, *Franklin D. Roosevelt*, and *Coral Sea*—were larger, barely able to squeeze through the Panama Canal. They each got the *Essex* upgrade—mirror landing lights (the "meatball"), angled decks, steam cats, the works (Project 110). Their angled decks were eventually slewed to port about 10.5 degrees, giving them a fractionally jauntier look than the *Essex* conversions.

All of the reconverted *Essexes* and *Midways*, for lack of an opposing carrier force, were designed to bear the brunt of the naval offensive against land targets, something the equally advanced but much smaller British carriers could not do very well. The *Essexes* were redesignated as antisubmarine platforms (CVSs) in 1953, somewhat of a downgrade from their previous strategic role. But the conversions, as welcome as they were to naval aviators, were not the "real thing."[6]

The real thing was the supercarrier, and when she arrived she was a magnificent quantum leap forward, as far removed from the *Essexes* and *Midways* as those ships had been from the Old Covered Wagon. On 12 July 1951 work resumed on what had been *United States*. Forrest Sherman's prodding, the "fall of China," and the Korean War had all played a part in regenerating the project. The keel was laid on 14 July 1952, and from that time forward the ship steadily took shape.

She grew into a giant: sixty thousand tons, four acres of flight deck, and more than two hundred thousand horsepower, which could drive her at the mandatory thirty knots (for creating wind across the bow) and more. Gone was the flush-deck concept; the angled deck made the conventional starboard island layout secure. In her was every advance made since World War II in carrier technology, advances gleaned from years of straight-deck, hydraulic catapult operation, advances that had been bought, in part, at the price of many lives.

Forrestal (CVA-59) was placed in commission on 1 October 1955. She would be followed by three sisters: *Saratoga* (commissioned a week later), *Ranger* (1957), and *Independence* (1959), each slightly different from the lead ship (as all naval ships usually were) but each, undeniably, a supercarrier. Dan Kimball, as secretary of the Navy in 1952, wanted a minimum of twelve of the *Forrestals* "if the Navy is to carry out its primary mission."

There were only four, but they were dandies. Each of the last three had to undergo serious budget battles, because they came, even stripped of their air groups, at a miminum of $250 million a copy. They were floating cities of five thousand or more men. They could handle more than one hundred aircraft, with any squadron mix desired—usually four fighter and fighter-bomber outfits, an attack squadron, tankers, early-warning planes, a few antisubmarine aircraft, and helicopters. They had four catapults, not two, and their combat information centers were electronic wonderlands, designed for air control and air interception.

"A have-not nation [?] with the overseas commitments of the United States is inviting disaster if it neglects sea power," bellowed Dan Gallery. "The *Forrestal* carriers will keep that sea power up to date." And up-to-date they were: 52,500 tons of structural steel; individualized, comfy squadron ready rooms; simultaneous launch and recovery capability; faster launch rates with the four steam cats; stronger arresting gear; and huge deck-edge elevators, a considerable improvement over the old centerline devices, mal-functions in which had often caused air operations to come to a screeching halt.

The Navy was increasingly self-conscious about "habitability." Each living space aboard the supercarriers was air-conditioned. The traditional gray paint was replaced by bulkhead and overhead colors that the Navy's interior designers (whoever they were) described as "soft and restful." Decks were made of a special resilient tile—easier to wax and buff. Two enormous galleys, fore and aft, fed each floating city, each of which was also served by a dry-cleaning plant, a laundry, three barber shops, a cobbler shop, three soda fountains, and four ship's stores.[7]

Men were still in uniform who had steered rickety box kites down the wooden roof of *Langley*. With the *Forrestals*, over three decades later, con-ventional carrier technology reached its highest plateau yet—but not without problems. The huge flattops sucked in manpower, and all of the supercarriers began their seagoing lives with from 30 percent to 50 percent green hands aboard. The new launching and recovery gear, as well as the new electronics, took time to learn. Their shipboard defensive armament was puny, compared with the porcupinelike gun nests aboard the older carriers, which meant a greater premium than ever on flight operations and aerial interception.

The bonuses, however, far surpassed the teething problems. The mirror landing system ("50 percent easier," said the skipper of a Cutlass squadron) let the aviator center an amber light in a green cross and fly a glide path right to the deck. "In twenty flying days of shakedown, we made 2030 landings," bragged *Forrestal*'s air boss, "and didn't scratch a flightdeck man, a pilot, or a plane." The angled deck did away with barriers, meaning "ready deck" at all times. The old hydraulic cats, in addition to their propensity for dieseling and other foibles, produced a heavy initial thrust and then dropped off rapidly. The steam cats gave constantly increasing pressure and better takeoff speed, providing a sliver of extra time for the jet planes to grab the air. *Forrestal*'s four cats could put a division of aircraft aloft in less than thirty seconds.

The supercarriers were "attack carriers," CVAs, which the Navy presented as "an orderly and necessary step in the progressive development of a proven weapons system." The "Attack Carrier Task Force," like Chick Hayward's jury-rigged composite squadrons that had gone before, was not competitive with the Strategic Air Command but supplemental—or so the Navy argued. "Smaller carriers could be built," wrote one analyst, "if we desired to sacrifice aircraft performance, seaworthiness, adequate logistic capacity, and all the other advantages that the larger hull of a modern carrier makes available to us."

To her advocates (and her initial press releases were uniformly warm and admiring), the supercarrier was a fundamental investment in national security. But no one was sitting on the oars. Only two years after *Independence* was commissioned came *Kitty Hawk* and *Constellation*, their main difference from the earlier four being their guided missiles. There would be two more *Kitty Hawks*, *America* (1963) and *John F. Kennedy* (1968).

The year of *Kitty Hawk* and *Constellation*, though, was also the year of a radical new weapons system, for on 25 November 1961 *Enterprise* was placed in commission, a nuclear-powered Goliath.[8]

—A dozen years, 1949 to 1961—from the death of *United States* to the birth of "Big E." Naval air, truly, was flying high.

☆

To a naval aviator, carriers were all very well, but he lived and breathed *aircraft*, and the same dozen years produced a bewildering array for him to master (or to master him). He saw himself (with some justification) as the cream of American manhood—coolheaded, physically superb, brainy, coordinated, capable of split-second decisions—and he had a love-hate relationship with anything he flew.

The aviators despised the glad-handing PR types from the manufacturing firms, the ones who gave the planes numbers and flashy names. All this was for the public, and confusing besides: in 1945 an "F-4" was a Grumman Wildcat; in 1955, a Douglass Skyray; in 1965, a McDonnell Phantom. The men who flew baptized the planes themselves—in carrier ready rooms, on the aprons of test centers, and in saloons ashore.

They always had. The old-timers remembered training in gaudy yellow Stearman N2S biplanes, and they nicknamed these frail assemblages of struts, fabric, and baling wire "Yellow Perils." World War II brought a rash of single-engine monoplanes, none of which escaped desecration. The Grumman TBF Avenger, which was a deadweight from the very beginning and was slaughtered at Midway, received and deserved the tag of "Turkey;" the reliable Chance-Vought F4U Corsair was "Hosenose," although its early landing safety record also earned the sobriquet "Bent-Wire Widowmaker;" the Vultee SNV Vindicator was the "Vibrator;" and all Navy blimps, platforms on their way out in the 1950s, were "Poopybags."

The newer planes received no quarter. A loving name—like "Spad," attached to the sturdy, trusty Douglas A1 Skyraider—meant that the aviators were truly satisfied. More often, however, the ready rooms were filled with chatter and complaints about "Fords" (F-4D Skyrays), "Cruds" (F-8 Crusaders), or "Flying Bricks" (F-4 Phantoms), each nickname highlighting an unwanted, unlovely, or dangerous characteristic.

The nicknames were not just for laughs, because anything that flew could kill you—quick. Naval aviators died by the dozens, even in peacetime—cracking up during qualifications at Pensacola, smashing into the deck during night carrier landings, stalling on launch, ditching at sea. Sometimes the plane failed, sometimes the man, sometimes no one ever knew—"cause unknown." Carrier aviation was the toughest flying anywhere, because if a four-acre flight deck looked huge to the man standing in its middle, to the man trying to land there the space was an unglued postage stamp, waffling in every direction, any hour of the day or night, in any weather.

Grampaw Pettibone knew all about this. Gramp was a cartoon character created by Captain Seth Warner back in 1943. Warner got the idea through the contemplation of his own flying sins. Robert Osborn drew the character, a feisty, bearded old geezer who appeared regularly in the *Naval Aviation News*, blowing his stack at each mishap. "Grampaw Pettibone was conceived in desperation," said Warner, "the offspring of frustration and of despair."

Gramp was fictional, but his examples of what aviator and plane could do to each other were not. Among many real-life horror stories, one of the best was about the jockey of an F-9F Panther, flying off *Essex*. He bounced on landing and, instead of allowing his plane to go into the waiting Davis barrier, tried to get aloft again. In doing so, the Panther caught the nylon tape with its extended landing hook and flew away, hook fouled, trailing the entire barrier. On the way up the deck, the Panther creamed another plane with its aviator inside, knocking off the canopy.

The deck handlers, now fully alerted to the fact that this was not business as usual, cleared the deck and installed a line of tractors behind a hastily erected second barrier to stop the Panther on the next pass. The plane, which had lost one flap and its left wheel on the first go-around, this time jammed its landing hook in the "up" position. The Panther whooshed past the arresting wires, the aviator rammed the throttle forward, and the plane sheared off its other two wheels on the tractors. Up the deck the Panther skidded on its belly, knocking off the one remaining flap and damaging both fuselage and wing tanks. Thus denuded, the plane roared off again, leaving havoc behind.

As the *Essex* deck crewmen tried to figure out their next move, the aviator's voice came over the radio: "This is becoming a rather rugged flight." He was ordered to try a belly landing on the beach, but he ran out of gas on the way in and ditched in the water. Gramp reported that the flier had turned in his wings.

Many were the errors: Aviators punched out of reeling aircraft, which then could plunge into occupied areas. The man at the controls sometimes got so locked in on his intentions that when something unexpected happened, he could not respond. A few simply daydreamed their lives away, a common mistake being shooting a landing with the wheels up. (In a prop plane, the flier's first clue that this had happened was the sight of his propeller blades bending backward toward his eyes.)[9]

—And the jets were faster, more unforgiving. The Navy's adventures with them began with the Ryan FR Fireball. The Fireball, like its younger cousin the Savage, was a hybrid, with a Wright Cyclone radial engine in the front and a General Electric jet engine in the rear. The fighter plane could mount guns, bombs, and rockets, and like all American combat aircraft was heavily armored.

But the Fireball was too late for combat. The plane got to the fleet in late 1945, with Fighter Squadron 66, but never proved itself. Either engine produced speeds over 300 miles per hour, but these speeds were already greatly exceeded by the faster conventionally powered monoplanes. Besides, the Fireball's jet engine was seriously underpowered, so much so that the conventional engine was used to get the plane off a carrier deck.

Still, jets were the future. The spiderlike McDonnell FH-1 Phantom was the first full jet to land and take off from a carrier—*FDR*, on 21 July 1946. By 1948 Fighter Squadron 17A was flying the FH-1 in the Atlantic and Squadron 5A (later VF-51) was using the North American FJ Fury in the Pacific. A host of questions arose, about operational altitudes; aviator safety; G forces; supersonic flight; heat, cold, and stress, on both man and machine; airframe endurance; instrument flight; tactics.

Jets could do many things that props could not, and at dramatically greater speeds, but their biggest bugaboo by far was restricted range and endurance. Jet engines gulped fuel like so many Draculas draining a vein. They liked high altitudes and high speeds, and in lower, thicker air, they labored to produce more thrust. In a single racetrack orbit off a carrier's port beam, early jets consumed eight times the amount of fuel that a reciprocating engine plane did during the same pattern. As jet engines became more efficient and metal alloys became both lighter and stronger, this ratio improved—but not by much.

Because jets were fuel hogs of colossal proportions, their flight plans had to be sketched with excruciating care. Even loafing along at moderately high speed and altitude, a jet swallowed over a ton of fuel an hour. Down near the deck, this consumption rate tripled. As a result, one-third the takeoff weight of a jet fighter was fuel. More fuel was spent getting to optimum altitude, between thirty thousand and forty thousand feet. This meant the jets' "stay time," or "loiter time," was, relatively, the wink of an eye.

The carriers had to be reconfigured to take jet fuels. A flattop operating both conventional and jet aircraft, as during the Korean War, had to have aviation fuel resupplied at a frantic rate. After Korea, fuel-mixing devices were installed on the carriers, allowing jets to use a mixture of aviation gas and the new jet fuel, JP-5. All jet-air groups meant that only enough avgas had to be carried for the helicopters. JP-5 was low in volatility and flash point; therefore its use required less bunker protection and gave carriers more storage space.

Jets were expensive. They needed special metals to withstand the scorching engine temperatures, closer airframe tolerances, and special fuels. A prop-driven Corsair cost around $80,000, a bargain at the price. But even a cheap, unproven jet ran to about $300,000 in the early fifties; the glitzier, bigger models were already up to $750,000 apiece.

But once the aviators got the hang of them, the jets flew like dreams. They were free of the troublesome torque produced by props, and the unchanging directional trim made them superior gun platforms. Jets were more "honest" near stall, with no treacherous torque roll to throw the airframe into a deadly spin. Although their landing speed was half again as high as that of conventional aircraft, they had no bulky engine or prop to block the view ahead, only a nicely tapered nose section sitting atop a tricycle landing gear.

The hydraulic catapults gave them trouble, though. If a jet's turbines could not suck in enough air at launch, the plane could plummet like a stone off the leading edge of the flight deck. The hydraulic cats tended to taper off the power at the moment the jets needed help most. The steam cats, with their steadily increasing launch force, gave the jets a more dependable leg up into the sky.

Jet fighters developed like dandelions in the spring, new generations breeding almost annually. By 1952 the Fury was already relegated to experimental and reserve duty after a service life of seven years. The F-9F Panther family, over 600 miles per hour worth of speed, proved itself in Korea, as did the twin-engine McDonnell F-2H Banshee. The tandem-seat Skyknight, the Navy's first jet night-fighter, came on line, as did the delta-wing Skyray. The Fury found a descendant in the FJ-2 Fury, a strengthened naval version of the USAF's F-86 (called the "Flying Barrel" by the fliers). And the slick, high-speed McDonnell F-3H Demon, the "Lead Sled," first flew in August 1951.

Jet attack planes multiplied, too. Here the propeller-driven aircraft made a last stand, because the jets did not like the lower altitudes and slower speeds that made for more accurate attacks. Among the props that survived (for a while) were the Martin AM-1 Mauler, used mostly to carry torpedoes and rockets; the AU-1 Corsair, specially modified for close support (the Marines loved them); and, above all, the Skyraider, that faithful stallion of attack aircraft. Some attack props were reconfigured for early-warning and antisubmarine work, the the AD-4W and the AF-2W Guardian. As to jets, the hybrid Savages held the line through the early fifties, but the future was with the Douglas A-3D Skywarrior ("the Whale"), the Navy's first pure jet attack plane, and the rest of its kind.[10]

☆

In 1950 the secretary of the Navy reported, somewhat too optimistically, that "the introduction of jet propelled fighters into carrier operations had been successfully accomplished." This secretary, of course, was Rowboat Matthews, who could not tell a jet from a golf cart. *Improvements* there certainly were: ejection seats, hard-shell helmets for fliers, new parachutes, stronger shoulder harnesses.[11]

The technology went forward as well, sometimes by plan, sometimes hit-or-miss. In fiscal year 1953 naval aviation's "modernization"—the proportion of modern aircraft in frontline aviation units—went from 28 percent to 56 percent. The Navy trumpeted the triumphs of the new marvels: a Skyray sped 752.9 miles per hour over a measured course; three F9F-6 Cougars flew nonstop from San Diego to New York in record-breaking time; the ZPG-2 airship (blimps were fighting a futile rearguard action) remained aloft for more than eight days; and the experimental D-558-2 Skyrocket, developed by the Navy and flown under the auspices of the National Advisory Committee for Aeronautics, blistered the sky at 1272 miles per hour.[12]

Then there were the oddities, the developmental paths that sometimes went places, sometimes not. The Convair XFY-1 was a flying pogo stick, a weird little stub with two counterrotating propellers on its nose, designed to test the concept of vertical takeoff and landing. Convair also produced turboprop seaplanes, while Lockheed turned out, among others, the turboprop R7V-2 Super Constellation and the WV-2 early-warning plane. Much attention was also given the Douglas A-4 Skyhawk in its developmental stages; the plane was initially dubbed the "midget A-bomber," but its fliers, with bows to its designer, affectionately christened the Skyhawk "Heinemann's Hot Rod."

By 1955 the aircraft inventory—partially experimental but mostly operational or intended to be so—was impressive. Naval aviation engineering was outstanding, at least in part because designers were forced to conceptualize within extremely tight operational limits. They felt themselves limited for physical reasons to speeds of Mach 2.5 and altitudes no higher than sixty thousand feet. Another limit was the increasingly longer lead time the newer airframes required. As a fleet average, five years would pass from the day a new requirement was issued by the deputy chief of naval operations for air to the initial airframe delivery. The aircraft engines, from dream to flying machine, took around seven years. And the avionics averaged nine years.

The power plants were the major operational problem, so much so that the Navy began to depend on engines developed by the Air Force, engines that had been designed to cover a larger range of aircraft requirements. But the aircraft that reached the fleet, most of them, did their jobs (eventually) very well indeed. An unlikely example was the Douglas F3D Skyknight, the blocky twin-engine jet night-fighter which proved as helpless as a beached whale in Korean daylight—enemy MiGs could climb faster than the Whale could dive. The portly plane also tended to smash hydraulic catapults while taking off. By 1952 the F2H Banshee ("Banjo"), equipped with a good radar in its nose, had stolen the Whale's night thunder. But as a land-based early-warning platform, a test vehicle, and an electronic warfare aircraft, the Whale—"over-used, over-aged, and over-awed by every other jet set speedster in the sky"—went on to have a productive, if somewhat unplanned, life.[13]

"Things look good," said one Navy flier in 1956, "but they were looking awfully bad before they looked good." In sum, ten to fifteen years passed before the fleet had learned how to fully integrate the jets into its operations—about a decade longer than Rowboat Matthews's claim. The late fifties brought the realization that the new age of carrier aviation had arrived. Arleigh Burke called the period one of "tremendous transition," but now the fliers knew where they were headed.

No unrestrained flood of aircraft occurred; research and development were far too good for that, and in some years, fewer aircraft were accepted for fleet use than in the previous year—21 percent fewer in 1959 than in 1958. But the planes were more burly, more heavily armed. By 1960 attack aircraft could carry, in addition to their bomb loads, Bullpup, an air-to-surface missile, and Zuni, a five-inch aircraft rocket that could be used against anything from tanks to small ships. Four Zunis could be carried for every Korean-vintage HVAR.

The fighters now sported air-to-air Sidewinder and Sparrow missiles, descendants of World War II's "Tiny Tim," an air-to-ground rocket used at Okinawa. Airborne missiles rapidly entered an evolutionary pattern that outpaced the aircraft themselves. In 1961 the newly integrated Bureau of Naval Weapons completed its first full year of operation, and the flow of technological weapons marvels, mostly under its auspices, never stopped.

Some people argued that in air-to-air combat maneuverability should be embodied in the guided missile, not the aircraft. Between 1956 and 1960 this idea reached its most extreme form with Eagle-Missileer. The F-6D Missileer was a relatively low-performance fighter carrying an exceptionally high-performance missile, the Eagle. This mix never really got off the ground, but the concept proved to be the grandfather of the highly successful F-14 Tomcat and its Phoenix missile.[14]

More stringent budgets, as well as technological advances like micronics, led designers to try to pack more and more options into every airframe. Like the carrier herself, naval aircraft tended to be exceptionally complex and multifunctional. Their costs soared accordingly, producing yet more budgetary austerity and even more rigorous attempts at packaging. In this way naval aeronautical design, while continuing to come up with exceptional aircraft, operated in a sort of technological prison. Always, the parameters of cost and time pressed in on the engineers, and they would often retool an existing airframe, like the Whale, for yet another task. In addition, they had to compete within the entire spectrum of military expenditures. Sometimes they lost money battles within their own service, particularly to high-visibility crash projects like Polaris.

Unsurprisingly, the number of aircraft in the active inventory shrank from 10,533 in 1958 to 8,863 in 1960, a loss of 16 percent in two years. Some of this drop represented the phaseout of the props, but making the airframes more multifunctional played a part as well. By 1962, for example, all naval fighter aircraft were expected to have some capability in close support work, in addition to their main chore of establishing local air superiority.

Of course, such design patterns meant that, in operational environments, aircraft designed for a variety of tasks might not be able to perform one specific task very well at all.

☆

All was not guns and roses. There were failures, even of planes that got to the fleet and, unlike the clumsy Whale, could not find alternative missions.

The most instructive example was provided by the McDonnell F3H-1 Demon.

Even during its R and D, the Lead Sled was a major headache. The Demon was supposed to be a do-everything airplane, an all-weather, carrier-based jet fighter. The Navy ordered fifty-six from McDonnell headquarters in St. Louis. Six of these crashed during tests; two pilots were killed. Of the remaining fifty planes, the Navy decided that twenty-one would be used only for ground training. The remaining twenty-nine got a more powerful engine (the original 7200-pound Westinghouse J40 could not handle the airframe weight) and went off to the fleet for carrier trials.

Ninety more aircraft were converted to F3H-2s, with the bigger engine and a modified airframe. By late 1955 Congress and budgetary watchdogs were fully alert, because even the grounded Lead Sleds were costing $1.3 million apiece. As of then, the plane had been in the R and D pipeline for six years, the engine for eight. As the months passed, the only predictable part of the Demon's performance was that the plane would crash like clockwork—eleven times, all told—and two more pilots lost their lives. The whole program had consumed $500 million.

Everything went wrong.The underpowered airframe was only a start. The airframe, engine, and components were all assembled and tested separately before marriage, and, as in many marriages, proved incompatible once joined. Responsibility for numerous design and testing gaffes was impossible to pin down. There were frequent "slippages" in production time, and by early 1956, of the grand total of 280 Demons ultimately on order, 220 had not yet been tested for fleet use.

There were the usual charges of incompetence and corruption, but what really went wrong with the Demon, other than its design, was that its birth passage was a bureaucratic and financial maze in which everyone played a part and no one was responsible. Aircraft design and construction were a *process*, but without a single guiding hand cases like that of the Demon resembled nothing so much as a group of youngsters working independently on an Erector set, each one attaching nuts and bolts every which way and each expecting a functional building. In April 1956 a Senate subcommittee wrote off the Lead Sled as a total loss, "except for the lessons learned." A few Demons got to the fleet, but the fliers' nickname for them told the story, and the plane never made its mark. [15]

But successes happened, too. In the fifties five combat aircraft came along, each destined for a durable, if not exactly untroubled, service life.

Edward Heinemann's Hot Rod, the Douglas A-4 Skyhawk, was the mightiest midget the Navy ever had. The Hot Rod packed the strength of a Skyraider and could carry nuclear weapons. In late 1955 the plane blazed a five-hundred-kilometer closed-course record of 695 miles per hour. Its success lay in its elegant simplicity of design; the Hot Rod was little more than a jet engine with an aviator riding along, held aloft by sturdy little wings so short they did not need folding during flight-deck operations— thus adding to the integral strength of the airframe. Its Wright J65 Sapphire engine was more than enough to power the low gross weight, only fourteen thousand pounds.

As in naval architecture, however, so in naval aircraft design: for something gained, something lost. The Skyhawk's main problem was stay time; like any jet, the plane gobbed fuel at low altitude and was notoriously short-legged. Those on the ground wanted their close air support to stay around, if not forever, at least for a good while. And this, despite its dependability in so many other areas, the little Hot Rod could not provide.

The new fighter thoroughbred was the Chance-Vought F-8U Crusader, the first production aircraft capable of exceeding 1000 miles per hour (unofficially, 1500 miles per hour—Mach 2). The Crud, an elongated tube of lightning, was maneuverable, reliable, and rakishly beautiful. VF-32 brought the plane to the fleet in 1957, and there the Crusader stayed (in thirteen different versions) for almost a quarter of a century. Squadron after squadron turned in its Banshees, Cougars, and Demons for the Crud. In all, 1261 F-8Us were built; they served with more than forty fleet and Reserve squadrons, and many ended up, still useful, in photographic reconnaissance roles.

Normally, the Crusader carried four 20-mm cannons and Sidewinders; its punch was good enough to rack up the best kill ratio of any American aircraft over Vietnam, earning the plane another nickname: "MiG Master." Flying the low-slung Crud was not for the squeamish, though; the plane often performed erratically at slow speeds, such as during carrier approaches. Ramp strikes were common in the early days, and the Crud always demanded a sure hand at the controls.

Then there was the Flying Brick. The McDonnell F-4 Phantom (really Phantom II) was "both the world's finest and ugliest combat airplane." The Brick had a droopy tail, upswept wing tips, a saggy nose radome for a snout, and twin engine intakes that produced an angry whine that could reverberate throughout a task force.

But the big, homely hog could *fly*. At over 1600 miles per hour, the plane became the fastest nonrocket aircraft anywhere and, as a bonus, proved maneuverable at speeds as low as 118 mph. The Brick joined the fleet in 1960, after beating out the Chance-Vought XF8U-3 as the next generation's fleet defense fighter in a much-debated competition, and stayed for twenty-six years. With the Brick came two new concepts in tactical naval aviation: a second man behind the aviator, a naval flight officer (NFO) to handle the radar intercepts and the fire control; and an aircraft completely armed with missiles, the Sidewinder and Sparrow.

More than 5200 Phantom IIs were built before McDonnell shut down the production line in 1978. The Navy used only 1171, or 22 percent, because the Air Force loved them too, and so did America's client states throughout the world. In fact, only the North American Sabrejet (5400) and the classic Chance-Vought F-4U Corsair (production of the Hosenose ended in 1953, with more than 12,000 planes) had bigger numbers than the Brick. And the plane proved itself in combat: all five American aces in Vietnam wore Phantoms.[16]

The Douglas A-3D Skywarrior was a real heavyweight, thirty-five tons of carrier attack aircraft to the Hot Rod's seven. Any landing of this second "Whale" was usually little more than a controlled crash. First designed as a nuclear bomber, the Skywarrior lost this role as the weapons were miniaturized and new strike tactics were developed but eventually found other tasks as an aerial tanker and a photo reconnaissance plane.

Finally, the meanest-looking aircraft in naval history: the A-5 Vigilante, which in embryo was considered to be *the* naval nuclear bomber. The original Viggie came with a sleek, elongated needle nose, twin engines, twin tails, Buck Rogers navigational and bombing gear, and an innovative bomb bay that ejected the nuclear weapon out the rear of the aircraft. The idea was for the Viggie to streak in on the deck, under enemy radar, then bolt to altitude and lob its bomb skyward. As the weapon described a high parabolic arc, the plane would roll back down low and scoot for home—as increasing air pressure triggered the detonation astern. Aviators, unconvinced, dubbed the maneuver the "idiot loop."

Unfortunately the Vigilante, though not difficult to fly, had its idiosyncracies. Its original stall speed was horrifying—195 miles per hour—and the number of fliers who actually looked forward to bringing the Vigilante onto a carrier deck at around 200 knots could be counted on the fingers of an amputee's hand. Only the use of blown flaps produced a landing speed of 140 miles per hour, still a pants-wetter for such a heavy aircraft. The plane's internal systems, particularly its inertial navigation, were constant worries. The men who flew the Viggie were selected only from second-tour applicants, and even then one landing signal officer turned in his wings because he did not want to fly the thing.

The plane's original mission had been scotched by the miniaturization of nuclear weapons and its own high-tech operational characteristics. By 1965 the Vigilante was beginning a new life as the RA-5C, a photo recon bird. Here the plane flourished, providing mapping surveys of both North and South Vietnam, designing route packages for aerial attacks, and bringing back excellent poststrike photo intelligence.

There were only 156 of them; the last went by the boards in 1979. They were Cadillacs, state-of-the-art airframes, and the best Vigilante epitaph was this: "When it worked, [it] had no equal in any other service."

☆

Other airframes evolved as well, for naval aviation, although centered on the carrier, included far more. Here, too, were false starts, fantastic successes, strange notions, and spectacular flops.

Experiments aboard *FDR* in 1947 showed the feasibility of using helicopters on carriers, especially as lifeguards. During the Korean War the Sikorsky HO3S, a light, four-seat whirlybird, gave a fine account of itself. The "Handy Andy" was remarkably versatile; helos rapidly became passenger platforms, airborne ambulances for medical evacuations, even stringers of telephone wire.

They could hover at will and putter along at speeds of up to ninety knots. The Handy Andy had three 48-foot blades (tilt-rotor) and an anti-torque rotor on the side of its waspy tail. They were extremely vulnerable to ground fire, as all subsequent generations of helicopters proved to be, but they could pop in and out at a moment's notice and also lugged an astonishing amount of weight, well beyond the dreams of their first designers.

In the fifties, helos learned a new role in antisubmarine warfare. In many ways they were the most versatile of airframes and thus, for the Navy, the most indispensable. They detected mines, spotted for gunfire, and became an air-sea rescue vehicle without parallel.

By 1960 helicopter utility squadrons were busy at sea, dashing about and hauling both people and cargo between vessels. "Vertical replenishment," which augmented the normal ship-to-ship transfers, entered the fleet on a routine basis. The whirlybirds became an important component of the hunter-killer antisubmarine warfare concept; they learned to sweep as well as find mines; and as helos became bigger and more powerful, the Gators and Marines began to experiment with "vertical envelopment"—helicopter-borne amphibious assault.[17]

If the helicopters were the Navy's utility infielders, the vertical-takeoff aircraft remained on the bench. There was a new acronym, V/STOL (for vertical/short-takeoff and landing), and the dream had remained alive ever since the adventures of the Flying Pogo Stick. The Pogo, a tail-sitter, never crashed, but its pilots had trouble figuring out how far they were from the ground, its engine gear box was notoriously unreliable, and any crosswind invited disaster.

The Ryan XV-13, another experimental bird, was a jet with no conventional landing gear. Fighter jocks loved the configuration, which produced a very high thrust-to-weight ratio. The plane landed by snagging a wire with a hook on its underbelly, a reverse twist on the old F9C-2 fighter, which had "landed" by hooking up with a trapeze slung below the dirigibles of the 1930s.

Neither tail-sitters nor wire-grabbers were much help, however, in getting off or onto a moving carrier deck at sea. In addition, V/STOL jets had limited ranges and payloads; sucked down enormous quantities of fuel in a hover (they relied on brute force to get themselves aloft); and because of the necessity of placing their engines near the plane's center of gravity, paid huge drag penalties once they were airborne. Then there was the blast of their downwash, the problem of hot engine gases recirculating back into their intakes (jets did not like to breathe hot intake air), and the simple truth that they were very hard to learn to fly.

The Marines, who wanted their close air support right now, loved the concept, though, and V/STOL stayed alive. Literally dozens of designs emerged following Pogo and XV-13: transports, gunships, antisubmarine platforms. There were air-cushion vehicles, surface-effect ships, hybrid helicopters. But none could do what the jet-powered V/STOL seemed to promise. Finally, twenty years after Pogo, the plane would reach operational reality as the British-American AV-8A Harrier, a sturdy, reliable, forgiving (once its pilot started moving forward) subsonic aircraft.

Naval land-based aircraft continued to surge ahead. Some airframes were adapted for at-sea photography; the Crusader had such a variant, the F8U-1P, and so did the Skywarrior, the A3D-2P. Bigger planes, like the later Neptunes, could do these chores as well. Powerful high-flying radars made land-based planes exceptionally keen early-warning systems.

By 1960 there were numerous radar barriers—electronic picket fences on land, at sea, and in the air—hedging North America against the menace across the pole. The best known were the Dew Line, stretching from Alaska to eastern Canada; the Mid-Canada and Pine-Tree lines farther south; and the Atlantic Radar Barrier, runing from Newfoundland to Iceland. The Navy manned a good share of the latter, staging twenty-two-man Lockheed WV-2s out of Argentia, Newfoundland. Lockheed Super Constellations were also used, along with some old Neptunes, all of them crammed with millions of dollars in radar and communications equipment. The planes did their own acquisition, plotting, and reporting, obediently flying designated patterns (usually at five thousand to eight thousand feet) for hour after hour.

In addition to airborne early warning—which carriers could do, too, with the WF Tracer—the land-based planes flew surface-surveillance, ice-patrol, search-and-rescue, and antisubmarine missions. In the latter role they had propeller-driven cousins at sea; the Grumman twin-engine S2F Tracker ("Stoof") was just entering its long service life as a subhunter, and the Tracer came with the same fuselage and an improbable flat, round radome perched atop—this flying pancake was the "Stoof with a Roof." The Tracer was also called "Willie Fud," and when its early-warning replacement, the exceptional, complex E-2 Hawkeye, came along, the son was baptized "Superfud."

Of critical importance, the Navy also developed a midair-refueling capacity using both carrier- and land-based planes. AJ-1 Savages got a brief lease on life by being fitted with tanker conversion kits in their bomb bays. The Skywarrior also became an airborne filling station. "Buddy packs" were designed for temporary use, plane resuscitating plane to stay aloft a little longer.[18]

But no electronic mission, magic means of propulsion, or refueling capacity could save one of the oldest loves of naval aviation—the seaplane. The type was a vestige of the days when scouting was all that aircraft did and carriers were but a dream. Most overseas routes were pioneered by flying boats, and the Navy always boasted that *its* fliers had been first across the Atlantic, eight years before Lindbergh. Over the years seaplanes became multiengined, stronger, and much heavier. They were still around in the fifties, but their future was dark.

There were the Convair A3Y-1 Tradewind and the Martin PB2M Mars, both four-engine seaplanes that could lift much larger amounts of cargo than anything flying off a carrier deck. The Mars, brainchild of the aviation pioneer Glenn Martin, was a kindly dray horse of a plane, a magnificently reliable, spacious transport aircraft correctly billed as the finest 75-cent ride in the military (food was served during the long flights, and officers paid 75 cents a meal). The $8 million giant, dubbed the "Old Lady," entered service in 1943 and carried everything: people, cargo, Christmas toys for kids. In 1948 a freighter bearing elephants and rare birds for American zoos broke down 1500 miles out at sea, and an Old Lady dropped twenty bales of hay and buckets of worms, in floating containers, alongside the distressed ship.

The Old Lady was much-loved, but she, like the Tradewind, the P5M Marlin, and others of the type, had come to the end of the line. Seaplanes required special handling and lots of harbor space, the latter commodity increasingly hard to come by. Their hulls had to be specially designed and manufactured, adding cost. They were slow, were prisoners of the weather at their bases, and, in comparison with equivalent land-based planes, were poor performers in everything but lift capacity.

They had their champions, though, and these made their last stand with the Martin P6M-1 Seamaster, a 600-mile-per-hour multiengine jet with a cruising ceiling of forty thousand feet and the characteristics, so its supporters said, of a B-47. "A fleet logistics seaplane is a must," urged one of them. Unfortunately, the first two Seamasters crashed, killing four men, and the program could not compete with front-burner items like Polaris for the Navy's attention. The jet engines, operating near corrosive salt water, gave no end of problems. In 1959 the Seamaster was killed, with only four planes flyable out of the thirty-two originally programmed. The last stand cost $400 million.

The greatest technological dream of naval aviation in the fifties was to somehow wed nuclear power to aircraft. The dream itself was irresistible: aircraft limited in operation only by crew endurance. Proposals abounded, mostly about how to cram a nuclear power plant into a seaplane; "such power for aircraft is now out of the dream stage," wrote one ardent advocate. But a serviceable airborne nuclear plant, even if one could be miniaturized, would still carry an inordinate weight, not to mention bringing along obvious radiation and other safety hazards.

A joint Navy–Air Force project called NEPA (Nuclear Energy for the Propulsion of Aircraft) spent a lot of time looking at possibilities, but the scientists eventually threw up their hands in despair. Nuclear submarines operated with weight-horsepower ratios of about 170 pounds per horse-power. An atomic plane would have to have a ratio of about 4 to 1, and the scientists never got close.[19]

☆

The failures and dead ends, as well as the undeniable excellence of many of the Navy's land-based aircraft, could not mask the fact that the flattop was the queen of the fleet. In the fifties naval strategy, fighter interception, tactical attack, amphibious assault, and antisubmarine warfare all orbited around her. She was sea control and power projection incarnate.

Yet as powerful, mobile, and flexible as she was, the queen never went to sea alone. Everywhere she moved, she went accompanied by a Praetorian guard.

CHAPTER SIXTEEN

PRAETORIAN GUARD

☆

By the 1950s the aircraft carrier and her Praetorian guard of escorts, originally formed even before World War II, had become the premier naval force anywhere. As global war had brought the emergence of the carrier over the battleship, so too had the ships of the guard found new duties. Only the Navy's minecraft had been employed in wartime for the specific tactical purpose that had originally been intended. Heavy cruisers, designed for fleet scouting, did nearly everything but; light cruisers meant to be destroyer leaders became anti-air warfare sentinels for the flattops; destroyers, conceived as defenders of the van and rear of the battle line against torpedo attacks, adapted to roles in antisubmarine and anti-air warfare. By V-J Day the upheaval in prewar tactical roles was practically complete.

In the postwar period these huge, powerful, do-everything task forces indicated that the Navy expected to wield influence overseas primarily through air strikes and amphibious operations. But this emphasis carried costs to other elements in the Navy. Small craft, so vital in the big war, went to the rubbish pile. All but four motor torpedo boats were sold, scrapped, or converted. Because small coastal vessels had such a low priority (coastal and riverine warfare historically had to be relearned, not having been kept alive), the Navy lagged behind in diesel technology, particularly in the development of a lightweight engine. The newer gas turbines, far more compact than steam plants and able to deliver more power per unit volume or weight than conventional gasoline engines, were also slower to reach the fleet than they otherwise might have been.

Although the bitter experience with mines in the Korean War rekindled interest in mine warfare, relatively few minesweepers were ticketed for harbor defense. Rather, the sweeps were most often lumped with amphibious assault forces, intended for an offensive role on the well-remembered model of World War II. Minecraft came in various sizes, from peewee minesweeping boats (MSBs) to oceangoing sweeps (MSOs). Their mine-hunting sonars, usually the UQS-1, were crude; things got better when the minecraft were fitted with SQQ-14 variable-depth sonars, but these basic underwater ears were limited to very short ranges, leading in turn to an exasperatingly low search rate.

Mine-hunting was in far worse shape than sweeping. Pressure mines, essentially unsweepable, could still be detonated safely if their presence was pinpointed, but the hunting itself, even with an entire pack of wooden-hulled hounds, was enormously expensive in both time and effort. The usual off-the-shelf solution was to run a guinea pig, usually a specially configured surplus merchant ship, over a swept area to check the success of a hunt or a sweep.

Few sailors or officers chose the mine specialty for a career. Despite the disasters off Wonsan and other Korean harbors, studies of mines, mining, mine-hunting, and minesweeping, while they went forward (twelve items in the mine program for 1953, for example), did so at a glacial pace compared with the cascade of improvements within the carrier arm. After all, the great Farragut himself had regarded mine warfare as "unworthy of a chivalrous nation."[1]

The development of general ordnance, not only mines but also torpedoes, guns, and guided missiles, accelerated greatly, as did the maturation of their fire control systems. But most of this energy was beamed at carriers, their Praetorian guards, and submarines. Inshore warfare, where the torpedo boats and the minesweepers lived, made up a rather minute portion of the grand design.

Torpedoes were now electrically powered (no telltale bubbling wake from steam drive) and, for the most part, homed in acoustically. They could be launched from submarines, surface ships, aircraft, even helicopters. The antisubmarine rocket system (ASROC), built by Honeywell, released an acoustic homing torpedo on entering the water. The submarine-launched rocket (SUBROC), a powerful technological marvel, was fired from a submerged torpedo tube; its solid-fuel rocket motor provided supersonic speed, and its inboard lightweight guidance system followed a ballistic trajectory to target after its airframe shed both rocket motor and housing. The warhead sank to a preset depth and hydrostatically exploded. The basic postwar antisubmarine torpedo, the Mark 37, was built by Northrop and featured, in its various modes, wire guidance and active-passive homing. This gave way to the actively homing, lightweight Mark 44. With the Mark 46, the Navy finally achieved a durable and dependable active-passive antisubmarine torpedo which could be launched from a wide variety of platforms. The fleet in time also came to be equipped with an active, wire-guided nuclear torpedo (the Mark 45 ASTOR Mod 1) and an antiship/antisubmarine active-passive wire-guided homing torpedo (the Mark 48).

This bewildering array of power was matched in its development, if at a slower pace, by the guns. The old 40-mm machine guns gave way to three-inch, rapid-fire anti-aircraft guns. The small-boy gun standard was now the five-inch, rapid-fire, dual-purpose (air and surface) gun mount. By 1955 these Mark 38s were completely automated, and soon they began to give way to the even more flexible five-inch Mark 54s. Gunnery fire control got more accurate (but never accurate enough), largely through the development of synchros, electromagnetic devices used for data computation and transmission. Mass production of synchros was made easier by new magnetic and plastic materials.

Most of this new ordnance bypassed the small boys. Inshore warfare was by no means dead, however. The underwater demolition teams (UDTs) and the explosive ordnance disposal (EOD) experts were still in business. The frogmen's talents were integrated with amphibious assault, while EOD types specialized in disarming everything—bombs, mines, any gadget that might blow up—on land or under water. "In the service everybody got pushed around and nagged at," the EODs liked to say. "But in our work nobody looks over our shoulders."[2]

But all of these elements—the small craft, minecraft, frogmen, EODs—despite the variety and usefulness of the skills involved, were inshore, for the most part did not directly involve high-seas clashes of navies, and thus were near the tag end of the Navy's shopping list. The new ordnance was going elsewhere. What counted most was what roamed out there on blue water—the carrier and her Praetorians.

☆

When *Forrestal* first put to sea in 1956, she represented, all by herself, almost $300 million. But she never steamed alone. As she passed through her shakedown at Guantanamo Bay, Cuba, she was surrounded by ships like the cruiser *Boston*, equipped with the new Terrier anti-aircraft missile; the tactical command ship *Northampton*, replete with the most advanced electronic and communications gear available; and the just-commissioned destroyer *Forrest Sherman*, lead ship of her class, the fastest can afloat, built especially to keep pace with *Forrestal*.

And more. Clustered about *Forrestal* at Guantanamo were twenty-six other warships: the refurbished antisubmarine carrier *Antietam*; three *Iowa*-class battleships; two eight-inch-gun cruisers, *Salem* and *Des Moines*; fifteen more destroyers; and two submarines. Naval leaders saw this aggregate as the modern task force, a billion dollars plus of oceanic striking power.

For each, a different configuration; for each, a different task—but all, ultimately, charged with protecting the queen. As far back as the sailing Navy, the inherent weaknesses in bureaucratic control of ship design had been apparent. Designs made by majority vote became merely "a hash of the opinions of many and the masterpieces of none." The ships of the Praetorian guard had such intrinsic weaknesses, and some, like *Antietam* and *Boston*, had been created for other roles, but all were now moons orbiting around the supercarrier's planet.

Of these satellites, the ones with the greatest problems staying in orbit were the biggest, the battleships. The four *Iowa*-class vessels, the three at Guantanamo and *Missouri*, were all that were left. Once they had been the pride of the battle line. "The carrier is essential to a balanced fleet," admitted one analyst during World War II, "but it is a fighter with a glass jaw and must be backed up with a long, gray line of battleships." "The fate of the nation," ran another wartime account, "rests upon the men behind the big guns." These were the remarks of amateurs. Many professionals, particularly naval aviators, could see the future more clearly. In 1945, Jack Towers predicted that the United States would never build another battleship.

They were still showboats, and any foul-up regarding them could generate reams of unfavorable publicity. At 0825 on 17 January 1950, *Missouri* ran hard aground on Thimble Shoal near Norfolk, grinding from twelve knots to a complete stop within full view of the window of her type commander, Rear Admiral Hoke Smith, Commander Cruisers, Atlantic Fleet. Smith turned and exclaimed to his staff, "Gentlemen, USS *Missouri* has just gone half a mile inland."

There she stayed for two embarrassing weeks, right under the eyes of Army brass at Fort Monroe. (The Air Force contributed a slogan: "The battleship is here to stay.") The Navy paid $130,000 to free her, over half going to an Army dredge. Her skipper, the unpopular Captain William Brown, was court-martialed, dropped 250 places on the captain's list, and spent his last four years of service commanding a Reserve district in Florida. A career-killing letter of reprimand was given the officer in CIC, and the navigator and operations officer were also reduced in numbers on the promotion list.

Missouri was the Navy's largest single peacetime salvage and left red faces throughout the gun club. Her ordeal was an all-too-public stubbing of the toe at a time when the reputation of the battlewagon was in precipitous decline. *Missouri* and *New Jersey* served off Korea, but now the battlewagons appeared to many to be antediluvian, "neither economically, politically, nor militarily rational."

Navymen thrashed about for ideas about their use. Mick Carney wanted to mount anti-aircraft missiles on them. For a while *Kentucky*—the fifth ship of the class and 72 percent completed—was seen, along with her sisters, as a supply ship. A few regarded them as perfect platforms for the new intermediate-range ballistic missiles. By 1957 they were being discussed as electronics-laden command ships, *Northamptons* with muscle. There were visions, growing more hysterical as the beloved behemoths steamed toward seeming oblivion, of battlewagon repair ships, battlewagon experimental rocket test ships, battlewagon landing support ships. If all else failed, said one expert, the *Iowas* could be used as target ships.

—None of this laundry washed. The Marines, who loved the huge sixteen-inch guns, were the most steadfast of their advocates, but they could not carry the day. Amphibious assault stood second to carrier strike warfare in the Navy's lexicon of priorities. The battleships offered undeniable prestige and the biggest naval guns anywhere. But they were expensive to operate, not as mission-flexible as the carrier, and, although they could provide most of their own air defense, needed help against the submarine.

By late 1957 they had been packed into mothballs, every one. For the first time in sixty years, the United States Navy had not a single battleship at sea, nor, just as Jack Towers had prophesied, would another ever be built. In their day they had been an awesome, if overrated, symbol of national defense; pride and tradition had kept the Blackshoes who ran the Navy glued to their burnished teakwood decks. They could light cities; carry more men, oil, and striking punch than any other ship except the carrier; and symbolize America around the world.

—But they had lost the precious power of self-defense, had been supplanted on the throne. And thus, for the moment anyway, they were gone.[3]

☆

Without the battleship to encumber its movements and divide its defensive attention, the guard became more intensively focused than ever on its central protective task. The surface threat to the queen, in the naval climate of the postwar world, was practically nonexistent. Not so the menace from underneath or above.

The Germans, toward the end of World War II, had developed advanced conventional U-boats (Types XXI—the 1600-ton, high-speed diesel-electrics—and XXVI—the famous "Walthers"). The Soviets captured a number of these, as well as some VIICs and IXCs, as they advanced along the Baltic coast. Shortly after V-E Day, the Navy estimated that the Russians had almost twenty of the most modern undersea craft anywhere, and by simple reproduction they could have had several hundred by the early fifties. The offensive use of the submarine was known to be a top priority of the Red Navy.

Accordingly, in June 1946 the chief of naval operations, Chester Nimitz, kicked off Project GIRDER, a major R and D initiative in antisubmarine warfare. Until the spring of 1950, GIRDER stood as the Navy's top R and D priority. In the shipbuilding program for fiscal year 1948, for example, the majority of vessels proposed were submarines and ships to find and kill submarines. In 1948, a General Board study, spearheaded by Arleigh Burke, downplayed strategic bombing and identified antisubmarine warfare as the first mission of carrier task forces.

There was good reason for this concern. All things being equal, a submarine could usually beat a surface ship, one-on-one. Against the Japanese in the Pacific, American submarines had sunk forty-seven destroyers, forty-two frigates, and nineteen submarine chasers—a grand total of 108 antisubmarine vessels for only twenty-three pigboats lost while going against them. This five-to-one ratio was not enjoyed by the German U-boats operating against the Americans, British, and Canadians in the Atlantic, but enormous exertion and a complete shake-up of Allied antisubmarine warfare policy had been necessary before the Battle of the Atlantic was won.[4]

The small escort carrier, with its extended aerial range, had been crucial in the Atlantic, and the type remained as the heart of one antisubmarine concept: the hunter-killer (HUK) group. HUK warfare involved both carrier- and land-based aircraft. Originally, the Navy envisioned six blue-water HUKs, each consisting of a light carrier, a *Norfolk*-class big destroyer (specially outfitted for antisubmarine work), and eight swift destroyer escorts.

A second concept revolved around the escorts themselves. Ocean escort of convoys, critical to any transatlantic scenario, would require for a full-scale conflict at least two hundred more destroyers or destroyer escorts. If air power was negligible or unavailable, these small boys would have to do the job on their own.

GIRDER also dreamed of a third concept, using submarines to hunt submarines. The study estimated that no fewer than 252 submarines would be needed. Of these, 62 would be "Guppies," capable of snorkeling, and 32 more would be new, fast, diesel-electric attack boats.

All this was a huge wish list, in the best military tradition, and budgetary reality eventually shattered GIRDER's dreams. The HUK groups, based mostly on the *Essex* conversions rather than the CVLs (which went to the boneyard with indecent haste), came to pass. Some existing *Fletcher*-class destroyers and a few Guppies went through an antisubmarine-warfare upgrade. But there was to be only one *Norfolk*. (A second "CLK," or heavy antisubmarine warfare ship, *New Haven*, was canceled in 1951.) The replacement design, the 3650-ton *Mitscher* class, numbered only four. The *Mitschers* were supplemented by the considerably less capable (but less expensive) *Forrest Shermans*. The new "antisubmarine submarines," or SSKs, were supposed to total fifty-four; only three (eventually named *Barracuda*, *Bass*, and *Bonita*) were ever built. Despite their large, bow-mounted sonar dome, the trio proved far too small and slow to accomplish their main mission design.

The Soviets were not the only reason the antisubmarine problem would not go away. As early as 1954, the secretary of the Navy was bemoaning the "wear and tear" on American subs and on the lightly constructed destroyers and escort vessels. Given the Navy's global commitments, the smaller the vessel, the more likely that the ship or sub was being steamed or dieseled to death.[5]

The combination of worldwide demands, hard budget choices, and a rapidly aging fleet made "modernization" mandatory, particularly in antisubmarine warfare. After the war the Navy's enormous covey of destroyers included smaller, 1620-ton *Bensons*, the much sturdier, 2050-ton *Fletchers*, the 2290-ton *Sumners*, and the 2425-ton *Gearings*. In 1945 there were hundreds of these cans still in commission.

But they were naval versions of Dorian Gray. Still youthful in years and appearance, they had been steamed very, very hard, and most of them were simply inadequate to bear the burdens of new technology. Many were dealt to foreign nations; among others, the Greeks, Turks, Brazilians, Argentines, Mexicans, and South Koreans soon sported American destroyers. The Taiwanese, in the 1950s, were perhaps the main recipients. Others of the prematurely elderly cans went to the breakers, were mothballed, or were pulverized as targets.

The remainder got antisubmarine upgrades: pairs of fixed "hedgehog" mounts were battened forward of the bridge (the hedgehog was an ahead-firing depth charge); longer-range three-inch 50s took the place of the old 40-mms; and lightweight Mark 32 or Mark 43/44/46 homing torpedoes were mounted, mostly amidships. The *Fletchers* received the most elaborate forms of this attention and thus had the greatest lease on their service life.

Despite the Dorian Grays, the postwar Navy had so many surplus destroyers that conversions were able to defer new designs. Thirty-six *Gearings* got air control updates (DDRs) but, like the other remaining cans, they were badly overloaded and suffered speed penalties, a real problem when the guard, to protect the queen, had to be able to stay with her at any speed.

The choice was between an ideal antisubmarine destroyer (which ideal, of course, transmogrified with each change in technology) and a destroyer suited to mass production, like the wartime designs. The destroyer escorts posed the same choice, in smaller packages. These, too, had been stamped out by the hundreds—*Buckleys, Cannons, Edsalls, Rudderows*, and *John C. Butlers*—during the war. The biggest, the *Rudderows*, displaced only 1450 tons. Eventually there would be several classes of destroyer escorts (DEs, renamed frigates, or FFs, in the sixties), but none of these—*Dealeys, Claud Joneses, Bronsteins*, or *Garcias*, was larger than thirteen ships (*Dealeys*).

These newer destroyer escorts showed the omnipresent strain inherent in budgetary choice. Antisubmarine warfare was very much an issue of sheer numbers; lots of ships were required to screen a task force or convoy, because sonars and antisubmarine weapons were extremely limited in both range and effectiveness. The *Dealeys* and *Bronsteins* were each built with single screws, and the *Claud Joneses* were diesel-powered, austere turkeys that could not come close to adequately performing their escort function. These escorts were far too slow to tackle the fifteen-knot Type XXIs or XXVIs. Most of the escorts could not hustle much over twenty knots; none of them could boast the required ten-knot speed advantage over the diesel-electric boats.

Numbers, then, were far from the whole story, but numbers were crucial, and the fleet never had enough *capable* antisubmarine platforms. The Navy's ability, with such ships, to conduct a major antisubmarine campaign was at best marginal.[6]

☆

There were eighteen *Forrest Shermans* in all. Essentially, they served as a transition between the numerous small destroyers of World War II—when guns and torpedoes predominated, ship-versus-ship scenarios came first, and antisubmarine warfare was a secondary task—and the big guided-missile destroyers of the modern naval world, which were multimission and had antisubmarine warfare as their main role.

They were driven by four husky, 1200-pounds-per-square-inch boilers, the earliest such in the fleet, and were readily identifiable by the jaunty, upward flare of their hurricane bows. Rather than the universal five-inch 38, they had the five-inch 54 dual-purpose gun, which would become the preeminent destroyer weapon for gunfire support and antisurface warfare. At 2800 tons, they were smaller than the *Mitschers*; at 407 feet in length, they were at first deemed too short for guided missiles. The dollars available could not build to the scope of classes like the *Fletchers* (175 ships) or the *Gearings* (105).

Their powerful boilers could propel them at thirty-three knots, more than enough to attend the conventionally powered queen, and even one boiler, supplying the main engines in cross-connected operation, could provide twenty knots in calm seas. To fight submarines, their primary weapon was the homing torpedo; initially, they also retained hedgehogs and the traditional stern-rack depth charges.

The main sensor for the *Forrest Shermans*, at first, was the SQS-4, the Navy's first major postwar sonar. Lower in frequency than the exasperatingly inefficient QHB "searchlight" sonar of World War II, the SQS-4 was advertised for a nominal detection range of ten thousand yards in the "active mode," in which sound echoes were bounced off an underwater body and were received back aboard, thus establishing bearing and range. This range was pure PR; the SQS-4s were rarely accurate beyond four thousand yards, even in good water, and eventually the class got the SQS-23, even lower in frequency and by far the Navy's most dependable sonar for surface vessels.

These postwar American destroyers were also roomier, 303 square feet per man compared with the 210 of the cramped *Gearings*. Their sailors (260 men in the crew) loved them, and like all cans they proved remarkably versatile. Four of them, along with two of the *Mitschers*, eventually got Tartar missile systems and became guided missile destroyers (DDGs), although their smaller size caused some problems.

They were rakishly handsome; everywhere they went, they did their jobs with flair. Arleigh Burke, a destroyerman's destroyerman, was their greatest champion. Despite the necessary compromises in their design, for the Navy of the fifties the *Forrest Shermans* were best in breed.[7]

For the *Forrest Shermans* and their kind, though, guns were of little help in solving the submarine problem. Only the most stupid skipper would surface during an attack if he did not have to, unless he was enveloped in the shroud of night, and even then the cans' improved gunnery fire control systems made such a move precarious at best.

The destroyers relied on their underwater weapons and the electronic ears that targeted a submerged enemy. Project SEAHAWK, an attempt to build a better antisubmarine platform from the keel up, died of "premature technology." So the newer miracles were packed on the existing platforms. For a while the SQS-4 guided standoff attacks with a rocket-assisted torpedo bearing the unfortunate acronym RAT. The sonar also provided data for the Mark 37 homing torpedo and a lightweight homer delivered by a drone helicopter, a system called DASH. Grandfather of the modern manned LAMPS, DASH was often hysterically ineffective.

In time, the SQS-23 had a better weapon, ASROC, which was destined for generations of service. Eventually an even lower frequency sonar, the SQS-26, entered the fleet, but the payback was considerable: the SQS-4 fit inside a one-hundred-inch dome, whereas the bulbous SQS-26 transducer was as big as a sixty-foot gondola, mounted partially underneath the hull. With this thing slung under its belly, a can was as lithe as a woman in the advanced stages of pregnancy, and its draft could increase twelve to fourteen feet.

The hedgehog gave way to a similar device, Weapon Alfa, which was so complex that its teething problems seemed interminable. And the defensive systems against the submarine multiplied, too; chief among these were Fanfare, a hydrophonic noisemaker that streamed behind the ship, and Prairie Masker, a device for venting air bubbles to confuse the lurking submarine's own sonar.[8]

The Navy's ultimate antisubmarine effort, however, came not from the cans or the HUK groups but from shore. This was the sound surveillance system, or SOSUS. The system was composed of giant strings of hydrophonic ears, laid on the ocean floor and monitored by carefully disguised stations on the beach. The first SOSUS hydrophones, manufactured by Western Electric, were laid along shipping channels off the Atlantic and Gulf coasts, beginning in the fifties. Called CAESAR, these ears were soon joined by the COLOSSUS line, extending along the Pacific coast.

Inevitably, SOSUS listened elsewhere as well. BARRIER consisted of two parts, one between Norway and Bear Island, the other linking Greenland, Iceland, and Scotland. BRONCO was strung from the southeastern tip of Hokkaido along the Kuriles to a point off the Aleutian coast. Still other SOSUS lines were laid in the approaches to China and Vietnam, on the Atlantic side of Gibraltar, throughout the Mediterranean, in the Indian Ocean, and off Hawaii.

The hydrophones were sealed in clusters inside massive tanks (as large as those used for refinery storage), linked by fiber-optic cables, and buried deep in the ocean floor. Each hydrophone was tuned to a specific frequency, listening for special components of a submarine's "signature:" engine noise, thumps from a cooling system, water flow around the hull, propeller wash, even the workings of the sub's own sonar.

All these individual noises, an underwater sound symphony, combined to form an individual audio fingerprint for every submarine. Eventually, these fingerprints became part of an enormous computerized data bank and were passed through the Fleet Satellite Communications System to the people who had to know: aboard the surface ships, with their sonar and towed sonar arrays; flying the helicopters, which came to be equipped with highly effective dipping sonars; and orbiting in the antisubmarine planes, which could drop acutely sensitive sonobuoys.[9]

And still, despite all their technology, the subhunters could never be completely sure. The submarine's technology did not stand still, either. The boats became quieter, faster, stronger-hulled, and able to go deeper and deeper into the sheltering depths of the ocean. Nuclear power, especially in its early stages, produced an entirely new (and loud) field of noise, but dampening began immediately. The boats could dodge, hide, drop to the safety of the ocean floor, and maneuver through underwater canyons that shielded them from probing sound waves. They could cover themselves with hidden carapaces like thermoclines, temperature gradients in the ocean that reflected or refracted sound waves from above.

So there were no permanent solutions. Antisubmarine warfare remained a constant concern, and ways to find, fix, and kill the deadly boats became an obsession for the Praetorian guard.

☆

The threat from the sky was worrisome too, and not only because of the tremendously different scale of speeds involved. Enemy submarines at least had been met and mastered in World War II. Although superficially the same was true of enemy air power, there continued to be deep, nagging concern.

The concern was there, in considerable part, because the Navy had a institutional nightmare, and its name was Okinawa. True, the amphibious assault there had been the capstone of the island-by-island campaign across the Pacific. But there also the terrifying kamikaze had come into its own, and the results had shocked naval leaders.

The predominant view of the woefully undertrained Japanese young-sters, strapped into their obsolete aircraft with a bomb aboard and told to go find the American fleet, was a vision in the purest samurai tradition: the last flowers of Japanese chivalry immolating themselves in the name of *ko-kutai*, the national polity. Any cultural analysis using this tragic sacrifice as a basis was certainly pertinent. But what the Navy got was a look, through bloody binoculars, at the future of anti-air warfare.

—For whatever else they were, the kamikaze were guided missiles, guided by the most sophisticated computing mechanism known, the Mark 1 Mod 0 human brain. True enough, most of the young men sent aloft in such desperation were dreadfully inept; many of them simply vanished into oblivion over the ocean on their flights toward Okinawa. Many more were splashed, as helpless as birds at a gander pull, by American interceptors; more disintegrated in a hail of American ack-ack; and some, unfamiliar with the controls of their aircraft, simply missed their targets.

But enough got through—hundreds, in fact. The damage they inflicted came close to canceling out the entire operation. The toll, in this crimson dawn of guided missile warfare, was bone-chilling. Off Okinawa, the kamikaze caused far more havoc than Pearl Harbor had. They damaged 368 ships and sank 36. The naval carnage included the deaths of 4907 officers and men, six hundred more lives lost than the Army total for the *entire* battle and two thousand more than the Marines.

Because the Japanese pilots were so inexperienced, they tended to go after the first thing they saw, and these most often were the guard's pickets at the farthest reaches of the formation, forty to seventy miles out. The pickets were radar-equipped destroyer escorts, diesel-powered little ships with around 150 men aboard. Their business was to warn the heavies of incoming raids, but they could barely defend themselves, especially against the saturation tactics of the kamikaze.

After the war six destroyer escorts—the merest token—were given radar updates and spent their time trying to keep anti-air warfare techniques alive. Some of them, like *Haverfield*, took part in barrier patrols far out in the North Atlantic. These escort pickets were a maze of electronic gear, little more than floating, pitching radar sets. But they were, at best, stopgaps— not big enough, not well-enough armed, and poorly equipped with communications.[10]

Very quickly, the Navy reached an important conclusion: anti-air warfare, courtesy of the kamikaze, had reached the missile age.

☆

There was a prehistory. As early as 1938, a radio-controlled Jenny had been sent creaking along at five thousand feet and seventy-five knots through a barrage of surface fire. Some gunclubbers took notice: a moving aerial target was extremely hard to hit; closing speeds multiplied alarmingly; and enough of these targets coalescing at the same time could saturate fleet defenses, befuddle radar, cause confusion by mingling with friendly interceptors, and generally raise billy hell with the air picture.

War raised their concern. In 1942 the Bureau of Ordnance requested the Office of Scientific Research and Development to work on a radar-controlled gliding bomb. There were experiments with assault drones, like the TDR-1 and the Gorgon program, although studies in King's office determined they were not ready for carrier use. And the wartime homing torpedo was an underwater version of a successful guided missile.

But the kamikaze brought home, with crashing force, the need for a weapon that sought aerial targets under its own power and guidance. In January 1945, even before Okinawa, the Bureau of Ordnance, in supersecrecy, started the Bumblebee program at Johns Hopkins University's Applied Physics Laboratory. Wall plaques there proclaimed that "the bumblebee cannot fly, by all recognized rules of aerodynamics." Twenty universities and corporations fed scientific brains and experimental data into Bumblebee, and under the press of the horrifying news from across the Pacific, the "Flying Stovepipe" moved rapidly from theory to drawing board to test.

Everything about Bumblebee was uncharted: propulsion, aerodynamics, radar, guidance and control, launch methods, warheads, telemetry. The program boomed along, though, and after only six months, in June 1945 on the sand dunes of New Jersey's Island Beach, Bumblebee's Thunderbolt engine was ignited successfully. And, in time (June 1947 for subsonic flight, March 1948 for supersonic), the "recognized rules of aerodynamics" were broken—Bumblebee flew.[11]

Missiles were different from guns. Missiles were not particularly effective, in their formative years, against surface craft; their guidance systems did not like the curvature of the earth. They were next to useless in shore bombardment, unless the idea was nuclear incineration. And the early missiles, because they relied on aerodynamic controls that were ineffective until the bird had been boosted nearly to top speed, were a poor bet for close-in aerial defense.

Most importantly, the guided missile was considered the equivalent of an all-weather fighter-interceptor, able to operate at night and in the worst of environments. In this sense the birds were believed to be superior to a carrier's fighter-interceptors, the ultimate answer to the saturation air raid from any or all points of the compass. Automation was the solution to saturation.

Bumblebee, conceived as a ramjet, led to the first operational generation of naval surface-to-air missiles. The urgency of the fleet air defense problem had become so acute by 1949 that the solid-fuel Supersonic Test Vehicle, developed as part of Bumblebee, was honed into a weapon.

This was Terrier, an 1100-pound, booster-launched beam-rider (meaning the missile tracked a path of electromagnetic radiation that continuously "lit up" the target). The initial service model was fired at sea in the spring of 1953. Terrier, with a range of about twenty-five nautical miles, first got to blue water aboard the converted cruisers *Boston* and *Canberra* and the fin-stabilized converted destroyer *Gyatt*. Eventually, Terriers armed cruiser conversions, destroyers, frigates, and the *Kitty Hawks*.[12]

Next came Talos, a liquid-fuel ramjet. Talos was son of Bumblebee, sharing some guidance systems with Terrier, but the two missiles were significantly different in many ways other than propulsion and required distinctly different handling systems. Talos had a forty-mile range and traveled at Mach 2. The ever-faster closing speeds led to later Talos upgrades that got out to seventy miles or so. Its development program pioneered atomic warheads in anti-aircraft missiles, although no one seemed to have thought much about why an atomic weapon was needed to shoot down an aircraft, or even a whole flock of them. Talos went aboard the cruisers *Galveston*, *Little Rock*, and *Oklahoma City*, as well as the one-of-a-kind nuclear-powered cruiser *Long Beach*.[13]

Finally came Tartar, completing the trio of "T-birds." Tartar's configuration and operating profile were similar to Terrier's. Tartar featured a homing-all-the-way radar seeker. This missile went aboard eight new destroyers in the late fifties and became a replacement for secondary batteries on several heavy ships.[14]

☆

The missile kingdom blossomed swiftly, principally along a slender, sandy beach and lagoon near Oxnard, California, called Point Mugu. On this 4200-acre promontory, supposedly, the Spanish-employed Portuguese *adelantado* Cabrillo had found his *mugu*, or "place of landing." Here, at the Naval Air Missile Test Center, the experimental birds zoomed seaward from their launching pads, writing the future with their vapor trails. "It appears," said Point Mugu's commander in 1953, with classic understatement, "that the work load assigned to the Center . . . will continue to increase. . . ."

At Point Mugu the experiments with relatively simple "command" missiles were played out. A radar operator, with both the invading aircraft and the missile on his screen, simply guided the missile to a point close enough to the plane that the proximity fuze in the missile nose would explode, shredding the aircraft. The "beam-riders" relied on a pencil of radio beam zeroed in on the plane. No matter how the incoming pilot jinked or evaded, as long as the beam had him, the missile (theoretically) would ride that beam until he was nailed.

There were "active homers," which contained their own radar brains, sending out electromagnetic pulses and steering themselves toward any target that returned echoes. There were "passive homers," which vectored toward any target that their sensors told them was emitting heat, light, or electromagnetic radiation. The new miracle of television made an early appearance in the missile kingdom. Missiles were developed that took pictures, relayed these to their controllers, and awaited a radio signal to send them blazing, at thirty miles a minute, into their targets. Already, in the early fifties, work was being done on magnetic navigation systems, star navigation systems, and terrain mapping—the Ur-story of the cruise missile.[15]

The anti-air missiles affected their host ships in critical ways. The tidal wave of data swept in, from Point Mugu; from the Naval Ordnance Test Station out at Inyokern, baking in the California desert; from the Naval Aviation Ordnance Test Station on windswept Chincoteague, Virginia, where the wild ponies roamed; and from the newly established Fleet Air Defense Training Center at Dam Neck, Virginia. The results of the experiments with the birds confronted ship designers with a "long series of unpleasant surprises and dead ends." Naval guidance systems often dictated a new topside arrangement, at no small expense. Stowage was an aggravating problem. Whatever their propulsion system, the birds were exceptionally thin-skinned and depended on highly volatile fuel; they had to be handled like so many fragile eggs.[16]

The kingdom also included experiments with antiship missiles, although these were still in their infancy, lagging far behind the T-birds in development. There were a one-thousand-pound infrared homing bomb (Dove) and a family of radar-guided winged missiles carrying homing torpedoes or bombs that would explode underwater. An early antiship missile, the Bat, went by the boards in 1948 because of its susceptibility to simple countermeasures.

Loon, little more than an updated German V-1, was test-fired from specially fitted submarines (SSGs), *Cusk* and *Carbonero*. Supposedly this missile had a range of 150 nautical miles and approximately a twenty-minute flight time, but in practice Loon was as crazy as its namesake. No one could discern its true altitude in flight, and its terminal ballistics were by guess and by God. At one point, *Carbonero* fired a series of test shots at a derelict building on San Nicolas Island, only to find that the entire island had been misplaced by three miles on her charts and that the poor Loon, in this case, was not to blame.

Regulus, a more successful program, was a virtual swept-wing turbojet fighter with an eventual seven-hundred-nautical-mile range and supersonic speed. Regulus II, twelve tons' worth, was designed for Mach 2 operation. The Reguluses used jet-assisted takeoff from surfaced submarine decks but could also be launched from anywhere, even an open stretch of beach. A few diesel boats got a lease on life by being retrofitted with Regulus in the fifties. Regulus I, which targeted eastern Soviet ports and cities to a range of about four hundred nautical miles, was stationed in Yokosuka in 1955 aboard *Grayback* and *Growler*.

Air-launched antiship missiles also got attention. Petrel, carried by the Neptunes, had a range of about twenty nautical miles and carried a Mark 21 homing torpedo. Puffin, never fully developed, was supposed to approach its target at low altitude, like Petrel, and then trace a high arc before entering the water as a 250-pound bomb. This "pop-up" flight profile would later become standard for many cruise missiles.

And there were more: dozens of missiles, hundreds of designs, thousands of ideas. "Very soon now," said one officer in the mid-fifties, "we of the

Navy must face up to the fact that the guided missile is a distinct and important competitor of our piloted naval aircraft."[17]

☆

The surface-to-air guided missile, the hoped-for solution to the fleet air defense problem, the end of the kamikaze-induced nightmare, received the most attention. The T-birds, in particular, seemed at first to be the answer to a fleet commander's prayers. With them, fire control could be applied more precisely and relatively late in the interception (which made for longer tracking time and, hence, for better targeting solutions); automatic guidance systems did away with botch-prone human voices talking to each other, usually on badly overstrained radio nets; and, for a given payload, the missiles were cheaper than manned aircraft and the aviator himself. In the mid-fifties, the cost of training the man in the cockpit ran to about $100,000, never mind the price of his plane. True, both man and plane could be reused, but the missilemen argued that the guided missile—simple, dependable, accurate—could be saved for its single, almost invariably successful, combat mission.

"A full scale marriage of seapower and missiles, strategic as well as tactical, will provide the United States with the best system of military force in the Missile Age," asserted one missileman, with typical hyperbole. The T-birds were only part of a weapons revolution. And the claims for this revolution, especially in the strategic guise, were sweeping. "Sea-based missile power can guarantee the world that the Soviet war machine would not survive. . . ."

As with the planes, there were false starts, like Bat and Puffin, and outright failures, like Loon. The classic among the failures was Corvus, and air-launched, rocket-powered missile designed to home on enemy radar installations—the grandfather of Shrike. Corvus, a Ling-Temco product, had a range of more than one hundred nautical miles, but the missile failed grade school at Point Mugu. Corvus had trouble hitting anything and was canceled in 1960 after an $80 million expenditure.

No matter; the missile kingdom kept hurtling forward, expanding apace with each passing year. To the Navy, the tactical missiles were fundamental, first for fleet air defense and second for extended-range attack from the air, from the surface, or from underwater. "The gun," avowed Rear Admiral John Clark (a gunman turned missileman and one of the commanders at Point Mugu), "is fast becoming obsolete as an effective air-defense weapon."[18]

Thus the cruiser, big enough to hold the new missiles and, with destroyers and frigates, to take on the antisubmarine warfare task, became the centerpiece of fleet air defense, the main missile shooter within the guard. In 1945 the cruiser had been a dual-purpose gunship, used both for anti-aircraft and antiship acton, the latter the residue of her old scouting role.

She was also the smallest warship with real effectiveness as an independent unit.

The missiles changed all that. Missiles were designed to help the Navy fight a high-intensity war, one in which the skies would be darkened with waves of enemy aircraft, radar screens cluttered with their echoes. A missile-shooting cruiser, whatever else she could do, had this as her primary function. Any other operating environment meant she was not doing the job for which she was specifically designed. Her station was out there on the periphery, on a series of concentric circles radiating out from the carrier at ZZ—the formation center.

The Navy, because cruisers were big ships (after the battlewagons departed, the biggest next to the carriers) and because most construction money was being funneled into the supercarriers, built no new missile-shooting cruisers in the immediate postwar era, with the exception of *Long Beach* (whose nuclear power plant was more a justification for her creation than was her main battery). The newly constructed missile ships were large and small destroyers. The rest of the missile-shooters in the guard were conversions, like *Boston*, *Galveston*, and *Gyatt*.

The conversions had their price. A large supply of cruisers was available for reconfiguration to missiles, but as in all naval architecture, for something gained, something lost. The earlier conversions were "single-ended:" missile mounts either astern or forward, guns left aboard at the other end. By 1956, with the *Albany*-class conversions, the Navy had its first all-missile ships. Some of these cruiser conversions came to be valued more as radar platforms, command centers, or admirals' barges than as missile shooters, and a few enjoyed a longer life simply by showing the flag (and in some of the glitziest ports in the world). *Oklahoma City*, the last of the conversions, hung around until 1979.

There was another, bigger cost. Particularly in the case of the much-publicized T-birds, the issue was whether these fancy new systems could hit what they aimed at. They had been built, as Vice Admiral Kleber Masterson noted, on "less than a shoestring." When Terrier, Talos, and Tartar "tested out" and were launched successfully, they usually worked. (When *Boston* gave an impressive demonstration of shooting down incoming aircraft with her missiles, a slotted box was placed at the head of her gangway bearing a sign reading "Naval Aviators Deposit Wings Here.") But bugs were everywhere in their systems, like a form of spreading electronic cancer. The crew of *Norton Sound*, a missile test ship, got used to Terriers flipping over, veering erratically off course, crashing into the sea. By 1962 an internal Defense Department report called the T-birds little more than scrap.

Galveston's experience with Talos was typical. The shipboard fire control system for the bird was almost impossible to keep on-line. Fire control systems that had worked beautifully on land at places like Dam Neck, with civilian technical representatives mother-henning every step of the way, came unglued on blue water. Mechanical failures led to electrical failures, a lockstep of frustration. New electronic components and intricate circuit designs that had performed flawlessly with guns were stubbornly resisted by missile rails.[19]

Still, the Navy plodded onward, committed now to the T-birds and the concept of surface-to-air missile defense. Originally, there were to be twenty-two Terrier ships, eight with Talos, and eight with Tartar. Talos, with the longest range, was also the most expensive—about $200,000 a copy. And costs like these *excluded* the costs of conversion. Tens of millions of dollars were in the birds (or *for* them, according to critics).

The ships' radar systems had to be redone, also. The Terrier-equipped *Canberra*, for example, got the new AN/SPQ-5 long-range, high-altitude missile-guidance radar, manufactured by Sperry. The early versions of this radar fell far short of designers' claims for multiple intercept capability; eventually, the Navy Tactical Data System would be needed to integrate fleet air defense. The Navy, grinding its own teeth through the T-birds' teething problems, kept sending the birds, and their allied systems, to the fleet.

For six years, from 1956 to 1962, the struggle with the unruly missile systems went on, as both the Defense Department and Congress got increasingly restless. The low point probably came in 1961, when the Navy staged a dog-and-pony missile show off the East Coast for President John Kennedy. He watched from a carrier bridge as a propeller-driven airplane drone was steered toward the fleet. The guard was alerted. One Terrier was fired . . . two . . . three. On came the drone, unscathed, which was hardly the condition of the missileers. The wretched failure led an appalled JFK, who had seen naval guns in action, to order that five-inch guns be installed aboard ships previously intended for all-missile armament. Interceptor training for the aviators got a new breath of life, too; when all else failed, they could *at least* see and attack, and maybe hit something.

The teething problems never really went away, but after 1962 they did diminish markedly. Eventually, by 1965, sixty-six ships carried the T-birds—only seven, however, with Talos. The T-birds were never to fulfill their designed role of surface-to-air missile warfare in a high-intensity conflict at sea. They were part of the price of the Navy's fixation with blue-water armageddon. In the only combat tests of the T-birds, *Long Beach* downed two MiGs over North Vietnam at different times in 1968, and *Chicago* bagged a MiG at forty-eight miles in 1972—all three kills credited to Talos.[20]

—And that was all.

☆

Thus was the Praetorian guard armed, against the threats from below and above. Without doubt, the ships of the guard were awesomely powerful defenders of the queen, but the Navy's technical experts knew there were always limits—sometimes very frustrating ones—as to how well these increasingly complex and expensive systems would work. The sonars, radars, torpedoes, guns, and missiles all needed sailors to man them, and like all technologies, none were "sailor-proof." In addition, stretching the outer edges of the technological envelope as they did, the systems were often smack up against the unyielding walls erected by the natural world, particularly in antisubmarine warfare. With all of these systems aboard, the guard, along with its carrier, was also extraordinarily defensive-minded, and terrifically noisy to boot, emitting electromagnetic and acoustic signals all over the place.

Nevertheless, by the mid-sixties the ships of the guard had reconfigured and rearmed. Along with the supercarriers they made up an altogether exceptional attack component of American military power—the carrier battle group. Of course, the enemy had to be willing to meet this formidable aggregation out on blue water, or the battle group would have to be put to other tasks.

For naval aviators and surface warfare specialists, then, the path was set for decades to come. But there existed a third important group in the Navy line, and its members too had not been standing still. These were the submariners. Out of their underwater world in the postwar years came the most exciting technological development of all, nuclear propulsion.

—Which was spearheaded by one of the most remarkable men in American naval history.

CHAPTER SEVENTEEN

RICKOVER

————— ☆ —————

T he Germans had shown what could be done, despite poor planning and chaotic production schedules, with advances in traditional submarine technology. Toward the end of World War II they developed what they thought was a true submarine, one capable of staying underwater for months. (They produced far too few of these Type XXIs, and far too late.) *U-977*, escaping to Argentina after the war, kept under the surface for sixty-six days.[1]

U-977 and her sisters were air breathers, technological mammals that needed oxygen to survive. Their innovation was the snorkel, a device enabling a boat to siphon in precious air without surfacing. The United States Navy immediately saw the advantages and, along with the British, rapidly incorporated as much German U-boat technology as possible. The later German boats had great selling points: they could dive more deeply; they had much greater battery capacity (more batteries meant additional hull volume); they had more powerful electric motors; and, of course, they had the snorkel.

The American evolution rapidly led to the *Tang* class, designed in 1945 and 1946 and in service by 1952. There were six members, designed from the keel up as state-of-the-art diesel-electric attack boats and armed with eight twenty-one-inch torpedo tubes. In addition, a major effort was begun to convert fleet submarines in the direction of the German technology, a program called Greater Underwater Propulsive Power. Acronym-happy as usual, the Navy shortened these conversions to "Guppies."

Guppies received new batteries and modified motors, and some of these conversions increased their underwater speed from ten to sixteen knots. Thus tricked up, the Guppies pulled off some highly publicized stunts. *Pickerel*, for example, crossed the Pacific from Hong Kong to Pearl Harbor without surfacing.

A few boats got a less ambitious conversion, in which a snorkel was installed and the bridge fairwater was streamlined. There were experiments with propulsion systems featuring high-test peroxide (on 16 June 1955 the

British submarine *Sidon* suffered an explosion from a hydrogen peroxide leak that killed thirteen men), Walther cycle engines, pressure-fired steam, and gas turbines. The main idea was to achieve longer underwater endurance times through some kind of conventional propulsion. A flurry of excitement surrounded a closed-cycle diesel (Project Gumbo), which was designed but never built.

There was also, for a brief moment, approval for a hunter-killer submarine (SSK). The idea was a small, dual-purpose (antiship, antisubmarine) attack boat that could lurk in harbor mouths and choke points to strike the enemy as he sortied. In 1949 Submarine Division 11 in the Pacific and Submarine Development Group 2 in the Atlantic began working on the problem of using subs to find, fix, and kill other subs (Project Kayo). By 1955 only the three 890-ton SSKs—*Barracuda*, *Bass*, and *Bonita*—were in commission.[2]

But none of these projects—the *Tangs*, the Guppies, the tinkering with different propulsion systems, the SSKs, even a stab at a midget sub, the *X-1*—held final answers. The SSKs, for example, sported huge sonar domes in their bows and had little trouble finding submerged submarines, but they proved far too small and slow to accomplish their mission. The lightweight diesel engines of the *Tang* class were consistent only in their defects; *Harder*, transiting from Belfast to her base in New London in 1953, ended up limping home in humiliation at the end of a submarine rescue ship's towline. Captain Edward ("Ned") Beach, who commanded one of the *Tangs*, called his boat an "inglorious failure."

The Guppies could do wonderful tricks; her skipper believed *Pickerel*, a converted *Tench*-class boat, "far and away the finest submarine in the world." They could stunt underwater like porpoises at play, cavorting at high speeds and steep angles that called for the greatest skill by diving officers and planesmen. But they, too, could be unreliable. *Cochino*, from the *Balao* class, was maneuvering north of Norway shortly after her conversion when she suffered a battery explosion and serious electrical fire. She eventually went down, costing the lives of a civilian technician and six men assigned from the *Tench*-class *Tusk* for rescue operations. *Stickleback*, another *Balao*-class conversion, lost power off Oahu during a practice attack on the destroyer escort *Silverstein* in 1958, surfaced, and was accidentally rammed by her quarry; all eighty-four aboard were saved, but $10 million worth of *Stickleback* sank in 1500 fathoms.

Then there was the marvelous snorkel itself. The diesels powering the conversions, when the boat was submerged, did not have an air intake large enough to suck in the required amounts. The engine exhaust discharged an incredibly high back pressure. When seas broke over the head valve of the snorkel the thing slammed shut, producing more than stuffiness in the ears and noses of the helpless crew. No Guppy conversion snorkeled for more than one hundred hours before wrecking its blower lobes. Persistent snor-keling developed potentially explosive concentrations of hydrogen within the hull.

Finally, the snorkel safety circuits were an overengineered nightmare. Aboard *Pickerel* the circuits were simply bypassed. To alert the controllermen to stand clear of the engines when the head valve was ducked, an ordinary glass milk bottle was installed, its open mouth fitted with a condom—the head of which was painted bright red. When the boat pulled a high vacuum, the condom stood to attention and the men responded immediately. "Their idling brains were more attuned to that frequency," the commanding officer dryly remarked. (When he heard of the condom idea, Arthur Radford, then commander of the Pacific Fleet, roared with laughter and had to see for himself; when he boarded *Pickerel*, he was the first four-star to welcome a returning boat since the war years.)

Many of the experiments related not only to operations but also to crew safety and comfort. Neoprene-coated nylon exposure suits were designed for submariners, some equipped with built-in water wings, detachable boots, and mittens. "Soft" interior paints were tried. Psychologists devised endless batteries of tests to find the perfect sub sailor. If the boats were to stay submerged longer (and endurance was what the submariners wanted; staying underwater meant increased safety and additional surprise), crew comfort had to be a priority. The objective was to create a boat whose only sub-mersion limits would be defined by crew fatigue.

On the eve of revolution, then, America's submarine force was tinkering with conventional technology. The snorkel had its problems, producing intense crew discomfort, ear and sinus complaints, and lack of sleep. True, subs could now recharge their batteries without really coming up for air. But the boats were still mammals, actually submersible torpedo boats rather than true submarines. With them, the dream of the true submarine, cut off from the oxygen blanket above the seas, could never be realized.

"Fleet-type subs of World War II, though still effective," wrote one observer, "are destined for the fate of the Model T Ford."[3]

☆

The progress of the age have [*sic*] changed our naval tactics, naval ships, naval machinery, and naval organizations; they have [*sic*] swept away many of the mouldy prejudices of an effete regime. The navy is no longer what it was; it has progressed, improved, and enlarged with the times, and if it is to continue in the same path it must be by the application of new inventions in mechanism and new discoveries in science.

—Thus wrote the great naval engineer Benjamin Franklin Isherwood, at the dawn of the Navy's conversion to steam and steel. Now an even greater revolution loomed: nuclear power.

As far back as 1939, the ad hoc Uranium Committee had reported to President Roosevelt that, among other possibilities, a controlled chain reaction could be "a continuous source of power in submarines." FDR read the report, which was then duly filed away for over a year. When interest in atomic power was revived, its wartime focus almost unavoidably became the atomic bomb: destruction before propulsion.

Excluded almost totally from the top-secret Manhattan Project, the Navy was decidedly unenthusiastic (at first) about the development of the bomb, not only because the service, apart from a few men like Deak Parsons and Fred Ashworth, had no part in the project but also because no one, in the early forties, could clearly see how the fleet could take on a nuclear attack role. Many officers, along with Fleet Admiral William Leahy, were aghast at the horrible destructive potential of atomic energy used in this way.

In war and peace alike, the Navy consistently prided itself not on its ability to destroy but on its flexibility and skills in precisely applying a precise amount of power—brain surgery in contrast to the wholesale butchery committed, according to this view, by the other services. Thus, although the Navy did eventually (and desperately) scramble for a role in the emerging national nuclear strategy, the search for "peaceful" applications of nuclear energy never died. The Uranium Committee's report was simply placed on hold for the duration.[4]

For the Navy, "peaceful" applications meant nuclear propulsion, and *any* kind of propulson meant the Bureau of Ships, formed in 1940 from the old Bureau of Construction and Repair and the Bureau of Engineerng. During the war BuShips had grown into a mammoth, highly effective organization, responsible for turning out the armada that made oceanic victory possible. Some of its people were naval architects, some engineers; at its wartime peak BuShips had a Washington staff of more than six thousand officers and civilians, operated 465 shipyards employing over one million people, and busily spent $17 billion constructing no fewer than 110,000 vessels.

BuShips was extraordinary in every way, not least in its ability to attract fresh, innovative minds, both military and civilian. Many of its officers had graduate degrees—a rarity then among the seagoing community—and the officer-civilian mix provided ship design and construction expertise that was unsurpassed. At the end of the war, BuShips was headed by the forward-looking Rear Admiral Edward Cochrane, an Annapolis grad with an advanced degree in naval architecture from MIT, and his deputy, the bluff and outspoken Rear Admiral Earle Mills, also Annapolis with a graduate degree in naval engineering from Columbia. Cochrane and Mills were the cream of the crop, the best the Navy had at what they did.

The man who had lost out in the auction to head the wartime bureau was Rear Admiral Harold Bowen, the obstreperous, cranky father of high-pressure steam in the Navy. Bowen's consolation prize was the directorship of the Naval Research Lab, from which post he supported preliminary naval research in atomic energy. "The prospects of harnessing atomic energy for the purpose of driving ships in the near future is [sic] an amazing possibility," he said. Bowen, personally chosen by Secretary of the Navy Forrestal in 1945 to head the new Office of Research and Inventions, had the great advantage of independence from the bureaus. But he was running an idea factory, while Cochrane and Mills had control of the nuts and bolts.

At war's end, a specially convened board of officers from the Pacific Fleet forwarded a host of recommendations to Ernie King concerning what types of ships should compose the postwar Navy. Most of the board's attention concentrated on submarines. The boats, even given their superb wartime record, still gave naval architects and engineers a real headache. Diesel-electrics, with their limited underwater endurance, had to be designed for efficient surface operation, but these same features worked against them the minute they submerged. The conventional submarine thus necessarily featured two propulsion systems. Diesel engines gave high speed and extended range—nice on the surface—but they needed air, and underwater the subs had to depend on battery-powered electric motors. The batteries needed periodic recharging and provided much lower speed and less endurance. The faster the subs went underwater, the quicker their batteries were bled. Recharging, while the sub was vulnerable on the surface, could take as long as six hours—in modern warfare the difference between safety and eternity.

The obvious answer was a single propulsion system for both surface and submerged operation. The goal was a true submarine, one capable of operating for extended periods at high speeds both on and below the ocean's surface. Chester Nimitz, a submariner, was only one of many fascinated by the idea, but in the fall of 1945, when he relieved King as chief of naval operations and restudied the report of his own Pacific Fleet board, nuclear propulsion seemed to be as remote as the Flying Dutchman, schooning along in the mists of a far-off future.[5]

Even during the war, however, the idea had not lain fallow. Ross Gunn, the Naval Research Lab's Yale-trained physicist who had heard Enrico Fermi's briefing on atomic fission in 1939, kept cobbling away at the notion of nuclear propulsion. Gunn pried $1500 from Bowen for preliminary research—a piddling sum, but a start. The physicist was also influential in getting bigger money, $100,000, for isotope separation experiments and a further $140,000 for studying physical constants and neutron multiplication, all this before Pearl Harbor. By 1941 the Navy was supporting nuclear research contracts and was conducting its own small isotope separation experiment at the Naval Research Lab.

Such amounts, though, were the merest raindrops against the deluge of money poured into the bomb. The lab grew increasingly isolated from the heart of nuclear research as Leslie Groves and the Army bulled ahead on the Manhattan Project. But the Navy's persistence in thermal diffusion experiments, under the direction of Carnegie's Philip Abelson, convinced Robert Oppenheimer and Groves that the process was the best way to produce the urgently needed uranium 235 quickly. Accordingly, in 1944 Abelson's schematic became the basis of the Oak Ridge nuclear facility in Tennessee, and the Navy thus made a small but measurable contribution to the creation of the uranium weapon, Little Boy.

With Oak Ridge, the Navy had its foot in the door opening to the postwar nuclear world. Cochrane selected Mills and Captain Thorvald Solberg (Annapolis, graduate degree from Columbia) to serve on a committee to study postwar atomic energy development. This committee, which got input from men like Gunn and Abelson, proposed in its final report to Groves that nuclear power be developed in the postwar Navy. Gunn, perhaps the greatest enthusiast, testified before the Special Senate Committee on Atomic Energy in 1945 that the main function of the atom should be "turning the world's wheels and driving its ships."

The Navy was interested in both nuclear weapons and nuclear power. Spike Blandy in OP-06 was forging ahead on the former, ginning up the Bikini tests. Under Blandy came the Division of Special Weapons, where Solberg found a home as head of the Atomic Power Section. Solberg and Parsons, who headed the section on guided missiles and atomic weapons, were convinced that nuclear propulsion would arrive in time, but only lots of time. Over in BuShips, Cochrane and Mills were of like mind and, in addition, believed nuclear power to be only one of several options for the postwar fleet. The drawdown tightened the bureau's purse strings, and the two admirals had other propulsion possibilities, like the closed-cycle system, appealing for their limited funds.

Bowen, in his idea shop, was relatively unharnessed and much more fixated on developing nuclear propulsion. There were turf wars; Solberg complained to Mills that Bowen was much too aggressive on the subject and was seeking to take over all atomic energy work within the Navy. Undaunted, as was his wont, Bowen went full steam ahead, releasing a report in March 1946 (authored by Abelson and his assistants) proposing construction of a nuclear-powered submarine within two years.

Bowen, by this time, had battled for seven years for a nuclear Navy, but his report was little more than a suggestion to plump down a nuclear reactor in a conventional submarine hull—by no means a finished design proposition. Much more would have to be done, and that meant BuShips, which was "soft" on nuclear power. Still, Cochrane and Mills, along with Solberg and Parsons, were convinced that even if the learning curve on nuclear power was steep, the climb had to be made. Accordingly, they took up Groves's suggestion that the Navy assign a small number of engineering officers full time to Oak Ridge to learn the fundamentals of nuclear technology.

The key role in recommending these men fell to Captain Albert Mumma, chief of the Machinery Design Division in BuShips. Mumma was also a Naval Academy graduate, with a rare advanced degree from the prestigious École d'Application du Génie Maritime in Paris. He had been a member of the wartime Alsos mission in Europe, ferreting about the ruins to see how far the Germans had gotten with their own nuclear development.

Mumma wanted Engineering Duty Only (EDO) officers for Oak Ridge, and he nominated outstanding men: Lieutenant Commanders Louis Roddis, Jr., first in his 1939 class at Annapolis and an MIT grad; James Dunford, an ambitious, exceptionally talented engineer; and Miles Libbey, another MIT grad who was already investigating the use of radioisotopes. A fourth officer, the strong-willed and truculent Raymond Dick, had etched an exceptional combat record. To head the project, which also included three brilliant civilian engineers from the Navy, Mumma recommended Captain Harry Burris, a BuShips insider who had expedited the production of steam propulsion plants for destroyer escorts during the war.

When Mumma bucked his choices up to Mills, who had the final call, the admiral had no trouble approving the list, all except one. Mills, with no ax to grind against Burris, thought he had a better man to head up the Oak Ridge team, an obscure, forty-six-year-old EDO captain who was not even eligible to command a Navy ship: Hyman George Rickover.[6]

☆

For all his life he was the outsider, the critic, the man looking in and standing apart. Some of this stance resulted from his heritage and his compulsive, explosive intellect, but the ways he did things were first and foremost his deliberate choice. Hyman Rickover gloried in his special solitude.

Even in 1946, on the brink of middle age, he appeared frail, even feeble. At five-foot-five, his figure tended from lean to emaciated, and his shock of prematurely white hair topped a quizzical, sagging face that gave him the look of a perpetually dissatisfied macaw. His head hung by a thread of a neck, his shoulders drooped, and his clothes—either naval or civilian— bagged about him in folds. "He hated the uniform," said Admiral Alfred Ward.

—A most unlikely naval officer, in every way. He was a child of the century, always advertising his birth year as 1900 (the beginning of the century of technology), although his school records showed that he was born in Makow, in Russian Poland, fifty miles north of Warsaw, on 24 August 1898, the son of Eliachako (Abraham) Rickover, tailor.

The Rickover family lived within the Jewish Pale, dominated by the intensely anti-semitic Russians. They were Poles, not Russians, but they were also Jews in a land where the dreaded pogroms might erupt at any moment. So, around 1899, Abraham emigrated to the promised land and, a few years later, sent for his family—his wife Ruchal, a daughter, Fanny, and six-year-old Hyman. A second daughter, Hitel (Augusta) was born in 1908.

Abraham Rickover was a model citizen in his adopted country; he worked hard and, for his generation of immigrants, did well—well enough to invest in an apartment building in Brooklyn. But the bad times of 1907 canceled his gains, and the Rickovers struck out for Chicago, a place Hyman would always call his hometown. There Abraham, perhaps with an eye to his progeny's future, deliberately avoided Maxwell Street, the first ghetto of Chicago Jewry, a place where Yiddish was the common language and where kosher butcher shops and matzo bakeries flourished on every corner. Instead, he settled his family in Lawndale, a well-proportioned middle-class suburb where many residents worked at the nearby McCormick reaper plant.

The Rickovers began in Lawndale on the edge of poverty, but Abraham kept on tailoring (an occupation he sustained all his long life), and the family inched into lower-middle-class respectability, Jewish division. Hyman grew up sheltered from most of the prejudices and terrors directed at his heritage, but he was an acutely sensitive and exceptionally intelligent boy, and these prejudices and terrors helped to mold him nonetheless, placing him on the outside in his new society from the beginning. Never, however, would he follow the tenets of his father's faith; some of his brother officers would come to believe he worshiped as an Episcopalian, and certainly by 1952 he regarded himself as one.

Hyman Rickover's recollections of his boyhood—fragmented, highly colored, concealing rather than revealing—suggested a life of hard work, dogged study, mildly punitive discipline, and what students of Puritanism would call an ethic of "deferred gratification." Maybe much of this was true. In school his grades ran from C's to A's, but by the time he was a senior at John Marshall High School, he was in full stride academically, with one C (typewriting), one B-plus (English), and the rest A's (including physics).

He graduated in 1918, as America's involvement on the Western Front grew to a crescendo. He worked part time as a Western Union messenger, bearing the black-bordered telegrams that meant emotional disaster for some families. On his route the young messenger often carried telegrams to the Chicago office of a Democratic congressman, Adolph Joachim Sabath, then well underway in his exceptional legislative career. (First elected in 1906, he served consecutively until his death in 1952.) Sabath's district centered in Lawndale, he was himself a self-made man and Jewish immigrant, and he was an ardent Wilsonian.

The congressman paved the way, but Rickover himself laid the bricks. Rickover would never be very clear about exactly what attracted an immigrant Jewish boy to the Navy, and indeed Jews had never found the Navy congenial (although an early example, Uriah Phillips Levy, had reached the then-highest rank of commodore in 1860). Perhaps his reason was the classic one: the service as the path upward, the way out. But more likely, Rickover saw the Navy as feeding his studiousness and his already pronounced technological bent.

The young man tried a cram preparatory course to get ready for his entrance exam to the Naval Academy, probably at "Bobby's War College"— the prep school run in Annapolis by Robert Lincoln Werntz, Class of 1884. After two weeks Rickover quit this hellish regimen, studied alone for two months in his boarding house room, and passed.

In the early summer of 1918 the young Polish-born Jew walked through the gates of Annapolis, a member of the Class of 1922.[7]

☆

All of the war-swollen regiment of midshipmen (they had been a "brigade" from 1903 to 1914 and would be a brigade again after 1945) could not be accommodated in Bancroft Hall, and Rickover spent his first few days at the Academy living in the musty old Marine Barracks. In addition, he went on the "binnacle list" and was sequestered in sick bay for several weeks. He quickly found that, compared with many of his classmates, he had had a poor academic preparation at John Marshall. The Naval Academy prized rote memorization and recitation, a type of "learning" that Rickover rapidly grew to loathe. He started in his plebe class running from behind.

Here began Rickover's lifelong hatred and contempt for the Naval Academy. (Irony of ironies, the building that one day would house the Division of Engineering and Weapons would be called Rickover Hall.) The Academy was an institution in which he could never, even if he had wanted to, become an insider. He could not afford the social swirl—dates, drags to hops, and the like. Whatever he was, he was decidedly not a WASP, and the Academy was not just a WASPish place: the school then was *quintessentially* WASP. He received frequent hazing, perhaps too frequent, even for a plebe. And academically behind the power curve, he had to hit the books hard, removing himself even further from his fellow mids and their easy, in-group affabilities. His late-night studying irritated some of them, and he took on the much-disdained Academy persona of the "grind."

The Class of 1922 called itself the "Disarmament Class," because the postwar cutbacks meant that many of them would not be commissioned. Competition for class standing, always fierce at Annapolis, thus became ferocious for Rickover and his peers, because those lower on the totem pole at the end would be graduated and released to civilian life. (The Academy did not award degrees until 1933).

Another Jewish midshipman in Rickover's class, West Virginian Leonard Kaplan, endured bitter hazing and was "sent to Coventry" for all four of his years at the Academy: no midshipman spoke to him or in any way acknowledged that he was alive. Kaplan and Rickover were two of around twenty Jewish midshipmen in the class, the largest number ever, but they were not unique in their ostracization, which may not have been entirely due to anti-semitism. A sagacious, forceful man, Edward Ellsberg, had been first in the Class of 1914, would go on to a exceptional career in naval salvage during World War II, and would later insist that he had experienced no anti-semitism in his years at the Academy.

The truth of what happened to Kaplan and Rickover at Annapolis was shaded by the memories of old men. But both, Kaplan by far the more seriously, were hurt by cruel forms of hazing and anti-semitism. Without doubt, these practices existed and scarred a few young men for life. There were suicide attempts by two members of the Class of 1923, both of whom were probably Jewish—enough to prompt a congressional investigation. But the hazing and prejudice varied from person to person, both in application and in results. Seven of the Jewish midshipmen in the Class of 1922 graduated, and two would reach flag rank.

Kaplan courageously kept an even keel and graduated. He was exceptionally bright, a scholarly competitor among competitors, and he stuck to his last during four years of horrible peer-group purgatory. Kaplan, not Rickover, was in serious competition for number one, and his graduation picture in the *Lucky Bag* for 1922, placed there by his archenemy and competitor for that position, appeared by itself on a perforated page next to an anti-semitic and thoroughly demeaning caricature—the easier to tear out of the yearbook. Kaplan graduated number two (the archenemy, first in his class, died the following year), and went on to a fine career, retiring in 1949 as an EDO captain.

In the years to come Leonard Kaplan's story—the Jewish outsider, the grind, Coventry, the duel for number one, the vicious attack symbolized by the perforated page—would get all mixed up with Rickover's, and pop psychologists would argue that the Academy had been completely responsible for the peculiar twists in the latter's personality. Without doubt the Academy shaped Rickover, beveling him along Navy lines, as the institution shaped almost everyone who passed through. But though his time at Annapolis confirmed his status as an outsider, the Academy years also disciplined him, introduced him to the arcana of naval technology.

He *was* a grind, "[looming] large through the chalk screens" (blackboards). "As water seeks its level, so has 'Rick' sought to bring himself up to the plane of a worth-while and credit-bestowing profession," his yearbook noted backhandedly. He was, alas, "neither a star on the gridiron nor a terror in the pool." He *had* to be a grind, to keep paddling upstream. Resolutely, he fought his way from the back of the academic pack. "I was impressed," said a classmate, "by his ruthlessness, his rudeness, and his obvious love of domination."

When the Class of 1922 graduated, Hyman Rickover stood 106th out of 539. He would be commissioned. He would enter the fleet.[8]

☆

Freed of the constrictions of the Academy and from what he regarded as the puerile concerns of his peers, Rickover found he liked the Navy, particularly its endless technological wonders and their related problems. He went first to the four-piper destroyer *La Vallette*, where he became the youngest engineering officer in the squadron, only a year after his graduation. Wardroom mates remembered him either curled up with a book or crawling through the can's cramped engineering spaces, studying the steam plant.

Early in 1925 he reported aboard *Nevada*, where he worked first in gunnery and then as electrical officer. On both the destroyer and the battleship, Rickover displayed an intense, even obsessive, interest in technology, in what made things work. He was, from early on, persistently and energetically oriented toward *results*, and if naval custom or protocol got in the way, that was too damn bad. By now he could walk through an engine room and sense, through the clamor and the strength-sapping heat, when a component was out of whack, when the vibrations of a metal jacket were not quite right, when boiler water was impure to the taste, when hot lube oil meant that a bearing was running hot. But, said his gunnery division officer aboard *Nevada*, he was "taciturn . . . not very good tempered . . . not . . . what is generally considered a good shipmate."

In 1927 he began a two-year course of graduate study in electrical engineering, first at Annapolis and then at Columbia, receiving his master's (then a rarity in the naval profession) in 1929. At the Naval Academy, Rickover like the other mids had relied on rote memorization to get him through the hoops. Columbia helped him to *think* his way through problems, introducing him to the delights of engineering analysis and further deepening his love of technology.

He was still a line officer, running with his year group, a lieutenant now. He requested submarine duty, figuring that the boats offered him the best chance for an early command. After sub school in New London, he was assigned to *S-48*, becoming the executive officer and qualifying for command in 1931. He found, however, that the seagoing life aboard the confined boats was not nearly as exciting as the intellectual challenges provided by the natural physics involved. In addition, he was on the outs with his skipper, already a familiar pattern. Also in 1931 he married Ruth Masters (a "real brain," said an officer who knew her), whom he had met at Columbia and who would receive her doctorate in international relations the next year.

After two years spent with the office of the inspector of naval material in Philadelphia, Rickover reported to *New Mexico* in 1935 as the assistant engineer. He became the chief engineer in all but name, since the real chief left him in charge. Carefully skimming the cream of new men reporting aboard, Rickover brought the old battlewagon from sixth place to first in the engineering competition, winning the much-coveted red "E," and this place she held for the next two years. Aboard *New Mexico* he was everywhere: reducing the expenditure of fuel oil; perking up the boilers to peak efficiency; rooting out more showerheads and faucets to turn off, more light bulbs to unscrew—anything to make the plant run better. The engineering plant was his life. And typical of his later pattern, he gave his younger engineering officers as much responsibility as they could handle—three of them would make flag rank. One of these, Rear Admiral Charles Loughlin, called his boss on *New Mexico* "the hardest working naval officer I have ever worked for in my life or I've ever known."

Rickover's reward was promotion to lieutenant commander in 1937 and assignment to his first (and only) command, the minesweeper *Finch*, remote and forlorn on the far-off China Station. *Finch* was a rustbucket, a collection of corrosion and peeling paint that was off the lower end of the modern technological scale. Rickover hated the duty, his crew hated his discipline and work ethic, and four months after stepping aboard he took the most critical step of his career. He applied for EDO status.

In 1916 congressional legislation had allowed a few officers, labeled "Engineering Duty Only," to specialize in engineering. They were line officers, but ineligible for command at sea. This was the Navy's reluctant admission that modern naval engineering was growing too complex for many generalists, but the service defended its traditional regard for the jack-of-all-trades officer by restricting the EDOs to specific duties and keeping their hands off the helm—the result of the deep fissures caused by the line-specialist controversy at the turn of the century. The EDOs' bailiwick lay in the design, construction, and maintenance of ships. They were usually more highly schooled than their fellow officers, an educational and technological elite. They used this self-esteem against the fact that they could never achieve the grail—seagoing command.

Rickover, especially if commands like the hapless *Finch* were to be his lot, eagerly grasped his chance to specialize. Everywhere he had been, he had gravitated to engineering, to the machinery, to the technology. He was relieved from *Finch* in indecent haste, in October 1937, and worked as an assistant production officer in the Cavite Navy Yard, slightly southeast of Manila, until May 1939. He traveled throughout Southeast Asia, as curious as ever about how things ran, but mostly he impressed the skippers who brought their ships in for overhaul with the demanding excellence of his work.

He left Cavite in the spring of 1939 as war gathered over Europe, an EDO headed for Washington and the Electrical Section of the Bureau of Ships.[9]

☆

Rickover arrived at BuShips as the Navy was gearing up for a massive shipbuilding program. There was much to do. The Electrical Section was responsible for the installation and maintenance of electrical equipment, covering everything from propulsion systems to searchlights, keel to signal bridge. Under Rickover the section mushroomed, hiving off subsections like atomic fission products: electrical design, procurement, degaussing, minesweeping.

He had been in place for over two years when war came to the United States. What had been a beehive became a positive swarm of activity, and Rickover found himself in the vanguard of the creation of the wartime armada. He worked out the plans for reconditioning the electrical systems of *California* and *West Virginia*, both badly damaged at Pearl Harbor. Both steamed again, and both stood in the line of battle at Surigao Strait. Under him the Electrical Section jealously kept control of its own design work and, typical of Rickover, took on even more projects, in areas such as mine locating and infrared signaling.

The section's production was prodigious and of exceptionally high quality. Special electrical cables were developed that would not leak water from flooded to dry spaces aboard ship. A casualty power system was created, a hydra of portable cables and fittings, so that a damaged ship could get electrical loads to her vital light and power circuits—steering gear, anti-aircraft batteries, fire pumps. Rickover's engineers continually improved circuit breakers and evolved wire insulation that could withstand higher temperatures. New cable shielding had to be devised; some of the old material gave off poisonous gases when burning.

Rickover was a hands-on manager. More precisely, he was a hands-*clamped*-on manager. He assiduously studied every damage report and visited every ship with battle damage that he could get to. From these trips he discovered that the war's more powerful mines were producing far more damage to electrical equipment than expected, and he fought vigorously for a shock-test program and better shock mounting for shipboard components.

For the first time in his career Rickover was at a pressure point in naval development, and his accomplishments in the Electrical Section sped him on his way. At the time of Pearl Harbor he was running a bit behind his class in promotions, which was a typical EDO pattern. On 1 January 1942 he was upped to commander, and a year and a half later, to captain. The section he led reflected his increased seniority. In 1938 only twenty-three people were there; by V-E Day Rickover was leading 343 officers, civil servants, and bright young engineers provided by civilian contractors.

Along the way, Hyman Rickover displayed full blown many of the attributes of his later career. His was the only section in BuShips that ignored ranks among workers. *Educating* personnel to their duties and the critical importance of those duties became a primary task, not one to be dusted off on rare occasions for a rah-rah win-the-war pep talk. Rickover fought hammer-and-tongs the Navy's policy of continually rotating officers and men to other duties, rightly regarding the loss of expertise as stupid, especially in wartime.

His zeal became legendary. He battled openly with some representatives from industry, stole others away from their civilian employers, stepped on tender bureaucratic toes all over the place. He was direct, acerbic, implacably *results*-oriented. When some importunate civilian seeking a contract would bring him an item that was supposedly shockproof, Rickover would immediately give the gear his personal shock test—either hurling the thing against the radiator in his office or tossing the equipment, fittings and all, out his window.

Rear Admiral Mills took notice, impressed by Rickover's effectiveness and boundless energy. Rickover knew no time clock, no weekends, no evenings off. Men working for him who could not keep the pace or stand the gaff were shunted out of the section. Rickover and the survivors shuttled back and forth cross-country by train and plane, endlessly checking, badgering, urging, expediting. "He never took anyone's word for anything," his senior engineer said of Rickover. "He was pretty tough [and] would take advantage of you if he could."

He was exasperating in the extreme—not "the kind . . . you brought to the bar," recalled one officer—but Mills was tuned to results. Rickover, traveling hither and yon in disheveled civilian clothes, was exasperated in his own right by what he regarded as a Navy that had gone to war ill-prepared and ill-managed. As always, his sensor systems illuminated the spot where *he* was—in the Electrical Section—and he struggled endlessly for better, more reliable, safer electrical equipment, run by men who *knew* what they were doing. He saw himself as a martyr, by which he meant someone who worked too hard in a righteous cause. "Most of the work in the world today is done by those who work too hard," he said. "The greater part of the remaining workers' energy goes into complaining."

Of course, he rubbed people, both Navy and civilian, the wrong way. His grating impatience with delays; his cantankerous distrust of all explanations, however plausible, that were not his own; his belief in the twenty-four-hour workday and the seven-day workweek—all stamped him indelibly as a dyed-in-the-wool son of a bitch, a seemingly reckless violator of bureaucratic channels who infuriated superiors and drove subordinates until they dropped or requested transfer to a more restful place—like a war zone.

All this was true, but like Ernie King (who had least had the authority of five stars to protect him), Rickover was an *American* son of a bitch, and amid the personality flail he was developing the management techniques that would later serve him and the Navy so well. Unlike many other naval officers he would delegate responsibility, piling as much work on a subordinate as the junior man could bear and then showing him, by exhortation and example, how he could handle more. He kept a close check on what was happening—information was to Rickover what water was to a dehydrated man—but when an individual showed that he could handle the program, Rickover would loosen the reins and let him gallop. As far as civilian contractors went, he decided early on that they were in the game only for a profit. They would cut corners and celebrate inefficiency if not ceaselessly watched and even harassed. Rickover's creed was to trust no one until he proved himself, then to constantly check on him.

To be sure, he was a real oddball. But his contributions to the war effort were unmistakable and brought him the Legion of Merit, the highest Navy award for an officer outside a combat area, as well as the Order of the British Empire (because many of the Electrical Section's design developments had been incorporated into the Royal Navy).[10]

The end of the war found this loner, outsider, and abrasive intellect on Okinawa. He had asked Mills for a war-zone job, but he first had to vector through the sprawling Naval Supply Depot at Mechanicsburg, Pennsylvania, where, in the span of a few short weeks, he reorganized the mail system; redesigned the mail room, right down to the proper location of chairs and desks; developed a depot organization chart eight inches in height and seventy-two inches in length; monitored the efficiency of the typing pool; and set up a salvage operation for scrap lumber. "He was ruthless," remembered a dumbfounded observer, "if he thought someone was trying to screw him or the Navy." When he left Mechanicsburg, after a brief tour that must have seemed like centuries to his victims, a harvest of discontented, thoroughly maddened souls in his wake, he left behind the TOBR Club—"tossed out by Rickover."

On Okinawa he did ship repair. "A more conscientious man never lived," asserted his boss, Vice Admiral Albert Fay. Still, a few of his officers griped about his unorthodox ways of doing things. (Some of his petty officers, because Rickover thought they knew what they were doing and some of his officers did not have a clue, were giving orders to the officers.) He was ordered to do things the Navy way—which, at times, he grudgingly did.

At war's end this "desk man" (at least as seen by the seagoing warriors) had seemingly reached the end of the line, shuffling papers in San Francisco's Nineteenth Naval District, shepherding much of the Pacific Fleet into mothballs. He was a captain with twenty-three years of commissioned service, and the EDO ranks were almost closed off for entry to flag level. Most of the Navy's concepts, methods, customs, traditions, and institutions were anathema to him. He preferred book reading to shore leave, problem solving to bellying up to the bar with his confreres, rumpled civvies to a spruced-up set of blues.

But something even his few friends had trouble understanding, Rickover *loved the Navy*: not what the service was—not by a long shot—but what the institution could become if only its men and ships could realize their potential. He deeply wanted to make the service better. This was why he remorselessly pinpointed flaws, harried everyone within ear- and memoshot, spoke with devastating frankness, and never put personal feelings before what he believed to be the mission (as defined, of course, by himself). Earle Mills sensed, even if he did not absolutely understand, this side of Rickover. And this was why, when the time came to choose a naval officer to head (but not be "in charge" of) the Oak Ridge group, he placed a proprietary, obsessive personality in a position to oversee the development of the Navy's "most advanced and potentially revolutionary technical effort."

Hyman Rickover reported to Oak Ridge at the end of June 1946.[11]

☆

Oak Ridge did things in a bureaucratically casual way, which was fine by Rickover. Officially his boss was Army Colonel Walter Williams, director of operations for the entire Manhattan Project, but Rickover quickly pilfered a private office at the lab, where he could hide from administrative chores and devote himself entirely to technical reports. All of the Navy team, officers and civilians alike, were free to attend informal lectures on nuclear physics, given by top men in the field, and to study documents.

Already Rickover, true to his compulsive personality, was obsessed by nuclear power, by the potential of the nuclear genie for revolutionizing naval propulsion systems and, thus, the entire Navy. At last he had found a compelling purpose greater even than his wartime work in the Electrical Section. This purpose would dominate the rest of his life. He did not have the training in advanced mathematics and nuclear physics enjoyed by some of his subordinates, but he readily vacuumed up every possible bit of information from the documents, classrooms, and corridors at Oak Ridge, becoming in the process more than a journeyman nuclear physicist and an exceptionally competent nuclear engineer. He pulled his little band into an effective task force of nuclear-power evangelists like himself and got permission from BuShips to prepare his group's fitness reports (always an important form of power in the Navy).

His method was direct: the group, effectively now "headed" by himself, would learn the esoteric terminology, read and abstract the technical reports, and think about the design of a shipboard nuclear power reactor. Everyone wrote his own technical reports, Rickover characteristically harping on clear, concise, correct, and relevant language. He was dreaming the future.

In the beginning neither Rickover nor anyone else, particularly in BuShips, was optimistic about quick development of a reactor for naval propulsion. The drawdown was in full swing, and budget cuts were the order of the day. Rickover himself estimated five to eight years to build a plant with existing resources. Apart from the scarce dollars there were problems galore in charting terra incognita. An effective shield would have to be designed to protect personnel from the enormous amounts of reactor-generated radiation; new materials would be needed, metals that could not only withstand high temperatures (such metals already existed) but would also have a low attraction for neutrons and thus could resist prolonged, intense neutron bombardment; a coolant had to be selected that could transfer heat effectively from the reactor to the propulsion equipment; and pumps, heat exchangers, and valves had to be designed, many from scratch, all leakproof and trouble-free.

To complicate matters, civilian industry was also in the picture, and the Navy would have to rely on private sources as well as its own expertise to help chart the nuclear world. General Electric had a solid claim on government funds with its Knolls Atomic Power Laboratory, which was meant primarily to develop atomic energy for civilian use. Westinghouse, a major supplier of propulsion equipment for the Navy, had like GE supplied electrical equipment for the Manhattan Project and was deeply involved in atomic research. As much as he might have wanted to, Rickover, and the Navy as well, would not be able to avoid dealing with civilians.

Then there was the new Atomic Energy Commission, created by the Atomic Energy Act of 1946. The commission had exclusive authority over national nuclear research and development, taking over the entire Manhattan Project from the Army on 1 January 1947. Any proposals for a naval nuclear reactor would have to clear the commission as well as the Navy.

Finally, the Navy itself: Initially, Rickover and his group at Oak Ridge, although fully realizing the special advantages that nuclear power would give a submarine, had considered a much broader spectrum of application, because installing a nuclear reactor in a surface ship appeared a bit easier than placing one in a submarine. But war-tested submariners had not been idle; in a series of conferences beginning in September 1946, some of these men had come to the conclusion that "we cannot expect surface and near surface detection to long remain in their present states of development. When the snorkelling submarine becomes readily detectable, nothing short of a deep-running true submarine will be acceptable."

—*A true submarine.* The sub officers assigned high priorities to new diesel construction and closed-cycle systems, but they also urged the design and development of submarine nuclear power plants. Chester Nimitz bought their package.[12]

Rickover was moving toward the center of this developing engineering effort like a force of nature, but he was as naturally unhappy that nuclear power was not being pursued with every ounce of the Navy's energy. On returning to Washington, he and the Oak Ridge group were assigned to evaluate GE's proposals for naval nuclear propulsion; for the first time, Hyman Rickover found himself in a position from which he could directly influence BuShips policy. GE suggested the possibility of building a liquid-metal-cooled reactor that could fit into a submarine hull. Rickover began urging that BuShips concentrate on the *entire* package, the whole nuclear submarine, that building a reactor was 5 percent theory and 95 percent engineering. He launched a fusillade of memos, most centering on the point that he and the rest of the Oak Ridge group understood engineering and that the civilians were suspect in this regard.

He had reluctant allies; Deak Parsons, now director of atomic defense for Nimitz, was supportive but cautious, seeing the engineering problems before the possibilities. Mills was not willing to give any nuclear project top priority, although he was happy to keep the nuclear fires simmering (which made Rickover simmer too, in a different way). Private industry, such as GE, was interested but lacked the spur of real economic motivation. Some of his own people felt that Rickover was chasing pie in the sky, that asking for a functional nuclear power plant in a submarine by 1950, 1955, or even 1960 was too much. The Atomic Energy Commission was still struggling to find its bureaucratic footing (its original estimate was that useful nuclear power would come in about twenty years) and was unwilling to commit to anything.

The Navy would have to provide what drive there would be toward nuclear propulsion. Hyman Rickover took this to be his task. [13]

☆

The Oak Ridge group came back to Washington, but after the GE study its members were sectioned off throughout BuShips. Moreover, the men were not in charge of the nuclear propulsion effort of the bureau; that job initially went to Albert Mumma. No one knew what to do with Rickover, acidic and hyperactive as usual and already beginning his customary rough-shod ride, now in hot pursuit of the dream of nuclear propulsion. Some BuShips officers did not want him in Washington at all, or even in the Navy.

He was saved by Thorvald Solberg, who had connections. Solberg had served on a committee with Leslie Groves, had helped Spike Blandy organize the Bikini tests, and had been on a military liaison group dealing with atomic energy. He urged Mills to keep Rickover at BuShips and in nuclear work; Mills, who after all had handpicked Rickover for Oak Ridge, agreed and appointed him as his "special assistant for nuclear matters."

Mumma did not have a chance. He was involved with far more than just "nuclear matters," and Rickover was a man possessed, driven by his dreams. At last Hyman Rickover was underway, cruising at formation center of the Navy's nuclear effort. He wasted no time. The Atomic Energy Commission had to be powered up on the naval nuclear propulsion issue. By constant badgering, Rickover got the topic on the agenda for all the commission's reactor planning meetings. He intensely studied the question of reactor types and came to the crucial conclusion that the use of pressurized water as both the moderator and heat-transfer medium in a power reactor was a better bet than GE's proposal of a liquid-metal-cooled reactor. He lobbied Nimitz and Secretary of the Navy John Sullivan through carefully crafted letters. He got endorsements from leading combat submariners, men like Captain Elton Grenfell and Commander Ned Beach, both holders of the Navy Cross and, in Beach's case, completely fed up with the *Tang* class.

Rickover's key document, bucked up to Sullivan on 5 December 1947, highlighted the Navy's need for a boat with unlimited submerged endurance at high speed (which meant nuclear power). With a sustained effort, Rickover said, an atomic submarine could be completed, out and about, by the mid-fifties. Sullivan signed off; Nimitz signed off; BuShips and the Atomic Energy Commission were asked to work out a mutually acceptable procedure for developing such a submarine.

—Ahead two-thirds. Rickover and the men he was assembling around him—he wangled back some of the Oak Ridge group—spouted ideas like roman candles. The possibility of the liquid-metal-cooled reactor, which Rickover did not favor, still had to be examined; metals like zirconium had to be studied as corrosion-resistant materials for the water-cooled reactor; a workable relationship with the commission had to be established. Hundreds of problems, thousands—and Rickover, the problem solver par excellence, was in his element.

The Navy's agreement with the Atomic Energy Commission proved to be critical in augmenting Rickover's rapidly expanding power. The Navy proposed that the commission establish BuShips as its agent for the nuclear propulsion project and that the bureau's unit would have dual status as both a commission and a bureau organization. The Atomic Energy Act clearly forbade an independent Navy project. The commission balked, wanting, like any nascent bureaucracy, to subsume the Navy's nuclear group. Rickover feared that Mills and Solberg, in charge of negotiations on the Navy's side, might sell the farm.

Rickover lobbied, wheedled, argued. His points were strong: first, if the commission was in charge, the Navy's nuclear submarine development would be in the hands of the commission's Argonne Laboratory near Chicago, not under naval authority; second, Argonne was oriented toward academic research and theory, and creating the nuclear sub was primarily a task for practical engineers; and third (although he did not put the case quite this way), leaving a bunch of civilian lollygaggers in control would lead only to endless delay and indecision.

Earle Mills, by April 1948, was at last convinced. Nothing would happen unless the dual-status proposal got off the ground. Argonne could train naval personnel in nuclear technology until the cows came home, and do this very well, but only BuShips and its established civilian contractors knew how to design and build boats. Both Mills and Rickover were aiming at a land-based prototype of a reactor that could power a submarine, whereas the commission and Argonne were painting on a much wider canvas, forwarding general advances in nuclear science and technology.

The breakthrough came in mid-July 1948, when Mills (reluctantly, since he knew the man had an almost unique talent for infuriating others) appointed Rickover as liaison to commission headquarters. In August, BuShips reflected the new order by establishing the Nuclear Power Branch (Code 390); here Rickover found a home, for a brief time under an easygoing director. Within six months he had almost all of the old Oak Ridge group back under his wing. After hard bargaining, this team was officially established in the commission's new division of reactor development.[14]

—Full speed ahead. In early 1949 the Atomic Energy Commission accepted the Nuclear Power Branch as its own Naval Reactor Branch—same men, two different titles. As the head of each one, Rickover emerged wearing two hats, military and civilian, giving him absolutely unparalleled bureaucratic leverage over any naval officer alive. Being both inside *and* outside the military, Rickover had immediate access to both organizations. He shamelessly began his lifelong tactic of using one to bring pressure on the other.

With blurring acceleration, his fingers began to play the keys of this remarkable bivalve instrument. Now, he had direct lines to both Navy field activities and civilian laboratories. Argonne and Westinghouse's Bettis Laboratory at West Mifflin, Pennsylvania, were mobilized to develop the pressurized-water reactor; Allis Chalmers got a contract to investigate the heat-transfer capability of a gas-cooled reactor using helium; Argonne and GE's Knolls Laboratory at Schenectady, New York, were set to work on the still-alive possibility of sodium as a liquid-metal medium for heat exchange.

So many questions, so much to do, never enough hours in the day. By spring 1949 Rickover had made his controversial decision, and convinced his superiors, that the pressurized-water reactor design was the way to go. (The liquid-sodium idea was not dead—the technology would power *Seawolf*—but Rickover had decreed the future.) Westinghouse and Argonne were given the task of developing the plant, called Mark I. Out in the wilds of Idaho, at the commission's newly established reactor test station near the town of Arco, the full-scale prototype, dubbed the Mark I Submarine Thermal Reactor (STR), began to rise from the high desert floor.

When Earle Mills, his most important sponsor, retired on 1 March 1949, Hyman Rickover was running the Navy's nuclear propulsion program. In fact, he was more than running the program; he was well on the way to becoming its czar.[15]

☆

If the organization existing in 1949 had been proposed to Harold Bowen back in 1945, that crusty flag officer would doubtless have responded with a volley of oaths that would have cracked wardroom coffee cups. The whole thing was unmilitary in the extreme. Involved were two federal agencies, one military and one civilian (the Navy and the Atomic Energy Commission); two relatively autonomous units within those agencies (the Bureau of Ships and the commission's division of reactor development); three civilian research organizations (Argonne, Westinghouse, and GE); and potentially countless civilian contractors and subcontractors.

On paper this was the worst of all possible worlds—technology by committee, each member speaking a different language. But at the core of the whole enterprise, where all the lines intersected, was a most remarkable man, relentlessly wheeling through eighteen-hour days and seven-day weeks, driving himself and everyone connected with him past exhaustion. At first Rickover's liaison position within the commission was less secure than his naval one (he promptly managed to enrage the commission's headquarters staff and lab personnel), but he rapidly made himself indispensable to both bureaucracies.

He had maneuvering room, and even as he rang up full speed ahead, he twisted and turned to give himself more. Rickover hated "management science," hated the kind of bureaucracy that assumed that once the boxes were outlined, the names filled in, and the lines of authority drawn, the thing would run by autopilot. No bureaucrat himself, he developed into the greatest bureaucratic infighter the Navy had ever known, largely because he knew that the *people*, not the organizational matrix, were what really counted.

Neither the Navy nor the commission could deny Rickover the key to any functioning bureaucracy—information—because of his unique position. He accumulated information like a magnet drawing iron flakes. He side-stepped red tape in one organization by the simple expedient of donning his other hat. By barging into unused interstices in both bureaucracies, he assembled a complement of brilliant, energetic, committed minds and a host of resources that neither bureaucracy could have provided on its own. And when one bureaucracy reached the stalling point on any issue, he could muster his forces in the other to get things revved up again.

Of course this *was* government bureaucracy, with players coming in from surprising angles, full of unexpected pitfalls, and never completely predictable. Rickover would endlessly carp over its shortcomings—if only all the world was on his wavelength—but he studied its intricacies as a shaman would pore over heaps of bones, and he incessantly schemed to make the unwieldy mass work for him. The outsider was still outside, but he had his hands all over the inside levers.[16]

And he pulled. Of prime importance were the Navy's relations with civilian contractors, the men who would have to breathe life into the dream. Rickover detested the Navy's bureau system and its reliance on purchase orders and contracts—paper before people. He believed that all that mattered was how written agreements were enforced. Through the contractual process, he firmly established his ultimate control. Engineering, not theoretical science, would drive the nuclear propulsion program, and he and his engineers, not contractors, would make the technical decisions. His general attitude toward contractors was akin to that of a suspicious housewife eyeing the butcher to make sure his thumb was off the scale. He demanded full value from every contractor.

Rickover and his men inspected contracting facilities from top to bottom, getting to know the key people involved, probing, questioning, suggesting—and, if they thought the situation required, they ordered. By now the Atomic Energy Commission, driven by political perspectives of the Cold War world, was stressing military applications of atomic energy, and Rickover at last had both bureaucratic masses—BuShips and the Commission—sliding in his direction. Thus, when contractors complained (and they did, loudly) of the abusive treatment they were getting from this little gnome in the Naval Reactors Branch, they usually met a stone wall.

He kept pulling. Another key to his increasing success was political. Navymen were supposed to be apolitical, to avoid politicians like the plague. But Rickover knew he needed political allies—powerful ones—and never hesitated. The fount of all progress was Capitol Hill, for only there, among Carl Vinson and his kind, did the money trees grow. Rickover frankly admitted, even gloried in, the fact that he was a political animal, a creature of Congress.

He began by romancing Senator Brien McMahon of Connecticut, the youthful and ambitious chairman of the Joint Committee on Atomic Energy. McMahon was ardently behind military uses for the atom. Rickover, in the winter of 1949–1950, quickly brought McMahon and the rest of the Joint Committee on board in support of the nuclear submarine.

McMahon was fated to die young, but the alliance formed then between the Naval Reactors Branch and the Joint Committee, crucial to Rickover's success and personal future, was destined to endure for decades. Rickover lost no time in extending his influence, walking through every congressional door that was opened even the least bit to his message. From 1950 on, Congress was his bottom line, and to the Hill he went when all else failed.

By the end of 1950, as the Korean War rolled on, the pieces were coming together. The basic elements of Rickover's altogether exceptional influence were just about in place. Technically, he and his hardworking staff in Washington set the goals and specifications for Argonne and the other labs. They scrutinized all the contracts. They microscopically checked the progress of each facet of work. The tentacles of the Naval Reactors Branch reached far afield, through the commission's division of reactor development to civilian field offices in Chicago, Pittsburgh, Schenectady, and Idaho Falls.

Rickover's emerging power was due to a combination of factors, of which his dual-hat role was the most important. Indeed, the only possible comparison with his bizarre military-civilian status had been that of General of the Army Douglas MacArthur, who as the Last Shogun had changed back and forth between his American and international hats as the situation suited him. But Rickover's unparalleled energy, pragmatism, and engineering-first approach also produced a bureaucratic freedom that was hard-earned and rigorously defended. He bossed or monitored an exceptionally diverse group of organizations and people; no single bureaucratic method could have done the job, even if Rickover was disposed toward methodology—and he most emphatically was not.

He was confident, determined, rigorous in his self-discipline, and, above all, convincing—the John the Baptist of naval nuclear power. His decisions were based on the best technical information possible, and he proved absolutely stellar in making, not avoiding, the hard decisions. Moreover, he sold these to the Joint Committee and, through its members, to much of the rest of the Hill. To the many politicians with questions and concerns about nuclear power, he made himself indispensable, the always-reliable expert, cultivating the allies he needed where he needed them.[17]

☆

Out near Arco, on the Snake River plain, the pressurized-water STR plant took form. Rickover, watching the project with a hawk's eye, insisted that the Mark I be both an engineering prototype and a shipboard prototype, designed to fit within a submarine hull. As he saw the dream evolve into the Mark I, he did not exactly mellow in anticipation. Jimmy Thach, who visited Arco during the preparations, called him "the most insulting human being I've ever known." Insulting to be sure, but also full of confidence; in late 1949 Rickover had even predicted an underway date for the first nuclear submarine: 1 January 1955.

Months of the most careful engineering went by. The Mark I at Arco began in wood and cardboard, a meticulous mock-up with dummies of every switch, pipe, and valve of an actual submarine. GE's Bettis Lab, working on the more complex sodium-cooled reactor, was doing the same thing with its Mark A prototype. The Arco prototype was fitted with actual steel sections of a submarine hull, and the reactor plant was connected with a steam generator and turbine. A sea tank, holding almost four-hundred-thousand gallons of water, was constructed around the hull section (nick-named the "McGaraghan Sea," after Commander Jack McGaraghan, its builder).

Meanwhile, the contract for the first nuclear submarine (to be powered by the Mark II, incorporating the lessons of Mark I) had been let—to Rickover's exact specifications—to the Electric Boat Company in Groton, Connecticut. (In 1952 the firm, with long experience in building submarines, a lineage that went back to the old Holland Company at the turn of the century, became the Electric Boat Division of General Dynamics Corporation.) As testimony to Rickover's growing political clout, Harry Truman spoke at the keel-laying ceremony on 14 June 1952. "The day that the propellers of this new submarine first bite the water to drive her forward," said the president, "will be the most momentous day in the field of atomic science since the first flash of light in the desert seven years ago." Rickover, clad in civvies, stood quietly nearby with his wife and their twelve-year-old son, Robert.

In March 1953, hafnium control rods were slowly lifted out of Mark I's core at Arco. The rods were there to absorb neutrons, preventing them from splitting uranium atoms and causing a premature fission chain reaction. As the rods were raised, there were periodic shutdowns, or "scrams," as sensitive instruments detected possible problems and lowered the rods back into the core. Slowly, though, amid much twidgeting with the controls, the rods kept inching upward. On 30 March, Mark I went critical.

Within two months the reactor plant was feeding steam to the main propulsion turbine. The dream was becoming substance. Full power came on 25 June—no problems. Rickover ordered a mock full-power trial, to simulate a submerged sub's run across the Atlantic. Over the strenuous objections of his officer-in-charge, Lieutenant Commander Edwin Kintner, he ordered the throttle kept wide open. ("Beyond forty-eight hours," remembered Kintner, "I could not accept responsibility for the safety of the $30,000,000 prototype.")

Rickover gambled and won; three times the plant had to be throttled back, but the turbines never stopped. At the end of ninety-six hours, in theory, the Mark I had driven a submarine 2500 miles from Nova Scotia to Ireland at an average submerged speed of twenty-six knots; no stopping, no refueling.

The men at Arco knew all about the gamble, about how many chances had been taken, how far the engineering envelope had been expanded. Rickover, a bear for safety standards, had pushed the parameters hard. "The fact that all the unknowns had turned out in our favor was a humbling experience," said a shaken Kintner.

"We must have had a horseshoe around our necks" was Rickover's observation. "But then Nature seems to want to work for those who work hardest for themselves."[18]

☆

—*Who work hardest for themselves.* By early 1953 Hyman Rickover was nearing mandatory retirement, still an EDO captain, after thirty-one years of commissioned service. The Flag Officer Board for 1952 selected thirty-nine men to wear the stars; Rickover was not among them. He had been turned down in 1951 as well.

His political allies, carefully cultivated over the years, now rose en masse. Members of the Joint Committee on Atomic Energy, particularly the young, promilitary senator Henry ("Scoop") Jackson, began agitating. On 12 February Representative Sidney Yates of Illinois attacked the "Navy brass" for their "convoy mentality" in failing to promote Rickover. Yates and Melvin Price, a member of the Senate Armed Services Committee, postponed congressional consideration (required by law) of the flag list. The question actually reached the desk of the newly inaugurated president, Dwight Eisenhower, who refused to intervene. The Armed Services Committee immediately announced hearings on the matter, convening 3 March.

Rickover's titular boss at the Bureau of Ships was now Rear Admiral Homer Wallin, a naval architect and the man who had supervised the herculean salvage job at Pearl Harbor. Wallin testified that Rickover was not that important to the nuclear power program and that there were other qualified Navymen to run nuclear propulson. This was all in good Navy form—we are a team here, no one person is indispensable—but did nothing to calm Rickover's supporters, who acted as if they were witnessing Salome's asking for the head of John the Baptist. Rumors flew that the Navy had asked Rickover to stay around after retirement to shepherd the experimental reactors through to completion. The "indispensable" argument raged on. Temperatures rose on all sides, until the flap over Rickover, fully debated in the national press, took on some of the dimensions of the Billy Mitchell case (although, unlike Mitchell, Rickover remained uncharacteristically sotto voce during the word-slinging).

The turning point was reached when some members of Congress threatened an investigation into the Navy's entire promotion system, a particularly sacred cow that the service would do almost anything to protect. Eisenhower's recent choice for secretary of the Navy, Robert Anderson, was a Texas Democrat allied with the likes of Sam Rayburn and Lyndon Johnson. A lawyer who knew nothing about the Navy, Anderson knew all about political pressure. He quickly caved in.

First, he convened a special board to select EDO captains for retention on active duty. One of them was to be "experienced and qualified in the field of atomic propulsive machinery for ships." Guess who. Thus saved, Rickover was eligible for the 1953 Flag Officer Board, which was directed to select one EDO of similar qualification. Guess who. On 30 July 1953, he was nominated for rear admiral by Eisenhower. As for Wallin, he was booted out of BuShips, all the way to Puget Sound Navy Yard.[19]

—Flank speed. Rear Admiral Hyman Rickover, now securely in place as head of the Navy's nuclear propulsion program, cracked the throttle wide open. No one could then know that he was destined to serve on active duty in flag rank, overseeing that program, *for twenty-eight more years*—in itself, more than a career for most Navy men and women and a record of naval longevity without precedent.

He had gone to Oak Ridge in 1946 as an unknown EDO. Already, seven hectic years later, he was being called "the father of the nuclear Navy." This title was preposterously unfair, for nuclear propulsion had many fathers, men like Ross Gunn and Harold Bowen, who had dreamed the dream; like Earle Mills and Thorvald Solberg, who had given the dream bureaucratic shape (and, in the case of Mills, saved Rickover for the program); like Philip

Abelson and dozens of other top-notch scientific minds; like many of the other Navymen at Oak Ridge, who contributed materially to design and development.

But Rickover, with his tireless energy and zeal, his endless bureaucratic maneuvering, his towering self-discipline, and his driven, obsessive intellect—Rickover was the one man, more than any other, who *influenced* the development of nuclear propulsion and the specific ways (the pressurized-water reactor, for example) in which he wanted that program to go. Perhaps only an outsider could have done what he did. He drew the complex lines of technology together, wrapped them around the rock-solid bollard of his personality, and moored the Navy to a nuclear-powered future. And maybe, as Vice Admiral Eli Reich said, he was the Navy's "evil genius," and the costs for his growing dominance might be high indeed.

During these seven years Rickover and his men had developed a new, abrasive, hands-on style of engineering administration. They had at their disposal top-flight industrial laboratories, technological squads of brains, influential members of Congress, and key players within the Atomic Energy Commission. With Rickover's promotion, a new sense of independence and confidence buoyed the entire program.[20]

Flank speed. Which was just as well, because up in Groton on the banks of the peaceful Thames River, the nuclear Navy was moving from dream to reality. There, on sheltered ways in Electric Boat's yard, the future was almost here.

—*Nautilus* was readying for sea.

CHAPTER EIGHTEEN

NUKES I

———— ☆ ————

H er name did not come from Jules Verne. Back in 1801, Robert Fulton had called his experimental boat *Nautilus* (from the Greek *nautilos*, "sailor," or perhaps the many-chambered, spiral-shelled tropical mollusk of the same name). Sir Hubert Wilkins had similarly christened the craft he used in 1931 in a bold attempt to penetrate beneath the Arctic ice. The United States Navy had used the name twice before; on *H-2* (1913) and on *SS-168* (1930), which completed fourteen war patrols before being decommissioned in 1945.

But Verne's classic fictional creation, along with her megalomaniac inventor, Captain Nemo, was stuck fast in public memory. The fictional *Nautilus* could cruise forty-three thousand miles at forty-three knots (a fairly good approximation of the capabilities of modern nuclear-powered attack boats), propelled by a "sodium Bunsen apparatus"—Verne did not say if this was what drove the monumental pipe organ in the crew's lounge. The name rang with adventure and daring; the cadence was that of the march of science.

Mick Carney, chief of naval operations, was not especially interested in pipe organs, but he could scarcely hold back his elation as the real world overtook the fictional. Diesel power was giving way to nuclear power. The potential energy in a lump of uranium the size of a golf ball equaled 465,000 gallons of oil, six million pounds of coal. "The revolution ignited aboard *Nautilus*," he exulted, "some day will literally sweep our present-day fleet— mightiest in the world though it is—off the seas and replace it with task forces of incredible speed, limitless cruising range, and crushing striking power." *Nautilus*, said Carney, "is but the Model T of our Navy of tomorrow." Maybe so, but the Model T was nonetheless the wonder of her day, and a quickly produced wonder at that. Her contract was awarded to Electric Boat on 21 August 1 1951. Harry Truman presided at her keel-laying ten months later, and she was launched on 21 January 1954. Now she was almost ready to go.

She was four thousand tons submerged, almost twice the displacement of old diesel-electrics like *Archerfish*. Outwardly, her shape was much the same as the conventional boats; only the clean knife-edge of her sail gave a hint that something unusual was going on below. Nominally, she was an attack submarine, armed with six 21-inch bow-mounted torpedo tubes (none in the stern), although no one intended to use her for anything but experimental "firsts." She had only conventional electronics, sonar, and communications equipment.

But at her core—literally—quietly thrummed the beat of revolution. The Mark II reactor, later redubbed the S2W ("S" for submarine, "W" for Westinghouse), had an uranium core of some 20 percent enrichment. The nuclear plant could drive her two small, outward-rotating propellers at a sustained speed of 22.5 knots underwater, a quantum jump beyond the best speeds of the diesel-electrics. (Just in case, she had a standby diesel and a snorkel, along with a bank of emergency batteries.)

With speed came endurance. Her first core would drive *Nautilus* 62,562 nautical miles; her second, 91,324; her third, 150,000—two "refuelings" in over 300,000 nautical miles. Here was revolution indeed.

She broke her commissioning pennant on 30 September 1954. Several admirals, at a Pentagon meeting the year before, had insisted that such a big submarine would be too lumpy to maneuver, make too large a target. And the smaller the hull, the lower the capacity of the reactor therein. But Hyman Rickover had fought all the way for *Nautilus*, stampeding over everyone in the way. Bob Moore, supervisor of shipbuilding at the Groton works and the man who did more than anyone else to put the boat together, was left with words for Rickover "not fit to print."

Rickover had important allies, Carney not the least of them, and he was also looking to a production-model reactor for the submarine fleet. In the process he won a critical battle: in November 1953 his shop gained responsibility for the development of the fleet reactor, although all hull and steam-machinery design still fell under the imprimatur of the Bureau of Ships. Here were the seeds of permanency; come what may, naval reactors would belong to Rickover, and any changes affecting their specifications or operations had to get by him.

And not only the reactors. Rickover had handpicked the officers and crew of *Nautilus*, beginning with Commander Eugene ("Dennis") Wilkinson, her popular, poker-playing skipper. Wilkinson was a Southern Cal grad (Rickover, then and always, had no great affinity for Annapolis products) who had taught high school chemistry and math for a few years in California before joining the Navy in World War II. As a submariner he made eight war patrols; afterward, he cycled through Oak Ridge in the wake of the Rickover team. He was Rickover's kind of man—dedicated, meticulous, thorough—and he had worked at both Argonne and Bettis helping to develop the Mark I. "I don't think there has ever been anyone in the Navy more technically proficient," Rear Admiral Charles Loughlin said of him.

But Rickover's massaging did not stop with merely selecting the people.

Wilkinson and the rest, all chosen from the best the submarine force offered, had to complete a one-year course in mathematics, physics, and reactor engineering at Bettis, then go into temporary exile out at Arco for hands-on training with the Mark I prototype. Only then, late in 1953, did they report to Groton, where they played key roles in testing plant systems and components. No precommissioning detail had ever studied their craft so well.

On 3 January 1955 they brought Mark II to full power. Two weeks later, the modish compartments of *Nautilus* were jammed with heavyweights, from Rickover on down. At 1100 the mooring lines were cast off, and Wilkinson, on the bridge with Rickover alongside, gave the command to back into the Thames. When the boat had barely cleared the pier, the engineering officer reported a loud noise in the starboard reduction gear; he switched to electrical propulsion. Rickover, with press boats expectantly hovering around, was not about to return to dock, as standard procedures required. *Nautilus* kept moving downriver on her port propeller, the gear was repaired (a loose locking pin on a retaining nut), and Wilkinson shifted back to steam propulsion. As the boat slipped past the breakwater into Long Island Sound, her signalman flashed a blinker to the escorting tug *Skylark:* "underway on nuclear power."

The future had arrived. No longer did subs need two propulsion systems—electric submerged, diesel on the surface. No more split-second timing on crash dives, to close the air-intake valves for the diesels. Indeed, no more familiar, reassuring throb of diesel engines. No more fear of surfacing, to face reconnaissance and attack from the air. Five-and-one-half years had passed since work had begun on the Arco prototype; Rickover's prediction of 1 January 1955 for "underway on nuclear power" had been just seventeen days off.

Once with the Atlantic Fleet, *Nautilus* performed like the thoroughbred she was. In the summer of 1955, she and some Guppies simulated attacks on an antisubmarine carrier and her escorts. The Guppies pressed the hunter-killer group hard, but *Nautilus* was well-nigh invulnerable. She could detect the surface ships at great ranges, whereas they did not have a clue as to her whereabouts. She was practically immune to air attack, perpetually snug beneath the surface. With her speed, she could overtake the surface force even when the ships were beating along at eighteen knots; the attack angles were superb. Admiral Jerauld Wright, the Atlantic Fleet commander, looked at the reports of the simulations and saw the handwriting on the wall. "It is urgent that countermeasures be developed for the true submarine," he wrote. "No future combatant submarine [should] be built that is not nuclear powered."[1]

Wilkinson stayed with *Nautilus* for the next two years. (He would go on to command *Long Beach* and ascend to flag rank.) In February 1957, with great celebration, he and *Nautilus*'s crew marked twenty thousand leagues on and under the sea, and Verne's fiction became truth, somewhere deep in the Atlantic off the continental shelf. All this on the submarine's first nuclear core. A few months later Wilkinson was relieved by Commander William Anderson. A sharp-featured Tennessean, Anderson was an Annapolis standout who had completed wartime patrols aboard such leading combat boats as *Tang* and *Wahoo*. After the war he had worked for a time as a staffer to the Atomic Energy Commission.

Among the first orders to the new skipper was one earmarked top secret: *Nautilus* would go to the North Pole.

☆

The Northwest Passage was the will-o'-the-wisp of Arctic explorers, a route across the roof of the world. Hundreds had tried, and almost all had failed. Many had left their bones to mark the way ("the hand of Franklin—pointing toward the Beaufort Sea," as the folk song went). The passage *did* exist, but the path was frozen in thick ice at most times, at others guarded by sentinel icebergs and floes that could grip and crush a ship, buffeted by sixty-knot winds, and shrouded in the thickest mists and fog.

No place for a surface vessel, but a submarine—a submarine might crack the passage, a submarine that did not need air and could go deep, not having to risk surfacing in leads or polynyas. In the late nineteenth century, the Philadelphia author Frank Stockton had created the fictional inventor Roland Crewe, who among other things designed an "artesian ray" that revealed the earth's inner structure and a shell that made tunnels by shooting holes through mountains. In his spare time, Crewe also invented a submarine that traveled to the North Pole under the ice. The actual breaching of the Northwest Passage—from Baffin Bay in the east, into Lancaster Sound, on through Queen Maud Gulf, and out past Cape Bathurst in the west—was not accomplished until the epic voyage of Roald Amundsen between 1903 and 1906. Another thirty-four years passed before another ship was able to repeat his triumph.

Anderson probably knew nothing of the fictional Crewe, but like Amundsen he had been bitten by the polar bug and had been studying Arctic geography and under-ice operations for over a year before he reported aboard *Nautilus*. The idea was in the air, and he knew what was coming.

The major advocates for the voyage were Waldo Lyon, an exceptionally competent physicist stationed at the Naval Electronics Laboratory; Rear Admiral Charles ("Weary") Wilkins, commander, Submarines Atlantic; and Robert McWethy, a World War II sub skipper and commander of Submarine Division 101 in New London, Connecticut. Hyman Rickover, not overly eager to risk such novel technology under the dangerous Arctic ice pack, was far from enthusiastic, but how *Nautilus* was used was beyond his control. The prime motive was more strategic than scientific, however; Arleigh Burke, Carney's replacement as chief of naval operations, was eager to test the nuclear boats against the frozen north. When missile-firing nuclear sub-marines became a reality, a premium spot for the boats to lurk would be underneath the Arctic Ocean, which dominated over three thousand miles of Russian coastline.

In San Francisco, Anderson met his crew. They were ensconced in unheard-of submarine luxury: ice-cream and soft-drink machines, built-in hi-fi system, juke box (five plays for a nickel), washer and dryer, nucleonics lab, machine shop, photographic darkroom, and a library with over six hundred volumes. The color scheme aboard had been conceived by a leading decorator. Each crew member had his own rack—no more "hot-bunking," a submarine tradition.

Rickover's handpicked crew members were top-notch, averaging twenty-six years of age (old by World War II standards), two-thirds of them married. They were far from sedate, however; one hospital corpsman, a "handsome drake," was accustomed to going ashore in civvies and introducing himself as "Major Keating of the Royal Algerian Balloon Corps." The major preyed on the unwitting, and witless, at the finest hotels and nightclubs, cadging free drinks and dallying with the ladies as he told of his adventures. In Bermuda he gave a grand dinner for two dozen people, who duly stuffed themselves and were duly stuck with the bill—the major had sailed away on *Nautilus* two hours before.

Anderson and his crew had to put up with lots of visiting firemen; everyone wanted to get aboard the new marvel. Naval officers were some-times given a turn at the controls. At one point, Anderson had a four-star running the stern planes, a three-star at the bow planes, and a two-star on the wheel. "By golly," cracked a passing seaman, "they always put the junior man on the helm."

But this was a well-knit crew, far from a bunch of skylarkers. They and their boat were no strangers to the Arctic; twice, in August 1957 and June 1958, *Nautilus* had probed tentatively under the ice packs, first in the Atlantic, then in the Pacific. Now her primary mission was to keep going, to cross from the Pacific to the Atlantic taking the shortest route—right through the pole—and blazing a new Northwest Passage.[2]

In July 1958 they left San Francisco quietly, 116 of them, having an-nounced to everyone that they were making a long underwater endurance cruise to Panama. Lieutenant Bill Lalor's wife had given him a shopping list of Panamanian items, and Anderson and his exec, Lieutenant Com-mander Frank Adams, had accepted dinner invitations with friends in the Canal Zone.

After a stopover at Oahu they left on 22 July, ostensibly headed for Panama. But after *Nautilus* nosed under, her gyroscope clicked to port, past 140, past 090, past 040, and headed almost due north, toward the Bering Sea. In addition to the tiny radioactive seed that was driving her so smoothly at a depth of three hundred feet, her crew had one more big ally: the fanciest piece of equipment aboard, the North American Aviation inertial guidance system, or N6A. (The crew called the thing "SFS," for Science Fiction Stuff.) The N6A was an electronic spy, immediately sensing the faintest roll, pitch, or yaw, each turn or change of speed. The data were fed to a computer, which read out the boat's position at any moment.

There were other dazzlers, soon to become routine: three Sperry gyro-compass systems, precision mechanisms; an automatic steering gadget that magically nudged *Nautilus*'s blunt bow along a narrow corridor in the sea; and no fewer than thirteen echo-sounding devices, including an upside-down sonar designed by Waldo Lyon, who was aboard. Lyon's invention aimed upward from a pressure-proof dome mounted on the outer hull and continuously painted a profile of the rugged ice ceiling above (a picture watched by the crew on closed-circuit television). *Nautilus* also carried a regular fathometer, bouncing pinging echoes off the bottom, to measure the soaring sea mounts and deep valleys over which the sub passed, and she sported automatic depth-control equipment that kept her within inches of ordered depth.

All the wonders, however, could not prevent one of the oldest foul-ups in steam engineering, a leak in the condenser system, which developed on the way to Seattle. The crew tried everything, until finally Anderson had a brainstorm. He sent several sailors, in civvies, to assorted gas stations around Seattle to buy up every $1.80 can they could of a product called Stop Leak, which motorists poured into automobile radiators. *Nautilus* received 140 cans of the stuff and, Stop-Leaked to the gills, proceeded on her way.

North she went, ever north—past the islands of the Bering Strait and into the shallow waters of the Chukchi Sea, only 150 feet deep. *Nautilus* measured some fifty feet from keel to sail, and her clearance here, as she headed under the retreating summer ice pack, was narrow indeed. For two days she tried to find a hole in the underwater fence and at last got into the great Barrow Sea Valley running north from the Alaskan coast. On 1 August, off Point Franklin, the navigator, Shepherd Jenks, took his last fix; then *Nautilus* dived and commenced her run of 1830 miles—straight for the pole.

Above her, tremendous icy rams jutted down as much as seventy-five feet, but in her deep trench she kept to a steady pace of twenty knots, four hundred feet down, her jukebox blaring "Purple People Eater" and crooning soft Hawaiian melodies. The ship's newspaper, the whimsically named *Pan-ama-Arctic-Pearl-Arctic Shuttleboat-News*, printed items gleaned earlier from the radio, such as the birth of an engineman's eight-pound baby girl.

In the reactor compartment, upper level shielded from lower by a deck covered in lead and polyethylene, the sealed pumps worked on, unheard by the crew. The pumps ceaselessly moved the primary water in a closed loop through the reactor and two heat exchangers. The water picked up the hot results of the controlled fission reaction and transferred the heat to unpressurized secondary water, which in turn boiled into steam. The steam, in its turn, powered two turbines driving the twin propellers and fed four turbogenerators, from which came the sub's lights, motors, and cooking electricity—her life's blood. Oxygen was kept at a uniform level by bleeding in from bottled stowage tanks around the hull. Burners and scrubbers reduced carbon monoxide and dioxide to very low levels. The temperature inside the hull was a constant seventy-two degrees; officers wore short-sleeved khakis and some of the crew lounged about in their skivvies.

2 August—eighty degrees north, six hundred nautical miles from the pole. Betting pools were organized, for everything from exact time at the pole to the appropriate nickname for transpolar veterans (grotesquely, the name PANOPO—Pacific to Atlantic via North Pole—was chosen). Everyone wrote letters, to be signed once the most northern spot on the planet was reached. Fifteen hundred would eventually be mailed.[3]

3 August, 1000—eighty-seven degrees north, and *Nautilus* passed the farthest point north ever reached by ship. Rapidly the distance dwindled; thirty miles, twenty, ten. . . . Anderson went on the 1MC to speak to the crew; the jukebox was shut off, and a hush fell over the entire boat. "Stand by," announced the skipper, glancing at the distance indicator as he spoke. At 2315, 3 August 1958, they were there: "For the United States and the United States Navy, the North Pole!" Cheers echoed through the crew's mess. Beneath them lay 13,410 feet of good water.

Electrician's Mate First Class James Sordelet came forward to reenlist for six years, the first man to re-up at the pole. A steak dinner and the "North Pole cake" were polished off with gusto. Santa Claus (another engineman in an outfit the quartermasters had rigged from some red flag material and cotton) appeared, a bit out of season.

They did not stop, but headed straight on, ever southerly now, into the open water of the Greenland Sea. In the early-morning hours of 5 August *Nautilus* surfaced, and the Northwest Passage through the pole had been forged at last. Onward she went, headed for Portland, England.

Anderson missed part of the ride; he was picked up by helicopter at sea and a plane carried him from Iceland to Washington, where Dwight Eisenhower decorated him with the Legion of Merit. (Rickover was not invited to the ceremony.) *Nautilus* received the Presidential Unit Citation, the first ever awarded in peacetime.

Her voyage was an underwater saga indeed, technology compounded by daring and courage. At first there were big notions, reworkings of the old visions of a commercial path to the Orient, giant submarines hauling commercial cargo. These would never come to pass, not only because of cost but also because the Arctic waited, as always, to confuse or kill the unwary and the unprepared. But *Nautilus* showed that under-ice Arctic operations were feasible, that the polar undersea area should be charted so missile-packing boats could roam at will beneath their frozen fortress.

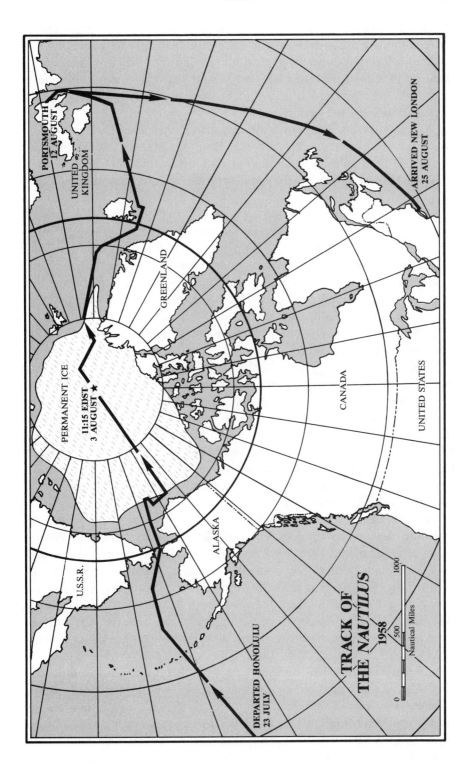

TRACK OF
THE *NAUTILUS*
1958

DEPARTED HONOLULU
23 JULY

PORTSMOUTH
12 AUGUST

ARRIVED NEW LONDON
25 AUGUST

11:15 EDST
3 AUGUST

PERMANENT ICE

UNITED KINGDOM

GREENLAND

CANADA

UNITED STATES

ALASKA

U.S.S.R.

0   500   1000
Nautical Miles

Nautilus and her technology were thus proved, and in spades. Further, her epic was a public-relations triumph of the first dimension, sealing the nascent nuclear Navy into the popular mind. Men like Cartier and Frobisher, Drake and Hudson, and the doomed Franklin had struggled in vain to find the Northwest Passage and a way to the South Sea. Now, Jules Verne's magic submarine lived again.

And more: from a certain position under the polar ice pack, a nuclear submarine could find herself 40 miles from Murmansk, 880 miles from Archangel, 1180 miles from Leningrad, 1420 miles from Moscow. *Nautilus* had done more than prove her technology; she was changing the world.[4]

☆

By 1958, she was not alone. The design and construction of nuclear submarines rested with the Bureau of Ships, of which Rickover's shop was only a part. But the clear superiority of the nuclear technology had been evident to most submariners, and to most of BuShips, almost ten years before. As a result, Rickover's key proposals—the pressurized-water reactor and the land-based prototype—became naval policy with bureaucratic backing.

Nautilus, however, was not a complete, integrated technology; her conventional hull shape worked against her increased speed and maneuverability. BuShips had long studied the problem, and even as *Nautilus* was abuilding, in late 1953, *Albacore* was placed in commission. The design people had considered two fundamental shapes for her: one was a sphere, which offered the least resistance but the most drag; the other, a needlelike configuration, provided minimum drag but had greater resistance because the needle's elongated length exposed more hull surface to water. The answer was a blend of sphere and needle, a blunt-nosed teardrop shape. The experimental, weaponless boat's hull was a body of revolution—any cross section of the hull was a circle.

Albacore was conventionally powered, fitted with a single screw to enable her to use her horsepower more efficiently. In addition to lacking a weapons system, she had neither fire control nor snorkel. Once submerged, she turned out to be as much airplane as submarine. Using a system of winglike, bow-mounted diving planes, an autopilot, and an artificial horizon, she cavorted through the depths like a sleek, barrel-smooth dolphin—banking at sharp thirty-degree angles, pirouetting, gliding smoothly over the ocean floor. After being retrofitted with silver-zinc batteries and contrarotating propellers, she reached the incredible underwater speed of thirty-three knots.

Submariners loved her. BuShips calculated that future boats, built along *Albacore*'s lines and powered by nuclear reactors, could theoretically reach underwater speeds of fifty knots or more, far faster than the most rapid surface ship, excepting only hydroplanes and surface-effect craft. *Albacore* proved that her new "hydrodynamic" shape was the answer, that submarines could be "flown" in three watery dimensions as an airplane flew in air.

She was a smashing success, but a different sort of experiment was not, generating a controversy that never went away. *Seawolf* was designed to test the sodium-cooled-reactor technology. The S2G ("G" for General Electric) reactor began to power *Seawolf* on 21 January 1957, and she was commissioned two months later. The technology had considerable potential, promising much greater operating temperatures and more efficient heat transfer.

At first things went well. The boat's first few thousand miles were trouble-free. She even gave a demonstration dive with Eisenhower aboard. Like *Albacore*, *Seawolf* was sheer experiment. In the fall of 1958, under the lead of the slightly built, crew-cutted Commander Richard Laning, a combat submariner with both Silver and Bronze stars, she spent sixty continuous days under the Atlantic, covering 14,500 nautical miles in the process, never once raising her periscope. Her crew, again specially chosen, passed the time playing bingo, watching daily movies, and working on hobbies such as painting, leather engraving, and model-building. At night the boat was darkened to maintain the rhythms of normal life. One petty officer said upon return to New London that the only things he had missed were "the birth of the hula hoop and the death of the Purple People Eater." "I have been asked about sex on such a cruise," quipped Laning. "Well, we do our best to leave it ashore."

He could not leave the liquid-sodium plant behind, of course; at least in public, he praised its performance. The reactor heat warmed the liquid sodium (which was not radioactive) in a sealed system. The hot sodium flashed into steam, which in turn drove the submarine. But the cost, to Rickover, was too high. The sodium had to be kept liquid constantly; if the material froze in its pipes, they would be ruined. The S2G was a constant worry and sprang at least one superheater leak.

Seawolf's experimental power plant was therefore judged to be not worth the trouble. At Rickover's request, Laning wrote a letter recommending that the sub's power plant be converted to pressurized water. "I've never regretted having to do anything," Laning would later write. In December 1958 *Seawolf* got a pressurized water-cooled S2WA reactor akin to that aboard *Nautilus*. Liquid sodium was dead in the United States Navy, to the rage of its proponents. (Unconfirmed reports of its use, in the French *Rubis* and Soviet *Alfa* classes, would occasionally surface.) Every future American naval reactor would be of the pressurized-water type. Laning himself later admitted that "politics" had resulted in "exaggerated condemnation" of the liquid-sodium reactor.[5]

Next came *Skate*. She was the lead boat of the Navy's first nuclear submarine class, propelled by the S3W/S4W reactor. Electric Boat was the lead yard, and Portsmouth and Mare Island were the follow-on yards. Rickover ensured this division of labor, after a scuffle with Albert Mumma inside BuShips; he would be the man to determine when a yard, Navy or civilian, was ready to build a nuclear ship.

Skate's price tag was $42 million. At first she conducted endurance cruises on the *Seawolf* model—*Skate*'s crew favored games of pinochle and acey-deucey—but her real business was to be a working boat, a nuclear attack submarine. Her performance was good, so good that her skipper, Commander James Calvert, said that driving her "was like playing chess in a dream—with all the queens to start with."

She was not without her own stunts, however. As *Nautilus* headed toward Portland after her trip beneath the Pole, she met *Skate* heading north. *Skate* actually cruised underneath the North Pole for several days, and the following March she came back, to punch through the frozen surface at the pole itself. While there, Calvert conducted an emotional burial service for Sir Hubert Wilkins, who had willed that his remains be taken to the North Pole in a submarine. (Somewhat less emotionally, *Skate*'s navigator called his boat the "first nuclear-powered ice pick.")

There would be three more like her—*Swordfish*, *Sargo*, and *Seadragon*—each of almost three thousand tons, twin-screwed, with eight 21-inch torpedo tubes. Together they composed the Navy's first class of nuclear-powered attack boats, and the Navy rapidly found that some people did not share its growing attachment to nuclear power. As *Skate* returned from her first polar cruise, for example. Denmark's prime minister announced that *Skate*'s scheduled call at Copenhagen would not be allowed. Denmark's grand old man of nuclear physics, Niels Bohr, had warned his government that, should the submarine have a serious harbor accident, dangerous radioactive materials might be released. England revealed that *Nautilus* was welcome in Portland but refused to let her venture up the Thames to London. Despite Rickover's dynamic emphasis on safety and the Navy's notion that these foreign strictures were only a kind of nuclear-age Luddite behavior, such concerns, particularly in Europe and Japan, would continue to dog the Navy's nuclear program.

In the meantime, though, still flank speed. *Triton* was a giant like her namesake (the son of Poseidon and Amphitrite), almost seven thousand tons, designed for high-speed surface operations as a radar picket for a task force. To complete this triple-decked leviathan cost $109 million, almost three times the price of *Skate*. *Triton* featured not one but two nuclear reactors.

Under the command of Ned Beach, a captain now and given the boat after service as Eisenhower's naval aide, *Triton* was assigned a mission to match her size. On 16 February 1960 she got underway on the "greatest shakedown cruise in naval history." Two-and-a-half hours out of New London she dove at the thirty-fathom line; for nearly three months she did not surface again. During this time, her ballast tanks holding the weight of water displaced by an entire World War I fleet submarine, she passed the Rocks of St. Peter and St. Paul, desolate outposts six hundred miles off the coast of Brazil; rounded Cape Horn; drove past Easter Island across the Pacific;

on the leg between Hawaii and Guam went near the spot where her fore-runner had been lost in 1943, victim of a Japanese depth-charge attack; passed on through the Philippines, the Makassar Straits, and the Indian Ocean; rounded the Cape of Good Hope; and passed St. Peter and St. Paul again.

Beach prosaically logged in: "First submerged circumnavigation of the world is now complete." (A critically ill sailor suffering from kidney stones had to put ashore at Montevideo.) All told, another Navy spectacular. Magellan had been at the mercy of the wind, current, and weather; for eighty-four days *Triton* had not once felt the fury of sea or sky, her crew sealed within a steel bubble of life support. She did not see, nor was she seen.[6]

Everything—nuclear power, teardrop hull, the complete technology—at last came together in *Skipjack*. She was both sinister looking and beautiful, every line suggesting power, grace, and speed. On returning from sea trials in 1959 her skipper, Commander William Behrens, Jr., joked "give her a Simoniz job and I'll buy her." Because a vendor could not meet standards for main coolant pumps for her new S5W reactor, her trials had been delayed for over a year, but once underway, *Skipjack* frolicked like *Albacore*. For the first time, nuclear propulsion and a streamlined hull had been combined in a submarine.

Her first keel was laid in 1955, but Sputnik went into orbit before her completion. The resulting strategic crash-dive by American planners led to lengthening her hull to produce the first Polaris missile submarine, *George Washington*. In her second incarnation, *Skipjack* went faster, around thirty-five knots, and dove deeper than any previous submarine. The men who ran her boasted that she was the smoothest-handling submarine anywhere.

Skipjack's technology was so good that the British were interested. True to form, Rickover did not want to share information (he even refused to let Lord Mountbatten, the First Sea Lord, aboard *Nautilus*), but he was over-ruled. The Atomic Energy Act was duly amended in March 1958, and the British purchased *Skipjack*'s S5W reactor system. Although the two countries continued to exchange information and Britain kept on with its own naval reactor project, America's strongest ally now had a leg up on a nuclear navy of its own. Rickover, dragging his heels all the way, even insisted that he personally control the assignment of British officers to nuclear power posts—a proposal that Mountbatten quickly killed.

There would be other experiments with nuclear submarines: *Halibut* was designed as a missile-shooter for Regulus II but armed with Regulus I. *Tullibee* was a single-screw hunter-killer in which Rickover substituted an electric-drive system for reduction gears (silence in submarine warfare was golden), in which the sonar was placed far forward, away from the boat's self-generated noise, and in which the torpedo tubes were amidships, angled outward from the centerline—*Tullibee* proved herself the quietest nuclear platform in the Navy. *Narwhal* was built to evaluate a quieter version of the S5G reactor. And *Glenard P. Lipscomb* had a turbine-electric propulsion system that sacrificed speed to reduce noise.[7]

But by 1960 the Navy had produced the four-boat *Skate* class and the six *Skipjacks;* nuclear propulsion was becoming assembly-line. The polyglot first generation of nuclear submarines, along with the playful *Albacore*, had accomplished wonders. The adventure of the sea, of the golden age of exploration, had been rejuvenated (*Nautilus, Skate,* and *Triton*); strategic formulations were being recast (*Nautilus, Skate,* a half dozen other boats); crew endurance had been tested (*Seawolf, Triton*); and a new underwater body had been born (*Albacore, Skipjack*). Above all, the nuclear Navy was a proven entity.

On 9 July 1960 the lead boat in yet another new class of nuclear attack submarines was launched. Her name was *Thresher*.

☆

The boats were called "Nukes." So, too, were the men who manned them. And Hyman Rickover chose the men. Building a fleet of nuclear ships required him to interact with many other "codes," or sections, in the Bureau of Ships and throughout the rest of the Navy. He adamantly insisted on his continuing responsibilities for all new nuclear power plants and for their safe operation at sea, and thus his influence, ever-broadening, ever more powerful, grew horizontally throughout the service.

In 1955 he had become Code 1500 in BuShips, but the numerical designation made no difference; what counted was the influence. In that year Albert Mumma became chief of BuShips, and he and Rickover clashed mightily at every level of the nuclear program. But Rickover won a decree from Mumma establishing Code 1500 as the "assistant chief for nuclear propulsion." Now Rickover was no longer subordinate to the assistant chief for building and maintenance—one more bureaucratic fetter broken.

Rickover was in complete control of contractual arrangements, fixed-price rather than cost-plus. He demanded that every manufacturer of reactor cores do all the work in company plants, saving the government millions of dollars. And he skillfully arranged that contracts were negotiated and administered, under his civilian hat, from within the Atomic Energy Commission, not only to position himself away from Mumma's control or that of anyone else who ran BuShips, but also to ensure that core fabrication would not fall within the Navy's sometimes deficient procurement system.

By 1960 Rickover had gained considerable vertical control as well, overseeing all phases of reactor design and production. He was virtually independent of the commission in his Navy hat and virtually independent of the Navy in the crucial contracting process. He had at his fingertips a completely novel administrative instrument.

The new technology demanded the utmost from its men; Rickover scorned "pump room fever," submariners wasting time on inconsequential trivia that rightfully belonged to professional study. He endlessly bullied the monthly Submarine Conferences along his own charted course, "a pure technician, uninterested in the strategic or political role of the new weapon, and not at all reluctant to discourage contrary thoughts by others."

"Man's work begins with his job, or profession," preached Rickover. This meant more than punching a timeclock: "One must guard against banality, ineptitude, incompetence, and mediocrity. . . . It is a device of the devil to let sloth into the world." For him, "the deepest joy in life is to be creative," and the enemy was "any man whose only concern about the world is that it stay in one piece during his own lifetime." To struggle against this enemy, and against apathy and indifference, was "to find purpose in life."

Rickover was an apostle with a guaranteed audience. From the beginning he modeled the Nuclear Reactors Branch on his experiences with the Electrical Section during the war, emphasizing complete thoroughness in training, knowledge, and safety. From the beginning the officers he drew to him were ordered to self-educate intensively in all phases of reactor technology. He micromanaged their formal courses of study. He got many of them assigned to MIT for advanced training, men like Edwin Kintner, who later oversaw the development of Mark I out at Arco. He prodded civilian engineers from Electric Boat to Oak Ridge. No one was exempt.

And Rickover's trainees trained others—reactor theory, shielding, basic physics and mathematics. He was a born teacher (as long as the instruction was done *his* way), and he devoted copious amounts of time to training. Every question, every problem left unresolved was never too small for him to give his fullest attention. He was far from claiming omniscience and constantly relied on the expertise of others (if they had the goods), but he was omnipresent; *his* way saturated the entire nuclear program.

In meetings with his juniors, Rickover expected every man to stand his ground and battle for his ideas. This type of intense training regimen was intended to produce intellectual self-reliance, and did so; he was culling some of the finest minds in the fleet, and together they boosted the nuclear Navy ahead by leaps and bounds. They were the ones who hounded the contractors, reported discrepancies, kept the technology moving forward.

And once he got them, he wanted to keep them. "The same man should have the job from its inception, through design, construction and operation," he maintained. He loathed the Navy's policy of periodic transfers and its cultivation of the "jack-of-all-trades" officer: "We should at once knock off this infernal rotation of military people." Of supreme importance to him, the country was misdirecting its youth, not training them to *think* within the demands of modern technology. The Naval Academy, unsurprisingly, was his favorite target: "Midshipmen are quite immature in their attitudes. . . . Instead of using these very impressionable years . . . to train them for a serious adult occupation, the Academy authorities treat them as adolescents, and they react accordingly."

This dire situation meant that once a midshipman graduated, "he will, in nine cases out of ten, stop thinking and studying." He would be stymied by "problems" with which a thinking man should be able to cope. "I view with horror the day the Navy is induced to place psychiatrists aboard our nuclear submarines," Rickover told a House Subcommittee on Appropriations. "We are doing very well without them because the men don't know they have problems. But, once a psychiatrist is assigned, they will learn that they have lots of problems."[8]

Hyman Rickover saw himself as an educator, a trainer of men, even before he was a naval officer. He would put the Nukes to school—his kind of school.

☆

Traditional submarine training involved rigorous physical and psychological screening procedures; standard drills in the decompression chamber; emergency escapes (hairy watery ascents wearing Momsen lungs); drilling in submarine architecture such as ballast tanks, fuel tanks, pumps, and valves; pinpoint written exams; and sea training aboard diesel-electrics stationed at New London for that purpose, boats like *Sarda*, *Toro*, *Dogfish*, and *Piper*. If the men did not wash out (and many did), boats were waiting for them in New London, Norfolk, Key West, San Diego, Pearl Harbor—and so were their much-prized dolphin badges. After about another year of tough on-board training, a young officer would find his gold dolphins at the bottom of a ten-ounce glass of whiskey. (The enlisted men's were silver.)

All this was very well, but Rickover, of course, had a better way. He had to fight the old Navy conflict between line officer and engineer, the former contemptuous of the greasy snipe, the latter disdainful of those who commanded but knew little of the machinery that drove their ships. In 1899 the old distinction between the line officer and the engineer had vanished, at least on paper, but the gap was still there. Rickover was out not to bridge the difference but to weld the gap shut, to make sure line officers *knew* their plants from the inside out.

Operational safety was Rickover's leitmotiv in this crusade. During the workup of *Nautilus*, for example, his organization prescribed the operating procedures and limits every step of the way. Only Rickover could break these when he wanted to, as he did the day *Nautilus* originally got underway on nuclear power. No one questioned his full authority over matters of operational safety. In 1957 an amendment to the Atomic Energy Act ensured that his strident voice in these matters would be heard and acted on throughout the nuclear Navy. By the next year, Code 1500 also had gained two other crucial areas of dominance: port entry for nuclear ships and, of utmost importance, the selection, training, and assignment of their personnel.

One experienced nuclear submariner put the matter this way: Nukes were to diesel-electrics as modern automobiles were to bicycles. Like bicycles, diesel-electrics were slow, short-legged, and very uncomfortable, especially if you stayed aboard them a long time; they were also relatively simple in design, easy to repair, and somewhat forgiving in actual practice— even at times rewarding the dexterity and daring of their operators. Nukes, by contrast, were fast, long-legged, and luxurious beyond previous submarine experience. But they, like automobiles, were extremely complex, required numerous highly honed skills for maintenance and repair, and needed to be operated with caution and precision.

Rickover was given to complaining that most submariners, conditioned to the more relaxed and free-lancing old ways, were too stupid and unimaginative to see the future. Indeed, most of them would be unceremoniously barred from the Nuke community. Rickover wanted new blood, his kind of blood, and he was transfusing from the keelplates up.

He was lucky that Vice Admiral James Holloway, Jr. was the chief of naval personnel from 1953 to 1958. Holloway's role in the drawdown back in the late forties was only one of several assignments that had given him considerable expertise in manpower matters. He saw clearly what Rickover was trying to do and agreed with the concept that all line officers aboard should be eligible for command. Therefore, the corollary ensued: all line officers aboard a nuclear submarine had to be nuclear-trained.

Holloway was charged by law with selecting and assigning naval personnel. He agreed to let Rickover interview and recommend candidates for nuclear training, but he reserved for BuPers the right to make selections. Rickover immediately rejected several applicants, just to let Holloway feel from which direction the wind was blowing, although he later accepted them. *Rickover* was the nuclear expert, the hurdle all Nukes had to clear, and in practice the wind blew constant from this quarter.

Then there was the traditional sub training at New London, also Holloway's bailiwick. Rickover got the academics there overhauled from stem to stern, adding elementary calculus, basic physics, electrical theory, thermodynamics, reactor systems, chemistry, metallurgy, even health physics. Officers got a more intense dosage than enlisted men. The nuclear power school at New London opened for business in January 1956 (Mare Island followed two years later); after shakedown, the attrition rates ran about 3 percent for officers and 10 to 20 percent for enlisted. "It's like getting a $20,000 education," said one sailor who lasted the course.

Everyone then went through prototype training, if not at Arco then at the various other prototypes that were becoming available. This particular aspect of training was the most obvious difference between the bicycle and the automobile. The six-month prototype ordeal was far from pleasant: the regimen was as realistic as possible, the instructors were driven men, and the attitude was one of no-nonsense determination. Prospective commanding officers like Bill Anderson and Jim Calvert were not spared; in fact, they underwent the most pressure. In the corridors of each of the nuclear power and prototype schools was the legend "In this school the smartest work as hard as those who must struggle to pass. H. G. Rickover."

Less formally, his motto was "Get 'em young and train 'em right."

☆

—Get 'em young. In 1957 Code 1500 required its Nuke enlisted men to be high school graduates and volunteers. They had to obligate for at least forty months. (Rickover would have preferred a lifetime.) Eventually, the nuclear power schools and prototypes began to turn these high-schoolers into reliable technicians.

—Get 'em young. Rickover bore in on his officer selectees, the men who would actually run the nuclear Navy. Beginning with *Nautilus*, he himself scrutinized records of individual officers and called them in for personal interviews. In the late fifties the cadre of officer Nukes was still small; he knew them all, had worked with some of them, like Wilkinson, for years, and had some kind of personal relationship—never intimate, seldom even friendly—with each man.

The first interviews featured Rickover's sudden, sharp probes from unexpected angles. Bill Anderson was asked: "Anderson. Name the books and authors you have read in the last two years. Don't mention anything you have read in the last month." When the amiable, easygoing Anderson (he had heard Rickover was looking for hard chargers) fumbled around, coming up with only one book, forgetting the author's name in the process, Rickover frowned and abruptly said good-bye. Anderson thought his goose was cooked, but with Rickover, as he and hundreds of other Nukes could testify, one could never tell. Anderson, like many in the first generation of Nukes, became a devout Rickover loyalist:

> . . . Everyone just naturally falls in behind Rickover and tries to keep up. The Admiral is instinctively one of the greatest leaders I have ever known. No one in [the Naval Reactors Branch] is ever ordered to do anything. All major decisions are made by a panel of Rickover's top experts. He inspires intense loyalty in the men and women around him.

Rickover was looking for people with a feel for technology, convinced that technical qualifications were supreme in the new naval universe he was doing so much to shape. Personnel selection was therefore crucial. As the Nuke community grew apace, the interview process took on the dimensions of a full-scale concert, Rickover always the unpredictable, terrible-tempered maestro. Usually the candidate would undergo three preliminary interviews with officers and civilians on Rickover's staff. These men tried to calm the candidate down (the ordeal was viewed by almost every victim as a trial by fire) and to sense whether he could handle the intense academic and practical program, which was now moving toward two years in duration before the graduates ever got to sea.[9]

The preliminary interviewers, who had the candidate's basic data before them, tended to concentrate on technical orientation, forcefulness, commitment to the Navy, and, above all, innate intelligence. Then in to see Rickover, who viewed with contempt anyone he thought was trying to softsoap his way through, to reap the rewards of the program (financial bonuses would eventually be involved) while trying to shaft the Navy. The admiral looked for some Nelsonian spark, some hint of originality, a clue that the candidate was imaginative and carried his own scissors for red tape.

At least, that was the politest face that could be given to being put on the rack by Hyman Rickover. In fact, the "interview," a Chinese water torture to be endured by would-be Nuke officers for a quarter-century, rapidly became the Nuke version of tales told round (nuclear) campfires: "When I was interviewed by Rickover. . . ."

The Rickover interview (the Nukes sarcastically called him the "KOG"—Kindly Old Gentleman) was a living autopsy, in which the candidate's flesh was metaphorically, systematically flayed, very slowly and in very small strips indeed. As with Anderson, a man might be asked about books he had read; Rickover would send his secretary to the library to check the answers. One commander's record showed he was his college's salutatorian; very nice, said Rickover, but why was he not number one? Rickover asked them about their hobbies; those unfortunate enough to admit to a singing voice would be ordered to perform on the spot.

The ordeal was often humiliating in the extreme, and meant to be so. A young Annapolis product named Jimmy Carter, asked about his class standing, proudly replied fifty-ninth out of 820. Did you do your best? asked Rickover. Carter gulped and shamefacedly replied, "No, sir, I didn't always do my best." Why not? asked Rickover. Carter, shaken, sat there for a while and then slowly left.

He interviewed midshipman candidates over Christmas break ("the man who stole Christmas"), advised young men not to marry, to give their all to the program and forget about chasing girls; and asked them who should be executed, a Nuke or a street cleaner. (Answer: the street cleaner, because anyone could sweep streets, but a street cleaner could never do the job of a Nuke.)

The KOG was a sardonic, pitiless inquisitor, not quite Dostoyevskian but close enough, the champion of the unexpected—anything to put the screws to a man. "Piss me off if you can," he told one candidate, whereupon the midshipman swept everything off the admiral's desk—ship models, souvenirs, paper—immediately producing a screeching little macaw. Some candidates never got that far, struggling to keep their balance in a chair whose front legs had been shortened. A few were ordered to stand in a nearby broom closet to contemplate their sins.

Part of this was sheer sadistic bullying, an ornery, contrary streak in Rickover's personality, a compulsive viciousness that fed on the weak and the unprepared. But part was his never-ending urge to find the best, to mold them in his image of excellence. And he did not stop with the youngsters. He needed them, they were the future, and most of them—Jimmy Carter, the mid who pissed him off, the veterans of the shortened chair and the broom closet—were accepted. But he needed more senior officers, too. No love was lost between Rickover and the veterans of the diesel-electrics, but he had to have some of them in the upper echelons of seagoing command, at least until his own breed could rise to the top. Thus men like Wilkinson, Anderson, Laning, Beach, and Behrens, in spite of their superior records, underwent their own trials by fire.

But many of the more senior men to pass before Rickover were unceremoniously jettisoned, and the rancor generated therefrom endured the passage of years. For command of one of the first nuclear submarines, he asked the Bureau of Personnel to send over the three best conventional sub skippers around; after he put them to the inquisition, he thought they were pretty bad. He asked for three more—same result. Finally he demanded the man who had sent him these six turkeys, and Jim Calvert showed up, to go on to command *Skate* and upward to flag rank.

With the nuclear Navy expanding apace, Nuke officers were urgently needed. The reservoir of qualified young diesel-electric submariners was steadily shrinking as the conventional boats went the way of the dinosaur. After the *Tangs* and the SSKs, conventional construction was not even desultory. There were the single-shafted "T" class (1953), *Mackerel* and *Marlin;* the twin-shafted *Sailfish* and her sister, *Salmon* (1955–1956); the Regulus II *Grayback* (1957); *Darter* (1956), an improved *Tang; Growler*, an improved *Grayback;* and the three "B-girls"—*Barbel, Blueback,* and *Bonefish.* With the launching of the experimental deep-diving submarine *Dolphin* in 1968, the United States Navy came to the end of the line with its diesel-electrics; everything was Nuke.

Thus the pressure on young men to go Nuke was stepped up. By the late 1950s Holloway and his successor at BuPers, Vice Admiral William Smedberg, allowed newly commissioned officers from the Academy and NROTC units to apply for direct entry into the Nuclear Power Program; previously, two years at sea had been required. By the early 1960s future ensigns were being "requested" to go to Washington to be pilloried by Rickover. Eventually, nonvolunteers from the surface forces had to be ordered to take Nuke training.

The surface nuclear Navy—*Enterprise, Long Beach, Bainbridge*—was growing as well, not as fast as the submarine Nukes but enough to cause alarm. These officers, junior and senior, had to pass through Rickover's office. One of them was a hotshot young commander named Elmo ("Bud") Zumwalt, who wanted command of *Bainbridge*, the Navy's first nuclear-powered destroyer. Two nuclear slots were open, the top job on *Bainbridge* and the exec's position on *Long Beach*, the first nuclear-powered cruiser.

Zumwalt was greeted by this observation from Rickover: "Everyone who interviewed you tells me you are extremely conservative and have no initiative or imagination" (irony indeed, in view of what was to come). Zumwalt was then exiled to the "tank," a room barren of everything but a bare table and a chair. Recalled, he was asked about his class standings and study habits. Shouting, Rickover asked Zumwalt to name one famous man who could argue either side of a question. Clarence Darrow, Zumwalt replied, in the Leopold and Loeb case.

"You are absolutely wrong!" the little macaw yelled. "I warn you here and now you better not try to talk to me about anything you don't know anything about. I know more about almost anything than you do and I know one helluva lot more about Darrow than you do. I warn you, you better stop trying to snow me!"

—Back to the tank. (A sympathetic officer handed Zumwalt a sandwich.) Then more questions, about the Naval Academy curriculum (a pet whipping post of Rickover's), about Plato, about anything. Back again to the tank. Then into the presence a third time: more raving, ridicule of Zumwalt's study habits, and personal questions about his family.

Zumwalt was selected, but deeply angered by this treatment and not wanting to risk the exec's slot on *Long Beach*, instead took command of the conventionally powered guided missile destroyer *Dewey*. Thus did a future chief of naval operations meet Hyman Rickover, inaugurating a grating tale that would be spun out over almost twenty years. Some of the candidates, of course, were without Bud Zumwalt's talent and drive; for them, being cursed and humiliated by Rickover produced lasting scars, perhaps even driving a few from the Navy.[10]

Rickover did not care; he was getting 'em young, and by 1960 his kind of men were coming out of the training pipeline and running the boats. Moving faster and deeper than ever before, the Nukes maneuvered their subs in icy blackness for weeks at a time, strapped into bucket seats, manning airplanelike stick-and-wheel controls while the rest of the crew clung to overhead straps like so many subway riders. Their psychological profiles were just short of cookie-cutter, tending to be uniform: "loves a challenge . . . strong taste for adventure . . . enjoys the discipline, efficiency and teamwork of a smoothly functioning, compact military group." Almost all of them were married, despite Rickover's strictures about chasing women; lots of children, low divorce rate. They were the products, not only of

Hyman Rickover but also of a program which turned them inside out to identify the physically healthy, emotionally stable, and psychologically motivated—something called "Submarine Medicine."

—And they knew they were changing the Navy.

☆

Nuclear power had the capacity "to do our military jobs with fewer ships, planes, and men." Rickover's shop preached the gospel not only of technology but also of efficiency. "[Nuclear power's] effect on sea power will be profound." "We stand with our backs to the end of an era at sea," wrote one submariner, "facing the beginning of another." An "entirely new era in the art of warfare at sea" had arrived, announced another, and whether the United States Navy was ready or not, the fleet must ride the wave.[11]

Hyman Rickover was not only riding the wave, he was generating the predominant proportion. The "Navy's authority on nuclear submarines" was up for promotion again in 1958; "the Rickover development team is a priceless national asset we cannot afford to lose," declared the *Saturday Evening Post*. The Joint Committee on Atomic Energy, infuriated by the White House snub of Rickover on the occasion of *Nautilus*'s polar exploits, chimed in. In 1958 Rickover became a vice admiral, with more security and leverage than ever.

The future seemed limitless. Nuclear or not, the submarine's main defense was still its ability to submerge, to hide in the ocean depths. The Nuke boats could do this indefinitely, and they vastly increased underwater load capacities to boot. They seemed ideal for exploitation of the Arctic, for strategic purposes and otherwise, and for loitering off an enemy's harbors, lurking unseen, potentially lethal.

For some, they sounded the death knell of the surface Navy. They were, in this view, the new "capital ships," heirs to all that was lasting in Mahanian thought. The time was quickly coming, predicted Vice Admiral Charles Momsen (he of the Momsen lung), "when the surface Navy will be turned into obsolete hulks by submarines." Momsen's was not a majority voice by any means, but his words held the edge of euphoria, of the overwhelming triumphs of a new technology:

> The lesson is clear. We must completely rewrite the textbooks on naval warfare. The entire Navy will have to go under water. That's where tomorrow's great sea battles will be fought and won. Otherwise, they will be most assuredly lost.

—*The entire Navy will have to go under water.* To be sure, the practice attacks indicated that the nuclear submarine had become a deadly menace to surface vessels. But the Nukes were far from a perfect technology. Their auxiliary machinery was extremely noisy, forcing Rickover into experiments like *Tullibee, Narwhal,* and *Glenard P. Lipscomb.* Communicating with them, absolutely critical in the case of the emerging Polaris fleet, was never a lock and was the more difficult the deeper they got and the faster they ran. Although reactor radiation proved, with Rickover's exacting safety standards, to be a minor menace, carbon monoxide poisoning was not. Any gas leakage, say of a refrigerant, during a long underwater cruise could produce respiratory problems (this happened aboard both *Nautilus* and *Seawolf*). And particularly foreboding in light of what was to come, the deeper water in which they operated produced enormous strains on interior piping.

Further, as *Nautilus*'s experiences with the British and *Skate*'s with the Danes proved, the Nukes were not universally welcomed. When Holy Loch, Scotland, was announced as the first overseas base for the Polaris boats, demonstrators in leaky dinghies and canoes unsuccessfully tried to impede entry of the submarine tender *Proteus* and the first of her brood, *Patrick Henry.* [12]

These were but teething problems to Rickover; once the safety and reliability of the technology was accepted, all would be well. His plate was full, anyway, well beyond preparing the follow-on reactor systems for the attack boats. Reactors for surface ships had to be designed. At least for the moment, the successes of *Nautilus* and her sisters had committed not only the Navy but also the entire nation to the development of light-water reactor systems.

Rickover was helping oversee the installation and running of the reactor at Shippingport, Pennsylvania, the nation's first civilian nuclear power plant. By 1958 Shippingport gave him an international reputation, among civilians as well as military men. Shippingport demonstrated not only the feasibility of using pressurized-water technology for civilian application; the reactor also showed the potential of "breeding," a process by which more nuclear fuel was produced than consumed. And everywhere—with the boats, the Nuke surface ships, the civilians—Rickover and his men stressed technological discipline, efficiency, and safety. He personally interviewed former naval enlisted men for employment at Shippingport, the only time he deployed his scathing technique against enlisted, with the exception of the crew of *NR-1,* a small nuclear-powered research submarine.

The ships themselves, the "Atomic Fleet" so hyped by the media, provided the Navy with a public relations bonanza. Naval officials admitted that the cost was high, but they argued that economies of scale would take hold once experimental phases had passed and classes of nuclear boats and ships were being produced. *Long Beach* was budgeted at $87.5 million, which could have underwritten an entire World War II carrier task force and then some. A nuclear-powered carrier striking force, already in the works, was estimated, very conservatively, to cost 40 percent more than a conventional force of the same size. But the extra price was being paid; by 1957 Congress had signed on for thirty seagoing reactors and six land-bound experimental prototypes.

The Atomic Fleet was to be backboned by atomic-bomb-carrying eighty-five-thousand-ton supercarriers, by fast-striking, guided-missile cruisers and destroyers, and by specially designed submarines for a smorgasbord of missions: high-speed attack, hunter-killer, radar-picket, guided-missile, the works. By 1958 over $2 billion had been spent or programmed for the research, development, and construction of this fleet. One officer estimated that "another $500,000,000-a-year for at least eight years ahead will be needed to bring it into full being."

Breathtaking numbers, matched by breathtaking results. "In a very real sense," said Under Secretary of the Navy William Franke in 1957, "we have begun construction of a new Navy as revolutionary . . . as were the first four steel ships of 'The New Navy' in the days of Chester A. Arthur."[13]

BuShips was on board; Albert Mumma, who never completely made his peace with Rickover (no head of the bureau ever would), nevertheless predicted that by 1963 the United States would be well on its way to a "complete nuclear fleet," with weapons to match. In 1958 work began on the gargantuan nuclear supercarrier *Enterprise*, a project initially budgeted at $314 million. The keel for *Long Beach* had been laid the previous December; she was expected to be the lead ship of a host of nuclear-powered, guided-missile cruisers. There was talk of nuclear submarine tankers, nuclear container ships, nuclear cruise liners.

By 1967, 2500 officers and 14,000 enlisted men had passed through the schools and prototypes and become Nukes. The Atomic Energy Commission and the Navy, together, had by that time invested $13 billion in the nuclear Navy, paying in the process for 223 reactor cores, of varying types and for varying purposes. Along the way, Rickover's team had established ties with over five hundred civilian contractors, ranging from Electric Boat to virtual backyard garages specializing in the tiniest component parts. By 1967, a decade after Franke sensed revolution, there would be three nuclear-powered surface warships and sixty-six nuclear submarines, with dozens more on the way.

Since that day in 1955 when Wilkinson had signaled "underway on nuclear power," said two analysts, "the Navy has never looked back, but has steamed full ahead on nuclear power." This was far from true; orders for conventionally powered surface ships of all types continued apace. But the submarine Navy *was* remade, and in a sensationally short time.

Perhaps "building a nuclear fleet surpassed the original development of the atomic bomb." Certainly the scope of the technology and the speed of its creation outlined the parameters of revolution. Almost seven years elapsed between the first test of a jet engine in England and the completion of the first operational jet fighters, and part of this occurred under the press of war. Rickover and his team, starting in a time of exceptionally austere budgets, had *Nautilus,* a far more complex technology, underway in six years. The support for the Naval Reactors Branch had been generous but never open-ended; by 1963 the total cost of the thirty naval nuclear reactors then operating was only 20 percent of the amount expended for naval shipbuilding and conversion in that year alone.

The Nukes were undoubtedly on their way. An enormous industry for supplying nuclear equipment had been born; the Naval Reactors Branch had pioneered in unprecedented methods for establishing precision machining, quality control, and production administration; and a technically trained manpower base, not just for the Navy but also for the growing civilian nuclear power industry in the United States, had come into being.

Hyman Rickover, Nuke of Nukes, bore Congress, the Joint Committee on Atomic Energy, much of the Atomic Energy Commission, and an increasing number of Navymen along in his wake, propelled by his integrity, technical honesty, and accent on people rather than bureaucratic process. By 1962, he had been in place in BuShips, increasingly independent and powerful, for fifteen years. During that time there had been seven secretaries of defense, nine secretaries of the Navy, seven chiefs of naval operations, six heads of BuShips, seven chiefs of naval personnel, and five chairmen of the Atomic Energy Commission. And Rickover would be in place for almost two more decades.[14]

The Nukes thus had longevity and technical expertise where longevity and technical expertise counted, and they had these things up to the gunwales. Above all, their proof was in the pudding—they were the technical success story par excellence of the postwar Navy.

STERN WATCH III

———— ☆ ————

I n the fifteen or so years after V-J Day, the technological Navy aged even
as the fleet was renovating itself. Stasis was an impossible technological
position to maintain, even if anyone had wanted to. If many of the *Essex*-
class carriers were still around, the supercarriers were on the scene; if propeller-driven planes were not quite obsolete, the jets had clearly won the
day; if the old destroyers still proudly sported their guns, the missile-shooters
had emerged; if some diesel-electrics would linger on, fading shadows of
their wartime glories, the Nuke boats now swept the field. And, of course,
there was the atomic bomb, by 1960 a component of the fleet's weaponry.

The technological development not only flashed forward but accelerated,
with bewildering speed. Some systems, such as the T-birds, were rushed
into operation before they were technically mature, such was the urge to
get them to sea. Others, like the supercarriers, were built more firmly on
what had gone before and were instant successes. The advent of truly reliable
electronic equipment, from radars through electronic countermeasures gear
to sonars, along with the introduction of the computer, was probably a more
radical development than any weapons system.

Much of this relentless advance, despite the speed, was conservative, in
the sense, say, that smaller aircraft carriers gave way to larger ones or that
guns made room for missiles. But much, like the computer and the Nuke
boats, was truly revolutionary. Technology, while spawned by men, proved
as ever to be a most potent creative force in itself.

—So potent, in fact, that the miraculous scientific achievements tended
to overshadow wider perspectives. C.P. Snow had posited the "two cultures,"
those of the arrogant scientist and the ignorant humanist, and had argued
that any government would subsidize that which best served its own interests. There was but the shortest step between government's basic interest
in science and support for the technology of war. Moreover, "[Science] . . . is
not wise," wrote the philosopher John Randall. "It does not discriminate
what is worth doing." But these were far from Navy views; better, constantly
better, was assumed to be the governing logic. One Tennessee congressman
had put the case back in 1882, while considering the Navy's first steel ships,

that a naval buildup should await that stage where "perfection . . . will present a model that we may safely adopt." Now there was no wait.[1]

Naval technology wore blinders, moving inexorably forward with its purpose largely confined to the "perfecting" of the weapons systems themselves. In the final analysis, however, all the ships, planes, missiles, and the rest were weapons *only*. They had the potential for causing more problems on the wider scale than they resolved on the narrower. "Man's moral nature dwindles as his machines increase in power," noted the architect Frank Lloyd Wright. "He has possession now of a means he has not been educated to exercise. He is more deadly now and no more competent morally than he was in the days of the Egyptians." Harry Truman agreed, saying that "machines are ahead of morals by some centuries."

Yet Truman oversaw, among other things, the beginning of the technological reshaping of the postwar Navy. Men made technology, and then found themselves virtual prisoners of their creations. "The maddening thing about a technological improvement," wrote the Civil War historian Bruce Catton, "is that it must be used to the limit. . . . We are made helpless by our own omnipotence."[2]

The crux of the matter was that military technology, so mysterious and so fearful, was yet so *necessary*. This was an old problem, as Thomas Hobbes, writing in an England recently riven by internal conflict, had glimpsed:

> Arts of public use, as fortification, making of engines, and other instruments of war, because they confer to defence, and victory, are power: and though the true mother of them be science, namely the mathematics, yet, because they are brought into the light, by the hand of the artificer, they be esteemed, the midwife passing with the vulgar for the mother, as his issue.

—"Because they confer to defence, and victory. . . ." Thus were the moral and technological joined, as Snow noted, in ageless debate. "Our trust is not in the devices of material equipment," claimed the Athenian statesman Pericles, "but in our own good spirits for battle." Of course, naval love of new technology for technology's sake was never total; many Navymen were repulsed by the idea of the atomic bomb; there was always an argument for smaller (and thus more) carriers; and the diesel-electrics continued to have their ardent champions. Some weapons were too vile for almost anybody; Fleet Admiral Leahy, thoroughly shocked, avowed that gas warfare would "violate every Christian ethic I have ever heard of and all of the known laws of war."

Yet even here, in the nightmare's world of chemical and biological weapons, the Navy played a part. In 1950 two minesweepers chuffed back and forth outside the Golden Gate Bridge making mock attacks on San Francisco (six of them), releasing clouds of a spray contaminated with *Bacillus globigii* and *Serratia marescens,* two supposedly harmless bacteria. Over 117 square miles of the Bay Area were judged "contaminated."

The following year, naval personnel deliberately contaminated ten wooden boxes with *Bacillus globigii, Serratia marescens,* and another wonder called *Aspergillus fumigatus* before the boxes were shipped from Pennsylvania to Norfolk, to test how easily disease "might" spread among people handling the boxes. (*Aspergillus fumigatus* was chosen because black workers in Norfolk were believed to be particularly susceptible to the strain.) There were also experiments with binary nerve gas weapons, devices that kept different chemical compounds apart in inert form until the firing of a shell fused them, forming a nerve agent. By the mid-sixties, a binary bomb had been designed.[3]

Lethality upon lethality, horror upon horror, all in the name of national defense, and victory. Only when the blinders were on, when the outside world was choked off, could the technology be most fully appreciated, pristine and creative, as Robert Oppenheimer had said of the A-bomb: "technologically sweet." "It is a 'stubborn and irreducible' truth of natural science," wrote an arch-critic of the Navy, the historian Charles Beard, "established as far beyond debate as anything known to man, that tools, implements, machines, and chemical substances will operate as calculated by their projectors and managers only when all the factors of material significance have been taken into the reckoning—that is, when no important factors of upsetting capacity are left out of the picture." World War II had spawned an enormous American industrial base, in electronics, petrochemical synthetics, steel, and nuclear power, among a multitude of such developments. Such overarching materialism, in the United States, unavoidably meant profit and private enterprise, capitalism unadorned, and therefore the concern of the Navy for the very latest in weapons technology radiated through the entire culture.

Unfortunately, what seemed to be the imperatives of technology—a stronger national military, the potential of victory if required—defined only what was *possible;* these did little to address what was *necessary* (outside the technology itself) or even *desirable.* This distinction was lost on the majority of Americans, the most materially conditioned people in history. Questions of morality, alternatives in imagination, differing social visions—all were downplayed or ignored in the process. "Psychological change always lags behind technological change," argued the eminent British military historian Sir Michael Howard, to which he might have added economic, political, and strategic change as well.[4]

Indeed, whereas military strategy had always followed weapons developments rather than the reverse, the sheer *pace* of the postwar changes ensured that operational planning would have to run even faster to try to stay even with technological reality. As far back as 1921, Bradley Fiske had groused that technological change had made naval officers mere "tiny parts" of the "modern military machine." One excuse for the postwar pace, of course, was the attempt to keep up with, or keep ahead of, the imagined or known achievements of the potential Cold War enemy, the Soviet Union—to achieve symmetry. Americans tended to do this by brute force; their economy and supreme abundance of their resources made this possible. As Alan Turing, the brilliant English expert on the German Enigma code machine and one of the fathers of the modern computer, saw the situation, their "tradition [was one] of solving one's difficulties by means of much equipment rather than by thought."

Thus emerged a new type of professional, like Hyman Rickover, a military technologist who was a bit of a scientist, a bit of an engineer, but fundamentally a military manager with a bank account of technical knowledge and a flair for drawing on this account, for dramatizing the imperative of technological "progress." The Navy, like the rest of the American military, made way for this new type (more so than did the Army, less so than the Air Force) because there seemed to be no alternative.[5]

The trick was to see technology as an ineluctable force for positive good. A leading historian of China, John King Fairbank, had an apt description: "Mechanists believe in both technological gadgetry and in ideology, the potent combination of material might with intellectual righteousness." Given the climate of the Cold War world, this was a "potent combination" indeed. Still, this belief, for many, could not suffice; all the destructive ingenuity came imbued with a "Faustian sense of foreboding," even guilt. Tolstoy, certainly no militarist the older he got, spoke to this sense:

> Success . . . in the technology not only of war but of all material advances as well has shown how clearly and how cheap these technological advances which are called culture are. It doesn't cost anything to copy them and even to invent new ones. What is invaluable, important and difficult, is a good life. . . .[6]

But, the response might come, technology is necessary to secure the good life, and military technology is necessary to defend what has been secured. For the Navy, if some moral connotation was necessary (and for the pure technician, such caveats were beside the point), then the atomic bombs, supercarriers, jet planes, guided missiles, and nuclear submarines were not so much a positive good as they were a necessary evil. And if they were necessary, they must be top of the line.

From such assumptions and by such methods were the tridents of Poseidon refurbished within the postwar Navy. The weapons arrived double-edged, dreaded yet applauded, appalling but obligatory. Struck off by the human mind and hand, for all their wizardry they were only as good as the people who operated them: the hands behind the shield.

PART FOUR

HANDS BEHIND THE SHIELD

Generally, management of many is the same as management of few. It is a matter of organization.

—Sun-Tzu, *The Art of War*

CHAPTER NINETEEN

FLAG PLOT

———— ☆ ————

With the Nuke boats coming on line, conventional diesel-electric submarines like *Barracuda*, the former *SSK-1*, had increasingly less to do. They wandered the byways and back alleys of naval operations, taking on an odd job here and there, unsuccessfully struggling to find a home in the modern Navy.

In the fall of 1965, *Barracuda* received such an odd job in Florida. She got underway and moved to a point twenty miles south of Key West, where her commanding officer, in full-dress uniform replete with decorations, gave the order to dive. The sub leveled off at periscope depth, stopped her engines, and hung suspended under the surface of the calm Gulf waters.

A small, canvas-wrapped signal-flare box, draped with the American flag, was brought forward to the torpedo room. The box was smartly placed in Tube One. A torpedoman removed the flag. A second gently pushed the box forward, and a third battened the hatch. A naval chaplain read the traditional prayer. "Shoot the tube," said the captain. Another grim-faced torpedoman pressed a button.

And so, as he had requested, the remains of Rear Admiral Hiram Cassedy, United States Navy—USNA 1931, combat submarine shipper (*Searaven* and *Tigrone*), Navy Cross, two Silver Stars, Bronze Star—were given over to the sea.

☆

Naval officers inclined, especially if they made a career of the service, to be an aristocratic lot, in the sense that the formal gap between them and the men they led tended to be greater than that in the other services. The Navy was, first and foremost, a *sea* service. Aboard ship its officers were sequestered from the sailors and, if the ship was properly run, were at an extra remove from them, because orders were passed on through chief petty officers. "Officers' Country" was as carefully marked off from the rest of the ship as a royal court from the rest of society. Officers ate separately, slept separately, lived separately. They tended to have a strongly ingrained idea of *order*, not in the modern sense of peace and serenity, but more in the sense that had prevailed in Puritan Massachusetts, where "everything was put in its proper place and held there by force if necessary." This idea made them archaic as well as conservative.

They lived by order and were the source of orders, and orders in the floating kingdom were meant to be *obeyed*. Never once in the storied history of the United States Navy had there been a successful mutiny (even the British could not claim this), which made Herman Wouk's *The Caine Mutiny* all the more unsettling to its naval readers. Naval officers were insulated from their men on the practical assumption that familiarity bred contempt.

This said, rapport between naval officers and their enlisted men was generally excellent. An incompetent officer was quickly found out and, if the sailors working for him were lucky, as quickly weeded out or shunted aside. Officers' skills were necessarily *public* aboard ship: if an officer mishandled his ship, the most lubberly sailor would know; if he could not find his way from one end of a gun turret to the other, the word quickly crept through the mess decks; if he was in his rack at all hours, the stewards would tug on the grapevine. Conversely, if his men knew that their officer was savvy, his way was greased.

Officers wore their ranks on their sleeves, right there for everyone to see, and with each accretion of gold braid, each inch or half-inch addition right on up to the broad band of flag rank, they were expected to gain—in maturity, responsibility, judgment, and wisdom. They ran, after all, an enormous, complicated seagoing enterprise, by far the largest of its kind in the world, an operation that spanned the widest spectrum of manufacturing, naval architecture, engineering, science, education, strategy, tactics, international law, diplomacy, medicine, finance, astronomy, hydrography, and social science. They worked routinely with other militaries, civilians, and foreigners. They were expected to know a bit about everything and a lot about many things. Above all, they were to be specialists in the art of getting men to follow—to be *leaders*.

In a simpler age, when the Navy's and America's ambitions in the world had both been much smaller, they had been obligated "to maintain the untarnished honor of the government and the nation." Their obligation came in the form of *duty*, and for most this was an almost visceral emotion. "Love of country," wrote Captain Caspar Goodrich, ought to "furnish an incentive to brave deeds and patient suffering" for naval officers.[1]

The broadening of the naval officer corps in the twentieth century had somewhat diluted the nationalistic idealism of the "band of brothers," but not their vaunted independence or their high-flown concepts of duty and service. Navy ships were independent in ways no Army or Air Force unit could attain, anchored to land as these services were. Naval officers were acutely aware of these differences, gloried in standing apart from the rest of the military crowd, and were proud of their refusal to indulge in what for most of them was "mere politics." For some of them, their profession glowed with a holy light. Captain Albert Niblack wrote his son:

> The naval profession is much like a ministry. You dedicate your life to a purpose. You wear the garb of an organized profession. You renounce your pursuit of wealth. In large measure, you surrender your citizenship, renounce politics and work for the highest good of the organization. In the final analysis your aims and objects are quite as moral as a minister's because you are not seeking your own good, but the ultimate good of your country. You train the men under you to be good and useful citizens and, like the minister, what you say must conform to the rules of the organization.

Thus imbued, Navy officers traditionally fought assignments to the Pentagon, billets usually welcomed by those in the other services as a chance to do a little politicking. There were indeed advantages to be gained by duty in the Puzzle Palace, advantages held in little regard by the Navy. Navymen usually did not do as well as the others in positions of allied or joint command; a comparison of Ernie King and Dwight Eisenhower merely proved the point. Naval officers tended to see shore duty, including educational assignments, as so much wasted time, a career-staller rather than a career-enhancer. Alone of the services, the Navy had no clear education track for promotion.

Its officers were relatively isolated, desiring sea duty and independence above all. They were, in a word, parochial, and they delighted in this condition. Unsurprisingly, they were thus great squabblers, not only with other services but with each other. Atlantic Fleet fought Pacific Fleet for resources; line fought staff; within the line the three "unions"—surface, aviation, and submarines—fought one another; some, like Hyman Rickover, fought everybody.

They were, in other words, institutionally arrogant. They had little time to waste on outsiders, the despised and pitied landlubbers; their emphasis was forever on operations and the chain of command. The hoariest of naval traditions, stemming from the days of John Paul Jones and Stephen Decatur, was that men properly organized and led could do anything. The Navy chain-of-command concept was thus not so much an organizational line of authority as an ethical bond, one that stressed constant, consummate integrity up and down the chain. The Navy tended to assume that such bonds were almost unknown in the wider world.

Ashore, then, the naval officer was out of his element. On dry land he found himself mired in bureaucracies where his ethical bonds seemed unshared and misunderstood. The fleet, out there on blue water, was what counted. The rest was endless trivia. Duty lay at sea, duty fostered by generations of naval tradition and accomplishment.

For the Navy, tradition was a palpable thing, replete with specialized language, rites of initiation, and sacred symbols. Tradition was "the altar at which the Navy worships." Its central icon was the concept of independent command at sea, something obviously not available to the other major services. Not for nothing did Bill Fechteler, from his four-star position as chief of naval operations, fondly regard his days in command of the battleship *Indiana* as the happiest of his life. Therefore, any attempt by outsiders to winnow away naval command and control, as in the unification controversy, was resisted as though the Huns were at the gates.

Navy officers were supremely confident of the *legitimacy* of their institution; none but they wielded the shield of the republic. General Quarters sounded when the Navy's *relevance* was called into question, as with the rebellion in gold braid. Independence and national stature really counted, and naval officers were not reluctant to convey these attitudes to the lubbers. "The naval defense of our country is our profession," as Rear Admiral Bradley Fiske had promised, "not that of Congress."

Such attitudes, naturally, led to much gnashing of teeth and drove other military men and political leaders half-mad; Harry Truman was actually intrigued with one tongue-in-cheek Army proposal, made during the unification controversy, that the only way to overcome Navy resistance was to abolish the War Department, transfer all its elements to the Navy, and redesignate the whole thing as the Department of Defense. Ernie King might have said, "Why not?"

In short, the Navy, of all America's services, had the clearest sense of its own identity and interests. Navymen knew what they wanted and had their priorities in line. If higher authority differed, then higher authority was usually seen as making a direct assault on the Navy's powerful, ingrained sense of self. Forced or unforced resignations had been the result, as in the case of Louis Denfeld, and they would happen again.[2]

—And of all the Navy's people, the ones who had the strongest sense of identity, who worshiped most steadily at the altar of tradition, and who cultivated the steeliest concepts of duty were the ones who had made the service their life, who had gone all the way to the top: the admirals—the men who lived in "Flag Plot."

☆

A ship had no room for large managerial organizations, no immediate resources beyond herself and her men. Vessels operating at sea were hard schools, perhaps the hardest of all, where the least mistake could be lethal, not only for the man who had tripped up but also for everyone else aboard. Patterns of conduct in the floating kingdom were the time-tested requirements of harsh necessity. The Navy accordingly preached responsibility and the delegation of authority—each man to his job. The strain was constant and, as a crucial part of the self-image, both invited and welcomed.

Of course, there were costs. "[The Navy] takes a man's best and most earnest work," groused the acerbic Admiral Richmond Kelly Turner, "and then not content with that, it takes his soul right out of him if he is not very careful—sucks him dry as a bone and then throws him aside to the dump heap. . . . A naval officer of sixty is an old, old man, incapable of doing the work a man of that age should do."

Few who felt the wrath of "Terrible Turner" would have agreed that the admiral fit his own description of an "old, old man," but even for this volcano of a naval leader the strain had its price: Kelly Turner took to booze in his later years, just as King had in his earlier ones. By no means every officer responded to pressure in this way; the point is that they were *expected* to respond, and to overcome.

The compensation came with the responsibility, the authority, and, above all, the *command*. "Democracies may do very well for the land," observed Raphael Semmes, who as skipper of the raiders *Sumter* and *Alabama* had bedeviled Union shipping during the Civil War. "But monarchies, and pretty absolute monarchies at that, are the only successful governments for the sea."

Much was given to the monarch of the floating kingdom, and much was demanded. Failure meant disgrace, and worse. Talking with his guide Martin, Voltaire's Candide, on reaching England, heard of Admiral Byng's execution on his own quarterdeck. Candide, ever the innocent, asked who the fat man was who had just been killed so ceremoniously. An admiral, replied Martin. Why? asked the curious Candide. "In this country," responded his friend, "it is a good thing to kill an admiral from time to time to encourage the others."[3]

—*To encourage the others.* No one held higher standards for himself than an admiral. (The name came from the Arabic *amir-al-bahr*—"commander of the seas.") To fail in duty was reprehensible, to fail in command (as poor Byng was accused of doing) utter disgrace. "Duty," intoned Bradley Fiske, "in whatever form it came, was sacred."

Naval officers had little patience with lubbers, particularly reporters, for these people could never understand their central concepts and their devotion to service, tempered in the mysterious school of the sea. Rear Admiral Thomas Selfridge, Jr., was speaking well beyond his generation in his belief that "service utility" was "the very essence of the Navy." Shirk this, shirk your duty, foul up your command, and if Byng's fate did not necessarily lie in wait (Americans proved to be a bit more tolerant of nautical mistakes than their British cousins), you would be a pariah still.

A few overcompensated by the most rigid, hectoring sort of command; the lore of the sea was replete with tyrannical skippers, from Captain Bligh to Captain Queeg. Rarely, however, did the real thing surface, and when this happened, the Navy usually responded with alarm and alacrity. In 1952, for example, the captain of *Reclaimer,* an auxiliary repair and salvage ship, was hauled before an investigating panel after seventy of his crew griped that he was a petty tyrant. (They called their ship the "USS *Ridiculous*.") The naval inquiry was closed-door, because the necessary side of duty and service was that the Navy, not outsiders, did its own dirty laundry.

Thus did the Navy police itself, endlessly carp about the highest standards, and constantly take its own temperature and pulse, "caught up in an anxiety largely of its own making." In a sense, the Navy was the "hypochondriac of the services." The public bought the Navy's standards, expected the maximum of its seagoing service, and, like the Navy itself, was highly intolerant of error—which in turn added to the self-imposed pressures.

The deep concern with duty, the intolerance for any margin of error in command, the exceptionally high degree of *expectation*, meant that the Navy's temporary custodians, the men in Flag Plot, were almost obsessively concerned with *self-image*.[4]

☆

In mid-1944, the Navy Department created a group for the express purpose of promoting certain views among selected segments of the public. In itself, this marked a break with tradition. The guarded insularity of the naval officer corps meant that they, of all American officers, were most inhibited in public discourse. Rear Admiral Tom Robbins, who oversaw much of SCOROR (the Secretary's Committee of Research on Reorganization), remembered that during the interwar period only two naval officers had reputations as effective public speakers, and these two unfortunates were run hither and yon making the few speeches on policy the Navy deemed worthwhile.

World War II cracked the dike. Even though Ernie King and others were operating at the very top of the wartime coalition and thus (in King's case, with decided reluctance) learning the fine art of public explanation, most naval officers toed the traditional line, virtually ignoring public relations. Secretary of the Navy Frank Knox, businessman that he was, established an Office of Public Relations on 1 May 1941, with field support at all the major shore facilities and fleet commands. But this office was charged only with "communicating" between Navy and public, not with producing a desired public impression.

The mid-1944 change moved the Navy into modern public relations once and for all. James Forrestal was the architect, and he made his point clearly to Annapolis graduates:

> The Navy must not be permitted [after the war] to relapse into one of its periods of neglect. That means that people must realize that it is an instrument of national policy, an instrument usable and to be used for the purpose of peace rather than war. If that point of view is to obtain and

retain currency, you will have to do your part in the creation and retention of public confidence in the Navy.

"Each of you . . . [should] consider yourself a purveyor of information about the Navy and about our national need for its continuance," urged Forrestal. "Never get tired of the repetition of this story, nor take it for granted that it is already known to your listeners." Historically, the Navy's image had usually been extremely favorable in the public mind, particularly since the Spanish-American War and Teddy Roosevelt's boosting of the Great White Fleet early in the century, but Forrestal foresaw threats to naval prerogatives that would call forth new techniques.

As always, the Navy would identify itself with the national interest; the congruence was adjudged perfect by any admiral who spoke on the subject. What was good for the Navy was good for the country. The converse did not necessarily hold, particularly when domestic politics came to the fore, and the dissonance gave some naval officers considerable problems. Beyond Forrestal's charge to the midshipmen lay certain specifics: preserving a strong naval force, recruiting the best people possible, maintaining naval pride and tradition, and promoting public interest in the Navy. When things went awry in any of these areas, the naval explanation was usually that the outsiders were at fault.

The postwar public relations structure of the Navy zeroed in on Forrestal's objectives. "Public relations should go beyond mere release of news," advised one of the Navy's new PR officers. "It should *create* news, foster ideas, get across in simple, easily understandable language what top command desires to say. . . . Public relations . . . is a vital secondary consideration in direct alliance with most naval functions."[5]

—Flag Plot would have to reorient toward the world outside. Forrestal set forth an "enlightened" public information policy for the postwar Navy. The Bureau of Naval Personnel was instructed to provide for an enlisted public relations specialty. Practically every major command was given its "Public Information Officer," or PIO (later "Public Affairs Officer," or PAO). "We can look forward," predicted one enthusiastic junior officer, "to having at our disposal a specially trained group of officers and men to do the Navy's public relations work. . . . Insofar as the citizen is concerned . . . it will make it very easy for him to get the information about his Navy *to which he is entitled.*"

"We in the Navy naturally want the truth presented fairly to the public." Accordingly, servants of "the truth" multiplied manyfold; by 1947 the Navy had six hundred people working in public relations, almost five hundred of them in uniform. The Director of Public Information in Washington set the policies. The district and fleet PIOs sought media pipelines wherever they could, in the press, radio, motion pictures, and the new wonder of television. Special events were staged; designated "visit" ships held periodic "open houses" when in port; "family cruises" of a day's duration were offered to Navy dependents and others; speakers were shuttled countrywide; biographies were shipped off to local newspapers. Every time Seaman Recruit Jones passed some milestone in his boot training, a press release duly went forth.

Forrestal, literally, had placed the onus of selling the Navy's viewpoint on everyone who wore Navy blue, but the real task belonged to Flag Plot. Public relations, an art most admirals scorned and performed with decided unease, was here to stay. Sometimes, however, the public did not seem to understand; more than a few naval officers, following the hearings before the House Armed Forces Committee in October 1949 during the rebellion in gold braid, were convinced that many in the press had overlooked or misunderstood much of the Navy testimony.

More than any other single event, the rebellion shaped the Navy's public relations in the postwar period, although the earlier unification controversy was important as well. The press and public response forced the admirals to come to grips with the fact that they and their beloved service had entered a new era, one in which the continuous repolishing of their time-honored image would no longer suffice. Naval men had their own argot and their own deep-seated eternal verities; they often assumed knowledge of their profession by the general public that simply was not there. Departure from these comfortable norms was difficult, and most of the inhabitants of Flag Plot felt they had better things to do than "sloganeer" and "propagandize."

But the world was changing. Appallingly, a Gallup poll helped move the Navy along the course charted by Forrestal. In 1949 the pollsters asked the question "If the United States should get into another World War, which branch of the armed forces do you think would play the most important part in winning the war—the Army, the Navy or the Air Force?" Only 4 percent answered "Navy."

—That hurt. Ready or not, the Navy had to accept that public relations was now mandatory. The real blitz had begun shortly after the war, and as good an example as any was the formation of the Blue Angels, the crack precision-flying team established in Jacksonville, Florida, in 1946. By 1954 the Blue Angels, then flying F9F-5 Panthers, had appeared before forty million people in eight years—by far the Navy's best-known and most popular public relations gambit.[6]

The idea with the Blue Angels, the news releases, and all the rest was to do what had previously been thought unthinkable and unnecessary: to "sell America" (and, by implication, everyone else possible) on the Navy. The shape of the postwar world and the new naval globalism meant that the stakes were high. Commander Daniel James put the case thus:

> We are engaged in a battle of persuasion with the most powerful sales force of all time which is selling Communism throughout the world. This sales

agency is selling its products without the use of any samples that could come under close scrutiny. . . . Like any clever sales group lacking an article of merit, an attack on the competition is a diverting substitute for a comparison of product. If the competition does not rise up to the challenge, bankruptcy is inevitable. . . . If we shrink away from the hard contest ahead, then the domination of the world by a more aggressive group is assured. Let not the future pages of history indicate that we had the better product but were the poorer salesmen.

"Our Navy has a fine 'product' to sell," wrote one PIO, "and a 'salesforce' which is not forced into their line of work but who sought that job voluntarily and have in most cases elected to stay with it throughout their lives." Thus the Navy found itself in "sales," to the horror of Flag Plot. Public relations, community relations, shows, stunts, attention-getters of every stripe—these did not belong to the sea; they ran across the grain, cutting like a rusty buzz saw.

And some of the news, unfortunately and unavoidably, was bad news. Planes crashed; ammo exploded aboard carriers; vessels ran aground (*Missouri*'s embarrassing stranding in Hampton Roads in January 1950 was the classic case); recruits dropped dead on drill fields; brig guards mistreated prisoners; paymasters absconded with payrolls; ships collided at sea. Bad news could not effectively be suppressed; "like murder, it will out," admitted another PIO. And so the Navy reluctantly found itself in the business of not only making the news but also slanting the news. "There is no choice whether or not to tell 'bad' news to the public. The only choice is how the news will be told." Always, the primary goal was to retain public confidence in the Navy, no matter how silly or god-awful the blunders.

The best way to do this was to drown bad news with good, to hope the razzle-dazzle of the Blue Angels would drive the *Missouri* grounding out of the media. One of the best examples of good news was the Navy's People-to-People Program, established in 1956. At one level, People-to-People tapped the altruistic best in the Navy, and in America. The program "aims at one target only—the making of friends for the United States." To this end, sailors on overseas deployments donated blood, made contributions to local charities, conducted sporting competitions, gave guided tours, provided first aid, showed American-made movies (always crowd-pleasers), gave away milk and staple foods—anything that indicated there was more to the tons of haze gray sitting out there in the harbor than guns, planes, and missiles.[7]

People-to-People worked, but this effort, like many others in a similar vein, remained in part an element of the Cold War duel for hearts and minds and thus was part of the Navy "product." In a sense the Navy had always had to sell itself, particularly in recruiting, but now the Cold War, coupled with naval globalism, meant a constant sales pitch abroad, while competition for the budget dollar and a share in national strategy meant a constant sales pitch at home.

—Huckstering was an almost entirely new role for Flag Plot. Admirals were not supposed to *sell*.

☆

What they were supposed to do, not least in their own eyes, was *fight*. However, years of "peace," for the United States Navy, far outnumbered years of "war," not only in the postwar era but throughout its history. Peace usually brought stagnation in combat technique, mothballing of ships and men, and the loss of lessons learned. Ship designers had few new problems to meet and little sense of urgency with which to meet them; young Turks who had risen fast in combat (in World War II young admirals often were simply recommended for their stars by their seagoing seniors, and were surprised when the good news came—no formality of selection boards) grew old and stale when the shooting stopped; and innovation was at least as much feared or ignored as welcomed.

The heating up of the Cold War and the dynamism of the naval technological revolution lessened some of these tendencies in the postwar period. Still, increasing age usually brought increasing conservatism and caution, and within the Navy, institutional forms and pressures made these inclinations persistently strong. "The bane of the Navy is a contented admiral," fumed one of them, Admiral Joe Richardson.

Lack of a shooting war made a continuous striving for excellence tougher to maintain. (This condition, especially because the Korean War was difficult to equate with any role for the nuclear attack submarine, made Hyman Rickover's achievement all the more remarkable.) With peace came routine: perfect drill, spit and polish, the elevation of privilege and form, dignity and ceremony. Innovation in the postwar Navy, despite its obvious presence and spectacular results, usually swam upstream.

Flag Plot was thus bifurcated. The admirals were expected both to guard tradition and to innovate. In either role, they saw themselves as both fighters and gentlemen, heirs to centuries of hard-earned seagoing laurels and the sacred precepts of John Paul Jones's ideas about their proper character.

The social side of this dual model was explicit but understated. Within the Pentagon, the "E-Ring" was the outermost of the huge structure's five rings; flag officers of all the services—the Lords of the E-Ring—had their offices there and thus had windows through which they could at least see outdoors. The Navy's part of the E-Ring was rich in softly lighted dark wood, elegant wainscoting, and brass door fittings. Along the corridors stretched immaculate glass cases filled with meticulously detailed ship models. Everything bespoke a club for proper gentlemen, institutional stability, and that sublime self-confidence that only time and tradition could provide.

The admirals thought of themselves as warriors first, and by some measures, they were. World War II, after all, had been the preeminent shaping factor in their professional lives, and many of them had climbed to flag rank through battle-zone accomplishment. But the combat casualties in Flag Plot had been surprisingly few. The age when the dashing young Decatur could swing aboard *Philadelphia*, cutlass in hand, to smite the wily Barbary pirates had long since passed.

Flag rank was established in the Navy in 1862; famous names like Jones, Decatur, and the first David Porter had never been admirals. David Glasgow Farragut was the first. No admirals perished in combat during the Civil War; eighty Union generals lost their lives to enemy fire, matched by eighty of the Confederacy. The Spanish-American War was too brief and one-sided to kill anybody of flag rank. In World War I no admirals were killed in action (two generals); in Korea, none of any service; in Vietnam, no admirals again (eight generals).

Only in World War II, when twenty-five American generals lost their lives in combat, did American admirals pay the ultimate price. There were five: Rear Admiral Isaac Kidd died aboard his flagship, *Arizona*, at Pearl Harbor; Rear Admirals Dan Callaghan and Norman Scott were killed during the three vicious days and nights of fighting in November 1942 known as the Naval Battle of Guadalcanal; Rear Admiral Henry Mullinnix died at Tarawa; and Rear Admiral Theodore Chandler lost his life at Lingayen Gulf in January 1945.

Over the years, then, five American admirals dead in combat, as against 195 generals. Such statistics had nothing to do with either courage or pugnacity, of which Flag Plot had plenty, but were a reflection instead of the nature of individual wars as well as the extended ranges of modern naval weapons and communications. Still, the Nelsonian image of the fighting commander on his quarterdeck was difficult to square with modern reality.

Nevertheless, they would be gentlemen always and warriors when they could. In addition, with their stress on order and authority, the men in Flag Plot tended to be strong political conservatives, and the Cold War only heightened the intensity of these feelings, producing an intense loathing of the Soviet Union, Communist China, and all their works.

If the men in Flag Plot could not actually fight, they would be prepared to fight, and the obvious enemy was "international communism." Admirals were almost to a man knee-jerk anti-Communists, especially in the two decades immediately following World War II. Many of them, like Savvy Cooke, were practically apoplectic over the "loss" of China, and many were deeply concerned over the "threat" at home. Fleet Admiral William Leahy called any State Department officials who might favor aid to the Chinese Communists "Pinkies," which was one short step removed from "traitors" in his lexicon, and Leahy was far from the exception within the Navy.

Anticommunism within naval ranks was not, however, produced by the

Cold War. The Office of Naval Intelligence (founded in 1882) routinely gathered information in the mid-thirties on radicals, "subversives," pacifists, and Communists through physical surveillance, "other surreptitious methods," and outright burglary—activities far outside its charter. ONI enlisted self-styled civilian patriots in its campaign, and in the Ninth Naval District, headquartered at Great Lakes, a naval-sponsored industrial intelligence service was created that infiltrated every business within the area under contract to the Navy to inform on suspected labor radicals, spies, or saboteurs. As late as 1949 Naval Intelligence was shadowing suspected figures like the great black entertainer Paul Robeson.[8]

—The roots of political suspicion ran deep and wide. "Pinkies" weakened national defense. Flag Plot maintained continuous guard, warriors against a new and insidious enemy.

☆

The admirals presided over a military society that was, like all militaries, a hierarchy and a pecking order. But the Navy's caste system had rather specialized distinctions. The differences among its varied components, branches, and activities were elaborately and painstakingly ranked. Line considered itself superior to staff. At the pinnacle of the line, after World War II, stood carrier aviation—at least by its own lights. Near the bottom came such specialties as mine warfare. New technologies, such as that represented by the Nukes, fought for preference, while old and somewhat discredited ones, like the battleships and the diesel-electrics, fought in vain to keep their positions on the scale.

Much of this caste bickering was only friendly teasing, but the jokes stopped when time came for officer assignment or promotion. Even within specialties, distinctions riddled the officer corps. Fighter jocks believed themselves superior to those who flew patrol planes, the tail hook over land-based air; attack submarines were thought better than ballistic-missile launchers; destroyers were preferable to the plodding Gators; and everything came before the dreadful auxiliaries. And yet, despite this crazy quilt of distinctions, Navy officers saw themselves as generalists—naval officers—first and specialists second.

Modern technology, of course, bred the specialist, but the old generalist ideal hung on, not only a relic but also an important criterion from the age of fighting sail, when an officer was expected to understand, in exquisite detail, every line, bolt, sail, gun, and piece of wood in his ship. The successful naval officer should know a bit of everything, be broad in his duties (this was part of the in-house prejudice against Rickover), and, above all, live the life of the sea. Most senior officers felt a certain contempt toward those who wandered off into other, proscribed areas—such as mere writing or theorizing. Alfred Thayer Mahan suffered from this prejudice all his professional life, and Ned Beach, a successful author even before he skippered *Triton* around the world, never made Flag Plot.

Reputations as well as successful tours of duty were the tickets of passage into Flag Plot or, more likely (since entrance was highly restricted by law), the padlocks of denial. The modern naval promotion system was a series of "great barrier reefs," or promotion boards, each of them staffed by naval officers only, all senior to the candidates. By the time the last barrier reef, the bar to Flag Plot, hove into sight, the aspiring captains usually had almost three decades of naval service under their belts. They had reputations, and most of them were known personally to one or more admirals on their boards. Reputations counted. "We of the Navy are worse gossips than a bunch of women," said Kelly Turner. "That and hard work is about all we do."

Behavior counted, too. Although the postwar Navy was decidedly less formal than its predecessor (the for-and-aft dress hat and the boat cloak had gone by the boards, for example, and the use of calling cards diminished markedly), the emphasis on etiquette remained stronger than in the other services. Naval ceremonies were encrusted with the weight of centuries of tradition; proper dress was a constant, except in the working environment aboard ship (Rickover scored low here as well); decorum and coolheaded judgment were highly prized. In 1954 the Navy decreed that ceremonial swords (dropped from naval attire in 1942) would once again be part of the full-dress uniform; form, in many cases, would precede function.

The gripes against these proprieties were never absent, of course, particularly among junior officers who felt that they had better things to do than present calling cards, provide polite conversation, or render a flashy sword salute. But conform to the Navy they would, for they were expected to be officers and gentlemen. A Navy wardroom on display was indeed a gentlemen's shrine: stiffly starched uniforms, snowy tablecloths, sparkling silver, hovering stewards. Only the liquor was missing, courtesy of Woodrow Wilson's temperance-minded secretary of the Navy, Josephus Daniels. Within this setting, naval gentlemen were unfailingly courteous to ladies of all ages (junior officers saved their sexual forays for liberty), polite in verbal discourse, and moderate in tone and temper.

Flag Plot preached these behavior patterns and ideals, the proper roles of an "officer and a gentleman." This carefully cultivated self-imagery was extremely powerful; much of the Navy *manner* was both accepted and admired by the public at large. There was a little hypocrisy here. Many officers drank to excess, even some of the residents of Flag Plot, like Kelly Turner; some chased women, like King; others had been unseemly brawlers in their youth, like Marc Mitscher. Some were hopeless politickers, shamelessly cultivating the favor of their seniors, and some naval wives were as bootlicking as their husbands. "Shoving juniors aside to pay homage to seniors is just an old Annapolis custom," resignedly wrote a junior officer.[9]

—All true, and yet the ideals, the careful cultivation of behavior, in practice *worked*. They were the varnish that coated the naval officer from the day he took his oath, the built-in gyrocompass that told him the right course to steer. The Navy's social standards were barnacled with time and tradition, and they were the institution's bonding cement. They helped define the naval officer, preserved his high standards, and provided him a constant mirror for judgment and self-assessment.

☆

The naval profession, then, demanded the utmost, and even though this might not always be given, the concern for officer quality was a constant. By the mid-fifties a decline in this quality was apparent, and there was more to the concern than the simple age-bemoaning-youth syndrome. Flag Plot grew alarmed. The evidence was clear: fleet operations and readiness were in decline, officer resignation rates were increasing, and the turnover of junior officers was high. The prosperity of Cold War America was enticing more young officers to ditch a Navy career for a gray flannel suit.

The prewar Navy had revolved around a relatively small, homogeneous cadre of highly motivated career officers, most of them produced by Annapolis. World War II, when nine of every ten officers were Reservists, seriously eroded this homogeneity. In the postwar period, naval officers came from many sources of commission and from a wide variety of educational and social backgrounds. Of necessity, the once-great selectivity of officer candidates was drastically reduced. Argument raged over whether this meant that officer quality had been reduced as well.

For the Navy not only needed good officers, the service needed good officers who would advance up the chain of command, make the Navy a career. The Navy's officer promotion system was based on the fitness report, written and signed periodically by an officer's reporting senior, usually his commanding officer. The "fitrep" system, painstakingly developed over decades, like any system evaluating thousands of people had its problems, loopholes, and procedures that could be abused. But all in all, the system was indeed extraordinary—probably the best and fairest large-scale personnel-evaluation system in existence.

"I believe in the Navy system," said Captain Slade Cutter. "I believe in the selection process. I believe that the Navy did the right thing when they passed me over for flag rank because you're selected for flag rank based upon your potential as a flag officer. . . ." But the fitreps were capable of distortion, and almost always on the high side. Many were the officers "two-blocked to the left"—ranked highest in every category—because skippers wanted to avoid morale problems and naturally desired to move their own men ahead as rapidly as possible.

Also, as Vice Admiral John Victor Smith noted, "There [was] an element of luck, in that you are lucky if you happen to work for someone who knows how to write a fitness report. Sometimes you get an officer who just cannot do it." And some reporting seniors lacked the expertise to properly evaluate some juniors—a skipper reporting on a chaplain in his command, for example—but were required to make the report anyway.

The ultimate result was an overall diminution in the discriminating selection of personnel. If almost everyone was near perfection, if everyone appearing before a promotion board walked on water, then proper assessment of personnel performance was proportionately difficult. Officers developed at different rates; different skippers judged certain traits more highly. Moreover, the Navy, in its assumption of an officer corps of uniformly high quality, was reluctant to use attrition, a kind of nautical Social Darwinism, to ensure this quality, doubly so because of the global demands placed on the postwar fleet.

There ensued a "conveyor belt" system of promotion, and the Navy was tied to the belt. Every officer was assumed to want to get ahead, to seek responsibility and gain promotion. The rewards of command and Flag Plot lay beyond. The most favored career path was that of the unrestricted line, out of which came the three unions of ship-drivers, aviators, and submariners. These were the people eligible for command at sea. In addition, the restricted line had several designations for specialists not eligible for command at sea, among them Engineering Duty Only, Aeronautical Engineering Duty Only, and Limited Duty Only. These last officers, the famous and highly valued LDOs, were former enlisted men worth their weight in gold on any ship. Finally, within the restricted line, there were special duty officers, with expertise in areas such as communications, cryptography, law (later a staff corps specialty), intelligence, public information (later public affairs), photography, psychology, and hydrography.

The conveyor belt also included the staff corps. Eventually there were eight of these. Four were connected with medicine: the Medical Corps, the Medical Service Corps, the Nurse Corps, and the Dental Corps. Beyond these were the Supply Corps (at times numbering as high as 10 percent of the line), the Judge Advocate General's Corps (the lawyers), the Civil Engineer Corps (out of which came the workaholic naval construction battalions, the "CBs"), and the Chaplain's Corps.

Most holders of flag rank belonged to the unrestricted line—Flag Plot numbered anywhere from 180 to 220 or so members for any given year, to run a Navy of 600,000 to 800,000—and the actual *power* was almost all in the unrestricted line. The restricted line and each of the staff corps claimed at most one or two admirals in each specialty.

Flag Plot was not a permanent sinecure. Flag officers came before a continuation board after thirty-five years of commissioned service and five years in grade (whichever came later); those continued remained until age sixty-two, when under statutory law they said good-bye. There were exceptions. Leahy was carried forward at the behest of two presidents, and he along with King, Nimitz, and Halsey wore five stars, which meant that all of them, technically, were on permanent active duty. Rickover, another exception, was proving to be practically immortal. And Rear Admiral Grace Hopper would stay around almost as long as the Nuke of Nukes because of her knowledge of computer logic.

Flag Plot, then, was alive with change, continuously taking in new blood and draining off the old. Sea daddies were very important, as always; positions as aides and flag secretaries counted for much; and slots for chiefs of staff never went begging—for someday your man might form part of a great barrier reef, and he might be able to guide you into safe harbor. One naval truism became more true the more senior one got: "You can't have a better assignment than your friends who are your seniors wish you to have."

There *was* a Navy "old boy network," but this network was much more open and fluid, more amenable to adjustment and correction, than such a phrase might suggest. Officer detailers, the men who sat in the ramshackle eight-winged Navy Annex on the Arlington hill overlooking the Potomac, by and by did an exceptional job of matching men with billets, although bickering with detailers remained one of the most time-honored of customs. There were many paths to Flag Plot, many "premium billets," and besides, the level of performance, almost always, was what really counted when confronting the last barrier reef.

The naval emphasis on the officer generalist was bound to clash with the modern age of specialization and technical expertise. The generalist was expected to have far more versatility and distinction in a far more diversified field than any civilian professional. "[The generalist's training]," judged one Reservist, *"has lacked the one essential that promotes maximum competence in those other pursuits:* specialization."

The postwar Navy's table indeed groaned under an impossible span of dishes: ship design; aerodynamics; every type of engineering under the sun—civil, mechanical, industrial, marine, aviation, electrical, steam, ballistics, nuclear; hydrography; legal specialties arcane enough to satisfy the most satirical penchant of Charles Dickens—international, admiralty, military, civil, criminal, commercial; quantum mechanics and atomic physics; protocol and personnel management; business administration; statecraft and politics—*et alii ad infinitum.* No one could even adequately sample such a menu, let alone digest its entirety.

"Why not provide for an officer who can follow a unilateral occupation of his own choosing, who can acquire more and more of a grasp on his job as he progresses, who can emerge in starred rank as a recognized authority in his sphere?" came the question. This was certainly the way of Rickover, of the staff corps, and of the restricted line. But the flag slots for these people were a precious few. The men of the unrestricted line, for their part, refused to admit that they knew a little about a lot. They believed that they knew a lot about the lot that counted—the seagoing Navy.

To further the generalist ideal, the naval policy of rotation of officers was set in concrete. Rickover was far from the only flag officer to blister the bulkheads with oaths against the practice, but no amount of urging or pleading availed. Kelly Turner himself argued against the wartime policy of the Bureau of Personnel that mandated yearly rotation between sea and shore duty; just when an officer was learning the ropes, off he would go to some Stateside desk, and in would come another eager greenhorn.[10]

The generalist bias undoubtedly had enormous costs, but the benefits were there, too, particularly when an unrestricted line officer reached Flag Plot. By then he would have long since become warfare qualified; was probably familiar with one or more areas of naval propulsion; was a specialist in some branch of naval weapons; was a master of a particular type of naval technology—ship, plane, or submarine—and many times a master of several; and, above all, would have been tested in command at sea, usually more than once. These were no small accomplishments, far superior to the breadth (and depth) of experience of most top civilian executives, and the Navy stubbornly clung to its ways.

☆

Unfortunately, not all naval generalists operated smoothly in harness, least so in Flag Plot. There had been a time, a century before, when all admirals looked alike to the uninitiated, when, as one wag said, "It was easier to lay up a ship than an admiral." Any officer, in that rigid system of seniority, might eventually ascend to flag rank if only he managed to live long enough. One, whose apparent sole distinction was the ability to run his ship aground no fewer than three times on his way from Annapolis to the sea, eventually retired as a rear admiral.

But modern admirals, while outwardly conforming to the generalist ideal, had had to become specialists despite themselves. Within the Navy had emerged, by the postwar period, the three great "unions:"—surface officers ("Blackshoes"), aviators ("Brownshoes"), and submariners ("Feltshoes," for the noise-muffling footwear they adopted aboard the boats, or, less politely, "bubbleheads"). Moreover, the vast bureaucratic hive that was the Navy tended to compartmentalize officers, to the point at which one's own special universe (Rickover's was a case in point) seemed to be all there was.

So tension and misunderstanding, to a certain degree, were built into the system. King spent much of his career cussing aviators and the Bureau of Naval Personnel. Jack Towers, one of the pioneers of naval aviation, was practically paranoid on the subject of nonaviators supposedly out to scuttle his specialty. Another aviator, Slew McCain, claimed that blackshoe Raymond Spruance had downgraded carriers to errand boys for Marines. Feltshoes were convinced that the money they deserved went instead to the glossy carrier forces. Blackshoe admirals who loved their battleships bemoaned their passing and blamed everyone but themselves.

Practically the only time these men of the unrestricted line banded together, apart from responding to threats from outside, was to deride the staff. This attitude, indeed, was as old as militaries; Wellington had preached the training of men for war as against "the futile drivelling of mere quill driving." But the interunion strife was always the most paramount. As late as 1952 surface admirals held 90 percent of the highest fleet posts, to the deep unhappiness of submariners and the utter frustration of aviators. Frederick Sherman, a Brownshoe who had commanded the stricken *Lexington* at Coral Sea, urged legislation requiring that the chief of naval operations and the fleet commanders be aviators. After all, legislation had been necessary to get aviators into the captain's chair on carriers in the first place. Sherman's position, while extreme, was indicative of these intraservice suspicions.

Two of the unions, however, were relative newcomers—the Brownshoes and the Feltshoes—and they found that they had much in common, particularly opposition to the more neolithic of the Blackshoes. Carriers and submarines had produced dramatically successful war records, particularly in the Pacific. The greatest technological jumps in the postwar period belonged to them. Many aviators and submariners had worked together on research and development projects, in nuclear ordnance, for example. In short, these two were more allies than rivals, except when debates over the budget dollar cropped up. Before 1970 they were the only two specialists in the unrestricted line to wear special insignia—wings for the aviator, dolphins for the submariner (the crossed swords and bows-on ship of the surface warfare officer came later)—and the only two to automatically draw hazardous duty pay in peacetime.

Together, as these two unions aged in service, their representatives entered Flag Plot in increasing numbers. After 1952 the Blackshoe proportion dropped dramatically. Eventually, about 35 percent of all flag billets would belong to Brownshoes, about half that percentage to Feltshoes. In other words, the new boys on the block together came to hold a preponderant majority. This development was, in sum, an internal revolution that not only reflected the technological changes within the Navy but would also change, forcefully, the way the Navy thought about its roles and about itself.[11]

☆

The great English admiral Robert Blake, during the bitter years of civil war in the seventeenth century, had been asked to declare himself against the Lord Protector, Oliver Cromwell. "It is not for us to mind state affairs," he rejoined, "but to keep foreigners from fooling us." This pose of political disinterest passed undiminished to the United States Navy.

"A sailor has no politics," Admiral George Dewey had pontificated. Like most avuncular pronouncements, this one was full of holes—not least, regarding Dewey himself. The victor of Manila Bay made a run at the Democratic nomination for the presidency in 1900, and made a fool of himself in the process. "I don't understand how I got the idea in the first place," he confessed to reporters as he threw in the towel.

Presidential politics were anathema to the Navy, and Dewey's embarrassing candidacy was the closest a career naval professional ever got to the Oval Office. Several former naval officers would serve in the postwar presidency—Kennedy, Johnson, Nixon, Ford, and Carter would make a run of five straight, and Bush would be the sixth—but only the Army, with Zachary Taylor, Ulysses Grant, and Dwight Eisenhower, could boast military professionals in the highest post.

This scarcely meant, however, that the Navy was devoid of politics, or of politicking. Many naval people followed national politics closely; Tommy Hart in 1916 wrote that "the nation's wants and ideas are fairly well represented by either party." But, he added despairingly, "we are *not* a real nation—just an enormous and rather unhealthy fungus mass." However, Hart's political remarks, like those of almost every other naval officer, were made privately. The intense public relations approach inaugurated by Knox and Forrestal meant that the Navy would be, more than ever, necessarily enmeshed both with Congress and with the in-house, interservice politics of the Defense Department. Moreover, at the intraservice level, politicking could be intense over union competition, research, budget battles, officer assignments, and promotion.

Flag Plot was gained through promotion, following decades of rigorously, consistently monitored service. In bizarre cases like Rickover's, the public had cause to believe that the Navy's promotion system was riddled with politics and factionalism. Congress, after all, had to approve all flag nominees. True enough, once he gained Flag Plot, a man found political temperatures rising. "The three- and four-star jobs are mostly political," noted Vice Admiral Truman Hedding. "Not all of them, but most of them."

More of the truth, however, lay in the opposite direction. Although reputation, emotion, friendship, and a host of other factors were never absent when the last barrier reef for promotion to admiral was formed, the essence was that the aspirant for flag rank "must convince six of nine old gentlemen sitting around a green-covered table that he *has* earned it." Hart, after his naval career had ended, was appointed to fill an unexpired senatorial term from Connecticut. He was asked which title he preferred, "admiral," or "senator." He did not have to think before replying: "It took me thirty years to earn the one—the other was given to me." The old gentlemen had given him, and everyone else who got past them, the title they would proudly bear to their graves: admiral. Congress almost always rubber-stamped the recommendations of the old gentlemen; Rickover's, again, was the great exception that proved the rule.

The public might talk loosely of an "aristocracy" in Flag Plot, of some kind of biological organism merely reproducing its own, but modern admirals were transients on active duty (by law) and, in addition, were almost always men, like Tommy Hart, who had *earned* their way in the school of the sea. Also, family connections were of no help in avoiding the shoals surrounding the barrier reef. For example, of the immediate postwar chiefs of naval operations, Ernie King was the son of a railroad shop foreman; Chester Nimitz's father ran a hotel; Louis Denfeld's was a professor; Forrest Sherman's sold schoolbooks; and Arleigh Burke's was a Colorado farmer. Only Bill Fechteler, whose father, Gustav Fechteler, achieved four stars, could claim a true "aristocratic" lineage, although Mick Carney's father had been a naval officer also.

Flag Plot was no aristocracy; the men who entered, with extremely few exceptions, nagivated on their own from all points of the social compass. A man like the Brahmin historian Samuel Eliot Morison might make rear admiral in the Naval Reserve in short order, but then Morison wrote "Dear Franklin" letters to the president of the United States. The men of Flag Plot were elitist, tremendously and rightfully proud of their accomplishments, but above all they saw themselves, correctly, as a *meritocracy* and zealously guarded their notions of what constituted naval merit.

And in the postwar period, they were getting younger. In 1941 active-duty flag officers averages 59.2 years or age—five years from mandatory retirement. By 1958 the retirement age had been lowered from 64 to 62, but the average age in Flag Plot was 54.1—eight years to retirement. Because of wartime rank inflation, combat promotions, and early and deep selections, the nation was getting more longevity from its admirals.

Of course, only the fortunate few got through the reefs. Multitudes broached and could not make the passage, with accompanying anger and recrimination. Not everyone treated rejection with Slade Cutter's aplomb. One captain who failed of selection bitterly commented that the old promotional emphasis on command at sea had been supplanted by emphasis on command of an LMD (Large Mahogany Desk)—which was partially true because, as in all walks of American life, the Age of the Manager had arrived.

There were always accusations that flag selection was little more than a popularity contest with political overtones, with high value being placed on social graces and connections. Cutter's comment that admirals were chosen not only for their past records but also for what they could *do* at flag rank had some merit. Sea daddies still counted, just as Marc Mitscher had once saved Alfred Pride from a bad fitrep (Pride went on to four stars). But the meritocracy almost always placed demonstrated expertise and well-rounded achievement first.[12]

The prewar Navy had practically sealed off Flag Plot to all but the Annapolis-educated (people who knew people), but now this was changing as well. Some of the vast numbers of Reserves who had entered during World War II stayed around, augmented to the regular Navy, and, in time, cleared the reef. The V-12 Program, which ran from 1943 to 1946, commissioned over three hundred thousand naval officers. Among them were six who rose to vice admiral, including the Navy's first black admiral, Samuel Gravely, Jr. Eleven more reached flag rank. The Naval Reserve Officers Training Corps (NROTC) began to add more aspirants in the 1950s, and a few inhabitants of Flag Plot eventually came from other sources, such as the Officer Candidate School in Newport and programs to commission enlisted men. In short, the educational background for the men in Flag Plot was broadening, even as the social base was widening.

Despite these trends the cohesion within Flag Plot was far more powerful than any centrifugal force. The Air Force, youngest and most rambunctious of the services, was much attached to its toys and gadgets and to the aura of gee-whiz and Buck Rogers. To the Navy, despite the fact that its playpen held a far more diverse set of toys, the playthings themselves did not generate the loyalty (although interest and pride in them was always high). Instead, the emotional engagement was with the Navy as an institution. Seagoing naval aviators, as an example, always had a higher affection for their service than for their aviation unit or for their aircraft, an affection that often did not hold true for their fellow officers in either the Army or the Air Force. When institutional loyalty was at stake, the Marines, of course, were a special case.

Still, the impact of new naval technology was slanting and narrowing this affection, this loyalty. Because the gadgets were so complex, the necessity for their mastery so compelling and demanding (*vide* Rickover), naval leadership and management were being transformed. Graduate education, of the type that once had made Rickover and his fellow EDOs so rare, was becoming more and more necessary, not only a useful "ticket" to be punched but also something of real value. And graduate education, to the naval traditionalist, seemed to lead not back to blue water but to the LMD. Thus did the naval technological revolution begin to reshape Flag Plot, creating new tensions within, such as that between the Operator and the Manager.[13]

One index of the merging of naval management with its civilian counterpart was the increasing flow of retired admirals out of Flag Plot into civilian executive positions. At one time, for a naval officer to go "into business" was permanently to soil his white gloves. Among the admirals of Dewey's generation, only one went into business on retirement.

But times had changed. Despite Kelly Turner's gripes, a man in his late fifties or early sixties was far from through. In the mid-1950s the base pay for a two-star admiral was about $13,000 a year; depending on his expertise and his "name value," an industrial position could reward him many times over. In 1956 Ben Moreell, father of the Seabees, was reported to be receiving $150,000 as board chairman of Jones and Laughlin Steel Corporation. Denfeld was a "consultant" to Sun Oil Corporation, Bill Halsey was president of International Telecommunications Laboratories, Earle Mills was president of Foster Wheeler Corporation, and Fechteler was a "consultant" to General Electric's Atomic Products Division (in which role he came perilously close to influence-peddling). Other admirals found retirement homes with companies dealing in electronics, automobiles, communications, aviation, oil, and construction.

Dwight Eisenhower would later label this close military-civilian association the "military-industrial complex," and scholars would regard the phenomenon with horror, but what was really happening provided, in the Navy's case, a lowering of the walls that had surrounded the service for generations. More and more, what the Navy found necessary in its own management policies was reflected in the civilian world of business and industry, and vice versa. The sea had always made the Navy special, not least in its own eyes, but now Flag Plot had to give more than casual attention to the ways of the shore. The rewards of service, once reserved for those who had spent a professional lifetime on blue water, now were being more widely distributed.

—The ideals were still there. So were the customs and traditions, the pride, the fierce love of blue and gold. But now there were more courses than ever by which a man could navigate the great barrier reef.

☆

Napoleon Bonaparte was a land animal, and so his judgment of admirals (some of his had served him ill) came as no surprise: "On the sea nothing is genius or inspiration; everything is positive and empiric. The admiral needs only one science, that of navigation. . . . An admiral needs to divine nothing; he knows where the enemy is and his strength."

Such plodding dray horses could indeed be found in the United States Navy at any time, including the postwar period. Few were "inspired," in the Napoleonic sense (who could be?), even fewer were "geniuses," and none outside the chaplains was in the business of divination. But they were far from men of "one science," and the achievement of Flag Plot capped a lifetime of something not to be taken lightly, a career of *service*.

Finally, though, they all had to leave Flag Plot behind (all but Leahy, King, Nimitz, and Halsey, that is; the five-stars were always on active duty). Some simply sat and remembered, a few wrote of their experiences, but most—because they were healthy, vital men who craved action of some kind—took other work. Some, inevitably, became entangled in their new positions with conflict-of-interest laws, an exceptionally hazy area of the legal world.

Admirals, unlike more junior officers, could usually get along on their retirement pay, but many chose not to. Further government service was made less attractive by the Dual Compensation Act, a much-amended legal maze that depleted by formula the retired pay of any regular officer working in government if his new salary exceeded a certain level. The act was a time-honored reflection of the national unease about men on horseback, but in the process the government denied itself the hard-won expertise of un-counted years of military service.

When the world of work was at last left astern, the men of Flag Plot could be found, for the most part, clustered about beloved duty stations— San Diego, Norfolk, and the like. Many settled around Annapolis. A few returned to the hills, prairies, or cities from which they had come, so long ago, as wide-eyed midshipmen-to-be. Their occasional critics could always charge them with being arrogant, unimaginative, and insensitive to the world around them. Some undoubtedly were. But, as individuals, their records were almost uniformly outstanding—far, far beyond the norm in the civilian sector.[14]

They were, after all, members of a naval generation of unalloyed triumph. Their country had given them the resources, the technology, and the men to wage victorious world war at sea, and they had responded magnificently. Of their accomplishments they were singularly, rightfully proud.

Proud of the uniform as well—when the time came for them to go, they were dressed for their last muster in their beloved blue and gold, the stripes climbing halfway to the elbow, and honorably shepherded to their final rest. Some chose the place of their youth, some chose Arlington. Some chose a final service at the imposing Naval Academy Chapel, modeled on London's St. Paul's Cathedral, from where their corteges would pace the short distance over the gently arched bridge spanning College Creek to the lovely little cemetery on a hill overlooking the west bank of the Severn.

The Severn led to Chesapeake Bay, and the bay opened to the sea. In the final analysis, even in the modern era, the sea bound them all together, made them special, gave their Navy both cohesion and purpose.

—And so, like Hiram Cassedy, to the sea some of them chose to return.

CHAPTER TWENTY

WARDROOM

———— ☆ ————

Through experience and tradition alike," pronounced Rear Admiral Charles Clark, "the qualities of the average American naval officer can safely be taken for granted." This was the reassuring voice of growing American naval professionalism—Clark had commanded the famed battleship *Oregon* during its much-heralded dash around Cape Horn to get to the Caribbean scene-of-action against the Spanish in 1898—and the voice, despite some croaks and stutters, remained confident throughout the twentieth century.

Stretching is an almost unbroken blue-and-gold line back to the middle of the previous century, Annapolis—except for a Civil War Naval Academy hiatus at Newport—produced these officers, men like the popular Clark (USNA 1864, graduated one year early). They were white, mainly Protestant, and overwhelmingly from the middle or upper-middle layers of society. They also tended to be parochial and overweeningly confident of themselves and of their service, seagoing Lords of Creation.

These men were both proud and jealous of their educational heritage. They were not about to admit rivals. In 1945, as the war drew to its cataclysmic climax, six bills were introduced in the House of Representatives, each proposing an additional Naval Academy—in places like southern California, San Francisco, Puget Sound, even Oklahoma. Annapolis grads responded to this threat of proliferation with the enthusiasm of sixteenth-century popes for Lutheran schismatics. Unsurprisingly, there would be no plural "naval academies" in the United States.

A few people without a college education became naval officers prior to World War II—a very few. The Navy led all the services in undergraduate time in the trenches. In 1947, at the time of service unification, 85 percent of all naval officers had attended college. The Army could claim only 77 percent, and in the upstart Air Force (where, the Navy claimed, any child could get a commission) only half the officers had a college background.[1]

The Navy's first personnel problem following the war, with the mass exodus back into civilian life, was choosing which officers to retain (and convincing these men to stay). "The candidate should possess a full measure of officer-like qualities," urged one commander. "With all credit due to the various Officer Procurement Centers, the huge number of war commissions has resulted in a percentage of poor officers." Rather than taking a large group that met minimum requirements, the service decided to admit a select few into the regular Navy, where one served at the pleasure of the president and had to resign his commission, unless special legislative or judicial action was taken. This was the standard elitist approach that the Navy, with the exception of World War II, had always followed. There were appeals that this new officer cadre be chosen "scientifically," with due emphasis on proper education.

At the peak of the wartime expansion, the Navy's career officer force (almost all Annapolitans) constituted less than 6 percent of its total officer strength. The first two years after V-J Day were exceptionally choppy sailing for naval officers, as the service tried to adjust its sights to the conflicting demands of the drawdown and the new naval globalism. The "officer problem" was a front-burner item for Chester Nimitz, and he dumped the hot potato into the lap of Rear Admiral Thomas Sprague, deputy chief of naval personnel and soon to be the first naval aviator to be fleeted up to the top personnel slot.

Tommy Sprague (not to be confused with Rear Admiral Clifton Sprague, who had commanded the outgunned Taffy 3, a vulnerable collection of escort carriers, in the courageous encounter with Japanese heavies off Samar in 1944) was USNA 1917, a veteran combat flyer who had commanded *Intrepid* during the Marshalls operation and a punishing raid against Truk. He had been in charge of CarDiv 22, the entire escort carrier group off Samar, and in helping fend off the Japanese sortie against the Leyte landing, he had won the Navy Cross. Now, he commanded a Navy team assigned to make sense of the postwar officer picture.

Sprague, working closely with congressional heavyweights like Carl Vinson, produced along with officers of the other services a landmark piece of legislation, the Officer Personnel Act of 1947. One of Vinson's sidekicks on the House Armed Services Committee, Dewey Short, described the bill as "about as interesting as a book of logarithms," which was true enough. But the handiwork of Tommy Sprague and the others charted the course for naval (and other American) officers for decades to come.

Unlike the Army, which clung stubbornly to its seniority system before World War II, the Navy had used merit selection for a quarter of a century before Pearl Harbor. The proof of its effectiveness was that the men who would run the naval war for the United States—King, Nimitz, Halsey, Spruance, Terrible Turner—were all at flag rank when the war began, and none of them had to be jettisoned. In addition, men who ascended to Flag Plot during the war—officers of the caliber of Mitscher, Radford, Forrest Sherman, and Close In Conolly—were all captains at the time of Pearl Harbor and walked smoothly into their flag leadership roles. The Navy did not need to reach down into the commander and lieutenant commander ranks to find young bloods who could win the war.

The Navy's merit policy actually went back to 1899, when a much-debated congressional "plucking bill" gave impetus for promotional flow by establishing an "up-or-out" process for the higher officer grades. The first real merit selection law came in 1916, applicable only to the Navy and the Marine Corps. (The Army insisted on maintaining its traditional seniority system, along with all the heartburn associated—such as in the huge jump that John Pershing made to general.) Board selection was required for commander and above; a second pass-over meant mandatory retirement. Under the 1916 law, promotion by seniority continued into the grade of lieutenant commander, but rising beyond meant running the great barrier reef.

Tommy Sprague and his peers, with a boost from a world war, flourished under the 1916 law, but by 1947 more was needed. The Officer Personnel Act of 1947 involved *all* the services. The act established a "promotion zone," which not only fine-tuned the advancement of officers but also allowed for the accelerated ("below zone") promotion of exceptional talent. For the first time, guidelines were established for normal duration in each officer grade: lieutenant (by the sixth year from commission); lieutenant commander (twelfth year); commander (eighteenth year); and captain (twenty-fifth year). The goal was to ensure that those selected for the stars would still have some spring in their step when they reached Flag Plot, not later than their thirtieth year of service.

The act also subjected rear admirals to mandatory retirement through the selection board process and established the new career categories of special-duty and limited-duty officers. All in all, Tommy Sprague and his fellow officers put the nation's officer personnel on a modern and reasonably equitable footing.

The Senate, however, almost rejected the bill. Only when James Forrestal threatened to refuse the post of first secretary of defense unless the Senate got on board was the act finally passed. With passage came the hardening of civilian-military lines within the new department; the officials who managed DOD were civilian appointees of the executive branch who came and went, leaving little corporate memory. Their situation contrasted mightily with that of the career military men subjected to the promotion requirements of the new law. And no legislation could guard against the occasional bad officer apple bobbing to the top. Even so, said Tommy Sprague, "the Good Lord Himself didn't do any better than eleven out of twelve."[2]

The Navy would take eleven out of twelve, but the act did nothing to address the other critical problems of officer recruitment, education, and training. Recruiting would continue to cherish elitist standards, even if the results sometimes were less than the Good Lord's ratio. Back in 1920, the so-called "Knox-King-Pye Board" had set the course for the education and training of naval officers. This board held as its major premise the notion that all naval officers should have a "well-rounded" education, and that superimposed on this amorphous entity should be a "specialty." These two concepts—the well-roundedness of the generalist and the highly concentrated knowledge of the specialist—would be in continuous conflict in the postwar Navy.

"There is no such thing as a typical officer in today's Navy," wrote Captain Robert Kelly in 1959. True enough; officers now came from a bewilderingly wide range of educational, professional, and even social backgrounds, in sharp contrast to the Annapolis-generated standard qualifications held by most officers of the prewar Navy. By 1956 only 55 percent of naval officers were "Regulars," products of either the Naval Academy or the new program of the Naval Reserve Officers Training Corps (NROTC). The rest were Reservists, who came from either the enlisted ranks or a clutch of Reserve-officer procurement programs and who served a standard set of years under contract.

Despite the increasing variety of the previous experience held by its officers, the Navy still hewed to its generalist self-image. One important index of this inclination was the minute scale of naval graduate programs. In 1927, 2 percent of the Navy's officers had been enrolled in technical postgraduate education. (Hyman Rickover was one of these.) By 1937 this figure had grown to only 3.5 percent, and by 1947, with the drawdown, only 1.5 percent of the officer corps was in graduate school. By 1957 this number had shrunk to a measly 1 percent, hardly a prescription for "specialization."

The proponents of specialization, which for the Navy meant *technical* specialization, were enraged. The Cold War provided the paramount rationale. Rickover was only the loudest of those who charged that America's schools were endangering the national security by allowing young people to fall behind the Russians in the things that counted—science, engineering, and mathematics. The postwar naval officer, in this line of thinking, *had to specialize*, or disaster was certain.[3]

—Thus the battle over *how* the quality of the Navy's officer corps would be ensured was joined. The battlegrounds would be those places where naval officers came from—specifically and foremost, the school on the banks of the Severn River.

☆

The United States Naval Academy celebrated its centennial in October 1945 in a panoply of self-congratulation that included a memorial service for the 729 alumni who had given their lives in the line of duty during those hundred years. Ironically, its future as virtually the nation's sole peacetime source of naval officers was in question. The plans for the postwar Navy envisioned a ten-to-one enlisted-officer ratio (500,000 to 50,000), and the Academy, by no stretch of the imagination, could supply such numbers.

By V-J day, James Forrestal had before him a plan to convert the Academy to a sort of two-year postgraduate school in "Navy" for young men who had completed at least three years of college. The idea was seductive, because the number of officers could be doubled (two years vice four) with existing facilities. But Forrestal and his BuPers chief, Louis Denfeld, balked; instead, they convened a special board, headed by Rear Admiral James Holloway, Jr. (the man who would soon ramrod the discharges of millions of naval personnel) to study the question of officer education.

Holloway's board rejected the grad school idea out of hand because of the importance placed on a four-year undergraduate program in a single institution. Likewise, those multiple proposals for other "naval academies" gave board members the shakes. "It was deemed wiser," remarked Holloway (USNA 1919), "that the Naval Academy at Annapolis, with its history and traditions, be the single institution representing . . . the ultimate in personal and professional standards, and a principal binding force . . . in the Navy as a whole." How Forrestal could have expected any other decision from a group loaded with "Boat School" graduates remained a mystery.

Forrestal soon appointed Holloway, a Blackshoe, as Academy superintendent. Known throughout the service, for his grand seigneur style, as "Lord Jim," Holloway had led Destroyer Squadron 10 during Operation Torch off North Africa in 1942 and had gone on to command *Iowa* in the latter months of the Pacific war. He was a personnel specialist without peer; Lord Jim did not seem to mind the paper shuffling, and he managed to fit his main recreation, golf, into his before-breakfast hours. Taking over at Annapolis in January 1947, he promoted a balanced and basic curriculum of mutually supporting courses—the generalist approach. He helped stave off a proposal to unify the service academies (a favorite notion of Dwight Eisenhower's) and, for the midshipmen, revoked a number of fossilized regulations—allowing First Class to own cars, for example.

The place was still the Naval Academy, however. When mids became twenty-one, they were allowed to drink, provided they obeyed an archaic state law forbidding them from drinking within a seven-mile radius of the nearby Maryland State House. (Many middie shenanigans turned on this single anachronism alone.) At first, Holloway also suspended the practice of marching the midshipmen across the Yard from Bancroft Hall to class, but the inevitable skylarking and lollygagging soon brought the marches back.

When Lord Jim departed in 1950, the Academy had shaken down to a relatively even keel. The Boat School had been adequate for turning out the five thousand line officers required by the prewar Navy, but now Annapolis had to maintain its traditional stability and esprit by incorporating change. Throughout the fifties the struggle between traditionalists and innovators went on. The curriculum was by no means static. The midshipmen had to be introduced to jet propulsion, electronics, and nuclear physics. Old favorites were still there, and claimed their victims: "steam" (naval engineering); "juice" (electrical engineering); "skinny" (physics and chemistry); and "bull" (history, government, and anything else smacking of the humanities). Amid the changes came concerns that the old ways were eroding. When Rear Admiral Walter Boone, USNA 1921, took over as superintendent in 1954, he was distressed to learn that ballroom dancing was no longer being taught.

By the mid-fifties the demands of the global Navy had produced a brigade size of about four thousand midshipmen, which called for another round of building and improvements in the Yard. The building program begun in 1957 inaugurated mighty tides of change, particularly in brigade curriculum and social composition. Enlisted personnel had been funneled into the Academy for years. Back in 1914 the Naval Academy Preparatory School (NAPS) had been established at the behest of Woodrow Wilson's populist-inclined secretary of the Navy, Josephus Daniels. By 1950, 160 enlisted men per year were allowed to compete for Academy appointments.

After some vicissitudes, including a six-year stint at Bainbridge, Maryland, NAPS settled in at Newport in 1949. (A previous school in San Diego had been closed in 1931.) NAPS was a one-year college prep course, and by no means all enlisted men, or other aspirants needing academic help, got through. Of course, if a student happened to be a 240-pound linebacker, his chances were markedly improved; NAPS was notorious for stashing the Academy's prize athletes. Those who failed the curriculum, usually from one-third to one-half of each class, mostly ended up back in the fleet to serve out their obligated service. The ones who got through, while often ranking toward the lower end of their Academy classes, were nonetheless highly (and rightly) valued by the Navy.

The changes at the Academy thus did not involve broadening its enlisted base. And these changes would occur not in place of but alongside tradition. Mister Joe Gish, the perennial plebe, would still throw a brace at the command of an upper-class and recite the days, hours, and minutes to June week. Like West Point, Annapolis still emphasized military engineering appropriate to the naval profession. The attrition rate remained remarkably constant over the years; no matter how hard the Academy's administrators worked on carefully judging the thousands of candidates for admission every year—and the Admissions Board worked very hard indeed—for every four inductees taken into a given plebe class, one of them (for whatever reason) would not be around in four years to get his commission. The three fundamental cornerstones were still there: mental, moral, and physical training.

So was the exhausting schedule; an Annapolis plebe followed a ninety-one-hour work week, interspersed with what the Navy, in all seriousness, called "mandatory sleep."

Everywhere he walked in the Yard, the midshipman was saturated with tradition. Monuments, paintings, ship models, mighty deeds, heroic names—none of these could he escape, even if he wanted to. And there, in the museum just inside Gate Three, was the glass case housing the graduation pictures of the men of Annapolis currently "on watch"—inevitably the chief of naval operations, fleet commanders, key players on the joint staffs and within the Pentagon. The old grads filled his history textbooks, their portraits lined the walls of Bancroft Hall, their memory rose towering in stone about the grounds, and their names were commemorated in the buildings in which he studied and the very sidewalks over which he marched to class. "The history of the past is the flesh-and-blood of the present," noted an old grad, Hanson Baldwin.

The Naval Academy, along with West Point, was the only truly *national* educational institution until 1955, when the Air Force Academy at Colorado Springs was opened. (The Coast Guard Academy up at New London never seemed to count.) But Annapolis was absolutely *unique;* there was literally no other school like the Boat School, anywhere. The public, looking only at Flag Plot and seeing USNA stamped on practically everyone who wore the stars, tended to see the Academy as a "school for admirals;" Annapolis saw itself as a school that trained junior officers for the Navy and the Marines. (Up to one-sixth of each class could elect to join the Corps.) Moreover, unlike West Point and Colorado Springs, Annapolis had included civilians on its faculty from the very beginning, usually around 50 percent of the teaching staff.

The Academy was a tremendous source of national pride, not least because of its makeup. The most common of the eight ways to get there was by congressional appointment, which ensured a truly national brigade matrix; every state and region had a stake in the midshipmen. Thus, adolescent peccadiloes that would be winked away at a civilian university could bring on a congressional investigation at Annapolis, arguably the most high-profile of all American schools. The superintendent was constantly under the gun, for his chain of command was a very short pipeline that led directly to the secretary of the Navy. The Naval Academy was the flagship of naval professional education, and its acute visibility made the place not only a national centerpiece but also an easy target for potshots from all quarters.

And the high profile was changing its shape. The mids were given greater personal freedom, beginning with Lord Jim's edict about their cars. Annapolis, the old saying went, was the place where one's God-given rights were taken away when one first walked through the gate, to be given back, one by one, as "privileges." Now, weekend passes and liberalized Christmas, spring, and summer leaves contrasted with the monastic confinement of the past. Smoking, strictly limited in the old days as to place and time, became much less subject to restrictions.

Forty years before, the young gentlemen of Annapolis, togged out in their "monkey jackets"—tight-fitting, brass-buttoned, choker-collared dress blouses—had been forced to endure ballroom instruction, of the type much-beloved by Admiral Boone, at the hands of a French dancing master who beat out the time with suitable Gallic vigor. The white-gloved young men danced with each other, and the plebes were not allowed to date at all.

By 1961 Bancroft Hall had its first "hostess" (the widow of a naval officer), young ladies routinely attended dances and hops, and even the lowly plebes could go to six "tea dances" a year with real live females. The women who were grist for the Academy's social mill were selected on an inbred basis worthy of a Kentucky thoroughbred stable. At any given time, about two thousand of them were on the "active" list, meaning they were deemed worthy of associating with midshipmen (black women were specifically provided for the occasional black middie).

But the real changes were going on inside the classrooms. At long last the cram-and-jam, stand-and-recite curriculum so loathed by Rickover and many other victims was being overhauled. Basic courses in math and science now emphasized fundamentals and analytics. Math, physics, and chemistry offerings were beefed up, and on the other side of the Yard the bull courses stressed theme writing and languages (the latter called "Dago" by the mids).

Formerly, a classic exam question in steam might have been: "Sketch and describe a Babcock and Wilcox boiler." Now, the old show-and-tell was replaced by questions that probed fundamentals of heat-transfer systems and thermodynamics. The Class of 1962 was the first to get the new curriculum. The courses remained heavily vocational; the firm conviction that the only sensible training was the kind that made the naval officer omni-competent aboard ship never went away. But the humanities approach was sneaking its nose farther and farther under the tent; during the early sixties a modern-drama seminar was studying the likes of Beckett, Ionesco, Albee, and Kopit.[4]

Change amid tradition—in a sense, this was always occurring at the Boat School, and the midshipmen, far more relaxed about such things than their elders, tended to take the changes in stride. Middies were less flamboyantly spartan than their counterparts up on the Hudson; the average midshipman salute was far from crisp, and Academy officers often referred patronizingly to their charges as "boys" or "lads." (At West Point, the cadets were "men.") A group of visiting Military Academy cadets was horrified by the shocking laxity they found in the Yard: dirty rifles, no continual room inspection, and private middie sea-lockers off-limits to prying officers.

The Naval Academy *was* less starchy than its sister institution, and with reason: the school successfully promoted a natural politesse among its future officers, the practice of staying aloof while remaining informal—the art of living in close proximity with enlisted men aboard ship. Still, its rigors far outstripped those of civilian institutions. Among these were compulsory chapel (detested by most mids, although some found the custom excellent for a Sunday-morning nap); constant ranking, in and out of the classroom—the pressure to perform and excel never went away; and constant reminders to do and learn. Over the urinals in Bancroft Hall were posted cards of signal flag hoists with the legend "Do You Know These?"

Despite the generalist, vocational emphasis of their education, many Academy alumni embarked on other career paths, proof that the age of specialization was not going away. Of the 765 graduates in the Class of 1962, fewer than half—375—actually went to traditional surface line assignments (and some of these would later go to submarines). Of the rest, 200 went Navy air, 58 chose the Marines, and 80 the Air Force. The balance went to staff positions or into the Army. "One is justified in wondering," mused one civilian critic, "whether the curriculum is in sound alignment with vocational realities."

The officer-civilian faculty members were not first-rate, in the sense that they could match a front-line civilian institution degree for degree and publication for publication. In 1963 only 15 percent of the 269 officers aboard had an advanced degree of any kind. The mids themselves were not in the upper echelon of Scholastic Aptitude Test scores; they came mostly from the second rank. Their lockstep schedule, from reveille to taps, usually precluded the pursuit of special academic interests. In many ways—because of the regimentation, the uniformity of curriculum, the weight of tradition—the midshipmen formed a "monolithic adolescent culture," one that was carefully controlled (and as cheerfully subverted whenever the mids thought they could get away with anything).

The Naval Academy was thus a "cultural steamroller." Regardless of the curriculum changes, which were important, there was only one major field of study at Annapolis: *Navy.* The midshipmen led a highly insulated life, yet one rich in promise and opportunity. They lived in confinement and constriction, yet were waited on by attentive messmen like little lords. They were fed according to carefully calculated dietetic principles, and their health was monitored constantly. Recreationally, the Academy was superior to any country club.

And these young people *traveled*, far more than their civilian peers, and sometimes to the ends of the earth. They first went to sea during Youngster Summer, often to exotic ports of call in Europe, the Middle East, or the western Pacific. They did aviation and Marine training on their Second Class cruise. As "Firsties," they might travel the world, this time as a junior member of the wardroom—their first entry into the fraternity of "officers and gentlemen."

In 1965 the changes initiated back in 1957 came to one kind of climax with the abandonment (to the horror of many alumni) of the lockstep program. Now, incoming plebes could "validate" (test out of) courses, choose electives, and have "majors" and "minors" in available subjects of study. The civilian faculty members, if not brighter, were becoming better educated; 29 percent of them now held a doctorate, and this percentage would increase dramatically in the years to come. Of the officers, 3 percent held Ph.D.'s in 1965. There was now a civilian academic dean (A. Bernard Drought, appointed in July 1964), charged with strengthening the program. Faculty research opportunities were increasingly encouraged.

None of this was accomplished without bitter alumni resentment. Many old grads bemoaned the "civilianization" of their beloved alma mater. One of them said remorsefully that the changes "will turn the Academy into a University"—which, to those who believed above all in the uniqueness of their educational heritage, was the last thing wanted or needed.

But the proof was in the pudding. Most midshipmen were not insane, and therefore did not especially enjoy their monastic years at the Boat School, but once they got their class ring (out in the fleet, their non-Academy wardroom mates called them "ring-knockers"), they were the most ardent alumni to be found anywhere. And they were loyal not only to their school but also to their service institution. In the mid-sixties about 80 percent of Academy graduates remained on active duty after their obligated four years of service (later extended to five), compared with 43 percent for graduates of NROTC programs and 33 percent for Officer Candidate School products. Their talents refracted through every branch of the service.

Annapolis was unabashedly elitist (in 1965, only one out of four applicants was admitted, and this ratio would become ever more exclusive), aggressively sectarian, and narcissistically in love with itself and the service of which the midshipmen were a part. But the Boat School was arguably the best-known and most popular national educational institution, its graduates were generally admired and respected far beyond their years, and the country, all in all, was being well-served.

One midshipman probably spoke for most when he said, "The sense of power and pride one feels one has attained as the result of one's training at the Naval Academy [makes] priceless possessions that one cherishes, but never mentions." The subject at Annapolis was Navy, and the mids were admonished to follow

> . . . laws of the Navy.
> Unwritten and varied they be
> And he that is wise will observe them
> Going down in his ship to the sea.[5]

☆

Despite all its changes, the Naval Academy, with its eight hundred or so graduates a year, could not come close to meeting the persistent demands of naval globalism. The Naval Reserve Officers Training Corps, which had been in existence since 1925 (initially operating at seven schools), had provided no more than a trickle of officers to the fleet before the war. In 1945, in the wake of the numerous wartime accelerated officer training programs, the NROTC Expansion Bill raised the maximum number of trainees from 7200 to 24,000—to be reduced to 14,000 one year after war's end. Twenty-five new NROTC units were established at schools around the country, and many people in the dying V-12 Program were phased into them.

But these numbers were in danger. After V-J Day the clampdown on the money spigot forced the Navy to send formal notices to all V-12 and NROTC units that they would be terminated as of 28 February 1946. If this was a bluff to shake money out of the congressional tree, the ploy worked. An emergency appropriations bill was the result, and NROTC units—barely—stayed in business.

Such hand-to-mouth measures, however, obviously would not do. Forrestal was acutely aware that naval officers in the polarized postwar world had to come from somewhere, in addition to the Naval Academy. Once the "Jacobs-Barker Plan," the two-year academy idea, had been deep-sixed, Forrestal asked Holloway's board—ten members, including two civilian educators—to come up with some answers.

Lord Jim and his board produced a proposal (ever after called the "Holloway Plan") that was eventually enacted into law by Congress. The NROTC program would stay on the books. Its young men would receive, however, far more than their predecessors had ever gotten from the prewar Navy: four years of tuition and fees, free books, and $50 a month in pocket money. Participating institutions, not the Navy, would set the academic standards. Candidates had to be accepted by both the Navy and the school.

The real architect of the Holloway Plan was Arthur ("Beanie") Adams, a former naval officer and provost at Cornell who had worked with both the V-7 and V-12 programs during the war. Adams selected the schools, did much of the lobbying, and organized the system of candidate selection and screening. Forrestal gave the proposal his full backing.

—And Carl Vinson moved the Holloway Plan into law. Lord Jim paid a visit to the Swamp Fox at the latter's Georgia farm in July 1946, pointing out that fall classes across the nation were starting in two months and the badly needed NROTC bill was dead in the water. The bill was on the House calendar the following week. Harry Truman (somewhat reluctantly, due to Army concern) signed the Holloway Plan into law (Public Law 729) in the middle of August.

Five thousand slots were available at fifty-two civilian colleges and universities in 1947, and about fifty thousand high-school seniors, graduates, and Navy and Marine enlisted men took a shot at what was to become one of the best scholarship opportunities anywhere in the country. After four years of *civilian* study (their majors were restricted, but not by much—no predentistry or forestry, for example), they were looking at *regular* Navy commissions (just like the Boat School grads), and their officer lineal, or seniority, numbers would be just behind the Academy graduates in the same year group. Holloway predicted that regular commissions would be split roughly fifty-fifty for the next few years between Academy and NROTC graduates (but he still believed that his alma mater was the surer if tougher way to make a career in the Navy).

The new plan included a "college" portion designed to train naval aviators and commission them as Reservists; the aviation aspect would later be broadened to include practically every officer specialty. More schools and a broader curriculum selection were available to the "college" people, but the scholarship benefits were much lower and the Reservist could be rejected for augmentation into the regular Navy. Holloway was looking toward a roughly equal opportunity for promotion between Boat Schoolers and other officers, because the disparity in this regard at the end of the war was brutally obvious: on V-J Day, although Reserves were then about 85 percent of total naval personnel strength, only two rear admirals and eight commodores (most of them specialists) were Reserves.

Lord Jim expected NROTC graduates to be less career-oriented than Annapolis products. "The Naval Academy is an undergraduate institution which no man should enter unless he wishes to make the Navy a life career," he said. The Boat Schoolers, after all, had paid their dues. Members of forty-six Naval Academy classes (1901–1946) had served in World War II, and 6.3 percent of all these graduates still in service had died in combat. Of the ten Academy classes immediately prior to Pearl Harbor—the ones that furnished the destroyer officers, submarine skippers, and aviation squadron leaders—12 percent of those still on board had been killed (16 percent in the Class of 1936 alone).

But Holloway was not in favor of "putting all our eggs in one basket insofar as methods of initial [officer] procurement are concerned," and hence the rejuvenated NROTC was an idea whose time had come. In 1947, with the fifty-thousand-officer Navy on hold because of the drawdown, eleven thousand officers came from Annapolis and the remaining nine thousand from other sources. Holloway preached "integration" and "synthesis" in the naval officer corps. He also voiced the ideal: "Assignment and performance are entirely dependent upon the intellect, the character, the industry, and the enthusiasm of the individual officer."[6]

NROTC instructors were duly cycled through "orientation" courses, initially conducted at Northwestern University. They were, within a few weeks, whipped through sessions on speech, practice teaching, administration, and educational psychology and then went forth to their assigned campuses. Approximately 140 Navy and Marine officers were assigned annually to the duty. At first the naval presence was welcomed on most participating campuses, and the Holloway Program was applauded nationally from the outset. "All concerned should benefit greatly from this plan," cheered *Collier's* magazine. "The Navy especially, because it will be in far closer touch than ever before with the nation's colleges and universities and their big research facilities and inquiring-minded faculties."

The initial budget was $15 million. In theory, Lord Jim's ideas were excellent: bright young men, seventeen to twenty-one years old, who otherwise could not get to college, now had a chance for a quality education and potential naval careers. A Holloway man, under the initial setup, would cost the government about $10,000—about half the price of the Annapolis middie. And the plan seemed perfectly consonant with the time-honored American ideal of citizen soldiers and sailors. In the mid-fifties NROTC units began to receive enlisted men from the fleet as part of the Naval Enlisted Scientific Education Program (NESEP), and their caliber was generally very high. "We had extraordinarily good men" in NESEP, remembered an officer connected with the program.

But not all was smooth sailing. Annapolis mids were quick to note that although the "Holloways" got the same commission as themselves, the "civilian students" were subject to naval discipline only three hours a week. There were fears that the Boat School's standards would have to be lowered to meet the competition. A popular chant arose on the banks of the Severn: "Keep your car, keep your gal, keep your pay—be an officer the 'Holloway!' "[7]

As time passed and the first groups of NROTC men reached the fleet, the criticisms redoubled in volume and became far more serious. "Creeping *rigor mortis*" was setting in, according to one "Professor of Naval Science" (the head man of an NROTC unit). Ten years after its inception, he said, "the Holloway Plan is dying."

The statistics coming in the door were positive: in a good year, the Navy received up to 30,000 applications for the scholarship and accepted about 2000 (1800 from civilian life, the rest from the fleet). Going out the door, however, the record was shabby. Of the seven NROTC classes entering after 1950 (about 2000 apiece), 1264 would be commissioned and 177 (college programmers) would augment to the regular Navy three years later—an atrocious 8.5 percent yield. And campus attrition in the last two years of a four-year curriculum doubled that of the first two: 44 percent for academics, 24 percent for "lack of motivation." Too many young men were taking the money and running. The Regular NROTC Class of 1953 was examined for its career potential after their sophomore year: 17 percent said yes to a career at the time, 30 percent said no, and 53 percent were undecided. When their time for election came up in 1956, only 13 percent of the entire class— Regulars and Reservists—stayed in the naval service.

Academy grads knew what had gone wrong. "Our Holloway Plan failed when it set base course toward public benevolence rather than enlightened Navy self-interest," wrote one. "We offered 'liberal education' to promising

American youth rather than opportunity to compete for the naval vocation."
Old Annapolitans were enraged that the Holloways were getting only a
"Cook's Tour of the naval service." The program required 120 to 130 credit
hours in liberal arts majors and 140 to 180 hours in engineering majors for
graduation, which included only 24 hours of naval courses. The Naval
Academy devoted twice as much time to naval subjects and required about
160 hours for a degree (always, regardless of major, a bachelor of science in
engineering). And the Annapolis midshipmen "lived Navy" twenty-four
hours a day.

These were unabashedly elitist outcries, but they had a point. Besides,
the NROTC units had often become outcasts on their own campuses, de-
nigrated by the professoriate both for the quality of the military instructors
(most with only a bachelor's degree) and of the instruction. Harold Dodds,
the president of Princeton, was only one of many educators arguing that
ROTC programs in general were substandard and unbecoming to both
military and collegiate vocations. And in the Navy's case, Public Law 729
provided for *civilian* educators to run the program from the Bureau of Naval
Personnel. "To them," claimed one exasperated critic, "the philosophy underlying the law is religious dogma; their own edicts based on the concept
are infallible." Professors of naval science from all around the nation railed
against this educational papacy, with few results.

Lack of *motivation* for the naval service seemed to be the key, but how
to adequately measure this intangible in a seventeen-year-old was another
question altogether. Things had changed from the simpler days of Rear
Admiral Stephen Luce's "School of the Ship" a century before: "The rem-
edy," Luce had written, "is to catch them while young and inure them to
ship life from the first."

The combination of a lip-service naval education within a predominantly
civilian environment was athwartship every seagoing tradition. Many naval
officers viewed the program with deep suspicion if not open hostility. Few
of them pressed their detailers for NROTC instructor billets, and indeed
the quality of NROTC instruction was often abysmally low. Further, with
the accelerating pace of naval technology in the postwar era, the "Holloways"
could no more than dip their toes in the mainstream of the modern Navy
before they were tossed in, complete with ensign's commission, to sink or
swim.

These problems never went away and were, indeed, endemic to the
concept itself. But the Holloway Plan, tinkered with but never altered in
the essentials, remained. Although quality of education and the amount of
"Navy" in the process were clearly important, the fundamental thing was
the production of naval officers. Lord Jim himself had hardly been a savant
during his years at the Academy. He graduated in the "five-fathom shot,"
the group near the anchorman; only the fact that his class graduated early
due to World War I saved him, he felt. ("I knew I would have bilged in

mechanics.") But Holloway always remained proud of his baby, which "has provided the navy with a splendid supply of junior officers and many successful senior ones ever since."[8]

—And so, this typically American solution to a naval manpower problem went its way, much-criticized and hardly "cost effective"—but, for all that, one of the finest scholarship opportunities in the United States.

☆

There were still other ways to become a naval officer. Up in Newport, the Officer Candidate School (OCS) had taken over the assembly-line creation of naval officers, a process made famous (or notorious) by the "Ninety-Day Wonders" of World War II. During the war, two hundred thousand officers, like Willie Keith of the fictional USS *Caine*, had been punched out in a few weeks at schools all over the country. In 1946 the postwar assembly line was consolidated at Newport, which could handle up to 2500 candidates at a time, in two overlapping sixteen-week curricula.

OCS was the device by which the Navy fine-tuned its officer supply. During Korea, for example, Newport spit out almost ten thousand line ensigns in less than three years. The school essentially crammed the four-year NROTC curriculum into those sixteen weeks and was the only place the Navy had for turning out officers *fast*.

By 1954 more than 40 percent of the junior officers on active duty had been run through Newport. By far the largest group of them were men who wanted to serve their military obligation as Naval Reserve officers for three years, rather than being Army fodder for two. Perhaps one hundred OCS grads a year had begun as naval enlisted men, and these were good bets for naval careers. But the bulk of these Reservists, who had the eventual choices of augmenting to the regular Navy, somehow extending their Reserve contract, or returning to civilian life, chose the third option. OCS people were older and more mature, usually equipped with an undergraduate degree from somewhere (some of them held sheepskins from institutions the anonymity of which was truly breathtaking), and often had a wife and kids. But this extra edge did not necessarily equate to a naval career and, in the cases of the family men, might even work against the option. In most Cold War years the "Wonders" left the service at an even more rapid rate than the "Holloways."

Despite the relatively poor career statistics, however, the Navy depended on Newport to keep its wardrooms manned. And still, Newport was not enough. In 1948 the Navy initiated yet another program, the Reserve Officer Candidate (ROC) School, at Newport and San Diego. Three years later the two groups were joined, at Treasure Island in San Francisco Bay. The ROCs were college students who drilled as enlisted men at their local Reserve Centers, capping off their student years with two summers of classroom and seagoing instruction at "TI."

The 1951 enrollment of ROCs was less than 1900, and the attrition rate from the program was enormous. The ROCs for all the 1951 summer session were selected from over 11,000 applicants from 486 different colleges. (Some of the ROC schools were even more bizarre than the Newport variety.) The training the ROCs received was, if anything, more frenetic and haphazard than the "Wonders" got back in Newport. After three years of operation the ROC School had produced a grand total of only 292 ensigns. A few ROCs would make the Navy a career, but in the 1950s the process was probably the least-satisfactory method of producing naval officers.

But the Navy had little choice. The wardrooms had to be filled—and kept filled. Fortunately, the School of the Ship did its work. For the first six months or so, the freshly minted Academy ensign would usually run ahead of his NROTC, OCS, or ROC contemporaries. But then, as Lord Jim had said, the merits and frailties of the individual took over, buttressed by further naval training.[9]

—And the Navy was not through educating its officers after their undergraduate diploma was delivered, not by a long shot. For all of them, whether from Annapolis or elsewhere, their naval education was only beginning.

☆

"Graduate school" was anathema to most of the men of the naval line. Advanced degrees were for restricted types: Aeronautical Engineering Duty Officers, Ordnance Engineering Duty Officers, EDOs, and the like. The line prejudice against such specialists was strong—implicit, for example, in the belief that "engineering duty types never go to sea" (which was false).

The statistics were grim reminders of this prejudice. In 1953 the Navy's Postgraduate School in Monterey, California, awarded only 167 degrees, bachelor's *and* master's. In one two-year period (1959–1961) the Navy lost six times this number of officers with graduate degrees, the great majority voluntary retirements or resignations. In 1960 the Cold War Navy mustered a grand total of 70,000 officers; of these, exactly 140 were enrolled in technical curricula leading to master's degrees. (Practically no one was interested in doctors' degrees.)

The Postgraduate School had had a troubled, checkered career since its inception back in 1904 as a special course in marine engineering conducted by the old Bureau of Engineering. The school moved to the Naval Academy in 1912, still emphasizing engineering technology, and proceeded to bounce from pillar to post for the next forty years. World War I shut down naval graduate training. Its postwar revivification changed its title from "Postgraduate Department" to "Postgraduate School." (Captain Ernie King was its first postwar head.) In the interwar period the curriculum broadened, but only to include newer branches of technology, such as radio communications and mechanical, electrical, and aeronautical engineering. Few line officers enrolled.

In the thirties the course of study expanded once more, to embrace such subjects as law, finance, supply, and business administration. Still, few line officers were in class. Then came World War II, and the school walked the plank again. With the postwar drawdown, its very existence was in question. Surviving by a hair, the school moved in the winter of 1951–1952 from its old quarters in the former Marine Barracks at Annapolis to the elegant Del Monte Hotel resort in Monterey, replete with beautifully manicured grounds and the spectacular California coastal scenery.

Monterey was plush—too damned plush for many naval officers, and the place immediately gained the "country club" cachet that had dogged the Naval War College in Newport. The officers assigned to Monterey, about a thousand a year in the sixties, underwent a crowded academic year of four ten-week terms. They were usually lieutenants and lieutenant commanders, many of them with restricted officer designators. Although one graduate claimed that Monterey "is a much more sensitive and progressive servant of the element of society it serves—the Navy—than are most technical schools," during the first two decades after the war the school was not a big-ticket item for naval line officers. This was partially because the Navy was being run by admirals who had gone through their salad years in the thirties and forties and who had usually not seen the need to have this particular ticket punched.

Furthermore, Monterey had trouble making its annual student quotas. Since 1960 an increasing number of officers—largely "liberal-arts types" from NROTC and OCS—lacked the undergraduate background needed to quality for the technically oriented program. And many young men who might have met the standards were using their badly needed technological expertise elsewhere, particularly in naval aviation and in Rickover's burgeoning nuclear power program.

Despite these problems, the increasing pressures for specialization and officer expertise in the 1960s bit in and took hold at Monterey. By 1970, 80 percent of all the Navy's postgraduate students (most of the rest were on special orders to civilian institutions) were at Monterey, which by then was awarding doctorates in certain fields. More and more, the men who commanded the ships, squadrons, and boats tended to have graduate experience.

Four out of every five instructors at Monterey were civilians, most of them with doctorates, many of them highly regarded in their fields. Their research money had increased sixtyfold in fifteen years, to about $2 million, and their research efforts, and those of their students, were sponsored by the likes of the Office of Naval Research, the Department of Defense, the Atomic Energy Commission, and the National Aeronautics and Space Administration.

The curriculum had been smoothed out, and Monterey now produced specialists in such areas as communications management, underwater physics systems, nuclear engineering effects, operations research and systems analysis, computer science, oceanography, and meteorology. In all this the Navy, despite itself, was admitting at last that the Age of the Specialist had arrived.

For those who yearned for a postgraduate dose of "Navy"—strategy, tactics, geopolitics, the good stuff—there was still the Naval War College, Admiral Luce's brainchild, established back in 1884. The ten-month curriculum at Newport, offered as "junior" and "senior" courses, featured seminars on such matters, and the better results saw the light of day in the *Naval War College Review*.

The Naval War College was now more than simply a place to which one took one's golf clubs in expectation of sharpening one's game for about a year. Chester Nimitz, as chief of naval operations, sent Raymond Spruance there in 1946 to upgrade the place. But Spruance allowed the war games to be dominated by surface tactics, as they had been before the war, and Nimitz had to assign Captain Charles Brown, a naval aviator, to add other dimensions to the curriculum. The school became an increasingly good ticket for everyone from lieutenant to captain, the quality of the instructional staff profited from an infusion of bright young civilians, and, in many ways, the stint in Newport was the most popular graduate training the Navy offered. Perhaps this was because the college was uncertified and offered no degree, only a certificate of completion (thus removing the onus of "civilianization"). [10]

Formal graduate education, despite inner reluctance and resistance, thus became increasingly standard in the postwar Navy. But for the line officer the *real* education remained hands-on, with the hardware. In this sense, his college days had given the green ensign only a passport to the real thing. Now, degree in hand and golden ensign bars gleaming, he was expected to learn his trade.

☆

The pick of the Navy's trade schools was at the Naval Air Station in Pensacola, Florida. There came the green ensigns, the former enlisted personnel and civilians (naval aviation cadets), the college boys—the young men who wanted Navy wings of gold. The aviation cadets, in particular, were "a super bunch of people," recalled Rear Admiral Francis Foley. For all of them, the course took about eighteen months; in 1950 each one of these aspiring eaglets cost the government $2000 a month to train.

They earned their wings; 30 percent would wash out of each class. Everyone began in preflight, or Ground School, for four months. They learned about weather, aviation regulations, communications, engineering, aerodynamics, aerial navigation. They underwent "the dunker," a device which might have done good service for the Spanish Inquisition, an actual cockpit that splashed them into the water and taught them how to survive a ditching at sea. At last, when they got to the flight line and the not-so-tender ministrations of their instructors, they found that the old Yellow Perils were history; in 1960 Basic Flight was conducted in changeable-pitch-propped SNJ "Texans"—slow, clumsy, and (relatively) safe.

The eaglets went through basic training at several outlying fields on the general theory that if they cracked up (and dozens did), they were likely to hazard no one's life but their own. "Solo" was the goal. There were usually twenty-eight weeks of flying, about 175 hours in the air. From the art of learning to fly in a straight line (harder than might be expected with the radial-engined Texan), the students progressed to instruments and radio-range flying. Then on to formation and night flying, cross-country hops, gunnery, and combat techniques.

At last, after almost a year, came a chance at a tailhook landing. In 1950 the light carrier *Wright* was used as an "ensign smasher" for carrier quali-fication; later, this duty fell for many years to the beloved second *Lexington*, old CVT-16. The rookie first practiced bounce landings on a carrier deck outline painted on a runway, until "he begins to believe that the man down there with the flags—the landing signal officer—has seen airplanes land before." Then, he hopefully tried to get on and off his carrier in one piece. (Most did, although a few "Dilberts"—shaken but still breathing—had to be fished from the drink.) Six good landings brought qualification—and the coveted wings.

After that ordeal, on to specialization: attack aircraft, interceptors, jets, patrol planes, helicopters. After almost two years the naval aviator entered the fleet with his squadron. And even then he would periodically be recycled through training, requalifying in old aircraft and learning the tricks of new ones. Naval aviators were in the prime of physical condition, razor-sharp aerial athletes, and by the time they were done, as of the early fifties, the Navy had spent $45,000 to train each of them, an individual cost that would soon skyrocket into six figures.[11]

These kind of men were hard to come by. About 2300 walked through the gates of Pensacola every year; one out of four failed the eye exam, and one out of eight, a "mechanical comprehension" test. The Navy could not guarantee them a career. In some years, as few as 3 percent of eligible naval aviators might be accepted for a regular commission, in other years as many as 25 percent. The danger was not the problem; indeed, the thrill of risking everything in the sky was part of the lure. (At Pensacola, one death occurred for every forty thousand hours of student flying.)

The problems for the aviation community were several, and on the ground. There was no all-out war, such as the conflict that had propelled tens of thousands of American youngsters, including a future president, George Bush, into naval aviation training during World War II. The draft law of the fifties required two years of active military service; the eaglets had to sign up for four years (later increased to five, then six). Jobs were plentiful on the outside for college-trained men, and the trainee at Pensacola, in 1953, earned the grand total of $109.50 a month. Above all, said Vice Admiral John Dale Price, chief of naval air training in 1953, "Flying today offers less of a challenge to the daring. Young men . . . tend to look upon flying as a vocation comparable to any other profession." The year before, naval aviation had attained only 70 percent of its quota.

Troubling—most troubling. Vice Admiral John Cassady told a Senate committee in 1952 that naval aviation, on the statistics, was twenty times more lethal than riding on scheduled airlines. But the danger had always been there, because flying the Navy way was the toughest flying in the world. When George van Deurs, later to rise to rear admiral, went through Pensacola in 1923, he and his buddies had been lured there by the risk and the skills involved. Within eighteen months of the day van Deurs got his wings, over a quarter of his Pensacola class was dead. Within four years, more than half of them were dead or permanently disqualified from flight.

Things were safer in the fifties, but naval aviation would never be "routine." And safe, money-making "routine" was what youths seemed to yearn for. There were over 1.5 million young men in the nation's colleges early in the decade, and almost no one seemed to want to fly. One aviation recruiter in San Francisco said that "there is less interest here in flying than in truck driving." Now, van Deurs and his generation were left to bemoan the fact that the pizazz required for naval aviation seemed to be in increasingly short supply.

By 1956 the Air Force, against its wishes, had been forced to provide civilian contract flight training for *its* badly needed pilots, but when this idea (NROTC flight training at civilian universities, for example) was broached to the Navy, the eagles recoiled in horror. "I find it difficult to even talk about the matter," said one. "I'm so dead set against the contract plan that I can't discuss it without emotion." To the naval aviator (and he had a point), Navy flying was entirely sui generis. Civilian training was not, could not be, the highly specialized and thoroughly unique *Navy* way. "[Our] system," said a Navy spokesman, "has produced the finest aviators in the world and the Navy considers it most unwise to shift to a different system."[12]

—So the Navy would train its own. Naval eagles would instruct naval fledglings. But the carriers were still out there, and their planes had seats that needed to be filled. By 1957 the Navy had to produce, somehow, 3300 aviators a year to fill those seats, culled, at standard depletion rates, from 4400 successful Pensacola applicants. Recruiting therefore became high-pitched and constant. Benefits replaced adventure and patriotism as the primary selling tools.

At Pensacola the new recruits found that training was becoming tougher, with newer airframes and more systems to learn. All-jet training was phased in earlier in the curriculum. (The multiengine aviators and the helo jocks would learn their trades later.) The venerable Texan went the way of all hardware in November 1955, replaced by the prop-driven T-34B Mentor. The Mentor was destined for a long service life at Pensacola, as was the jet-powered Lockheed TV, the Navy version of the USAF T-33. The dependable, piston-engine T-28B came on line also, the staple of the basic course for years to come.

As good as they were, the successful students at Pensacola could no longer do their job while alone in the air, unless they flew the single-seaters, like the Crusader or the Skyhawk. Even the simplest fleet aircraft were now loaded with avionics and electronics, and more brainpower and split-second decision-making were required aloft than ever before—in the WV-2 Constellations flying the North Atlantic barrier patrols, the P2 and S2F sub-hunters, the Skywarriors and Vigilantes, the F-4 Phantoms.

Aircrew and ground-duty sections in postwar naval aviation suffered from heavy turnover, poor morale, and excessive training costs. The money for these much-needed specialists was far better in the rapidly expanding civilian aviation industry. The Navy's partial solution, in the early sixties, was to make some of them officers, to put a new aviation specialist—the Naval Aviation Officer (later, Naval Flight Officer)—in the air. The NAOs got the same preflight training as naval aviators and then began to specialize in electronics, ordnance, and individual mission-oriented aircraft. They became the indispensable "second-seaters" in postwar naval aviation, to such a degree that many analysts claimed they were the key people in the plane. The aviator, this argument went, only drove, while the NAO made the aircraft do what the thing was supposed to do.[13]

Aviator or NAO, the man would need about two years before he was of any use to the Navy, and the same theme predominated at the Submarine School up in New London. The coming of the Nukes meant more officer schooling, not less, and Rickover's men, after specialized courses, prototype training, and all the rest, reached the fleet in about the same time as the fliers. The lapse of many months—necessary training before a man could be trusted in a cockpit or on the diving planes—only increased the pressure to recruit and retain these technically qualified officers.

—Only the Blackshoes kept to the School of the Ship, and this would change in time, with the formation of Surface Warfare Schools on each coast in the seventies. But in the immediate postwar years, ship-drivers learned their trade at sea. They would be funneled back ashore for specialized training in such subjects as damage control, communications, and law (every ship had a "legal officer," a much-detested collateral duty among junior members of the wardroom), but their primary school remained the bridge, the engine room, and the gun mount.

The Navy paid consummate attention to the vocational training of its line officers, but the strains of specialization were clearly splitting the much-honored generalist ideal apart at the seams.

☆

Two centuries before, the "unrestricted line" had been all there was. A sailing warship was an entity unto herself. She had no real staff suport aboard, previous little ashore, and virtually no communications network. Her officers were responsible for everything: operations, navigation, gunnery, disbursing, supply, logistics, morale, justice, intelligence, medical services—the works. Over the years the Navy shared in the trends of management everywhere, marked by increasing specialization and by a continuing devolution of authority and responsibility.

In 1776 the first naval physician had been ordered aboard John Paul Jones's *Alfred.* In 1799 the first naval chaplain was commissioned. The first engineer appeared in 1836, followed six years later by the founding of the Medical Corps. The restricted line—engineering and aeronautical engineering only—came in 1916. Thus the Navy, like a beehive, added to and subsectioned itself, and these trends only accelerated after 1945.

The Officer Personnel Act of 1947 mandated that about 32 percent of the total line officers on active duty would be specialists. About half of these were staff, and the rest were engineering, special-duty, and limited-duty officers. By rejecting a combination of these as a "Technical Corps" in 1959, the Navy stated that the restricted line structure would remain essentially the same.

The EDOs (line officers said the acronym meant "Easy Duty," "Extremely Dumb," or "Every Day Off") were creatures of the Bureau of Ships. In the early fifties there were only about nine hundred of them in the entire Navy, but their technological expertise made them indispensable. Most of them had graduate degrees in engineering specialties like chemical, electrical, electronics, mechanical, metallurgical, petroleum, nuclear, diesel, and gas turbine. Like all other members of the restricted line, they could not succeed to command at sea. Together with the aeronautical engineers and the Special Duty Officers—intelligence, cryptography, hydrography, and the like—they were lumped together under the 1947 act.

The postwar civilian economy offered considerable rewards to these specialists, and the ranks of the Navy's EDOs were bled white. From 1953 to 1962 the number of uniforms in BuShips was reduced by 48 percent. The hemorrhage was greatest at the critical midmanagement grades of captain and commander. Few dedicated career men would continue to work at Navy salaries when they could as much as triple their incomes on the outside, and even fewer young specialists were willing to take on the necessary postgraduate training. Most line officers, although more amenable to getting their tickets punched at Monterey or Newport, were disinclined to specialize in the restricted line.

The inadequate input and excessive attrition among the EDOs and AEDOs was not as severe among the other Special Duty Officers, if only because skills in naval intelligence, cryptography, and hydrography were not in great demand in the civilian marketplace. The picture was even brighter among the Limited Duty Officers. These men, former enlisted, were almost always career professionals, had years of experience in a specialized rating before they broke bread in the wardroom, and, by the mid-sixties, made up about 20 percent of the junior officer strength of the Navy. Many other officers griped about the fact that the LDOs were required to have only a high-school equivalency certificate, but most of these "Mustangs" had some kind of advanced education.

In many ways the LDOs were valuable symbols of a democracy's Navy, living proofs of an open wardroom. Their hard-won expertise simply could not be matched by callow, inexperienced junior officers from other commissioning programs, and the generally high morale and career orientation of the Mustangs made the glaring problems of specialization, as with the EDOs, seem all the more acute.[14]

☆

The Navy's problems with officers did not end with recruiting, training, and retaining of specialists. If an officer stayed around long enough, he could eventually learn at least to partially protect himself from running aground on most bureaucratic shoals and could even learn to manipulate his part of the Navy a bit from within. A Navy maxim held that "a cruise in Washington is worth two around Cape Horn."

But many junior officers were not bothering to stay around for that particular cruise. They were leaving after their obligated service, and in hordes, placing the Navy ever more firmly on the endless treadmill of recruiting and training. Some left for civilian occupations, some because they found Navy life intolerable, some for both reasons and for family obligations as well.

Periodically the Navy, with its well-honed penchant for taking its own pulse, would scrutinize the problem. Over and over, junior officers said they were *not* leaving because of low pay. Other factors were clearly at work. From beginning to end, many looked upon their required service as but an interlude; their civilian friends would ask them, not about their next duty station, but "how long do you have to do?" Some felt there was little prestige anymore in a naval career; Jones, Decatur, and Farragut were long since dead. Now, being a naval officer no longer seemed to have the splendor of the big-money professions of the postwar period—law, engineering, architecture, and business. Officers questioned about their reasons for leaving often cited the "challenge and competition" of civilian life, as against the Navy's system of "growing old together," with the occasional rejection of the less fit.

Most young officers liked the travel, the liberty ports, the fast-paced rhythms and exacting responsibilities of life at sea. Watch-standing, fleet operations, and handling men carried their own intrinsic rewards. But many young officers groaned (audibly) under the endless cascade of paperwork—the instructions, forms, reports, check-off sheets—which could drive sane men mad and which never diminished but only multiplied. Even training exercises tended to be canned, humdrum, and boring. "Gundecking," the outright forging of documents impossible to keep up with on a daily basis, was common throughout the fleet. Line officers tended to look on "paperwork" as something the sand crabs ashore did, or should be doing, but in fact much of their shipboard time was spent in the Arctic whiteout of a paper blizzard. "The line officer is the backbone of the fleet," pleaded one commander. "His career must not be subordinated to that of the staff or specialist groups, no matter what their special problems."[15]

One "special problem" concerned every midgrade officer in the postwar period and more junior men as well. This was "The Hump," which technically was described as a "gross maldistribution of officers on the lineal list by year groups." By the mid-fifties, 28 percent of the Navy's total unrestricted line officers came from just four year groups, 1942 through 1945 (about half of these Regulars). These were the wartime commissions who had stayed in, and now they formed a human tsunami headed straight for the rocky cliffs of the Officer Personnel Act.

This group, mostly lieutenant commanders and commanders, was absolutely critical to the Cold War Navy. Out of its ranks would come the destroyer captains, squadron leaders, boat skippers. Their experience was highly valued (most of them were veterans of two wars), especially when over 40 percent of all naval officers had less than four years of commissioned service. The Hump, to make matters worse, had been heightened by recalled Reservists during Korea.

Above The Hump, those officers who had been part of the relatively small procurement in the pre-Pearl Harbor days were flying free; the naval buildup of the fifties meant better selection. From fiscal 1950 through 1953 the selection rate for captain was a fantastic 90 percent, and in 1949 *100 percent* had gotten the eagles. Thus, the grades of commander and captain were filled by officers who had undergone very little of the Navy's boasted winnowing, whereas the men below, trapped in The Hump, would fall before selection boards like flies on an electric mesh.

Many in The Hump were aviators, and the morale problems generated by their bleak outlook, such as the increasingly slender chance of squadron command, led directly to the loss of men with a decade or more of flying experience, including those with dozens of combat missions. The heavy weight of job stagnation loomed over them all; "to the junior officer, the hump appears to have all [challenging] assignments sewn up in a hammock." Of course, the farsighted among the younger men could see that when The

Hump's survivors retired, in the sixties and seventies, that would greatly buck up their own promotion possibilities—like a glacier calving an iceberg. But few were interested in staying around that long.

The Hump slashed the veins of the officer corps, provoking a career bloodbath. "I hold [senior officers] responsible," charged one irate lieutenant commander, "on the simple ground of lack of leadership—moral leadership, the kind of leadership that has made our Navy great." The Navy could not simply order its officers to ride out the storm, for many of them were destined by law to be driven ashore and out of uniform. "Morale [is] near the lowest ebb reached in the last fifty years."

Commander Bud Zumwalt, the future chief of naval operations, spent two successive tours working on the problems of The Hump. Zumwalt was a Humpster, one of eight thousand Regulars at the lieutenant commander and commander level who had to be fitted into two thousand captain vacancies during the following decade. On his advice, and the advice of more senior officers finally awake to the wardroom's screams of anguish, the Navy did the only realistic thing. The service chose the middle course of spreading the increased forced attrition through the widest imaginable span of pay-grades and specialties, as well as trying to dampen the promotion flow as equitably as possible—slow, increasing pressure on the brakes.[16]

Bud Zumwalt survived; many other fine, career-oriented officers did not. The bloodbath passed almost unnoticed by the public, which was much more energized by the "tombstone" provisions of the "Hump Act" signed by Dwight Eisenhower in 1959. This act greased the skids, providing "cash readjustment payments" for officers retiring before their thirty years were up and granting last-gasp promotions to some (which, when approved by the executive, meant extra retirement pay). But this was no solace at all for the thousands forced out before even their twenty years were up.

No one ever accepted responsibility for The Hump, and in fact the creature was the unavoidable product of maintaining a pyramidal hierarchy amid the pressing demands of naval globalism. This personnel disaster, when at last the Hump Act had done its work, provoked much soul-searching but did little to ensure that such a catastrophe could not happen again.

The Hump was part of the systaltic nature of naval requirements for manpower. This neither lessened the anguish nor prevented the suspicion that the Academy was looking out for its own. The Commander Board for fiscal 1960 selected 73 percent from Boat School grads, the rest from other sources of commission. (So what, said one non–Naval Academy captain; "the Naval Academy produces better naval officers *as a group* than any other source.") Indeed, the "old school tie" seemed to help very little when the great barrier reef approached, at least until Flag Plot hove into sight.[17]

☆

—So, the wardroom of the sixties was partially, painfully purged. The Navy, like all militaries, rightly insisted on a pyramidal command structure—one man at the top and increasing numbers at each descending level. But as one admiral said, "The Navy does not propose now [1960], nor at any time, to have its officer corps made up of anything but the best elements of the nation's citizens." Some junior officers, while agreeing, went so far as to propose a system of "open promotion" of the best officers in each rank. Everyone realized, as a lieutenant remarked, "in an organization charged with defense of the nation and of the free world, there is no room for mediocrity."

Mediocrity there certainly was, inevitable in any large, exceptionally fluid organization. The wardroom had its share of apple-polishers, bootlickers, ticket-punchers, dancers and prancers, careerists of all kinds—as well as incorrigible loafers. And virtue was not always rewarded.

Sometimes the mediocre got the rewards. Once, the story went, a German general had divided his officers into four classes: the clever, the stupid, the industrious, and the lazy. Every officer, the general believed, had two of these qualities. The clever and lazy, because they would figure out the easy way, were perfect for command; the clever and industrious were born staffers. The lazy and stupid were by-products with whom one had to live. The dangerous ones were those who combined stupidity and industry—they were a positive menace should they rise to the top.[18]

The Navy, despite its vicissitudes with its officers, usually did not reward laziness and stupidity. Simply put, men with these qualities were almost always weeded out by the School of the Ship and the endless training regimen. Naval wardrooms, to the contrary, were full of very good men indeed, men who operated what was by far the superior navy in the world.

Even after all those years, if frayed a bit around the edges and despite the wardroom's revolving door, Charles Clark's axiom still held. Like so much else concerning its innards, the Navy was obsessed with the maintenance of high officer quality, and the nation was being well-served.

—In large part, because one fundamental duty of any naval officer was *to lead*.

CHAPTER TWENTY-ONE

MESS DECKS

T ales about sailors are universal, eternal, and not very complimentary. "No man will be a sailor who has contrivance enough to get himself into a jail," Samuel Johnson erupted. "Being in a ship is being in a jail with the chance of being drowned." Besides, said the Great Cham to his adoring Boswell, "a man in jail has more room, better food, and commonly better company." He that would go to sea for pleasure, said the proverb, would go to hell for a pastime.

The Royal Navy in Johnson's time dealt mostly with the scourings of the waterfront and made impressment the order of the day. As a result, discipline in His Majesty's fleet was quick and fierce. This tradition, the absolute *necessity* of physical punishment aboard ship, was transferred almost intact to the infant American Navy. "I believe there never was so depraved a set of mortals as sailors are," wrote William Bainbridge. "Under discipline they are peaceable and serviceable—divest them of that and they constitute a perfect rabble."

The social gulf between the perfect rabble and their officers was an unbridgeable chasm, bringing to mind Macaulay's vintage comment about the navy of Charles II: "The seamen were not gentlemen, and the gentlemen were not seamen." Not all American captains rowed with Bainbridge's oar; some tried to uplift their charges with compulsory church services and the like. ("Sailors ought never to go to church," gibed H.G. Wells. "They ought to go to hell, where it is much more comfortable.") But the social divide, like the discipline, crossed the Atlantic in practically pure form.[1]

Despite the United States being a self-advertised democracy, however, many skippers in the early years evolved a rather warm, paternalist view of their men. This, too, had been an English trait. "Our seamen are like forward children not knowing how to judge for themselves," ran one eighteenth-century observation, "but on account of their great use to the nation, are to be cherished as the first born of a fond parent." American naval leaders built on paternalism rather than participatory democracy. Raphael Semmes, weaned to command in the pre–Civil War Navy before he went raiding for the Confederacy, was typical. "Seamen are very much like children," he asserted, "requiring the reins to be tightened upon them from time to time." And again: "The sailor is as improvident, and incapable of self-government as a child."

The children needed constant discipline, but also required affection and respect, at least from the better officers. Many naval men, going back to the sainted John Paul Jones, were paternalists in the most positive sense. "The care . . . of our seamen," Jones wrote to Robert Morris shortly after *Ranger* arrived in France late in 1777, "is a consideration of the first magnitude." "Those men under [naval officers] should be looked after in every way whatever," urged Alfred Thayer Mahan.[2]

But the children could get rambunctious, escape the bounds of discipline, lose control. Constant watchfulness was needed, for entire industries, existing only to pluck poor Jack, thrived in seaport towns. Sailors, of course, saw the situation somewhat differently. "O ye moralists!" exclaimed Seaman Jacob Hazen about 1839. "Talk not of the temptations of a city, the corrupting tendency of brothels, the demoralizing influence of theatres and public exhibitions, for city life with all its evil accompaniments, is a career of godliness in comparison with that which is endured on board a man-of-war." Reformers throughout the nineteenth century were particularly concerned about the innocent, youthful recruits lodged in "that Pandemonium, the birth-deck [*sic*] of a receiving ship, there to remain long enough to be inducted into vices of the most disgusting character."

Of the "vices of a most disgusting character," although homosexuality was not unknown, two stood out, then and forevermore—alcohol and women. Booze and the American sailor went hand-in-hand throughout the nineteenth century. Excessive drinking in the early Navy was the "foremost of crimes;" before 1815 three times as many officers were dismissed from the fleet for alcohol abuse than for "money problems," such as fraud, embezzlement, or theft, and ten times as many were sacked for drinking than for brutality of some sort.

William Keeler, the acting paymaster of the well-known *Monitor*, wrote his wife that "there are three great evils in both our army and navy which if corrected would render them much more efficient—the first is whiskey, the second is whiskey & the third is whiskey." Charles Wilkes, a naval explorer and rigid disciplinarian, deplored the life he saw on shipboard and on the beach: "No school could have been worse for morals and none so viciously constituted." Wilkes despised the drinking even among officers, whom he characterized as "debauching and drunken blackguards." Franklin Buchanan, who became a Confederate admiral, commanded *Vincennes* in 1843 and informed the secretary of the Navy that "the crime of drunkenness causes all the insubordination and consequent punishment to officers and men."

Later, as superintendent of the Naval Academy, Buchanan went even further, remarking that "dissipation is the cause of all insubordination and misconduct in the Navy." Semmes did not even like the idea of sailor liberty. "This giving of 'liberty' to them is a little troublesome, to be sure, as some of them will come off drunk, and noisy, and others, overstaying their time, have to be hunted up in the grog-shops, and other sailor haunts, and be brought off by force."[3]

Boozing was bad enough, but the women. . . . Waterfront prostitutes were a staple in every port in the world, with many sailors their eager customers. Officers were not immune, either. The early Navy "was noteworthy neither for its chastity nor its continence," and these tendencies did not vanish, even in the Victorian Era. Life at sea was hardly conducive to sexual morality ashore; traditionally, when any Navy ship left its Atlantic port and headed seaward, the word was passed: "Cape Hatteras is abeam; all men are now bachelors." "The sailor's heart is capacious enough to love the whole sex," Semmes said. The sailor was, above all other men, "susceptible of female influences."

No one kept statistics in the nineteenth century, but there was no doubt that many sailors did more than drink while on the beach. For a greenhorn, his first visit to a bordello or tryst with a streetwalker was a rite of passage; for a veteran, these were precious customs, even rewards. Some sailors who indulged were married, some were not—but all had passed Cape Hatteras.

When numbers began to be kept, the traditional paternalist philosophy of "boys will be boys" was found to have its costs. In 1906, a meeting of the American Society for Social and Moral Prophylaxis (progressivism was in full swing) was informed that soldiers and sailors, lacking the restraining influence of home and family, "appear to be set apart as a class above others to suffer from sexual unrest."

Josephus Daniels, Wilson's secretary of the Navy, was bombarded by letters from parents worried that their seaman recruit sons would be seduced, and worse; they would come home brimming with "sexual unrest." Daniels agreed about the problem (he called a lecture to a group of surgeons "Men Must Live Straight If They Would Shoot Straight"), and he asked for civilian help to protect his lads from the "harpies of the underworld." The secretary backed up his words with action; when, during World War I, the commander of the Naval Hospital at Mare Island, California, reportedly asserted that "immoral conditions at Vallejo didn't make a damn bit of difference," he found himself summarily relieved.

The Navy, by that time, was known to exhibit high rates of venereal disease. After a visit to a particularly welcome (and infected) liberty port, some ships had 10 percent or more of their crews on the binnacle list for VD. Daniels was urged to try the obvious, issuing contraceptives to the men and ordering their use. This brought the following salvo from the secretary:

> The use of this [preventive or prophylactic] packet I believe to be immoral; it savors of the panderer; and it is wicked to seem to encourage and approve placing in the hands of men an appliance which will lead them to think that they may indulge in practices which are not sanctioned by moral, military, or civil law, with impunity, and the use of which would tend to subvert and destroy the very foundation of our moral and Christian beliefs and teachings with regards to these sexual matters.

—More than a bit preachy, and with little consequence. Though one reformer claimed that the "army and navy which is the least syphilized will, other things being equal, win" World War I, and though the General Medical Board of the Council of National Defense endorsed continence for the duration, nothing seemed to work. "I believe there is a well defined purpose on the part of the German government to break down the morale of the American troops through liquor and vice," suspiciously avowed the commandant of the Mare Island Navy Yard. The Navy fought on, in 1917 even forcing the closing of New Orlean's fabled Storyville, the mecca of prostitution in the South.

And still American sailors fornicated away. (They had been seen surreptitiously changing into civilian clothes before going to Storyville.) The interwar Navy, somewhat relieved to get out from under Daniel's strictures, did little to attack the VD problem. The mass influx of enlisted men during World War II merely introduced more whitehats to more exotic places in which to become infected. By that time, according to Lieutenant Commander Leo Shifrin, "the average enlisted man attaches [little importance] to venereal infections. Most of them think as little of a gonorrheal infection as they do of the ordinary common cold."

Most of the time, officially, the Navy threw up its hands at the problem. The better skippers tried to ensure that their men got some kind of prophylaxis, but the common theme was to let their men do their own business on the beach, as long as they did not unduly jar public order. At times, this attitude resulted in the virtual industrialization of sin. Shortly after V-J Day, a block-long line of sailors was seen patiently waiting their turn at a Tokyo whorehouse. On entering the lobby they would select a prostitute (over one hundred on duty)—dirty, heavily painted, clad in gaudy rayon pajamas—pay ten yen to the concierge, and go upstairs. Afterward, Navy corpsmen on duty at the place would administer prophylaxis. The VD incidence among the women in this bagnio was 100 percent.

This was extreme but not untypical, certainly for men who had spent long wartime months at sea. Many officers only winked at this expected bawdy aspect of the sailor's image. At the same time, official policy was deeply troubled by the perpetual linkage of sailors, booze, and women.

The realization that its sailors, mostly youthful and virile, needed to let off steam, coupled with the obvious attendant problems of discipline, disorderly conduct, and disease, had always made the Navy hypocritical on these twin subjects. Daniels may have been preachy, but he had tried his best to uplift the fleet—and had failed dismally. In 1940 the artist Paul Cadmus presented his painting *Sailors and Floozies*—which showed two gobs and a Marine cavorting drunkenly with three tarts—at the Golden Gate International Exposition in San Francisco. The work was quickly removed at the behest of the director, who said "There's too much smell about it. It's not a masterpiece. It's just unpleasant." Unrepentant, the artist responded that "nobody expects or wants the Navy to be made up of Lord Fauntleroys and Galahads. The picture portrays an enjoyable side of Navy life. I think it would make a good recruiting poster. I will raise my prices."

Lord Fauntleroys and Galahads they were not, but most sailors were not the roistering rogues of legend and popular imagination, either. In the nineteenth century the Navy was thought by many to be the last refuge of the drunken or incompetent, and the service even then was extraordinarily sensitive to this image, even though its leaders knew that sailors had to come from *somewhere*. Enlistees were screened (sometimes) for signs of alcoholism or drug addiction. The rum ration went by the boards in 1862, and beer was prohibited aboard ships and on naval stations in 1899. Daniels, to the everlasting mortification of naval officers, abolished their wine mess in 1914.

All this did little to stop the truly thirsty. Sailors taped flasks inside their trouser legs, hid bottles in crannies aboard ship, and bought booze hidden in baskets of fruit by bumboat men. In addition, the men could see their officers drinking on the beach, stumbling aboard drunk after taps, at times even drinking on the sly in their staterooms—the young Ernie King was such an example. In fact, abuse of alcohol permeated the entire Navy, not just the enlisted ranks. Rear Admiral Kemp Tolley remembered that he and his wardroom mates used to smuggle gallons of rotgut Caribbean rum aboard *Florida*.

Still, things got better as the years passed. Teddy Roosevelt's Great White Fleet quadrupled the number of Navy enlisted, to forty-four thousand, and they were no longer drawn from the gutters of seaport towns but came instead from across the nation. The tier of states starting with the two Dakotas and running down through Oklahoma was thought at one time to provide the highest per capita number of sailors for the fleet, on the general theory, as someone said, that these farmers had never seen salt water and were too damned dumb to know what was in store for them. Regardless, with the turn of the century, sailors' behavior ashore, although always potentially rowdy and never close to the ideals of Emily Post, improved noticeably, particularly in American liberty ports, where the local press was always waiting to take a potshot at the Navy.

Discrimination against American sailors in "nice places," like dance halls and recreation centers, accordingly became more rare. Drunkenness could still land a bluejacket in the brig, but boozing was far behind unauthorized absence as an infraction of regulations. Drinking by all hands was so common as to be *expected*. As late as the 1950s Captain John Noel remembered a fistful of drunken admirals: "These flag officers stumbling around from one naval air station to another were really a scandal." "We all drank too much," said Kemp Tolley of his service in the thirties. "It was a way of life."

As to women, some officers also participated in whorehouse activity and were skirt-chasers; to this extent they were accomplices rather than regulators of the enlisted men. The machismo mentality ran throughout the fleet, the exclusive preserve of neither the wardroom nor the mess decks. Daniels had not been able to make the slightest dent in this self-image. In 1921, after his departure from office, the Navy Department stopped regarding the failure to take prophylaxis as disobedience, and the following year the Medical Corps once again gave contraceptives to liberty-bound sailors.[4]

What counted was shipboard performance. Corporal punishment may have been outlawed, but the naval discipline was still there. That, plus naval paternalism, ensured that a "good man" would be allowed his occasional sinning, so long as he did his job.

And do his job he did, to the extent of helping win a world war. By 1945, people everywhere knew the swaggering American sailor, in his tightly fitting, thirteen-button, bell-bottom trousers, Dixie cup rakishly askew, payday in hand—on the beach and looking for action.

☆

"In the American Navy," Josephus Daniels had written, "every sailor carries an admiral's flag in his ditty box." This was a populist, democratic ideal, to be sure, but the Navy's World War II enlistees were largely happenstance sailors, with the consuming desire to get out and get home. Late in the war, the popular correspondent Ernie Pyle (shortly to be killed on the tiny island of Ie Shima during the Okinawa campaign) visited a light carrier in the Pacific. He spent his time, as was his custom, chatting with the crew. "Very few of the boys have developed any real love for the sea—the kind that will draw them back to it for a lifetime," he concluded. "Some of course will come back if things get tough after the war. But mostly they are temporary sailors, and the sea is not in their blood."

—*Temporary sailors*. And the postwar Navy needed Regulars, men who would stay around, half a million of them. A career sailor would endlessly make the assertion, to whoever would listen, that the Navy was great for officers and lousy for enlisted men. But as one boatswain's mate first class said, an American sailor was seriously interested in only four things: enough liberty, enough chow, enough pay, and not too much work. To the outsider, the isolation of "Officers' Country" seemed a recipe for social rebellion, but sailors knew that, for the most part, they had little personal contact with their officers, and that the people really in a position to give them grief were other enlisted men, the "lifers"—their chiefs, the master-at-arms, an ob-noxious first class.

They knew, these lifers, that their officers were better educated than they were, but they conceded not a whit on the grounds of native intelligence and shrewdness. There was no real "caste system" in the Navy, despite appearances, because enlisted men, apart from the racial issue, had no sense of social inferiority, or any other kind. They expected to be treated with respect, and by the better officers they always were. The enlisted had their special preserves and privileges, too, as jealously guarded as the officers guarded theirs. Woe betide the inexperienced junior officer who entered the Chief's Mess without first knocking and requesting permission to enter, and scorn would follow that officer who walked through the mess decks without removing his cover.[5]

After the drawdown, the Navy shakily made its way back to a strength of about six hundred thousand enlisted personnel, a figure maintained throughout the fifties. The revolving door was whirling here as well. Most men enlisted for a four-year hitch; after that, they either "re-upped," usually for six years (and became candidates for a career of twenty years or more) or returned to civilian life. In the fifties, about 175,000 replacements were needed annually, a yearly turnover of about one-third of the enlisted force. Reenlistments varied from 14 percent to 32 percent per year. These numbers were bleak. In 1956 Secretary of the Navy Charles Thomas was forced to admit that the Navy's experience level, particularly in the group of men with four to ten years under their belts (the second and first class) "is below that desired."

About 8 percent of the enlisted were chief petty officers, a good lead-ership ratio, and about 40 percent were unrated, in the three lowest pay-grades, at any given time. The problem of specialization was affecting the enlisted ranks, too, and those with test scores in the upper half were being steered to hot new ratings like electronics technician and data processing technician, whereas the bottom half would be more likely to end up in traditional ratings like boatswain's mate and signalman.

The rating structure itself was becoming exceptionally intricate and complex. The sailing Navy had offered little by way of special training. In 1826 the service began placing receiving ships (those "Pandemoniums" for "vices of the most disgusting character") in major ports to house men awaiting transfer to seagoing vessels. While aboard these hulks, the recruits learned the rudiments of handling masts, yards, and sails, and then, without further ado, they were sent to sea.

Before World War II a sailor's "rating" referred to what he did—seaman, fireman, gunner—and to what he was paid—third class, chief. The enlisted rating structure, although somewhat slow to change, usually faithfully mir-rored the skills the Navy needed. In 1801, with only 2500 enlisted men, the Navy already had twenty-one ratings, ten of which were in what was later called the "seaman branch" (boatswains, gunners), four in what became the "artificer branch" caring for the ship (armorers, carpenter's mates), and the rest in odd jobs such as clerks, cooks, and stewards.

Steam power revolutionized the enlisted ratings, producing skills needed to deal with the novel intricacies of iron and steel. Now came machinists (1866), boilermakers (1869), and oiler and water tenders (1884). Electricity in its turn produced electrician's mates (1898)—even though the Navy had used electrical power for a full decade by then—and radiomen (1921). After World War I, aviation ratings became a separate branch; by 1930, 9 percent of all ratings were "airedales."

The Navy was positively Darwinian in its rating structure. Along the way, old specialties were sloughed off as new ones were added. The sailmaker and his loft ashore vanished, although the rating remained until 1939, a vestigial example, making boat covers and awnings. The captains of the maintop and mizzentop went by the boards in 1893. Other ratings transmuted; carpenter's mates, for example, with no more wooden ships to keep in trim, became damage controlmen, with part of their old specialty continued in shoring techniques. Still others changed their techniques but not their specialty. Gunner's mates were in business with a smoothbore cannon or a five-inch 38.

During and after World War II, electronics changed the enlisted rating structure once again, and with remarkable speed. Now came, in dazzling array, the new rating badges of fire control technicians, electronics technicians, radarmen, and sonarmen. And specialties hived off subspecialties; the cryptologic technician rating, for example, had at one time no fewer than six different subspecialties.

More schooling than ever was needed for these new ratings, and the fleet was continuously short of the modern skills, such as those of the electrical and electronics specialists. "Personnel allocations for the 864 active fleet ships are austere," wrote Secretary of the Navy William Franke in 1959. "Austere" was hardly the word; shortages were constant in a number of critical ratings, and remained so.

And once assigned, these people never stayed put. The Navy's policy in the postwar period was periodic rotation for enlisted as well as officers. In the prewar Navy some enlisted men could camp on a single ship for practically an entire career; now, they were rotated every two or three years. Ensuring equitability between sea and shore assignments for over half a million men was no small task. In this respect the Navy was a constantly moving human stream—on assignment, heading toward an assignment, on leave, and so forth.

In 1940 over 89,000 of the Navy's 116,000 enlisted personnel had been assigned afloat. Now, due to the growing shore infrastructure, a far greater percentage had to be ordered to the beach. There had been for years the Shore Duty Survey (SHORVEY), a list of people due to go on sea duty.

In the fifties this was joined by the Sea Duty Survey (SEAVEY), a list of men eligible for shore duty. In its wisdom, the Navy figured that for each rating, there were X billets ashore and Y billets at sea or overseas. The ratio of Y to X determined the sea-to-shore rotation for that rating. Of course, the needs of the Navy predominated, and some ratings were cursed by long periods at sea; signalmen were a classic example.

But in general, SEAVEY-SHORVEY kept the human stream moving and, with the introduction of data processing machines, gave skippers some idea of who was reporting aboard. Previously, a duffel bag reading, say, "Gunner's Mate Second Class," would show up on the quarterdeck with a human being attached. Now, the sailor's new command got his enlistment data, age, evaluation history, career history, and family information.[6]

The increasing complexity of the enlisted world could be handled, at least in part, by the machines and by the personnelman rating, but the monitoring of the human stream occurred only after the tap had been turned on. Getting people into uniform in the first place was a crucial naval problem.

☆

The logical place to get postwar sailors was from the fleet's three million or so war-trained Reserves. But, as Ernie Pyle had noted, these people were coming home to stay. Many enlisted men doubtless had the bitter edge of one Reserve officer, a veteran of two years in the Pacific, who wrote in 1945:

> I wouldn't stay in the goddam Navy if I starved to death on the outside. . . . The man 30 or older who wants to stay in is a rare exception. If a man has ever held a responsible civilian job, all he wants is to get out. The younger men, who might otherwise have some thought of staying in, are convinced that the Reserves will get the undesirable assignments after the war. They see themselves holding down the Kwajaleins and the Pelelius while the Regular Navy sails the ships and gets the good shore assignments. . . .

—Which meant that the postwar Navy, despite its massive wartime size, had to recruit frantically just to keep itself afloat. By 1948 Tommy Sprague in the Bureau of Naval Personnel had naval recruiters blanketing the nation's high schools, looking for the 131,000 new hands the Navy needed that year for what were being sold as "eighty skilled trades." The pitch, instead of being career-oriented, was in the direction of learning a skill that could then be marketed on the outside, once the sailor veteran returned to "real life." By using such an orientation, or "soft sell," the Navy was slowly drawing a razor across its own throat, but recruiters could see little alternative, now that the press of wartime patriotism had been lifted.

The Navy's postwar recruiters, usually chiefs or first class petty officers, were no longer the traffickers in human flesh who had filled out the Royal

Navy's press gangs two centuries before. Sprague urged them to become part of their localities, and indeed, most recruiters found that the Navy was the object of considerable affection throughout the country, particularly in the interior. This public warmth toward the service was the recruiter's hole card, which he played along with the old standbys of travel and adventure, but across the table were the attractions of civilian life and the obvious drawbacks of the sea service: low pay, family separations, discipline. Many recruiters labored like Sisyphus to make their monthly quotas, and the demand for more bodies was never-ending.

For a decade after V-J Day, the Navy proudly proclaimed itself an all-volunteer service, in spite of the Selective Service Act of 1948. The Navy's Korean War had been fought by volunteers, Reservist recalls, and Regulars. But the continuing problems of recruiting, plus the sagging reenlistment rate dourly noted by Secretary Thomas, led the Navy to ask for fifty-six thousand men from the nation's draft boards by mid-1956. The action put the Navy directly in the line of fire of antidraft critics. "We accept without question the post–World War II thesis," said one of these, "that military service is a part of a boy's maturing process, like getting drunk and losing his virginity"—two examples, unfortunately, that were precariously close to those activities in which the sailor traditionally indulged himself.

Conscription did not mean the end of recruiting. Indeed, the Navy had always recruited, going back to that October day in 1775 when the Continental Congress had set up the Marine Committee and instructed its members to recruit men for the ships of the Continental Navy. Over the years recruiting had had many ups and downs, reflective of the Navy's national role, economic factors, and a host of other variables. But, always, recruiting was mandatory, and no more so than after World War II when, out of ten first-cruise sailors, only *two* would ship over—a revolving door whirling at even greater speed than that for the officers.

By 1956 about 260 officers and 3500 enlisted personnel were assigned full-time to recruiting duty—the complement, almost, of a supercarrier. They operated out of forty-three main stations and 385 substations in every state, plus Hawaii and Alaska. To aid them, they had batteries of standardized written tests, physical qualification standards, and even psychiatric screening, which had been around since 1941. "We have the beginnings of a psychiatric science of manpower," bragged four Navy medical men.[7]

Science of manpower or not, no measurement known could determine a man's aptitude for the Navy. That proof lay in the reenlistment rates. If a man re-upped after his first hitch—20 percent did—then the Navy's chances of keeping him markedly improved. In the 1950s, 80 percent re-upped a second time, 90 percent of those a third (after about sixteen years of service), and 95 percent of those a fourth—by which time they were lifers.

But as one chief quartermaster succinctly noted, "We have no proof whatsoever . . . that the one man in five who initially reenlists is the best of the five for the Navy." Moreover, even second- and third-time reenlistees were leaving the Navy at a fearsome rate. There were several reasons: civilian life beckoned, very strongly to those with the new electrical and electronics skills; veteran's benefits like the GI Bill were, ironically, too good for many to pass up; the forced move to conscription produced many sailors who simply put in their time and got out; and, for the married men, the family pressures were always there.

☆

Still, while they were in, they were "Navy." They learned Navy talk, apart from its exquisite and imaginative profanity "easily the most bewildering language in the world." The obscenity itself, which had to be heard both in quantity and volume to be believed, was unequaled anywhere else, and indeed quickly lost its obscene character because of its high utility—the *lingua obscena* of the sea. "A petty officer who cannot swear well, cannot use the nuances of obscenity, is incapable of giving an order adequately," claimed the author Eugene Burdick, himself a Navy veteran. The regulations banned "excessive obscenity," whatever that was, but no one paid the slightest attention.

All sailors displayed a surface contempt for the Navy and things naval, a contempt as old as navies themselves. Every sailor hated the Navy—his officers, his food, his pay, his living conditions, his work, his lack of liberty. He was contemptuous of a taut ship and a slack ship alike. Always, he could make more, do more, *be* more, on the "outside." Even the lifers strummed this tune. Only the experienced ear could hear the murmurs running underneath the contempt, the language of deep respect and even downright love. Even those who got out as quickly as they could usually carried a bit of "Navy" with them, despite all their efforts to the contrary.

The major reason for the seeming paradox was the sailor's life. He existed in a world of delicately balanced teamwork, each man to his job, each job done responsibly. Everyone, from the Old Man on down, depended on everyone else; any dissonance in the finely strung wires of a naval command echoed and reechoed throughout the entire structure. Thus, and often despite themselves, sailors took an inordinate *pride in craft*, knowing that, without them and their particular skills, the thing of which they were all a part would be diminished, even be unable to run. Because of this pride, there was always an "Old Navy," the halcyon days of yore, and the lifers would endlessly pronounce on the fact that the Navy, *their* Navy, was slowly corroding.

The griping came with the uniform. Some loathed the officer corps and the stuffiness of rank; others, although not using the name, despised the paternalism, the Navy's traditional belief that enlisted men could not think for themselves. John Paul Jones himself had said that "a Navy is essentially and necessarily aristocratic," but no sailor in a democracy ever swallowed that one whole.[8]

So most of them left as soon as they could, taking their gripes with them. By 1955 the Navy's overall reenlistment rate had fallen to 8.1 percent. The sailors were mustered out, by the hundreds, at places like Norfolk and San Diego. They got a last-ditch pitch ("YOUR CAREER—QUESTIONS CONCERNING"), in which they were asked if what lay ahead of them in civilian life would provide them with thirty days' annual leave, free medical care, retirement after twenty years, a free life-insurance policy, or worldwide travel. They cheerfully answered no—and as cheerfully went over the side.

Some hated the "chicken regs," the nattering little regulations that marked the furthest compass of naval paternalism. Others felt they had been misused—sent to radio maintenance school, for example, only to be put to work pushing jet planes around on a carrier deck. The phrase "needs of the Navy" cut little ice with nineteen-year-olds who might have been promised the moon by desperate recruiters.

"The Navy has lost its sex appeal," moaned one admiral. Even before the turn to conscription, many men enlisted simply to avoid the Army's draft—"shotgun volunteers." Their junior officers, mostly Reservists planning to get out themselves, were poor salesmen for keeping them in. Thus, America's naval personnel, particularly those on the lower rungs of the officer and enlisted ladders, were excessively mobile and dissatisfied. The problem was most acute in those places where large numbers of men were constantly required, like the supercarriers. In the last six months of 1957 *Forrestal* had to replace 60 percent of her crew.

Much of this the Navy lumped under that intangible something called "morale," a quality much derided by sailors well before Ensign Pulver had been appointed laundry and morale officer. For many whitehats, morale was as far away, or as near, as the next beer and the next woman. Nevertheless, the statistics suggested that something was haywire. In the mid-fifties the overall population of naval brigs was almost twenty thousand—enough to man every submarine in the service. One-third of the brig inmates at Great Lakes were actually striving to win bad-conduct discharges just to get out of uniform. Every year in the fifties enough sailors were deserting to man twelve guided-missile cruisers, and enough were dishonorably discharged to man twenty destroyers. Many enlisted men had mental problems, real or faked; naval hospitals were flooded with neuro-psychiatric cases.

In May 1958, Secretary of the Navy Thomas Gates, Jr., issued General Order 21, a high-profile official response to obvious problems with personnel. This document really said nothing new and was in fact full of ideas that most good military men took for granted: leadership by example, the importance of character, the need for fair and equitable management. General Order 21 had been percolating ever since 1950, and indeed the secretary's new creation, whatever else people might read in, was undeniably an authentic Cold War document. "Morals" and "morale" were primary worries for the American military, which like the public at large vastly overrated the "brainwashing" that had supposedly been inflicted on American prisoners during the Korean War.

But General Order 21 was mostly meant for internal consumption. The new post of "special assistant to the chief of naval personnel for leadership" was created. Captain John Miner was the first incumbent. Slowly, Miner and his staff began to edge their way into the forest of personnel problems, using experienced chief petty officers as their guides. Nothing changed overnight, but the startling numbers concerning desertions, reenlistment rates, and the like began to improve with the new decade.

Some sailors had to be "pre-selected for morale." The average Navy man on sea duty saw his family about ninety days out of the year. General Order 21 could not change the Navy's pace or scope of operations, but many commanders did begin seriously to come to grips with morale issues. Although the major offenses declined somewhat, the technical drain continued. By 1961 the fleet was keeping only 10 to 15 percent of its technicians.[9]

—Which only negated one of the oldest of naval aphorisms. A griping sailor was not necessarily a happy sailor.

☆

They all needed to be trained, every man jack of them. At the beginning of the twentieth century, so powerful had been the idea of the School of the Ship, only four training activities had been located ashore: the Naval Academy, the Naval War College, and two recruit training programs at Newport and San Francisco. Beginning in 1879 a tiny office devoted to apprentice training had been tucked away in the Bureau of Equipment and Recruiting. Transferred to the Bureau of Navigation ten years later, the "training office" stayed there until World War II, the almost-ignored stepchild of BuNav, which was actually the personnel bureau.

The Navy's pre–World War II training establishment consisted of seventy-five schools, through which about ten thousand sailors were cycled annually—about one-thirtieth of the fleet. The bulk of the Navy's sailors were still in the School of the Ship. The war crushed this comfortable, slow-paced routine. The ships were needed in combat zones, and their men had to be ready when they walked over the brow. Naval training was driven ashore, where for the most part the establishment remained.

Naval schools sprang up everywhere—colleges, factories, hotels, commandeered country estates, trade schools. By 1944 the Navy was running almost one thousand schools ashore, with an average *daily* attendance of 303,000. Many of these schools disbanded or combined at war's end, but the fragmented training structure created by the draft and the frenetic pace of wartime hung on. Aviators, submariners, and surface sailors had all developed independent training fiefdoms, and over on the staff side—supply, medical, and the like—the story was the same.

Duplications in subject material were everywhere, the waste in time and talent was atrocious, and training costs per man were spiraling steadily upward, but the barons of the fiefdoms, such as the deputy chief of naval operations for air, were reluctant to admit that much of their training was not as highly specialized as they liked to think. An electron was an electron and had no idea whether its antics were taking place on an aircraft, a submarine, or a ship.

Several boards recommended streamlining and unifying the ramshackle and redundant mess of naval training, but not until 1971 was a chief of naval training (later naval education and training—CNET) established in a three-star billet at Pensacola. Until then, the fiefdoms held sway, and naval training—at least at its grass roots, where seamen, firemen, and airmen got the basics—was nowhere near the standard of efficiency on which the Navy had always prided itself.

There *was* centralization up at Port Washington, New York, however. There the Naval Training Device Center, child of the fertile brain of Rear Admiral Luis De Florez, had been in business since the beginning of World War II. The center produced a bewildering variety of training aids, from packs of signal cards to attack center mockups for submarines (the latter at $15 million a copy). In the new world of the cathode ray tube, specialized simulations of every possible kind of naval maneuver in any element—air, sea, or both—became the center's specialty. The training may have been redundant, but the regimen and the instructors were usually of high quality. The shore-based schools stressed both a hands-on and a team approach, minimizing the chances for disaster at sea.

By 1950, sixty-one thousand sailors were moving through seventy-seven schools. The Korean War caused recruits who normally would have gone to their commands straight out of boot camp to be sent directly to schools; 90 percent of the basic technical school (A School) enrollment came from the boots. This process remained after Korea, so that the first time a sailor saw his ship or squadron, he might already have a third class crow on his arm as an A School graduate.[10]

Navy "boots" were a classic image—scared eighteen-year-olds struggling with a seabag full of newly issued, ill-fitting clothes, embarrassed as shorn sheep by their first whitewall haircuts. Most of them reported to Great Lakes or San Diego, where they were trained in companies of fewer than one hundred men by a chief or a first class. Their rites of passage, in addition to enduring fusillades of cursing, included military drill, physical training, learning the "Navy way" (there was a right way, a wrong way, and a Navy way), seamanship, ordnance, gunnery, damage control, and what the Navy called "character guidance."

Boot camp was supposed to take thirteen weeks, but the revolving door often speeded the process to eleven, ten, or even nine weeks. (By comparison, the much smaller but highly professional Canadian navy devoted twenty weeks to its "preentry" training.) Here was where a battery of standardized tests began to separate the boots into "mental categories" that, to a degree unknown to them at the time, would tend to determine their nautical futures.

There were five of these categories, and those scoring in the two lowest were usually shunted directly to the fleet, there to man the deck divisions and parts of engineering. From these groups came most of the Navy's morale and discipline problems. These boots might not have been able to do well on tests, but they were not stupid; a few months of seagoing experience convinced many of them that they were consigned to be naval equivalents of hewers of wood and drawers of water, and they liked the prospect not one bit.

Up to 50 percent of boot camp graduates were in these lower categories; many of them could read at only a fifth-grade level. Men who fell below a fourth-grade reading level were placed in a special remedial reading school. (If one could not read instructions on how to safely operate equipment, one could swiftly be dead.) But officers who had to confront these illiterates in the fleet testified that the extra training resolved little.

Practically all of the higher mental groups qualified for an A School and would eventually reach the fleet with some technical training. This process, culling boot camps with mental tests, amounted to a sort of technical segregation of enlisted personnel, with the least mentally fit, by test results, becoming the immediate problems of seagoing commands. Thus, modern technology created serious stresses within the Navy's personnel structure, stresses that were increased by the fact that training commands were low-profile, usually only a captain's slot. (Their Army and USAF opposite numbers wore two or three stars.)

In addition, except for the Training Device Center, boot camps and other training schools got physically seedier and seedier, the old temporary wartime barracks moldering away as they continued to be used, the classrooms stifling and overcrowded, the living and berthing conditions reminiscent of a cattle roundup. As a rite of passage the boot camp was supposed to have shock value, but part of the shock was souring too many recruits on the service from the very beginning.

For those at the upper end of the "mental categories," though, opportunity beckoned, just as the recruiting posters said. The wonder-world of electronics was particularly attractive, with its fantastic array of tubes, scopes, condensers, and complex circuitry. By 1952 the surface Navy ran fifty-four A Schools, designed to make a sailor an instant specialist in any field from lithography to photography, pattern-making to storekeeping. Most of these courses lasted several months, further delaying the time before which a man could be of some use to the fleet. In time, B and C Schools were available for petty officers to get up to speed on developments in their specialties.

A typical A School was the Fire Control Technician's School near the nation's capital, which offered a forty-four-week curriculum. During his first twelve weeks the aspiring FT studied electricity, electronics, and radar fundamentals. He learned to build simple receivers and circuits. In the next eight weeks he met his first fire control system (in the 1950s, usually the relatively simple Mark 63), which he tore apart and repaired. Then on to other systems, to mechanical power drives, mathematical computers, stable elements, battery alignments.

The A Schools were short on theory and long on practical repair and troubleshooting. The Naval Air Technical Training Command, the aviation fiefdom, ran its own. Every Navy plane required fifteen or twenty technicians, and by 1951 the air side had thirty A Schools. Airman apprentices received indoctrination in aviation history, types of planes, safety precautions, taxi signals, carrier flight deck operations, cockpit familiarization, and engine repair.

There were thirteen aviation ratings (later fourteen), and the airman would be sent to the appropriate A School, like the fourteen-week Aviation Machinist Mate's School in Memphis. There, his basics would include engine parts, nomenclature, and operation; transmission systems; fuel and ignition systems; and lubrication. Then he would specialize—in reciprocating, turbo-prop, or jet engines. He learned by taking engines apart, right down to the cotter pins, and putting them together again.

Some of the airmen would actually fly, others stay on the ground. The more electronics that were packed into a plane, the more valuable these aviation specialists became—to civilian aviation as well as to the Navy. The drain on these highly trained young men was horrendous, and many of them left the Navy just as they were beginning to get the feel of the flight deck.

Submariners were all volunteers. They went through Sub School at New London. As a group they averaged nineteen years of age and were more highly educated than their enlisted peers. Almost all had a high school degree. (The Navy average for enlistees was between ten and eleven years of schooling, although conscription produced more whitehats with some college experience.) Each sub volunteer was given the Thematic Apperception Test, in which he was shown a series of pictures and asked to write a story about each. Navy psychiatrists analyzed the results, watching for indications of excessive anxiety, abnormal shyness, work difficulties, unusual fears, "shunning of women after puberty" (considered to be *most* unsailorlike), and "abnormal attachment to mother."

Then they got their escape-tank training. Fifteen men at a time were enclosed in a small lock, wearing their Momsen lungs. The lock was flooded, and they had to escape one-by-one through a hatch leading to the bottom of a one-hundred-foot tower filled with water. Then they had to ascend—

slowly, to prevent the bends—holding onto a rope. About 8 percent failed this exercise.

The Sub School took eight weeks (compared with six months for the prospective submarine officer), and New London supplied about 1600 men a year to the boats in the 1950s. The training emphasis was on calmness, routine, and working together in exceptionally confined spaces. (Later, the psychiatric aspects of the New London approach would contribute to the astronaut program.)[11]

Fewer and fewer men were going to the diesel-electrics, and for most of the Sub School graduates, the nuclear training cycle came right after basic. Hyman Rickover's stress on safety and thorough understanding of the nuclear plant meant that when a nuclear-qualified submariner reported aboard his first command, he was already almost two years out of boot camp. These men, with the lure of the growing civilian nuclear power industry and the long undersea deployments of the Polaris force, would also prove difficult for the Navy to retain.

The surface, aviation, and submarine sailors provided the overwhelming bulk of the enlisted ranks. They fed the boilers, typed the letters, fueled the planes, baked the bread, repaired the torpedoes. By far the most public attention, however, went to naval esoterica, and of these, the most highly publicized, by a long shot, were the Underwater Demolition Teams—the famous "frogmen."

The frogmen had been born of necessity. At Tarawa, the Japanese had studded the island's approaches with steel rails set in concrete, and when Marine landing craft had raced toward the beach, these and the lurking coral reefs had impaled many of them, leaving their heavily laden men sitting ducks for enemy fire. The Marines took Tarawa, but they waded past the bodies of hundreds of their comrades to get there.

In response, Lieutenant Commander Draper Kauffman and others designed the Underwater Demolition Teams. The UDTs spearheaded practically every amphibious landing after Tarawa, in all theaters. Their numbers grew to more than 3000. They were an athletic, daring, devil-may-care elite, trained to go in ahead of the assault forces, chart the approaches, and clear the beaches and offshore waters of mines and other obstacles. At Guam the chief bottleneck was a coral reef, three hundred yards offshore. Using ten thousand pounds of explosives, frogmen blasted a passage through. When the first wave of sweaty, overburdened Marines, ducking machine-gun fire, hit the beach, they found a crudely lettered sign: "Marines, welcome to Guam. Beach open courtesy of UDT. USO two blocks to the right."

In short, the frogmen had cachet, and they really did live with danger. (At Normandy, where they were not allowed to do preliminary reconnaissance because of the surprise factor, 41 percent of them were killed). At war's end there were thirty-four UDT teams with 3500 frogmen. Most of the teams were decommissioned during the drawdown; only a handful survived. They were at Inchon, charting the harbor and fixing buoys on shoals and submerged rocks. The public loved them, and while their operating techniques were secret, the Navy was never loath to publicize their derring-do, even assisting in the making of a commercial film, *The Frogmen* (1951)—Richard Widmark in swimming trunks.

In the 1950s, UDT consisted of five 112-man teams, one hundred enlisted men and twelve officers apiece (the highest proportion of officers to men in the Navy). Three of the teams were based at Coronado, California (just south of San Diego), and two at Little Creek, Virginia. All were volunteers, all got extra pay, and all had exceptional physical skills and endurance. They did not have to be swimmers—the Navy taught them to swim the Navy way. They could swim fifty yards underwater and usually stayed under about a minute when working (usually in depths of twenty feet or less). In the fifties they got aqualungs, extending their underwater endurance.

All of them—officers and enlisted—got the same ten-week training, featuring the notorious "Hell Week." The workday for Hell Week was officially eighteen hours (graduates of UDT School knew this to be an outright lie on the short side), punctuated with distance runs, cold-water swims, hikes, exhausting calisthenics, hazing, physical combat, and unexpected explosions and attacks. Hell Week wiped out about 40 percent of the candidates. The rest became a highly polished team; nowhere else in the Navy did officers and men function so completely together.

After Hell Week came eleven more weeks of training in such lethal arts as the use of TNT, ammonium nitrate, and bangalore torpedoes, as well as instruction in judo and in what to do with their sheath knives (one cut, under right chin, across jugular vein). Then they had six months of probationary service with a unit before they could call themselves UDT men.

They wore mythical fins—no insignia, because the Navy did not want these five hundred unusual specialists to be easily identified. (The SEALs, who would come along later, would be much more splashy and even higher-profile.) Frogmen tended to be hell-for-leather, more than a bit on the primitive side, and UDT unit orders had interesting angles not found elsewhere, such as to "leave sharks alone" and not to use submarine running lights as slingshot targets. When asked if they, the sun-bronzed ones in swimming trunks, were in the Navy, they would answer "Hell, no! I'm UDT!" Peacetime did not lessen the need for their skills; they found work in salvage, cartography, ordnance disposal, and underwater repair. Always, they had the air of raffish discontinuity with the normal world. When Vice Admiral Frank ("Spike") Fahrion, commander of the Atlantic Fleet amphibious force, inspected UDT 21, he called the team's commander over and quietly said, "I'm glad they're on our side."

The age limit for recruits was thirty-two, but once in, a man stayed until he could no longer cut the mustard. (One UDT chief in 1959 was forty-seven.) UDT sailors came from all ratings, but they tended to be markedly adventurous and, unlike the uxorious submariners, markedly fond of what could politely be called the "bachelor life." By the end of the fifties the frogmen were qualifying as parachutists, working with astronauts (for ocean recovery techniques), conducting Arctic swims, and being snatched from the water by jet-propelled recovery boats.[12]

For those who liked life underwater but thought the frogmen a bit excessive, there was Navy Diving School. Enlisted divers were also the physical cream of the crop, and they did both hard-hat and scuba work. (The naval stereotype of a diver was a sailor with a size 54 jumper and a size 3 hat.) Their major business was marine salvage, because saving a damaged ship was far less expensive than building a new one. But they also did harbor clearance and routine underwater maintenance. No Navy ship of any size was without its qualified divers.

And for those sailors who liked loud noises, there were the Explosive Ordnance Disposal units (EODs). Their school at Indian Head, Maryland, had a curriculum covering everything from Civil War cannonballs to nuclear weapons. The nineteen-week basic course was followed by "practical training"—exhuming five land mines, removing cranky unexploded bombs from bomb bays, exploding live ordnance; they had to be, for their lives depended on their skills.[13]

The frogmen, divers, and EODs were among the cream of the Navy's enlisted, elite units with specialized training not readily marketable on the outside. For this reason, along with their soaring esprit de corps, these people tended, unlike the more prosaic seamen, firemen, and airmen, to be career sailors, among the Navy's most highly valued men.

☆

There were others, though—the rotten apples, the discipline cases, the rule-breakers. Whether naval discipline was soft or harsh, there were always "cases." Many skippers in the sailing Navy had been quick with corporal punishment. Matthew Perry, "Old Bruin," the man who opened up Japan, routinely cursed, struck, and kicked his men. Two of his sailors caught urinating on deck had their grog stopped, got thirteen lashes apiece, and had "their face and eyes [filled] with excrescence of man and . . . [rubbed] . . . well in."

Flogging and other physical brutality had been abandoned long before the twentieth century, but not without protest from senior Navy officers. In 1850, during the debate over outlawing flogging, the secretary of the Navy had polled his officers on the subject. Of eighty-four men replying, only seven wanted to discontinue flogging.

Officers feared the lack of corporal punishment because they knew that discipline was the bedrock of naval law, which recognized both criminal and military infractions. The latter had more to do with obedience to regulations than violation of the law of the land, and most sailors ran aground on these reef points. Penalties in this regard were generally at the discretion of the commanding officer, the person offended against (the captain was charged with maintaining good order on his ship and was responsible for punishment)—a decided departure from civilian practice.

Over the years, whether a sailor confronted a captain's mast, a deck court, or some form of court-martial, his chances of getting off scot-free were slim. Only 2.9 percent of bluejackets appearing before general courts-martial from 1904 to 1939 were acquitted. Masts were the most common form of punishment (they could be used for praise and commendation, too—but rarely were), usually hearing cases of disobedience, drunkenness, and absenteeism. A few cases could be highly imaginative. Jack Kerouac, a future leader of the "beat generation" of the fifties, enlisted in the Navy in 1942 and then feigned insanity. He was discharged for having "indifferent character."

The incorrigible ones ended up doing hard time, some emerging with dishonorable discharges. But the Navy began to learn to invest more time in rehabilitating brig cases, because some of these people were of potential help to the service. The brig cases were the ones whom standard shipboard punishment, like reduction in rate or forfeiture of pay, could not handle. Advising and analysis began to accompany punitive action. At the Naval Disciplinary Barracks on Terminal Island, off San Pedro, California, 74 percent of the inmates in 1945 came from broken homes. Increasing attention to details such as these at least slightly improved the Navy's rehabilitation process and decreased recidivism.

Of the millions of World War II sailors, only forty thousand did hard brig time. By 1948 the Navy was returning about two thousand whitehats a year from the brig to active duty. Many of these men had tested in the lower mental groups, and for most of the offenders the story was *cherchez la femme;* "woman trouble is at the heart of many a sailor's downfall," wrote one observer. Not everyone could be saved, by any means. At Norfolk's Camp Allen in the late forties, about 35 percent of the men received their bad-conduct discharge as ordered.

After the war the Naval Retraining Command moved into the full-time business of rehabilitation; as difficult as retaining personnel had become, the service could afford to lose only the minimum. In a naval equivalent of a reformatory, sailors convicted of absence without leave, thievery, sexual offenses, or violation of any one of hundreds of Navy regs ("Rocks and Shoals") were run through a daily routine of work details, formations, exercises, and lectures. Their average time served was six months, and about half returned to duty. The others got a bad-conduct discharge or one under "less-than-honorable" conditions. All would remember the tender ministrations of their Marine keepers.

The major postwar change was the inclusion of psychiatric counseling in the regimen. One psychologist designed a "social integration scale," ranking his charges from I-1 to I-7. (I-1s were in mental hospitals, I-2s were egomaniacs.) Other sailors found themselves labeled "nonconformists," fodder for "group dynamics," talking about their parents, venting their frustrations about women or authority, and role playing with their fellow inmates. During the decade ending in 1955, about 48,000 men passed through the Retraining Command; 14,000 returned to duty.[14]

—The Navy, still discipline-conscious and far from "coddling" its sailors (as some old-timers always charged), was trying mightily, and necessarily, to save as many of its people as possible.

☆

The Navy's revolving door also meant that far more attention had to be given to the good sailor, to the quality of his life at sea and ashore. In the prewar Navy the comfort of the men had been practically the last concern. Now, as new ships were built, the "habitability" spaces grew larger and more livable. Ashore, barracks construction tried to emphasize "sizeable reduction of the gross area per man, without reducing each man's actual living space." Life in the Navy was always crowded, privacy always at a premium, but these were problems that had to be addressed.

Recreational opportunities provided part of the answer. The Navy had always rigorously supported sports and physical conditioning. As only one example, baseball—after a slow start—was a staple from the late nineteenth century onward. Naval ships fielded their own nines, the Naval Academy had a team as early as the late 1860s, and Navy teams played games overseas as well. (The Japanese may have gained much of their love for the game from American sailors.) A few whitehats, like Sam Rice, went on to the major leagues, in Rice's case to 2404 games, a .322 lifetime batting average, and a twenty-year career.

The postwar Navy kept up the accent on physical competition and also sought to broaden recreational opportunities for the fleet. The new supercarriers, like *Kitty Hawk*, were in part designed for recreation, and one officer and nine enlisted men were assigned full time to organize play. Movies, television, radio; parties, picnics, tours; volleyball, softball, fishing expeditions—everything possible for the sailor's comfort and relaxation. (Well, not quite; as *South Pacific* had made clear, "We ain't got dames!")

Every ship had a "Special Services" organization, usually funded by the take from soft drink and candy machines. Intership athletic competition, as always, was commonplace. *Kitty Hawk* fielded football, bowling, softball, basketball, rifle, pistol, and chess teams. Larger vessels had spaces in which sailors could work on their hobbies or crafts. Weight-lifting rooms came into vogue. Crew morale was everywhere a top item, and recreational opportunities abounded. One of her officers called *Kitty Hawk* a "transient recreation district."

Submarines were a tougher proposition, but even aboard the boats there were table games, hobbies, and the usual movies to while away the time on the long patrols. Submariners, selected in part for their emotional stability, generally had far fewer conduct offenses than other whitehats, anyway.[15]

Another change in the postwar Navy came with a vastly strengthened library program. Nothing could force a sailor to read, and those in the lower mental groups had trouble reading in the first place, but every command had a "library" of some sort, even if the title described a few battered books thrown in the skipper's drawer. The supercarriers sported libraries of three thousand volumes or more, complete with Dewey decimal system. Big shore bases could boast sixty thousand books. Many sailors, of course, confined their reading to dog-eared, smudgy-paged pornographic works gleaned in smut peddlers' stalls from Naples to Hong Kong. But there was always a good run on quality fiction, as well as books on the sciences, hobbies, military history, and politics.

Librarians and doctors also experimented with "bibliotherapy programs" at naval hospitals, using reading for both therapy and diagnosis. Literacy training, involving special classes under professional teachers, became commonplace at many naval installations as the service struggled to bring its sailors some kind of comprehension of modern technology. Literacy units were etablished at each of the Navy's training centers—Bainbridge, Great Lakes, and San Diego. Classes ran about eight weeks, and instructors claimed an improvement of about one grade in reading level per student.

Most bases also featured U.S. Armed Forces Institute (USAFI) courses in six thousand high school and college subjects. At any given time, thousands of sailors were working on their high-school equivalencies or on undergraduate subjects. Indeed, more sailors than ever were convinced of the value of a premium education; no one wanted to be doomed to the tedious round of never-improving routine that had trapped the illiterate sailor aboard the nineteenth-century man-o'-war. The crew of the destroyer *John S. McCain* even contributed a full scholarship to the University of Hawaii for a penniless Okinawan. (The ship earmarked its bingo and ice cream machine profits for this use.)[16]

The days when bluejackets would be paraded on the main deck for compulsory church services had long since passed, but the Chaplain's Corps was still in business, and its business was not only spiritual guidance but also morale. About four thousand men received special religious instruction during 1952, with almost six hundred being baptized. Numerically, this was but a drop in the bucket, evidence of the Navy's intense secularization, but the emphasis on moral training, despite the obvious roadblocks inherent in sailor life, remained strong. "Men with good morals are better fighting men," bluntly stated Rear Admiral Francis Olds.

The postwar Navy also established a Lay Leaders program, in which sailors trained by the squadron chaplain would conduct services on those many ships without a "sky pilot." Chaplains were scarce (there were only 238 Catholic chaplains in the Navy in 1959), and the Lay Leader stopgap was necessary and at least partially effective. Eventually a new rating, Religious Program Specialist (RPS), was created to help out even more. The overall irony of religious faith within military life was not lost on critics, however. "It is not only the pacifist who says that war is becoming an obsolete institution," observed the *Christian Century*. "How then can character be built by promoting moral allegiance to an institution whose moral basis is so dubious? Can character be character when it is promoted within the confines of such a structure?"[17]

—Such questions zipped right by the average whitehat. His main index of morale, if not morals, was what had always been his main index: food. Navy chow—its amount, quality, and accessibility—was everyone's province. The Navy prided itself on being a "good feeder." Pastries, cakes, sweet rolls, and breads rolled out of Navy ovens by the ton. Freezers were crammed with precooked, precut meats (called "prefabricated" by the Navy), vegetables, and fruit. Subs carried a "submarine provision load" of food which, the service proudly announced, took up 25 percent less space and produced 65 percent less garbage. (At least one boat rebelled against this bland fare, and her cook ended up serving round after round of chicken cacciatore.)

The Navy's cookbook contained over six hundred recipes, usually whipped up for anywhere from twenty-five people to thousands. At the Navy Supply Base in Bayonne, New Jersey, dietitians endlessly experimented with sailor palates. As a rule, fish, carrots, asparagus, beets, and spinach were slow movers, while whitehats tended to love the standards: steak, meat loaf, turkey, fried chicken, hamburgers, stews, peas, and beans. Every once in a while, Filipino mess cooks would bring forth some exotic dishes not in the cookbook, like the dangerous "gilly-gilly," complete with chicken head. The cost to feed the Cold War Navy was around $282 million a year in the fifties, which meant big business for dozens of industries and which sometimes led to whopping miscalculations, as when the Navy admitted to a stockpile of hamburger meat that could feed the fleet for sixty years.

Griping about his chow was the sailor's time-honored right. One yeoman third class stationed at Bainbridge even tried to lead a rebellion in the name of better cuisine: "What the dietician for this naval training center and his assorted mess cooks do to the food is a crime. . . . A man is almost forced to survive on the packaged dry cereal, packaged half-pint milk, bread, butter, salt, sugar, and pepper (the only edibles the cooks can't alter)." But for the most part, the griping went hand-to-mouth with eating, and eating well.[18]

—A bit too well, in fact. By the sixties the Navy was forced to adopt a weight-reduction program and inaugurate physical conditioning standards.

☆

At the summit of the Navy's enlisted ranks stood the Navy chief, gold hashmarks running up his left sleeve like a ladder to infinity—an enduring and exceptionally valuable institution. Chiefs were people with hard-earned privileges: they were the only enlisted to wear khaki; they had their own, very exclusive mess aboard; they had their own clubs ashore. Their decades of service made them unparalleled advisers, to juniors and seniors alike. They were the Navy's hands-on experts, on boilers, guns, radars, typewriters, anything. With their grizzled countenances, sulphurous language, and thorough knowledge of their craft, they spelled one word: experience.

The chief went back to the late nineteenth century. He was part of the Navy's response to the industrial era, in that he was a rough analogue of a shop foreman. But he was much more: father-confessor to young sailors, instant disaster for whitehats who stepped out of line, guiding light to junior officers, barometer of weather below decks for captains, and repository of sea stories and tales of when life was really good (in the Old Navy). Above all, he, beyond all other enlisted men, was depended on to get things done. "We were the glue," said Jackson Parker, a chief machinist who ascended all the way to rear admiral. "The backbone of the Navy is the chief petty officer."

Postwar chiefs were badly shaken by the drawdown and by the influx of thousands of inexperienced sailors with whom they were supposed to do something. Chief Machinist Richard McKenna, who went on in retirement to write the best-seller *The Sand Pebbles*, about prewar life on the China Station, noted in 1948 that chiefs were being subjected to an "apparently endless series of transfers" and often plunked into duty assignments that had nothing to do with their skills. "The corps spirit of the chief petty officers is waning," McKenna claimed.

Two years later a commander wrote that the chiefs' morale was "among the highest in the service." The truth was probably somewhere between his and McKenna's estimates, but for the Navy the most important factor was that these enlisted lifers made the Navy run, and if they were unhappy, something was fouled up. As Tommy Sprague said, "The officers say what to do, the chiefs decide how to do it."

Usually, a chief took from twelve to sixteen years to make his pay grade, E-7, the top of the heap. In 1950 two-thirds of the chiefs, despite wartime accelerated promotions, had been in service more than a decade. Most of them were paid around $250 a month, about twice the amount earned by most of the enlisted men working for them. The pay differential was important, but in the decade after the war the chief, as McKenna had sensed, felt his importance and independence beginning to erode.

In the prewar Navy, when the average whitehat never got to Officers' Country and seldom even *saw* an officer short of inspection, the chief's word had been practically all there was. The chief exercised a considerable amount of unwritten Navy law, and often he himself would punish or restrict his sailors without appeal to higher authority. A rotten chief (and there were some of these) could be a holy terror for his men, but in general, officers were more than content to let their chiefs hold sway on the mess decks. Fewer men went to captain's mast, and the smart skipper usually backed his chiefs right down the line. Clearly this was a system capable of abuse, but chiefs took great pride in "handling their own."

The sudden need for expertise in World War II introduced Reservists who had worked in supervisory capacities in civilian life willy-nilly into the Chiefs' Mess. These "slick-arm" chiefs (no hash marks on their sleeves connoting years of service) were in many instances militarily inept and scorned by their saltier counterparts. After the war, as McKenna noted, the Navy found itself so top-heavy in E-7s that many chiefs had to be assigned to billets usually held by junior petty officers.

To cap all, the administrative organization of the Navy was overhauled and changed by concepts embodied in the *Uniform Code of Military Justice* (1951). Modern psychological approaches to leadership frowned on "negative discipline," and if the old-school chief specialized in anything, he specialized in hands-on punishment, quick and to the point. Now, the chief who dispensed a little mess-decks justice with his fists or the sole of his shoe was liable to mast himself. Throughout the Navy, chiefs were complaining that they were losing prestige, were being reduced to figureheads. Most of the chiefs of the fifties had entered the service at a time when *their* chiefs had been Gods Almighty—kicking ass and taking names—and they wanted that role for themselves.

More politely put, chiefs wanted to be disciplinarians, strong supervisors, and advocates for their men. The current of modern leadership techniques was not running their way, however. Only in submarines, with their institution of "chief of the boat," did some of the old ways survive.

A partial solution was found in 1958. The Committee on Professional and Technical Compensation strung out the enlisted ranks for the entire military at the upper end. For the Navy the result, the "Kilday Bill," provided two new pay grades: E-8 (senior chief) and E-9 (master chief). In 1958 the Navy had sixty-four ratings and 47,200 chiefs at the tops of these ratings. The new "superchiefs" were chosen by selection boards, on the officer model; 922 senior chiefs and 149 master chiefs were selected that first year.

By ratio, there were still fewer chiefs than officers. In 1958, for every 100 chiefs there were 137 commissioned officers, 10 warrant officers, and 1125 sailors. But the superchiefs got big jumps in pay and were, in their turn, highly valued members of their units. Critics charged that the Kilday Bill simply diluted the Chiefs' Mess and did nothing to address the problem of erosion in enlisted leadership, which was true enough, but the Navywide response to the new grades was uniformly positive.

—The Navy's chiefs were far from finished. But their cherished independence was deeply shaken. They now had to live in a seagoing environment where suggestion and persuasion counted for more than outright force and coercion, where they had to understand as well as drive their men.

☆

The sailor in the Cold War Navy was usually aboard only for his first hitch. Turnover on the mess decks was fierce. The lifers, as always, set the tone and the standards for the service. And these were high—given the numbers of people coursing through the personnel system, exceptionally high. Despite the endless griping about the officers, the work, the liberty, the chow, and everything else under the sun, the ships still steamed, and the Navy, stretched to the seams, was still able to do what the country asked the service to do.

This was possible because of the whitehats. They maintained, with their perpetual training, the finest quality of any enlisted naval force in the world, the highly professional navies of Great Britain, Canada, and Australia not excepted. They were far from the *canaille* who had manned the sailing navies and who had given Samuel Johnson such pause. They needed to be led intelligently and with compassion; this given, they responded magnificently. The naval enlisted force, despite its obvious problems, was effective almost all the time, which, for an institution of half a million men, was remarkable in itself.

Rear Admiral Robley ("Fighting Bob") Evans, chosen by Teddy Roosevelt in 1907 to take the Great White Fleet around the world, had spoken for the century when he came to describe his sailors.

"You don't need armor," Fighting Bob had said, "when you have men like mine."[19]

CHAPTER TWENTY-TWO

ASHORE

T he Navy was the sea service, and ashore was not the sea. The dedicated, zealous line officer, though he might welcome service ashore for family reasons, regarded the duty professionally as a sentence to purgatory. "You could lose your reputation ashore," Vice Admiral George Dyer remembered, "but you could not make it there." The satisfactions of seagoing duty and command lay beyond the coastline, out on salt water. Besides, to the true old salt, the beach might provide respite but was a bore. "A naval officer's periods of shore duty are like the country without a history," complacently wrote Rear Admiral Charles Clark, "the happier for having little to record."

—All very well, but the modern Navy required a vast, and constantly growing, amount of support ashore, most of this provided by the various staff corps and in-house civilians. Behind every sailor who went to sea stood dozens of men and women, in and out of uniform, who worked on land.

The Supply Corps went through severe changes in the wake of World War II. "The Navy is now Big Business," noted one supply captain, and he urged that every technique of modern business be applied to naval affairs. This meant supply officers who were experts in management, logistics, accounting, industrial production, contracting, and tax policy—people who could navigate around every corner of the increasingly sophisticated business world.

Although the Navy, in relative economic terms, had always been Big Business, things were much simpler in the early days. Sea dogs like Thomas Truxtun, Edward Preble, and Stephen Decatur saw themselves as fighting sailors, not as businessmen. To enable them and their kind to concentrate on their primary task, which was command at sea, they had the aid of the ancestor of the supply officer, the purser, who was outside the early Navy's four-step ladder of promotion: midshipman, lieutenant, master commandant, and captain. Pursers were at first drawn mostly from the counting houses of successful waterfront mercantile firms. Their duties were to guard and distribute the ship's "purse" but also to haggle over the going rate for cordage, blocks, rum kegs, round shot, clothing, tar, pitch, turpentine, salt junk, and hardtack.

As time went on and "supply" became largely a settled staff job ashore (the Supply Corps was established in 1892), each ship was usually given at least one such officer, the paymaster. Supply officers, looked at through the jaundiced binoculars of the line, tended to quickly become superannuated and, to put the case mildly, set in their ways. Most of them—half-derisively and half-affectionately called "porkchops" from the shape of their staff insignia—came into the Navy from civilian jobs in finance or the like. They tended to be older than the fresh-caught midshipman-turned-ensign.

Annapolis would annually offer up only four or five who chose the specialty, but "for every recruit the Corps thus gained, two or three elderly men retired for age, blood pressure, or a heart murmur." The porkchops congregated in the old BuSandA, the Bureau of Supplies and Accounts. "His mission in life," Vice Admiral Ruthven Libby said of one of these men, "was to study the *Supplies and Accounts Manual* exhaustively so that he could find a reason for saying that anything you needed to run your department you couldn't have."

World War II blew the placid, stodgy Supply Corps, with its few hundred specialists, wide open. The Navy Supply Corps School, hitherto a mossy backwater, expanded its program dramatically. Many inductees were run through a hastily organized graduate curriculum at Harvard, cramming in subjects such as fuel studies, foreign resources, accounting, transportation, government policy, production organization, and statistical controls. Newly minted supply officers scattered by the thousands all over the world, on every naval front, and rapidly made themselves indispensable. (Mr. Roberts, despite all his bellyaching about not being assigned to a destroyer, was doing important work in supply.) By 1945, almost twenty thousand supply officers were on active duty, twice the number of the entire officer corps of the prewar Navy.

The postwar Supply School was begun in Bayonne, New Jersey, but was later moved to Athens, Georgia—another gift to their state from Representative Carl Vinson and Senator Richard Russell. More Annapolis and NROTC grads began to choose the specialty, either from inclination or because medical problems disqualified them for the line. Every ship, no matter how minuscule, had its Supply Department, and many young officers would cut their porkchop teeth on "independent duty," usually a destroyer. From pay to toilet paper, no naval command, afloat or ashore, could operate without them. Their training was now far more elaborate, and their business methods were in many ways indistinguishable from those of the civilian sector—with which, through contracts, purchasing, and the like, they dealt constantly.

Supply meant not only the traditional beans, bullets, and black oil but also the infinitude of things that made the modern Navy run. The supply officer, barred from command at sea though he might be, became far more important in the postwar period than he had ever been before.[1]

Unlike the supply officers, the Navy's lawyers seldom went to sea. Most of them came into the service complete with law degree, although in the postwar period a very few ensigns were handpicked to go to law school at the Navy's expense. The lawyers worked for the Judge Advocate General's (JAG) Corps and provided all the Navy's legal services, except those aspects of commercial law specifically relegated to the General Counsel of the Navy.

A Navy lawyer always had a full plate, and as modern American society became ever more complicated and litigious, the plate overflowed. Supply officers, with their management and financial skills, often left the service to sample the rewards of civilian life; legal officers, with even more money potentially available on the outside, usually did so just as soon as their obligated service was up. The turnover in the junior ranks of Navy lawyers was at a turnstile pace.

While they were in uniform, their "practice" was wide indeed. They did the routine paper-shuffling of administrative law; civil law, including claims and legal assistance; litigations; investigations; international and admiralty law; and, most importantly for the common sailor, military justice under the *Uniform Code of Military Justice* issued in 1951.

Must of their work was novel, in rapidly developing areas like the application of new weapons and surveillance systems; arms control; nuclear safety issues; and, most novel of all, "space law." These were tidbits that could not be gathered on the outside, and the novelty kept a few topnotchers in uniform. For the career Navy lawyer, there was plenty of challenge and intellectual excitement.

At the deckplate level, however, naval justice remained the province of the commanding officer, although his punitive sanctions were nowhere near the scope of those available to Truxtun, Preble, and Decatur. The skipper still had his captain's mast; he could still bust a sailor in rate, dock his pay, and confine him aboard. (When an officer was thus slapped on the wrist, he was confined aboard "in hack.") To aid him, the captain had a legal officer—on the heavies a trained lawyer—but on most commands an unfortunate junior officer cannoned through a "legal course" in the arcane areas of investigations, punishments, summary courts-martial, and defendants' rights.

Critics—and they had good points—were fond of deriding the Navy's concepts of seagoing justice, particularly since the formal accuser—the captain—was also the judge, in violation of centuries of hard-won Anglo-Saxon jurisprudence. But shipboard punishment was the Navy's way, quick and hopefully effective, and while the service's legal system had to carve out a far larger sphere for defendants' rights in the postwar period, the conviction rate, for everything from captain's mast to general courts-martial, remained exceptionally high, well above 90 percent across the board. Once charged, a sailor was almost always punished, unless his misconduct was an innocuous first offense.

The legal system, fostered by time-honored concepts of seagoing law and custom, was meant to serve the demands of military discipline and obedience. The system, as sailors experienced Navy law, was a thing apart from the legal niceties of civilian law and could be brutally unfair, particularly in the cases of racial minorities and homosexuals. But Navy law suited the Navy just fine, even though the increased concern for individual rights in the new code "put a great strain on the line officers who had to administer men and to run a ship."

A third staff corps was the "God Squad"—the Chaplains' Corps. By no means all sailors were religious, but the broad ocean had a wondrous way of instilling awe, fear, and the sense of a Higher Presence. Many who went to sea felt that their life was in God's hands. When Jonah, in the Old Testament, boarded a ship at Joppa to sail to Tarshish, "there was a mighty tempest at sea, so that the ship was likely to be broken. Then the mariners were afraid and cried every man unto his own god."

Every man unto his own god was the Navy way, and, ideally, a god for every man. Religious belief could be devilishly hard to find aboard ship and in sailor haunts ashore, but chaplains, who had been around since the Navy's earliest days, by 1945 represented every Protestant denomination and included many Catholic priests and a few Jewish rabbis. To this extent America's Navy was ecumenical, trying to serve the religious needs of the greatest possible number of sailors. A chaplain, said a member of the corps, stayed away from "narrow, sectarian and dogmatic preaching."

—But there were never enough chaplains to go around. Only a few hundred served the fleet's religious needs at any given time, and many of these properly ordained men were assigned to Navy chapels ashore. At sea the heavies had their own chaplains, but all other ships had to depend on the Navy version of circuit riders—squadron chaplains who rotated among ships in their pastoral care. Compulsory chapel service was a thing of the past, and so were the days when a ship's crew would be mustered on the fantail on Sunday morning, hangovers or not, to hear the word of God. The Navy was pronouncedly secular in its ways, but the service prided itself on being on God's side (the converse was also believed to be the case), and more than lip service was given to religion.

A glimpse of the numbers can be gleaned from the Pacific Cruiser-Destroyer Force in the 1950s. There, on an average Sunday, thirty-five Catholic Rosary prayer services (total attendance 350) and as many Protestant services (400 attending) would be held. The mathematics worked out to no more than 10 or so men per service, far from what one chaplain called an "impressive total," but the word of God was in the fleet, for those who wanted to hear the message.

The lack of chaplains led to the Lay Leader Program. The lay leaders, either officers or enlisted, were not clergymen. They did not administer sacraments aboard Navy ships, except for baptism in extremis and prayers for the dying, according to the accepted form of the appropriate church. In a pinch, they did religious counseling, although these cases, if at all possible, were referred to the squadron chaplain or a cleric ashore. The lay leaders' prime function was to conduct divine services. They got a boost from their squadron chaplains and, in time, were supported by the new rating of religious programs specialist. In this stopgap way the Navy's religious needs, never very severe, were at least partially met. Ashore, where family problems came to the fore, the chaplains found a steady stream of work in what amounted to full-time counseling and emotional therapy.

A fourth staff corps, another that seldom got to sea, was the Civil Engineer Corps (CEC). These engineers, many but not all university-trained in civil engineering, were the Navy's builders, fixers, and professional maintenance men. They kept hundreds of naval stations and installations running, and their enlisted personnel sported construction specialties from electricity to plumbing to concrete work. Every ship had its "engineering" department, but these had been line officer positions since 1899.

During World War II, under Rear Admiral Ben Moreell, the CEC spawned the justly famed construction battalions—the Seabees—and this institution plowed into the postwar world intact, a fundamental aspect of the new naval globalism. Every member of the CEC, officer and enlisted, regardless of previous training and experience, went through the CEC School at Port Hueneme, California, just as the chaplains learned the Navy way at Chaplain's School in Newport. Most, but not all, of the CEC officers would cut their teeth with the Seabees, who did construction jobs for the Navy all over the world.[2]

The Navy's shore establishment could not run without the CEC. Indeed, three of these four staff corps—Supply, JAG, and CEC—grew tremendously in importance in the postwar period, concrete evidence that the Cold War Navy required a huge logistic, management, and administrative infrastructure.

—By no means all of the officers and sailors were out there riding around on haze gray.

☆

The other four staff corps—Medical, Medical Service, Nurse, and Dental—dealt with the health of the fleet. The Navy's health care, a bastion of socialism in an institution that prided itself on its individualism, was very good indeed in flagship hospitals like those at Bethesda or San Diego. For the service as a whole, however, medical and dental care was at best marginal, as had always been the case.

The problem had many facets, but at the core lay the unwillingness of medical professionals to put on the uniform, particularly for a career in which the earnings differential between what the Navy offered and a lucrative civilian practice was spectacular. In the ten years following V-J Day the nation's medical schools graduated almost forty-seven thousand doctors, and the merest handful of these entered the Navy. Only a fraction of this fraction stayed for the long haul. All the services had the same problem: highly trained medical people had little relish for military life.

World War II propelled tens of thousands of physicians into uniform; the Navy's V-12 College Training Program alone turned out over eleven thousand. But at war's end came a mass exodus, and only 450 of the wartime doctors accepted an appointment in the regular Navy. Until 1950 there was no assurance whatsoever of an adequate supply of medical officers, and in many areas of the Navy the constantly reiterated claim of reasonable medical care was a farce. In December 1948 the American Medical Association urged 7610 newly minted doctors under twenty-six years of age to volunteer for active duty. Only thirty-three signed on with the Navy, and then only for two years.

Some relief came in September 1950, three months after North Korean tanks rolled across the 38th parallel, with the passage of Public Law 779, the "doctors' draft law." The Navy itself did not resort to Selective Service for any physicians, but the pressure of the draft led some medical men into the fleet anyway. Still, the statistics were appalling. In the eight years from 1946 to 1954, the regular Navy's Medical Corps lost one-quarter of its strength. The lifers were leaving. By 1953 only 1458 regular Navy physicians were in uniform, along with 2800 Reservists expected to provide health care across the board for six hundred thousand Navy people, their dependents, and countless retirees.

Furthermore, most of the medical "draftees" were a surly lot. The majority of them, according to one medical flag officer, "put on a uniform with reluctance [and] accept the ordeal as a sentence to be served. They carry out their work in an unhappy frame of mind." Most of them were fresh from medical school, some with residencies under their belts. They learned the Navy way in the Naval Medical School at Bethesda and were then dispersed to naval hospitals or ships, where many of them did squadron circuit riding on the order of the God Squad. In most cases these young physicians at sea did general practice, felt themselves denied the right to specialize, and counted bitterly both the dollars and the training they were missing on the outside.

The quality of naval medicine varied from the exceptially high (U.S. presidents were treated at Bethesda) to the mediocre and worse. Griping, particularly among dependents forced to endure long waits and indifferent treatment, was all too common. The rare scandal, of course, got the ink, as when the General Accounting Office found that some Navy doctors stationed at Twenty-Nine Palms, a Marine base in southern California, were receiving kickbacks from civilian doctors who were treating dependents and being paid by the government. Generally, however, basic health care was being provided across the board—but barely.

By 1955 the crisis within the Medical Corps was full-blown. The Korean War had frozen the resignation of regular Navy doctors; from 1953 to 1955, the two years following the freeze, one out of every five resigned. Despite Public Law 779, the lifers continued to go over the side. In 1953 only sixteen new medical officers were commissioned. Lack of public recognition for the uniform (the "ego factor") was part of the reason many people gave for this sorry state of affairs, but dollars and cents were by far predominant. In 1951 the average civilian physician had an income of $25,000, a figure that would escalate sharply in years to come. A Navy lieutenant commander in that year netted nearly $9000 less than the average civilian specialist, and that gap would widen also.

This, for the Navy, was a completely new situation. Before 1941 commissions in the Medical Corps had been eagerly sought, and entrance had been highly competitive. But the erosion in earning power of these highly trained medical professionals had turned into a landslide. By 1951 Navy doctors received only 51 percent of the remuneration of civilian physicians doing comparable work.

Although engineers, tempted by higher salaries, were leaving the CEC and although skilled supply specialists and lawyers could also make more on the outside, nowhere was the civilian-military earnings gap so wide as in the Medical Corps or so costly for the Navy. The best that could be offered was this assessment by a naval flight surgeon: "When all disadvantages and advantages are compared it leads to the conclusion that a naval medical officer must decide whether or not he can accept the reduced financial status in exchange for the pride to him of wearing the uniform."

—The numbers indicated that this was not much of an appeal. In 1954 a career incentive program was set up, providing improved residency training, higher specialty pay, and more stable assignments. Slowly the situation improved; by 1960 the Navy was commissioning between two hundred and three hundred doctors a year. Nevertheless, the drain at the end of their obligated service continued to be tremendous.

But those who stayed were practicing good medicine. In the late 1940s, about twenty-two of every one thousand active-duty personnel were hospitalized each day of the year; by 1959 this figure had fallen to fourteen and would continue to shrink. These numbers were significant in a worldwide health empire so vast that patients were practically invited to fall through the cracks.

The Medical Corps, by 1960, was running twenty-six naval hospitals, thirty-one station hospitals, and dozens of dispensaries—a total of sixteen thousand beds. Counting civilians, these beds were more than three-quarters occupied. And some Navy physicians, particularly if they stayed aboard and moved up in ranks, were at the frontiers of their profession: aviation and submarine medicine, radiobiology, clinical medicine, and space medicine.

Much of naval life was dangerous. People died, on and off duty, carelessly, accidentally, for reasons unknown. In fiscal 1961, 1400 Navy people (0.002 percent of the whole) died on active duty. Vehicles were the biggest killers (35 percent), followed by aviation (25 percent) and other injuries (22 percent). Only 18 percent of this largely youthful, male population died of disease. With some justification, the secretary of the Navy could say proudly that "excellent health conditions prevailed throughout the naval forces."[3]

Naval medicine, of course, was not a local but a worldwide practice. Out in the boondocks, in addition to the circuit riders, the Navy had three Medical Research Units (NAMRUs) doing research and treatment on a heroic albeit unrecognized scale. NAMRU-2, for example, was a twelve-person outfit, led by a captain, which roamed Asia in everything from jeeps to light planes. The men of NAMRU-2 collected mosquitoes from traps set in dunghills, snakes from jungle underbrush, and snails from paddy fields. They fought cholera in East Pakistan (the future Bangladesh), studied "black-foot" (an arterial disease that could lead to gangrene) in Formosa, did research on parasites that attacked the intestinal tracts of African and Asian field workers, and examined the effects of German measles on pregnant women and their fetuses.

Technically, the NAMRUs existed solely to investigate and develop cures for diseases that might impair the Navy's effectiveness. In actuality, the Navy's medics overseas treated all comers and were not overly concerned about the legal niceties. They were among America's finest goodwill ambassadors, and cheap. The cost of NAMRU-3's operations in Cairo cost the average American taxpayer 15 cents a year.

The Navy's sprawling medical enterprise, with thirty-seven thousand employees and nearly two million patients a year by 1960, was run by the surgeon general of the Navy. His office oversaw the Navy's medical responses to emergencies, and these could happen at any time—cholera in Thailand, yellow fever in the Sudan, hurricanes in Texas. All the hospitals, dispensaries, and medical facilities on almost one thousand ships belonged to him. So did the twenty-eight research labs, the Preventive Medical Units, the NAMRUs, and all the rest. Under him, the Navy handled one of the largest health care programs anywhere, short of a national socialized medical program. By the 1960s the service was also participating in reformed dependent medical care, the Civilian Health and Medical Program of the Uniformed Services (CHAMPUS).

Besides the doctors, the surgeon general's medical personnel included the Medical Service, people like pharmacists and hospital administrators, the Nurse Corps, and the dentists. There were 376 dental activities in 1959, many centered on dental care for recruits (12 surface restorations, 7 cavities, and 1.5 extractions per boot). Over a hundred ships had their own dental facilities. The quality of the general dental program was not high; the emphasis was placed on preventive dentistry, sailors were hard to track during months and years of overseas duty, and dental skills, like medical ones, were compensated for much better on the outside.

With all these problems—pay, morale, and treatment facilities not only scattered around the world but many highly mobile as well—naval medicine and dental care, given the nature of the organization, could not be expected to be uniformly excellent. What was surprising, rather, was that so much of the care was proper and consistent. The four health-related staff corps contained some of the very best of the Navy's professionals, and most of the career people were nothing short of outstanding.[4]

☆

To the traditional Navyman, ashore was where civilians were—sandcrabs on the beach. By the mid-1950s the Navy had become the third-largest employer of civilian personnel in the federal government. In 1956 almost 400,000 civilians were on the Navy payroll, ranging from the leaf-rakers who manicured the well-groomed lawns of the Naval Academy to astrophysicists winkling out the secrets of space at the Naval Research Laboratory. About 75,000 civilians were women. Cutbacks diminished the numbers to a total of 346,000 by 1960.

The Navyman tended to see the sandcrabs as operating under the principle of dual supervision: three civilians set off to do a task; one works, and the other two sit on their butts and supervise. There was an element of truth to the stereotype, partially because in the lower civilian pay-grades, as in the uniformed service, the personnel turnover was terrific. The Navy had an annual civilian separation rate of almost 20 percent in the 1950s. And the civilian presence, like that of the staffers, was worldwide. About 30,000 civilians worked for the Navy overseas, and many of these were foreign nationals. In terms of direct support of the fleet, the Bureau of Ships had the most—134,000 in 1956—followed by the Bureau of Aeronautics (81,000) and the Bureau of Ordnance (55,000).

In consonance with the difficulties experienced by the naval line and staff officer corps, severe civilian shortages existed in engineering and scientific skills. Federal pay scales simply could not compete with those of a flourishing private sector. There were incentive rewards ("beneficial suggestions," or "bennysugs," could bring a small amount of cash, a plaque, and a handshake), and the Navy paid its civilian workers $2 million in 1956 alone for these. The major problem was somehow to keep civilian wage scales close to those in private industry, which meant congressional approval and proved to be, in the case of many badly needed technological skills, a hopeless task.

In addition, the Navy had to pick its way through the ever-shifting maze of Civil Service regulations, try to hire the "best qualified" people, ensure their training and opportunity for advancement, monitor and evaluate their performance, and strive to keep them on board. The Government Employee Training Act (1959) set the hurdles but did not stop the pernicious phenomenon of "grade creep," by which a civilian inched upward on the pay scale while still doing the same job.

All this was a long way from, say, 1803, when the secretary of the Navy operated with a chief clerk and two assistants—period. Despite the Civil Service, political considerations were omnipresent, for two reasons: the higher civilian levels in the Navy Department were for the most part politicized, and a large reduction in the civilian work force, particularly if geographically concentrated, could wreak havoc with a local economy and bring anguished screams from Congress.

"The skills and competence of civilian personnel continue at a high level," asserted Secretary of the Navy William Franke in 1960. But, as he admitted with considerable understatement, "as can be expected in a dynamic technical age, a number of specialized fields are advancing faster than sufficient personnel can be trained in them, and shortages of qualified people recur and persist in the sciences, engineering, and some highly skilled trades." Put another way, the Navy was far from able to sustain and improve its in-house technology on its own, which meant expensive contracting to think tanks, universities, and private enterprise. In this way, the Navy's increasing dependence on sophisticated technology made the service, paradoxically, less rather than more self-reliant.[5]

The public was mistaken to see the Navy as only uniforms and ships. For every two Navymen out there on blue water, a civilian was working directly for Navy pay, doing tasks in naval support. Beyond the civilians in direct support were literally millions more Americans in contractual relationships with the Navy. In this way alone, the service was a long way from being isolated from the country at large. The fleet, despite the traditional viewpoint of admirals like Dyer and Clark, was indeed bound to the shore.

☆

The Navy, to use later popular terminology, was almost by definition macho and sexist, an overweeningly male service in which masculine "virtues" were encouraged, celebrated, and rewarded. In fact, uniformed military women did not appear until the early twentieth century, when the mildly feminist accent of Progressivism led to the first tentative steps. The Army Nurse Corps was established in 1901, followed by the Navy Nurse Corps in 1908—the latter a virtually all-female preserve. The nurses, however, were initially civilian employees and did not receive full military status with men, nor did they get equal pay or equal benefits until World War II.

World War I brought a breakthrough—of sorts. Josephus Daniels, ever the reformer, found that nothing legally prohibited women from serving in the newly created Naval Reserve. Seizing this opportunity, he ordered their enlistment. Beginning in 1917, about twelve thousand women became, officially, members of the "Naval Coast Defense Reserve." Unofficially, they were yeoman-Fs, or "yeomanettes." (Even so, they did better than their unfortunate Marine counterparts, who were called "Marinettes.") On 21 March 1917, Loretto Perfectus Walsh enlisted as a chief yeoman at the Naval Home in Philadelphia, thus becoming the first female sailor two weeks before America declared war on Germany.

The yeomanettes did clerical chores ashore, serving as telephone operators, typists, and stenographers. A few did cooking, translating, drafting, camouflage preparation, and even electrical work. Of critical importance, they received the same pay and allowances as men similarly placed.

At first, the Navy did not know what to do with them. According to naval regulations, all yeomen were required to be assigned to a ship, but these women were prohibited by their enlistment law from serving aboard ship. In typical fashion, the Navy solved this problem by administratively assigning all women in the service to a tugboat permanently mired in the mud of the Potomac River.

The previously male-only Navy had no program for women's physicals (naval doctors and the female enlistees approached each other in considerable confusion). At first there was no women's uniform. (The enlistees devised their own, supplemented with articles from their own wardrobes.) Everyone was bewildered about where social etiquette left off and military etiquette began.

Undaunted, the women made their way, and most officers ashore came to fully recognize their importance. Most of the griping against them issued from male yeomen who protested the idea of sharing their precious rating badges with mere women. "The yeoman branch," insisted an editorial in *Our Navy*, "like all other branches of the Navy, is and always was a MAN's branch—a *seagoing* man's branch."

Nevertheless, the women were seen by the higher-ups as an entirely special, wartime-induced group. The yeomanettes were regarded essentially as civilians, to the degree that courts-martial for punishing female offenders were severely limited. (The Navy "cannot deal with women as with men," Daniels noted in his diary.) The women were usually disciplined, on the rare occasions when discipline was required, under civil service rules.

When the war ended, so did the temporary role of the yeomanettes. Many of the women wanted to stay on, and some Navymen agreed. One magazine for enlisted men appealed in doggerel:

Don't fire 'em, Josephus;
To our plea don't be deaf.
The Navy won't be any fun
Without the Yeomen (F).

—But fired they were. The Naval Appropriation Act of July 1919 required that all women be discharged. Some men even wanted to prevent them from receiving "honorable" discharges, but after much bureaucratic hassling, those who merited the discharge received their documents. The women were also issued the Victory Medal and, like the male enlisted, were paid the $60 gratuity for wartime service. In 1924, however, Congress attempted to exclude women from the "adjusted compensation bill" (the famous Veteran's Bonus Act, which caused so much trouble in the depths of the Depression). Only strong protests and fierce lobbying secured an amended bill that included the female veterans.

Following this unpromising foray into the masculine world of blue and gold, naval attitudes toward women hastily retreated to the traditional. Retired Rear Admiral Bradley Fiske, but for Daniels's opposition the man who might have been the first chief of naval operations, had won his reputation as a naval reformer by rattling the cages of conventional wisdom. But the masculine conventional wisdom about women was proof against new attitudes. Fiske doubtless spoke for the overwhelming majority of his male generation when, in 1925, he announced that women had a "seemingly insatiable desire to interfere in matters they do not understand." Wars, according to Fiske, were made to comfort and protect women, even against their will. "War they understand least, and from it they instinctively recoil. There is danger in this situation. Women now have the vote, and they outnumber the men. . . . In spite of themselves we must protect the ladies!"[6]

—This was the predominant strain, a potent sexual prejudice. Despite the exceptional service rendered by the yeomanettes in World War I, the Navy Department, even in the face of the crucial need for people in the bleak early days of World War II, at first resisted the drive to enlist women. As late as February 1942, with news of assorted Allied disasters pouring in from around the world, the chief of the Bureau of Navigation, the man who handled naval personnel matters, wrote that the department did not intend to seek legislation permitting the acceptance of women in either the Navy or the Naval Reserve. "Many admirals," acidly commented one woman, "would prefer to enroll monkeys, dogs, or ducks."

The Navy's urgent personnel needs soon changed all this. Shortly after BuNav had issued its sexual ukase, Carl Vinson's House Naval Affairs Committee reported favorably on a resolution that proposed amending the Naval Reserve Act of 1938 to include a "Women's Auxiliary Reserve." The legislation became law on 3 June 1942, specifically providing that women were to serve *in* the Navy, not merely *with* the Navy. Unlike the yeomanettes, they were to be subject to the existing laws and regulations governing the Naval Reserve. They would be led by one lieutenant commander (Mildred McAfee, the forty-two-year-old president of Wellesley College, took charge), supported by thirty-five lieutenants and a few more junior officers. When McAfee made the rounds of the bureaus to get suggestions and reached BuAer, Jack Towers barked, "Where have you been all this time? We've been clamoring for these [women] and nobody's ever listened to us."

The Navy, acronym-happy as usual, forgot about the "Women's Auxiliary Reserve" (WAR) and tortuously decreed the females were "Women Accepted for Volunteer Emergency Service," thus producing the salty WAVES (few of whom would get close to salt water). The acronym was actually the brainchild of Elizabeth Reynard, a professor of English at Barnard College, and came just in time; the press had begun to refer to the women as "goblettes."

Like the yeomanettes, the WAVES succeeded brilliantly. In their first year, sixteen enlisted training schools and the Naval Reserve Midshipman's School were established. (There would never be such a thing as a "midshipwoman.") Enrollment rapidly tripled the size expected by the Navy.

The women did everything they were allowed to do, and more. "They can be just as trustworthy as the man from Annapolis for the special duties they can discharge," admitted Fleet Admiral Leahy. They were trained in gunnery, blind flying, aerology, aviation ground crew procedure, navigation, aviation control (six hundred worked in Navy control towers), and naval communication, in addition to doing the clerical work pioneered by the yeomanettes. Their tasks freed enough men to crew a major task force, including two large carriers, a battleship, two heavy cruisers, four light cruisers, and fifteen destroyers.

Mildred McAfee's puny original organization rapidly swelled to giantess size. By July 1944 the WAVES numbered 72,000, and McAfee was a captain. A year later they totaled 86,000; they were 18 percent of all naval personnel assigned to stateside shore establishments. Collectively, by the end of the war they had sprung 50,000 men for duty afloat or overseas and had taken over 27,000 jobs in the Navy's enormously expanded shoreside operations. Among the 6500 WAVES stationed in the nation's capital, for example, were women who helped design vessels for BuShips and others who worked in previously nonfeminine pursuits such as hull construction, deck equipment, turbines, air conditioning, and salvage.

The accomplishments of WAVES did little to eradicate the Navy's traditional sexism. McAfee had been commissioned as "an officer and a gentleman in the United States Navy." She was not without barbed defenses of her own, noting the similarities between Navymen and the author of the Eighty-eighth Psalm: "Thy wrath lieth hard upon me, and thou hast afflicted me with all thy Waves."

The women, indeed, had tougher requirements to meet than the men. They all had to be at least twenty years old, of "high moral character," and in good health, in addition to passing rigorous verbal, mathematical, and physical exams. The officers had to have a college degree or two years of college with two years of work experience; enlisted personnel had to be high school graduates or to have completed two years of secondary schooling with two years of work experience. If the men had had to meet the same standards, the wartime fleet would have been substantially weakened.

As in World War I, all was not smooth sailing. McAfee barely squelched a proposal for a uniform featuring comic-opera stripes and red, white, and blue insignia. An experimental hat with a perky, upturned brim proved to be a miniature bathtub during rainy-day drills. Finally Mainbocher, the well-known couturier, designed a stylish navy-blue uniform with light-blue stripes, throwing in a white dress uniform for summer use. Occasionally WAVES would wear dungarees or slacks for dirty work or sports, but most of the time their dress standards were sharp and flawless.

At first, WAVES were prohibited from marrying anyone in the armed forces. Since every healthy, eligible man seemed to be in uniform, many women were driven from recruiting stations by this stupid provision alone. Next, they were permitted to marry men in services other than the Navy. Finally, near the end of the war, common sense took hold, and the women, after completing training, were allowed to marry naval officers or enlisted men.

Regulations governing pregnancies were enormously restrictive. The law prohibited WAVES from having dependent children under the age of eighteen, so McAfee's force was composed overwhelmingly of single women and childless married women, along with a few older women (some of whom were proud retreads from World War I). WAVES, either married or single, who became pregnant were honorably discharged from the service. A late wartime policy change allowed women whose pregnancies had ended before their resignation had been accepted to remain in uniform. Husbands, however, were never counted as dependents, which also hampered recruiting and led to some resignations.

Despite these restrictions, the performance of WAVES, like that of the yeomanettes a generation before, was stellar. Their discharge rate was relatively low, and disciplinary problems, though not unknown, were far more rare than in the case of men. Most of the women who were involuntarily released from service had been found unsuitable or simply inept; few had committed the more serious offenses to which some male sailors were prone.

The original law prohibited WAVES' service abroad. In late 1944 they were permitted to serve in Alaska and Hawaii (although Chester Nimitz did not want them at Pacific Fleet headquarters) and at Caribbean bases under American purview. Those assigned overseas eventually numbered four thousand, almost all of them replacing men sent to sea. War's end found eighty-six thousand WAVES stationed at over nine hundred shore stations stateside and in the few allowed overseas locations.

Among them was a truly remarkable person. Grace Murray was the daughter of an insurance broker, born in New York City in 1906. When her father lost both legs through hardening of his arteries, he told his children that if he could walk with two wooden legs and two canes, they could do anything.

His daughter took him at his word. Grace became a Phi Beta Kappa student, earning a BA in mathematics and physics from Vassar in 1928 and master's and doctor's degrees in math from Yale. In 1930 she married Vincent Foster Hopper, a childless union that ended in divorce in 1946. Grace Murray Hopper taught mathematics at Vassar until 1943.

She needed a weight waiver to join the WAVES—at 105 pounds she was sixteen pounds shy of the minimum—but her mind was too good to lose. She was first in her training class and was commissioned as a lieutenant junior grade in June 1944. After her commissioning she laid flowers on the grave of her great-grandfather, Rear Admiral Alexander Wilson Russell. "It's all right for females to be Navy officers," she reassured him.

Assigned to work in Cruft Laboratory at Harvard, she confronted a glass-encased, fifty-one-foot-long contraption whose 3300 electrical relays were clacking along, opening and closing. This was the Navy's Automatic Sequence Controlled Calculator, or Mark I. Grace Murray Hopper had found her destiny. "The Mark I was the prettiest gadget I ever saw," she said.

She became an expert in "coding" Mark I. After the war, forty years old, she was forced into the Naval Reserve (thirty-eight was the artificially restrictive limit). But she stayed at the lab, eventually programming Mark III, which produced solutions fifty times faster than Mark I. She began to pioneer in computer languages; her mind was all over the development of UNIVAC and COBOL (Common Business Oriented Language). She also kept up her Reserve affiliation until 1961, when, Commander Grace Murray Hopper now, she was placed on the retired list.

—But she was not through. In 1967, at the age of sixty-one, she was recalled to active duty, where she would remain until her retirement as a rear admiral in 1986. Before her death in 1992 she was recognized Navywide for teaching the service to "talk computer" and by her country as well (thirty-seven honorary doctorates).

Grace Murray Hopper was a signal example as Mildred McAfee presided over a quiet feminist revolution, one proving that women could do much work formerly thought to be exclusively male. She led with loose reins. "I was director," she remembered, "never commander." She believed in encouraging individuality while maintaining order and discipline, and her monument was the wartime work of the WAVES. Enlisted women served in ratings as diverse as aviation machinist's mate, control tower operator, keypunch operator, parachute rigger, and radioman (as with "midshipman," there would never be enlisted ratings of "women" in the Navy). These ratings embodied the world of heretofore-male work being experienced by their civilian counterpart, "Rosie the Riveter." In all, thirty-eight of the sixty-two enlisted ratings were open to female Reservists.[7]

But this was a revolution with limits. At war's end the decampment of WAVES from the service matched that of the men. And some of the remaining male officers did not mind a bit. "I don't think [the WAVES] served any great purpose," reflected Vice Admiral Charles Wellborn. "They weren't really necessary."

Necessary or not, most of the women were back in civilian life by the middle of 1946. Only a small nucleus, under the command of Captain Jean Palmer, McAfee's relief, remained to agitate for a permanent women's role in the peacetime Navy. Soon Palmer herself was gone, replaced by Captain Joy Bright Hancock, a former yeomanette. When Hancock took charge, the WAVES had shrunk to a meager 9800.

For two years they hung on, until finally legislative sanction appeared with the Women's Armed Services Integration Act, which Harry Truman signed into law on 12 June 1948. The WAVES' status as a "Women's Reserve" was abolished (although the acronym remained in popular usage). Women (exclusive of nurses) became a part of the regular Navy and Naval Reserve. The act established a ceiling for enlisted women at a mere 2 percent of total enlisted strength and for female officers at 10 percent of female enlisted strength. A separate promotion system for women was created. Of critical importance for the future, this landmark legislation explicitly excluded women from service aboard combat aircraft and from duty aboard Navy ships, with the exception of hospital ships (soon there would be none of those, anyway) and transports. However, women were not statutorily exempted from participating in ground combat.

The personnel ceilings proved a restrictive cap indeed. During the next two decades the representation of women in the entire American military, including nurses, never exceeded 1.5 percent of the whole. For the same length of time, women were denied promotion to the higher officer grades. Not until 1967 was the 1948 act amended to allow women to be promoted to the permanent rank of O-6 (Navy captain) and to receive stars as flag officers.

Still, under Hancock until 1953 and then under Captain Louise Wilde, the women haltingly inched ahead. Recruitment programs began to include women; both officers and enlisted women were sworn into the regular Navy; the women's uniform was redesigned to parallel that of the male officers. One of the five female doctors on active duty in the early 1950s became the first ordered to report aboard ship. During Korea a few female Reservists were recalled to serve alongside their male counterparts, although, with the exception of nurses, no military women served on the peninsula itself.

But male prejudices were far too strong to be diluted by any of this change. Women remained cloistered in clerical and service fields. As late as 1973, 89 percent of all Navy enlisted women were concentrated in five occupational areas—health care, administration, communication, supply, and data processing. The way to blue water, though not completely closed, was painfully restricted. "It's just not natural to have women aboard fighting fleet units," said Vice Admiral Raymond Peet in a tone suggesting some eternal law was in peril of being breached. "The idea of women aboard combatant ships," added Admiral Roy Johnson, "simply makes no sense at all."

By 1980 only three thousand of the Navy's forty-five thousand enlisted women were at sea. (At any given time, almost half the enlisted men were afloat.) Over thirty years after the "Integration" act, women were aboard major auxiliaries (destroyer and submarine tenders, repair ships), minor auxiliaries (salvage ships, fleet ocean tugs, submarine rescue ships), research ships (guided missile test and deep submergence support ships), oceanographic units, and old CVT-16, *Lexington*, the ensign-smasher down in Pensacola. But frigates, destroyers, cruisers, carriers, submarines, and battleships saw them not.[8]

In short, the personnel ceilings of the 1948 act, when added to the duty restrictions placed on women, wrote military (and Navy) sex discrimination into law in the United States. Navy women throughout the 1950s and 1960s did what men believed to be "women's work"—and little more. They were "girls," regardless of age. ("The girls are of high caliber," said a member of the Great Lakes training staff of his female boots in 1949.) The Navy promoted "integration" by issuing quotes about its women in traditional masculine vein, such as that by the third class photographer's mate who told a Chicago radio station that the Great Lakes women were "tops in brains, and tops in looks, too!"

—And there were always the same arguments from biology, most crudely put by the second class machinist's mate who said he had no desire to work alongside a female sailor who would "trip off the line every twenty-eight days." More seriously, the average strength variance between the sexes *was* a real problem, but one enormously exaggerated by men inordinately proud of their muscles.

For example, women were moved into the parachute rigger rating during World War II because the dominant men believed that women were "naturals" for the sewing required in repairing parachute and lifesaving equipment, and that they would carefully fold the parachute silk for packing—just as Mom did with their clothes for summer camp. Unfortunately, the shorter women, who worked in pairs on opposite sides of the wide rigging table, were often unable to reach the center with enough purchase to complete the closing of the pack. Parachute riggers, the Navy decreed, had to be at least five feet six inches in height. Still, some women could not close the packs by themselves. (A tool was eventually designed, for both men and women, that closed the packs with ease.)

Such biological "examples" were powerful arguments against using women in combat, and they seemed to many men to be an unanswerable piece of pragmatism. But in a rapidly advancing age of technology, these "two-hundred-pound hay bale theories" (only a masculine gorilla equipped with strength to heft such a load should be allowed in combat) held less and less water, particularly for the Navy. In addition, the vastly expanded range of modern weaponry blurred the edges of the traditional "battle area"—on land or at sea—to the point of obliteration. Women in and out of uniform, wherever they might be, were vulnerable.

But the Navy, through the three decades after V-J Day, continued as a mighty fortress of masculinity and male prejudices. The worst aspect, by far, was the assumption of sexual superiority by many Navymen and the concomitant assumption by some men that a woman in uniform was sexually available. One woman who served in the 1950s encapsulated the problem:

> When you're a woman wearing a Navy uniform, you are assumed *not* to be a lady, and all kinds of men think they have a right to make comments on your body, and announce whether they would like to fuck you. By putting on a Navy uniform, you have made a certain kind of statement about yourself in their minds. That made me indignant. I didn't see any reason why I shouldn't be able to walk along the street without that kind of harassment. Even if men considered it a compliment, it was still harassment. I wasn't free to move.

—Extreme perhaps, but fully reflective of a masculine world that admitted women only at its periphery, and then with the greatest reluctance. For everyone, male or female, who balked at outright sex discrimination in the Navy's workplace, there were many more who agreed with Bradley Fiske that war was "man's business." Perhaps the best summary of the uneasy sexual halfway house in which the Navy and the military found themselves in the postwar period was made by an Army officer, Major General Jeanne Holm, in 1975: "It would be no exaggeration to say that probably the most significant accomplishment of the women in the line of the services from 1953 to 1966 was sheer survival."[9]

—The sexual discriminations within the Navy would provide a long trail of social gunpowder into the future. In 1992 they would cause an explosion, bringing down several admirals and causing the forced resignation of a secretary of the Navy.

☆

The Navy had another sexual problem, one that the service seldom addressed—and never in public. The jokes about homosexual sailors went back at least to the ancient Greeks, and there were scattered bits of evidence suggesting that some male seafaring communities—pirate havens, for example—were held together at least in part by homosexuality. But professional navies took a far less tolerant view. In the eighteenth-century Royal

Navy, sodomy ranked ahead of murder and theft as a horrid crime, often bringing the death penalty.

The American Navy inherited the Royal Navy's intense homophobia. Any suggestion of homosexuality, male or female, in its ranks not only meant vice unbounded; the practice was thought to fundamentally corrupt good order and discipline. A sailor having sex with a woman was doing what came naturally; with another sailor, the act became unspeakable and was swept under the rug as quickly and quietly as possible. Besides, with males rogering each other in shipboard bunks or showers, the phrase "band of brothers" took on a sinister and most unwelcome tinge.

Homosexuality and the resultant homophobia had existed from the Navy's beginnings. The Navy took its full-blown homophobia not only from the British but also from its surrounding society. Decatur, in 1812, forwarded to Secretary of the Navy Paul Hamilton an account of the sexual escapades of Midshipman William Cutter, calling the young man "this monster." "Take Midshipman William Cutter's warrant from him," Hamilton flared back. "Inform him that his name has been stricken from the roll of Navy officers. He does not deserve a trial. His offense is of such a character that I do not wish to disgrace the files of the department with a record of it."

The practice apparently was far more feared than indulged in. Cutter's was the only known, direct case of officer homosexual behavior in the pre-1815 Navy. Much homosexual activity, however, was necessarily covert and never officially discovered, so the fears remained. Here is how the sailor Jacob Hazen described the school ship *Columbus* in 1839:

A den where some two hundred boys are collected together, exposed to every kind of sinful vice—where swearing, gambling, cheating, lying, and stealing, are the continual order of the day; where drunkenness, obscenity, and self-pollution, stalk unrestrained; and where crimes abound of even so deep and black a dye that it fires the cheek with shame to name them, and which yet escape the just punishment their heinousness deserves. . . .

—To a later generation, service aboard *Columbus* might sound like lots of fun. If discovered, those practicing homosexuality were almost always discharged, some (before 1850) after undergoing the lash. No one knew the amount or frequency of homosexual behavior, in the Navy or anywhere else in American society, but early punishment records did not suggest unnatural vice unrestrained. In the years 1836 through 1847 the Navy reported that sixty vessels administered 5936 floggings. Of this prodigious total (a hundred floggings per ship meant a trip to the grating about once a shipboard week during those two years), only five were for clearly homosexual offenses. In 1848, 424 floggings were reported (pressure was developing for reform), and only one of these involved an obvious homosexual case.

Beyond the legal records, though, some men indulged with other men, either by proclivity or because they were denied women by seagoing life—according to a character in *Fanny Hill*, a case of "any port in a storm." Herman Melville, who shipped as a seaman aboard *United States* in 1843, later used his naval experiences to write his classic *White-Jacket*. He was talking about homosexuality when he observed "What too many seamen are when ashore is very well known; but what some of them become when completely cut off from shore indulgences can hardly be imagined by landsmen." Melville called the Navy's ships "wooden-walled Gomorrahs of the deep."

The heightened recruiting standards and increasing professionalism of the new steam-and-steel Navy may have diminished the practice. At any rate, between 1904 and 1939, the cases that reached general courts-martial were usually those of unauthorized absence, along with drunkenness and "scandalous conduct" (most often, brawling). Prosecutions involving clear homosexual offenses were negligible.

The Navy dismissed homosexuals from the service as quickly as possible. The most spectacular instance involved a rear admiral in the Pacific Fleet. In 1911 Edward Barry was forced to tender his resignation after supposedly fondling a quartermaster aboard his flagship, *West Virginia*. His resignation was accepted under "less than honorable" conditions, which meant no pension, and Barry apparently spent his declining years (he died in 1938) dodging creditors. The most sordid was a campaign against homosexuals in the Newport area shortly after World War I, which involved ordering some sailors to have sex with gay men to entrap them. (Both Daniels and his assistant, Franklin Delano Roosevelt, approved.) The Navy, without a doubt, fully shared the homophobia of the rest of the culture, but the special circumstances of shipboard life produced an acute revulsion against the practice that was never eroded, not even by the more flexible sexual patterns in the American life-style that developed after World War II.[10]

If Alfred Kinsey's famous report on male sexuality translated to the naval service and if his statistics were anywhere near the mark, something like sixty thousand officers and sailors in the postwar navy would have had some homosexual experience. In the 1950s the Navy's number of enlisted undesirable discharges for homosexuality varied from a low of 483 in 1950 to a high of 1352 in 1952. From 1950 through 1965, 17,392 enlisted men were so released, an annual average of 1087. These statistics, however, certainly did not mean that about one-third were being "caught." One officer claimed he had seven homosexuals in a department of twenty-seven men.

Much was hidden, much unsuspected. The Navy was uninterested in genetic, environmental, cultural, or other explanations of homosexuality but believed, in the case of some sailors, that the practice might be "cured." One man, talking about his "Gay career in the Navy" in the 1940s, was asked if he had been sent to a naval psychiatrist for such treatment. The man's answer was classic: "Well, yes, but the psychiatrist was Gay, and all he did was have an affair with me instead of psychoanalyzing me."

No one bothered to ask if even the admitted homosexuals—men and women—were doing their jobs well. If found, they were to be purged. In the Senate, Kenneth Wherry of Nebraska, a man of supremely small-caliber mind (Wherry had wanted to elevate Shanghai until "it was just like Kansas City"), led the crusade against military homosexuals: "We should weed out all of them—wherever they are on the government payroll." In 1952 the commanding officer of a ship was relieved of his command and subsequently resigned ("NAVY OUSTS SEX OFFENDER," shrieked the headlines), and twenty-four enlisted men at Newport were administratively discharged under conditions "less than honorable." (The "unnatural vice" also had an unnatural administrative tail).

One sidebar to Joe McCarthy's anti-Communist witch-hunt was a campaign against homosexuals; political and sexual aberrancy were thought by many to go hand-in-hand, and the fear of Commie blackmail of highly placed homosexuals permeated the most frigid days of the Cold War. During the Army-McCarthy Hearings in 1954 an Army counsel reported he had tried to divert McCarthy's crowd from investigating the Army by providing as "bait" evidence against alleged homosexuals in the Air Force and the Navy.

Such gamesmanship was hardly necessary. When the Navy found a homosexual, even if he or she happened to be a 4.0 sailor, that person was gone. There were even cases of charging chronic malcontents or malingerers with homosexuality because this singular charge was the greasiest skid out of the service. The administrative field board was the favored method, a bureaucratic quickstep that produced an honorable or even less-than-honorable discharge without lawyers or judicial proceedings mucking things up.

The majority of homosexuals dismissed from the Navy probably received "undesirable" discharges. One seaman was held in the brig for a considerable time, awaiting trial, for homosexual activities. When the accusation was found not to hold water, he was given an undesirable discharge anyway. "Homosexuals and other sexual deviates," pronounced the secretary of the Navy in 1964, "are military liabilities who cannot be tolerated in a military organization" (which would have been news to Alexander the Great). The Navy, avowed Admiral Charles Duncan, "is simply not the place for the homosexual. Whatever rights he may have in society have no bearing on his place in the structure of the military."[11]

The severe injustices dealt out to sexual minorities—lesbians and male homosexuals—merely underscored the Navy's sexual bottom line, which was that of an institution designed by males, for males, to do the work of males. Women and homosexuals were beyond the pale. Shielding the republic was the job of men—"real" men.

☆

Ashore also lay a Navy within the Navy—the Naval Reserve. Postwar America was awash, to a previously unknown extent, with veterans. In 1940 there had been only 4.2 million veterans, about 7 percent of all men. By 1947 there were 18.2 million, one-quarter of the male population. Aid to veterans became a huge budget item. The cumulative total spent on the nation's veterans from George Washington's day to 1933 had been $16.2 billion; almost exactly that amount was spent on veterans' aid from 1946 to 1948 alone.

The veterans formed an immense, experienced military manpower pool, and the Navy wanted its share. An overabundance of sailors, hanging about seaport towns, had characterized the Navy of the nineteenth century; expanding naval manpower pools in a hurry had been a relatively simple process, even if many of the Jack Tars were foreign nationals. A technologically oriented Navy, however, required a wide variety of skilled manpower that kept its skills sharp.

There had been various state naval militias, and an Office of Naval Militia was nudged into the Bureau of Navigation in 1911, but a truly national Naval Reserve was not created until the Naval Reserve Force Act of 1916. Uniforms, pay provisions, and a training program were set forth for the "citizen sailors." Previous regular Navy experience was not, and was never to be, required, although most Reservists through the years claimed considerable time on active duty.

Thousands of Naval Reservists served in World War I (four won the Medal of Honor), but practically all Reservists were disenrolled in 1921, victims of public apathy and budget cutbacks. A reorganization took place in 1925, and by 1938 the Naval Reserve numbered about twenty-two thousand. The Navy launched its V-7 Program in 1940 to obtain more Reservists for the expanding fleet. A host of other programs followed in the wake of Pearl Harbor, and the giant armada of victory of World War II was crewed— 90 percent—by Naval Reservists. There were over three million of them in Navy blue on V-J Day.

—Most of these sailors went home, gladly, in the drawdown. But the Navy was interested in their hard-won skills and wanted them aboard, even if they were only drilling on weekends in places like Paducah, Peoria, or Sioux Falls and going on active duty only two weeks out of the year.

After the creation of the Department of Defense in 1947, a report of the Committee on Civilian Components (the Gray Board) was highly critical of the relationship of the various armed services with their respective Reserve components. The board made the obvious observation that the military effectiveness of World War II's combat veterans would decline with age and that restocking was needed. Indeed, almost the only resource the Naval

Reserve had in the immediate years after the war was the savvy its sailors had gained in wartime. Everything else—useful implementing legislation, money, facilities, and equipment—was practically nonexistent.[12]

The Selective Service Act of 1948 helped, providing for a flow of manpower into Reserve units. Korea interrupted this process, and many Reserve units were sped willy-nilly, without much preparation, to the theater of operations. At one time Reservists made up 35 percent of all the American military in Korea, and some naval vessels were almost wholly manned by them, just as in World War II. Korea was not a true test of the Naval Reserve system, however; the personnel situation was very much catch-as-catch-can, and the entire Reserve was never fully mobilized.

The partial Korean mobilization, elements of which were either comic or chaotic, depending on one's viewpoint, highlighted obvious deficiencies in Reserve training, organization, and mobilization potential. The upshot was the keystone Armed Forces Reserve Act of 9 July 1952. This piece of legislation created a military Reserve, including the Naval Reserve, in three categories: a Ready Reserve of units and individuals subject to presidential recall in a national emergency; a Standby Reserve of trained personnel who could be selectively recalled by Congress when the Ready Reserve cupboard emptied; and a Retired Reserve of "former military persons" who could be recalled only by Congress.

In February 1958 Chief of Naval Operations Arleigh Burke established the Selected Reserve within the Navy Ready Reserve. The Selected Reserve was designed for a quicker response time and was divided into "Category A" drillers, who were paid for drills, did at least two weeks active duty each year, and were deemed ready to instantly go to work when mobilized, and "Category B," who were also in the Ready Reserve but did not have precut orders telling them where to go when the balloon went up.[13]

With these legislative and administrative improvements, the Naval Reserve, within ten years, had shaken down to a reasonably even keel. How deeply that keel cut water was another question altogether. Before the war, prejudice against Reservists in the regular Navy was intense. "It would take two or three civilians in uniform to do one young regular officer's job," sneered Admiral Joe Richardson.

Then came the war, and the flood of Reservists. Regular Navy officers, unless they wore blinders, were forced to pay tribute to the Reservists of World War II. Vice Admiral Charles Lockwood, for example, was quick to admit their value to his Pacific Fleet submarines; three-quarters of the men who rode the boats were Reservists, and eleven of Lockwood's subs were commanded by a "USNR," not a "USN." "They were eager to learn," remembered Lockwood, "and their zeal and fighting spirit were all that could be desired."

—But other memories were not so rosy. Of the 310,000 or so wartime naval officers, only about 10,000 were Regulars—most of these, like Joe

Richardson, proudly wearing their Academy "Navy rings." Among the other 300,000 were many who claimed that the Navy was little more than an insiders' club, for ringknockers only, and, faced with what they considered patent discrimination, refused to compete for regular commissions at war's end. One Reserve officer, Lieutenant Commander Jimmie Val Alen (a tennis singles champion before the war), put some of these feelings into verse:

> You've heard of the English Old School Tie,
> Of the Fly Club and the Pork;
> Of the boys of El Morocco,
> "21" Club and the Stork.
> For loyalty some rate Bones as tops
> And others Scroll and Keys,
> But the Brotherhood of the Navy Ring
> Makes a monkey out of these.
>
> The Masons have a hand shake
> And the Elks all wear a tooth,
> The New York A.C.'s emblem
> Is the wing-ed foot of youth;
> Crusaders wore St. George's Cross
> Of which the poets sing,
> But the whole lot lumped together
> Don't rate half the Navy Ring.
>
> Aladdin had his wondrous lamp
> And Samson had his hair,
> One gave the owner boundless wealth,
> One strength beyond compare.
> But the Navy Ring's fantastic charm's
> By far the best of all,
> For it sheds a dazzling brilliance
> Where there is no light at all. . . .

The problem, of course, was that the global postwar Navy needed its Reservists more than ever, needed them for orderly, rapid mobilization. In 1945 Navy planners foresaw the need for a postwar Reserve of 8750 officers and 135,000 enlisted for the surface Navy alone. The air side, one estimate held, would need over sixty carrier and over seventy land-based Reserve squadrons. Everyone gave lip service to a strong Naval Reserve; Ernie King and Louis Denfeld, as chiefs of naval operations, urged Reservists to keep their skills polished and hew to the colors.[14]

The reality fell far short of the ideal, and the "anti-ringknocker" sentiments were not the crux of the problem. In the broadest sense the Naval

Reservists, like the nation's other Reserve forces, were being trained to refight World War II, fleet actions and all. Large conventional wars, however, were not to be in the Navy's future, not against other navies, at any rate.

The numbers, however, were impressive on paper; when the Korean War began, over 1.1 million Naval Reservists were on the muster rolls, 17,000 of these on continuous active duty. By then, the navy within the Navy could have made a respectable nautical force for practically any other country in the world. There were 316 Naval Reserve training centers, twenty-one Naval Reserve air stations, and 104 ships assigned exclusively to Naval Reserve training. By the middle of 1951, 182,000 Naval Reservists were on active duty for the Korean "emergency." The Naval Air Reserve program alone contributed four thousand officers. "The Naval Reserve . . . is now in sound condition," boasted Secretary of the Navy Francis Matthews.

—Like many of Rowboat's claims, this one was full of hot air. True, Ready Reserve organization in the 1950s had shaken out on a unit scale—ships' companies, aviation squadrons, construction battalions—and their recall was easier. The old Naval Militias, never much more than collections of naval hobbyists anyway, withered and died. By 1961 thirty-eight Naval Reserve escort ships and eighteen antisubmarine aircraft squadrons could be mobilized, and mobilized effectively, for the Berlin Crisis. (In 1968 six Reserve fighter and attack squadrons and two construction battalions would be mobilized for Vietnam.)

But the numbers and the useful recall of select units masked serious difficulties. Apart from the painful reorientation from civilian to military life, a Reserve call-up put men (and women) into uniform who, year after year, were falling further behind the Navy's ever-accelerating technological curve. This situation was particularly true of submariners, most of whom could not beg a ride aboard the boats after the nuclear revolution, but surface sailors trained on five-inch 38 guns knew nothing of Talos, Tartar, and Terrier. Those used to a 600-pound steam system were dumbfounded by 1200-pound superheaters and gas turbines. An old-time radar operator could be mystified by the intricacies of the Navy Tactical Data System. And, of course, the skills that Reservists did have tended to gather cobwebs in civilian life.

By 1954 the Ready Reserve had shrunk to about 140,000; these units would level out at a total of about 100,000 to 120,000 during the years to come. They trained as best they could, the units in coastal sites having perhaps the best opportunities. Inland, things were much more dicey—units in Denver trained with a five-inch 38 gun well after that particular weapon had left the fleet. But the Reserve was losing its skilled petty officers, people like electronics technicians, minemen, radarmen, radiomen, and sonarmen. In 1953 the secretary of the Navy reported that only 10 percent of experienced petty officers released from active duty were affiliating with the Reserve.[15]

The Naval Air Reserve probably had the best training. In 1946 Arthur Radford, then deputy chief of naval operations for air, placed Eddie Ewen in charge of the Naval Air Reserve program with the announced purpose of keeping Navy fliers in the Reserve. The Air Reserve's groups, squadrons, and units, unlike much of the surface side, were organized on the regular Navy model, with fighter, bomber and torpedo squadrons featuring unit integrity and clearly assigned mission areas. The goal, said one observer, was that "all new models which are to be used in the regular Navy will be made available to the Air Reserve."

At first this promise was kept, because there were plenty of planes to go around after the cornucopia of wartime production had been emptied. Naval Reserve squadrons flew the familiar birds of World War II—Hellcats, Corsairs, Avengers, Helldivers, Seahawks, and the rest. By 1950 jets like the Phantom and Fury were being phased in. The fliers flourished. When Korea began, the Naval Air Reserve had thirty-two thousand officers and men, organized into 311 squadrons—theoretically enough to man the flight decks of fifty-five mothballed carriers. They flew about 2200 aircraft (the regulars had about 5000), and they were good. In 1949 they had the Navy's lowest accident rate—with even minor scrapes counted as "accidents," 6.13 per 10,000 flight hours. Also, the petty officer situation on the air side was far healthier than that in the rest of the Naval Reserve.[16]

But as time went on, the soaring unit cost of newer Navy aircraft limited production numbers, and the regular Navy had first call. Air Reservists, more and more, found themselves doing transport and VP (antisubmarine) work, while the hot new tickets—Skyhawks, Vigilantes, and Intruders—tended to stay on the active-duty side. The technological gap was never as great as in the other specialities, however. Air Reservists, with their unit activity and plentiful hardware, performed with credit when called upon, but they, too, were as a group falling behind.

The larger picture, though, gave the greatest concern. With the minds of Navy planners set on a huge conventional conflict, World War II at sea revisited, numbers were given the utmost importance. Although statistics varied over the years, the chances were far less than fifty-fifty that any individual, officer or enlisted, would affiliate with the Naval Reserve upon leaving active duty. Even then, many of these men and women would stay around only long enough to earn a little money to supplement their education or help them get their families started. In 1954, throughout the entire American military, only 695,000 Ready Reservists out of a total of 2.2 million were participating in training programs. For a big conventional war scenario, American mass against Soviet mass, training less than one-third of the potential backup force was ample cause for worry.

Generically, the Naval Reserve, filled with experienced personnel, could do quite well. That is, training in subjects like damage control and health care was at a consistently high level. Seabee Reserve units specialized in important community projects. Also, old sea dogs could teach young Regulars new tricks; a chief electronics technician, say, who ran his own civilian television repair shop could easily guide youngsters fresh out of A School through the mysteries of a shipboard cathode ray tube.

But the Naval Reserve, like the other Reserve forces, was at the low end of the budgetary totem pole. The two- or three-star admiral in charge, almost always a Regular, had usually failed to be selected for higher rank and was on his way out. Reservists had nowhere near the clout on Capitol Hill as the active side. In any budgetary or other compromise, the short end of the fiscal stick usually pointed in the Reserve direction. And many Ready Reserve units unfortunately proved, under the strain of mobilization for Korea, Berlin, and Vietnam, to be less effective than expected.

Finally, active-duty naval personnel, particularly some higher-ranking officers, were not without their prejudices against Reservists. "One Navy" was the slogan, but without the development of its own internal organizations and its own considerable lobbying effort in the three decades after V-J Day, the Naval Reserve "would have been emaciated" by its parent service. This simmering mutual animosity within "One Navy" would eventually cool somewhat, but the back-and-forth suspicions, criticisms, and recriminations were endemic to the structure and would never completely vanish.[17]

—Which was far from saying that the Naval Reserve was unnecessary or unwanted. Despite its variegated states of training, rocky financial support, manpower problems, and uneasy relationship with the regular Navy, the Naval Reserve persisted. Indeed, in the latter years of the century, Reservists would prove to be more important than ever.

☆

Charles Clark and George Dyer, like the general run of their fellow officers of the line, derided and dreaded shore assignments, merely tolerating the staffers and others who mostly stayed on the beach. Some staffers even shared their credo; Lieutenant Commander Joe O'Callahan, a Catholic chaplain who won the Medal of Honor for his actions aboard the badly wounded carrier *Franklin* off the coast of Japan, wrote that "sea duty to any naval man is naturally preferable to shore duty."

"While the Shore Establishment can lose a war, it can't win a war," Joe Richardson had proclaimed. In fact, sea and shore were mutually interdependent, and never more so than in the postwar era. Although the Navy had always relied on its shore establishment, no matter how minuscule, the growing complexities and enormous logistics needs of the modern service elevated the shore to a level of importance never seen before.[18]

The bulk of Navy supply work, finances, business management, construction, legal work, and building maintenance, not to mention the operation of hundreds of schools, took place ashore. The long chain of activities that fed, paid, sheltered, prayed for, and gave medical care to sailors started and often remained ashore. Sailors were formally trained ashore, and to the shore they rotated for welcome duty after long overseas deployments. Ashore also was the Naval Reserve, which—ill-funded, partially trained, and largely ignored though several of its segments might be—remained a potent naval force. The Cold War Navy relied completely on its shore support.

Navy women became a permanent part of the shore establishment during World War II and began a long, tedious struggle to get to sea in meaningful roles. To the service's discredit, however, the Navy during the postwar years remained a rock-solid pillar of male supremacy, hypermasculine attitudes, and male-oriented sexual discrimination—against both women and homosexuals.

These patterns of discrimination did not stand by themselves. Alongside them must be placed the Navy's attitudes to still other minorities—the ones whose skins were not white.

CHAPTER TWENTY-THREE

OUTSIDERS

☆

T he United States Navy was a racist institution. Without ever admitting the fact directly, the service had a standard argument: the fleet was only a reflection of the nation, and besides, the Navy was not in the business of social reform. There was certainly an element of truth to this defense, but the argument itself was no excuse. The Navy's authoritarian, hierarchical structure abetted and exacerbated racial problems even as all hands were trained to stress group cohesion and teamwork. By harboring both overt and covert racism within its structure and in many instances encouraging racist practices, the Navy worked against the best interests of both itself and the country at large.

☆

Shortly after World War I, the fleet experimented with a destroyer, *Rizal*, manned wholly by enlisted Filipinos, supervised by white officers. There was some talk of a similar ship for blacks. Nothing could have more appropriately symbolized racial segregation afloat. Nonwhites were kept apart, a virtual servant caste—permanently on the outside. The *Rizal* experiment, unsurprisingly, failed; her officers cited training and language problems, but in fact practically no officer in the Navy was keen to take on an all-minority crew.

Different skin color had long implied menial status in the Navy. The fleet had a long-standing tradition that Chinese recruited from the Asian littoral made the best servants, and many ships on the distant Asiatic Station depended heavily on Chinese manpower for a wide variety of tasks, from preparing food to slinging coal. On some ships, as Richard McKenna memorialized in his novel *The Sand Pebbles*, the Chinese were indispensable to the running of the vessels themselves.

But the Filipinos had a "special relationship" to the Navy. In 1907, after a vicious American campaign had squelched the Filipino bid for independence in the wake of the Spanish-American War, the Navy created a citizenship requirement for its enlistees. But this was sometimes waived for the Chinese and, more importantly, for the Filipinos. Special regulations allowed for recruitment from America's new insular possessions.

Young Filipino men rapidly took to the Navy uniform. Almost all of them were messmen, but they were well paid (by the standard of their homeland) and had the promise of a "career," after which they dreamed of living like lords back home on their pension checks. By 1914 the number of Filipinos in the Navy had surpassed that of blacks. Many officers believed that the "Little Brown Brothers" were "superior servants," always smiling, always eager to help.

In the thirties, after the Roosevelt administration had scheduled the Philippines for independence, Filipino enlistments declined. The Navy took up some of the slack by signing on Chamorros, natives of Guam. Officers loved them. After World War II and the arrival of Philippine independence, in 1946, a special agreement between the two countries allowed the enlistment of Philippine citizens as messmen. They were always servants, with an occasional musician thrown in. In 1920 the Bureau of Navigation had succinctly stated that its policy was not "to rate Filipinos in any branches other than the messmen and musician's branches."

So, the Little Brown Brothers waited on tables, did dishes, cleaned officers' staterooms, and tootled away on their instruments. But naval service, despite its decidely menial nature, still held its attractions for them, even after V-J Day. Every year about one hundred thousand young Filipino men applied—men like Johnny Mabanta, who made more money as a third class steward's mate then he had as a second lieutenant in the Philippine army. Under the Filipino Immigration and Naturalization Bill of 1946, only one hundred Philippine citizens were allowed to enter the United States annually (by contrast, Poland had a quota of 6524), so naval service was an accepted way to taste the sweets of American life. Most Filipinos, for years after the liberation of their islands from the Japanese, continued to have the deepest admiration for Uncle Sam.

Until the mid-sixties, Filipino sequestration as officers' servants continued. Only then were they allowed to break into other ratings, such as machinist's mate. In addition, the Immigration Act of 1965 abolished the national-origins quota and provided for an annual admission of 170,000 immigrants from the Eastern Hemisphere, 120,000 from the Western. In the next twenty years 665,000 Filipinos entered the United States, and by 1988 they were the largest Asian group in the country. Many of these newcomers were professional people, driven to immigrate by the repressive, corrupt regime of Ferdinand Marcos, and many more were propelled by simple economic factors. In 1968 the per capita income in the Philippines was $180, compared with $3980 in the United States.

Thus, despite the swelling numbers of Filipino immigrants, the exodus was largely peopled by members of the islands' middle class, and the attraction of Navy life remained for many Filipino young men, particularly those from the remote backwoods of places like Mindoro and Leyte. The service still provided a way out of the slough of despond in their home islands, and after the sixties, they could make their way to the top of the enlisted ranks in a wide variety of ratings. Even as some Filipinos grew to hate the United States for its economic imperialism and thoughtless support of Marcos, Navy duty remained popular.

But the Filipinos were in every way special cases: foreign nationals, Little Brown Brothers, "natural servants." In only a few instances could they become American citizens as a result of their Navy duty, and their very existence in uniform after 1946 depended on international agreements. Many white officers could actually argue, with some credence, that Filipinos were being "uplifted" and "bettered" by their naval service, an argument at least as old (and loathsome) as the Social Darwinism of the late nineteenth century.[1]

—Such an argument was no justification, either, for the treatment accorded American Negroes by the Navy.

☆

By the beginning of World War II, the Navy's racism had become practically generic. Not every white naval officer or petty officer was a racist, by any means, but before the war the officer class was lily white and mostly middle class, with all the ingrained prejudices of such a social background. "Our melting pot may have melted the charge but the mass in the crucible is really a mess," wrote Admiral Tommy Hart in 1941. "The good sound material [is] so cluttered with dross and slag that its effectiveness is badly compromised. And, the damage is probably irreparable." Much of the Navy's racism was paternal and benign but no less galling for all that. Racial slurs were common and could override a lifetime of accomplishment, as when a naval officer dismissed the Nobel laureate Enrico Fermi as a "wop."

America's black underclass, the major victim of such racism, had always provided seagoing men. Colonial privateers in King George's War often sailed with blacks on board. Caesar Tarrant, a black man, was given 2700 acres of Ohio land for his services as a pilot for the Virginia navy during the Revolutionary War, and blacks served aboard various Revolutionary warships and privateers. But peace, and ominous news of racial warfare in Haiti, led to the tightening of southern slave codes and the exclusion of blacks from local militias. In 1798 they were barred from the infant Navy and Marine Corps.

Such a restriction was impossible to enforce, because recruiting of whites, never mind white *Americans*, was always a problem in the catch-as-catch-can Navy of the nineteenth century. Officers often enlisted free blacks (among the crewmen taken at gunpoint from *Chesapeake* by the British warship *Leopard* in the notorious 1807 incident was a black man), and blacks fought at sea with distinction in the War of 1812. "They are as brave men as ever fired a gun," enthused Stephen Decatur about the Negroes in his command. "There are no stouter hearts in the service."

Negroes usually acted as cooks in the sailing Navy, but the necessary massing of people within the wooden walls precluded spatial segregation, and with the numerous all-hands evolutions under sail, "integration seems to have been an accomplished fact." Despite laws barring naval use of slaves, some southern officers took their retainers to sea. A few slaves apparently served as crewmen aboard *Java* (their masters pocketing their pay), and some slaves were used as laborers in naval yards. Herman Melville wove a slave character into the fabric of *White-Jacket*, one who was allowed to wear civilian clothing and be disciplined by his master, the purser (who of course allocated his slave's seaman wages to himself). Black sailors did not exactly abound in either the Navy or the merchant marine, but they were there in significant numbers; the colored Seaman's Home in New York City, founded in 1839, averaged about 450 black boarders a year.[2]

The Union Navy enlisted black "contrabands" for its blockading squadrons during the Civil War, giving them full rations but paying them less than the normal seaman's wage. Rear Admiral David Dixon Porter began substituting former slaves for white firemen and coal heavers on his Mississippi River flotillas in 1862, "reducing the expenses in that way." Sketchy wartime muster rolls indicated that as many as one out of four Union sailors may have been black, a total of thirty thousand men.

But their participation in emancipation's war did not bring seagoing equality; rather, the reverse was the case. The steam-and-steel Navy featured compartmented ship structures that encouraged segregation at sea. The nation at large was plunging into the racially demeaning era of Jim Crow, and the Navy joined in without hesitation. Although the service continued to enlist blacks on what was claimed to be a "fully integrated basis," black sailors were limited to service in the ranks, making their way as seamen, gunner's mates, or messmen.

In the late nineteenth century two black sailors won the Medal of Honor, yet a strong current of racial prejudice coursed through the service. White sailors, said one of them, would "growl like a dog in a manger" about sharing watches, quarters, and meals with Negroes. When the great black leader Frederick Douglass was appointed minister to Haiti in 1889, he was to travel by naval ship to his new post. One captain resigned, another declared his ship unfit for the duty, and a third requested a transfer—all to avoid sharing their table with a black man.

Five black youths were appointed to the Naval Academy between 1872 and 1897, after which a degrading racial curtain descended almost for half a century. Three—James Conyers, Alonzo McClennan, and Henry Baker—passed the entrance exams. All underwent vicious hazing and social ostracism. None graduated. Not until 1936 was another Negro admitted to Annapolis, and not until 1949 was a black man commissioned from that school.

Two thousand blacks served in the victorious Navy of the Spanish-

American War, ironically helping to usher in the new imperial age with its hegemony over darker-skinned peoples. Twenty-two Negroes died alongside 244 whites in the explosion that demolished *Maine*. The first shot at Manila Bay (the "You may fire when ready, Gridley" shot) was actually fired by John Jordan, the black chief gunner aboard Dewey's flagship, *Olympia*. Robert Penn, a black fireman first class, won the Medal of Honor by helping extinguish a dangerous coal fire in a boiler room on *Iowa*.

—All to no avail. Even before the victory over Spain, the Navy had begun to restrict blacks to the messman's branch (later the Steward's Branch), established in 1893. Soon, black men were permitted to enlist only as messmen and could become only officers' cooks or stewards—shipboard menials. In time, the John Jordans and Robert Penns disappeared from the service. In all this bias, institutional hypocrisy was not absent; the new restrictions were put in place "apparently by verbal instructions to the recruiting service rather than by written orders."

Many officers were convinced that blacks aboard ship produced racial disorder by their very presence and that the best solution, ensuring that most important of naval requirements—discipline—was to ban them from the service. Some officers contended that blacks were inferior sailors, that whites would not take orders from black petty officers, and that any chance of shipboard racial equality, especially when the society at large was lynching thousands of blacks, was the merest will-o'-the-wisp. A white petty officer with twenty years' service wrote that "among the many causes of discontent and desertion in the Navy the presence of the Negro is one of the most potent."

With these biases firmly in place, officially and otherwise, the numbers of black men in the triumphant Navy of Empire rapidly dwindled toward the vanishing point.[3]

☆

Race had been a decidedly secondary consideration within the wooden-walled Navy; any able-bodied seaman who was experienced and agile and could scramble to the topmost yardarm had been welcome. The men of the new Navy were, of course, products of the national upsurge of Jim Crow, but shipboard life stratified blacks by regulation and custom as well as deep-seated prejudice. Whites refused to eat or bunk with them in the confined yet separated spaces of the new steel warships.

Now, racial violence simmered just beneath the surface, frequently breaking out of the straitjacket of regulations. *Boston* experienced a "miniature race war;" *Charleston* had a brawl that was triggered when "a negro threw a bowl of coffee into a white man's face;" and the ancient frigate *Independence* featured "nothing less than an attempt to kill an insolent negro boasting that he could 'lick any white son of a bitch in the ship.' " By design, progressively fewer blacks were becoming petty officers, and when they did, they could give orders only to members of their own race and Filipinos—in other words, messmen like themselves.

White officers, many of them, led by racist example. Few were as outspokenly pompous as Rear Admiral John Grimes Walker, who ostentatiously donned gloves before he shook hands, on social occasions, with members of the Haitian government. But officers were far too quick to blame blacks, and blacks alone, for "racial unrest" aboard ship. Negroes were the classic outsiders, disruptive simply because they were apart, unassimilable. When black and white sailors got into a racial melee in Cherbourg during the cruise of the Great White Fleet, officers universally blamed black "impudence" for the ruckus. Some officers read, and believed, the pseudoscientific humbug of the turn of the century, which claimed to "prove" black inferiority. Looking about their ships, they could see that this was "true," because all around them were blacks in inferior positions.

And the Navy was changing its social makeup in those early years of the twentieth century. Recruiters were bringing in American citizens, white boys from Iowa farms, Georgia dirt roads, and Pennsylvania mill towns. Farm hands and grocery clerks needed to be taught, quickly and well, how to operate boiler stops, gun sights, and electrical switchboards. The new Navy depended on a growing influx of young, white volunteers who were products of national Jim Crowism. So, rather than risk alienating potential white recruits, who were considered to be smarter and more amenable to discipline than blacks, the Navy, with no regrets, turned its back on the black man. The few Negroes who were accepted were blatantly segregated from their shipmates and shunted to the mess decks.

Racially separate ships were proposed from time to time—spiritual if not ethical forerunners of *Rizal*—but such propositions were too expensive, and besides, few self-respecting white officers would hear of such an assignment. Instead, the Navy's blacks literally became what, in the white-dominated world beyond the waterfront, they were thought to be—the mudsills of society. When the Great White Fleet reutrned home in early 1909, its few remaining black petty officers were sent to shore duty. "Every one of us was transferred," recalled Charles Parnell. "We knew that the end of a colored man being anything in the Navy except a flunkey had arrived."

Negro seamen became as rare as hen's teeth, a Negro petty officer rarer still. Navy parades, such as the National Naval Review in New York City in 1912 featuring six thousand sailors, were bereft of a single black face. The operating Navy, apart from the mess decks, was being thoroughly bleached. On the eve of World War I, two enlistees passed the test to become specialists in the new technology of "wireless." The white man was accepted; the black man was told that he was "eligible for the mess service only."

—Nowhere was this intense racial bias written down; everywhere in the fleet such social stigmata were understood and, what was more important, acted on. Blacks had made up 5 percent of the enlisted cadre of the

Great White Fleet; during World War I only 6000 of the 238,000-man enlisted force—fewer than 3 percent—were black. About two dozen black women served as yeomanettes. (All of them did their typing and filing in a single socially segregated office in the Navy Department.) Most of the black Navymen who got overseas went as stevedores in longshoremen's battalions, working in French ports. Army segregation was cut from similar cloth. The captain of *Virginia* refused to carry the black 367th Infantry back to the United States after the war. A minuscule number of blacks hung on in the petty officer grades, most with assignments as water tenders, electricians, or gunner's mates.

After war's end, in the summer of 1919, the Navy refused to accept any more initial enlistments of blacks, finding that smiling Filipino messmen were much more conscious and accepting of their proper "place." When enlisted openings did occur after the retirements of black petty officers, whites were promoted to fill the slots.

The results were as desired: a nautical version of racial purification. By the depths of the Depression, 1932, the Navy had just 441 blacks on active duty, about 0.5 percent of the enlisted personnel of the diminished peacetime service. In that same year the question of enlisting black men was raised again. The discussion within the Bureau of Navigation led some officers to contend that the Little Brown Brothers were superior servants, and that enlisting Negroes would "be a distinct step backwards."

However, the ultimate judgment within BuNav was that black enlistment should go forward, but with hypercritical selectivity in recruiting. Blacks from northern urban areas—many of the northern ghettos dated from World War I, when southern blacks had ventured north in search of war work—were undesirable; as one officer wrote, they tended to be "independent, insolent, and over-educated." Recruiting in the South for the "unspoiled young Negro" was the better way to go; "by training and environment the Southern colored man has inherited a servant's point of view and is usually contented and happy in that position." Enlistment of blacks, properly submissive ones, was resumed on 4 January 1933, two months before FDR entered office. The Negro boots were immediately shunted to the new mess attendants' school at Hampton Roads.[4]

The economic pinch on the outside was so severe that many black men welcomed even these narrowly defined tasks. By June 1940 four thousand blacks, almost all messmen, were in uniform, about 2.3 percent of the total enlisted force. A dwindling band of black gunner's mates, torpedomen, and other technical specialists persisted, because black *reenlistment* in these ratings had never been prohibited.

The Navy's obvious but unspoken racial policy was too blatant and too gross to pass unnoticed. The Negro press by 1940 was in full cry against such cruel and unfair practices; not far behind came civil rights organizations and some white liberals. No one made so much as a dent in the Navy's armor; when thirteen black messmen sent a letter in that year to a black newspaper criticizing their working conditions, they were promptly given "undesirable" discharges—no small thing in a country not yet steady on its economic feet. The racism continued to extend into every corner of Navy life; the Naval Academy even refused to allow a black member of the Harvard lacrosse squad to play against the middies.

When pressed by black leaders, white liberals, and other racial reformers about its glaring racism, the Navy had a standpat policy statement:

> After many years of experience, the policy of not enlisting men of the colored race for any branch of the naval service, except the messmen's branch, was adopted to meet the best interests of general ship efficiency.

FDR's new secretary of the Navy, Frank Knox, declared that the racial problem was impossible to resolve; "southern" and "northern" ships were not possible, and close living conditions aboard ship precluded racial integration.[5]

—Order, discipline, racial exclusion. In 1940, Adolf Hitler was building a new order based on the same principles.

☆

The Navy enforced its segregation by occupation, by the deliberate maintenance of a menial, servant class. Even Franklin Roosevelt, the Navy's best friend and a pragmatic reformer on so many nonracial issues, could not see a way out. FDR felt that political caution, in the face of his failure to purge conservative southern Democrats in the off-year elections of 1938, was the best way to get what parts of his program he could through Congress; race reform was a sure way to wave a red flag in the face of these southern bulls.

In September 1941, with America fighting an undeclared naval war in the Atlantic and waiting for the Japanese ax to fall in the Pacific, FDR met with a group of black leaders outraged by the Navy's adamant racial policy in the face of looming worldwide conflict. The best the president had to offer was the possibility that "good Negro bands" could be assigned aboard battleships, so that blacks and whites could learn to be harmonious shipmates (in more ways than one).

Then came Pearl Harbor. On that bloody Sunday morning Dorie Miller, a black steward's mate aboard *West Virginia*, dragged his wounded skipper off the bridge and, despite no formal training, manned a machine gun and bagged two Japanese planes. The Navy praised Miller, a Texas sharecropper's son, to the skies—he was the perfect symbol of American democracy at war—and he won the Navy Cross. Eventually there would be a "Dorie Miller Trophy," awarded for improvement of Navy racial policy. But no one bothered to mention that when he died two years later in the torpedoing of the escort carrier *Liscome Bay*, Dorie Miller was still waiting on officers' tables and cleaning up officers' staterooms. Leonard Harmon, who lost his life on *San Francisco* during the Naval Battle of Guadalcanal, became the second black messman to win the Navy Cross.

Navy blacks eventually made up 4.8 percent of the enlisted force in World War II. But even if every one of them had had the courage of Dorie Miller and Leonard Harmon, the walls of prejudice could not have been breached by combat fortitude alone. The Navy even kept blood from black donors separate from that of whites. Rear Admiral Ross McIntire, FDR's personal physician as well as Chief of the Bureau of Medicine, told Knox in January 1942 that "it is my opinion that at this time we cannot afford to open up a subject such as mixing blood or plasma regardless of the theoretical fact that there is no chemical difference in human blood."

The bigotry ran all the way to the top. Part of Ernie King's obsession with the Pacific theater was his insistence on defending Australia and New Zealand because they were "white man's" countries. Many high-ranking officers felt that dissatisfied black sailors were little more than bait for Communist agitators and Japanese saboteurs. Negroes were denied all billets in the Office of Naval Intelligence during the war, with the exception of three minor clerical jobs. Captain Leo Thebaud, the director of Naval Intelligence, thought racial minorities in the United States needed to be kept under surveillance (in violation of his outfit's charter). When black inmates rioted at Portsmouth Naval Prison, intelligence officials were convinced that the men were Communist pawns.[6]

So black sailors went to war segregated and suspect. Their own black press labeled them "seagoing bellhops." With bitter memories of the *Rizal* experiment, the Navy Department at first ignored the idea of an all-black ship (which would mean black officers). FDR agreed with Knox that naval integration was an impractical idea in wartime (almost all his numerous acquaintances in Flag Plot were telling him so), although he still liked the idea of black Navy bands. So did Rear Admiral Charles Snyder, the inspector general of the Navy, who offered the opinion that "the colored race is very musical and they are versed in all forms of rhythm." Major General Thomas Holcomb, commandant of the Marine Corps (which was lily white from the lowliest buck private on up), said that black desire to enter naval service was only an effort to "break into a club that doesn't want them."

But the demand for manpower was too great. The Navy, reeling from the shock of the Japanese and German oceanic onslaughts, had to give way. On 7 April 1942 Knox announced the Navy would accept 277 black volunteers a week (the service was not yet drafting anyone), with the Navy's first annual goal set at 14,000 Negroes in uniform. Black sailors, however, would still be segregated, limited to the petty officer ranks, and, except as stewards, barred from sea duty.

Stewards—here black men were "attentive colored boy[s] hovering in the background, ready to bring another cup of coffee or a second helping of ice cream or strawberries." Or, true to their race, they would supposedly "[get] out their razors" to defend their ship. In 1942 the Navy managed to find one black worthy of a Reserve commission—a student from Harvard Medical School. The search for the *one* worthy black man among all those stewards led the black poet Langston Hughes, in "The Black Man Speaks," to chant mockingly:

> . . . Jim Crow Army,
> And Navy, too—
> Is Jim Crow Freedom the *best*
> I can expect from you? . . .

—Jim Crow Freedom *was*, at the start, "the best." The only exceptions, and these were pathetic indeed, were trite tales of black heroism in the Miller or Harmon mold, which lauded and demeaned blacks at the same time. Such an example was the "Mess Boy of Squadron X," a gooey story of a Negro who shot down two Japanese planes and subsequently wrote his "Azalea" that "a little colored boy from down in Texas got a chance to do his bit, for which I am mighty glad."[7]

And still the Navy acted surprised when blacks, after Knox's announcement, failed to swamp the recruiting stations. In 1942 Negro seventeen-year-olds, prime targets of military recruiters, chose the Army over the Navy at a ten-to-one ratio—not that the army's racial record was that much better but that the Navy's was so bad. Historians at the Bureau of Naval Personnel, heads in the sand, attributed this mass rejection to the Negroes' "relative unfamiliarity with the sea or the large inland waters and their consequent fear of water."

To the contrary, youthful blacks had the Navy's racial number as the "exclusive preserve of white America." Only when blacks were assigned to recruiting duty did the tide begin to turn. By 1 February 1943 the Navy contained over 27,000 Negroes (still only 2 percent of the total enlisted). Of these, 6600 were in the general service (theoretically eligible for all ratings), 2000 in the newly formed Seabees (almost all as laborers), and over two-thirds of the total (19,200) in the Steward's Branch.

The Navy's first draft call came that same month. The quota system for blacks (1200 per month for general service and 1500 as stewards) still held. Any more Negroes, said Knox, would invite the horror of racially mixed crews, which, as the secretary reminded Roosevelt, was "contrary to [your] program." "Most decidedly we must continue the employment of negroes in the Navy," FDR responded. "I do not think it the least bit necessary to put mixed crews on ships. I can find a thousand ways of employing them without doing so."

—The "thousand ways" were mostly servile, and black enlisted strength throughout the war never got above 5 percent of the whole, in a nation which was around 10 percent black. Knox told Roosevelt that the Navy would continue to segregate Negroes socially and by occupation. In the twenty-seven new Seabee battalions, almost all the blacks were stevedores; blacks manned harbor craft and served in local defense forces; they dominated billets for cooks and port hands. But they were generally not, except as servants, aboard combat ships.

Under these conditions racial tension within the Navy expanded like steam in a heating kettle. For the most part blacks found themselves restricted to laborers' jobs ashore, concentrated in large and all-too-obviously segregated groups, denied prestige assignments, and given the sketchiest chances for promotion. All the while they were being told that they were fighting democracy's war.

The rapid wartime expansion of the officer corps meant that more wardroom coffee would have to be poured, more stateroom beds made; by mid-1944 over thirty-eight thousand black sailors (enough to crew thirteen *Essex*-class carriers) were serving as cooks, stewards, and bakers. Ashore, about half the Negroes in the navy were in billets inside the continental United States.

No black women had been enlisted. The WAVES, initially, were exclusively white, and so was the Nurse Corps. When even Eleanor Roosevelt started checking on this sorry state of affairs and learned that the Nurse Corps was five hundred people short, she received a reply from BuMed that since enough white nurses were in the training pipeline, "the question relative to the necessity for accepting colored personnel in this category is not apparent."

Soon enough, the kettle began to boil. In June 1943 over three hundred blacks assigned to the Naval Ammunition Depot at St. Julian's Creek, Virginia, rioted after being placed in segregated seating at a radio show. The next month over seven hundred, belonging to the 80th Construction Battalion, staged a protest over segregation on a transport vessel in the Caribbean. The Navy's answer to these and other early warnings was the old standard: leadership, not policy, was the problem. At least one commanding officer was relieved.[8]

—As far as black America was concerned, democracy's war, not only within the Navy but also across the board, was segregated by skin color.

☆

There were those, however, including key civilians within the Navy Department, who clearly saw the stupidity, injustice, and viciousness of the Navy's racial policy, stated and unstated. In the midst of war, they began to slowly nudge the service in the direction of integration, to the point that the Navy, which had begun the war with the most restrictive racial practices of any branch (except for the Marines, which with its all-white cadre had no need for restriction), ended the conflict as arguably the most advanced.

Two essential points were made by these men (among them Adlai Stevenson, future governor of Illinois and two-time presidential candidate): first,
the old liberal concern of equal opportunity for Negroes and second (carefully couched in pragmatic terms that could be understood even by admirals),
the optimum use, of the nation's manpower, not simply *white* manpower.
FDR, moving beyond his love for black bands, helped a bit by insisting that
blacks be assigned to duties other than messmen.

The break came in August 1943 with the formation of the Special
Programs Unit within the Bureau of Personnel, a group charged with overseeing the Navy's policy for Negroes. Captain Thomas Darden headed the
outfit, aided by Lieutenant Commanders Donald Van Ness and Charles
Dillon. A third lieutenant commander, Christopher Sargent, was not assigned to the unit but, because of his connections, became the bureaucratic
lightning rod for the Navy's changes on racial policy. Sargent was a Reservist, a blueblood with impeccable associations (he was independently
wealthy and a member of Dean Acheson's law firm), and he weaved like a
halfback through the obstacles in BuPers, arguing, chivvying, pleading for
a more sane racial policy.

Slender and bespectacled, Sargent (who died shortly after war's end)
was the *aristos* as moral crusader, convinced that social customs that had
been shackled in peacetime rust could be changed dramatically in war. He
even hoped that the Navy's racial revolution (for that was his goal) would
somehow bridge the racial gap in postwar American society, that the service
would for once lead rather than follow national racial mores.

With Sargent applying leverage all over BuPers, Darden and his team
gathering information and laying plans, and Stevenson and others making
high-pressure points at the upper end of the scale, the members of the
Special Programs Unit began to work on the logjam. They opened more
overseas billets for blacks, created new specialties for blacks in the general
service, started black shore patrol units, established a remedial training
center for black illiterates, argued for a more efficient use of black A School
graduates (getting them aboard combatants, for example), and, in December
1943, got a BuPers directive that, with few exceptions, no black sailor could
be assigned to such civilian tasks as stevedoring and maintenance work in
the continental United States.[9]

The only real way to break the logjam, however, was to open up slots
for Negroes in the fleet. By early 1944 the Special Programs Unit had a
reluctant nod from King. BuPers assigned 196 black enlisted men and forty-
four white officers and petty officers to the newly commissioned destroyer
escort *Mason*. A lesser mix, whites again topmost, went to a patrol craft,
PC-1264. On both vessels, black petty officers and some black officers
(among them Ensign Samuel Gravely, Jr., who in 1971 was to become the
Navy's first black admiral) were later phased in.

Only four other segregated ships, all of them patrol craft, were added.

These six ships were racial sons of *Rizal*, and they were not the answer. With the phasing out of most of the whites, segregation simply moved outward from the compartment to the skin of the entire ship. *Mason* passed her shakedown cruise, but BuPers observers thought her black petty officers had trouble maintaining discipline. Even the Special Programs Unit admitted the truth of the charges. *Mason* steamed anyway, on escort duty in the Atlantic, and she proved two things: blacks could handle any rating, and black and white sailors could work aboard without racial friction.[10]

The most ticklish question for the Navy, however, was that of black line officers. *Mason* and the five patrol craft initially had none assigned—because none existed. There were three routes to a commission: Annapolis, the Ninety-Day-Wonder programs, and the V-12 Program. Stevenson, whom Knox, not without some exasperation, called his "New Dealer," was an invaluable ally for the Special Programs Unit; he would have liked to use every available avenue to produce black officers. But Annapolis, the school that three years before would not allow a black man from Harvard to sully its lacrosse field, was the most sacred of cows, and in the entire V-12 Program in 1943, a program churning out tens of thousands of officers, there were exactly twelve Negroes, participating at integrated civilian colleges throughout the country.

Late in that year, goaded by Stevenson, Knox got BuPers to recommend that the Navy commission twelve line and ten staff officers from a selected list of black enlisted men. Ernie King again signed off, but Knox revealed his grasp of this hot potato when he minuted to BuPers, "After you have commissioned [these] officers . . . I think this matter should again be reviewed before any additional colored officers are commissioned."

On 1 January 1944 sixteen blacks (twenty-two were apparently too many) reported to Great Lakes for officer training. They were segregated from other officer trainees and at first were not allowed to use the officer's club. The racial slights they received ranged from the indifferent through the casual to the savage. "We went through living hell," said George Cooper. All sixteen passed the course, but in the final week three of them were suddenly returned to the ranks, BuPers having arbitrarily decided to pare the sixteen down further. Another man, the only one without a college degree, was commissioned as a warrant officer because of his outstanding work. The remaining twelve were commissioned as line officers in the Naval Reserve on 17 March.

This baker's dozen were the "Golden Thirteen" (a name coined later by one of them, Dennis Nelson)—the first black line officers in Navy history. They were also, unfortunately, perfect examples of naval tokenism. All of them were in good health, businessmen and professionals in civilian life, far more qualified for naval leadership roles than many of the Ninety-Day white hotshots pouring into the wardrooms of the fleet. Yet six of the new black ensigns were assigned to training duty at Great Lakes, four went to yard and harbor craft, and two ended up on the faculty of all-black Hampton Institute. All carried in their service records the label "Deck Officers Limited—Only," a tag usually given to the naval equivalent of the lame, the halt, and the blind.

Soon they were joined by scattered black graduates of the V-12 Program, no more than seventy-five all told. Some of these men had actually been admitted to the program nine months before the Golden Thirteen had gone to Great Lakes, and for some of them, like the earnest, quiet Sam Gravely and the deliberate, precise Carl Rowan, who later became a prominent journalist, V-12 was a "turning point" in their lives. But they were far too few to make any impact. By 1 June 1945 there were exactly thirty-eight black officers in the Navy, two of them women. All were Reservists, and they were 0.0013 percent of the naval officer corps. In short, they were shunned, shooed off to dead-end jobs, and worse: Gravely, shortly after being commissioned, was arrested by the shore patrol for impersonating an officer.

Although all but five black officers eventually got overseas, they had no real authority. The only exception was Ensign Dennis Nelson, who commanded a logistics support unit of both whites and blacks on Eniwetok. Only one black officer reached the rank of full lieutenant by war's end (the fictional Willie Keith, a Ninety-Day Wonder, ended up as the last captain of the *Caine*), and only one black was admitted to the Naval Academy in wartime, in the summer of 1945.

In short, this brazen treatment of a deserving racial minority did not so much illuminate the Navy's racial awareness—although this had increased slightly—as cast a harsh spotlight on the rocky road ahead. Adding to the problem, for the tens of thousands of enlisted Negroes, was the fact that BuPers was fond of choosing white southerners as their officers, on the theory that people from such backgrounds had a natural "understanding" of the racial question.[11]

—Thus the first halting, highly discriminatory steps. They were far from leading to any meaningful, fairly defined racial goal in democracy's war.

☆

Good businessman that he was, James Forrestal knew inefficiency when he saw inefficiency, and if he was far from a racial liberal of the Stevenson or Sargent stripe, he was fully aware of the head of steam being built up on racial issues, both inside and outside the Navy. When he took over the Navy Department upon Knox's death, he moved quickly. After weeks of jawboning, he at last got the support of King and the mandarins at BuPers.

In July 1944 segregated advanced training schools went by the boards. Recruit training, however, run mostly by southern-born white officers—the ones who "understood" the racial question—remained segregated. A month later blacks were assigned to twenty-five auxiliaries with full integration, although their numbers were limited to 10 percent of each crew. In April 1945 all auxiliaries were opened to them, still with the 10 percent cap.

The month before, Forrestal brought Lester Granger, head of the National Urban League, on board as his adviser on racial policy. (The secretary had himself been a league member for many years.) Granger, an eloquent, persuasive man, spent the next half-year, past war's end, traveling fifty thousand miles and visiting sixty-seven naval facilities throughout the world. Forrestal acted on practically every one of his suggestions for the better treatment of black sailors. Even before Granger's arrival, Forrestal had finally shoehorned a few black women into the WAVES. Frank Knox had told Mildred McAfee that black WAVES would be enlisted "over [my] dead body." Now they were.

But Lester Granger walked the point. He quietly advised local base commanders on how to deal squarely with their black charges. He became the node where the Navy Department, civil rights organizations, and the black press intersected. He got Forrestal to inaugurate an informal committee to oversee the Navy's treatment of Negroes. Much of the Navy's halting progress was due to Granger's gentle but insistent prodding.[12]

—All was not progress. Indeed, there was disaster along the way. On 17 July 1944 at Port Chicago, California, an ammo-handling depot up the Sacramento River from Mare Island, two ammunition ships exploded, obliterating Port Chicago and killing 320 people, including 202 black sailors in stevedoring battalions. This single catastrophe accounted for 15 percent of all black naval casualties during the war. The survivors claimed their job was too dangerous and refused to go back to work—the battalions were segregated—and in the largest mass mutiny trial in America's history fifty of them, all black men, were convicted and sent to the brig. Only after a nationwide outcry by black organizations and patient work by Granger and Thurgood Marshall (whose greatest legal work lay ahead) were the sentences set side and the men returned to duty. They received "clemency" and discharges "under honorable conditions," but the blot of "mutineer" remained on their records.

Six months later, on Guam, a riot broke out between black sailors and white Marines. A series of Christmas Eve shootings left a black and a white dead. In the aftermath, two truckloads of armed Negroes descended on a Marine camp, another riot followed, and forty-three blacks were arrested. Both whites and blacks were convicted, some of them receiving up to four years in prison. Again, only the efforts of civil rights leaders like Walter White, national secretary of the NAACP, produced the release of the black men, in early 1946. They had been victims of racial discrimination from the moment they set foot on Guam, and their unit had been cursed with abysmal white leadership.

Finally, in March 1945, blacks at Port Hueneme, California, went on a hunger strike to protest discrimination in a Seabee battalion. No violence ensued, but this mass protest, involving a thousand men, was a preview of things to come. They continued to work but did not eat for two days. The Navy, abhorring as usual the resulting negative press coverage, promptly adopted Solution One: the unit skipper was relieved, and the whole outfit was shipped overseas.

These ventings of steam got Chester Nimitz a bit steamed, too. All three incidents occurred in his sprawling Pacific command, he was busy fighting a war, and he did not want to be bothered by racial outbreaks far from the battlefront. As he made clear to one of his captains, "when we say we want integration, we mean *integration.*" In the weeks following the Guam riots, Forrestal and King agreed on a policy of total integration in the general service; Negroes were to be assigned as individuals to all branches and billets.

A world war and four bitter years of institutional racial discrimination had been needed to gain even this much. In all, 166,195 Negroes wore a Navy uniform in World War II; in 1945, more than 90 percent of those still in service were messmen. There were 10,914 Navy nurses, all told; only 4 were black. And, on V-J Day, the regular Navy contained 7066 blacks, all enlisted—2.14 percent of the total cadre.

The young James Baldwin would write, in *The Fire Next Time*, that the war "marks for me a turning point in the Negro's relation to America: to put it briefly, and somewhat too simply, a certain hope died, a certain respect for white Americans faded."[13]

☆

Peace came, and racial discrimination in the Navy stayed. Forrestal, Nimitz, Granger, and all the rest, men with the best intentions, could not make much of a dent in deeply ingrained racial attitudes that had been hardening for decades. The escort carrier *Croatan*, assigned in December 1945 to return servicemen from Le Havre, refused to board 123 black men in an Army quartermaster truck company (shades of *Virginia* after World War I). One black officer and five black enlisted men were reluctantly given a ride back home. The resulting brouhaha, although not entirely the Navy's fault, led to less-than-flattering coverage by the press of both races, protests by black unions, an appeal by the NAACP, and a formal investigation by Forrestal.

Exasperated, the secretary had already written six months before that "we are making every effort to give more than lip service to the principles of democracy in the treatment of the Negro and we are trying to do it with a minimum of commotion." *Croatan* was not the "minimum of commotion" Forrestal desired. Granger's informal Committee on Negro Personnel was telling the secretary that a no-nonsense integration policy had to come, soon, and that some of Forrestal's much-loved PR bonfires needed to light up the black community. Indeed, Granger's to-do list was long and stark: enlisting and commissioning a "significant number" of Negroes in the regular Navy, indoctrinating commanders in their racial responsibilities, eliminating racial discrimination in shipyards and other shore facilities, and broadening employment opportunities in the Navy Department for black civilians.

Above all, Granger and his committee zeroed in on the Steward's Branch as the overwhelming symbol of the Navy's racial biases. They called for the assignment of white stewards and for allowing black stewards who qualified to transfer to the general service.

Granger harped in particular on the issue of morale. Horrible morale among blacks lay at the heart of the Port Chicago mess and the Guam riots, and Granger's reports from the field to Forrestal reflected the suspicions of the Special Programs Unit: the performance of blacks was directly affected by their sense of discrimination and segregation. Naval bases widely and routinely practiced segregation, despite official disclaimers, and this was not a regional phenomenon limited to the South. The experiences of the Golden Thirteen at Great Lakes were all too typical. There was segregation in housing, mess halls, and work crews; Navy shore patrols enforced segregation in civilian bars, even where the practice was forbidden by state law. On southern naval bases, "colored" and "white" signs were as common, and rank, as weeds.

The Committee on Negro Personnel did not as a group go so far as Granger: they recommended only a "gradual integration" of the service, in the name of efficiency. Fearing "concentration" of Negroes (the discipline-and-order bogey again), the committee counseled the easy course, integrating the small number of black specialists in the Regular Navy and leaving the vast number of black sailors right where they were—in the Steward's Branch, waiting on tables just like Dorie Miller and Leonard Harmon.

This was, at best, partial integration. Still, the absurdity of operating both a black and a white Navy, on the *Mason* model, was readily apparent. Civil rights leaders, after V-J Day, pressed more strongly than ever for total service integration. "Democracy's war" had been won, and the bill from racial minorities was long overdue.

The handwriting could be read even by the Bureau of Naval Personnel, that great bastion of the racial status quo. Its chief, Louis Denfeld, at least believed that Negroes in the peacetime Navy should lose none of their wartime gains. On 27 February 1946 came BuPers Circular Letter 48-46: "Effective immediately all restrictions governing types of assignments for which Negro naval personnel are eligible are hereby lifted. Henceforth, they shall be eligible for all types of assignments in all ratings in all activities and all ships of the naval service." There was also a directive to redistribute personnel so that no command would be more than 10 percent Negro. Somehow this percentage, possibly based on the wider population, seemed an appropriate racial "ceiling."

The directive, however, pointedly ignored the virtually all-white officer corps and the composition of the now-infamous Steward's Branch. There was no administrative machinery to enforce the new policy. Equal opportunity across the board for black Navymen remained an illusion. Still, these tentative steps forward were enough to shake the bushes and bring sniper fire from southern segregationists. "White boys are being forced to sleep with these negroes," Congressman Stephen Pace of Georgia raved to Forrestal. Indeed, the secretary's failure to put teeth in his, and the bureau's, racial directives ensured that a chasm separating official words and naval practice would remain.[14]

—For the postwar Navy's and America's blacks alike, between the ideal and the real fell the shadow of the promise.

☆

Carl Vinson was the Navy's mightiest legislative champion, but like Pace and practically every other southern politician, he was no friend of blacks, stubbornly believing that the only reasons the wartime military was segregated was because of its sheer size. After the off-year elections in 1942, the hardening alliance between Republicans and southern Democrats meant that racial reform in the military would find precious few voices of real support on Capitol Hill.

And the Hill was not the only problem for black sailors. They had no real base of support in either the Pentagon or the Navy Department once the civilians and civilians-in-uniform, like Sargent, went home. Negroes and whites at every level in the Pentagon were "openly antagonistic." White supervisors there commonly refused to refer to Negro subordinates by title, the kind of casual paternalism that rasped like a file.

One black yeoman generalized that Negro leaders everywhere "functioned more or less on sufferance." And when he himself reported aboard his first ship, a destroyer, at war's end, he heard his chief yeoman tell the executive officer, "Sir, a nigger yeoman first class has come aboard, and there's gonna be trouble!" (There was; the chief raised such a fuss that the black petty officer was quickly transferred to the nearest receiving station.)

That black yeoman, Felix Paul, spoke for everyone of his race, bedeviled as they were by political and social bigotry, bureaucratic malaise, and sheer racism:

> I found the Navy in many ways a great disappointment. I tried to get duty overseas, but never got the break. I tried like hell. I served twenty-eight months for an average of $73.60 a month, at a time when money was circulating freely and a man with training could do well in civilian life.
>
> I maintained an average of 4.0 in Conduct, Proficiency in Rate, and Ability as a Leader of Men. This is the highest possible mark in the Navy. And yet, I never got higher than yeoman first class, and many considered that excellent for a Negro.[15]

By the end of 1945, the Navy already had two hundred or more ships with "racially mixed" crews, but the statistics hid the virulent racism experienced by Felix Paul and most of the other blacks in the service. Circular Letter 48-46, in effect, imposed a racial quota on the entire Navy. (No more than 10 percent of the entire enlisted force could be black.) And after his appointment as secretary of defense, Forrestal became more aloof than ever, seeking to moderate interservice differences rather than imposing his will through the service secretaries. Any racial change, he firmly believed, had to begin with the slow, deliberate education of all concerned. "Slow" and "deliberate" were terms that black America had heard before, and would hear again.

As late as 1948, 80 percent of the blacks serving in the Navy were stewards—certainly slow and deliberate enough as a pace of change. Roughly 0.5 percent of all WAVES who stayed in were black. Only one of every four black nurses from the war remained on active duty. Even Sam Gravely left the Navy (but would soon return).

Dennis Nelson of the Golden Thirteen hung on, at the special insistence of Secretary of the Navy John Sullivan. Bright and brash, a complete dandy with a twinkle-eyed smile surmounting his pencil mustache, Nelson projected himself in a way that many black men, like the much more self-contained Gravely, did not. Taking over much of the work of the disbanded Special Programs Unit (gone by June 1946), Nelson fought valiantly from his lowly position as a junior officer to broaden the scope of racial integration, his only weapons a pipeline to the secretary and his own flamboyant personality. In 1949 he at last won consideration of chief cooks and stewards as Navy chief petty officers in their own right—an important if mostly symbolic step, and eventually, in 1951, he produced an important source work, *The Integration of the Negro into the U.S. Navy*.

In the immediate postwar years, despite the efforts of Nelson and a few other naval reformers, the proportion of enlisted blacks in the Navy leveled off at about 4.3 percent of a much-diminished force. By mid-1948 only Nelson and two other black officers remained on active duty. Sullivan, despite his support for Nelson, callously said that the Navy "naturally" excluded black officers as Regulars, just as Negroes were commonly placed as stewards.

In 1948 more than eight out of every ten black men in the Navy trained and worked apart from whites, consigned to the servile hell of menial tasks and led by black noncoms whose claim to advanced petty officer rank was largely ignored by their white peers and white seniors. This crude racism was somewhat concealed by the extremely high reenlistment rate in the Steward's Branch, traditionally the best in the Navy. Men like Stephen Pace and Carl Vinson could look at these figures and legitimately ask what the clamor was all about. The truth, of course, was that the Navy's stewards, largely denied professional careers on the outside, could upon retirement make comfortable livings in hotel, restaurant, and club work—augmented by their government checks. The stigma had to be accepted; Secretary Sullivan, despite Nelson's tutelage, was of the opinion that messmen's duty was a haven for those unable to compete for billets and promotion in the rest of the Navy.

Dennis Nelson shouldered the Steward's Branch as his special cross. A lowly lieutenant in the department's Office of Public Relations (he would retire as a lieutenant commander, his flamboyance as well as his race perhaps standing in the way of higher rank), Nelson fired off memos right and left to admirals and buttonholed Sullivan and his successors every chance he got. Eliminate the branch as racially separate, pleaded Nelson; change the distinct steward's uniform to conform with that of other sailors; give the branch's petty officers commensurate authority; above all, do not call these grown men "boys."

His pleas mostly echoed in the void. As late as March 1953, of twenty-three thousand blacks in the Navy, about half were still in the Steward's Branch. Even more disheartening was the situation of black officers. Not one Negro was granted a Regular commission in the first eighteen months after the war. In March 1947 Ensign John Lee, a V-12 grad assigned aboard an auxiliary, became the first black to receive such a commission, and in January 1948 Lieutenant Edith DeVoe made the same transition in the Nurse Corps. Nelson himself became a Regular in January 1950.

Other breakthroughs occurred, on an exasperating, gut-wrenching individual scale. Wesley Brown, in 1949, became the first black man ever to graduate from the Naval Academy. He was only the sixth Negro to enter in the school's 104-year history. In October of that year Jesse Brown, no relation, began his path to golden wings as the first black naval aviator; he was commissioned seven months later. Yet in 1947, just fourteen Negroes were among the nation's 5600 NROTC students. Not a single black served on any state's NROTC selection committee. Only six NROTC candidates, a farcical number, won Reserve commissions in 1948. And still the Navy argued that its black officers were integrated and being assigned without discrimination.[16]

—Black Americans, with resounding good reason, were ignoring the postwar Navy. Dennis Nelson himself spoke before 8500 potential black officer candidates throughout the country in 1948, and a special recruiting team met with at least that many the following year, but fewer than ninety applicants from both groups even bothered to show up to take the competitive examination. Lester Granger saw irony in black unwillingness to enlist, despite the widely publicized promises of racial equality in the service, but in fact the Navy's racial chickens were coming home to roost.

The Navy's track record on race relations was simply too long and too shoddy to bear examination, and now, when the service was honestly trying to improve, at least in an official sense, its racial past dragged like a fouled anchor. Young blacks knew about the wartime labor battalions bossed by whites (the analogy with the despised plantation system was not lost); about the Port Chicago mutiny, the Guam riots, the Port Hueneme strike; about the lack of openings in technical specialties and the dearth of black officers; and, above all, about that detested symbol of racism, the Steward's Branch.

The Navy's claims that the service had made great advances in racial *policy* were to a considerable degree true (the Marine Corps's odious attitude about race, for example, made the Navy look like the NAACP), but "progress" was at best sporadic and riddled with hypocrisy. Harry Truman, assuming a vigorous civil rights stance in the complicated 1948 presidential campaign, helped by issuing Executive Order 9981 on 26 July. Although deliberately vague, the order decreed "equality of treatment and opportunity for all persons in the armed services without regard to race, color, religion or national origin." Truman, who did not really want to go as far as the Democrats' liberal civil rights plank that year, managed to muddy the racial issue by stating that the new policy should go into effect "as rapidly as possible." He refused to set a time limit for true integration but said he expected his order to abolish segregation in the armed forces.

The president was far too sanguine. Although well meaning, particularly in the context of a campaign in which the segregationist Dixiecrats fielded one of their own, Strom Thurmond of South Carolina, 9981 was far from a Magna Carta for blacks in the military. Truman nevertheless had come a long way from the comfortable racial assumptions of most of his fellow border-state Missourians, that blacks "prefer[red] the society of their own people." When Omar Bradley, another Missourian, announced that the Army "is not out to make any social reform," the president publicly rebuked him.[17]

The Navy response to 9981, though, was less than overwhelming. Circular Letter 48-46, the equality guarantee, was mostly theoretical; since 1946 the Navy's racial problems had been connected less with stated policy than with actual practice. By 1949 racial quotas in recruiting had been abolished, but their absence, given black lack of interest in the service to begin with, was academic. In December 1949 the Navy admitted that fewer than seven thousand black sailors were serving in what the service called "racially integrated" assignments.

More PR was lathered on. Wesley Brown, fresh from the banks of the Severn, spent much of his time as a junior officer making speeches about the opportunities for blacks as naval officers. In the 1950s the number of black officers in the Navy would increase sevenfold, a deceiving statistic because blacks would still, in 1960, be less than 1 percent of the Navy's total officer strength, well below the Army and the Air Force percentages. Through the 1950s, no black officer rose to command a ship; Lieutenant Commander Sam Gravely would be the first, taking over the destroyer escort *Falgout* in 1961.

Executive Order 9981, in sum, was only as good as the Navy's inclination to thoroughly carry out presidential policy. Most blacks viewed the service's claims about racial improvements to be nothing more than blue-and-gold-colored cant. As late as 1961, the chief of naval presonnel reported that black audiences were booing and hissing Navy recruiters making their pitch. In fact, Truman's "rapidly as possible" never happened. The Steward's Branch was folded into the Navy's rating structure, but the branch remained almost 65 percent black as late as 1952, when Truman was finishing his elected four-year term. (The rest of the branch was mostly Filipinos under contract.)

The hot specialty ratings were hardly flooded with blacks, either. In 1950 only 114 Negroes were assigned to submarines, even fewer to naval aviation. On paper the Navy looked good and always claimed to be ahead of the power curve on 9981. But in practice the record was both "business as usual" and despicable.

Forrestal's successors as secretary of defense let the individual services set their own paces of integration. This was fine with the Navy, the corporate memory of which included the steadfast denial of blacks' entrance to the Naval Academy in the first third of the twentieth century, official segregation in the offices of the Navy Department (1913), and even a proposal for separate lavatories for the races in the Pentagon's design. (FDR personally killed this plan.) Some naval officers stationed in the District of Columbia were close to being white supremacists, and retired officers of high rank included many who firmly believed that part of the ethos of the Navy was the maintenance of its racial purity.

—And not only the old but also the young. Wesley Brown said of his Academy plebe year that he developed "a feeling they were trying to run me out of the place." He roomed by himself in Bancroft Hall. Courageously, Brown hung on, made white friends and allies, and graduated in the top half of his class—he would retire as a lieutenant commander in the Civil Engineer Corps. Brown's experience in the Yard, at best bittersweet, was no grand racial open sesame for the future. In the twenty years following his graduation, only fifty-four blacks entered and only thirty-five (fewer than *two* a year) graduated.

The Navy was evading and avoiding responding to 9981 with a "salvo of self-congratulation, lauding past accomplishments and ignoring the future." Truman's aides, in the climactic days of the 1948 campaign, had created the President's Committee on Equality of Treatment and Opportunity in the Armed Forces, mercifully called the Fahy Committee after its chair, Charles ("Whisper") Fahy, a soft-spoken Georgian. This committee, convening in January 1949, issued pronouncements right and left, with painfully limited results. Everyone, of course, said the right things. The under secretary of the Navy, at the end of the year, wrote that "racial tolerance is spreading and it is only a question of time until it will no longer present a problem within the Navy."

"Only a question of time" . . . "as rapidly as possible." The Fahy Committee accurately pinpointed the Navy's racial failures at the grass-roots level, but ingrained service racism, combined with black distrust, kept Negro enlistments shockingly low.[18]

—For blacks, all this was simply the same old white man's shell game.

☆

Then came Korea. The Negro leader A. Philip Randolph, a veteran of countless racial protests, threatened to call a black boycott of the armed forces if the foot-dragging continued. But no uprising occurred, and most of the Navy's blacks who participated in the Korean conflict served in their familiar menial roles.

—But not Jesse Brown. In 1950 he was a long way from Hattiesburg, Mississippi. There, as a boy, he had raised up from picking cotton and watched in fascination as airplanes buzzed overhead. Through intelligence and sheer tenacity he enrolled at Ohio State, studying architecture while working nights loading railroad boxcars. He enlisted in the Naval Reserve and began to realize his dream by taking flight training. When he got to Pensacola, as an aviation officer candidate, he was crudely taunted, so much so that he secretly married, against regulations. With the support of his new wife, his high school sweetheart, and with his own skills, he became the Navy's first black aviator on 21 October 1949.

A year later, Ensign Brown had a Med cruise under his belt and was flying Corsairs off *Leyte* with Fighter Squadron 32, striking deep into North Korea. He was quiet, and he made his share of ensign's flying mistakes. But he was becoming, in the words of a squadron mate, "damned good." He was accepted by his fellow aviators even before he flew his first combat mission, on 13 October 1950. By early December he had flown nineteen more missions and had received the Air Medal for his close support work, bombing, and strafing.

On 4 December VF-32 flew again, in support of UN troops retreating down the frozen slopes of North Korea in the face of the Chinese onslaught. Brown was launched as part of a four-plane sortie that crossed the coastline and trolled along at 500 feet, 150 knots, looking for targets of opportunity. After about an hour of this dangerous work, Brown's plane was hit by ground fire. His Corsair struck in a clear, snow-covered area surrounded by forested mountains, far behind the southward-surging enemy lines near the Chosin Reservoir. The engine tore loose. His mates, orbiting overhead, saw that Brown had slid back his canopy and was waving. Smoke was curling from the forward section of the plane.

One of Brown's escorts, Lieutenant Junior Grade Thomas Hudner, wondered why Brown did not clear out of the cockpit. Finally, Hudner wheeled over and, flaps down, landed bumpily on an icy upgrade about a hundred yards from the downed aircraft. Leaving his own damaged plane, Hudner scrambled to Brown's side, where he found the black aviator's legs pinned inside the broken fuselage. Brown was conscious, but he was badly injured and probably bleeding internally.

Chinese lurked nearby—they had shot Brown down in the first place. Frantically, Hudner pulled at his companion's imprisoned body. No go. He threw handfuls of snow at the smoke venting from the cowling. Nothing worked. He straddled the canopy, tugging at the helpless man with all his might. Still no go. Brown was fading in and out of consciousness.

Forty-five minutes passed. The two remaining members of the orbiting sortie had to head for home plate. The rescue helicopter clattered in. Its pilot, Marine First Lieutenant Charles Ward, quickly found that the whirly's small fire extinguisher was useless. He took his turn hammering at the bent fuselage with an ax. Nothing. As Hudner and Ward tried everything they could, Jesse Brown probably drew his last breath. Still they worked on furiously, until dark.

Hudner's plane was unflyable, and Ward's helo was not equipped for darkness or foul weather. Distraught, the two men flew out to Yonpo, leaving Brown and his plane to the worsening weather. (Hudner would win the Medal of Honor for his selfless courage.)

Days later, when the weather cleared, several planes from VF-32 vectored to the crash site. The aviators saw Brown's body, now stripped of clothing, still in the cockpit. Slowly they turned, flew in low over the spot, and toggled off their canisters of napalm.

—The body of the Navy's first black eagle was cremated in the cockpit of his own plane.[19]

☆

Twenty-three years later, Captain Tom Hudner, Jesse Brown's widow, and Rear Admiral Sam Gravely stood by as the destroyer escort *Jesse L. Brown*, the first Navy ship honoring a black man, was placed in commission. In a way, they were honoring not only Brown's courage and skill, but also all the black men and women who served through the Korean War and beyond.

—Because Ensign Jesse Brown, fighter jock, was a great racial exception. The proportion of blacks in the Navy stayed around 4 percent through the Korean War, even though their absolute numbers increased to thirty-nine thousand with the wartime naval expansion. Some of the new recruits went into corpsmen's or dental technician's specialties, but in 1955, eighteen months after the Korean truce was signed, the Navy was still ordering 50 percent of its blacks to steward duty.

This was the turning point. In 1956, with the last of the Korean War three-year enlistments expiring, 75 percent of the thirty-seven thousand blacks in the 591,000-person force received assignments to general service.

In 1953, Dennis Nelson had reported that "the entire situation has undergone a startling and refeshing change." He admitted the problems with the Steward's Branch ("there is no regulation which forbids white men from being assigned . . . but it just doesn't happen") but noted with pride the increasing numbers of black officers (sixty in 1953).

These people were scattered all over the place, as doctors, dentists, chaplains, engineers, WAVES, nurses, and line officers. Negro line officers were aboard *Missouri, New Jersey, Wisconsin, Saint Paul, Roanoke,* four carriers, and a host of smaller combatants. Usually, like Jesse Brown, they were the only blacks in their respective wardrooms not waiting on tables. "The Navy takes the position at this reporting," noted Nelson with more than a trace of sarcasm, "that it has no segregation hence nothing on which to report or comment."

If words were all there were, then the official position was true. President Dwight Eisenhower, no proponent of rapid racial change, unintentionally took note of the problem when, shaking hands with a Newport Navy chaplain who had just delivered a sermon on the need for new civil rights legislation, remarked that "you can't legislate morality." Eisenhower, like so many Americans, had his own hidden racism; the president was fond of passing on the latest "nigger jokes" gleaned from his cronies at the whites-only Augusta National Golf Club in Georgia.

But even within his own rather conservative administration, currents were moving beneath the ice. Attorney General William Rogers had served aboard an aircraft carrier in World War II, had seen black men fire machine guns against kamikaze attacks, and had watched them then go below to serve meals to white officers. Rogers worked on the Justice Department's supporting brief in the landmark case of *Brown* v. *Board of Education of Topeka* in 1954, and as the head of the department he had pressed for the appointment of southern Republican judges who were sensitive to civil rights issues.[20]

Interest at the top, sparse enough even with the involvement of men like Rogers, was necessary because the second line of defense in racial bigotry lay with attitudes, practices, and prejudices that could not be cured overnight by a circular letter from the Navy Department or a stroke of the pen from a well-meaning secretary. In the south, in 1953, shore stations were still segregating black and white civilian employees. When the new secretary of the Navy, Robert Anderson, orally asked local commanders to put an end to separate racial facilities, several of them, citing "local custom," said they would ignore the request unless they got written orders (which were immediately forthcoming). Charleston and Norfolk were rapidly desegregated (at least Charleston so reported), and by the end of 1953 Eisenhower, who in these cases had ridden herd on Anderson, was boasting that segregation in the Navy "was a thing of the past."

The president was premature. His secretary of defense, Charles Wilson

("Engine Charlie" of General Motors, not to be confused with "Electric Charlie" Wilson of General Electric, who had served on Truman's committee for civil rights) had to launch a campaign to bring integration to Defense Department schools operated on federal property for the dependents of servicemen. One-third of these schools were in states that maintained segregated educational systems. Progress was slow, because some school districts used local tax revenues to build schools on land donated by the federal government. Not until 1963 did the last of the segregated districts succumb to court decisions and a threat to terminate all federal aid to local systems.

Navy shipyards in the South were also segregated; the signs and notices of apartheid were on drinking fountains, toilets, dressing rooms, and shower facilities. Rear Admiral Wesley Hague, chief of the Navy's Office of Industrial Relations, had sent out a notice in January 1952 that left these pernicious situations to the local commander's "judgment," saying that segregation in these yards would continue if "the station is subject to local laws of the community in which located, and the laws of the community require segregated facilities."

This was enough to infuriate Dennis Nelson, by now a permanent (and effective) racial gadfly about the Pentagon. He mobilized the Urban League and the NAACP, got Anderson turned around (the secretary, on assuming office, had offhandedly endorsed Hague's witless notice), and, by early 1954, earned the satisfaction of seeing the signs come down and integration take place, at least officially, in all the Navy's shipyards.[21]

With official integration of the Navy's shore stations, schools, and shipyards, the long and tortuous pursuit of racial equity seemed to be over.

☆

—But racism, first and foremost, dwelt in the minds and hearts of men, screened from paper manifestos by the deep-seated prejudices of a lifetime. In 1955 *Midway* visited Capetown, where her nonwhite sailors were summarily informed that, while on liberty, they must abide by South Africa's harsh apartheid laws. The Navy officially turned down a request by the NAACP that the fleet's ships steer clear of South African ports. The stop at Capetown, said the Navy, satisfied "an operational logistic requirement"— operations *über alles.*

Minds and hearts were slow to change, and so were racial attitudes. As Eisenhower prosperity rolled on, the American civil rights movement made exasperatingly slow headway—with the notorious "all deliberate speed" of the Supreme Court's obiter dictum in *Brown* v. *Board of Education*, with the internationally embarrassing Little Rock incident in integrating Central High, and with the badly diluted Civil Rights Act of 1957.

When John Kennedy became president, the Navy's paper policy on race and equal treatment was firmly in place. Yet when Kennedy was inaugurated in January 1961, Negroes continued to predominate in the Steward's Branch, and the evidence of black exclusion was right before his eyes in the inaugural day parade. When the one-hundred-man naval honor guard marched past, not a single black face was in the ranks.

In 1962, 5.2 percent of the naval enlisted strength and an infinitesimal 0.2 percent of the officer corps were black. In 1964 blacks were reenlisting at about twice the rate of whites, a reflection not of some newfound racial equality but of black sailors' estimates of their chances for gainful and respectable employment on the outside. Blacks in command were as scarce as zebra's spots; by 1965, after Sam Gravely, only three other black officers with command experience were on active duty.

At Pensacola in the early sixties, blacks were never used for guard duty at the main gate, lest they offend passing whites. The base housing there segregated black Navy families in slovenly rundown shacks literally below the railroad tracks, flimsy structures that would have shamed even a Snopes. At Charleston, despite all the directions from on high, the Navy still segregated Negro personnel on base. And in 1953 a worried Carl Vinson introduced a bill to outlaw any integration activity by military officers.

Wearing very soft shoes indeed, the Navy tried to shuffle past staunch congressional allies like Vinson without giving offense, while at the same time trying to clean up such obvious racist cesspools as Pensacola and Charleston. This kind of act resulted, more often than not, in the treatment of the whole area of naval civil rights as just another public relations problem, pointing always to the directives already in place. In addition, the service was leery, for the traditional reasons of discipline and good order, of pressing for closer contact between the races aboard ship. Nevertheless, spokesmen were continually forced to admit that the Navy's "community relations" concerning racial issues left much to be desired.

A memo by a special assistant to the secretary of the Navy in 1963 confessed that after all the paper policy, America's Negroes continued to avoid the naval service in overwhelming numbers because "they have little desire to become stewards or cooks." The chief of naval personnel hoped for "palatable evolutionary progress" rather than "bitter revolutionary change," which he apparently felt were mutually exclusive goals with nothing in between.[22]

Kennedy's secretary of defense, Robert McNamara, was a systems man; he assumed that when the dots were all lined up and connected, things would happen. Later McNamara would reflect on the failure of his own racial directives: "I was naive enough in those days to think that all I had to do was show my people that a problem existed, tell them to work on it, and that they would then attack the problem. It turned out of course that not a goddamn thing happened."

Black tokens, like the skipper of the radar picket *Finch*, Lieutenant Commander George Thompson (an OCS grad), might be given photo spreads of several pages in *Ebony*; healthy black reenlistment rates would be publicized to "prove" black satisfaction with the racial climate in the Navy; notices and instructions issued by the ream would continue to gasconade from the Navy Department concerning equal opportunity and the service's commitment to integration. There were indeed many well-meaning white people in support of naval civil rights, people who detested racial prejudice in any form.

Yet blacks had learned, by and large, to avoid naval service, and with good reason. In this way, the fleet was largely cut off from a premium source of the nation's manpower. For this damage, and for such facts as its minuscule percentage of black officers, by far the smallest of any of the services (except the Marines), the Navy had only itself, and its racial history, to blame.

Dennis Nelson had begun his study of racial integration in the Navy by saying that "the United States Navy has made no attempt to settle national racial problems nor can it be expected to." But this was never the point, only a rather squalid standard around which the evasive, the recalcitrant, and the indifferent could rally. Instead, the Navy's racial problems, within its own house, were addressed only with the greatest reluctance and with decidedly mixed success. Such an approach guaranteed that decades-deep racial wounds would continue to fester.[23]

As the sixties, that decade of marvelous fruition of the long-deferred civil rights dream, unfolded, the Navy's racial policy was on a far-from-even keel. Heavy seas lay ahead.

STERN WATCH IV

———— ☆ ————

The postwar American Navy was the navy of a democracy. Just as a democracy could torment and confound the purist with its imperfections and inequities, so too did the fleet fall far short of idealist goals for its variegated personnel. The people problems were everywhere: in the shortages of critical skills, like those of aviators and electronics specialists; in the reduced manning levels of a fleet stretched out across the globe; in the revolving door of junior enlisted men and officers; in the treatment accorded sexual minorities; and, above all, in the self-defeating racism infecting attitudes toward nonwhites.

In the broadest sense, however, two of the Navy's signal virtues were that the service was *open*, open to white men anyway, and that Navy and nation had a well-worn symbiotic relationship—each needed the other. In this context, like Antaeus when touching the earth, the fleet continually renewed itself from the nation and returned naval veterans to civilian life.

This constant two-way transfusion was not without its own problems, two conspicuous examples being the inordinate amount of training and retraining time required and the cozy relationship between some retired naval officers and military contractors. But the alternative, a Navy (and a military) completely ingrown and almost totally sequestered from the country at large, was unthinkable. Although critics argued that civilian life was being "militarized" by this transfusion, such assertions in the long view were difficult to prove, and the opposite may have been the case as well—witness the reforms of the *Uniform Code of Military Justice* in 1951.

In addition, and again with the caveat concerning white men, the service was open internally, far more so than expected by the outside world. Personal merit probably accounted more for upward mobility in the Navy than anywhere else in comparable American life. In World War II over twenty thousand enlisted personnel had been advanced to the wardroom by 1943, fifty-eight thousand in all by 1945. This practice, through the warrant, limited-duty, and direct commissioning programs, continued in the postwar era.[1]

The sea was a harsh school; naval duty had a relentless way of separating the wheat from the chaff. The men who reached the top, whether in Flag

Plot or in the Chief's Mess, generally deserved to be where they were. They knew what they were about and were, above all, consummate professionals.

In this context, among the naval career sailors, the country was resoundingly well-served, during the Cold War years, by the hands behind the shield. In the wardroom, on the other hand, the issue was more problematical. The revival of the draft, which would last for a quarter century after 1948, meant that many of the Navy's fresh-caught officers would be most reluctant catches indeed, struggling against the net until the day of their release. The reluctant draftee was most often seen in the ranks of the young professionals—doctors, dentists, engineers—but he was no stranger in the line community, either.

These people served their mandatory two or three years and speedily departed, many bitter that a gaping hole for national service had been torn in their upwardly mobile, professionally achieving lives. When possible, the Navy made use of their undoubted skills. But exasperatingly, just as the line officer learned to drive his destroyer, he was gone; just as the doctor began to fit smoothly into his medical routine, he vanished to the verdant uplands of civilian practice; just as the engineer was becoming competent to function on his own in a Seabee battalion, off he went.

A second group of officers gave the Navy a fair try but eventually left anyway. They did their jobs without more than the average amount of griping, and then they too were gone. A few of these might connect with the Reserves, but the pickings there were slim indeed.

This left the career officers, no more than 10 to 20 percent of the whole in any given year. They alone could not man the ships or the shore stations, because the global fleet in the postwar era had exploded the tightly woven integrity (and, more negatively, the insularity) of the prewar "band of brothers." The career people made their way upward as best they could, remorselessly subjected to winnowing at every level.

The survivors—the men in Flag Plot—were very often exceptional leaders, managers, or both. Some were worried that the managerial officer was supplanting the warrior, a constant complaint in the postwar period. Although officer warriors were by no means giving way to the managers and the systems men, more and more room had to be made for the latter, with their sorely needed skills.

More than a few senior officers, who had learned their trade in the earlier years of the century, were rigid, unthinking, unbending individuals who tended to confuse stubbornness and ignorance with a thoughtful ethical stance. They were likely to believe in eternal verities (communism was evil, blacks were inferior) that could, and did, make them in a military sense inimical to the best interests of their service. Despite this, the Navy was, on the whole, well led in the Cold War era. The cream was rising to the top.

The men and women of the enlisted cadre were of finer quality than ever before. They were better educated and more intolerant of poor leadership than their prewar fellows. Historically, American soldiers or sailors needed to be led with intelligence and good judgment rather than by the knout; this axiom became even more the case as the Navy grew more technically complex, thus requiring significantly higher standards from its enlisted personnel.

But the revolving door was spinning along the mess decks as well. The Navy relied on continuous training, both at sea and ashore, to maintain the edge required on the shield of the republic. The revolving door ensured that training would become not just a way station to some kind of professional expertise but a constant, growing concern at every level of the organization.

With the increasing extension of training time, the crucial new technological expertise was rapidly used up, as a thirsty man in the desert drains the last drop of water from his canteen. The hot-rock A-4 aviator came through a two-year training pipeline; then he acclimated himself to a replacement air group and a carrier squadron; then he flew operationally for two years; then, perhaps, he was gone. Hundreds of thousands of dollars and countless man-hours of training went with him. All this money and time were not wasted, but neither was this system by any standard the most effective use of taxpayer money. The nuclear specialist had much the same training time, with only a solid two years of responsible duty to show for all the recruiting and training effort. These were some of the costs of maintaining democracy's Navy—but they were heavy ones.

By the 1950s the Navy found itself snared in a vexatious circle from which the service was never to break free. Increasing technological complexity was unavoidable, so that more and more time was required to train both officers and enlisted personnel. Democracy's Navy could not tolerate too many years of required service. Thus, no sooner trained—almost—than gone. The technology only got more complex, the training cycles only lengthened, the revolving door only kept spinning.

These binding constraints made the Navy's attitude toward sexual and racial minorities all the more conspicuous. Sexism and racism were rampant in the larger society, to be sure, but the Navy's oft-stated position that the service was not in the business of social reform was beside the point; of course, its business was national defense. In the conduct of this business, however, the Navy needed the best people available—not the best white men.

The worst blotch on the Navy's personnel record, by far, was its deep-seated institutional racism. When forced to the wall, during and after World War II, a "fair percentage" of white officers and sailors accepted integration. A middle group seriously dragged its feet, delaying the most elemental reforms—such as integrated restrooms in naval shipyards. A third group was quietly intolerant, resisting racial change whenever possible. But never loudly. After 1946 the paper trail supporting integration fell into place, and overt racism was never the Navy's way. Instead, the way of the resisters was the way of the home-grown anthropologist admiral who told Frank Knox in 1942 that "the white man is more adaptable and more efficient" than the Negro and, by implication, therefore better for the Navy.

When Lieutenant Dennis Nelson, in 1951, asserted that "the Navy is the first of the military services to treat minority groups within the service as first-class citizens with no encumbering reservations," he missed the mark by a mile, preferring perhaps to assess the distance previously covered rather than to measure the long, arduous road ahead. The "encumbering reservations" were hidden deep inside individuals. They were hard to isolate, harder to change. In fact, scattered throughout the Navy, these reservations were the most effective brakes to the achievement of true civil rights in the Navy for a good quarter century after V-J Day.[2]

This observation should not conflict with the Navy's *relative* performance in civil rights, which was much better as compared with both the other services and its own past. Among the nation's military services, "the Navy was the acknowledged pioneer in integration." The general service began to be integrated when, in wartime, the Navy painfully realized that any alternative to integration was woefully inefficient. The policy of full integration first announced in February 1946 would, however, take decades to mature. In the interim, the service's traditional racial attitudes, while noticeably softening, would continue to war with its equally traditional pragmatism and desire for efficiency.[3]

This war would be fought on many fronts: in *Leyte*'s wardroom, where Ensign Jesse Brown became a hero to the black stewards; in the halls of the Pentagon, where Dennis Nelson restlessly roved in his ceaseless quest for black civil rights in the Navy; in naval shipyards, schools, shore stations everywhere; above all, in the minds and hearts of the Navy's people.

Here was a struggle that, in its implications for simple human justice and fair play, was arguably the most historically important in the Navy's history. But all the Navy's personnel, in the two decades after World War II, had to look outward, to the world, as well as inward, to themselves. Because the Navy indeed had a worldwide role to play.

—And there was a Cold War on.

PART FIVE

COLD WAR NAVY

He who intimidates his neighbors does so by
inflicting injury upon them.

—Sun Tzu, *The Art of War*

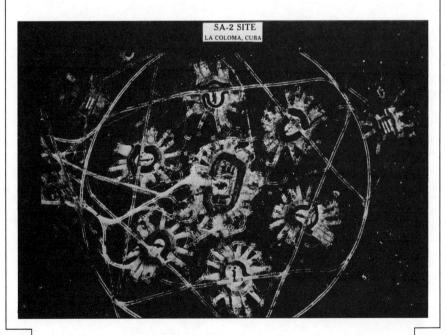

SA-2 SITE
LA COLOMA, CUBA

CHAPTER TWENTY-FOUR

TOPSIDE III

————— ☆ —————

T he Cold War Navy was master of the world's oceans. Wherever the bows of America's haze-gray warships cut water, they went unchallenged by any other naval power. These warships were potential and actual instruments of war, the calculated expression of national force, but they were also powerful pieces on an ideological chessboard, part of their purpose being to check, and possibly roll back, international communism.

This omnipotent fleet was a mailed fist that wore a velvet glove called "international peace," to which end the Navy, in the minds of Americans, anyway, policed the globe. Analysts were fond of calling this period one of *Pax Americana*, modeled on the Royal Navy's *Pax Britannica* of the nineteenth century. As things developed, "international peace," in the years following V-J Day, meant anything short of all-out nuclear war.

American leaders found that overwhelming naval hegemony did not automatically provide peace and stability. The lack of any real naval opposition gave naval and military planners unexpected but very real headaches, because Mahan's dictum that the business of navies was to fight navies had now come into serious question. Always a clumsy giant on the international scene in the twentieth century, the United States now faced the crucial problem of exactly how its naval strength should be used, and to what ends.

Americans quickly discovered that despite their country's economic might and far-flung military power, the Cold War years were seldom calm. Instead, crisis succeeded crisis, unsettling confrontations to which Americans often felt the need to respond.

—There was plenty of *Americana*. But precious little *Pax*.

☆

At first glance the newly elected president, Dwight David Eisenhower, would have been expected to cut the Navy little slack indeed. Here, after all, was a career Army officer, a five-star general whose professional life had been molded by a brother, but rival, institution. And there had been times in his career when his sulphurous temper (he was not always the Smilin' Grampa of fifties newsreels) had been fixed on things naval.

In the early days of World War II, after Eisenhower had been called to Washington by George Marshall to do war planning but before he had been assigned to lead the invasion of North Africa, he quickly became exasperated with his Navy counterparts' "non-cooperation." "What a gang to work with," he seethed. Ernie King he regarded with particular horror as a petty, rank-conscious, stubborn autocrat—"the antithesis of cooperation," he wrote, "a deliberately rude person, which means he's a mental bully." Then followed the famous comment that victory might be speeded up if only someone could be found to shoot King.

Later, King would become one of Ike's strongest supporters, but Eisenhower's first real introduction to joint operations in wartime did not augur well for his relationship with the Navy. Ordered to the European Theater, he unavoidably knew little of the conflict half a world away; he disparagingly referred to the Pacific as "the Navy's private war." On the eve of his greatest military moment, the Normandy invasion, he was still worrying over the proper number of landing craft (a Navy responsibility) and complained, in disgust, "How in hell can we win this war unless we crack some heads?"

This said, Eisenhower, who was an innately conciliatory man and a team-builder, cracked very few heads. Through his direction of the greatest wartime coalition in history, he came to understand and respect naval power to a far greater extent than any other Army officer, with the possible exception of Douglas MacArthur. Ike knew precisely what had enabled him to get into North Africa, Sicily, Italy, and France, and in the British admiral Sir Andrew Cunningham he found an authentic heir to the Nelson tradition—dignified yet dashing, graceful, courageous, a shining standard for any officer. He called Sir Andrew a "real sea dog" and gave his British and American naval subordinates full credit for the successes that had begun with Operation TORCH and culminated in Operation OVERLORD.

After the war, during his interlude as president of Columbia University ("interlude" because he never caught on there, and because five-star flag officers were on active duty for life), Eisenhower was appalled by the rebellion in gold braid. "Our present Navy can scarcely be justified on the basis of the naval strength of any potential enemy," he wrote to his lifelong friend from Abilene, Navy Captain Everett ("Swede") Hazlett. (Ike had at first wanted to go to the Naval Academy, like Swede, but no slots were available.) Eisenhower thought that *United States*, the proposed supercarrier, would have no other use than as a supertarget. And like his loyal comrade-in-arms, Omar Bradley, he did not favor the idea of a strong Marine Corps, regarding the gyrenes as fiscally and militarily redundant.

Here Eisenhower foreshadowed the strict financial conservatism he would try to follow during his two terms as president. Called back to active duty as Supreme Allied Commander, Europe, by Harry Truman in 1951, he showed an earnest commitment to balanced budgets and lower taxes. This meant, at the very least, holding the line in military spending, even with the Korean War on, and possibly supporting drastic military cuts, not only for NATO (always his primary military concern) but also across the board. Thus, for him, the Navy's supercarrier, strategy and tactics aside, was simply too expensive. This line of thinking included his own branch, as Ike advocated leaner infantry divisions and fewer heavy tanks.

The conservatism carried over into his presidency. "You can't provide security just with a checkbook," he chided Congress. He inherited a tripled annual military budget from Truman, $50 billion, cut this to $40 billion, and managed to hold roughly to that figure, with strenuous effort, for the rest of his time in office. "Reasonable defense posture is not won by juggling magic numbers—even with the air of great authority," he told the American people. "There is no wonderfully sure number of planes or ships or divisions—or billions of dollars—that can automatically guarantee security."

—These were wise words, ones that should have been well heeded by later administrations, and the president who had spent most of his adult life in the military was at his best when he thought of what military spending meant in a deeply divided Cold War world. On 16 April 1953, shortly after Stalin's death, the recently inaugurated Eisenhower addressed the American Society of Newspaper Editors and laid out for them the costs of the garrison state:

> Every gun that is made, every warship launched, every rocket fired signifies, in the final sense, a theft from those who hunger and are not fed, those who are cold and are not clothed. . . .
>
> The cost of one modern heavy bomber is this: a modern brick school in more than thirty cities.
>
> It is two electric power plants, each serving a town of sixty thousand population.
>
> It is two fine, fully equipped hospitals.
>
> It is some fifty miles of concrete highway.
>
> We pay for a single fighter plane with a half-million bushels of wheat.
>
> We pay for a single destroyer with new homes that could have housed more than eight thousand people. . . .
>
> *Is there no other way the world may live?*

These words, obviously, did not cheer the Joint Chiefs of Staff. From the beginning, Eisenhower's commitment to budgetary conservatism and his frank estimate of the appallingly inhumane nature of the Cold War overrode his military considerations. For fiscal 1954 he made substantial cuts in both the Army and Navy budgets; the latter went from the Korea-swollen $11.2 billion to $9.7 billion, and naval personnel were cut from 920,000 to 870,000. Navy and Air Force chieftains quickly went before Congress to demand more money.

The split between the Joint Chiefs and the president over money was nasty and public, despite the fact that Eisenhower had the Atomic Energy Commission turn over its control of nuclear weapons to the Defense Department. Ike, ever the conciliator, wanted the Chiefs to speak with one voice on military issues; what he got was internecine bickering, the uniformed equivalent of cats fighting in a sack. In the face of the president's direct order, the Army and Navy Chiefs continued to supply statistics to reporters "proving" that more money needed to be spent on conventional forces. For his part, Eisenhower kept harping at the Chiefs to present a single opinion. They only kept on bickering.

Every Chief agreed that the money allotted the other services was more than adequate but that his own branch was being shortchanged. Eisenhower wrote Swede Hazlett that he had no trouble blue-penciling Pentagon requests for more money because he knew the game so well, but "some day there is going to be a man sitting in my present chair who has not been raised in the military services and who will have little understanding of where slashes in their estimates can be made with little or no damage." Then, he continued, "if that should happen while we still have the state of tension that now exists in the world, I shudder to think of what could happen in this country."

Always, he tried to hold the line against the Pentagon's kicking and storming. His basic proposition was that a healthy economy needed a "proper" military posture and a balanced budget. By 1959 he was forced to bare knuckles, scolding the Joint Chiefs that "the military in this country is a tool and not a policy-making body; the Joint Chiefs are not responsible for high-level political decisions."

For their part, the generals and admirals wanted to be at the cutting edge of technological development, continuously demanding the largest nuclear arsenal, premium delivery systems, the best of everything. Eisenhower's difficulties holding the line (he was not always able to do so) were paralleled by his opposition to some specific force structures. At one time, for example, he proposed reducing the American contribution to NATO and wondered if the maintenance of the Sixth Fleet in the Mediterranean was necessary.[1]

Of course, this warrior-president was far from antimilitary; he supported a strong, *necessary* defense and made the customary presidential visits aboard naval ships. (A ride aboard the recently commissioned *Saratoga* produced a fanfaronade of napalm drops, missile launchings, and over-the-shoulder simulations of A-bomb tosses.) But he resisted what he felt was too much. He did not want nuclear carriers; they were not needed in a little war, he said, and they "would be useless in a big war." When the strategic missile revolution, including the Polaris boats, was underway, Eisenhower waspishly snapped, "How many times do we have to destroy Russia?"

His view was far broader and a degree wiser than that of most military men. He was demonstrably uneasy about the ever-accelerating pace of development of the new wonder weapons. "Science seems ready to confer upon us, as its final gift," he gloomily forecast, "the power to erase human life from this planet." He was first dismayed, then horrified, by the Cold War arms race. "This is not a way of life at all, in any true sense," he observed. "Under the cloud of threatening war, it is humanity hanging from a cross of iron." Nuclear weapons truly terrified him; perhaps for this reason he advised Atomic Energy Commission officials in 1953 to keep the public "confused" about different types of radiation hazards.

These were deeply held feelings that did not dissipate but only grew in intensity under the unrivaled pressures of his office. In his famous farewell address in 1961, he noted that the costs of building a huge garrison state to defend freedom threatened to deny that which was to be defended. He identified, in words that immediately passed into the lexicon, the "military-industrial complex," and he warned about its "unwarranted influence." He worried about the potential domination of the nation's intellectual life by this terrible Moloch. In retirement, he still insisted that "this combination [military, scientists, armaments industries] can be so powerful and the military machine so big it just has to be used."

The supreme irony of Eisenhower's presidency, given his heartfelt opinions, was his utter inability to do anything substantial about these concerns. At times he was knowledgeable and masterful within his administration, but his years in power were also characterized by considerable bureaucratic and intellectual confusion surrounding military policy. The Cold War was a novel experience for everyone, not least the military planners. During Ike's time in the Oval Office, Americans tried to come to grips with their increasing vulnerability in a bipolar nuclear world. Now, for the first time in their history, they could be attacked suddenly, and ruinously, from abroad. While they still exercised much of their traditional control over their destiny, Eisenhower's countrymen slowly came to realize that their safety "now depended in large part on the good behavior of the country they had identified as their mortal enemy."

The president and his administration found this problem—*guaranteeing* national security—to be insoluble. The best they could hope for was some set of policies that would minimize "national insecurity," and even this, certainly in the psychological sense, was not achieved. To compound the irony, Americans ended up paying for a military that was expected both to deter strategic nuclear warfare and to dampen limited conflict. Eventually, to this end, weapons budgets would be greatly increased, and Americans would be more vulnerable than ever.

Such dilemmas were probably intractable, certainly in the deep-freeze years of the Cold War, but Eisenhower was not helped by the occasional flares sent up by the men around him, men like Secretary of State John Foster Dulles, a messianic Cold Warrior who saw the U.S.-Soviet standoff as the Wars of Religion revisited. In 1956 Dulles informed an interviewer that "the ability to get to the verge without getting into war is the necessary art. If you cannot master it, you inevitably get into war. If you try to run away from it, if you are scared to go to the brink, you are lost."[2]

—Such "brinksmanship" terrified most intelligent people, and in truth the nuclear saber-rattling of some of his subordinates was not Eisenhower's way. But he could find no knife to cut the ever-tightening Gordian knot of bipolar nuclearism. Against an almost hysterical background of ideological conflict, the Cold War confrontation of incredibly lethal giants became, against his will and best efforts, the ultimate nightmare of his presidency.

☆

From the Navy's perspective, Eisenhower's relatively tight purse-strings were a major migraine, but the smothering bureaucracy of the Department of Defense was a disease. The number of people in the Office of the Secretary of Defense quadrupled in the 1950s, and although 80 percent of the senior civilians in the Pentagon had some military experience (not surprising, with a world war only a decade astern), this was no guarantee that naval requests would be rubber-stamped.

In fact, the Defense Department was moving obtrusively, in the manner of dominant bureaucracies, into the routine administrative activities of all the services. Sometimes these forays were stimulated by queries from congressional committees of the Bureau of the Budget, but always the results were centripetal, accreting power to the Pentagon. The never-ending demands for reports, interfering policy direction, and even detailed supervision rapidly drove Navymen, traditionally insular and suspicious of outsiders, up the wall. Eventually this scream of anguish was produced from a Navy captain: "The Navy itself, as a recognizable, distinct official entity, is threatened with eclipse by a burgeoning, all-powerful Department of Defense."

The department was indeed a monster, rapidly mushrooming beyond the control of even the most watchful secretaries and presidents. By the mid-fifties the department owned property valued at $160 billion and had become, by any yardstick, "the world's largest organization." In Eisenhower's eight years, more than $350 billion was spent for the military. By fiscal 1962, appropriations for defense, space, and international aid (the last two closely related to defense) gobbled up 63 cents of every budget dollar. Critics estimated that 77 cents of every budget dollar was spent for past wars, the Cold War, and preparations for future war.

By 1960 the military assets of the United States were triple the *combined* assets of United States Steel, American Telephone and Telegraph, Metropolitan Life Insurance, General Motors, and Standard Oil of New Jersey. The Defense Department's paid personnel were also triple the number of employees of all these corporations. In fiscal 1960, the department let $21 billion worth of contracts (86.4 percent of these without competitive bidding). More than 1400 retired officers, from the rank of O–4 up, were employed by the top one hundred corporations, many of which feasted at the rich table of military contracts. Overall, the department employed 3.5 million people, almost 1 million of them civilians, on an annual payroll of $12 billion.

—Here was the heart of the garrison state. By the end of the Eisenhower years, 7.5 million people depended directly on the military for their jobs. An estimated 25 percent to 35 percent of *all* economic activity in the country hinged on military spending. The country was prosperous, to be sure, and Ike's time would be fondly remembered in the tempestuous future—but part of the bargain was surely Faustian.

Eisenhower's choice to oversee the unprecedented mass that the Defense Department had become was Charles Wilson of General Motors. The president was fond of wealthy men, admiring them not only as what he believed to be self-made paragons but also as locker-room hail-fellows-well-met. His Cabinet choices were derided by the press as "eight millionaires and a plumber." The plumber, Secretary of Labor Martin Durkin—the only Democrat and only Catholic in the group—was soon gone, and Ike was left with his millionaires, of whom "Engine Charlie" was a conspicuous example.

Wilson reportedly was the highest paid executive in American business. Although Ike initally found him narrow and simplistic (these views would become even more negative), he still thought of Engine Charlie, with all that GM experience, as an obvious choice to run the vast Pentagon empire. "We both can't [run the department]," Eisenhower told Wilson, "and I won't do it. I was elected to worry about a lot of other things than the day-to-day operations of a department."

Unfortunately for Eisenhower's peace of mind, Engine Charlie's mouth often operated without a clutch. Before his confirmation hearing with the Senate Armed Services Committee he told reporters, "I've got a feeling that I'm going to be pretty pleased and surprised at how easily these boys can be handled."

The "boys" quickly dragged him over the coals to such an extent that Wilson stripped his gears, blurting that there was no conflict between his General Motors stock holdings (he had given up a $600,000 annual salary, plus perks, for the $22,000 paid the secretary of defense) and his prospective position: "For years I thought that what was good for our country was good for General Motors and vice versa."

—This one remark, somewhat distorted, dogged Wilson throughout his years in the Pentagon, but his foot-in-mouth proclivity was the least of his problems. He could never quite grasp the Pentagon's levers of control (if they existed). He "was never convinced that he knew enough about all the details of the military services to make any significant change in the distributions of the budget," recalled Admiral Charles Griffin. "He wasn't too sure of himself."

Against his better judgment, Eisenhower was soon intervening directly in the operation of the Defense Department. Vice Admiral Robert Salzer, then in the maw of the Pentagon bureaucracy, remembered "a very definite aura of Presidential involvement." The president could seldom find a good word to say about Wilson (this from a man who had let George Marshall be pilloried by Joseph McCarthy during the 1952 presidential campaign), and he would always deride the secretary to his White House staff. But Ike, the great conciliator, could scarcely bring himself to fire a man, particularly one of his own choosing; just as he never dismissed his vice president, the repellent and opportunistic Richard Nixon, so too he never rid himself of Engine Charlie.

Wilson was completely helpless trying to swim in the shark's tank of bitter interservice rivalries caused by new strategies, new weapons systems, and competition for the budget dollar. He was, for Eisenhower, by far "the most time-consuming Cabinet officer," forever dumping his problems into the president's lap. Ike, who of course knew more about the Pentagon than about his other departments, came to spend hours nattering around with its budget and manpower details. "I have got a man [Wilson] who is frightened to make decisions," he complained to Secretary of the Treasury George Humphrey. "I have to make them for him."

Engine Charlie survived until October 1957, when he at last resigned. His managerial talents, which may have been marginal at best, even with General Motors, cut no ice within the Pentagon. And managing was all he had been brought on board to do. "He didn't know anything, really, about foreign affairs," claimed Hanson Baldwin; "strategy he knew nothing about and paid very little attention to."

Wilson was indeed the millionaire as hail fellow, along with Dulles and Attorney General Herbert Brownell, talking back to Eisenhower and cracking jokes with him. But for the military, and especially the Navy, he was a cipher. Research, for example, mystified him. "Basic research," proclaimed Engine Charlie, "is when you don't know what you are doing." One of the Joint Chiefs called Wilson "the most uninformed man, and the most determined to remain so, that [sic] has ever been Secretary."[3]

☆

Eisenhower's Defense Department thus clanked along, riven with rivalries and suspicions, with no firm hand on the wheel. Ike *wanted* a strong secretary of defense. After his election victory, he asked Nelson Rockefeller to chair a committee aimed at reforming the department—clarifying lines of authority, giving the secretary more say in service missions, providing for more effective scientific and industrial planning, and ensuring maximum economies. Also, during his first months in office, the president issued a directive empowering the secretary to designate an appropriate service as his "executive agent" through which the secretary could issue operational directives to the field forces. In theory this would make the civilian secretary a deputy commander in chief who could directly control the operations of unified commands.

Paper lines of authority were one thing; the men who moved along them quite another. With Wilson in charge, and later under his successor, Thomas Gates, Jr., the Navy had little trouble avoiding civilian control, at least from within the Defense Department bureaucracy. The chief of naval operations acted as the secretary's executive agent, but that was where the theory ran aground. The men in uniform retained, for the time being, direction and control of fleet operations.

Increasingly dissatisfied with the Pentagon's independent-minded behavior, Eisenhower, accustomed to a single chain of command, criticized the Navy's bilateral system in which the secretary of the Navy managed nonmilitary matters while the chief of naval operations handled the military side. At first, however, the president could make little dent in a practice that the Navy claimed had proved its worth in two world wars.

The president kept prying away at the lid; the first product of his labors emerged with the suggestions of the Rockefeller Committee, Reorganization Plan 6 (1953). The secretary of defense was given the power to appoint six new assistant secretaries, which further undercut the independence of the service secretaries. Indeed, the last vestiges of the 1947 unification, in terms of three semiautonomous departments, were wiped out. Additionally, the secretary of defense gained the authority to name the director of the Joint Staff, a group that had been expanded after the 1949 reorganization from 100 to 210 officers.

A much-debated "single chain of command" strengthened the chairman of the Joint Chiefs but not the individual chiefs themselves. Eisenhower, with sour memories of the way he thought the Joint Chiefs had functioned during World War II and unimpressed with the conflicting advice he was getting from his own Chiefs, directed them to focus on *joint* issues, using an enlarged staff closely tied to the civilian side of the Office of the Secretary of Defense. The result was a deepening ambiguity about the roles of the individual Chiefs, because Reorganization Plan 6 minimized their command responsibilities.

This accretion of power on the civilian side of the Pentagon, coupled with Wilson's lack of leadership, still allowed the Navy to run free with its cherished bilateralism for a few more years. But the trend in Eisenhower's presidency was ominous for the admirals: more and more real authority, not only on paper but concerning nuts and bolts as well, was moving away from them in the direction of the civilians.

The Navy dug in its heels. The Gates Board (chaired by Under Secretary of the Navy Thomas Gates, Jr.) responded to Reorganization Plan 6 the following year. Gates and his men said flatly that the ongoing trend toward centralization within the Defense Department required no changes in the Navy's way of doing business. Bilateralism (the Navy used the term "bilinear") was defended as pragmatic, realistic, and ideally suited for the fleet. The concept simply meant that certain naval functions could best be handled by the Navy's civilians and that certain ones—particularly strategy and the movement of units—were the proper province of the uniforms.

The Gates Board observed that unlike its sister services, the Navy was an *inherently* divided and decentralized organization, held together by continuing "consultation" among its leaders, both uniformed and civilian. The board was attempting a high-wire act of exceptional delicacy and dexterity, trying to balance the new, augmented executive duties of the secretary of the Navy with the service's traditional decentralization. Under Reorganization Plan 6, the secretary and the chief of naval operations *both* had access to the secretary of defense and the president.

Confusion and conflict were practically guaranteed: if the secretary of the Navy delegated specific authority to the chief of naval operations, as Robert Anderson did with Mick Carney, the problem could be finessed, and bilateralism could proceed on its traditional way. But if a secretary claimed his statutory prerogatives, as Charles Thomas was prone to do, the question of who was the president's principal naval adviser (in this case, Thomas or Carney) was confused at best and could be complicated further if the chairman of the Joint Chiefs of Staff, like Arthur Radford, was a naval officer.

For the moment, Admiral Carney's adamant claim to his command and advisory duties as chief of naval operations (which had been codified in Public Law 432 of 5 March 1948) held sway. The Gates Board's proposals for some sort of collegial leadership by committee never flew.[4]

—So much depended on the men involved—on their tempers, experience, and views of the naval service. The Navy, and its vaunted traditions of bureaucratic independence, had been placed on notice. Things would be different the next time "reform" reared its head.

☆

Since the two service reorganizations of 1947 and 1949, the Navy Department had kept essentially the same internal organization. The secretary of the Navy remained the department's chief executive, and the chief of naval operations, double-hatted as a member of the Joint Chiefs of Staff, continued as the secretary's main adviser and "quasi-coordinator" of the bureaus. The secretary was thus required to direct eight people and their organizations: the Chief of Naval Operations and his office, the commandant of the Marine Corps, and the six bureau heads. Since Forrestal's time as secretary of the Navy, the chief of naval operations and the bureau heads were expected to "coordinate" their efforts.

There was, in short, still plenty of maneuvering room for an activist secretary of the Navy, especially given Engine Charlie's weak grasp on the Pentagon. The marching orders were clear. "Today," went one typical piece of naval puffery, "the citizen of a democracy fringing the Iron Curtain views seapower as a safeguard to his freedom. The communist glowers at it as a frustrator of his aggressive schemes."

Certainly the fleet was expected to be everywhere—to be ready, versatile, mobile, and able to meet any threat. Although the mighty armada of World War II had dwindled drastically, Eisenhower found when he took office that American naval power was far and away dominant on the world's oceans. Twenty-nine carriers of all types were in commission, joined by 4 battleships, 19 cruisers, 300 destroyers and destroyer escorts, 105 submarines, 115 minecraft, and a host of auxiliaries and amphibious warfare vessels. The Navy owned 13,000 aircraft of all types. Over 100 combatants were under construction, a figure that did not include the experimental, revolutionary *Nautilus*, and 550 more were in the Reserve Fleet.

—This was the Cold War Navy. In 1953 the fleet operated about 1130 vessels of all types, a number that had been constant since the end of the Korean upsurge in 1951. The Eisenhower budgeting plans were, however, already forcing difficult choices. The combined cost of the first three *Forrestals*, for example, devoured about 20 percent of the total shipbuilding and modernization funds. The Navy, as the vice chief of naval operations, Wu Duncan, noted, was faced with a policy of "dubious temporizing."

A fleet that was expected to be ready, versatile, and mobile had to be seaworthy, and corners were being cut everywhere—in the yards, in maintenance, in upkeep, in overhaul. Even vessels that had been "modernized" usually kept their most important internal organs—their propulsion machinery—and these organs were under serious strain. In the words of one financial analyst, only eight years after V-J Day the American Navy was "drifting toward obsolescence."[5]

Wu Duncan had hit the nail on the head. There were problems and prospects aplenty for any secretary of the Navy willing to take a few turns and heave on the line. Unfortunately, the office continued to feature the same revolving door that had characterized the previous presidency. Harry Truman had had four secretaries in less than eight years—Forrestal, John Sullivan, Rowboat Matthews, and Dan Kimball. Eisenhower, in his two terms, would have four more.

Ike's initial choice was Robert Anderson, a leading Texas Democrat-for-Eisenhower who was chummy with Democratic politicos of the likes of Sam Rayburn and Lyndon Johnson. Anderson was a farm boy, born in central Texas in 1910, and he knew nothing about the sea. "I have never paced the deck of a battleship," he frankly admitted on being selected. "I come from Texas where it doesn't even rain."

—But Anderson was no Rowboat Matthews. The new secretary was intelligent, patient, and urbane, a thoughtful moderate on most issues. "A very religiously proper individual" was how Vice Admiral Bernard Austin (who worked for him) described Anderson. His record showed head-of-the-class at the University of Texas Law School (1932), high school teaching, a stint in the state Senate, and various state offices. Meticulously dressed and groomed, alert-eyed behind wire-rimmed glasses, he limped slightly from a childhood bout with polio and thus missed uniformed service. He spent the war as a civilian adviser in the War Department and became a member of numerous boards and businesses in the years following.

Like his pals Rayburn and Johnson, Anderson had matriculated in the rough school of Texas politics. He was a man who knew people and who had a fairly good handle on the political process; he prepared himself for his new task by nightly readings of the contents of his stuffed briefcase, and his confirmation hearings consisted of three minutes of perfunctory questioning.

The actual duties of office, he found, were less perfunctory. First came the hot potato of the Rickover promotion issue. Anderson, who had never paced the deck of a battleship, still knew a political land mine when he stumbled across one, and he speedily arranged for Rickover's special board. Next came the annual budget battle. The new secretary did not protest overmuch at the Navy's slightly reduced slice of the pie. The fiscal 1954 budget held $9.5 billion for Anderson's shop, the smallest total since 1951.

Although he had to be prodded, Anderson eventually moved decisively to abolish racial segregation at southern naval installations. He tramped through naval shipyards, inspected the naval base at Port Lyautey, and cruised with the Sixth Fleet. He also tinkered with the department's organization table, moving the commandant of the Marine Corps from a position analogous to that of the bureau chiefs to one on the level with those of the assistant secretaries.

Of greater importance, Anderson saw early on that, even in the bipolar nuclear age, the superpowers might still be forced to rely on conventional weapons, particularly in the case of a nuclear standoff. He accordingly urged a military policy based on both conventional and nuclear capabilities, which of course was right up the Navy's alley. With his continuation of bilateralism within the department, he made friends with the service's senior officers.

Anderson was developing, from the Navy's perspective, into a Good Guy—but he was in office for little more than a year. His performance as secretary was uniformly praised. Arthur Radford called him a "man who instills confidence in his subordinates and associates by his dedicated effort," while Mick Carney, who called a spade a spade, described him as a "considerate gentleman but 'his own man' in [his] approach to all problems." These comments smacked a bit of the fitness report style, but Captain Slade Cutter, never one to mince words, praised Anderson as "brilliant."

Anderson's brief tenure was the result of the increasing weight of the Pentagon bureaucracy pressing down on the Navy Department. Just as the Texan was really getting his sea legs he departed—bumped upstairs to be

Wilson's deputy secretary of defense. As in the case of Forrestal, if a secretary of the Navy was any good—he was soon gone.

"The Navy is a peculiar institution," Dan Kimball had once mused. "The Admirals tell you nothing, but they sure know to to make a Secretary feel good." Part of Radford's and Carney's remarks was surely in this vein, but when the Navy lost a political smoothie and adept manager like Robert Anderson, there was real loss as well.

His replacement, Charles Thomas, knew the Navy intimately. Born in 1897 in Truman's home town of Independence, Missouri, Thomas grew up in Los Angeles and was educated at the University of California at Berkeley and at Cornell. In 1916, still a student, he joined the Naval Reserve, his heart set on aviation training. Just as he reported to San Diego for Basic Flight School, World War I ended and he was demobilized. But his navalist seeds had been planted.

During the interwar years he developed into an entrepreneur, working in investments and commerce in the desert Southwest. Shortly after Pearl Harbor, he came to Washington as a special assistant to Artemus Gates, the assistant secretary of the Navy for air. Within a year he was Forrestal's assistant, handling aircraft procurement and inventory management for the rapidly expanding wartime fleet. Late in the war he did a detailed survey of the Navy's enormous base complex in the western Pacific, traveling thirty-three thousand miles in the process. Thomas proved to be intelligent and energetic, a thoroughly capable executive. After the war his townsman Truman awarded him the Presidential Medal of Merit, the highest civilian award for wartime service.

Thomas was certainly bipartisan enough, but he was also a dedicated Republican moderate. Ever alert for new opportunities, he went into civilian avaiation in postwar southern California and prospered during the explosive growth of the Los Angeles basin. As a politician he was always the well-meaning amateur, but he was an early supporter of Eisenhower and was not loath to use his own vivid personality and his pocketbook to help not only local Republicans (among them an unknown Navy veteran named Richard Nixon) but also, eventually, the general himself. In 1952, Thomas helped raise almost half a million dollars for Eisenhower's successful California campaign.

Such dedication had its rewards, and the new president appointed Thomas under secretary of the Navy. After relieving Anderson, Thomas devoted most of his time to managing the Navy Department. He was content, for the most part, to let his service chiefs, first Carney and then Arleigh Burke, run the operations side, but he proved to be far more jealous of his prerogatives than Anderson had been.

The secretary became particularly involved in personnel issues. He was on-scene at the *Bennington* tragedy in a matter of hours, visiting every injured man. He pressed for better pay and allowance. He interested himself in the higher-ups, too, seeking younger blood among the leadership. Horacio Rivero, who went on to four stars, was a prime example, selected for Flag Plot at age forty-five.

Bald, sharp-nosed, incessantly active, Thomas was usually studiously polite. But he could turn caustic in a hurry, especially over what he regarded as bullheaded stupidity or mistakes. "He had very little faith in the military," observed his aide, Vice Admiral Andrew Jackson. "He didn't trust anybody with a uniform on."

And they did not always have to wear a uniform. Thomas blasted the contractors on *Nautilus* when she developed teething problems on her initial trials. But most of his impatient wrath was reserved for admirals. He griped that the deputy chief of naval operations for air was not displaying "aggressive thinking." After some Naval Academy entrance exams were compromised, he delivered a stern warning to the chief of naval personnel. Thomas's reach was far indeed; he even reprimanded the Navy inspector general for slackness in investigating a stevedoring dispute on Guam.

At a higher level, Thomas oversaw a $7 billion buildup of the navy's stockpile of strategic war materials (mostly nuclear arms). He fought valiantly, and without much success, against the remorseless budgetary pruning of personnel (800,000 in 1954, 682,000 in 1955). Always he wanted more—money, machines, men—and he supported, so long as he felt his prerogatives unthreatened, the Navy's bilateral organizational concept. He even spoke wistfully of razing the hoary Main Navy Building and housing the department's functions under one roof. (Main Navy, an architectural nightmare, would not disappear until 1968 and, as to one roof, the department was spread out all over Washington.)

Thomas also attempted, as Anderson had, to eradicate the Navy's segregation patterns, but with limited success. He also had to try, somehow, to stem the leakage of junior officers and experienced petty officers into civilian life. He got reenlistment incentives increased and was one of the first Navy civilians to realize that family problems were a crucial component of sailor morale. His lasting interest in naval aviation was also evident; while never trying to preempt the Air Force's strategic role, he was an adamant advocate of the supercarriers. "Any enemy who launches an attack against a modern carrier task force with its mobility, aircraft, new missiles and other equipment," he told a Senate subcommittee, "will be attacking the toughest target in the world."

Like Anderson, Thomas was a zealous Cold Warrior and an adherent of conventional forces. "The sum total of little aggressions," he warned, "could bring total defeat as surely as the loss of a global struggle." Technology was his answer: "The age of technology has come to sea and the consequences are truly colossal." "To retain the obsolete," he chanted, "is to invite defeat." He believed wholeheartedly in the critical importance of the Cold War technological race and worried that America was "falling behind the Commmunist world in quantitative training of scientists." Military power, he argued, was probably the most important aspect of national power, and technological advance was at the root of military power.

—With civilians like Thomas in charge—intent, capable, committed to the Cold War Navy and its technology—the Navy's contribution to international polarization not only supported the continuance of *Pax Americana*. In the words of one critic, such impassioned advocacy also produced a full-fledged *Pax Americana Technocratica.* [6]

☆

Technology, particularly its cutting edge, had always held allure, especially for impressionable young males. When Arthur Radford was fourteen, back in 1910, an uncle took him to see an international air show at Chicago's Grant Park. Many of the daring heroes of the air were there—Americans, Frenchmen, Englishmen—all cavorting aloft in their rickety crates. Young Arthur was enchanted with the planes and their designs, which in fact were only a short remove from chaos.

Some of the planes had wheels, some used skids; some engines "pushed," some "pulled," some seemed to do nothing at all; the number of wings, not to mention their size and shape, appeared to be based on the whim of the designer. The French exhibited an umbrellalike kite, the English offered a bewildering assortment of models, and the leading Americans, the Wright brothers and Glenn Curtiss, were represented as well.

Arthur was disturbed when the foreigners carried off most of the prizes (his chauvinism was virtually ingrained), but the machines, and their pilots, held him in thrall. In his mind these early aviators became avatars, god-heralds of the life he wanted to live. He was, in a word, completely smitten by the very *idea* of flying. Rapidly he collected everything he could about the birdmen, covering the walls of his bedroom with pictures of planes and aerial daredevils.

When Arthur arrived in Annapolis a little more than two years later, after schooling in Grinnell, Iowa, he was a precocious sixteen, still dreaming about being an airman. Even as he crammed his way through Bobby's War College that spring of 1912 (Hyman Rickover would follow him at Werntz's six years later), he would duck out every chance he got and scoot down to the Severn, where he could gaze at an early, cumbersome symbol of naval aviation—a lone Curtiss seaplane tied to its moorings.

Young Radford was so eager to fly that he would bail out of bed before sunrise to get to the siding, impatiently waiting for the plane's godly lieutenant to show up. The youngster would hang around, watching the maintenance procedures and hoping for the invitation that never came, to take a ride in an aircraft.

Annapolis was not interested in instructing midshipmen in naval aviation. There were no aeronautics courses per se, nothing to feed his desires. Radford began running way back in the pack at the Academy, a gangly, callow kid who never had much punch with the books. But his dream, for a naval commission and for flight, was fierce to the point of obsession; each year he inched up in the academic standings until, in 1916, he graduated in the upper half of his class (fifty-ninth out of 178).

Only a corporal's guard was being taken into the Navy's new "flying program," so Ensign Radford went the way of all fresh-minted braid—to sea. He served aboard *South Carolina* and *Chicago*, with early stints as flag secretary and aide. After World War I the Navy sent out its first call for Academy graduates to take flight training at Pensacola. Most of the Navy's fliers in the war had, like James Forrestal, been hastily commissioned Reservists. Now a flight path was being prepared for a few selected Regulars.

Radford jumped at the chance and would have been in the first class out of flight school except that his ship was off Central America when the group convened. But he made the second, and in 1920 he gained his golden wings, Naval Aviator 2896. Thus he embarked on what could justly be called the great love of his life. For the next two decades he lived naval aviation, not marrying until 1939.

Fledglings flew anything and everything in the 1920s. Radford rode seaplanes off battleship turret catapults, took up any land plane he could get into the air, and coached frightened students frozen at their biplane controls in the skies over Pensacola. He was part of the team that worked up the reconverted *Langley*, the Navy's first "carrier," and aboard the Old Covered Wagon he received his landing qualifications in 1923.

Naval aviation was a most dangerous trade, particularly in those early years; Radford's friends and Pensacola classmates were dying or being injured in droves. Flying biplane fighters, he learned his craft inside and out, profiting from his mistakes and those of others. By 1931 he was in command of the famed Fighting One, flying off *Saratoga*.

These fighter jocks were an elite, as they were well aware—none more so than Arthur Radford. Always he was curious and daring, pushing the outer envelope of this exciting and lethal new technology. He practiced aerial gunnery, in-flight refueling, and aerobatics; went aloft in balloons; tested parachutes—anything to improve his first love, make her ever more perfect in his eyes.

And he rose in his profession, even as he developed into a vocal protagonist for naval air power. He was not alone; men such as Jack Towers and Marc Mitscher were carrying the standard too, and by the 1930s some naval aviators were beginning to rise into the decision-making ranks of the Navy. Radford was not that high, not yet, but he was committed, active, and mouthy—to a battleship admiral, one of those aviation "zealots."

Cycling in and out of Washington on tours of duty, always thinking about his true love, Radford became convinced that seaplanes, those ungainly descendants of that lone Curtiss back on the Severn, while still useful for long-range reconnaissance and transportation, could never provide an adequate offensive punch at sea. Only carrier-borne strike aircraft could do that. *Lexington* and *Saratoga*, the converted battle-cruiser hulls allowed by the Washington Disarmament Conference (1921–1922), were the experimental platforms for these ideas. As the Depression-era carriers came off the ways—first little *Ranger*, then *Yorktown* and *Enterprise*, finally *Wasp* and *Hornet*—Radford and his fellow aviators fostered new techniques and pleaded for more powerful planes, preaching the gospel of naval aviation.

They were looking at the vast spaces of the Pacific, and at the startling growth of Japanese carrier aviation. The months before Pearl Harbor found Radford a captain in the naval outback, commanding a sleepy air station on Trinidad. With war, he was placed in charge of the Navy's aviation training. He went at the job like a crazed lumberjack, felling every obstacle that got in his way. He began with a rigorous preflight program at a handful of universities. He set up inland centers hundreds of miles from tidewater. Along the way he got women integrated into aviation ratings. By 1943 Radford's schools were turning out thousands of superbly trained and conditioned naval aviators, coming through a pipeline that the Japanese, for all their head start, could no longer match. By early 1944 Japanese carrier air was beginning to meet its master, and much of the reason lay with Arthur Radford.

Bellicose, exceptionally well-organized, fixated on aircraft carriers (although he was never to command one or, for that matter, any naval ship), Radford at last got two stars and the seagoing assignment he wanted: at Tarawa he commanded a Task Group. He organized and trained the Navy's first night-fighter teams (Butch O'Hare, the hero of Coral Sea, was killed accidentally by his own comrades on one of these missions) and was awarded the Distinguished Service Medal. He proved himself again and again—at Tarawa, Iwo Jima, Okinawa—an exceptional combat commander.

After the war, Radford's stentorian promotion of naval aviation spearheaded the rise of the "carrier admirals," of whom he was the most conspicuous example. He supported service unification, although he testified against the original draft for a "merger." He very much feared that the Air Force wanted control of naval aviation, and he fought the slightest indication of that direction with every weapon he had. As commander in chief, Pacific, and head of the Pacific Fleet, his no-holds-barred remarks during the rebellion in gold braid—"He was really the guiding light of that operation, the only senior officer who was," avowed Arleigh Burke—marked him publicly, after Towers's retirement and Mitscher's death, as the premier champion of naval air power in all its guises; for the Air Force, with its parochial claims to strategic predominance, he was Public Enemy No. 1.

Radford had developed one other great passion, in addition to naval aviation. He had become a virulent anti-Communist, an ardent "Asia firster" who told a congressional committee in 1952 that Red China must be destroyed, even at the cost of a fifty-year war on the Asian mainland. His strategic analysis included the Soviet Union, where he saw a "three-pronged threat" that was military, political-economic, and psychological, but his military background and imagination were in the Pacific—where his beloved carriers could roam.

In his mid-fifties now, he looked "exactly as a four-star admiral should look:" leathery skin, jutting jaw, steel-gray hair, level-eyed stare. He was an awesome, commanding, unforgettable presence, a man so meticulous that, according to his aides, he could reach into his dresser and pack his bags in the dark. He seldom smiled (perhaps embarrassed by his irregular teeth), but he could be awkwardly charming and, when not blistering the bulkheads with his formidable brand of invective, could disarm both military and civilian alike. Captain Steve Jurika, who knew him well, called Radford a "smooth, suave, personable extrovert." Physically he seemed hewn of granite (his numerous critics charged that this configuration was true of him mentally as well); at the age of fifty-seven, as curious as ever about new technology, he strapped on a single-seat F-80 Shooting Star—and flew.

As the Korean War flared, he supervised the quickstep American buildup in the Pacific, becoming convinced in the process that only a strong military hand could clean out Asia's Communist infection. He decided that the tragedy of Korea, like the unseemly squabble over service unification, was the result of too much civilian meddling. (During the unification battle, General Eisenhower got such a bitter taste of Radford's temper—always cold, cutting, and insistent—that he swore never again to sit at the same council table with him.) Liberals saw Radford as a menacing militarist symbol who could be, in the context of the Cold War, infinitely more dangerous than the enemy he so detested.

Radford was at the Wake Island Conference on 15 October 1950 and supported MacArthur's plan to crush any Chinese intervention in Korea by bombing their Manchurian bases. He was disgusted with Truman's creation of an enemy sanctuary north of the Yalu—more civilian meddling. He sailored on with the war, feeling his hands tied by ridiculous civilian restraints, but he believed that his public pronouncements, on both air power and communism, had canceled his chances for any other duty assignment. He expected to go from his flower-banked headquarters on Makalapa Heights into retirement.

When President-elect Eisenhower, paying off a campaign promise, went to Korea in November 1952, Radford joined him at Iwo Jima. Here Raddy was on his best behavior, and Eisenhower not only sat at the same table with him but also decided to name him chairman of the Joint Chiefs of Staff when Omar Bradley's tour ended in August 1953. When Pacific strategy was discussed, according to a junior officer, Radford "could take the general and lead him around by the nose."

—Perhaps Ike saw in Radford the same type of gruff old sea dog he had so admired in Sir Andrew Cunningham—you might not like what you got, but what you got came straight and with the bark on. At any rate, during the rest of the trip Radford and Charles Wilson, who had come along, spent the time arguing with Eisenhower for an Asia-first policy. Eisenhower, whose experience was as solidly European as Radford's was Pacific-oriented, countered that NATO was the key to American defense and that a strong Europe would be essential to Asian stability.[7]

Eisenhower chose Radford not because of the admiral's geopolitical and strategic views but in spite of them. He told Radford, in no uncertain terms, that as chairman he should issue a statement divorcing himself "from exclusive identification with the Navy." Radford's loyalty would be given to national defense and to the Defense Department; henceforth he was to be be "champion of *all* the services, governed by the single criterion of what is best for the United States."

Radford thus came on board, after William Leahy (whose relationship with both Roosevelt and Truman had always been more personal than statutory) the second of four postwar Navymen to chair the Joint Chiefs; Thomas Moorer would follow in the seventies, William Crowe in the eighties. At Eisenhower's behest the Joint Chiefs immediately undertook a basic strategic study, looking at nuclear options, service roles, and military aid, a study punctuated on 12 August 1953 when the Soviets exploded their first hydrogen bomb. The Chiefs urged a continuation of force levels and a $35 billion annual military budget.

Radford, to the amazement of his critics, *did* heed Eisenhower's marching orders; as chairman his views broadened, indeed taking in the entire world beyond the Pacific. His bashing of the Air Force's strategic bombing concepts dwindled to the vanishing point; indeed, in people like Curtis LeMay, the boss of the Strategic Air Command, he found brothers under the skin. The fight for naval aviation was won anyway; the supercarriers were coming on-line, carrier air was moving into all-jet wings and nuclear ordnance, and naval aviation's place in the national arsenal was assured. But here, in the highest military position in the gift of the United States, Admiral Arthur Radford's venomous anticommunism got full play, in the process scaring the daylights out of many.

Raddy was never a loose cannon on the deck of American military policy, but there were times when he was not securely bolted down, either. On five occasions during 1954, the admiral recommended that Eisenhower intervene in France's Indochinese imbroglio, even to the point of using atomic bombs against China. He was not alone; some of the Joint Chiefs, almost the entire National Security Council, and many of the upper echelon in Dulles's State Department were saying the same thing.

Force was the answer, Radford believed. He urged the nuclear weapon first in April, as the French struggled in vain to hold Indochina at Dien

Bien Phu; again in May, as the badly positioned fortress fell; a third time in June, when the French feared that the Red Chinese air force was about to enter the Indochina War; fourthly in September, as the Red Chinese began to shell the offshore islands of Quemoy and Matsu; and finally in November, when China announced that captured American fliers would be given prison terms.

To his lasting credit, Eisenhower resisted these suggestions, but such moderation did nothing to change Radford's mind. He hated communism to the core of his being. "We cannot trust the Russians on . . . anything," he said. "The Communists have broken their word with every country with which they ever had an agreement." The same thing went for the Chinese, because in Radford's view the Communist world was a monolithic, aggressive giant. If there was to be some kind of mutual disarmament among the Cold War powers—the sort of thing Eisenhower was questing for with ill-thought-out notions like the "open skies" proposal—then Radford insisted on an ironclad inspection setup. In the meantime, Americans should keep their powder dry—even their nuclear powder.[8]

Where the Communist menace was concerned, Arthur Radford was pure obsidian. The story went around Washington that the journalist Fletcher Knebel had gone to the Pentagon for an interview, come under the icy, unblinking stare, and listened to Raddy hold forth on the world's problems and the appropriate solutions.

—Thoroughly shaken, Knebel had returned home, to immediately begin writing. Not on the interview. On a story about an impending military takeover of the United States—*Seven Days in May*.

☆

"Radford's plans were as sharp and clear as the designs of a new-model Cadillac," said Engine Charlie Wilson in a characteristic phrase. "You could draw up a budget on them, and you would know precisely where you were going." In terms of general American strategy, Radford believed that a strategic reserve should be concentrated on the North American continent. Local defense, in both Europe and Asia, should be left to the forces on the spot. And Asia, both he and Wilson believed, was the pivot on which the Cold War would turn.

Bradley, the previous chairman of the Joint Chiefs, was the embodiment of NATO, the containment idea, and limited war. Radford personified nuclear saber-rattling, Asia, and sea and air power. Yet the new chairman, with Eisenhower as the moderate court of last resort, was never to *make* American military policy. He *contributed* more than his share, however, and thus did his part to shape the much-hyped strategic dynamism of the new administration.

Radford's contributions lay in the across-the-board military emphasis aimed at the defeat, not just the containment, of communism. When he felt he could speak even more bluntly, after his retirement in 1957, he called for "total victory over the Communist system—not stalemate." His ideas had not changed, only his situation. "The massive power providentially given us," he informed the Daughters of the American Revolution, "is frustrated by an abstract idealism that is apart from reality and does not recognize the basic conditions for the effective use of power."

Raddy was sure he had the handle on the "basic conditions." If he was more rigidly doctrinaire than some, he was also the archetypal Cold Warrior. This individual came in both military and civilian guises (the future would show that some civilians could be both more doctrinaire and more blood-thirsty than those in the military); believed that international communism was monolithic, expansionist, and evil; and generally regarded anything even remotely tinged with pink as akin to the Black Death.

Many Navymen, like Radford, insisted on *action*. "The minute we be-came satisfied with the status quo," warned the admiral, "we have started down the road to defeat. . . ." *Defeat*; for the victors of World War II the word, the very thought, was unbearable. Admiral Felix Stump, Radford's relief in the Pacific, later told a Los Angeles audience that "World War III has already started, and we are deeply involved in it." Stump called for the use of tactical nuclear weapons if necessary. Rear Admiral Chester Ward, formerly the judge advocate general of the Navy, loudly opposed what he categorized as any "priority on peace." "The side will win," he predicted, "which uses the most effective weapons and uses them first."

Radford, Stump, and Ward, all of whom made such public remarks from retirement, after they had ceased to affect policy, were *not* the lunatic fringe. They were, instead, indicative of the Cold War mind-set, a reflexive militance that was not entirely military but was shared by much of the civilian leadership as well. But there were extremes. Some naval stations, overzealously following what were perceived to be their cues, set up pro-grams for lectures on subjects such as anticommunism and "Americanism" (whatever that was). "Operation Abolition," at the Sand Point Naval Air Station, even wormed its way into the Seattle school system. At Glenview Naval Air Station the anti-Communist crusade, which corralled base per-sonnel, Naval Reservists, and civilians from the Chicago area, preached a line indistinguishable from the right-wing rantings of the John Birch Society. The Navy's "Project Alert" put on a five-day school of anti-Communism in Los Angeles, the major theme of which was that a "no win" policy in the Cold War meant defeat.

"If we *think* the enemy is about to strike us," cried Ward, "we should strike first." In Chicago, naval units cosponsored a rally entitled "Peace Is War!" The militant mind-set, at this point, clearly capered into Never-Never Land, and yet the unabashed militance and paranoic fears, despite the best efforts of Eisenhower and other strategic moderates within the administra-tion, were reflected to a certain degree in American strategy.[9]

As chairman, Radford flatly stated that, given the obvious Communist threat, the military had to plan for every possible contingency, ranging from limited through conventional to all-out nuclear war. Against the opposition of the Army chief of staff, Matthew Ridgway, the admiral pressed for "more bang for the buck"—a crude but effective argument that anticipated using nuclear weapons whenever they were "technically advantageous." By this means the military budget could be dramatically cut and manpower needs lessened as well.

Ridgway well knew the value of ground troops in conventional war from his experience in Korea; he was no convert to Radford's idea. But Secretary of the Treasury George Humphrey was, believing that only American nuclear striking power "kept peace in the world." *More bang for the buck*—"All the rest of these soldiers and sailors and submarines and everything else," Humphrey went on, "comparatively speaking, you could drop in the ocean, and it wouldn't make too much difference."

Nothing more measured Radford's increased distance from his beloved Navy (and naval aviation) than his support of this new strategy, which was bound to elevate the Air Force at the expense of the other services. Radford believed in maximizing the American nuclear threat, and he always opposed nuclear test-ban negotiations.

The increased reliance on strategic air power was codified in NSC 162/2, adopted 30 October 1953. The document stated that the United States had to maintain a strong military posture, "with emphasis on the capability of inflicting massive retaliatory damage by offensive striking power." Thus "massive retaliation" entered the strategic lexicon. "In the event of hostilities," 162/2 summed up, "the United States will consider nuclear weapons to be as available for use as other munitions." Any battlefield, anywhere, could become a nuclear battlefield.

This policy inaugurated Eisenhower's "New Look," reducing military spending and force levels while relying on strategic power, particularly that provided by long-range nuclear bombers. The Army, as Ridgway had feared, took the big hits, losing almost 30 percent of its division strength. The Navy, with Anderson applying bandages to the cuts as best he could, lost only a handful of frontline combatants, but the fleet had to say good-bye to almost 100,000 sailors. The Air Force was the big gainer, planning an increase from 115 to 137 wings and adding 30,000 men. The new strategy owed much to Radford's ideas—reducing American forces overseas and backing up allies with stateside mobile reserves. The Air Force would act as the primary deterrent against Communist attack, and George Humphrey was pleased with an annual military budget that, at first, was lessened by $4 billion, to $31 billion.

Essentially, Eisenhower, in accepting NSC 162/2 and the accompanying budgetary arguments, had chosen a strategic policy of deterrence rather than one of containment, but the thunderclouds of nuclear war only grew more ominous. The policy's backers hoped that limited wars would be deterred by the Big Threat. But much of this deterrence strategy, especially when paced by the drum-beating about "massive retaliation," was deliberately ambiguous and contributed to *insecurity*. To his discredit, Ike thought the ambiguity beautiful; no one "would undertake to say exactly what we would do under all that variety of circumstances," he said.[10]

—Thus the balance of terror between the superpowers was twisted in the most positive direction possible. "All that variety of circumstances" was what primarily concerned the Navy, and its new chief of naval operations.

☆

"Two years isn't very long to get your stamp on anything," Bill Fechteler wistfully recalled—but two years was all he had. Since Ernest King, no postwar chief of naval operations had served longer. Fechteler had tried to maintain Forrest Sherman's course and speed, but the office fitted neither his personality nor what ambition he had.

Robert Anderson assured Fechteler that while Eisenhower, in bringing Radford in as chairman of the Joint Chiefs, wanted a housecleaning, Fechteler's "performance of duty had not been criticized by anyone in any respect." Soft words, but the exit door was open. Fechteler asked for his successor's old command, Allied Forces Southern Europe, and he spent his final three uniformed years in the Neapolitan sunshine, retiring in 1956.

They had been Naval Academy classmates, Bill Fechteler and Mick Carney—lifelong friends. This was always Carney's way—loyal, tough, persistent to the end (he would live to be almost one hundred). As Robert Bostwick Carney, he had been born to the Navy in 1895 in Vallejo, California, where his father, Lieutenant Commander Robert Emmett Carney, was stationed. He was only seventeen when he entered the Academy in 1912, fresh out of Central High in Philadelphia—an older man to his classmates Radford and Fechteler, who was also a mere sixteen.

Jug-eared, with a prematurely wizened pixie face, the slightly built Carney got along quietly during his years at Annapolis. But his natural reserve could not conceal either his ambition or his urge to command. He graduated with distinction in 1916 and, like Radford and Fechteler, went straight to the fleet. He was aboard *Fanning*, a destroyer stationed on the Queenstown patrols out of Ireland during World War I, and was a part of her sinking of *U-58* and the capture of the German crew. He also married young, in 1918, and fathered two children.

The interwar period brought Carney a typical Blackshoe melange of assignments, though his poor eyesight precluded his going Radford's way. He taught navigation at the Academy. ("What a wonderful guy," one of his students remembered.) As he rose in rank, he commanded no fewer than four destroyers, learned his weapons as gun boss aboard the cruiser *Cincinnati*, and served as exec on *California*. His shore tours, in addition to the

Annapolis duty, included a useful stint in the Office of the Secretary of the Navy.

By 1941 he was a captain, nothing very special but definitely running with his class. In February, under Vice Admiral Arthur Bristol's command, he helped organize a special surface and air escort force for convoys that, until April 1942, guarded more than 2600 ships in the North Atlantic while losing only 6. There were never enough escorts to go around, however, and Carney learned to make do with what he had. Bristol moved him up, from operations officer to chief of staff, and he earned the Distinguished Service Medal for his work on his demanding specialty, antisubmarine warfare.

With the war, Carney got the Pacific. He commanded the light cruiser *Denver* in the Solomon Islands and was twice decorated for heroism. He was upped to Flag Plot on 26 July 1943, still indistinguishable among the harvest of new admirals produced by combat.

His big break came with assignment as Bill Halsey's chief of staff. With the Third Fleet, Carney was in the thick of planning and executing many of the major operations of the Pacific war. At Leyte Gulf, he won the Navy Cross. His performance as a planner (his last wartime task was ginning up the first proposed landing on the Japanese mainland) was superb. Carney stood at Halsey's side aboard *Missouri* as the Japanese surrendered.

Three stars came a year later. Carney served as deputy chief for logistics, earning a reputation as a capable budgeteer during inordinately tough times for the Navy. Then he moved to command the Second Fleet in the Mediterranean. He was among the top echelon now, a man with a distinguished combat record who had proved he could also drive a desk, his burning ambition not yet satisfied. (He watched the rise and fall of his fellow admirals like a seer peering at tarot cards.)

In 1950, four stars on his collar, he became commander in chief of U.S. Forces, Eastern Atlantic and Mediterranean—the cumbersomely titled predecessor of NATO's naval command. There he impressed General Eisenhower enormously, so much so that he was named to the joint command in Naples. There he was when the summons came from the new president to relieve Fechteler.

Mick Carney was the fifth chief of naval operations in six years. He had served for ten years at flag rank before assuming his new post, longer than any of the chiefs before him. Although his appointment was unexpected, stemming almost solely from his association with Eisenhower, there were no doubts about either his competence or his experience. He was a veteran planner and administrator who knew well the entrails of the Pentagon bureaucracy, a "brilliant man" who could dictate finely crafted speeches off the top of his head, an officer with "very high standards." He could not tolerate confusion and abominated things done backwards, exploding about a "tonsillectomy through the rectum." His humor was honed to a sharp edge. When Joe Taussig, Jr., as a young naval officer wanting to do things the right way, asked for his daughter's hand in marriage, Carney immediately asked if that was all he wanted.

Carney's major problem was tailoring the Navy for the New Look. While he was a Blackshoe and a licensed gunclubber, he had seen firsthand what carrier air power could do and had indeed planned numerous air strikes with Halsey. He was thus quick to argue that the nation's offensive striking power should include carriers, and he got the rest of the Joint Chiefs to endorse this policy early in 1954. Under Carney the Navy responded to NSC 162/2 by separating itself from the concept of massive atomic striking power as much as possible. Eventually, by 1958, the service would argue that carrier forces were ideal for "limited war"—"the nation's primary cutting tool for that purpose."[11]

Carney was convinced that Americans had to "hedge our strategic bets;" his view of the New Look was broad and pragmatic as well as forward-looking. The new chief created an important ad hoc agency, the Long-Range Objectives Group (OP-93, in Navyese), designed specifically to help the Navy weather political and planning crises. OP-93 was the son of OP-23, where Carney had worked alongside Arleigh Burke during the Navy's trials in the B-36–supercarrier controversy, and both Carney and Burke, with vivid memories of the emotional swordplay that had flared then, wanted updated, closely reasoned studies of the nation's naval needs.

—To this end OP-93, small and lean but headed by a rear admiral reporting directly to the chief of naval operations, was given marching orders to study "subjects of interest to the Navy for the period from the present extending through approximately 10-15 years in the future," including tasks and responsibilities, technology, composition of forces, and optimum direction of weapons development. A small group of civilian scientists under contract with the Massachusetts Institute of Technology was also brought under OP-93's umbrella; called the Naval Warfare Analysis Group, this outfit was to provide au courant brainpower.

The Long-Range Objectives Group concluded that in the emerging bipolar nuclear world, neither superpower would be able, or would want, to initiate and sustain a nuclear conflict. Future wars would be confined to Eurasian peripheries, and on the littoral of these peripheries (Korea and Indochina were conspicuous examples in 1954) lay the Navy's future.

These ideas were decidedly non-Mahanian, an attempt to come to grips with an international situation in which no navies existed that could contest the seas with the Americans. Increasingly powerful *nonnuclear* forces were needed. OP-93 was boosting not nuclear weapons technologies (most of which were being fed in the direction of the Air Force) but such developments as long-range missiles, anti-aircraft missiles, and vertical takeoff aircraft—anything to extend naval striking power. The planners also gave considerable attention to that Carney favorite, antisubmarine warfare.

In the upshot, OP-93 conducted very few of these long-range studies.

The group instead was inexorably sucked into daily policy-making and crisis-planning; its expertise was simply too good for Carney and other naval leaders to pass up. Burke had said that OP-93 was to be free from "the hampering aspects of day-to-day administrative problems," but the nature of the Cold War, as seen by naval leadership at any rate, ensured that OP-93 was seldom able to gaze, unhampered, into the Navy's future.[12]

☆

The vital necessity of command of the sea was readily recognized in the context of the Cold War. Nevertheless, as one authority noted in 1954, the Navy of the future would "probably face conditions varying greatly from those of the past." Uncertainties abounded about the shape that future seapower would take. The pre–World War II situation of a multiplicity of oceanic navies had been reduced to that of *one* superpower.

While the Navy worked hard to extend its striking power against the shore, the fleet was also configured, as always, for battle at sea. Professionals like Mick Carney could see the elements of shadowboxing outlined clearly. Mahan no longer seemed pertinent in his teachings about capital ships, and certainly his geopolitical and strategic concepts were in deep trouble as well. But his basic question, about what a Navy was for, was ever-green. The problem lay not so much in preparing for a blue-water enemy (in the 1950s there was none) as in figuring out the best use of the overwhelming naval power the United States possessed.

After Reorganization Plan 6 in 1953, joint war plans diluted the Navy's vision of fighting wars, dispersing military tasks among the three services much like a seasoned politico balancing handouts to the folks back home. The New Look did orient the Navy's supercarriers toward nuclear strikes, but the Navy remained, strategically, a nuclear stepsister to the Air Force's giant new B-52s. Limiting the Navy to strikes against Soviet maritime targets also subtracted from more traditional naval missions, such as local sea control.

In addition, the development of the Sound Surveillance System supported a naval version of the Maginot Line mentality, the notion that all would be well once the early-warning hydrophonic ears were in place and listening. This defensive-mindedness would only be reinforced as the USSR began to deploy increasing numbers of nuclear ballistic-missile and attack submarines. Whereas Forrest Sherman and his planning staff had visualized direct operations against the Soviets in the Far Eastern littoral, events would direct the Navy's attention elsewhere in the western Pacific for the next twenty years.

—All this eroded the reasonably firm naval strategy that had been cobbled together shortly after World War II. And there were practical, everyday problems. The Eisenhower hold-the-line budgets, coupled with the struggle

Getting the A-bomb to sea: A P2V Neptune, using jet-assisted takeoff, launches from USS *Franklin D. Roosevelt* (CV-42), c. 1949.

The arrival of the supercarrier: USS *Forrestal* (CV-59) takes shape in her Newport News drydock, 1 December 1954.

A naval aviation success story: The first of nearly 3000 Douglas A-4 Skyhawks takes off on its maiden flight, 22 June 1954.

The Praetorian guard: USS *Forrest Sherman* (DD-931), lead ship of her class, steams with USS *Boston* (CAG-1) off Guantanamo, Cuba, March 1956.

The missile kingdom: USS *Boston* (CAG-1) launches a Terrier missile during fleet exercises, 29 June 1961.

Hyman Rickover, at the controls of USS *Sam Houston* (SSBN-609), June 1961. To his right is Edward Teller, arch-advocate of nuclear weaponry.

Underway on nuclear power: USS *Nautilus* (SSN-571) on her initial sea trials, January 1955.

VSHIPS 1111 (REV. 11-54)

SHIP'S POSITION

U. S. S. *NAUTILUS*

): COMMANDING OFFICER

(Time of day)	DATE
1915 U	3 August 1958

TITUDE	LONGITUDE	ETERMINED AT
90° 00.0'N	Indefinite	—

NGA ☒	D. R. ☒	MK 19 ☒	RADAR ☐	VISUAL ☐

T	DRIFT	DISTANCE MADE GOOD SINCE (time) (miles)
—	—	Honolulu 4844

STANCE TO	MILES	ETA
North Pole	Zero	—

UE HDG.	ERROR				VARIATION
80°	MK 19 GYRO 3 E MK 23 GYRO 0°				170 E

GNETIC COMPASS HEADING (Check one)

☐ STD	☐ STEER-ING	☒ REMOTE IND	☐ OTHER	M 244	G 359

VIATION	1104 TABLE DEVIATION	DG: (Indicate by check in box)
26E	3° W	☐ ON ☒ OFF

MARKS

NGA DR
σ = 0
N = 0

NGA
$n_x = 0$
$n_y = 0$
$n_z = 1$

ESPECTFULLY SUBMITTED (Reviewer)

LT Shepherd M. Jenks, USN

The most famous position report in naval history: "*Nautilus* 90 North," 3 August 1958.

Nukes: The watch crew in the control room of USS *Nautilus* (SSN-571) as she passes under the polar ice pack, August 1958.

The sea bound the men of Flag Plot, and to the sea some of them ultimately returned: A Navy public relations composite photograph.

Members of Flag Plot in Yokosuka, March 1952. Left to right: Rear Admiral Ralph Ofstie, Vice Admiral Harold Martin, Vice Admiral Robert Briscoe, and Rear Admiral George Dyer.

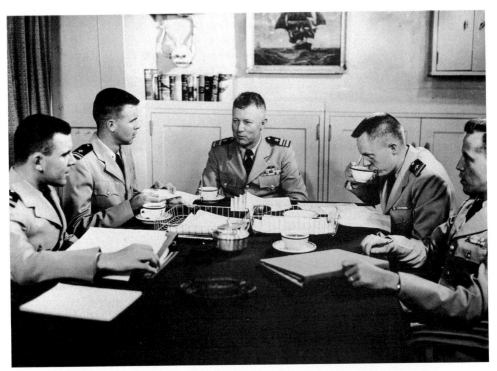

The officers of USS *Carronade* (IFS-1) in their wardroom, 1955. Retention of officers was a major problem for the cold war Navy.

Officers and men in the main battery plot of USS *Missouri* (BB-63) off Korea, May 1951. The acceleration of modern technology was undermining the generalist ideal for naval officers.

A Navy boot with non-optional accessories, 1945.

Metalsmith shop aboard USS *Forrestal* (CV-59), February 1956. The cold war Navy had great difficulty maintaining its skilled enlisted personnel.

The backbone of the Navy: These seven chief petty officers from Fleet
Aircraft Service Squadron 6, Naval Air Station, Jacksonville, Florida, had
210 years of combined naval service when they retired in April 1950.

Naval Air Station, Pensacola, Florida, April 1951. The quality of medical
care in the cold war Navy varied widely.

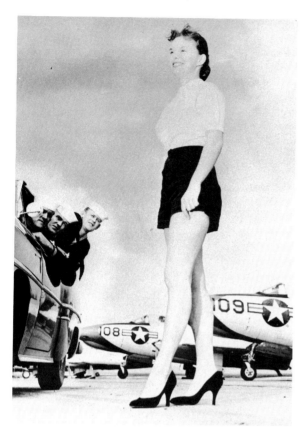

Hospital Corpsman Donna Marie Locher poses for Navy photograph at the Memphis Naval Air Station, March 1958. The cold war cultivated an intensely male, macho, and (to a later generation) sexist personality.

A steward striker adjusting the magazine rack in wardroom number two, USS *Ranger* (CVA-61), February 1958. By this time, blacks were beginning to break out of the odious steward rating.

Dwight Eisenhower, with his naval aide Captain Evan Aurand, aboard USS *Canberra* (CAG-2), 27 March 1957.

Rear Admiral Arthur Radford, commander, Carrier Division 6, relaxing at Ulithi, 29 March 1945. Radford championed naval aviation for three decades before becoming Chairman of the Joint Chiefs of Staff (1953-1957).

USS *Ford County* (LST-772) takes on Chinese Nationalist soldiers and supplies prior to evacuating the Tachen Islands, February 1955. The Formosa Strait had become a cold war "hot spot."

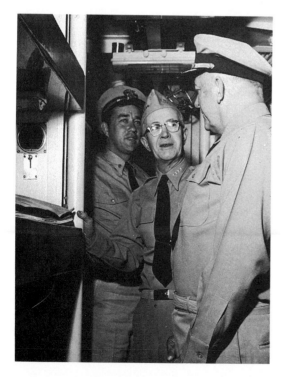

Admiral Robert ("Mick") Carney, Chief of Naval Operations (1953-1955), aboard USS *Nautilus* (SSN-571), flanked by Commander Eugene Wilkinson, the sub's first skipper, and Vice Admiral Robert Briscoe, 10 May 1955. Eisenhower did not reappoint the outspoken Carney for a second term.

Commodore Arleigh Burke, going to school with Marc ("Pete") Mitscher (left) on the subject of naval aviation: Aboard USS *Randolph* (CV-15) off Okinawa, June 1945.

Admiral Arleigh Burke, Chief of Naval Operations (1955-1961) and habitual pipe smoker.

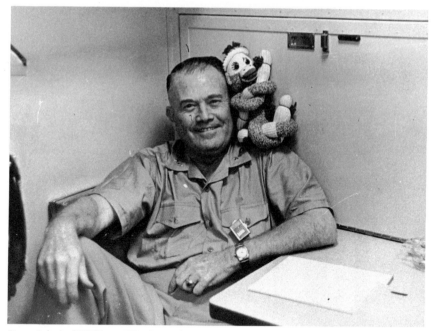

Rear Admiral William ("Red") Raborn, Jr., aboard USS *George Washington* (SSBN-598), with "Kluge," a Lockheed technician's lucky monkey, on his shoulder. By this date (1960), Raborn had cut the estimated time for the Polaris project in half.

"From out of the deep to target. Perfect." The first Polaris launch, from USS *George Washington* (SSBN-598), 20 July 1960.

Naval diplomacy in the
Persian Gulf: Rear Admiral
John Quinn, commander,
Middle East Force, meets
with Sheikh of Bahrain,
4 February 1956.

Vice Admiral Charles
("Cat") Brown aboard
his Sixth Fleet flagship,
USS *Des Moines* (CA-134)
in the Mediterranean,
c. 1957. Thomas Gates, Jr.,
Secretary of the Navy
(1957-1959), is to his left.

The worldwide naval resupply effort: First lines are over from USS *Forrestal* (CVA-59) to USS *Denebola* (AF-56) in the characteristically placid waters of the Mediterranean, August 1962.

The antisubmarine warfare package: Task Force Alfa, in this case centered on USS *Randolph* (CVS-15), 1960.

John Kennedy on the mess decks of USS *Northampton* (CLC-1), 13 April 1962. Kennedy's obsession with Communist insurgency played into the Navy's claims of operational mobility and flexibility.

Robert McNamara, Secretary of Defense (1961-1968), shielding his eyes, visits USS *Stribling* (DD-867), Washington, D.C., 13 July 1961. McNamara's changes were resisted throughout the Pentagon, particularly by the Navy, and his abrasive style was abhorred by all.

The cold war Navy at work: A motor whaleboat from USS *Joseph P. Kennedy, Jr.* (DD-850) approaches the freighter *Marucla* at the height of the Cuban Missile Crisis, 26 October 1962.

Admiral Alfred ("Corky") Ward, commander of the Second Fleet during the Cuban Missile Crisis.

of an aging fleet coping with global missions, eroded American naval power as well. The public, responding to full-blast naval PR, gave its appreciation to the new wonders: the nuclear submarines, supercarriers, guided-missile cruisers. But by the late fifties the fleet had been reduced from 409 warships to 376 (a loss of 8 percent) and from 558 ships of other types to 436 (a 22 percent loss).

Overall, the Cold War Navy of the fifties, in terms of numbers of ships, *shrank* 16 percent while its missions remained as demanding as ever. Radford, horrified, was forced to admit that he would rather have ten destroyers half-manned than five destroyers fully manned. True, the new wonders could do more things, but they could not be everywhere at once, and flexibility and mobility were the leitmotivs coming out of OP-93.

In 1959 the Navy's Board of Inspection and Survey found an astounding 72 percent of the fleet's ships to be in some way unsatisfactory. Cuts in personnel did not help; after Anderson's and Thomas's battles, between 1957 and 1960, the Navy's active-duty strength was further pared away, from 677,000 to 618,000. The planners estimated that personnel levels were at least 4 percent too low, an enormous understatement in light of the fact that many of the shortages came among junior officers and in key electrical and electronics ratings. The amphibious forces, essential for any projection of naval power against Eurasian shores, were being especially degraded.

In horse-barn terms, the Navy's ships were being steamed hard and not put up at all, save in mothballs. Programs like Fleet Rehabilitation and Modernization, introduced in 1959 and aimed primarily at the indefatigable destroyers, helped a bit, but aging ships, under this or any other resuscitation process, only got older.[13]

Thus the New Look—strategically, politically, economically, and in every other way—did not fit the Navy at all. The New Look's economically minded military posture focused on nuclear deterrence. And the strain, particularly for the Navy, was omnipresent; NSC 162 had warned that the United States should be prepared to "continue, for as long as necessry, a state of limited defense mobilization." The Air Force, primary strategic custodian of the New Look, waxed prosperous, expanding to its promised 137 wings and increasing to almost one million men. Air power, massive and decisive, was to be the major component of the administration's deterrent strategy.

The Navy marched halfheartedly to this strategic cadence. The resulting war plans, for all the services, were terrifically rigid and inflexible, the precise opposite of the Navy's version of its optimum roles. If the Joint Chiefs were to instruct the Pacific Fleet to bomb Russia, for example, targeting and range-payload considerations would probably have led to Navy-delivered nuclear ordnance falling on Chinese cities. There seemed to be no way of modifying the all-out, castastrophic nature of war plans keyed to major nuclear responses.[14]

The problem was that events in the real world seldom cooperated. As an instructive instance, on 4 September 1954 a Navy Neptune patrolling the Soviet east coast (exactly where was disputed) was fired on by two Russian MiGs. Technically, there was an act of war here somewhere, either in the violation of airspace or in unwarranted aggression over open water. Clearly this was no cause for a nuclear riposte, but exactly what form retaliation *should* take under the New Look was a matter for serious concern. The Neptune case was buried under squabbling orations in the United Nations.

A year later, on 22 June 1955, the Russians, tormented by American snoopers, finally shot down a Navy patrol plane over the Bering Strait. The Soviet Union, to America's surprise, actually paid half the damages and issued a statement of regret. This was all the more amazing since the plane had clearly been violating Soviet airspace. Eisenhower warned Radford to keep all American flights outside the fifteen-mile limit, at least during the period of increasing thaw leading to the Geneva Conference of 1955.[15]

Such instances were symptomatic of the inherent difficulties of the New Look, which relied on crude threat to a degree that undercut its viability as a useful strategy. And this was apart from the interservice bickering thereby generated; the Navy–Air Force strategic rivalry had now entered Round 2. Under the pressure of nuclear strategic planning, the Navy obediently conjured up dozens of "strategic targets," some of them little more than East European cornfields that could barely be reached by carrier-launched F-4s from the Mediterranean. The Navy's liaison admiral to the newly installed Strategic Air Command headquarters in Omaha acted as an undercover agent to inform the Navy's high command about any USAF ploy to enlarge its own strategic role. When two missile-launching tests from the submarine *Patrick Henry* failed, there was celebrating in SAC headquarters.

In the meantime, Navy and Air Force targeters blanketed the Soviet Union with nuclear bull's-eyes; one militarily insignificant Russian provincial city was threatened with four times the nuclear ordnance needed to obliterate the place. The interservice strife and competition were wasteful and time-consuming; men of the caliber of Charles Wilson could never come close to stopping the wrangling. Herbert York, one of Eisenhower's civilian weapons procurement specialists, estimated that such rivalries resulted in the funding of twice as many nuclear missile programs as were actually "needed."

Both sides, Navy and Air Force, were to blame. On the Navy's part, massive retaliation seemed to be no strategy at all but simply a reflexive sledgehammer that could accomplish little but the creation of a nuclear wasteland. Captain William Moore attended an SAC briefing in 1954 during which the Air Force explained what massive retaliation would mean in practice. Moore heard plans to saturate the USSR with up to 750 nuclear weapons. He recalled that "no aspect of the morals or long-range effect of such attacks [was] discussed, and no questions on it were asked." He reflected that "virtually all of Russia would be nothing but a smoking, radiating ruin at the end of two hours."

As "strategy," this was little more than "overkill." Eisenhower himself preferred targeting Soviet military capability rather than the country's urban-industrial base, but the service targeters' competition ensured that the USSR was nuclear boresighted from one end to the other. Vice Admiral Ruthven Libby was only one of many Navy planners who believed that their service should "stake out a claim" to strategic bombing, in response to "unremitting attempts by the Air Force to exercise absolute control over all air operations."[16]

Both Army and Navy were nettled by Air Force targeting policy, because the inclusion of enormous numbers of Soviet military targets and more marginal target areas made large-scale destruction inevitable and probably unnecessary. In addition, Army and Navy force requirements, under such battle-ax schemes, were almost impossible to estimate.

An alternative concept was that of "broken-backed" war, in which an initial nuclear exchange would exhaust stockpiles on both sides. Then, amid the radioactive ruins, both sides would revert to the conventional weapons and strategies of the prenuclear age (an idea, along with the later brouhaha over the fictitious "missile gap," beautifully satirized in the "mineshaft gap" of Stanley Kubrick's black film comedy, *Dr. Strangelove*). The broken-backed idea, which enjoyed a brief strategic heyday, was again right up the Navy's alley, although men like Captain Moore could still see the moral bankruptcy behind such a notion.

So the interservice rivalry ground on, infecting strategic thought with a seemingly permanent irrational imbalance. The Air Force, Radford had said, possessed in the B-36 only a high-visibility target for jet interceptors. The Navy, rejoined the now-retired USAF general, Carl ("Tooey") Spaatz, was in its supercarrier program only building easy targets for Russian submarines. Spaatz had no doubt where the military dollar should be invested for the best return—and that place was in the heavy bomber wings.[17]

☆

As the debates, name-calling, and targeting went their way, the Cold War strategists, from Eisenhower on down, were beginning to learn that the nuclear Big Stick made little impression indeed on the world's trouble spots. Turmoil here, turmoil there—and not all the unrest was amenable to the use of military force. Nuclear saber-rattling calmed the storms not one whit.

The Navy under civilians like Anderson and Thomas and admirals such as Carney and Burke, persisted in its arguments for a more flexible and adaptable national strategy.

Americana, but little *Pax*. The first geopolitical lesson in this dangerous, post-Korea Cold War arena came from an area long familiar to the Navy— the western Pacific.

CHAPTER TWENTY-FIVE

WESTPAC I

—————— ☆ ——————

Westward from the Hawaiian Islands the muscle of American naval power stretched forth—past Midway, Guam, Wake Island, and other storied battlegrounds of World War II. The Navy after the Korean War found itself pressed close against the East Asian littoral, an era containing the gateways to over half the world's population.

By 1953 the United States had become deeply involved in the Western Pacific. Korea was certainly one pretext, but after the Panmunjom truce, the Navy stayed on, pledged to support South Korea, Japan, Formosa, and the Philippines. Although America had historically maintained a presence in these remote waters—up to nine thousand miles from home—the vessels had usually numbered only a corporal's guard. Never before had American warships remained in WestPac in such numbers.

The North Atlantic, measured along a great circle, was a bit over three thousand miles wide; the Pacific, from San Francisco to Subic Bay and beyond, spanned almost three times that distance. The Pacific Fleet had to somehow keep up with this demanding geography, because Asia, multifaceted and often bewildering, had become a major focal point of the Cold War. Not a few Navymen, in fact, regarded the Pacific as the single most important key to the future. Thus Arthur Radford:

> . . .You become aware of the Communist planning, begun years ago, that has won most of Asia for the Soviets. You think of the methodical pattern of upheaval that has followed World War II. You picture the elaborate apparatus that extends from Moscow to communities all over Asia, a system of youth organizations, political commissars, and study centers devoted solely to the Communist idea. And you wonder, how then to regain a friendly Asia?

—*How then?*

☆

The post-Korea Navy was all over WestPac, showing the Stars and Stripes practically anywhere its ships could steam. In early 1954, for example, the heavy cruiser *Rochester*, eight-inch guns tampioned, touched in one cruise the cities of Manila, Singapore, Bangkok, and Saigon ("the Paris of the East," enthusiastically wrote one crew member, "a busy, prosperous metropolis"), hit Iwo Jima for a flag ceremony, and visited Korea and Japan to boot.

Port calls such as these were eye-openers for the Navy; the palmy routine of the Far East was gone. "For good or for evil, the old order has changed," observed Commander John Noel, *Rochester*'s exec. "The days of colonialism in Asia are definitely over. Economic logic must surrender to the fierce and long suppressed forces of nationalism and racism."

"Economic logic"—pure Marxism—was not about to surrender. China loomed, its power and its capacity for mischief seemingly undiminished by the horrible pounding its troops had taken in the Korean War; the Soviets, as always, fished in waters roiled by nationalism, ethnic rivalries, and revolution; insurrections (some Communist-led, some not) popped up all over the map. The colonial powers—Great Britain, France, the Netherlands—were in rapid, inglorious retreat, and a new world was being born. "In the struggle against the spread of Communism in the Far East," warned one Naval Reservist, "there is a very real danger that the West, and its thermonuclear deterrent, may be outflanked and isolated by the gradual transfer of enormous territories, populations, and resources from the western to the eastern orbit without the detonation of a single weapon of mass destruction."

Many Navymen were convinced, like Radford, that a major part of the fight against communism would be for control of the sealanes that carried the fabled trade of Asia. "Without sea supremacy in the Far East nothing else would matter very much," one authority glumly concluded. The Soviet Union depended heavily on its seaborne transport in the Far East, and Red China, while no naval power, featured a rich and varied coastal traffic. In addition, WestPac was strewn with shipping "choke points," such as the Tsushima Strait and the Strait of Malacca, ideal pressure spots for the application of naval force.[1]

The heritage of carrier air power and Marine amphibious assault in World War II had given the Navy strategic predominance in the Pacific. In 1947 the commander in chief of the Pacific Fleet had donned a second hat as commander in chief, Pacific (CINCPAC). The two commands would not be divided until 1958. Under this arrangement CINPACFLT reported to himself, as CINCPAC. Under his operational control, through the Korean War and after, came the Seventh Fleet in the Western Pacific. CINCPAC was the big player, dominant among all the services; by 1957 he had swallowed the Army's Far East Command and controlled Air Force assets throughout the Pacific.

All the threads thus led back to Pearl Harbor. There, the major concern was to augment the conventional-warfare strength of the Pacific Fleet, especially its capability to project power ashore, following the well-remembered model of World War II. CINCPAC's premier task was preparing to counter aggressive Communist military actions on the Asian rim.

For this task, he was given the sharpest tridents available. Most of the new carriers, the attack aircraft, the amphibious assault ships, and the logistic support vessels (critical in the vast reaches of the Pacific) went to CINCPAC. Within a decade after Korea, the Pacific Fleet totaled 434 commissioned ships. Among these were 13 attack and antisubmarine carriers, 7 cruisers, 117 destroyer types, and 43 submarines.

CINCPAC bossed an amphibious assault force of seventy-two vessels. He controlled forty-three coastal and oceangoing minesweepers. His naval air force was organized into ten attack carrier wings, five antisubmarine carrier air groups, and thirty-one separate squadrons. His aircraft were the best in the inventory: F-4 Phantom IIs, F-8 Crusaders, A-4 Skyhawks, and A-3 Skywarriors. The sturdy, dependable A-1 Skyraider still flew, and the all-weather A-6 Intruder was coming on-line.

Over 110 auxiliaries and dozens of naval and Marine bases tied this far-flung force together. By himself, CINCPAC commanded a more powerful navy than that of any other country. There were, of course, problems, most of these related to the enormous ocean that was his domain. There were never adequate numbers of crucial aircraft types; sealift was always in short supply; large-caliber guns (desirable for shore bombardment, loved to the point of passionate distraction by the Marines) were being phased out, not only with the last of the *Iowa*-class battleships in 1957 but even with the eight-inch cruisers like *Rochester*. Stocks of ordnance and spare parts were perpetually low. And throughout, "the material condition of the Pacific Fleet remained marginal."[2]

Still, an awesome naval force patrolled the new American lake, right up to the Asian rim. "How then to regain a friendly Asia?" Radford had asked—as if the United States had once "possessed" such a friend. In the Cold War, if one was not a "friend"—he was an "enemy."

☆

Japan, not yet an economic colossus, was nevertheless recovering rapidly from its wartime devastation, and the benign American presence and financial aid were not the least reasons. Immediately after the 1951 signing of the San Francisco Peace Treaty, which brought American occupation of Japan to an end, the two countries agreed to a security pact. The preamble said that the United States, "in the interests of peace and security, is precisely willing to maintain certain of its armed forces in and around Japan, in the expectation, however, that Japan will increasingly assume responsibility for its own defense against direct or indirect aggression." The way was paved for the Japanese to reenter the family of nations; in 1956 Japan became the eightieth member of the United Nations, and two years later the last American ground troops left the country. (By 1969 even the much-contested Okinawa prefecture would be part of Japan once again.)

The security pact with Japan was but a prelude to "WestPac pactomania." Washington quickly signed a series of security agreements with the Philippines, New Zealand, and Australia, shortly followed by defense treaties with South Korea (1953) and Nationalist China (1954). Ultimately the Southeast Asia Treaty Organization would attempt to combine the noncommunist states in the region.

For Japan, American support was the arterial necessity for renewed economic health. For more than two decades following the security agreement, the average American military subsidy ran to $500 million annually. The Japanese were vitally interested in the West, and particularly in the United States, for the hard currency needed for their economic revival. The United States, through expensive military procurement programs, helped to modernize Japan's high-technology and export sectors in particular. Japan, unarmed by treaty and nonmilitant by its new constitution, achieved its economic miracle on the shoulders of American defense procurements abroad.

Yokosuka continued to see the most of the Navy, although Sasebo and a few other ports prospered from the fleet as well. As many as 25,000 sailors at once, some fresh from patrols and the Korean bomb line, would descend on Yoko, turning the place into a steamy, artificially lit wonderland from noon till midnight. The Enlisted Men's Club ashore would play host to as many as 27,000 sailors *a day*. "The men try to squeeze 48 hours into 12," explained the club's manager.

Yoko's businessmen saw the neon light. The tawdry, scattered gin joints and whorehouses of 1946 blossomed in this hothouse atmosphere into a Japanese version of Las Vegas, a garish strip a mile long and three blocks wide. Street signs were in English, and enterprising merchants installed loudspeakers that incessantly bellowed familiar stateside phrases. Sailor dollars, converted to yen to avoid problems with the black market, flowed in the millions into Yoko and beyond, throughout the entire Japanese economy. The United States Navy did more than its share in jump-starting prostrate Japan.

"We get on fine with the Japanese there," beamed Radford. The Japanese were now "friends." So were the twenty million or so war-ravaged South Koreans, although their economy was as yet in shambles. Sailors found Pusan or Inchon, after the scented delights of Yoko, to be small beer indeed as liberty ports.

While the Navy had numerous contracts with local merchants and vendors, in Japan and throughout Asia, almost all of the fleet's big chores, from repair to resupply, were done in-house. Virtually everything was afloat, from barracks to electronic repair shops to hospitals. Even small craft could be cradled in the wells of landing ships and hauled at a moment's notice to wherever events might dictate.

Thus the Navy might have home ports in the Far East, but the fleet was never truly "home." The closest Navymen came in this regard was in the Philippines, where the American naval presence after the war developed exceptional dimensions. Following the American defeat of the *insurrectos* after the Spanish-American War, Filipinos had embarked on a love-hate odyssey with the United States—so far away, yet so tantalizingly near. "Three centuries in a Catholic convent," went one brisk summary of Philippine history, "and fifty years in Hollywood."

Most Filipinos deeply admired the United States, partly for the Hollywood glitter but mostly for what they understood to be the good life there. Hundreds of thousands were emigrating to America: nearly 300,000 annually requested authorization just to visit. For many, the most precious treasure would become a "green card," a permit to reside in the United States. The waiting list in the Philippines for immigration visas was decades long.

The Navy thus found a friendly, receptive atmosphere in the archipelago. The year after Philippine independence, 1947, Filipinos had signed an agreement allowing the Americans to keep all their bases in the islands, ranging from military cemeteries to the plush Camp John Hay in the delightful resort town of Baguio, high in the mountains of Luzon. Of crucial importance, the Air Force retained Clark Air Base, and the Navy kept Subic Bay Naval Base.

Subic would become the Navy's largest overseas base, the core of its Asian presence. The majority of Filipinos, who in the fifties were eager to be part of America's global strategy, welcomed the bluejackets. Subic Bay itself had caught the eye of George Dewey as far back as 1900, when he pleaded for an "impregnable naval base" there. The Army thought Subic was vulnerable from the land and proposed Manila Bay for the fleet outpost, a suggestion the Navy quickly rejected. The compromise settled a small naval station at Subic, while the Army got Fort Stotsenburg, grandfather of Clark Field.

During World War II, Manuel Quezon, the Filipino patriot-in-exile, wrote Franklin Roosevelt that despite the geographical position of the Philippines, "we are with the West." And so they were. The American Joint Chiefs, after the liberation of the islands, asked for twenty-three Navy and thirteen Army bases. "They could have had anything," wrote one commentator. As American bases peppered the islands, the Filipinos extracted nothing more in return than a vague American pledge to defend the archipelago.

The formal 1947 agreement gave the United States ninety-nine-year leases on twenty-two bases, including Clark and Subic. The Americans also gained extraterritoriality—the right to try Americans—and got jurisdiction over Filipino workers on the bases as well. Olongapo, the community adjoining Subic Bay, rapidly became a premier sailortown, an ever-replenished swill-bucket that slopped over with bars, whorehouses, and massage parlors—an Asian smorgasbord for every social and sexual persuasion. The prostitutes and their pimps were part of gang rackets, which in turn were protected by corrupt politicians.

The bases, and particularly Subic, poured a stream of American currency into the Philippine economy. The islands quickly became used to the presence of the Golden Calf, which not only brought a raffish prosperity to sinkholes like Olongapo but also helped enrich the upper crust of the entire country, the interlocking oligarchy of families that actually ran the Philippines. (The islands were never to solve the problem of prosperity for a majority of their citizens.)

While some Filipinos were rankled by the fact that they, as allies, had to deal with tougher basing terms than the Americans imposed on their former enemies, the Japanese, the economic and military boost given by the American presence, not to mention the continuing dream of the good life across the Pacific, were too good to pass up. For their part, most Americans, including the Navy, continued to patronize their Little Brown Brothers—independent now but still needing a benevolent guiding hand. Near the end of his life Senator Robert Taft, son of the man who had once been governor of the Philippines, declared that the islands should by right be an American outpost in the Pacific. "The fact that they have a completely independent, autonomous government is, I think, a good thing," graciously conceded "Mr. Republican." "But certainly we shall always be a big brother, if you please, to the Philippines."

Big Brother saw nothing wrong in intervening directly in Philippine elections. Several days before the 1953 presidential vote, for example, an American light aircraft carrier and a covey of destroyers materialized in Manila Bay, which seemed to confirm the rumors spread by one of the candidates, Ramon Magsaysay, that his opponent, Elpidio Quirino, was about to commit polling fraud on a magnificent scale. When the voting began, Magsaysay and his Nacionalista party bosses were guarded at the Subic Bay Naval Base. (Magsaysay won in a landslide, taking 68.9 percent of the vote; the naval exercise was stage-managed by the Central Intelligence Agency's Far East Division.)

Big Brother's Navy grew to depend on Subic Bay. As the docks were built, supply buildings reared, channels dredged, and communications nets laid, the fleet moved in to stay. There was also a green hell of a golf course, carved out of mountainous jungle by the Seabees, featuring chattering monkeys and an occasional python. The base had everything the Navy needed in the Far East: central location, amid a friendly government and people, with a solid infrastructure of logistic support.[3]

—Which was just as well, because right across the South China Sea from Subic, the French were in the process of losing Indochina.

☆

Back in 1950, Harry Truman had approved a small, $15 million aid package for the newly formed but still dependent states of the Indochinese peninsula—Vietnam, Laos, and Cambodia—in the hope that their governments could crush Communist insurrections, particularly the guerrilla forces led by Ho Chi Minh in the hills of northern Vietnam. As a symbol of support, two destroyers, *Stickell* and *Richard B. Anderson*, showed up in Saigon in March 1950. Seventh Fleet himself, Vice Admiral Russell Berkey, a somewhat stuffy Blackshoe experienced in cruiser operations, flew his flag aboard the former. As a further gesture, sixty aircraft off *Boxer* treated the city to a tight-formation flyover.

Thus began the indirect American assistance to the beleaguered French, bogged down in a seemingly endless rice-paddy war. Berkey's ships and planes around Saigon were symbolic; the money was real. By 1953 the United States was underwriting almost 80 percent of the French military budget in Vietnam. The cost soon spiraled to over $3 billion—25 percent of the pre-Korea budget for the entire Defense Department.

In early 1954 the French committed their military strength—and international prestige—to a string of posts in northwestern Vietnam centered on Dien Bien Phu. In April, as the tenacious Viet Minh fighters tightened their stranglehold on the French, Radford placed American carriers in the area on twelve-hour alert. Mick Carney notified Vice Admiral William Phillips, in command of the potential strike force, that there were no plans for intervention but that everyone in Washington was aware of "the grave consequences that could result from loss of Indochina to the Communists."

"You have a row of dominoes set up," remarked Eisenhower at a press conference on 7 April, "and you knock over the first one and what will happen to the last one is the certainty that it will go over very quickly." Thus, a rapid response seemed in order, a test of the New Look.

Radford outlined such an American response to Paul Ely, the visiting French chief of staff. The plan, Operation VULTURE, had been drawn up by both French and American officers in Saigon. Sixty American B-29s, some of them possibly equipped with atomic bombs, would fly from Clark to plaster the area surrounding Dien Bien Phu. They would be joined by some 150 planes off Phillips's carriers.

VULTURE was Raddy's brainstorm; no other member of the Joint Chiefs, not even Carney, supported the plan. Eisenhower and Dulles were insistent that any American intervention be part of a joint venture—which meant the British. Radford kept plugging, although he admitted to congressional leaders that an air strike did not preclude the later use of ground forces. The French cabinet, for its part, asked that VULTURE be implemented as the only way to avoid defeat at Dien Bien Phu, and in Indochina. They also asked for support from American carrier air.

For Eisenhower, this was too much, well beyond his ill-thought-out "domino theory." He had already chewed out Radford on 5 April for misleading Ely and had told the chairman of the Joint Chiefs, in no uncertain terms, that VULTURE was "politically impossible." The opposition fusillades had started; a youthful Massachusetts senator, John Kennedy, warned that a war in Indochina would be "dangerously futile and self-destructive," and Texas's Lyndon Johnson, the Senate majority leader, in an irony of ironies fulminated against "sending American GIs into the mud and muck of Indochina on a bloodletting spree."

—Still, the temptation was great. General Nathan Twining, head of the Air Force, regretted that the United States had not dropped at least "three small tactical A-bombs" around Dien Bien Phu. "Those commies [would have been cleaned] out of there and the band could play the 'Marseillaise' and the French would come marching out of Dien Bien Phu in fine shape." Even Ike had second thoughts. He was tempted to order "a single strike, if it were almost certain this would produce decisive results." He added, "Of course, if we did, we'd have to deny it forever."

Only death and taxes were certain. Rear Admiral Arthur Davis, a pioneer in naval dive-bombing and now a Pentagon planner, warned that any dream of potential involvement in Indochina was foolish: "One cannot go over Niagara Falls in a barrel only slightly." Eisenhower, with good reason, took heed of his own caution and the advice of men like Davis and Matt Ridgway, refusing the drastic recommendations of Radford and the later second thoughts of Twining. Lack of allied support was the key. "Unilateral action by the United States in cases of this kind would destroy us," Ike said. "If we intervened alone in this case we would be expected to intervene alone in other parts of the world."

The decks of Phillips's carriers were hot. One admiral and his staff, flying in Dakota transports at night, even reconnoitered the entrenched camp of Dien Bien Phu, looking for targets. But America's naval aviators never flew, and neither did VULTURE. The British got cold feet as members of a prospective allied coalition, everyone was nervous about possible Chinese intervention, and nuclear saber-rattling by Radford and others did not help. In early May, Dien Bien Phu at last fell, the Geneva Accords followed, and shortly the French were gone in humiliating retreat, their imperial gamble in the Far East a disastrous failure. Radford would go to his grave believing that somehow, if American and allied force had been applied, then and there, the later catastrophe in Vietnam might have been avoided.

But even Radford, who "liked to consider himself as the defender of the Western world," saw dangers in unilateral American action. He and the rest of the members of the Joint Chiefs considered Indochina militarily unimportant—certainly less important than the Soviet and Chinese littoral—and thus not worth major risk. Carney feared Chinese intervention and that haunting American nightmare, war on the Asian mainland. Thus VULTURE, designed as a cheap and relatively easy solution to a monumentally complex problem, could not fly because of one massive roadblock: the plan could not guarantee the much-desired solution and might indeed lead to something infinitely worse.

With Vietnam divided into northern and southern halves as a result of the Geneva Accords, signed between the French and the Viet Minh on 20 July 1954, the 17th parallel, at first intended to be only a temporary dividing and restraining line, rapidly hardened into an international boundary. The Eisenhower administration prevented a plebiscite on Vietnam's political future, scheduled for 1956, from ever being held.

The accords, to which the United States was not a signatory, permitted civilians on either side of the 17th parallel to migrate to the other—which gave the Navy a big transportation headache. The resulting humanitarian sealift, which the Navy billed as the Passage to Freedom, went almost unrecognized back home but was a huge operation nonetheless. Eisenhower directed Carney to organize a ferry service from the north to Saigon and other southern ports. The Navy responded magnificently. Some 800,000 Vietnamese, for one reason or other, chose not to sample the delights of Ho's new Communist regime in North Vietnam. They were about 5 percent of the northern population, many of them educated members of the middle class. About 311,000 went south on Navy ships. In addition, Navymen rescued hundreds of Vietnamese who had desperately put to sea in small boats to flee to South Vietnam.

Passage to Freedom was naval humanitarianism at its best, but the obvious success of the Communists in hewing North Vietnam out of the French Empire remained a bitter memory. In 1956 Radford and the chief of naval operations recommended that the northern port of Haiphong, gateway to the capital of Hanoi, be mined and that American forces be landed in the area, ostensibly to "protect" naval forces cruising the South China Sea. Once again Eisenhower refused to raise the military ante.

The major diplomatic fallout of the crisis was the Southeast Asia Treaty Organization (SEATO), cobbled together by John Foster Dulles and signed at a conference in Manila on 8 September 1954. America already had security pacts with Japan, the Philippines, Australia, New Zealand, and South Korea. SEATO was a device to move the Far Eastern defense perimeter right up to the shores of the People's Republic of China. Most of the signatories to this alliance for local defense and American deterrence in Southeast Asia were, significantly, non-Asian nations—the United States, Great Britain, France, Australia, and New Zealand. Only Pakistan, Thailand, and the Philippines, from the immediate area, came on board. As a sign of the new world taking shape, the infant independent nations of India, Burma,

Indonesia, and Ceylon refused to align themselves, considering SEATO nothing more than provocative neocolonialism.

A special protocol extended SEATO protection to "South" Vietnam, Laos, and Cambodia, at either their invitation or consent. Unlike NATO, the SEATO pact, while anti-Communist to the core, did not involve assignment of any additional military or naval forces to the region, nor did the agreement list precise commitments in case of armed aggression. Each member was to act, in such cases, "in accordance with its constitutional processes."

Despite these caveats, which filled SEATO with logical gaps through which a Thai elephant could stroll, the agreement, to have any teeth at all, had to rest on American naval power. This power had gone unused at Dien Bien Phu. In fact, the entire debate over American intervention in Indochina in 1954 was a gross example of the supreme inadequacy of the New Look as an operational strategy, and this less than a year after its heralded introduction. No sooner had the Eisenhower administration promoted this dynamic method for enforcing containment—by the nuclear big stick—than the idea was challenged.

—And found lacking.[4]

☆

China was the problem. The gateway to Mao Tse-tung's kingdom of perpetual revolution was Hong Kong, a British Crown Colony that, for many sailors, was the supreme liberty port in the Far East. There they could sample all the basic bluejacket delights, a bit pricier but also a bit more high-toned than those found in the stews of Olongapo, and there they could run across such institutions as Mary Soo.

She was a Chinese woman of indeterminate age, squatly built and featuring a three-foot pigtail. Her racket was removing garbage leftovers from visiting Navy ships, in return for which cash crop she and her minions (she controlled over a dozen sampans and scores of Chinese girls) would repaint the ships' sides. Mary Soo was a marketing monopolist of no mean proportions, amassing and reselling garbage by the ton while jawboning with American sailors. Scuttlebutt said she was one of the richest women in Hong Kong (doubtful) and that she ran her own restaurant where Navy refuse was recycled, tasting better than in its original form at the mess tables (less doubtful).

"I no rich," said Mary. "I sleep on sampan. I sell garbage for pigs. I no marry. I take care of Mary." She was not alone. Everyone in Hong Kong scrambled to take care of themselves. Navy ships would barely have set the stoppers on their anchor chains when they were immediately assaulted, not just by Mary Soo's ramshackle fleet but by sampans bearing nursing women, squalling children, and vendors toting every imaginable type of merchandise to unload on unsuspecting sailors. Silk with 40 percent rayon, teak statuettes carved from packing crates, onyx made out of deodorant jars, "my sister"—everything was for sale. Some skippers had to order their fire hoses and extinguishers turned against the eager mobs just to keep their decks clear.[5]

Hong Kong was an entrepreneurial paradise and an entrepreneurial hell, freewheeling capitalism at its best and worst. The place represented exactly the kind of thing Mao and his fellow revolutionaries in Peking were pledged to stamp out. Hong Kong might have been the historic gateway to China (Canton lay only a few miles up the sluggish Pearl River), but the gateway was now sealed. Sailors on liberty could ride the ferry from Victoria Island over to Kowloon and travel up to the border. From there they could gaze on the tranquil rice paddies to the north, studded with abrupt, strangely shaped mountains—but they could go no further.

China, then, was the problem. "All over Southeast Asia the people are uneasy," Radford had said in 1952. "They are all afraid of Communist aggression from China." He, and most other Navymen, believed (both during and after Korea) that the best way to prevent the spread of communism in Asia was to prevent the Chinese "from going any further." Still, he conceded, "Communist China is an enemy only in the sense that they [*sic*] are now acting on orders from Moscow." Some Navymen, however, stopped short of agreeing with some of Raddy's solutions—he had recommended blockading the Chinese coast during the Korean War (a monumental if not impossible task), and he conceived of taking action "directly against Communist China by employing naval air power."

From retirement, Ernie King also supported the blockade idea. Naval advocates of a blockade were far too sanguine, particularly where the long and deeply indented Chinese coastline was concerned. The two most successful naval blockades in history—England's against Napoleon and the Union's against the Confederacy—were conducted virtually in the backyard of the blockading power, and (after 1805 in England's case) against vastly inferior naval forces. Pro-blockaders were also far too sanguine about how badly China's economy—localized, fragmented, and only marginally industrial—could be hurt by such a tactic.

But Mao's regime, particularly after Korea, was hypersensitive to instances of "imperialist aggression," and all the talk about a blockade did not help. In July 1954 a Chinese plane downed a Cathay Pacific Airlines DC-4 off Hainan Island in the South China Sea. Two Skyraiders and a Corsair off *Philippine Sea* were searching for survivors when they were jumped by two Chinese La-7s, low-wing, single-seat, propeller-driven planes. The La-7s were promptly splashed, but incidents like this one did nothing to lessen the tension along the Chinese coast.[6]

As Mao saw the world, there was still unfinished business—across the Formosa Strait.

☆

When Chiang Kai-shek and his defeated Nationalist forces were driven off the mainland in 1949, they managed to cling to several offshore islands even as they settled down on Formosa. Two of these island garrisons, in particular, were crucial to Chiang in his vow to reconquer the China he and his un-principled, poorly led coterie had lost. The Matsu group, rocky and barren, sat just ten miles out from the port of Foochow. The larger and more habitable Quemoy group lay within short gunnery range of the port of Amoy.

The Nationalists not only kept these toeholds; they assiduously strength-ened them. The offshore islands were impossible for Peking to ignore; their continued control by the Nationalists amounted to a two-fingered salute. For his part, Eisenhower was asked what the United States would do if China or the Soviet Union were backing a hostile army based on Staten Island.

The problem, however, was not so much that of geographic analogy as of the "Two Chinas." As late as 5 January 1950, Truman had pledged the restoration of Formosa, "stolen" by the Japanese, to the "friendly" China—the Nationalist one. He also swore, however, that no American military aid or advice would be given the new Nationalist government of Formosa.

Chiang had Formosa, hardly a springboard for the reconquest of the mainland that the Republican right claimed, but Mao had the mainland. Dean Acheson, to most Republicans a loathsome symbol of all that was wrong with American international policy, on the same day that Truman made his pledge said that as far as he knew, "no responsible person in the Government, no military man has ever believed that we should involve our forces in [Formosa]." Events soon decreed otherwise. On 14 January 1950, all American consular property in Peking was seized, and a month later Mao and the Soviets culminated a "Treaty of Friendship, Alliance, and Mutual Assistance."

Then came Korea. Truman's critics began screaming for him to "unleash Chiang," as if somehow a man whose forces had fallen through their own rottenness, incompetence, and lack of popular support could now, like a suddenly maniacal bulldog, tear his victorious opponents to bits. On 27 June 1950, three days after the North Koreans had pushed south over the 38th parallel, Truman ordered the Seventh Fleet into the Formosa Strait, to somehow keep the two Chinas apart. At this, the China lobby grew even more rabid.

As the war ground on to its unsatisfying end, the Seventh Fleet doggedly kept patrolling the strait, as much to keep the Nationalists out as the Red Chinese in. After Korea, Eisenhower kept the Navy's commitment "to pre-vent any attack on Formosa" intact. But Peking's agenda would not be complete, seemingly, without the incorporation of those offshore islands.

In July 1954, Mao launched a propaganda campaign pledging their "liberation."

On 3 September, five days before the SEATO pact was signed in Manila, shore batteries near Amoy harbor opened fire on Nationalists unloading landing craft at Quemoy. A sporadic bombardment began, one which was to last for nine months—as the United Nations debated and the Americans pondered their options. Chiang had every reason to hold on to these rocky fragments off the coast of his homeland. He feared a drop in Nationalist morale if the islands were lost; they were his oft-announced stepping-stones to a reconquest of the mainland; their inlets gave him sanctuary for guerrilla raids; they tied down local Communist troops; and they were excellent points from which to harass and even blockade Foochow and Amoy.

For Eisenhower, the Nationalist hold on the islands was probably a bigger pain in the neck than that suffered by Mao. The president kept the Seventh Fleet as a tripwire across the Formosa Strait but at increased risk, because Peking still held about sixty-two Americans under detention, of whom twenty-two were military captives from Korea. The Joint Chiefs declared the islands essential to the defense of Formosa (how this conclusion was reached was never quite clear) and added that the Nationalists needed American assistance to hold them.

—And American assistance they would get. After three months of the shelling, on 2 December 1954, Chiang won a formal Mutual Defense Treaty with the United States (ratified two months later), although the agreement said nothing about Quemoy or Matsu. Chiang's island regime, still putatively one of the wartime "Big Five" in the United Nations, thus gained a limited legitimacy. But American policy was deliberately ambiguous; if the Seventh Fleet were to actually defend the offshore islands in the course of defending Formosa, the Navy would be scuppers-deep in what was, essentially, still a Chinese civil war.

The stakes were not long in being raised. On 10 January 1955, one hundred Red Chinese aircraft attacked the Nationalist-held Tachen Islands, well offshore and about two hundred miles north of Formosa. Ichiang Island, near the Tachens, was actually occupied by four thousand of Mao's troops, in itself remarkable proof that the Navy's Formosa Strait patrol could not be everywhere at once. Radio Peking promptly bragged that the fall of Ichiang had showed a "determined will to fight for the liberation of Taiwan" (as Formosa was now, once again, beginning to be called).

Eisenhower quickly riposted; two weeks later Congress whipped through the Formosa Resolution by whopping bipartisan majorities, 410–3 in the House and 85–3 in the Senate. This resolution, which would set a most unfortunate precedent for the enlargement of executive authority in Far Eastern military affairs and elsewhere, gave the president the power to use American forces to defend Formosa and the nearby Pescadores against armed attack. Ike was authorized to secure and protect "such related positions and territories of that area now in friendly hands . . . as he judges to be required or appropriate."

"*As he judges*"—Democrat Walter George of Georgia, who as chairman of the Foreign Relations Committee shepherded the resolution through the Senate, reassured his colleagues that "I believe that President Eisenhower is a prudent man." No one recalled that James Madison had sapiently written, in Federalist Number Ten, that enlightened statesmen would not always be at the helm.

In the interim the Tachens, less than eight miles from occupied Ichiang and only fifteen miles from the mainland, could no longer be "secured or protected" without a major (and unwanted) commitment of American forces. Far from straining at his leash, Chiang could not even defend his front doorstep. Accordingly, the Seventh Fleet, on 5 February, was ordered to evacuate Nationalist forces from the area.

There followed a miniature replay of the Indochina sealift, in which the Navy moved over 20,000 troops and civilians down to Formosa. In the meantime, American naval forces from all over the world began to converge on the strait. On 9 February, a Skyraider covering the evacuation was shot down twenty miles southeast of the Tachens. Eisenhower celebrated the rescue of the crew and downplayed the incident itself.

Now the crisis reached harrowing proportions, providing yet another demonstration of the weakness of the New Look as strategy. Probably the only things that averted a direct shooting war were Eisenhower's prudence and restraint, coupled with Mao's lack of seapower. Peking, never of a navalist bent, depended on fast coastal patrol vessels to guard its various ports, prevent smuggling (still very much a way of life in the Far East), and stop the escape of defectors—this last, in the wake of the POW imbroglio in the final months of the Korean War, a consummate loss of face. The Red Chinese navy also had a few cast-off Russian diesel submarines. In 1955, when the Soviets abandoned Lü-shun, they also handed over two destroyers and five newer-model subs. All this was certainly nonthreatening in naval terms, but the president was chilled by the prospect of sliding into another war with the Red Chinese with little support from America's allies and with equally little chance of endorsement from the American public.

Chiang, for his part, rebuffed an idea to create a "maritime zone" in the strait, which meant in practice that the Seventh Fleet would have had to blockade the China coast from Wenchou in the north to Swatow in the south.[7]

☆

For four years, from 1950 onward, the Seventh Fleet had been asked to "neutralize" the Formosa Strait, patrolling vigilantly to keep two antagonists from each other's throats. This was a considerable strain that the Navy could have done without. On 26 March 1955, Mick Carney, perhaps reacting to the pressure, made an off-the-record statement (immediately leaked to the press) predicting a Chinese attack on Quemoy and Matsu in April and indicating that the Joint Chiefs advocated an all-out attack on Mao's forces in response.

By that time the Formosa Strait patrol had practically become institutional. The Navy had to be both wary and ready—the La-7 incident in July 1954 was proof. (Later, in August 1956, Chinese fighters shot down a Mercator plane from VQ-1 out of Iwakuni, Japan, on a night mission, killing the entire crew.)

Shortly after assuming office, Eisenhower had made a dramatic statement that the Seventh Fleet would "no longer be employed to shield Communist China," as if Chiang's defeated forces would now suddenly spring back onto the mainland in all their righteous fury. In fact, the Navy (operating under secret orders from Truman) had encouraged and even abetted Nationalist raids against the Chinese coast for some time.

In sum, the Navy was not engaged in any "neutralization patrol" at all, and Carney's slip of the tongue only punctuated the point. Chiang, for his part, had declared, "Give us the tools, and we will finish the job of reconquering Red China." Right-wing Republicans, in particular, were obsessed with the idea that the Seventh Fleet was such a "tool."[8]

CINCPAC himself, Admiral Felix Stump, was not far from believing the same thing. A slender balding naval aviator, Stump had commanded the second *Lexington* and a carrier division during World War II, winning two Navy Crosses along the way. Captain Steve Jurika, who worked for him, remembered Stump as "very, very understanding . . . very kind." But CINCPAC was a naval version of Dulles, the son of a Baptist preacher, "strong-minded and strong-willed," according to his staff chaplain. With Stump, strong-mindedness usually won out over understanding. "If he [could] run over you," said Admiral Charles Duncan, "you're dead." "A frightening personality to people who don't know him," recalled his intelligence officer, Rear Admiral Samuel Frankel.

Most of his juniors never had a chance to "know" Stump, and since everyone in the Pacific was junior to CINCPAC, the "frightening personality" was often on display. Stump was a virulent anti-Communist, totally committed to victory in the Cold War. "It is always serious," he proclaimed, "when additional millions of helpless human beings become Communist slaves."

With the Korean War ended, Stump kept a light cruiser, half a dozen destroyers, and some auxiliaries near the peninsula, operating as they chose so long as they stayed clear of the three-mile offshore limit recognized by the United States. But they, and the rest of the Seventh Fleet, kept their weapons cocked, especially since CINCPAC's passionate attention to the

Communist menace was being increasingly drawn to the Formosa Strait. "If a man approaches you with a pistol in his hand," Stump argued, "you don't have to wait until he shoots you before you try to stop him."

But the Formosa Strait was a bit more complicated than the OK Corral. By September 1954, four navies were shouldering one another throughout its hundred-mile-wide swath. In the strait itself, a handful of American destroyers prowled up and down the mainland coast (usually, despite Stump's three-mile claim, outside the internationally recognized limit of twelve miles). They endlessly scanned the hundreds of junks that daily sailed from mainland ports and fishing villages, while their sensitive radars probed the infinitude of jagged inlets and river mouths. Just to the south, in the rough oceanic triangle formed by Formosa, Hong Kong, and the Philippines, carrier task forces maneuvered on the flat, glassy sea.

The flattops had their combat air patrols up from dawn to dusk. Navy Neptunes and Mariners cruised lazily above the coast, watching for ship or troop concentrations. Bogeys produced air-raid alarms back on Formosa. Far to the north, along a great arc running from Vladivostok through Dairen and south to Tsingtao, American submarines stood silent watch on Russian and Chinese shipping. Occasionally, the boats would keep an eye on Hainan as well.

The Royal Navy was passing through, escorting British merchant ships from Hong Kong to Communist ports in the north. (Unlike the United States, Great Britain had diplomatically recognized Mao's regime.) Nationalist Chinese warships flitted back and forth, occasionally bombarding shore targets and conducting hit-and-run raids. Chiang's "navy" was composed of American cast-offs: two 1650-ton destroyers, six destroyer escorts, some antiquated Japanese vessels, and a few gunboats. This mosquito fleet was just big enough to cause trouble and not big enough to do anything about the results.

Mao's "navy" in 1954, before the Soviet gifts, was really no navy at all, only a motley collection of thousands of junks. Some people feared the specter of a junk armada, each one carrying fifty soldiers, descending upon Formosa. Navy planners could afford to scoff at this scenario, but in the meantime the junk traffic in the strait was a pounding headache, because the junks could easily carry raiding parties and saboteurs, sowing mines to boot.

All these seagoing forces, packed into a very tight stretch of water, meant serious problems for Vice Admiral Alfred ("Mel") Pride, commander of the Seventh Fleet. He was another pioneer of naval aviation, flying off the old *Langley* back in 1922 when such stunts were truly death-defying. Mel Pride was not a zealot of Stump's caliber; he was a low-key, salty New Englander, crisply mustachioed and dignified. His way to the top had been most unusual; no Naval Academy graduate, he had attended Tufts University and begun his naval career as a second class machinist's mate during World War I. "Thoroughly competent" was the assessment of John Noel.

Pride flew his flag aboard the cruiser *Saint Paul*, but his real concern, in addition to maintaining his destroyer patrols, lay in making sure his carrier air wings, aboard *Yorktown* and *Hornet*, were prepared. His trigger finger was not quite as itchy as Stump's. "I'm not out here to start World War III," he said. "But we're ready."

"Ready" meant Task Force 72, the Formosa Strait patrol. Everyone in the task force knew the most unrealistic part of their mission was keeping the Nationalists from attacking the mainland. "We were the best allies the Communists had," in the words of one naval aviator. Staying out of the civil war, and yet keeping a finger on the trigger, was a constant worry; often the aviators could see cannon fire erupting among the islands and would fly over fierce ground skirmishes. By September 1954, Task Force 72 had been operating for over four years, and some of its aviators were now on their third six-month tour of duty.

With such a crowd in such confined space, the United Nations rocked to a cross fire of charges and countercharges concerning rights of passage, maritime boundaries, and freedom of the seas. The Soviets managed to accuse the United States Navy of "piracy." As the name-calling went on, the incidents at sea piled up—and the guns stayed cocked.[9]

The Seventh Fleet's orders continued to be those of preventing an assault on Formosa. But thanks in large part to the Formosa Resolution, Pride's ships did not have clear orders about whether Quemoy and Matsu were in their defensive area. In addition, there was that twelve-mile limit, and the water depth between the offshore islands and the mainland was very shallow. Chiang's mouth, at least, was "unleashed," and he endlessly announced that the fall of the two island groups would be but a preliminary to the invasion of Formosa. Eisenhower was told that Nationalist morale would fall if no attempt was made to defend Quemoy and Matsu.

Thus Dulles was far from alone when he fervently wished for an end to "this horrible business." Radford, backed by all the Joint Chiefs except Ridgway, recommended putting American forces on Quemoy and Matsu, bombing the mainland as an exclamation point. Pride's carrier air wings had to plan for sorties over mainland Chinese cities. Eisenhower, again to his credit, once more rejected Raddy's advice. The Mutual Defense Treaty with Chiang included only Formosa and the Pescadores, omitting Quemoy and Matsu. The Seventh Fleet was ordered to "act defensively."

On New Year's Day 1955, Chiang predicted "war at any time," and indeed the United States came closer to using atomic weapons in the Formosa crisis than during the Indochina affair. But the Tachen evacuation proved to be the intermediate solution. Mick Carney protested the abandonment of the Tachens and the Formosa Resolution itself. For him, the whole thing was a turn-tail retreat. Instead of evacuating the Tachens, argued the chief of naval operations, the United States should defend them—as the easier and wiser course of action. This was a job for Pride's Seventh Fleet.

Eisenhower rounded on his top naval adviser, told him there was no relationship between the Tachens and Formosa, and ordered him to get on with the evacuation. Carney did so. The president had told reporters that "any invasion of Formosa would have to run over the Seventh Fleet," but Quemoy and Matsu were a different matter altogether. He was having trouble, however, holding his fractious military team together. With the exception of Ridgway, his Joint Chiefs were ready for a shooting war. Radford admitted that the offshore islands were not vital to the defense of Formosa, but he insisted that their loss would have "bad, possibly disastrous, psychological effects" on Chiang's troops.

But Ike, like Mel Pride, was not about to start World War III. Carney's orders sped down the line through Stump in Hawaii to Pride aboard *Saint Paul*, culminating with Rear Admiral Lorenzo Sabin, Commander Amphibious Forces, Western Pacific. Sabin, a Texan, was a Blackshoe and a veteran amphibious specialist. Vice Admiral George Dyer, no mean judge of character, called him a "thoroughly capable naval officer."

Sabin had a huge force at his disposal: five attack carriers, four heavy cruisers, twenty destroyers, and four attack transports, plus assorted amphibious vessels. Indeed, the Tachens operation featured every element of full-scale amphibious assault except the assault force itself. "In no combat engagement of World War II," reflected the hawk-faced Sabin, "did I have such a comforting feeling of personal security as I did when I surveyed the armada guarding my flagship in this one."

Sabin, however, was never to understand the thinking behind what he called the "giveaway" of the Tachens. His was not to reason why. His force was within easy gun range of the Chinese mainland, all his battle stations were manned, guns loaded and ready, combat air patrols aloft. Pride had sent him into these tight waters by saying that "the Commies will start World War III when and where they wish, if they wish, and no minor move by us will make any difference at all."

The "minor move" attracted the eyes of the world. Leading American press lights, men like Joe Alsop, Homer Bigart, and Keyes Beech, were on hand; so too were writers from *Time* and *Life*. Something new showed up— CBS Television sent a team. The news services were all there, and so were the newsreels. For the folks back home, the Tachens operation *was* reduced to the face-off at the OK Corral.

But there was no photogenic war, only a sad procession of thousands of Nationalist Chinese filing aboard American ships. (Chiang had to be cajoled, at the last minute, into ordering his troops to cooperate.) The whole process, which Mao's men carefully watched but with which they did not interfere, took almost a week. In an eighty-five-hour period, 27,000 people were evacuated by sea, along with 8600 tons of equipment, 100 vehicles, and 166 heavy guns. Underway replenishment sustained everyone. All through the night of 11 February, Navy demolition teams did their work, and the islands were lit by the detonations of the fortifications and minefields that had been created by the Nationalists in expectation of the attack that never came. The next morning the work was completed; Sabin and his armada steamed away to the south.[10]

Whether the Tachens evacuation was a needless giveaway, as Carney, Sabin, and many other Navymen believed, or whether the move was a necessary diplomatic ploy, Peking may have been influenced. At any rate, the evacuation, though certainly no rollback of communism, was a classic demonstration of American seapower, carried out in the very shadow of a potential enemy. Peking may have been angered and abashed, but the Red Chinese leadership may also have been apprehensive. "The betting here, at this time," said *U.S. News & World Report* in a cheerleading stance typical of most American press coverage, "is that Communist leaders are aware of the fleet's power and are unwilling to start a fight with an antagonist that so far overshadows any force they can throw against it."

Seventh Fleet, including Task Force 72, was about the strength of the Sixth Fleet in the Mediterranean, but the Med was a pond compared with WestPac. Pride and Sabin were also operating ships manned at about 60 percent to 70 percent of their wartime complements; many officers and men were standing double duty. Morale was generally high, but the fingers stayed off the triggers. "Sure, I want to get home," admitted one aviator aboard *Yorktown*. "But I don't want to miss anything either. If trouble comes, I hope it will be before we leave."[11]

Trouble—the kind of trouble Eisenhower feared—did not come (although Stump predicted a Red Chinese attack on the offshore islands in early March, which may have influenced Carney's later, leaked prediction). Patrol planes still droned up and down the strait. Seaplanes and their mother-hen tenders—in their last major operation—worked out of the Pescadores. Formosa, crammed now with over 8.5 million people, suggested a loaded lifeboat surrounded by bristling American naval power. Carrier combat air patrols flew day and night, and destroyers still restlessly darted about.

The cans had the toughest job. Aboard them shipboard routine went on—hammers chipping away, gun mechanisms hissing as the barrels slewed to track a "skunk," blowers roaring, propeller shafts relentlessly pounding. Ordinarily, four-destroyer squadrons were assigned the patrol, for two or three months at a time, but at any given moment only two were actually in the strait, policing separate, sixty-mile-long north-south sectors, some fifteen miles off the mainland. Another destroyer might be sampling Hong Kong on R and R and getting worked over by Mary Soo and her girls, while the fourth ship, acting as the squadron flag, might be moored to a buoy in Kaohsiung Harbor, Formosa.[12]

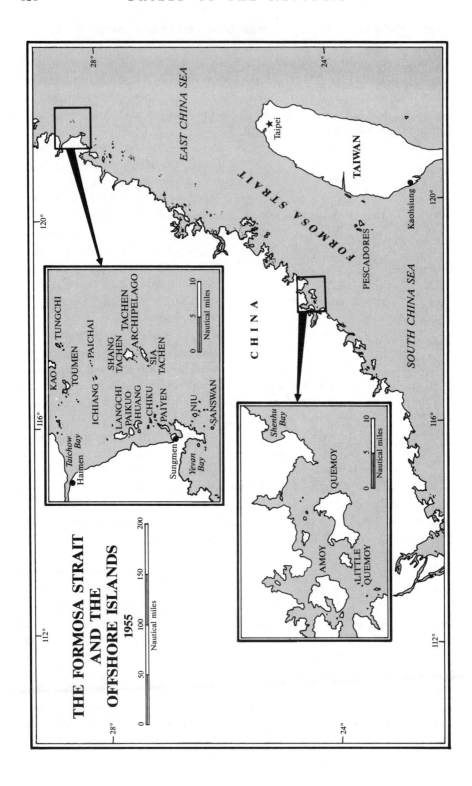

THE FORMOSA STRAIT
AND THE
OFFSHORE ISLANDS
1955

Nautical miles

Such a routine—exhausted off-duty officers and men tumbling wearily into their racks, radars endlessly searching, guns tracking back and forth—seemingly could have gone on forever.

☆

—But the diplomats found a way. The Red Chinese, perhaps influenced by the smoothness of the Tachens evacuation and certainly influenced by the parade of American naval power, suggested (via Chou En-lai on 23 April at the Bandung Conference) that they were willing to begin direct discussions with the United States. Dulles had ignored an earlier suggestion in February; the contretemps in the Formosa Strait might have been a "horrible business," but the thought of negotiating with godless Communists was more horrible still. However, allied pressure was strong for ending the crisis, and American public opinion, balanced on tenterhooks for eight months, was also restless. In early May an American pollster reported 70 percent approval of the talks.

The crisis petered out in the aftermath of Bandung, a conference featuring the anticolonialist rhetoric of the new, "nonaligned" nations. Washington and Peking did not actually get to the Geneva conference table until 1 August 1955. The talks did not resolve the issue of the offshore islands, nor did they really address the fate of Nationalist Formosa. But the diplomats adapted a face-saving formula to stop the shelling of Quemoy and Matsu and thus to end the crisis. Eisenhower sent a private message to Chiang, reassuring the Nationalist leader that America was still committed to the defense of Formosa.

By the end of May 1955, shooting had stopped in the Formosa Strait. Chiang's troops remained ensconced on Quemoy and Matsu. At month's end, also, Peking released four American fliers, and during the summer all other prisoners were freed. The American naval presence in the strait diminished—but the destroyer patrol stayed in place.

Eisenhower had kept his hand off the nuclear trigger. But his approach to the crisis had been deliberately ambiguous and even downright scary. At a press conference on 16 March he was asked about the possible use of tactical atomic weapons. "Yes, of course they would be used" in the event of war, he replied. "In any combat where these things can be used on strictly military targets and for strictly military purposes, I see no reason why they shouldn't be used just exactly as you would use a bullet or anything else."

Such words were manna to Radford, and Carney was also looking for an excuse to use American naval power. Eisenhower even admitted to his diary that Carney might be right, that only military force could deal with the recklessness and indifference of Peking. But in the end he took his own counsel and rejected the advice of almost all his "experts," including most of his military leaders. That advice ran the gamut, from liquidating Chiang to joining the Nationalists in some sort of Far Eastern jihad against communism.

Eisenhower's policy, fumbling and stumbling at times, rested in the last analysis on American force and the announced willingness to use that force—which meant naval power. In the process, the atomic saber was rattled, which in turn rattled the world. People were forced to reflect on whether flyspecks such as Quemoy and Matsu were worth nuclear holocaust, or even worth the tension that came with the threat of nuclear weapons. The policy, as the administration twisted and turned in the toils of Dulles's "horrible business," was, in the words of one authority, "awkward, illogical, incomplete, ethically questionable, and legally dubious." But, and not in the least because Navy ships and planes were muzzle to muzzle with Mao's forces, locked and loaded, the policy worked.[13]

—Once again, however, the New Look had proved, as a strategy, to be bankrupt—and terrifying.

☆

The waters of the Formosa Strait never completely cooled; they merely simmered. By late 1957 the Navy's presence, close against the Asian littoral, had become routine. From the Kamchatka Peninsula in the north to North Vietnam in the south, the Seventh Fleet, sixty thousand men strong, tracked Soviet subs and destroyers, which at times steamed serenely through its bailiwick, and kept constant watch on Chinese coastal traffic.

By this time, the Seventh Fleet belonged to Vice Admiral Wallace Beakley, an aviator and an expert on antisubmarine warfare who had also been seasoned in naval diplomacy. He had swum to safety from Forrest Sherman's sinking *Wasp* when she was torpedoed during World War II. Wally Beakley, blue-eyed and blunt-nosed, was a perfectionist who delighted in both a good dry martini and a fast set of tennis. At Annapolis he had been distinguished not only for his brightness but also for his proclivity for sleeping in every morning. But he improved; by World War II, as a captain, he had convinced even Ernie King of his abilities. (Highly professional and cooperative, a despondent Beakley would later, after the loss of his crippled wife, commit suicide.)

At the moment, his units, on any given day, could be found peacefully feasting on the delights of the liberty ports throughout the area—particularly Hong Kong, Manila, Keelung, Inchon, Yokosuka, and Singapore. "We have to fly the flag for our friends to see," said Beakley, "but we must not show it too often. Our friends must see the flag often enough to be reassured that we are here."

Under Beakley, Task Force 72 still patrolled the Formosa Strait, looking for signs of trouble. Task Force 77, carrying the latest atomic weapons for its new A-3D Skywarriors, continued as the fast carrier attack force. Task Force 70, the Hunter-Killer Group, was poised to deal with Soviet submarines. Task Force 73 resupplied the fleet, Task Force 75 was trained for surface strikes, and Task Force 76 provided amphibious lift. Ashore, Task

Force 79 consisted of seventeen thousand Marines, stationed on Okinawa and with powerful support from the 1st Marine Air Wing, also armed with atomic weapons.

The Seventh Fleet proudly advertised itself as "the world's largest operating fleet." In addition to his A-3Ds and the Marines, Beakley's midget A-4s could pack an atomic punch, and so too could the new Regulus I missiles. Also on line were *Thetis Bay*, the first ship specially configured for helicopter assaults, and *Carronade*, a rocket-firing little dragon on an LST hull. All this power had done much, in the previous three years, to neutralize North Korea's highly dangerous four-hundred-thousand-man army; to check Red China's three-million-man army and 2000-plane air force; and to monitor the Soviet Union's considerable military presence in the Far East, which included three tactical air armies, mounting 1700 jet fighters and more than 800 bombers.[14]

"Commanding the Seventh Fleet is a marvelous job," enthused Beakley. "There's no time to be bored." Both Chinese sides soon made sure of that. The Nationalists had steadily and cheekily increased their strength on both Quemoy and Matsu until, by August 1958, Chiang had one hundred thousand troops (over 30 percent of his total force) shoehorned onto the offshore islands. On 24 August, after protesting numerous times, Peking began, once again, to shell the islands. The bombardment was desultory but still obnoxious; there was no evidence of any impending assault from the mainland. At times the volume of fire reached fifty thousand rounds a day.

Eisenhower dusted off his domino metaphor. The fall of Quemoy and Matsu, he said, would "lead to the loss of Formosa," and then "the future security of Japan, the Philippines, Thailand, Vietnam, and even Okinawa" would be threatened. "United States vital interests would suffer severely." The president authorized the Seventh Fleet to provide protection to Chiang's convoys trying to resupply the islands, under the three-mile-limit restriction. (When the American escorts, usually two cruisers and four destroyers, would peel off, Mao's forces would start shelling the convoys as if by signal— and the Nationalist ships would usually turn and scoot away without delivering their cargoes.)

About two hundred miles over the horizon, the seventeen ships of Task Force 77, centered now on *Midway* and *Lexington*, prowled at the ready. F-8U Crusaders from the carriers swept along the Chinese coast at a thousand knots, their Sidewinder missiles inscribed with obscene messages to the Communists. "We make lots of big radar blips," joshed one of *Midway*'s aviators. The Formosa Strait had not been easy on *Midway*—the year before she had lost two fliers and three planes to accidents within a week. On the deck of each carrier, poised over the special weapons bay, stood a single A-3D Skywarrior—waiting for the word from Washington.

The word never came. At first, on 6 September, the Joint Chiefs recommended that Beakley be given wider freedom of action, up to and including air strikes on the Chinese mainland. Rebuffed by Eisenhower, the Chiefs then said, "The islands are not defensible and probably not required for the defense of Formosa." The scenario was déjà vu; no one wanted World War III to start over such insignificant patches of real estate, and not a single NATO ally was prepared to support the defense of Quemoy and Matsu. For his part, Beakley ordered his command, "If the Communists shoot, shoot back."

Under pressure again from the Americans, Chiang grudgingly issued a statement renouncing the use of force as an acceptable means of getting back to the mainland. Peking responded with a short cease-fire, then unaccountably announced that its men would shell Nationalist convoys on odd-numbered days of the month only, thus permitting resupply operations on even days. Eisenhower, not without cause, wondered "if we were in a Gilbert and Sullivan war."

Eventually Chiang reduced his garrisons on the islands (the cost of continuously resupplying so many mouths was astronomical), Mao stopped firing, and this second crisis went the way of the first. There was no war, no retreat, no loss of face—only the casualties of the shelling and the still-smoldering hatreds of Mao, Chiang, and their peoples.[15]

The comic-opera aspects of this second crisis could not, however, obscure the reality. Wally Beakley's force of 125 warships, as large as Halsey's or Spruance's striking fleets in World War II, and armed with atomic weapons, had been nose-to-nose once again with a prospective enemy, over eight thousand miles from the continental United States. Kansas-born Harry ("Don") Felt, a fervent naval aviator who had relieved Felix Stump as CINC-PAC, was as staunchly anti-Communist as his predecessor. (In fact, vocal and intense anticommunism was transmitted intact from Radford through Stump to Felt and beyond, to Oley Sharp and others who would command in the American lake, almost as though the walls at Makalapa Heights harbored a virus.) Felt recalled that he and his staff had believed that the use of tactical nuclear weapons in the second crisis would *not* start World War III. They planned for such use in the Formosa Strait because "we didn't have a plan to do it any other way."

Fortunately, and due largely once again to Eisenhower's resistance to the advice he was getting from many of his military men, this strategic rigidity was never to become operational reality. By 1959 WestPac had cooled down once more, and the Seventh Fleet had resumed its routine patrols—which included Task Force 72's omnipresent destroyer watch.

The sailors got back to creating what the Navy euphemistically called "good will." Every day, over 25,000 of them went ashore somewhere in WestPac, payday resting heavily in their wallets. "They leave behind a lot of friends," said one observer—which was true. They also left behind a lot of money. Over eighty ships of the Service Force were necessary to sustain them out there—1100 officers and 19,000 men for this task alone. They spent their time at sea practicing skills and conducting exercises, such as SEATO drills involving as many as sixty ships.

Seventh Fleet had demonstrated neither too much nor too little seapower but just enough to maintain the desired status quo in the Formosa Strait. Nationalist Chinese morale and self-confidence soared; whether this was the best use of American naval force remained, however, a moot point. The offshore islands once again moved to the back pages, and then they vanished from the world's attention. Political purposes and the more extreme proposals of some naval leaders aside, the crises in the Formosa Strait showed definitively what superior naval force could do.

The Navy's presence off the Asian littoral had become perpetual. Seventh Fleet's staff coined a motto: "We have no schedule, and we adhere to it!"[16]

☆

Mick Carney was not around for the second Formosa crisis. His warning about a Red Chinese attack on the offshore islands back in March 1955 had angered Eisenhower, even though, when asked at a press conference if his chief of naval operations would be reprimanded, the president had cryptically responded, "Not by me." Observers noted that Secretary of Defense Wilson quickly directed military personnel to submit all their speeches, press releases, and "other information" to his office for clearance.

In fact, Ike was thoroughly tired of the nattering among his Joint Chiefs, of their obvious reluctance to play team ball. Carney was only one of the offenders. But he, in addition, had no friend in Engine Charlie Wilson. Army General James Gavin, "Jumpin' Jim" from World War II and one of Eisenhower's Pentagon planners, asserted that Wilson treated the Chiefs like "recalcitrant union bosses"—which, in some circumstances, they were.

Carney's two-year appointment was up in August 1955, but he no longer had friends in high places. Secretary of the Navy Charles Thomas, who long had thought that Carney was excluding him from key decisions, told him in May that he would not be reappointed. Mick Carney would go into retirement with his head held high, a speech he gave to students at the Naval War College his fitting naval epitaph. "Be frank and fearless in your considered counsels," he said. "No valid exception can be taken to forthright and mature opinion; there need be no inconsistency between honest belief and loyal compliance with the dictates of constituted authority."

The matter of his relief was handled cloak-and-dagger. The man in question was hustled secretly into Washington to be briefed by Radford, Wilson, and Thomas—perhaps, the bewildered individual thought, for some sort of joint staff position. On 10 May, Thomas resummoned him to the Pentagon and offered him Carney's post.

The man was amazed; ahead of him on the Navy Register were no fewer than ninety-two admirals, more than eighty of whom were possible candidates for the job he had been offered. Besides, he deeply admired his longtime friend Carney. (Thomas, who also liked Carney, thought that Mick had relied too much on old, mossback cronies who lacked imagination and vigor, opposing change at every step.)

In a state of shock, the successor left Thomas's office and, "with his heart in his boots," immediately sought out Carney. Riding home with him that evening, he unleashed his volley of misgivings. He would not last two years in the job; he would be the sixth man in the slot since King had left in 1945. He had little experience with high-level policy-making. He was unsure of his own competence. He did not really know Thomas, or Wilson, or Eisenhower (who had actually selected him). He was afraid he had been chosen "because they thought I might be a push-over."

If that was what they were thinking, Carney responded, then "they are due for a hell of a surprise."[17]

—Indeed they were. On 17 August 1955, Arleigh Albert Burke became the fifteenth chief of naval operations.

CHAPTER TWENTY-SIX

BURKE

T he high plains of Colorado were a far remove from salt water. There were analogues, though, between this windswept, semiarid land and the ocean. Living on each was tough, and each tolerated rather than accepted the presence of man. Oscar Burke, second son of a Swedish baker's apprentice who had emigrated to America in 1857, learned this lesson well. He bounced around eastern Colorado in the late nineteenth century, working as a cowboy and a miner before homesteading with his wife, Clara. The Burke farm prospered, and the place was close enough to Boulder so that Clara could teach grade school in town.

Their first son, Arleigh Albert (his name probably cribbed from one of Clara's heroes, Sir Walter Raleigh), arrived on 19 October 1901, the first of six children. Oscar never interfered with the education of his offspring, but young Arleigh—chunky, blond, blue-eyed, a pure Swede (the family's original name was Björkgren)—was assigned, like his brother and four sisters, endless farm work. From these chores, which Oscar commanded be finished *on time*, Arleigh had punctuality and independent problem solving pounded into him from his earliest years. The five-room farmhouse required order and system; there was a wood stove that demanded to be incessantly fed, and there was neither indoor plumbing nor electricity.

The parents were frugal but friendly, each a promoter of proper planning and rules of conduct. "I've got land, I've got kids," Oscar used to boast, "and I owe no man a dime." Arleigh learned his three Rs at Baseline Elementary School, a new red-brick structure built on land donated by his father. As he rose through the grades, the boy made one early decision: the tedium and backbreaking work of the family farm were not for him. By the eighth grade, he was writing papers in praise of military training and preparedness.

He entered high school in Boulder in the fall of 1915, riding in on horseback each day from the farm. Oscar and Clara wanted him to go to college but, typically, urged him to pay his own way. So Arleigh, while hating the work, hired himself out to neighboring farms. He also trapped muskrats along the tumbling Bear and Boulder creeks, cleaning, stretching, and drying the skins to be sent on to furriers in Denver, St. Louis, and Chicago. At a dollar a pelt, he began to wonder if he would ever accrue enough for college.

With the coming of World War I, military life was in the air. Arleigh got the bright idea that West Point, with its free board, tuition, and small salary, was the answer. A neighbor arranged an interview for the youngster with the local congressman, Charles Timberlake. This gracious old gentleman informed Arleigh that all his Military Academy slots were filled or promised, far into the future.

A teacher told Arleigh that the Naval Academy offered a similar deal (young Burke had never heard of the place). Timberlake again turned him down, with the same reasons. Arleigh worked at odd jobs during the summer of 1918, scheming always about college. Then, unaccountably, Timberlake's Naval Academy appointees for 1919 withdrew, and the congressman announced that he would appoint the top two scorers on the entrance examination.

Not for the last time, the problems confronting Arleigh were enormous. His school, like so many others across the nation, shut down during the terrible influenza epidemic of 1918 and 1919. For $100 a month, he got himself into a prep school for the Academy, improbably located in Columbia, Missouri, for a three-month cram course. There, for room and board, he did kitchen and cleaning work. His courses were all memory-jamming, based on the generations-old tradition of naval education.

To cap all, the evening before Timberlake's exam day in April 1919, a Rocky Mountain snowstorm blew in. Arleigh rode into Boulder, stabled his horse, and spent the night sleeping next to the animal. The next morning he showed up for the test—one of the few candidates to do so. He had, more or less, memorized what answers he could back in Columbia, and his characteristic tenacity paid off. His appointment came by mail.

Arleigh was almost broke by the time the train deposited him in Annapolis, hungry and alone, a hick farmboy from the high-plains outback. As he passed through the entrance gate, he got his first sense of a few of the traditions that would wrap themselves around his life; stately academic buildings stood to his left, the imposing mass of Bancroft Hall to his right. A gray-haired jimmylegs at the gate gave him some advice: "Keep your back straight and your mouth shut. There's no room for wise guys at this Academy."

—This was all the wisdom he got, and all he ever needed. On 26 June 1919, Arleigh Burke took his place with the 708 other midshipmen in the Class of 1923.[1]

☆

Burke was used to long, sweaty hours of labor, to monotony and regimentation. He took to plebe summer like a duck to water. He found the Navy was his kind of place, one in which "the rules were strict, known, and observed." His stocky, muscular build, the product of years of farm work, discouraged harsh hazing by upperclassmen, but he accepted the lesser indignities, such as push-ups, with his usual good humor.

There was, however, a streak of Scandinavian melancholy in him. All his life, spells of depression would occasionally clamp down, and the homesickness and sequestration of plebe year did not help. Things began to look up when he was introduced to Roberta Gorsuch, the Kansas-born daughter of a Washington businessman. Together, they made a rather odd couple, he with his ragged country mannerisms and Bobbie a shy but determined mite barely five feet tall.

Plebe year passed, and Burke survived. He did not like the more brutal forms of hazing for those entering after him, such as banging away with broom handles on upturned rear ends. He supported, instead, "constructive hazing," with plebes learning naval knowledge or skills—the kind of regimen followed today. His own grades were just average or barely above; by his own admission, to keep them even at this level he had to "work like hell."

Arleigh Burke thrived on working like hell. He boxed, wrestled, and fenced amid attention to the books. As much as possible, he squired Bobbie to balls and other doings about town. With his peers he was reasonably popular, good-humored and open when the black moods were not upon him. His fellow mids nicknamed him "Satchel" during plebe year, for his excessively padded posterior; when the movie star Billie Burke visited the Academy, this tag passed into blessed oblivion and he began to be called "Billie."

His wrestling produced Burke's favorite Academy story. As a junior he won his class numerals in the sport. Eager to get them sewn on his sweater, he sped to the tailor shop, which was located next to the "natatorium," or swimming pool. Told he could have the sweater back the next day, Burke again dashed to the tailor's at the appointed hour. In his haste, he took a shortcut through the swimming pool dressing room.

—He had forgotten about ladies' day at the pool. Shrieks and screams accompanied his embarrassed lunge for the exit. The next morning a chillingly calm request appeared in the order of the day: "Will the midshipman who entered the woman's dressing room about 1000 yesterday please report to the commandant." Burke lay low—very low. The outside door to the dressing room was quickly nailed shut.

The story was consonant with Burke's standing at the Academy. While affable and hardworking, he made little impression. He held no regimental rank, no student office. He would be recalled as neither influential nor colorful. He was not a cipher, but he was no standout, either. At the end, in June 1923, he was *respectable*, graduating seventy-first in a class drastically reduced by resignations to 413 men.

Graduation day was his wedding day; he and Bobbie began Navy life together walking out of the chapel under the crossed swords. She became, in every way, his ally and support. They would remain childless, and her attention was to be centered on him, on his career and his comfort. "Wonderful woman," he would later say about her while she was in earshot. "All the attributes of a perfect wife. Warmth, understanding, stamina."

He might as well have said "perfect Navy wife." For the young couple, stamina was what really counted. The bride and groom immediately took the train to the West Coast, where his first assignment, *Arizona*, waited. Burke was eager to begin serving in what he was already calling "my navy."[2]

☆

Four out of every five Academy grads went to battlewagons; Burke was just another ensign. He spent five years aboard *Arizona*. On her he did navigation, learned steam engineering, and began his technical training in gunnery, first as a turret officer in the big fourteen-inch mounts, then as head of the plotting room. Over all the junior officers loomed the shadows of tight money, a return to American isolationism, and a seriously contracting fleet in the wake of the Great War and the Washington Disarmament Conference. In 1922, Burke and his classmates had been warned that 50 percent of them might never wear Navy blue; those that remained would be lucky to make lieutenant commander.

Burke's running mates vanished like raindrops in the desert. By 1928, the year he left *Arizona*, only 269 of his class remained on active duty; by 1933 only 230 were left (a number that probably would have been even lower but for the Depression); by 1940 there were only 193—a drop of more than 50 percent in seventeen years and of 73 percent from those who had first walked through the gate with him back in 1919. Burke's formative professional years were ones of desuetude for the Navy.

Ensign Burke made his way as he was accustomed, gaining a reputation for amiability, efficiency, and hard work. Establishing a pattern for his entire career, his nose-to-the-grindstone attitude aboard *Arizona* only earned him tougher assignments. The topper of these, in the winter of 1924, was the chore of cleaning the battleship's double bottoms. Hercules, confronting the Augean Stables, could not have been more dismayed. The men assigned to Burke for the job were real roughnecks, sailors who were being punished by being sent into the Navy's version of the underworld to scrape rust and drain bilges.

Burke, as either Hercules or Orpheus, went at the job with both anger and determination; anger that he always seemed to get the nasty assignments (the first lieutenant had suggested that being assigned to lead Navy hardcases into the bilges was a compliment), and determination to see the thing through by sweating away amid reeking paint fumes in near-suffocating conditions, right alongside his bilge rats. The double bottoms got cleaned, and his stock rose aboard *Arizona*.

—That is, until a hooker, posing as a sailor, was smuggled aboard in New York. The sailors, quick to sense a good deal, nicknamed her "Blackie" and connived to give her practically the run (and the business) of the ship, outside Officer's Country. Blackie was not discovered until *Arizona* reached the Canal Zone, when a chief, waiting in line to use the scuttlebutt, noticed that the dungaree-clad figure bending over before him was not cut along standard sailor lines.

Then all hell broke loose. Henry Wiley, commanding the Battle Fleet, took the whitehats' prank seriously; twenty-three of the plotters were court-martialed, and some served up to ten years at the Naval Prison in Portsmouth, New Hampshire. Wiley also commanded that each officer of the battleship, for lack of vigilance, would have a derogatory fitness report. For Burke, who had sensed the presence of a woman aboard but had thought the whole rumor too ridiculous to be true, this was to be the only black mark of his career. William Veazie Pratt, who commanded BatDiv 4 with his flag on *Arizona*, thought the censure itself ridiculous; when he became chief of naval operations in 1930, he ordered the derogatory reports expunged, and Burke got well again.

Burke left *Arizona* with the hard-won reputation of an eager beaver. He was not just a workaholic; that type was common enough among younger officers struggling to make their mark. What was altogether exceptional about him was the way he merged "my navy" with himself, not in a possessive or proprietary way but by way of complete *identification*. Arleigh Burke and his institution—and all that that institution meant to him—were indistinguishable. His comfortable, supportive family life only fed this identification; Bobbie, in the best sense, was the perfect "Navy wife."

He was not distinguished by brilliance, intuitive flashes of insight, or dazzling displays of expertise. His work habits were the only ones he knew, those of a Colorado farmhand—basic, direct, no frills—and he would be there until the last cow came home.

"Arleigh Burke will be dead before he's fifty," predicted one of his *Arizona* shipmates, "or he'll be the chief of naval operations."[3]

☆

After a short tour aboard the auxiliary *Procyon*, Lieutenant Junior Grade Burke requested postgraduate study in ordnance. At the Postgraduate School in Annapolis and then at the University of Michigan, he studied fuels, explosives, and chemistry, spending almost sixty hours a week in class and on homework. His master's in engineering came from Michigan, in 1931, a degree as rare among naval officers then as a doctorate today. He was now a gunclubber, like most of his peers, and oriented toward command of a warship.

During the depths of the Depression, Burke worked in every facet of naval ordnance: as an inspector of explosives, as main battery officer aboard the heavy cruiser *Chester*, as an analyst of fleet target practice, and in ammunition research and development at the Bureau of Ordnance. He always asked for battleship duty, at least until 1934, but *Arizona* was to be his only battlewagon. His chief at BuOrd, Rear Admiral Harold ("Betty") Stark, a future chief of naval operations and a man of measured praise, wrote that Burke "with additional experience in a position of responsibility [would] become an officer of exceptional value to the service."

—*Position of responsibility*. In 1934 Burke had started pestering the Bureau of Navigation, in charge of officer assignments, for destroyer duty. He wanted to broaden his experience. After three years of job-mongering through the warrens of BuNav, he got his wish. In May 1937, a senior lieutenant, he became the exec of *Craven*, one of the sleek new cans replacing the aging four-pipers of World War I.

So Arleigh Burke came to the destroyer Navy. Aboard *Craven* he did administration, navigation, and a score of the kinds of odd jobs that fall to any second-in-command. He got upped to lieutenant commander in August 1938. His skipper, Lieutenant Commander Watson Bailey, was also new to destroyers; Bailey was a submariner with three years of postgraduate work in diesel engineering.

Together the two men commissioned *Craven*, and together they began to learn the ways of the destroyer Navy. After trials and a shakedown cruise through the Panama Canal to Ecuador, they took *Craven* to the Pacific Fleet. Lieutenant Commander Burke was there, in June 1939 as Europe began to boil, when he received orders to his first command, the new destroyer *Mugford*.

Burke had originally been slated to command the old four-piper *Perry*. As an experiment, however, BuNav had selected five officers from the Class of 1923 to test the command abilities of men approximately five years younger than those usually ordered to command new destroyers. Burke was one of the five, but he was still no standout. Six of his peers had already commanded destroyers, and thirty-one more, including submariners and aviators, had also held command.

Mugford, two years old in 1939, was the flagship of Commander Francis ("Red") Whiting, commodore of Destroyer Division 8, Squadron 4, Destroyers, Battle Force. Red Whiting, unlike Watson Bailey, knew his cans rivet by rivet. He gave Arleigh Burke a graduate education not only in destroyers but also in leadership. Arrive before you are due, preached Whiting. Plan, prepare, move fast, hit hard.

In his first months aboard, Burke, under Whiting's unblinking eye, ran *Mugford* through a full round of multiple-ship maneuvers, simulated torpedo attacks, night attacks, and night gunnery. Red Whiting did not kid around; DesDiv 8 ran through everything at high speed and under simulated battle conditions. Burke got *Mugford* assigned as the squadron gunnery school, and everyone improved his shooting. In addition, Burke's command scored high in communications and engineering competition and won the coveted Destroyer Gunnery Trophy for firing an unprecedented perfect score in short-range battle practice—thirty-six rounds, thirty-six hits.

His engineering officer, Harry McIlhenny, knew that his skipper had good officers and men under him, but Burke "was the catalyst that welded the team and made it click." In fact, Arleigh Burke had fallen in love with the destroyer Navy; he would later admit to Whiting that his tour aboard *Mugford* "was one of the happiest times of my life." Under Whiting's tutelage, he really began to bend his natural talents—for hard work, planning, even innovation—to the improvement of his very own command. "In my opinion," wrote Whiting on Burke's final fitrep, the departing skipper of *Mugford* "is one of the outstanding officers of his time. . . . He is a leader of the highest type—in fact words fail to speak too highly of him. I predict he will go far in the Navy."

In July 1940 Burke went as far as Washington, as inspector of anti-aircraft and broadside gun mounts at the Naval Gun Factory. Yet his tours aboard *Craven* and *Mugford* had shaped him fundamentally. He was loyal, to the last breath, to the tradition-rich institution of the Navy. He believed, in the most personal and committed way, in the worth of Navy life and in the importance of Navy missions. Although an occasional challenger of established ways and a sometime innovator, he would never wield a knife to tear the basic fabric of the institution he loved so much.

Thus Arleigh Burke was a conservative, in the classic guise of an earlier Burke, Edmund, and in this lay his greatest strength. The Navy was his sea anchor; the service bolstered him, rewarded him with advancement and command, and provided him both direction and purpose. There was always a bit of the dull plodder in him, but by the time he left *Mugford* he was established well beyond such prosaic terms. He found that he loved being in charge, running his own show. As his fellow Coloradans might say, he had "sand." Burke would stay the course, through the bad times as well as the good. He might bitch and bellyache, as he had done when ordered to descend into *Arizona*'s bowels with a gang of sailor reprobates, but always he rolled up his sleeves and did the job. "He might have been endowed with gifts beyond other men, but that is not important," observed Robert Speck, his gun boss aboard *Mugford*. "He developed the numerous ones he had to a superb degree by continuous persistent application with a firm determination to do anything he did very well."

The downside of his relentless drive was the killing pace he set for his officers and men. He could flash a look of grim fury at a miscreant who fouled up, on the bridge or anywhere else. When he was tired, as he so often was, or when the black moods were upon him, his wrath could be terrible. He was impatient with the half-cocked and the lazy, and could not stomach the inane. He could be ruthless with those who did not measure up to the demands of "my navy." "If you've got power," he later said to Red Whiting, "use it and use it fast."

These attitudes traced the backbone of a born combat leader, but they were in danger of ossification at the Naval Gun Factory. Burke chafed under the routine of endless rounds of inspections. The day after Pearl Harbor, he asked for sea duty in the Pacific. Every week thereafter, he forwarded the same request to his superior, Rear Admiral Theodore Ruddock, and every week thereafter Ruddock turned him down. "Arleigh," Ruddock told him, "You've been trained for this job, and I can't spare you."

Coral Sea was fought; then Midway; then Guadalcanal. Burke, staked down in a bureaucratic prison, stewed and schemed. Finally, a friendly secretary named Delores abetted him, and a thoroughly badgered Ruddock let him go. In February 1943 he finally reached the South Pacific, a commander now, with orders to take charge of Destroyer Division 43 with his pennant aboard *Waller*, a spanking-new *Fletcher*-class destroyer of 2050 tons.[4]

—And there, amid the dangerous, inky-black waters of the southern Solomons, the farm boy from Colorado caught fire.

☆

Fortune favored him; indeed, "Burke luck" became legendary in the Navy. Early 1943 was a period of minor operations in the South Pacific. Carriers, the new prima donnas of naval power, were a scarce commodity for both sides. Of the six American fast attack carriers at the time of Pearl Harbor, *Lexington* had gone down at Coral Sea, *Yorktown* at Midway, and *Wasp* and *Hornet* during the six-month struggle for Guadalcanal. The venerable *Saratoga* had twice been crippled by Japanese torpedoes but, patched up once again, was back in the South Pacific at the beginning of the year. *Enterprise*, the sixth carrier, accompanied her, but Big E had undergone heavy air raids at three different times; her Air Group a shambles, she would shortly depart for stateside. For their part, the Japanese had lost a light carrier at Coral Sea, four veterans of the Pearl Harbor strike at Midway, and one more flattop off Guadalcanal.

In short, the area was wide-open for small-unit naval actions, and as the only games in town, these could mean disproportionate press coverage. Burke knew he was lucky to be in such a place at such a time. He was well aware, in addition, of the narrow margin afforded by chance, when one's only allies were swift decision and the gods. As a destroyer squadron commander, he once asked a green officer of the deck what the difference was between a good officer and a poor one. The young man rattled off all the leadership qualities he had ever heard of, until Burke cut him short. The answer, he said, "is about ten seconds."

But chance could be wooed by preparation, and this was Burke's strong suit. His destroyers now had electronic eyes, and "radar plot"—Combat

Information Center, or CIC—had become the electronic brain of each. Japanese radar was well behind in development, installed only on the emperor's largest combatants. The new electronic brains could also be knit together, and American crews were relentlessly drilled in plotting, communication, night-attack tactics—anything that could provide the necessary edge in small-unit action.

Arleigh Burke got down to business. Now the lessons learned at Red Whiting's side were pounded home, in waters where the right spadework could mean the difference between life and death. He drafted a paper he called "Employment of Destroyers," in which he discussed destroyer tactics at night against enemy surface craft, planning and initiation of attack, delegation of authority. His preaching was in Whiting's vein as well: preparation, initiative, and audacity—always audacity.

In June 1943 he moved to command Destroyer Division 44, his pennant aboard *Conway*. To his disgust, the division was assigned to convoy supplies and reinforcements to Guadalcanal, now rapidly becoming a backwater of the war. But the Japanese still filtered into the area. On 20 July Burke took over Task Group 31.2 in addition to DesDiv 44. As "ComDesSlot," he would be given all of Halsey's Third Fleet destroyers available for independent missions in the waters of the Central Solomons.

There, the Tokyo Express was operating again, on a shorter route now, and Burke, moving his pennant to *Maury*, was eager for action. He quickly indoctrinated his destroyer skippers in his concept (gleaned, he said, from the tactics of Scipio Africanus in the Punic Wars) of fighting his ships in mutually supporting divisions.

But the Japanese did not cooperate. On 3 August, Burke was relieved by Commander Frederick Moosbrugger. The sweetener was a spot promotion to captain, with command of Destroyer Squadron 12. Three days later, using Burke's battle plan, Moosbrugger fought a four-destroyer Tokyo Express in Vella Gulf. He sank three, while the six cans of Task Group 31.2 emerged unscathed. Burke heartily congratulated "The Moose," but he itched for some action of his own.

His chance came in October, with command of the newly formed DesRon 23, the largest unit of new destroyers in the Solomons. The squadron was all *Fletcher*-class, all commanded by skilled regular line officers, all with the latest gear. Burke's new command was part of Rear Admiral Aaron Stanton ("Tip") Merrill's Task Force 39, which was headed for Bougainville.

Burke summoned his skippers to his new flagship, *Charles S. Ausburne*. He gave them their doctrine, tersely summarized by five lines on the cover page:

> If it will help kill Japs—it's important.
> If it will not help kill Japs—it's not important.
> Keep your ship trained for battle!

Keep your material ready for battle!

Keep your boss informed concerning your readiness for battle!

One of his captains, an offbeat character named Herald Stout, had a logo painted on one of the torpedo tubes of his command, *Claxton*. Burke liked the image—a diminutive Indian clad only in headband, outsized G-string, and moccasins, firing an arrow into Tojo's rear end. From that time forward, the ships of DesRon 23 became the "Little Beavers," named after Red Ryder's cartoon sidekick.

On the night of 1–2 November 1943, the Little Beavers fired an arrow into Tojo's rear end. They supported Tip Merrill's cruisers in the Battle of Empress Augusta Bay, driving off a strong enemy force that was attacking the American beachhead on Bougainville. The battle was a melee. At one point Burke had the Little Beavers launch twenty-five torpedoes, none of which hit home. At another, he mistakenly turned his fire on one of his own ships, Commander Bernard ("Count") Austin's *Spence*. Austin, horrified, got on the TBS (talk between ships) radio, yelling "Cease firing! Cease firing! Goddammit, that's me!"

"Were you hit?" Burke shot back.

"Negative," The Count replied. "But they aren't all here yet!"

"Sorry," responded Burke as he returned to the fray. "But you'll have to excuse the next four salvos. They are already on their way."

—The Count's thoughts the next few moments were probably unprintable, and indeed he would always be lukewarm on the subject of Arleigh Burke, but Austin survived, and so did the Little Beavers. While there were innumerable problems with radar-controlled gunfire at Empress Augusta Bay, and while American torpedo shooting was dreadful, Merrill and Burke had proved that the Imperial Japanese Navy no longer owned the night. The Japanese lost a cruiser and a destroyer, in addition to seventeen attacking planes shot down by Merrill's force. "It was an organized hell," was Tip's analysis—but the Little Beavers, like those salvos which had missed Count Austin, were on their way. Burke received the Legion of Merit, the first of four.

On 24 November DesRon 23 was refueling. For days Burke had reported that the Little Beavers were being forced to proceed at thirty knots, five below flank speed, due to lack of upkeep. Now he received orders to get to sea; the Tokyo Express was running again, on its way to resupply Bougainville and Buna. The ships with him included *Spence*, his accidental target from earlier in the month. Burke was allowing her to steam cross-connected (when in combat, regulations stipulated that a ship's boilers be "split," so that if some were knocked out, the others could still provide propulsion). By thus defying higher authority, *Spence* could crank up enough steam to do thirty-one knots.

Once underway, Burke was asked by radio for data on his command. He replied, including—to the merriment of SoPac headquarters at Nouméa, the people to whom he had bitched about his thirty-knot speed—the phrase "proceeding at 31 knots" (in order to keep Count Austin with him). From that moment forward, he was "31-Knot Burke," a partially derisive nickname that was picked up by the press back home. The public thought thirty-one knots was hell-for-leather speed, and Burke's image as a hotshot destroyerman (which he was) became set in concrete.

The Little Beavers headed for Cape St. George, off New Ireland. There Burke's five destroyers tangled with a five-destroyer Tokyo Express on a dark, overcast night, sinking three without taking a scratch. All the preparation, the drill, and the can-do morale was paying off. The Naval War College would later call Cape St. George "an almost perfect action"—that virtual impossibility in combat.

Arleigh Burke's battle plans had underlain Vella Gulf, contributed at Empress Augusta Bay, and won at Cape St. George. From November 1943 to March 1944, he led the Little Beavers into no fewer than twenty-two engagements with the Japanese. They gave far more than they took. DesRon 23 won the Presidential Unit Citation, and Burke gathered in the Navy Cross and other awards. With his snazzy new nickname and his derring-do, he was high-profile now, very high-profile; *Time* made him a cover boy ("Arleigh Burke—King of the Cans"), a most unusual recognition of a mid-grade officer. Other excellent surface-ship tacticians, men like Moosbrugger and the charming, able Merrill, got little notice.

None of this was Burke's fault, but the publicity inevitably caused some resentment among a few of his peers and superiors. He paid little attention; he was eager to get on with the destroyer war. By March 1944 the Little Beavers were a smoothly running machine, arguably the best DesRon anywhere. Then came orders from the Bureau of Naval Personnel: report as chief of staff to Commander Carrier Division 3.

Burke was bewildered. "I know nothing of carriers or planes or little of big ships any more," he wrote a friend. "Fate is a darn funny thing."[5]

☆

Commander Carrier Division 3, and Task Force 58, was a living legend, Rear Admiral Marc ("Pete") Mitscher. He was pleased with his current chief of staff, a seasoned aviator captain named Truman Hedding. But Ernie King, far away in Washington, had decreed that aviator commanders select nonaviators as their chiefs of staff. BuPers had offered Mitscher four names, Burke's last on the list. A disgusted Mitscher let Hedding choose his own relief, and Hedding chose Burke, his old classmate from postgrad school.

—Burke luck. Now he, a Blackshoe among Blackshoes, was propelled into the fast lane, as a key planner and operator for the greatest carrier strike force in history. "What in hell am I doing here?" he groused to Hedding when he reported for duty. "I don't know anything about carriers. Destroyers are my navy."

At first, the destroyerman and his admiral circled each other like a pair of wary pit bulls. Mitscher looked like anything but what he was: a consummate aerial tactician and the absolute nemesis of Japanese naval air and surface power. Bald, with a huge-billed khaki fishing cap constantly surmounting a face creased by an infinitude of wrinkles, this frail little man customarily spoke in the mildest of tones, barely above a whisper.

The facade was not a fake, but the real man lay hidden behind. In fact, Pete Mitscher was a good hater and a natural fighter. His way into Annapolis had been greased by his wealthy Oklahoma father, but once at the Academy he quickly gathered in more demerits than the maximum, then managed to get involved in a serious hazing scandal that led to his removal from school. His father greased the skids again, and Pete graduated in 1910, two years after his original class. As a younger man, Mitscher was surly and instinctively combative, and age made him a veteran of decades of battling for naval air power. He wanted to be surrounded by his own—people who wore wings.

—Which Arleigh Burke did not. Mitscher, who detested the TBS, began to use the voice radio himself, as "Bald Eagle," his call sign. This hardly increased Burke's confidence; Hedding had been entrusted with radio messages. Finally Burke, during one torpedo plane attack, grabbed the TBS and issued his own orders for the formation to avoid. The laconic response from Mitscher was "Well, it was about time, Captain Burke."

Slowly, painfully, the two men knit together. Mitscher, a sleepless man himself, quickly saw that his new chief was steady as a rock. Burke used his work ethic to saturate himself with the arcana of flight plans and operations. He began rising well before dawn, trying to beat Mitscher to the flag bridge; at night, he retired only after Bald Eagle went to his rack. Burke was always hustling, always trying to stay a step ahead of his boss.

Mitscher could never forgive him for his lack of wings, but ever so slowly, he began to listen to Burke's advice. For his part, Burke was seeing a master of carrier warfare in operation, planning, fighting, correcting mistakes, always pushing the might of Task Force 58 ever closer to the shores of Japan. Because each of them could so readily assess the talents of the other, the ice began to thaw.

They were together for twenty-seven consecutive months, until July 1945. During that time, Task Force 58 (38 when under Halsey's overall command instead of Spruance's) fought the Battle of the Philippine Sea and the Battle of Leyte Gulf (where Burke correctly believed that the Japanese carriers to the north were decoys). The force covered both the Iwo Jima and Okinawa operations. Burke was in the middle of everything—watching, learning, planning, executing. At Philippine Sea he saw Mitscher, who like himself had no children of his own, turn on the lights of his carriers to shepherd home his beloved aviators, whom he had adopted as so many foster sons.

Along the way, Burke developed a deep fondness for his admiral, one sustained rather than strained by Mitscher's numerous quirks. The two were an odd team, from opposing points of the naval compass. Burke's Scandinavian toughness and unflagging energy saw him through the endless cycles of planning, flight operations, aerial defense, enemy attack. Mitscher, whose body was refueled mostly by coffee and cigarettes, got by on sheer willpower. After Philippine Sea, he started calling his chief of staff "Arleigh." They even began to chat about nonmilitary topics, such as Pete's obsession, fishing.

Mitscher came to rely on his destroyerman. Bald Eagle was probably the man who, confronted with a blank fitness report bearing Burke's name, simply scrawled across the paper, "This is the best damned officer in the Navy." He recommended Burke for commodore, an honorary title that Burke received despite the lack of a favorable endorsement by Chester Nimitz (who had possibly noted all the publicity surrounding the Squad Dog of the Little Beavers).

By Iwo Jima, Burke had mastered his boss's style and usually, with Mitscher overseeing, conducted operations himself—a Blackshoe ordering up naval aviators—incomparable training for flag rank. He would still have exchanged his gold-encrusted commodore's hat for a destroyer command, but he was broadening, extending himself every day, constantly widening the scope of "my navy."

By Okinawa, Mitscher, a skeletal presence weighing only 100 pounds, with watery, sunken eyes peering out over baggy sockets, had to be physically carried by Burke up and down the steep ladders of his flagship. Pete's voice, usually never above a whisper, now could hardly be heard. Some visitors thought that Blackshoe Arleigh Burke was running the entire task force. But Mitscher's keen, precise mind burned as brightly as ever; Burke was his trusted subordinate, never the man who made the decisions. Those still rested with Bald Eagle.

And so they sailored on together, on to V-J Day. In June 1945 Mitscher recommended Burke for rear admiral, the real thing this time, citing his combat skills, his leadership, and his altogether exceptional combination of surface and carrier warfare. The promotion did not come then, not in a field cluttered with deserving, combat-proven captains. But Burke indeed was ready for higher command. He had planned for and led ships in tactical confrontation, planned at the strategic level, and maneuvered the largest naval force ever known in some of its most crucial actions. He, a Blackshoe, had worked naval aviation from the inside.

For himself, however, Burke was considering bringing down the curtain in 1945. Always ambitious, he was nevertheless exhausted from the long months of combat and strain, while acutely aware of Burke luck. He expected a tombstone retirement promotion to rear admiral. His tone, writing to a friend, was almost elegiac and reminiscent, scarcely the hard-driving, forward-looking voice of 31-Knot Burke:

> I like this Navy, but I hope I can tell when I am no longer pulling my weight in the boat. At that time, when either I or the Navy believe I can't contribute anything more, I hope to be able to retire in some nice, peaceful, warm climate.

—"But not on a farm," he hastily added. "I had all the farming I wanted when I was a kid."[6]

☆

This daydream was rapidly blown away by the troubling winds of the postwar world. After three months back in BuOrd as director of research, where he learned about the secrets of the atomic bomb and helped establish the Navy's early guided-missile programs, Burke was ordered in November 1945 to form a staff for Mitscher's new and embarrassingly minuscule Eighth Fleet.

His scope broadened once more, not only in planning for the Navy's new Mediterranean presence but also in studying the drastically changed international environment. In September 1946 Mitscher took over the Atlantic Fleet, and Captain Arleigh Burke was again his chief of staff. Burke in peacetime was no different from Burke in wartime. Bobbie, in their family car, would wait patiently at the flagship's pier for her husband, who sometimes kept her there until 2100, when he would at last descend the gangway with his usual sheaf of papers to work on at home.

Pete Mitscher's powerful will at last burned out in early 1947. With Bald Eagle's death, Burke lost one of his best friends and teachers. Now he began to loose his formidable energies on the problems facing "my navy" as a whole. He wrote a memo on deteriorating naval morale, in the process opposing service unification. This caught the eye of Secretary of the Navy Forrestal, who, after thinking about appointing Burke as his aide, sponsored him instead for the General Board. Burke and other combat veterans brought young blood to the superannuated institution; for fifteen months, he and a few brother midgrade officers analyzed naval shipbuilding programs, projected force requirements in tune with the Joint Chiefs' initial postwar long-range plans, and examined the Navy's shore establishment.

In these first years after V-J Day, Arleigh Burke—still only a captain—moved onto center stage of Navy planning and policy-making. In January 1948 he began a lengthy study of the shape of the Navy for the next decade, including military, political, and economic factors both at home and abroad. At a time when national security policy was adrift and in danger of foundering, Burke's analyses (and his pessimistic conclusions—there was not enough Navy for all its assigned tasks, he said) were hard-edged and incisive. For example, he identified the Soviet submarine force as the most significant potential enemy of the Navy, and this assessment would come to be written in Pentagon stone.

He gladly fled Washington in July 1948 for command of the light cruiser *Huntington*, but the brouhaha over the supercarrier and other problems brought him back six months later to head OP-23, from which vantage point he found himself up to his neck in the rebellion in gold braid. By now Burke's worldview was far more broad and inclusive than that of most captains; he saw both "my navy" and national defense issues in global perspective. He was thus quick to defend the Navy's turf, again in an extremely high-profile way for a captain.

But Burke's stance during the rebellion, and the machinations of OP-23, raised his head very far out of the weeds indeed. Forrestal was dead, and Louis Johnson's scythe was waiting. Johnson's faithful minion, Rowboat Matthews, swung the blade. The 1949 Selection Board had unanimously recommended Burke for rear admiral. Matthews reconvened the board and, with Johnson's approval, removed Burke's name. This was illegal; by law the list of selectees had to be submitted unaltered to the president.

—Burke luck: his friend and classmate, Captain Robert Dennison, was Harry Truman's naval aide. Bob Dennison managed to call Truman's attention to the injustice. Forrest Sherman, the new chief of naval operations, weighed in, and by the end of the flap Arleigh Burke was a rear admiral (he made his number on 15 July 1950). Johnson and Matthews ended up by arguing that this happy solution had been their idea all along.

Sherman knew a front-runner when he saw one, and he assigned Rear Admiral Burke as C. Turner Joy's deputy in the Far East; Burke was actually the chief's on-the-spot troubleshooter. He helped get Japan's flattened maritime power off the ground, commanded Cruiser Division 5 off the Korean coast, and, in July 1951, began duty alongside Joy at the Korean truce talks. Like all the other Americans, Burke soon felt trapped "in a conference which seems to have no ending." He fumed over the procedural delays, the endless propaganda barrage (from both sides), the nit-picking negotiations that took place while, all around the negotiators, thousands of men were dying. He took his frustrations out on his relief, Ruthven Libby, selling Libby his secondhand blanket and making 50 cents on the deal.

Burke came back to the Pentagon in November 1951 as director of OP-30 (Strategic Plans). He spent two years in the billet, giving a lot of attention to the Pacific at a time when most military men were concentrating on building up American forces in Europe. Mick Carney sent him to sea again, as commander of Cruiser Division 6 in the Mediterranean, in April 1954. In early 1955 he became commander of the Atlantic Fleet destroyer force, a job that for him was unalloyed joy. Carney figured that Burke's next step would be to three stars as a fleet commander, thus completing his seasoning for a four-star command.

Dwight Eisenhower thought differently. By 1955 the reputation of 31-Knot Burke, within the Navy, was pure gold. Any enemy of Louis Johnson and Rowboat Matthews was secure within the service. Those few who had worked directly under him, while high in their praise, had a different perspective. They knew him to be a resounding whip-cracker who operated on the general principle that the best work was done through overwork. Rear Admiral Henry Miller, who fell under Burke's lash in OP-30, remembered him as a "driver" with "tons of energy." Burke "never let up," said Miller. "He was absolutely dedicated to the Navy [and] knew no hours."

He was fifty-four years old. He had never held fleet or oceanic command. But he indeed was "absolutely dedicated"—and he was chief of naval operations.[7]

☆

Burke met with the secretary of defense. Engine Charlie Wilson told him the Navy had a problem: "There must be better cooperation between the military and the civilians." He talked with the president (he had actually briefed the general six years previously on carrier warfare, but Eisenhower did not recall); Ike was impressed with his relative youth and outstanding record. The president, like Wilson, expected him to be a team player.

Burke's appointment was greeted with huzzahs within the Navy, everywhere but in Flag Plot. There, several older admirals griped about his "premature appointment" and lack of "top policy experience." Burke, who had a streak of humility running through his high-voltage work habits, conceded the essentials of these criticisms; for this reason, he did not immediately clean house in his own bailiwick, OPNAV, replacing Carney's appointees with his own men only as officers senior to him completed their tours of duty. He would impress the men in Flag Plot with his work ethic, or he would not impress them at all.

He began with the Navy's severe manpower shortage. Burke blamed the GI Bill of Rights, which he knew made civilian life—educational expenses, low-interest loans, unemployment benefits—more attractive to servicemen. The Navy, unlike the Army and Air Force, did not use the peacetime draft. Congress had proposed the extension of the draft law until 1959, but the Navy, still priding itself on its peacetime voluntarism, was not included. Carney had wanted to continue the voluntary policy.

But the Navy could not stanch the bleeding of its highly trained personnel back into civilian life. Burke, after talking with Vice Admiral James Holloway, his BuPers chief, concluded that "my navy" needed 56,000 draftees—right away. Charles Thomas opposed the move, and Burke asked to see the president. This was his legal right, but the secretary of the Navy probably wondered why he had supported exchanging Carney for Burke. Along with Wilson, away they went to the White House.

There the new chief of naval operations, all of one week in office, asked Eisenhower to rescind his own public statements about the Navy side of the draft and reverse both his secretary of defense and secretary of the Navy. Whatever the three men in civilian clothes had expected, here was no pushover. Eisenhower kept him after Wilson and Thomas had left and chewed him out royally, one military man to another. "Admiral," said the grim-faced Ike, "you put me in a hell of a spot! Don't you ever again embarrass your commander in chief like this!"

Burke got his 56,000 men, and the Navy returned to the peacetime draft. But, he concluded, the price of standing his ground in this initial test of bureaucratic turf would be a short tenure. Like Fechteler and Carney, he would do his two years, then get the heave-ho. In fact, however, the Navy draft incident was the start of a growing rapport between the five-star in the White House and the four-star in the Pentagon. Eisenhower quickly came to realize that Arleigh Burke was nobody's man but his own, fiercely independent, all-Navy, and one stubborn bastard. He also realized that his new chief of naval operations could be counted on to give straightforward, no-nonsense advice, the kind every president always needs but so seldom gets—and this was far more important than staying on the team.

Soon, on selected afternoons, the two of them—the Kansas-bred West Pointer who had wanted to go to the Naval Academy and the Colorado-bred Annapolitan who had been eager to go the Military Academy—could be found in the White House sipping their old-fashioneds around 1700. Together they would roam the world, chatting about naval problems, military problems, anything under the sun. Eisenhower solicited advice from many others, of course, but few of his advisers shared Burke's depth of experience or combat record. And none worked with his steely ferocity. The two men became friends and, for Burke, the president "had a hell of a lot of character." "Kind of lazy," he continued (anyone who fell short of his gospel of perpetual work was "lazy" to Burke), "but the man had integrity and he had good judgment, and he had high standards."

—And he had chosen Burke. "The day of the gray-beards in the Navy is past," exulted Admiral Jocko Clark. The Joint Chiefs certainly bore the tinge of youth. Nathan Twining, head of the Air Force, was fifty-eight, but he had been a four-star for years and, like most Air Force generals, looked closer to the bassinet than to the Pentagon's E-Ring. Maxwell Taylor, who had replaced Ridgway as head of the Army in Eisenhower's house-cleaning, was a boyishly handsome fifty-four. Out in Omaha at the Strategic Air Command, the owl-faced, cigar-chomping Curtis LeMay was forty-nine, another four-star. Burke himself seemed to be in the swing of things, with his leap-frog promotion. He even sent out quite a few letters to rear admirals, asking them to retire to make way for younger blood.

But Burke's ascendancy, while connoting youth and opportunity, was in fact a direct infusion of *energy*—which could come from anyone, at any age. "I've worked for seven different admirals in my eighteen years service," said one chief yeoman, "and have never seen a man turn out as much work as Admiral Burke."

Now, the whole shebang really *was* "my navy." He had the national press for a bully pulpit, and he wasted no time. "If the day should ever come when the United States Navy cannot control and exploit the sea," Burke predicted, "our country will be at the mercy of the enemy who can." Thus, the Navy literally had to be ready for anything: "We have to be able to defeat any threat whatever against our control of the seas."

Burke was in no doubt about the threat. He had seen communism up close at the Korean truce talks and, like almost every other naval officer, was prepared to contest its expansion. He knew the Chinese and North Korean navies to be nonentities, but the Soviets presented a clear danger. "I think the Russian objectives haven't changed since the time of Lenin," he asserted. "They will use every tactic, every method, every procedure that they think will win."

Still, Burke did not have the almost maniacal fixation on communism of men like Radford and Stump. The new chief sounded almost like FDR when, speaking of the balance of terror that had emerged between the superpowers, he noted that "we are so fearful that we sometimes, perhaps, don't do the smaller things that would be very effective."[8]

☆

The "smaller things," which were to say practically anything that could be done through seapower, were what Burke intended for "my navy." Every morning, promptly at eight bells, there he was at his daily briefing—still pear-shaped at five foot eleven and two hundred pounds, with his lumpy face under the wavy, blond hair suggesting the careless product of a drunken potter, a faint tinge of salt-spray green on his braid. The manner was open and congenial, the smile ready and warm, all complemented by an occasional reflective puff on his pipe, a pause to smack the dottle out against his Academy ring.

Men who worked for Burke saw another side. At each press interview, he would have aides peering in through one-way peepholes in self-defense. They knew they were sure to be assaulted by memos and questions without number, all stemming from their boss's seemingly casual conversations. He constantly ragged admirals for study papers, position papers, thoughts on any problem. His mind was like a vacuum cleaner gone berserk, but with some kind of total purpose. And he did not simply pick the brains of the top echelon: he also gave regular stag dinners for youthful lieutenants in his graceful Observatory Hill quarters off Massachusetts Avenue. After dinner and some of Bobbie's patient, delightful conversation, he would fire up his pipe and set the young men talking. The next morning the memos would fly forth to his aides.

After his morning briefings, he would attack the mountains of dispatches on his desk, making marginal notations in green pencil. (No one else in OPNAV was to use green.) He had as many as twenty conferences a day. His work in the Pentagon went on until about 2100; then he took his packed briefcase home with him. "The only man who had his work done by Friday," he liked to say, "was Robinson Crusoe." The pace would have killed a dray horse, but Arleigh Burke, as always, thrived. He refueled when he could, passing up bread, butter, and potatoes in his never-ending war against his weight, but he could never resist ice cream. ("He doesn't seem to mind getting fat on ice cream," observed Bobbie.)

His management style, shotgunning problems great and small within OPNAV and throughout the fleet, inevitably made waves. His quick temper and intolerance of mistakes and foolishness rubbed senior officers the wrong way; subordinates got confused by his habit of bypassing channels and, too often, did not clearly understand what the human dynamo at the top expected of them; everyone felt the boss had a tendency to get bogged down in trivia. "The most difficult man I ever worked for," recalled Raymond Peet of his time of trials with Burke. "In the early morning . . . he was usually pleasant and helpful, but as the evening wore on he got mean and difficult to work with." "Sometimes hard to live with," added Alfred Ward, another veteran of Burke's shop.

Characteristically, Burke tried to hold all the reins, and aides fretted without the authority they felt they needed to do their jobs. Burke ran a team, but he was a mule skinner rather than a coaxer; he had told Red Whiting years before how he would use power, and he was not kidding. Persuasion, bargaining, and compromise, while there, were low on his scale of virtues. Most of his staff felt ambiguous about his human qualitites. At times he could be almost chummy, and at others the black moods, or something, would make him testy and snappish. "He was not warm and personal to his staff," said Peet. An in-house study of his own leadership style (which Burke, in yet another memo, commissioned) concluded that the chief "has caused a lot of uncertainty within the staff" but that his men had been kept on their toes and had been productive.

Burke was Burke—he just kept bulldozing along. His methods were fierce and unrelenting, but his perspective was pragmatic, flexible, diversified. His restless mind was ranging the globe, and everything—*every-thing*—counted. "There is no task more vital—in this nuclear missile age—than keeping close surveillance and control of all activities that take place on the 100 million square miles of world oceans," he proclaimed. "This is the job of the United States Navy."[9]

—Which indeed seemed to be everywhere. In William Tenn's science-fiction tale "Project Hush," the idea is to get a manned rocket to the moon before the Russkies. Three carefully selected Army men accordingly blast off, land on the northern tip of Mare Nubium near Regiomontanus, dutifully plant the American flag, set up their base, and begin to explore. Soon they discover another base, of different design. There are thoughts of Russians, Chinese, Martians—someone has beaten them. A scout comes back with even more depressing news—the earlier base, he reports, was "owned and operated by the Navy. The goddam United States Navy!"

Burke was not yet ready for the moon—not quite—but everything else was fair game. He put the Navy's emphasis on mobile striking forces; the United States, by 1957, had mutual defense pacts with forty-two countries, and the fleet's task of ocean patrol had become almost infinite in scope. Thus an enormous complex of ships and bases had to be kept constantly alert and ready for any contingency.

By the end of 1956 Burke knew that the Soviet Union's growing nuclear capability would soon produce a nuclear standoff between the superpowers. He believed wholeheartedly in the maintenance of a strong American nuclear establishment, but he reasoned that, given the standoff, the future would see conflicts beneath the nuclear threshold, so-called limited wars. He had been an early critic of massive retaliation as a strategy. As director of OP-30, in December 1953 he had prepared a wide-ranging critique of that policy for Carney.

The Eisenhower administration, despite the lessons of Indochina and the Formosa Strait, still clung to the New Look, primarily for fiscal reasons. Burke ceaselessly pressed for reemphasis on naval flexibility in countering communist aggression, in whatever form. He and other naval officers, like Don Felt and Charles Griffin, began to warn that limited conventional attacks and localized "brushfire" wars were the likeliest possibilities for the future, that the New Look was a threadbare and dangerously incomplete guide for national strategy. The Navy's answer, as always, was across-the-board flexibility.

Repeatedly, America's Cold War military was being confronted with conflicts in which nuclear weapons, tactical or otherwise, had little or no utility. (The destabilization and paranoia provided by the threat of their use was hardly positive.) At every point—concerning Korea, Indochina, Formosa—their use had been discussed and, for a variety of reasons, rejected. Burke feared that "in emphasizing the nuclear general war, the nation will lose sight of the necessity to maintain adequate strength to combat limited wars in areas remote of this country—limited wars requiring the United States' control of the seas."

Flexibility meant money, and Burke was being asked to do more with less. From 1957 to 1961, fleet strength declined from 409 warships to 376, from 558 other types to 436. The partial solution was technological, cramming more wonders into a single platform, but even a supercarrier or a nuclear submarine could not be in two places at once. Still, as Burke and other senior naval officers pounded away with their concern, the national strategic posture began to shift from the New Look to the much more costly idea of "flexible response," which would be accepted by the Kennedy administration. At the end of Burke's tour, naval forces to support this flexibility on a worldwide scale did not exist in required strength—but not for his lack of trying.

In 1958 Burke wrote his British opposite number, Lord Louis Mountbatten, that "nuclear retaliatory forces will not solve the myriad other problems with which we are confronted. . . . If we go too far on the megaton road we will, I think, have found that the free world will have been lost by erosion, and perhaps not even military erosion."[10]

☆

Erosion—this the farm boy in Burke detested, the strength-sapping erosion that could wreck the future. Everything and everyone had to be keyed up, on line all the time, ready to go. "There is never a convenient place to fight a war when the other man starts it," he said in 1958. He got his message of preparedness and flexibility out any way he could. He fully supported the Navy's public relations effort, although he scolded admirals who gave too many news conferences and "showed too much gold."

Concerning Congress, Burke shifted the old Office of Legislative Liaison from the judge advocate general to the purview of the secretary of the Navy, under whom a rear admiral now dealt directly with members of Congress and their staffers. The Defense Department, for obvious reasons, wanted to minimize lobbying by the individual services on Capitol Hill. Burke would have none of this, and by 1960 the renamed Office of Legislative Affairs had emerged as a potent lobbying tool not only with Congress but also with the executive branch and the civilian world. He wanted everyone to get the message.

Like Radford, Stump, and many others, Burke was not reluctant to use the bogeyman—unreasoned fear of communism—to underscore his points. He was militant and outspoken but usually stopped just short of being an alarmist. He admitted that Russia was developing a "capacity" to destroy America, "and we can't do anything about it either." But underneath the nuclear threshold still steamed the old warrior. The United States, he informed a congressional committee, could "destroy any enemy who attacks us regardless of when or how he does it."

Such doomsday remarks needed to be taken in the context of Burke's ideas about limited war and operational flexibility. He took his business to be, properly, the readiness of the fleet because, he announced, the Soviet

Union was the "sponsor, instigator, and supporter of aggression by proxy." This "proxy" could cause the erosion, the notion that as long as nuclear war was averted, all would be well.[11]

Even as he struggled to keep "my navy" ready for anything, however, Burke faced enormous problems within the larger structure of the Department of Defense. In late 1957 an advisory group to the National Security Council, named for its chairman, H. Rowan Gaither, Jr., of the Ford Foundation, made various recommendations for improving the nation's strategic capabilities. The top-secret Gaither Report found America's active defenses inadequate and its passive defenses insignificant.

By 1959, in the Gaither Report's gloomy scenario, if the Russians were to launch a surprise attack with intercontinental ballistic missiles, up to three-quarters of Curtis LeMay's B-52 bombers would be caught on the ground; there would be no real American "second-strike" capability. This nightmare so frightened three of Gaither's group that they recommended immediate preventive war, before time ran out. Indeed, Gaither was forecasting catastrophe, the virtual end of Western civilization.

The report presented a catalog of Communist horrors: a rapidly expanding Soviet gross national product; 1500 Russian nuclear weapons; a phalanx of 4500 bombers, 300 submarines, and uncounted (for good reason—they were not there) ballistic missiles. Gaither himself pleaded with Eisenhower to add $10 billion to the $38 billion military budget and spend $30 billion more on a crash program of fallout shelters—one for every person in the country, at a cost of $100 a unit. Even with the shelters in place, Gaither sermonized, half the population would perish in a nuclear exchange.

This was high-level panic, based on exceptionally shaky evidence and even shakier assumptions. Eisenhower rejected the report: "I can't understand the United States being quite as panicky as they are," he calmly said. The demands for more bombers, more bombs, more shelters reached fever pitch nonetheless, and *Sputnik*, the Russian satellite launched on 4 October 1957, did not help. But the president's common sense held firm, and panic military spending did not become the policy of his administration.

Still, the Gaither Report, especially after being leaked, was influential, doing its part in feeding the paranoia of the Cold War. There would be, the report predicted, nothing but "a continuing race between the offense and the defense. . . . There will be no end to the moves and countermoves." Eventually, under John Kennedy and his secretary of defense, Robert McNamara, its recommended national security program would be largely played out: the enormously expensive missile complexes, both on land and at sea; the hardening of missile sites; a highly mobile, fully mechanized Army; the vast expansion of military research and development.

In the midst of all these suggestions (some of which he supported) and cataclysmic warnings (none of which he believed), Burke found a recommendation to streamline and centralize the nation's military establishment.

This, for him, was an old alarm bell from the days of the unification struggle, and now the klaxon was sounding loud and clear once again. "These are proposals," he resoundingly declared in a speech that made headlines around the nation, "all leading toward more and more concentration of power, more and more autocracy by military power and military decision, more and more suppression of differences in judgment, and more and more of what is described as 'swift efficiency of decision' as a substitute for debate and discussion of the military aspects of national policy."

—These were remarks that were self-serving for "my navy," to be sure, but Burke meant them. Unfortunately, Eisenhower was all for another Defense Department reorganization; he had supported unification a decade before. Here was a difference the two men could not work out over a couple of old-fashioneds.

Burke fought the Defense Reorganization Act of 1958 tooth and nail. He told the Senate that concentrating power in the hands of the secretary of defense could lead to merger of the services or creation of a national general staff, either one of which would undermine the cherished independence of his beloved Navy. In the House, Carl Vinson unsuccessfully tried to keep the heat off by sponsoring his own, much-diluted reorganizaton bill.

Neil McElroy, who had replaced Wilson as secretary of defense, called Burke's testimony "regrettable," but both he and Eisenhower, amid a flurry of Burke resignation rumors, backed the admiral's right to speak his mind. This was a battle, however, that Burke—and the Navy—lost.[12]

He went down fighting. Letters sped out to influential flag officers, politicians, friends of the Navy, and makers of public opinion. His staff was mobilized as though a bureaucratic Trafalgar was at hand. Burke ordered his deputy for plans and policy to develop a counterproposal for reorganizing McElroy's office the Navy way. He spoke directly with Eisenhower, begging him not to submit any bill that would, as this one did, strip the chief of naval operations of actual operational authority. Vinson and Paul Kilday, a Texas Democrat and the second-ranking majority member of the House Armed Services Committee, chimed in by insisting that the secretary of defense be forbidden to merge the services, create a single chief of staff, or establish a general staff. The bill would result in a "Prussian general staff," cried the Swamp Fox. "Nonsense," retorted Eisenhower.

The Defense Reorganization Act of 1958 was not all that Burke and the Navy had feared; there was no merger and no general staff. But from the perspective of the Navy brass, what emerged was bad enough. Indeed, this act marked the most fundamental change in lines of military command and authority in the postwar period.

Now, the three service secretaries were, on paper, out of the loop. The new chain of command ran from the president to the secretary of defense to the Joint Chiefs of Staff. From the Joint Chiefs, the chain ran directly to the field, to either unified commands, such as the Navy's CINCLANT or CINCPAC, or to specified commands, such as the Air Force's Strategic Air Command. Of critical importance, the individual Joint Chiefs now did not act as their service's delegated representatives. Burke, for example, could by himself order not a single ship or squadron. He was only one of a small group of military experts advising the civilian leadership.

Burke had always regarded the Joint Chiefs as more political than military, a raw little Darwinian universe of catch-as-catch-can for scarce resources. Turf wars were an inevitable part of doing business. Even Arthur Radford had a tendency, despite his broad marching orders from Eisenhower, to assume that he knew what was best for the Navy. Burke, despite their friendship, had to defend "my navy" at times against the wishes of his chairman, a member of the same service.

Burke constantly drove his staff to keep ahead of the other services, particularly the always-malign Air Force. Before 1958 several major staff committees served the Joint Chiefs, in areas like strategic plans, logistics, intelligence, advanced studies, and military assistance. The reorganization remodeled the Joint Staff along Army lines, with nicely numbered directorates: J-1 (Personnel), J-2 (Intelligence), J-3 (Operations), J-4 (Logistics), and so on. This whole idea, which was meant to ameliorate the turf wars, was alien to Navy staffing concepts. The coming of the joint officer, or "purple-suiter," was anathema to the blue-suiters, and the Navy rapidly developed an aversion, which Burke fully shared, to assigning its best officers to joint work (which, after all, was the loathed "Prussian" tradition). Burke once chided Bernard Austin, by this time his operations deputy, "Count, you're too damn joint in your views."

As to the chairman himself, the reorganization act gave him a vote in the deliberations of the Joint Chiefs and also strengthened the size of his staff, up to four hundred officers. In all of this, the operational posture and independence of the Office of the Chief of Naval Operations, and for good measure the Navy's cherished self-image of independent action, were fundamentally weakened.

Burke fought these changes in vain. His real pain, however, lay in the augmented military role of the civilian secretary of defense. Now, subject to a veto by either house of Congress, the secretary could alter service functions. He could reorganize a service's supply and logistics activities (an opportunity McNamara would not overlook). And he could assign weapons system development to a single service. (Within eight months of the act's passage, the Air Force requested that SAC be given operational control of the Navy's future fleet of Polaris submarines, an incredibly wrongheaded proposal that Burke had to battle for fifteen more months to scotch.)

Constitutionally, all this was in good form, providing more powerful, direct control by civilian authority. Managerial specialists could applaud as well; the chains of command were clearer, and the system *appeared* to be better organized. In terms of naval professionalism, however, the Defense Reorganization Act of 1958 cut the legs out from under the chief of naval operations, effectively isolating him as an individual from the *operational*, as opposed to administrative, chain of command. By previous law, the chief executed the decisions of the Joint Chiefs. A series of strong Navy chiefs— King, Nimitz, Sherman, Carney, and Burke—had increasingly taken over operational control of naval forces, without real protest from a series of bureaucratically weakened secretaries of the Navy.

Now Eisenhower, the team man, the conciliatory military professional who abhorred turf wars, had created conditions whereby a secretary of defense (because of delegated authority) could issue orders through the chairman of the Joint Chiefs to the operating forces. Secretaries also could (and would) bypass the chain completely and issue operational instructions to field commanders. Moving in the other direction, the secretary of defense was now in a position to filter the recommendations of the Joint Chiefs before he took them to the president. Personalities and friendships could still play a role, and sipping old-fashioneds together could still count for much—but the line diagrams now did not run the Navy's way.

Nothing could have been more calculated to infuriate Arleigh Burke, a naval professional to the very core. The Joint Chiefs were now largely confined to an advisory role. Burke found himself only a member of a committee. One of their number, the Army's handsome and urbane Max Taylor, would later gripe that "the Joint Chiefs cannot command anybody, unless they're lucky enough to have a stenographer." Proponents of the act argued that the Navy's old way impeded responses to crises, was not truly unified, and undercut sound joint planning. All this was true—but whether the new arrangement would make the nation's military policy and actions *more effective* was another question.[13]

☆

By the time the reorganization act became law, Charles Thomas had resigned, and there was a new secretary of the Navy. Before the act, this office had been charged with providing strategic direction to the naval combatant forces of the nation, and, for the most part, its holders had let activist chiefs of naval operations, from King to Burke, run with the ball. Now the secretary had become a *fonctionnaire*, a bureaucrat who was to provide an organized, trained, equipped, and ready naval force to the unified and specified commanders, operating under the aegis of the secretary of defense.

The new man was Thomas Sovereign Gates, Jr. Charles Thomas, nearly sixty years old, had submitted his resignation at the beginning of Eisenhower's second term, recommending that his fifty-year-old under secretary take over. Gates's middle name was a good indicator of his style; lanky and good-looking, he was a liege lord. He came from the Philadelphia Main

Line, an investment banker and partner with the Morgan-allied Drexel and Company. The son of a former president of the University of Pennsylvania, he had served as a naval intelligence officer in World War II, winning two bronze stars for combat duty aboard aircraft carriers (*Ranger* and *Monterey*) in both oceans. A management and financial expert, he was appointed as under secretary of the Navy in October 1953.

Once in Washington, Gates contracted a bad case of Potomac fever (he would replace McElroy as Eisenhower's third secretary of defense). He became a good friend of the president, and later would be close to both Richard Nixon and Gerald Ford. Rich and affable, the new secretary exuded the easy air of one born to lead. His conviviality carried a hint of the macho; he loved wine, women, and warplanes, not necessarily in that order. One associate recalled that "Gates liked living and liquor better than anybody I knew." (After the tragic death of his son in a hunting cabin fire, his drinking would become a chronic problem.)

But underneath the glossy exterior of the Main Line smoothie was a blunt, no-nonsense manager. Gates quickly closed some useless Navy bases and took the political flak. When a balky traffic light caused trouble near a Navy arsenal in Virginia, a "special study" was generated and the ponderous results dropped onto his desk. "Turn off the damn light," he scrawled across the top page. He was not above playing politics with officer assignments and promoting the men he wanted promoted.

Tom Gates respected Arleigh Burke. As under secretary, he had supported Burke's relief of Carney, and he quickly recommended Burke's reappointment as chief of naval operations in 1957. (Burke would be reappointed again in 1959; his six years of service in the post would be a record.) To Gates, the Navy had four principal tasks: nuclear deterrence, flexible response, continental defense, and provision of reserve forces. He was serious about naval resources, too, right down to the preservation of forests. He brought a powerful combination of experience, both naval and business, to his job. "Our naval supremacy is vital to our national security," he said, and he and Burke matched strides through the bitter battle over the Defense Reorganization Act of 1958.[14]

The organization man within Gates was dissatisfied with the daily hassles that had overcome Carney's Long-Range Objectives Group (OP-93). The reorganization act made accurate and timely naval planning all the more imperative. To this end, Gates put a variety of planning issues before another group, the Naval Research Advisory Committee, a technically oriented outfit. These men found that the Navy was unable to plan adequately for future weapons systems and for naval warfare in general. Gates and Burke promptly formed the Naval Long-Range Studies Project and gave its control to the hard-charging Rear Admiral Edwin Hooper, who was plucked from his destroyer command in the Caribbean to head the project.

Hooper and his team settled in at Newport and got to work. (As the

Institute of Naval Studies, they moved to Cambridge, Massachusetts, in 1961.) Their original focus (which, like that of OP-93, rapidly became technological) was international political, economic, and social trends—the kind of thinking that Burke devoured. Hooper's shop became dominated by civilians, another sign of growing civilian input into the Navy, but unlike OP-93, the Naval Long-Range Studies Project was at least partially responsible for more articulate and reasoned naval positions in national security policy debates.

The old Progress Analysis Group, formed back in 1950, was now used by Gates and Burke for the hard sell. Burke used *this* outfit to funnel Navy materials to Congress. He also used these officers to keep him current on what his fellow admirals were thinking. Between 1955 and 1958, the Progress Analysis Group was headed by a real up-and-comer, Captain John McCain, Jr., son of the famed McCain of World War II carrier fame. The younger McCain became Burke's Burke, his eyes and ears, and by the end of 1958, despite the severe setback of the reorganization law, he and his men had helped give Burke a generally favorable image in Congress.

—Which was necessary, because the Defense Reorganization Act of 1958 left the Navy in a bureaucratically unstable position, rolling in heavy seas. In 1959 the Franke Board (chaired by Gates's under secretary, William Franke) reported that the continuing trend toward centralization in the Pentagon required no basic changes in the Navy's internal organization or ways of doing business. The board, in essence, recommended retention of the Navy's treasured bilateral system of parallel civilian and military administration (although, in consonance with the reorganization act, General Orders 5 and 9 were changed to eliminate the operational command authority of the chief of naval operations).

This was fine by Gates and Burke, who worked smoothly in harness, and indeed the Franke Board, in its naval standpattism after a major legal change, was merely the Gates Board of 1954 revisited. But there was a crucial difference, one that would, a quarter century later, bear unexpected fruit in the person of John Lehman. The Defense Reorganization Act of 1958 made the secretary of the Navy a de facto line manager for the secretary of defense. There was nothing to prevent an activist secretary of the Navy, with the confidence of the secretary of defense, from running roughshod over a dissenting chief of naval operations, or naval establishment, on questions of naval research, development, and acquistion or even on matters of strategy and deployment of naval power.

For the moment, though, the personalities in place kept the remnants of bilateralism intact and meshing nicely. The Dillon Board Report of 1962 did recommend some centralizing reforms after Burke's watch, mostly relating to the Navy's management of material. The Navy's commitment to its tradition of organizational decentralization was weakened somewhat, but the commitment was still there.[15]

☆

—So was Arleigh Burke's, right across the board. Both he and Gates now *approved* more than they *decided;* the real decision making within the labyrinth of the Navy's command structure occurred more and more during the collective process of staffing, review, agreement, and approval. This diluted responsibility, and Burke worried about the process—unavoidable in any complex organization. The gain, when there was gain, came from the collective expertise.

And from the man at the top. Burke may have been cosseted more than he liked by civilian control, but he still *led*, and in spades. He was frank in admitting the Navy's problems—too few ships, too few men, too much ocean, too much political interference—but he sailored on with every weapon he had at hand, because that was the only way he knew. He still had access to the media. He got his ideas out to traditional pro-Navy bodies, like the Navy League, and these broadcast the need for a strong navy throughout the nation.

"We're powerful," Burke told his countrymen. "Why be fearful?" The words were the measure of the man. "The major deterrent," he said, "is in a man's mind. Stamina, guts, standing up for the things we say—those are deterrents."[16]

By 1960, "my navy" underwrote American foreign policy for what the Cold Warriors euphemistically called the "Free World." The fleet was expected to be diplomatic yet forceful, deterrent yet combative, supporting as well as protective. "The acceptance by the United States of its position of world leadership and the adoption of the principle of 'collective security,'" in the words of one naval officer, "are tied inextricably to the continued freedom of movement on the sea."

Burke's overriding problem in helping ensure the "freedom of movement on the sea" was that he was running, ostensibly, a *peacetime* Navy. Yet "my navy" was one of increasingly devastating superweapons, hopefully deterrent; of naval, air, and ground forces surpassing half a million men and women, hopefully trained for the widest possible scope of emergencies; and of increasing civilian control, hopefully capable of comprehending military logic and necessity. He ran a navy constantly balanced on the knife-edge of war.

Up at the Naval War College in Newport they went over the edge, wargaming through electronic warfare simulators and computer analysis. They got down in the grass with antisubmarine warfare, anti-air warfare, oceanic resupply, anything that could win at sea. Machine-men were in charge, programming, calculating, planning. "While the game technique may not be entirely free from error and cannot guarantee foreseeing future development by our enemies," they said, "it does provide a means for refining the basis of decision by clearly stating expected outcomes on the basis of clearly stated assumptions."

Burke, too, operated in a world "not entirely free from error," one in which "expected outcomes" were dicey at best. He had to balance the disparate might that made up the nation's seapower—the sailors, ships, shipyards, weapons, bases—and somehow make that might serve the policies of his nation, as conflicted or obscure as those policies might be. In the balance, he succeeded. He lost one major bureaucratic struggle—over Pentagon reorganization—and he won, eventually, one major strategic one—the move to "flexible response."

Further: he was integrating exceptional new technology into the fleet; promoting coordination and efficiency at every turn; advancing talented younger officers like Hooper and the junior McCain to positions of responsibility. Above all he was reinvigorating "my navy," burnishing its enthusiasm and sense of purpose. He spoke forthrightly to his countrymen about the Navy's Cold War roles and duties, critically influenced programming and budgeting, and contrived at every turn to make his considerable political skills really count. Beyond all other chiefs of naval operations, with the possible exception of Ernie King, he used all his powers, and his incredible energy, to the limit.[17]

But Burke wanted even more for "my navy." To this end, almost as soon as he had taken office, he embarked the service on one of the greatest strategic revolutions in its history. The task would be enormous, the pressure terrific. As usual, he knew the man for the job.

—Arleigh Burke summoned Red Raborn to Washington.

CHAPTER TWENTY-SEVEN

POLARIS

———— ☆ ————

Missiles—seaborne missiles. These were part of Arleigh Burke's dreams for "my navy." His missiles were not tactical air-defense weapons on the limited scale of Terrier, Tartar, and Talos. Burke, like many before him, dreamed of giant missiles that could span vast distances, carrying warheads of enormous destructive power—true intercontinental strategic weapons.

The Germans had dreamed the dream. In the early days of World War II, *U-511* had actually fired two dozen short-range rockets while submerged, but her successful test was an army affair; the German navy refused to sign on. (Later, when the *Kriegsmarine* tried to duplicate *U-511*'s success, the experiments fizzled.) The famous land-based V-1s and V-2s performed better, but their guidance systems, such as they were, proved erratic in the extreme.

The V-1 "buzz bomb" was really a short-range, winged, pilotless airframe, driven by pulse-jet engines that could propel the device about 150 miles at three hundred knots. Its crude guidance system got the V-1 into the general area intended for its one-ton warhead. Launched from ski-ramp sleds in the Low Countries, V-1s proved to be nasty little brutes. More than eight thousand of them pasted England during the war, leaving over twenty thousand people dead or wounded and damaging thousands of buildings.

The postwar Navy slightly improved the V-1 technology, called the result Loon, and reconfigured the *Balao*-class submarine *Cusk* to launch the missile from the ocean surface. No one could figure out how to stow Loon below decks, but after radio-controlled guidance had been added, its tests off the California coast in 1947 were reasonably successful.

V-2s were different. These big, vertical-standing rockets had a true suborbital, parabolic, ballistic trajectory. They had also been used against England, falling indiscriminately and without warning on civilian populations—true terror weapons. Toward the end of the war, the Germans were developing a gimcrack idea to launch the V-2 against American cities. The V-2 had extremely limited range; most of its fuel was expended in its climb into the stratosphere. The plan was to tow the missile, in a hydrodynamically designed container, behind a submarine. Once at the launching point, the container would be erected for firing. When the Russians overran the German rocket base at Peenemünde on the Baltic, this paper project went down the drain.

—But not the V-2. In the late summer of 1945, a few young U.S. Navy officers drafted a proposal for the Bureau of Ordnance. They dreamed of a long-range missile, on the loose model of the V-2, that could be launched from surface ships as well as submarines. That fall, their proposals were rejected; ballistic missiles, in 1945, were not in the Navy's crystal ball.

Still, thoughts of a big naval missile persisted. For two years the dream simmered, and on 6 September 1947 a V-2 was launched from the deck of *Midway*, steaming off Bermuda. The rocket was powered by a highly unstable mixture of liquid oxygen and alcohol, which alone gave the Navy's fledgling missileers something to think about. In addition, its guidance system was preset to a large chart grid, almost akin to an oceanic game of pin-the-tail-on-the-donkey. There was no such thing as "pinpoint accuracy," the overused (and inaccurate) characterization of the next generation of missiles. This first test did nothing to convince the Navy brass, either; *Midway*'s V-2 almost smashed into the carrier's bridge while lifting off the deck.

The idea of vertical sea launch was thus put on hold, and V-1 became the Navy's notional missile for the next decade. If Loon was son of V-1, then Regulus I was the grandson. First flight-tested by its contractor, Chance-Vought of Dallas, in 1950, Regulus I was a success story, the Navy's first operational attack missile. Designed to be launched from either surface ships or surfaced submarines, Regulus I had a range of five hundred miles and a subsonic speed of six hundred miles an hour. The missile was catapulted off a sled by a pair of conventional solid-fuel rockets; once in the air, a turbojet engine cut in.

Although Regulus I was periodically launched from carriers and cruisers, its very presence aboard made Blackshoes nervous. In a storm or in heavy seas, with its jet engine whining, its jet gas pumping, and the high explosive in its nuclear warhead ready to go, the missile "was probably more hazardous to us than it could have been to any enemy," said Robert Wertheim, then a launcher officer. Regulus I, however, did find a home on reconfigured diesel submarines. *Tunny* fired the first shot, in 1953, and the next year the missile became operational. Eventually *Barbero* was equipped, and then *Grayback*, *Growler*, and the nuclear-powered *Halibut*.

By this time, 1957, Regulus II had been test-fired. This was a Mach 2 nuclear-capable missile with a one-thousand-mile range and a cruising altitude of sixty thousand feet, a significant leap over its predecessor. Its guidance system and attack profile were also much more sophisticated. In September 1958, *Grayback* fired the first (and last) Regulus II from an operational platform. Again, naval aviators, in particular, were nervous; they did not want this big missile mounted on their carriers. In December, Secretary of the Navy Thomas Gates directed that all Regulus work be stopped. The broad support base within the Navy for the Regulus program had broken down.[1]

—The generations of V-1, seemingly, had reached a dead end.

☆

The progeny of V-2 had lived on, but just barely. At White Sands, New Mexico, the Navy (with carefully hoarded funds) staged a model V-2 launch in 1949 from a steel mock-up of a warship deck built in the sand. Engineers lashed a V-2, loaded with its volatile mix of liquid oxygen and alcohol, to a tripod and ignited the engines.

The idea was to see what would happen if something went wrong during a missile launch at sea. A leg of the tripod was yanked away. (The entire drill was called Operation PUSHOVER.) The big rocket immediately crashed onto the steel deck; the thermal shock of the liquid oxygen spilling out cracked steel plates and split supporting I beams. "One look at that mess," said one officer, "and a shudder ran through every ship in the Navy." A liquid-fuel Viking research rocket was successfully launched from the missile test ship *Norton Sound* in May 1950 and got to a height of 105 miles; its developers began to talk of Viking as a weapon. But the liquid-fuel problem was scary, and this proposal went nowhere.

Instead, the path for solid-fuel propellants was being blazed at the Ordnance Test Station in the wasteland of Inyokern, California. Commander Levering Smith and a group of talented engineers were creating a series of increasingly heavier and more advanced solid-fuel missiles. In 1951 their two-stage Big Stoop flew successfully three times.

Further development of Big Stoop, with its puny initial range of only twenty miles, was choked off. The Defense Department's missile development funds were being increasingly funneled to the Air Force. In the winter of 1953–1954 a secret study committee, chaired by James Killian of MIT, recommended that development of a true intercontinental ballistic missile (the Air Force's Atlas) be accelerated. The Killian Committee also called for Army development of an intermediate range ballistic missile (Jupiter, around 1500 miles) and for some similar missile that could be launched from ships. Dwight Eisenhower, on 13 September 1955, decided to implement the Killian Committee's recommendations, believing that haphazard, almost outlaw missile programs had gone on long enough and that strategic missiles needed to be part of a national policy design.

Thus, the Navy was directed to design a sea-based support system for Jupiter. By then, the autumn of 1955, the Office of Naval Research had in hand a study jointly done by General Dynamics' Electric Boat Division and Convair Pomona. Entitled "Strike Submarine Missile Weapons Study," the document admitted that little was known about combining missiles with ships and submarines in a design system, as opposed to shooting missiles off existing platforms such as *Cusk*, *Midway*, *Tunny*, and *Grayback*. Both solid and liquid propellants were discussed, as well as a variety of configuration options. This study, an early example of systems analysis, indicated (on paper) the feasibility of submarine-launched missiles while emphasizing the necessity for a solid propellant and some kind of shipborne inertial navigation system.

The Key West Agreement, back in 1948, had reserved the development of intercontinental ballistic missiles to the Air Force, although the Army was allowed to go ahead with its intermediate Jupiter. The Navy, knowing Loon was no strategic weapon and that its V-2 test aboard *Midway* had been more frightening than reassuring, did not protest. Until 1955, the Navy had no formal role in ballistic missile development. All the generations of V-1 had been advanced tactical weapons; although Regulus II could reach one thousand miles inland, its flight profile was still low enough for the missile to be intercepted by conventional weapons. The V-2 experiments aboard *Midway* and at White Sands had been bootstrapped; many Navy officers argued that better places existed for their funds. Finally, the last thing the Air Force wanted, particularly after Key West, was competition from another service in the development of an intercontinental ballistic missile.

The Navy's marching orders to develop a sea-based support system for Jupiter were thus consonant with recent history but ran counter to the findings of the "Strike Submarine Missile Weapons Study." For good measure, they still left the service trailing the Air Force and its pending "intercontinental" weapon. The Army, not to be left out, had argued that *its* artillery expertise should mean its leadership of any missile program, because missiles were only artillery writ large, fired from fixed positions on land. But the Air Force's argument, that ballistic missiles were strategic weapons and extensions of air power, rightly belonging to the Strategic Air Command, held sway in 1955.

There were specific problems with Jupiter. The missile required liquid fuel. The knee-knocking V-2 launch aboard *Midway*, along with the kinetic results of Operation PUSHOVER, had convinced Navy missileers like Levering Smith that the liquid fuels needed for the big rockets were far too dangerous to be carried around on surface ships or submarines. Liquid oxygen, used to burn the fuel inside the missile cylinder, was a constant menace. If the stuff was spilled, the slightest spark of static electricity could cause an explosion. One drop on an oily deck could blow a man's foot off.

Solid fuels were the answer, but in 1955 none existed that could hurl a big missile even the 1500 miles that then defined intermediate range. Liquid fuels had a higher specific impulse (producing greater thrust) than solid fuels. The fuel problem was a tight corner, which the Navy began to turn with two powerful arguments, one generic and one specific.

The generic argument was simple, and effective. Over 70 percent of the globe was encased in salt water, more than 350 million cubic miles of ocean. A "launch platform" (read submarine) could hide in any one of these cubes and, even with only a 1500-mile range, could deliver its missile well inside the coastline of an enemy (read Soviet Union). The ocean, with its beguiling opacity, thus could become, unlike a fixed site on land, an ideal sanctuary for missile shooters. The sea could shield a true strategic force.

Even more so if that force could go deep and keep station indefinitely. By 1955 the nuclear submarine, in the shape of *Nautilus*, was a proven entity. The Navy's specific argument was to marry solid-fuel missiles to nuclear submarines. These platforms could be highly mobile and practically undiscoverable, and they could strike with deadly suddenness—a fundamental physical and psychological deterrent.

At first the Navy, under Mick Carney, tried to sell the idea as only a "tactical" missile to strike enemy submarine bases, navies doing in navies— which masked the essentially strategic nature of such a weapon. This was Pentagon politics, because the Key West Agreement had made intercontinental ballistic missiles the province of the Air Force, but the masking was bad politics, ensuring an interservice battle royal when the real purpose of the weapons system became apparent.

Any Navy ballistic missile program had to be authorized by the secretary of defense, and Charles Wilson was chary about duplicating missile-development programs. The Air Force argument, of course, was that *any* Navy ballistic missile program would be redundant and thus wasteful. "The Navy was really in danger of being read out of its ballistic missile altogether," remembered one Pentagon official. "There just wasn't enough money in the defense budget."

In the negotiations over exactly how to implement the Killian Committee report, the Navy's ball was carried by Rear Admiral John ("Savvy") Sides, a longtime friend of Burke's. Savvy Sides was a dreamer, too, an ordnance veteran with mine-warfare and destroyer experience and, as much as any man, the father of Regulus. Vice Admiral Paul Stroop called him "outstanding." Sides fought in vain for a solid-fuel missile. What he got, in a Wilson decision issued on 17 November 1955, was an order to join the Army on Jupiter development. Wilson also decreed that all such missile development would not be specially funded but would have to be carved out of the Navy budget.

Hobbled by these two constraints, Secretary of the Navy Charles Thomas and Burke (only weeks on the job as chief of naval operations) created a special organization independent of any Navy bureau. The head of the new entity, called the "Special Projects Office," would be given extraordinary authority. He would report only to the secretary of the Navy (which, in the bilateral system, meant Burke as well). He would have poaching rights on every shred of naval and technical expertise he could cumshaw.

This altogether unprecedented position was an indication of how far the Navy was willing to go to establish itself in the strategic missile field.

There were reasons for Sides's nickname. He was savvy about ordnance and savvy about men. As Burke and his aides culled through service records, Sides kept advancing one name. He said his former director of guided missiles was the right man for the job—tough and smart, an intense leader and meticulous planner. Burke and Thomas soon concurred.[2]

—And so Red Raborn came to Washington.

☆

"They couldn't have chosen a better person," the seasoned submariner Roy Benson would later say. William Francis ("Red") Raborn, Jr., was born in Texas in 1905 and grew up in Marlow, Oklahoma. Until he got to Annapolis, he had never been near the ocean in his life. (When he first glimpsed a lighthouse in Chesapeake Bay, he thought he had seen a ship.) Red, who was short and blocky, proved to be an undistinguished mid, finishing in the bottom half of the Class of 1928.

After tours aboard *Texas* and a destroyer, he put in for flight school. At Pensacola he met Bill Halsey, then qualifying as an aviator in a special program designed for Blackshoes being sent to command carriers. Raborn's aggressive, pugnacious personality matched that of the older man, and perhaps he took from Halsey some of that go-ahead, bulldoglike tenacity for tackling any problem in any situation. The two men also shared a deep love of the naval service; even the occasional scraps their dogs got into around Pensacola could not ruin their friendship, which lasted the rest of their lives.

Raborn got his wings on 16 April 1934. As a naval aviator, he flew Grumman biplanes with Fighting 5-B off *Lexington* and the SOC-1 Curtiss seaplane off the cruiser *Portland*. After a tour as a flight instructor back at Pensacola, he was serving with Patrol Squadron 11 at Pearl Harbor when the Japanese struck. By now he was a specialist in aerial gunnery, teaching the skill to the horde of eager-beaver aviators coming into uniform. Eventually he was given Navywide responsibility for training aerial gunners and established over forty gunnery schools. He got to the shooting war in the Pacific in 1944 as exec of *Hancock*, a brand-new *Essex*-class carrier.

In April 1945, near Hansei Island, "Old Hannah" was creamed by a single kamikaze. Eighty men died. Red Raborn won the Silver Star for his life-saving and damage-control efforts. A gaping forty-foot hole in the flight deck was repaired in less than two hours, and Old Hannah's strike aircraft, out on sorties when the kamikaze hit, were able to return to home plate safely.

Gunnery assignments and duty in BuOrd followed after the war, along with promotion to captain. Korea brought Raborn his first command, a demothballed *Commencement Bay*–class escort carrier named *Bairoko*—eleven thousand tons of trouble. Practically every officer and sailor aboard was as green as spring grass; only one man was qualified to stand watch under way as officer of the deck—the skipper. Raborn somehow got this early edition of McHale's Navy, carrying two squadrons of jet fighters, to Japan. Along the way, suffering through a howling williwaw off Wake Island, his crew began to learn how not to kill themselves, or their shipmates, at sea. *Bairoko* spent a quiet war, assigned to hunter-killer operations against enemy submarines. Since there were none of these to be found, Raborn at least got the chance to train his men.

He came home to a tour at the Naval War College, then became Savvy Sides's deputy for guided missiles. From OPNAV he gained his second command, a tragic tour. Red Raborn was the captain of *Bennington* when she suffered her disastrous hydraulic catapult explosion. Damage Control Central was lost with the blast, and once again, as he had done aboard Old Hannah, Raborn directed damage control operations personally. Cleared by a court of inquiry following the catastrophe, he was commended and awarded a Bronze Star.

Duty as assistant chief of staff for operations to CINCLANTFLT followed, a responsible assignment. Normally such a stain as *Bennington* on a skipper's record, whether his fault or not, would have barred the way to Flag Plot. But Raborn was picked up for rear admiral in July 1955.

The hair that gave him his nickname had receded a bit, but the face was blunt and forceful, all angles and planes, the eyes capable of staring intensity. His manner was always brisk; subordinates were never sure if he was frowning through a smile or vice versa. He was scrupulous and decisive, a clean-desk man. "Everything he went about he devoted all of his time to," recalled David McDonald, a future chief of naval operations.

Unlike Burke, Raborn never took a stuffed briefcase home, regarding this (although he would never tell Burke) as a sign of managerial inefficiency. Burke, for his part, saw Raborn as an immediate (and obedient) source of high voltage for Special Projects. "Red would do what I wanted him to do," Burke told George Miller, one of his OPNAV planners.

At home, the can-do carapace sloughed off. Then, in his white frame house across the Potomac in Arlington, purchased after his move up from Norfolk, Raborn would doff his blues and outfit himself in gardening togs. As Pete Mitscher had loved fishing, so Red Raborn loved plants—watering, weeding, tending—hour after hour. He had married Leah Barnes a year out of the Academy, and she had given him two children, but they divorced in 1953. His new wife, a retired commander in the Navy Nurse Corps whom he called "Admiral Mildred," described her husband as a "Japanese farmer." Raborn had a grape arbor, apple trees, honeysuckle bushes, azaleas, over a hundred kinds of roses—an entire botanical wonderland to administer. (At times, getting home after dark, he would simply turn on the outdoor lights and do some nightime gardening, waging ceaseless war against a healthy community of beetles.)

The garden was a necessary release, and Raborn certainly needed the relaxation. A fresh-caught admiral who had never commanded more than single ships, he was no expert in missiles—despite his well-spent time with Savvy Sides. What he could do was get things done, and Thomas and Burke were gambling that their new head of the Special Projects Office could accomplish one gigantic task.[3]

—To bring the Navy into the strategic missile age.

☆

Burke gave Raborn a letter that would become famous (and notorious) as "Red Raborn's hunting license." The letter promised Raborn all the support possible within the Navy and, when that had been expended, Navy backing all the way up the civilian ladder. Burke was acutely sensitive to the problems that the new technology, particularly the liquid-fuel–solid-fuel difficulty, would entail. "Anytime it looks as though you're batting your head against a technological wall," he told Raborn, "if you see the job isn't technically feasible, it will be cut off dead."

Burke also warned his new appointee about something Raborn already knew. The job was a field of land mines—technological, political, bureaucratic, strategic—and Raborn was not to go charging around like a bull elephant, but instead was to use every power of persuasion he could muster. He could have a staff of forty officers—his choices—from anywhere in the Navy.

But Raborn, Burke said, was to steer clear of Hyman Rickover. Burke and Rickover, near contemporaries, had much in common: both were driven to their tasks, ruthless with the men working for them, obsessively pushing for a better Navy. But Rickover wore the technological blindfold and had trouble seeing other aspects of the Navy from underneath its folds; Burke had thoughts and ambitions that were Navywide, incorporating every facet of the institution. Burke believed that Rickover, in his Navy hat, had done a fine job with nuclear propulsion, but he knew all about Rickover's studied contempt for the traditional navy—"my navy," to Arleigh Burke—and about Rickover's relentless lobbying end-runs with Congress.

Burke could see that Raborn's omnibus hunting license and Rickover's perpetual penchant for empire-building were bound to clash. Therefore, Rickover would not be allowed in the ballistic missile program except in the most basic and functional way—supplying already-proven nuclear reactors for missile platforms. In the meantime, Raborn was to treat Rickover with kid gloves.

Finally, Burke advised Raborn that he had to act *fast*. If the Special Projects Office failed to meet a series of deadlines, the program might be canceled; the Navy's already tight purse could not be allowed to spring a continuous leak. Raborn and his outfit would receive credit if they succeeded, Burke told him, placidly puffing away on his pipe. If they did not, said the chief of naval operations, "it will be your neck."

—Thus encouraged, Red Raborn took over his new assignment on 5 December 1955. He moved into the slapdash "W" Building, a "temporary" structure that, like most of its kind, had fossilized into permanency just off Constitution Avenue, in the backyard of Main Navy. His first offices were two cramped spaces near the storeroom. No one knew Raborn's project existed. He had, officially, been given ten years, until 1965, to make something happen: to create a ballistic missile system for the Navy.

Raborn did not intend to take that long. Now the contacts he had made as Savvy Sides's deputy began to pay off. He brought Commander William Hasler, chief of BuOrd's missile research branch, with him. Bill Hasler got the thankless job of developing the Navy variant of Jupiter. Raborn snared Edward Mernone, a budget officer in the bureau; Mernone became, officially, the head administrator; unofficially, his finger was in every pie. As his own deputy, Raborn picked the highly experienced John Colwell, who immediately began to snaffle likely officers for the project.

—And on board they came, some of the Navy's very best minds. The quiet, retiring Missourian Levering Smith, absolutely unflappable, a captain now, arrived from White Sands and took charge of the propulsion branch. "The finest scientist in uniform," a fellow officer said of him. Smith had been mostly a destroyerman until January 1948, when, on making captain, he switched to Engineering Duty (Ordnance) and became a full-time missileer.

Captain Frank Herold, an electronics specialist, found his orders to the Naval Research Laboratory canceled. Raborn wanted him for missile fire control and guidance. Hasler himself, studying the Jupiter in Huntsville, Alabama, got an assistant, Commander Roderick Middleton, another missileer who was speedily detached from command of the destroyer *Benham*. Commander Dennett ("Deke") Fla, a marine engineer, found himself heading the launching branch. Commander Paul Backus, a destroyer officer, became Raborn's Cerberus, a strong-willed personality who guarded Raborn from outside intrusions and acted as the connection between Special Projects and OPNAV. Civilians came too; most were technical specialists from BuOrd, a few from outside the government.

All of them were drawn to Washington in a rush, most without their families. BuOrd was hit the hardest. When one staffer, inundated by unexpected detachment orders, called over and asked, "Who the hell does the Red Rooster think he is?," he found out. Raborn flashed his hunting license, and the men he wanted sprouted up like dragon's teeth.

By February 1956 Raborn had his basic team, exceeding his given number of forty by ten. Others would come later (including a budget management specialist, Gordon Pehrson). And the vacuuming did not stop with people; "If they wanted it, they got it," recalled Admiral Charles Duncan, "whether it was toilet paper, paint, rags, or BOQ space." By June, Mernone had found them all a new home, on the third floor of the venerable Munitions Building next to Main Navy.

—There, inside a "Management Center" guarded by a padlocked steel door, Red Raborn and his team got cracking.[4]

☆

All around them were the mines. At the highest level, Eisenhower and Wilson were determined to limit the number of missile programs. The Navy itself, in the world outside Burke's immediate purview in OPNAV, was uncertain about the Special Projects Office, because its cost came directly out of the service's financial hide. Then there were the internecine turf wars: the Naval Research Laboratory had been experimenting since 1945 with high-altitude rockets; the Bureau of Aeronautics had developed Regulus I and was working on Regulus II; the Bureau of Ordnance itself, now denuded of some of its best people, had proposals in the works for the Triton cruise missile (to replace Regulus) and for a ballistic missile. All believed they were being shouldered aside by the Special Projects Office, an unnecessary bureaucratic overlap envied for its key to the candy store.

Not a few people felt that the Navy's existing deterrent forces, centered on the new supercarriers, were deterrent enough. Many submariners loathed the idea of their boats being used as ballistic-missile platforms, seeing Special Projects as an intruder on their preserve. Raborn, a Brownshoe, had to be especially convincing with this audience.

There were four ballistic programs. Three (Atlas; its backup, Titan; and the Thor land-based intermediate-range ballistic missile) belonged to the Air Force. The fourth would be either the Army Jupiter or the fruit of Raborn's men. This was how things were early in 1956; Wilson's order for a joint Army-Navy IRBM program boxed the Navy in very tightly indeed. The best Burke could gain was a commitment from Wilson to fund the Navy portion of the Jupiter work from Wilson's own Defense Department pocketbook.

With men like Levering Smith and Bill Hasler aboard, people with experience in solid fuels and the conviction that Navy rockets could be powered in no other way, the Navy from the very beginning told the Army in Huntsville that a solid propellant was its goal. Wernher von Braun, the expatriate German rocket scientist, who now worked for the Army team, sneered that if the Navy fired a solid-fuel missile from the Atlantic coast of Europe, its farthest reach into the continent would be the Simplon railway tunnel in Switzerland.

Undaunted, Burke and other senior Navy officers, acting on their own, got a solid-fuel ballistic missile design ginned up by the Aerojet-General

Corporation and Lockheed's Missile and Space Division; the results were ready even before Raborn and his team moved into the Munitions Building. Raborn's shop, meanwhile, uneasily went ahead under its original marching orders, planning to test a liquid-fuel Jupiter on a surface ship. They were also planning to build a "Jupiter S," a solid-fuel variant. The problem with Jupiter S, in the state of the art at the time, was that the missile would have to be gargantuan—forty-four feet high, ten feet in diameter, and 160,000 pounds in weight. A submarine designer, given the task of sketching a home for this monster, could come up only with a blueprint for an 8500-ton boat carrying merely four missiles in a housing awkwardly attached to the sail.

Here matters stood by the summer of 1956—either a liquid-fuel Jupiter, with its attendant seaborne perils, or the unwieldy Jupiter S. Then, a group of scientists meeting on Nobska Point at Woods Hole, Massachusetts, advanced the possibility of a new lightweight missile. Project NOBSKA led to further studies, and one by a panel on the Strategic Use of the Underseas recommended that the Navy construct a solid-fuel ballistic missile with a weight of between eight and fifteen tons (a weight reduction of over 80 percent from the Jupiter S), a low-yield nuclear warhead, and a range of between 1000 and 1500 miles.

Both Burke and Raborn saw their window of opportunity. Between them, with the various studies in hand, they knew they could gain considerable internal Navy support for the new missile. Burke, in particular, was willing to bet the house, and Raborn's men were more than willing to get out of the lesser-of-two-evils choices surrounding Jupiter. Also, Raborn had been trying to give a moniker to the missile project, one he liked for its historic navigational connotations. Now he could apply the name to the Navy's very own strategic missile: Polaris.

The Army, naturally, was shocked and angered at the sudden notice of divorce. (Army brass decided to continue alone in competition with the Air Force to provide the initial American strategic missile.) Burke and Raborn had moved the Navy off the reservation, outside the four missile programs, and now they had to bring Eisenhower and Wilson with them.

They did. The Navy prepared a proposal indicating that Polaris would come in at two-thirds of Jupiter S's development cost—a savings of $500 million. Burke, the political shrewdie, then voted with the Air Force on the Joint Chiefs to assign *land-based* IRBM responsibility to the USAF instead of the Army. (To the Army, this was insult after injury, akin to moving in with the lover next door after the divorce.) In late November 1956, Engine Charlie Wilson, impressed with all the promises of cost-cutting, gave the Air Force control over land-based missiles with ranges over two hundred miles; the Army was left with battlefield tactical weapons. And days later, he authorized the Navy to terminate all collaborative efforts with the

Army—the divorce was decreed in court—and to initiate, on its own, a fleet ballistic missile program.[5]

Polaris, at last, was underway.

☆

Already, the developments highlighted by Project NOBSKA were beginning. In June 1956, scientists in Alexandria, Virginia, mixed an additive of powdered aluminum with the gum slurry that hardened into a rocket grain propellant; the result was a 15 percent boost in specific impulse. Later that summer, the Atomic Energy Commission's Livermore Laboratory developed a lightweight nuclear warhead of substantial yield. Nuclear guru Edward Teller, one of the fathers of the hydrogen weapon, claimed that miniaturization would reduce the nuclear core of the next generation of warheads from 1600 to 600 pounds.

Increase in thrust, reduction in weight—things were moving. Raborn and his men began with an exceptionally crude idea: Polaris had to be able to reach Moscow from a position at sea and cause a reasonable amount of damage. This implied at least a nine-hundred-mile range and a half-megaton yield.

As to the platform, the preferred concept was to pack missiles two abreast inside a submarine pressure hull. The missile size had to be limited by the two-inch, HY-80 steel pressure hulls of nuclear submarines. The specifics of the "reentry vehicle" and payload were, at best, educated guesses. The Bureau of Ships produced designs varying from four to thirty-two missile tubes, hull length being the major problem. Sixteen was the compromise eventually reached.

As to guidance, the potential for targeting error was enormous. The sub had to know its own location in its cube of water, precisely; the missile had to be fired, somehow, underwater, get its bearings in the air, and fly; data were needed on the exact target location and the required missile trajectory; and compensation had to be made for reentry conditions, such as winds over the target. Any computer or set of computers that could do all this, in 1957, would have had to be almost as large as the host boat itself; for this reason, Raborn knew that the Navy would have to accept less navigational and targeting accuracy than land-based missiles could achieve.

The myriad problems of physics began to be solved, usually by compromise with the ineluctable demands of the natural world. The human problems were something else again. Some naval officers, true to their innate conservatism, rejected new technologies out of hand; Polaris would create a new species of officers and sailors, missilemen Nukes, and there was opposition. Carrier advocates generally were leery of what they regarded as unnecessarily drastic change. "The carrier admirals just don't like the idea of going to sea in pig boats," noted Representative Clarence Cannon. When the Blue-Gold concept—two rotating crews for each Polaris boat—was advanced, some decried this operational necessity as a violation of the naval tradition of one captain, one crew. Raborn's looting of the entire Navy for talent did nothing to calm the waters.

Then there was the money. As Special Projects swelled in size and its tentacles projected into practically every nook of the country's science, Raborn's group, like some broadening whirlpool, sucked in more and more Navy funds. The original argument—the $500 million saved as against Jupiter S, proved to be pocket change. Burke had to rob Peter to pay Paul. The Triton cruise missile program was axed, then Regulus II, then the $400 million jet seaplane, Seamaster. The costs of Polaris mushroomed to a titanic 10 percent of the entire Navy budget; ships that otherwise would have steamed went into mothballs. Part of the noticable Navy drawdown in the late 1950s was directly due not to increasingly antique platforms but to Polaris. Other shops were screaming at their cutbacks and loss of programs; Burke had bet the house, and he resolutely kept channeling money Raborn's way.

But the basic threat to Polaris came from the Air Force. Raborn knew who his major enemy was; he trained his dachshund, Heinz, accordingly. "Heinz," he would ask, "would you rather be an Air Force dog or a dead dog?" Heinz would obediently flop over on his back, stubby paws in the air. "Heinz," Raborn would continue, "how about the Navy?" Heinz would be propped up, sitting, in his lap, Red raising the dog's right paw in an obedient salute.

The Air Force and the Navy, with the Army out of the ICBM picture, were now direct competitors for national ballistic-missile allocations. The sons carried on the wars of their fathers. No one was yet willing to accept what, in the early sixties, became the "strategic triad" of national deterrence—manned bombers, land-based missiles, and sea-based missiles. The Air Force was not loath to remind Congress of what Burke, Raborn, and the men of the Special Projects Office already knew: Polaris was an exceptional technological gamble, playing with cards largely unknown. Everywhere—in propulsion systems, guidance systems, submerged communication with submarines—Polaris was not merely expanding the envelope: the program was deliberately, and with enormous risk to itself and to the Navy, stepping outside.

The Air Force liked the big megatonnage carried by its bombers and land-based missiles; Polaris was a runt by comparison, carrying only a relatively low-yield warhead. The Air Force stressed targeting accuracy and the ability to recall its manned bomber wings; the Navy could offer neither. When the Navy budgeted $300 million for forty-eight to sixty Polaris missiles, the Air Force claimed that 1600 of its newly conceived Minutemen could be had for the same cost. When forty-five Polaris boats were proposed, the Air Force thought sixteen to twenty would be plenty. Some USAF officers deliberately spread misinformation about the project, and each Polaris test failure produced a round of "I told you so's" in the Air Force's arc of the Pentagon E-Ring.

Heinz could salute all he wanted (or whenever his master could prop him up), but Raborn knew he had to address the naysayers the only way he could: by succeeding. He emphasized the uniqueness of the Polaris system. He fired up his men with his own unquenchable zeal. The Special Projects Office operated at fever pitch, on a wartime basis. Raborn's officers wore Navy blue, at a time when Burke did not want too much gold shown around Washington and most Navy personnel there wore civvies; they worked a five-and-a-half-day week, even when the work load occasionally slackened; their messages were red-stamped and often hand-carried. Urgency ran through Special Projects like an electric current. Polaris flags, similar to Navy "E for Excellence" flags, flew above the laboratories and factories participating in the program.

Raborn did not skimp on the public relations; in fact, he laid on the publicity with a trowel (another pinprick to the Air Force's amour propre). Special Projects' PR budget was hidden in contractor budgets and administrative overheads, but there was little doubt that Red Raborn had the largest PR slush fund in the Navy. And he was the lead cheerleader. More often than not he was on the road, visiting those labs and factories to exhort and praise. One contractor's plant, having fallen behind on its delivery schedule, got the Raborn treatment. After he had swept through, 250 workers "spontaneously" drew up and signed a pledge to rededicate themselves to their tasks. These high-tech American Stakhanovites were to be found in the wake of every Raborn visit.

The Head Evangelist had a pat speech when he went to the vineyards. The Russians were threatening everyone with their ballistic missiles, he would say. (The USSR successfully tested an ICBM in 1957.) But Polaris, through deterrent strength, would nullify the threat. He would ask the members of his audience to grasp the backs of their necks. "Those are the necks that will be saved when Polaris is developed," he would tell them.

Raborn used his stable of technical experts like a maestro conducting an orchestra. When Congress asked questions, there would be a civilian or naval scientist with the answers, down to the last gram and erg. After the first year of the program, recalled Vice Admiral Kleber Masterson, "the congressional committee used to sit there watching in awe." Aerospace contractors like Lockheed did the bulk of research and development, and Raborn would continuously harass them for the latest data. He had ordnance specialists, procurement specialists, management specialists, theoretical physicists, ballistics experts—the gamut, practically, of American science and administration. He would call them together occasionally, particularly the civilians, for revival meetings, at which time company presidents and shop heads would be cozened into public committal to delivery dates. They all thus put their business and personal reputations on the line, and the big names—General Electric, Westinghouse, Lockheed, Electric Boat, Sperry Rand—were in the lead.

Per Burke's instructions, Raborn made his peace with Rickover. That eccentric little genius had every American contractor who could build nuclear submarines beholden to him. He could not be bypassed. The deal with Rickover was that he, and the Bureau of Ships, would have a say in decisions regarding the characteristics of Polaris boats, their construction scheduling, and their crews. This alliance was critical, because many senior submariners loathed the very idea of Polaris, one even telling his junior officers that their naval careers would be finished if they had anything to do with the project.

For his part, Rickover promoted Polaris, calling the system an "underwater satellite," and "ideal mobile platform." While admitting that Polaris would not be cheap, Rickover declared that any enemy searching for such a weapon "would be in the position of a man trying to find a black cat on a vast and empty plain on a moonless and starless night."

Within the Navy, reflecting a tune currently popular in the musical comedy *Damn Yankees*, there was a saying about the Special Projects Office: "Whatever Lola wants, Lola gets." But Raborn/Lola, craftily, never asked for the moon; after his initial turf raids, he was solicitous in moderating his *public* demands (while still ladling out the PR). His bureaucratic infighting behind the scenes, however, was wondrous to behold.

Arleigh Burke, with all the political adroitness he could muster, was careful to point out that Polaris "is an extremely attractive system," but that America should never rely on sub-launched missiles exclusively. The chief was aboard as long as Raborn *produced*. Raborn knew he needed friends, like Burke, and allies, like Rickover. Above all, he knew he needed *method*.[6]

☆

The Special Projects Office saw its mission as far more than simply rustling up some missile equipment for submarines; from the beginning, these men were thinking about a novel ballistic missile *system*. In effect, they pioneered the Navy's later "systems" approach. When they thought about Polaris, they thought about handling, launching, fire control, navigation, test equipment; about submarines, tenders, test ships, floating drydocks, resupply vessels; about personnel, supply, shore facilities, ancillary services. And they thought about how all these things fit together—symbiotically.

Yet they were no czars of some evolving missile kingdom. They had budgetary influence, to be sure, but at the edges (Rickover was one edge) their control was fuzzy. Rickover controlled the submarine reactors; the Bureau of Ships controlled the submarine systems and support ship designs; the Bureau of Ordnance did some contract management and housekeeping; BuShips and the chief of naval communications controlled the critical comm gear; the Atomic Energy Commission oversaw warhead development. No one, seemingly, had a fix on the defensive systems for the Polaris boats.

Raborn could be Lola, then, but he had to be a very diplomatic Lola, all the while keeping Special Projects zeroed in on its system focus. In the process, he inadvertently weakened the strength of the Navy's old and cumbersome bureaus. Special Projects had only one technological objective and a zealous taskmaster in charge. The bureaus were warrens of conflicting internal work assignments that severely curtailed their efficiency. They were specialized by *function;* Raborn was committed to a *project.* As Polaris took shape, the way Raborn and his men operated began to erode the Navy's confidence in the bureaus.

Raborn's shop became the node where all the problems—ship mainte-nance, equipment design, tactical procedures, crew morale—came together, to be solved in conjuction, systematically. The alternative—jury-rigging and ad hoc decision making—was far more the historical norm for the American military. For example, such was the rush to drop the first atomic bombs on Japan that the physical size of these weapons was determined not by what was technologically possible but by what could get through the bomb-bay doors of the B-29.

To allow bomb-bay dimensions to be determinants of weapons para-meters was *asystematic.* Polaris was an integrated system, in conception and execution, although there was debate about who actually ran the project, the Navy or the major contractors. Certainly, Special Projects by itself could not have *created* Polaris; Raborn and his men, left to themselves in the Munitions Building, would only have been able to dream great dreams. But Special Projects, more than any other entity, was the heart of the emerging system. Raborn's shop, paradoxically, was dominant because Special Proj-ects depended on a multiplicity of contractors, not some single (and hence more powerful) source. Eventually dozens of firms, large and small, would help make Polaris a reality.[7]

There was, however, a Polaris equivalent to those B-29 bomb-bay doors. This was the compromise of sixteen missiles per submarine. Burke's plan-ning staff got a list of active Soviet targets from the Joint Strategic Targeting Agency. The staffers estimated the number of Polaris missiles, with the expected ranges and warheads, needed to take out these targets. Input from other services was ignored; the Navy was apparently going to war alone. The magic number of missiles required turned out to be a suspicious one: 656. Division by sixteen produced a basic requirement of forty-one Polaris submarines.

The Navy raised this preferred number to forty-five to provide a margin for error and, cynics said, to provide five nicely balanced Polaris squadrons of nine boats each. The four extra submarines would eventually vanish, leaving the magic number of forty-one as the Navy's irreducible minimum.

So many systems, so much money. The first supplementary defense bill to include Polaris had funded only three submarines, but that would change. The Special Projects whirlpool steadily devoured Navy funds: $18 million in fiscal 1956, $89 million in 1957, $511 million in 1958. From fiscal 1959 through 1964, the costs of Polaris to the Navy were between $1 billion and $2 billion a year, around 10 percent of total Navy appropriations. The Navy was getting only about 28 percent of Eisenhower's military budgets, compared with the Air Force's 48 percent, and this made the shoe pinch even more tightly. The entire Polaris construction program would eventually cost over $10 billion, the amount publicly admitted.

And construction was not the end. These "weapons systems" were designed for a useful life of twenty years. A Polaris submarine, circa 1960, cost between $110 million and $150 million simply to build—$30 million to $50 million more than one of Rickover's nuclear-powered attack submarines. The Polaris boats had to be crewed, supplied, and periodically overhauled. Their intended posture of continuous readiness would mean support bases, new communications nets, a complete logistics tail, realistic exercises. In the upshot, the cumulative operating costs of Polaris would turn out to be in the billions, too, almost the equivalent of the costs of research and development.

For the Navy, all this was big fiscal pain, even though Polaris proponents could ask about the price of national security and provide the expected positive answer. To bring the Polaris boats on line, rags were tied around boiler pipe joints in destroyers, naval research on guns and gun mounts temporarily vanished, and the supply of new cruisers and hunter-killer submarines dwindled to a trickle. The Navy paid through the nose for the program. The price (economists would say "opportunity cost") was cancellation of some other programs, increasing decrepitude in the conventional fleet, and a slowdown in the arrival of new equipment.

This huge price was a measure of Arleigh Burke's determination. The money kept flowing toward Special Projects to such an extent that, in the end, when the forty-one boats were operational, nearly $700 million was left in the kitty to allocate to other Navy projects. As one of Raborn's officers noted, "Polaris was never nickeled and dimed." Raborn the evangelist always preached frugality, but his goal was getting the boats to sea; he privately told his branch chiefs that "they would not get medals for saving money." He did not quite have financial carte blanche, but he came closer than any other officer in Navy history. The money was not squandered, but in such a project there were inevitable pockets of inefficiency and contractor peculation, and there the Navy paid through the nose as well.

Everyone hoped that some kind of method would help cut costs. Gordon Pehrson, the civilian management specialist, with his assistants came up with something called the Program Evaluation and Review Technique, the kind of dazzling Navy acronym—PERT—that could have been designed by an admiral. PERT had four basic features: delineating a series of steps (called "events") leading to a specific goal, or "end item;" estimating of the time involved to reach each event (there were three of these estimates—most optimistic, most pessimistic, and most likely); a way of calculating a probability curve for the expected time of completion; and, finally, establishing the "critical path," defined as the longest expected time sequence through the network of events. The critical path was the key, since the end item could not be realized until its events had been completed.

PERT, programmed for computers, was all about *time*. Originally, the method had no device for considering cost in dollars. (A later "PERT/ COST" system partially corrected this.) Further, PERT could not do quality control. (Eventually, a "reliability management index" would prove only partially successful in this regard.) The Special Projects Office was very proud of PERT, and indeed the idea was trumpeted far and wide as a management revolution.

Much of PERT's vaunted effectiveness was a myth. The system was not in full operation until the early sixties and had little to do with getting the first boats to sea. Some of its component parts either were tried unsuccessfully or succeeded for the wrong reasons. Raborn's shop may have been proud of PERT, but nobody trusted such a flowchart; up-to-date information was gotten by the simple expedient of picking up a telephone and calling the relevant contractor or branch. In cases of serious hang-ups, a flying squad, often led by the Red Rooster himself, would descend on the miscreants by plane.

Eventurally, PERT and its offshoots hardened into reasonably clear guidelines for action, but in the early years they bred more confusion than anything else. Contractors had differing ideas over "events" and project milestones; there were false starts, redoubling back along the "track;" everyone was pushing the "urgent" button and trying to jump past bottlenecks. Despite the much-ballyhooed PERT, advertised as a "space age management technique," Special Projects had little time to waste on a mass of formal documents or nicely wired communications channels. Robert Wertheim, who had become the head of Raborn's Re-Entry Body Section, said his boss "Made no use of [PERT] at all."

By 1964 there would be nearly a thousand books and articles about PERT, most of them extolling the virtues of their subject. Pehrson at first called his brainchild a "management breakthrough." Variants of the system were in use by the Army, Air Force (high praise), and the National Aeronautics and Space Administration. However, as far as the Special Projects Office was concerned, PERT was more for external than internal use. Only a small portion of the early Polaris program was even on PERT. Many people in Raborn's shop opposed the system in the first place, and contractors did not cotton to being told what they should do, and when, by some computer readout. Everyone knew that the worst place to be was on that "critical path," so deception and obfuscation were often rewarded.

Still, Raborn was eventually forced to sell the system as a key reason behind the miracle of Polaris, although he and everyone else connected with the program knew this to be manifestly false. PERT became part of Special Projects' PR effort. "PERT did not build the Polaris," reasoned one analyst, "but it was extremely useful for those who did build the weapon system to have many people believe that it did."

The PR was lathered on, the computers hummed, the brightly colored flowcharts cascaded out of Special Projects. Most of the uninitiated were convinced. But PERT's loudest proponents, the ones who were not using the system, forgot the most basic principle of the arts of stewardship and oversight: good people make good management—not the reverse. In Special Projects, people, more than anything else, were the method.[8]

—And Red Raborn had some very good people indeed.

☆

Polaris was not some sort of spontaneous generation. The project owed much to the fabulous success of *Nautilus*, to the guidance and navigation expertise gained when the Air Force canceled its contract with North American Aviation for the Navaho cruise missile, and to the studies in reentry physics already begun by the Air Force and Army. But much of Polaris was—had to be—sui generis. Rear Admiral Charles Martell, a proven Pentagon bureaucrat who played a key role in merging the Bureau of Ordnance and the Bureau of Aeronautics to form the Bureau of Weapons in 1959, would say, "Of course, Special Projects is the best thing the Navy has ever done organizationally—and, of course, we must never repeat it." Martell and other old-timers well knew that Raborn's crash project was dooming the hoary organizational verities of the bureaus.

To successfully deploy Polaris required the carefully timed weddings of at least a dozen exotic technologies. Technological trends already in the works were dramatically accelerated—in solid-propellant motors, reentry vehicles, and submarine navigation systems. Developments in subsystems had to be satisfactorily fused with the larger whole, uncertainties in result were always present, and schedules were constantly being expanded and sped up simultaneously. A prime example of the symbiotic nature of the program was the missile itself. When the project really took off, in 1957, the initial system was called the A-2 missile. The interim, or working concept, system was the A-1. The combination of the two was to be incorporated into the follow-on A-3.

The program's fetish was reliability. Raborn, so aides said, did not want to become known as the admiral who had built an underwater fleet filled with useless telephone poles. Reliability was expensive, tended to be highly ritualistic, and, so Polaris's critics claimed, was heavily lubricated with Special Projects' particular brand of PR. But the proof was in the pudding;

no Polaris submarine patrol would ever be aborted because of technical failure.

—The subsystems took shape, came together, became systems—which in turn began to interlock. Launcher Handling had Westinghouse as the prime contractor. Then there was Fire Control (General Electric), Guidance (General Electric), Navigation (Sperry Rand, RCA, and the Applied Physics Laboratory), Instrumentation Testing (Lockheed, Interstate Electronics), Missiles (Lockheed), Rocket Motors (Aerojet-General, Hercules), System Testing (Applied Physics Laboratory), and Ship Installation (Bureau of Ships, Vitro). For every system, there were competitive contractors asking for a piece of the action, and sometimes succeeding. Levering Smith, a rear admiral now, monitored the technical branches and their contractors; Red Raborn monitored Levering Smith.

Raborn was in the middle of everything. He told any person even remotely connected with the project—contractors, workers, wives, even children—that failure would mean a national disaster. (One ranking naval officer avowed that "Polaris couldn't fail because the wives wouldn't let it.") The Red Rooster was a premium blend of snake-oil salesman and charismatic leader; "our religion," he later said, "was to build Polaris."

The acolytes brought forward a finless missile controlled by swiveling engine nozzles, missile stabilization systems for fueling, and two test ships, *Compass Island* (to test the missile's navigation system) and *Observation Island* (to launch test missiles from the ocean surface). Polaris, they concluded, would be shaped like a magnum of champagne, twenty-eight feet long, weighing twenty-eight thousand pounds, with a range of 1500 miles. At this range, all of the Soviet Union, except for a small area around Kazakh in Central Asia, could be targeted.[9]

Raborn went with most of this, except that he chafed under the delivery date of 1965. *Sputnik* was a shock, and the orbiting of the minuscule eighteen-pound Russian satellite shifted Special Projects into even higher gear. From October 1957 onward, Raborn was keyed to 1960 rather than 1965; he would saw Burke's marching orders in half. The necessary compromises were made: the range of Polaris would decline to 1200 miles; bulkier navigaton and fire-control systems would have to be accepted, for the moment; a somewhat less powerful solid propellant would be used (materials that could withstand the higher temperatures produced by the ideal solid propellant were not yet ready); and an even lighter warhead would be fitted.

The word went out to the two thousand major contractors and six thousand subcontractors. The entire hive accelerated, engulfing what had been expected to be the beginnings of PERT. ("Pretty crude stuff," even Pehrson had to eventually admit of his management tool.) Lockheed developed a scheme for expelling Polaris from its underwater tube on a bubble of compressed air. Practice launches were conducted at the San Francisco

Navy Yard, the dummy missile being snagged at its apogee by a crane. An underwater launch off San Clemente was successfully conducted early in 1958.

The solid-propellant problem was more intractable, threatening to put brakes on the entire project. A small propellant plant blew up in 1956, followed by explosions in two more propellant mixers the next year (the first of which killed a man). Finally, a rubbery composition evolved, one that was mixed in huge vats, poured into rocket casings, and allowed to harden. Aerojet, the prime contractor, claimed that the stuff was so safe that engineers used hollowed-out chunks for ashtrays. Its technical name was "castable polyurethane propellant," and the Navy would eventually buy hundreds of thousands of pounds per month.

Polaris had two motors; at the end of each was a nozzle through which the hot gas produced by the propellant escaped. The "jetavator," a metallic ring that cut into the gas streams and deflected their flow, linked the two big motors and the missile's brain.

The brain had three parts—navigation, fire control, and missile guidance. Inertial navigation, using gyroscopic motion, was the only way to go. Gyros for a shipboard system had to last for months or years, and gyros tended to "drift" over time. The Ships Inertial Navigation System (SINS) went back in its development to 1948, but even by 1957 the system was not good enough to be mounted in *Nautilus* for her first probe under the polar icepack. In 1958 Sperry took over as the prime contractor and immediately found itself locked into Raborn's time-vice. With incredible speed, a solution, requiring highly miniaturized computers utilizing the new transistors, was found.

Polaris, like all ballistic missiles intended for use in the Northern Hemisphere, was aimed along an angle created by the relationship of the target to the geographic North Pole. In addition to its inertial guidance (there were three inertial navigators in each Polaris submarine), the missile contained a "stable table," which was a round, gyro-controlled platform, continuously adjusted to be aligned horizontally with the Earth's center. If the stable table was at a tilt when Polaris was fired, the missile would become confused—its guidance system would have a false reference point—and Moscow might become Paris.

The brain had to constantly adjust for six submarine (or ship) motions: pitch, roll, and yaw (the classic three), but also for surge (wave motion), sway, and heave (all motions of the entire frame in three dimensions). The Earth's rotation and atmospheric influences had to be accounted for. The submarine had to be naturally buoyant both before and after launch. Information coming from the inertial navigators had to be refined before being fed to the missile's guidance system.[10]

Sperry and other contractors created a true electronic prodigy, a brain that could do all this, and they did their job within two years. Now, all the systems and subsystems had to jell together—aboard an operational submarine.

☆

In Groton, Connecticut, Electric Boat was in the midst of a string of triumphs: first *Nautilus*, then *Seawolf*, *Skate*, and *Skipjack*. The hull of another *Skipjack*-class, *Scorpion*, was taking shape in 1957. Her reactor and control-room sections were almost complete.

The post-Sputnik acceleration of Polaris, and Raborn's new deadline of 1960, led to yet another compromise—the most breathtaking of all. *Scorpion* was designed as a nuclear attack submarine, 250 feet long. Raborn evangelized Electric Boat, brought Secretary of the Navy Gates on board, and, by the end of 1957, had the contracts he wanted. *Scorpion*'s hull sections would be pried apart, much like the magician's trick of sawing a lady in half. In her midriff would be inserted a 130-foot missile bay, sixteen tubes in tandem. Raborn wanted this lash-up hybrid delivered to the fleet by the end of 1959.

Scorpion's reactor was designed to drive a 2830-ton attack boat; the lash-up, rechristened *George Washington*, would weigh 5400 tons. Rickover concluded that *Scorpion*'s reactor would do the job, with slight loss of speed. So the hull was bisected and the missile bay inserted, rather like cutting a cigar in two and plunking a matchbox down in the middle. *George Washington* would have a slightly humped back over her rectangular midsection.

Electric Boat had crackerjack submarine builders. Across the top of a large brick warehouse in its yard spread row after row of faded signs, seventy-four in all, each bearing the name of a submarine the company had produced during World War II. Across nineteen of the plaques were the large-lettered words LOST IN ACTION. EB's men were exceptionally competent designers, technicians, jury-riggers; by 1944 they had been launching a brand-new 1500-ton submarine every two weeks.

—But they had never seen anything like *Scorpion/George Washington*. Mistakes were made; several parts of the boat had to be ripped out and redone. Some jobs were repeated three times. Valves got placed bass-ackward, pipes were run where they were not supposed to be. Through all the turmoil *George Washington* somehow took shape, and nearby the keel of Hull 153 was laid down on 27 May 1958: her twin, *Patrick Henry*. Electric Boat, after teething on these two, would eventually build fifteen more Polaris submarines—more than any other shipyard.

On 9 June 1959 *George Washington*, her sixteen missile tubes fitted with the precision of pistons in an automobile engine, slid down Electric Boat's ways. Only eighteen months had passed since the welders' torches had first sliced into the hull of *Scorpion*. Next door, *Patrick Henry* was rapidly taking shape. And Raborn had even more abuilding, despite the unproven missile technology: *Theodore Roosevelt* at Mare Island, *Robert E. Lee* at Newport News, and *Abraham Lincoln* in Portsmouth, New Hampshire. Together, these five hybrids, all launched before June 1960—would be called the *George Washington* class.

But *George Washington* herself was the one that counted. She went to sea on 17 November 1959 and charged over her initial hurdles beautifully. Rickover conducted the reactor trials, spending the time, as was his wont, calmly reading a book in the control room. Raborn was not aboard; he thought that he and the KOG ("Kindly Old Gentleman"), the sardonic name many officers had fastened on Rickover, should not come into needless conflict. Reactors were the KOG's province.[11]

And the missile systems were Raborn's. *Compass Island* had spent three years at sea testing the navigation equipment. The underwater launcher off San Clemente had fired over sixty dummy missile shots. *Observation Island* had been shooting off Polaris shots right and left. Twelve out of seventeen tests of live "birds" from the new rocket complex at Cape Canaveral had succeeded. (The first Polaris shot broke up and fell into the nearby Banana River, leading Raborn to crack, "You can't have high points without low points.") On 6 January 1960, a guided Polaris flew downrange for the first time—exactly seven days later than Raborn's hurry-up schedule back in late 1957 had called for. Soon the missile was achieving accuracies of less than one mile at long ranges; one nine-hundred-mile shot landed 400 yards from bull's-eye. "Polaris has been a good boy," crowed Tom Gates.

At last the time came for the good boy to be married to *George Washington*, to see if the pair could strut their stuff. Under the command of the crew-cutted, square-jawed Commander James Osborn, the sub was an engineering marvel, crammed with seventy miles of cable and twenty-four miles of piping. Theoretically her main battery, those sixteen missiles in her added midsection, could deliver an explosive yield greater than all the bomb tonnage delivered by all the air forces, Axis and Allied, of World War II (including that dropped on Hiroshima and Nagasaki). The vessel was in fact a microcosm of American applied technology: turbine and rocket propulsion, nuclear power and warheads, and sophisticated electronics systems. On board were state-of-the-art developments in fluid dynamics, hydraulics, metallurgy, ceramics, and plastics.

Jim Osborn, who could chomp a cigar to pieces and spew out multisyllable erudition at the same time, conned his boat about twenty-five miles east of Cape Canaveral Lighthouse on 18 July 1960. Raborn and Smith rode aboard, along with a score of contractors. Osborn took *George Washington* down to 250 feet; people aboard the watching observation vessels could see only the tip of her telemetry mast slicing through the royal-blue sea.

The countdown began, marred by several "holds." *George Washington* had two tubes loaded; Osborn switched to the second missile. More holds; there were instrumentation problems and communications glitches. Finally the telemetry batteries ran down, and everyone went home.

—They all came back two days later. This time, after the sub went under, there were only two brief holds. Then the muzzle doors—the hatches on deck—electronically swung open. A barrier of strong, thin plastic stretched across the opening, preventing seawater from rushing in. Once the doors were clear, Osborn gave the order to fire. The fire-control button was pressed.

Immediately, a charge of compressed air shattered the plastic and blew the twenty-eight-thousand-pound bird out of its tube. Polaris quickly rode its air bubble one hundred feet to the surface, vaulting sixty feet above the waves like a just-hooked white marlin. Observers gasped as the missile broke through at an angle, seemingly wildly out of control. Suddenly Polaris's powerful rocket engines cut in; the missile instantly righted itself and began to ride a steady white arc of flame into the summer sky. Seconds later the bird was at seventy thousand feet, traveling at fourteen thousand miles an hour; the dummy warhead separated on schedule and was on its ballistic way, one thousand miles into the South Atlantic. The second missile flashed off successfully two hours later.

Osborn sent a signal to Eisenhower, who was vacationing up at Newport. The message was terse and precise, like Osborn himself. "Polaris—from out of the deep to target. Perfect."[12]

☆

By mid-1961, *George Washington* had completed three Polaris patrols off the Soviet coastline. Based out of Holy Loch, Scotland, and mother-henned by the submarine tender *Proteus*, she pioneered in the Blue-Gold crew concept, each 133-man crew riding her for sixty to seventy days at a time—all underwater. The exec of her Blue Crew called her a "space station in the sea."

She and her sisters coming on line were not all that popular. There was a strong pacifist movement to have them banned from British shores; some Labourites, clergymen, and intellectuals chimed in. The leader of the Presbytery of Glasgow asked, "Is it a worse problem that communism shall dominate the world than that the world shall be subjected to the horrors of nuclear war?"

—A reasonable question, and these concerned, impassioned people also worried over nuclear accidents and Soviet retaliation in kind—fears that would follow Polaris wherever its boats and crews appeared. Hundreds of demonstrators would periodically gather at Holy Loch in protest. Some American officers and men had to stumble through massed sitdowns at pierside just to get back to their boats. Other protesters rowed in the way of submarines returning from patrol, and a few even tried to board *Proteus*.

But most Scots, and the rest of the British citizenry, were not anti-Polaris, accepting the boats as what Arleigh Burke and Red Raborn had advertised them: powerful and necessary forces of strategic deterrence. Aboard them were men of a new Navy. Their business was never to use their weapons; if they did, they had failed. The rest of the Navy called them, and their boats, "boomers," but no one wanted to hear the sound. Each man was a volunteer, the veteran of psychological tests; each one received special "incentive pay."

"There is little of the sailor about them," wrote one observer. "They are not sailors but highly trained technicians, seagoing specialists who, as long as they remain on [Polaris] duty, will probably not see an overseas bar or a waterfront skin show." (These conditions did not make the boomers any more pure—only more cloistered.) Their time was spent tending the sixteen gray-green tubes stretching in paired columns down the 130-foot length of the missile compartment. The men called their charges "Sherwood Forest."

But Robin Hood and his Merry Men never gallivanted in such a setting. Between the lid of each tube and each missile's brain lay the reentry vehicle— the nose cone. At the base of each white-skinned nose cone was a slotted metal disk, a keyhole that had to be turned to arm the nuclear warhead. The captain of each Polaris boat was the sole possessor of the key.[13]

The ultimate horror of all this was not lost on anyone, certainly not on Eisenhower, Burke, or Raborn. The dream came sheathed in nuclear nightmare. But Burke and Raborn, like the thousands of other people behind Polaris, regarded the fruit of the Special Projects Office as a *necessary* horror. The politicians agreed. John Kennedy's first budget tripled production of Polaris submarines and the Air Force's Minuteman. By 1964 the Polaris A-3 would be on line, outfitted with a system called Claw. Multiple warheads would separate from their rocket after launch, just as the single warhead had done in *George Washington*'s initial tests. But now the several warheads would be guided to their earthly targets by a single guidance system— multiple (but not independent) reentry vehicles, or MRVs.

And, despite the deeply felt fears of some of their people, British leaders liked Polaris, too. Royal Navy officers remembered with disgust how they had been manhandled by Rickover concerning the issue of the transfer of *Skipjack*'s S5W reactor system. But Burke was a different matter. His friendship with Lord Mountbatten meant that a handpicked Royal Navy Officer, with missile experience, had been a part of Special Projects almost from the beginning.

Mountbatten pushed for a British Polaris fleet, and an Admiralty study in 1959 indicated that the system was the least-vulnerable nuclear deterrent. The price tag, for a British economy that was continuously reducing military expenditures, was something else again. So the British accepted Skybolt, an American-built, air-launched, medium-range ballistic missile, as an alternative. Skybolt, however, was bedeviled with both developmental and financial problems, in addition to being clearly inferior to both Polaris and Minuteman.

In the Nassau Agreement, which the British patched together with the

Americans late in 1962, a future British Polaris force was assigned to NATO but was "available for national use in time of emergency." The Americans agreed to match the number of British Polaris boats assigned to NATO. The British, not without rancor, abandoned the doomed Skybolt project and began to purchase Polaris A-3 missiles from the United States, producing the warheads themselves. The Polaris Sales Agreement was accordingly signed on 6 April 1963, and the missile system went international. Beginning with the launching of HMS *Resolution* in 1966, the British would build three more Polaris boats— *Renown, Repulse*, and *Revenge*.

In December 1959, in the heat of Special Projects' work, Burke had commissioned a fourteen-member civilian-military panel (Project Poseidon) to study the Navy's problems in broad scale. The group's general recommendations were the expected: more fast-track technology requiring more money. As to Polaris, the experts believed the combination of the nuclear-tipped missile with the nuclear submarine "to be one of the most outstanding engineering achievements of our nation during the past decade."[14]

☆

For the United States Navy, the operational reality of Polaris meant much more than an "outstanding engineering achievement." In 1958, Clarence Cannon, chairman of the powerful House Appropriations committee, had claimed that the Americans lagged behind the Russians in the space race, intercontinental ballistic missiles, submarines, tanks, rifles, radar, and rocket fuels—a doleful list, consonant with the Gaither Report, that was a thermometer of the fever of post-*Sputnik* panic. Now came Polaris—silent, deadly beyond imagination, a seemingly omnipotent trump card in the Cold War.

Hanson Baldwin called the Polaris-carrying submarine the "new battleship," the capital ship of the future. Relieved to have what seemed to be an impregnable nuclear deterrent force on line at last, many commentators (but not Baldwin) forgot that the Polaris boats were completely useless in any conventional conflict. Instead, imaginative accounts appeared of the Polaris fleet holding Russia hostage from its bastions under the polar ice cap, warheads targeted on sites as far away as Magnitogorsk and Lake Baikal. Naval professionals knew there was no such thing as an ultimate deterrent weapon, but the marriage of Polaris with the nuclear submarine, which the Navy called the Fleet Ballistic Missile Weapons System (FBM), "possesses inherent invulnerability to a considerably higher degree than any other system conceived"—such was the opinion of the author of the Naval Institute's Prize Essay for 1959.[15]

Burke's Naval Warfare Analysis Group (NWAG) sought to place Polaris in strategic context. Unsurprisingly, NWAG-5 ("National Policy Implications of Atomic Parity") tried to shoulder the Air Force, with its manned bombers and land-based missiles, to one side to make room for the

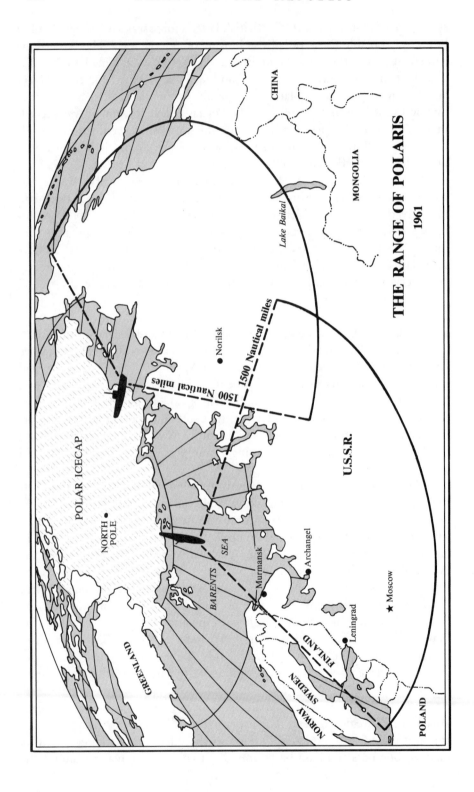

THE RANGE OF POLARIS
1961

FBM. Because Polaris could not compete with the bomber wings in operational flexibility or with land-based missiles in targeting accuracy, NWAG-5 advanced "generous adequacy for deterrence alone" as doctrine. This Pentagon doublespeak meant the ability to destroy major urban areas. The Navy, which had publicly abhorred city-busting as atomic strategy ever since Hiroshima and Nagasaki, now was forced into promoting rather than denigrating the nuclear sledgehammer.

Some admirals, but not the politically sensitive Burke, thought the FBM made every Air Force strategic system redundant if not obsolete. A few believed that, in the future, *all* strategic weapons should go underwater, where the boomers would be the sole custodians of national strategic security. Burke got behind NWAG-5 nevertheless, tried to dampen these extremist arguments, and instructed retired naval officers to speak out on the Navy's strategic shift whenever possible. When General Thomas Power, who had relieved Curtis LeMay as commander of SAC (LeMay had become the Air Force's vice chief of staff), heard of Burke's ploy, he wrote to General Thomas White, the Air Force chief, that "we would be well advised to match this action in concept and to exceed it in distribution." The wars of the fathers ground on.

The FBM would never supplant the Air Force's strategic weapons systems, but Burke was committed to achieving a place in the strategic sun for the Navy—and this Raborn and his team had achieved. At their most benign, said one analyst, the FBM and other strategic systems "can play their most effective role as a protective umbrella which, although inactive itself, keeps the enemy from using them [his own nuclear weapons] and thus allows other and milder forms of military power to carry out their respective missions." Burke and other Navy moderates were also careful to make sure that the FBM did not undercut the strategic importance of the Navy's cherished operational flexibility, centered, in particular, on the aircraft carrier.

Navy ideas of "finite deterrence," hazy as they were, never amounted to much in national strategy. By the late 1950s, the Eisenhower administration had long since muted the crude "massive retaliation" concept to pianissimo, however; Burke's struggle for operational flexibility, paradoxically, was succeeding in the shadow of the FBM. The Polaris system was widely praised as being a stabilizing force in international affairs. Even the necessary inaccuracy of FBM guidance systems was put forward as a positive; Polaris would be incapable of alarming the enemy, the argument went, because the system could not adequately threaten his means of retaliation. Therefore, the Cold War, thanks in large part to the FBM, had arrived at a condition of "stability" (others would say "balance of terror") based on invulnerable retaliatory forces.[16]

This was entirely too much sugarcoating. In fact, both the Navy and the Army had already gotten Eisenhower to approve the nuclearization of their nonstrategic arsenals. Naval "operational flexibility" would include nuclear weapons. Naval units began to be equipped with low-yield tactical nuclear weapons (less than twenty kilotons), such as the Mark 57 nuclear depth charge. Such tactical weapons, John Foster Dulles smoothly claimed, "can utterly destroy military targets without endangering unrelated civilian targets." This was hogwash, but soothing hogwash, and in addition, tactical nukes were relatively cheap. NATO had agreed as early as 1954 to integrate tactical nuclear weapons into its military system. The FBM, far from being some kind of capstone of nuclear development, was a crucial component of nuclear proliferation.

Moreover, the "missile gap" scare of the late 1950s boosted production of hundreds more nuclear ballistic missiles. USAF Atlas-Titan production went from 80 to 255; Minutemen from 400 to 450 (with an additional 90 mobile missiles for fiscal 1962); Polaris expanded to a force of 304 missiles on nineteen submarines, and then kept on going. The "missile gap," which had been a major bogeyman of the Gaither Report, died a quiet death during the Kennedy administration. Intelligence estimates in 1961 indicated that the United States held a "very considerable advantage in strategic deterrent strength."

But by that time *George Washington* was on patrol somewhere in the Atlantic depths, having departed from Charleston for her maiden voyage on 15 November 1960—less than five years after Red Raborn had been given his marching orders and a time frame of ten years. Her FBM sisters were marshaling in her wake. (*Ethan Allen* would conduct the first Pacific patrol in 1964.) John Kennedy (the Cold Warrior par excellence) and his secretary of defense, Robert McNamara, quickly accelerated the production of American strategic weapons systems, missile gap or not. The laying of Polaris keels was stepped up, from five to twelve per year. This was fine by the Navy, which hewed to its original magic number of forty-one FBMs; McNamara agreed, and forty-one there would be.

The five lash-up *George Washington*s would be joined by the five members of the *Ethan Allen* class, the first submarines built as Polaris launchers from the keel up. In May 1962 *Lafayette* slid down the ways, the progenitor of thirty more like her, at eight thousand tons one-third bigger than *George Washington*. The thirty-one *Lafayette*s would bring the Polaris fleet right to the magic number. All told, the Kennedy build-up produced a strategic force of 600 B-52s, 1000 Minutemen, 54 Titans, 126 Atlases (until 1965), and 656 Polaris missiles on those forty-one nuclear submarines—Burke's and Raborn's original estimate to a T. The missile gap did not create this buildup, nor did the new strategic ideas of "flexible response." The fears of a youthful, untested administration that, above all else, wanted to appear tough on the tough questions, were responsible.[17]

Thus, the FBM was enshrined in the nation's strategic posture. The placement of Polaris on submarines had been intended to ensure Navy control and entry into the strategic game as much as to contribute to the country's deterrent force. The Joint Strategic Target Planning Staff at SAC headquarters near Omaha (which now included a three-star admiral) was ordered to create the Single Integrated Operational Plan (SIOP), and there the FBM was further cemented into place. The SIOP would remain the primary strategic warfare document of the United States, and Joint Plans included the "strategic triad:" manned bombers, land-based missiles, and—the FBM.

SAC tried desperately to get control of Polaris (by promoting an overall "United States Strategic Command," to be dominated by guess who) and failed. Burke won this fight, but even he had trouble addressing the one critical technical problem involving the FBM that remained unsolved, one that no form of control could do much about—communication. The Navy scarcely mentioned the problem in all the ballyhoo over Polaris, and with reason. World War II submarines, once they had slipped the leash and were off on patrol, had been as good as on another planet so long as they remained underwater. This situation had not changed, because underwater physics had not changed either. Radio waves did not like water, and there was no reasonable way to communicate with a submerged submarine from any realistic distance.

Low-frequency signals were the answer—very low frequency. A submerged submarine, with its small whip antenna sticking out of the water, could get such a signal, on the five- to fifteen-kilocycle band. A submerged sub in the Mediterranean received a VLF signal from Annapolis, loud and clear, in 1959. Enthusiastically, the Navy began construction of an enormous VLF station in Cutler, Maine, on a 2800-acre peninsula. Cutler was a monster, featuring arrays of two 980-foot masts, each surrounded by concentric circles of six 875-foot towers and six 790-foot towers. Each array spread out over an area of eleven Pentagons. The whole produced two million watts.

But Cutler, as the Navy soon knew, was not the answer. The basic idea behind the FBM was anonymity, and a big submarine just beneath the surface trailing an antenna was not anonymous. Work pressed ahead on communications satellites, but even with these in place a boat had to be near the surface to receive an ultrahigh-frequency (UHF) downlink burst. The solution seemed to be extremely low frequency (ELF) transmission, sending signals, at the sacrifice of time and volume, through the earth itself, which would require enormous power and an incredibly large communications grid. The search for a suitable site for such a grid would plague the Navy for decades.[18]

With this potentially critical flaw, the FBM boats went on line. By October 1962, a watershed month in American history, nine FBM submarines were at sea—144 missiles all told. The Soviet Union had no comparable weapon. At the same time, the United States had about 226 ICBMs

(Minuteman, Atlas, and Titan) to the Russians' 75, and 1350 long-range bombers (600 B-52s and 750 B-47s) to the Russians' 190 (70 Bears and 120 Bisons).

And there they were, big as *Juneau*-class cruisers, eventually forty-one of them—silent, submerged, virtually undetectable, lethal almost beyond human imagination. Their missiles had terrifyingly short flight times, and they could at best hit only the general areas of cities. They were, in a phrase, "floating embodiments of deterrence's central message," and they had placed the Navy firmly at the center of American strategic planning once and for all. With them, the nuclear arms race, at least temporarily, reached some sort of "logical plateau," where any kind of preemptive attack by the Russians would automatically bring disaster raining down on their homeland.

☆

Red Raborn became a vice admiral. Polaris, he said, was not merely another missile project. The missile was "an entirely new combination of striking power, mobility, self-sufficiency and concealment." Polaris, indeed, was all of these, and more: Polaris was a *revolution*.

Along with Burke, Raborn had done more than any other man to make that revolution. The Blackshoe and the Brownshoe had created a strategic submarine weapons system. Like Rickover, Raborn proved to be a consummate bureaucratic politician. He fused a policy consensus (the Navy's desire to be a key player in national strategy) with technological opportunity. He was innovative, defensive (vis-á-vis the Air Force), and moderate—all at the same time. And he brought the Navy's greatest peacetime crash project of the twentieth century to a resounding completion.

The pace of Special Projects became more routine, ossified, bureaucratic. Raborn was relieved by Rear Admiral Ignatius Galantin early in 1962, and FBM development passed into the permanent control of submarine officers (many of whom had opposed the system in the first place). Levering Smith would be the first missileer to reach Flag Plot, on his way to vice admiral and forty-five years of commissioned service, not finally retiring until 1977.

The FBM program did not miss a beat. *Ethan Allen* fired the first improved A-2 missile in October 1961; on 6 May 1962 she also fired a live nuclear warhead from the depths of the Pacific Ocean, a warhead that flew unerringly downrange and obliterated its ocean target. In 1964 *Daniel Webster* fired the first A-3; by 1966, with the launching of *Will Rogers*, the forty-one boat group was complete.[19]

Raborn, upon his retirement, was appointed by Lyndon Johnson as director of central intelligence—a disastrous tour. The CIA, he found, was no Special Projects Office, and he—the no-nonsense, publicity-conscious, cheerleading admiral—was no spymaster. But by then, his monument was already in place, out there in its cubes of salt water.

All along, Raborn knew that his managerial and technological miracle was no sole solution to the Cold War or even a single basis for American strategy. He knew that Polaris would go bankrupt in its purpose the instant its armed nuclear warhead began to ride that bubble of compressed air toward an enemy target. And he knew that not even the marvels of Polaris could dampen conventional struggles throughout the world.

—In places like the Mediterranean.

CHAPTER TWENTY-EIGHT

MED I

———— ☆ ————

B y 1956 the United States had wired together a number of peacetime military alliances with the rest of what American leaders were pleased to call the "Free World." This "pactomania" included the Rio Treaty with Canada and most of the Latin American countries, which committed the American military to a defense of the entire Western Hemisphere; the ANZUS Treaty with Australia and New Zealand, which brought obligations in the southwestern Pacific; and the Southeast Asia Treaty Organization, which was aimed at somehow containing communism along the Asian littoral.

On the other side of the globe, the Baghdad Pact of 1955, sponsored by the United States and including Great Britain, Turkey, Iraq, Iran, and Pakistan, became the Central Treaty Organization (CENTO) in 1959; its purpose was to try to bank the fires in the volatile Middle East. America, by 1970, would be a member of four regional military alliances and a participant in a fifth. In that year the United States would have mutual defense treaties with no fewer than forty-two nations and would be furnishing military or economic aid to almost one hundred.

All these alliances were *over seas* and thus placed a tremendous burden, both potential and actual, on the United States Navy. By diplomatic agreement, the Navy's responsibilities had become worldwide. In the strategic terminology of 1956, however, the most important alliance was still the first one—the North Atlantic Treaty Organization.

In January 1952, Admiral Lynde McCormick, commander of the Atlantic Fleet, had put on another hat as Supreme Allied Commander, Atlantic (SACLANT). The British had not liked the idea of an American unified commander at all. "Should we have fallen so far into the walks of humanity," Winston Churchill had pleaded from the opposition benches, that Albion could produce "no British admiral capable of discharging this function?" They apparently had.

Along with the Supreme Allied Commander, Europe (SACEUR), at that time Dwight Eisenhower, McCormick reported to NATO's Standing Group, headquartered in Washington. NATO's collective strategy was based on the presupposition that Western Europe was the "strategic pivot of the world." Many American naval leaders, like Ernie King and Arthur Radford, did not buy this assumption for one minute, but both Harry Truman and Eisenhower were Europe-centered. Under these two presidents, and those to follow, NATO would remain the linchpin of American alliances.

NATO strategists knew that their combined land power could not match that of the Soviet-dominated Warsaw Pact, formed in 1955 in response to NATO. Therefore seapower, and Allied technological superiority, were critical in NATO planning. The planning, moreover, had to be both thorough and complex, for McCormick's command responsibilities as SAC-LANT were huge: from the North Pole to the Tropic of Cancer (23 degrees 27 minutes north latitude) and from the eastern shores of North America to the coastal waters of the British Isles and the continent of Europe. Inside his zone lay such diverse locales as iced-over Jan Mayen, Spitsbergen, the Azores, Madeira, Bermuda, and the windswept Faeroes.

Lynde McCormick was, according to a SACLANT subordinate, a "delightful, smart clean-cut gentleman." He was an unusual combination, a submariner who had also skippered *South Dakota*, and was well enough thought of to have been acting chief of naval operations after Forrest Sherman's untimely death. But even an experienced hand like McCormick was manacled by SACLANT's marching orders. In peacetime, McCormick did not command so much as an oil barge. On occasion he would gather in some Allied fleet elements for maneuvers, but these would generally be designed to test concepts rather than to train the ships and men of a permanent standing force. The first of these efforts came in the fall of 1952 (Operation MAINBRACE), involving 160 Allied ships—of which 9 carriers and 36 destroyers were American.

Any NATO-sponsored naval force, these exercises proved, came with plenty of problems attached. Common doctrines was dreadfully slow in developing; combined schools were evolving well behind any reasonable power curve; every participating navy had its own forms of organization, administration, and communication—individual cat's cradles that somehow had to be blended. In the event of conflict, 80 percent of the heavy combatants would have to be supplied by the United States—a huge scheduling problem. There were basing problems, supply problems, equipment problems. Even common military ideas were found to be difficult to express in consonance.

NATO, to be effective, had to be a seapower alliance. In the upshot, its effectiveness rested on the ability of sealift to reinforce Western Europe in the event of a land offensive by the Warsaw Pact. McCormick, who had both commanded submarines and hunted them, was an authority on antisubmarine tactics. He gave NATO's seaborne posture an antisubmarine warfare accent that the organization was never to lose.

Russia had about 500 conventional submarines available in the mid-fifties, so NATO believed, about half of them capable of long-range cruising. (Hitler's U-boat arm, at its World War II peak, had mustered around 440.) The Russian subs could get into the Atlantic through the narrow passages of the Baltic and the much wider ones to either side of Iceland, and into the Mediterranean from the Black Sea. They would target the same shipping that the U-boats had: the vital resupply convoys from the Western Hemisphere. And the Russians, NATO knew, were beginning to convert some of their boats to guided missiles.

The destroyer was the classic enemy of the submarine. By 1955 SACLANT had available, from his own Atlantic Fleet Destroyer Force, two hundred middle-aged cans of World War II vintage. Only six Atlantic Fleet destroyers were of post-1945 construction. When Admiral Jerauld Wright took over as SACLANT, destroyers and antisubmarine warfare were major concerns.

Jerry Wright was tall and handsome, a bachelor as late as his lieutenant commander years in a service that liked its more senior men married and family-oriented. From time to time, while he was stationed on the West Coast in the 1930s, his good looks and tailored manner had even gotten him dates with a few movie stars. His sea time had been spent mostly aboard destroyers and cruisers. By the time he reached flag rank ("just as naturally as he might walk," in Rear Admiral Joshua Cooper's admiring words), he had developed into a powerful, superlatively organized leader, an officer who was not only effective as a naval politico and diplomat but also popular with his juniors.

Wright knew antisubmarine warfare like a book (he had written a fair share of that book himself). He continued McCormick's program of weaving NATO's ASW picture together. Seven other nations were potential naval contributors—Canada, Great Britain, France, Norway, Denmark, the Netherlands, and Italy—and he arranged for anything new in ASW to be tested and evaluated in the Atlantic.

The Americans had begun the conversion of several *Essex*-class carriers into ASW platforms; by 1959 Wright had five of these in the Atlantic. Great Britain made two of its four flattops available. (The other two remained, overly hopeful symbols of a dying imperialism, "East of Suez.") The French contributed three, and the Canadians and Dutch one each. The quality here was very good, and the U.S. Navy's sturdy, twin-engine S2F Tracker was proving its worth as a dependable ASW aircraft.

But the destroyers were a constant concern. Altogether, the eight naval nations of NATO had some 450 cans and escorts available, but their small hulls could not take major sonar or weapons conversions. Fully 75 percent of them were of World War II vintage. Early in 1958, the commander of the Atlantic Fleet's Antisubmarine Defense Force had to admit that his destroyers were "soft spots," most of them "approaching the end of their useful life." The small American *Forrest Sherman* class, while modern, could not begin to fill the breach. By mid-1958, the Americans had only 25 new destroyer leaders, destroyers, and destroyer escorts available, out of their total of some 300 destroyer types in both the Atlantic and Pacific fleets.

Some of the slack was taken up by the Canadians, who converted practically their entire navy into a superb ASW force. About half of the Royal Navy's seventy-five ASW ships were new. France's ASW program was modest but continuing; the French were asking for more military assistance for carriers and destroyers, even as they were indicating increasing dissatisfaction with their NATO roles. Norway and Denmark together contributed twenty-two destroyer types, while the Dutch were small in numbers but fairly efficient. Even the Portuguese, not counted on for a significant naval role in the alliance, gave a mite in ASW. In the Mediterranean, the Italians built ten modern ASW platforms, fully up to their excellent standard of marine construction. Even those quarrelsome neighbors Greece and Turkey (not assigned Atlantic roles in NATO) came up with twenty-eight ASW vessels.

Still, Wright had to *integrate* these forces with ASW submarines, land-based patrol planes, sonar development, and the mounting of new weapons systems. Superior Allied technology would have to win any new Battle of the Atlantic, and this technology would have to be understood and used synergistically by all hands.

Progress in these areas was painfully slow. Wright's chief of staff, Vice Admiral H. Page Smith, confessed that "it is economically impossible for the NATO countries to build anti-submarine forces in the ratios that we found necessary in the past . . . to defeat Hitler's U-boats in the Atlantic." Progress would have to come, Smith said, through research and development breakthroughs in ASW techniques.

As NATO saw the situation, the Russians could use their seapower in two ways: first, as support in the Baltic on the right wing of Warsaw Pact forces as they moved westward across the central European plain, and second, to attack the Allied transatlantic lifeline with their submarines. Thus NATO needed strong coastal defense forces, skilled in mine, harbor, and riverine warfare, as well as (in the words of one analyst) "a force capable of operating on the high seas—anywhere on the globe—and ready to meet anything the opponent might throw against it."

These were tall orders; Lynde McCormick and Jerry Wright could not come close to meeting them. At one level, NATO seapower was all *concept*—a constant mental game played across millions of square miles of North Atlantic. At another level, SACLANT had to deal with all the usual difficulties confronting allied forces, magnified now because no war-bred urgency existed.

Unsurprisingly, most of the Atlantic Fleet's officers and men were far removed from all this, except when they were swept into the occasional, and more than occasionally fouled-up, NATO exercise. For them, Europe was not the NATO alliance but duty, training, and some of the best liberty anywhere—Copenhagen, London, Amsterdam, Villefranche.

—*Villefranche*. That was on the Mediterranean, a sun-spackled spot on the French Riviera, a place so good that Sixth Fleet himself stationed his flagship there whenever possible. In "Villa," sailors could be coddled at Madame Germaine Brau's quayside restaurant, take a trip into the breath-taking French Maritime Alps, or tumble a complaisant whore in one of the Riviera's many seaside hotels.

NATO planners schemed and worried, but their version of World War III was on paper and in the mind. Events, as usual, stole a march on the planners, and this meant that much of America's Cold War effort came to center, not on NATO and some grand design of Allied strategy, but on the Mediterranean—where no single "strategy" could suffice for long.[1]

The Med, of course, featured the delights of Villa and a harvest of other great liberty ports. But the historic sea, as the Navy well knew, was also the gateway to the Middle East.

☆

By the mid-fifties, the United States found itself bobbing in the unpredictable crosscurrents of Middle Eastern politics, factionalism, and power struggles. From 1950 to 1955, over $30 million in American arms was funneled into the region. The new state of Israel (with which the United States never had an alliance, but with which its relationship was always close and always rocky) got almost $8 million. Saudi Arabia claimed the lion's share, over $20 million, but Egypt, Syria, Iraq, Lebanon, and Jordan all got some tokens. American military missions were sent to Saudi Arabia, Iran, and Iraq. Turkey was a steady customer for American aid.

These sums and missions were mere drops in the bucket compared with what was to come, but they heralded the ascendancy of the region on the world scene. When Pakistan, even farther to the east, joined both NATO and SEATO in 1954, half the globe became interlinked in agreements for which the United States was the keystone and guarantor. In 1955 the Baghdad Pact locked NATO, SEATO, and the Middle East into a chain of anti-Soviet military agreements.

The American connection with the Baghdad Pact was informal, a sponsor's role, but this distancing act could not fool the rest of the world. And no ringmaster, however generous or benign, could have coaxed the fractious Middle East into jumping through any kind of syncopated anti-Communist hoop. The Achilles heel of Arab unity was that the Arab states preferred to fight among themselves before they acted effectively against outsiders. But to many Arabs the United States was only the latest outsider, the most recent intruder in a clash of arms with the West that went back at least to 1500.

The Arabs did enjoy one common enemy, although they could never agree about how to do away with Israel. Particularly after the victorious Israeli war for independence in 1948, the Arab states loathed the very idea of a Jewish homeland. Israel, with its strong, vocal lobby in Congress, resented any American arms deals with Arabs. The Joint Chiefs had opposed the partition of Palestine, on the basis of American "strategic interests" (oil). In NSC 47/2 (September-October 1949), the National Security Council said that Israel and its Arab neighbors should reach an accord on their own and that the "Eastern Mediterranean and the Near East" were critically important for American security.

The American signals to both Israelis and Arabs were thus mixed, and they would remain so. Elsewhere, no one trusted Iraq. The Iranians, not being Arab and composed mostly of Shiite Muslims, were suspect. States such as Egypt were white-hot with the fervor of nationalism. Politically, the region was all about power: who held power, who challenged for power, who was in danger of losing power. In international terms, the Middle East was pure witches' brew.

Because the area was bound by salt water—the Mediterranean Sea, Suez Canal, Red Sea, Arabian Sea, and Persian Gulf—the Navy was there. As early as 1800, *Essex* hd been sent round the Cape of Good Hope to protect growing American trade in the Indian Ocean. By 1833, a two-ship American squadron had taken a diplomatic mission to the fiefdom of Muscat (modern Oman). Commercial treaties were cut with Persia (Iran) by the 1850s, and in 1879 *Ticonderoga* became the first American warship to poke its bullnose through the Strait of Hormuz, visiting Bushire and Basra. Naval imperialists of the stripe of Robert Shufeldt and Alfred Thayer Mahan, writing in the late nineteenth century, already saw the region not only in a trading context but also as a buttress against Tsarist Russia's historic impulse to expand southward.

By 1945, the United States had 150 years of commercial relations with the Persian Gulf States and had already established a very limited military presence in Saudi Arabia and Iran, the last country a "crisis" situation until Soviet forces withdrew from the northern one-third. Strategic considerations and Cold War bipolarism made American interest even stronger, but even these paled alongside the predominant fact of power in the modern Middle East: oil.

Everyone knew about the importance of oil. The Navy's concern was especially acute. The Taft and Wilson administrations had created three naval oil reserves for the new oil-burning fleet, two in California and one in Wyoming. (The Wyoming reserve, Teapot Dome, created a pungent political scandal in the 1920s.) By 1940, the United States produced almost two-thirds of the world's oil, with an unused capacity of around one million barrels *a day*. In World War II, American oil went to the front right along with the Army and Navy, providing in particular the fleet's long legs across the Pacific. By late 1944, Japan's air forces were consuming only 21,000 barrels a day—just one-sixth of the amount available to the Americans on Guam alone. By the end of the war, the Allies had consumed almost seven billion barrels of oil, six billion of which were produced by the United States. In 1945, America was daily producing 4.7 million barrels of the stuff.

In all of this the Middle East—Iran, Iraq, and the Arabian Peninsula— was a cipher. In 1940, the region produced but 5 percent of the world's oil, compared to 65 percent produced by the United States. But the region, almost overnight, began to be tapped by the greedily thirsty West. By 1950, 60 percent of the world's known oil reserves were in the Middle East. Europe was well on its way to converting from a coal-based economy to an oil-based one; the United States, with its fascination for gas-guzzling automobiles and its perpetual penchant for mobility, ran on oil; even Japan, westernizing at a ferocious pace, based its economic revival almost solely on oil.

American and NATO strategists were keenly aware of the importance of Persian Gulf oil. By 1945, specialized refined products—high-octane avgas, Navy diesel, and "NSFO" (Navy specialized fuel oil)—were being produced all over the Gulf, at Abadan, in Bahrain, and at Ras Tanura in Saudi Arabia. But after the war, few forces, including naval ones, were available for permanent stationing in the area.

Already in 1947, with the diminution of the British presence in the Med and the Truman Doctrine providing aid to Greece and Turkey, the Navy had become predominant in the eastern Mediterranean. But there was not enough Navy left over for the Persian Gulf, and this grated. Despite the nascent revolution in nuclear power, the Cold War Navy ran on oil.

Throughout World War II, the national oil industry's historic boom-and-bust cycle had been high on the production curve. But demand soon outstripped supply in the postwar period. Quickly, the oil "problem" became acute. "The Marshall Plan for Europe could not succeed without access to the Middle East oil," James Forrestal wrote in his diary. "We could not fight a war without access to it and . . . even in peacetime our economy would be unable to maintain its present tempo without it." Forrestal wanted the State Department to "promote the expansion of United States oil holdings abroad, and to protect such holdings as already exist, i.e., those in the Persian Gulf area." In the late 1940s, Americans were discovering that their domestic production could not slake their continuously escalating thirst for (cheap) oil. The country was about to become a net importer of oil, and this fact alone moved the oil lands of the Middle East into the center of the Cold War strategic picture. Forrestal did not care which oil companies developed the Middle Eastern reserves, especially those in Arabia, as long as they were "American."

The Truman Doctrine coincided with oil concessions being granted by the Saudis to four major American oil companies. Strategic and economic interest in the area became almost totally fused. By 1948 the "Great Game" played by the powers (mostly the British) for generations—the resistance to Russia's southward expansion—had merged with the strategic considerations raised by the importance of the region's oil for the industrialized nations. In 1946, 77 percent of Europe's oil came from the Western Hemisphere; five years later, well over 50 percent came from the Persian Gulf. The Middle East, half a world away from the United States, was firmly established as crucial to European and American security.

The Navy certainly felt the postwar oil pinch. From 1946 to 1950, between 30 percent and 42 percent of petroleum products used by the fleet came from the Persian Gulf. Gulf oil was easy to refine, and its products were easily swallowed by complex modern engines. During fiscal 1947, for example, 55 percent of the fleet's special fuel and 52 percent of its diesel fuel came from refineries in Saudi Arabia and Bahrain. And in 1948, America's East Coast cities ran so short of oil that the Navy was ordered to hand over one million barrels for their use.

Each month, Navy and chartered tankers moved up to five million barrels of oil and oil products from the Persian Gulf into the Med or the Pacific, for direct use by the thirsty ships of the Sixth and Seventh fleets. If the Gulf spigot were to be turned off, the Navy would not go dry. (The fleet still had massive oil reserves in the continental United States.) But the Navy's vessels would have to dramatically contract their presence around the globe, and the fleet's oil costs would have increased.

In January 1948, for these reasons, Task Force 126, U.S. Naval Force, Persian Gulf, was established. Initially this was only a tanker force, commanded by whatever officer happened to be senior in the Gulf at the time. By the following year, renamed first the Persian Gulf Forces and then the Middle East Force, the Navy's presence in the Gulf became permanent. Beginning in 1951, a rear admiral (Don Felt was the first) took command.

At times, a carrier task force or other units of warships would pop inside the Strait of Hormuz to show the flag. But, for the most part, the Gulf command was a seaplane tender (a type no one could find much other use for) like *Duxbury Bay* or *Valcour* and a couple of destroyers. This little group, painted a dazzling white to withstand the blazing tropical sun and one-hundred-degree heat over water, spent its time visiting small ports and making courtesy calls on the indigenous desert nobility.

Sometimes the nobility would be piped aboard: sheikhs in glimmering Arab ceremonial dress, curved, gold-encrusted daggers in their sashes; handfuls of fierce-looking, ceremonially scarred bodyguards in brilliant white robes; an occasional Western-educated Arab or an Englishman, mad for the desert, to do the translation. Ashore, naval officers sweltering inside their dress whites would dive into heaping platters of roast sheep, chicken, and rice, washing their hands afterwards, as their hosts did, with great ceremony.

There was more than a hint of Kipling to all this, but while the sunbaked naval diplomacy was quaint, romantic, and even bizarre, COMIDEAST-

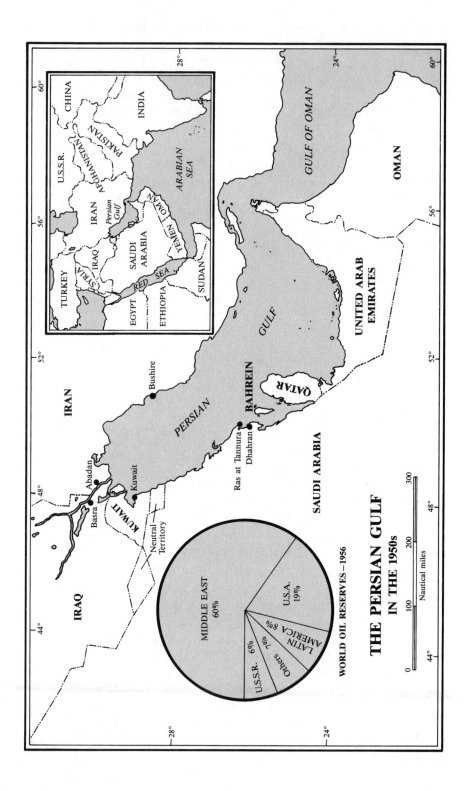

THE PERSIAN GULF
IN THE 1950s

WORLD OIL RESERVES—1956

MIDDLE EAST 60%

U.S.A. 19%

LATIN AMERICA 8%

Others 7%

U.S.S.R. 6%

FOR had real strategic purpose. On paper, his flea-bite fleet embraced a lot of blue water: the Red Sea, the Persian Gulf, the Arabian Sea, and practically all the Indian Ocean north of the equator. On land, he was expected to maintain American friendship with all the countries, sheikdoms, and emirates facing the Red Sea, Persian Gulf, Arabian Sea, and the western bay of Bengal as far as the frontier of Burma. The handful of white ships thus did a lot of steaming. Their officers and men visited plenty of bazaars and mosques. Arab women, in their cloistered seclusion, were a different story, and duty with MIDEASTFOR did not rank high on the scale of Navy social values.

At sea, most shipboard work was done in the early morning; only essential watches were stood in the oven of afternoon. Temperatures in berthing and messing spaces rose to 115 degrees. The humidity was choking. Both officers and enlisted men slept topside on cots. Even sick bays were moved onto the main deck. Crews were fed in the open air, on the fantails of their ships. The uniform aboard (except when the desert nobility showed up) was shorts and undershirts. Shower waters, when the showers ran, was usually scalding.

Ashore, conditions improved a bit. The Navy operated out of Bahrain, then the major British base in the Gulf. On the beach, sailors could get a rare beer (the disgusting British habit of serving room-temperature beer had never seemed more uncivil), play softball with American oil company personnel, and wait for the irregular mail run. The duty was never very great, but the naval presence, by 1951, was permanent, a sweaty reminder of the price of global strategy—and of oil.

The Persian Gulf had become a region "too important to surrender, but too distant to defend."[2]

☆

"I thought it a good idea for the United States to get into the picture," Fleet Admiral William Leahy wrote, "so that we, particularly our Navy, would have access to some of King Ibn Saud's oil." "There are 400,000 Jews and forty million Arabs," Forrestal noted in 1948. The Arabs were going to push the Jews into the sea, "and that's all there is to it," he concluded. "Oil. That's the side we ought to be on." But Saudi oil, and that of the other desert barons, was only the beginning of the incredibly complex mosaic of the Middle East.

Another overlay came with areas that had little oil but had crucial strategic leverage because of their location and other factors. By the 1950s the colonial powers were in retreat, either voluntarily or enforced. Their war-induced economic weaknesses had accelerated the process of decolonization to the point that nationalism had emerged as a potent, unpredictable force.

Great Britain, ever since Disraeli's masterful purchase of controlling shares in the Suez Canal ("Madame, you have it," he informed Queen

Victoria) had controlled the canal and Egypt for three-quarters of a century. But the world was now spinning faster. In 1952 a cabal of Egyptian officers deposed the sybaritic King Farouk, who was left to astonish the Riviera with his coterie of sloe-eyed girlfriends and his bulging girth.

By 1954 Egypt had come under the dictatorial control of a charismatic Arab nationalist, Colonel Gamel Abdel Nasser. He was only thirty-six, the first Egyptian to independently rule his native land since invading Persians had overthrown the last of the pharaohs in 525 B.C. Nasser had a visceral hatred of imperialism; he wrote that when, as a boy, he had seen airplanes overhead, he would shout: "O God Almighty, may a calamity overtake the English!"

Now the "calamity" had come; Nasser's new Egypt had no place for a European-dominated Suez Canal. Most of the canal's considerable earnings went to European shareholders (including the largest, the British government). The canal operation itself was a too-perfect symbol of clinging imperialism, what with its British and French pilots, crisply clad in starchy white uniforms and knee socks, expertly shepherding dozens of ships daily through the vital choke-point in which ran the life's blood of industrial Europe. Nasser, boss of a densely populated strip of a country (Egypt, as always, was really the sliver of the Nile and its delta), hoped for complete control of the canal and its colossal revenues—manna for his desperately poor nation.

The British considered the canal, in the words of Foreign Secretary Selwyn Lloyd, "an integral part of the Middle East oil complex, which was vital to Britain." Nasser knew, because of increasing leverage gained by the oil-producing states, that desert kingdoms like Saudi Arabia, with but a fraction of the mouths Egypt had to feed, received 50 percent of the profits from their oil. But Egypt did not get 50 percent of the profits from the canal. Anthony Eden, the British prime minister, told the Soviet leaders Nikolai Bulganin and Nikita Khrushchev that the Russians must not fish in these troubled waters. "I must be absolutely blunt about the oil," Eden said, "because we would fight for it. . . . We could not live without oil and . . . we [have] no intention of being strangled to death." Eden told Eisenhower that "Nasser can deny oil to Western Europe and we shall all be at his mercy."

The Americans found themselves caught in the toils of a profound dilemma. As the prime sponsor of the Baghdad Pact, they had pleased no committed Arab nationalist, least of all Nasser. Egypt blamed the United States for thus heightening the always tense intra-Arab antagonisms and for being a front for renascent Western imperialism. The British were critical of what they called America's failure "to put its weight behind its friends, in the hope of being popular with its foes." Bulganin and, after his downfall, Khrushchev, *did* fish in these troubled waters, and Nasser had good reason to go for their bait (a weapons deal). By early 1956, Eisenhower's administration was hopelessly ensnared, despite its announced policy of anti-imperialism, in seething rivalries among Arabs, between Arabs and Israelis, and between Arabs and the British—their firmest historical allies.

To make things worse, the old forces providing some sort of stability in the eastern Mediterranean were crumbling. The French had left Syria and Lebanon after World War II, although they chose to hang on in Indochina and Algeria—with disastrous results. Israel's sudden independence had introduced a new player with strong, Holocaust-based claims on Western consciousness. American petroleum companies, led by the giant consortium ARAMCO, were now active in an area long the preserve of British, French, and Dutch corporations. Any Soviet move into the Middle East—and Nasser's arms deal certainly seemed to Eisenhower and his people like a harbinger of such a move—would threaten not only the Suez Canal but also the rapidly improving economic health of Europe.[3]

There were thus many important competing interests at stake in Nasser's plans. The Egyptian leader had a dream, the Aswan Dam—a structure that could control the Nile, make the desert bloom, feed his people—and be funded from canal tolls. On 26 July 1956, speaking in the same public square in Alexandria in which he had first participated in an anti-British demonstration as a boy, Nasser harangued the crowd with the name of the Frenchman Ferdinand de Lesseps, the builder of the canal. The reviled name was the code word; as Nasser spoke, the Egyptian army moved. By the time his speech was done, Egyptians were in control of the Canal Zone.

The resulting Suez Crisis was the most unsettling event during Eisenhower's two terms. To him, the Suez Canal was "the world's foremost public utility;" he was concerned not so much with Nasser as with the effect of the canal seizure on Western Europe and the possibility that the Soviets might intervene. Throughout, the president kept his sword in its scabbard, telling the press on 8 August that "I can't conceive of military force being a good solution." The crisis required restraint, tact, and a considerable level of diplomatic skill. Nasser's seizure of the canal, after all, seemed to portend only the most negative results for the West.

Eisenhower's policy required a hard stance toward an old friend. He told Eden on 31 July that the United States was opposed to using military force—*anyone's* military force—against Nasser. The president took this step with regret and remorse, yet he later wrote, "I felt that in taking our own position we were standing firmly on principle and on the realities of the twentieth century."[4]

☆

The Navy also had to deal with these "realities of the twentieth century." In 1956 the Sixth Fleet was far and away the strongest military force in the Mediterranean, a floating powerhouse operating four thousand or more miles from its homeport in Norfolk. Its mission, at first simply defending sea lines of communication, had changed to providing air support on the right flank of NATO's armies. The fleet was earmarked for CINCSOUTH, the NATO command in Naples, but in 1956 its nuclear ordnance, by American law, belonged to the Joint Chiefs, not to any unified command. Its punch was built around Task Force 60, composed of the attack carrier *Coral Sea*, with one hundred planes, and the ASW carrier *Randolph*, with eighty planes. The heavy cruisers *Salem* and *Macon* were on line, along with twelve destroyers.

And the warships were not all. Task Forces 61 and 62 were amphibious ready groups, capable of putting ashore a fully armed Marine battalion. Task Force 66, centered on the ASW carrier *Antietam*, was a hunter-killer group. Sixth Fleet also had available dozens of attack transports, attack cargo ships, tankers, and repair vessels. The fleet was powerful, flexible, mobile—ready to go.

What Nasser thought of such naval might steaming about on his doorstep was anyone's guess. "The genius of Americans," he supposedly said, "is that [they] never make clear-cut stupid moves, only complicated stupid moves which make us wonder at the possibility that there may be something to them which we are missing." On 31 July, Arleigh Burke was among those meeting with Eisenhower to decide what to do. By then, the Americans knew that the British were aiming to "break Nasser," even if this meant military action. Ike felt that Eden's government was badly behind the times, overtaken by the "realities"—the ebb tide of decolonization and the flood tide of nationalism. Burke, however, said that "the JCS are of the view that Nasser must be broken," that the United States should support any military action by the British.[5]

With such divided counsel, America seemed ready for one of its "stupid moves," but during the Suez Crisis the prize for stupidity went elsewhere. Eisenhower rejected the advice of Burke and the rest of his Joint Chiefs. For weeks the diplomats sought a way out, primarily through the United Nations, and failed. By early October, the British and French (who were also vitally interested in the canal) had cut a backdoor deal with the Israelis, who were more than nervous about Nasser's belligerent version of pan-Arabism.

The plotters decided that Israel would attack Egypt on 29 October, striking the Gaza Strip (a favorite launching pad for anti-Israeli terrorism) and Sharm al-Sheikh, on the Gulf of Aqaba. For their part, the Europeans would register surprise and horror, then issue an ultimatum to both Israel and Egypt for both sides to withdraw ten miles from the area of the canal within twelve hours. Nasser, of course, would refuse the ultimatum, at which point England and France would send already-poised troops to seize the waterway, using the pretext that the canal had to be neutralized during the fighting. Thus the world would be presented with a clever fait accompli.

October 1956 was a month of extreme pressure for Eisenhower. There was a presidential campaign on; Poland was once again trying to throw off the Soviet yoke; and in Hungary, for a brief and marvelous moment, "freedom fighters" began to take over the streets of Budapest. Understandably, with all this upheaval, when news of the ultimatum reached the White House, he hit the ceiling. He knew that armed conflict was coming (American temporizing and appeals to all sides had been unable to accomplish a thing) and when the Israeli attack jumped off on schedule, his language was barracks-room. Two days later, still according to plan, the British began bombing Egyptian bases. "Bombs, by God!" Eisenhower yelled. "What does Anthony think he's doing?"

Anthony thought he was preserving the remnants of empire and British security. But the United States, and its Navy, would not help him (even though Burke would have had things otherwise). The senior American officer in the Med was Admiral Walter ("Freddie") Boone, commander in chief eastern Atlantic and Mediterranean. Freddie Boone had been the officer so distressed by the fact that ballroom dancing was no longer taught at the Naval Academy during his tour there as superintendent; indeed, as a childless man himself, he was almost totally disconnected from the younger generation. He could still be shocked, for example, by the most minor midshipman misdemeanors. Charles Loughlin, an Academy subordinate, called Boone's assignment to Annapolis "the worst case of detailing I've ever seen."

But Boone, a bespectacled aviator who sported the slightest wisp of white mustache, rose fast. By 1956 he sported four stars. With the Israeli onslaught, he traveled under Burke's orders to Turkey, his primary mission to protect American citizens wherever they seemed to be threatened. Boone flew his flag aboard *Cambria*, flagship of the amphibious ready group, and immediately began to oversee the work of the Sixth Fleet. The commander of that outfit had just received a brief message from Burke: "If United States citizens are in danger, protect them. Take no guff from anyone."

—Which was all right by Vice Admiral Charles ("Cat") Brown, who had never taken guff from anyone in his life. Cat Brown—a baby sister had tagged him with the nickname—was a pistol. At the Naval Academy, as a member of Freddie Boone's class, he had set remarkable standards for boozing and generally uncontrollable behavior. He was accordingly invited to take his act elsewhere, but his father, a Democratic wheelhorse back home in Tuscaloosa, Alabama, moved heaven and earth to get him readmitted— a virtual replay of Pete Mitscher's rescue a decade before.

Upon graduation (far, far down) in 1921, Brown went where he thought the action—and the danger—was. He flew off *Langley*, set aerial gunnery records in his biplane crates, and learned to hate shore duty. He developed into a gritty, stubborn naval aviator. In his last scheduled carrier landing, aboard the old *Saratoga* in 1941, his tail hook missed the arresting wire, and he crashed into the landing barrier. Thoroughly shaken up, he was not about to let his wings get tarnished that way; he got another plane, took off, and touched back down to a perfect landing.

By Pearl Harbor, Brown's naval reputation combined aviation savvy with his penchant for practical jokes. He was slightly built but whalebone-tough; his weatherbeaten face featured a mouth creased in an almost permanent wry half-smile, one that seemed to tell the world that life itself was just some sort of cosmic jest. He began World War II in a dangerous combat role—on Ernie King's staff in Washington. Impressed, King sent him to command the escort carrier *Kalinin Bay* in the Pacific. From there, Brown went to command *Hornet* and became chief of staff to CarDiv 1 as American carriers moved from Leyte Gulf to the shores of Japan. After the war, more staff work and carrier division command came his way, culminating with his third star and assignment to command Sixth Fleet.

Everyone had a story about Cat Brown. Mel Pride's was about the time Rear Admiral Brown and Rear Admiral ("Artie") Doyle were due to turn over their flagships in a ceremony at Gibraltar. Doyle sent a message to Brown, his relief, to be aboard Doyle's carrier at 1000 sharp for the turnover; as a joke, he added, "You'll have to wear shoes." At the appointed hour Doyle had his crew mustered smartly, the honor guard and sideboys paraded. At the first shrill of the boatswain's pipe Cat Brown hove into sight over the rail—carrying his shoes in his hand.

Brown was salty and profane, yet he managed to be warm and engaging at the same time, his crackling phrases volleying forth in almost constant salvos. "A good commander to be at sea with," recalled Vice Admiral Charles Melson. Brown read nightly from his well-thumbed King James version of the Bible. He was no religious bigot, though, often quoting the Koran to Turkish friends. A fundamentalist, he preferred the Old Testament, with its blood-soaked tales of treachery, redemption—and revenge. His hobby, he said, was "reading classics," and indeed, by the time he took over Sixth Fleet, the Academy's former bad boy had become an extraordinarily well-read man. He was already by nature an aggressive one. "I cannot tell you how exciting it is," he wrote upon taking command of Sixth Fleet, "to hold in my two hot hands a large part of the striking power of the Navy."

The Israeli attack on 29 October, if Eisenhower had not rejected Burke's recommendations, would have given Cat Brown's two hot hands something hot to do. The attack found the Sixth Fleet undertaking landing exercises in Suda Bay, Crete. Brown reboarded his Marines, beached his landing equipment, and quickly took station in the pocket of the eastern Med—with two carriers, two cruisers, and two destroyers. He radioed Burke that he was ready "to furnish protection if needed for the ships on evacuation duty."

Other forces began to assemble. Rear Admiral Paul Dudley and the men of Hunter-Killer Group 2, centered on *Antietam*, were enjoying the delights of Rotterdam when the Israelis jumped off; by 2 November, on his own hook, Dudley had his command heading east through the Strait of Gibraltar. Two diesel boats, *Hardhead* and *Cutlass*, had been exercising in the Adriatic; they armed their torpedoes and took up war patrols off Cyprus and Alexandria.

Brown immediately sent a small force to Haifa, taking aboard some 150 refugees. All embarked safely, although the Israelis sank an Egyptian destroyer, *Ibrahim el-Awal*, in the midst of the operation. Three destroyers were detailed to Gaza, a tense area by 31 October. Egyptian and Israeli troops were locked in combat for that fingertip of sand pointing from the Sinai toward Israel. UN truce officials were in the middle of the shooting, and they needed to be evacuated.

The greater share of the sealift, however, came at Alexandria. Brown detailed Amphibious Squadron 6 to the seaport to pick up endangered Europeans and Americans. Captain Frederick Laing, its commodore, had three amphibious vessels and two destroyers. With these, he was planning to take on one thousand passengers. His ships flew extra-large American flags, illuminated at night and horizontally draped to alert any approaching aircraft. Aboard the attack transport *Chilton*, the flagship, Marines prepared to establish a defensive perimeter around Alexandria. Crews stood by for General Quarters. Just over the horizon, behind Laing, steamed *Coral Sea* and *Randolph*. Cat's cats were at the ready.

The ships of Amphibious Squadron 6 arrived off Alexandria before dawn on 31 October. The Egyptians challenged them but let pilots come aboard to guide the Americans into the inner harbor. No evacuees. Laing radioed Brown, "No sweat here yet." At the insistence of the Egyptians, Laing ordered his two accompanying destroyers to withdraw thirty miles out to sea.

That night, air raids commenced. Laing had his ships blacked out. American sailors, for the next two nights, watched as British land-based fighter-bombers and French carrier planes attacked Alexandria and, 120 miles to the southeast, Cairo. The skies were lighted with bomb and shell flashes (anti-aircraft fire passed immediately over *Chilton*). Laing was cut from the same cloth as Cat Brown. "If anybody got tough and gave me any more trouble than I was already having—like lead bullets—," he later said, "I was going to toss a few back and then go back to sit around a long green table."

In the middle of the fireworks the refugees began to arrive, after tedious, dangerous auto and bus convoys from Cairo. Eventually, 1528 people were taken aboard—964 Americans, 138 UN personnel, and 426 American embassy workers and tourists (the latter cursing their vacation timing). One woman heard Egyptian anti-aircraft fire whistling overhead as she boarded *Chilton* and still managed to exclaim, "I have never felt safer anywhere."

At 1600 on 2 November, Laing got his arks to sea, in column, an Egyptian minesweeper in the van. As they gingerly made their way through what he thought might be a minefield, the sailors and passengers could see the entire panorama of the harbor—Farouk's palace, the lighthouse, the long sweep of breakwater to the north—while overhead yet another air raid zoomed in, headed for the military airport at Dikheila, off to the west. Brown had designated points along Laing's sea chart to guide their way: Points Abraham, Isaac, and Jacob. For his own position at ZZ, Brown modestly reserved the code name of Point Moses.

Laing dispatched his two destroyers to Port Said for some more passengers. (No one there wanted to embark, and *Charles S. Sperry* and *Allen N. Sumner* quickly rejoined.) He then headed his charges for Suda Bay. Every ship was jammed to the sponsons; officers and men gave up their racks. Everyone was accommodated, although naval ships were not designed for children. (*Chilton* alone carried seventeen babies under the age of nine months.) The cooks broke out special food, corpsmen sterilized baby bottles, and the ships' laundries were awash in diapers. Older kids, to their delight, were given Marine-guided shipboard tours. Unheard-of calls went out over the IMCs. "Now hear this," came the plea aboard *Thuban*. "A small boy with light hair, about three years old, has lost his family. Will his mother please call for him?" Sailors became "baby-watchers," and at 2200 came a novel form of taps: "Now hear this. You look tired. Go to bed."

They reached Suda Bay in the wee hours of 4 November, dirty, tired— and safe. "They left in high spirits and perfect health," crowed Cat Brown. "Exodus III, 8." The curious could refer to the verse, which said, "I have taken heed of their sufferings, and have come down to rescue them from the power of Egypt, and to bring them up out of that country into a fine, broad land; it is a land flowing with milk and honey. . . ."

Almost seven thousand Americans had been caught in the operational area when the Israelis attacked; three thousand of these were taken out by the Navy. Indeed, Navy ships were almost the only way out of Egypt. Aircraft evacuated about 20 percent of the people in the area, but Egyptian airfields soon became unusable, due to bomb damage. No ground forces were available other than the embarked Marines, and Eisenhower was not about to land them in the midst of a shooting war to which the United States was not a party.

Cat Brown's hot hands stayed cool; his ships had not gone to war, but they had probably saved lives. These evacuations were yet another telling example of the flexibility, adaptability, and usefulness of American sea-power. "In delicate international situations [the Navy] can whisper," Brown said. "But behind the whisper is great strength and, if need be, the Navy can raise its voice or it can roar. It is not limited to a choice between roaring and staying silent."

Quite so, but perhaps the most telling commentary on American policy had come at the beginning of the crisis, when Brown had asked Burke,

"Who's the enemy?" Burke had then told him not to take any guff, but he later confessed, "I didn't know who the damned enemy was."[6]

☆

In a sense, the "damned enemy" was the Middle East itself, with its tangled crosscurrents of hatred, suspicion, and ambition. Trying to please some faction or state in the region automatically enraged others. Beyond these unpromising generalities, the Suez Crisis put the United States and its oldest allies at loggerheads. The Navy played a small role. But Cat Brown's warships were not idle; they were edgy, on guard, aggressively gathering intelligence and patrolling. On the night of 4 November, ships of the Sixth Fleet illuminated some of the Anglo-French squadron, and shortly afterward a few of Brown's aircraft made dummy runs on French vessels. Eventually two of his submarines, probably *Hardhead* and *Cutlass*, were caught shadowing the Europeans too closely and ordered to surface. A flurry of traffic passed between Brown and his putative NATO allies, until at last the American warships slacked off a bit.

The Anglo-French gamble had dismally misjudged world reaction and, more critically, the American response. On 4 November, the Sunday when Brown's ships were lighting up the British and French, John Foster Dulles took an American cease-fire resolution before the UN General Assembly. The Soviets did not cast a veto, and by a vote of 64–5 the United Nations called on Great Britain, France, and Israel to halt their invasion of Egypt.

The Israelis' attack had been swift and decisive. Within days they occupied both the Gaza Strip and Sharm al-Sheikh. The Europeans did not do so well. On 5 November, after six days of bombing and shelling Egyptian bases, and heedless of the UN vote, their paratroopers dropped on the canal. The following day, their ground troops landed. By then the Soviets had already threatened retaliation on Great Britain and France. Bulganin suggested to Eisenhower that the USSR and the United States join together in military action against the aggressors.

In response, leery of any deal with the devil, Ike placed American forces (including the Sixth Fleet) on worldwide alert. He had just won reelection in a cakewalk over Adlai Stevenson, and he could now turn his full attention to the crisis. He would not fight as an ally of the Soviets, nor would he fight as an ally of the Europeans. The United States, in effect, was turning its back on its three most important comrades-in-arms against Hitler. But there was no doubt about who the potential enemy was. Eisenhower later revealed that "we just told [the Russians] that this would be, well, we just told them, really, it would be global war if they started it, that's all."

For the British, the combined pressure was too much. The Americans orchestrated a run on the pound that threatened their already weak currency reserves. Harold Macmillan, the chancellor of the exchequer, told the Cabinet even as his country's troops were moving into Egypt that there was no alternative to giving in. The Egyptians and Israelis had already ceased fire. Eden, in ill health throughout the crisis, was near exhaustion. Both angered and saddened by the quick and rather ruthless behavior of the Eisenhower administration, the British agreed to a cease-fire at midnight on 7 November (which meant a 500-million-pound loan from the International Monetary Fund to prop up the shaky sterling). The French, with at least equal resentment, were thus forced to withdraw as well.

Cat Brown "categorically" denied that his units had been "deliberately maneuvered" so as to impede or embarrass the British and French vessels. (The key word here may have been "deliberately.") Never short of a sparkling turn of phrase, however, he told journalists shortly after the European withdrawal that "I cannot ignore the volcano on which I sit. Without vigilance, tomorrow could be my Pearl Harbor."

As Brown continued to sit on his volcano, almost reveling in his new celebrity, UN peacekeeping forces began to arrive in Egypt. Eisenhower wrote his wartime comrade, the British general Lord Hastings Ismay, of "the sadness in which the free world had become involved." In fact, out of the entire Suez mess only Nasser emerged a clear winner. His stock in the Arab world was higher than ever. The two old colonial powers, Britain and France, were left defeated and humiliated, their shoddy connivings with Israel now public knowledge. Nasser controlled the Suez Canal, although he had blocked the waterway with wrecked ships. Once the canal was cleared, by April 1957, Egypt operated the shore stations, collected the tolls, and guided the shipping. Emboldened, Nasser kept up his preaching of Arab nationalism. Soviet aid kept coming; from 1954 to 1971, Egypt would account for 43 percent of all Russian assistance to Third World nations.

In mid-May 1957, the British terminated the gasoline rationing they had commenced during the crisis. Europe was still dependent on oil for only 20 percent of its energy needs, although that figure was dramatically shifting upward, as Eden and other leaders well knew. Eden, broken in health and shattered in spirit by Suez, left office, to be replaced by the urbane, conciliatory Macmillan. Years later, the *Times* of London would appropriately say of Eden that "he was the last prime minister to believe Britain was a great power and the first to confront a crisis which proved she was not."

The temporary blockage of the canal focused attention on the longer route between the Middle East and Europe, around the Cape of Good Hope. The Japanese soon made this way viable by building tremendous supertankers. For Great Britain, the former indispensable belt buckle on their empire had been ripped away, and they were now more dependent on the outside world than ever before. The Suez Crisis was thus a preview of a new world economic order, the death knell of the British Empire, and a mighty boost for Nasser and his pan-Arab ideas.

For the United States Navy, Suez marked the third time in two years that its ships had engaged in a major humanitarian sealift, the other instances being Indochina and the Formosa Strait. Many naval officers, like Burke, wanted to do even more, to throw their weight on the side of their old allies. One (Rear Admiral George Miller) even called the American failure to come to their aid "the great strategic blunder of this century."

Blunder or not, Suez sputtered to a melancholy conclusion for every non-Arab state concerned. The Navy's role had been both positive, in the sense of rescuing people, and passive, in the sense of not being drawn into a many-sided conflict. Beyond this, Suez focused attention on such issues as strengthening amphibious and logistic forces, prepositioning supplies and munitions, and on-the-spot cooperation with other navies. Suez had been a brief flare-up in terms of military time; the question of the Sixth Fleet's ability to endure such a situation, for months rather than weeks, drove planners to reconsider these issues. Finally, despite Cat Brown's disclaimers, some of the Sixth Fleet's actions during the crisis, to the British and French at least, had been recklessly cavalier. While Brown's stock with the American public was high, the question of deliberately inviting trouble in the midst of someone else's combat remained of the utmost pertinence.[7]

☆

By 22 December 1956, British and French troops had been removed from Egypt. The immediate problem, prolonged conflict that would perhaps have drawn in the superpowers, was averted. But Eisenhower saw a bigger problem. "Russia's rulers have long sought to dominate the Middle East," he told Congress in a special message on 5 January 1957. "This was true of the Czars and it is true of the Bolsheviks. . . ."

Ike asked for $200 million in economic assistance for Middle Eastern countries threatened by such domination. He also wanted military aid for the same countries. Lastly, he asked Congress to permit the president to use armed force to protect nations in the area that might ask for such help against "overt armed aggression from any nation controlled by International Communism."

Together, this package was called the Eisenhower Doctrine and in itself was a major step along the road toward what would come to be called the "Imperial Presidency." The implications for the Navy, and for the Sixth Fleet, were obvious.

Even at the time, however, the "doctrine," like most Cold War manifestos from either side, was seen to be full of logical holes. Nasser's Egypt and Syria, the nations seemingly most susceptible to Communist influence, were highly unlikely to request aid from "imperialist" America. And they were touchy about anyone else; by 1958, Nasser was arresting Egyptian Communists. Small, oil-poor nations like Jordan and Lebanon were more likely to be shredded to pieces by Arab nationalism than by international communism. Most moderate Arab leaders, while liking the idea of American naval power lurking just offshore (the Saudis were an excellent example) wanted the United States at more than one remove. Truman's former secretary of state, Dean Acheson, archly and correctly called Eisenhower's requests (as approved by Congress) "vague, inadequate, and not very helpful."

But Eisenhower and his men were Cold Warriors, deeply worried about Soviet advances on a worldwide scale. In particular, they were concerned about Soviet designs on Persian Gulf oil. The Russians were oil-sufficient from their own production, but Ike feared that they planned "to seize the oil, to cut the canal and the pipelines of the Middle East, and thus seriously to weaken Western civilization." The House passed the Eisenhower Doctrine by 355–61, but the Senate (led, in an ironic move, by Lyndon Johnson) denied specific presidential authority to use troops, substituting instead a statement that the United States was "prepared" to use force if the president "determines the necessity thereof."

This stance, and American politicking at the United Nations, eventually produced an Israeli evacuation of the Sinai in March 1957. The Eisenhower Doctrine, fuzzy and open-ended, remained—a self-created invitation to American meddling in the Middle East. From 1957 onward, American influence increasingly replaced that of the British and French in the region, and the major military share of this influence belonged to the Sixth Fleet. The costs of this sea change were almost incalculable: the temporary entanglement with eons-old rivalries that the United States, with all its armed might, could not begin to solve; and the elevation of the Middle East from a simple headache to a continuous, pounding migraine.

No country in the Middle East was "Communist" or "Communist-dominated." In fact, rulers of lands like Iran and Saudi Arabia both loathed and feared communism. Israel was already staunchly (and messily) democratic. Most regional politicians in the Arab world were also deeply suspicious about both democracy and communism, because theoretically both these political beliefs were about *sharing* power. Arabs were more concerned, as their culture taught them, about *gaining* and *holding* power.

To these ends, Arab leaders would deal with anyone. Egypt got Soviet arms, including MiG fighter planes. Syria also received military assistance from the USSR. Others, like the Saudis and other rulers along the Persian Gulf, took what they could get from the United States. Critics of the Eisenhower Doctrine were quick to point out that, to the Arab world, enticing arms deals offered by either superpower could be seen in terms of a clever merchant working both sides of the street. And there was that frustrating, opaque quality of the doctrine itself. Eisenhower, groused Senator J. William Fulbright, "asks for a blank grant of power over our funds and armed forces, to be used in a blank way, for a blank length of time, under blank conditions with respect to blank nations in a blank area. . . . Who will fill in all these blanks?"

Certainly the Eisenhower Doctrine was more propaganda than concrete promise, but the idea was potent propaganda and came with both money and military weaponry attached. Syria, Egypt, and Jordan (at first) rejected the implied offer out of hand. Undeterred, the Eisenhower administration, "with all the subtlety of temperance crusaders in a distillery," began to romance Middle Eastern states into some kind of anti-Soviet, anti-Nasser posture. The romance never bloomed; most Arab leaders perceived very little Soviet threat, seeing instead only more neo-imperialism, Western meddling, and clumsy attempts at carving out new spheres of influence.

But the idea remained, given sanction by Congress. In April 1957 pro-Nasser politicians in Jordan, alerted by what they regarded as the dangers of the Eisenhower Doctrine, won elections and put pressure on the young King Hussein to back away from Jordan's historic ties with the West, particularly with Britain and the United States. Hussein, inexperienced and frightened, did a complete turnabout and cried that his kingdom was threatened with communism. In response, he got $10 million in American aid and Cat Brown's Sixth Fleet, which belligerently moved deep into the eastern Mediterranean.

Hussein, threatened not by Communists but by his own Arab nationalists, won the day. Jordan moved into the American orbit, and Brown steamed away. But this first use of the doctrine had nothing to do with communism and everything to do with local Arab nationalism and power politics. Here was a lesson not lost on other rulers throughout the region, like the shah of Iran and the Saudi royal family.

Jordan, an artificial country of thirty-seven thousand square miles created after World War I, with its 1.5 million people struggling to make a living in their barren desert, was thus exalted in the United States as a Cold War triumph. When *Forrestal*, its flight deck stocked with gleaming new A-3D Skywarriors, showed up, along with *Lake Champlain*, *Wisconsin*, two cruisers, and a flotilla of destroyers and submarines, America patted itself on the back for its "quick action." Hussein had not asked for the United States Navy, but the Sixth Fleet undeniably bolstered his position and his power—at the cost of intensified Arab nationalism.

—None of these international complexities computed with Cat Brown. He called the presence of his ships off the Levantine coast "a hell of a good drill."[8]

☆

The Sixth Fleet was the master of the Med. From the Rock to the Levant, Cat Brown's ships steamed at will, tethered to no local base. They produced awe ("Dios mio! She's a floating Gibraltar!" blurted a Spaniard as *Forrestal* slid by, heading for points east), respect—and apprehension. The last feeling derived from the fact that the fleet was poised, always in a ready position. Its warships and planes had a striking range of over 1400 miles, nuclear weapons, guided missiles, and amphibious assault forces. And Suez and Jordan had proved that this power would be used, if not exactly in the Nelsonian tradition.

But the Sixth Fleet was an ambassador, too. Its ships had ninety-two ports of call sprinkled about the Med, and its sailors were indeed welcomed almost anywhere. Much of this welcome was sincere friendship, but as always throughout the region, money—and power—talked.

"This is the best job in the Navy," said Brown of his billet, "and also one of the toughest. We have to be ready to handle anything at any time— from a brush fire to the big blowout." Brown's men were, for the most part, excellent diplomats, gregarious and free-spending American kids abroad. "If the American sailors were to go away tomorrow, I would weep," avowed Madame Brau from her restaurant in Villefranche, "but next year a million Frenchmen would weep with me." In 1956 alone the Americans made 1450 port visits, from the lovely Spanish island of Majorca to the dusty Turkish town of Izmir.

The port visits were ideal for letting off steam, but the real work of the fleet came at sea. And there, all was not routine. Even without the various crises erupting around the region, life at sea with the Sixth Fleet was po- tentially and actually dangerous. *Ticonderoga* (the lineal descendant of the first American warship through the Strait of Hormuz) had several people killed during "routine" night flight operations in 1955. *Essex* lost four men during her 1958 cruise. There was no relief from the danger, because training had to be conducted.

Brown's big worry was Soviet submarines, either slipped into the sea through the Dardanelles or supplied to countries like Egypt. The Sixth Fleet's ASW posture was high ready. Few if any Russian subs were in the Mediterranean in 1957, but the Navy trained for tactical threats and, amid the rollicking port visits, the Russian subs would have to do. (One sailor was quoted in his belief that the two greatest threats were Russian subs and that lethal Greek beverage, ouzo.) Any redeploying of American naval strength, then, as in the Jordanian crisis, could be blatantly palmed off as normal operations and training. The mission of the Sixth Fleet, as cleverly put forth by *Time*, was "not to apply the [Eisenhower Doctrine], but to deter an outbreak of gunplay that might make it necessary for the U.S. to apply the doctrine."

So the Sixth Fleet steamed, supported the anti-Communist status quo, and endlessly trained. Its Marines could be inserted almost anywhere in the Mediterranean, practically overnight. Its heavily armed strike aircraft could hit points beyond the Baku oil fields and Soviet naval bases on the Black

Sea. Naval planes, if called upon, could roam over a considerable portion of the Warsaw Pact nations: Bulgaria, Romania, Hungary, Czechoslovakia, East Germany, and most of Poland. This was small solace, however, to the rebellious Poles and Hungarians, who had seen their revolt ruthlessly smashed in late 1956 without so much as a glimmer of American military aid.

Day and night the fleet cruised in a state of wary alert, a relaxed yet watchful, prowling cat. Its radar eyes ceaselessly scanned surface and sky, its sonar ears listened in the depths (mostly to sea creatures). Occasionally a hunter-killer group would join up, and everyone would play the ASW game. When things got tense, land-based planes cruised at high altitudes above the fleet, transmitting their extended radar picture to the ships far below. As Cat Brown (seldom had a man's nickname been so appropriate) assessed his command, "We can operate indefinitely at sea." Underway replenishment kept its ships mobile, sustained by an umbilical cord of thousands of miles, stretching all the way back to the continental United States. "We do not run on a short leash," Brown bragged. "We run free."[9]

☆

—All the way to the coast of Lebanon. After World War II, the Lebanese had gained their independence from French rule. The tiny country, pressed between the desert and the sea, had long been a nexus of Middle Eastern commerce and banking. Independence found its citizens neatly divided between Maronite Christians and Sunni Muslims. A bartered political agreement split power between the Maronites, who got the presidency and the foreign ministry, and the Muslims, who controlled the Parliament. Craftily, since their country had no defenses beyond their own skill and guile, the Lebanese had pursued a neutralist foreign policy, at least until the Suez Crisis.

At that time, President Camille Chamoun had publicly supported the Eisenhower Doctrine, thereby alienating almost every Muslim in Lebanon. A presidential election was due in 1958, and Chamoun began maneuvering for a constitutional change to permit his reelection. By May of that year, Nasser was rousing the Lebanese Muslims via Radio Cairo, and the Syrians were shoveling in troops and supplies from across the mountains. On 13 May, Chamoun asked Eisenhower about the American response if Lebanon requested help.

Ike saw the kicker in the question. He cautiously temporized, replying that America would intervene only if a second *Arab* state backed Lebanon's request and if Chamoun clearly renounced another term for himself. He felt that American involvement "should be a last resort." As a precaution, however, a few more ships were added to the Sixth Fleet, and Burke stepped up the fleet's round of training.

Then, with the suddenness of a desert thunderstorm, a bloodbath washed over Iraq. On 13 July, army rebels entered the royal palace in Baghdad and massacred young King Faisal II and the Crown Prince Abdulillah. For good measure, the rebels killed the pro-Western prime minister, Nuri as-Said, the next day, and then let a street mob tear his body apart. Eisenhower was shaken by this sudden, violent coup, so typical of emerging nations, and his concern over equivalent "anti-Western" trouble in Lebanon deepened.

The Iraqi coup had happened so fast that no outside military force could have responded. But the violence unsettled Chamoun; he urgently requested American troops for his country. This time, Eisenhower made his decision quickly. "How soon can you start, Nate?" he asked General Nathan Twining of the Air Force, his JCS chairman, on the morning of 14 July. "Fifteen minutes after I get back to the Pentagon," Twining replied. "Well, what are we waiting for?" rejoined the president of the United States. Eisenhower and his advisors feared that Iraq was but the start of what Brown had called a "brush fire," the beginning of a Nasserite blaze that could devour Lebanon, Jordan, even Saudi Arabia.

Cat Brown was still at the helm of the Sixth Fleet, and he had his marching orders from the Joint Chiefs within minutes. Late on 14 July, when he began to move (his flagship, *Des Moines*, hotfooted out of Villefranche at thirty knots just before midnight), Brown had three carriers (including the spanking-new *Saratoga*), a second heavy cruiser (*Boston)* along with *Des Moines*, more than twenty destroyers, and about fifty supply, support, and amphibious vessels. His Marine Battalion Landing Teams had been augmented by recent exercises to 2500 men. Sixth Fleet also had its usual suite of nuclear weapons; depth charges that could be delivered by planes, helicopters, and surface ships; tactical weapons for use of Marines ashore; and a profusion of air-to-ground and air-to-air ordnance.

By midafternoon the next day, 15 July—a little over twenty-four hours after Eisenhower had given Twining the "go"—the first wave of Marines in Operation BLUEBAT hit the beach of Beirut. They incongruously waded ashore past bikini-clad bathers, who apparently remained uninformed of (or unimpressed by) the menace to their country. As the Marines slogged inland (this was hardly Guadalcanal or Iwo Jima), vendors sold soft drinks to the ranks. Overhead, a wave of fifty jets off *Essex* zoomed across the city. Just over the horizon, as he had done off Alexandria and during the Jordanian crisis, Cat Brown prowled.

During the night of 15 July, for the first time in eight weeks, no shots were fired in Beirut. Marine units kept landing; they occupied the airport and guarded the approaches to the city. Off they went into the countryside on jeep patrols, Marine helos whickering above. They freed the Lebanese army from the task of urban crowd control, allowing that scant force to partrol the Syrian border.

The first U.S. Army units arrived on 19 July. By the end of the month,

Marine and Army personnel had stretched a cordon around Beirut. By early August, 15,000 troops—7000 Marines and 8000 Army—were part of the cordon, the majority of them having arrived by naval transport.

In addition, the Middle East Specified Command, which under Freddie Boone had been alerted during the Suez Crisis, was activated on the first day of the intervention. This command now belonged to Admiral James Holloway, Jr., and Lord Jim had Navy, Army, Marine, and Military Sea Transportation Service (MSTS) units from which to draw. Holloway got himself to Lebanon in time to ride with Ambassador Robert McClintock in an open car, leading the Marines into downtown Beirut. In the first three weeks of the Lebanese intervention, Holloway's planes flew over three thousand sorties and gave Brown's carriers combat air patrol.

In sum, Eisenhower's "go" signal produced a massive American naval and military effort at a moment's notice. The eastern Med was piled high with American shipping; at one point Holloway had thirty-eight MSTS vessels alone detailed for the intervention. By the middle of August, MSTS had lifted over five thousand men, along with eighty thousand tons of cargo and thousands more tons of heavy equipment, to Lebanon.

The Soviet Union screamed in outrage. Even before the intervention, Russia had accused the United States of plans to "invade Lebanon and enslave the Arab people." But rhetoric was about all the Russians could apply. Their feeble response was a token deployment of a few diesel submarines into the area, boats that were quickly staked out and trailed by Brown's hunter-killer groups.

American seapower had delivered—all the way from the Norfolk docks, North Carolina beaches, and Mayport airfields—right to the shores of Lebanon, and beyond.[10]

☆

The entire Lebanese intervention, said one observer, "had a smooth picnic look about it." As in any military operation, however, the ants came along. Naval communications were badly snarled; the weight of traffic from the forces assembled off Lebanon immediately produced circuit overload. Hydrographic material for inshore operations was minimal. Aerial intelligence was unable to give an immediate picture because of the brief lead time. Holloway and Brown had plenty of advance intelligence information, but the short fuse for BLUEBAT meant that many of their commanders could get no meaningful updates.

Arleigh Burke, back in Washington, had gone sleepless on the first night of the intervention. He had given Eisenhower the traditional ringing "affirmative" when asked if the Navy could pull off BLUEBAT. With no military opposition in Lebanon worth noting, Burke now saw "my navy" humming along at an almost perfect pitch, glitches and all.

Lebanon was a classic, and expensive, Cold War demonstration of American seapower. BLUEBAT, which bore a price tag of about $200 million, was an operation of "catalytic force" but of no well-defined objective. The Marines crossed the beaches in order to buy time, and time was what they bought. Nikita Khrushchev demanded an immediate summit conference (a demand that sank amid a welter of sterile diplomatic exchanges), the Soviet Black Sea Fleet ominously "exercised," and neighboring Arab governments looked on nervously. In diplomatic terms, the Middle East had become "unstable" again. The Americans were buying time, they told the world, in order to "stabilize" the situation.

Chamoun's request had given American intervention an aura of legitimacy. Congress had acquiesced; after the Eisenhower Doctrine, that body could do little else. Lebanon was the underlining of a point already obvious to people like Nasser: the United States, despite its endlessly preached revolutionary and democratic idealism, was a status quo power; American leadership tended to see "instability" in the Cold War world as threatening in its very nature.[11]

The United States had no treaties with Lebanon. Eisenhower himself confessed that his doctrine was inapplicable there; although the Syrian military was a concern, and Nasser kept Radio Cairo blasting away, Lebanon was not being invaded by anyone. But, Ike later revealed, "my mind was practically made up . . . we had to move into the Middle East, and specifically into Lebanon, to stop the trend toward chaos." Thus, for the only time in his presidency, the president loosened his tight rein on American military power.

Lebanon was a curious instance of the use of force. There was no evidence of Russia or Egyptian involvement in Lebanon or, for that matter, in the coup in Iraq. A new Lebanese president, General Fouad Chehab, was elected on 31 July with support from both Muslim and Christian elements—Chamoun had announced that he would not seek the unconstitutional second term even before the intervention. By mid-August American troop levels were below twelve thousand, and by the end of October the Marines and Army were gone.

The real target of BLUEBAT was Nasser, who was seen from Washington as the arch "destabilizer." The Lebanese intervention was actually traditional American gunboat diplomacy, this time carried out thousands of miles from its usual locale in the Caribbean and indirectly aimed at the Egyptian leader, to demonstrate American will in support of the status quo. Eisenhower linked the causes of BLUEBAT to Greece in 1947, Czechoslovakia in 1948, Mao's victory in China in 1949, and the North Korean attack in 1950. All these analogies were specious; there was no Communist "threat" in Lebanon. Nasser himself had gotten the message. He had flown to Moscow in July, only to be told that the Soviets had no intention of really moving into the Middle East.

No shots were fired by Americans in Lebanon. But all of Eisenhower's tergiversations could not hide, from Arabs at least, the fact that brutal Western power politics were on display. BLUEBAT solved no problems and created no realignments. Ambassador McClintock, after his ride into Beirut with Holloway, was nevertheless of the opinion that the interests of the world were involved in Lebanon, "through the maintenance of peace." To McClintock, a career diplomat with a distinguished record, the American landing was "a case history in the use of limited war and the practice of applied diplomacy." "This American action left indelible impressions in Arab minds," he wrote.

> The Americans were mighty but they kept their might in check. They came faithfully when called by a friend but they left without harming him. The old "imperialists" had not acted like this. This was an inverse imperialism, if indeed imperialism was the word for the occasion. And so the tale ran, not only in the souks and bazaars and the coffee houses, but in the villas of the statesmen and in the map rooms of the General Staffs. The word ran also to the New Nations, the Uncommitted Countries fiercely determined to preserve their newly-won sovereignty against all comers.

—Many in the souks and bazaars and coffee houses would certainly have agreed with this glowing, brotherly assessment, but Arab nationalists might be pardoned if they could not quite see the "inverse imperialism." The United States Navy was the operational agent in Lebanon; the Sixth Fleet and the Middle East Specified Command had been thoroughly prepared by Brown, Holloway, and Burke. Cat Brown, on Burke's instructions, had been moving about the Med on hurry-up exercises and unscheduled movements for months. By the lights of these naval officers, what they were doing bore not the slightest taint of imperialism.

Lebanon in 1958 was the last time that the chief of naval operations was allowed by law to maneuver and position fleets, and Arleigh Burke had done a masterful job. The British and French, obvious imperialists, had failed at Suez by hurriedly and secretly jury-rigging a military ploy for shabby political ends and then advancing into a powderkeg. The Sixth Fleet, by contrast, operated out of idealism (albeit the idealism of international stability), was thoroughly prepared and trained, and moved into an area where no other force was ready or able to intervene. Suez, said Burke, "had given our . . . people a very good idea of how *not* to conduct such an operation."

The Lebanese gambit also had more than a slight air of carnival, of conspicuous excess. Lord Jim's biggest problem, for example, seemed to be keeping away from the horde of VIPs who descended on him. He proudly remembered that when his forces pulled out on schedule, on 24 October, they left behind a constitutionally elected president, a united army, peace in the area, and "a few legal beagles to pay for damage to the olive groves."[12]

—But this was not quite all. The Sixth Fleet had fully lived up to

Burke's prediction to Eisenhower: if the Eisenhower Doctrine was to be effective, the Sixth Fleet would be the primary force behind that effectiveness. Overwhelming naval power had given the Americans a tremendous degree of control, a degree the British and French had never come close to enjoying at Suez. Nevertheless, behind the overt success of Lebanon lay a fundamental confusion in American Middle Eastern policy.

In the midst of the landings on 15 July, one Marine had taken in the tranquil, sun-drenched spectacle on the beach and exclaimed, "It's better than Korea, but what the hell is it?" "It" was in fact Arab nationalism, and years would pass before most American policymakers would even begin to come to grips with its multiple meanings for the Middle East.

The Eisenhower Doctrine, when the idea did not dismiss Arab nationalism altogether, confused individuals like Nasser and movements like pan-Arabism with Communist or pro-Communist ideals. The Cold War tent in the Middle East was meant to cover only red camels (an extremely scarce breed). BLUEBAT did nothing to repel "international communism;" the red camel was never really in the Middle East to begin with. The heavy-handed intervention in Lebanon doubtless won a few friends, as men like McClintock believed, but for many Arabs the Sixth Fleet's sortie against the Lebanese coast only made America the new (and extremely useful) imperial villain in the region.

Nasser would flourish, even linking Egypt to Syria in a short-lived pan-Arab dream, the United Arab Republic. The USSR would find new grounds for its anti-imperialist message, new markets for its arms. Israel would continue to be at dagger's point with nearly every Arab neighbor. Only Jordan, Lebanon, and Saudi Arabia, hardly major military powers among the Arab states, maintained cordial relations with the United States. Lebanon, in fairness, would be granted a reprieve of almost two decades before internal tensions ripped the place wide open, but the price of American intervention, in terms of U.S. policy goals (anti-Communist "stability" for the entire region), was exceptionally high.

That sunny promenade by the Marines on Beirut's beaches only inflamed Arab nationalists. Middle Eastern "stability," in American terms, was not threatened by communism or anything close to communism but by this very nationalism and by traditional power struggles that had nothing whatsoever to do with any "ism" at all. The best that could be said of Eisenhower's policy was that he had a clear view of what was at stake for the West in terms of Persian Gulf oil. But this view played right into the hands of Arab nationalists, who were preaching resistance to American neo-imperialism in many of McClintock's souks, bazaars, and coffee houses and made nonsense of his notion of "inverse imperialism."[13]

In the long run, then, the Sixth Fleet's triumph (and in a narrow, operational sense the Navy operation off Lebanon *was* a triumph) came loaded with problems and burdened by crucial misunderstandings, on the part of both Arabs and Americans. Seldom in American history had such a faulty policy been so militarily well served.

☆

The Sixth Fleet was a compromise force. Among its fifty or so ships, two thousand aircraft, and thirty thousand men, the preparation for a worst-case, Soviet-centered scenario predominated. But the fleet's potential tasks ranged from nuclear attack to dampening the ardor of an Arab street mob. American sailors in the Mediterranean were expected to be both fighting men and friendly men, and this last mission involved everything from guided tours of ships to sponsorship of orphanages to band concerts. From Barcelona to Athens and back to Algiers, everyone around the rim of the sea spoke at least two words of English in common: "Sixth Fleet."

From the time *Missouri* steamed past Gibraltar in 1946, the American naval presence in the Mediterranean had mostly involved leisurely circling the great sea several times a year, displaying powerful warships to over two hundred million people. At times, the fleet's presence had more purpose. Before the Italian elections in 1948, for example, American warships anchored ostentatiously in the country's main ports. (Whether this action influenced the Italians was moot; however, the left-wing parties got less than one-third of the vote.) In addition, the crises in Suez, Jordan, and Lebanon put an edge on fleet operations. Not an American shot had been fired in anger in any of these instances, but the Sixth Fleet had played a crucial role, just the same, in every one.

Officers and men still enjoyed the duty, to be sure. The Med, on most days, remained a most friendly and forgiving sea. Some of them even forgot to behave like sailors. When four thousand liberties were granted one weekend, only two resulted in disciplinary action. Given his own checkered past, Cat Brown could be forgiven when, conducting shipboard church services himself one morning, he looked out at what he called a "sea of angelic faces" and asked himself, "Are these my hoary sailors?"

—They were, and they were playing their naval roles superbly. They could have their ships off any trouble spot in a few days, land their Marines in a few hours, or have aircraft over a target in a few minutes. Normally they did not belong to NATO, but they were NATO's seaborne right flank, and they trained accordingly. They were a mixture of nearly all the arms and capacities of American naval power, a compromise Navy tailored for the widest possible range of tasks.

In the wider perspective, however, the Sixth Fleet was regarded by U.S. policymakers as America's own Rock of Gibraltar, a force supporting stability. But the struggles between Arab and Jew, Muslim and Christian, Greek and Turk, and nationalist and Westerner, plus many more deep, historically conditioned hostilities, could not be resolved by naval power. At best, naval power could help clamp a lid on a problem for a short time.

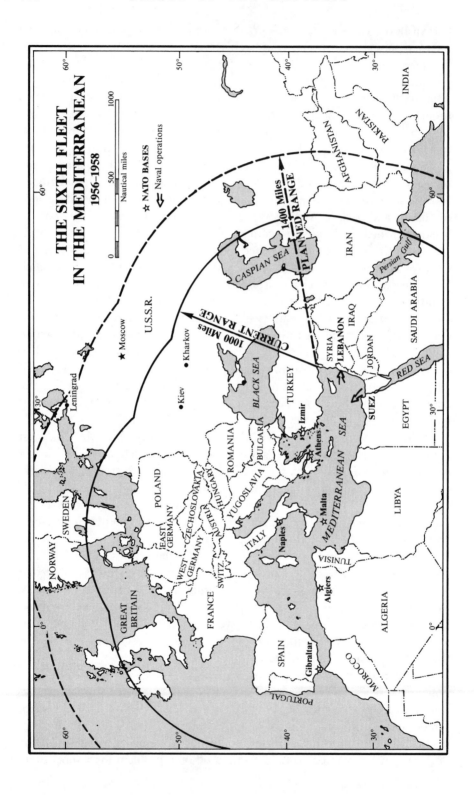

THE SIXTH FLEET
IN THE MEDITERRANEAN
1956–1958

★ NATO BASES
Naval operations

Nautical miles
0   500   1000

And while these same policymakers almost willfully confused Arab nationalism with communism, the Navy's preference for the status quo was blatantly evident to all. If a line were to be drawn bisecting the Mediterranean from west to east, from Gibraltar to Lebanon, by far the greatest share of the Sixth Fleet's beloved port visits took place north of that line. To the south, along the Arab rim of the sea, the haze-gray warships more often showed up with their planes in the air and their guns trained. These "visits," and their purposes, were not lost on Arab leaders, and in this way the Sixth Fleet did its part in perpetuating suspicion and stowing away hostages for the future.

"We are haunted by memories," Cat Brown wrote home, "of epic battles and fabled heroes from the days of Byzantium and Constantinople down to bloody Gallipoli of only yesterday. Phoenicians, Greeks and Romans, Saracens and Venetians and Crusaders, all have fought here in their time. What future tales of human heroism, suffering and folly have these storied waters yet to tell?"[14]

CHAPTER TWENTY-NINE

STRETCH

───── ☆ ─────

I n the Free World—among the nations allied against Moscow's imperial-
istic schemes for world enslavement—control of the seas rests mainly
today with the United States Navy," ran one typically fervent Cold War
editorial. "America's blue-gray ships and planes and her men in blue are
the mainstay in protection of the sea lanes that are the life arteries of the
free lands."

Certainly the Navy did not disagree with this estimate of its purpose.
The American public received the Navy's own version through the chief of
information (CHINFO), a position established in 1950, after the rebellion
in gold braid. CHINFO, a rear admiral, was the Navy's public relations
tsar; he worked jointly for the secretary of the Navy and the chief of naval
operations. Thus serving two masters, CHINFO could find himself in
trouble if the civilian and military sides could not agree on an appropriate
PR slant. But this happened rarely, and besides, for the major PR items,
chiefs like Mick Carney and Arleigh Burke preferred to use their own long-
standing organizational and personnel networks. CHINFO took care of the
rest, fighting the Cold War alongside the fleet.

Every senior commander had his own public information (later public
affairs) officer. The PR men sought to gain good will from the American public, using every possible media avenue. Like everyone, the Navy
loved good news, but the institution loathed bad news like the very devil.
Bad news could lose votes, lose money, lose public support. As a result,
and without a doubt, the Navy was in the business of managing its news.
At the height of the Cold War, fortunately for the service, public criticism of this practice barely existed. Most of the nation was still "on the
team."

"The Navy is a real neophyte in this public relations profession," sighed
Rear Admiral Edmund Taylor, CHINFO in 1957. But even as Taylor was
speaking, to an audience of students at the Naval War College, his words
no longer held true. The prewar attitude exemplified by Ernie King—
"there's no need of public relations, our good deeds will speak for themselves"—had gone by the boards. Navy PR, ever since the bitter lessons of

the unification battle and the controversy over *United States*, had become very slick indeed. The best Navy PR people told the truth, or as much truth as they were allowed to tell. A few others, however, produced merely the advertising garbage of Madison Avenue, dealing mostly in evasion, half-truths, propaganda, and lies.

Despite the Navy's growing PR professionalism, then, and regardless of the overwhelming support of the service by the American people, the *product* of naval public relations (because the bad news never went away) was a decidedly mixed bag. In 1954 a set of "public information objectives," seven in all, had been decreed by both civilian and uniformed leadership. Three of these, concerning seapower, present naval roles, and future naval roles, were educational and general in nature. Two, career service and the Naval Reserve, dealt with personnel. One, on the need for fleet modernization, was economic and technological. The seventh, and the one that would come to dominate the Navy's PR effort, was strictly related to the Cold War: "Awareness of Growing Soviet Naval Strength."[1]

There was much PR to be done; after Korea, America's naval presence was expected to be capable of immediate response to practically any crisis. Cold War naval publicity thus tended to extoll the wonders of technology, particularly the new, the novel, and the powerful. The supercarrier's capabilities and missions received numerous instances of favorable coverage; naval training, of both officers and men, was covered on a continuous basis; Rickover's nuclear shop had its own beautifully greased PR machinery. Always, the emphasis (per Madison Avenue) was on "the latest thing," with little or no attention being given to the *purposes* or *uses* of whatever that thing happened to be.

In 1953, the paid manpower of the Department of the Navy was 1.6 million people, around 1 percent of the nation's population. Then there were the dependents, the Navy veterans, and those who relied on naval largesse or naval pensions. By the time these numbers were tallied, perhaps as much as 10 percent of the entire population was intimately and directly "pro-Navy," an enormous advantage for any public relations effort.

Beyond these figures lay the intangible but all-important aspects of national pride and patriotism. Navy PR tried never to forget the taxpayer. Hundreds of warships and thousands of Navy planes were in operation; public relations endlessly sought to prove their "worth." Of far greater emotional importance, the number of American families with "someone in the Navy" or "discharged from the Navy" or "going into the Navy" ran into the millions.

The Navy's gigantism was a compelling factor in its considerable public support. Naval supply catalogs in the fifties held 1.3 million items, roughly ten times the inventory of Sears; naval lawyers handled 100,000 cases a year, dwarfing the caseload of any law firm; naval records alone accumulated at the rate of 400,000 cubic feet annually. The Navy was a rent-collecting landlord for more than 24,000 families, employed no less than ten Nobel Prize winners, supervised two hundred industrial plants, and owned four oil fields outright.

—To cover all this activity, and much more, 1.6 million news releases were fired off every year (about one per employee), a considerable portion of them to hometown papers telling of the local boy's success in boot camp and the like. By the mid-fifties, well before Taylor's speech at the Naval War College, CHINFO was not missing a beat. The public was endlessly reminded of the never-ending strains of Navy deployment, "Communist acts of aggression" (usually presented almost as one word), problems with maintaining a strong reservoir of trained personnel, and growing fleet obsolescence. The Navy's PR effort could praise or boost to the skies, but CHINFO could never appear smug or self-satisfied—always, there was more to do.

Therefore, the Navy itself, with the best intentions, was a prime culprit in leading the American people always to expect more of their national seapower and their naval service. The good news spoke for itself. Disasters, such as those aboard *Bennington* in 1954 or on *Leyte* the year before (another hydraulic catapult explosion, which took thirty-seven lives), were presented as the tragedies they were but also as reminders of the need for improvement and the need to do more.

"The overall material condition of the Fleet is satisfactory," pronounced Secretary of the Navy Charles Thomas in 1955. Just two years later, Under Secretary William Franke was feverishly warning that "Soviet Russia is making her bid for world domination in all phases of national effort. . . . The increasing Soviet use of the oceans as a Cold War battleground is simply another tactic in furtherance of the announced Communist objective of ultimate world domination."

—With such a menace on the loose, satisfactory material condition alone would never suffice. Americans, continued Franke, must "retain our capability for *all* types of war." Any erosion in this capability was more than worrisome. By 1959, over 80 percent of the active fleet consisted of aging ships of World War II vintage or even older; Thomas's assessment of only four years before no longer held. For fiscal 1959, the Board of Inspection and Survey found that 72 percent of the ships inspected had been "unsatisfactory."[2]

So the Navy, despite its undoubted predominance, was under enormous and partially self-imposed pressure. The service had to live up to its own pride and publicity, to provide constant, worldwide defense against an insidious enemy, and to move forward in every possible area of improvement. The strain was continuous, and telling. By the late 1950s the Cold War Navy—materially, logistically, financially, geographically, technologically, and tactically—was operating at full stretch.

☆

"Supply," in the form of the purser, went back to the earliest days of the Navy, but the modern Naval Supply System, inaugurated in 1947, made the full stretch possible. The system centralized inventory management and, by 1957, was using fancy communications nets and automatic data processing to get everything from socks to spare parts out to the fleet. Supply handled petroleum, medical needs, food, clothing—the gamut of the basics, and far more. Supply personnel cataloged, disposed of excess property and parts, and prepared "allowance lists" for every naval command.

Meanwhile, logistics programs were shifting in emphasis from conventional equipment to special weapons systems, nuclear power, and ever-more-direct support of contractor production. Millions of line items of repair parts and general stores inventories moved through the system every day, drawn to their naval users by a network of transportation and communications capillaries unrivaled in their complexity.

Naval supply was always good for a joke, all the way from *Mr. Roberts* to the latest horror story of a ship left immobile through lack of necessary spare parts. Screwups were inevitable, as much a part of the system as anything, but what sometimes got lost in the joking and the screaming was the fact that Navy supply *worked*, and worked amazingly well.

Always, Navy supply people tried to *provide*—faster, more efficiently, on time. They experimented with new textiles, improved food service, and cranked up the loading speed on cargo-handling systems. They gloated in their victories over time and space: at-sea cargo replenishment, increased to one hundred tons per hour from twenty; time for loading twelve tons of refrigerated cargo, reduced from six hours to twenty-seven minutes; sales of excess material, up to $65.6 million. In the mid-fifties, they began to experiment with a technique that would change the shape and pace of underway replenishment—helicopter cargo lifts for "vertical replenishment," or VERTREP, at sea.

These were the most prosaic of victories, but no less important for that. The Navy's largest inland supply depot was located in Mechanicsburg, Pennsylvania, and was typical in its range of services. Its very location inland was a register of the fact that, even before Pearl Harbor, the demands placed on the Navy's supply personnel had far outstripped what coastal shipyards could provide. There had once been a day when almost all the Navy's support functions could be conducted at water's edge; those times were gone. Mechanicsburg's Naval Supply Depot had been commissioned in 1942; by the end of the war, the facility was storing and distributing material for the entire Navy, all the way around the world.

Mechanicsburg was the hub of the Navy's supply grid. From its depot, supplies and equipment could be moved to any point on the Atlantic coast in a few hours, by rail or air. Inland, there were direct rail connections to Erie, Pennsylvania, Detroit, and Chicago, where the training base at Great Lakes was a major consumer. Mechanicsburg was the Navy's largest storage point for reserve stocks of ships' parts and the leading center for procurement and control of every item of naval material. Furthermore, the installation was critical for the economic health of the surrounding region, characteristic of the Navy's impact on the hinterland. Civilian employment alone ran to 2500.[3]

More and more, the Navy's supply officers were being forced to learn the techniques of industrial management on an enormous scale. Already in 1953, the gross physical assets of the Department of the Navy were valued in the books at $47 billion, a figure about 2.5 times the combined assets of General Motors, United States Steel, AT&T, and the Pennsylvania Railroad. Civilian direction and control of the Navy's management, through the under and assistant secretaries, was being strengthened; experienced managers like Franke and Tom Gates were now the norm. But the everyday nuts and bolts, in places like Mechanicsburg, belonged mostly to the Supply Corps.

The contracting load alone was mind-boggling. In 1954, after the post-Korea drawdown, the Navy still placed contracts for materials, services, and supplies totaling almost $5 billion. Many contractual arrangements involved land as well. As a landlord, the service controlled 1.1 million acres of landed property in the continental United States, 1.4 million acres of public domain land "withdrawn for naval purposes," and 210,870 acres for the Naval Petroleum Reserves. Over 100,000 acres, scattered throughout the Caribbean and the Pacific, also belonged to the Navy.

Such monumentalism was a problem in itself. As both a landlord and a contractor, the Navy struggled to give small businesses a fair share. Small operations could build neither supercarriers nor nuclear submarines, but they could provide cardboard boxes and radio headsets. In 1955, for example, small companies received over $800 million of prime contract awards, about 24 percent of the net procurement sum. An additional 16 percent went to "first tier" subcontractors. Generally speaking, then, the Navy did not ignore small business, despite the frequent cries from Capitol Hill that the little guy was being shortchanged. Watchdog members of Congress, eager to appease constituents, made sure that naval contracting policy reserved a slice of the government pie, no matter how slender, for as many people as possible. Big-ticket and highly complicated items, on the other hand, were increasingly becoming the province of single-source suppliers.

Comptroller organizations, to keep track of all this money, multiplied throughout the Navy. Managers were making decisions that drastically affected what the operators could do. In addition, the operators (line officers) were having to devote much more of their time to managing their money and the rest of their assets. The Navy continually audited both itself and its contractors, and the occasional scandal (pounced on with relish by the press) could not diminish the fact that the flow of the huge money stream was being channeled remarkably well.

Where the money went could be seen from this typical example, for fiscal year 1957:

BUDGET CATEGORY	AMOUNT (IN MILLIONS OF DOLLARS)	PERCENTAGE
Personnel	3,080	30
Operations and maintenance	2,475	25
Major procurement and production	3,755	35
Public works	370	4
Reserves	226	2
Research and development	523	5
DOD establishment	25	—
Working capital funds	− 103	− 1
Undistributed	47	—
	10,398	100

In short, almost 60 percent of the Navy's funds (the first two categories plus public works) were spent in simply *operating*. Active contracts accounted for the bulk of the remainder. By 1959, about fifteen cents of every dollar spent by the federal government was chargeable to the Navy and Marines, which came to twenty-eight cents of every Defense Department dollar. Polaris, that voracious devourer of naval funding, would distort the operations and maintenance portion of the budget for years to come.

Such numbers inevitably led to the creation of "supermanagers" to try to handle this incredible infrastructure of supply, contracting, accounting, and financing. "We are now in an era," remarked one such individual, Rear Admiral Ralph Shifley, in 1965, "in which operationally oriented officers of the Navy came to realize more than ever before how closely operational success is tied to success in solving logistical problems."

Public Law 432, back in 1948, had formed the Office of Naval Material. But its chief had had no responsibility for material programs, only for "procurement policy formulation and enforcement." These shackles were the result of generations-old turf wars on the part of the bureaus, whose leaders instinctively resisted any imposition of central authority on them with every bureaucratic fiber of their being.

But the Special Projects Office and its brainchild, Polaris, in addition to skewing the Navy's internal budgeting procedures, also represented a major program that ran unbridled by the bureaus—unbridled, indeed, by anyone short of Burke and Red Raborn. Polaris was crash management with a "robbing Peter to pay Paul" budget, not institutionalized management within a larger, subordinating structure. Thus, after the dust surrounding Special Projects had settled and Raborn had checked out, a way to manage naval "projects," of which Polaris was the spectacular first instance, had to be found.

On 2 December 1963, the chief of naval material became the Navy's quintessential supermanager. General Order No. 5 gave him responsibility for most of the material, development, and procurement capacity of the Navy. Specifically, "NAVMAT" (as he was universally known throughout the service) now bossed the four material bureaus—Supplies and Accounts, Naval Weapons, Yards and Docks, and Ships.

The bureaus were not quite ready to fold their tents and sulk away. In fact, NAVMAT at first left them practically unchanged, seeing himself simply as a coordinating overlay. The first chiefs of naval material bent over backward to ensure that their people avoided stepping on sensitive bureau toes. But the bureau system was on its way out, and its usher was the new "projects" approach.

By 1965, seven project managers reported directly to NAVMAT. These men ran the Fleet Ballistic Missile Program, the Surface Missile Systems, the ill-fated F-111B–TFX Project, Antisubmarine Warfare, Ships Instrumentation, Carrier All-Weather Landing Systems, and a catch-all acronym, REWSON (Reconnaissance, Electronic Warfare, Special Operations, and Naval Intelligence Processing Systems). In short, the cream of naval technology now rose straight to the top, to NAVMAT, short-circuiting the bureaus on the way. NAVMAT accounted for two-thirds of the Navy's entire budget within two years of the issuance of General Order No. 5.

NAVMAT became the Navy's logistician supreme. Basically, the goal of his office was to ensure that a far-flung naval force operating at full stretch could solve most of its logistics problems on the spot—and keep operating. On average, ships took between 60 percent and 80 percent of their operating requirements from their own storerooms (or the storerooms of those ships in company). At the same time, a fantastic 92 percent of allowance items were never used. Toilet paper, for example, was forever needed, but a nuclear trigger, never. NAVMAT wanted a ship to be able to fulfill 90 percent of its own parts and supplies requirements for ninety days.

The incipient waste in such a system was colossal, but the waste was rarely that of fraud or peculation. Rather, problems came in the process of simply *moving* items along the chain of production, assembly, storage, transportation, and use. At one time in the early sixties, for example, critical spare parts worth $600 million were lost in the Navy's own logistics system. They had not vanished forever, but neither were they available on demand and thus could not be part of that desired self-sufficiency of 90 percent.[4]

☆

Everything demanded money, and supplies. Ashore, for example, naval air stations were the most expensive items, consuming some 20 percent to 25 percent of everything on the beach. These were followed, in rough descending order, by supply depots, hospitals, and naval stations. Then came ammo and mine depots, communications stations, and naval districts, trailed by experimental stations, laboratories, shipyards, naval schools, and training centers.

Most of these shore stations operated in relative public anonymity. Some of them, however (hospitals and shipyards being conspicuous examples), had a significant civilian impact well beyond their budget portions. Naval medicine was an acute financial problem all by itself, made more so by the continuously accelerating costs of medical technology and health care. In 1957, the Navy ran 262 medical facilities containing more than eighteen thousand beds; the occupancy rate was 70 percent to 80 percent. Full research programs were being funded in both medicine and dentistry, as well as specialty programs in aviation, submarine, and preventive medicine. The shortage of medical talent from the immediate postwar period had been partially resolved, but naval medicine persisted as a classic example of a budget item that could not better itself simply by swallowing more money.

"It is becoming apparent," admitted the somewhat exasperated Franke in 1960 (after he had become secretary of the Navy), "that the planning for shore activities is not sufficiently responsive to the changing operational demands on the modern Navy and its needs for support." A lot of money— $20 billion a year by 1961—was being spent ashore, and the stickiest problems were where civilian work met naval requirements most directly, in the shipyards.

As a business proposition, Navy shipyards were unparalleled. They looked like industrial corporations, operated like industrial corporations, and turned out the same categories of goods and services as industrial corporations. But they were not. These businesses were run by naval officers, who were required neither to pay taxes nor to make a profit. No shareholders haunted their dreams. They knew not the need to advertise.

By 1962 the Navy owned eleven shipyards, a total investment of $1.5 billion. These yards turned out more than $1 billion of "goods and services" a year. Together they employed ninety-eight thousand people, and much of their highly specialized equipment (rolls that could bend three-inch steel, for example) was hard to find elsewhere.

The New York Naval Shipyard, known throughout the fleet as the "Brooklyn Navy Yard," was the largest of the eleven, and there much of the strain of the Navy's full stretch could easily be seen. "Brooklyn" stood on 292 acres of the most expensive land anywhere, employed 12,800 personnel, and sported an annual payroll of $100 million. At every turn, the place featured specialists: masters of the yard's great 350-ton hammerhead crane; machine and metal experts, working to exact tolerances in eighteen shops; men to run the seven graving docks and two shipbuilding ways. (The oldest graving dock, built of hand-fitted Vermont granite blocks in the first two decades of the nineteenth century, needed the least maintenance.)

Talent like this could not be invented overnight; Brooklyn's expertise was both valuable and busy. In 1962 the yard was modernizing destroyers through the Fleet Rehabilitation and Maintenance Program (FRAM), in which the cans each got an antisubmarine rocket system (ASROC), a helicopter drone (DASH—a miserable failure), new air and surface radar systems, and new sonar equipment. In addition, the yard was building the first eight of ten ordered landing platform docks (LPDs) for amphibious assault. In short, Brooklyn was both sustaining and creating, just as a shipyard should.

Up to 1947, line officers had been commanding officers of Navy shipyards, with Engineering Duty Only officers as their operating managers. Then the EDOs began to command the yards, and with them came their engineering and managerial skills. Brooklyn, for example, prided itself on its tightfistedness, constantly striving to be meticulous in its cost accounting. (One day after the yard helped in a rescue from a forced-down civilian helicopter, the helicopter's owners got a bill for services rendered.) But for all their efficiencies, both great and small, yards like Brooklyn were showing the strain of maintaining the Cold War Navy.

There were always problems with civilian unions. Mildly put, naval officers were inexperienced in union negotiations; one of the reasons the EDOs ascended to command was a history of continuous strife between tough union bosses and stubborn line officers. At one time, Brooklyn's skippers had to deal with no fewer than fifty-three unions. Perhaps the labor problems stemmed at least in part from the fact that the yard's famed fringe benefit of the 1800s—a twice-a-day issue of grog to all hands—was no more.

But if naval shipyards were not industrial corporations, they still had "competition"—the civilian shipyards. Here was the crux of the Navy's shipyard problem. This was an ancient debate, over who could best build and maintain the Navy's ships. The Navy stressed that part of its costs were strictly "military," such items as security, medicine, and recreation, and thus that its shipyards' price tags only *seemed* inflated. Neither side could claim a wage victory; indeed, both private and Navy yards paid about the same wages. But the Navy yards prided themselves on *service* rather than *profit*. "We have unimpeachable integrity," proudly proclaimed Rear Admiral Schuyler Pyne, who ran Brooklyn in the late fifties.

The civilians countered that, because of the market economy, the bottom line belonged to them. A private yard, they said, could build a ship more cheaply than a Navy yard. (Everyone admitted, however, that maintenance was another matter.) Navy yards paid no taxes, were not required to show a profit, and had no funded debt. There were no shareholders to answer to. They were, according to the critics in the private sector, fat and lazy.

The Navy's policy was to place shipbuilding and repair projects in such a way as to keep as many government and private yards going as possible. In 1962, for example, civilian shipbuilders had a collective $5 billion backlog in new construction for the Navy. Part of this was sheer political reality, bowing to the frequent winds from Capitol Hill. But there was rationale in back of the approach also: maintaining the widest possible pool of expertise in shipbuilding and ship repair. Regardless, both these aspects, by their very size and substantial economic impact, spelled pork barrel politics in capital letters. Waste was everywhere, and if a single shipyard like Brooklyn could boast of its efficiencies, monumental inefficiencies were nevertheless built into such a dual system.[5]

Places like Brooklyn were where the Navy began, and where the fleet came to be renewed. If the ships could not steam, the missions could not be accomplished; if the missions could not be accomplished, national policy could not be fulfilled. Big problems and delays in shipbuilding and ship repair thus radiated like blood poisoning out onto blue water, multiplying the difficulties of a service already stretched to the limit.

☆

From the shoreline seaward, the elasticity in the stretch was sustained by the ships and people no one thought much about and everyone depended on—the Service Forces. In the early days of World War II, Ernie King, exasperated as usual, had groused, "I don't know what the hell this logistics is that Marshall is always talking about, but I want some of it." Eventually he got lots of "it;" the old Fleet Train became a worldwide resupply service, without which victory anywhere overseas would have been impossible. These vessels brought the oil, ammunition, general stores, and spare parts. The tenders provided havens for repair, thousands of miles from home. The service ships were indispensable to a mobile, widely scattered naval force.

In the mid-1950s, however, the Navy's motley collection of service ships, as necessary as they were, came last in line—at budget time, off the drawing boards, at Brooklyn and the other yards, everywhere. Most of the attention went to the warships and the dazzling new systems. As of 1955, the Navy had never built a logistic support ship designed from the keel up for the specific purpose of replenishment at sea. The policy was "do the best we can with what we have," and what the Navy had was a rapidly deteriorating collection of hastily built World War II cargo and tanker hulls based on civilian models and civilian needs. The designs of amphibious assault craft— the LPDs, LSDs, LSTs, and the like—were just as old, but these were specific designs for specific missions, and thus capable of longer life.

The service ships were not. More specifically, the Navy's improvised transfer-at-sea rigging was cumbersome, rather like pairing a ballerina and a weightlifter on stage. (The job would eventually get done, but efficiency would certainly suffer.) Fuel transfer pumps could carry only a marginal load. There was little room topside to shunt cargo before breaking bulk and stowage. Distribution of storage tanks was haphazard and inflexible. Ammo ships, for example, were ancient merchant designs intended for leisurely up-and-over lifting and discharge of bulk cargo at pierside. These vessels (AEs), as well as general stores (AKs), aviation stores (AVBs), and reefer ships (AFs), were all crude adaptations, not *mission-oriented*, like warships. The tankers (AOs) did a little better, but their fuel capacities and pumping rates were extremely limited.

The merchant designs meant that problems of watertight integrity, damage control, and electrical circuitry abounded. Hatch openings varied; winch locations (and operating limits) were a throw of the dice; deck stowage was improvised at best. Booms broke, guys parted, hose couplings came undone, and personnel got dunked during highline transfer. The United States Navy did underway replenishment better than any other navy in the world, but like Samuel Johnson's dog walking on its hind legs, the miracle was that any replenishing at sea got done at all.

By the mid-fifties there was some talk of reconfiguring the *Iowa*-class battleships as do-everything replenishment platforms, but this came to nothing. As of 1957 there were five Service Squadrons—two each in the Pacific and the Atlantic and one in the Mediterranean. They were composed of the same old workhorses, doing everything from carrying the mail to marine salvage. They were the principal logistics agents of their fleet commanders (Task Force 73 for Seventh Fleet, for example), and their responsibilities knew no end. One ServRon commander realistically remarked that his title should be "Vice President in Charge of Things and Stuff."

The ServRons had proven their worth time and again, mostly in the humble duties of transfer at sea but also in dramatic moments like the Indochina sealift and the Tachens evacuation. But they were the first to lose out in the Navy's intramural budget battles. This meant, among other things, that their ships' boats (used for some cargo and personnel transfer) were grossly inadequate; that their radio shacks were mostly bad jokes, when everything in underway replenishment depended on up-to-date communication; that they were mostly blind (with closets for combat information centers), feeble (three-inch guns at most), and deaf (no sonar); and that their own internal supply discipline—the way they acquired, stored, and moved their cargo—left much to be desired.

"Unless action is taken, and taken soon, to provide adequate and timely logistics support," warned one supply officer, "we will have at best a one-shot Navy." Piecemeal changes were being made: mechanized cargo handling, endurance loading, the introduction of air and electric winches, and the advent of the Coordinated Shipboard Allowance List (COSAL) for support of technology. But without proper platforms, the changes were patchwork at best. "Our current capability for underway replenishment is barely adequate," judged Captain Morton Lytle, a veteran submariner, in 1959. "In some areas it is woefully inadequate."

The development of nuclear power might reduce the need for oilers, but the increasing size and complexity of the Navy's big warships—nuclear and nonnuclear alike—meant that underway replenishment was becoming ever more critical. The proper solutions—specifically designed replenishment ships big enough to handle a variety of loads and fast enough to run with the heavies—were on the boards but not yet available.

One of these was the Fast Combat Support Ship (AOE), initially created to carry 177,000 barrels of fuel oil, 1500 tons of ammo, and 500 tons of stores. The lead ship, *Sacramento*, was commissioned in 1963. At almost 20,000 tons, with a twenty-six-knot top speed (Sacramento and her sister, *Camden*, received steam turbines originally built for the canceled battleship *Kentucky*) and with helicopters embarked, she revolutionized underway replenishment. The AOE would become, arguably, the Navy's most successful ship design of the postwar period.

A second type, the Combat Stores Ship (AFS), also appeared in 1963, in the shape of *Mars*. The AFS combined into one hull two-thirds of a reefer (AF) load, all of a General Stores Issue Ship (AKS) load, and all of an Aviation Supply Ship (AVS) load. *Mars* and her sister, *Sylvania*, also made brilliant debuts, one in each ocean.

The Navy's dozens of oilers were in pretty sad shape, led by the dowagers of the group, *Cimarron* and *Platte*—both launched in 1939. World War II produced a huge crop of oilers, most of them smallish, at around 5300 tons. The five immediate postwar oilers, starting with *Mispillion* (AO-105), literally felt the stretch in the early sixties, being lengthened ("jumboized") to accommodate more fuel. Oilers built in the 1950s, starting with *Neosho*, grew to over 11,000 tons, but the basic designs were still merchant hulls. Real solutions in this area were far over the horizon. The big ship, the Replenishment Fleet Oiler (AOR), did not come along until the late sixties. The little, "low-mix" ship, the second *Cimarron* class, would not arrive until the eighties.

In the fifties, saviors of the caliber of *Sacramento*, *Mars*, and the AOR were years away. All hands recognized the importance of logistics, especially the operators, but Brooklyn and the other yards could not produce AOEs, AFSs, and AORs overnight. And since the demands placed on the Cold War Navy were merciless and unremitting, something else had to be found.[6]

☆

The "something" was the Military Sea Transportation Service (MSTS). Actually, the Navy's need for quasi-civilian assistance went back at least to 1898, when Commodore George Dewey found himself in Hong Kong with warships enough to go against the Spanish squadron in Manila Bay but no auxiliary support. Teddy Roosevelt, then the mercurial assistant secretary of the Navy, authorized the purchase of a collier and a supply ship from the British. With this necessary logistical backing, Dewey sortied to victory and fame.

The Navy's rather undistinguished "collier service" lasted until 1905, when the Auxiliary Service was established. During World War I, the Cruiser and Transport Force ferried doughboys to Europe, while the Naval Overseas Transportation Service actually "transported" fuel, dry cargo, and ammo. In place of these two outfits after the war came the Naval Transportation Service, which steamed through World War II and lasted until 1 October 1949.

On that date, MSTS was born. Completely unknown or little understood by the American public, MSTS operated by Department of Defense directive under naval command. Its force contained both commissioned and noncommissioned ships, regular Navy personnel and civilians. In the beginning, MSTS combined the Naval Transportation Service and the Army Transport Service, with a total operating fleet of ninety-two vessels. The new service was also authorized to charter commercial ships.

On paper, MSTS looked like a patchy thing of many parts, impossible to make work or even coordinate. But the organization proved itself in spades in Korea. In the first seven months of the conflict, MSTS added dozens of ships and carried over seven million tons of dry cargo, twenty-five million barrels of petroleum, oil, and lubricants (POL), and over 700,000 passengers to the western Pacific. By the middle of the war, the MSTS fleet had grown to 215 ships, and its amount of charters from 6 to 230. These were no small numbers and, politics aside, MSTS helped make the United Nations effort in Korea possible.

After the war, MSTS settled into its Washington headquarters as a worldwide operation with four area and three subarea commands. Its blue-and-gold-banded stack markings were identifiable anywhere. Its fleet had transports, tankers, cargo vessels, and a host of smaller craft. But these ships had all the problems of the Navy's own Service Squadrons, plus the added handicaps of possessing no terminal facilities of their own and the inability to manage inland traffic leading to pierside. MSTS operated on water, and *only* on water.

Still, MSTS made a critical difference, largely because its ships took over roles, such as personnel transport, for which naval bottoms intended for other use would otherwise have had to be detailed. MSTS ships served exceptionally well in carrying refugees in connection with the UN's International Refugee Organization—sixty-three thousand people in the first six months of 1950 alone. Some of their sealifts were truly heroic: during the Hungnam evacuation in Korea, for example, *Meredith Victory*, a chartered cargo ship built to accommodate twelve passengers, took on fourteen thousand Korean civilians—who stood patiently, packed shoulder-to-shoulder, during their wintry, three-day trip to the south, and safety.

All the ships, equipment, and personnel of MSTS belonged to the Navy (unlike the Air Force's Military Air Transport Service, to which the Navy contributed planes, equipment, and personnel), but MSTS provided ocean transport for *all* of the Defense Department. In every respect MSTS was a hybrid, a mix of Navy and civil service personnel, subject to both naval and civil service regulations, relying heavily on commercial shipping. In 1953, 74 percent of its budget was paid directly to private shipping interests and ship repair companies.

This hybrid force totaled almost thirty thousand people in the mid-fifties, 61 percent civil service and twenty-four thousand afloat. Each ship had a military department; clashes between civilian crews and their military customers were far from unknown. Yet whatever friction there was in the gears got greased, because everywhere MSTS operated, its ships provided the margin for sustained naval operations. The bulk of the Navy's Persian Gulf POL, for instance, traveled in the blue-and-gold-striped vessels.

These added platforms meant extra expense. But MSTS itself was designed as a break-even operation. In the 1950s, its costs ran around $400 million a year. The Army, Navy, and Air Force paid MSTS out of their own appropriated funds at established tariff rates for cargo and passengers.

In sum, MSTS was necessary, effective, and fairly efficient, managing to substantially reduce its operating costs per cargo-ton and passenger-mile. The service was opposed by maritime unions and by those who, as in the case of civilian shipyards, believed that private enterprise could do the MSTS assignments more efficiently and less expensively. The last point was moot, but the Defense Department was not about to give up military control of this exceptionally useful pool of sealift.

On the downside, MSTS undeniably contributed to the further deterioration of an already weak American merchant marine. Also, its shipping space was often misallocated, with blistering arguments over passenger priority and optimum use of cargo stowage space. Still, MSTS had rapidly become a fixture in national maritime planning. By the late fifties, the organization was experimenting with Arctic operations, heavy-lift gear, and roll-on-roll-off (RO-RO) cargo ships.

MSTS vessels, after their work around Korea, Indochina, and the Tachens, were involved in the Suez Crisis and Lebanon. They would steam again at the time of the Berlin Crisis in 1961 and the Cuban Missile Crisis the following year. The motto of MSTS was "Service to the services," and from 1949 onward, no deployments of American troops were delayed because of a shortage of ocean transportation.[7]

In a world of seemingly endless crises, this augmented sealift, coupled with the flexibility and durability provided by underway replenishment, was no small boon to the United States Navy. Without the dependable if glamorless ServRons and the strange hybrids of MSTS, most of the missions of the fleet in the Cold War would have been sheer impossibilities.

☆

Part of the Navy's stretch was geographical and geophysical—through space and the elements. Since the days of Matthew Fontaine Maury, back before the Civil War, the Navy had needed as much weather data as possible, and by the 1950s the Naval Weather Service had outposts scattered about the world, both at sea and ashore. By 1957, Captain Paul Drouilhet had his weathermen serving the entire Navy, not just a few key stations. While the number of fleet weather centrals had been reduced from fourteen to five, their tasks had been broadened, and through more effective communication, their information load had increased as well.

Now, naval weathermen provided optimal ship track routing (OTSR), an invaluable guide for navigators; antisubmarine warfare environmental prediction (ASWEPS); determination of radar propagation patterns; and even ice forecasts. The Navy, with its limitless mission profile, needed to know the entire world's weather. The bureaucratic proof of the increasing importance of climatology came in 1958, when the weather command function within the Office of the Deputy Chief of Naval Operations for Air (OP-05) was upgraded to divisional status (OP-58).

Those ice forecasts came in handy because, in addition to the under-ice adventures of nuclear submarines at the North Pole, the Navy was moving south again, in a big way. Navymen were no strangers to the Antarctic (the exploits of Richard Byrd before World War II still registered with many Americans), and the eighteen-month International Geophysical Year in 1957 and 1958 provided yet another opportunity. A dozen countries, in celebration of the IGY, announced that they would establish one or more bases on the globe's last politically undivided continent. The United States, not to be outdone, wanted coastal bases and a glamor post smack on the South Pole itself. Civilian scientists needed to be freed for full-time work, so the Navy became the lead service in providing ship, air, and land transport, as well as providing site construction and base maintenance.

The result, Operation DEEP FREEZE, was accompanied by the somewhat withdrawn Byrd himself, now a retired rear admiral. "Commander" in name only, the sixty-eight-year-old admiral was able to spend only a few weeks in the Antarctic. (He died in Boston in March 1957.) DEEP FREEZE was no sideshow; the Antarctic enterprise sucked in men and material, draining naval resources from more "worldly" missions.

Rear Admiral George Dufek, commander of Task Force 43, was, like Byrd, an experienced Antarctic hand (he had been ducked in frigid water during a highline transfer on an earlier trip). Dufek, like King, was one of that rare breed: both a qualified submariner and an aviator. He first joined Byrd in the Antarctic in 1939, spending hours in exploratory flying over the icy wastes. He fought World War II in the Atlantic Theater, participating in the campaigns of North Africa, Sicily, Italy, and southern France before taking command of *Bogue*, in one of the new hunter-killer groups. After the war he managed to get to the Arctic and, as part of Operation HIGHJUMP, to the Antarctic again with Byrd.

A second projected Antarctic trip (HIGHJUMP II) was canceled in 1948. Despite a command tour aboard *Antietam* off Korea, Dufek's last years on active duty were routine. He seemed to be on his way out as a captain. His Antarctic experience, and the IGY, resuscitated him. Task Force 43 needed a rear admiral.

Dufek led his men in setting up a permanent base at the South Pole, on the continent's incredibly harsh high central plateau, and in putting in the large American base at McMurdo Sound. Each Antarctic summer, Fleet Weather Central McMurdo came on the air with forecasts of such accuracy that regular flight schedules to and from New Zealand and South Africa became possible.

The Navy, in the shapes of *Nautilus* and her nuclear sisters, had come to the North Pole in well-fed, snugly heated comfort. In Antarctica, a two-hundred-man crew of Seabees (handpicked from eleven thousand volunteers) worked wonders building five snowbound, partially underground towns, one right at the South Pole. Dressed in insulated thermosuits, the Seabees were rather like human experiments themselves. They whirled over the barren, snow-clad landscape in helicopters, bounced along wind-drifted ridges in their Army Weasels and Snocats, and piloted snorting mechanical sled trains along flag-marked trails where a sudden blizzard could leave a man snow-blind, then lost, then dead.

Their tricky buildings, prefabbed much like oversized Lincoln Log kits, went up at the rate of one a day. All the while, Navy and MSTS ships kept showing up at the continent's edge, after weeks spent steaming to the bottom of the world. The vessels could never get close enough to land for a real mooring—the ice was too thick. Crews chopped holes in the fifteen-foot ice carapaces and froze tethering points, called "deadmen," in them. Once the ships were moored fast to the deadmen, supplies could be unloaded and transferred to the sled trains.

Antarctica featured the granular glacial ice called névé. The Navy's initial transportation solution across this unpromising material was a squat, ugly-looking tracked vehicle, a cross between a jeep and a tank, called Ontos (Greek for "the thing"). Ontos was originally designed for the Marine Corps (which in time would want nothing to do with the thing). Meantime, Navymen hoped that Ontos would be the Antarctic's version of a dune buggy, useful for reconnaissance. Unfortunately, the first Ontos delivered got fifty feet from shipside and promptly dug its own grave in the névé. Weasels and Snocats, providing about the same luxury as a ride in a drying-machine tumbler, became the vehicles of both necessity and choice.

Always, the Navy and the civilian scientists had to fight the ice, a constantly moving, pressurized glacial mass from which great chunks sometimes calved to form icebergs, often hundreds of square miles in area. When one piece, 220 miles long and 15 miles wide, broke off, part of the base camp Little America IV went along. The snow-covered ground was inherently treacherous; gaping fissures could open without warning, threatening to swallow men and machines alike.

Despite the harrowing obstacles, the IGY went off as scheduled. Indeed, the naval presence in the Antarctic region, thanks to veteran polar explorers like Dufek, became routine—so much so that a special ribbon was created to signify duty there. No such ribbon represented Arctic service, perhaps because the naval presence there was so transient. But there too, in the form of *Nautilus*'s successors—*Skate, Sargo,* and *Seadragon*—the Navy's presence was becoming almost commonplace. In the Arctic, however, the scientific cooperation of the IGY was not in evidence, giving way to geopolitical and strategic considerations. By the late 1950s the Navy was routinely taking the measure of the Arctic, and within a few years Polaris submarines were utilizing Arctic waters as part of their cover.[8]

The Navy's reach had come to encompass, quite literally, the ends of the earth.

☆

The never-ending avalanche of technological development placed the Navy under yet more pressure. The familiar silhouettes of the warships of World War II—spare, clean, with almost engraved personalities—were vanishing fast. In their place came clutter and obfuscation, the look (not the actuality) of cabinets of bric-a-brac. There now were missile rails, ASROC launchers, festoons of radars—the latter a forest of mushrooms, mattresses, and dishes. Ceaselessly they bobbed, rotated, trained, scanned. Modern Navy ships, Hanson Baldwin waspishly noted, "looked like some futuristic doodlings of a naval designer gone mad."

The designers had not gone mad, but they had gone bigger, more powerful, and more wide-ranging than ever. By 1957 the last of the battle-wagons, *Wisconsin*, had been wrapped in mothballs, joined by dozens of escort and light carriers, gun cruisers, and smaller ships of bewildering variety. One ship remained predominant: the carrier.

During the 1950s, around fifteen attack carriers (then called CVAs) were generally available. Eleven CVAs had been used in Korea. During the most frigid years of the Cold War, American carriers steamed to practically every crisis point like iron filings drawn to a magnet: the Formosa Strait (1954–1955 and 1958), Suez (1956), Jordan (1957), Lebanon (1958), the Congo (1960), Central America (1960), Laos (1961), the Dominican Republic (1961), Thailand (1962), and Cuba (1962). Indeed, one key index of how important a "crisis" was to American policymakers was whether they dispatched a carrier to the scene.

These ships and their mix of squadrons were expected to perform a gamut of tasks. They provided air cover for opposed amphibious landings (Inchon), gave close air support (Korea), covered unopposed landings (Lebanon, Formosa, Thailand), and prepared for blockades (Nicaragua, Guatemala, Cuba). They covered evacuations, provided a nuclear strategic deterrent, transported munitions and equipment, and gave the United States a well-recognized "military presence."

—But there were only fifteen of them, and they could not be everywhere at once. To illustrate, when the shelling of Quemoy and Matsu began in August 1958, America's attack carriers were dispersed as follows: two in the eastern Mediterranean, one in the eastern Atlantic, two on the East Coast, one in East Coast overhaul, four on the West Coast, two en route to the western Pacific, and three congregated near the Formosa Strait. Clearly, the attack carriers could handle a single "crisis." But two or more "crises," or a war and a "crisis," might provide a different story.

The attack carriers got bigger and took on more missions, but their very size and expense still limited their numbers to around fifteen. By January 1959, the four *Forrestals*—the lead ship, *Saratoga*, *Ranger*, and *Independence*—were all on line. Two improved *Forrestals*—*Kitty Hawk* and *Constellation*—were commissioned in 1961, as was the nuclear-powered leviathan *Enterprise*. But for every supercarrier at sea, an attack carrier went to the boneyard or was reconfigured for antisubmarine warfare. Lesser carriers were assigned lesser crises, as when *Wasp* was stationed off the Congo in the summer of 1960 to cover the evacuation of American nationals if necessary.

Fifteen attack carriers scattered around the globe were only the most obvious examples of the stretch. Naval aviation ceaselessly sought more speed, maneuverability, and range. As the aircraft became more complex, so did their maintenance and repair. Obsolescence was virtually built in; during 1957 alone, two thousand naval aircraft were declared obsolete. Increasing unit expense, mostly attributable to aspects like metallurgy and avionics, meant that smaller quantitites of high-performance planes could be ordered. Navy funding in 1958 bought 587 fewer aircraft than in the previous year.

Some aircraft designs, like the jet-powered Martin P6M Seamaster, were wiped out by Polaris or their own conceptual deficiencies. Others, like long-range, conventional-engine seaplanes, went the way of the dinosaur, along with their tenders. The Navy had some rivalry between its carrier and land-based aviation, but the latter could be supplemented by smaller carriers in an ASW role. Still, fewer airframes were being packed with more expensive sensors and weapons, and even a Mach 2 A-5 Vigilante, like its carrier deck, could be in only one place at one time.

The six- and eight-inch-gun cruisers were also being laid up right and left. Most of those that remained, like *Boston* and *Canberra*, were being equipped with Terrier, Tartar, and Talos missiles. Their new mission was to run with the carriers and provide fleet air defense. In the 1950s, however,

what was to be defended against was decidedly problematic, and so reconfigured cruisers, like the carriers, were assigned a host of widely varied
missions connected with "crises." As individual units, these ships were
conditioned by their officers and men to run as efficiently as possible; Programmed Integrated System Maintenance (PRISM), the ancestor of the
Navy's excellent Preventive Maintenance System, was created in 1953
aboard *Des Moines* by Chief Fire Control Technician C.E. Satterwhite. But
as a collective group, the Navy's dwindling number of cruisers and hundreds
of senescent small boys felt the strain of Cold War deployments as well.[9]

Most of the stretch was hidden from the American public, partially
through service pride and publicity, partially because the Navy did not
want to be seen crying wolf, and partially because the service had been *too*
successful in selling the capacities of its new technological marvels. "The
Navy [is] more formidable than ever and far more vital to the nation's
survival," applauded *Newsweek* in 1956. "It's a Jules Verne and Buck Rogers
Navy," enthused Baldwin, and with the same mission: "to control the seas,
deny their free use to the enemy, to use them freely ourselves." And, lest
the point be lost, Baldwin added that "this is a mission of immutable permanence, for as far into the future as man can see."

Visions of modern war multiplied naval roles in every dimension—sea,
air, and land. The Navy was expected to wage every facet of air war,
including strategic bombing; fight the submarine; blockade enemy coasts;
attack enemy shipping; engage mines; conduct amphibious assault; resupply
itself; and, for good measure, support the other services. These roles contained cosmic, indeed infinite, dimensions. (Outer space would soon be
added.) And only excruciatingly finite men and machines were available to
fill them.

The Navy was thus caught in the prop wash of its own highly advertised
versatility and flexibility. As the "prepared for everything, do anything"
service, the Navy had imposed much of the pressure on itself. Its officers
and men were keyed to operate at unprecedented levels of efficiency; its
"day's work" took place all around the world, and from top to bottom; its
ships, bragged *Life*, "can respond to crises, large or small, with anything
from a helping hand to a clenched fist."

—So the strain went unnoticed by most Americans. But strain there
was, and the Navy paid a huge price under its pressure, even if measured
only by the turnover in highly skilled officer and enlisted personnel. In
fairness, however, many people thrived on the never-ending, pressure-filled
routine, and other rewards came as well. There were always those like
Seaman John Dunworth, aboard the eight-inch-gun cruiser *Newport News*,
who could say, "I joined the Navy . . . looking for adventure, and I want
my money's worth."[10]

☆

Much of the "money's worth" lay in research and development. By the late 1950s, the old civilian office of the coordinator of research and development, which dated back to mid-1941, had become that of the assistant secretary of the Navy for research and development. His uniformed assistant now wore three stars, as deputy chief of naval operations for development. Thus fortified, Navy R and D continued its unmatched policy of advancing an amazing variety of basic research projects, to the extent that applause came from distinguished civilian scientists of the caliber of Robert Bucher, Lee DuBridge, and Enrico Fermi.

The projects, in their plenitude, were also an index of the Navy's stretch. Aviation, surface propulsion, aerology, antisubmarine warfare, mines, amphibious assault, medicine, supply, and earth satellites were only a few of the areas in which the Navy evinced intense interest and for which the service opened its wallet. William Franke noted with pleasure that the IGY's worldwide scientific effort seemed merely to parallel the Navy's own research program. There were experiments and studies in nuclear and molecular physics, astronomy, astrophysics, mathematics, chemistry, psychology, and operations research. Nevertheless, "additional scientific research is now even more essential," Franke ominously warned.

In particular, naval weaponry received the most emphasis. Families of guided missiles proliferated like protozoans; rockets and munitions evolved in accuracy and lethality; Polaris mutations blossomed; underwater weapons developed into a subset of devastation all their own, with nifty acronyms like SUBROC (an antisubmarine underwater and aerial guided missile) and RAT (rocket-assisted torpedo).

Nuclear weapons loomed large at the top of the list; the Navy called these appallingly sinister devices Special Weapons. With the Korean buildup, Eisenhower probably inherited an arsenal of around 1500 nuclear weapons, relatively few of these belonging to the Navy. By 1959, the Atomic Energy Commission was believed to have produced around 4500 more, ranging in yield from a few kilotons to many megatons—a rate of production of more than two per day. The three huge production plants for atomic material—at Oak Ridge, Tennessee, Paducah, Kentucky, and Portsmouth, Ohio—together used six million kilowatts of electrical energy when they ran full blast. In the mid-1950s, this load amounted to 12 percent of the electrical demand of the entire United States. In 1955, Eisenhower ordered some of these weapons dispersed overseas, to "limit the effects of surprise attack." Arthur Radford protested; he was especially concerned with storage in areas like England, from where, perhaps, "we could not use [nuclear weapons] freely in case of attack."

The proliferation and miniaturization of nuclear weapons meant that the Navy's proportionate share of the devices increased. The Navy, of course, had no storage problems on foreign soil. Attack carriers routinely carried nuclear weapons by the mid-1950s. Nuclear mines and depth charges were designed, and the *Gearing*-class destroyer *Agerholm* made the only test-firing of a nuclear depth charge, on 11 May 1962. A nuclear projectile for the eight-inch naval gun, to match the Army's gun weapon, was developed, although on second thought this was considered not a very good idea and was never deployed. Polaris boats carried nuclear megatonnage as their raison d'être.

To this degree, at the end of the Navy's worldwide stretch lurked dooms-day. Out there, at the very fingertips of naval power, was lethal force un-matched in earlier generations. Even Cold War politicians (Senator Mike Mansfield of Montana was a case in point) could have second thoughts about so much power, so ready to use, so far from home.[11]

Beneath the nuclear threshhold, R and D burst forward along paths both well-worn and new. Among the former, mine warfare enjoyed a brief renaissance in the wake of the Korean disaster. The major lesson from Wonsan had been that even fields of primitive contact mines, primitively laid, could bring naval operations to a standstill. Furthermore, the loss of minesweepers to magnetic mines off Wonsan called forth a new ship design, which emerged as the 172-foot *Aggressive* class, designated ocean mine-sweepers (MSOs) in 1955. The *Aggressives* featured wooden hulls, improved degaussing, and enhanced electrical-generating capacity for magnetic sweep-ing. They were, in the 1950s, the "Cadillacs of the international mine fleet."

Coastal minesweepers (MSCs) were also built, 159 of them. They were 144 feet in length, with controllable-pitch propellers and separate engines to generate more power for magnetic sweeps. All but 20 went overseas under the Military Defense Assistance Program (most of them to NATO allies). But only one new minehunter, *Bittern*, was commissioned. Experiments also began with helicopters towing minesweeping gear in "precursor sweeps."

During these halcyon days for a usually neglected arm, the Navy de-veloped a complete program of new ocean, coastal, and small-boat mine-sweepers; converted some minehunters; and reactivated several mine-warfare vessels. By the late fifties, the total strength of the mine community came to 333 ships (180 of these new, 93 on active service).

In 1951, the Office of Naval Research contracted with Catholic Uni-versity to form the Mine Advisory Committee of the National Academy of Sciences. Many of the ideas of the next few years were initiated or examined by this group: mine countermeasures, precision navigation, high-resolution sonar, helicopter minesweeping. One brainstorm, the experimental mag-netic, acoustic, and pressure sweep (XMAP), was supposed to be a mine-warfare smorgasbord. Tug-towed, the device was expected to be able to counter any type of mine in a single sweep. XMAP swept up plenty of money but little else, and was finally discarded in 1961. Pressure mines, in particular, were proving to be the modern mineman's bugaboo; they were virtually unsweepable.

Briefly, also, mine warfare attracted high-quality officers and men, people who came to love the loosey-goosey life-style on the small ships and gloried in the additional early responsibility. But their MSOs had major problems with brittle, unreliable, aluminum and stainless steel nonmagnetic diesel engines; the wooden construction added to fire hazards (any fire aboard a minesweeper was an instant life-and-death situation); and the minesweepers could do only fourteen knots in an era when the Navy was getting faster and deploying ever forward. Furthermore, the flurry of mine-warfare developments had been shock-produced by Korea, rather than being part of a continuous evolution. There was no sustained naval commitment to mines or mine countermeasures.

Everyone, right up to Burke, mouthed the platitudes about the necessity of a strong mine-warfare capability. But like the ServRons, the mine community stood at the end of the budget line. After 1958, the Polaris ax bit deeply into the minemen's budget. Mine warfare receded once again into a naval backwater, where "it had a slightly fetid smell," as Vice Admiral Robert Salzer recalled. "People were not working very hard."

Unlike XMAP, however, some Navy R and D really did limn the future. Experiments were conducted with "surface effects" platforms, hovercraft skimming over the water on a cushion of air. The idea had its skeptics, but its zealots kept pushing (and would for years to come). Underwater demolition teams looped, rolled, and dived in the Mark VI MiniSub, a scaled-down underwater version of a jet fighter. Novel forms of munitions and propulsion and dozens of other items of interest all struggled to get their day in court. Some never got attention. Some, like XMAP, were dismal failures. And some, like the hovercraft, would not emerge until the next generation. Almost all, however, took up some of the Navy's time—and money.

Of all the technological developments short of nuclear power and Polaris, the one with the greatest operational impact was doubtless the sound surveillance system (SOSUS). Cable-laying ships first began to install the strings of underwater hydrophonic ears in the 1950s, literally "bugging" the world's seaways and shipping choke points. The strings were planted along the American coasts and the approaches to the Panama Canal, then strewn off Iceland, the Aleutians, and eventually a considerable portion of the Soviet coastline. By the mid-sixties, no Russian submarine could leave the Barents Sea or the Sea of Okhotsk without lighting up SOSUS, which in turn fed its data through shore stations to the fleet commanders and the Pentagon.

SOSUS tentacles were eventually strung for thousands of miles, from the Bering Strait to the Baja Peninsula, from North Cape to Cuba. Technicians listened twenty-four hours a day, tuned in to the sounds of the sea, marine mammals, anything that made noise in the depths. SOSUS was a technological success story, one of the few postwar developments that eased the stretch by making possible a more knowledgeable positioning of American naval forces.[12]

—For, above all, those technicians were listening for the sounds of Russian submarines.

☆

The oceans were a greater mystery than outer space. Seawater was opaque to electromagnetic radiation, was corrosive, and was heavy (which meant instrumentation problems at greater depths). Everything eventually wore out underwater; SOSUS repair, for example, became a mini-industry. The only viable enemy the Navy could perceive in the 1950s moved in this element. So, of all the tactical factors that increased the Navy's stretch, antisubmarine warfare received the most attention.

In the opinion of one theoretical physicist writing in 1959, "the modern submarine in its various roles in limited and all-out war represents the greatest present military threat to the United States." No one knew exactly how many submarines the Russians had, exactly what these submarines could do, or what they were *supposed* to do. But the Russian boats numbered in the hundreds. The Soviets were beginning to produce nuclear submarines to go with their German-inspired, top-of-the-line diesel-electrics. All, nuclear or diesel-electric, could benefit from the shielding properties of the sea. Most of the successful World War II ASW techniques—air search, sonar ranging, electronic countermeasures, and the like—had been now largely invalidated by higher underwater speeds and greater endurance. Radar could no longer be counted on for detection. Even if an enemy sub was fixed and within the greatly extended range of modern sensors and weapons, its destruction was still highly problematical. Even a nuclear depth charge had a kill radius of only about a mile—the merest bubble amid the vastness of the sea.

The technology of detection (of which SOSUS was an important part) was the key to successful antisubmarine warfare. ASW, to be effective, also had to be an *integrated* art, not only of machines and weapons but of men as well—involving surface, air, and underwater platforms. The balancing and interplay of all these elements, dedicated to the task of finding, fixing, tracking, attacking, and destroying the submarine, was what ASW was all about.

Destroyers were the classic enemies of the submarine. Sonarmen aboard the new *Forrest Shermans* boasted that they could hear shrimp feeding, guppies mating, or subs snorkeling at ranges of tens of thousands of yards. This was "passive," or listening, sonar. "Active" sonar sent out sound waves from the ship's transducer dome (usually, but not always, bow-mounted) and timed the return echo, or "ping," to estimate the range and bearing on the unknown underwater object. When the cans attacked, they had depth-charge guns (Weapon Able, later Weapon Alfa) that lofted packages of explosives hundreds of yards ahead of the ship, where they would sink until hydrostatically detonated. Homing torpedoes with sonar brains ("active homers") were also available. ASROC, with its Mark 44 torpedo (later the Mark 46), was coming on line.

Some destroyers had their after mounts removed to make room for helicopter platforms. Helos were beginning to be integrated into the ASW game in the late fifties; their dipping, or variable depth, sonar (VDS) enabled surface forces to hear under thermoclines in the ocean. VDS was installed on some surface vessels as well. Fixed-wing aircraft, flying from both shore bases and carriers, featured the extended-boom magnetic anomaly detector (MAD gear) and were becoming regular participants in the hunt. Finally, although the SSKs were not produced in any great quantity, the notion of an "antisubmarine submarine" persisted, since only a sub could truly sense and catch another sub under all those thermal layers.

Thus, a considerable arsenal was being directed to the ASW problem— but nothing was working very well. As commander of the Atlantic Fleet in 1957, Jerry Wright readily admitted that antisubmarine warfare was his number one concern. This was no secret to the rest of the Navy either, and early in 1958 Burke flew to Norfolk to meet with Wright, who knew the other side of the game well. In 1942, Wright had been a "co-commander" of a British submarine that had helped smuggle Mark Clark into North Africa as part of the cloak-and-dagger preliminaries for Operation TORCH. Four other top ASW commanders gathered for the conference. At the meeting, Burke, the master destroyerman, wanted to know why the Navy's antisubmarine warfare effort, despite all the high tech, was so weak and ineffective.

In response, a tanned, lanky, big-eared admiral stood up and began a litany. The equipment was obsolescent, he said; there were no antisub submarines, and the personnel were leaving faster than they could be trained. The chief of naval operations sat patiently, palm wrapped around his warm pipe, listening. At the end of the spiel, Burke replied with characteristic directness: "Jimmy Thach made an unfortunate speech—he just talked himself into a job. . . ."

—Here was the old Navy game; let the griper provide the solution. As he had done thirty months before with Red Raborn, Burke unerringly tapped the right man. Rear Admiral John Smith ("Jimmy") Thach was an outstanding naval aviator with more than six thousand hours of flight time. At the Naval Academy he had followed his older brother, James Harmon Thach, Jr., who became a vice admiral and responded to the nickname "Jimmy." The younger Thach was at first "Little Jimmy," but the adjective quickly dropped away; there was, as things turned out, nothing "little" about his exploits in the cockpit.

The second Jimmy Thach was an undistinguished mid, a varsity wrestler with a trick shoulder, but after his graduation in 1927 a ride in a yellow twin-engine H-16 fixated him on naval aviation. In 1930 he joined Fighting 1, the famed High Hats, then skippered by Radford. The High Hats barnstormed the nation in Curtiss F8C4 Helldivers, stunting through loops, snap rolls, and high wingovers with their planes tied, wingtip to wingtip, with Manila rope. They flew all the stunt scenes in the movie *Hell Divers* (1931), Radford himself acting as the flying stand-in for Clark Gable.

Thach matured quickly as a naval aviator. When he left the High Hats, he became an ace test pilot. He could fly anything, make the clumsiest planes do tricks. He flew patrol duty in the Aleutians in drafty Martin PBM-1s ("the bearskin flying suits stank like hell," he remembered), was catapulted (like Raborn) in SOC-1s off the cruiser *Cincinnati*, and patrolled the Canal Zone in PBYs. Promoted to the command of *Saratoga's* Fighting 3, he would invite his green aviators to mock dogfights, challenging them to "stay on my tail." Then, insouciantly munching an apple in his cockpit, he would give them the advantage of altitude and usually evade their attacks with little sweat.

Like all great aviators, Thach had more than a touch of arrogance, but he was also *thinking* all the time about what he was doing in the air, and about what the other guy was trying to do. In the early days of World War II, as skipper of Fighting 3 (now aboard the old *Lexington*), Thach devised a two-plane gunnery maneuver based on interlocking fields of aerial fire (the Thach weave) that brought down nineteen out of twenty attacking Japanese Bettys at Coral Sea. When a Mark II Zero was downed practically unscathed at Dutch Harbor, the plane was put back into operation, and he refined his tactics against this once-feared foe.

Thach went on to become a carrier task force operations officer, first for Pete Mitscher, then for Slew McCain. He was, by all accounts, the Navy's finest aerial tactician in World War II, and at the end, he stood there aboard *Missouri* to watch the Japanese surrender. After the war, he command *Sicily* during Korea and served in the Pentagon as the senior naval member of the Defense Department's Weapons Systems Evaluation Group.

Burke ordered Thach to organize a new unit "to write the book on ASW tactics." As he had done with Raborn, Burke delivered a caution: Thach's book, he said, was "to have a happy ending." Wright immediately issued a new directive to his command: "The primary mission of every combat ship in the Atlantic Fleet is antisubmarine warfare. Everything else is secondary."

For his task, Thach had his flagship, *Valley Forge*, eleven other major combatants, an S2F Tracker squadron, a helicopter squadron, two submarines, some blimps, and five thousand men. Thach ordered his artist yeoman to draw a command insignia, a large "A" with a jagged bolt of lightning flaring across. He directed that the insignia be in black and white—no gray. In ASW, said Thach, "we want everything to be black and white.

It's either a friendly sub or an enemy sub and you either sink it or you don't."

Task Force Alfa, formed on 1 April 1958, had as its mission to experiment with new ways to get at Soviet "goblins" (the underwater term for unidentified contacts, analogous to "bogeys" for air contacts and "skunks" for surface contacts). Burke gave them full support; "If Alfa wants beefsteak for breakfast," he intoned, "give 'em beefsteak." Thach had a different metaphor. "This is like a chess game," he reasoned. "Each piece has a different value. By playing them together, by using the submarine—which has the biggest ears—and the aircraft—which has the longest punch—and the airship—which has the quietest touch—you win your game."[13]

The hunter-killer concept had long preceded Task Force Alfa, dating back to the stationing of escort carriers with transatlantic convoys in 1943. No element in Thach's experimental group was really new, either, with the possible exception of the antisubmarine submarine, and that idea ran smack up against an almost insurmountable problem: underwater-to-surface communication, which was only barely possible—sometimes—when the sub was close to the surface (with a device called Jezebel) but got hairier the deeper the sub went. The antisubmarine submarine, both because of lack of numbers and the technological problems, turned out to be, despite Thach's chess-game metaphor, a no-show. Blimps were also on their way out in the late fifties. So Task Force Alfa was left, for the most part, with a sub-hunting quartet composed of destroyers, helicopters, carrier fixed-wing aircraft, and land-based air.

Work was especially needed on combined ASW tactics, the successful integration of these different platforms, sensors, and weapons systems through doctrine, timing, and, above all, communication. Under Thach, Task Force Alfa became uniformly offensive-minded; the accent in hunter-killer was on the "hunt." "If I can find him and identify him," said Jimmy Thach, "I can kill him."

—That was the critical problem: underwater detection. There would be, unlike the miracles of Raborn's Polaris project, no magic breakthroughs in antisubmarine warfare—only incremental gains at best. Every means of underwater detection (sound, electrical, magnetic, and electromagnetic) was severely limited in both range and capability. Sonar, the Navy's primary underwater ear, was notoriously unreliable. Passive sonar was an aural vacuum cleaner that registered practically every noise in the sea, a bewildering cacophony that even highly trained technicians had trouble sorting out. Active sonar often had its sound waves deflected or distorted by thermoclines, the water's surface, or the ocean bottom. In addition, pinging was extremely limited in its effective range, particularly in what sonarmen commonly called "bad water." "Good water" might produce useful pings out to four or five thousand yards.

Thach's experiments with Task Force Alfa, carried out in rigorous at-sea conditions, showed the Navy how far an ASW program had to go to be credible and effective. Slowly, both newer sonars and the MAD gear began to show improved range. More reliable electronic equipment started to arrive. Synthetic trainers and automatic data displays made their appearance. In the midst of all this, Thach was preaching doctrine—all hands on the same page—and reliable communications.

As the doctrine and communications took hold, the carrier-based Grumman S2F Trackers and the Sikorsky HSS-1 helicopters with their dipping sonars began to prove their worth. Both could also sow sonobuoys (floating sonar miniplatforms with communications antennas). The Tracker, the Navy's first all-weather carrier-based ASW plane, was a hunter-killer all by itself. The plane carried MAD gear, sonobuoys, and a complete arsenal of bombs, torpedoes, depth charges, and rockets; a pair of powerful, 1525-horsepower, nine-cylinder Wright engines gave the bulb-nosed, wide-winged Tracker tremendous lift and exceptional endurance at the required low altitudes.

The Navy even experimented with "sniffer gear" to sense exhaust fumes from a sub's snorkel, much like the exhaust-gas analyzer used by a mechanic tuning up an automobile engine. Sniffers, of course, were useless against nukes, and experiments began with both heat and radiation sensors, which were to become much more important as time went on.[14]

Thach worked his men hard. "We pay overtime," he proclaimed with a typically wry twist, "after twenty-four hours a day." His own naval generation was haunted by the specter of Hitler's submarines, the bitter memory of what a relative handful of U-boats had been able to accomplish in the Atlantic. Now Soviet subs were seemingly popping up all over the chart; in the last six months of 1957, there were 186 separate reports of what might have been Russian boats in the western Atlantic. Nikita Khrushchev, with his penchant for bombast, did not help any when he boasted that "our submarines can block American ports and shoot into the American interior, while our rockets can reach any target. America's vital centers are just as vulnerable as NATO bases."

So Task Force Alfa got its beefsteak, working overtime to detect those Russian submarines and keep them in constant contact for up to four days (after which time a diesel-electric would be forced to surface for lack of oxygen). An Alfa search area, whether involving an active Russian sub or a games-playing American one, resembled Times Square at rush hour. Up to eight destroyers could be converging on a "datum" (the last known position of the submarine) in two diamond formations, an inner and an outer screen; HSS-1s could be scurrying about on all sides, dunking their sonars and then resolutely moving on to a new location; S2F Trackers could be vectoring close overhead, MAD booms extended, pulling up at the last moment to avoid destroyer masts. Communication nets could be constantly crackling with updated information.

After six months of work in 1958, Task Force Alfa—which previously would have counted itself lucky to have held a submarine contact for as long as thirty minutes—was successfully following submarines for up to eight hours. This was far from four days, but eight hours could mean the difference between a sighting and a kill. "They're much, much better," judged Lieutenant Commander Joe Bonds, the skipper of one of their games-playing foes, *Sea Leopard*.

Alfa's track record was mixed, but not for any lack of trying on the part of Thach and his men. The basic reason was well—if backhandedly—stated by the admiral's chief of staff, Captain Thomas McGrath. "A most encouraging feature," McGrath summarized, "is that there is so much room for progress."

This understatement withheld several factors. For one thing, despite Burke's promise of beefsteak, there was never enough money. (As the Navy was trying to persuade Congress to increase the budget for ASW, the cartoon hero Buzz Sawyer was effortlessly chasing a Soviet nuclear submarine off the American coast.) For another, practically all the prodigious assets of Task Force Alfa were necessary to find, fix, and track a *single* diesel-electric submarine. What hundreds of coordinated underwater locusts could do to any ASW effort boggled the mind. And experiments with *Nautilus* and her sisters had strongly suggested that fast-running and deep-diving nuclear submarines were able to toy with surface and air ASW forces just about any time they chose. Some analysts admitted that the only instance in which a nuke could be found was when the boat signified itself by releasing a weapon—a gloomy prognostication for the ASW art.

In 1960 a veteran submariner, Commander George Steele, confessed that "after six years of operating nuclear submarines, we still do not have at sea a weapon system able to cope with even one of them." This admission certainly increased confidence in the invulnerability of the Navy's fleet ballistic missile submarines but did nothing to substantiate the intense focus on ASW. Still, the effort was well worth making. Task Force Alfa had not been on the wrong track; barring breakthroughs in new sensor systems, Thach and his men had been on the *only* track, one strewn with obstacles and frustrations every step of the way.[15]

Antisubmarine warfare would remain of intense interest to the United States Navy, and the art would always present fundamental problems in integrated tactics. But antisubmarine warfare carriers (CVSs), like Thach's Happy Valley, were aging, World War II hulls; during the 1960s, these pillars of the HUK groups began to be decommissioned. No dedicated ASW carriers would take their places. Instead, the ASW function was added to CVAs. As a result, these supercarriers would take on more missions than ever, and their squadron mix in the carrier air wing would be ever more critical.

Despite the Navy's clear recognition of a significant potential naval threat, the laws of physics and the budgets of man provided enormous roadblocks. The considerable effort in antisubmarine warfare, while producing some increased effectiveness, in the end only added to the dimensions of the stretch.

☆

In 1961, when Burke stepped down after his record-breaking six years as chief of naval operations, he left to his successor and to the incoming Kennedy administration a naval force certainly without peer, but also without rival. "My navy" was predominant across the board—in geographical spread, technological development, and operational flexibility. Never had its vaunted claim to be shield of the republic, the first line of national defense, held more truth.

Concealed, however, was the ominous reality of a service under the most severe strain. Its tensions were caused by budget decisions, both internal and external; mission demands on a global scale; and a "can-do" orientation that mandated omnibus patterns of response to provide any level of naval presence or naval force. For the most part, guided by Navy public relations, Americans saw only the successes—from pole to pole, from the Med to WestPac.

—These successes were both many and merited, but they disguised a deeper—and troubling—Cold War reality.

CHAPTER THIRTY

TOPSIDE IV

———— ☆ ————

I n early 1961, for the first time in the nation's history, a former naval
officer moved into the White House. The two Roosevelts had had experience as naval bureaucrats, but not until the inauguration of John
Fitzgerald Kennedy did a man with an operational naval background reach
the presidency. The Harvard-educated Kennedy had been a Naval Reservist
in World War II. A possibly apocryphal story about him in this regard
surfaced in the 1950s. He had been kept on the rolls of the Naval Reserve
after the war, but as he moved ahead in politics, first as a representative
from Massachusetts and then as senator, he had found little time for drill
participation. A naval promotion board duly rejected him. (The Army and
Air Force routinely lubed the promotion rails for their politico reservists.)
When Kennedy wrote the department asking why he had not been promoted, the Navy (so the story went) replied with a routine form letter stating
that he had failed to meet basic requirements for participation. —So much
for political clout.

Nevertheless, both Kennedy's interest in the sea and his operational
experience were honestly earned. Born in 1917 to wealth and privilege, the
second son of a remarkably aggressive and upwardly mobile Boston Irishman, Joseph Kennedy, young Jack learned early to love seafaring and its
lore. His older brother, Joseph junior, with whom he competed intensely,
taught him to sail. He began a cherished collection of scrimshaw, parts of
whales' teeth etched and sometimes dyed with sailing ship designs. He
favored seascapes in art and was quick to decorate his presidential offices
with naval paintings, ship models, and naval flags. He also treasured a plaque
given him by Hyman Rickover (one naval officer who really did know how
to cultivate politicians), on which was inscribed the famous prayer of Breton
fishermen: "O, God, thy sea is so great, and my boat is so small." To his
delight, his wife, Jacqueline, rummaging in the White House basement,
found a magnificent desk hewn from the timbers of HMS *Resolute*, presented
by Queen Victoria to Rutherford Hayes back in 1878. Refurbished, the
desk made its way to Kennedy's office within a month of his inaugural.

Even before Pearl Harbor, the young man who would become "JFK" tried to get into the Army, but he was rejected because of a chronically bad back. He and his father, by now a multimillionaire and former ambassador to England, pulled every wire they could grab, including one leading to Captain Alan Kirk, then director of Naval Intelligence, to get him and his older brother into a Navy uniform. (After the war, his younger brother Robert also did a brief stint as a naval enlisted man.) The wires led to the right places; Jack was on the reserve roles when the Japanese struck. He should not have been; his back should have disqualified him from naval service.

More of Kennedy senior's wire-pulling—which involved none other than James Forrestal—and his own remarkable energy got JFK from behind a desk, in the office of Naval Intelligence, to sea duty. (While at ONI, he was almost cashiered because of his love affair with Danish-born Inga Arvad, a woman who had friends among the Nazi leadership.) He chose torpedo boats, the most exciting and dangerous assignment he could find. In the Pacific, learning his trade in this fast-and-loose mosquito fleet, he went through the Solomon Islands, Tulagi, and Rendova. The PT Navy in these waters divided itself informally into Ivy Leaguers and the "Weed League"— those from schools like Georgia Tech—and in the intramural chaffing, Kennedy gave as much as he took. The pounding his back took aboard the PTs forced him to wear a corset. Like so many of the reserve officers of his generation, he rose to command one of the eighty-foot cockleshells—*PT-109.*

In early August 1943, in the midst of the darkness of the Ferguson Passage, *PT-109* was sliced in half by the Japanese destroyer *Amagiri*, dumping Kennedy and his crew into waters ablaze with burning gasoline. Thus commenced an adventure during which the young skipper towed one of his crew ashore by means of a lifebelt gripped between his teeth, kept his men alive during days and nights of excruciating peril, and cheered them on until rescue finally came.

The saga of *PT-109*, which JFK's longtime friend, the journalist Robert Donovan, enshrined in a best-selling book, outlined the Kennedy mystique: the preoccupations with daring, courage, and will, the intrinsic nobility of suffering and enduring, the studied nonchalance of accomplishment, and the inherent morality of "a man who does what he must." Kennedy's religious upbringing and his own physical pain also had given him a certain sensibility about death and duty and about how the two might be related; to make the first palatable, the second must be done.

A surface casualness masked the deeper concerns. Part of the young JFK was sheer rakehell, with women, ships, anything that came along—a common characteristic of privileged young men. He was fond of racing *PT-109* against other boats, for example, at least until one such contest in the Russell Islands, when his reverse gear failed and his pygmy command plowed into a gasoline dock, earning him the attention of his squadron leader.

Much more seriously, Navymen could see in the famous *PT-109* incident something other than what the saga, perpetually embellished as JFK rose to power, implied. *PT-109* was the *only* patrol craft ever hit by a Japanese destroyer during the Pacific war. That particular night, Kennedy's command was part of a three-boat picket line that was *expecting* Japanese destroyers. Yet when the collision came, at 0200 on 2 August, two of Kennedy's men were asleep, and two were lying on deck. Visibility was almost one mile. Kennedy was radioed about a bow wake heading toward him; he gave no response. His squadron commander, Thomas Warfield, was later to describe him as "not a particularly good boat commander."

Kennedy's recommendation for a Silver Star was "for the survival phase," pointedly remarked his commanding officer, Albin Cluster, "not the preceding battle." Only the three officers present received medals, although several enlisted men had performed heroically as well. Kennedy eventually received the lesser Navy and Marine Corps Medal, and then, apparently, only through a second intervention by Forrestal. Within the Navy the loss of *PT-109* was "something of a scandal." "Kennedy had the most maneuverable vessel in the world," recalled one PT squadron leader. "All that power and yet this knight in white armor managed to have his PT boat rammed by a destroyer. Everybody in the fleet laughed about that."[1]

Kennedy emerged from his wartime service an authentic and becomingly modest hero. "Modest" he should have been; he had been callow, reckless, and careless in command, although his heroism was never in question. On his chest was the Navy and Marine Corps Medal; in his heart was a burning desire, ceaselessly stoked by his hyperambitious father, to succeed in politics. The death of his older brother (on a typically macho bombing mission over Europe) had left him as the focus of the patriarch's passionate politicking. He was ideal as a novitiate in Boston politics: young, rail-thin and handsome, Irish to the last blarney, a war hero and a bachelor. He campaigned tirelessly. "My story about the collision is getting better all the time," he told friends. "Now I've got a Jew and a nigger in the story, and with me being a Catholic, that's great." Voting matrons may well have provided his edge at the ballot box; he entered Congress in 1946.

Kennedy shone neither as a congressman nor as a senator; his roll-call record was poor, and he initiated few bills of merit. In his third term in the House, he was among the bottom four members in attendance. The backlog of business in his office was perpetual. In fairness, during this period he was diagnosed with Addison's disease, a condition in which the adrenal cortex produced insufficient hormones. This debilitating affliction he hid from the public, which knew only the story of the bad back.

In 1952 Kennedy defeated another Massachusetts scion, Henry Cabot Lodge, Jr., for a Senate seat. This was not so much a reward for merit as a recognition of his *political* skills, in the cultivation of which (the *how* of getting elected) he was proving a veritable prodigy. (He never lost a political race, only his premature bid for the vice presidential nomination in 1956.)

After his landslide reelection to the Senate in 1958, only his religion seemed to limit his political future. In the presidential campaign of 1960 against Richard Nixon, he defused the Catholic issue enough to win convincingly in the electoral college, 303–219. His popular margin, a little over one hundred thousand in the more than sixty-eight million votes cast, was something else again, and did much to make him exceptionally cautious on domestic issues, particularly civil rights.

Kennedy came to the presidency with his love of the sea undiminished. He had paid little attention to naval affairs while in Congress (most of his time was spent in affairs both political and personal), but the attachment was still there. When he visited a Navy ship overnight, he liked to pace the deck in the darkness: "I want to feel the salt on my face." He preferred to keep Navy chiefs around him as physical therapists, directing his exercises in the heated water of the White House pool. JFK was even tolerant of Navy pomp and could walk a reviewing line with the best of them. "He almost converted me to being a Democrat," confessed Slade Cutter—"which was unthinkable."

But in the sense of marking him for his conduct of the presidency, the Navy had influenced him little if at all. Rather, the shaping elements in this regard he shared with most of his generation. They were branded with the "lessons" of appeasement, the coming of World War II, and the rise of the Soviet superpower. To JFK's way of thinking, and those of most of the men with whom he surrounded himself, only toughness could face down international communism. As a senator, he had continually sought increases in military spending. He backed away from the Joe McCarthy fracas; disgracefully, he was the only Senate Democrat who failed to vote or pair on the McCarthy censure. His frail health was no excuse.

For Kennedy, there was no substitute for strength in international affairs, nor for the ultimate willingness to use that strength; anything less would be a retreat from America's proper role in the world. Communism was the enemy—insidious, vicious, immoral, and attempting to advance on a global scale, wherever democracies or struggling new states were weakest. A powerful United States was the sine qua non, the necessary bulwark of the "free world."

—These were vague, superficial, sometimes mistaken, and (as time would show) downright dangerous ideas. But to JFK and many in his generation, now risen to national leadership, they were the hard-earned lessons of the years of Hitler's rise and fall. The mantle of the Third Reich, in terms of raw international aggression, had descended on the Kremlin. Much of Kennedy's conduct of foreign affairs was to be diplomacy and the use of military force by analogy.

Kennedy's rhetoric on these international issues was full-blown. "I wasn't the vice president who presided over the communization of Cuba," he trumpeted during the campaign against Nixon, as if the Republican candidate had been right out there in the Sierra Maestra planning guerrilla operations alongside Fidel Castro. The Eisenhower years, said JFK, might be judged as "the days when the tide began to run out for the United States. These were the times when the Communist tide began to pour in." In Congress, he had always been an ardent Cold Warrior, but occasionally, particularly under the pressure of his presidential campaign, he sounded like a younger clone of John Foster Dulles. "The enemy is the Communist system itself—implacable, unceasing in its drive for world domination," he informed his fellow Americans in 1960. "For this is not a struggle for the supremacy of arms alone—it is also a struggle for supremacy between two conflicting ideologies: Freedom under God versus ruthless, godless tyranny."

Then there was the famous Inaugural Address, much admired in its day but later, with a generation of historical perspective, to appear in a far different and more baleful light. Kennedy characterized his generation as "tempered by war" and "disciplined by a hard and bitter peace." Lest anyone doubt the new administration's commitment, he then pronounced the cadenced, moving (and in retrospect, highly frightening) words: "Let every nation know that we shall pay any price, bear any burden, meet any hardship, support any friend, oppose any foe to assure the survival and the success of liberty."

There was substance underneath these oratorical vapors. These men of Kennedy's "New Frontier" would be activists, hands-on leaders. (Their court historian, Arthur Schlesinger, Jr., would later call activism their "besetting sin.") Taking their tone from their leader, they styled themselves as tough, talented, quick, precise—people who made *decisions*, who got things *moving*. Kennedy set the pace, profanely. ("Kennedy uses profanity with the unconcern of a sailor," wrote Fletcher Knebel, "which he was and is.") The journalist David Halberstam would call them the "best and the brightest," a description with which most of the New Frontiersmen, not sensing the deep irony, would have agreed in 1961.

—But never publicly. Energy counted, but so did style, the cool detachment of a duck gliding with seeming effortlessness over the pond while, underneath the surface, its webbed feet were paddling frantically. The people JFK brought to Washington were rapidly labeled, particularly by a nervous conservative press, as proto–New Dealers, meaning that they favored the passionate involvement of government in everyday life, with the goal of setting things right for average citizens. But in fact, the New Frontier, while spawning notable programs in housing and education at home and the Peace Corps abroad, had as its bedrock ideal the international opposition to communism.

The members of the Kennedy administration were not exactly buccaneers; indeed, practically all of their foreign policy would be conducted amid clouds of the loftiest ideals. But their stress on deeds rather than reflection, on commitment rather than detachment, was worrisome, even at the time. Adlai Stevenson, the twice-defeated Democratic nominee against Eisenhower and Kennedy's much-derided chief delegate to the United Nations—and a meddlesome old fud to many of the New Frontiersmen—told a friend that "they've got the damndest bunch of boy commandos running around . . . you ever saw."

In a military sense, the boy commandos proved to be particularly enamored of counterinsurgency doctrines and intrigue. Kennedy, like some other presidents before him, was not above trickery and deceit—he secretly taped 325 White House conversations. Eventually, he would create an oversight committee to handle, among other things, paramilitary operations of the Central Intelligence Agency in Southeast Asia, charging its members to recognize subversive insurgency as "a major form of politico-military conflict *equal in importance* to conventional warfare."

For the New Frontiersmen, helping nations and peoples threatened by the Communist menace to save themselves was worth any tactic. Special Forces were elevated to new importance; "We are not just saving them for the junior prom," said Walt Rostow, a Kennedy adviser. Under JFK, the Special Forces of all services increased fivefold, about parallel with their capacity for interfering in other countries' affairs. They were to be a primary avenue by which the American experience—politically, economically, socially, ideologically—would be projected onto others. That this experience would be salutary for all concerned went without debate inside the New Frontier. The Navy's part in all this came in January 1962, with the formation of the first two Sea, Air, Land (SEAL) teams.

"Communist insurgency," rather than a conventional Russian assault into Western Europe, became a crucial operational bellwether for the new administration. The operating assumption, seldom even debated, was that the United States had the obligation to cope with such insurgencies *everywhere;* "Globalism gone rampant," chided one critic. Schlesinger, a not unbiased witness, was nevertheless devastatingly accurate when he assessed the New Frontier's fascination with counterinsurgency, a doctrine he called "a mode of warfare for which Americans were ill-adapted, which nourished an American belief in the capacity and right to intervene in foreign lands, and which was both corrupting in method and futile in effect."

Militarily, Kennedy's administration, while casting itself as the inheritor of twentieth-century American liberalism, would prove to be the most unabashedly militant of the century, at least until Ronald Reagan showed up in Washington. Under JFK, an arms race of unprecedented proportions continued, at a rate of $17 billion in additional appropriations (including a bomb shelter craze that he encouraged); the American nuclear arsenal (despite the significant accomplishment of the Test-Ban Treaty of 1963) increased by 150 percent; and tactical nukes in Europe were increased 60 percent. Traditional diplomacy atrophied, while force majeure quickened.

American military power became everywhere overcommitted, around the globe.

Always, the threat of communism (which was indeed significant, but hardly overwhelming) was exaggerated. The more-than-occasional distinctions among Communists, insurgents, and nationalists (a single individual, indeed, could be all three) were reduced to almost nothing. A "victory" for "Communists" anywhere, in true zero-sum logic, was construed as a "loss" for the United States. "Who is the man in your administration," the exasperated economist (and ambassador to India) John Kenneth Galbraith asked Kennedy in 1962, "who decides which countries are strategic?"

To Kennedy and his men, inaction was worse than a crime; not to *act* was to forgo the commitment, the decision, the victory. "Kennedy's style of toughness was more appropriate to the football field than to diplomacy," judged a diplomatic historian. But here was a style made for military, including naval, intervention, to the utmost reaches of American power.

JFK was fond of watching displays of that power, aboard the cruiser *Northampton*, from high on the island of the new nuclear-powered *Enterprise*, or watching ordnance fireworks out at China Lake. The fondness was telling. The New Frontier would not be without its liberal domestic triumphs, but the greatest irony of his administration was that the handsome young prince who succeeded the aged five-star general in the Oval Office, the media darling who brought Camelot to the Potomac, would prove to be the most ardent Cold Warrior of them all.[2]

☆

Back in the fifteenth century, in the dimly lit dawn of military professionalism, the English *condottiere* Sir John Hawkwood had been careening about Italy, in search of booty or someone who would pay his mercenary's price. When certain citizens of Florence made so bold as to advise him on military affairs, as the tale was told, Hawkwood rounded on them with the words, "Go and make cloth, and let me manage the army."

Sir John was probably not the first military man, and certainly far from the last, to loathe civilian interference in his violent specialty. The rise of Western democracies, with their increasingly firm convictions of civilian and participatory rule, merely compounded the problem from the military perspective. In the postwar United States, the line between civilian authority and military specialization was blurred somewhat by the fact that most civilian officeholders within the Department of Defense were military veterans themselves. In addition, most of them came to the department from walks of life that valued the military virtues of order, planning, and discipline. Between 1940 and 1967, seventy of the ninety-one people who held the top jobs in what some called the "permanent military establishment" had been businessmen, corporate lawyers, and bankers.

Tom Gates was part of this pattern, a civilian imbued with militarism.

As secretary of defense, he revered the cast-iron ideology of the late John Foster Dulles and loved to monkey around with covert activity. Gates put his stamp on an early blueprint for the Bay of Pigs, authorized (with Eisenhower's final concurrence) the disastrous final flight of the U-2 spy plane in May 1960, and preached constantly about the Soviet threat. Like his predecessor, Neil McElroy, Gates was a Cold War hard-liner. Also like McElroy, he mostly let the Navy alone, having complete confidence in Arleigh Burke. Thus the implicit civilian-military tensions within the Pentagon were largely masked during McElroy's and Gates's tenures.[3]

Kennedy, with his selection of a new secretary of defense, changed all that. Robert Strange McNamara, who would manage to make military men yearn for the days of the inept Engine Charlie Wilson, was not a member of the so-called eastern, Ivy League establishment. He was of the new suburban West, educated in California's public schools and graduated from Berkeley with high honors. Success at Harvard's Graduate School of Business followed, and he was on the faculty there, an assistant professor of accounting, when World War II came.

McNamara was an absolute demon with numbers, a man who truly *believed* in the power of statistics, particularly as a management tool. As a young Army Air Corps officer, he was deemed to have too much talent for the cockpit (and not enough eyesight); he joined a small group of statistically minded technicians in the Pentagon. There, he and his fellow number-crunchers developed exceptional new methods of control for dealing with large numbers of units, the kind of control that was mandatory to manage the flood of wartime aviation production. Borrowing calculators from an insurance company (ENIAC and its fellows did not yet exist), he set up a statistical unit that kept daily track of the Corps's warplanes, fuel, bombs, and ammunition. In the process, he came to the attention of a *real* member of the establishment, Robert Lovett.

Lovett, who was connected with most of the movers and shakers in the country, regardless of political persuasion, was impressed by Bob McNamara's intensity, his ability to throw a relentless, pitiless spotlight on problems. After the war, Henry Ford the younger (whose mother owned a house near Lovett's on Hobe Sound, Florida) asked Lovett for the names of some top men to inject into his car company, which had sunk into severe debility at the hands of his exceptionally aged and eccentric father.

So McNamara came to Ford Motors, as part of a youthful, supercharged management "team." He began as a cost accountant, a middle manager, but he had a flair for the automobile business, at least from the numbers side. He shortly moved into the controller's office and, by 1960, had become president of the corporation. He made his way by his command of statistics and of the new wonders of computer technology. McNamara was the manager as pure technician, and, at Ford at least, this approach seemed to work and brought him outstanding rewards.

When Kennedy was casting around for a secretary of defense, Lovett, by now an Elder Statesman, thought of McNamara—whom he viewed as an iconoclast, just the right type to sail the fresh breezes of the New Frontier. Here, after all, was the president of one of the leading corporations in America, a man who had joined both the ACLU and the NAACP, who chose to live in the university town of Ann Arbor rather than cloistering himself in Grosse Point, the elegant Detroit suburb that was a haven for Ford executives. In Ann Arbor, McNamara even belonged to a study group that debated subjects such as the fine arts, existentialism, and Communist China. Further, Lovett, as a former secretary of defense himself, was concerned with the Pentagon's ever-expanding sprawl and growing unwieldiness; McNamara, at forty-five seemingly at the peak of his powers, might be the man to bring order and system to the jungle.

Lovett therefore recommended McNamara to JFK's headhunter brother-in-law, Sargent Shriver. (JFK found that McNamara had even read and admired Kennedy's Pulitzer Prize–winning book, *Profiles in Courage*, although he probably did not inform McNamara that this work, like his earlier *Why England Slept*, had largely been the creation of other minds.) Kennedy worried that McNamara, whom he did not know, might be an Irish Catholic; still sensitive to the concerns of the just-finished campaign, he was loath to pepper his administration with his coreligionists. When he found that the Ford man was a Protestant who usually voted Republican, the way was clear.

As secretary of defense, McNamara would prove to be far more the management technician than the global strategist or innovator. With his no-nonsense glasses and his slicked-back dark hair, he certainly looked the part. He would never critically examine the presuppositions underlying the nation's global commitments, at least not until very late in the day, when the horrors of Vietnam were being driven home to him. In terms of strategy and policy, he took what had been shaped by the Truman and Eisenhower years and strove to make these policies more efficient and more workable. The presuppositions, in a manner unusual for a man of the inquiring mind he had shown in Ann Arbor, he simply accepted.

In the management of things military, however, McNamara would prove to be very much a citizen of Florence, one who, in addition, worshiped the logic inherent in numbers. Lovett, perhaps, had forgotten the definition of a statistician he had supplied Truman in 1952: "a man who draws a straight line from an unwarranted assumption to a foregone conclusion."[4]

☆

Bob McNamara came to the Pentagon almost as a statistician Christ out to cleanse the temple. Later, when a White House staffer told him flat-out that America's Vietnam venture was doomed, he would shoot back, "Where is your data? Give me something I can put in a computer. Don't give me your poetry." (The best response to this ludicrous mind-set came, fittingly, from a Vietnamese general: "Ah, *les statistiques*," he said. "We Vietnamese can give [McNamara] all he wants. If you want them to go up, they will go up. If you want them to go down, they will go down.")

—All this was redolent of the Russian fabulist Ivan Krylov's tale, in which a monkey, a goat, a donkey, and a bear concluded that, if they could only sit in the right order, they would be able to play beautiful music. To McNamara, the numbers themselves made beautiful music, and his Pentagon would echo to their continuous crunching and recrunching.

In fairness, the people of all the services, the Pharisees in the Navy included, needed lessons in statistical controls, if only to rein in the colossal waste a bit and give a firmer texture to budgetary decision making. Mc-Namara was not on board to coax military men along, however; he entered the Defense Department with all the finesse of a buzzsaw, trailing in his wake a corps of pink-cheeked statisticians and economists, quickly nick-named the "Whiz Kids." Some of them had been in the Pentagon prior to the new administration; others had been with McNamara at Ford. Even to his critics (who blossomed immediately, particularly among the uniforms), McNamara was the very model of the assertive, shirt-sleeved, probing, self-starting manager. He constantly quizzed subordinates, generated new ideas and goals (efficiency-oriented, rather than strategic), and fired those he deemed incompetent.

As he began his first sweeps through the temple, McNamara proved himself a workaholic, a man reluctant to delegate, and a manager who did not simply step on toes: he *stomped* on them. His tools were the lexicon of the brave new world of postwar management orthodoxy: systems analysis, game theory, and linear and dynamic programming. This meant that the numbers, whatever they were, wherever they came from, and however they were gathered, bowed in the direction of "cost-effectiveness," which in au-tomobile manufacturing and sales was readily discernible most of the time. In terms of a commodity called "national defense," the concept's usefulness was altogether another matter.

—But not to McNamara and the Whiz Kids. As the buzzsaw cut its new patterns, McNamara lumped together functions he considered common to all the services, items like supply, procurement, intelligence, and research and development. He looked upon national defense as a product, one whose component parts could be streamlined in the production process. In part he was absolutely correct; some of this drastic reshuffling was sorely needed. But McNamara overlooked legitimate differences in the individual services (indeed, he pooh-poohed them), and he also badly underestimated the worth of *useful* service traditions, as opposed to deadening or obfuscatory ones.

The Navy saw the shape of the new patterns immediately and was quick to react. Unhappy admirals complained that their service had singular prob-lems (planes that had to be specially crafted for carrier landings, for example) as well as singular advantages (operational flexibility and mobility) that were going unrecognized or unappreciated by the new analysts. But Kennedy's aides had warned McNamara that the Pentagon Pharisees were running an organizational and fiscal monster that needed to be harnessed for the national good. And in the long run, McNamara's management techniques would indeed make the place more cost-conscious. Still, for the Navy in particular, McNamara's lack of understanding of naval policies and traditions meant a near disaster.

To begin with, the Navy's leaders were almost totally illiterate in the language of systems analysis. A Whiz Kid (about the age of a lieutenant) would ask them to demonstrate the "effectiveness" of a proposal, and they not only had trouble responding but also seldom knew *how* to respond. Then there were many problems, such as measuring the cost-effectiveness of a fleet ballistic missile submarine, that would not readily yield to systems analysis. "The opinions of competent military professionals," wrote Captain Paul Ryan, "sometimes could not be packaged in neat mathematical units."

The Whiz Kids, undaunted, proved adept at creating assumptions, many of which blithely ignored such factors as weather, training status, and logistic support—aspects a naval professional would instinctively think of. The assumptions, in turn, marked numerical signposts for naval programs. For years, the Navy had used a much looser form of logic, called the "estimate of the situation," and the Postgraduate School at Monterey was beginning to turn out graduates in operational research. But McNamara and the Whiz Kids flew by the numbers all the way, using marketplace concepts such as "opportunity cost" and "marginal utility" as statistical gods, quantitative analyses that would, *of themselves,* drive strategic and planning decisions.

McNamara thus frequently overrode the advice of his naval professionals. He did this with the best of intentions; if the numbers did not crunch, national defense would somehow be "weakened." Despite the Navy's continued confidence in its seat-of-the-pants analytic method, Navymen had to increase their in-house analytic skills in self-defense—which was by no means a negative development. Weapons systems began to be evaluated in new ways, and procurement policy underwent a huge (and long overdue) overhaul. Congress, which had previously received the military budget in short-term, annual bites, now got multiyear national defense plans that really helped in predicting costs and even in assessing effectiveness, to a limited degree. As a not unimportant side effect, more naval officers began to speak an alien tongue, at least enough to refute the conclusions of Pentagon systems analysts from time to time, and in their own language. To do so, however, members of this nouveau naval managerial class had to spend more time at their desks and less time on the underway bridge.

—Thus ran the warfare in the trenches. Back at headquarters, McNamara and his staff, an activist bunch if there ever was one, broadened the Defense Department's managerial power enormously, largely because of their prerogative to create paper on demand—administrative studies and reports and reams of computer-usable data. He who controlled the creation of the paper controlled the questions asked, and thus the solutions. To the military, and the Navy especially, this was not just creeping civilian intrusion onto uniformed turf, it was trampling intrusion. But unlike Sir John Hawkwood, the Navy could not simply tell its civilian superiors to stuff the whole thing. In uniform, the admirals simmered with rage but remained loyal servants. In retirement, they rent the air with tirades against the civilians, tirades such as this by Admiral John Hyland:

> The professional Navy is kibitzed and closely controlled in the details of procurement, of operations, and the advancement [assignment and promotion] of relatively senior officers. This [control] comes not only from the Defense Department but from the Congress and its professional committee staffs, most of which have developed a certain superficial competence. They all have the ability to say "no" or to block or delay action; but none of them have to take any responsibility for the things they do.

—"Certain superficial competence" or no, part of the turf wars between McNamara's Pentagon and the Navy was clearly a matter of *style*. ("McNamara [could] look like a complete ass . . . if he tried hard," said Captain John Noel.) McNamara was no respecter of service tradition or custom, and in these areas, much-beloved by Navymen, the buzzsaw really hurt. He referred to the situation he found in the temple as "chaotic;" with characteristic lack of modesty and equally characteristic confidence in his precious numbers, he would assure the American public that the problems had been "corrected." He believed that, within the span of a few months, he and his Whiz Kids had really mastered everything his officers had learned about strategy, tactics, and military management in collective lifetimes of professional service. This intransigent hubris was perhaps best displayed when he declared that the chief problem of his uniformed critics was "ignorance."

The Navy's Pharisees might have been many things, but they were not ignorant men. The name-calling got out of hand on both sides, which did little to distinguish mature adults trying to do their jobs as best they could. McNamara's proclivity for rubbing Pentagon fur the wrong way, sadly, obscured many of his real achievements, the chief of which was probably his introduction of the Planning-Programming-Budgeting System (PPBS). This analytical track divided the executive phase of the military budget into three clearly defined cycles, offered input and evaluation at every stage, and lengthened the decision process from twelve to eighteen months.

But even in this case, Pentagon leaders proved more wary than cooperative. McNamara's gloves-off approach tended to create enemies rather than alliances. The Joint Chiefs of Staff quickly learned to band together against their civilian superior. McNamara met frequently with them, but the Chiefs came to feel that these meetings found McNamara, rather than listening, to be trolling for one or more of them to side with him on a particular issue. Therefore, they downplayed their own turf wars in the face of a man they perceived to be a common foe.

This meant, in terms of recommendations, that the Chiefs would defer as a group to the individual chief concerned. For example, if the Navy recommended fifteen attack carriers as the operational minimum and the Army only twelve, everyone knew that McNamara, worshiping at his shrine of cost efficiency, would invariably choose the lower number. Therefore, on the principle of mutual back-scratching, the Chiefs would collectively go forward with the higher number. In this way, McNamara and his Whiz Kids found their arrogance and number crunching actually working against what they were trying to do, and the country was ill-served to boot.

The Chiefs also learned to stonewall McNamara, in hopes that they could eventually get the president's ear, take their case to powerful friends on Capitol Hill, or—at the very least—establish a "military position," as opposed to the one set by the civilians in the Defense Department. Things got so bad that McNamara ordered the Chiefs not to reveal their differences with him unless pressed by Congress. And if that happened, they were to give the secretary's side of the case as well. Naturally, the volume of leaks from the E-Ring redoubled.

For the Navy specifically, the McNamara era brought excruciating pain. Nothing was sacred to the Whiz Kids. They questioned whether modern supercarriers were worth their enormous cost. Rumors abounded that each new one would be the last. Navy planners were directed to "modernize" their ships, making do with what they had, rather than to count on new construction. Shipbuilding contracts received a thorough (and badly needed) working-over. The Whiz Kids even put a cap on the most sacred of Navy cows, stopping the building of the Polaris boats at forty-one rather than at the Navy's announced goal of forty-five.[5]

The cocksureness of the Whiz Kids, most of them too young for World War II and a few of them too young even for Korea, left older people, for the most part, splenetic. This was a feud among generations, levels of experience, and types of expertise, as well as being one of both style and substance. The crusty House speaker, Sam Rayburn, who had seen many bright young men come and go during his time in Washington, reflected that "I'd feel a whole lot better about them if just one of them had run for sheriff once."

Admirals (who had never run for sheriff, either) simply seethed. Some of the Whiz Kids, fumed Vice Admiral John Victor Smith, were "really detestable types." While naval operations historically relied heavily on operations research, and while excellent operations analysts were billeted in key positions throughout the service, the Navy itself had practically no tolerance for *outside* evaluation, either by service requirements or systems analysis. Such evaluation was "amateur," by definition, and therefore axiomatically flawed. As surely as the morning sunrise, the Navy *knew* that its forces were at their most effective when used as the Navy alone saw fit. This fiercely parochial cast of mind was the product of centuries of deeply felt naval experience and tradition.

As far as McNamara was concerned, the Navy would learn his language and play his game, dragging its webbed feet all the way. Always, however, the service was suspicious of outsiders and pragmatic in its responses to threats from these sources. In this view, McNamara was the ultimate outsider, a man who did not belong in the temple, a dangerous bureaucratic gorilla who could carelessly harm sacred institutions and programs with his thrashing about. "Poor man," Admiral Horacio ("Rivets") Rivero, Jr., said of McNamara. "Brilliant, [but] he could never believe he could be wrong."

Certainly Rivero's service never collectively saw itself in error. The Navy would continue to hold that its institutional judgments were infallible. This cleansing of the temple would be but a passing wind. In the end, as McNamara and his coterie hung on, these hopes would fade; "We'll never recover from McNamara," moaned Vice Admiral Ruthven Libby.

Still, the Navy's reluctant, foot-dragging responses could wear down even the most dedicated of men, which Bob McNamara certainly was. While he was speaking of the world situation, he might just as well have been talking about the armed services in general and the Navy in particular when he wearily admitted, "There is no strategy; there is only crisis management."[6]

☆

An activist secretary of defense, particularly one as dominating and domineering as McNamara, left any secretary of the Navy in a fairly tight straitjacket. Eisenhower's last appointee, William Franke, had been a faithful public servant under both Truman and Ike, a New York financial expert with a background in accountancy. He lacked the messiah complex about numbers that animated his fellow accountant McNamara. He was fair-minded and levelheaded; he helped keep Gates's and Burke's commitment to Polaris on an even keel, along with Burke chose top hands for fleet command assignments, and proved a competent, workmanlike administrator.

But Franke was no boat-rocker; he could never have fit in with Camelot's athleticism, derring-do, and panache of commitment. JFK's first secretary of the Navy turned out to be a purely political choice—John Connally, Vice President Lyndon Johnson's friend and protégé. Like Johnson, Connally was a Texas wheeler-dealer to whom politics was mother's milk.

Connally's saving grace, which was slight, was that he had some Navy experience. Born in Floresville, Texas, in the same year as JFK, he graduated from the University of Texas in 1941 with a law degree; that same year he gained a commission in the Naval Reserve. He started out taking junketing trips with his fellow reservist manqué Johnson, but unlike Johnson he did the long haul. Assigned to *Essex*, he served as radio and radar officer and flight director officer, going through most of the big campaigns in the Pacific from the Gilberts to the Ryukyus. No less an officer than Rear Admiral Tommy Sprague, boss of Task Group 38.1, sang his praises.

After the war, he became a quintessential man-on-the-make. Charming and drawlingly handsome, he emitted the aura of the new Southwest—a combination of oil, old leather, and fresh money. Connally had a nose for power. He was Johnson's Senate administrative assistant for a time, then became the attorney for an ultraconservative Texas oil millionaire, Sid Richardson. With this troglodyte as a mentor, Connally shifted rightward politically, supporting Eisenhower in 1952. He never left the Democrats, however, managing Johnson's campaign against Kennedy in the 1960 primaries. With Johnson, somewhat surprisingly, in as vice president, the time had come for the political payoff.

To get McNamara as his secretary of defense, JFK had agreed to let him have the last word on high civilian appointments within the department. McNamara nixed Kennedy's first choice for the Navy secretary, Franklin Roosevelt, Jr. (which would have made for a nice historic trio of Navy Roosevelts), but he approved of Sam Rayburn's recommendation, Connally. Johnson supposedly kept his hands off this brokering, but the Rayburn intervention was an indicator of Connally's connections—which were first-class.

Once in office, Connally started fast. He had absolutely nothing in common with McNamara and the Whiz Kids; his experience was with deal making, not with number crunching. But from his own perspective, he could see that the temple needed some cleansing. So he chided naval officers for being too resistant to new ideas, urged the more rapid promotion of younger men, and put out feelers about creating simpler, less-sophisticated ships.

—But all this was a smoke screen. Burke did everything he could to familiarize Connally with his new job; three days after taking office, Connally told Burke he was planning to run for governor of Texas. As Connally said of himself, "I've been called an opportunist, and I do move from place to place and from thing to thing and I enjoy it." By December 1961 he was gone, on his way to the governor's chair in Austin and that dreadful afternoon two years later in Dallas, riding with Kennedy in the presidential limousine.

From the Navy's perspective, Connally was a horrible appointment, the worst secretary since Rowboat Matthews. Unlike Matthews, however, Connally was no incompetent. He was, rather, a restless, opportunistic political and financial operator, out to advance himself at any cost—at the furthest remove from any reasonable concept of public service. The Navy could not afford, and certainly did not need, this sort of pure political animal as its civilian head.[7]

His replacement was an altogether different sort of Texan. Fred Korth was eight years older than Connally; he had graduated from the state university in the depths of the Depression and gone east to finish law school at George Washington University. Korth spent World War II in the Army Air Corps, like McNamara serving mostly inside the continental United States (in Korth's case, doing transportation work). Like Franke, he became a capable Washington bureaucrat, the exact opposite of a high roller like Connally. He rose through the civilian ranks in the Department of the Army, where he was civilian aide to Secretary Elvis Stahr, Jr., when JFK tapped him for the Navy job.

Korth was able, and he was zealous. But in his new assignment he was thrown between the Scylla of the hyperactive McNamara, on the one hand, and the Charybdis of unhappy admirals, on the other. Superficially, with his slight stoop, his white hair severely brushed back (McNamara's similar haircut was at least inky-black), and his thick, black-rimmed glasses, he certainly resembled somebody's ineffectual pushover. He was nothing of the sort, understanding his position—that of middleman in a time of inordinate civil-military tension—with acute insight.

Therefore, Korth both appeased and offended. When he reorganized the Navy's business side, commencing the better coordination of four bureaus that led to the creation of the Bureau of Naval Material, some admirals, he said, "screamed like . . . gut-shot panther[s]." Likewise, when McNamara crunched some numbers and recommended a military pay raise, Korth fired off a blistering letter to his boss protesting the increase as inadequate.

Frustration and discontent, through no fault of his own, were thus built into Korth's job. At times, notably in the interservice flail over the TFX airplane, he earned the dubious distinction of alienating everybody. JFK himself was never overly fond of his second secretary of the Navy, grousing about his "propensity to write too many letters."

Korth *was* a chronic letter writer (the habit, along with the TFX imbroglio, would eventually lead to his dismissal), but this was a direct result of his gregarious, friendly, outgoing nature. His bonhomie made friends for him on Capitol Hill—which McNamara, as suspicious of usurpers as a Shakespearean king, regarded as an end run. Carl Vinson, in his final years as chairman of the House Armed Services Committee and as devoted to the Navy as ever, liked Korth so much that he took him home to Milledgeville, Georgia, to meet the rest of the Vinson clan. Under different circumstances, Korth's frankness, booming voice, and earthy humor, coupled with his considerable bureaucratic skills, might have made him an excellent secretary of the Navy. With McNamara and the admirals flanking him port and starboard like wary sharks, he never had much of a chance.[8]

☆

Arleigh Burke had been winning his spurs as a combat destroyer commander in the South Pacific when Ensign John Kennedy was still wet behind the ears. Now, almost twenty years later and with his epochal third term as chief of naval operations almost over, "my navy" was about to lose its most ardent and committed voice.

He had been firm as a rock for his service. On Capitol Hill, testifying about supercarriers, nuclear propulsion, or Polaris, Burke had earned congressional trust not only by his reputation, but by his sincerity and his depth of knowledge. Across the board, he knew more about "my navy" than any man alive.

Old friends like Vinson and Rayburn could still be counted on in the House. (In time, a nuclear-powered supercarrier would bear the name of the former, a fleet ballistic missile submarine that of the latter.) There were newer allies as well, men like Mendel Rivers of South Carolina, busy building up Charleston as a Navy town, and F. Edward Hebert of Louisiana, industriously packing his entire state with Navy offshoots. In the Senate, Richard Russell of Georgia, as chairman of the Armed Services Committee, had reached a position where Kennedy's secretary of state, Dean Rusk, called him "the second most powerful man in Washington." Like Vinson, Russell had advanced through the pernicious legislative seniority system; also like Vinson, he had the deep-seated virus of southern racism and was a commanding roadblock to civil rights legislation. But, like Vinson again, he was indispensable to the military; he could move congressional mountains to get appropriations through. Both men were expert in camouflaging controversial items, like CIA expenditures, in military budgets.

Largely because of Burke, the Navy enjoyed generally good rapport with these men and most of the rest of Congress, although even Burke could not sway curmudgeonly Clarence Cannon, chairman of the House Appropriations Committee. "A carrier is the most expensive machine the world ever saw," Cannon announced. "It consumes more skilled labor, more strategic material, and more steel than any human contrivance the sun has ever shone upon. And yet in war it would be worse than useless."

The first two-thirds of Cannon's catechism were true. Burke worked mightily to convince all concerned that the last third was not. His labors, indeed, extended beyond the supercarriers to every weapons system the Navy possessed. By 1961 his repositioning of "my navy" was practically complete. The Long-Range Objectives Group had ranked the service's primary missions, in order, as nuclear deterrence, deterring or fighting limited wars, and antisubmarine warfare. Polaris was the answer to the first mission, the operational flexibility of the carrier strike force the answer to the second, and the renewed attention to hunter-killer ASW the answer to the third. This repositioning, as Burke intended, would guide the Navy's shipbuilding for the decade to follow.

Burke had also wrestled with the Single Integrated Operational Plan (SIOP) proposed late in Eisenhower's second term. The Air Force expected to be the master player. Burke, ever the canny infighter, packed a planning meeting with forty naval officers, each one imbued with the gospel of naval strategic independence; the Air Force responded by labeling Polaris a strategic power grab. After much screaming back and forth, the much-rehashed SIOP landed on Kennedy's desk early on, where the document got only minor revisions. Burke's machinations (one naval officer remembered that the only time he ever heard Burke yell "bullshit!" was over some Air Force suggestion about the SIOP) had gotten the Navy control of its own strategic weapons systems. The SIOP would stay in place, mercifully unused, until canceled by Jimmy Carter.

During Burke's tenure, the position of chief of naval operations had undergone considerable pounding from the outside. The biggest hammer-blow, of course, had been the Defense Reorganization Act of 1958, which vested operational command in the unified and specified commanders. The chain of command, to Burke's disgust, now ran directly from the president through the secretary of defense to these commanders, bypassing the service chiefs. Burke, legally, could not "command;" he could only "supervise," and that only as part of a management team called the Joint Chiefs of Staff.

More and more authority, even before the advent of the dark specter of McNamara, was accruing to Defense Department civilians, and Burke railed mightily, if Canute-like, against this trend. Even so, he proved that an activist, savvy chief of naval operations retained plenty of maneuvering room. The office was still far more substance than shadow. The chief was, for all the bureaucratic battering, still the professional head of the Navy, and the legal and psychological implications could be stretched practically to infinity. He was the Navy's leading voice, after all, and his position meant far more than words. For example, Burke had his hand in every key naval development of the Eisenhower years, from strategic planning and systems programs to doctrine and combat tactics to the design and production of individual platforms. The chief of naval operations was also a charter member of the nation's "board of strategy," the Joint Chiefs of Staff. Here, in a small group where personalities, minicoalitions, and exceptionally refined politicking could go a long way, a service chief could also accomplish much. Burke's achievement of the development of Polaris and the creation of a SIOP satisfactory to the Navy were only two of the more conspicuous examples.

These two hats worn by the chief of naval operations produced conflicts as well as solutions. There was never enough time to wear both hats well, and even a man with Arleigh Burke's bruising energy felt the strain. Some of his duties, under the 1958 act, he delegated to his vice chiefs, but this never seemed to diminish the load. If the Navy's leader concentrated on his role as one of the Joint Chiefs, he risked slow alienation from his power base, his own service; if he became merely a megaphone for his service, his parochialism ill-served the Joint Chiefs, the administration, and the country. The chief of naval operations could seldom satisfy his admirals and his executive leadership at the same time, particularly in matters of budget.

Not even rocklike Burke could successfully stand athwart the path of bureaucratic centralization. In his own lifetime, the nation had gone from an annual federal budget of around $1 billion (deemed monstrous at the time) to one of over $100 billion; when he left office, one out of every four American families depended directly on some kind of federal, state, or local government payroll. Modern communications smoothed the way for this centralization and also made possible what had once been thought unattainable: tighter bureaucratic control of the Navy's traditionally far-flung and decentralized organization.

Relatively speaking, these trends benefited the executive branch, while the legislative branch waned. Men like Vinson, Rayburn, Rivers, Hebert, and Russell were still kingmakers, to be reckoned with especially at budget time, but the day-to-day operational power lay more and more within the Defense Department.

As Burke stepped down, the Defense Department, which had begun in 1947 as the "National Military Establishment" with one secretary and three "special assistants," had become a prodigious hive of the following: a deputy secretary of defense; eight assistant secretaries; twenty-six deputy assistant secretaries; one director of research and engineering; five deputy directors of same; and no less than 3950 (as of 1 June 1962) civil service posts in the GS-14 to GS-18 range. The Joint Chiefs of Staff had increased from one hundred officers to four hundred—officially, that is; hundreds more, forbidden by law to be directly assigned, were under orders to the "Organization of the Joint Chiefs."

More and more, this hive pumped out and controlled the paper. In the modern management world, that usually computed to control of policy, force levels, mission assignments, even operational details. McNamara's Defense Department (most of which Burke was mercifully spared, through retirement) also relied less than previous civilian leadership on military experience and judgment; the new yardsticks were cost-effectiveness, quantitative analysis, and computers—all of which made Burke's skin crawl. Command and control became more tightly centralized, but in the direction of the department's civilians. The trend was toward military conformity rather than service individualism and independence, and this trend was most threatening to the Navy, of all the services. (To the horror of Burke and every other Navyman, there was even a short-lived attempt to develop a standard military uniform for the *entire* American military.)

All this Burke loathed, but there was more; in-house, considerable power might remain for the chief of naval operations, but now he had to politick even with his unified and specified commanders, men theoretically junior to him in seniority. In addition, the chief's precise authority over the Navy Department's various bureaus was still, more than a century after their inception, legally fuzzy. Burke showed his impatience here with his "projects" approach, spearheaded by Polaris, and with the creation of the Bureau of Naval Weapons in 1959, the uniting of the squabbling sisters, the Bureau of Aeronautics and the Bureau of Ordnance.

—All these trends, changes, and pressures were draining. Burke had scrapped for "my navy" every step of the way. But he was tired. Six years at the helm was a lifetime, even for a man of his incredible powers. Already, before the election of 1960, he had submitted his resignation. Kennedy, like most naval men of his generation, revered Burke; he offered to reappoint him to a fourth term and renewed the offer several times.

Burke said no. He thought his service needed new leadership, and besides, the Bay of Pigs fiasco in the spring of 1961 had not raised either the young president or the Pentagon civilians any higher in his estimation— to the contrary. While preferring not to be directly involved, he dutifully prepared a list of fifty officers he believed qualified to take his place. Connally insisted he pare the list, so Burke shaved his choices to eight or so, leaning over backward so that the successful candidate would not have to bear the stigma of being "Burke's man." Frustrated with the numerous forces surrounding him and his office, he resolutely sailored out his term, declining Kennedy's offer of an ambassadorship to Australia. "I felt there was nothing more I could accomplish," he morosely wrote.

> I was spinning my wheels. I would submit recommendations, I would explain and explain and explain and nothing would happen. And what the hell, I could go out and grow roses or sugar cane or sit on the front porch, and at least I could watch the sun come up in the morning under pleasant circumstances. But of that job was nothing more I wanted to continue.

—His time had come. There was a White House ceremony and one more award, a Distinguished Service Medal. Then, on 1 August 1961, for the last time on active uniformed service, Arleigh Albert Burke snapped a final, crisp salute—to his successor. At fifty-nine he went over the side for good—walking into a long, richly deserved, and much-honored retirement.[9]

☆

There was feverish handicapping on the question of Burke's relief. In the spring of 1961, after he had said no to JFK for the last time, and before he had pared his list of possible successors, no fewer than fifty admirals were trotted past Connally for scrutiny. *Newsweek* took the trouble to evaluate the race, rating Vice Admiral John Hayward ("Chic Chick") at 2–1, Admiral Robert Dennison ("Denny Boy") at 3–1, Red Raborn ("Red Rooster") at 6–1, and so on. (Savvy Sides came in at 15–1, Jimmy Thach at 40–1, and Rickover at 50–1; the rambunctious Cat Brown trailed at 100–1.)

Kennedy's choice was another 2–1 shot, Vice Admiral George Anderson, Jr. Anderson was the son of a Brooklyn realtor, born in 1906 and raised as a Catholic. Exceptionally bright, he graduated from the Jesuit-run Brooklyn Preparatory School at sixteen. As Burke left Annapolis in the spring of 1923, Anderson arrived as a member of the Class of 1927. He zipped through, graduating twenty-seventh in his class, and was not yet twenty-one when he became an ensign. He did three years aboard *Cincinnati*, then went into flight training. The wings came in 1930, and during the Depression years he passed through a variety of aviation billets afloat and ashore: cruiser planes, flight testing, service aboard *Yorktown*, and flying chilly patrols with Patrol Squadron 44 out of Seattle.

Anderson proved tactful as well as forceful, a thinker as well as a doer. He showed aptitude for planning. He was assigned to the Plans Division of BuAer when World War II came, working on the development of naval aircraft. In this job he meshed smoothly with a host of newly spawned wartime agencies, so much so that he was personally commended by Eisenhower, then in the Army's War Plans Division.

In March 1943 Anderson went to the new *Yorktown* as navigator and "tactical coordinator." He got into several air actions and reaped a harvest of decorations. After *Yorktown* he spent the bulk of the war, from late 1943 to the end, as a plans officer for CINCPAC and as an assistant to Nimitz's deputy, Vice Admiral John Towers.

After the war Anderson moved, again with typical smoothness, to a variety of billets with a joint or international flavor. His experience, as he moved up the ranks, looked more outward, from the Navy, than inward, toward the intrinsic service. He served as a member of the Joint Planning Staff, the American-Canadian Permanent Joint Board of Defense, and the Brazilian–United States Defense Commission. He took time to attend the newly established National War College. At sea, he commanded the escort carrier *Mindoro* and the attack carrier *Franklin D. Roosevelt*.

He was a comer. Ike remembered him, and as Supreme Allied Commander in Europe he made Captain Anderson his senior officer for plans and operations. When as president he appointed Arthur Radford as chairman of the Joint Chiefs, Raddy asked for and got Anderson as his special assistant. Flag rank duly followed, in the summer of 1954.

Anderson moved on to command the Taiwan Patrol Force, then became CINCPAC Felix Stump's chief of staff. In July 1958, holding this three-star billet, he took the most unusual step of reverting to two stars to get a carrier command, CarDiv 6 in the Mediterranean. No sooner had he taken over than his carriers were off Lebanon, where he performed so flawlessly that he quickly got back his third star and took command of the Sixth Fleet. In that role he shone, both as a naval commander and as a naval diplomat. "A tough boss who did not suffer fools gladly," was John Noel's estimate of him.

Unsurprisingly, Anderson's name was on Burke's short list. His operational background was astoundingly broad: battleships, carriers, both patrol and fighter squadrons. He had held a wide variety of commands in a variety of theaters. Moreover, his staff work had been remarkable for its quality and breadth—naval, joint, and international alike. He had worked intimately with allied military leaders in Europe, the Pacific, and the Western Hemisphere. Finally, the Navy liked him—for his tact, his deep love of the customs of the service, and (not least) that willingness to voluntarily give up his third star.

Kennedy, McNamara, and Connally made their choice. Square-bodied George Anderson, bluff-faced and white-haired, was the third aviator, the first Catholic, and the first graduate of the National War College to become chief of naval operations. He was vaulted over ten senior admirals to reach the position. Kennedy appointed him to a two-year term, with the thought that Anderson would replace General Lyman Lemnitzer of the Army as chairman of the Joint Chiefs when Lemnitzer stepped down, after a planned four-year term, in 1963.

If anyone had ever been specifically tailored to be chief of naval operations, George Anderson was that man. The supreme irony of his years in the Navy's highest office would be that this polished and thoughtful naval officer, a man who had made a career of operating smoothly and effectively with others, would have almost nothing but difficulties and personality conflicts during his tenure.

His problem, in two words, was Robert McNamara. The secretary of defense was a detail man, right down to the last period on the last inconsequential piece of paper. (He bragged that he—personally—made several thousand decisions a year.) McNamara had quickly gotten into the habit of overruling the recommendations of the Joint Chiefs without either explanation, discussion, or consultation (Burke's Parthian shot about "nothing happens"). For McNamara, the musicians were seldom in the right order.

George Anderson, McNamara's Navy musician, never found his proper chair. He was all for analysis, cost-effective and otherwise, but he wanted that analysis to temper rather than replace military experience. For him, McNamara's task was to lay out broad policy; the Navy's business was to use its expertise to carry out that policy. Anderson insisted, moreover, that no gatekeeper should bar his way to either the president or Congress; no recommendation by a service chief should be "dulled in any way in transition."

—There was a brief honeymoon between the two men: Anderson instructed his staff to be more accommodating with the other services; McNamara raised the Navy's budget 21.4 percent for fiscal 1962 and pushed more money at Polaris. But McNamara's obsession with detail grated the Navy, with its less rigid hierarchy and its decentralization, probably the most of all the services. McNamara and Anderson, coming at naval problems from decidedly differing points of the compass, were not destined to be bosom buddies. McNamara, in this early phase of his stewardship, was exceptionally autocratic and arrogant; Anderson was not without these qualitites and, despite his diplomatic training, could be a real mossback in cases where he believed the prerogatives of the Navy to be threatened.

The sweetness and light ended in the fall of 1961, after Anderson supported McNamara's decision to make the scheduled nuclear follow-on to *Enterprise* a conventionally powered carrier (which turned out to be *America*). One squabble after another ensued, as the Harvard-educated statistician and the Jesuit-trained naval officer feuded openly. They quarreled over military compensation, the Nuclear Test-Ban Treaty, the production of the TFX fighter, and the bureaucratic politics of the Air Force's B-70 bomber. (Both men wanted the plane killed, but Anderson would not publicly support McNamara—another case of mutual back-scratching by the Joint Chiefs.)[10]

—These were but preliminaries. There would be bigger rounds ahead.

☆

George Anderson took over a Navy stretched to the limit. One of the reasons he was so ready to grapple with McNamara was that he felt unable to surrender *anything* and still do his job. He led 627,000 officers and sailors worldwide, and his experienced personnel, both in the wardroom and on the mess decks, were still leaking away to civilian life. No one could find the hole in the dike, much less supply the plug. Fred Korth confessed that "the problem of getting enough motivated, dedicated, and skilled officers and men has yet to be solved."

In 1961 the Navy had 350,000 civilians as well, meaning that Anderson stood at the head of a million-person operation. He was acutely conscious of morale throughout his vast domain, and by his lights McNamara and his crowd were part of the problem, not part of the solution.

The good news with the Navy's hardware, as the Kennedy administration got underway, was that the nukes were taking shape: the attack boats were coming off the ways, Polaris submarines were moving out on patrol, and the surface vessels, in the shape of *Enterprise* and the first nuclear-powered cruiser, *Long Beach*, were at sea. In addition, there was other new construction to be thankful for. Six *Forrestals* were in commission (although the Navy, because of their missile batteries, would call the last two of these the *Kitty Hawk* class), and a new generation of assault landing ships (landing platform helicopter—LPH), led by *Iwo Jima* and *Okinawa*, was likewise.

But Anderson was well aware that the bulk of the nine-hundred-ship fleet was growing old, and simultaneously ("block obsolescence"). McNamara's cost-cutting simply made the pinch hurt more. Ships were normally estimated to have a useful life of twenty years or so, although this figure increased the larger or more important the vessel. When Anderson relieved Burke, the twentieth anniversary of Pearl Harbor was only months away. By the end of 1963 and Anderson's first-two-year term, only 43 percent of the fleet had been built since V-J Day; the rest of the ships dated from the war years or before. Despite programs like Fleet Rehabilitation and Modernization, and despite the dazzling new construction, Anderson had to guard his assets jealously.

These assets, as usual, were spread out all over the place. When Anderson took over, the four fleets were operating in their customary waters— the First in the eastern Pacific, the Second in the western Atlantic, the Sixth in the Mediterranean, the Seventh in the western Pacific. The ships and men were conducting exercises, showing the flag, doing resupply and support, and carrying out humanitarian rescues. The Navy was seemingly everywhere, and the nation apparently expected this omnipresence as a matter of course—an omnipresence given an exclamation point by Rear Admiral David Tyree, the "Antarctic Project Officer," when he helped craft the Antarctic Treaty of 1961, which ensured the use of the region for "peaceful purposes."[11]

☆

"Pacific" was supposed to be peaceful, too. Out there, CINCPAC was lord of the largest military domain in the world. His command encompassed eighty-five million square miles of the earth's surface, a practically infinite jurisdiction riddled with insoluble problems, ancient rivalries, and trouble spots galore.

In 1961, CINCPAC was Admiral Harry ("Don") Felt ("Our Harry," at 20–1 in *Newsweek*'s handicapping). To help him run his domain, Felt had the Pacific Air Forces (thirty-five squadrons of 650 combat planes), Army Pacific, and the Pacific Fleet, led by Savvy Sides. Felt commanded 61,000 airmen, 81,000 soldiers, and naval forces amounting to 400 ships and 1800 aircraft. CINCPAC had the cream of America's war-fighting assets.

Felt was a prime example of a unified commander who had grown in importance as the service chiefs had been diminished by the Defense Reorganization Act of 1958. Unlike Anderson, Felt could actually *operate* his command. To him, Makalapa Heights, not Anderson's Pentagon, was where the action was. And Don Felt was action personified.

His days began at full throttle; then he picked up the pace. Arleigh Burke, according to some accounts, got nastier as the day went along; Felt began nasty and did not improve much. A former aide called him "mean as hell." Small and feisty, Felt was tough as a hickory knot, and about as pliable. Like Burke, he did not know the words *weekend* and *evening*. Like McNamara, he was a demon for facts and figures. His favorite saying was a paraphrase from Finley Peter Dunne's Mister Dooley: "Trust everybody, but cut the cards."

Felt was a classmate of Burke's, but at Annapolis he had racked up a considerable number of demerits and had graduated well back in the pack. Bored stiff with battleship and destroyer assignments, he put in for flight training. He proved to be a born hot rock. His wife, Kathryn, described her husband's life, once he got his wings, as "just fly, fly, fly."

—And he flew—with Scouting Squadron 3-B, off *Minneapolis* and *Houston*, and as skipper of Bombing 2 aboard *Lexington*. After Pearl Harbor he commanded the Air Group aboard *Saratoga*, leading the first American carrier strike of the war and earning a Distinguished Flying Cross. A Navy Cross quickly followed, awarded for sinking some Japanese ships at Torpedo Junction, off the Eastern Solomons. By the end of the war, as a captain, he was commanding the escort carrier *Chenango* off Okinawa.

Don Felt was dedicated, enthusiastic, a naval warrior to the core. He was also a rabid anti-Communist. "I hope we don't let the Russians in," he wrote Kathryn at the time of the Yalta Conference. "We don't need them." His postwar rise was rapid: command of *FDR* and Naval Forces MidEast. As a carrier commander, he was fond of picking up his radio handset and, using his call sign, bellowing at one of his miscreant small boys: "This is Jehovah! What do you think you're doing, you stupid bastard?"

Felt came under Burke's wing in the Navy's War Plans Division; when Burke took over the top spot, he jumped Felt over a score of senior admirals to make him vice chief of naval operations, with his fourth star. (Burke joked that he had learned in the South Pacific the value of a "no" man and that that was why he kept Felt around for two years.) "The majority of naval officers in the Pentagon when told that Admiral Felt wanted to see them would practically start quivering in their boots," remembered David McDonald, a future chief of naval operations. "Many people were afraid of him . . . he was pretty rough," added the seasoned submariner Red Ramage.

When Felix Stump retired in 1958, Felt jumped at the CINCPAC assignment. He simply barbecued Makalapa Heights, dragooning everyone onto his endless work schedule and chewing out his admirals and generals right and left. "Feltgrams" blistered the command. ("Advise me ASAP.

Resp'y, F.") He worked under a continuous sense of urgency, convinced that his enormous fiefdom could catch ablaze at any time. "We are the fire brigade," he said.

Felt's chief fireman in 1961 was a classmate of Anderson's, Vice Admiral Charles ("Don") Griffin ("Donny Boy," at 4–1), commander of the Seventh Fleet. Griffin's 160,000 men were even more alert than usual that summer, as Anderson took over from Burke; many Navymen believed that the current Berlin Crisis might provide the Soviet Union ample opportunity for some sort of "blackmail pressure" in East Asia. Griffin's 165 ships were thus individually tracked by both Anderson in the Pentagon and Felt at Makalapa Heights.

Don Griffin, a raw-boned, lop-eared aviator, was acutely conscious of the stretch of his command. "I've never seen a military commander say he had everything he wanted," he admitted. "It is just not in the nature of the beast." But he knew his force was more than considerable, right up to its carrier-borne nuclear punch. Many of the smaller countries in his bailiwick could not afford to be brave, and Seventh Fleet's presence, sometimes, could hearten hesitant allies or impress nervous neutrals.[12]

—Sometimes. Laos—small, remote, and practically unknown to most Americans—was a nervous neutral, a sliver of Southeast Asia that had been suffering for years through a complex, three-sided civil war, including an insurrection by the Soviet-backed Pathet Lao. Burke, the staunch anti-Communist, had been all for American intervention, early on. "Threats to our national welfare such as these must be localized and stamped out where they occur—that is, far from home," he wrote Representative Samuel Stratton in 1959. "We have strong mobile forces for handling this type of situa-tion. . . . We have the power *now* and stand ready to use it."

The Pathet Lao was far from threatening America's "national welfare," then or ever, but Burke nevertheless had been adamant, arguing (alone among the Joint Chiefs) that failure to act in Laos would result in the eventual "loss" of Southeast Asia. But Laos was landlocked; seapower (as opposed to air power) could not get at the country directly. This made little difference to Burke, or to Felt, who knew he had the air power to cremate the Pathet Lao (if he could find its guerrillas amid the Laotian hills and jungles). "[Anticommunism] . . . is what counts most in the sad Laos situation," avowed CINCPAC. "We must support [the Laotian anti-Communist leaders] with all their faults," Burke added, although "we must control them as much as we can."

Military aid was rushed to Laos, which was not a member of SEATO. The Seventh Fleet was alerted. President Ngo Dinh Diem of neighboring South Vietnam, then undergoing the revival of an insurrection in his own country, approved. In 1960 the South Vietnamese were sent some landing craft to beef up their own Mekong River patrols. But Laos continued to be a too-convenient channel through which the North Vietnamese Communists persistently ran men and supplies into South Vietnam, encouraging the Pathet Lao on the way.

Thus Laos was a continuous, bleeding sore, and—because of its unfortunate location and the reluctance of both Eisenhower and Kennedy to become fully committed in such a backwater—a place difficult for Burke and Felt to apply bandages. Burke had gotten Seabee units, based in Bangkok, into Laos as early as 1957, and the Seabees had done their customary fine work, building and repairing roads and runways.

But Eisenhower had temporized, assessing Southeast Asia with his typical caution, and the Laotian situation had reached critical mass when Kennedy came into office. JFK moved the carriers of Griffin's Task Force 77 into the South China Sea and landed a detachment of Marines by helicopter in Thailand, not far from the Laotian capital of Vientiane. Further than this, the young president, still smarting from the Bay of Pigs, was not willing to go, seeking a political rather than a military settlement. The Joint Chiefs, for their part, were contemplating the use of nuclear weapons in case of direct involvement by the Chinese.

George Anderson, also new to his office, was willing to take an extra step. He advised McNamara: "A strong warning to North Vietnam accompanied by quick strikes at Communist forces in Laos, following our firm measures in South Vietnam and commitment of U.S. forces in Thailand, may convince the Communists that further aggression could provoke larger scale U.S. intervention, which would pose an unacceptable risk for them."

—Here was a preview of the immediate American future in Southeast Asia, tweaking the levers of military power until the enemy realized his "unacceptable risk." Burke, Anderson, and Felt, in the name of anticommunism, were far too ready to use military force in areas of the world where no possible threat existed to the United States. They, but hardly they alone, helped set the tone for the grimly confrontational international politics of the early sixties.

Laos, however, soon receded to its accustomed back burner. Kennedy, scorched by the failure at the Bay of Pigs, kept Laos at a distant remove. A Geneva Conference in 1962 got all the players—the Americans and North Vietnamese, in particular—to agree to get out of Laos. A Navy amphibious group stood off Bangkok to take out Marines. Kennedy and his diplomatic troubleshooter, Averell Harriman, brokered a deal that produced a cease-fire between the right-wing Laotian government and the Pathet Lao. A "neutral" government (native Communists sharing authority with moderate neutralists) was established. By December 1962 Laos was off the front pages.

The Navy leadership had wanted to go into Laos directly, to apply an ounce of prevention. In a strictly military sense, Burke, Anderson, and Felt were quite right. Certainly the North Vietnamese never came close to living up to the Geneva deal. Their Group 559 had infiltrated twenty thousand cadre into Laos since 1959, over what was coming to be known as the Ho

Chi Minh Trail, and they showed no signs of stopping. The Kennedy administration responded by sending CIA operatives into the Laotian hills to train Meo and other tribesmen. The CIA budget for Laos was "only" $20 million to $30 million annually. "Signing of Geneva Agreement will not end struggle," observed Felt. "Laos will continue to have pivotal role in future of SE Asia."

—Felt was also right on this score. Indeed, top-ranking naval officers were infuriated by what they regarded as a cut-and-run strategy in Laos by the political leadership. Naval forces had been deployed in the South China Sea, Don Griffin had ostentatiously conducted fleet exercises, aerial reconnaissance flights had been laid on, Marines had landed, and military aid had been given. And Laos was still a superhighway for North Vietnamese infiltration. The Joint Chiefs, with the exception of Anderson, had finally determined that Laos, in terms of a ground war, was not worth an American commitment. [13]

Laos, however, was a wake-up call for the Navy in general and CINCPAC in particular. Should naval force ever be required in Southeast Asia, the admirals—after Laos—would want that force applied correctly and overwhelmingly, against people they perceived as the Communist enemies of their country.

☆

John Kennedy, to his credit and despite his hyperkinetic Cold War rhetoric, had avoided real American military involvement in Laos. He had been chastened by the Bay of Pigs and, concurrently with the Laotian settlement, was involved in the greatest crisis of his presidency. Here, in the closest and most critical "American lake," the issues of communism and American security had far more import than anything suggested by a remote patch of Southeast Asian real estate.

—And here, in the sunny Caribbean, the United States Navy would have its finest hour in the Cold War.

CHAPTER THIRTY-ONE

CARIBBEAN I

—————— ☆ ——————

S omeone, perhaps speaking from experience, once defined an emergency as a time when several things needed to be done, and each one had to be done first. Such a definition, of course, assumed that there was agreement on what had to be done.

Latin America and its host of problems were rarely high on the things-to-do list of American policymakers, who were usually content if order was maintained, trade and tourism with *el Norte* were conducted properly, and local *caudillos* did not get too far out of hand. If these conditions existed— then there was no emergency.

American money or indifference had propped up many Latin American dictators and their militaries. Back in 1944 Congress passed the Surplus Property Act, allowing "friendly" nations to buy, at bargain-basement prices, warships that otherwise would have been mothballed or made into razor blades. Harry Truman choked off Lend-Lease right after V-E Day, and the next year a feisty, Republican-dominated Congress rejected the president's proposal to continue naval cooperation with Latin America beyond the old naval mission system.

Thus, Latin American navies, despite the Surplus Property Act, had to make do with some British and Canadian *Flower*- and *River*-class escorts for a while. But postwar Communist expansion changed all that. The Mutual Defense Assistance Act of 1949 not only provided military grants to NATO members but also authorized sales of military equipment practically any-where that communism seemed a threat—which included Latin America. To get their ships, Latin American countries had only to ratify the 1947 Inter-American Treaty of Reciprocal Assistance (the Rio Treaty) and pay cash on the barrelhead for delivery.

The United States, long the dominant foreign power in the region, asked only for the original cost of the item. Of course, the warships were tools of mutual interest, along with other military hardware a means of keeping the lid on the discontent caused by the enormous social and economic inequities that tarnished practically every Latin American nation. Through bilateral agreements in January 1951, Argentina, Brazil, and Chile each got two prewar American cruisers. The price tag, including ammunition, spare parts, and rehabilitation costs, was a mere $4 million apiece. The cruisers were obsolescent in state-of-the-art navies but were still useful to these countries; indeed, the ex–USS *Phoenix* (*General Belgrano*) steamed for Argentina until 1982, when modern naval conflict, in the shape of the nuclear-powered HMS *Conqueror* and her spread of Mark 8 torpedoes, caught up with the weary old craft during the Falklands War.

The naval bonds to the south grew steadily tighter. By 1956, every Latin American country with an American naval mission except Venezuela had signed a bilateral defense agreement with the United States. (Argentina had no naval mission or agreement, the muddled legacy of Peronism.) Midshipmen from Latin American countries had been attending the Naval Academy even before Pearl Harbor. Joint antisubmarine warfare exercises had been conducted since 1950, when Brazilians and Americans went through a few drills together. By the late 1950s, the United States had assigned Latin American navies the hemispheric military role of antisubmarine warfare. In 1959, Latin American naval officers meeting in Panama recommended that their respective navies hold exercises with the dominant Americans on a regular basis. Their own serious squabbling (there had been at least twenty-four major territorial disputes since independence was gained from Spain and Portugal in the early nineteenth century) tended to preclude the obvious multinational exercise on the NATO model.

The result was a public relations acronym, UNITAS, supposed to stand for United Interamerican Antisubmarine Warfare Exercise—which did not quite fit. Neither did a press release from CINCLANT, saying that the word was a Latin one meaning "unity." Regardless, an American task force began to circumnavigate South America annually on a "UNITAS cruise." While a carrier might join up for a short time, the United States Navy customarily devoted only a few destroyers, a vintage submarine or two, and some ASW aircraft to the exercises.

The combined Americans did get a chance to do combined ASW. Doctrines and methods were established, English became the common operational language, and, in time, more young Latinos began to show up at the Naval Academy. But the ancient castoffs crewed by the Latin Americans simply could not conduct modern antisubmarine warfare; they lacked the sensor systems, the training stations ashore, and the integrated air element. Vice Admiral Charles Minter described everything he saw from the southern neighbors during one UNITAS cruise as "pretty antiquated." Naval professionals on all sides knew that UNITAS was primarily a political and social drill, useful perhaps (Argentina and Brazil drew closer together in naval affairs, for example) but hardly likely to improve the ability of Latin American navies to deal with modern submarines. The harsh fate of *General Belgrano* merely underscored the point.

—What mattered most to the Big Gringo was stability and "friendship." The United States had a long and decidedly checkered career in intervening directly in Latin American affairs. The "good neighbor" policy of the 1930s marked a high point. But when international communism was added to the normal social and economic leaven after World War II, Americans moved beyond their normal dollar diplomacy and resumed the kind of interference, this time through subterfuge rather than overt military action, that had distinguished their prewar forays into Haiti, Nicaragua, and the Dominican Republic—to mention only a few choice instances.

Guatemala was the prime example of the new mix. In 1953 Milton Eisenhower returned from a fact-finding trip to Latin America and informed his brother the president that Guatemala had "succumbed to Communist infiltration." The Central Intelligence Agency was then swaggering through its heady buccaneering years, fresh from engineering a successful coup in Iran that had placed the shah back in power. In the spring of 1954, Dwight Eisenhower unshipped the CIA's leash in the direction of Guatemala. He also ordered an airlift of fifty tons of small arms to neighboring Nicaragua and Honduras, both ruled by anti-Communist dictators. After calling for a meeting of the Organization of American States to preserve the diplomatic niceties, he also declared a naval blockade of Guatemala—which was an act of war.

The Soviet Union responded by trying to ship ammunition to the revolutionaries in Guatemala (not all of whom were "Communists"), but the freighter concerned was seized by U.S. Army officers in Hamburg. This was a violation of a principle—freedom of the seas—that Americans had gone to war to defend twice in the past, in 1812 and 1917. Eisenhower, who liked history but loathed communism, simply intensified the naval blockade. American bombers flown by CIA pilots tweaked up a bombing "offensive." The result was the resignation of the Guatemalan president and the establishment of a military dictatorship.

Guatemala was a case study of American reaction to the specter of "communism" in the Western Hemisphere. The connection of the word with tiny Guatemala provoked U.S. defiance of international law, the direct threat of American military action, the use of CIA aerial cowboys against a foreign country, and the U.S. sponsorship of exactly what Guatemala (or any other Latin American nation) did not need—more right-wing repression.

The Navy, an institutional bastion of anticommunism, saw Guatemala as another day's work, in terms of fleet assets the merest shrug of the shoulders. Arthur Radford and the Joint Chiefs prepared contingency plans (which were never used). Mick Carney, the chief of naval operations, had his planes carrying out aerial surveillance against any further Soviet attempts to resupply Guatemalan rebels. Another country was safely in America's corner.[1]

The Big Stick in Latin America was alive and well—and a good share of that stick floated on the sea.

☆

When Eisenhower shut down the Guatemalan "emergency," Fidel Castro was doing hard time—fifteen years—on Cuba's Isle of Pines for his leadership role in an attack on Santiago's Moncada Army Barracks on 26 July 1953. The young lawyer had appeared in his own defense, delivering a five-hour harangue (a form of public address that would prove to be his specialty) that proposed land reform, industrial confiscation, and summary measures against waste and fraud.

Cuba certainly needed a change. The huge Caribbean island and its six million people had been in the grip of the despot Fulgencio Batista and his cronies since 1952, and Batista's malign influence had been felt throughout the island for more than a quarter century. The lot of most Cubans, despite the fact that Cuba historically displayed one of the highest levels of median income in Latin America, was one of callous injustice, casual (and thus unfeeling) corruption, debt, hunger, and sickness—all adding up to a sense of hopelessness.

Batista was nothing if not politically opportunistic, however, and in one of his forgiving moments (which usually occurred under international pressure) he released some political prisoners in 1955. Among them was Castro, who made his way to Mexico. There he joined forces with his brother Raul and the Argentine Marxist Ernesto ("Che") Guevara; together the three revolutionaries and a Spanish anarchist began to train eighty men in guerrilla tactics.

When this impudent little band attempted to "invade" Cuba late in 1956, Batista killed or captured most of them. Castro, with twelve followers (the Christ parallel was not lost on some Cubans), escaped southeasterly into the remote Sierra Maestra. From there, undaunted, he began to recruit his third revolutionary force.

The mountains nurtured them, and Batista's own ineptitude, plus their growing guerrilla skills, kept them alive. By the beginning of 1958 the heavily bearded Castro, trademark cigar jutting from his mouth, had become an international curiosity, certainly to Americans. He was saying all the right things, and at his customary length. Castro was fighting, he claimed, to do away with the dictatorship, hold honest elections, and protect property that should be protected. He was no Communist, he said of himself, only an honest Cuban patriot with the best interests of his country at heart. Whether Fidel was merely cunning, a savvy political temporizer, an unscrupulous liar, or a stereotypical subversive Commie would remain a matter of debate, but even in the 1950s what he wanted was crystal clear: power in Cuba.

—And power in Cuba he got. At the end of 1958, buoyed by a frenzy of Cuban expectation, he and his *barbudos* came down from the hills. On

New Year's Day 1959, they took power, ninety miles from the American mainland. The United States, where key newspapers like the *New York Times* had been favorable to his movement, promptly recognized the new government. The major American oil companies, hoping to continue business as usual, advanced Castro $29 million because the fleeing Batista regime had left the cupboard bare.

Once installed in Havana, however, Castro wasted no time. Allies and even old friends were sacked; some never emerged from prison. In the months that followed, as the Eisenhower administration got increasingly edgy, his rhetoric became even more strident. "Cuba has never had an honest election and a truly free press," Fidel now explained. "Therefore, Cuba has no right to have them under me." American property worth almost $1 billion was expropriated; the oilmen kissed their money (and much else) good-bye.

Embittered Cuban exiles descended on the United States in the thousands, most of them clustering around Miami. Diplomatic relations between the United States and Cuba were severed on 3 January 1961, in the waning days of Eisenhower's presidency. By April, Castro was openly declaring himself a "Communist;" a "Communist revolution" was going on in Cuba.

—Nothing could have been more calculated to resurrect the ancient chauvinism of the internationally incredible Monroe Doctrine, to deepen American worries over hemispheric defense, and above all to create problems about possible Russian bases in and Communist subversive doctrines passing through Cuba. The Cuban exiles, many of them, played on these American fears. Some of the exiles were political right-wingers who had been cozy under Batista, opponents of Castro from the very beginning. Others had opposed Batista but had found Castro's brand of repression more of the same under an ideological cover. Still others had once been avid Castro supporters but were now, after two years, deeply disillusioned with the Cuban "revolution."

Arleigh Burke, for one, had thought Castro was a Communist even when the Fidelistas were holed up in the Sierra Maestra. For Burke, and for "my navy," this meant that the enemy had arrived in the Antilles. As early as 1959, Richard Nixon, for another, was urging Eisenhower to do something about Castro. By the time Castro took power, the CIA was developing the conviction that this particular revolution was bad news, the direct insertion of communism into the heretofore sacrosanct Western Hemisphere.[2]

Militant American anticommunism, the clear excesses of Castro's regime, and the increasing clamor of the exiles for redemption made a potent brew. There were 113 Cuban exile groups by early 1961. Not all of these were significant, by any means, but they were all active, vocal, and avidly anti-Castro.

—And Washington was listening.

☆

Afterward, no one wanted to touch the Bay of Pigs operation. This monument to bungling on an outrageously colossal scale became the stuff of professional comedians. No one wanted the responsibility, certainly not John Kennedy, who eventually shouldered the blame. The Bay of Pigs had many fathers, but the one most accountable was the most intangible, the hardest to grasp: militant, almost unthinking opposition to communism.

Little over a year passed between Castro's triumphal entry into Havana and the beginning of American attempts to unseat him. On 17 March 1960, Eisenhower authorized the CIA to organize, equip, and train a force of Cuban exiles for "possible" action against the Castro regime. The exiles already had a loose conglomeration of their groups pasted together (none too solidly), and the CIA at first simply provided direction. Then came funding and—finally—planning and control. Washington made the decisions; the nascent rebels found that they possessed almost no autonomy.

The pace of the Cuban exiles' move to the operational front burner was in direct proportion to Castro's actions. On 23 May he ordered American and British oil companies to refine Soviet oil (they refused). Three days later Eisenhower canceled all American aid programs to Cuba. Castro replied by seizing the oil companies. On 5 June, Eisenhower withdrew the Cuban sugar quota, a central prop of the island's economy. Castro kept on confiscating.

The CIA's door into Guatemala had been kept ajar, and there, in June 1960, the exiles were established on training bases provided by a wealthy coffee planter who happened to be a brother of the Guatemalan ambassador to the United States. An airstrip for training the rebel air force was built. This outfit consisted of sixteen World War II vintage B-26 bombers and nine transports—five C-46s and four C-54s. There would also eventually be a navy: five ancient freighters and three World War II landing craft (utility), LCUs.

The initial idea, on which President-elect Kennedy was briefed on 17 November 1960, was to filter the trained exiles into Cuba in driblets, first to form an intelligence network, then to coalesce into sabotage groups, psychological-warfare units, and, at last, guerrilla bands, ready to give Castro a dose of his own medicine. Throughout all this, the United States would play the innocent bystander.

There were two problems with this proposal: first, the exiles had transferred their intramural bickering from Florida to Guatemala and, as of November 1960, were far from combat-ready in any form. Second, the CIA and other American intelligence sources had badly underestimated what Castro and his associates had been able to do with their newfound power. With extreme rapidity, and with some Soviet aid, they had developed a militia and a conventional armed force of no little consequence. Their intelligence service, relying heavily on revolutionary ideology and terror, was already one of the best in Latin America. By November 1960, the few exiles already inserted into Cuba were spending more time trying to survive than in being clandestine agents.

Although the clandestine stuff certainly appealed to Kennedy's mindset, the amateurish aspects of the pending operation were all too obvious, even to the CIA. On 29 November, Kennedy received another briefing and another proposal, and with this second briefing the debacle was really set in motion. Now a more substantial force, not just a few isolated bands, would be landed to seize a beachhead. The CIA, by itself, was proposing an amphibious operation against a hostile shore, of the type that had taken the Navy and Marine Corps years and tens of thousands of casualties to master in World War II.

As the second proposal was presented to Kennedy, the notion seemed to be that popular resistance within Cuba would rise up, defectors from Castro's militia and military would miraculously materialize, and the combined anti-Castro forces would succeed in an exultant ground swell of redeemed democracy. The thought that Cubans would actually *fight* for some despicable Communist government never crossed anyone's mind. Kennedy himself seemed to believe that a mass of people would be surreptitiously delivered to the beach and then would quickly infiltrate inland to do their work.

There were two major amphibious plans. The original idea was to capture the small town of Trinidad, nestling in the foothills of the Escambray Mountains on the south coast. The Joint Chiefs, who at all times were on the fringes rather than at the center of the planning, wanted a less conspicuous location. Inchon had been the great exception that proved the rule: no amphibious planner wanted to hit an urban area from the sea, especially if other choices were available.

The second plan settled on the Bay of Pigs, one hundred miles west of Trinidad, which led into a sparsely populated and swampy interior. Here vision was piled upon dream: the swamps and limited road network would somehow impede the Cuban forces more than the rebels; an airdrop would capture a vital crossroads; a beachhead would be quickly established and defended; the surrounding area would quickly rise to the anti-Castro colors. The Joint Chiefs, though neither the Trinidad plan nor the Bay of Pigs plan belonged to them, with the information they were given assessed both locations as feasible.

The go-ahead was given for the Bay of Pigs—initiated by Eisenhower, triggered by Kennedy, and driven throughout by virulent anticommunism. Down in Guatemala, American advisers replaced the original instructors. New equipment, including tanks and heavy artillery, began to stipple the grounds of the coffee plantation. Recruiting was stepped up. Tables of organization materialized, along conventional military lines. The president of Guatemala gave his full cooperation, and his neighbor, President Luis Somoza Debayle of Nicaragua, kindly provided the airfield for the B-26s. Ships of the United States Navy patrolled Guatemalan waters to provide security, although no one was quite clear against what.

The 2506 Brigade took shape, composed of 1453 idealistic anti-Castro Cuban exiles. One of them, Carlos Santana, died during the early days of training, and his serial number gave the brigade its name. As 1960 drew to a close, the pressure to act intensified. Tons of Soviet equipment were pouring into Cuba; nature and diplomacy alike abhorred vacuums, and Nikita Khruschchev was fishing in Caribbean waters. In addition, Castro had sent eighty Cuban pilots to Czechoslovakia for jet fighter training. Soon, however, American military personnel who reviewed 2506's progress reported that the Cubans were well-trained and capable of their task.

But the Bay of Pigs was a cross-wire operation from the get-go. To begin with, the fervently anti-Castro Cubans in exile, many of them as blood-thirstily anti-Communist as only men who considered themselves betrayed nationalists and patriots could be, were convinced that the new Kennedy administration would not, could not, let the operation fail. The rebels knew that the initiative for their training and mission had come from the highest echelons in Washington; if worst came to worst, American military strength would be directly applied. For his part, however, JFK, as fuzzy as he was about the actual design of the operation, was clarity itself on the question of direct American involvement. This was to be an exile operation—to them the risks, to them the credit for success or the ignominy for failure. There would be no Americans on the beach; officially, there would be no Americans anywhere near the place.

Kennedy was only fooling himself. The multiarmed Cuban Revolutionary Council, as well as every man in 2506, fully expected that, should the brigade falter, American Marines out of the U.S. naval enclave at Guantanamo Bay in Cuba would come hotfooting to the rescue. Allen Dulles, director of central intelligence, told Kennedy that the brigade had a better chance of success, by itself, than the Guatemala operation seven years before. On the training grounds in Guatemala, though, the exiles were being fed the line that American help would be there in the event of trouble. A final message sent from Guatemala by the American project chief radiated confidence "in the ability of this force to accomplish not only initial combat missions but also the ultimate objective of Castro's overthrow."

Only weeks into his activist presidency, Kennedy was being pressured for a decision. His defenders would later look for scapegoats everywhere but in the White House. In actuality, the design of the Bay of Pigs scenario fed right into the youthful president's urge for commitment, his militant anticommunism, and his love of clandestine activity.

The Joint Chiefs, who would later deny the bungled operation left partially on their doorstep, were ambiguous, were divided among themselves, and were not functioning with all the necessary information, some of which the CIA kept close to its vest. The Chiefs did say that ultimate success "would depend on either a sizeable uprising inside the island or sizeable support from the outside." Kennedy, in disallowing participation by American armed forces, was banking heavily on some kind of uprising by the Cuban people—knee-jerk anticommunism. The possibility that any kind of program calling itself "Communist" might actually gain popular favor somewhere was never considered.

The president was nervous and uncertain, reserving the right to call off the whole thing as late as twenty-four hours before D day, which was set for Monday morning, 17 April 1961. As the days ground down, JFK approved the switch to the Bay of Pigs site and, critically, decided that 2506 would go in during darkness rather than daylight. Even crack amphibious assault troops would have choked on this menu.

—And 2506 Brigade, while filled with dedicated, brave fighting men, was no amphibious assault outfit. They were invading Cuba, one of the largest islands in the world, against a hostile, and growing, force. They had fewer than 1500 men, no rehearsal, five tanks, minimal artillery, and no naval gunfire support. Only four of their battalions were reasonably trained; the other two were latecomers, completely green. (Some of the men assigned to these had never even fired their weapons.) Air support was contingent on sixteen old, temperamental B-26s operating from a mainland base over seven hundred miles away. Their navy was the five freighters, manned (as things turned out) by incompetent, cowardly crews, most of them non-Cuban, and the three antique LCUs. A more damning list of negatives for an amphibious assault could scarcely be imagined.

Just before they left Central America to hit the beaches of their homeland, the rebels heard Kennedy's public announcement that American armed forces would not intervene in Cuba under any conditions. Many of them believed that this was only a cover story; when push came to shove, the Americans would be there.[3]

☆

Burke had wanted forceful opposition to Castro from the beginning. His equation was simple: Castro was a Communist; he would invite Soviet forces into Cuba; the Soviets would gain a bastion right in the heart of the Western Hemisphere, and on the cheap. To Burke, Cuba after the revolution was a nest of rattlesnakes, in need of thorough eradication; for him, some of the men around Castro, as he told the National Security Council on 10 March, "were even worse than Castro."

Burke's hatred of Castro went back at least to June 1958, when thirty American Marines (some of them "half drunk") on a tour of Batista's Cuba had been hijacked by Raul Castro (Fidel had not authorized the raid). Burke advocated sending an entire American division into the Sierra Maestra in pursuit, but three weeks of diplomacy and some veiled threats to ship Batista more weapons got the Marines back unharmed. To the admirals, this was just caving in. "You can't blame Castro for being contemptuous of the United States," fumed Dan Gallery, to whose command the Marines belonged. For his part, Burke was convinced that the *barbudos* were no more than Commie bandits, and when the Joint Chiefs were ordered only to advise on the Bay of Pigs operation rather than shoulder the burden of a rational military plan, he foamed at the bit.

David Shoup, commandant of the Marine Corps, told his fellow Chiefs that "if this kind of operation can be done with this kind of force, with this much training and knowledge about it, then we are wasting our time . . . [with] our [regular] divisions; we ought to go on leave for three months out of four." Burke described the CIA plan (not all of which he even saw) as "weak" and "sloppy," with no proper logistic or communications annexes.

Unlike Allen Dulles, whose baby this very much was, Burke thought the chances of success for 2506 Brigade were much less than 50 percent. The Chiefs accepted (not "approved") the Bay of Pigs site with extreme reluctance. To their lasting discomfiture, they never informed either Kennedy or Robert McNamara about their qualms over the entire operation, particularly the last-minute improvisations. Whenever the Chiefs asked for details, they were told they were not involved. "We were told it was a CIA operation and you [the military] stay the hell out of it," Burke remembered. Also in his own defense, Burke said that "you had to pound on the table to be heard in the Kennedy Administration." But the Chiefs could not get off scot-free; they had the *duty* to pound, to give the president the best military advice they could. To their discredit, they did not. Instead, they signed off on an operation that each of them knew was fraught with peril.

Down in Norfolk, Admiral Robert Dennison, commander of the Atlantic Fleet, had had inklings since September 1960 that something was afoot. Twinkle-eyed, with a huge shock of hair topping a face lined with expectancy and care, Bob Dennison was an exceptionally acute naval officer, a man so engaging and skilled that during the tension-filled days leading up to war in 1941, he had acted as liaison between Admiral Thomas ("Terrible Tommy") Hart, commander of the Asiatic Squadron, and the imperial Douglas MacArthur—pleasing both men.

Dennison was a Pennsylvanian, a member of Burke's Class of 1923. Rare among line officers, he was exceptionally oriented toward formal education; he possessed a master's from Penn State (1930) and a doctorate in engineering from Johns Hopkins (1935). At sea, he went into submarines, qualifying aboard the old *S-8* in 1925. An indefatigable worker, he developed fast. His command tours were mixed and highly successful: the rescue ship *Ortolan*, the submarine *Cuttlefish*, and the destroyer *John D. Ford* (where William Mack, his gunnery officer, assessed him as an excellent ship-handler).

After refereeing between Hart and MacArthur, Dennison served as a staff officer for both submarines and amphibious craft, did war plans for the Joint Chiefs, and was a special adviser to Under Secretary of the Navy Forrestal. His lack of combat command in World War II did nothing to impede his career and indeed sped him onward. After the war he commanded *Missouri*, where he so impressed the visiting Harry Truman that he became the president's naval aide—from which post he helped save the promotion of his friend and classmate Burke to Flag Plot.

Unsurprisingly, an admiral's flag came with the duty in the White House. Then came command of Cruiser Division 4, relief of Burke as director of strategic plans, command of First Fleet, and deputy chief of naval operations for plans and policy. In February 1960, wearing four stars, he took over as CINCLANT.

By this time Bob Dennison was known everywhere as an exceptionally able thinker, patient yet incisive with seniors, juniors, and peers alike. He floated on a sea of pure praise seldom seen in naval history. "Probably the best teacher I had during all the time I was in the Navy," judged Draper Kauffman. Kemp Tolley, not an easy man to please, remembered him as a "real diplomat and a wise man." To Henry Miller, Dennison was a "brilliant man, more relaxed than Admiral Burke, and a great leader." "Just a magnificent man to work for," gushed Charles Loughlin. Robin Quigley, who worked for him as an ensign in strategic plans, saw him as "rather cold on the surface," but from her lowly position, she soon perceived him with "tremendous respect and awe." The only person Steve Jurika could find with whom to compare Dennison was that foremost of planners and thinkers, Forrest Sherman.

Fortunately for the Navy and the country, this paragon, as CINC-LANT, was in the right place at the right time. In September 1960, a subordinate informed Dennison of a most unusual request: the CIA, for purposes unknown, wanted the landing ship (dock) *San Marcos*, then in Puerto Rico, and assorted smaller craft. Dennison raised hell and was duly told about the exiles and their pending operation. To CINCLANT, the whole thing was a "hot potato," a "very risky and probably . . . unsuccessful operation." On 7 February, as the exiles rounded out their training, Dennison was told by General Lyman Lemnitzer, chairman of the Joint Chiefs, that CINCLANT's naval forces would not be used to evacuate 2506, should the need arise. Then Kennedy himself told Dennison the same thing. Deeply worried, Dennison complained until he was finally allowed to send a cruiser, a few planes, and a Marine battalion to reinforce the naval base at Guantanamo Bay, which was in obvious peril.

During the final days before the invasion, Dennison found his rules of engagement being refined to the point of exactitude. CINCLANT could not convoy the ships of the brigade, except loosely at night. His carriers were to operate no closer than fifty miles to Cuba, his aircraft no closer than fifteen miles, and no more than four aircraft were to be on station at any one time. He could fire only if about to be directly attacked. Should the brigade's motley collection of ships have to be protected in such a manner, the whole operation would be automatically scrubbed. What Dennison did not have was the CIA invasion plan, and therefore he had no information on which to base an evacuation, should one suddenly be required. All the fine-tuning "didn't satisfy me one damned bit," he concluded.

To CINCLANT, the pending invasion was a military operation without the military; the whole shebang was taking place in his water, on his watch, but without any real advice from him and beyond his control. Like Burke, Dennison was too good an officer to leave things like that. He readied Rear Admiral John Clark's Carrier Division 16, built around *Essex*, for a possible aerial umbrella. In addition, he and Burke had the Marine battalion destined for Guantanamo fully combat-loaded, which meant the Leathernecks could be quickly landed onto a beach of their choosing.

Early in April, *San Marcos* at last played her role, delivering the three LCUs to a pre–H hour rendezvous with the brigade's shipping. By this time, everyone in the Caribbean knew something was up. The brigade's movement from its training base to its embarkation point at Puerto Cabezas, Nicaragua, had not exactly been a secret, and to top things off, the CIA had laid on air strikes from the Nicaraguan bases on Saturday, 15 April. The strikes damaged some of Castro's aircraft; they also alerted Fidel, in no uncertain terms, that the wind had shifted, and gave him forty-eight hours to prepare.

The original plan, formulated way back in mid-1960, had been to use American naval air in support of the landing if Castro's air force was not destroyed by the initial strikes. Now, naval air was off the table, and John Clark, although in the area, was virtually handcuffed.

On 17 April 1961, 2506 Brigade went in—alone.[4]

☆

At 0430 that morning, Kennedy turned down an eleventh-hour suggestion for naval air cover from three miles offshore to twelve miles. JFK kept to the fifteen-mile barrier, which meant that the unloading invasion ships and their beached landing craft had no aerial roof. So long as *Essex* and her seven destroyers kept station, Clark could provide the brigade with early warning—but that was all. *Independence* was also in the area, and some of her planes were controlled by *Essex*'s primary flight control. In actuality these boundaries would be broken by American ships, planes, and crews, but with intentional duplicity—a form of subterfuge that riled Burke, Dennison, and everyone else right down the chain of command.

The men of 2506 never knew that in the event of their detection and attack while at sea, the Navy had orders to abandon the operation and convoy their fleabite armada without further ado to Puerto Rico. Further

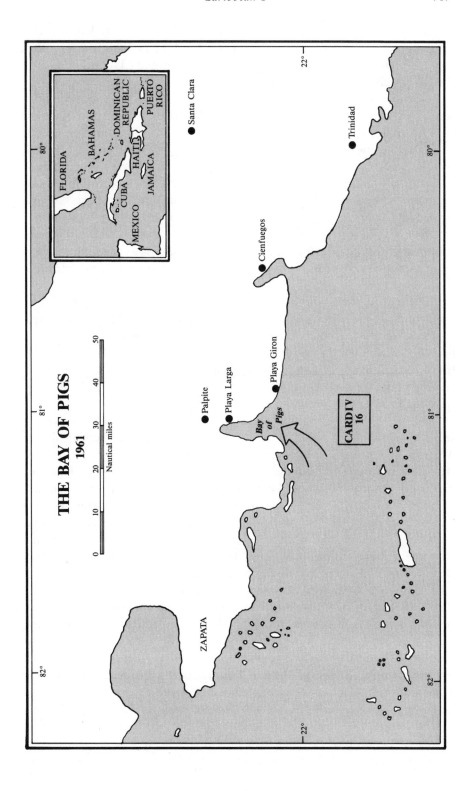

THE BAY OF PIGS
1961

Nautical miles
0 10 20 30 40 50

FLORIDA
BAHAMAS
MEXICO
CUBA
JAMAICA
HAITI
DOMINICAN REPUBLIC
PUERTO RICO

Santa Clara
Trinidad
Cienfuegos
Playa Giron
Playa Larga
Palpite
Bay of Pigs
ZAPATA

CARDIV 16

confusion came regarding the Navy's role after the exiles were landed. The entire operation was called Pluto by the CIA, which perhaps had forgotten that Walt Disney's dog was friendly but rather stupid. The exiles named the naval side Bumpy Road.

—And a bumpy road they had. The American destoyer *Eaton* led the way in but did not support them directly. American frogmen, in violation of JFK's order, were first ashore, disguised as Cubans. They fired the initial shots. But no one had thought to inform the prospective Cuban "insurgents" that their salvation was on the way. The CIA and Navy were using different (and mutually unknown) radio circuits. Unexpected coral reefs popped up, delaying or stopping landing craft (thirty-six small aluminum boats), which were badly operated in the first place. On the beaches there was another surprise: immediate, fierce resistance. Overhead, as the creaky freighters crammed with troops, ammunition, and high-octane aviation gasoline jostled in no particular order for position, the remnants of Castro's pygmy air force showed up.

The Cuban planes did a highly creditable job. Three rocket-equipped T-33s and two Sea Furies forced one ship to ground and blew up another, *Rio Escondido*, aboard which, in violation of every principle of combat loading, had been stashed all the brigade's vital enciphering gear. By 1400, with the troops ashore taking a pasting, Washington allowed the remaining ships and landing craft to retreat to about fifteen miles offshore; there, at least, they were under *Essex*'s air umbrella.

During the second night of the invasion two of the brigade's surviving ships, *Atlantico* and *Caribe*, panicked and fled deeper into the Caribbean. The remainder, ordered in again by the Navy, were so reluctant to move that they never resupplied the beleaguered brigade during the hours of darkness. Aboard one of the slowpokes, *Blagar*, a mutiny erupted that had to be put down by force. Airdrops of munitions for the brigade were so widely dispersed that most of them ended up in the hands of Castro's men.

Late in the evening of 18 April, the CIA (in the person of Richard Bissell, the deputy director of plans, who more than any other person had brainstormed the operation) finally begged for naval air support. Lemnitzer joined Burke in supporting the plea. Burke also proposed immediate use of the 1500-man Marine battalion aboard *Essex*, as well as sending in the destroyers for close-in gunfire support. McNamara and Secretary of State Dean Rusk, in Kennedy's presence, argued against further American commitment. The result was a diluted compromise in perfect consonance with the expanding weirdness of Pluto. Clark was ordered to have *Essex* provide a one-hour, six-plane cover, which did little more than try to interpose between the brigade's B-26s (some of which, again against the president's orders, were being flown by Americans) and Castro's air force. *Essex*'s combat air patrol was ordered to shoot back only if attacked.

By this time the brigade was being demolished piecemeal, on land and from the air. Rusk opposed letting unmarked American landing craft move close inshore to pick up the bedraggled remnants now fleeing seaward for their lives, as if this cold-blooded disregard of endangered men would somehow stave off international criticism of American involvement. One of JFK's advisers even suggested that sailors manning the landing craft wear civvies. This nonsense was beside the point; the CIA's planners had only the foggiest conception of evacuation by sea, and in any case they had not clued in Burke or Dennison, whose ships would have to do the work. Aboard *Essex*, the flight schedule changed minute to minute. Some of her planes returned with bullet holes. The Blue Blasters of Attack Squadron 34, flying A-4D2 Skyhawks, eventually logged 768 flight hours and 512 accident-free arrested landings. They operated under yet another bizarre rule of engagement: "If an unfriendly aircraft is shot down, every effort shall be made to hide the fact that such action has occurred."

At the sorry end, on 19 April, only two American destroyers were authorized to sniff around for swimmers, but no closer than two miles at night or five miles during the day. (Presumably, after fighting steadily for two days and nights, any survivors of 2506 heading to sea would be swimmers of Olympic quality.) A few subs went in at periscope depth, looking to tow survivors to safety. Only a handful was picked up from the water and from small keys off the coast.

—One last screwup remained. On the morning of 19 April an incoming B-26 raid against Castro's howitzer batteries, which were pounding the brigade to shreds, arrived an hour before its scheduled air cover from *Essex*. Four American "volunteers" in the bombers were shot down (probably by Castro's surprisingly efficient anti-aircraft) and killed. This brought the brigade's air losses to nine B-26s, more than half its "air force," and the remaining Cuban pilots were wisely refusing to fly.

Forewarned by the Saturday raids, Castro had managed to throw twenty thousand men and numerous tanks against the brigade at the point of landing, and quickly. Of greatest importance, there was no "uprising," spontaneous or otherwise; the intelligence surrounding Pluto was noteworthy for its sheer wish fulfillment and imbecility. About 1200 of the men of 2506 Brigade vanished into Castro's prisons; most of the rest lost their lives. They had fought well against impossible odds, killing some 1250 of Castro's men and wounding about 2000 more.

"I'll take the defeat," JFK told his advisers the night of 19 April, "and I'll take all of the blame for it." That was big of him; Kennedy apologists would insist that he had been misled by *both* the CIA and the Joint Chiefs, and later on he would speak to his confidants as if the Chiefs had hoped to sucker him into finally approving American force when Operation Pluto was in extremis. This was far from the truth. The Chiefs, while not *responsible* for Pluto, were expected to *advise*, and with only the sketchiest information from which to work. When the operation began to fall apart, the Chiefs responded like the military men they were, offering military solutions for a military imbroglio. Besides, there was only one man who could have pressed the "stop" button on Pluto, and Kennedy never pressed.

Most of Castro's prisoners from the brigade were ransomed back two years later for $53 million in food and medicine and another $2.9 million for Castro, who claimed the sum as payment for sick and wounded Bay of Pigs survivors already released. This holdup marked a fitting end to the fiasco.

The Bay of Pigs left Burke apoplectic: Pluto ran squarely against the grain of thirty-eight years of commissioned naval service, against everything he had tried to make "my navy" capable of doing in six years as chief of naval operations. The dismal failure of Pluto went far toward making him decline Kennedy's renewed offers of a fourth term in office. In response to Burke's recommendation that *Essex*'s jet fighters take on the Cuban air force, Kennedy had said, "Burke, I don't want the United States involved in this." At that Burke, who had never been much for admiring the emperor's new clothes in any situation, snapped back, "Hell, Mr. President, but we *are* involved." Burke always felt that Kennedy had "chickened out" on the aircraft issue. He left office with little but disdain for the young president and thorough contempt for McNamara, whom he called JFK's "bagman" at the Department of Defense.

The Bay of Pigs was a perfect disaster on every count, one that saddened Navymen everywhere. (A "real debacle," said Red Ramage.) The bungled operation, grist for cartoons if human lives had not been sacrificed, accomplished the following negatives: an overwhelming propaganda coup for communism; a powerful boost to Castro, who could now claim (correctly) that *yanqui imperialismo* had been exposed; and a bitter lesson to Latin Americans that the United States would oppose any social or economic reforms that might lessen its vaunted hegemony in the region, particularly if they bore the odious "Communist" label.

There was one further, and crucial, negative: JFK developed a scathing distrust of his military men, who, he remained convinced, had led him down the garden path. In a postmortem with Eisenhower at Camp David, Kennedy told the ex-president that the two great powers had neutralized each other in nuclear terms, but that in force levels and "communications," the United States was relatively weak. JFK smoldered over the bad advice that he believed he had received from the uniforms. Eisenhower recorded that his young successor "did not seem to think that our great sea power counteracted this situation completely."

Kennedy's militant anticommunism remained in place; on 20 April 1961, the day after he took the rap for the Bay of Pigs, he showed his first substantial interest in Vietnam by establishing a special task force headed by Deputy Under Secretary of Defense Roswell Gilpatric to study the situation. (Gilpatric reported back a week later, with the Bay of Pigs fresh in memory, with the ringing words, "Come what may, the United States intends to *win* this battle.")[5]

An inherently dangerous combination was developing: civilian distrust of military leadership, a military increasingly convinced of its improper use, and an increased civilian willingness to use military force in what the civilian leadership regarded as "proper" instances. While there was plenty of blame to go around for the Bay of Pigs, the civilian side (particularly the inexperienced president and the CIA) had to shoulder the lion's share. Supposed to be a "clandestine military operation," Pluto was both a military operation that failed to be clandestine and a clandestine operation that failed to be military.

—And, cutting right to the bone, was that insidious and obnoxious Communist government in Havana, more secure now than ever before.

☆

The Cuban situation, especially after the Bay of Pigs, was well-nigh irresistible for Khrushchev. In June 1961 he took the measure of the young American president at a face-to-face meeting in Vienna and, in all probability, interpreted Kennedy's reluctance to go forward with military force at the Bay of Pigs as a measure of his "realism." Ideological "spheres of interest," to the Soviet leader's way of thinking, were now possible in the Cold War world. All Russia asked was its proper share.

The Soviet Union could also read the strategic handwriting on the wall. Since World War II, the Russians had lived under the ominous shadow of American nuclear force. First, the Soviet Union had been ringed with strategic bomber bases. Next came sites for sixty Thor medium-range missiles in Britain. After that came more sites for Jupiter missiles, thirty in Italy and fifteen in Turkey. Short-range Matador and Mace tactical cruise missiles were deployed in West Germany.

Although the Russians themselves had deployed medium- and intermediate-range missile systems in response, to target European areas, nuclear superiority lay heavily in favor of the United States. The Kremlin knew there was a "missile gap," all right, but the gap favored the Americans, and to a considerable degree. The deployment of Polaris was the last straw; by the spring of 1962 the United States Navy had enough nuclear-tipped missiles at sea to wipe out every key city in the Soviet Union.

Khrushchev—coarse, theatrical, unpredictable—was fond of talking about America's experts on the Soviet Union, the so-called "Kremlinologists." "They don't understand the Politburo," he chuckled. "They are from a highly educated nation and they look upon us as being equally highly educated. They don't know that we are dominated by an unimaginative and unattractive bunch of scoundrels."

—"A bunch of scoundrels" they may have been, but the Old Bolsheviks who led Russia, hardened survivors of world wars, civil wars, and Stalin's purges, were also seasoned realists, particularly in geopolitics. After the Bay of Pigs, they saw a sight previously unthinkable: a functioning Communist government in the Western Hemisphere, right in the middle of the Caribbean, the most prized of America's lakes. Moreover, this new Cuba had just repelled an American-sponsored invasion. Indeed, Castro's revolution had flushed the American presence completely out of Cuba—except for the naval enclave at Guantanamo Bay.

"Gitmo," on Cuba's southeast coast, was such a capacious haven that Columbus, when he anchored there in April 1494 during his second voyage of discovery, had labeled the spot Puerto Grande. Sheltered by dust-blown, scrub-covered mountains from the seasonal hurricanes that came storming up the Antilles, offering a protected anchorage of fifteen square miles of water, the bay was indeed exceptional. The Navy used Gitmo as an advance base during the Spanish-American War and liked the place so well that, in spite of the fact that American postwar occupation of the island (a product of the Platt Amendment of 1902) galled the Cubans, the service argued for a continued naval presence.

The price was dirt cheap, fully consonant with the nascent age of American imperialism. When Cuba's new government attained independence in February 1903, Theodore Roosevelt cajoled its leadership into leasing Guantanamo and another site, Bahia Honda, in perpetuity for a measly $2000 yearly in gold. (Bahia Honda, fifty miles west of Havana on the north coast, was abandoned nine years later.) A congressional investigating group quickly appropriated $100,000 for a naval base, a joint Cuban-American commission set up the exact boundaries of the reservation, and by 10 December 1903 the Navy had its Caribbean treasure. The United States had complete jurisdiction within the base.

For the immediate future, however, the Navy had slight use for Guantanamo. The old coaling station at Hospital Cay would spring to life each winter, when the fleet came south for maneuvers. Then the three hundred or so officers and men assigned to Gitmo could see their bay lined with battlewagons and cruisers. For the rest of the time, though, except for a flurry during World War I, the base slumbered under the Caribbean sun. Even though FDR abrogated the Platt Amendment (which allowed the United States to militarily intervene at any time and which was bitterly resented by Cubans), Guantanamo remained American.

World War II woke the base up. On 7 December 1941, Gitmo had two airfields, a tank farm, a hospital, assorted repair shops, and barracks. During the war the base's services grew ever more dense, and the reservation boundaries were suddenly constraining. In the Cold War period, Guantanamo continued to flourish, for several reasons: its crucial Caribbean location; its usefulness for training, particularly in antisubmarine warfare, at any time of year; and its value as a logistics concentration and staging point.

The Soviets knew all about Gitmo, and about the confluence of CINC-

LANT assets there. At one time or another almost every ship in the Atlantic Fleet would be run through Guantanamo Bay for what the Navy called refresher training and what sweaty sailors undergoing the weeks-long ordeal called "REFTRA." The Soviets also knew that water was critical there; rainfall totaled only twenty-five inches a year, practically a drought for the Caribbean, and almost 20,000 of the base's 28,821 acres were arid hills and salt flats—the rest was bay surface. The area was so dry that when the Navy built a radar station atop a four-hundred-foot hill, a cable had to be run all the way to the beach to find soil moist enough to ground the gear properly.

Water was the base's Achilles' heel. By 1962 almost four thousand Cubans from surrounding towns were working there, and the United States, despite the formal cessation of trade, was thus injecting around $7 million annually into the Cuban economy. Castro could turn his Cubans off at any time, just as he could turn off the water, every drop of which came from the Yateras River, four miles outside the base. The Cuban government ran the pumping station. Guantanamo's storage tanks held a three-week water supply, and there were contingency plans to use Navy tankers to bring in water in case Castro acted.

In the post-Pluto climate, Guantanamo Bay, for all its hustle and bustle, was at risk as a naval base. Castro, of course, steadily and loudly demanded its surrender. Outside the twenty-one miles of fence ringing its land side, Cuban soldiers, armed with Russian and Czech automatic weapons and tanks, stood wary guard. Rear Admiral Edward O'Donnell, who commanded the base in 1961, said, "If anyone attacks, we'll fight." His Marines had orders to hold the base at least two or three days. After the Bay of Pigs, 6300 Americans were inside the fences, counting dependents.

Some naval officers yearned for the day when fast-moving nuclear-powered ships would enable them to get rid of albatrosses like Gitmo; even in 1961, beer, softball, and sunshine—not the strategic location—were the main attractions there for sailors. O'Donnell knew that the Navy's dependence on shore facilities like his command was declining, but after Pluto, Guantanamo Bay had escalated from sunny naval training base to glaring Cold War symbol. In November 1961, Castro cleared a network of military roads sloping down from the surrounding hills, and Cuban gun emplacements and observation posts speckled the heights. In February his novice blue-shirted militiamen outside the fences gave way to 3500 fresh young troops in battle fatigues, trained up in those same hills by Russian and Czech advisers.

In turn, the base itself was augmented by almost a thousand Marines.[6]

☆

The Russian "scoundrels" appreciated the importance of Guantanamo Bay as a symbol, but to them a Communist Cuba was the far greater prize.

Khrushchev loved to play with symbols. "Berlin is the testicles of the West," he once declaimed. "Every time I want to make the West scream, I squeeze on Berlin." But the Russians could not get at the United States directly from Berlin.

At the same time that Castro was moving his recently trained troops into position above Gitmo, American intelligence began to get reports of increased numbers of Russians visiting Cuba. Most of them, although the Americans could not have known, were advance men, charged with selecting locations for Soviet missile emplacements. The Cubans provided their visitors with excellent data and large-scale topographic maps, produced in the late 1950s by an American constructor. The same maps would eventually be used by American analysts to plot all new Soviet construction on the island.

The decision to implant the missiles had already been made in the upper reaches of the Politburo, probably between November 1961 (when the latest Soviet gambit over Berlin failed) and February 1962. American experts later estimated that the unfolding Russian operation would have taken at least six months of planning, and Castro himself later revealed that the decision to place Soviet missiles in Cuba was made "at the beginning of 1962."

The Soviet supply effort was huge: an initial provision of conventional weapons, such as three varieties (15, 17, 19) of MiG aircraft, tanks, artillery, and electronic equipment; defensive armament, such as surface-to-air missiles, coastal defense missiles, and KOMAR patrol boats; protective shields for the missile emplacements; advanced aircraft like the MiG-21 and the medium-range Il-28 Beagle bomber; and medium-range ballistic missiles. There was to be a final phase, the shipment and emplacement of nuclear-tipped intermediate-range ballistic missiles. Khrushchev later said the idea for this buildup came to him during a visit to Bulgaria in May 1962, but the massive size of the supply effort suggested that he was off by at least half a year. The month of May might have been the time he gave the go-ahead for the crucial move, which was the emplacement of the nuclear missiles.

The Soviet decision was a breathtaking gamble born of strategic desperation, one to which Castro and his coterie gave their willing assent. The Kremlin's thinking was conditioned by an excruciating feeling of strategic inferiority, in the sense that Russia was surrounded by the nuclear weapons of the West. For a nation invaded three times from the West since 1812, each time with catastrophic results, a nation concentrated to the point of paranoia to meeting the challenges of the world outside its borders, the Cuban situation was heaven- (or Lenin-) sent. Now America's overwhelming advantage in nuclear bases and weaponry would prove as temporary as its monopoly of the atomic bomb had been in the 1940s.

Through the spring and summer of 1962, rumors of the enormous Russian effort continued to leak out of Cuba. Kennedy may have had some solid evidence as early as July. Aerial monitoring of Cuban-Russian signals traffic was almost constant. In July alone, naval surveillance detected thirty Soviet merchantmen arriving in Cuba, a 50 percent increase in one month. On 29 August 1962 a U-2 reconnaissance flight was assigned to photograph the entire island. Although clouds obscured much of the east, what got onto film shook the CIA's photo analysts. Before them in grainy black-and-white enlargements were eight Soviet surface-to-air-missile sites scattered along Cuba's northwest coast. The sites, joined by a road network in the familiar Russian "Star of David" pattern, were clearly designed to provide strategic area defense of the entire island. They also featured the latest guidance radar, the NATO-code-named Fruit Set (Model C).

The same day, the Navy spotted a KOMAR boat at sea near the port of Mariel. Eventually seven were found, and more Cuban patrol craft were being converted to missile shooters. On 7 September JFK sent a memo to Secretary of the Navy Fred Korth: "I would like to get a report on the ability of our destroyers to deal effectively with the new motor torpedo boats of the KOMAR class that the Cubans now possess."[7]

—By that date, the American leadership had a far greater "emergency" on its hands than ever before, and the United States Navy was up to its gunwales in what came to be called the Cuban Missile Crisis.

☆

As early as 1960, Eisenhower had authorized "off-course" Navy reconnaissance planes, ostensibly headed for Guantanamo, to photograph suspected Soviet missile sites in Cuba—with no luck. The Cubans had not been amused by a succession of constantly "straying" aircraft. The afternoon following the epochal U-2 mission, 30 August 1962, a Grumman S2F, manned by three Reservists on a training mission, was fired on by two Cuban patrol craft fifteen nautical miles off the port of Cardenas. "What in the hell are reservists doing training so close to Cuba?" screamed John Kennedy. "Have we run out of training space in the United States?"

The president's outburst aside, the evidence from the U-2 was both harrowing and convincing. Something out of the ordinary run of arms trading was occurring in Cuba. Responding to a Defense Department order by Gilpatric, the Navy in early September transferred Fighter Squadron 41 and its twelve F-4B Phantom IIs from Oceana, Virginia, to Key West. VF-41 contained some of the Navy's hottest rocks; the squadron immediately began to concern itself with Cuban pilots flying MiG-21 Fishbeds.

The Phantoms did not have long to wait. On 8 September two MiG-17s jumped two S2Fs out of Key West and made simulated firing runs, again over international waters. Two F-4Ds scrambled to help, but the MiGs fled before they arrived. When Vice President Lyndon Johnson heard about the incident, he exploded: "Next time they appear, shoot their asses out of the sky."

The incidents with the S2Fs, along with the U-2 information, worried Rusk, badly burned diplomatically by the Bay of Pigs and now twice shy. He several times raised the issue of violating Cuban airspace. Attorney General Robert Kennedy, the president's younger brother, responded, "Let's sustain the overflights and the hell with the international issues." No satellite imagery was yet available, and side-look cameras operating from offshore were unsatisfactory. To find out accurately what was going on in Cuba, the United States *had* to violate Castro's airspace.

Yet partially due to Rusk's concerns and partially due to bad weather, the U-2s did not fly for several critical weeks in September. JFK was involved in an off-year election. Although Republicans were harping on the issue of "communism in the Western Hemisphere" in the campaign, and although the Soviets had publicly admitted that they were sending "arms" and technicians to Cuba, Berlin was the major issue as October arrived. All the while, the Soviet supply effort went on, even including nine short-range Luna rockets (NATO-code-named Frog). The Frogs were armed with approximately ten-kiloton warheads and had a range of twenty to twenty-five miles. (Their existence in Cuba would not be revealed for thirty years.)

George Anderson, Burke's successor as chief of naval operations, would later testify that he knew in September that the Soviets were putting offensive missiles in Cuba (not simply the air-defense SA-2s), but how he had gotten this information was never made clear. Regardless, he and Bob Dennison began to act. They had a Marine option available; indeed, the Corps, never overly subtle in its public relations, had announced that there was going to be an amphibious brigade exercise (PHIBRIGLEX) in the Caribbean in the fall of 1962, the central feature of which was to be a Marine invasion of the mythical Republic of Vieques to liquidate its equally mythical dictator, "Ortsac."

Dennison had to deal with real dictators who spelled their names front-to-back. On 1 October, still with no real information beyond the month-old U-2 flight, scattered bits of intelligence, and solemn, self-serving Russian pronunciamentos, he began to prepare an air-strike plan against the known Cuban bases—312 OPLAN. The Kennedy administration, which gave Dennison the green light, was clearly and properly doing its military preparation for any contingency. Dennison was told to have 312 OPLAN at "maximum readiness" by 20 October.[8]

In addition to 312, the air-strike option, McNamara and the Joint Chiefs also developed two others: 314, concerning airborne and amphibious assaults after eighteen days of preparation, and 316, an air assault after five days of preparation and an amphibious landing three days later, aimed at the "removal of the threat of Soviet weapons." Dennison, besides ginning up 312, was ordered to update his contingency plans for Cuba, which had been on paper ever since the Bay of Pigs. On 3 October, CINCLANT promulgated an operations order (still contingency) for the blockade of the island. The plan, as befitted such an imposing piece of real estate, was exceptionally complex, including a blockading group and other groups for cover, logistics, and ASW. As time went on, the blockade plan would undergo considerable modification and get thoroughly worked over by legal specialists.

Every service was involved in the contingency planning. Army plans extended to the company level; jump zones were chosen for the airborne; known beach obstacles and fortifications were carefully charted. The Air Force began to target every known military installation on the island. Dennison threw in a plan for the mining of all Cuban harbors. The United States, at least partially forewarned, intended to be forearmed and not surprised. Any response to the Russian initiative would be no "clandestine military operation."

PHIBRIGLEX-62 was scheduled for the 15th to the 20th of October. The attack on the evil "Ortsac" was built around Amphibious Squadron 8, with thousands of Marines loaded aboard fifteen assault ships. The task force also included four carriers and twenty destroyers. The Navy was fully prepared to "exercise" in naval air bombardment, live ship fire, amphibious assault, and combat support ashore. "Ortsac" himself was convinced that the much-publicized exercise was but a prelude to an actual attack on Cuba, and he began to alert his forces accordingly. As he did so, UNITAS III, the third annual ASW exercise with Latin American navies, was nearing completion.

In sum, the largest part of Bob Dennison's striking power was, as of 15 October 1962, either at sea or ready to go.

☆

—On that day, another U-2 flight brought back the first hard evidence of *offensive* missile sites in Cuba. These were SS-4s (Sandals), medium-range nuclear ballistic missiles. Unlike the SA-2s, which were for air defense, or the Frogs, which could barely reach offshore, the SS-4s were rated at a range of 1100 miles, an arc that included within the United States such targets as Washington, Dallas, Atlanta, New Orleans, three major naval bases, eighteen SAC bomber and tanker bases, and an ICBM base. Also included in the SS-4 strike profile were Puerto Rico and the Panama Canal.

Full alert. The Navy, with its well-developed low-altitude jet reconnaissance capability, received new orders. Light Photographic Squadron 62, under Commander William Ecker, flying F8U-1P Crusaders and based at Cecil Field outside Jacksonville, got the task of close-in recce. VFP-62's aviators had operated around the world, off the decks of twenty-two different carriers. They were the best in the business at what they did, which was to zoom in at lower than five hundred feet to provide a hundred-mile swath of photographic coverage. Their targets this time were tough, hidden in karst hills and tucked among pockets of scrub pine. By 16 October the unit had a list of possible sites and had begun to fly its missions.

The same day, JFK first met with the group of special advisers, dubbed the Executive Committee (EXCOM), that in differing combinations was to offer up recommendations throughout the crisis. Its members included top administration officials—Rusk, McNamara, the trusted Secretary of the Treasury C. Douglas Dillon, Lyndon Johnson, and Robert Kennedy; national security specialists—John McCone of the CIA, McGeorge Bundy, the national security adviser, Gilpatric, and Paul Nitze, the assistant secretary of defense for international security affairs; and other assorted Wise Men, chief among them Dean Acheson and the chief UN delegate, Adlai Stevenson. Indicative of the president's distrust of the military, there was only one military man among the EXCOM—General Maxwell Taylor, the polished paratrooper who had recently relieved Lemnitzer as chairman of the Joint Chiefs of Staff. The group was formally established on 22 October by National Security Memorandum 196.

The EXCOM, almost all civilians, began by debating what to do, mostly in military terms. Acheson, whose militance as a Cold Warrior had increased in direct proportion to the length of his absence from office, wanted a "demonstration" of American military superiority, something that PHIBRIGLEX-62 was fully prepared to do. Taylor, speaking for the unanimous Joint Chiefs, believed that the emplacement of the SS-4s was a major effort by the Soviet Union to change the strategic balance of power. He proposed a full panoply of military responses—an air strike, an airborne assault, and an invasion—to wipe out the missile sites. Outside the EXCOM, the airstrike option was fiercely promoted by that arch-hawk Curtis LeMay, now chief of staff of the Air Force. (LeMay had once been asked what he would do about the problem of a Communist Cuba. His reply was terse: "Fry it.")

Robert Kennedy, much despised by most of the country's top military men as an officious, loud-mouthed meddler, had one great virtue in this unprecedented situation: he was his older brother's trusted confidant. "The United States," he said, "would be damned in the eyes of the world forever should such a military operation [an air strike] be undertaken." (At this point he made his famous statement that his brother would not go down in history as the American Tojo.) Acheson thought that Bobby behaved "like Captain Bligh on the foredeck."

The younger Kennedy was indeed, at this time in his life, a cocky and hard-to-take scattershot artist who was obviously riding on his older brother's coattails. But he was asking the right questions. When he pressed Taylor for reassurances that an air strike could eradicate all the missile sites, the general had to honestly reply that "it was reasonable to conclude that there would be a retaliatory strike, however minimal, against the United States."

—With this, the boundaries of the debate within the EXCOM were set, the lines drawn between the misleadingly labeled "hawks" and "doves." In fact, both factions proposed the use of military force; the arguments were over the possible methods of application. The first meeting was inconclusive, but on the next day, 17 October, the group presented JFK with three specific courses of action, or "tracks." Track A was political pressure, to be followed by a military strike if no satisfaction was forthcoming. Track B was essentially the Taylor–Joint Chiefs plan, a military strike without prior warning, to be accompanied by soothing international messages about the "limited" nature of the action. Track C was political pressure again, this time to be accompanied by congressional action, up to and including a declaration of war, and—a naval blockade.

The blockade idea began to gather support within the EXCOM. Few of the civilians had much idea of what a blockade actually entailed, particularly under international law, but some of them began to see that the notion was less dangerous, more reversible than an all-out military strike. A blockade, by any name, would also serve a psychological, tactical objective: to show the Soviet Union the partial extent of American will.

As the advisers batted ideas back and forth, the Joint Chiefs sent two naval officers over to the CIA's interpreting center to see what could be done. The Navymen were concerned with the effective range of the MiG-21s. First, they drew a five-hundred-mile arc centered on Cape Maysi, the eastern tip of Cuba. Then, when the photo interpreters showed them the military buildup in the Havana area, they struck a second five-hundred-mile arc, with the Cuban capital at the center.

LeMay and the rest of the Air Force leadership hated the blockade idea, certainly from keenly felt interservice rivalry but also because the option was clearly not the whole hog. George Anderson strongly argued for invasion. Robert Kennedy, however, seized on the blockade notion, and so too did his brother, who was concerned about the air-strike option not only on moral grounds but also on the realistic premise that an air strike would probably kill some of the Russians manning the sites and exacerbate rather than resolve the crisis. Also, JFK knew that an air strike had to be totally successful, and that was a guarantee neither Taylor, LeMay, nor General Walter Sweeney, commander of the Tactical Air Force, could give.

On the morning of 18 October, by a vote of 11–6, the EXCOM approved the option of a naval blockade of Cuba.[9]

☆

By 1330 that afternoon, Dennison's CINCLANT plan had been reworked yet again to include the new blockade option. A Gallup public opinion poll taken a week later would show that 81 percent of those respondents aware of the crisis favored the blockade, with only 4 percent opposed. The blockade would be directed against Soviet "offensive" weapons inbound to Cuba and would operate within the charter provisions of the Rio Treaty and the Organization of American States. When Dennison and Taylor briefed JFK, Anderson, in a telling commentary on the new civilian-military power relationships since the Defense Reorganization Act of 1958, was not present.

The president chose the word *quarantine* rather than *blockade* to describe the American intention—the establishment of the latter, under international law, was an act of war.

The United States did not intend a blockade, in any case. A true naval blockade, of the kind the Union Navy had clamped on the Confederacy during the Civil War, penalized all seaborne traffic, including ordinary and neutral maritime commerce, directed at a specific state or area. "Quarantine" was a far hazier notion. "No one knew exactly what a quarantine meant," Rusk admitted. Acheson was more blunt: "To hell with international law. . . . If you're troubled with what the books may say about the blockade, then change the name."

"A naval quarantine for collective regional purposes need not be legally founded on belligerency," analyzed one naval lawyer, but the term was unfortunate nevertheless, because *nothing* would be "quarantined" by the Navy's actions. What would occur was *selective interdiction* on the high seas, and for those who were historically minded would run directly counter to age-old American claims for "freedom of the seas."[10]

Furthermore, the United States Navy had not the slightest idea (nor did any other navy) about how to conduct such a "quarantine." But the service knew how to interdict, sifting acceptable ships through a blockade net like sand through a sieve. Anderson and Dennison planned such an interdiction action, under control of higher authority. Anderson reassured JFK on the morning of 19 October that all references to the action would be changed to "quarantine"—as if this somehow changed the legal and international ramifications of what the United States was about.

Already the naval forces were moving, rerouting, and coalescing into powerful formations. On 17 October, Vice Admiral Alfred ("Corky") Ward, commander of Dennison's Amphibious Forces and thus deeply involved with PHIBRIGLEX-62, was called by a CINCLANT staff captain, who told him he would be relieved of command the next day. Ward blurted, "What have I done wrong?"

A good question; Corky Ward had done little wrong in his distinguished career. From Mobile, Alabama, he graduated from the Naval Academy (where he had edited the *Lucky Bag*) in the most dismal year of the Depression, 1932. He was a gunclubber, serving in destroyers and cruisers and then aboard *North Carolina* from 1941 to 1944. In 1940 he received a master's degree in engineering from MIT. He finished World War II at the Naval Gun Factory in Washington.

In the decade following V-J Day, Ward rose steadily—Destroyer Division 102, the Strategic Plans Division (where he worked closely with Dennison), Amphibious Squadron 8, a planner for CINCLANT, Cruiser Division 1, assistant chief of naval operations for fleet ops. From the last post he went to command the Atlantic Fleet's Gators. Throughout his career,

Ward had been immersed, unlike people such as Louis Denfeld or even Dennison, in seagoing assignments. His competence had been recognized from his midshipman days onward; he had been deep-selected for Flag Plot.

Anderson and Dennison, seeing a possible shooting war on the Caribbean horizon, wanted a long tenure of command for Second Fleet. Corky Ward was their man. From 18 to 20 October, as Ward hustled to prepare himself, Second Fleet oilers, ammunition ships, and reefers were putting to sea, fully loaded, from Atlantic ports. His replacement as the amphibious commander, Horacio Rivero, was readying his Gators. Surface combatants were clearing breakwaters all along the coast. Less ostentatiously, attack submarines were silently gliding toward station. Ward, feeling his fleet sliding out from under him, ran through a quick change-of-command ceremony in Norfolk on the 20th aboard his flagship, *Newport News*, then joined Dennison for a flight to Washington. Airborne, Ward heard for the first time from his boss about the Soviet missiles in Cuba.

Ward was told that his ships would carry out the interdiction. By the 21st, Russian-speaking naval officers were beginning to board designated Second Fleet vessels. Above Ward, the chain of command, decided on three days before, ran from the Joint Chiefs (responsible for the overall planning) to CINCLANT, the pertinent unified command. Under Dennison were Ward and Army and Air Force commanders. Anderson was assigned to act for the Joint Chiefs in all matters relating to the blockade, an ad hoc arrangement to directly use the naval expertise on the Joint Chiefs of Staff.

The entire American military establishment was shifting into high gear. Rear Admiral Rhomad McElroy, in charge of Key West, found overnight that his base (normally the drowsiest of commands) had become the locus of swarms of strike, reconnaissance, and air defense planes. VF-41 was maintaining continuous patrol off Cuba's north shore. VFP-62 was setting up shop; its photo lab went into one of McElroy's hangars. Boca Chica, home of the Key West Naval Air Station, was soon stuffed to the gills with seventy-six fighters, fifty-seven attack aircraft, and ten patrol planes.

Down at Guantanamo, Patrol Squadron 56 arrived from Norfolk, with orders to locate and track all Cuba-bound shipping. The PatRon joined twenty-four other assorted naval attack aircraft—not many, but then they would not have far to fly to their targets. From Gitmo and all along the Atlantic and Gulf coasts, picket ships put to sea, headed for assigned barrier stations in the Atlantic and the Gulf of Mexico.

Ward, back from Washington, briefed his subordinates and caught up with his widely scattered, rapidly moving command. Task Force 135, bult around the newest carriers in the Navy, *Enterprise* and *Independence*, was on its way to station off the south coast of Cuba with an underway-replenishment group and fifteen destroyers. If word came down, its mission was strike. Task Force 136 was the interdiction force, composed of *Essex*, *Newport*

News, and *Canberra*, along with an underway-replenishment group and nineteen destroyers. Corky Ward was not only at sea in force; he intended to remain there.

The operations order for Task Force 136 featured the five-hundred-mile arc to the northeast, centered on Cape Maysi. The "quarantine line," which in practice was an extremely general guide, consisted of twelve destroyer stations, sixty miles apart, along the arc. *Canberra* and her two escorts anchored the northern end, *Newport News* and her two the southern. *Essex*, with five destroyers, served as a backstop, taking station farther west, behind the arc.

There also was, in a bid toward Rio Treaty solidarity, Task Force 137, which formed late with little. This force was composed of the American destroyer *Mullinnix*, along with two destroyers apiece from Argentina, Venezuela, and the Dominican Republic. (Brazil, for strange reasons of its own, said that its navy would participate but chose to do so through destroyer patrols off its own coast—perhaps in case Khrushchev decided to ship missiles to Rio de Janeiro.)

By 22 October, Ward was able to tell Dennison that over 150 naval vessels, all of them belonging to the United States Navy, were on station. Everything had been accomplished in the span of less than a week, an absolutely remarkable example of planning and execution. Forty-six of the ships, along with 250 naval aircraft and thirty thousand men, were directly involved in locating shipping either inbound to or outbound from Cuba. In Florida, naval aircraft were part of a force of 156 planes that were fully combat-loaded, prepared to strike Cuban targets immediately. Both the Navy and Air Force were ready to conduct continuous strike warfare. Planners for the Joint Chiefs estimated that almost 1200 sorties could be flown the first day.

On the afternoon of the 21st, Anderson had briefed JFK on the whole setup: intercept codes, linguists, station positions, shots across the bow, minimum force, shots fired at rudders, boarding if necessary. He was confident; he knew the Soviet navy could not adequately cover its merchant shipping so far from home. As he ended his two-hour briefing and was putting his charts away, he found Kennedy at his side with the words, "Well, Admiral, it looks as though this is up to the Navy."

George Anderson did not miss a beat. "Mr. President," he replied, "the Navy will not let you down."[11]

☆

On the evening of the 22nd, Kennedy went before the television cameras and, in a speech that riveted the nation, told the American people of the crisis, the "quarantine" decision, and, most horrifyingly, of his resolve to respond directly against the Soviet Union in the case of an attack from Cuba.

Now, the Cuban Missile Crisis engaged the world, and the nuclear peril suddenly appeared more stark and terrifying than ever before.

The offensive weapons, said JFK, could not be allowed to remain on Cuban soil. Those that were there must be removed; those in transit would be stopped. These weapons were defined as MRBMs and bombers, such as the Il-28s, which could strike the United States directly. Defensive weapons were those that could not, like the air-defense SA-2s.

As the president spoke, things were not going too well. Ward had decreed that amphibious training exercises be conducted in Florida in as realistic an environment as possible; rehearsals were de rigueur for naval amphibious operations. Hollywood Beach, near Fort Lauderdale, a tourist trap festooned with hotels, motels, restaurants, and bars, was the unlikely site selected by harried staffers. By the time Marines and Army personnel sauntered ashore, several hours late, the noonday sun was out and sunbathers were gaping from the shade of their beach umbrellas. Some of the "amphibious assault force" spent their time fraternizing with the bikinis, in a replay of the Lebanon landing four years before; others cheerfully posed for tourist cameras; a considerable number could find nothing better to do than invade the bars. "We had one helluva time rounding up that group for reembarkation," remarked a landing party officer. Corky Ward said the drill was the closest thing to the Keystone Kops he had ever seen.

Down at Guantanamo were over nine hundred families, about 2800 women and children, living on base. McNamara, against advice that this would add to a panic atmosphere, insisted that they be evacuated—and they were. The Navy rounded up a transport, a seaplane tender, a refrigerator ship, and a landing ship, and, even before Kennedy went on the air, Ed O'Donnell had the dependents aboard. In a reprise of the evacuation from Egypt in 1956, the civilians found accommodations aboard a bit unusual, but they all eventually got to Norfolk. Guantanamo was left with 120 airplanes, 5750 Marines, 155 tanks, a Hawk missile battery, three gunfire support ships—and Task Force 135, lurking just over the horizon. When Stevenson had suggested in the EXCOM that the base be closed down as part of a trade to get the Russian missiles out, he had gotten nowhere. Gitmo would be held.

After JFK's speech, the public focus shifted to the conduct of the "quarantine." Chatting with his younger brother and some other advisers the day following his television address, Kennedy mentioned Barbara Tuchman's best-selling account of the beginning of World War I in Europe, *The Guns of August*—a work he had just read. Tuchman's history was replete with the blunders that had triggered the cataclysm. JFK wished that a copy could be sent "to every Navy officer on every Navy ship right now." Then, perhaps remembering his own career in uniform, he added, "but they probably wouldn't read it."

Unknown to the public, behind-the-scenes diplomacy and intelligence-gathering were going on around the clock. From the Navy's perspective, VFP-62 went through the workout of its squadron life. Bill Ecker's sixteen Crusaders got fancy new camera mounts (custom-designed in Lieutenant Cecil Ogles's garage) and began flying their hair-raising, low-level reconnaissance missions. Their take was superb: screaming in right over the missile sites at low altitude, cameras humming steadily, the aviators jotted notes on military activity around the designated targets. The squadron painted a dead hanging chicken on the fuselage of each plane after every successful mission—a reference to Castro and his entourage, who on a visit to the United Nations had insisted on cooking chicken in their rooms, to the outrage of hotel managers and the delight of the tabloids.

VFP-62 brought back the goods. Now the photo interpreters began to assemble the entire picture—sites, launchers, transporters, generators, cranes, trailers, air compressors, even decontamination shower units (a tip that nuclear materials had arrived or were on the way). The briefing boards for both the EXCOM and the Joint Chiefs became cluttered with detail. When Kennedy was shown the work of VFP-62 and other units, he could not believe that planes flying so low and so fast could register such images.

—But they could. By the end, VFP-62 had a Presidential Unit Citation.[12]

☆

The Crusaders and camera-carrying P2V Neptunes also ranged far out to sea, hunting for missile-laden freighters. When the planes found them, they photographed them, roaring in at masthead height to do so. Not only did the photo analysts reap a fresh and rewarding harvest of material, but the skippers aboard the merchant vessels (by no means all of the ships or the men aboard them were Russian) knew, in no uncertain terms, that they were being monitored—and they had radios.

By the day of Kennedy's speech, American intelligence estimated that approximately ten thousand Russians were in Cuba. (The Russians later said that over forty thousand of their personnel had been there.) Among them, clearly marked from the air by their unit symbols and insignia implanted in flagstone and flowers around garrison positions, were infantry, motorized rifle, and airborne outfits. As soon as VFP-62 and other surveillance crews got them on film, they were targeted. The presence of nuclear warheads themselves was uncertain. Almost thirty years later, a Russian general would say that twenty warheads had arrived in Cuba during the crisis. Twenty more, he added, had been aboard the Soviet merchantman *Poltava*.

—None of this, of course, was known by the Navymen out on the interdiction line. The line, despite debates among the Joint Chiefs, remained at five hundred miles until moved closer to Cuba on 29 October. On 23

October the line began to do business. The ships were in direct contact with Anderson's Flag Plot, Room 6D624 of the Pentagon, and Anderson was hooked into CINCLANT, the White House, McNamara, and Korth. Here, in Flag Plot, the positions of the American warships on the line were meticulously plotted and updated on a large wall chart of the Atlantic and Caribbean. The chart also showed the positions of all foreign merchant shipping in the quarantine zone. Navy and Air Force eyes tried to be everywhere: the Puerto Rico Trench, pathway to Havana; the Straits of Florida; Caicos Passage in the Bahamas; the Mona and Windward passages, routes to Cuba's southern ports.

Shipping companies around the world, fearful for their cargoes, were bombarding the Navy for instructions. Diplomats deluged the State and Defense departments with questions. Flag Plot fielded all such queries and requests on the fly, but Anderson was concentrating on Soviet and Soviet-contract shipping. He had *Oxford*, loaded with electronic snooper gear, stationed just off Havana to intercept Russian signals; concerned, JFK ordered *Oxford* a bit farther out to sea.

Anderson's chief military concern was not the unarmed merchantmen but Russian submarines. Intelligence from a variety of sources, including snoopers like *Oxford*, said that four or five *Foxtrot*-class diesel boats had left Murmansk on 27 September, headed for the Atlantic. The *Foxtrots* were long-range attack submarines, suspected of being armed with nuclear-tipped torpedoes. Also, a Soviet refrigerator ship and the auxiliary oiler *Terek* had showed up in the Atlantic, as had the ubiquitous Soviet intelligence trawler (in this case, *Skval*). The trio was ideal for supporting submarine operations.

By the day of Kennedy's speech, the subs and their surface shepherds were already about six hundred miles from the interdiction line, the first time, to the Navy's knowledge, that Russian boats had ventured so close to American home waters. One of the *Foxtrots* surfaced that morning in the mid-Atlantic to recharge batteries, and a long-range *Zulu*-class diesel sub was seen several hundred miles to the north near *Terek*. The mission of these boats was unclear to the Americans (and indeed may have been unclear to the Russian skippers themselves), but Anderson took no chances. He sicced his destroyers, patrol aircraft, and helicopters on the submarines and put American subs in trail of the oiler. Orders were cut to sink *Terek* and the Russian boats on command. *Skval* was also steaming on borrowed time; if conflict occurred, the Navy had orders to sink all Soviet intelligence collectors, wherever found.

McNamara was a frequent visitor to Flag Plot. Like Anderson, he was aware that no Soviet submarine had ever been known to visit a Cuban port. On the evening of the 23rd, as the line began to operate, McNamara learned that at least seven freighters capable of carrying missiles or missile equipment were en route to Cuba. Two (*Poltava* and *Krasnograd*) were ships with hatches large enough to carry eighty-foot missiles in their holds. Some of the freight-

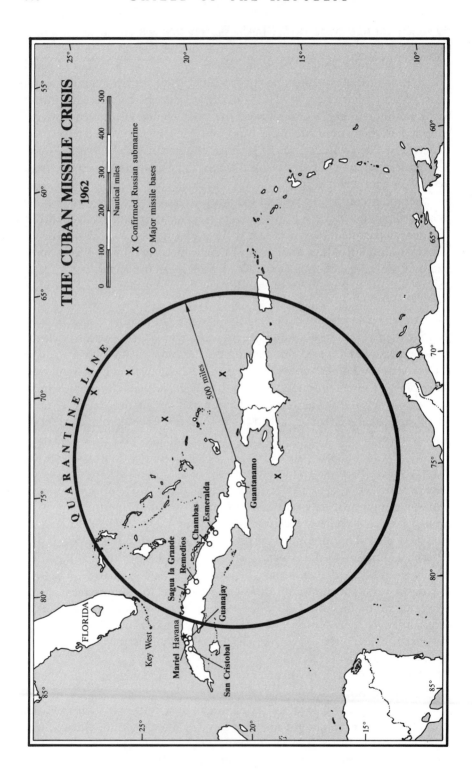

ers were also carrying deck cargo; one had thirteen Il-28 bombers crated topside.

That evening, interest zeroed in on *Poltava*. She was brand-new, at 12,500 tons the lead ship of her cargo class. *Poltava* had two trucks lashed on deck, both with unique and oddly offset truckbeds. Each bed was offset to take a large metal ring, which analysts identified as a launch support ring for the SS-5 Skean missile. (The SS-5 was a finless, single-stage IRBM with a range of 2200 miles.) *Poltava* accordingly became a prime Navy target; *Newport News* and two destroyers were detailed to stop her if ordered.

Anderson was on edge. That afternoon the British ambassador, David Ormsby-Gore, had met with his longtime friend JFK to urgently request that the interdiction line be retracted to a position closer to Cuba, so that Khrushchev could have more time to react to Kennedy's speech. Anderson, acutely conscious of the combat range of the MiGs in Cuba, got irate at the suggestion; only if the president so ordered, he rumbled.

—The president did not so order (not until the 29th), and the Soviet freighters doggedly continued to plod forward. To Anderson and LeMay, Khrushchev was erratic and unpredictable; direct force was the only way— Anderson said "unsheathing the cold blue steel of power"—to confront him. From his Second Fleet command, Corky Ward read all the Joint Chiefs as being wary of Kennedy in this regard. No American military man wanted to be "the Kimmel and Short of this generation" (a reference to the admiral and lieutenant general who were sacked from their Pearl Harbor commands after the Japanese attack). LeMay, as usual, was the most outspoken. "The Russian bear has always been eager to stick his paw in Latin American waters," he complained. "Now, we've got him in a trap, let's take his leg off right up to his testicles. On second thought, let's take off his testicles, too."

Meanwhile, as the freighters drew ever nearer, all of the Joint Chiefs had to think about unified defense. On 24 October they issued Defcon 2— the second highest order of military alert, with a readiness posture to strike Russia, Cuba, or both. As they did so, a *Foxtrot* moved closer to some of the Soviet merchantmen; Anderson put more destroyers in trail. Suddenly word was flashed that some of the Soviet ships had been observed to be either turned about or to be dead in the water; by noon Navy intelligence specialists assigned to the National Security Agency were refining data suggesting that sixteen of the eighteen ships under observation, some with the extra-large hatches, were definitely either heading back or standing still. One of them was *Poltava*.

The secretary of defense had not been told this information (nor had JFK) until the material, in the way of intelligence guesstimates, took firm shape. Enraged, McNamara barged into Flag Plot "like a madman," chewing out every naval officer in sight. Anderson was summoned, got McNamara off to the side, and was summarily told that the secretary was not pleased with the Navy's performance. This got Anderson's back up, and he rejoined that he, the chief of naval operations, would be responsible for the Navy's actions. With that, McNamara stormed away. Captain Isaac ("Ike") Kidd—the son of the rear admiral who had died at Pearl Harbor—was on duty in Flag Plot, and he later claimed that a shouting match ("angry words") never happened.

They were all under enormous—and intensifying—pressure. That evening some of the EXCOM, with coolheaded Admiral Claude Ricketts, Anderson's vice chief, in attendance, reviewed the day's developments. The Russians were now showing caution. JFK directed Ward not to board or stop any Soviet vessel bound for Cuba but to keep them all under surveillance. No interception of a Soviet ship had yet been necessary.

Meanwhile Defcon 2, like some great, cresting wave, surged onward. McNamara set seven days as the time when American forces would be ready to invade Cuba. LeMay had 1436 bombers and 134 ICBMs on constant alert; one-eighth of his bombers were airborne at all times. Anderson recapitulated his orders for a constant watch on the submarines. He was supremely confident that Dennison, Ward, and the other naval commanders closer to the scene knew their duty.

A letter arrived from Khrushchev (his second to Kennedy during the crisis) saying that "you, Mr. President, have challenged us." The Soviet leader seemed to be pleading (not demanding) that Soviet ships be allowed through the Navy line, that his country not be totally humiliated. These were mixed signals; some American military leaders thought that he had capitulated, asking that a few merchantmen be let through to save face. Others thought that new threats (such as over Berlin) were to come and that the Russian was stalling. "We should rub their noses in it a little," gloated Robert Kennedy.

McNamara, awash on every side from incoming streams of information, some of which was partial or conflicting, was naturally frazzled. Here was a true, unparalleled "emergency," with *many* things needing to be done, and each one had to be done first. On the evening of the 24th, tense and tired, he was back in Flag Plot again, and again he got into an argument with Anderson. This time the subject was naval hold-down procedures on the Soviet submarines. Some of the destroyers had strayed from the line during their prosecution of contacts, and McNamara wanted to know why. When the secretary asked how the Navy knew that these were Russian subs, Anderson, the consummate naval professional, gave an impolitic answer: "Trust me."

McNamara was again incensed by what he took to be Anderson's casual attitude. He insisted that Anderson send out a special order detailing submarine surfacing and identification procedures, which turned out to be both redundant and ineffective, since the Russian submarines failed to heed warning orders (for whatever reason) and surfaced only when forced to, as had the *Foxtrot* in mid-Atlantic, because of foul air and uncharged batteries.

In the upshot, the Navy certainly played its part in unnerving the submarines, pinging on them with active sonar and, in at least one case, dropping practice depth charges (which could be particularly unsettling to ears trapped inside a pressure hull). During the last two days of October, the radar picket destroyer *Charles P. Cecil* dogged one Soviet boat almost continually for thirty-six hours, until the exhausted Russian, his batteries bled, at last surfaced and was identified. One sub skipper got so rattled from such treatment that his boat surfaced displaying not one false pennant number (a common Soviet practice), but *two*—a different one on each side of his sail. "Our ASW forces flushed all . . . Soviet submarines en route to the Caribbean within a matter of a couple of days from the word 'go,' " proudly declared Red Ramage, exaggerating only slightly.

Anderson, who knew what his ASW people could do, thought that his civilian boss was emotionally overwrought and confused. When he tried to reassure McNamara that the interdiction was going according to plan, McNamara shot back, "What plan?" Anderson handed him the big black notebook containing the Oplan; "It's all there," he said. McNamara impatiently pushed the book aside.

The secretary may have mistaken Anderson's self-control (such, at least, was Anderson's view of himself in these instances) for a cavalier approach to an unprecedented emergency that had all their nerves frayed. Anderson, after the fact, supported this notion a bit when he summarized the Cuban Missile Crisis as a chance, with all those Russian submarines about, for American ASW forces to "exercise their trade [and] perfect their skills." But, like Dennison and Ward, he knew what the Navy's men were capable of doing. In fact, all the Soviet *Foxtrots* in the Atlantic would eventually surface for battery recharging. Each time they did, they found American destroyers alongside and, frequently, naval patrol planes lazily orbiting overhead. One destroyer, moving up to a surfaced *Foxtrot* amid a billow of submarine diesel smoke, could not resist flashing, "Do you need help?" The Russians on the bridge responded by frantically shaking their heads negatively and trying fruitlessly to shoo the can away.

Dean Acheson gave plaudits rarely, but he would describe the Navy's performance throughout the crisis as "flawless." This was not quite the case; as in any naval operation, there were plenty of glitches and unanticipated moments. But the chain of command was clear, and so was its unity. JFK could talk directly from the White House to the skippers of the intercepting destroyers, and only he could decide which ship or ships would be stopped or boarded.

The second McNamara-Anderson confrontation highlighted not only the tension the men in Flag Plot were under but also the Navy's considerable and hard-won ASW skill. Out there on the line, the months of drill by Jimmy Thach and others with HUK Group Alfa and its fellows was bearing fruit. The merchantmen were another matter. Some were allowed through, like the tanker *Bucharest* (trailed for days with on-and-off orders to board her) and the East German passenger liner *Völkerfreundschaft*. Some Soviet shipping, despite the preponderance of American naval power, may simply have slipped through undiscovered.

Anderson knew that the ocean was a big place. At a Joint Chiefs meeting on the 24th he asked for Air Force help in locating Soviet vessels. LeMay, emitting clouds of smoke from his omnipresent cigar (practically all that he and his nemesis Castro had in common), boasted that his boys would locate all Soviet shipping in the search area within four hours. The results were unilluminating. Several Air Force B-52s and RB-47Ks and sixteen KC-97 tankers began flying search patterns in the mid-Atlantic. Soon they began to radio back their reports, identifying American, British, and Greek freighters as Russian. Their classic gaffe came when they reported several ships as Russian, due to the telltale red star on their stacks. These turned out to be Texaco tankers on their routine rounds.

"What in hell does a SAC bomber crew know about ships at sea?" exploded one of Dennison's staff officers, "much less a SAC tanker crew." Even in the midst of the greatest nuclear crisis in the nation's history, the wars of the fathers raged on.[13]

☆

At an EXCOM meeting on the 25th, a test case for the effectiveness of the interdiction developed. The candidate for boarding was *Marucla*, a vessel perfectly symbolizing the interlocking universe of international shipping. *Marucla* began life as an American-built Liberty hull; in October 1962, resolutely plodding her way westward through the Atlantic, she was owned by Panamanians, registered in Lebanon, crewed by Greeks, and under Soviet charter. She had taken on her nonmissile cargo at Riga. These factors made her a good bet for proving the strength and validating the purpose of the interdiction while not directly inflaming Soviet leadership. JFK accepted the EXCOM's recommendation.

At 2100 that evening, *Essex*'s planes pinpointed *Marucla*. In a graceful gesture, Vice Admiral Wallace Beakley, the former Seventh Fleet commander who was now Dennison's chief of staff, suggested to Ward that the namesake ship for the president's older brother be involved. Joe Kennedy, Sr., had persuaded Forrestal to name a destroyer after his eldest son, a posthumous holder of the Navy Cross, and Robert Kennedy had served on the can as a seaman. And so Commander Nick Mikhalevsky, skipper of *Joseph P. Kennedy, Jr.*, got orders to join *John R. Pierce* and be the on-scene commander for the intercept operation.

Through the night, the two cans trailed *Marucla*. Ward wanted a daylight boarding operation. Mikhalevsky notified the Greeks by radio of his intent to stop and board at first clear light; *Marucla*'s skipper replied that he would cooperate.

The nation's press would write some very purple prose about the high drama out on the high seas as the world held its collective breath; the naval professionals on the spot simply went about their business. At 0650 on 26 October, *Kennedy* signaled *Marucla*, "Heave to; stop at once!" *Marucla* obediently went dead in the water; back in Flag Plot, sailors painstakingly plotted her position—26-30 north, 74-30 west.

Half an hour later, *Kennedy* sent over her boarding party—all in dress whites and all unarmed—led by the two destroyers' execs, Lieutenant Commander Dwight Osborne of *Pierce* and Lieutenant Commander Kenneth Reynolds of *Kennedy*. As they climbed up *Marucla*'s Jacob's ladder, they were met by the fully compliant, English-speaking crew members.

Their mission took three hours. They examined the ship's manifests, looked at records, viewed the deckload of twelve trucks, and went below to inspect an indiscriminate assortment of precision instruments, truck and machine parts, rolls of paper, and sulfur. By 1030 they were back aboard their respective destroyers. Ward was radioed that no prohibited cargo had been found. *Marucla* was allowed to proceed.

That was that. *Marucla* was a mutually instructive test case proving that the United States Navy could enforce this particular national policy and showing the Soviet Union that point with sharp-edged clarity. Naval interdiction, however, was only as effective as its directing hand. That very afternoon, the Swedish freighter *Coalangatta* refused to respond or stop at a destroyer's challenge. Ward consulted Washington; *Coalangatta*, under Soviet charter, had left Leningrad on 9 October with general cargo. The *Marucla* point having been made, Ward was ordered to let the stubborn Swede proceed, and proceed she did.[14]

☆

By 27 October, everything was at full boil. Several Polaris submarines that had earlier sortied from Holy Loch had reached their assigned stations. SAC's B-52 bombers were flying designated patterns high above the Arctic, ready to snap their tethers at the "go" signal. That day, the first Minuteman ICBM was placed on alert. (By 30 October, nine Minutemen and all the on-station Polaris boats were locked and loaded, ready to launch.)

Some EXCOM members were proposing a positive response to a Soviet proposal: withdrawal of the Russian missiles in Cuba in return for the removal of the already-obsolete Jupiters in Turkey. The pending deployment of more Polaris submarines in the Mediterranean made this look like a feasible option. JFK, who thought he had ordered the Jupiters removed the year before, was furious when he found out the missiles were still on Turkish soil. In any event, Polaris boats were not scheduled to deploy to the Mediterranean until 1 April 1963, and the Turks wanted, in the bargain, some F-104 fighters as reassurance. Thus the Jupiter option was shelved, for the moment.

Kennedy, apart from this initiative and diplomatic feelers reaching him from a wide (and unusual) variety of sources, was naturally concerned that the military would somehow get away from him, specifically that individual Navy ships on the interception line might provoke an incident that would trigger nuclear holocaust. McNamara, to a considerably more emotional and unsettled degree, shared this concern. The smooth professionalism displayed by the men of *Kennedy* and *Pierce* had not assuaged him.

—And the unswerving approach of the Soviet tanker *Groznyy* toward the Navy's waiting pickets only thrummed his nerves the more. *Groznyy* was an eight-year-old, *Kazbek*-class tanker, converted in 1960 for the specific task of conveying liquid ammonia to Cuba. She had 566 tons of this stuff aboard as she trudged onward; the Americans thought she, rather than the Greek-crewed *Marucla*, might be the Soviets' own test case for the interdiction process.

As if to show Acheson that its performance was not completely flawless, the Navy had lost track of *Groznyy*. She was rediscovered on the morning of the 27th by one of LeMay's RB-47K reconnaissance aircraft (perhaps having run out of Texaco tankers to spot), placidly steaming along the Puerto Rico trench toward Cuba. Dennison and Ward quickly got a destroyer alongside her, but the tanker ignored the can's signals.

The destroyer skipper radioed Dennison for instructions, and CINC-LANT queried Flag Plot. *Groznyy*'s skipper, after *Bucharest* and another Soviet-crewed tanker, *Vinnitsa*, had been let through, may have thought he had carte blanche to proceed; no one ever knew. In any case, *Groznyy*'s refusal to respond to the destroyer touched off the third and ultimate confrontation between McNamara and Anderson.

Standing beside the chief of naval operations in Flag Plot, McNamara (who later had the chutzpah to call the entire interdiction process "a communications exercise, not a military operation") asked what would happen should *Groznyy* keep going. Anderson's marching orders were clear; they were the ones he had explained in detail on the afternoon of the 21st to the president. He responded that if the tanker did not stop, a shot would be fired at her rudder. At that, McNamara "blew his cork." No shots would be fired without his express permission, he said, and that would come only after the president's specific approval.

—By now, Anderson was up to his hawsepipes with McNamara. "The Navy has been handling quarantines and blockades since John Paul Jones," one version recounted that he testily (and somewhat inaccurately) rejoined, "and if you people will let us handle it, we'll handle it right." (Anderson denied saying the "John Paul Jones" part.)

"You people" was not the crowd with which to lump Robert Strange

McNamara. He exploded, "I don't give a damn about John Paul Jones, but there will be no firing on Soviet ships!" And all at once, there they were, the secretary of defense and the chief of naval operations—jaw to jaw, bristling like bullterriers, the awesome imperatives of their respective positions flooding each of them with self-righteous wrath.

McNamara broke the impasse. "Is that understood?" he demanded. Then he stormed out once again.

By now, *Groznyy* had attracted a swarm of destroyers, each, on Dennison's orders, with her guns loaded. CINCLANT commanded them to clear their guns by firing out to sea. The reports of the rounds were relayed back to shore as direct shelling of the tanker. *Groznyy's* skipper, awake at last, frantically radioed Moscow for instructions. Whatever these were, the tanker quickly reversed course and steamed back beyond the interdiction line, where she lay dead in the water, thoroughly shaken, for several days. (Eventually, she was allowed to proceed.)

Anderson, more than a bit steamed himself, took off in a huff (perhaps mistakenly, but certainly to get away from McNamara, at least for a short while) to attend a football game between Navy and the University of Pittsburgh. Along the interdiction line, the Navy kept broadcasting special warnings to approaching ships. Non-Cuban trade was being allowed through with little difficulty, and a system of port clearances from the United States was put into effect.

About this time, Dean Rusk found himself riding in a State Department elevator with Acheson, Under Secretary of State George Ball, and two hefty security agents. As the elevator made its way to his seventh-floor office, Rusk, referring to his two guards, said to Acheson and Ball, "You know, the only decent advice I have had this past week has come from these two fellows." One of the "fellows," a former Pittsburgh Steeler lineman, Bert Bennington, retorted, "The reason for that, Mr. Secretary, is that you have surrounded yourself with nothing but dumb fucks!"[15]

☆

The "dumb fucks" were trying, as best they could, to avert thermonuclear war. Civilian-military tensions were built into the American command setup, and one amazing aspect of the crisis was that men like McNamara and Anderson, with their enormous turf responsibilities, were not at each other's throats more often. "We didn't . . . [have] a lot of wild men in the Pentagon," McNamara would eventually say. But that was years down the line; at the time there was at least a slight aura of civilian suspicion cast over the uniforms. To most, LeMay was an obvious wild man, tolerated by JFK for his skills and dynamic leadership. Anderson, who had earlier showed an aggressive aspect when he had planned to strike Soviet bases north of Iran in a Pentagon war game, was also suspect.

But as even Paul Nitze noted, when the secretary was monitoring the military, "McNamara was overdoing it." In the early days of the crisis, Anderson remembered, "McNamara was Alice in Wonderland—and arrogant. He once told me he was a person of integrity. I said, 'Not the type of integrity that we're used to.' "

Anderson would say that the handling of the crisis had depended "on the personalities involved." This was, at best, only partially true, and the overblown emphasis on his clashes with McNamara obscured equally significant aspects. For one thing, McNamara later made partial amends; Anderson recorded in his official diary on 1 November that ". . . last night Mr. McNamara had expressed to me a high degree of satisfaction with the performance of the Navy and Marine Corps units; thus echoing the President's words."

More importantly, the days between McNamara's ultimate blowup on the 27th and his "attaboy" on the 31st had seen the defusing of the crisis. And these, like the preceding days, were ones of consummate, highly skilled military professionalism, which depended not on personality but on rigorous training, finely honed discipline, and the most painstaking devotion to duty.

The two letters from Khrushchev to Kennedy, both in the president's hands by 26 October, indicated some confusion and exceptional tension within the Politburo. (The anti-Khrushchev cabal would succeed in removing him from power two years later, ostensibly over an issue of agricultural policy.) The first letter presented a soft line: The Soviet offer to remove the offensive weapons from Cuba in return for the end of the interdiction and an American promise not to invade Cuba. The second letter, arriving only hours after the first, took a harsher stance, requiring the removal of the Jupiters from Turkey as part of the solution.

Publicly, JFK acted on the first letter, and this began the untangling of the Gordian knot. Privately, he got the strategically redundant Jupiters removed as soon as possible. Khrushchev, under increasing pressure from his own leadership, responded on 28 October, promising "to discontinue construction of the [missile] facilities, to dismantle them, and to return them to the Soviet Union."

—The solution, at last, was thus a diplomatic one. But the Russians, everywhere they looked, could see American intent graven in brutal strokes: in the readied missile wings, the manned bomber fleets aloft, the deployed Marine and Army units. And above all, they could see that intent far out in the Atlantic, in the hundreds of haze-gray warships, silent submarines, and watchful Navy planes efficiently and effectively going about their designated tasks.[16]

☆

The Cuban Missile Crisis encompassed the most telling example of the use and value of seapower in the twentieth century. Here were no great fleet actions, no dramatic duels at sea—only the calm and calculated exercise of overwhelming naval superiority. Seapower was the difference, the vital balance needed between the political impotency of doing nothing and the probably irreversible consequences of military attack. Seapower, under the sure hand of civilian authority and the guidance of exceptional naval men like George Anderson, Bob Dennison, and Corky Ward, was America's trump card, one that may well have prevented nuclear war.

In this single, harrowing moment, the United States Navy fully justified every dime spent on its machines and men. Anderson called the entire marshaling of America's military might a "magnificent testimonial" to skill and professionalism, both civilian and military, and he was right. By 4 November, every suspect Soviet ship had peacefully turned back.

During the following week, the Navy busied itself identifying ships outbound from Cuba with dismantled weapons aboard. American destroyers positioned themselves just outside Cuban ports; low-flying reconnaissance aircraft and helicopters took pictures of everything that moved off the island; ships that had covered their deck cargoes with tarpaulins were politely asked to remove these for visual inspection. (All, even the obstinate Soviet freighter *Volgoles*, eventually did.)

There were some more glitches and misunderstandings as the vast Soviet logistical process heaved into reverse, but everyone was breathing easier now. A helicopter from *Wasp* hovered over a departing Russian vessel to take pictures. The Russians aboard, many stripped to the waist to get an unaccustomed November suntan, were smiling and waving greetings. A Navy captain aboard the helo spontaneously took off his Navy tie clasp and lowered the tiny emblem on a line to the Russians below. As the helicopter, its pictures taken, began to lift away, the Russians motioned for its return. The line was again lowered; when the crew winched up again, they found a bottle of vodka attached.

The whole reverse process took weeks, but by 15 December the Navy could report that the last offensive weapons (in the form of fifteen crated Il-28s) had left Cuba. The Navy had kept its eye on these weapons, most of them, almost every step of the way, and now the haze-gray warships ushered them back home, into the Mediterranean and the Baltic. "I want to report to the boss when they are all back in Russia," said George Anderson—and so he did.

Well before, on 18 November, Kennedy had lifted the "quarantine." At the height of the crisis, 183 Navy ships had taken part. Anderson, speaking for the entire fleet, had earned the right to bust his buttons. "Again," he said, "the U.S. had turned to seapower to wield the iron fist in a velvet glove and again the Navy and ships of the Atlantic Fleet had shown this confidence was not misplaced." Reservists who had been summoned to duty were released, and Guantanamo's evacuated dependents got their emergency relocation expenses.

—There had been excruciating moments. Major Rudolf Anderson, Jr., of the Air Force had been shot down in his U-2 over Cuba. (A false rumor held that Castro himself had fired the surface-to-air missile that killed him; Fidel had been in Havana at the time.) Anderson was the only person to lose his life during the crisis. A USAF plane out of Alaska, flying what the Air Force said was a routine weather mission to the North Pole, had locked in on the wrong navigational star and soon found itself over Siberia. The Soviets had scrambled their fighters but, listening to the worried American pilot's plain-voice radio chatter, decided he really *was* lost and let him go his way. Dennison's order to clear the guns in the *Groznyy* affair had caused palpitations. There were enough such incidents to lead Acheson, still miffed that his idea for an immediate air strike on Cuba had not been accepted, to tartly claim that the outcome of the crisis, because of JFK's halfhearted actions, "was just plain dumb luck."

Dumb luck maybe; military professionalism, to be certain. The only unhappy allied militaries were those that had been summoned late into Task Force 137. Its patrol stations were not established till 7 November, but the combined force did observe and report on 153 ships—few of them Soviet—to the end of the quarantine. The Latin Americans were there for a show of unity; even the usually diplomatic Dennison noted that their participation "didn't mean a damn thing."

What meant a damn was the strategic balance of forces. Beyond being overwhelmed by American naval might at the operational point of the crisis, the Soviets were made to perceive their overall strategic inferiority in no uncertain terms. As events reached a crescendo in late October, Russia could summon up 44 ICBMs, 97 diesel-submarine–launched ballistic missiles (SLBMs), and a few hundred medium bombers, the last of little use because they would have had to stage through forward bases of extremely limited capacity in the Arctic. Against these, the Americans had, on-line and ready, 156 ICBMs, 144 SLBMs (all Polaris), and 1300 strategic bombers, the medium-range variant of which could be supported in flight by 1000 airborne tankers. In short, the United States had several thousand nuclear weapons loaded and cocked. No country, short of madness, could have gone into the maw of such a beast, and the Soviet leaders, whatever else they may have been, were not madmen.

Fidel Castro, yoked to the Soviet Union now by ideology and economic necessity, was of a different mind. The Maximum Leader was both embarrassed and enraged. He described Nikita Khrushchev as a man lacking *cojones*. "I gave [the Russians] my heart," Castro moaned, "but now I wouldn't give them the cockles off my ass."[17]

☆

The Russians probably had little use for Castro's cockles, but they still had something infinitely superior: a significant toehold in the Caribbean. As they retreated, they left behind a 2800-man combat brigade (the presence of which would not be made public until the administration of Jimmy Carter, although the brigade was detected some years earlier). They also left an equal number of "military advisers" and about 2100 technicians at the Lourdes intelligence facility, from where the Soviets and Cubans continued to electronically eavesdrop on American military, space, maritime, and even telephone communications. (The Americans, courtesy of ITT's work for Batista, would continue as before to tap into Castro's landlines.)

None of this Russian remnant was known at the time to American leadership, many of whom basked in the afterglow. The most famous quote belonged to Dean Rusk. When news arrived that several of the Russian missile-carrying freighters were turning around and heading back, he exultantly said to his colleagues, "We are eyeball to eyeball, and the other fellow just blinked." Publicly, Kennedy refrained from gloating; privately, he said of Khrushchev: "I cut his balls off."

Many Americans may indeed have seen the crisis as some kind of High Noon on the Atlantic, in which forcing the other guy to back down was the vindication of some sort of macho nuclear superiority. But many more probably were simply relieved and grateful beyond rejoicing. Impending nuclear terror was hardly the time for proclamations of victory, superiority, or—in Rusk's and Kennedy's cases—forms of posturing that were more excusable in the world of cinema fiction.

Kennedy got most of the credit for the solution to the Cuban Missile Crisis. His conduct throughout was measured, thoughtful, and moderate—without a doubt, the high point of his conduct of the presidency. This said, Kennedy's Cold War mentality, along with that of scores of American policymakers going back to Truman, had done much to shape the preconditions of the crisis. These policymakers, reacting to communism instinctively, as to a goad, had surrounded the Soviet Union with a phalanx of nuclear-tipped terror. They had overthrown or attempted to overthrow governments or movements they believed to be "Communist" in practically every corner of the globe. In this context, and given the deep-seated Soviet fears of strategic inferiority, a nuclear "emergency" between the two countries was probably only a matter of time.

The Soviet Union, for its part, was scarcely innocent. Khrushchev and his henchmen made an absolutely stupid assessment of the historic American relationship to Latin America, in general, and to Cuba, in particular. This they compounded by a decision to try *secretly* to change the nuclear balance of power. While perfectly reasonable in a traditional world of diplomatic balance of power buttressed by conventional weaponry, their attempt to introduce nuclear missiles into Cuba was doomed to be opposed because the missiles were nuclear, America had never been in anyone's boresight before, and the Caribbean was an American lake.

Still, surrounded by American nuclear might, as they were, and deeply paranoid about the world beyond their borders, as they were, the Russians could not resist Cuba. "That Castro is crazy," later insisted Anastas Mikoyan, an Old Bolshevik and Khrushchev's deputy premier. But "you Americans must understand what Cuba means to us Old Bolsheviks," he went on. "We have been waiting all our lives for a country to go Communist without the Red Army, and it happened in Cuba. It makes us feel like boys again!"[18]

We have been waiting all our lives. . . . They wanted to be a "superpower," too, and they certainly had the nuclear megatonnage for the role. But in the Cuban Missile Crisis a true superpower was matched against, at best, a semi-superpower. Both Americans and Russians had found out, at a time of unparalleled danger, that all the old rules went by the boards, that Dean Acheson had been right—international law *had* gone to hell.

And that meant that the crisis was conditioned by sheer brute force, both implied and actual. Each country had its nuclear-tipped missiles, its huge bomber wings, its massive armies. But the Russians conveyed their precious cargoes toward Cuba with a flimsy escort of a few submarines, a couple of surface support ships, and an intelligence trawler. Along their heading, they ran athwart the mightiest Navy in the world.

They had badly misread American will. Of crucial importance, up to the point when the haze gray got in their way they had probably never understood, coming from an historic land power as they did, what applied seapower could do.

—Now they knew. The lesson would not be forgotten.

STERN WATCH V

☆

On 17 October 1962, as the EXCOM was reviewing the known Russian missile sites in Cuba, General Maxwell Taylor, its only military member, argued adamantly that the Soviet Union was making a major effort to alter the world's balance of power. His feelings were reflected in an EXCOM memo sent that night to John Kennedy:

> Nevertheless it is generally agreed that the United States cannot tolerate the known presence of offensive nuclear weapons in a country 90 miles from our shore, if our courage and our commitments are ever to be believed by either allies or adversaries. Retorts from either our European allies or the Soviets that we can become as accustomed as they to accepting the nearby presence of MRBMs have some logic but little weight in this situation.

"Some logic but little weight"—here was the language of raw, unadulterated power. Both the United States and the Soviet Union had, already in 1962, the capacity to wreak nuclear havoc on their sworn enemy, and enough warheads left over to obliterate the rest of humankind in the bargain. But neither side could use shame or bluff to force the other into surrendering anything considered vital. Americans had urged self-determination within the Soviet bloc since the Red Army rolled westward in the final two years of World War II; when courageous Hungarians rose in 1956, the United States did nothing. Nikita Khrushchev had, by 1962, issued ultimatums for three years over the issue of divided Berlin, threatening everything from rockets to Russian infantry if the West did not give way.

Yet neither Hungary, Berlin, nor even the Cuban Missile Crisis, as emotionally unsettling as each was at the time, produced nuclear war. By 1962 nuclear diplomacy, if that was even a proper descriptive phrase for nuclear saber-rattling, was bankrupt as a counter in international affairs. No rational political leader could run the risk of nuclear retaliation. Thus, while the Russian attempt to place nuclear missiles in Cuba produced a corresponding nuclear threat from the United States, the bipolar nuclear

821

world (always given the presence of rationality) had produced a stalemate game.

Stalemate ensued despite the strategic imbalance of forces precisely because of the impossibility of guaranteeing, as American military men found at the time of the Cuban Missile Crisis, that *all* the targets would be taken out before a retaliatory salvo could be fired. No thoughtful military man would ever make such a guarantee. Civilian and military leadership on both sides, for the best of reasons—national survival—therefore had a vested interest in never pressing the nuclear button.

In the Caribbean in October 1962, the United States used its nonnuclear superiority—sea and air power—to force the Soviet Union to back down. This result certainly did not mean that nuclear conflict over the Soviet missiles had been *impossible*. "If shooting starts over Cuba, the U.S. is ready," bragged the *U.S. News & World Report* even as the Russian ships were headed home. Cuban and American troops continued to stare at each other over the no-man's-land surrounding the Guantanamo base, and any sort of conventional shooting could well have escalated to nuclear proportions.

But more and more in the Cold War era, such escalation seemed increasingly unlikely, although no one, rational or otherwise, would say nuclear conflict was impossible in *every* instance. As close to the nuclear abyss as the Cuban Missile Crisis seemed to nudge the world, the entire episode constituted powerful evidence of nuclear stalemate.

Senator J. William Fulbright of Arkansas had once told Kennedy that "the Castro regime is a thorn in the flesh, but it is not a dagger in the heart." This was true enough, but JFK still wanted Castro and his Communist revolution out of the Western Hemisphere. His administration, after all, launched Operation Mongoose, a bag of dirty tricks trying to sabotage Cuban property and discredit Castro. Kennedy aided exile groups working against Castro, engineered the expulsion of Cuba from the Organization of American States, and urged other Latin American countries to break diplomatic ties with Havana. "My God," said Richard Helms of the CIA, "those Kennedys keep the pressure on about Castro."

—So they did, to the point of continuing a shadowy and half-farcical plot begun during the Eisenhower years to actually assassinate Fidel. Robert McNamara remembered that "we were hysterical about Castro at the time of the Bay of Pigs and after." Castro had every reason to be suspicious about American policy, every reason to shop for support wherever he could.

Furthermore, the American "success" in the Cuban Missile Crisis escalated the forceful, tough-talking stance—making the other guy blink— practically to an American diplomatic canon. Nonmilitary solutions to diplomatic problems were pushed more and more to the periphery of policy decision making. Kennedy even went so far as to tell Hugh Sidey of *Time* that "the country rather enjoyed the Cuban quarantine. It was exciting, it was a diversion, there was the feeling that we were doing something." Mil-

itary force, however, was not *nuclear* force, and indeed a cogent argument
could be made that the use of nuclear weaponry rendered every previous
notion of military combat null. Kennedy, in his conversation with Sidey,
added that "it might have been a different story if there had been thousands
killed in a long battle."

There were, of course, those who saw no difference between military
and nuclear force, viewing the latter as a simple and obvious extension of
the former. When JFK invited the Joint Chiefs of Staff to the White House
to thank them for their support during the Cuban Missile Crisis, Curtis
LeMay came in at a rant, shouting "We lost! We ought to just go in there
today and knock 'em off!" "We have been had!" cried George Anderson.
Robert McNamara, who was present, noted that Kennedy was "absolutely
shocked. He was stuttering in reply."[1]

Probably not even the majority of military men, however, thought like
Iron Eagle or the chief of naval operations. By 1962 the American military
was beginning to come to grips with the hard concept of nuclear stalemate;
"hard" because, for the first time in its history, the United States was now
targeted, round the clock, by a foreign power—one with nuclear weapons.
The Soviet leaders, despite their sometimes crude blustering, had long since
realized the same thing, that their country was a perpetual nuclear bull's-
eye.

Because of the stalemate, which had occurred not because of the respective *numbers* of nuclear weapons, warheads, or delivery systems but
rather because of the *nature* of these weapons, the sides in the Cuban Missile
Crisis were woefully mismatched. A semi-superpower with no means to
extend its power *over seas* had sought to do so, against a true superpower
with a complete conventional as well as nuclear arsenal. The result was a
humiliating disaster for the Soviet Union, a misleading triumph for the
United States.

The crisis was far more than a potentially nuclear face-off. The American selective interdiction of ocean traffic bound for Cuba showed, in vivid
and unmistakable terms, that seapower had an absolutely critical place in
modern diplomacy and military affairs. Indeed, given the nuclear stalemate
and American hegemony over the world's oceans, the United States Navy
could be said to have been the crucial fulcrum for balance-of-power questions
wherever the land met the sea, and beyond.

☆

"We're a gr-reat people," Mister Hennessy observed earnestly, over his customary glass. "We ar-re," replied Mister Dooley. "We ar-re that. An' the
best iv it is, we know we ar-re."

—Americans had always known. The Cold War period was no different
in this regard. What had changed was the customary American feeling of
security behind the wide ocean moats, far from the ancient quarrels of

Europe or Asia. Now the ingrained notion of American superiority was riven with considerable tension and even bore elements of national paranoia, mostly directed at an ill-understood bogeyman called "international communism."

The bogeyman could appear in any guise—as Khrushchev, Castro, or a remote Third World guerrilla leader. Sometimes he could do real damage, starting needless insurrections, causing wars, or robbing people of individual rights, liberties, and dignity. More often, though, the bogeyman was only a mask covering age-old inequities and problems involving health, food, economic need, social injustice, and political oppression.

Americans seldom bothered to look behind the mask. Bathed in their own postwar prosperity, they simply assumed what they had always assumed, that American solutions were the best solutions for the problems of the world. If American solutions were resisted, then usually, and unfortunately, force would have to be used, for the nation's cause was just. In his *Biglow Papers* back in 1848, James Russell Lowell had grasped the point, apropos the Mexican War:

> Thet our nation's bigger'n theirn an so its rights air bigger,
> And thet it's all to make em free thet we air pullin' trigger. . . .

Almost a century later, Will Rogers remarked, "It takes quite a sense of humor for these people to understand us shaking hands with one hand and shooting with the other."

—These historic assumptions were alive and well in the Cold War, now given a far darker aspect by the American obsession with the "Communist menace" and national security. (There was, after all, no "National Security Council" until 1947.) Few Americans, in such a world, could see themselves and their nation, draped in the glossiest of democratic and individualistic ideals and rhetoric, as anyone's villain. Why they might be distrusted, despised, or even hated for "pullin' trigger" was beyond their comprehension.

The aging Negro leader William Edward Burghardt DuBois was a double minority in Cold War America, a black man who, in despair, turned to communism late in life. Almost no one was listening to him as he raged that "drunk with power, we are leading the world to hell . . . and to a Third World War."[2]

DuBois's estimate of the destination could be debated, but if Americans were not drunk with their power, they were certainly blinded and confused, to the point at which many of them, including their leaders, confounded the exercise of power with justice and some kind of moral imprimatur. The United States indeed had many friends in the international arena, honestly won, but even these friends could sometimes stand appalled as the nation's awesome strength was applied and misapplied around the globe.

This strength was an exceptional mix of economic gigantism, social ideology, and political will. The production of military technology was the node at which these lines of force most conspicuously intersected. Critics were fond of pointing to the ethical problems that abounded here, as in the case of Rear Admiral Lloyd Harrison, onetime chief of the Bureau of Aeronautics, who insisted that Navy contracts on the McDonnell F-3H jet fighter be continued despite the loss of eleven of the planes in test flights and the deaths of several pilots. Offered a post at McDonnell five months before his retirement, Harrison became a vice president of the company, smoothly arguing that his advocacy of the plane had had nothing to do with gaining his civilian position.

Ethical problems, moreover, were the least of the worries generated by this potent Cold War mix. Military technology and its uses were usually developed in the context not only of national defense but also of anticommunism, which meant a good product, a good purpose, and a good sell. Such a noble cause generated clouds of paranoia, inside which questions about who was a "real American" and who was not were hotly debated. Vice Admiral Robert Goldthwaite, in a Christmas letter to his command in 1960, advised his men to write the John Birch Society (a leader in right-wing dementia) for information, in order to "identify public officials and policies displaying softness toward communism." Goldthwaite's sailors were urged to "demand a more patriotic attitude . . . join a citizens group dedicated to upholding American principles and resisting socialism-communism . . . demand that the nation take the offensive in the cold war with the objective of victory over communism."

In retirement, Arleigh Burke, among other things, was a founder and director of the Center for Strategic and International Studies. From this post, he clearly identified the enemy: the "communist movement and its advocates." America's earlier policies, Burke believed, "envisaged two major territorial powers facing each other in the traditional way. From this basic error derived such territory-centered policy proposals as containment, roll-back, and withdrawal." Things had changed, Burke continued:

> The American policy [at the think tank] envisages the destruction of an ideological movement. This policy depends, not on any particular form of power, but on all forms of power. It is oriented to a world order guaranteed by the power of the United States in cooperation with the wider base of power of the North Atlantic Community. With the North Atlantic Community as its core, the free world can defeat communism and bring peace and order to the whole world.[3]

Nothing in history had *ever* brought "peace and order to the whole world," but then nothing had seemed, to Cold Warriors like Burke, as cosmic as the Manichean struggle between the Russian-led forces of darkness and the

American-led forces of light. In such a high-stakes confrontation, any use of power would be reasonable, any critic of such a policy a backslider or worse. Naval investigators, for example, routinely investigated even the lowest-ranking inductees on questions of their political affiliation, racial attitudes, or sexual preferences. The right to privacy was no barrier when ideological conflict loomed.

According to a famous formulation by the maverick sociologist C. Wright Mills, America was manipulated throughout the Cold War by a "power elite," which, if existing, certainly had men like Burke at its core. The "military establishment," according to Mills, had become "the largest and most expensive feature of government," managed with "all the grim and clumsy efficiency of a great and sprawling bureaucracy." The elite prospered in the shift from domestic-centered economic affairs in the Depression years to international-centered ideological and political affairs in the Cold War.

The power elite had three dominant institutional orders, contended Mills. The military was joined by political and economic structures. There was an "interchangeability of positions" among the three orders (Lloyd Harrison of the Navy and McDonnell being a pertinent example). "Insofar as the power elite is composed of men of similar origin and education, of similar career and style of life," Mills wrote, "their unity may be said to rest upon the fact that they are of similar social type, and to lead to their easy intermixing." All this was part of the new corporate-military-industrial-educational-Cold War "system."

Mills's ideas, which were extraordinarily influential in the 1960s, hazily suggested a camarilla of elites, conspiring away for profit and mutual advantage. There was, indeed, plenty of evidence about the interlocking nature of his three orders. In 1964, for example, one U.S. senator (Republican Hugh Scott of Pennsylvania) was a member of the Naval Reserve. So were nineteen members of the House of Representatives, ten Republicans and nine Democrats, in ranks ranging from captain to lieutenant. Similar examples could be multiplied manyfold.

But a major leap in logic had to be taken to assume that such people, whether found in politics, economic and business life, or the military, operated in consonance with an elitist program. The politicians who were Naval Reserve members, while sometimes agreeing on Navy issues, almost never agreed on anything else. Mills's analysis of the "power elite" was simplistic and failed to account for the numerous (and sometimes effective) countervailing forces in American life.

Still, in a world deemed to be constantly menaced by communism, the military demanded to be constantly fed. While Dwight Eisenhower did not keep raising the Korea-inspired Truman military budgets, he did not lower them substantially, either. And when Kennedy took office, the budget lid was ripped off. The huge military expenditures occurred mostly in the name of anticommunism, which in terms of international purpose held Americans (not just "elites") together more than any other single issue.

Military spending alone became a form of national unity in the postwar United States. Until Vietnam, any "elites" that may have existed did not so much manipulate anything (although some in power, of course, did so) as they reflected a loose national consensus. The congruence between political, economic, and cultural leadership, on the one hand, and the dominant middle class, on the other, concerning the subject of communism was simply too strong.

Kennedy's administration publicly announced that the recession of 1960 would be fought by "priming the pump" with military orders. The easy way was also the most politic way; the House Armed Services Committee reported out a bill authorizing $808 million for new construction projects at 790 military installations spread throughout *each* of the fifty states. Cold War pork was some of the tastiest of all, and many Americans (not just "elites") ate at the trough.

—As Carl Vinson happily reassured his fellow members of Congress, "There is something in this bill for everyone."[4]

☆

The object of all this expenditure, all this mustering of military might, was supposedly the Soviet Union—which had problems of its own. The Russian bosses, claiming leadership of the Communist bloc (never monolithic after Yugoslavia's defection in 1948 but perceived to be so by most American policymakers), wanted desperately to hold the United States hostage to nuclear force, just as they knew themselves held hostage by the Americans.

Khrushchev and his supporters, to this end, thus devised a reckless gambit depending on secrecy and surprise. Had they chosen to reach an open diplomatic agreement with Cuba to station Russian missiles on the island, men such as Robert McNamara and McGeorge Bundy believed the United States might not have been able to make an issue of the deal. Next, compounding his folly, Khrushchev chose a four-star general of the army, Issa Pliyev, as the overall Soviet commander in Cuba. Pliyev may have been politically safe, but he had had no experience with ballistic missiles, air defense, or tactical concealment. (The Russian military units displayed their presence to American reconnaissance flights as if auditioning for the Metropolitan Opera.) Pliyev's major claim to fame seemed to be that he had led the last cavalry charge in history—a Soviet-Mongolian force cantering against the startled rear guard of the retreating Japanese Kwantung Army in Manchuria in August 1945.

How the Russians expected to convey such a missile load (forty-eight planned SS-4s, thirty-two planned SS-5s) to Cuba without being discovered taxed the imagination of the most credulous. But they did. When Khrushchev heard of the American interdiction plan, his first violent reaction was to order his charter ships to somehow bull their way through. Only his fellow Old Bolshevik Anastas Mikoyan was able to persuade him to back down. The Russians, amazingly, had sent a series of unarmed merchant vessels bearing the most politically destabilizing material imaginable across thousands of miles of ocean without any real naval protection.

The idea was always that the ships would arrive safely. The forty thousand or so Russians sent to the island were there for defense against American attack; they originally did not know their destination or the reasons for their trip. (Some arrived with winter clothes and skis.) The Russian leaders, in short, fell victim to a mind-set that moved immediately from the "go" decision to establishing the missile sites in Cuba. They simply *were not thinking in naval terms.* Khrushchev's fury with the blockade included words like "banditry" and "the folly of degenerate imperialism," stereotypical Russian phrases that nevertheless strongly suggested that what was going on, out there in the broad Atlantic, was beyond the bounds of acceptable conduct. He had earlier told some visiting Cubans: "You don't have to worry; there will be no big reaction from the U.S. And if there is a problem, we will send the Baltic Fleet."

When the problems arose, the Russian responses were often ludicrous. The Baltic Fleet (or indeed any other appreciable body of Soviet ships) never reached the Atlantic. The merchant captains were reportedly ordered to scuttle their vessels if attempts to stop and search them were made. This obviously did not go down well with the Greeks, Swedes, and others who were the contract skippers. As a final, hapless touch, Soviet personnel were said to have been ordered to dance on deck as American reconnaissance planes buzzed over, hoping to confuse the imperialists by acting like tourists.

From a naval standpoint, this was the supreme irony of the supposedly supreme superpower confrontation of the Cold War: the semi-superpower simply could not *conceive* of the naval effort necessary to support its strategy, much less mount such an effort; the superpower *relied* on a naval effort to check that strategy. This was a distinction that literally made a world of difference.

The Russians had been thinking about naval matters for some time, but in a country where the army, in military terms, had always reigned supreme, the navy had received relatively little support from either the political leadership or the command economy. However, as early as the Twenty-first Party Congress in 1959, the Soviet naval missions and naval force structure had been redesigned, mostly in an effort to counter the threat of American carrier-launched, nuclear-capable attack aircraft. From 1960 onwards, Soviet naval discussion was fairly unanimous in outlining the Soviet navy's major missions, the main American targets being the attack aircraft carrier and the Polaris submarine.

Moreover, the basic surface ship and submarine designs that would spark the renaissance of the Soviet navy in the next two decades had already been planned *before* the Cuban Missile Crisis: the ASW helicopter-carrying carrier *Moskva* (1957–58); the *Kara* command missile cruiser (1960–61); the *Kresta I* missile cruiser (1957–58) and the *Kresta II* (1960–61); the *Yankee* nuclear fleet ballistic missile submarine (1957–58); the *Charlie* nuclear guided-missile submarine (1957–58); the *Victor* nuclear attack submarine (1957–58); the *Krivak* missile destroyer (1960–61); and the *Kotlin AAW* SAM-AAW destroyer (1960–61).[5]

—Practically none of these were ready, however, in October 1962. When the Russians ran smack into the United States Navy in the Atlantic, they did so unsuspecting, practically unarmed, and—in the end—undone.

☆

The Cold War Navy thus brilliantly justified its existence, in a most unusual way. The Navy was configured for battle at sea, a replay of its epic adventures of World War II. In the absence of any appreciable enemy navy in the post-1945 period, American naval planning by default centered on the only enemy possible in the emerging bipolar world. The Russians were well aware of the American abilities in power projection—the carrier strikes, the amphibious assaults, and, eventually, the nuclear fleet ballistic missile submarine—and they began to plan accordingly, if belatedly and somewhat fitfully. In this negative sense, with the Cuban Missile Crisis a spur and not a primary cause, the United States Navy could be said to have summoned its main postwar opponent into being.

But in the seventeen tension-filled years between the Japanese surrender aboard *Missouri* and the Cuban Missile Crisis, this opponent could not keep the seas with the American fleet; indeed, no navy in existence, certainly not the severely contracting Royal Navy, could even come close. One of the defining characteristics of these most frigid of Cold War years was American naval hegemony. And this hegemony held not only in areas of traditional American naval concern—the littorals, the western Atlantic, the eastern Pacific, the Caribbean—but on a truly global scale.

The Cold War Navy was supreme on any part of salt water American policy chose. This supremacy ensured the American entry into the Mediterranean and the Persian Gulf; underwrote NATO and SEATO; made the conduct of the Korean War possible; and underlay American rule in Japan, American influence in the Philippines, and American domination of the vast Pacific basin.

Before World War II, the Shield of the Republic had been held close, at times lapsing into desuetude, at times showing a feeble presence in far-off waters to protect trade. Never had the Navy been expected to carry out major diplomatic or military missions far from home with forces on the spot; indicatively, Tommy Hart's puny Asiatic Squadron had been designated for little more than sacrifice on the eve of Pearl Harbor.

Following the war, the new internationalism of the United States meant an equally new and ultimately crucial role for its Navy. Now, the Shield of the Republic was held at tremendous length. Enormous stretches of land were the only barriers to its extensions, and, with the advent of Polaris, even those fell. No serious military analyst really believed the continental United States to be in peril of armed invasion; that had not happened since the War of 1812, a notable failure of the Shield (although James Knox Polk would have argued the contrary in 1846, concerning the Mexicans). Instead, national defense was now seen as a function of international order. Since power abhorred a vacuum, the world's only superpower took on the self-imposed task of upholding its version of that order.

Among the country's military forces, the Air Force possessed the primary strategic weapon. While its tactical air power was no small matter and featured both skilled pilots and state-of-the-art warplanes, this tacair required fixed overseas operating bases and a considerable logistics structure to operate, as in Korea. The USAF's heavily promoted nuclear punch was its fundamental strategic design, and early in the Eisenhower administration this concept was seen to be severely flawed in the context of maintaining international order.

The Army, usually on the shorter end of the budget stick, could in no way match the sheer size of the Soviet ground forces. Army personnel relied on mobility, technological advantage, NATO ground allies, and the ability to get firepower quickly to the point of contact. But the Army, too, depended on fixed bases, fretting particularly over the vulnerability of its NATO European installations. Beyond NATO or its several Pacific garrisons, the Army owned units with heavy equipment that were tough to get to most trouble spots, while light-loaded troops, like the elite airborne outfits, could not sustain themselves in the field for long.

The major war of the period, the Korean conflict, featured American combined arms used in a limited, conventional fashion. But among these combined arms, each of which had an important part to play, only the Navy possessed the potent combination of mobility, flexibility, striking power, and logistical staying time for the task of international policeman. In the absence of any appreciable blue-water enemy, this was a role for which the Navy auditioned and one which the service received, practically by default.

Such a force—thousands of ships, hundreds of warships, hundreds of thousands of men and women—was far too tempting as an international instrument not to be used. Truman (in the Mediterranean, the Persian Gulf, Korea) stretched the fleet to the fullest; so did Eisenhower (Suez, Formosa, Lebanon); and so did Kennedy (Laos, the Cuban Missile Crisis). As these successive political leaders and their policymakers utilized their Navy, they found its abilities to be indispensable to their ideas of international order. Accordingly, the lines of civilian control became ever stronger and more immediate; by the time of the Cuban Missile Crisis, destroyers far out in the Atlantic could be maneuvered directly from the White House.

From one perspective, this was all to the good, upholding and making more direct the authority vested in the civilian side by the Constitution. As command, control, and communications technologies proliferated and intelligence information cascaded in at a far greater rate and in far greater volume than ever before, the "C^3I" moved ahead quantum leaps in effectiveness. The Bay of Pigs, where the American military mostly stood aside, was the disastrous exception that proved the rule.

From two other perspectives, however, the dramatically increased centralization of civilian authority over far-flung military forces in the modern age contained built-in problems. The Navy bitterly resisted this centralization, clinging desperately to its cherished independence afloat. There was nothing even remotely suggestive of Fletcher Knebel's "Seven Days in May" syndrome about all this. Rather, Navymen were absolutely convinced that their type of hard-won professionalism could only be gained in the school of experience; they resisted with every fiber of their professional being what they regarded as intrusions on their service prerogatives or their traditional roles (the unification controversy, the rebellion in gold braid). When defeated, as in the battle over the Defense Reorganization Act of 1958, they only grudgingly got into line. They had the right to be a bit smug when a collective Joint Chiefs command arrangements of the Cuban interdiction was deemed unworkable. George Anderson had to be specifically assigned to oversee the operation, a naval professional leading other naval professionals.

Secondly, and admittedly more difficult to assess, was the nonetheless pertinent issue of the *use* of so much naval power. The haze-gray warships owned the seas. They could be instantaneously vectored to whatever spot the controlling political authority desired them to be, and for whatever purpose. (Many times, they were on the spot already.) For example, whether Korea should have been contested, particularly in the way the conflict was actually conducted, was certainly debatable; that the Navy made the American conduct of the war possible was not.

Many naval operations had been highly laudable, even approaching that rarest of all international commodities—altruism. The Navy's ships had rescued hundreds of thousands of people, in the Far East and the Middle East, from the jaws of war. Countless humanitarian missions—saving flood or typhoon victims, fighting epidemics, building schools and hospitals, shipping food, cleaning up after disasters of every kind—were gold stars on the Navy's Cold War record. Its personnel were welcomed in a wide variety of ports throughout the "friendly" world, and not just for their payday money. The Navy proudly called its sailors "ambassadors of goodwill," and while the occasional lapse got most of the press coverage, for the most part the whitehats really were.

—None of this could be forgotten. At the same time, the practically irresistible temptation to use this unparalleled force was omnipresent. Two examples were most pertinent. The American incursion into Lebanon in 1958 was highly criticized, and rightly so. The whole operation was possible only because of the presence of American seapower, in the form of the Sixth Fleet, and thus, in an indirect way, the very dominance of its Navy helped entangle the United States in the blood feuds of the Middle East, a snare from which the nation has yet to emerge. On the other side of the world, American naval force, the Seventh Fleet this time, helped keep the corrupt Chiang Kai-shek regime propped up in Taiwan and thus played, again, an indirect role in keeping Communist China and the United States at logger-heads for more than three decades.

In each of these instances, and in many others, the Navy was simply attempting, with all its training, tradition, and skill, to accomplish tasks ordered by higher authority. The fleet was an *instrument*, arguably the most potent and responsive military means ever possessed by any nation for the day-to-day conduct of international affairs. Navymen did not make policy so much as they advised about and executed policy.

Of course, sailors had their own opinions about the international situations in which they could find themselves suddenly immersed. Their usual concerns, though, were far more prosaic. They served in combat, stood lonely watches, endured raging northers, and moved silently far under the ocean's surface. They operated round the clock off carriers, oversaw steaming boilers, flew long, boring patrol missions, and waded knee-deep through supply accounts. Their duty stations were as varied as the world itself—after all, their matchless recruiting slogan had been the appeal to which millions of American youths had responded throughout the century: "Join the Navy and See the World!"

—The Cold War Navy, more than any other military force in history, saw the world. When orders came, the haze gray got underway.

☆

On the cool, moonless night of 26 April 1952, Task Group 88.1 was underway as well, steaming blacked-out toward Gibraltar and a rendezvous with the Sixth Fleet. The main body was 1200 miles east of Boston. Fifty miles to the northwest steamed Task Unit 88.1.1, composed of the thirty-eight-thousand-ton carrier *Wasp* and her two escorts. One of these, the destroyer-minesweeper *Rodman*, was stationed one thousand yards off *Wasp*'s port bow.

The other escort, the destroyer-minesweeper *Hobson*, was off the carrier's starboard quarter at three thousand yards. The ships were galloping along on course 102 degrees true through freshening, four-foot swells at twenty-five knots, prepared to crank up to twenty-seven when ordered by Captain Burnham McCaffree, skipper of *Wasp* and commander of the Task Unit.

Earlier in the evening, *Hobson* had received a "signal in the air" that had ordered her, upon execution, to take plane guard station on *Wasp*'s port beam at one thousand yards as the carrier turned into the wind to recover her planes from a nighttime exercise. All hands in the Task Unit were standing by for the "execute."

Hobson and her sister DMS were former *Benson-Livermore*–class destroyers converted to the minesweeping function (just like the fictional *Caine*). *Hobson* had been commissioned in 1942; she displaced 1630 tons and, on this particular evening, carried a crew of 236 men. Her skipper, Lieutenant Commander William Tierney, had been aboard a bit more than a month. He had served on several ships during World War II, had gone into civilian life after the war as a deck officer in the merchant marine, and, after returning to uniform, had been exec of an Atlantic Fleet destroyer during two deployments to the Med. Tierney was a seagoing officer with almost a decade of experience; *Hobson* was his first command.

Earlier in the day, *Hobson* and the other destroyers in the entire Task Group had received a message from Rear Admiral Chester Wood, the screen commander. Wood's message said, in part, that all destroyers should expedite getting on station, even "at the expense of an occasional mistake."

Tierney showed his officer of the deck, Lieutenant William Hoefer, his plan for the change of station. The skipper would first turn starboard, with *Wasp*, to course 130 degrees true; then, *Hobson* would turn to port with full rudder until she reverse-paralleled *Wasp* at a range of one thousand yards, clearing the carrier on *Hobson*'s starboard beam. Hoefer was aghast; at one point in *Hobson*'s projected port turn, she would be headed straight at the carrier, at twenty-seven knots. The two men had heated words, then Tierney stalked out to his bridge chair on the starboard wing. *Hobson* would make the maneuver her captain wanted, to expedite getting to her new station.

"Execute" came over the bridge radio at 2221—new speed twenty-seven knots, new formation course 260 degrees true—a sweeping turn by the carrier to starboard, with the escorts expected to solve the courses to their new stations by the most expeditious (and safest) method. Both *Hobson* and *Rodman* rogered the signal.

Tierney called in from the starboard wing: "Right standard rudder. Come right to 130. All engines ahead flank." Hoefer, with the conn, gave the proper response: "Captain, do you have the conn?" Tierney shot back, "I have the conn."

Hobson pirouetted smoothly to starboard, leaning gently away from her turn to 130 true. She held this course, inside *Wasp*'s own, longer arc, for ninety seconds. Then Tierney ordered "Left standard rudder, new course 090." *Hobson* obediently slewed to port, coming to her new heading in the general direction of the still-turning *Wasp*. The two ships, the carrier displacing twenty-three times the amount of salt water as the can, were now closing at a relative speed of over fifty knots.

Aboard the carrier, the Combat Information Center reported to the bridge that *Wasp*'s surface search radar was down. At the same moment, McCaffree noted with seaman's eye that his new relative wind was not quite right; he ordered the flattop eased to a new course of 250 true. The new course was passed by radio to both escorts; neither acknowledged.

Now, *Wasp* and *Hobson* were racing toward each other in the inky blackness on almost reciprocal courses. Still, they would have passed abeam to port (not starboard, as Tierney had planned) at a few hundred yards—a close shave, but the kind the Navy had practically every day at sea.

Then, *Hobson*'s skipper, perhaps wanting to increase the range of his intended starboard-to-starboard passage, suddenly ordered, "Left standard rudder." *Hobson*'s own CIC thundered up on the 21MC: "Lost contact due to short range! Do we intend to pass astern of the carrier?"

In these last moments, William Tierney suddenly realized what he had done. "Left full rudder!" he screamed. "Hard left! All ahead emergency flank!"

The bridge clock read 2225, and *Hobson*'s time had run out. *Wasp*'s bow slammed into her at twenty-seven knots, about twenty feet aft of her second stack on the starboard side. The shock bowled the little DMS over on her port beam; for an instant she was draped across the carrier's huge bow— then she skidded off, her keel slicing through *Wasp*'s forward compartments like a razor.

Hobson snapped in two. One of her main shafts, wrenched from her guts like a toothpick, stayed fast for a moment in the gaping mouth carved in the carrier's bow. Within four minutes, both her sections disappeared beneath the sea. She took 175 of her men down with her; 150 of them had been sleeping in stern compartments and never had a chance. Sixty-one survived; *Hobson*'s captain was never seen again.

No one was killed or injured aboard *Wasp*. Aft of her bow extended a jagged slit about ninety feet long and fifteen feet deep. Twelve feet of the gash lay below the waterline, and the carrier was shipping water. Parts of her keel and forefoot had been ripped off, and the full length of the six-hundred-foot starboard anchor chain was now being dragged along like the tail of a kite, carrying at its bitter end a piece of hull plate—the only part of *Hobson* left.

—*Wasp* staggered back to port. *Hobson*, with three-quarters of her crew, lay in her grave—2600 fathoms deep in the North Atlantic.

☆

—Human error, to be sure. Rotten luck, of course. A deep blow to the Navy's pride and professionalism, without a doubt. The dead Tierney was found to be at fault by a naval court of inquiry; Hoefer and most of the bridge crew survived, to give testimony.

But there were other meanings here. *Hobson*'s catastrophic end cost the

United States Navy more lives than any other single instance of combat or shipboard emergency in the half century following World War II. And the disaster happened during a simple change-of-station evolution that the fleet practiced dozens of times, at all hours, every day throughout the world.

The word for this was "routine"—but, in fact, nothing the Navy did could *ever* be counted routine, simply because of the nature of its business. As had been said so often, the sea was a cruel mistress, and the sea was the element on, under, and over which the Navy served.

The Navy was a *service*, in the most severe meaning of the word. The fleet existed to *serve* national policy, in all its grandeur, mediocrity, folly, and "routine." To serve well meant that every sailor, from the lowliest seaman to the most senior admiral, had to be both *responsible* and *accountable*.

Such were the ancient lessons of the sea, pertinent now no less than in centuries past. The Navy relied on responsibility and accountability above all else. Responsibility and accountability lay at the core of its vaunted independence; they drove its officers and men to higher posts and more authority; they went with the blue-and-gold uniform like a tight-fitting suit of armor.

The Navy's senior people, far more than those in almost any other walk of life, could not avoid their responsibility and accountability, even if they tried (and no one could imagine trying). They not only served; they tried to serve according to the highest canons of naval professionalism, and they expected to be summoned to the long green table if they made mistakes. To these senior people much was given: authority, immense symbolic reward, high station in life, important posts of leadership. And of them, much was expected.

The expectation was there, much more than in any other profession, because of the roles they were called upon to play in the international arena, and because the sea was there, too—the waiting, unforgiving sea. In a flash— through mistake (nothing at sea or in port was *ever* "sailor-proof"), misunderstanding, carelessness, a bad roll of the dice—everything could be lost, even when things were at their most "routine." The lucky survivors of *Hobson* knew this; so did the men of *Bennington* and *Leyte;* so too did those who remembered the hundreds of dead aviators, the smashed-up flight deck crews, the engineers burned in boiler flarebacks, the men washed overboard into churning seas, the electrocutions. Dozens of Navymen perished at sea every year, in ways so "routine" that only the dead man's hometown newspaper even bothered to report the fact of his passing.

The Navy operated routinely on, under, and over an element that *could take lives.* This was why safety was drummed into its people, why there was never enough time for training, why responsibility and accountability had to form its collective backbone. The Navy's *Hobson's* choice meant that you acted on your best information with all the training and skill you possessed; then you stood tall for judgment. This had been the necessary way of the sea since men first ventured forth in ships, and this was the way of the United States Navy.

A few people fell short of these ideals; a very few, like William Tierney, fell tragically, fatally short. But so many more served capably or even brilliantly, doing their duty. And they did that duty so well, from V-J Day through the Cuban Missile Crisis, that they shaped the history of the world.

To this end, some of the Soviet leaders in 1962 might well have immersed themselves in historical study. Napoleon was especially pertinent; he had had words to explain their chagrin and humiliation. The French emperor had been bedeviled by the Royal Navy throughout his stunning, stormy career. After all the battles were over, Napoleon had had this to say about His Majesty's fleet: "Wherever there is water to float a ship, we are sure to find you in the way."[6]

In like manner the Shield of the Republic, for whatever purpose, was "in the way." The Navy's ability to keep the seas, to project power, and to establish the American presence abroad was among the most significant international facts of the postwar world.

—And so, in the wake of its outstanding conduct in the Cuban Missile Crisis, the incomparably powerful instrument that was the Cold War Navy steamed on, at its triumphant peak.

NOTES

---- ☆ ----

All ranks and rates are those of American naval personnel, unless otherwise iden-tified. The quotations at the beginning of each part are from Sun Tzu, *The Art of War*, trans. Samuel B. Griffith (New York: Oxford University Press, 1963), as follows:

Part I	Page 21
Part II	Page 167
Part III	Page 285
Part IV	Page 431
Part V	Page 569

ABBREVIATIONS USED IN NOTES

AAF	Army Air Forces
AH	*All Hands*
AN	*American Neptune*
ASH	*Aerospace Historian*
CEC	Civil Engineer Corps
CHC	Chaplain's Corps
CSN	Confederate States Navy
FA	*Foreign Affairs*
HDHUSMC	Historical Division, Headquarters, U.S. Marine Corps, Washington, D.C.
JFS	*Jane's Fighting Ships*
MA	*Military Affairs*
MC	Medical Corps
MH	*Military History*
MM	*Mariner's Mirror*
MR	*Military Review*
NH	*Naval History*
NHD	Naval History Division, Department of the Navy, Washington, D.C.
NL	Nimitz Library, United States Naval Academy
NT	*Navy Times*
NWCR	*Naval War College Review*

NYT	*New York Times*
RN	Royal Navy
SC	Supply Corps
SDR	Secretary of Defense, Annual or Semi-Annual Report
SM	*Shipmate*
SNR	Secretary of the Navy, Annual or Semi-Annual Report
USA	United States Army
USAF	United States Air Force
USCG	United States Coast Guard
USMC	United States Marine Corps
USMCR	United States Marine Corps Reserve
USNI	United States Naval Institute
USNIP	United States Naval Institute *Proceedings*
USNR	United States Naval Reserve
WP	*Washington Post*

☆

PROLOGUE

[1]Rear Admiral George Van Deurs, Oral History, USNI, II (1974), NL, 560; Captain Roland W. Faulk, CHC, Oral History, USNI (1975), NL, 153; Captain T.H. Suddath, "Cessation of Hostilities with Japan Within the Third Fleet," *SM*, 33, n. 7 (July–August 1970), 4; D. Clayton James, "American and Japanese Strategies in the Pacific War," in Peter Paret, ed., *Makers of Modern Strategy from Machiavelli to the Nuclear Age* (Princeton: Princeton University Press, 1986), 718; Emmett K. Perryman, Jr., "The End: Japan, August and September 1945," *SM*, 41, n. 6 (July–August, 1978), 23.

[2]Faulk, Oral History, 142, 155; E.B. Potter, *Bull Halsey* (Annapolis: Naval Institute Press, 1985), 354–355; LeRoy W. Vance, "When New York Welcomed the *Missouri*," *SM*, 9, n. 10 (October, 1946), 11, 16–17; CINCPACFLT Action Report, "Surrender and Occupation of Japan, August–December 1945," Appendix I, 11 February 1946, NHD, 93; Gordon Newell and Vice Admiral Allen E. Smith, *Mighty Mo: The USS Missouri, A Biography of the Last Battleship* (Seattle: Superior Publishing Company, 1969), 43.

[3]"USS *Missouri* (BB-11), Tokyo Bay, 1908," *SM*, 36, n. 7 (July–August, 1973), 17; Robert O. Dulin, Jr., and William L. Garzke, Jr., *Battleships: United States Battleships in World War II* (Annapolis: Naval Institute Press, 1985), 129; Newell and Smith, *Mighty Mo*, 41; War Diary, USS *Missouri* (BB-63), 2 September 1945, NHD, 1; Douglas MacArthur, *Reminiscences* New York: McGraw-Hill Book Company, 1964), 270; E.B. Potter, *Nimitz* (Annapolis: Naval Institute Press, 1976), 393.

[4]Potter, *Bull Halsey*, 356–357; Vance, "When New York Welcomed the *Missouri*," 16; Faulk, Oral History, 145–146; Admiral Stuart S. ("Sunshine") Murray, Oral History, USNI, II (1974), NL, 447–449; Rear Admiral Brooke Schumm, "Tokyo Bay, August 1945," *SM*, 42, n. 6 (July–August, 1979), 28; Vice Admiral

Charles A. Lockwood, *Sink 'Em All: Submarine Warfare in the Pacific* (New York: E.P. Dutton & Co., 1951), 361; *NYT*, 2 September 1945, 4; Thomas B. Buell, *The Quiet Warrior: A Biography of Admiral Raymond A. Spruance* (Boston: Little, Brown and Company, 1974), 369.

⁵Captain Henri Smith-Hutton, Oral History, USNI, II (1976), NL, 516, 518–519; War Diary, USS *Lansdowne* (DD-486), 2 September 1945, NHD, 2–3; *JFS*, 1944–1945, 480–481.

⁶Samuel Eliot Morison, *History of United States Naval Operations in World War II*, I: *The Battle of the Atlantic, 1939–1945* (Boston: Little, Brown and Company, 1975), 154, 415; V: *The Struggle for Guadalcanal, August 1942–February 1943* (Boston: Little, Brown and Company, 1975), 131–136, 205, 226–227; VIII: *New Guinea and the Marianas, March 1944–August 1944* (Boston: Little, Brown and Company, 1975), 405, 415; Battle Reports, USS *Lansdowne* (DD-486), 11 December 1943, 16 January 1944, 21 February 1944, 2 March 1944, NL; James, "American and Japanese Strategies," 725; *Time*, 10 September 1945, 30; *Newsweek*, 10 September 1945, 29.

⁷Samuel Eliot Morison, *History of United States Naval Operations in World War II*, XIV: *Victory in the Pacific, 1945* (Boston: Little, Brown and Company, 1975), 366–367; Admiral Robert B. Carney, " 'Under the Cold Gaze of the Victorious,' " *USNIP*, 109, n. 12 (December, 1983), 47; D. Clayton James, *The Years of MacArthur*, II: *1941–1945* (Boston: Houghton Mifflin Company, 1975), 790; Toshikazu Kaze, *Journey to the Missouri* (Hamden, Conn.: Archon Press, 1969 [1950]), 9; MacArthur, *Reminiscences*, 272; *NYT*, 2 September 1945, 2; War Diary, USS *Piedmont* (AD-17), 12 October 1945, NHD, 1; Vice Admiral Eli T. Reich, Oral History, USNI, I (1982), NL, 241.

⁸*JFS*, 1944–1945, 511; Captain C.A. Bartholomew, *Mud, Muscles, and Miracles: Marine Salvage in the United States Navy* (Washington, D.C.: Naval Historical Center and Naval Sea Systems Command, 1990), 164; Rear Admiral Worrall Reed Carter, *Beans, Bullets, and Black Oil: The Story of Logistics Afloat in the Pacific During World War II* (Washington, D.C.: Government Printing Office, 1953), 163, 180, 185, 328–329; Smith-Hutton, Oral History, II, 519–520.

⁹Lockwood, *Sink 'Em All*, 361, 256–258; Theodore Roscoe, *Pigboats: The True Story of the Fighting Submarines of World War II* (New York: Bantam Books, 1958), 440–441; Brian Johnson, *Fly Navy: The History of Naval Aviation* (New York: William Morrow and Company, Inc., 1981), 327; Clay Blair, Jr., *Silent Victory: The U.S. Submarine War Against Japan* (New York: J.B. Lippincott Company, 1975), 988–991, 777–780; *JFS*, 1944–1945, 486–487; Samuel Eliot Morison, *History of United States Naval Operations in World War II*, XII: *Leyte, June 1944– January 1945* (Boston: Little, Brown and Company, 1975), 410–411; Ship's History, USS *Archerfish* (SS-311), n.d., NL, 3–6; Captain Joseph F. Enright and James W. Ryan, *Shinano! The Sinking of Japan's Secret Supership* (New York: St. Martin's Press, 1987), 153.

¹⁰Gary E. Weir, *Building American Submarines, 1914–1940*, Contributions to Naval History . . . No. 3 (Washington, D.C.: Naval Historical Center, 1991), 115–117; A. Russell Buchanan, *The United States and World War II*, II (New York: Harper and Row, 1964), 580–581; Lockwood, *Sink 'Em All*, 27, 299, 350–351; War Patrol Report Number Seven, USS *Archerfish* (SS-311), 12 September 1945,

NHD, 17; Paul R. Schratz, *Submarine Commander* (Lexington: University Press of Kentucky, 1988), 178–179; Vice Admiral Roland N. Smoot, Oral History, USNI (1972), NL, 196–197.

11Schratz, *Submarine Commander*, 184; Commander Third Fleet Operations Report (16 August 1945–19 September 1945), 6 October 1945, NHD, 15; Samuel Eliot Morison, *History of United States Naval Operations in World War II*, II: *Operations in North African Waters, October 1942–June 1943* (Boston: Little, Brown and Company, 1975), 266–271; X: *The Atlantic Battle Won, May 1943–May 1945* (Boston: Little, Brown and Company, 1975), 35; XI: *The Invasion of France and Germany, 1944–1945* (Boston: Little, Brown and Company, 1975), 57; Vice Admiral Daniel E. Barbey, *MacArthur's Amphibious Navy: Seventh Fleet Amphibious Force Operations, 1943–1945* (Annapolis: Naval Institute Press, 1969), 216; *JFS*, 1944–1945, 521; Commander Kendall King, "LSTs: Marvelous at Fifty," *NH*, 6, n. 4 (Winter, 1992), 37–41; Eric Larrabee, *Commander in Chief: Franklin Delano Roosevelt, His Lieutenants, and Their War* (New York: Simon and Schuster, Inc., 1987), 444–445; Vice Admiral George C. Dyer, *The Amphibians Came to Conquer: The Story of Admiral Richmond Kelly Turner*, II (Washington, D.C.: Government Printing Office, 1971), 964, 1032, 1105; Thomas B. Buell, *Master of Sea Power: A Biography of Fleet Admiral Ernest J. King* (Boston: Little, Brown and Company, 1980), 308–311, 405–406.

12Action Report, *LST 656*, 26 August 1944, NL; Admiral John S. Thach, Oral History, USNI, II (1977), NL, 474, 482–483; Clark G. Reynolds, *Admiral John H. Towers: The Struggle for Naval Air Supremacy* (Annapolis: Naval Institute Press, 1991), 510–511; War Diary, USS *Cowpens* (CVL-25), 2 September 1945, NHD, 1–2.

13*JFS*, 1944–1945, 461; James H. Belote and William M. Belote, *Titans of the Seas: The Development and Operations of Japanese and American Carrier Task Forces During World War II* (New York: Harper and Row, 1975), 169–170; Samuel Eliot Morison, *History of United States Naval Operations in World War II*, VII: *Aleutians, Gilberts and Marshalls, June 1942–April 1944* (Boston: Little, Brown and Company, 1975), xxvii, 92, 116–117, 141, 208, 326, 330; VIII: *New Guinea and the Marianas, March 1944–August 1944* (Boston: Little, Brown and Company, 1975), 36, 174, 238, 268, 273; XII: *Leyte, June 1944–January 1945* (Boston: Little, Brown and Company, 1975), 90, 100–102, 309–310; XIII: *The Liberation of the Philippines, Luzon, Mindanao, the Visayas, 1944–1945* (Boston: Little, Brown and Company, 1975), 54, 70, 181; XIV: *Victory in the Pacific, 1945* (Boston: Little, Brown and Company, 1975), 21; Vincent Davis, *Postwar Defense Policy and the U.S. Navy, 1943–1946* (Chapel Hill: University of North Carolina Press, 1966), 185; Faulk, Oral History, 150–152.

14Faulk, Oral History, 153–154; Fleet Admiral William F. Halsey and Joseph Bryan III, *Admiral Halsey's Story* (New York: McGraw-Hill Book Company, 1947), 282–283; *Time*, 10 September 1945, 30; Carney, " 'Under the Cold Gaze of the Victorious,' " 49; *NYT*, 3 September 1945, 3; Potter, *Bull Halsey*, 358–359; Richard P. Hallion, *The Naval Air War in Korea* (New York: Zebra Books, 1988), 17–21; Belote and Belote, *Titans of the Seas*, 173–174.

15Hallion, *The Naval Air War in Korea*, 20–21, 18; Carney, " 'Under the Cold Gaze of the Victorious,' " 50; *Newsweek*, 10 September 1945, 29; *Time*, 10 September

1945, 29; War Diary, USS *Lansdowne* (DD-486), 2 September 1945, NHD, 3; Potter, *Nimitz*, 396; James, *The Years of MacArthur*, II, 791–792; War Diary, USS *Missouri* (BB-63), 2 September 1945, NHD, 1; Suddath, "Cessation of Hostilities with Japan within the Third Fleet," 5; Vance, "When New York Welcomed the *Missouri*," 17; *NYT*, September 1945, 1.

[16]*SNR*, FY 1945, A-13, A-31, A-14, A-16, A-47, A-17; Paul Kennedy, *The Rise and Fall of the Great Powers: Economic Change and Military Conflict from 1500 to 2000* (New York: Vintage Books, 1989 [1987]), 357–359; R. Ernest Depuy and Trevor N. Dupuy, *Military Heritage of America* (New York: McGraw-Hill Book Company, 1956), 637; Rear Admiral Thomas L. Gatch, "The Battlewagon Fights Back," in Lieutenant William Harrison Fetridge, ed., *The Second Navy Reader* (Indianapolis: Bobbs-Merrill Company, 1944), 120; J.F.C. Fuller, *A Military History of the Western World*, III: *From the American Civil War to the End of World War II* (New York: Da Capo Press, 1987 [1956]), 596–597; Correlli Barnett, *Engage the Enemy More Closely: The Royal Navy in the Second World War* (New York: W.W. Norton & Company, 1991), 879; Bernard Brodie, "New Tactics in Naval Warfare," *FA*, 24, n. 2 (January, 1946), 210, 223.

CHAPTER ONE

[1]Herodotus, *The Histories*, trans. Aubrey de Selincourt (New York: Penguin Books, 1984), 488–489; *King John*, Act 2, Scene 1; *King Richard II*, Act 2, Scene 1; Edward Mead Earle, "Adam Smith, Alexander Hamilton, Friedrich List: The Economic Foundations of Military Power," in Peter Paret, ed., *Makers of Modern Strategy from Machiavelli to the Nuclear Age* (Princeton: Princeton University Press, 1986), 223; Sir William Blackstone, *Commentaries* (1765–1769), I, Book I, Ch. 13; Leonard D. White, *The Republican Era: A Study in Administrative History, 1869–1901* (New York: Free Press, 1965), 157–161; Charles A. Beard, *The Navy: Defense or Portent?* (New York: Harper & Brothers, 1932), 12.

[2]Beard, *The Navy*, 87; Mary Klachko and David F. Trask, *Admiral William Shepherd Benson: First Chief of Naval Operations* (Annapolis: Naval Institute Press, 1987), 65; John Edward Weems, *Peary: The Explorer and the Man* (Los Angeles: Jeremy P. Tarcher, Inc., 1987), 308; Kenneth L. Moll, "A.T. Mahan, American Historian," *MA*, 27, n. 3 (Fall, 1963), 131.

[3]John Shy, "Jomini," in Paret, *Makers of Modern Strategy*, 179; Archer Jones, *The Art of War in the Western World* (Urbana: University of Illinois Press, 1988), 89; Alfred Thayer Mahan to James R. Soley, 29 October 1892, in Robert Seager II and Doris D. Maguire, eds., *Letters and Papers of Alfred Thayer Mahan*, II (1890–1901) (Annapolis: Naval Institute Press, 1975), 81; Robert Seager II, *Alfred Thayer Mahan: The Man and His Letters* (Annapolis: Naval Institute Press, 1977), 555; William E. Livezey, *Mahan on Sea Power* (Norman: University of Oklahoma Press, 1981 [1947]), 342–343, 345, 347; Earle, "Adam Smith, Alexander Hamilton, Friedrich List," 233, 237; Alfred Thayer Mahan, "Preparedness for Naval War," in *The Interest of America in Sea Power* (Freeport, N.Y.: Books for Libraries Press, 1970 [1897]), 199, 214; Scott G. McNall, *The Road to Rebellion: Class Formation and Kansas Populism, 1865–1900* (Chicago: University of Chicago Press, 1988), 94.

⁴Livezey, *Mahan on Sea Power*, 334–335; Alfred Thayer Mahan to Stephen B. Luce, 22 January 1886, in Seager and Maguire, *Letters and Papers of Alfred Thayer Mahan*, I (1847–1889), 623; Alfred Thayer Mahan to editor of *NYT*, 22 May 1912, in *ibid.*, III (1902–1914), 459; Mahan to Samuel A. Ashe, 27 January 1876, in *ibid.*, I (1847–1889), 441; Alfred Thayer Mahan, *Sea Power in Its Relations to the War of 1812*, II (Boston: Little, Brown and Company, 1919 [1905]), 216; Klachko and Trask, *Admiral William Shepherd Benson*, 69, 73; Earle, "Adam Smith, Alexander Hamilton, Friedrich List," 237; Edgar Stanton Maclay, *A History of the United States Navy from 1775 to 1898*, I (New York: D. Appleton and Company, 1898), 163; Vice Admiral George C. Dyer, *On the Treadmill to Pearl Harbor: The Memoirs of Admiral J.O. Richardson* (Washington, D.C.: Naval History Division, 1973), 89; Alfred Thayer Mahan to Stephen B. Luce, 22 January 1886, in Seager and Maguire, *Letters and Papers of Alfred Thayer Mahan*, I (1847–1889), 623; Gerald E. Wheeler, *Prelude to Pearl Harbor: The United States Navy and the Far East, 1921–1931* (Columbia: University of Missouri Press, 1963), 113–114, 121.

⁵Livezey, *Mahan on Sea Power*, 358; Seager, *Alfred Thayer Mahan*, 171–172, 291–292, 474; Wheeler, *Prelude to Pearl Harbor*, 116; Russell F. Weigley, ed., *The American Military: Readings in the History of the Military in American Society* (Reading, Mass.: Addison-Wesley Publishing Company, 1969), 97; William N. Still, Jr., *American Sea Power in the Old World: The United States Navy in European and Near Eastern Waters, 1865–1917* (Westport, Conn.: Greenwood Press, 1980), 141–142; Philip A. Crowl, "Alfred Thayer Mahan: The Naval Historian," in Paret, *Makers of Modern Strategy*, 475; Charles C. Bates and John F. Fuller, *America's Weather Warriors, 1814–1985* (College Station: Texas A&M University Press, 1986), 41.

⁶R. Ernest Dupuy and Trevor N. Dupuy, *Military Heritage of America* (New York: McGraw-Hill Book Company, 1956), 194–198; Crowl, "Alfred Thayer Mahan," 472–473; Walter Millis, "Sea Power: Abstraction or Asset?," *FA*, 29, n. 3 (April, 1951), 371, 373; Crowl, "Alfred Thayer Mahan," 452–453; Vincent Davis, *Postwar Defense Policy and the U.S. Navy, 1943–1946* (Chapel Hill: University of North Carolina Press, 1966), 163, 14; Carl H. Builder, *The Masks of War: American Military Styles in Strategy and Analysis* (Baltimore: Johns Hopkins University Press, 1989), 76.

⁷Shy, "Jomini," 173–174; Davis, *Postwar Defense Policy*, 188–189, 129–130; David MacIsaac, "Voices from the Central Blue: Theorists of Air Power," in Paret, *Makers of Modern Strategy*, 632; Captain M.R. Browning, "Battleship Tactics," *MR*, 25, n. 9 (December, 1945), 11; Robert O. Dulin, Jr., and William H. Garzke, Jr., *Battleships: United States Battleships in World War II* (Annapolis: Naval Institute Press, 1976), 4–5, 27, 114, 175.

⁸Dulin and Garzke, *Battleships*, 155; Russell Spurr, *A Glorious Way to Die: The Kamikaze Mission of the Battleship* Yamato, *April 1945* (New York: New Market Press, 1982), 14, 34; Atsushi Oi, "Why Japan's Antisubmarine Warfare Failed," in David C. Evans, ed., *The Japanese Navy in World War II in the Words of Former Japanese Naval Officers*, 2nd ed. (Annapolis: Naval Institute Press, 1986), 414; Mitsuru Yoshida, "The Sinking of the *Yamato*," in *ibid.*, 474; Toshiyuki Yokoi, "Thoughts on Japan's Naval Defeat," in *ibid.*, 505–507; Minoru Nomura, "Ozawa in the Pacific: A Junior Officer's Experience," in *ibid.*, 305; Paul S.

Dull, *A Battle History of the Imperial Japanese Navy (1941–1945)* (Annapolis: Naval Institute Press, 1978), 316.

[9]Dulin and Garzke, *Battleships*, 44, 46, 73–76, 84–85, 61, 94, 143–144, 190–191, 168; Samuel Eliot Morison, *History of United States Naval Operations in World War II*, XII: *Leyte, June 1944–January 1945* (Boston: Little, Brown and Company, 1975), 240–241; Dan van der Vat, *The Atlantic Campaign: World War II's Great Struggle at Sea* (New York: Harper & Row, 1988), 362; W.H. Russell, "Mahan's Doctrine and the Air Age," *MA*, 20, n. 4 (Winter, 1956), 227–229; Livezey, *Mahan on Sea Power*, 364–366.

[10]Toshikazu Ohmae, "The Battle of Savo Island," in Evans, *The Japanese Navy in World War II*, 242; Yoshida, "The Sinking of the *Yamato*," in *ibid.*, 478; Yokoi, "Thoughts on Japan's Naval Defeat," in *ibid.*, 509; Spurr, *A Glorious Way to Die*, 36–37; Kennosuke Torisu and Masataka Chihaya, "Japanese Submarine Tactics and the *Kaiten*," in Evans, *The Japanese Navy in World War II*, 440; Rikihei Inoguchi and Tadashi Nakajima, "The Kamikaze Attack Corps," in *ibid.*, 436–437; Brian Johnson, *Fly Navy: The History of Naval Aviation* (New York: William Morrow and Company, Inc., 1981), 11.

[11]Klachko and Trask, *Admiral William Shepherd Benson*, 156; J.F.C. Fuller, *A Military History of the Western World*, III: *From the American Civil War to the End of World War II* (New York: Da Capo Press, 1987 [1956]), 461–462; Harry H. Ransom, "The Battleship Meets the Airplane," *MA*, 23, n. 1 (Spring, 1959), 21–27; Thomas C. Hone, "Battleships vs. Aircraft Carriers: The Patterns of U.S. Navy Operating Expenditures, 1932–1941," *MA*, 41, n. 3 (October, 1977), 133–141; Livezey, *Mahan on Sea Power*, 358, 363–364; Seager, *Alfred Thayer Mahan*, 535–538.

[12]Torisu and Chihaya, "Japanese Submarine Tactics," 440; Rear Admiral Edward Wegener, Federal German Navy, "Theory of Naval Strategy in the Nuclear Age," *USNIP*, 98, n. 5 (May, 1972), 190–207; Commander James A. Barber, "Mahan and Naval Strategy in the Nuclear Age," *NWCR*, 24, n. 7 (March, 1972), 78–88; Livezey, *Mahan on Sea Power*, 370–371, 378; Thomas C. Kennedy, "Charles A. Beard and the 'Big Navy Boys,' " *MA*, 31, n. 2 (Summer, 1967), 65–73; Captain Ernest M. Eller, "Will We Need a Navy to Win?," *USNIP*, 76, n. 3 (March, 1950), 237–247; Rear Admiral John D. Hayes, "The Influence of Modern Sea Power, 1945–1970," *USNIP*, 97, n. 5 (May, 1971), 279.

[13]Paul Kennedy, "The Influence and the Limitations of Sea Power," *International History Review*, 10, n. 1 (February, 1988), 5; Walter Millis, ed., *The Forrestal Diaries* (New York: Viking Press, 1951); Mahan, *Sea Power in Its Relations to the War of 1812*, II, 99, 131; Mahan, "Preparedness for Naval War," 198; Wheeler, *Prelude to Pearl Harbor*, 83; Rear Admiral S.S. Robison, *A History of Naval Tactics from 1530 to 1930: The Evolution of Tactical Maxims* (Annapolis: Naval Institute Press, 1942), 451–452, 895; Dupuy and Dupuy, *Military Heritage of America*, 7, 18.

[14]Still, *American Sea Power in the Old World*, 144; Oliver Warner, *A Portrait of Lord Nelson* (New York: Penguin Books, 1987 [1958]), 143, 148, 263, 348, 151, 179–180, 153; Samuel Eliot Morison, *John Paul Jones: A Sailor's Biography* (Boston: Little, Brown and Company, 1959), 226–242; Mahan, *Sea Power in Its Relations to the War of 1912*, II, 133–148; Alfred Thayer Mahan, *Admiral Farragut* (New

York: Haskell House, 1968 [1892]), 278–279; Tamara Moser Melia, *"Damn the Torpedoes:" A Short History of U.S. Naval Mine Countermeasures, 1777–1991*, Contributions to Naval History . . . No. 4 (Washington, D.C.: Naval Historical Center, 1991), 4; Edward Luttwak, "The Strategy of Survival," *American Heritage*, 39, n. 5 (July–August, 1988), 77–85; Dupuy and Dupuy, *Military Heritage of America*, 119.

CHAPTER TWO

[1]Vincent Davis, *Postwar Defense Policy and the U.S. Navy, 1943–1946* (Chapel Hill: University of North Carolina Press, 1966), 10–11; Clark G. Reynolds, *Admiral John H. Towers: The Struggle for Naval Air Supremacy* (Annapolis: Naval Institute Press, 1991), 371; Hanson Weightman Baldwin, Oral History, USNI, I (1976), NL, 361–363; Memorandum, Vice Admiral F. J. Horne to Admiral E. J. King, 2 August 1943, Box 198 (A16-3[5]), NHD; Robert William Love, Jr., "Ernest Joseph King, 26 March 1942–15 December 1945," in Robert William Love, Jr., ed., *The Chiefs of Naval Operations* (Annapolis: Naval Institute Press, 1980), 147; Vice Admiral Paul D. Stroop, Oral History, USNI (1970), NL, 75; Memorandum, Admiral C. C. Bloch to Vice Admiral F. J. Horne, 10 June 1943, Box 197 (A16-1[3]), NHD; Admiral Charles Donald Griffin, Oral History, USNI (1973), NL, 55–56; Admiral H. E. Yarnell to Vice Admiral F. J. Horne, 14 June 1944, Box 198 (A16-3[5]), NHD; Yarnell Diary, Admiral Harry E. Yarnell Papers, NHD.

[2]Davis, *Postwar Defense Policy*, 4, 113–114, 179; "Basic Post-War Plan No. 1," 7 May 1945, Box 197 (A16-1[3]), NHD; Letter, Ernest J. King to Secretary of the Navy, 3 March 1945, Box 197 (A16-1[3]), NHD; Memorandum, Captain A. D. Douglas to Admiral R. S. Edwards, 20 March 1945, Box 202 (P16-1), NHD.

[3]Davis, *Postwar Defense Policy*, 180–181, 95, 70, 76; "Synopsis of Statement by Vice Admiral Forrest P. Sherman, USN, Deputy Chief of Naval Operations (Operations) Before the Committee on Naval Affairs, United States Senate, on H.R. 4421, February 14, 1946," Box 197 (A16-1[3]), NHD; Ronald Steel, *Pax Americana* (New York: Viking Press, 1967), 4; Joseph Zikmund, "James V. Forrestal, 19 May 1944–17 September 1947," in Paolo E. Coletta, ed., *American Secretaries of the Navy*, II: *1913–1972* (Annapolis: Naval Institute Press, 1980), 732–733; E. E. Larson, Memorandum, "Navy Basic Demobilization Plan No. 2," 12 October 1944, Box 198 (A16-3[5]), NHD; "Navy Basic Demobilization Plan No. 2, Revision No. 1," 16 March 1945, Box 213, NHD, 1.

[4]Richard Smoke, *National Security and the Nuclear Dilemma: An Introduction to the American Experience*, 2nd ed. (New York: Random House, 1987), 30; Alexander L. George and Richard Smoke, *Deterrence in American Foreign Policy: Theory and Practice* (New York: Columbia University Press, 1974), 21; Rear Admiral John D. Hayes, "Patterns of American Sea Power, 1945–1956: Their Portents for the Seventies," *USNIP*, 96, n. 5 (May, 1970), 337–339; Hoffman Nickerson, "The Navy in U.S. National Strategy," *USNIP*, 73, n. 2 (February, 1947), 149; Commodore Ernest M. Eller, "Sea Power and Peace," *USNIP*, 73, n. 10 (October, 1947), 1161–1173; William B. Willcox, "The Future in Relation to American Naval Power," *Yale Review*, 35, n. 1 (September, 1945), 100–118.

[5]James K. Eyre, Jr., "The True Meaning of Post-War Naval Preparedness," *USNIP*, 72, n. 2 (February, 1946), 234–235; "Navy Basic Demobilization Plan No. 2, Revision No. 1," 5; Captain K. C. McIntosh, "The Road Ahead," *USNIP*, 71, n. 11 (November, 1945), 1283–1293; Seaman First Class Peter Marsh Stanford, "The People's Navy: Prospects of an American Sea Power," *USNIP*, 71, n. 12 (December 1945), 1455–1467; Rear Admiral Charles R. Brown, "American National Strategy," *USNIP*, 76, n. 4 (April, 1950), 355–363; Bertram Vogel, "Military Lessons Learned and Not Learned," *USNIP*, 74, n. 6 (June, 1948), 723–731; Lieutenant Commander Ralph E. Williams, Jr., "Power and America's Promise of Peace," *USNIP*, 75, n. 5 (May, 1949), 505–513; Captain Whitaker F. Riggs, Jr., "A Suggested Guide for Amateur Military Critics and Prophets," *USNIP*, 74, n. 8 (August, 1948), 935–949; Davis, *Postwar Defense Policy*, 187; Zikmund, "James V. Forrestal," 733.

[6]Edward Luttwak, "The Strategy of Survival," *American Heritage*, 39, n. 5 (July–August, 1988), 82; "How Naval Battles Are Fought," in Lieutenant William Harrison Fetridge, ed., *The Navy Reader* (Indianapolis: Bobbs-Merrill Company, 1943), 240; Major Guy Richards, USMCR, "The Navy's Stake in the Future," *USNIP*, 74, n. 2 (February, 1948), 183–195; Eyre, "The True Meaning of Post-War Naval Preparedness," 236–237; Captain R. A. Hall, "The Peacetime Duties of the Armed Services," *USNIP*, 72, n. 6 (June, 1946), 787; Vogel, "Military Lessons Learned and Not Learned," 731; Commander M. A. Peel, Jr., "War-Making Must Be in the Hands of Those Who Hate War," *USNIP*, 74, n. 5 (May, 1948), 537–547; H. H. Holly, "Wherein Lies Our Strength?," *USNIP*, 74, n. 7 (July, 1948), 837–841; Lieutenant William H. Hessler, "Geography, Technology, and Military Policy," *USNIP*, 73, n. 4 (April, 1947), 379–389; Zikmund, "James V. Forrestal," 733.

[7]Peel, "War-Making Must Be in the Hands of Those Who Hate War," 543; "Role of the United States Navy in Diplomacy: Editors' Views," *U.S. News & World Report*, 18 October 1946, 40; Robert McLintock, "The United Nations and Naval Power," *USNIP*, 73, n. 6 (June, 1947), 637–647; Davis, *Postwar Defense Policy*, 192–196; Robert Leckie, *Delivered from Evil: The Saga of World War II* (New York: Harper & Row, 1987), 782.

[8]Lieutenant Colonel Robert E. Cushman, Jr., USMC, "Amphibious Warfare: Naval Weapon of the Future," *USNIP*, 74, n. 3 (March, 1948), 301–307; Major General Charles L. Bolte, USA, "The Role of Land Forces in Future Warfare," *USNIP*, 75, n. 1 (January, 1949), 21–31; Davis, *Postwar Defense Policy*, 130–131; Leckie, *Delivered from Evil*, 932; W. Barton Leach, "The Stupidity of a Big Navy," *American Mercury*, 62 (May, 1946), 527–531; DeWitt John, "The Navy Is Changing—Fast," *Christian Science Monitor*, 26 October 1946, 2.

[9]William H. Harbaugh, *The Life and Times of Theodore Roosevelt*, Rev. ed. (New York: Oxford University Press, 1975 [1961]), 486; Anton Antonov-Ovseyenko, *The Time of Stalin: Portrait of a Tyranny* (New York: Harper & Row, 1981), 183; Cajus Bekker, *Hitler's Naval War* (New York: Zebra Books, 1974), 384–387; Jak P. Mallmann Showell, *The German Navy in World War II: A Reference Guide to the Kriegsmarine, 1935–1945* (Annapolis: Naval Institute Press, 1979), 55; Commander Marc Antonio Bragadin, *The Italian Navy in World War II* (Annapolis: Naval Institute Press, 1957), 324–325, 359–360.

[10]*JFS*, 1944–1945, iv, 338–345; Paul S. Dull, *A Battle History of the Imperial Japanese Navy (1941–1945)* (Annapolis: Naval Institute Press, 1978), 343–350; J.F.C. Fuller, *A Military History of the Western World*, III: *From the American Civil War to the End of World War II* (New York: Da Capo Press, 1987 [1957]), 504; Norman Friedman, *The Postwar Naval Revolution* (Annapolis: Naval Institute Press, 1986), 55–56; Rear Admiral Paul Auphan and Jacques Mordal, *The French Navy in World War II* (Annapolis: Naval Institute Press, 1959), 383.

[11]Humphrey Carpenter, *W. H. Auden: A Biography* (Boston: Houghton Mifflin Company, 1982), 308; Friedman, *The Postwar Naval Revolution*, 14, 36; Stanford, "The People's Navy," 1464; Paul M. Kennedy, *The Rise and Fall of British Naval Mastery* (New York: Charles Scribner's Sons, 1976), 324; Leach, "The Stupidity of a Big Navy," 528; Davis, *Postwar Defense Policy*, 178, 95–96; D. Clayton James, "American and Japanese Strategies in the Pacific War," in Peter Paret, ed., *Makers of Modern Strategy from Machiavelli to the Nuclear Age* (Princeton: Princeton University Press, 1986), 723; Douglas MacArthur, *Reminiscences* (New York: Da Capo Press, Inc., 1985 [1964]), 183.

[12]Melvin A. Conant, Jr., "The Navy Question," *American Mercury*, 63 (September, 1946), 381–382; Davis, *Postwar Defense Policy*, 220; Major General Leslie R. Groves, USA, to Ferdinand Eberstadt, 6 September 1945, OP-23 Files, A1/2–A1/5, NHD; "Navy Basic Demobilization Plan No. 1," 17 November 1943, Box 213, NHD; "Basic Demobilization Plan No. 1, Subsidiary Plans," 22 May 1944, Box 213, NHD; Memorandum, Admiral R. S. Edwards to Fleet Admiral Ernest J. King, 8 February 1945, Box 197 (A16-1[3]), NHD; Memorandum, Captain A. D. Douglas to Admiral R. S. Edwards, 19 January 1945, Box 197, (A16-1[3]), NHD; Commander Malcolm W. Cagle and Commander Frank A. Manson, *The Sea War in Korea* (Annapolis: Naval Institute Press, 1957), 18–19.

CHAPTER THREE

[1]William Bradford Huie, *The Case Against the Admirals: Why We Must Have a Unified Command* (New York: E. P. Dutton & Company, 1946), 74; Robert Leckie, *Delivered from Evil: The Saga of World War II* (New York: Harper & Row, 1988), 53–56; Eric Larrabee, *Commander in Chief: Franklin Delano Roosevelt, His Lieutenants, and Their War* (New York: Simon & Schuster, Inc., 1987), 3; Clark G. Reynolds, *Admiral John H. Towers: The Struggle for Naval Air Supremacy* (Annapolis: Naval Institute Press, 1991), 311; Admiral Robert Lee Dennison, Oral History, USNI (1975), NL, 90–91; Vice Admiral Bernhard H. Bieri, Oral History, USNI (1970), NL, 136; Richard Hough, *The Greatest Crusade: Roosevelt, Churchill, and the Naval War* (New York: William Morrow and Company, Inc., 1986), 156–157.

[2]Larrabee, *Commander in Chief*, 11, 24, 28, 32, 66, 142; Rear Admiral Kemp Tolley, Oral History, USNI, II (1984), NL, 597; Vice Admiral Charles A. Lockwood, *Sink 'Em All: Submarine Warfare in the Pacific* (New York: E. P. Dutton & Company, 1951), 202; Rear Admiral Thomas H. Morton, Oral History, USNI (1979), 218–219; Robert J. Donovan, *Conflict and Crisis: The Presidency of Harry S Truman, 1945–1948* (New York: W. W. Norton & Company, 1977), 23; Admiral Charles K. Duncan, Oral History, USNI, I (1978), NL, 240.

[3]Rear Admiral Schuyler Neilson Pyne, Oral History, USNI (1972), NL, 167; Bradley F. Smith, *The War's Long Shadow: The Second World War and Its Aftermath—China, Russia, Britain, America* (New York: Simon and Schuster, 1986), 158–159; Duncan, Oral History, I, 450; Donovan, *Conflict and Crisis*, 140; Walter Millis, ed., *The Forrestal Diaries* (New York: Viking Press, 1951), 88–89; Captain Roland W. Faulk, CHC, Oral History, USNI (1975), NL, 160–161.

[4]Clay Blair, *The Forgotten War: America in Korea, 1950–1953* (New York: Anchor Books, 1989), 4; Margaret Truman, *Harry S Truman* (New York: Quill, 1972), 159–160, 153, 155, 333; Robert J. Donovan, *Tumultuous Years: The Presidency of Harry S Truman, 1949–1953* (New York: W. W. Norton & Company, 1982), 16; Admiral Stuart S. ("Sunshine") Murray, Oral History, USNI, II (1974), NL, 506–508; Admiral Harry E. Yarnell Papers, Diary, 28 April 1944, NHD; George H. Lobdell, "Frank Knox, 11 July 1940–28 April 1944," in Paolo E. Coletta, ed., *American Secretaries of the Navy*, II: *1913–1972* (Annapolis: Naval Institute Press, 1980), 677–727; Leonard D. White, *The Republican Era: A Study in Administrative History, 1869–1901* (New York: Free Press, 1965), 154–157; Millis, *The Forrestal Diaries*, xvi–xxiv; Joseph Zikmund, "James V. Forrestal, 19 May 1944–17 September 1947," in Coletta, *American Secretaries of the Navy*, II, 729–730; Vice Admiral Felix L. Johnson, Oral History, USNI (1973), NL, 237–238; Vice Admiral William R. Smedberg, III, Oral History, USNI, I (1979), NL, 324–327.

[5]Leckie, *Delivered from Evil*, 870; Larrabee, *Commander in Chief*, 195–198; Millis, *The Forrestal Diaries*, 335; Paul B. Ryan, *First Line of Defense: The U.S. Navy since 1945* (Stanford: Hoover Institution Press, 1981), 6–7; Truman, *Harry S Truman*, 15; Thomas G. Patterson, *Meeting the Communist Threat: Truman to Reagan* (New York: Oxford University Press, 1988), 8, 44; Fred J. Cook, *The Warfare State* (New York: Collier Books, 1964), 82–83; Rear Admiral Thomas H. Robbins, Jr., to Rear Admiral Allan E. Smith, 20 May 1947, OP-23 Files, A1/1-1, NHD; Vincent Davis, *Postwar Defense Policy and the U.S. Navy, 1943–1946* (Chapel Hill: University of North Carolina Press, 1966), 65; Reynolds, *Admiral John H. Towers*, 515.

[6]Captain John F. Tarpey, "Uncle Carl," *USNIP*, 108, n. 1 (January, 1982), 38–45; Robert Greenhalgh Albion, *Makers of Naval Policy, 1798–1947* (Annapolis: Naval Institute Press, 1980), 252; Nick Kotz, *Wild Blue Yonder: Money, Politics, and the B-1 Bomber* (New York: Pantheon Books, 1988), 74–75; Reynolds, *Admiral John H. Towers*, 316; Vice Admiral George C. Dyer, *On the Treadmill to Pearl Harbor: The Memoirs of Admiral J. O. Richardson* (Washington, D.C.: Naval History Division, 1973), 463.

[7]Eliot Janeway, "The Man Who Owns the Navy," *Saturday Evening Post*, 15 December 1945, 17, 101–102; Rear Admiral Ralph Kirk James, Oral History, USNI (1972), NL, 208; Vice Admiral Paul D. Stroop, Oral History, USNI (1970), NL, 67–69; Rear Admiral Malcolm E. Schoeffel, Oral History, USNI (1979), NL, 288; Smedberg, Oral History, I, 371–373; Vincent Davis, *The Admirals Lobby* (Chapel Hill: University of North Carolina Press, 1967), 197; Admiral Charles Donald Griffin, Oral History, USNI, I (1973), NL, 311.

[8]Davis, *Postwar Defense Policy*, 184–185; Thomas B. Buell, *Master of Sea Power: A Biography of Fleet Admiral Ernest J. King* (Boston: Little, Brown and Company,

1980), 24, 87; Arthur T. Hadley, *The Straw Giant, America's Armed Forces: Triumphs and Failures* (New York: Avon Books, 1987), 33; Vice Admiral Kleber S. Masterson, Oral History, USNI (1973), NL, 29.

[9]Robert William Love, Jr., "Ernest Joseph King, 26 March 1942–15 December 1945," in Robert William Love, Jr., ed., *The Chiefs of Naval Operations* (Annapolis: Naval Institute Press, 1980), 137–179; Vice Admiral George C. Dyer, Oral History, USNI (1973), NL, 466, 468; Larrabee, *Commander in Chief*, 193, 174; Yarnell Papers, Diary, 21 September 1943, NHD; Ed Cray, *General of the Army, George C. Marshall: Soldier and Statesman* (New York: Touchstone Books, 1991), 10–11, 301; Forrest C. Pogue, *George C. Marshall: Statesman, 1945–1959* (New York: Viking Penguin, 1987), 5–8; Captain Stephen Jurika, Jr., Oral History, USNI, II (1979), NL, 711; Ambassador William J. Sebald, Captain, USNR, Oral History, USNI, III (1980), NL, 1580; Vice Admiral J. Victor Smith, Oral History, USNI (1977), NL, 138–139.

[10]Albion, *Makers of Naval Policy*, 3; Charles Oscar Paullin, *Commodore John Rodgers: Captain, Commodore, and Senior Officer of the American Navy, 1773–1838* (Annapolis: Naval Institute Press, 1967 [1909]), 103; White, *The Republican Era*, 162–171; Samuel P. Huntington, "The Making of the American Military," in Russell F. Weigley, ed., *The American Military: Readings in the History of the Military in American Society* (Reading, Mass.: Addison-Wesley Publishing Company, 1969), 128; Zikmund, "James V. Forrestal," 734–736; Thomas W. Ray, "The Bureaus Go On Forever . . . ," *USNIP*, 94, n. 1 (January, 1968), 58; Davis, *Postwar Defense Policy*, 103–104; Thomas C. Hone, *Power and Change: The Administrative History of the Office of the Chief of Naval Operations, 1946–1986*, Contributions to Naval History . . . No. 2 (Washington, D.C.: Naval Historical Center, 1989), 5–28.

[11]Ryan, *First Line of Defense*, 8; Millis, *The Forrestal Diaries*, 237; Davis, *Postwar Defense Policy*, 117–118.

CHAPTER FOUR

[1]Frank Knox to Admiral Ernest J. King, Serial 0915913, 26 August 1943, in Admiral Harry E. Yarnell Papers, NHD; Stephen E. Ambrose, "The Armed Services and American Strategy, 1945–1953," in Kenneth J. Hagan and William R. Roberts, eds., *Against All Enemies: Interpretations of American Military History from Colonial Times to the Present* (Westport, Conn.: Greenwood Press, 1986), 306; Admiral Harry E. Yarnell Papers, Diary, 21 August 1943, NHD; Vincent Davis, *Postwar Defense Policy and the U.S. Navy, 1943–1946* (Chapel Hill: University of North Carolina Press, 1966), 75; Commander Horace V. Bird, "Let's Take Off Our Shells," *USNIP*, 74, n. 5 (May, 1948), 619–622.

[2]Walter Millis, ed., *The Forrestal Diaries* (New York: Viking Press, 1951), 115–116; Commander M. A. Peel, Jr., SC, "War-Making Must Be in the Hands of Those Who Hate War," *USNIP*, 74, n. 5 (May, 1948), 537–547; Davis, *Postwar Defense Policy*, 28–29, 218.

[3]Bird, "Let's Take Off Our Shells," 622; Davis, *Postwar Defense Policy*, 170; Vice Admiral Ruthven E. Libby, Oral History, USNI (1984), NL, 2–3; Captain

Slade D. Cutter, Oral History, USNI, II (1985), NL, 556; Vice Admiral George C. Dyer, Oral History, USNI (1973), NL, 226.

[4]Rear Admiral Arthur H. McCollum, Oral History, USNI, II (1973), NL, 754–755; Stephen T. Ross, "Chester William Nimitz, 15 December 1945–15 December 1947," in Robert William Love, Jr., ed., *The Chiefs of Naval Operations* (Annapolis: Naval Institute Press, 1980), 181–191; E. B. Potter, *Nimitz* (Annapolis: Naval Institute Press, 1976), 61–62, 126–127, 401, 413; Ed Cray, *General of the Army, George C. Marshall: Soldier and Statesman* (New York: Touchstone Books, 1991), 628.

[5]Chief of Naval Operations Letter Serial 002540, 8 August 1945, "Assumptions to Be Used in Demobilization Planning," Box 197, A16-1(3), NHD; *Newsweek*, 1 October 1945, 56; Davis, *Postwar Defense Policy*, 212–213 [emphasis in original]; Millis, *The Forrestal Diaries*, 100.

[6]*New York Herald Tribune*, 13 April 1947; Vice Admiral Charles A. Lockwood, *Sink 'Em All: Submarine Warfare in the Pacific* (New York: E. P. Dutton & Company, 1951), 353; R. Ernest Dupuy and Trevor N. Dupuy, *Military Heritage of America* (New York: McGraw-Hill Book Company, 1956), 647; Davis, *Postwar Naval Policy*, 214–215; Vice Admiral Felix L. Johnson, Oral History, USNI (1974), NL, 219–221; "The Navy's Demobilization Program," Navy Department, 15 December 1945, 4, NHD.

[7]Vice Admiral Lawson P. Ramage, Oral History, USNI (1975), NL, 196; H. F. Sipe, "Bringing 'Em Home," *SM*, 9, n. 1 (January, 1946), 22–23, 30–31; Rear Admiral Charles J. Wheeler, Oral History, USNI (1970), NL, 343; Vice Admiral Charles S. Minter, Jr., Oral History, USNI, I (1981), NL, 178–192; Commander Edward P. Stafford, *The Big E: The Story of the USS Enterprise* (New York: Dell Books, 1962), 501–503; Admiral James L. Holloway, Jr., and Jack Sweetman, "Demobilization and Change: Naval Personnel Problems, 1945–47," *SM*, 45, n. 10 (December, 1982), 14–16; "The Navy's Demobilization Program," 12–13; *Washington Star*, 13 March 1946; *SNR*, FY 1947, 7; Rear Admiral Malcolm F. Schoeffel, Oral History, USNI (1979), NL, 264; Memorandum, Commander M. C. Mumford to Admiral Sherman, 7 December 1945, in "Demobilization Planning: An Outline of Basic Considerations," August, 1949, following book V, 31, NHD.

[8]Davis, *Postwar Defense Policy*, 202; Brian Johnson, *Fly Navy: The History of Naval Aviation* (New York: William Morrow and Company, 1981), 347; Rear Admiral Joseph Muse Worthington, Oral History, USNI (1975), NL, 334–335; Captain Stephen Jurika, Jr., Oral History, USNI, II (1979), NL, 675; Millis, *The Forrestal Diaries*, 196; Rear Admiral Joshua W. Cooper, Oral History, USNI (1975), NL, 249; *New York Herald Tribune*, 19 January 1946; Admiral Harry D. Felt, Oral History, USNI, I (1974), NL, 173; *Newsweek*, 4 March 1946, 30, 32–34; Vice Admiral William R. Smedberg, III, Oral History, USNI, I (1979), NL, 382; Rear Admiral Charles E. Loughlin, Oral History, USNI (1982), NL, 140; Vice Admiral Eli T. Reich, Oral History, USNI, I (1982), NL, 248.

[9]*Newsweek*, 4 March 1946, 32–34; Vice Admiral Charles Wellborn, Jr., Oral History, USNI (1972), NL, 267–268; Chief of Naval Operations Letter Serial 00221923, 17 May 1945, "Material for Placing Ships in the Inactive Status," Box 199 (L9-1), NHD; Chief of Naval Operations Letter Serial 2705, 17 April

1944, "Preservation and Readiness of Inactive Ships," Box 199 (L9-1), NHD;
"Naval Vessels Preserved," *Science News Letter*, 49 (26 January 1946), 53; Lieu-
tenant David Felix, "America's Fighting Ships in Hibernation," *Travel*, 87
(August, 1946), 14–16, 34; *SNR*, FY 1948, 10; *Life*, 9 September 1946, 31–35.

[10]Herbert L. Zorn, "Putting the Navy's Inactive Fleet in Mothballs," *SM*, 10, n. 6
(June, 1947), 21–22; Mel Fredeen, "Scrapping Our World War II Navy,"
USNIP, 105, n. 2 (February, 1979), 63–73; Stafford, *The Big E*, 503–504; Letter,
James W. Cheevers (executive secretary, Historic Naval Ships Association of
North America, Inc.) to author, 7 April 1989; Robert O. Dulin, Jr., and William
H. Garzke, Jr., *Battleships: United States Battleships in World War II* (Annapolis:
Naval Institute Press, 1976), 121.

[11]Dulin and Garzke, *Battleships*, 208–209; Captain Clinton H. Sigel, "The Reserve
Fleet," *USNIP*, 77, n. 7 (July, 1951), 681–689; "Demobilization Planning," 14
January 1946, book I, 11; *SNR*, in *SDR* (1 January–30 June 1950), 116–117;
Clinton H. Whitehurst, Jr., "The National Defense Reserve Fleet: Past, Present,
and Future," *USNIP*, 103, n. 2 (February, 1977), 26–34.

[12]Commander George J. Lappan, "Going Home," *NH*, 3, n. 1 (Winter, 1989), 26–
30; Joseph Zikmund, "James V. Forrestal, 19 May 1944–17 September 1947,"
in Paolo E. Coletta, ed., *American Secretaries of the Navy*, II: *1913–1972* (An-
napolis: Naval Institute Press, 1980), 733; Peel, "War-Making Must Be in the
Hands of Those Who Hate War," 537–538; *SNR*, FY 1947, 4; "BUPERS Pro-
gress Report," Chart 3, 31 August 1945, 7, in "The Navy's Demobilization
Program;" "Demobilization Planning," 16 January 1946, book V, 27; Captain
C. A. Bartholomew, *Mud, Muscles, and Miracles: Marine Salvage in the United
States Navy* (Washington, D.C.: Naval Historical Center and Naval Sea Systems
Command, 1990), 195, 202–203, 237; Davis, *Postwar Defense Policy*, 218; Millis,
The Forrestal Diaries, 374–376; Ross, "Chester William Nimitz," 188.

CHAPTER FIVE

[1]Samuel P. Huntington, "The Making of the American Military," in Russell F.
Weigley, ed., *The American Military: Readings in the History of the Military in
American Society* (Reading Mass.: Addison-Wesley Publishing Company, 1969),
123; Charles A. Beard, *The Navy: Defense or Portent?* (New York: Harper &
Brothers, 1932), 8; Samuel P. Huntington, "Interservice Competition and the
Political Roles of the Armed Services," in Harry L. Coles, ed., *Total War and
Cold War: Problems in Civilian Control of the Military* (Columbus: Ohio State
University Press, 1962), 178–210; Dan van der Vat, *The Atlantic Campaign:
World War II's Great Struggle at Sea* (New York: Harper & Row, 1988), 276–
277; Vice Admiral Charles A. Lockwood, *Sink 'Em All: Submarine Warfare in
the Pacific* (New York: E. P. Dutton & Company, 1951), 82, 261, 289; Clark G.
Reynolds, *Admiral John H. Towers: The Struggle for Naval Air Supremacy* (An-
napolis: Naval Institute Press, 1991), 470.

[2]Walter Millis, "Military Problems at the Close of World War II," in Weigley, *The
American Military*, 114–116; Vincent Davis, *Postwar Defense Policy and the U.S.
Navy, 1943–1946* (Chapel Hill: University of North Carolina Press, 1966), 233–
234; Arthur T. Hadley, *The Straw Giant, America's Armed Forces: Triumphs and*

Failures (New York: Avon Books, 1987), 79–81; Rear Admiral Malcolm F. Schoeffel, Oral History, USNI (1979), NL, 243–256; Letter, Ferdinand Eberstadt to James Forrestal, 14 October 1946, OP-23 Files, A1/2-1/5, NHD; Senate Committee on Naval Affairs, "Unification of the War and Navy Departments and Postwar Organization for National Security" (Washington, D.C.: Government Printing Office, 1945), 3–7.

³Jeffrey M. Dorwart, "Forrestal and the Navy Plan of 1945: Mahanian Doctrine or Corporatist Blueprint?," in William B. Cogar, ed., *New Interpretations in Naval History: Selected Papers from the Eighth Naval History Symposium* (Annapolis: Naval Institute Press, 1989), 209–223; Davis, *Postwar Defense Policy*, 234; Huntington, "Interservice Competition," 182–183; John Brook Penfold, "Peace Insurance— Double Indemnity," *USNIP*, 72, n. 3 (March, 1946), 377–383; Chief of Naval Operations Letter Serial 002650D, 9 April 1945, "Estimated Cost of Universal Military Training," Box 197 (A16-1[6]), NHD; Letter, Fleet Admiral Chester W. Nimitz to Clifton A. Woodrum, Chairman, House Select Committee on Postwar Military Policy, 22 May 1945, Box 197 (A16-1[6]), NHD; Captain James E. Hamilton, "The Navy and Universal Military Training," *USNIP*, 74, n. 5 (May, 1948), 563–571; CNO Letter Serial 067P10, 29 December 1945, "Post War Navy of 58,000 Officers and 500,000 Enlisted," Box 202 (P16-1), NHD; Walter Millis, ed., *The Forrestal Diaries* (New York: Viking Press, 1951), 15, 385, 59–60.

⁴Bradley F. Smith, *The War's Long Shadow: The Second World War and Its Aftermath— China, Russia, Britain, America* (New York: Simon and Schuster, 1986), 154–155; Huntington, "Interservice Competition," 182–183; Millis, *The Forrestal Diaries*, 447; H. Struve Hensel, "Changes inside the Pentagon," *Harvard Business Review*, 32, n. 1 (January–February, 1954), 98–108; Davis, *Postwar Defense Policy*, 143–146; Eric Larrabee, *Commander in Chief: Franklin Delano Roosevelt, His Lieutenants, and Their War* (New York: Simon & Schuster, Inc., 1988), 216; Reynolds, *Admiral John H. Towers*, 487.

⁵Davis, *Postwar Defense Policy*, 66, 236–240, 72; Memorandum, Lieutenant Olive Dunham to Director, EXOS Administrative Division, 24 January 1946, OP-23 Files, A1/1-1, NHD; "Annual Report, Officer in Charge, Secretary's Committee on Unification," 17 September 1948, OP-23 Files, A1/1-1, NHD; Vincent Davis, *The Admirals Lobby* (Chapel Hill: University of North Carolina Press, 1967), 285–286, 268–273; Captain Stephen Jurika, Jr., Oral History, USNI, II (1979), NL, 681–682; Letter, Rear Admiral Thomas H. Robbins, Jr., to Captain F. J. Cleary, 11 August 1947, OP-23 Files, A1/1-1, NHD; Memorandum, Lieutenant Olive H. Dunham, 10 January 1947, OP-23 Files, A1/1-1, NHD; General Vernon E. Megee, USMC, Oral History, HDHUSMC (1973), NL, 109–110; A. A. Vandegrift and Robert D. Asprey, *Once a Marine: The Memoirs of General A.A. Vandegrift* (New York: Ballantine Books, 1966), 308; Philip A. Crowl, "Alfred Thayer Mahan: The Naval Historian," in Peter Paret, ed., *Makers of Modern Strategy from Machiavelli to the Nuclear Age* (Princeton: Princeton University Press, 1986), 444; Letter, Rear Admiral Thomas H. Robbins, Jr., to Rear Admiral Charles R. Brown, 15 January 1948, OP-23 Files, A1/1-1, NHD.

⁶Herman S. Wolk, "The Birth of the US Air Force," *Air Force Magazine*, 60, n. 9

(September, 1977), 68–72, 75–78; Vandegrift and Asprey, *Once a Marine*, 314–315; Alexander L. George and Richard Smoke, *Deterrence in American Foreign Policy: Theory and Practice* (New York: Columbia University Press, 1974), 23, 58–59: Bertram Vogel, "A Reply to the Extremists," *USNIP*, 73, n. 5 (May 1947), 545–548; Paul R. Schratz, *Submarine Commander* (Lexington: University Press of Kentucky, 1988), 172.

7Davis, *Postwar Defense Policy*, 153–155; William Bradford Huie, *The Case Against the Admirals: Why We Must Have a Unified Command* (New York: E. P. Dutton & Company, 1946), 15, 115–116; Vice Admiral Fitzhugh Lee, Oral History, USNI (1972), NL, 185–187; William Bradford Huie, "The Backwardness of the Navy Brass," *American Mercury*, 62, n. 270 (June, 1946), 647–653; William Bradford Huie, "Navy Brass Imperils Our Defense," *American Mercury*, 67, n. 295 (July, 1948), 7–14; William Bradford Huie, "Rough Selling for the Navy," *Nation's Business*, November, 1948, 39–41, 74–75; William Bradford Huie, "Why We Must Have the World's Best Air Force," *Reader's Digest*, 54 (March, 1949), 27–34.

8Memorandum, Rear Admiral Thomas H. Robbins, Jr., to Vice Admiral Arthur Radford, 17 July 1946, OP-23 Files, A1/1-1, NHD [emphasis in original]; Davis, *Postwar Defense Policy*, 149–150; Huie, *The Case Against the Admirals*, 35, 70–71; Hoffman Nickerson, "The Navy in U.S. National Strategy," *USNIP*, 73, n. 2 (February, 1947), 156; Bertram Vogel, "Military Lessons Learned and Not Learned," *USNIP*, 74, n. 6 (June, 1948), 723–731.

9David Lawrence, "Why Punish the Navy?," *U.S. News & World Report*, 19 April 1946, 32–33; Davis, *Postwar Defense Policy*, 169; Millis, *The Forrestal Diaries*, 119, 60, 62, 159–170; Hadley, *The Straw Giant*, 76; Joseph Zikmund, "James V. Forrestal, 19 May 1944–17 September 1947," in Paolo E. Coletta, ed., *American Secretaries of the Navy*, II: *1913–1972* (Annapolis: Naval Institute Press, 1980), 736–741; Ernest K. Lindley, "Mr. Truman and the Navy," *Newsweek*, 22 April 1946, 33; Robert J. Donovan, *Conflict and Crisis: The Presidency of Harry S Truman* (New York: W. W. Norton & Company, 1977), 200–202.

10Zikmund, "James V. Forrestal," 740–741; Millis, *The Forrestal Diaries*, 200–206, 223–231; Michael A. Palmer, *Origins of the Maritime Strategy: American Naval Strategy in the First Postwar Decade*, Contributions to Naval History . . . No. 1 (Washington, D.C.: Naval Historical Center, 1988), 35–40; Letter, Fleet Admiral William F. Halsey to James Forrestal, 12 September 1945, OP-23 Files, A1/1-1, NHD; Captain John F. Tarpey, "Uncle Carl," *USNIP*, 108, n. 1 (January, 1982), 40–41; Memorandum, Captain J. A. Roberts to Rear Admiral Arthur Radford and Rear Admiral Forrest Sherman, 23 November 1945, OP-23 Files, A1/1-1, NHD.

11Letter, Rear Admiral Thomas H. Robbins, Jr., to Vice Admiral Thomas C. Kincaid, 23 December 1946, OP-23 Files, A1/1-1, NHD; Memorandum, Rear Admiral Thomas H. Robbins, Jr., to Vice Admiral Forrest Sherman, 30 October 1946, OP-23 Files, A1/1-1, NHD; Lee, Oral History, 194–195; Memorandum, Rear Admiral Thomas H. Robbins, Jr., to "Admiral Miller," 1 July 1946, OP-23 Files, A1/1-1, NHD; Admiral John S. Thach, Oral History, USNI, II (1977), NL, 495–500; Millis, *The Forrestal Diaries*, 147, 152–153; Commodore Dudley W. Knox, "Development of Unification," *USNIP*, 76,

n. 12 (December, 1950), 1309–1315; George Fielding Eliot, "How to Lose a War," *USNIP*, 76, n. 7 (July, 1950), 707–714; Letter, Vice Admiral W. H. P. Blandy to Chief of Naval Operations, Serial 045, 19 December 1946, Burke Papers, Folder 98-C, NHD.

[12]Reynolds, *Admiral John H. Towers*, 398; James Coates and Michael Kilian, *Heavy Losses: The Dangerous Decline of American Defense* (New York: Penguin Books, 1986), 126; Wolk, "The Birth of the US Air Force," 77; Lieutenant Commander Charles Moran, "Security by Enactment," *USNIP*, 74, n. 4 (April, 1948), 403–415; Millis, *The Forrestal Diaries*, 37; Stephen E. Ambrose, "The Armed Services and American Strategy, 1945–1953," in Kenneth J. Hagan and William R. Roberts, eds., *Against All Enemies: Interpretations of American Military History from Colonial Times to the Present* (Westport, Conn.: Greenwood Press, 1986), 307; Major General Wilburt S. Brown, USMC, Oral History, HDHUSMC (1967), NL, 264–265; Mark S. Watson, "Two Years of Unification," *MA*, 13, n. 3 (Fall, 1949), 193–198; Eugene E. Wilson, "A Basis of Unity," *USNIP*, 76, n. 9 (September, 1950), 961–967; Rear Admiral David L. Martineau, "1947— A Very Good Year," *USNIP*, 103, n. (9 September, 1977), 25–31.

[13]Lieutenant Commander Allan N. Glennon, "The Perennial Fallacy," *USNIP*, 86, n. 12 (December, 1960), 55–61; Paul B. Ryan, *First Line of Defense: The U.S. Navy Since 1945* (Stanford: Hoover Institution Press, 1981), 9–11; Eugene S. Duffield, "Organizing for Defense," *Harvard Business Review*, 31, n. 5 (September–October, 1953), 29–42; Millis, *The Forrestal Diaries*, 390–394; Commander E. John Long, "A Year of Unification," *SM*, 11, n. 9 (September, 1948), 7–8, 23-24; *SDR* (1948), 79–80; Hadley, *The Straw Giant*, 87–92; Ambrose, "The Armed Services and American Strategy," 307; Coates and Kilian, *Heavy Losses*, 138; Hensel, "Changes Inside the Pentagon," 103–104; Roger D. Launius, "Military Unification's Precursor: The Air Force and Navy Strategic Airlift Merger of 1948," *Air Power History*, 39 (Spring, 1992), 22–33.

[14]Ambrose, "The Armed Services and American Strategy," 307; Ryan, *First Line of Defense*, 11; Hensel, "Changes Inside the Pentagon," 104; Duffield, "Organizing for Defense," 34–35; Davis, *The Admirals Lobby*, 160–162; Rear Admiral Raymond D. Tarbuck, Oral History, USNI (1973), NL, 253–254.

CHAPTER SIX

[1]Stephen Howarth, *To Shining Sea: A History of the United States Navy, 1775–1991* (New York: Random House, 1991), 475; Captain F. Clifton Toal, SC, "Navy Transportation Logistics," *USNIP*, 75, n. 7 (July, 1949), 777–785; Rear Admiral John D. Hayes, "Patterns of American Sea Power, 1945–1946: Their Portents for the Seventies," *USNIP*, 96, n. 5 (May, 1970), 337–352; "Military Sea Transportation Service," *USNIP*, 77, n. 12 (December, 1951), 1327–1335; *SNR*, in *SDR* (1 July–31 December 1949), 176–178.

[2]*Life*, 1 April 1946, 34–35; Charles C. Bates and John F. Fuller, *America's Weather Warriors, 1814–1985* (College Station: Texas A&M University Press, 1986), 143–144; Captain R. S. Quackenbush, "Operation Highjump," *SM*, 10, n. 7 (July, 1947), 13–14, 28–29; Vincent Davis, *The Admirals Lobby* (Chapel Hill: University of North Carolina Press, 1967), 209–210; Richard A. Stubbing, *The Defense*

Game: An Insider Explores the Astonishing Realities of America's Defense Establishment (New York: Harper & Row, 1986), 261; Thomas H. Etzold, "From Far East to Middle East: Overextension in American Strategy since World War II," *USNIP*, 107, n. 5 (May, 1981), 69; Robert L. Scheina, *Latin America: A Naval History, 1810–1987* (Annapolis: Naval Institute Press, 1987), 141, 146; Jorge Ortiz Sotelo, "Captain Davy and the U.S. Naval Mission in Peru, 1920–1930," in William R. Roberts and Jack Sweetman, eds., *New Interpretations in Naval History: Selected Papers from the Ninth Naval History Symposium* (Annapolis: Naval Institute Press, 1991), 57–66; Walter Millis, ed., *The Forrestal Diaries* (New York: Viking Press, 1951), 115; *SNR*, in *SDR* (1 January–31 December 1951), 163.

[3]Richard Drinnon, *Facing West: The Metaphysics of Indian Hating and Empire Building* (New York: Schocken Books, 1990), 249; James MacGregor Burns, *The American Experiment*, II: *The Crosswinds of Freedom* (New York: Vintage Books, 1990), 194; Millis, *The Forrestal Diaries*, 175–176; Carl H. Builder, *The Masks of War: American Military Styles in Strategy and Analysis* (Baltimore: Johns Hopkins University Press, 1989), 133; Merrill Bartlett and Robert William Love, Jr., "Anglo-American Naval Diplomacy and the British Pacific Fleet, 1942–1945," *AN*, 42, n. 3 (July, 1982), 203–216; Dean Rusk and Richard Rusk, *As I Saw It*, ed. Daniel S. Papp (New York: Penguin Books, 1991), 123; William Roger Louis, *Imperialism at Bay: The United States and the Decolonization of the British Empire, 1941–1945* (Oxford: Oxford University Press, 1986), 18–19, 84–85, 6–7, 115–116, 261–273, 366–377, 448–449, 485; Fleet Admiral William D. Leahy, *I Was There* (New York: Whittlesey House, 1950), 258, 314.

[4]Millis, *The Forrestal Diaries*, 21, 45, 214; Margaret Truman, *Harry S Truman* (New York: Quill, 1984 [1972]), 250; Thomas G. Paterson, *Meeting the Communist Threat: Truman to Reagan* (New York: Oxford University Press, 1988), 58; *SNR*, in *SDR* (1 July–31 December 1949), 182–183; Harold L. Ickes, "The Navy at Its Worst," *Collier's*, 31 August 1946, 22–23, 67; Louis, *Imperialism at Bay*, 72–73, 75; Michael Schaller, *The American Occupation of Japan: The Origins of the Cold War in Asia* (New York: Oxford University Press, 1985), 54–57.

[5]George F. Kennan, *Memoirs, 1950–1963* (New York: Pantheon Books, 1972), 42–43; Clark G. Reynolds, *Admiral John H. Towers: The Struggle for Naval Air Supremacy* (Annapolis: Naval Institute Press, 1991), 516, 520–522; Millis, *The Forrestal Diaries*, 176; Schaller, *The American Occupation of Japan*, 27; Roger Dingman, "The U.S. Navy and the Cold War: The Japan Case," in Craig L. Symonds, ed., *New Aspects of Naval History: Selected Papers Presented at the Fourth Naval History Symposium, United States Naval Academy (1979)* (Annapolis: Naval Institute Press, 1981), 291–312; Rear Admiral Kemp Tolley, Oral History, USNI, II (1984), NL, 799–800, 806; Robert J. Donovan, *Tumultuous Years: The Presidency of Harry S Truman, 1949–1953* (New York: W. W. Norton & Company, 1982), 78, 146–147; Chief Aviation Mate M. D. Ingram, "The United States Navy in Japan, 1945–1950," *USNIP*, 78, n. 4 (April, 1952), 379–383; Admiral Alfred M. Pride, Oral History, USNI (1984), NL, 229.

[6]Martin E. Holbrook, "Our Dilemma in Japan," *USNIP*, 76, n. 1 (January, 1950), 23–25; Forrest C. Pogue, *George C. Marshall: Statesman, 1945–1959* (New York: Viking Penguin, Inc., 1987), 108; Etzold, "From Far East to Middle East," 69;

Eric Larrabee, *Commander in Chief: Franklin Delano Roosevelt, His Lieutenants, and Their War* (New York: Simon & Schuster, Inc., 1988), 543; Barry Rubin, *Secrets of State: The State Department & the Struggle over U.S. Foreign Policy* (New York: Oxford University Press, 1987), 54; Paterson, *Meeting the Communist Threat*, 58–59; Donovan, *Tumultuous Years*, 70; Millis, *The Forrestal Diaries*, 105; Vice Admiral J. Victor Smith, Oral History, USNI (1977), NL, 179.

[7]Donovan, *Tumultuous Years*, 79–80, 86; Captain Glyn Jones, CHC, Oral History, USNI (1978), NL, 111–119; Darrell Berrigan, "Is Our Navy Trapped in China?," *Saturday Evening Post*, September 25, 1948, 26–27, 145–147; Vice Admiral Ruthven E. Libby, Oral History, USNI (1984), NL, 153–154; Captain E. M. Eller, "United States Disaster in China," *USNIP*, 75, n. 7 (July, 1949), 739–751; Commander Robert C. Wing, "Political and Legal Aspects of Nationalist China's 'Port Closure,' " *USNIP*, 76, n. 5 (May, 1950), 499–505; Lieutenant Edward E. Wilcox, "Back Door in the Pacific," *USNIP*, 76, n. 2 (February, 1950), 187–189; Schaller, *The American Occupation of Japan*, 209; Captain James R. Hansen, "Last Evacuation of Foreign Devils From Chefoo," *SM*, 49, n. 3 (April, 1986), 21–23.

[8]Michael A. Palmer, *Origins of the Maritime Strategy: American Naval Strategy in the First Postwar Decade*, Contributions to Naval History . . . No. 1 (Washington, D.C.: Naval Historical Center, 1988), 4–6, 2–3, 7, 12–15, 17–19.

[9]Palmer, *Origins of the Maritime Strategy*, 24–31, 33–35.

[10]Ernest R. May, *Imperial Democracy: The Emergence of America as a Great Power* (New York: Harper Torchbooks, 1973), 7; Larrabee, *Commander in Chief*, 499; Louis, *Imperialism at Bay*, 549, 503; Eric Grove, *Vanguard to Trident: British Naval Policy Since World War II* (Annapolis: Naval Institute Press, 1987), 3, 20; Correlli Barnett, *Engage the Enemy More Closely: The Royal Navy in the Second World War* (New York: W. W. Norton & Company, 1991), 880; Paul Kennedy, *The Rise and Fall of the Great Powers: Economic Change and Military Conflict from 1500 to 2000* (New York: Vintage Books, 1989), 367–368; Frank Uhlig, Jr., "The Atlantic Ocean—Sea of Decision," *USNIP*, 80, n. 3 (March, 1954), 275–279; William N. Still, Jr., *American Sea Power in the Old World: The United States Navy in European and Near Eastern Waters, 1865–1917* (Westport, Conn.: Greenwood Press, 1980), 3–4, 6.

[11]Palmer, *Origins of the Maritime Strategy*, 11, 21–24; Stephen G. Xydis, "The Genesis of the Sixth Fleet," *USNIP*, 84, n. 8 (August, 1958), 41–50; Vice Admiral George C. Dyer, *The Amphibians Came to Conquer: The Story of Admiral Richmond Kelly Turner*, II (Washington, D.C.: Government Printing Office, 1971), 1124–1125; Millis, *The Forrestal Diaries*, 141, 144–145, 171, 210–211, 184–185 [emphasis in original]; Marx Leva, "Barring the Door to the Med," *USNIP*, 113, n. 8 (August, 1987), 83–88; Truman, *Harry S Truman*, 344–345; Paterson, *Meeting the Communist Threat*, 24–25; Vincent Davis, *Postwar Defense Policy and the U.S. Navy, 1943–1946* (Chapel Hill: University of North Carolina Press, 1966), 224–225.

[12]*U.S. News & World Report*, September 13, 1946, 22–23; Leva, "Barring the Door to the Med," 88; Ensign E. J. McNulty, "European Strategy Re-Evaluated," *USNIP*, 77, n. 6 (June, 1951), 631–636; *Life*, May 26, 1947, 38–39; Rear Admiral Thomas H. Morton, Oral History, USNI (1979), NL, 278; Bradley F. Smith,

The War's Long Shadow: The Second World War and Its Aftermath—China, Russia, Britain, America (New York: Simon and Schuster, 1986), 238–239, 259; Grove, *Vanguard to Trident*, 37.

[13]Pride, Oral History, 149; Demaree Bess, "Our Big Stick in the Mediterranean," *Saturday Evening Post*, 8 May 1948, 15–17, 140–141, 143; Demaree Bess, "Our Navy in Striped Pants," *Saturday Evening Post*, 15 May 1948, 30, 169–172; *Life*, December 6, 1948, 86–88; Commander Anthony Talerico, "Sea of Decision," *USNIP*, 76, n. 9 (September, 1950), 941–949; William H. Hessler, "The Versatile Sixth Fleet," *USNIP*, 78, n. 5 (May, 1952), 469–477; Lieutenant Leon B. Blair, "Mediterranean Geopolitics," *USNIP*, 77, n. 2 (February, 1951), 135–139; "Navy Squadrons in Berlin Airlift," *USNIP*, 75, n. 8 (August, 1949), 931–939; Journalism Chief Brendan P. Mulready, "Berlin Airlift Proved Unification Can Work," *USNIP*, 76, n. 3 (March, 1950), 283–287; Millis, *The Forrestal Diaries*, 454; *SDR* (1948), 69–70.

[14]Ed Cray, *General of the Army, George C. Marshall: Soldier and Statesman* (New York: Touchstone Books, 1991), 624–625; Paterson, *Meeting the Communist Threat*, 47, 32, 93; Donovan, *Tumultuous Years*, 51–52, 176–177; Reynolds, *Admiral John H. Towers*, 519, 547; Joel J. Sokolsky, *Seapower in the Nuclear Age: The United States Navy and NATO, 1949–1980* (Annapolis: Naval Institute Press, 1991), 11, 13–16; Robert McClintock, "The Atlantic Alliance," *USNIP*, 75, n. 8 (August, 1949), 857–863; Admiral W. F. Boone, "NATO—Keystone of Defense," *USNIP*, 85, n. 4 (April, 1959), 23–43; Grove, *Vanguard to Trident*, 48, 54–55; Vice Admiral George C. Dyer, Oral History, USNI (1973), NL, 463–464; Etzold, "From Far East to Middle East," 69; Kennedy, *The Rise and Fall of the Great Powers*, 378–379; Vice Admiral Brian B. Schofield, RN, "The Role of the NATO Navies in War," *USNIP*, 87, n. 4 (April, 1961), 65–69; Vice Admiral Jerauld Wright, "The North Atlantic Treaty Organization," *USNIP*, 77, n. 12 (December, 1951), 1253–1265; Admiral Robert B. Carney, "The Principles of Sea Power," *USNIP*, 79, n. 8 (August, 1953), 817–827; Smith, *The War's Long Shadow*, 151–152, 158, 164; *SNR*, in *SDR* (1949), 208–209.

CHAPTER SEVEN

[1]Walter Millis, ed., *The Forrestal Diaries* (New York: Viking Press, 1951), 554–555, 547, 550, 325, 343; Joseph Zikmund, "James V. Forrestal, 19 May 1944–17 September 1947," in Paolo E. Coletta, ed., *American Secretaries of the Navy*, II: *1913–1972* (Annapolis: Naval Institute Press, 1980), 742; Townsend Hoopes and Douglas Brinkley, *Driven Patriot: The Life and Times of James Forrestal* (New York: Alfred A. Knopf, 1992), 453–468; Paolo E. Coletta, "John Lawrence Sullivan, 18 September 1947–24 May 1949," in Coletta, *American Secretaries of the Navy*, II, 747–780; Captain Slade D. Cutter, Oral History, USNI, I (1985), NL, 57–58; Admiral Robert Lee Dennison, Oral History, USNI (1975), NL, 111.

[2]Coletta, "John Lawrence Sullivan," 752; Paolo E. Coletta, "Louis Emil Denfeld, 15 December 1947–1 November 1949," in Robert William Love, Jr., ed., *The Chiefs of Naval Operations* (Annapolis: Naval Institute Press, 1980), 193–206; Michael A. Palmer, *Origins of the Maritime Strategy: American Naval Strategy in*

the First Postwar Decade, Contributions to Naval History . . . No. 1 (Washington: Naval Historical Center, 1988), 40–47; Hanson Weightman Baldwin, Oral History, USNI, II (1976), NL, 471.

[3]Coletta, "Louis Emil Denfeld," 194–197; Paul Y. Hammond, "Super Carriers and B-36 Bombers: Appropriations, Strategy and Politics," in Harold Stein, ed., *American Civil-Military Decisions: A Book of Case Studies* (Birmingham: University of Alabama Press, 1963), 465–480; Eric Larrabee, *Commander in Chief: Franklin Delano Roosevelt, His Lieutenants, and Their War* (New York: Simon & Schuster, Inc., 1988 [1987]), 304; Arthur T. Hadley, *The Straw Giant, America's Armed Forces: Triumphs and Failures* (New York: Avon Books, 1987), 94–95.

[4]Vincent Davis, *Postwar Defense Policy and the U.S. Navy, 1943–1946* (Chapel Hill: University of North Carolina Press, 1966), 120–121, 96–97, 123–129, 199–201, 203, 205; Clark G. Reynolds, *Admiral John H. Towers: The Struggle for Naval Air Supremacy* (Annapolis: Naval Institute Press, 1991), 323; Admiral Charles M. Cooke, "Soldiers Need Wings," *FA*, 27, n. 4 (July, 1949), 576–585; Millis, *The Forrestal Diaries*, 9, 354–355, 466–467, 513–515.

[5]Nick Kotz, *Wild Blue Yonder: Money, Politics, and the B-1 Bomber* (New York: Pantheon Books, 1988), 73, 232; Alexander P. De Seversky, *Victory Through Air Power* (New York: Simon and Schuster, 1942), 10, 25, 162, 172, 175, 97, 119; Admiral Harry E. Yarnell Papers, Diary, 21 August 1943, NHD.

[6]De Seversky, *Victory Through Air Power*, 24, 48, 118, 182, 123–152, 306–307, 155, 166, 259, 212, 329; William Bradford Huie, "Rough Selling for the Navy," *Nation's Business*, November, 1948, 41; Vincent Davis, *The Admirals Lobby* (Chapel Hill: University of North Carolina Press, 1967), 194–195, 196–197; Huie, "Rough Selling for the Navy," 39–41, 74–75; William Bradford Huie, "Why We Must Have the World's Best Air Force," *Reader's Digest*, 54 (March, 1949), 27–34; Paul B. Ryan, *First Line of Defense: The U.S. Navy since 1945* (Stanford: Hoover Institution Press, 1981), 11; Carl H. Builder, *The Masks of War: American Military Styles in Strategy and Analysis* (Baltimore: Johns Hopkins University Press, 1989), 72.

[7]Huie, "Why We Must Have the World's Best Air Force," 33; Lieutenant Commander Edward L. Beach, "Our Duty Lies Before Us," *USNIP*, 75, n. 1 (January, 1949), 79–83; Robert J. Donovan, *Tumultuous Years: The Presidency of Harry S Truman, 1949–1953* (New York: W. W. Norton & Company, 1982), 57; Captain Brown Taylor, "Controversy in Retrospect," *USNIP*, 88, n. 7 (July, 1962), 39–51.

[8]Davis, *Postwar Defense Policy*, 228–229; Ryan, *First Line of Defense*, 12; Rear Admiral R. A. Ofstie, "Strategic Air Warfare," *USNIP*, 77, n. 6 (June, 1951), 591–599; Hammond, "Super Carriers and B-36 Bombers," 480; Rear Admiral Daniel V. Gallery, Oral History, USNI (1976), NL, 142–143.

[9]Captain Paul R. Schratz, "The Admirals' Revolt," *USNIP*, 112, n. 2 (February, 1986), 64–71; Kenneth J. Hagan, "The U.S. Supercarrier: Strategic in Origin, Tactical in Use," in Jean Pariseau, ed., *International Colloquium on High and Low Intensity Conflicts Since the Second World War* (Ottawa: n.p., 1989), 39–40; Phil Gustafson, "Why the Navy Wants Supercarriers," *Popular Science Monthly*, January, 1949, 114–120.

[10]Clay Blair, *The Forgotten War: America in Korea, 1950–1953* (New York: Anchor Books, 1987), 14–15; Vice Admiral Ruthven E. Libby, Oral History, USNI

(1984), NL, 163–165; Ryan, *First Line of Defense*, 12–13; Hammond, "Super Carriers and B-36 Bombers," 492; Donovan, *Tumultuous Years*, 60; Rear Admiral Schuyler Neilson Pyne, Oral History, USNI (1972), NL, 334; Schratz, "The Admirals' Revolt," 65; Admiral John S. Thach, Oral History, USNI, II (1977), NL, 497; Hadley, *The Straw Giant*, 95.

[11]Schratz, "The Admirals' Revolt," 65–66; Donovan, *Tumultuous Years*, 64; Coletta, "John Lawrence Sullivan," 774; Blair, *The Forgotten War*, 15; Vice Admiral Fitzhugh Lee, Oral History, USNI (1972), NL, 191–200; Dennison, Oral History, 186–188; Memorandum, A.A. Burke to Admiral Carney, 18 May 1949, Burke Papers, Folder #98, NHD; Paolo E. Coletta, "Francis P. Matthews, 25 May 1949–31 July 1951," in Coletta, *American Secretaries of the Navy*, II, 783–827; Taylor, "Controversy in Retrospect," 43.

[12]Jeffrey G. Barlow, " 'The Revolt of the Admirals' Reconsidered," in William B. Cogar, ed., *New Interpretations in Naval History: Selected Papers from the Eighth Naval History Symposium* (Annapolis: Naval Institute Press, 1989), 224–243; Schratz, "The Admirals' Revolt," 66; Davis, *The Admirals Lobby*, 287; Letter, Admiral A. W. Radford to Captain Arleigh Burke, 20 June 1949, Burke Papers, Folder #98, NHD; *Newsweek*, 14 November 1949, 29; "Revolt of the Admirals," *Air Force Magazine*, 32 (December, 1949), 22–27; Taylor, "Controversy in Retrospect," 40, 44; Captain John F. Tarpey, "Uncle Carl," *USNIP*, 108, n. 1 (January, 1982), 42; *U.S. News & World Report*, 14 October 1949, 23.

[13]Donovan, *Tumultuous Years*, 105–106, 110–111; Baldwin, Oral History, II, 457; Taylor, "Controversy in Retrospect," 44–46; "Statement of Captain John G. Crommelin, U.S. Navy, in Regard to B-36 Investigation," Burke Papers, Folder #98, NHD; Letter, Captain Arleigh Burke to Rear Admiral C.R. Brown, 15 September 1949, Burke Papers, Folder #98-A, NHD; *Newsweek*, 17 October 1949, 23; John Crommelin, "The General-Staff Concept," Burke Papers, Folder #98, NHD; John Crommelin, "Creed," Folder #98, NHD; Ryan, *First Line of Defense*, 13–14; Blair, *The Forgotten War*, 21–23; Schratz, "The Admirals' Revolt," 66–67; Tarpey, "Uncle Carl," 42; Palmer, *Origins of the Maritime Strategy*, 51; *U.S. News & World Report*, 14 October 1949, 22–23; *U.S. News & World Report*, 28 October 1949, 53–79; *Newsweek*, 17 October 1949, 23–27; *Life*, 17 October 1949, 48–49; *Time*, 17 October 1949, 21–23; *Aviation Week*, 17 October 1949, 12–14; Hammond, "Super Carriers and B-36 Bombers," 514–537; Baldwin, Oral History, II, 472; Lee, Oral History, 215–220.

[14]Ryan, *First Line of Defense*, 14; Davis, *Postwar Defense Policy*, 254–255; Dennison, Oral History, 200–203; Keith D. McFarland, "The 1949 Revolt of the Admirals," *Parameters*, 11, n. 2 (June, 1981), 53–63; Phillip S. Meilinger, "The Admirals' Revolt of 1949: Lessons for Today," *Parameters*, 19, n. 3 (September, 1989), 81–96; Commander Edward P. Stafford, "Saving Carrier Aviation—1949 Style," *USNIP*, 116, n. 1 (January, 1990), 44–51; Tarpey, "Uncle Carl," 42; Hammond, "Super Carriers and B-36 Bombers," 549–551.

[15]Donovan, *Tumultuous Years*, 58; Hadley, *The Straw Giant*, 96; *Newsweek*, 7 November 1949, 26–28; Coletta, "Louis Emil Denfeld," 199; *Time*, 7 November 1949, 20; Palmer, *Origins of the Maritime Strategy*, 48; Admiral Charles Donald Griffin, Oral History, USNI, II (1973), NL, 187–194.

[16]Palmer, *Origins of the Maritime Strategy*, 48; Admiral Louis E. Denfeld, "Reprisal:

Why I Was Fired," *Collier's*, 18 March 1950, 13–15, 62, 64; *Collier's*, 25 March 1950, 32–33, 46–47, 50–51; *Collier's*, 1 April 1950, 36–37, 42, 44; Schratz, "The Admirals' Revolt," 67; Donovan, *Tumultuous Years*, 113; Davis, *The Admirals Lobby*, 288–289; Dan van der Vat, *The Atlantic Campaign: World War II's Great Struggle at Sea* (New York: Harper & Row, 1988), 372–373; Rear Admiral D. V. Gallery, "Don't Let Them Cripple the Navy!," *Saturday Evening Post*, 29 October 1949, 36–37, 44, 46, 48; Rear Admiral Daniel V. Gallery, "If This Be Treason—," *Collier's*, 21 January 1950, 15–17, 45; Gallery, Oral History, 129–134, 208–209.
[17]Palmer, *Origins of the Maritime Strategy*, 52; *Newsweek*, 17 October 1949, 25; Hadley, *The Straw Giant*, 96; Coletta, "Francis P. Matthews," 806; Blair, *The Forgotten War*, 22; Ryan, *First Line of Defense*, 14.

STERN WATCH I

[1]Samuel Taylor Coleridge, *Table Talk and Omniana* (London: H. Milford, 1917), 434.
[2]Thomas G. Paterson, *Meeting the Communist Threat: Truman to Reagan* (New York: Oxford University Press, 1989), 22; Fred J. Cook, *The Warfare State* (New York: Collier Books, 1962), 81–82; Judith Schachter Modell, *Ruth Benedict: Patterns of a Life* (Philadelphia: University of Pennsylvania Press, 1983), 277.
[3]John Selden, *Table Talk*, ed. S. W. Singer, 3rd ed. (London: John Russell Smith, 1860), 210.

CHAPTER EIGHT

[1]Admiral John S. Thach, Oral History, USNI, II (1977), NL, 515; David F. Long, *Gold Braid and Foreign Relations: Diplomatic Activities of U.S. Naval Officers, 1798–1883* (Annapolis: Naval Institute Press, 1988), 374–380; James A. Field, Jr., *History of United States Naval Operations: Korea* (Washington: Government Printing Office, 1962), 1–15; Peter Lowe, *The Origins of the Korean War* (New York: Longman, 1986), 6, 9; Burton I. Kaufman, *The Korean War: Challenges in Crisis, Credibility, and Command* (New York: Alfred A. Knopf, 1986), 6–7, 17; Vice Admiral Ruthven E. Libby, Oral History, USNI (1984), NL, 143.
[2]Kaufman, *The Korean War*, 16–21; Field, *Korea*, 16–34; Michael Schaller, *Douglas MacArthur: The Far Eastern General* (New York: Oxford University Press, 1989), 162–163; John C. Donovan, *The Cold Warriors: A Policy-Making Elite* (Lexington, Mass.: D. C. Heath and Company, 1974), 125–126; Walter Isaacson and Evan Thomas, *The Wise Men: Six Friends and the World They Made* (New York: Touchstone Books, 1988), 507; Herbert P. Bix, "Regional Integration: Japan and South Korea in America's Asian Policy," in Frank Baldwin, ed., *Without Parallel: The American-Korean Relationship since 1945* (New York: Pantheon Books, 1974), 192, 195–196; Michael Schaller, *The American Occupation of Japan: The Origins of the Cold War in Asia* (New York: Oxford University Press, 1987), 256; Lowe, *The Origins of the Korean War*, 118–119; Robert J. Donovan, *Tumultuous Years: The Presidency of Harry S Truman, 1949–1953* (New York: W. W. Norton & Company, 1982), 136–138; Michael Carver, *War Since 1945* (Atlantic Highlands, N.J.: Ashfield Press, 1990), 154.
[3]Bruce Swanson, *Eighth Voyage of the Dragon: A History of China's Quest for Seapower*

(Annapolis: Naval Institute Press, 1982), 183–187; Donald W. Mitchell, *A History of Russian and Soviet Sea Power* (New York: MacMillan Publishing Co., Inc., 1974), 472–473; Admiral Stuart S. ("Sunshine") Murray, Oral History, USNI, II (1974), NL, 598; Donovan, *Tumultuous Years*, 158–161; Field, *Korea*, 36–37.

⁴Neil Sheehan, *A Bright Shining Lie: John Paul Vann and America in Vietnam* (New York: Vintage Books, 1989), 132; *SNR*, in *SDR* (1 January–30 June 1950), 107, 139; Richard P. Hallion, *The Naval Air War in Korea* (New York: Zebra Books, 1988), 54–57, 67; Carver, *War Since 1945*, 155; Vice Admiral William R. Smedberg III, Oral History, USNI, I (1979), NL, 453.

⁵Kaufman, *The Korean War*, 30, 305; Clay Blair, *The Forgotten War: America in Korea, 1950–1953* (New York: Anchor Press, 1989), 75, 71; Carver, *War Since 1945*, 155, 157; Donovan, *Tumultuous Years*, 262–263, 216–217, 255; Commander Seventh Fleet Operation Order 7-50 (1 July 1950), NHD; Dean Rusk and Richard Rusk, *As I Saw It*, ed. Daniel S. Papp (New York: Penguin Books, 1990), 166; Edward J. Marolda, "Invasion Patrol: The Seventh Fleet in Chinese Waters," in *A New Equation: Chinese Intervention into the Korean War*, Colloquium on Contemporary History, No. 3, 20 June 1990 (Washington, D.C.: Naval Historical Center, 1991), 13–27; Jonathan D. Spence, *The Search for Modern China* (New York: W. W. Norton & Company, 1990), 529; Lowe, *The Origins of the Korean War*, 153–154, 163; Field, *Korea*, 40–42; David Rees, *Korea: The Limited War* (Baltimore: Penguin Books, Inc.), 275; Schaller, *The American Occupation of Japan*, 204, 266–267.

⁶Field, *Korea*, 42–50; Clark G. Reynolds, *Admiral John H. Towers: The Struggle for Naval Air Supremacy* (Annapolis: Naval Institute Press, 1991), 530–531; General Headquarters Far East Command, Operations Instruction No. 6 (1 April 1950), NHD, 4; Officer Biography, Vice Admiral James H. Doyle, File 166, NHD; Colonel Robert D. Heinl, USMC, "The Inchon Landing: A Case Study in Amphibious Planning," *NWCR*, 19, n. 9 (May, 1967), 53–54; Commander Malcolm W. Cagle and Commander Frank A. Manson, *The Sea War in Korea* (Annapolis: Naval Institute Press, 1957), 30–33, 36–39; Clark G. Reynolds, *Famous American Admirals* (New York: Van Nostrand Reinhold Company, 1978), 172–173, 341–342; John A. Giles, "The Navy Strikes in Korea," *Flying*, 47, n. 5 (November, 1950), 15, 46–48; *SNR*, in *SDR* (1949), 203–235; *SNR*, in *SDR* (1 July–31 December 1949), 165–188; Vice Admiral Kleber S. Masterson, Oral History, USNI (1973), NL, 80; Rear Admiral Joshua W. Cooper, Oral History, USNI (1975), NL, 235; Libby, Oral History, 168-169; *SNR*, in *SDR* (1 January–30 June 1950), 107, 109–110; *SNR*, in *SDR* (1 January–30 June 1951), 145; Rees, *Korea*, 365; Joseph C. Goulden, *Korea: The Untold Story of the War* (New York: McGraw-Hill, Inc., 1983), 67; Far East Command, Operations Instructions No. 1 (27 June 1950), NHD.

⁷Field, *Korea*, 102–108, 68–81; Far East Command, Operations Instructions No. 2 (3 July 1950), NHD; War Diary, USS *Mount McKinley* (AGC-7), 16–31 July 1950, NHD; Giles, "The Navy Strikes in Korea," 46.

⁸Field, *Korea*, 81–85, 90–100, 108–121; Goulden, *Korea*, 103; Cagle and Manson, *The Sea War in Korea*, 48–51; Giles, "The Navy Strikes in Korea," 46; Thach, Oral History, II, 532; Commander Seventh Fleet Operations Order 10-50 (18

July 1950), NHD; Letter, Commander Seventh Fleet to Commanders, Carrier Divisions 3 and 1, Serial 0027 of 1 August 1950, NHD; Report of Operations, USS *Valley Forge* (CV-45), 16–31 July 1950, NHD.

[9]Field, *Korea*, 121–146; Cagle and Manson, *The Sea War in Korea*, 70–71; Thach, Oral History, II, 535–536; Commander Seventh Fleet Operation Order 13-50 (3 August 1950), NHD; Action Report, USS *Valley Forge* (CV-45), 4–21 August 1950, NHD.

[10]Field, *Korea*, 146–170; Letter, Commanding Officer, USS *Juneau* (CL-119) to Chief of Naval Personnel, Serial 015 of 14 July 1950, NHD; Blair, *The Forgotten War*, 172; Lieutenant Colonel J. D. Hittle, USMC, "Korea—Back to the Facts of Life," *USNIP*, 76, n. 12 (December, 1950), 1289–1297.

CHAPTER NINE

[1]Colonel Robert D. Heinl, USMC, "The Inchon Landing: A Case Study in Amphibious Planning," *NWCR*, 19, n. 9 (May, 1967), 56; Commander Malcolm W. Cagle, "Inchon—The Analysis of a Gamble," *USNIP*, 80, n. 1 (January, 1954), 49; Vice Admiral George C. Dyer, *The Amphibians Came to Conquer: The Story of Admiral Richmond Kelly Turner*, II (Washington, D.C.: Government Printing Office, 1971), 730.

[2]Michael Schaller, *Douglas MacArthur: The Far Eastern General* (New York: Oxford University Press, 1989), 188; James A. Field, Jr., *History of United States Naval Operations: Korea* (Washington: Govenment Printing Office, 1962), 172; Clay Blair, *The Forgotten War: America in Korea, 1950–1953* (New York: Anchor Press, 1989), 87–88; Heinl, "The Inchon Landing," 61, 56; General Douglas MacArthur, *Reminiscences* (New York: Da Capo Press, Inc., 1985 [1964]),346–347; Cagle, "Inchon," 47; Brigadier General Victor H. Krulak, USMC, "The Inchon Operation: It Couldn't Happen—But Did," *SM*, 21, n. 9 (September, 1958), 8.

[3]Field, *Korea*, 174–177; Charles C. Bates and John F. Fuller, *America's Weather Warriors, 1814–1985* (College Station: Texas A&M University Press, 1986), 156; MacArthur, *Reminiscences*, 347–351; Krulak, "The Inchon Operation," 10; Heinl, "The Inchon Landing," 60; Vice Admiral Arthur D. Struble, "What Can We Learn From Korea?," *U.S. News & World Report*, 17 August 1951, 26–27; Schaller, *Douglas MacArthur*, 192; Rear Admiral Charles Adair, Oral History, USNI (1977), NL, 529–531; Joseph C. Goulden, *Korea: The Untold Story of the War* (New York: McGraw-Hill, Inc., 1983), 192–196; Blair, *The Forgotten War*, 223–233; Commander Malcolm W. Cagle and Commander Frank A. Manson, *The Sea War in Korea* (Annapolis: Naval Institute Press, 1957), 75–89; Commander Joint Task Force 7 and Commander Seventh Fleet, "Inchon Report," 5 April 1951, NHD, I-A–I-D.

[4]Blair, *The Forgotten War*, 263–264, 251–252, 267–269; Goulden, *Korea*, 204–205; Field, *Korea*, 178–183; Burton I. Kaufman, *The Korean War: Challenges in Crisis, Credibility, and Command* (New York: Alfred A. Knopf, 1986), 78–82; MacArthur, *Reminiscences*, 353; Vice Admiral Bernard L. Austin, Oral History, USNI (1971), NL, 404–408; Hanson Weightman Baldwin, Oral History, USNI, I (1976), NL, 45–46; Admiral U.S. Grant Sharp, Oral History, USNI,

I (1970), NL, 108–115; Vice Admiral Gerald E. Miller, Oral History, USNI, I (1983), NL, 96–97, 150–160; Captain Glyn Jones, CHC, Oral History, USNI (1978), NL, 171; Commander Task Force 77, Action Report (25 June 1950–19 January 1951), 19 March 1951, NHD, 1-1-1-13; Vice Admiral Edward Coyle Ewen, Officer Biography, NHD; Heinl, "The Inchon Landing," 62; Cagle and Manson, *The Sea War in Korea*, 88–89.

⁵Krulak, "The Inchon Operation," 11–12; Field, *Korea*, 183–198; Major Robert A. McMullen, USMC, and Captain Nicholas A. Canzona, USMC, "Wolmi-Do: Turning the Key," *USNIP*, 82, n. 3 (March, 1956), 291–296; Blair, *The Forgotten War*, 269; Cagle and Manson, *The Sea War in Korea*, 89–94; Admiral John S. Thach, Oral History, USNI, II (1977), NL, 552; Action Report, USS *Gurke* (DD-783), 13–21 September 1950, NHD; Commander Joint Task Force 7 and Commander Seventh Fleet, "Inchon Report," I-E; Krulak, "The Inchon Operation," 12; Commander Task Force 77, Action Report, 3-I-3-IV; Goulden, *Korea*, 210.

⁶Krulak, "The Inchon Operation," 12; Field, *Korea*, 198–202; Blair, *The Forgotten War*, 272–273; Cagle and Manson, *The Sea War in Korea*, 94–101; Sharp, Oral History, I, 115–121; Thach, Oral History, II, 552–559; Commander Joint Task Force 7 and Commander Seventh Fleet, "Inchon Report," I-F; Commander Task Force 90, Action Report (6–21 September 1950), 22 October 1950, NHD, 26–27; Arthur T. Hadley, *The Straw Giant, America's Armed Forces: Triumphs and Failures* (New York: Avon Books, 1987), 112; Schaller, *Douglas MacArthur*, 198; Commander Task Force 90, Action Report, Appendix II; Goulden, *Korea*, 217; David Rees, *Korea: The Limited War* (Baltimore: Penguin Books, Inc., 1964), 77–97.

⁷Field, *Korea*, 202–218; Action Report, USS *Rochester* (CA-124), 13–26 September 1950, NHD; Action Report, USS *Missouri* (BB-63), 15–17 September 1950, NHD; Commander Joint Task Force 7 and Commander Seventh Fleet, "Wonsan Report," 5 April 1951, NHD, I-C.

⁸Field, *Korea*, 219–229; Blair, *The Forgotten War*, 287–288, 331; James I. Matray, "Truman's Plan for Victory: National Self-Determination and the Thirty-Eighth Parallel Decision in Korea," *Journal of American History*, 66, n. 2 (September, 1979), 314–333; Schaller, *Douglas MacArthur*, 199–201; Captain Richard T. Spofford, Officer Biography, NHD.

⁹Cagle and Manson, *The Sea War in Korea*, 118–120; Blair, *The Forgotten War*, 332–333, 335; Robert C. Duncan, *America's Use of Sea Mines* (Washington: Government Printing Office, 1962), 8–9, 13–15, 35, 38, 84–87, 90; Colonel Paul L. Bates, USA, "Naval Mines," *MR*, 33, n. 1 (April, 1953), 48–56.

¹⁰Cagle and Manson, *The Sea War in Korea*, 125–127, 134; Field, *Korea*, 229–233; Rear Admiral Kenneth L. Veth, Oral History, USNI (1980), NL, 247–248, 275; Tamara Moser Melia, *"Damn the Torpedoes:" A Short History of U.S. Naval Mine Countermeasures, 1777–1991*, Contributions to Naval History . . . No. 4 (Washington, D.C.: Naval Historical Center, 1991), 40, 67–70; Gregory K. Hartmann, *Weapons That Wait: Mine Warfare in the U.S. Navy* (Annapolis: Naval Institute Press, 1979), 78, 80; Blair, *The Forgotten War*, 343; Vice Admiral J. Victor Smith, Oral History, USNI (1977), NL, 229–230; Baldwin, Oral History, II, 510–511.

¹¹Field, *Korea*, 233–237; Blair, *The Forgotten War*, 343–344, 365–367; Commander Sheldon Kinney, "All Quiet at Wonsan," *USNIP*, 80, n. 8 (August, 1954), 861; George Fielding Eliot, "Now Russia Threatens Our Sea Power," *Collier's*, 24 September 1953, 32–36; Cagle and Manson, *The Sea War in Korea*, 142, 144, 148; Letter, Commanding Officer, USS *Pledge* (AM-277) to Secretary of the Navy, Serial 39 of 29 October 1950, "Report of Sinking of USS *Pledge* (AM-277) on 12 October 1950," NHD; Commander Joint Task Force 7 and Commander Seventh Fleet, "Wonsan Report," I-D, I-E; Vice Admiral Allan E. Smith, Officer Biography, NHD; Commander Mine Squadron THREE [Spofford], "Report of Sinking of USS *Pirate* (AM-275) and USS *Pledge* (AM-277), 19/29 October 1950, NHD; Commander Malcolm W. Cagle and Commander Frank A. Manson, "Wonsan: The Battle of the Mines," *USNIP*, 83, n. 6 (June, 1957), 598–611; Herbert P. Bix, "Regional Integration: Japan and South Korea in America's Asian Policy," in Frank Baldwin, ed., *Without Parallel: The American-Korean Relationship since 1945* (New York: Pantheon Books, 1974), 194.

¹²Field, *Korea*, 237–262; Cagle and Manson, *The Sea War in Korea*, 154–164, 150–151; Hartmann, *Weapons That Wait*, 81; Melia, *"Damn the Torpedoes,"* 73–82; Rees, *Korea*, 125; Heinl, "The Inchon Landing," 52–53, 70–71; Cagle, "Inchon," 50–51; Krulak, "The Inchon Operation," 12, 14; Eliot, "How Russia Threatens Our Sea Power," 32; Commander Joint Task Force 7 and Commander Seventh Fleet, "Wonsan Report," VI-D-1; Richard P. Hallion, *The Naval Air War in Korea* (New York: Zebra Books, 1988), 110; Commander Task Force 77, Action Report, 3-III-1.

CHAPTER TEN

¹Commander Malcolm W. Cagle and Commander Frank A. Manson, *The Sea War in Korea* (Annapolis: Naval Institute Press, 1957), 112; Robert J. Donovan, *Tumultuous Years: The Presidency of Harry S Truman* (New York: W. W. Norton & Company, 1982), 303; Joseph C. Goulden, *Korea: The Untold Story of the War* (New York: McGraw-Hill, Inc., 1983), 284–285; Burton I. Kaufman, *The Korean War: Challenges in Crisis, Credibility, and Command* (New York: Alfred A. Knopf, 1986), 137.

²Michael Schaller, *Douglas MacArthur: The Far Eastern General* (New York: Oxford University Press, 1989), 207, 212–213; James A. Field, Jr., *History of United States Naval Operations: Korea* (Washington: Government Printing Office, 1962), 263–274.

³Kaufman, *The Korean War*, 110–111; Field, *Korea*, 274–285; Cagle and Manson, *The Sea War in Korea*, 178.

⁴Clay Blair, *The Forgotten War: America in Korea, 1950–1953* (New York: Anchor Books, 1989), 542–545; Cagle and Manson, *The Sea War in Korea*, 181, 189–192; Vice Admiral James H. Doyle, "December 1950 at Hungnam," *USNIP*, 105, n. 4 (April, 1979), 44–55; Field, *Korea*, 285–316; Action Report, USS *Missouri* (BB-63) (23–24 December 1950), 10 January 1951, NHD; Close Air Support Report, USS *Princeton* (CV-37) (21–22 December 1950), 26 December 1950, NHD; Goulden, *Korea*, 378–381; David Rees, *Korea: The Limited War* (Baltimore: Penguin Books, Inc., 1964), 165–166.

⁵Field, *Korea*, 317–345; Vice Admiral Fitzhugh Lee, Oral History, USNI (1972), NL, 211–212; Rees, *Korea*, 193; Commander Task Force 77, Action Report (25 February–4 April 1951), 16 February 1951, NHD; Action Report, USS *Manchester* (CL-83) (17 March 1951), 1 April 1951, NHD.

⁶Kaufman, *The Korean War*, 144–149; Blair, *The Forgotten War*, 654, 734; Cagle and Manson, *The Sea War in Korea*, 491–492.

⁷"Life Lines for Korea," *USNIP*, 79, n. 3 (March, 1953), 310–315; *SNR*, in *SDR* (1 January–30 June 1951), 154–155; *SNR*, in *SDR* (1 January–30 June 1952), 148; *SNR*, in *SDR* (1 January–30 June 1953), 227–229; Donald Robinson, "Stingiest Man in the Navy," *Collier's*, 4 August, 1951, 36–37, 43–44; *Newsweek*, 16 April 1951, 34–35; "Sea Power at Cost," *Fortune*, April, 1951, 79–80; Kaufman, *The Korean War*, 156; Blair, *The Forgotten War*, 127; *SNR*, in *SDR* (1 January–30 June 1952), 164–165; Ed Rees, *The Seas and the Subs* (New York: Duell, Sloan and Pearce, 1961), 178; Rear Admiral Joshua W. Cooper, Oral History, USNI (1975), NL, 309–312; Admiral Charles K. Duncan, Oral History, USNI, I (1978), NL, 342–344.

⁸Richard P. Hallion, *The Naval Air War in Korea* (New York: Zebra Books, 1988), 295–296; Andrew Hamilton, "We're Back in Business—the Seabees," *Popular Mechanics*, 95, n. 5 (May, 1951), 110–114, 270; Historical Report, Attack Squadron 702 (20 July–31 December 1950), 13 February 1951, NHD; Historical Report, Attack Squadron 702, (1 January–31 December 1951), 15 January 1952, NHD; Commander Task Force 77, Action Report (19 April–19 May 1951), 19 June 1951, NHD; Field, *Korea*, 345–361; Action Report, USS *Thompson* (DMS-38) (14–15 June 1951), 17 June 1951, NHD.

⁹Field, *Korea*, 408–427; Cagle and Manson, *The Sea War in Korea*, 281–284, 288–289, 293–294, 305–306, 370–373; Robert R. Simmons, "The Korean Civil War," in Frank Baldwin, ed., *Without Parallel: The American-Korean Relationship since 1945* (New York: Pantheon Books, 1974), 166; Vice Admiral George C. Dyer, Oral History, USNI (1973), NL, 505.

¹⁰Cagle and Manson, *The Sea War in Korea*, 203–204, 336–337, 349, 352–353; Donovan, *Tumultuous Years*, 345.

¹¹Blair, *The Forgotten War*, 867; *U.S. News & World Report*, 23 January 1953, 73–74; Field, *Korea*, 324, 428; "*Iowa*-Class Battleships Off Korea," *USNIP*, 78, n. 7 (July, 1952), 785–789; Vice Admiral Charles L. Melson, Oral History, USNI (1974), NL, 164–175; Vice Admiral William R. Smedberg III, Oral History, USNI, I (1979), NL, 450–451; Cooper, Oral History, 326–329; Action Report, USS *Missouri* (BB-63) (17–22 December 1952), 25 January 1953, NHD; Arthur T. Hadley, *The Straw Giant, America's Armed Forces: Triumphs and Failures* (New York: Avon Books, 1987), 115; *Time*, 5 May 1952, 31; Action Report, USS *Saint Paul* (CA-73) (April 1952), 3 May 1952, NHD; Rees, *Korea*, 366–370.

¹²Commander Malcolm W. Cagle and Commander Frank A. Manson, "Wonsan: The Battle of the Mines," *USNIP*, 83, n. 6 (June, 1957), 610–611; Cagle and Manson, *The Sea War in Korea*, 208–209, 216–217, 218–221, 194, 201–203; Captain C. A. Bartholomew, *Mud, Muscles, and Miracles: Marine Salvage in the United States Navy* (Washington, D.C.: Naval Historical Center and Naval Sea Systems Command, 1990), 212; Charlotte Knight, "Men of the Minesweepers," *Collier's*, 10 November 1951, 13–15, 66–68; Lieutenant Colonel Harry D. Ed-

wards, USMC, "A Naval Lesson of the Korean Conflict," *USNIP*, 80, n. 12 (December, 1954), 1337–1340.

¹³"Frogmen in Korea," *Collier's*, 21 February, 1953, 50–51; James Berry, "Operation Fishnet," *USNIP*, 116, n. 12 (December, 1990), 107–108; Action Report, USS *Diachenko* (APD-123) (23 July–1 August 1952), 4 August 1952, NHD; Clay Blair, Jr., "The Mission of the 'Pregnant *Perch*'," *Life*, 5 November 1951, 141–142, 145–148; Paul R. Schratz, *Submarine Commander: A Story of World War II and Korea* (Lexington: University Press of Kentucky, 1988), 288–289, 292–299, 302; Rear Admiral William D. Irvin, Oral History, USNI (1980), NL, 308–309; Cagle and Manson, *The Sea War in Korea*, 365–366; *SNR*, in *SDR* (1 January–30 June 1951), 187; Dyer, Oral History, 510–513; Vice Admiral J. Victor Smith, Oral History, USNI (1977), NL, 229–233.

CHAPTER ELEVEN

¹Commander Malcolm W. Cagle and Commander Frank A. Manson, *The Sea War in Korea* (Annapolis: Naval Institute Press, 1957), 310, 331–332; Joseph C. Goulden, *Korea: The Untold Story of the War* (New York: McGraw-Hill, Inc., 1983), 559, 565, 579, 585; Clay Blair, *The Forgotten War: America in Korea, 1950–1953* (New York: Anchor Books, 1989), 253; Robert J. Donovan, *Tumultuous Years: The Presidency of Harry S Truman, 1949–1953* (New York: W. W. Norton & Company, 1982), 320.

²Burton I. Kaufman, *The Korean War: Challenges in Crisis, Credibility, and Command* (New York: Alfred A. Knopf, 1986), 150; Michael Schaller, *The American Occupation of Japan: The Origins of the Cold War in Asia* (New York: Oxford University Press, 1985), 196; Donovan, *Tumultuous Years*, 265–267; James A. Bell, "Defense Secretary Louis Johnson," *American Mercury*, 70, n. 318 (June, 1950), 643–653.

³Paolo E. Coletta, "Francis P. Matthews, 25 May 1949–31 July 1951," in Paolo E. Coletta, ed., *American Secretaries of the Navy*, II: *1913–1972* (Annapolis: Naval Institute Press, 1980), 819–822; Kaufman, *The Korean War*, 56–57; Captain John F. Tarpey, "Uncle Carl," *USNIP*, 108, n. 1 (January, 1982), 42–43; K. Jack Bauer, "Dan Able Kimball, 31 July 1951–20 January 1953," in Coletta, *American Secretaries of the Navy*, II, 829–830; Captain Slade D. Cutter, Oral History, USNI, II (1985), NL, 575; Admiral David Lamar McDonald, Oral History, USNI (1976), NL, 136–146.

⁴Clark G. Reynolds, "Forrest Percival Sherman, 2 November 1949–22 July 1951," in Robert William Love, Jr., ed., *The Chiefs of Naval Operations* (Annapolis: Naval Institute Press, 1980), 209–210; "The Navy's 'Box of Brains'," *Reader's Digest*, May 1951, 15–19; Vice Admiral Edwin B. Hooper, Oral History, USNI (1978), NL, 145; Captain Stephen Jurika, Jr., Oral History, USNI (1979), NL, 679–680; Rear Admiral Francis D. Foley, Oral History, USNI (1988), NL, 211–212.

⁵Reynolds, "Forrest Percival Sherman," 210–211; "The Navy's 'Box of Brains'," 17–18; Admiral Charles Donald Griffin, Oral History, USNI (1973), NL, 114; Vice Admiral Truman J. Hedding, Oral History, USNI (1972), NL, 87–94; Letter, Forrest P. Sherman to Admiral Harry Yarnell, 8 September 1943, Forrest P. Sherman Papers, Box 4, Series 2, NHD; Clark G. Reynolds, *Admiral John*

H. Towers: The Struggle for Naval Air Supremacy (Annapolis: Naval Institute Press, 1991), 442, 478.

[6]Vice Admiral Herbert D. Riley, Oral History, USNI, I (1972), NL, 295–296; Reynolds, "Forrest Percival Sherman," 211–216; "The Navy's 'Box of Brains'," 19; Vice Admiral George C. Dyer, Oral History, USNI (1973), NL, 476–477; Rear Admiral Joshua W. Cooper, Oral History, USNI (1975), NL, 270–274, 287–295; Rear Admiral Frederic Stanton Withington, Oral History, USNI (1972), NL, 97; Rear Admiral Thomas H. Morton, Oral History, USNI (1979), NL, 270–272; Rear Admiral Kemp Tolley, Oral History, USNI, II (1984), NL, 715–716, 725–726; Michael A. Palmer, *Origins of the Maritime Strategy: American Naval Strategy in the First Postwar Decade*, Contributions to Naval History . . . No. 1 (Washington, D.C.: Naval Historical Center, 1988), 53–54; Vincent Davis, *The Admirals Lobby* (Chapel Hill: University of North Carolina Press, 1967), 224–225; *Newsweek*, 14 November 1949, 29; General Clifton B. Cates, USMC, Oral History, HDHUSMC (1973), NL, 215; Captain Henri Smith-Hutton, Oral History, USNI, II (1976), NL, 713–714.

[7]Palmer, *Origins of the Maritime Strategy*, 63–69, 54–58; Reynolds, "Forrest Percival Sherman," 216–217.

[8]Palmer, *Origins of the Maritime Strategy*, 69–72; Reynolds, "Forrest Percival Sherman," 217–218, 221–226; *U.S. News & World Report*, 10 March 1950, 30–35; Rear Admiral Joseph Muse Worthington, Oral History, USNI (1975), NL, 381; Vice Admiral Fitzhugh Lee, Oral History, USNI (1972), NL, 165; Blair, *The Forgotten War*, 219–220, 84–85, 623–624; Michael Schaller, *Douglas MacArthur: The Far Eastern General* (New York: Oxford University Press, 1989), 224; Memorandum, J. H. Thach, Jr., to Chief of Naval Operations, "Naval Assistance to the Republic of China," undated [but 1951], Forrest P. Sherman Papers, Box 5, Series 1, NHD.

[9]Schaller, *Douglas MacArthur*, 232, 238, 242–243; Donovan, *Tumultuous Years*, 353–354; Goulden, *Korea*, 385, 399–400, 408, 487–490; Message, JCS 86736 of 24 March 1951 to CINCFE Tokyo, Japan, Forrest P. Sherman Papers, Box 4, Series 2, NHD; JCS 98134 of 6 December 1950, Forrest P. Sherman Papers, Box 4, Series 2, NHD; Forrest P. Sherman, "Reasons for the Relief of General MacArthur," Memorandum for the Record, undated [but 1951], Forrest P. Sherman Papers, Box 5, Series 1, NHD; Reynolds, "Forrest Percival Sherman," 218–219.

[10]*U.S. News & World Report*, 30 March 1951, 20; Eric J. Grove, *From Vanguard to Trident: British Naval Policy Since World War Two* (Annapolis: Naval Institute Press, 1987), 103–105, 137–150; Stanley G. Payne, *Franco's Spain* (New York: Thomas Y. Crowell Company, 1967), 38, 44, 68; Gill Robb Wilson, "Key to Destiny," *Flying*, 50, n. 6 (June, 1952), 9–11, 62.

[11]*Newsweek*, 8 October 1951, 42, 45–46; James P. O'Donnell, "Eisenhower's Navy Is Ready!," *Saturday Evening Post*, 13 October 1951, 19–21, 134, 136–137, 139; "Sixth Fleet," *Collier's*, 10 May 1952, 50–51; Holman Harvey, "Our Friendly Fleet in the Mediterranean," *Reader's Digest*, January, 1953, 111–113; "Our Calculated Risk," *Flying*, 49, n. 5 (November, 1951), 48–51, 155; Milton Lehman, "Not as the Conqueror Comes," *Nation's Business*, December, 1951, 36–38, 76–78; Admiral Alfred M. Pride, Oral History, USNI (1984), NL, 213–

214; Rear Admiral Malcolm F. Schoeffel, Oral History, USNI (1979), NL, 309–315; Commander H. B. Seim, "The Navy and 'Fringe' War," *USNIP*, 77, n. 8 (August, 1951), 835–841; E. B. Potter, "Arleigh Burke Buries the Hatchet," *USNIP*, 116, n. 4 (April, 1990), 57–60.

[12]William H. Hessler, "Air-Sea Power on the Asian Perimeter," *USNIP*, 77, n. 10 (October, 1951), 1019–1027; Vice Admiral Arthur D. Struble, "Korea and Command of the Sea," *Vital Speeches of the Day*, 18, n. 3 (15 November 1951), 85–88; Peter Marsh Stanford, "Limited War: A Problem in Maritime Defense," *USNIP*, 77, n. 12 (December, 1951), 1311–1317; Reynolds, "Forrest Percival Sherman," 231–232; Smith-Hutton, Oral History, II, 731–732; Memorandum, Major Sherman A. Smith, USMC, to Admiral Lynde D. McCormick [Acting Chief of Naval Operations], 27 July 1951, Forrest P. Sherman Papers, Box 10, Series 5, NHD.

[13]Vice Admiral Bernhard H. Bieri, Oral History, USNI (1970), NL, 45–46; Bauer, "Dan Able Kimball," 830; Gerald Kennedy, "William Morrow Fechteler, 16 August 1951–17 August 1953," in Love, *The Chiefs of Naval Operations*, 235–241; Smith-Hutton, Oral History, II, 715; *U.S. News & World Report*, 5 October 1951, 24–29; Palmer, *Origins of the Maritime Strategy*, 73–78; Admiral Charles K. Duncan, Oral History, USNI, I (1978), NL, 306, 357–359; Cutter, Oral History, II, 365–366, 576; Walter Isaacson and Evan Thomas, *The Wise Men: Six Friends and the World They Made* (New York: Touchstone Books, 1988), 555–556; Rear Admiral Charles Adair, Oral History, USNI (1977), NL, 552–554; John C. Donovan, *The Cold Warriors: A Policy-Making Elite* (Lexington, Mass.: D. C. Heath and Company, 1974), 47–49; Reynolds, *Admiral John H. Towers*, 337; Memorandum, Director of Naval Intelligence to Chief of Naval Operations, "Intelligence on Korea and the Far East," 28 May 1951, Forrest P. Sherman Papers, Box 5, Series 1, NHD.

CHAPTER TWELVE

[1]James A. Field, Jr., *History of United States Naval Operations: Korea* (Washington: Government Printing Office, 1962), 427–436; Commander Malcolm W. Cagle and Commander Frank A. Manson, *The Sea War in Korea* (Annapolis: Naval Institute Press, 1957), 66–67, 73–74, 222–223.

[2]George F. Kennan, *Memoirs, 1950–1963* (New York: Pantheon Books, 1972), 92–93; "Naval Aviation's Roles and Goals," *Flying*, 49, n. 6 (December, 1951), 14–15, 45–47, 53–54; Vice Admiral John Howard Cassady, "Air Navy's Quarterback," *Flying*, 49, n. 5 (November, 1951), 54–55, 142; *U.S. News & World Report*, 18 January 1952, 28–33; Admiral Donald B. Duncan, Officer Biography, NHD; Admiral John H. Cassady, Officer Biography, NHD.

[3]*Aviation Week*, 25 February 1952, 23–28; *Time*, 22 December 1952, 16–17; *U.S. News & World Report*, 12 December 1952, 23–25; Cagle and Manson, *The Sea War in Korea*, 374–375, 386–387; Richard P. Hallion, *The Naval Air War in Korea* (New York: Zebra Books, 1988), 90–91, 295.

[4]*Time*, 25 June 1951, 24–25; James Michener, "The Forgotten Heroes of Korea," *Saturday Evening Post*, 10 May 1952, 19–21, 124, 126, 128; "Naval Air Power in Action," *Flying*, 49, n. 5 (November, 1951), 43–45, 174–175; Charles C.

Bates and John F. Fuller, *America's Weather Warriors, 1814–1985* (College Station: Texas A&M University Press, 1986), 163–165; Commander Task Force 77, Action Report (14 July–10 August 1951), 2 September 1951, NHD; USS *Essex* (CV-9), Storm Damage Report, 10 January 1952, NHD.

5*Aviation Week*, 21 April 1952, 18, 21–22, 24, 26, 28; Vice Admiral John Perry, Officer Biography, NHD; Hallion, *The Naval Air War in Korea*, 206; USS *Essex* (CV-9), Action Report (18 August–21 September 1951), 30 September 1951, NHD; "Wings of Gold Don't Rust," *Flying*, 49, n. 5 (November, 1951), 104–105, 145–146; *Life*, 26 November 1951, 100–101; Lieutenant W. H. Vernor, Jr., "Standby Squadron," *USNIP*, 78, n. 7 (July, 1952), 729–739; Captain Stephen Jurika, Jr., Oral History, USNI, II (1979), NL, 809–810; Fighter Squadron 884, Historical Report (1 July–31 December 1951), 30 January 1952, NHD; Attack Squadron 702, Historical Report (1 January–31 December 1951), 15 January 1952, NHD.

6Ed Rees, *The Seas and the Subs* (New York: Duell, Sloan and Pearce, 1961), 45–46; USS *Boxer* (CV-21), Action Report (10 March–2 May 1952), 19 May 1952, NHD; Hallion, *The Naval Air War in Korea*, 62–63, 294–295, 172–175; USS *Essex* (CV-9), Report of Damage (16 September 1951), 7 October 1951, NHD; USS *Essex* (CVA-9), Action Report (5 September–1 November 1952), 1 November 1952, NHD.

7Hallion, *The Naval Air War in Korea*, 219, 81–84, 299–300, 119–120, 188–194, 118–119; USS *Essex* (CV-9), Action Report (18 July–4 September 1952), 4 September 1952, NHD; Fighter Squadron 172, Historical Report (1 July–31 December 1951), 28 January 1952, NHD; Commander Task Force 77, Action Report (25 June 1950–19 January 1951), 19 March 1951, NHD, 5-1.

8Admiral John S. Thach, " 'Right on the Button'," *USNIP*, 101, n. 11 (November, 1975), 54–56; Hallion, *The Naval Air War in Korea*, 68–75, 125–129; Clay Blair, *The Forgotten War: America in Korea, 1950–1953* (New York: Anchor Books, 1989), 577, 597; USS *Boxer* (CV-21), Action Report (26 July–24 August 1951), 27 August 1951, NHD; Arthur T. Hadley, *The Straw Giant, America's Armed Forces: Triumphs and Failures* (New York: Avon Books, 1987), 112.

9*Aviation Week*, 19 May 1952, 75–76; Burton I. Kaufman, *The Korean War: Challenges in Crisis, Credibility, and Command* (New York: Alfred A. Knopf, 1986), 221–223, 251–252; Hallion, *The Naval Air War in Korea*, 111–113, 160–165, 282; *Life*, 27 July 1953, 22–23.

10Hallion, *The Naval Air War in Korea*, 113–117, 138–140, 148–149; Cagle and Manson, *The Sea War in Korea*, 239–240, 224–225, 228, 230–231, 267–270, 277–280, 252–254, 256; USS *Boxer* (CV-21), Action Report (3 September–5 October 1951), 8 October 1951, NHD; Jurika, Oral History, II, 827–830; USS *Essex* (CV-9), Action Report (1–31 October 1951), 6 November 1951, NHD.

11Hallion, *The Naval Air War in Korea*, 144–145, 194–200; Field, *Korea*, 335–336, 347; USS *Princeton* (CV-37), Action Report (23 February–6 April 1951), 6 May 1951, NHD; Blair, *The Forgotten War*, 851–852

12USS *Boxer* (CV-21), Action Report (9 June–8 July 1952), 23 July 1952, NHD; Kaufman, *The Korean War*, 276; Hallion, *The Naval Air War in Korea*, 195–200; Joseph C. Goulden, *Korea: The Untold Story of the War* (New York: McGraw-Hill, Inc., 1983), 619; Commander Malcolm W. Cagle and Commander Frank

A. Manson, "Post Interdiction Carrier Operations in Korea," *USNIP*, 83, n. 7 (July, 1957), 699–712; Field, *Korea*, 436–439, 442–444; Vice Admiral Paul D. Stroop, Oral History, USNI (1970), NL, 238; *Aviation Week*, 29 September 1952, 17.

¹³Cagle and Manson, *The Sea War in Korea*, 440–441, 467, 474, 391–397; *U.S. News & World Report*, 2 January 1953, 24–25; Hallion, *The Naval Air War in Korea*, 202–204; Field, *Korea*, 445; Vice Admiral Truman J. Hedding, Oral History, USNI (1972), NL, 160.

¹⁴Hallion, *The Naval Air War in Korea*, 226, 302–303, 307–311, 289–291; Michael Schaller, *Douglas MacArthur: The Far Eastern General* (New York: Oxford University Press, 1989), 193; Goulden, *Korea*, 416–417, 628–629; Stroop, Oral History, 247; Field, *Korea*, 446–459; USS *Boxer* (CVA-21), Action Report (1–27 July 1953), 10 August 1953, NHD.

¹⁵Gerald E. Wheeler, "Naval Aviation in the Korean War," *USNIP*, 83, n. 7 (July, 1957), 762–777; Lieutenant Colonel S. B. Folsom, USMC, "Korea—A Reflection From the Air," *USNIP*, 82, n. 7 (July, 1956), 733–735; Cagle and Manson, *The Sea War in Korea*, 274–277, 439; Captain Paul Gray, Officer Biography, NHD; Brian Johnson, *Fly Navy: The History of Naval Aviation* (New York: William Morrow and Company, Inc., 1981), 354; David Rees, *Korea: The Limited War* (Baltimore: Penguin Books, Inc., 1964), 185; *SNR*, in *SDR* (1 January 1951–30 June 1951), 150–151; *SNR*, in *SDR* (1 January 1952–30 June 1952), 173; Hallion, *The Naval Air War in Korea*, 286–289, 298–299; Barrett Tillman and Commander John B. Nichols III, "Fighting Unwinnable Wars," *USNIP*, Supplement (April, 1986), 78–86; Commander Sheldon Kinney, "All Quiet at Wonsan," *USNIP*, 80, n. 8 (August, 1954), 859–867.

STERN WATCH II

¹*Newsweek*, 12 January 1953, 36–38; Michael Schaller, *Douglas MacArthur: The Far Eastern General* (New York: Oxford University Press, 1989), 252; Michael Carver, *War Since 1945* (Atlantic Highlands, N.J.: Ashfield Press, 1990), 169; Burton I. Kaufman, *The Korean War: Challenges in Crisis, Credibility, and Command* (New York: Alfred A. Knopf, 1986), 271.

²Kaufman, *The Korean War*, 303; Arthur T. Hadley, *The Straw Giant, America's Armed Forces: Triumphs and Failures* (New York: Avon Books, 1987), 75; Paul Kennedy, *The Rise and Fall of the Great Powers: Economic Change and Military Conflict from 1500 to 2000* (New York: Vintage Books, 1989), 384.

³Peter Hayes, Lyuba Zansky, and Walden Bello, *American Lake: Nuclear Peril in the Pacific* (New York: Penguin Books, 1986), 41; Seyom Brown, *The Faces of Power: Constancy and Change in United States Foreign Policy from Truman to Reagan* (New York: Columbia University Press, 1983), 52–53.

⁴James A. Field, Jr., *History of United States Naval Operations: Korea* (Washington, D.C.: Government Printing Office, 1962), 362–407; Commander Malcolm W. Cagle and Commander Frank A. Manson, *The Sea War in Korea* (Annapolis: Naval Institute Press, 1957), 527–531.

⁵R. Ernest Dupuy and Trevor N. Dupuy, *Military Heritage of America* (New York: McGraw-Hill Book Company, 1956), 689; Lieutenant Commander Samuel S.

Stratton, "Balance Sheet on Korea," *USNIP*, 80, n. 4 (April, 1954), 367–373; Commander Malcolm W. Cagle, "Errors of the Korean War," *USNIP*, 84, n. 3 (March, 1958), 31–35; Cagle and Manson, *The Sea War in Korea*, 493–494; Kaufman, *The Korean War*, 351–357.

[6]Craig L. Symonds, *Navalists and Antinavalists: The Naval Policy Debate in the United States, 1785–1827* (Newark: University of Delaware Press, 1980), 42, 113–114; Carver, *War Since 1945*, 170.

[7]Neil Sheehan, *A Bright Shining Lie: John Paul Vann and America in Vietnam* (New York: Vintage Books, 1989), 131; Eric Larrabee, *Commander in Chief: Franklin Delano Roosevelt, His Lieutenants, and Their War* (New York: Touchstone Books, 1988), 631; Philip West, "Interpreting the Korean War," *American Historical Review*, 94, n. 1 (February, 1989), 80–96.

CHAPTER THIRTEEN

[1]Lewis R. Farnell, *The Cults of the Greek States*, IV (Oxford: Clarendon Press, 1907), 13–14, 60–63 [I am indebted to Professor Phyllis Culham of the Department of History, United States Naval Academy, for this reference]; Max Horkheimer, *Critique of Instrumental Reason: Letters and Essays since the End of World War II* (New York: Seabury Press, 1974), vii; Martin van Creveld, *Technology and War: From 2000 B.C. to the Present* (New York: Free Press, 1989), 5.

[2]Richard Smoke, *National Security and the Nuclear Dilemma: An Introduction to the American Experience*, 2nd ed. (New York: Random House, 1987), 12–13, 15–19; Jon Winoker, ed., *The Portable Curmudgeon* (New York: New American Library, 1987), 17, 18, 15; Van Creveld, *Technology and War*, 225, 303–304; Michael Geyer, "German Strategy in the Age of Machine Warfare, 1914–1945," in Peter Paret, ed., *Makers of Modern Strategy from Machiavelli to the Nuclear Age* (Princeton: Princeton University Press, 1986), 541, 543, 548, 586.

[3]R. Ernest Dupuy and Trevor N. Dupuy, *Military Heritage of America* (New York: McGraw-Hill Book Company, 1956), 693 [italics added]; Harvey M. Sapolsky, *The Polaris System Development: Bureaucratic and Programmatic Success in Government* (Cambridge: Harvard University Press, 1972), 235; Van Creveld, *Technology and War*, 274–275; *SDR* (1948), 64–65; Carl H. Builder, *The Masks of War: American Military Styles in Strategy and Analysis* (Baltimore: Johns Hopkins University Press, 1989), 34.

[4]*Business Week*, 28 July 1962, 58; *Aviation Week*, 30 March 1959, 40–41; Edward Luttwak, "The Strategy of Survival," *American Heritage*, 39, n. 5 (July–August, 1988), 85; Rear Admiral Edward A. Ruckner, Oral History, USNI (1977), NL, 328–340; *SNR*, in *SDR* (1 July 1958–30 June 1959), 265–273; *SNR*, in *SDR* (1 July 1959–30 June 1960), 293–300; *SNR*, in *SDR* (1 July 1960–30 June 1961), 260–265.

[5]Van Creveld, *Technology and War*, 218–219, 242, 276; *Henry V*, Act II, Chorus I; David F. Noble, *America by Design: Science, Technology, and the Rise of Corporate Capitalism* (New York: Oxford University Press, 1979), 148–150, 272, 125–126; Vincent Davis, *Postwar Defense Policy and the U.S. Navy, 1943–1946* (Chapel Hill: University of North Carolina Press, 1966), 93.

6*SNR*, in *SDR* (1 January–30 June 1953), 203–207; Dorothy F. Deininger, "Books for the 'New Navy'," *Library Journal*, 81, n. 9 (1 May 1956), 1086–1092; Vincent Davis, *The Admirals Lobby* (Chapel Hill: University of North Carolina Press, 1967), 176–178; *Newsweek*, 11 February 1946, 89; S. David Pursglove, "Thinking Factories," *Popular Mechanics*, 118, n. 5 (November, 1962), 87–92, 204, 208, 210; Officer Biography, Vice Admiral Harold G. Bowen, NHD; Officer Biography, Rear Admiral Luis De Florez, NHD; Clark G. Reynolds, *Admiral John H. Towers: The Struggle for Naval Air Supremacy* (Annapolis: Naval Institute Press, 1991), 357–358; Ralph M. Hogan, "Manpower for Research and Development," *Science*, 4 August 1950, 133–137; Hanson Weightman Baldwin, Oral History, USNI, I (1976), NL, 321–322; Captain Joy Bright Hancock, Oral History, USNI (1969), NL, 47–48, 106; Vice Admiral Andrew McBurney Jackson, Jr., Oral History, USNI (1978), NL, 95; *Annual Report of the Office of Naval Research* (FY 1947), II, III, NHD.

7Officer Biography, Captain Robert D. Conrad, NHD; Luther J. Carter, "Office of Naval Research: 20 Years Bring Changes," *Science*, 22 July 1966, 397–400; "The Office of Naval Research," *Science*, 10 September 1948, 277; John E. Pfeiffer, "The Office of Naval Research," *Scientific American*, 180, n. 2 (February, 1949), 11–15; "Research Guarantees Superiority," *Flying*, 49, n. 5 (November, 1951), 110–111, 179; *SNR*, in *SDR* (1 January–30 June 1953), 223–226; Jack Alexander, "Dreamers on the Payroll," *Saturday Evening Post*, 19 November 1960, 38, 89–90, 92; Rear Admiral Henry L. Miller, Oral History, USNI, I (1973), NL, 113–126; Lawson M. McKenzie, "After Six Years—A Study of the Impact of the Physics Branch Program," *Science*, 28 August 1953, 227–232; *Aviation Week*, 3 June 1957, 131–133, 135, 137.

8*Missiles and Rockets*, 1 January 1962, 13–18, 38–39; *Missiles and Rockets*, 26 March 1962, 124–125, 140; John G. Hubbell, "The Navy's Amazing Problem-Solvers," *Reader's Digest*, 76, n. 456 (April, 1960), 137–140, 142; Thomas R. Henry, "Science HQ of the Navy," *Popular Mechanics*, 88, n. 4 (October, 1947), 89–92, 264, 268; *Science*, 20 August 1948, 177–178; *Aviation Week*, 3 June 1957, 351; "The U.S. Naval Research Laboratory," *USNIP*, 84, n. 12 (December, 1958), 112–117; *Annual Report of the Office of Naval Research* (FY 1947), II, 79–96; *Time*, 31 August 1959, 49; *Newsweek*, 31 August 1959, 54; *Aviation Week*, 24 August 1959, 34–35; *Science News Letter*, 29 August 1959, 131.

9Captain C. O. Holmquist and R. S. Greenbar, "Navy's 'In-House Research Laboratories,'" *USNIP*, 88, n. 2 (February, 1962), 68–75; Michael Day, "The Navy's Chamber of Horrors," *Popular Mechanics*, November, 1950, 133–137, 264, 266; Lieutenant Junior Grade Howard Norman Kay, "The Navy's Scientific Wonderland," *USNIP*, 78, n. 4 (April, 1952), 389–397; Rear Admiral Miles H. Hubbard, "The Design of Naval Weapons," *USNIP*, 91, n. 10 (October, 1965), 38–45; "The Naval Ordnance Laboratory," *USNIP*, 92, n. 10 (October, 1966), 104–119; Captain Frank F. Rigler, "NOL," *SM*, 33, n. 2 (February, 1970), 2–4; Joseph P. Smaldone, *History of the White Oak Laboratory, 1945–1975* (Silver Spring, Md.: Naval Surface Weapons Center, 1977), 1–24, NHD; Minchen Strang, "The Navy in the Desert," *USNIP*, 107, n. 9 (September, 1981), 65–71; *Life*, 6 January 1967, 31–32, 34–35; J. D. Gerrard-Gough and Albert B. Christman, *History of the Naval Weapons Center, China Lake, California*, II: *The Grand Experiment at Inyokern* (Washington, D.C.: Naval History Division, 1978), 203–273.

[10]"The U.S. Naval Weapons Laboratory, Dahlgren, Virginia," *USNIP*, 94, n. 10 (October, 1968), 89–100; "The Naval Air Engineering Center," *USNIP*, 93, n. 9 (September, 1967), 92–105; "Naval Air Development Center," *USNIP*, 96, n. 8 (August, 1970), 76–89; " 'Pax River:' The Naval Air Test Center," *USNIP*, 95, n. 12 (December, 1969), 93–106; "ONR London: Two Decades of Scientific Quid pro Quo," *Science*, 4 November 1966, 623–625; [Frederic] Withington, "The Outcome of the Electronic Revolution in the Navy," *USNIP*, 89, n. 11 (November, 1963), 66–75; Archer Jones, *The Art of War in the Western World* (Urbana: University of Illinois Press, 1987), 598.

[11]Samuel Freedman, "Radio-Radar-Sonar in NAVAL Applications," *Radio & Television News*, 45, n. 4 (April, 1951), 31–34, 82; Oliver E. Allen, "The Power of Patents," *American Heritage*, 41, n. 6 (September–October 1990), 49, 59; Commander E. I. Battey, "Naval Reserve Offers New Electronic Training Opportunities," *Radio & Television News*, 45, n. 4 (April, 1951), 35–38, 128–131; *Aviation Week*, 8 February 1960, 31; *SNR*, in *SDR* (1 January–30 June 1950), 130; *SNR*, in *SDR* (1 January–30 June 1951), 171–172; *Aviation Week*, 25 January 1960, 33; U.S. Navy Electronics Laboratory, Command History (1 June 1940–31 December 1958), n.d., NHD; *Business Week*, 22 August 1953, 66; *Missiles and Rockets*, 8 February 1965, 14–15.

[12]Thomas D. Nicholson, "Sky Reporter," *Natural History*, 74, n. 6 (June–July, 1965), 42–44; Robert S. Strother, "The Nation's Window on the Stars," *Reader's Digest*, 80, n. 479 (March, 1962), 222–223, 225–228; E. John Long, "Giant 'Ear' to Eavesdrop on 'Invisible Stars,' " *Nature Magazine*, 44 (October, 1951), 406–407; Edward F. McClain, "A High-Precision 85-foot Radio Telescope," *Sky and Telescope*, 32, n. 1 (July, 1966), 4–6; Gaston Burridge, "Arizona's New Big Eye," *Arizona Highways*, 35 (October, 1959), 2–5; Paul D. Hemenway, "The Washington 6-inch Transit Circle," *Sky and Telescope*, 31, n. 2 (February, 1966), 72–77; E. John Long, "Most Accurate Clocks in the World," *Science Digest*, 35, n. 3 (March, 1954), 6–9; "The Navy Hunts Cosmic Rays," *Popular Mechanics*, 99, n. 3 (March, 1953), 103–105, 266; *SNR*, in *SDR* (1 January–30 June 1950), 127; *SNR*, in *SDR* (1 January–30 June 1951), 169–170; *Aviation Week*, 20 December 1954, 54; *Missiles and Rockets*, 25 September 1961, 45; *Aviation Week and Space Technology*, 9 July 1962, 46, 51, 53; Admiral Robert Lee Dennison, Oral History, USNI (1975), NL, 475.

[13]Commander Charles P. Rozier, "Iron Brains and Iron Ships," *USNIP*, 85, n. 3 (March, 1959), 56–61; Commander M. Eckhart, Jr., " 'The Wit to See,' " *USNIP*, 90, n. 8 (August, 1964), 34–41; Louis A. Gebhard, *Evolution of Naval Radio-Electronics and Contributions of the Naval Research Laboratory* (Washington, D.C.: Naval Research Laboratory, 1979), 384–386; A. Prentice Kenyon, Oral History, USNI (1973), NL, 132–136; Rear Admiral Frederic Stanton Withington, Oral History, USNI (1972), NL, 163–164; Richard W. Turk, "Robley D. Evans: Master of Pugnacity," in James C. Bradford, ed., *Admirals of the New Steel Navy: Makers of the American Naval Tradition, 1880–1930* (Annapolis: Naval Institute Press, 1990), 88; David F. Long, *Gold Braid and Foreign Relations:*

Diplomatic Activities of U.S. Naval Officers, 1798–1883 (Annapolis: Naval Institute Press, 1988), 11–14, 416–417; James C. Bradford, "Henry T. Mayo: Last of the Independent Naval Diplomats," in Bradford, *Admirals of the New Steel Navy,* 275; William N. Still, Jr., *American Sea Power in the Old World: The United States Navy in European and Near Eastern Waters, 1865–1917* (Westport, Conn.: Greenwood Press, 1980), 13; Mary Klachko and David F. Trask, *Admiral William Shepherd Benson: First Chief of Naval Operations* (Annapolis: Naval Institute Press, 1987), 11–12; James C. Bradford, Preface to Bradford, *Admirals of the New Steel Navy,* xvii; Rear Admiral S. S. Robison, *A History of Naval Tactics* (Annapolis: Naval Institute Press, 1942), 838; Captain J. A. Morrison, "Technical Aspects of Naval Communications," *Radio & Television News,* December 1950, 50–51, 94, 96, 98; *SNR,* in *SDR* (1 January–30 June 1950), 116; *SNR,* in *SDR* (1 January–30 June 1952), 150–151; Rear Admiral John H. Redman, "Naval Communications," *Radio & Television News,* December 1950, 47–49, 120, 122–124, 126.

CHAPTER FOURTEEN

[1] Baron de Montesquieu, *The Spirit of the Laws,* trans. Thomas Nugent (New York: Harper Publishing Company, 1949), xix; Ronald E. Powaski, *March to Armageddon: The United States and the Nuclear Arms Race, 1939 to the Present* (New York: Oxford University Press, 1987), 4; Richard Rhodes, *The Making of the Atomic Bomb* (New York: Touchstone Books, 1988), 293–295, 551; Officer Biography, Rear Admiral Stanford C. Hooper, NHD.

[2] Officer Biography, Rear Admiral Garrett Lansing Schuyler, NHD; Laura Fermi, *Illustrious Immigrants: The Intellectual Migration from Europe, 1930/41,* 2nd ed. (Chicago: University of Chicago Press, 1971), 183–184; Walter Isaacson and Evan Thomas, *The Wise Men: Six Friends and the World They Made* (New York: Touchstone Books, 1988), 274; Powaski, *March to Armageddon,* 19; J. F. C. Fuller, *A Military History of the Western World,* III: *From the American Civil War to the End of World War II* (New York: Da Capo Press, 1987 [1956]), 627–628; Rear Admiral Frederic Stanton Withington, Oral History, USNI (1972), NL, 37–38.

[3] Powaski, *March to Armageddon,* 30; Ronald Schaffer, *Wings of Judgment: American Bombing in World War II* (New York: Oxford University Press, 1988), 164–166; Forrest C. Pogue, *George C. Marshall: Statesman, 1945–1959* (New York: Viking, 1987), 11; Vincent Davis, *Postwar Defense Policy and the U.S. Navy, 1943–1946* (Chapel Hill: University of North Carolina Press, 1966), 177; Arthur T. Hadley, *The Straw Giant, America's Armed Forces: Triumphs and Failures* (New York: Avon Books, 1987), 81.

[4] Vice Admiral Frederick L. Ashworth, "Rear Admiral William S. Parsons and the Atomic Bomb," *SM,* 49, n. 6 (July–August, 1986), 24–26; Al Christman, "Deak Parsons: Officer-Scientist," *USNIP,* 118, n. 1 (January, 1992), 56–61; Rear Admiral Malcolm F. Schoeffel, Oral History, USNI (1979), NL, 351; Withington, Oral History, 131; *Time,* 25 August 1958, 17; Officer Biography, Rear Admiral William Sterling Parsons, NHD.

[5] Captain Slade D. Cutter, Oral History, USNI, I (1985), NL, 174; Admiral Charles K. Duncan, Oral History, USNI, I (1978), NL, 304–307; Rear Admiral Joshua

W. Cooper, Oral History, USNI (1975), NL, 301; Officer Biography, Admiral William Henry Purnell Blandy, NHD; Lloyd J. Graybar, "The Buck Rogers of the Navy: Admiral William H. P. Blandy," in William R. Roberts and Jack Sweetman, eds., *New Interpretations in Naval History: Selected Papers from the Ninth Naval History Symposium* (Annapolis: Naval Institute Press, 1991), 335–349; Paul Boyer, *By the Bomb's Early Light: American Thought and Culture at the Dawn of the Atomic Age* (New York: Pantheon Books, 1985), 232; Officer Biography, Admiral Horacio Rivero, NHD; Vice Admiral Edwin B. Hooper, Oral History, USNI (1978), NL, 136; Davis, *Postwar Defense Policy*, 242–246; Captain Thomas M. Daly, "Crossroads at Bikini," *USNIP*, 112, n. 7 (July, 1986), 64–74; Walter Millis, ed., *The Forrestal Diaries* (New York: Viking Press, 1951), 150; Rear Admiral Robert H. Wertheim, Oral History, USNI (1981), NL, 49–50.

[6]Vice Admiral E. L. Cochrane, "Crossroads and Ship Design," *SM*, 9, n. 9 (September, 1946), 9–11, 18; Lloyd J. Graybar, "Bikini Revisited," *MA*, 44, n. 3 (October, 1980), 118–123; Colonel Harry A. Toulmin, Jr., AAF, "Is Bikini a Fair Test?," *Flying* (July, 1946), 17, 84, 86, 88; Boyer, *By the Bomb's Early Light*, 83.

[7]Rear Admiral Draper L. Kauffmann, Oral History, USNI, I (1982), NL, 295–314; Daly, "Crossroads at Bikini," 70–73; Graybar, "Bikini Revisited," 120–122; James P. Delgado, "What's Become of *Sara?*," *USNIP*, 116, n. 10 (October, 1990), 45–50; Ed Rees, *The Seas and the Subs* (New York: Duell, Sloan and Pearce, 1961), 63–64; Powaski, *March to Armageddon*, 44; Boyer, *By the Bomb's Early Light*, 314–318, 228, 84–90; Waldo K. Lyon, Oral History, USNI (1972), NL, 11–14; David Alan Rosenberg, "American Postwar Air Doctrine and Organization: The Navy Experience," in Colonel Alfred M. Hurley, USAF, and Major Robert C. Ehrhardt, USAF, eds., *Air Power and Warfare*, Proceedings of the 8th Military History Symposium, United States Air Force Academy, 18–20 October 1978 (Washington, D.C.: Office of Air Force History, 1979), 249.

[8]Peter Hayes, Lyuba Zarsky, and Walden Bello, *American Lake: Nuclear Peril in the Pacific* (New York: Penguin Books, 1987), 68; Boyer, *By the Bomb's Early Light*, 91–92; Barton C. Hacker, "Radioactivity on Film: Operation Crossroads at Bikini, 1946," *Film and History*, 19 (February, 1989), 14–18; Charles C. Bates and John F. Fuller, *America's Weather Warriors, 1814–1985* (College Station: Texas A&M University Press, 1986), 135–137.

[9]C. Sharp Cook, "The Legacy of Crossroads," *NH*, 2, n. 4 (Fall, 1988), 28–32; Commander Frank I. Winant, Jr., "The Lesson of the ADU," *USNIP*, 74, n. 9 (September, 1948), 1067–1079; Captain C. A. Bartholomew, *Mud, Muscles, and Miracles: Marine Salvage in the United States Navy* (Washington, D.C.: Naval Historical Center and Naval Sea Systems Command, 1990), 199–200.

[10]David Alan Rosenberg, "U.S. Nuclear Stockpile, 1945 to 1950," *Bulletin of the Atomic Scientists*, 38, n. 5 (May, 1982), 25–30; David Alan Rosenberg, "The Origins of Overkill: Nuclear Weapons and American Strategy, 1945–1960," *International Security*, 7, n. 4 (Spring, 1983), 11–18; Rosenberg, "American Postwar Air Doctrine," 250, 252, 254, 256, 261–262; Powaski, *March to Armageddon*, 43; Boyer, *By the Bomb's Early Light*, 344–345; Millis, *The Forrestal*

Diaries, 460–462; Robert J. Donovan, *Tumultuous Years: The Presidency of Harry S Truman, 1949–1953* (New York: W. W. Norton & Company, 1982), 100; Howard Ball, *Justice Downwind: America's Atomic Testing Program in the 1950s* (New York: Oxford University Press, 1986), 16; Richard Smoke, *National Security and the Nuclear Dilemma: An Introduction to the American Experience*, 2nd ed. (New York: Random House, 1987), 55; Rhodes, *The Making of the Atomic Bomb*, 765, 769.

[11]Millis, *The Forrestal Diaries*, 350–351.

[12]Millis, *The Forrestal Diaries*, 464; Fleet Admiral Chester W. Nimitz, "Atomic Age Navy," *Collier's*, 11 May 1946, 12–13, 66, 69; Schaffer, *Wings of Judgment*, 192–198; Powaski, *March to Armageddon*, 52.

[13]Powaski, *March to Armageddon*, 50–51; Captain W. D. Puleston, "The Probable Effect on American National Defense of the United Nations and the Atomic Bomb," *USNIP*, 72, n. 8 (August, 1946), 1017–1029; *U.S. News & World Report*, 1 February 1946, 28.

[14]John Philips Cranwell, "Sea Power and the Atomic Bomb," *USNIP*, 72, n. 10 (October, 1946), 1267–1275; Walmer Elton Strope, "The Navy and the Atomic Bomb," *USNIP*, 72, n. 10 (October, 1947), 1221–1227; Lieutenant Colonel William R. Wendt, USMC, "Outlaw the Atomic Bomb?," *USNIP*, 75, n. 3 (March, 1949), 334–335; Lieutenant Commander H. B. Seim, "Atomic Bomb— The X-Factor of Military Policy," *USNIP*, 75, n. 4 (April, 1949), 387–393; Lieutenant Commander Richard B. L. Creecy, "Military Applications of Atomic Energy," *USNIP*, 76, n. 7 (July, 1950), 743–751.

[15]Rear Admiral W. S. Parsons, "Atomic Energy—Whither Bound," *USNIP*, 73, n. 8 (August, 1947), 895–905; Fred Kaplan, *The Wizards of Armageddon* (New York: Touchstone Books, 1984), 232–234.

[16]Stephen E. Ambrose, *Eisenhower*, II: *The President* (New York: Simon and Schuster, 1984), 93; Vice Admiral Eli T. Reich, Oral History, USNI, II (1982), NL, 532–533; Davis, *Postwar Defense Policy*, 132, 252–253, 256; Commander Edward P. Stafford, "Flight of the Truculent Turtle," *USNIP*, 118, n. 8 (August, 1991), 45–48; Officer Biography, Vice Admiral John T. Hayward, NHD; Chuck Hansen, "Nuclear Neptunes: Early Days of Composite Squadrons 5 & 6," *American Aviation Historical Society Journal*, 24, n. 4 (Winter, 1979), 262–268; Letter, Commanding Officer, Composite Squadron 5, to Chief of Naval Operations, "Report of Heavy Load Take-off and Operational Tests of P2V-3C Airplanes," 18 March 1949, NHD; Richard P. Hallion, *The Naval Air War in Korea* (New York: Zebra Books, 1988), 35; Hayes, Zarsky, and Bello, *American Lake*, 69; Rear Admiral Henry L. Miller, Oral History, USNI, I (1973), NL, 155–161; Composite Squadron 5, Historical Report (1 July–31 December 1949), 30 December 1950, NHD; Composite Squadron 6, Historical Report (6 January–31 December 1950), 22 February 1951, NHD; Rosenberg, "American Postwar Air Doctrine," 264–265.

[17]Kaplan, *The Wizards of Armageddon*, 182; Rees, *The Seas and the Subs*, 74–75.

[18]Donovan, *Tumultuous Years*, 156; Powaski, *March to Armageddon*, 59; Bill Stapleton, "Navy vs. the H-Bomb," *Collier's*, 23 July 1954, 19–25; Ambrose, *Eisenhower*, II, 168–170; Robert L. O'Connell, *Of Arms and Men: A History of War, Weapons, and Aggression* (New York: Oxford University Press, 1989), 298; *Time*, 13 De-

cember 1954, 15; *U.S. News & World Report*, 25 May 1956, 37–39; Norman Friedman, *The Postwar Naval Revolution* (Annapolis: Naval Institute Press, 1986), 19.

[19]Martin Van Creveld, *Technology and War: From 2000 B.C. to the Present* (New York: Free Press, 1989), 292; Hayes, Zarsky, and Bello, *Amercian Lake*, 338; Friedman, *The Postwar Naval Revolution*, 213; Captain Stephen M. Millett, USAF, "The Capabilities of the American Nuclear Deterrent, 1945–1950," *ASH*, 27, n. 1 (Spring/March 1980), 27–32.

[20]Schaffer, *Wings of Judgment*, 202–203; Jeffrey G. Barlow, "The Navy and the Bomb: Naval Aviation's Influence on Strategic Thinking, 1945–1950," in *A Time of Change: National Strategy in the Early Postwar Era*, Colloquium on Contemporary History, No. 1, 7 June 1989 (Washington, D.C.: Naval Historical Center, 1989), 31–40.

[21]Colonel Irving D. Roth, USA, "Atoms and Sea Power," *MR*, 33, n. 6 (September, 1953), 3–8; Colonel George C. Reinhardt, USA, "Sea Power's Role in Atomic Warfare," *USNIP*, 79, n. 12 (December, 1953), 1279–1287; Commander Malcolm W. Cagle, "Philosophy for Naval Atomic Warfare," *USNIP*, 83, n. 3 (March, 1957), 249–258; Lieutenant Commander Carl H. Henn, Jr., "Sustaining an Air-Atomic Navy," *USNIP*, 83, n. 5 (May, 1957), 471–478; *Business Week*, 23 February 1957, 114, 117–118, 120.

CHAPTER FIFTEEN

[1]Norman Polmar, *Soviet Naval Power: Challenge for the 1970s*, Rev. ed. (New York: Crane, Russak & Company, Inc., 1974), 97; David Alan Rosenberg, "American Postwar Air Doctrine and Organization: The Navy Experience," in Colonel Alfred F. Hurley, USAF, and Major Robert C. Ehrhardt, USAF, eds., *Air Power and Warfare*, Proceedings of the 8th Military History Symposium, United States Air Force Academy, 18–20 October 1978 (Washington, D.C.: Office of Air Force History, 1979), 247, 253; Norman Friedman, *The Postwar Naval Revolution* (Annapolis: Naval Institute Press, 1986), 22–25, 47–48; David MacIsaac, "Voices from the Central Blue: The Air Power Theorists," in Peter Paret, ed., *Makers of Modern Strategy from Machiavelli to the Nuclear Age* (Princeton: Princeton University Press, 1986), 647; "News from the Navy," *Popular Science*, 163, n. 3 (September, 1953), 114–115.

[2]Friedman, *The Postwar Naval Revolution*, 101–108, 84–93; Peter Hayes, Lyuba Zarsky, and Walden Bello, *American Lake: Nuclear Peril in the Pacific* (New York: Viking Penguin, Inc., 1986), 45–47; Paul B. Ryan, *First Line of Defense: The U.S. Navy Since 1945* (Stanford, Cal.: Hoover Institution Press, 1981), 111–114.

[3]Robert L. O'Connell, *Of Arms and Men: A History of War, Weapons, and Aggression* (New York: Oxford University Press, 1989), 130–131, 192–194; USS *Antietam* (CV-36), Action Report (18 February–22 March 1952), 2 April 1952, NHD, 3; Commander Paul W. Gill and Commander Richard A. Teel, "A Brighter Future for Carrier Aviation," *USNIP*, 79, n. 11 (November, 1953), 1177–1184; Lieutenant Dorothy L. Small, "Catapults Come of Age," *USNIP*, 80, n. 10 (October, 1954), 1113–1121; Admiral Charles Donald Griffin, Oral History,

USNI, I (1973), NL, 259–260; Admiral Alfred M. Pride, Oral History, USNI (1984), NL, 197–198; Commander John J. Dougherty, "The *Bennington* Disaster, 26 May 1954," *SM*, 47, n. 4 (May, 1984), 23–24; Captain Slade D. Cutter, Oral History, USNI, II (1985), NL, 576.

[4]Commander Malcolm W. Cagle, "Naval Aviation at Mid-Century," *USNIP*, 77, n. 6 (June, 1951), 605–608; Captain Frederick W. Oliver, "Our Navy Girds for the Atom Age," *Popular Mechanics*, 96, n. 5 (November, 1951), 81–85, 236, 242, 244; *SNR*, in *SDR* (1 January–30 June 1953), 208; *SNR*, in *SDR* (1 January–30 June 1954), 194–195; *SNR*, in *SDR* (1 January–30 June 1955), 179–181; *Aviation Week*, 15 March 1954, 56–60.

[5]*Aviation Week*, 18 February 1957, 27; Frank A. Hecht, "The Proper Growth of Naval Aviation," *Vital Speeches of the Day*, 18, n. 15 (15 May 1952), 476–477; Admiral Arthur W. Radford, "Naval Power Reaffirmed," *Flying*, 49, n. 5 (November, 1951), 34–42; John F. Floberg, "Sea Power's Sunday Punch," *Collier's*, 4 October 1952, 18–21; Cagle, "Naval Aviation at Mid-Century," 608; Rear Admiral Apollo Soucek, "Why We Need a Navy in the Air Age," *Coronet*, 35 (March, 1954), 41–44.

[6]*SNR*, in *SDR* (1 January–30 June 1955), 179–180; Oliver, "Our Navy Girds for the Atomic Age," 85; Brian Johnson, *Fly Navy: The History of Naval Aviation* (New York: William Morrow and Company, Inc., 1981), 347–353; Eric J. Grove, *Vanguard to Trident: British Naval Policy Since World War II* (Annapolis: Naval Institute Press, 1987), 56.

[7]Rosenberg, "American Postwar Air Doctrine," 263; *Time*, 16 June 1958, 17; Johnson, *Fly Navy*, 357–359; *SNR*, in *SDR* (1 January–30 June 1952), 191–193; Ernest K. Lindley, "Shackle on the Navy," *Newsweek*, 19 May 1952, 34; Hanson W. Baldwin, "Electronic Queen of the Fleet," *Science Digest*, 33, n. 3 (March, 1953), 53–56; Rear Admiral D. V. Gallery, "Sea Power—Keystone of Air Power," *Reader's Digest*, May 1953, 29–35; Lieutenant Junior Grade W. J. Aston, "Jet Age Carrier," *USNIP*, 82, n. 5 (May, 1956), 529–539; Admiral Roy L. Johnson, Oral History, USNI (1982), NL, 160–180.

[8]*Aviation Week*, 27 January 1958, 70–72, 75; Barrett Gallagher, *"Forrestal* Class Appraisal," *Flying*, 60, n. 5 (May, 1957), 32–33, 56, 58; Commander Albert H. Vito, Jr., "The Attack Carrier—Mobile Might," *USNIP*, 87, n. 5 (May, 1961), 37–47; Commander Albert H. Vito, Jr., "Lone Carrier—Fact or Fancy?," *USNIP*, 88, n. 4 (April, 1962), 49–55; Johnson, *Fly Navy*, 359; Stephen E. Ambrose, *Eisenhower*, II: *The President* (New York: Simon and Schuster, 1984), 495–496.

[9]Captain G. G. O'Rourke, "Of Hosenoses, Stoofs, and Lefthanded Spads," *USNIP*, 94, n. 7 (July, 1968), 56–61; John A. Linkletter, "Cantankerous Gramp—The Navy Flier's Conscience," *Popular Mechanics*, 118, n. 2 (August, 1962), 86–89, 196; Captain Rosario Rausa, USNR, "Naval Aviation's 'Gramps'," *USNIP*, 118, n. 9 (September, 1991), 109–111.

[10]"Fireball," *SM*, 8, n. 12 (December, 1945), 40, 76–77; Lieutenant Commander Malcolm W. Cagle, "The Jets Are Coming," *USNIP*, 74, n. 11 (November, 1948), 1343–1349; Fighting Squadron Seventeen Able, Historical Report (1 January–31 March 1948), 1 April 1948, NHD; Fighting Squadron Five Able, Historical Report (1 January–31 March 1948), 1 April 1948, NHD; Commander

Harvey P. Lanham, "The Jets Come of Age," *USNIP*, 77, n. 4 (April, 1951), 371–377; "The Navy's Jet Fighters," *USNIP*, 78, n. 6 (June, 1952), 659–665; "The Navy's Attack Planes," *USNIP*, 78, n. 8 (August, 1952), 897–903; Fritz Leiber, "Navy Fliers Aim Higher," *Science Digest*, 35, n. 6 (June, 1954), 24–28; Gerald E. Wheeler, "Naval Aviation in the Jet Age," *USNIP*, 82, n. 11 (November, 1957), 1214–1233.

[11]*SNR*, in *SDR* (1 January–30 June 1950), 112–113, 127–130; *SNR*, in *SDR* (1 January–30 June 1951), 148–149; *SNR*, in *SDR* (1 January–30 June 1952), 155–157.

[12]*SNR*, in *SDR* (1 January–30 June 1953), 213–217; *SNR*, in *SDR* (1 January–30 June 1954), 199–206; *SNR*, in *SDR* (1 January–30 June 1955), 185–191.

[13]*Business Week*, 13 November 1954, 30–31; *Aviation Week*, 15 November 1954, 18–19; *Aviation Week*, 14 March 1955, 84–88; James J. Haggerty, Jr., "I Flew with the Foul-Weather Fighters," *Collier's*, 19 February 1954, 48, 50–52; O'Rourke, "Of Hosenoses, Stoofs, and Lefthanded Spads," 61; Friedman, *The Postwar Naval Revolution*, 100.

[14]*Aviation Week*, 12 March 1956, 84–88; *Aviation Week*, 25 February 1957, 84–87; *SNR*, in *SDR* (1 July 1958–30 June 1959), 246–248; *SNR*, in *SDR* (1 July 1959–30 June 1960), 272–279; *SNR*, in *SDR* (1 July 1960–30 June 1961), 236–246; J. D. Gerrard-Gough, "Tiny Tim: The Navy's Unused Sunday Punch," *ASH*, 21, n. 3 (Fall, 1974), 160–168; Friedman, *The Postwar Naval Revolution*, 101; *Aviation Week and Space Technology*, 9 April 1962, 89, 93–95; Ron Westman and Howard A. Wilcox, "Sidewinder," *American Heritage of Invention & Technology*, 5, n. 2 (Fall, 1989), 56–63.

[15]*Aviation Week*, 9 March 1959, 78–83; *Aviation Week*, 13 March 1961, 78–81; *Aviation Week*, 12 March 1962, 74–77; *Aviation Week*, 3 October 1955, 12–13; *Aviation Week*, 10 October 1955, 16–17; *Aviation Week*, 31 October 1955, 12–13; *Aviation Week*, 12 March 1956, 341; *Aviation Week*, 30 April 1956, 32.

[16]Wheeler, "Naval Aviation in the Jet Age," 1214; Lieutenant Commander Peter B. Mersky, "The Crusader: Farewell to the Fleet," *USNIP*, 108, n. 6 (June, 1982), 56–61; Frank Harvey, "World's Meanest Flying," *Popular Science*, 171, n. 1 (July, 1957), 52–56, 192, 194; Commander Peter Mersky, "Phantom, Farewell," *NH*, 2/3/4 (Summer, 1988), 37–44; O'Rourke, "Of Hosenoses, Stoofs, and Lefthanded Spads," 59; L. W. Reithmaier, "Phantom II—Record Breaking Fighter," *Flying*, 70, n. 5 (May, 1962), 62–63, 96, 98, 104, 106, 108.

[17]Wheeler, "Naval Aviation in the Jet Age," 1217; O'Rourke, "Of Hosenoses, Stoofs, and Lefthanded Spads," 61; Lieutenant Commander Peter B. Mersky, "Vigilante Fadeout," *USNIP*, 106, n. 8 (June, 1980), 63–69; *Aviation Week*, 14 July 1958, 54–55, 57, 59, 61, 63, 67; Lieutenant Edward L. Barker, "The Helicopter in Combat," *USNIP*, 77, n. 11 (November, 1951), 1207–1221; Commander Malcolm W. Cagle and Commander Frank A. Manson, *The Sea War in Korea* (Annapolis: Naval Institute Press, 1957), 134–135, 336–337; Commander Charles J. Burton, "The Helicopter in the Fleet," *USNIP*, 86, n. 1 (January, 1960), 45–50.

[18]Captain Gerald G. O'Rourke, "The Wondrous World of Jet V/STOL," *USNIP*, 98, n. 11 (November, 1972), 33–41; R. M. Braybrook, "V/STOL: Stalled?," *USNIP*, 100, n. 9 (October, 1974), 32–40; Commander George Cornelius, "Air

Reconnaissance—Great Silent Weapon," *USNIP*, 85, n. 7 (July, 1959), 35–42; *Aviation Week*, 3 April 1961, 63, 65, 69, 71, 73; *Aviation Week*, 1 November 1954, 21–22.

[19]*Aviation Week*, 16 July 1956, 61, 63; Lieutenant Commander Andrew Serrell, "Mars, No Bettah Da Kine," *USNIP*, 83, n. 8 (August, 1957), 857–861; Commander L. B. Liebhauser, "Capital Ship for an Air Navy," *USNIP*, 83, n. 9 (September, 1957), 961–969; Lieutenant D. P. Kirchner, "The Future of the Seaplane," *USNIP*, 87, n. 5 (May, 1961), 54–63; *Aviation Week*, 31 August 1959, 32; Commander C. T. Dugin, "Nuclear Power and the Seaplane," *USNIP*, 82, n. 1 (January, 1956), 18–23; Commander Arthur D. Struble, "Toward a Nuclear-Powered Seaplane," *USNIP*, 83, n. 11 (November, 1957), 1168–1173.

CHAPTER SIXTEEN

[1]Wayne P. Hughes, "Fleet Tactics: A Weaponry Revolution," in David Curtis Skaggs and Robert S. Browning III, eds., *In Defense of the Republic: Readings in American Military History* (Belmont, Cal.: Wadsworth Publishing Company, 1991), 393–394; Norman Friedman, *The Postwar Naval Revolution* (Annapolis: Naval Institute Press, 1986), 201–211, 175–187; Edgar Stanton MacLay, *A History of the United States Navy from 1775 to 1898*, II (New York: D. Appleton and Company, 1898), 404.

[2]Edwyn Gray, *The Devil's Device: Robert Whitehead and the History of the Torpedo*, Rev. ed. (Annapolis: Naval Institute Press, 1991), 248–249, 270; *SNR*, in *SDR* (1 January–30 June 1953), 218–222; *SNR*, in *SDR* (1 January–30 June 1954), 207–211; *SNR*, in *SDR* (1 January–30 June 1955), 192–195; Milton Lehman, "He Plays Tag with Death," *Saturday Evening Post*, 26 April 1952, 20–21, 100–102.

[3]*Aviation Week*, 19 March 1956; Howard I. Chappelle, *The History of the American Sailing Navy: The Ships and Their Development* (New York: Bonanza Books, 1988 [1949]), 425; "Heavyweight Sluggers of the Sea," in Lieutenant William Harrison Fetridge, ed., *The Navy Reader* (Indianapolis: Bobbs-Merrill Company, 1943), 50; Roger Kafka, "Behind the Big Guns," in Fetridge, *The Navy Reader*, 369; Clark G. Reynolds, *Admiral John H. Towers: The Struggle for Naval Air Supremacy* (Annapolis: Naval Institute Press, 1991), 513; Malcolm Muir, Jr., "Hard Aground on Thimble Shoal," *NH*, 5, n. 3 (Fall, 1991), 30–36; Captain C. A. Bartholomew, *Mud, Muscles, and Miracles: Marine Salvage in the United States Navy* (Washington, D.C.: Naval Historical Center and Naval Sea Systems Command, 1990), 204–209; Lawrence C. Allin, "An Antediluvian Monstrosity: The Battleship Revisited," in William B. Cogar, ed., *Naval History: The Seventh Symposium of the U.S. Naval Academy* (Wilmington, Del.: Scholarly Resources, Inc., 1988), 287–289; "Farewell to the Battleship," *Life*, 11 November 1957, 46.

[4]Commander David D. Lewis, *The Fight for the Sea: The Past, Present, and Future of Submarine Warfare in the Atlantic* (New York: Collier Books, 1961), 223–225; David Alan Rosenberg, "American Postwar Air Doctrine and Organization: The Navy Experience," in Colonel Alfred F. Hurley, USAF, and Major Robert C. Ehrhardt, USAF, eds., *Air Power and Warfare*, Proceedings of the 8th Military History Symposium, United States Air Force Academy, 18–20 October 1978 (Washington, D.C.: Office of Air Force History, 1979), 250, 257; Vice

Admiral Charles A. Lockwood, *Sink 'Em All: Submarine Warfare in the Pacific* (New York: E. P. Dutton & Co., Inc., 1951), 349.

[5]Friedman, *The Postwar Naval Revolution*, 47–49; *SNR*, in *SDR* (1 January–30 June 1954), 164, 191–198; *SNR*, in *SDR* (1 January–30 June 1955), 181.

[6]Friedman, *The Postwar Naval Revolution*, 143–145; Norman Friedman, "Destroyers for Mobilization," in Department of History, U.S. Naval Academy, eds., *New Aspects of Naval History: Selected Papers from the 5th Naval History Symposium, 1981* (Baltimore: The Nautical and Aviation Publishing Company of America, 1985), 199–206.

[7]Commander Daniel G. Felger, "Retrospective on the *Forrest Shermans*," *USNIP*, 113, n. 5 (May, 1987), 162–175; "Notes from a Navy Cruise," *Atlantic Monthly*, 202, n. 1 (July, 1958), 88–89; John C. Niedermair, Oral History, USNI (1978), NL, 297–299.

[8]Friedman, *The Postwar Naval Revolution*, 60–68, 75–82; *Missiles and Rockets*, 8 November 1965, 18; Friedman, "Destroyers for Mobilization," 205; Rear Admiral Thomas H. Morton, Oral History, USNI (1979), NL, 246; Admiral Charles K. Duncan, Oral History, USNI, I (1978), NL, 324–329; Admiral Charles Donald Griffin, Oral History, USNI, II (1975), NL, 524.

[9]William E. Burrows, *Deep Black: The Startling Truth Behind America's Top-Secret Spy Satellites* (New York: Berkley Books, 1988), 172–174; Vice Admiral John L. Chew, Oral History, USNI (1979), NL, 402–403.

[10]Vice Admiral George Carroll Dyer, *The Amphibians Came to Conquer: The Story of Admiral Richmond Kelly Turner*, II (Washington, D.C.: Government Printing Office, 1971), 1104; Lieutenant Commander Everett A. Parke, "The Unique and Vital DER," *USNIP*, 86, n. 2 (February, 1960), 89–95; Commander W. D. Brinckloe, " 'Paul Revere' Ships Join the Lookout," *Popular Mechanics*, 103, n. 6 (January, 1955), 89–91, 242.

[11]Captain W. D. Brinckloe, "Missile Navy," *USNIP*, 84, n. 2 (February, 1958), 23–29; Rear Admiral Delmer S. Fahrney, "Drones and Guided Missiles: Their Development in the U.S. Navy," *SM*, 46, n. 1 (January–February, 1983), 28–31; Richard P. Hallion, *The Naval Air War in Korea* (New York: Zebra Books, 1988), 292–293; Reynolds, *Admiral John H. Towers*, 434–435; Commander Todd Blades, "The Bumblebee *Can* Fly," *NH*, 2, n. 4 (Fall, 1988), 48–52; Vice Admiral Kleber S. Masterson, Oral History, USNI (1973), NL, 206–210, 264.

[12]Friedman, *The Postwar Naval Revolution*, 68–69, 71, 93–98; Brinckloe, "Missile Navy," 26; *SNR*, in *SDR* (1 January–30 June 1950), 130–131; *SNR*, in *SDR* (1 January–30 June 1951), 172; *SNR*, in *SDR* (1 July 1960–30 June 1961), 229–230; Masterson, Oral History, 314, 248–252; Rear Admiral Malcolm F. Schoeffel, Oral History, USNI (1979), NL, 340–344; Rear Admiral Arthur W. Price, Jr., Oral History, USNI (1980), NL, 224–229; Vice Admiral Eli T. Reich, Oral History, USNI, I (1982), 462–463.

[13]Friedman, *The Postwar Naval Revolution*, 71; *SNR*, in *SDR* (1 July 1958–30 June 1959), 241–242; Brinckloe, "Missile Navy," 27; Masterson, Oral History, 251; Schoeffel, Oral History, 344; Vice Admiral John Barr Colwell, Oral History, USNI (1974), NL, 224–227; Ensign J. A. Lynch and J01 M. D. Buoncuore, "The Cruiser with the Supersonic Sting," *Popular Mechanics*, 111, n. 1 (January, 1959), 140–142.

[14]Brinckloe, "Missile Navy," 26; Rear Admiral Ralph Kirk James, Oral History, USNI (1972), NL, 378; Office of the Chief of Naval Operations, "Annual Progress Report of the Guided Missiles Program," 1 October 1955, NHD, 24.

[15]"Mugu Guides the 'Birds'," *Flying*, 49, n. 5 (November, 1951), 124–125, 152; *SNR*, in *SDR* (1 January–30 June 1952), 150; Admiral Alfred M. Pride, Oral History, USNI (1984), NL, 172–174; Historical Report, U.S. Naval Air Facility, Point Mugu, California (26 January–30 June 1946), 30 June 1946, NHD; Annual Progress Report, U.S. Naval Air Missile Test Center, Point Mugu, California (1953), NHD; Office of the Chief of Naval Operations, "Annual Progress Report of the Guided Missiles Program," 24–28.

[16]Friedman, *The Postwar Naval Revolution*, 71; Office of the Chief of Naval Operations, "Annual Progress Report of the Guided Missiles Program," 11–14.

[17]Friedman, *The Postwar Naval Revolution*, 82–83; Commander John T. Bothwell, "The Barnstorming Days of Submarine Missiles," *USNIP*, 116, n. 12 (December, 1990), 52–57; David K. Stumpf, "Blasts From the Past," *USNIP*, 119, n. 4 (April, 1993), 60–64; Lieutenant Commander Allan P. Slaff, "Time for Decision," *USNIP*, 82, n. 8 (August, 1956), 809–813; Brinckloe, "Missile Navy," 27; *Aviation Week*, 16 December 1957, 31–32; Peter Hayes, Lyuba Zarsky, and Walden Bello, *American Lake: Nuclear Peril in the Pacific* (New York: Viking Penguin, Inc., 1986), 71; Admiral Arleigh Burke, Oral History, USNI (1973), NL, 89–93.

[18]Slaff, "Time for Decision," 812–813; Lieutenant Roy L. Beavers, Jr., "Seapower and Geopolitics in the Missile Age," *USNIP*, 85, n. 6 (June, 1959), 41–46; *Aviation Week*, 25 July 1960, 35; *U.S. News & World Report*, 20 July 1956, 115–117; Officer Biography, Rear Admiral John E. Clark, NHD.

[19]Friedman, *The Postwar Naval Revolution*, 110–113, 132–133, 135, 60; Blades, "The Bumblebee *Can* Fly," 50–51; Commander Eugene E. Wilson, *Kitty Hawk to Sputnik to Polaris* (Palm Beach, Fla.: Literary Investors Guild, 1967), 152; *Science News Letter*, 7 June 1958, 357; *Aviation Week*, 12 March 1956, 341; Masterson, Oral History, 336–337, 381, 397; Vice Admiral Raymond E. Peet, Oral History, USNI (1984), NL, 143–144; Rear Admiral Edward A. Ruckner, Oral History, USNI (1977), NL, 271–274, 558–559; Rear Admiral Francis D. Foley, Oral History, USNI, II (1988), NL, 812–813.

[20]*Aviation Week*, 16 July 1956, 34, 37; *Radio & TV News*, 58, n. 1 (July 1957), 37; Friedman, *The Postwar Naval Revolution*, 70; Blades, "The Bumblebee *Can* Fly," 52; Vice Admiral Lawson P. Ramage, Oral History, USNI (1975), NL, 451–453; Admiral U.S. Grant Sharp, Oral History, USNI, II (1976), NL, 440–41, 457.

CHAPTER SEVENTEEN

[1]Dan van der Vat, *The Atlantic Campaign: World War II's Great Struggle at Sea* (New York: Harper & Row, 1988), 340; Heinz Schaeffer, *U-Boat 977* (New York: Ballantine Books, 1966 [1952]), 117–124.

[2]Norman Friedman, *The Postwar Naval Revolution* (Annapolis: Naval Institute Press, 1986), 188–200; Vice Admiral Charles A. Lockwood, *Sink 'Em All: Submarine Warfare in the Pacific* (New York: E. P. Dutton & Co., Inc., 1951), 377; Michael

A. Palmer, *Origins of the Maritime Strategy: American Naval Strategy in the First Postwar Decade*, Contributions to Naval History . . . No. 1 (Washington, D.C.: Naval Historical Center, 1988), 62–63; Edwyn Gray, *The Devil's Device: Robert Whitehead and the History of the Torpedo*, Rev. ed. (Annapolis: Naval Institute Press, 1991), 216–217; Chairman, Submarine Conference, "The Type XXI Submarines" ("Guppy Study"), 10 June 1949, NHD, 8–10; Commander Submarine Development Group 2 to Commander Submarine Force, U.S. Atlantic Fleet, "Report of Arctic Cruise of Submarine Development Group 2, July–September 1949," 24 September 1949, NHD; Chairman, Submarine Conference, to Chief of Naval Operations, "Report of Submarine Conference on 20 April 1949," n. d., NHD, 3–10.

3*Newsweek*, 11 March 1957, 34; *Time*, 24 August 1953, 11–12; Paul R. Schratz, *Submarine Commander* (Lexington: University Press of Kentucky, 1988), 245–246, 251, 266–267, 274–275; *Newsweek*, 9 June 1958, 36; Richard G. Hewlett and Francis Duncan, *Nuclear Navy, 1946–1962* (Chicago: University of Chicago Press, 1974), 346; "Spray Suit Keeps Sub Crews Dry," *Popular Science*, 162, n. 3 (March, 1953), 130; *Science News Letter*, 13 December 1952, 374–375; "It's Cold Inside," *New Yorker*, 27 (10 March 1951), 23–24; Allan C. Fisher, Jr., "Our Navy's Long Submarine Arm," *National Geographic Magazine*, 102, n. 5 (November, 1952), 613–636; Letter, Commander T. W. Hogan to Chairman, Submarine Conference, "Study of Advantages of a Nuclear Propelled Submarine over a Closed Cycle Submarine," 27 April 1949, NHD.

4Dean C. Allard, "Benjamin Franklin Isherwood: Father of the Modern Steam Navy," in James C. Bradford, ed., *Captains of the Old Steam Navy: Makers of the American Naval Tradition, 1840–1880* (Annapolis: Naval Institute Press, 1986), 315; Richard Rhodes, *The Making of the Atomic Bomb* (New York: Touchstone Books, 1986), 317; Ed Rees, *The Seas and the Subs* (New York: Duell, Sloan and Pearce, 1961), 64–69.

5Rear Admiral Schuyler Neilson Pyne, Oral History, USNI (1972), NL, 337–338, 309–310; Hanson Weightman Baldwin, Oral History, USNI, I (1976), NL, 321; Officer Biography, Vice Admiral Edward L. Cochrane, NHD; Officer Biography, Vice Admiral Earle W. Mills, NHD; Officer Biography, Vice Admiral Harold G. Bowen, NHD; Hewlett and Duncan, *Nuclear Navy*, 6–14; "Atomic Powered Navy," *Science News Letter*, 4 May 1946, 275.

6Hewlett and Duncan, *Nuclear Navy*, 15–33; Vice Admiral Ruthven E. Libby, Oral History, USNI (1984), NL, 235–236; Officer Biography, Rear Admiral Thorvald A. Solberg, NHD; Officer Biography, Rear Admiral Albert G. Mumma, NHD.

7Admiral Alfred G. Ward, Oral History, USNI (1972), NL, 248–249; Patrick Tyler, *Running Critical: The Silent War, Rickover, and General Dynamics* (New York: Harper & Row, 1986), 21–22; Norman Polmar and Thomas B. Allen, *Rickover: Controversy and Genius* (New York: Simon and Schuster, 1982), 27–40; Francis Duncan, *Rickover and the Nuclear Navy: The Discipline of Technology* (Annapolis: Naval Institute Press, 1990), 8; Officer Biography, Admiral Hyman George Rickover, NHD.

8Polmar and Allen, *Rickover*, 41–59; Duncan, *Rickover and the Nuclear Navy*, 8; United

States Naval Academy *Lucky Bag* (1922), NL, 94, between 326 and 327; Baldwin, Oral History, I, 103–106; Rear Admiral George W. Bauernschmidt, Oral History, USNI (1970), NL, 165–166; Officer Biography, Captain Leonard Kaplan, NHD.

[9]Rear Admiral Charles J. Wheeler, Oral History, USNI (1970), NL, 139–141; Officer Biography, Admiral Hyman George Rickover; Duncan, *Rickover and the Nuclear Navy*, 8–11; Polmar and Allen, *Rickover*, 60–96; Libby, Oral History, 43–45; Pyne, Oral History, 19; Rear Admiral Charles E. Loughlin, Oral History, USNI (1982), NL, 24–30, 256; Vice Admiral William P. Mack, Oral History, USNI, I (1980), 115; Rear Admiral William D. Irwin, Oral History, USNI (1980), NL, 100–106.

[10]Duncan, *Rickover and the Nuclear Navy*, 11–12; Polmar and Allen, *Rickover*, 97–107; Admiral Edwin J. Roland, USCG, Oral History, USNI, II (1977), NL, 436; Officer Biography, Admiral Hyman George Rickover.

[11]Rear Admiral Ralph Kirk James, Oral History, USNI (1972), NL, 170; Paul B. Ryan, *First Line of Defense: The U.S. Navy Since 1945* (Stanford, Cal.: Hoover Institution Press, 1981), 27–28; Polmar and Allen, *Rickover*, 107–111; Rees, *The Seas and the Subs*, 76; Hewlett and Duncan, *Nuclear Navy*, 34–35; Officer Biography, Admiral Hyman George Rickover.

[12]Admiral James S. Russell, Oral History, USNI (1976), NL, 352; Hewlett and Duncan, *Nuclear Navy*, 35–43; Polmar and Allen, *Rickover*, 123–129; *Duncan, Rickover and the Nuclear Navy*, 12–13.

[13]Hewlett and Duncan, *Nuclear Navy*, 43–51; Polmar and Allen, *Rickover*, 129–134; Officer Biography, Admiral Hyman George Rickover.

[14]Polmar and Allen, *Rickover*, 134–143; Hewlett and Duncan, *Nuclear Navy*, 52–82.

[15]Polmar and Allen, *Rickover*, 143–144; Hewlett and Duncan, *Nuclear Navy*, 82–87.

[16]Hewlett and Duncan, *Nuclear Navy*, 88–100.

[17]Hewlett and Duncan, *Nuclear Navy*, 100–120; Duncan, *Rickover and the Nuclear Navy*, 13; Polmar and Allen, *Rickover*, 147–149; Michael Schaller, *Douglas MacArthur: The Far Eastern General* (New York: Oxford University Press, 1989), 156.

[18]Admiral John S. Thach, Oral History, USNI, II (1977), NL, 611–612; Polmar and Allen, *Rickover*, 149–153; Rees, *The Seas and the Subs*, 82–89; Commander E. E. Kintner, "Admiral Rickover's Gamble: The Landlocked Submarine," *Atlantic Monthly*, 203, n. 1 (January, 1959), 31–35; Ronald Schiller, "Submarine in the Desert," *Collier's*, 5 February 1954, 88–91; Captain Sherman Naymark, " 'Underway on Nuclear Power:' The Development of the *Nautilus*," *USNIP*, 96, n. 4 (April, 1970), 56–63.

[19]Captain Slade D. Cutter, Oral History, USNI, II (1985), NL, 371–372; Admiral Stuart S. ("Sunshine") Murray, Oral History, USNI, II (1974), NL, 639–642; Captain C. A. Bartholomew, *Mud, Muscles, and Miracles: Marine Salvage in the United States Navy* (Washington, D.C.: Naval Historical Center and Naval Sea Systems Command, 1990), 58; K. Jack Bauer, "Robert Bernerd Anderson, 4 February 1953–2 May 1954," in Paolo E. Coletta, ed., *American Secretaries of the Navy*, II: *1913–1972* (Annapolis: Naval Institute Press, 1980), 843–845; Rees, *The Seas and the Subs*, 91; Hewlett and Duncan, *Nuclear Navy*, 186–193; *Time*,

10 August 1953; 18; Polmar and Allen, *Rickover*, 153; Duncan, *Rickover and the Nuclear Navy*, 13–14; John C. Niedermair, Oral History, USNI (1978), NL, 283; Officer Biography, Vice Admiral Homer N. Wallin, NHD.

²⁰Libby, Oral History, 235–236; Vice Admiral Eli T. Reich, Oral History, USNI, II (1982), NL, 924–926; Hewlett and Duncan, *Nuclear Navy*, 193; Schiller, "Submarine in the Desert," 89; Pyne, Oral History, 330–332.

CHAPTER EIGHTEEN

¹Richard G. Hewlett and Francis Duncan, *Nuclear Navy, 1946–1962* (Chicago: University of Chicago Press, 1974), 177–178, 204–209, 215–224; Admiral Robert B. Carney, "Atomic Victory Depends on the Navy," *Nation's Business*, 42, n. 2 (February, 1954), 38–39, 58, 60–51; *SNR*, in *SDR* (1 January–30 June 1952), 152–153; David Miller and John Jordan, *Modern Submarine Warfare* (New York: Military Press, 1987), 42–43; Captain Slade D. Cutter, Oral History, USNI, II (1985), NL, 373–378, 562–565, 394–397; Rear Admiral Ralph Kirk James, Oral History, USNI (1972), NL, 287; Lieutenant Commander Dean L. Axene, " 'School of the Boat' for the *Nautilus*," *USNIP*, 81, n. 11 (November, 1955), 1229–1235; Rear Admiral Charles E. Loughlin, Oral History, USNI (1982), NL, 315; Officer Biography, Vice Admiral Eugene P. Wilkinson, NHD; Captain Sherman Naymark, " 'Underway on Nuclear Power:' The Development of the *Nautilus*," *USNIP*, 96, n. 4 (April, 1970), 56–63; Richard Boyle, "1960: A Vintage Year for Submariners," *USNIP*, 96, n. 10 (October, 1970), 35–41.

²*Newsweek*, 18 February 1957, 30; Commander William R. Anderson and Clay Blair, Jr., *Nautilus 90 North* (New York: World Publishing Company, 1959), 44–49, 52–60, 213; Van Wyck Brooks, *The Confident Years, 1885–1915* (New York: E. P. Dutton & Co., Inc., 1952), 38; Pierre Berton, *The Arctic Grail: The Quest for the North West Passage and the North Pole, 1818–1909* (New York: Penguin Books, 1989), 537, 548; Officer Biography, Vice Admiral Charles W. Wilkins, NHD; Commander William R. Anderson, "The Arctic as a Sea Route of the Future," *National Geographic*, 115, n. 1 (January, 1959), 21–24; Lieutenant William G. Lalor, Jr., "Submarine Through the North Pole," *National Geographic*, 115, n. 1 (January, 1959), 1–20; Dr. Waldo K. Lyon, Oral History, USNI (1972), NL, 26–27, 99–104.

³Lalor, "Submarine through the North Pole," 3, 6, 14, 16; Lieutenant Shepherd M. Jenks, "Under the Ice to the North Pole," *Reader's Digest*, 74, n. 442 (February, 1959), 103–106; Wesley S. Griswold, "How *Nautilus* Hit the Bull's-Eye at the Pole," *Popular Science*, 174, n. 1 (January, 1959), 161–164, 252; Vice Admiral Lawson P. Ramage, Oral History, USNI (1975), NL, 316–319; Lyon, Oral History, 105–111; Anderson and Blair, *Nautilus 90 North*, 133–135.

⁴Lalor, "Submarine Through the North Pole," 16–20; Anderson and Blair, *Nautilus 90 North*, 222–223; Jenks, "Under the Ice to the North Pole," 105–106; Lyon, Oral History, 112–121, 131–163; *Business Week*, 16 August 1958, 32–34; *Newsweek*, 18 August 1958, 25–26; *Time*, 18 August 1958, 9-10; *Life*, 18 August 1958, 20–21; *Life*, 1 September 1958, 57–60, 63–64, 66, 69–70, 72; *Science News Letter*, 24 August 1958, 115; "*Nautilus*, Nemo, and the Northwest Passage," *America*, 23 August 1958, 527; Commander Robert D. McWethy, "Significance of the

Nautilus Polar Cruise," *USNIP*, 84, n. 5 (May, 1958), 32–35; Lieutenant Commander James T. Strong, "The Opening of the Arctic Ocean," *USNIP*, 87, n. 10 (October, 1961), 58–65; Lyon, Oral History, 64, 102.

[5]Commander Henry Jackson, "USS *Albacore:* The 'New Look' in Submarine Design," *BuShips Journal*, 2, n. 11 (March, 1954), 2–4; John C. Niedermair, Oral History, USNI (1978), NL, 287–294; Hewlett and Duncan, *Nuclear Navy*. 153–186; Ed Rees, *The Seas and the Subs* (New York: Duell, Sloan and Pearce, 1961), 109–111, 106; Cornelius Ryan, "I Rode the World's Fastest Sub," *Collier's*, 1 April 1955, 25–29; Patrick Tyler, *Running Critical: The Silent War, Rickover, and General Dynamics* (New York: Harper & Row, 1986), 56–57; Miller and Jordan, *Modern Submarine Warfare*, 40–41, 43; Cutter, Oral History, II, 398–399; Letter, Senior Member, Sub-Board of Inspection and Survey, Naval Inactive Ship Maintenance Facility, Portsmouth, Virginia, to President, Board of Inspection and Survey, "Survey of ex–USS *Albacore* (AGSS-569)," 4 January 1980, NHD; Ship's History, USS *Albacore* (AGSS-569), 29 January 1957, NHD; Officer Biography, Captain Richard B. Laning, NHD; Letter, Commanding Officer, USS *Seawolf* (SSN-575) to Commander in Chief Atlantic Fleet, 27 September 1957, NHD; Francis Duncan, *Rickover and the Nuclear Navy: The Discipline of Technology* (Annapolis: Naval Institute Press, 1990), 50–51; *Newsweek*, 8 April 1957, 32; *Newsweek*, 13 October 1958, 30–31; *Time*, 20 October 1958, 23; Captain Richard B. Laning, "Sixty Days Out of This World," *Look*, 23 December 1958, 22–26; Allene Talmey, "A Masterpiece of Space Planning: The *Seawolf*, Atomic Submarine," *Vogue*, 133 (15 January, 1959), 44–47, 98; *Life*, 18 February 1957, 61; Captain Richard B. Laning, "The *Seawolf*'s Sodium-Cooled Power Plant," *NH*, 6, n. 1 (Spring, 1992), 45–48; Captain Richard B. Laning, "The *Seawolf:* Going to Sea," *NH*, 6, n. 2 (Summer, 1992), 55–58.

[6]Hewlett and Duncan, *Nuclear Navy*, 298–301; Officer Biography, Vice Admiral James F. Calvert, NHD; Rees, *The Seas and the Subs*, 114–118, 120–123; "Our Newest A-Sub: The *Skate*," *New York Times Magazine*, 2 February 1958, 10–11; *Time*, 25 August 1958, 17; Lieutenant Commander William H. Layman, "*Skate* Breakthrough at the North Pole," *USNIP*, 85, n. 9 (September, 1959), 32–37; *Life*, 20 October 1958, 18–19; *Time*, 1 September 1958, 24; Lyon, Oral History, 131–132, 178–179, 240–241; *Time*, 25 August 1958, 17; "Nuclear Navy," *New York Times Magazine*, 24 August 1958, 8–9; Eliot Tozer, "Twin Reactors to Drive World's Biggest Sub," *Popular Science*, 173, n. 1 (July, 1958), 88–91, 202; Officer Biography, Captain Edward L. Beach, NHD; Boyle, "1960: A Vintage Year for Submariners," 36–37.

[7]Officer Biography, Vice Admiral William W. Behrens, Jr., NHD; Duncan, *Rickover and the Nuclear Navy*, 17–18, 23–34; Rees, *The Seas and the Subs*, 112; Hewlett and Duncan, *Nuclear Navy*, 267–270; Eric J. Grove, *Vanguard to Trident: British Naval Policy since World War II* (Annapolis: Naval Institute Press, 1987), 230–233; Miller and Jordan, *Modern Submarine Warfare*, 60; Letter, Commanding Officer, USS *Tullibee* (SSN-597) to Commander in Chief Atlantic Fleet, 19 April 1962, NHD.

[8]Hewlett and Duncan, *Nuclear Navy*, 258–267, 271–296, 121–152; Paul R. Schratz, *Submarine Commander* (Lexington: University Press of Kentucky, 1988), 222, 231; Admiral H. G. Rickover, "Thoughts on Man's Purpose in Life . . . and

Other Matters," *USNIP*, 100, n. 12 (December, 1974), 67–72; "Rickover Looks at the U.S. Navy," *U.S. News & World Report*, 3 July 1961, 74–75.

⁹John G. Hubbell, "The Making of a Submariner," *Reader's Digest*, 66 (May, 1955), 25–35; Hewlett and Duncan, *Nuclear Navy*, 340–361; Vice Admiral John Barr Colwell, Oral History, USNI (1974), NL, 351–352; Captain John W. Crawford, Jr., " 'Get 'em Young and Train 'em Right'," *USNIP*, 113, n. 10 (October, 1987), 103–108; Commander James F. Calvert, "What We Don't Know Can Hurt Us," *USNIP*, 85, n. 1 (January, 1959), 55–59; *Time*, 12 May 1961, 63A–63B; Anderson and Blair, *Nautilus 90 North*, 27–29, 38.

¹⁰Crawford, " 'Get 'em Young and Train 'em Right'," 106–107; Rees, *The Seas and the Subs*, 99–102; Norman Polmar and Thomas B. Allen, *Rickover: Controversy and Genius* (New York: Simon and Schuster, 1982), 267–275; Captain John W. Crawford, "Passing Rickover's Muster," *NH*, 6, n. 1 (Spring, 1992), 35–38; Lyon, Oral History, 183–184; Admiral William R. Smedberg III, Oral History, USNI, II (1979), NL, 724–725; Elmo R. Zumwalt, Jr., *On Watch: A Memoir* (New York: Quadrangle, 1976), 85–96.

¹¹Evan M. Wylie, "No Sky, No Sun, No Moon," *Coronet*, 45 (December, 1958), 45–50; "Medicine Under the Sea," *Science Digest*, 42, n. 2 (August, 1957), 9–13; Commander E. B. Roth, "Atomic Power—Where Will It Pay First?," *USNIP*, 79, n. 10 (October, 1953), 1091–1101; Lieutenant George P. Steele II, "Nuclear Energy and Sea Power," *USNIP*, 79, n. 12 (December, 1953), 1314–1319; Commander G. W. Kittredge, "The Impact of Nuclear Power on Submarines," *USNIP*, 80, n. 4 (April, 1954), 419–425.

¹²*U.S. News & World Report*, 25 October 1957, 60, 62; *U.S. News & World Report*, 21 March 1958, 68–72, 75–76; *Saturday Evening Post*, 22 February 1958, 10; Hewlett and Duncan, *Nuclear Navy*, 361–362; Strong, "The Opening of the Arctic Ocean," 58–65; Hanson W. Baldwin, "New 'Battleship'—the A-Submarine," *New York Times Magazine*, 16 March 1958, 13, 100–101; Paul Cohen, "The Future of the Submarine," *FA*, 38, n. 1 (October, 1959), 110–120; Lieutenant Commander Carvel Hall Blair, "Arctic Submarine Material," *USNIP*, 85, n. 9 (September, 1959), 39–45; Vice Admiral C. B. Momsen and Peter Maas, "The Coming Death of the Surface Navy," *Look*, 13 May 1958, 21–25; *Time*, 14 April 1958, 71–72; *Life*, 17 March 1961, 44–45.

¹³Hewlett and Duncan, *Nuclear Navy*, 225–257; Duncan, *Rickover and the Nuclear Navy*, 190–231; *Business Week*, 15 September 1956, 154, 156, 158, 160; Captain Morton H. Lytle, "Replenishing the Nuclear Navy," *USNIP*, 85, n. 10 (October, 1959), 56–61; *Time*, 12 August 1957, 38; Commander Craig Hosmer, "Nuclear Power for the Navy," *USNIP*, 84, n. 5 (May, 1958), 57–64; *SNR*, in *SDR* (1 January–30 June 1956), 197–206; *SNR*, in *SDR* (1 January–30 June 1957), 230–240; *SNR*, in *SDR* (1 January–30 June 1958), 240–243; *Newsweek*, 1 September 1958, 38.

¹⁴Michael Day, "Atomic Revolution in the Shipyards," *Popular Mechanics*, 109, n. 2 (February, 1958), 97–102, 274, 276, 278, 280; *SNR*, in *SDR* (1 July 1958–30 June 1959), 249–253; *SNR*, in *SDR* (1 July 1959–30 June 1960), 272–279; *SNR*, in *SDR* (1 July 1960–30 June 1961), 236–246; Hewlett and Duncan, *Nuclear Navy*, 194–204, 209–215, 377–391; "The Naval Nuclear Propulsion Program," *SM*, 30, n. 5 (May, 1967), 4–10; Captain Carl O. Holmquist and Russell S.

Greenbaum, "The Development of Nuclear Propulsion in the Navy," *USNIP*, 86, n. 9 (September, 1960), 65–71.

STERN WATCH III

[1]Norman Friedman, *The Postwar Naval Revolution* (Annapolis: Naval Institute Press, 1986), 212–218; Otto Friedrich, *Before the Deluge: A Portrait of Berlin in the 1920s* (New York: Fromm International Publishing Corporation, 1986), 235; John Herman Randall, Jr., *The Making of the Modern Mind: A Survey of the Intellectual Background of the Present Age* (New York: Columbia University Press, 1976[1926]), 99; B. Franklin Cooling, *Benjamin Franklin Tracy: Father of the Modern American Fightng Navy* (Hamden, Conn.: Archon Books, 1973), 58.

[2]Brendan Gill, *Many Masks: A Life of Frank Lloyd Wright* (New York: Ballantine Books, 1988 [1987]), 497; Richard Rhodes, *The Making of the Atomic Bomb* (New York: Touchstone Books, 1986), 683; Bruce Catton, *Waiting for the Morning Train: An American Boyhood* (Detroit: Wayne State University Press, 1987), 37–38, 220.

[3]Thomas Hobbes, *Leviathan: Or the Matter, Forme and Power of a Commonwealth Ecclesiastical and Civil*, ed. Michael Oakeshott (New York: Collier Books, 1962 [1651]), 73; Thucydides, *History of the Peloponnesian War*, II, ed. Rex Warner (Suffolk, England: Bungary, 1954), 39; Robert Harris and Jeremy Paxman, *A Higher Form of Killing: The Secret Story of Chemical and Biological Warfare* (New York: Hill and Wang, 1982), 117, 156–157, 231–232.

[4]Charles A. Beard, *The Navy: Defense or Portent?* (New York: Harper & Brothers, 1932), 70, 185; William Greider, *Secrets of the Temple: How the Federal Reserve Runs the Country* (New York: Touchstone Books, 1989), 324; David F. Noble, *America by Design: Science, Technology, and the Rise of Corporate Capitalism* (New York: Oxford University Press, 1979 [1977]), 258; John Keegan, *The Price of Admiralty: The Evolution of Naval Warfare* (New York: Viking Penguin, Inc., 1989), 50.

[5]Benjamin Franklin Cooling, "Bradley Allen Fiske: Inventor and Reformer in Uniform," in James C. Bradford, ed., *Admirals of the New Steel Navy: Makers of the American Naval Tradition, 1880–1930* (Annapolis: Naval Institute Press, 1990), 140; Robert O'Connell, *Of Arms and Men: A History of War, Weapons, and Aggression* (New York: Oxford University Press, 1989), 301; Andrew Hodges, *Alan Turing: The Enigma* (New York: Touchstone Books, 1984 [1983]), 364; Morris Janowitz, "Military Career Patterns and the Military Mind," in Russell F. Weigley, ed., *The American Military: Readings in the History of the Military in American Society* (Reading, Mass.: Addison-Wesley Publishing Company, 1969), 142–143.

[6]John King Fairbank, *Chinabound: A Fifty-Year Memoir* (New York: Harper Colophon Books, 1983 [1982]), 458; O'Connell, *Of Arms and Men*, 122–123; A. N. Wilson, *Tolstoy* (New York: Fawcett Columbine, 1988), 473.

CHAPTER NINETEEN

[1]*Time*, 8 November 1965, 36; Officer Biography, Rear Admiral Hiram Cassedy, NHD; Eugene Burdick, "The United States Navy," *Holiday*, 24 (October, 1958),

54–59, 92, 94, 96–99, 101–102; David Hackett Fischer, *Albion's Seed: Four British Folkways in America* (New York: Oxford University Press, 1989), 189; B. Franklin Cooling, *Benjamin Franklin Tracy: Father of the American Fighting Navy* (Hamden, Conn.: Archon Books, 1973), 66; Peter Karsten, *The Naval Aristocracy: The Golden Age of Annapolis and the Emergence of Modern American Navalism* (New York: Free Press, 1972), 35, 194–203.

[2]Tristram Coffin, *The Armed Society: Militarism in Modern America* (Baltimore: Penguin Books, 1964), 64–65; Arthur T. Hadley, *The Straw Giant, America's Armed Forces: Triumphs and Failures* (New York: Avon Books, 1987), 68–69; Thomas C. Hone, *Power and Change: The Administrative History of the Office of the Chief of Naval Operations, 1946–1986*, Contributions to Naval History . . . No. 2 (Washington, D.C.: Naval Historical Center, 1989), 65, 131; Carl H. Builder, *The Masks of War: American Military Styles in Strategy and Analysis* (Baltimore: Johns Hopkins University Press, 1989), 18–19, 29, 31–32, 36–37.

[3]James A. Field, Jr., *History of United States Naval Operations: Korea* (Washington, D.C.: Government Printing Office, 1962), 25; Vice Admiral George C. Dyer, *The Amphibians Came to Conquer: The Story of Admiral Richmond Kelly Turner*, II (Washington, D.C.: Government Printing Office, 1971), 1110; Admiral Raphael Semmes, *Memoirs of Service Afloat during the War between the States* (Secaucus, N.J.: Blue & Grey Press, 1987 [1868]), 412; Voltaire, *Candide, or Optimism* (New York: Appleton-Century-Crofts, 1946 [1759]), 85.

[4]Karsten, *The Naval Aristocracy*, 250–253; *Nation*, 19 April 1952, 359; Builder, *The Masks of War*, 21.

[5]Vincent Davis, *Postwar Defense Policy and the U.S. Navy, 1943–1946* (Chapel Hill: University of North Carolina Press, 1966), 80–82, 85–86; Karsten, *The Naval Aristocracy*, 386; Lieutenant W. H. Long, "Public Relations and the Peacetime Navy," *USNIP*, 71, n. 12 (December, 1945), 1469–1472 [emphasis in original].

[6]Lieutenant Junior Grade P. W. Rairden, Jr., "Navy Public Information," *USNIP*, 73, n. 1 (January, 1947), 47–53 [emphasis added]; Fred J. Cook, *The Warfare State* (New York: Collier Books, 1964 [1962], 106; Commander Richard Lane, "The Navy and Public Opinion," *USNIP*, 77, n. 3 (March, 1951), 285–287; Lieutenant Commander R. L. "Zeke" Cormier, "I Lead the Blue Angels," *Flying*, 55, n. 2 (August, 1954), 16–18, 42–43.

[7]Commander Daniel V. James, "Sell America," *USNIP*, 79, n. 5 (May, 1953), 523–527; Commander Richard A. Velz, "Wanted—Naval Officers and Their Families," *USNIP*, 80, n. 1 (January, 1954), 71–75; Lieutenant Commander Edmund L. Castillo, "The Art of Getting *Off* the Front Page," *USNIP*, 85, n. 3 (March, 1959), 37–43; Lieutenant William A. Platte, "The U.S. Navy's People-to-People Program," *USNIP*, 86, n. 7 (July, 1960), 55–60.

[8]Howard I. Chappelle, *The History of the American Sailing Navy: The Ships and Their Development* (New York: Bonanza Books, 1988 [1949]), 18–19, 362; Vice Admiral George C. Dyer, *On the Treadmill to Pearl Harbor: The Memoirs of Admiral James O. Richardson* (Washington, D.C.: Government Printing Office, 1973), 470; Builder, *The Masks of War*, 34–36; Russell K. Brown, *Fallen in Battle: American General Officer Combat Fatalities from 1775* (Westport, Conn.: Greenwood Press, 1988), 173–181; Robert J. Donovan, *Tumultuous Years: The Presidency of Harry S Truman, 1949–1953* (New York: W. W. Norton & Company, 1982), 68; Athan

G. Theoharis and John Stuart Cox, *The Boss: J. Edgar Hoover and the Great American Inquisition* (New York: Bantam Books, 1990 [1988]), 210; Jeffrey M. Dorwart, *Conflict of Duty: The U.S. Navy's Intelligence Dilemma, 1919–1945* (Annapolis: Naval Institute Press, 1983), *passim;* Martin Bauml Duberman, *Paul Robeson: A Biography* (New York: Ballantine Books, 1990), 376.

⁹Builder, *The Masks of War*, 25–26; Dyer, *The Amphibians Came to Conquer*, I, 22; *Business Week*, 16 January 1954, 32; Lewis H. Conarroe, "Buttering the Navy Brass," *Collier's*, 21 June 1947, 24–25, 91–93.

¹⁰Lieutenant Commander R. G. Alexander and Lieutenant W. L. Read, "Let's Get Rid of the Conveyor Belt!," *USNIP*, 83, n. 9 (September, 1957), 938–943; Captain Slade D. Cutter, Oral History, USNI, II (1985), NL, 499; Vice Admiral William P. Mack, Oral History, USNI, I (1980), NL, 237–240; Vice Admiral J. Victor Smith, Oral History, USNI (1977), NL, 255; Captain Glyn Jones, CHC, Oral History, USNI (1978), NL, 317–321; Commander Ralph Gerber, "The Choice of a Career within the Navy," *USNIP*, 79, n. 6 (June, 1953), 621–627; Dyer, *The Amphibians Came to Conquer*, II, 1144, 1056; Lieutenant Maynard Kniskern, "Officer Specialization and the Post-War Navy," *USNIP*, 72, n. 9 (September, 1946), 1035–1041 [emphasis in original].

¹¹Robert H. Ferrell, *American Diplomacy: A History*, Rev. ed. (New York: W. W. Norton & Company, Inc., 1969), 347; Hadley, *The Straw Giant*, 33–34; Dyer, *The Amphibians Came to Conquer*, II, 601; *Aviation Week*, 17 March 1952, 17–18; Davis, *Postwar Defense Policy*, 132–134.

¹²Antonia Fraser, *Cromwell: Our Chief of Men* (London: Methuen, 1985), 537; Stanley Karnow, *In Our Image: America's Empire in the Philippines* (New York: Ballantine Books, 1990), 162; Ronald Spector, *Admiral of the New Empire: The Life and Career of George Dewey* (Baton Rouge: Louisiana State University Press, 1974), 111–116; James Leutze, *A Different Kind of Victory: A Biography of Admiral Thomas C. Hart* (Annapolis: Naval Institute Press, 1981), 54 [emphasis in original], 317; Vice Admiral L. S. Sabin, "Deep Selections," *USNIP*, 86 n. 3 (March, 1960), 46–54 [emphasis in original]; *Newsweek*, 19 November 1945, 64–65; Admiral Alfred M. Pride, Oral History, USNI (1984), NL, 234–235; Vice Admiral Truman J. Hedding, Oral History, USNI (1972), NL, 187.

¹³James G. Schneider, *The Navy V-12 Program: Leadership for a Lifetime* (Boston: Houghton Mifflin Company, 1987), 299, 341–342; Builder, *The Masks of War*, 23–24; Captain W. D. Brinckloe, "Is the Versatile Line Officer Obsolete?," *USNIP*, 85, n. 6 (June, 1959), 27–34.

¹⁴Cook, *The Warfare State*, 52, 200–201; *U.S. News & World Report*, 27 April 1956, 55–56; Robert B. Holtman, *The Napoleonic Revolution* (Philadelphia: J. B. Lippincott Company, 1967), 57; Captain Joseph K. Taussig, Jr., "The State of Retired Officers," *USNIP*, 94, n. 3 (March, 1968), 72–79; Neil Sheehan, *A Bright Shining Lie: John Paul Vann and America in Vietnam* (New York: Vintage Books, 1989), 285.

CHAPTER TWENTY

¹Rear Admiral Charles E. Clark, *My Fifty Years in the Navy* (Annapolis: Naval Institute Press, 1984 [1917]), 141; Vincent Davis, *Postwar Defense Policy and the*

U.S. Navy, 1943–1946 (Chapel Hill: University of North Carolina Press, 1966), 135; Arthur T. Hadley, *The Straw Giant, America's Armed Forces: Triumphs and Failures* (New York: Avon Books, 1987), 82.

[2] Officer Biography, Admiral Thomas L. Sprague, NHD; Commander Herman Reich, "Officers for the Post-War Navy," *USNIP*, 71, n. 9 (September, 1945), 1029–1031; Rear Admiral David L. Martineau, "1947—A Very Good Year," *USNIP*, 103, n 9 (September, 1977), 25–31; Samuel Eliot Morison, *History of United States Naval Operations in World War II*, XII: *Leyte, June 1944–January 1945* (Boston: Little, Brown and Company, 1975), 125, 420.

[3] Commander John S. McCain, Jr., "Where Do We Go from Here?," *USNIP*, 75, n. 1 (January, 1949), 47–51; Captain Robert B. Kelly, "The Education of the Line," *USNIP*, 85, n. 12 (December, 1959), 48–52; Diane Ravitch, *The Troubled Crusade: American Education, 1945–1980* (New York: Basic Books, Inc, 1983), 228.

[4] Officer Biography, Admiral James L. Holloway, Jr., *NHD;* Jack Sweetman, *The U.S. Naval Academy: An Illustrated History* (Annapolis: Naval Institute Press, 1979), 202–215; Rear Admiral Roy S. Benson, Oral History, USNI, II (1987), NL, 588–589; Commander William P. Mack and Commander H. F. Rommel, "NAPS Comes of Age," *USNIP*, 76, n. 10 (October, 1950), 1107–1113; Hanson W. Baldwin, "The Academies: Old Ideals, New Methods," *New York Times Magazine*, 16 April 1961, 32–33, 84, 86, 88, 90, 92.

[5] David Boroff, "Annapolis: Teaching Young Sea Dogs Old Tricks," *Harper's Magazine*, 226, n. 1352 (January, 1963), 46–52; Luther J. Carter, "Naval Academy: Lockstep Program Is Abandoned," *Science*, 150, n. 3699 (19 November 1965), 1008–1012; *Newsweek*, 8 November 1965, 66; Sweetman, *The U.S. Naval Academy*, 215–226; Tristram Coffin, *The Armed Society: Militarism in Modern America* (Baltimore: Penguin Books, 1964), 68–69; Baldwin, "The Academies," 92; Clark G. Reynolds, *Admiral John H. Towers: The Struggle for Naval Air Supremacy* (Annapolis: Naval Institute Press, 1991), 14; Admiral Charles K. Duncan, Oral History, USNI, II (1981), NL, 1225–1231.

[6] James G. Schneider, *The Navy V-12 Program: Leadership for a Lifetime* (Boston: Houghton Mifflin Company, 1987), 304–308; *Time*, 20 January 1947, 79–80; "The Holloway Plan: The Navy's College Training Program," *Personnel and Guidance Journal*, 25 (February, 1947), 292; Rear Admiral James L. Holloway, Jr., "The Holloway Plan—A Summary View and Commentary," *USNIP*, 73, n. 11 (November, 1949), 1293–1303; Duncan, Oral History, I (1978), 220–223; Vice Admiral William R. Smedberg III, Oral History, USNI, I (1979), NL, 394–396, 418–419.

[7] Homer C. Rose, "Educational Team Helps Train Naval Officers," *Industrial Arts and Vocational Education*, 42 (June, 1953), 198; Homer C. Rose, "Civilian Educators Help Train Naval Officers," *Industrial Arts and Vocational Education*, 42 (December, 1953), 329–330; "Maybe This Is for You," *Collier's*, 25 October 1947, 110; Captain John V. Noel, Oral History, USNI (1987), NL, 111–112; *Newsweek*, 15 September 1947, 89.

[8] Brigadier General William B. McKean, USMC, "Demise of a Dream," *SM*, 21, n. 1 (January, 1958), 2, 4–6; Lieutenant Peter H. Smith, "The NROTC Plight," *USNIP*, 91, n. 10 (October, 1965), 64–67; Admiral James L. Holloway, Jr., and

Jack Sweetman, "A Gentleman's Agreement," *USNIP*, 106, n. 9 (September, 1980), 71–77.

⁹R. L. Johnson, Jr., "Weariest Sailors in the Navy," *Saturday Evening Post*, 23 October 1954, 28–29, 81–82, 84; "The ROC School, Treasure Island, California," *USNIP*, 77, n. 10 (October, 1951), 1093–1101; Benson, Oral History, II, 484–485.

¹⁰Vice Admiral Raymond E. Peet, Oral History, USNI (1984), NL, 52–53; Commander John G. Carl, "The Technical PG Quandary," *USNIP*, 89. n. 9 (September, 1963), 42–45; *SNR*, in *SDR* (1 July 1960–30 June 1961), 222; Lieutenant Commander Frank H. Featherston, "P. G. School," *USNIP*, 89, n. 12 (December, 1963), 62–71; Rear Admiral Robert W. McNitt, "The Naval Postgraduate School: Sixty Years Young," *USNIP*, 96, n. 6 (June, 1970), 68–78; Reynolds, *Admiral John H. Towers*, 518; Rear Admiral Edward K. Walker, Oral History, USNI (1985), NL, 268–269; Rear Admiral Raymond D. Tarbuck, Oral History, USNI (1973), NL, 36–37; Rear Admiral John S. Coye, Jr., Oral History, USNI (1983), NL, 137–140; Vice Admiral Kleber S. Masterson, Oral History, USNI (1973), NL, 188–191; Admiral Alfred G. Ward, Oral History, USNI (1972), NL, 151–155.

¹¹Rear Admiral Francis D. Foley, Oral History, USNI, II (1988), NL, 549; Lieutenant Commander Robb White, "$2,000 a Month Pilots," *USNIP*, 76, n. 6 (June, 1950), 641–645; *Life*, 21 May 1951, 119–120; "Annapolis of the Air," *Collier's*, 19 May 1951, 30–31; "Training Navy Pilots," *Flying*, 49, n. 5 (November, 1951), 99–101, 168–169; Rear Admiral Arthur W. Price, Jr., Oral History, USNI (1980), NL, 111–114.

¹²*U.S. News & World Report*, 6 February 1953, 35, 37–38; Rear Admiral George van Deurs, "The Admiral Sounds Off," *Flying*, 3, n. 1 (July, 1953), 22, 64; "Navy Rejects $7 Million Saving," *Nation's Business* (December, 1956), 28–29, 78–79.

¹³James R. Greenwood, "Navy's New Training Program," *Flying*, 60, n. 5 (May, 1957), 34–36, 80–82; Commander H. C. Hogan, "NAO—The Navy's Newest Career Opportunity," *USNIP*, 87, n. 3 (March, 1961), 62–67.

¹⁴Lieutenant Commander Edgar K. Lofton, "A Modern Navy for Modern Defense," *USNIP*, 86, n. 11 (November, 1960), 56–61; Commander Ralph Gerber, "The Engineerng Duty Officer in the Navy Today," *USNIP*, 78, n. 3 (March, 1952), 293–297; Charles R. Peck, "Engineering Duty Officers: The Dwindling Muster," *USNIP*, 91, n. 12 (December, 1965), 46–54; Lieutenant Commander John T. Rigsbee, "Is Experience Enough?," *USNIP*, 88, n. 10 (October, 1962), 41–45.

¹⁵Harold D. Langley, *Social Reform in the United States Navy, 1798–1862* (Urbana: University of Illinois Press, 1967), 23; Commander Russell S. Crenshaw, Jr., "Why We Are Losing Our Junior Officers," *USNIP*, 83, n. 2 (February, 1957), 127–132.

¹⁶"The Problems of the 'Hump'," *SM*, 20, n. 4 (April, 1957), 5–7, 15; Lieutenant Commander John A. Chastain, "Inside the Hump," *USNIP*, 85, n. 7 (July, 1959), 48–58; Commander E. R. Zumwalt, Jr., "Beyond the Hump," *USNIP*, 85, n. 7 (July, 1959), 59–65.

¹⁷*Newsweek*, 7 September 1959, 34; Vice Admiral A.E. Jarrell, "Lessons Learned from the Hump," *USNIP*, 86, n. 8 (August, 1960), 79–86; Captain John H.

Hitchcock, "Discrimination in Selections: Fact or Fancy?," *USNIP*, 86, n. 9 (September, 1960), 72–75 [emphasis in original].

[18]Rear Admiral Ray C. Needham, "Officer Evaluation and Promotion," *USNIP*, 86, n. 3 (March, 1960), 60–69; Lieutenant J. W. Hopkins, SC, "Digging Out Buried Talent in the Navy," *USNIP*, 86, n. 5 (May, 1960), 67–71; Colonel David H. Hackworth, USA, *About Face: The Odyssey of an American Warrior* (New York: Touchstone Books, 1990 [1989]), 201, 347–348.

CHAPTER TWENTY-ONE

[1]James Boswell, *The Life of Samuel Johnson* (London, 1791), 86: N.A.M. Rodger, *The Wooden World: An Anatomy of the Georgian Navy* (Annapolis: Naval Institute Press, 1986), 60; Craig Symonds, "William S. Bainbridge: Bad Luck or Fatal Flaw?" in James C. Bradford, ed., *Command Under Sail: Makers of the American Naval Tradition, 1775–1850* (Annapolis: Naval Institute Press, 1985), 112; Thomas Babington Macaulay, *History of England*, I (London, 1849), ch. 3; Philip Ziegler, *Diana Cooper* (New York: Harper & Row, 1987 [1982]), 164.

[2]Rodger, *The Wooden World*, 118; Admiral Raphael Semmes, CSN, *Memoirs of Service Afloat* (Secaucus, N.J.: Blue & Grey Press, 1987 [1868]), 283, 420; James C. Bradford, "John Paul Jones: Honor and Professionalism," in Bradford, *Command Under Sail*, 24; Alfred Thayer Mahan, "A Distinction between Colonies and Dependencies," in Robert Seager II and Doris D. Maguire, eds., *Letters and Papers of Alfred Thayer Mahan*, III (Annapolis: Naval Institute Press, 1975), 596.

[3]Harold D. Langley, *Social Reform in the United States Navy, 1798–1862* (Urbana: University of Illinois Press, 1967), 41, 110; Christopher McKee, *A Gentlemanly and Honorable Profession: The Creation of the U.S. Naval Officer Corps, 1794–1815* (Annapolis: Naval Institute Press, 1991), 447; Robert W. Daly, ed., *Aboard the USS Monitor, 1862: The Letters of Acting-Paymaster William Frederick Keeler, U.S. Navy, to His Wife, Anna*, Naval Letters Series, I (Annapolis: Naval Institute Press, 1964), 8; Geoffrey S. Smith, "Charles Wilkes: The Naval Officer as Explorer and Diplomat," in James C. Bradford, ed., *Captains of the Old Steam Navy: Makers of the American Naval Tradition, 1840–1880* (Annapolis: Naval Institute Press, 1986), 67; Charles M. Todorich, "Franklin Buchanan: Symbol for Two Navies," in Bradford, *Captains of the Old Steam Navy*, 92, 98; Semmes, *Memoirs of Service Afloat*, 237, 159.

[4]McKee, *A Gentlemanly and Honorable Profession*, 442; Paul R. Schratz, *Submarine Commander* (Lexington: University Press of Kentucky, 1988), 250; Semmes, *Memoirs of Service Afloat*, 116, 238; Allen M. Brandt, *No Magic Bullet: A Social History of Venereal Disease in the United States since 1880* (New York: Oxford University Press, 1987), 52–53, 57–59, 68, 114, 62–63, 73–75, 164; *Newsweek*, 12 November 1945, 82, 84; "1940: Fifty Years Ago," *American Heritage*, 41, n. 5 (July–August, 1990), 38; Frederick S. Harrod, *Manning the New Navy: The Development of a Modern Naval Enlisted Force, 1899–1940* (Westport, Conn.: Greenwood Press, 1978), 11, 51, 156–157, 160–162, 117, 136; Rear Admiral Kemp Tolley, Oral History, USNI, I (1983), NL, 128–130; Captain John V. Noel, Oral History, USNI (1987), NL, 164–167.

[5]Vice Admiral George C. Dyer, *The Amphibians Came to Conquer: The Story of Admiral*

Richmond Kelly Turner, I (Washington, D.C.: Government Printing Office, 1971), 53; Ernie Pyle, "On Board a Fighting Ship," in Edward K. Eckert, ed., *In War and Peace: An American Military History Anthology* (Belmont, Cal.: Wadsworth Publishing Company, 1990), 295; Edmund A. Gibson, "More about the 'Caste System,' " *USNIP*, 75, n. 9 (September, 1949), 1005–1009.

[6]*SNR*, in *SDR* (1 January–30 June 1956), 186–196; *SNR*, in *SDR* (1 January–30 June 1957), 220–229; Harrod, *Manning the New Navy*, 10–11, 97–100; *SNR*, in *SDR* (1 July 1958–30 June 1959), 233; *SNR*, in *SDR* (1 July 1959–30 June 1960), 260; *SNR*, in *SDR* (1 July 1960–30 June 1961), 223; Vice Admiral George C. Dyer, *On the Treadmill to Pearl Harbor: The Memoirs of Admiral J. O. Richardson* (Washington, D.C.: Government Printing Office, 1973), 55; Captain B. H. Shupper, "Modern Enlisted Personnel Distribution," *USNIP*, 85, n. 4 (April, 1959), 91–96.

[7]*Time*, 13 August 1945, 20; Rear Admiral T. L. Sprague, "Navy Recruiting Policy for Secondary Schools," *School Life*, 30, n. 4 (January, 1948), 11–12; Rear Admiral Jackson K. Parker, Oral History, USNI (1987), NL, 125–127; Chief Boatswain's Mate Raymond F. Marshall, "Reflections of a Navy Recruiter," *USNIP*, 75, n. 4 (April, 1949), 405–413; "Navy Fishes for Volunteers—Drafts, Too," *Business Week*, 24 September 1955, 30; *Newsweek*, 26 September 1955, 37–38; Tristram Coffin, "The Threat of Militarism," in Russell F. Weigley, ed., *The American Military: Readings in the History of the Military in American Society* (Reading, Mass.: Addison-Wesley Publishing Company, 1969), 160; Chief Journalist O. S. Roloff, "One Hundred and Eighty Years of Naval Recruiting," *USNIP*, 82, n. 12 (December, 1956), 1301–1308; "Psychiatric Screening Works in Navy Program," *Science News Letter*, 13 November 1954, 311.

[8]Chief Quartermaster W. J. Miller, "Reenlistment: A Key Factor in a Strong Navy," *USNIP*, 80, n. 4 (April, 1954), 403–412; Eugene Burdick, "The United States Navy," *Holiday*, 24 (October, 1958), 54–59, 92, 94, 96–99, 101–102; *Life*, 5 November 1945, 35, 41.

[9]Milton Lehman, "Why Are They Quitting?," *Saturday Evening Post*, 30 July 1955, 34–35, 70, 72, 74; "What about the Navy?," *America*, 19 October 1957, 59; John G. Hubbell, "To Give Our Young Men a Goal," *Reader's Digest*, 76, n. 457 (May, 1960), 37–42; *Newsweek*, 27 February 1961, 27, 30.

[10]Vice Admiral Malcolm W. Cagle, "The New Naval Training Command," *SM*, 35, n. 3 (March, 1972), 7–10; John G. Hubbell, "How Our Troops Are Trained for Combat," *Reader's Digest*, 79, n. 474 (October, 1961), 57–61; *SNR*, in *SDR* (1 January–30 June 1950), 120; *SNR*, in *SDR* (1 January–30 June 1951), 182–183.

[11]Captain W. J. Catlett, Jr., "Recruits and Basic Leadership Opportunities," *USNIP*, 83, n. 11 (November, 1957), 1159–1167; Paul Lee, "From Boot to Electronic Whiz-Kid," *Popular Mechanics*, 97, n. 3 (March, 1952), 123–127, 278, 280; "20 Techs behind the Pilot," *Flying*, 49, n. 5 (November, 1951), 77–78, 139; *Newsweek*, 21 December 1953, 86–88; "Men under Pressure," *Look*, 28 December 1954, 57–60; *Newsweek*, 22 September 1958, 74.

[12]T. L. Bosiljevac, *SEALS: UDT/SEAL Operations in Vietnam* (New York: Ivy Books, 1990), 5–6; Edwin Muller, "Exploits of the Navy's Frogmen," *Reader's Digest* (April, 1952), 105–108; Andrew R. Boone, "How You Become a Frogman,"

Popular Science, 160, n. 5 (May, 1952), 135–138; Bill Stapleton, "Navy Frog-men—Top Skin-Divers of Them All," *Collier's*, 27 May 1955, 84–89; *Life*, 12 September 1955, 141–142, 144, 146; Theodore Roscoe, "The Navy's Frogmen: Underwater Astronauts," *New York Times Magazine*, 9 August 1959, 18, 49, 51; Frank Harvey, "Navy Jetboat Snatches Frogmen on the Run," *Popular Science*, 177, n. 2 (August, 1960), 50–52; John G. Hubbell, "Hell Week at Little Creek," *Reader's Digest*, 77, n. 464 (December, 1960), 81–86.

[13]Captain C. A. Bartholomew, *Mud, Muscles, and Miracles: Marine Salvage in the United States Navy* (Washington, D.C.: Naval Historical Center and Naval Sea Systems Command, 1990), 395; "Initial Success—or *Failure*," *USNIP*, 88, n. 12 (December, 1962), 93–105.

[14]Langley, *Social Reform in the United States Navy*, 150, 181; Harrod, *Manning the New Navy*, 115–128; Barry Miles, *Ginsberg: A Biography* (New York: Perennial, 1990), 45, 54; Don Eddy, "How to Make Bad Boys Good," *American Magazine*, 140 (September, 1945), 32–33, 138, 140; Fred B. Barton, "Mending Broken Gobs," *Rotarian*, 72 (June, 1948), 22–25; *Time*, 25 July 1955, 32, 35; J. Douglas Grant and Marguerite Q. Grant, "A Group Dynamics Approach to the Treatment of Nonconformists in the Navy," *Annals of the American Academy of Political and Social Science*, 322 (March, 1959), 126–135.

[15]"Enlisted Men's Barracks," *Architectural Record*, 112 (September, 1952), 188–196; Harold Seymour, *Baseball*, III: *The People's Game* (New York: Oxford University Press, 1990), 300–305, 310–315, 352–354; Lieutenant Junior Grade Ronald C. Hallberg, "Recreation Afloat," *Recreation*, 58 (November, 1965), 439–442; E. M. Waller, "Recreation Forty Fathoms Down," *Recreation*, 53 (February, 1960), 56–58.

[16]Helen E. Hendrick, "Libraries Ashore and Afloat," *Wilson Library Bulletin*, 27 (June, 1953), 831–832; Helen Hendrick, "Booking a Voyage," *Library Journal*, 83, n. 12 (15 June 1958), 1884–1886; Ruby Hannah, "Navy Bibliotherapy," *Library Journal*, 80, n. 10 (15 May 1955), 1171–1176; Howard S. Dewey, "The Navy Is Grateful to Schoolmarm Brady," *Coronet*, 32 (August, 1952), 104–107; R. M. Foster and J. F. Ballard, "The Navy's Literacy Training Program," *School Life*, 36, n. 2 (November, 1953), 31–32; *Time*, 8 August 1960, 66.

[17.]Clyde E. Weaver and Chalmer E. Faw, "A Day with the Navy," *Christian Century*, 69 (2 July 1952), 777–778; "Laymen Take Hold," *America*, 101 (4 July 1959), 483.

[18]"Submariners Eat Better," *Science News Letter*, 59 (19 May 1951), 307; "Navy Chow Maid," *American Magazine*, 153 (January, 1952), 50; *U.S. News & World Report*, 20 May 1955, 77–81; *Newsweek*, 17 September 1951, 21–22.

[19]Parker, Oral History, 92; Rear Admiral Draper L. Kauffman, Oral History, USNI, I (1982), NL, 345–348; Chief Machinist's Mate Richard M. McKenna, "The Post-War Chief Petty Officer: A Closer Look," *USNIP*, 74, n. 12 (December, 1948), 1481–1485; Commander Joseph L. Miller, "The Navy Has No Foreman's Problem," *USNIP*, 76, n. 3 (March, 1950), 265–267; Chief Personnelman Don A. Kelso, "The Role of the Chief Petty Officer in the Modern Navy," *USNIP*, 83, n. 4 (April, 1957), 386–391; Captain Slade D. Cutter, Oral History, USNI, I (1985), NL, 265–266; Master Chief Journalist William J. Miller, "New Horizons in the Enlisted Navy," *USNIP*, 85, n. 11 (November, 1959), 34–38; John

D. Alden, *The American Steel Navy: A Photographic History of the U.S. Navy from the Introduction of the Steel Hull in 1883 to the Cruise of the Great White Fleet, 1907–1909* (Annapolis: Naval Institute Press, 1989 [1972]), 280.

CHAPTER TWENTY-TWO

[1] Vice Admiral George C. Dyer, *The Amphibians Came to Conquer: The Story of Admiral Richmond Kelly Turner* (Washington, D.C.: Government Printing Office, 1971), 42; Rear Admiral Charles E. Clark, *My Fifty Years in the Navy* (Annapolis: Naval Institute Press, 1984 [1917]), 126; Vice Admiral Ruthven E. Libby, Oral History, USNI (1984), NL, 48; Captain K. C. McIntosh, SC, "Ships and Shoes and Sealing Wax," *USNIP*, 75, n. 2 (February, 1949), 135–147.

[2] *SNR*, in *SDR* (1 July 1960–30 June 1961), 266–267; Captain John V. Noel, Oral History, USNI (1987), NL, 158–159; Captain Roland W. Faulk, CHC, Oral History, USNI (1975), NL, 14–15; Captain Glyn Jones, CHC, Oral History, USNI (1978), NL, 205–210; Captain John H. Shilling, CHC, "Church Call Without a Chaplain," *USNIP*, 85, n. 5 (May, 1959), 70–73.

[3] Rear Admiral Lamont Pugh, MC, "Doctors for the Armed Forces," *USNIP*, 80, n. 1 (January, 1954), 33–45; Tristram Coffin, *The Armed Society: Militarism in Modern America* (Baltimore: Penguin Books, 1964), 78; Commander Philip B. Phillips, MC, "The Navy's Medical Problem," *USNIP*, 81, n. 4 (April, 1955), 391–399; *SNR*, in *SDR* (1 July 1958–30 June 1959), 254–257; *SNR*, in *SDR* (1 July 1959–30 June 1960), 280–286; *SNR*, in *SDR* (1 July 1960–30 June 1961), 247–251; Admiral Charles K. Duncan, Oral History, USNI, I (1978), NL, 438–440; III (1983), NL, 1333–1334.

[4] *Time*, 5 October 1959, 70; Arturo F. Gonzalez, Jr. "Worldwide Disease Busters: The Navy Medics," *Today's Health*, 42 (September, 1964), 36–38; William R. Vath, "He's the Navy's Top Doctor," *Today's Health*, 40 (October, 1962), 32–33, 76–82; Noel, Oral History, 115–118; *SNR*, in *SDR* (1 July 1958–30 June 1959), 255; *SNR*, in *SDR* (1 July 1960–30 June 1961), 249; *Time*, 8 April 1966, 47.

[5] *SNR*, in *SDR* (1 January–30 June 1956), 243–246; *SNR*, in *SDR* (1 July 1958–30 June 1959), 274–275; Christopher McKee, *A Gentlemanly and Honorable Profession: The Creation of the U.S. Naval Officer Corps, 1794–1815* (Annapolis: Naval Institute Press, 1991), 19; *SNR*, in *SDR* (1 July 1959–30 June 1960), 301–303; *SNR*, in *SDR* (1 July 1960–30 June 1961), 269–271; Rear Admiral Roy S. Benson, Oral History, USNI, II (1987), NL, 820–822, 853–854.

[6] Martin Binkin and Shirley J. Bach, *Women and the Military* (Washington, D.C.: Brookings Institution, 1977), 5; Frederick S. Harrod, *Manning the New Navy: The Development of a Modern Naval Enlisted Force, 1899–1940* (Westport, Conn.: Greenwood Press, 1978), 64–67 [emphasis in original]; *WP*, 4 December 1990, A17; "Women in the Navy," *SM*, 45, n. 2 (March, 1982), 14–15.

[7] Harrod, *Manning the New Navy*, 67; Clark G. Reynolds, *Admiral John H. Towers: The Struggle for Naval Air Supremacy* (Annapolis: Naval Institute Press, 1991), 381, 482; "Women in the Navy," 14; Binkin and Bach, *Women and the Military*, 7; Fleet Admiral William D. Leahy, *I Was There* (New York: Whittlesey House, 1950), 166; Lieutenant E. Louise Stewart, USMCR, "Women in Uniform," in

Lieutenant William Harrison Fetridge, ed., *The Second Navy Reader* (Indianapolis: Bobbs-Merrill Company, 1944), 333–338; Captain Mildred McAfee, Oral History, USNI (1971), NL, 35–41; Lieutenant Commander Mary Jo Shelly, Oral History, USNI (1970), NL, 21, 30–33, 64–65; Susan H. Godson, "The Waves in World War II," *USNIP*, 107, n. 12 (December, 1981), 46–51; *Newsweek*, 31 July 1972, 12–13; "Education Directly Related to Duties of WAVE Personnel," *Education for Victory*, 3, n. 19 (3 April 1945), 20–21; Vice Admiral Gerald E. Miller, Oral History, USNI, I (1983), NL, 103–104; Patricia J. Thomas, "From Yeomanettes to WAVES to Women in the U.S. Navy," in David R. Segal and H. Wallace Sinaiko, eds., *Life in the Rank and File: Enlisted Men and Women in the Armed Forces of the United States, Australia, Canada, and the United Kingdom* (New York: Pergamon-Brassey's, 1986), 98; Captain Rosario M. Rausa, USNR, "Grace Murray Hopper," *NH*, 6, n. 3 (Fall, 1992), 58–60.

[8]Vice Admiral Charles Wellborn, Jr., Oral History, USNI (1972), NL, 224–227; Captain Joy Bright Hancock, Oral History, USNI (1970), NL, 72–76, 111–114, 131–134; Godson, "The Waves in World War II," 51; "Women in the Navy," 14–15; David R. Segal, *Recruiting for Uncle Sam: Citizenship and Military Manpower Policy* (Lawrence: University Press of Kansas, 1989), 118–120; Martha A. Marsden, "The Continuing Debate: Women Soldiers in the U.S. Army," in Segal and Sinaiko, eds., *Life in the Rank and File*, 64–65; Thomas, "From Yeomanettes to WAVES to Women in the U.S. Navy," 104–105, 107; Binkin and Bach, *Women and the Military*, 10–12; Rear Admiral John S. Coye, Jr., Oral History, USNI (1983), NL, 197–202; Vice Admiral Raymond E. Peet, Oral History, USNI (1984), NL, 71–72; Admiral Roy L Johnson, Oral History, USNI (1982), NL, 17–18; Rear Admiral Charles Adair, Oral History, USNI (1977), NL, 483–485.

[9]Lieutenant Robert A. Rogers III, "These Boots Wear Skirts," *USNIP*, 75, n. 9 (September, 1949), 1023–1027; "Women Are Very Efficient Sailors," *Flying*, 49, n. 5 (November, 1951), 114–115, 152; Jonathan Katz, *Gay American History: Lesbians and Gay Men in the U.S.A.* (New York: Harper & Row, 1985 [1976]), 439 [emphasis in original]; Binkin and Bach, *Women and the Military*, 12; Duncan, Oral History, III, 1310–1312; Noel, Oral History, 134–136.

[10]N.A.M. Rodger, *The Wooden World: An Anatomy of the Georgian Navy* (Annapolis: Naval Institute Press, 1986), 227; B. R. Burg, *Sodomy and the Pirate Tradition: English Sea Rovers in the Seventeenth-Century Caribbean* (New York: New York University Press, 1983), *passim*; McKee, *A Gentlemanly and Honorable Profession*, 438; Harold D. Langley, *Social Reform in the United States Navy, 1798–1862* (Urbana: University of Illinois Press, 1967), 172–174; Herman Melville, *White-Jacket, or The World in a Man-of-War* (Chicago: Newberry Library, 1970 [1850]), 375–376; Harrod, *Manning the New Navy*, 117; Katz, *Gay American History*, 50; Vice Admiral Roland N. Smoot, Oral History, USNI (1972), NL, 118–121; Rear Admiral Edward Buttevant Barry File, National Personnel Records Center [I am indebted to Professor William Cogar of the Department of History, United States Naval Academy, for this reference]; Lawrence R. Murphy, *Perverts by Official Order: The Campaign Against Homosexuals in the United States Navy* (New York: Haworth Press, 1988), *passim*.

[11]Faulk, Oral History, 273–277; Katz, *Gay American History*, 114, 96, 101–104; *New*

York Times, 31 August 1952, 32:6; Coffin, *The Armed Society*, 80; Colin J. Williams and Martin S. Weinberg, *Homosexuals and the Military: A Study of Less Than Honorable Discharge* (New York: Harper & Row, 1971), 49, 108–109, 25; Captain Stephen Jurika, Jr., Oral History, USNI, II (1979), NL, 802–807; Duncan, Oral History, III, 1302–1305.

[12] Bradley F. Smith, *The War's Long Shadow: The Second World War and Its Aftermath— China, Russia, Britain, America* (New York: Simon and Schuster, 1986), 141; William R. Kreh, *Citizen Sailors: The U.S. Naval Reserve in War and Peace* (New York: David McKay Company, Inc., 1969), 193–195, 217–222; Abbott A. Brayton, "American Reserve Policies Since World War II," *MA*, 36, n. 4 (December, 1972), 139–144; Rear Admiral I. M. McQuiston, "History of the Reserves Since the Second World War," *MA*, 17, n. 1 (Spring, 1953), 23–27; Benson, Oral History, II, 568–570.

[13] Rear Admiral Francis D. Foley, Oral History, USNI, II (1988), NL, 583–588; Brayton, "American Reserve Policies Since World War II," 140–141; McQuiston, "History of the Reserves Since the Second World War," 25; Lieutenant Commander William Thompson, "The Selected Reserve: Ready for the First GQ," *USNIP*, 88, n. 1 (January, 1962), 69–77.

[14] Vice Admiral George C. Dyer, *On the Treadmill to Pearl Harbor: The Memoirs of Admiral James O. Richardson* (Washington, D.C.: Government Printing Office, 1973), 64; Vice Admiral Charles A. Lockwood, *Sink 'Em All: Submarine Warfare in the Pacific* (New York: E. P. Dutton & Co., Inc., 1951), 392–393; "Trade Winds," *Saturday Review of Literature*, 10 November 1945, 28–29; Memorandum, Commander C.F. Adams, Jr., to Captain H. O. Larson, "Proposed Post War Naval Reserve," 23 October 1945, Box 202 (P16-1), NHD; Captain Howard G. Copeland, "A Post-War Naval Reserve," *USNIP*, 72, n. 6 (June, 1946), 813–823; Captain Charles J. Merdinger, Oral History, USNI (1974), NL, 21–22.

[15] Brayton, "American Reserve Policies Since World War II," 141, 143; *SNR*, in *SDR* (1 January–30 June 1950), 123; *SNR*, in *SDR* (1 January–30 June 1951), 184–185; *SNR*, in *SDR* (1 January–30 June 1954), 185-187; *SNR*, in *SDR* (1 January–30 June 1953), 192–193.

[16] Frances Hansford, "The Navy's Air Reserve," *Flying*, 45, n. 6 (June, 1946), 22–23, 80; Charles L. Black, "A Report on the Naval Air Reserve," *Flying*, 49, n. 3 (March, 1950), 16–17, 46–47; Norman Sklarewitz, "Navy's Trial Enlistment," *Flying*, 52, n. 5 (May, 1953), 34–35, 60–61.

[17] Commander D.J. Carrison, "Reserves—What Kind?," *USNIP*, 81, n. 5 (May, 1955), 528–533; Brayton, "American Reserve Policies Since World War II," 143–144; *Look*, 24 August 1954, 15; Duncan, Oral History, II (1981), NL, 748–751.

[18] Father Joseph T. O'Callahan, *I Was the Chaplain on the* Franklin (New York: MacMillan Company, 1961 [1956]), 3; Dyer, *On the Treadmill to Pearl Harbor*, 177–178.

CHAPTER TWENTY-THREE

[1] Admiral Charles K. Duncan, Oral History, USNI, III (1983), NL, 1294–1295; Frederick S. Harrod, *Manning the New Navy: The Development of a Modern Naval*

Enlisted Force, 1899–1940 (Westport, Conn.: Greenwood Press, 1978), 53, 60–62, 222, n. 72; Stanley Karnow, *In Our Image: America's Empire in the Philippines* (New York: Ballantine Books, 1990), 17; Martin Binkin and Mark J. Eitelberg, *Blacks and the Military* (Washington, D.C.: Brookings Institution, 1982), 18; Ronald Takaki, *Strangers from a Different Shore: A History of Asian Americans* (New York: Penguin Books, 1990), 417, 419, 432–436; Vice Admiral Raymond E. Peet, Oral History, USNI (1984), NL, 336–338.

[2]James Leutze, *A Different Kind of Victory: A Biography of Admiral Thomas C. Hart* (Annapolis: Naval Institute Press, 1981), 204; Richard Rhodes, *The Making of the Atomic Bomb* (New York: Touchstone Books, 1988), 295; Bernard C. Nalty, *Strength for the Fight: A History of Black Americans in the Military* (New York: Free Press, 1989), 8, 14, 20–21, 26–27; Peter Olsen, "The Negro and the Sea," *Negro History Bulletin*, 35, n. 2 (February, 1972), 40–44; Jack D. Foner, *Blacks and the Military in American History* (New York: Praeger Publishers, 1974), 21; Harold D. Langley, *Social Reform in the United States Navy, 1798–1862* (Urbana: University of Illinois Press, 1967), 92–95.

[3]Nalty, *Strength for the Fight*, 32–33, 63, 71–72; Olsen, "The Negro and the Sea," 41; Foner, *Blacks and the Military*, 67–68, 83, 103–106; Harrod, *Manning the New Navy*, 55.

[4]Nalty, *Strength for the Fight*, 78–86, 122–123; Foner, *Blacks and the Military*, 105–106, 124; Olsen, "The Negro and the Sea," 41; Richard M. Dalfiume, *Desegregation of the U.S. Armed Forces: Fighting on Two Fronts, 1939–1953* (Columbia: University of Missouri Press, 1969), 22; Harrod, *Manning the New Navy*, 60, 168; Lieutenant Dennis D. Nelson, *The Integration of the Negro into the U.S. Navy* (New York: Farrar, Straus and Young, 1951), 7.

[5]Morris J. MacGregor, Jr., *Integration of the Armed Forces, 1940–1965* (Washington, D.C.: Center of Military History, 1980), 4–6; Nalty, *Strength for the Fight*, 85–86; Dalfiume, *Desegregation of the U.S. Armed Forces*, 29–30, 38; Harrod, *Manning the New Navy*, 62.

[6]Nalty, *Strength for the Fight*, 184–186; Binkin and Eitelberg, *Blacks and the Military*, 42; MacGegor, *Integration of the Armed Forces*, 36, n. 47; Nelson, *The Integration of the Negro*, 24–26; Eric Larrabee, *Commander in Chief: Franklin Delano Roosevelt, His Lieutenants, and Their War* (New York: Touchstone Books, 1988), 632; Jeffrey M. Dorwart, *Conflict of Duty: The U.S. Navy's Intelligence Dilemma, 1919–1945* (Annapolis: Naval Institute Press, 1983), 188, 222–223, 225.

[7]MacGregor, *Integration of the Armed Forces*, 58–67; Foster Hailey, "Pilots, Man Your Planes!," in Lieutenant William Harrison Fetridge, ed., *The Navy Reader* (Indianapolis: Bobbs-Merrill Company, 1943), 78; John Field, "Life and Death of the U.S.S. *Yorktown*," in Fetridge, *The Navy Reader*, 155; Arnold Rampersad, *The Life of Langston Hughes*, II: *I Dream a World, 1941–1967* (New York: Oxford University Press, 1988), 50 [emphasis in original]; Lieutenant F. T. Greene, "Mess Boy of Squadron X," in Lieutenant William Harrison Fetridge, ed., *The Second Navy Reader* (Indianapolis: Bobbs-Merrill Company, 1944), 259–262.

[8]MacGregor, *Integration of the Armed Forces*, 67–75; Olsen, "The Negro and the Sea," 41; Nalty, *Strength for the Fight*, 188–190; Foner, *Blacks and the Military*, 166–169; Dalfiume, *Desegregation of the U.S. Armed Forces*, 53–56.

[9]Dalfiume, *Desegregation of the U.S. Armed Forces*, 101–103; Nalty, *Strength for the*

Fight, 190; MacGregor, *Integration of the Armed Forces*, 75–77; Nelson, *The Integration of the Negro*, 38–73.

[10] MacGregor, *Integration of the Armed Forces*, 77–80; Foner, *Blacks and the Military*, 171; Nalty, *Strength for the Fight*, 193; Captain Slade D. Cutter, Oral History, USNI, II (1985), NL, 497; Commander Norman H. Meyer, "Shipmate Jim Hair," *NH*, 6, n. 2 (Summer, 1992), 35–36.

[11] Paul Stillwell, ed., *The Golden Thirteen: Recollections of the First Black Naval Officers* (Annapolis: Naval Institute Press, 1993), *passim;* George Cooper, Oral History, USNI (1989), NL, 20–28, 38–54, 69–73, 138–173; MacGregor, *Integration of the Armed Forces*, 80–82; Foner, *Blacks and the Military*, 170–171; James G. Schneider, *The Navy V-12 Program: Leadership for a Lifetime* (Boston: Houghton Mifflin Company, 1987), 152–154, 159; Nelson, *The Integration of the Negro*, 12, 94–112; Carl Rowan, "Those Navy Boys Changed My Life," *Reader Digest*, 72, n. 429 (January, 1958), 55–58; Vice Admiral William R. Smedberg III, Oral History, USNI, II (1979), NL, 748–751; Stephen Howarth, *To Shining Sea: A History of the United States Navy, 1775–1991* (New York: Random House, 1991), 416.

[12] Foner, *Blacks and the Military*, 171–172; Nalty, *Strength for the Fight*, 193–195; Dalfiume, *Desegregation of the U.S. Armed Forces*, 101–102; MacGregor, *Integration of the Armed Forces*, 84–92, 95–97; Lester Granger, "Racial Democracy— The Navy Way," *Common Ground*, 7 (Winter, 1947), 61–68.

[13] Robert L. Allen, *The Port Chicago Mutiny: The Story of the Largest Mass Mutiny Trial in U.S. Naval History* (New York: Warner Books, 1989), 64, 139; MacGregor, *Integration of the Armed Forces*, 92–94 [emphasis in original], 98; Foner, *Blacks and the Military*, 172, 175; Nalty, *Strength for the Fight*, 195–196; Nelson, *The Integration of the Negro*, 76–93; John Patrick Diggins, *The Proud Decades: America in War and Peace, 1941–1960* (New York: W. W. Norton & Company, 1989), 277–278.

[14] Admiral Charles Donald Griffin, Oral History, USNI, I (1973), NL, 144–147; Donald J. Mrozek, "The *Croatan* Incident: The U.S. Navy and the Problem of Racial Discrimination after World War II," *MA*, 44, n. 4 (December, 1980), 187–191; MacGregor, *Integration of the Armed Forces*, 128–129, 143–151, 166–170; Nelson, *The Integration of the Negro*, 20–21.

[15] Martin Bauml Duberman, *Paul Robeson: A Biography* (New York: Ballantine Books, 1990), 337; Capitola D. Newbern, "Pentagon Melting Pot," *The Survey*, 82 (November, 1946), 289–291; Felix L. Paul, "Yeoman, First Class: Negro," *Survey Graphic*, 36 (August, 1947), 444–446, 453.

[16] Cooper, Oral History, 48–50, 190–191; Nalty, *Strength for the Fight*, 208–211, 238, 218–221; MacGregor, *Integration of the Armed Forces*, 234–248; Binkin and Eitelberg, *Blacks in the Military*, 30, n. 65; Nelson, *The Integration of the Negro*, 113–122; Admiral Robert Lee Dennison, Oral History, USNI (1975), NL, 234–235.

[17] MacGregor, *Integration of the Armed Forces*, 248–252, 291–314; Stephen E. Ambrose, "The Armed Services and American Strategy, 1945–1953," in Kenneth J. Hagan and William R. Roberts, eds., *Against All Enemies: Interpretations of American Military History from Colonial Times to the Present* (Westport, Conn.: Greenwood Press, 1986), 313.

[18]MacGregor, *Integration of the Armed Forces*, 412–427, 331–334, 396; Constance McLaughlin Green, *The Secret City: A History of Race Relations in the Nation's Capital* (Princeton: Princeton University Press, 1969), 117, 173, 257, 278; Penny Vahsen, "Blacks in White Hats," *USNIP*, 113, n. 4 (April, 1987), 65–71; JO3 Colleen C. Riddick, "First Black Academy Grad Goes Back to Sea," *SM*, 45, n. 6 (July–August, 1982), 37–38; Nalty, *Strength for the Fight*, 242–243, 245–246, 250; Dalfiume, *Desegregation of the U.S. Armed Forces*, 180, 195, 199–200; Nelson, *The Integration of the Negro*, 158–168.

[19]Duberman, *Paul Robeson*, 343; John E. Weems, "Black Wings of Gold," *USNIP*, 109, n. 7 (July, 1983), 35–39; Richard P. Hallion, *The Naval Air War in Korea* (New York: Zebra Books, 1988), 129–131; Commander Malcolm W. Cagle and Commander Frank A. Manson, *The Sea War in Korea* (Annapolis: Naval Institute Press, 1957), 176–177; Nalty, *Strength for the Fight*, 265.

[20]Nalty, *Strength for the Fight*, 264–265; Lieutenant Dennis D. Nelson, "A Report on Military Civil Rights," *Negro History Bulletin*, 16, n. 4 (January, 1953), 75–78; Taylor Branch, *Parting the Waters: America in the King Years, 1954–1963* (New York: Touchstone Books, 1989), 213, 236.

[21]*Time*, 31 August 1953, 10; Stephen E. Ambrose, *Eisenhower*, II: *The President* (New York: Simon and Schuster, 1984), 126; Nalty, *Strength for the Fight*, 268; MacGregor, *Integration of the Armed Forces*, 490–491, 498, 483–487.

[22]"*Apartheid* and the Navy," *Commonweal*, 61 (28 January 1955), 446; MacGregor, *Integration of the Armed Forces*, 481, 508–509, 522–529, 568–572, 542, 551, 539, 561–563; Branch, *Parting the Waters*, 399–401.

[23]MacGregor, *Integration of the Armed Forces*, 579; David R. Segal, *Recruiting for Uncle Sam: Citizenship and Military Manpower Policy* (Lawrence: University Press of Kansas, 1989), 112; "Guardian of Western Coastline," *Ebony*, January 1965, 40–42, 44–46; Nelson, *The Integration of the Negro*, xii.

STERN WATCH IV

[1]Vice Admiral George C. Dyer, *On the Treadmill to Pearl Harbor: The Memoirs of Admiral James O. Richardson* (Washington, D.C.: Government Printing Office, 1973), 62, n. 13.

[2]Lieutenant Dennis D. Nelson, *The Integration of the Negro into the U.S. Navy* (New York: Farrar, Straus and Young, 1951), 181–182, 188.

[3]Morris J. MacGregor, Jr., *Integration of the Armed Forces, 1940–1965* (Washington, D.C.: Center of Military History, 1980), 614–615.

CHAPTER TWENTY-FOUR

[1]Stephen E. Ambrose, *Eisenhower*, I: *Soldier, General of the Army, President-Elect* (New York: Touchstone Books, 1983), 141–142, 145, 284, 149–50, 179, 486, 513–514; Paul A. Carter, *Another Part of the Fifties* (New York: Columbia University Press, 1983), 32, 261–262 [emphasis in original]; Admiral Arleigh Burke, Oral History, USNI, II (1980), NL, 245–246; Ambrose, *Eisenhower*, II: *The President* (New York: Touchstone Books, 1983), 223–226, 389, 515–516, 549–551; Admiral Charles K. Duncan, Oral History, USNI, III (1983), NL, 1400–1402.

[2]Rear Admiral Draper L. Kauffman, Oral History, USNI, I (1982), NL, 452–453; *Time*, 17 January 1957, 18; Ambrose, *Eisenhower*, II, 456, 495–496, 43, 94–95, 612–613, 632; Paul Boyer, *By the Bomb's Early Light: American Thought and Culture at the Dawn of the Atomic Age* (New York: Pantheon Books, 1985), 188; H. W. Brands, "The Age of Vulnerability: Eisenhower and the National Insecurity State," *American Historical Review*, 94, n. 4 (October, 1989), 963–989; Lawrence Freedman, "The First Two Generations of Nuclear Strategists," in Peter Paret, ed., *Makers of Modern Strategy from Machiavelli to the Nuclear Age* (Princeton: Princeton University Press, 1986), 745, n. 24.

[3]Captain J. V. Noel, Jr., "The Navy and the Department of Defense," *USNIP*, 87, n. 11 (November 1961), 23–31; Fred J. Cook, *The Warfare State* (New York: Collier Books, 1964), 30–33; Admiral Charles Donald Griffin, Oral History, USNI, I (1973), NL, 341–342; Vice Admiral Robert S. Salzer, Oral History, USNI (1981), NL, 193–194; Ambrose, *Eisenhower*, II, 23, 40–41, 90, 345, 440–441; Carter, *Another Part of the Fifties*, 274; Hanson Weightman Baldin, Oral History, USNI, II (1976), NL, 523; Colonel David H. Hackworth, USA, *About Face: The Odyssey of an American Warrior* (New York: Touchstone Books, 1990), 353.

[4]Paul B. Ryan, *First Line of Defense: The U.S. Navy Since 1945* (Stanford, Cal.: Hoover Institution Press, 1981), 23; Clark R. Mollenhoff, *The Pentagon: Politics, Profits and Plunder*, Rev. ed. (New York: Pinnacle Books, 1972), 55; H. Struve Hensel, "Changes inside the Pentagon," *Harvard Business Review*, 32, n. 1 (January–February 1954), 105–108; Eugene S. Duffield, "Organizing for Defense," *Harvard Business Review*, 31, n. 5 (September–October 1953), 35–38; Thomas C. Hone, *Power and Change: The Administrative History of the Office of Chief of Naval Operations, 1946–1986*, Contributions to Naval History . . . No. 2 (Washington, D.C.: Naval Historical Center, 1989), 29–34; Arthur T. Hadley, *The Straw Giant, America's Armed Forces: Triumphs and Failures* (New York: Avon Books, 1987), 128; Vincent Davis, *The Admirals Lobby* (Chapel Hill: University of North Carolina Press, 1967), 165.

[5]Captain R. P. Smyth, "The Navy Department: The Fulcrum and the Balance," *USNIP*, 93, n. 5 (May, 1967), 70–78; "The Navy," *Flying*, 52, n. 3 (March, 1953), 53–62; "Eisenhower's Navy," *Fortune*, September 1953, 76, 80.

[6]K. Jack Bauer, "Robert Bernerd Anderson, 4 February 1953–2 May 1954," in Paolo E. Coletta, ed., *American Secretaries of the Navy*, II: *1913–1972* (Annapolis: Naval Institute Press, 1980), 843–855; Vice Admiral Bernard L. Austin, Oral History, USNI (1971), NL, 433–434; "A Texan Takes Over the Navy," *Fortune*, August 1953, 80, 82; Rear Admiral Charles Adair, Oral History, USNI (1977), NL, 570–573; Captain Slade D. Cutter, Oral History, USNI, II (1985), NL, 575, 386–388, 575–576; Vice Admiral Andrew McBurney Jackson, Jr., Oral History, USNI (1978), NL, 193; John R. Wadleigh, "Charles Sparks Thomas, 3 May 1954–1 April 1957," in Coletta, *American Secretaries of the Navy*, II, 857–874; *Time*, 22 March 1954, 29; *U.S. News & World Report*, 20 July 1956, 112–114; Admiral Horacio Rivero, Jr., Oral History, USNI (1978), NL, 262; *SNR*, in *SDR* (1 January–30 June 1956), 251–254; John C. Donovan, *The Cold Warriors: A Policy-Making Elite* (Lexington, Mass.: D. C. Heath and Company, 1974), 53; Admiral David Lamar McDonald, Oral History, USNI (1976), NL, 175–177.

[7]Officer Biography, Admiral Arthur W. Radford, NHD; "The Chairman of Joint Chiefs of Staff is an Aviator," *U.S. Air Services*, 38, n. 9 (September, 1953), 4–6; Clark G. Reynolds, *Admiral John H. Towers: The Struggle for Naval Air Supremacy* (Annapolis: Naval Institute Press, 1991), 428, 448–449; Edgar Kemler, "No. 1 Strong Man: The Asia-First Admiral," *Nation*, 179 (17 July 1954), 45–47; Captain Stephen Jurika, Jr., Oral History, USNI, II (1979), NL, 718–721; Captain Joy Bright Hancock, Oral History, USNI (1971), NL, 56, 53, 62; Robert J. Donovan, *Tumultuous Years: The Presidency of Harry S Truman, 1949–1953* (New York: W. W. Norton & Company, 1982), 286–288; Ambrose, *Eisenhower*, II, 30, 33; Burke, Oral History, IV (1983), 588; Stephen Jurika, Jr., ed., *From Pearl Harbor to Vietnam: The Memoirs of Admiral Arthur W. Radford* (Stanford, Cal.: Hoover Institution Press, 1980), 240–245; Griffin, Oral History, I. 334, II (1975), 618–619.

[8]Ambrose, *Eisenhower*, II, 90 [emphasis in original], 120–121, 177–178, 205–206, 229, 402; Seyom Brown, *The Faces of Power: Constancy and Change in United States Foreign Policy from Truman to Reagan* (New York: Columbia University Press, 1983), 69; Robert A. Divine, *Eisenhower and the Cold War* (New York: Oxford University Press, 1981), 34–36; Frederick H. Hartmann, *Naval Renaissance: The U.S. Navy in the 1980s* (Annapolis: Naval Institute Press, 1990), 292.

[9]Kemler, "No. 1 Strong Man," 47; David Rees, *Korea: The Limited War* (Baltimore: Penguin Books, 1970), 404; Tristram Coffin, *The Armed Society: Militarism in Modern America* (Baltimore: Penguin Books, 1964), 128–130; Cook, *The Warfare State*, 277–278, 303–304, 318–319 [emphasis in original], 328–329.

[10]Divine, *Eisenhower and the Cold War*, 36–39; Brown, *The Faces of Power*, 71–73; Ronald E. Powaski, *March to Armageddon: The United States and the Nuclear Arms Race, 1939 to the Present* (New York: Oxford University Press, 1987), 82.

[11]Gerald Kennedy, "William Morrow Fechteler, 16 August 1951–17 August 1953," in Robert William Love, Jr., ed., *The Chiefs of Naval Operations* (Annapolis: Naval Institute Press, 1980), 235–241; Officer Biography, Admiral Robert Bostwick Carney, NHD; Paul R. Schratz, "Robert Bostwick Carney, 17 August 1953–17 August 1955," in Love, *The Chiefs of Naval Operations*, 243–261; Rear Admiral Edward K. Walker, Oral History, USNI (1985), NL, 27–28; David Alan Rosenberg, "American Postwar Air Doctrine and Organization: The Navy Experience," in Colonel Alfred F. Hurley, USAF, and Major Robert C. Ehrhardt, USAF, eds., *Air Power and Warfare*, Proceedings of the 8th Military History Symposium, United States Air Force Academy, 18–20 October 1978 (Washington, D.C.: Office of Air Force History, 1979), 268–269, 271; Cutter, Oral History, II, 458–459, 575; Vice Admiral Felix L. Johnson, Oral History, USNI (1974), NL, 48–49, 171; Vice Admiral John L. Chew, Oral History, USNI (1979), NL, 169–176.

[12]Schratz, "Robert Bostwick Carney," 247; Davis, *The Admirals Lobby*, 289–291; Norman Friedman, *The Postwar Naval Revolution* (Annapolis: Naval Institute Press, 1986), 20, 49–55; Samuel P. Huntington, "National Policy and the Transoceanic Navy," *USNIP*, 80, n. 5 (May, 1954), 483–493; Rivero, Oral History, 298–301.

[13]Donald W. Mitchell, "Seapower in the Twentieth Century," *Current History*, 26, n. 153 (May, 1954), 271–276; Michael A. Palmer, *Origins of the Maritime Strategy:*

American Naval Strategy in the First Postwar Decade, Contributions to Naval History . . . No. 1 (Washington, D.C.: Naval Historical Center, 1988), 78–83; Edward J. Marolda and Oscar P. Fitzgerald, *The United States Navy and the Vietnam Conflict*, II: *From Military Assistance to Combat, 1959–1965* (Washington, D.C.: Naval Historical Center, 1986), 8–13; Duncan, Oral History, III, 1416.

[14]Daun Van Ee, "From the New Look to Flexible Response, 1953–1964," in Kenneth J. Hagan and William R. Roberts, eds., *Against All Enemies: Interpretations of American Military History from Colonial Times to the Present* (Westport, Conn.: Greenwood Press, 1986), 325–326; Powaski, *March to Armageddon*, 63; Fred Kaplan, *The Wizards of Armageddon* (New York: Touchstone Books, 1984), 275–276.

[15]Carter, *Another Part of the Fifties*, 61–62; Ambrose, *Eisenhower*, II, 249.

[16]Nick Kotz, *Wild Blue Yonder: Money, Politics, and the B-1 Bomber* (New York: Pantheon Books, 1988), 45–47, 56; Ronald Schaffer, *Wings of Judgment: American Bombing in World War II* (New York: Oxford University Press, 1985), 207; David Alan Rosenberg, "The Origins of Overkill: Nuclear Weapons and American Strategy, 1945–1960," *International Security*, 7, n. 4 (Spring, 1983), 3–71.

[17]Freedman, "The First Two Generations of Nuclear Strategists," 751; Michael Carver, "Conventional Warfare in the Nuclear Age," in Paret, *Makers of Modern Strategy*, 783; *Newsweek*, 16 April 1956, 32–33.

CHAPTER TWENTY-FIVE

[1]Admiral Arthur W. Radford, "Our Navy in the Far East," *National Geographic Magazine*, 104, n. 4 (October, 1953), 537–577; Commander John V. Noel, Jr., "Showing the Flag in Southeast Asia," *USNIP*, 81, n. 2 (February, 1955), 179–191; USS *Rochester* (CA-124), "Report of Visit to Manila, 31 January–3 February 1954," 10 February 1954, NHD; USS *Rochester* (CA-124), "Report of Visit to Singapore, 7–10 February 1954," 18 February 1954, NHD; USS *Rochester* (CA-124), "Report of Visit to Bangkok, 12–15 February 1954," 20 February 1954, NHD; Maurice H. Hellner, "Sea Power and the Struggle for Asia," *USNIP*, 82, n. 4 (April, 1956), 353–361.

[2]Peter Hayes, Lyuba Zarsky, and Walden Bello, *American Lake: Nuclear Peril in the Pacific* (New York: Penguin Books, 1987), 77–78; Edward J. Marolda and Oscar P. Fitzgerald, *The United States Navy and the Vietnam Conflict*, II: *From Military Assistance to Combat, 1959–1965* (Washington, D.C.: Naval Historical Center, 1986), 277–281, 295–297.

[3]Edward Behr, *Hirohito: Behind the Myth* (New York: Vintage Books, 1990), 377–378; Michael Schaller, *The American Occupation of Japan: The Origins of the Cold War in Asia* (New York: Oxford University Press, 1985), 294, 296–297; Radford, "Our Navy in the Far East," 540, 552; Stanley Karnow, *In Our Image: America's Empire in the Philippines* (New York: Ballantine Books, 1990), 9, 13, 330–335; Sterling Seagrave, *The Marcos Dynasty* (New York: Fawcett Columbine, 1990), 151; Raymond Bonner, *Waltzing with a Dictator: The Marcoses and the Making of American Policy* (New York: Vintage Books, 1988), 32.

[4]Officer Biography, Admiral Russell S. Berkey, NHD; Vice Admiral William P. Mack, Oral History, USNI, I (1980), NL, 201–203; Captain Thomas H. Dyer,

Oral History, USNI (1986), NL, 104; Admiral Charles Donald Griffin, Oral History, USNI, I (1973), NL, 229–230; Ship's History, USS *Stickell* (DD-888), 17 July 1951, NHD; Paul B. Ryan, *First Line of Defense: The U.S. Navy Since 1945* (Stanford, Cal.: Hoover Institution Press, 1981), 17–19; Arthur T. Hadley, *The Straw Giant, America's Armed Forces: Triumphs and Failures* (New York: Avon Books, 1987), 168; David W. Tarr, *American Strategy in the Nuclear Age* (New York: MacMillan Company, 1966), 72, 74, 76–77; Robert A. Divine, *Eisenhower and the Cold War* (New York: Oxford University Press, 1981), 40–51; Officer Biography, Admiral William Kearney Phillips, NHD; Officer Biography, Admiral Arthur C. Davis, NHD; Jules Roy, *The Battle of Dien Bien Phu* (New York: Pyramid Books, 1966), 240–241, 244–245, 271–272; Commander Seventh Fleet, "Report of Operations (1 December 1953–30 June 1954)," 15 September 1954, NHD.

5"The Navy's Girl in Hong Kong," *Collier's*, 1 October 1954, 60–61; Paul R. Schratz, *Submarine Commander: A Story of World War II and Korea* (Lexington: University Press of Kentucky, 1988), 264–265.

6*U.S. News & World Report*, 22 February 1952, 54–59; *U.S. News & World Report*, 16 January 1953, 16–18; *Aviation Week*, 2 August 1954, 15; Letter, OP-33 to OP-03, "Chronological Record of the Hainan Affair, 23–28 July 1954," 29 July 1954, NHD; Letter, Commander Task Group 70.2 to Commander First Fleet, "Report of Operations of Task Group 70.2 during Period 23–29 July 1954 in Connection with Search for Survivors of British Air Cathay Airliner and Air Action Incident Thereto Involving Two Chinese Communist La-7 Type Aircraft," 7 August 1954, NHD; Letter, Commander Task Group 70.2 to Commander First Fleet, "Report of Training and Operations of Task Group 70.2 for the Period 20–31 July 1954," 23 August 1954, NHD.

7Letter, Commander Seventh Fleet to Chief of Naval Operations, "Narrative of Operations Following the Chinese Communist Attack on Quemoy, 3–30 September 1954," 15 October 1954, NHD; Commander Albert J. Ashurst, "The Formosa Resolution, 1954–1955, 1958," *NWCR*, 20, n. 7 (February, 1968), 56–64; Paul A. Carter, *Another Part of the Fifties* (New York: Columbia University Press, 1983), 66–75; Robert Accinelli, "Eisenhower, Congress, and the 1954 Offshore Island Crisis," *Presidential Studies Quarterly*, 20, n. 2 (Spring, 1990), 329–348; Rear Admiral Samuel B. Frankel, Oral History, USNI (1972), NL, 359–361; Jonathan D. Spence, *The Search for Modern China* (New York: W. W. Norton & Company, 1990), 561.

8Alexander L. George and Richard Smoke, *Deterence in American Foreign Policy: Theory and Practice* (New York: Columbia University Press, 1974), 194, 291; Richard P. Hallion, *The Naval Air War in Korea* (New York: Zebra Books, 1988), 285; Stephen E. Ambrose, *Eisenhower*, II: *The President* (New York: Simon and Schuster, 1984), 47; *Newsweek*, 9 February 1953, 30; *Time*, 9 February 1953, 16.

9Officer Biography, Admiral Felix B. Stump, NHD; Captain Stephen Jurika, Jr., Oral History, USNI, II (1979), NL, 949–950; Captain Roland W. Faulk, CHC, Oral History, USNI (1975), NL, 321–322; Admiral Charles K. Duncan, Oral History, USNI, I (1978), NL, 507–513; Frankel, Oral History, 346–354; *U.S. News & World Report*, 27 August 1954, 24–27; *U.S. News & World Report*, 1

October 1954, 35–38; Officer Biography, Admiral Alfred Melville Pride, NHD; Captain John V. Noel, Oral History, USNI (1987), NL, 100; Admiral Alfred M. Pride, Oral History, USNI (1984), NL, 215–217, 221–231; Ship's History, USS *Saint Paul* (CA-73), 5 August 1955, NHD; Ship's History, USS *Hornet* (CVA-12), 26 September 1955, NHD; Ship's History, USS *Yorktown* (CVA-10), 16 November 1955, NHD; *Life*, 4 October 1954, 28–29; Lieutenant Brooks Honeycutt, "On Guard Off Formosa: Is This Where Our Next War Starts?" *Look*, 30 November 1954, 23–25; *Department of State Bulletin*, 27 December 1954, 996–1003; Vice Admiral Truman J. Hedding, Oral History, USNI (1972), NL, 168–169; Rear Admiral Etheridge Grant, Oral History, USNI (1971), NL, 58–59.

[10]Ambrose, *Eisenhower*, II, 212–214, 231–233; Divine, *Eisenhower and the Cold War*, 55–61; Vice Admiral L. S. Sabin, "A Sledge Hammer to Crack a Nut," *SM*, 30, n. 3 (March 1967), 4–7; Officer Biography, Vice Admiral Lorenzo Sherwood Sabin, Jr., NHD; Vice Admiral George C. Dyer, Oral History, USNI (1973), NL, 265; Letter, Commander Seventh Fleet to Chief of Naval Operations, "Tachen Islands Visit, 14 August 1954," 25 August 1954, NHD; Commander Seventh Fleet, "Report of the Evacuation of the Tachen Islands, 6–13 February 1955," 10 April 1955, NHD.

[11]Ryan, *First Line of Defense*, 19–21; *U.S. News & World Report*, 4 February 1955, 23; *U.S. News & World Report*, 18 February 1955, 44–46.

[12]"Patrolling Troubled Formosa Strait," *National Geographic Magazine*, 107, n. 4 (April, 1955), 573–588; "With the 7th Fleet . . . Off Formosa," *Look*, 5 April 1955, 17–19; William L. Worden, "Cold War in the Formosa Strait," *Saturday Evening Post*, 14 May 1955, 27, 115–116, 118.

[13]Divine, *Eisenhower and the Cold War*, 61–66; Accinelli, "Eisenhower, Congress, and the 1954–1955 Offshore Island Crisis," 341–344; Ashurst, "The Formosa Resolution, 1954–1955, 1958," 62; Carter, *Another Part of the Fifties*, 74; Ambrose, *Eisenhower*, II, 235–244.

[14]Officer Biography, Vice Admiral Wallace M. Beakley, NHD; *Life*, 23 December 1957, 52–57; *Newsweek*, 17 March 1958, 42, 44; *Newsweek*, 22 September 1958, 47–48; Rear Admiral Francis D. Foley, Oral History, USNI, II (1988), NL, 738–739; Rear Admiral Charles D. Loughlin, Oral History, USNI (1982), NL, 268–269; Hanson Weightman Baldwin, Oral History, USNI, I (1976), NL, 42–43; Captain Henri Smith-Hutton, Oral History, USNI, II (1976), NL, 467–468; Rear Admiral John S. Coye, Jr., Oral History, USNI (1983), NL, 149–150.

[15]Ambrose, *Eisenhower*, II, 482–485; Captain Edward F. Baldridge, "Lebanon and Quemoy—The Navy's Role," *USNIP*, 87, n. 2 (February, 1961), 94–100; *Time*, 22 September 1958, 22–24; Harold H. Martin, "On the Prowl With '31 Knot' Burke," *Saturday Evening Post*, 18 January 1958, 36–37, 86–88; Ashurst, "The Formosa Resolution, 1954–1955, 1958," 62–63; *U.S. News & World Report*, 19 September 1958, 31–33; Divine, *Eisenhower and the Cold War*, 66–70.

[16]Officer Biography, Admiral Harry D. Felt, NHD; William H. Hessler, "The Seventh Fleet Is Ready," *Reporter*, 8 June 1961, 30–31; A. M. Rosenthal, "On Patrol with the Seventh Fleet," *New York Times Magazine*, 1 October 1961, 27, 82–83; *U.S. News & World Report*, 19 September 1958, 31; Hayes, Zarsky, and

Bello, *American Lake*, 57; Franc Shor, "Pacific Fleet: Force for Peace," *National Geographic Magazine*, 116, n. 3 (September, 1959), 283–335; *U.S. News & World Report*, 23 October 1961, 66–67; Baldridge, "Lebanon and Quemoy," 100.

[17]Paul R. Schratz, "Robert Bostwick Carney, 17 August 1953–17 August 1955," in Robert William Love, Jr., ed., *The Chiefs of Naval Operations* (Annapolis: Naval Institute Press, 1980), 260–261; David Alan Rosenberg, "Arleigh Albert Burke, 17 August 1955–1 August 1961," in Love. *The Chiefs of Naval Operations*, 263–265; Ambrose, *Eisenhower*, II, 274.

CHAPTER TWENTY-SIX

[1]E. B. Potter, *Admiral Arleigh Burke: A Biography* (New York: Random House, 1990), 3–10; David Alan Rosenberg, "Arleigh Albert Burke, 17 August 1955–1 August 1961," in Robert William Love, Jr., ed., *The Chiefs of Naval Operations* (Annapolis: Naval Institute Press, 1980), 265–266; David Alan Rosenberg, "Officer Development in the Interwar Navy: Arleigh Burke—The Making of a Professional, 1919–1940," *Pacific Historical Review*, 44, n. 4 (November, 1975), 505.

[2]Potter, *Admiral Arleigh Burke*, 10–21; Harold H. Martin, "On the Prowl With '31 Knot' Burke," *Saturday Evening Post*, 18 January 1958, 86; Rosenberg, "Arleigh Albert Burke," 266; Rosenberg, "Officer Development in the Interwar Navy," 505–509; Rear Admiral Ernest M. Eller, Oral History, USNI, I (1986), NL, 43–44, 47–48.

[3]Rosenberg, "Arleigh Albert Burke," 266–267; Potter, *Admiral Arleigh Burke*, 22–39; Rosenberg, "Officer Development in the Interwar Navy," 508–511.

[4]Rosenberg, "Arleigh Albert Burke," 267–268; Potter, *Admiral Arleigh Burke*, 40–67; Rosenberg, "Officer Development in the Interwar Navy," 509–526; Rear Admiral Edward A. Ruckner, Oral History, USNI (1977), NL, 18, 25–26; Rear Admiral Edward K. Waller, Oral History, USNI (1985), NL, 124–125; Captain Stephen Jurika, Jr., Oral History, USNI, I (1979), NL, 138–144.

[5]Potter, *Admiral Arleigh Burke*, 67–111; Rosenberg, "Arleigh Albert Burke," 268–269; Vice Admiral Raymond E. Peet, Oral History, USNI (1984), NL, 32; Rear Admiral Frederic Stanton Withington, Oral History, USNI (1971), NL, 56–57; Vice Admiral Bernard L. Austin, Oral History, USNI (1971), NL, 261–265; Admiral Charles K. Duncan, Oral History, USNI, I (1978), NL, 210–211; Vice Admiral John Barr Colwell, Oral History, USNI (1974), NL, 88–92; Vice Admiral Felix L. Johnson, Oral History, USNI (1974), NL, 146–147.

[6]Vice Admiral Truman J. Hedding, Oral History, USNI (1972), NL, 61–64, 70–72, 80–82; Admiral Charles Donald Griffin, Oral History, USNI, I (1973), NL, 129; Jack Sweetman, *The U.S. Naval Academy: An Illustrated History* (Annapolis: Naval Institute Press, 1979), 151, 155–156; Potter, *Admiral Arleigh Burke*, 112–258; Rosenberg, "Arleigh Albert Burke," 269–270; Colonel Francis Fox Parry, USMC, *Three-War Marine: The Pacific-Korea-Vietnam* (New York: Jove Books, 1987), 239–240; Vice Admiral Gerald F. Bogan, Oral History, USNI (1970/1986), NL, 109–110.

[7]Griffin, Oral History, I, 178–180; Admiral Robert Lee Dennison, Oral History, USNI (1975), NL, 194–200; Admiral John S. Thach, Oral History, USNI, II

(1977), NL, 838–839; Potter, *Admiral Arleigh Burke*, 259–383; Rosenberg, "Arleigh Albert Burke," 270–275; Rear Admiral George W. Bauernschmidt, Oral History, USNI (1970), NL, 227; Vice Admiral Ruthven E. Libby, Oral History, USNI (1984), NL, 181–182, 196.

[8]Potter, *Admiral Arleigh Burke*, 384–399; Admiral Arleigh A. Burke, Oral History, USNI (1973), NL, 6–10, 228–231; Duncan, Oral History, III (1983), 1387–1388; Admiral J. J. ("Jocko") Clark, "31-Knot Burke," *Flying*, January 1956, 22–23, 53–54, 56; Admiral Arleigh Burke, "Today's Ships Pack a Substantial Atomic Wallop," *U.S. News & World Report*, 6 January 1956, 84–86; *U.S. News & World Report*, 4 May 1956, 82–88, 90, 92, 94; Rosenberg, "Arleigh Albert Burke," 275–276; Rear Admiral Roy S. Benson, Oral History, USNI, II (1987), NL, 814.

[9]*Time*, 21 May 1956, 25–32; Thomas C. Hone, *Power and Change: The Administrative History of the Office of the Chief of Naval Operations, 1946–1986*, Contributions to Naval History . . . No. 2 (Washington, D.C.: Naval Historical Center, 1989), 48; Admiral Arleigh Burke, "The Future of the Navy," *Vital Speeches of the Day*, 15 October 1956, 9–12; Potter, *Admiral Arleigh Burke*, 400–418; Vice Admiral Paul D. Stroop, Oral History, USNI (1970), NL, 307–308; Peet, Oral History, 121–128, 139–140, 177; Admiral Alfred G. Ward, Oral History, USNI (1972), NL, 81–91, 157–164; Vice Admiral William Peden Mack, Oral History, USNI, II (1980), NL, 816–818; Rear Admiral George H. Miller, Oral History, USNI (1975), NL, 237–240.

[10]Paul A. Carter, *Another Part of the Fifties* (New York: Columbia University Press, 1983), 231–232; *Business Week*, 2 March 1957, 126, 128, 130; Edward J. Marolda, "The Influence of Burke's Boys on Limited War," *USNIP*, 107, n. 8 (August, 1981), 36–41; Edward J. Marolda and Oscar P. Fitzgerald, *The United States Navy and the Vietnam Conflict*, II: *From Military Assistance to Combat, 1959–1965* (Washington, D.C.: Naval Historical Center, 1986), 3; Rosenberg, "Admiral Arleigh Burke," 280–281; Austin, Oral History, 198–201; Admiral Roy L. Johnson, Oral History, USNI (1982), NL, 248–249.

[11]David Rees, *Korea: The Limited War* (Baltimore: Penguin Books, 1970), 36; Vincent Davis, *The Admirals Lobby* (Chapel Hill: University of North Carolina Press, 1967), 282–283, 258–259, 262–263; Fred J. Cook, *The Warfare State* (New York: Collier Books, 1964), 22; Harry L. Coles, "Strategic Studies Since 1945: The Era of Overthink," in David Curtis Skaggs and Robert S. Browning III, eds., *In Defense of the Republic: Readings in American Military History* (Belmont, Cal.: Wadsworth Publishing Company, 1991), 468.

[12]Richard Smoke, *National Security and the Nuclear Dilemma: An Introduction to the American Experience*, 2nd ed. (New York: Random House, 1987), 94–97; Stephen E. Ambrose, *Eisenhower*, II: *The President* (New York: Simon and Schuster, 1984), 434–435; Lawrence Freedman, "The First Two Generations of Nuclear Strategists," in Peter Paret, ed., *Makers of Modern Strategy from Machiavelli to the Nuclear Age* (Princeton: Princeton University Press, 1986), 756; John C. Donovan, *The Cold Warriors: A Policy-Making Elite* (Lexington, Mass.: D. C. Heath and Company, 1974), 143; Potter, *Admiral Arleigh Burke*, 423–425.

[13]Hone, *Power and Change*, 42–44; Captain John F. Tarpey, "Uncle Carl," *USNIP*, 108, n. 1 (January, 1982), 38–45; Rosenberg, "Arleigh Albert Burke," 275; Paul

B. Ryan, *First Line of Defense: The U.S. Navy Since 1945* (Stanford, Cal.: Hoover Institution Press, 1981), 23–26; James Coates and Michael Kilrain, *Heavy Losses: The Dangerous Decline of American Defense* (New York: Penguin Books, 1986), 126–127; "The Navy Objects," *New Republic*, 7 July 1958, 3–5; Austin, Oral History, 461–463; Clark R. Mollenhoff, *The Pentagon: Politics, Profits and Plunder*, Rev. ed. (New York: Pinnacle Books, 1972), 55; Potter, *Admiral Arleigh Burke*, 425; Rosenberg, "Admiral Arleigh Burke," 287–288; Admiral Harry D. Felt, Oral History, USNI, II (1974), NL, 359–362, 465.

[14]Captain R. P. Smythe, "The Navy Department: The Fulcrum and the Balance," *USNIP*, 93, n. 5 (May, 1967), 70–78; John R. Wadleigh, "Charles Sparks Thomas, 3 May 1954–1 April 1957," in Paolo E. Coletta, ed., *American Secretaries of the Navy*, II: *1913–1972* (Annapolis: Naval Institute Press, 1980), 857–874; John R. Wadleigh, "Thomas Sovereign Gates, Jr., 1 April 1957–7 June 1959," in Coletta, *American Secretaries of the Navy*, II, 877–893; Ron Chernow, *The House of Morgan: An American Banking Dynasty and the Rise of Modern Finance* (New York: Touchstone Books, 1990), 542–543; *Time*, 11 March 1957, 18; Griffin, Oral History, 379–380; Stroop, Oral History, 301–303; Thomas S. Gates, Jr., "Naval Supremacy Vital to Our National Security," *Vital Speeches of the Day*, 1 December 1956, 114–117; Colonel Clayton O. Totman, USMC, "The Navy and Conservation," *American Forests*, 64 (September, 1958), 16–18, 52–53, 55; Peet, Oral History, 134; Captain John V. Noel, Oral History, USNI (1987), NL, 163.

[15]Davis, *The Admirals Lobby*, 291–303, 165–170; Hone, *Power and Change*, 45–55; Vice Admiral Edwin B. Hooper, Oral History, USNI (1978), NL, 298–299.

[16]Hone, *Power and Change*, 55; Admiral Arleigh A. Burke, "Missiles and the Defense Organization," *Vital Speeches of the Day*, 24, n. 8 (1 February 1958), 244–247; John Davis Lodge, "Peace Is a Product of Strength," *Vital Speeches of the Day*, 25, n. 3 (15 November 1958), 66–69; *U.S. News & World Report*, 3 October 1960, 70–76.

[17]Captain Daniel J. Garrison, "The Role of the Navy in the Cold War," *USNIP*, 85, n. 6 (June, 1959), 57–63; Lieutenant Commander L. K. Pomeroy, Jr., "The Navy and National Policy," *USNIP*, 86, n. 4 (April, 1960), 90–97; Anthony E. Sokol, "Sea, Land, Air, and Missile Power," *USNIP*, 86, n. 5 (May, 1960), 27–35; Commander John B. Davis, Jr., and Dr. John A. Tiedeman, "The Navy War Games Program," *USNIP*, 86, n. 6 (June, 1960), 61–67; Captain Cassius D. Rhymes, Jr., "Balanced Sea Power and Cold War," *USNIP*, 86, n. 9 (September, 1960), 76–82; Rosenberg, "Arleigh Albert Burke," 298, 319.

CHAPTER TWENTY-SEVEN

[1]Captain Dominic A. Paolucci, "The Development of Navy Strategic Offensive and Defensive Systems," *USNIP*, 96, n. 5 (May, 1970), 204–223; David K. Stumpf, "Blasts from the Past," *USNIP*, 119, n. 4 (April, 1993), 60–64; Vice Admiral Lawson P. Ramage, Oral History, USNI (1975), NL, 206–207, 327; Ship's History, USS *Cusk* (SSG-348), NHD; William F. Whitmore, "The Origin of Polaris," *USNIP*, 106, n. 3 (March, 1980), 55–59; James Baar and William Howard, *Polaris!: The Concept and Creation of a New and Mighty Weapon* (New

York: Harcourt, Brace and Company, 1960), 10–18; Clay Blair, Jr., "Our Hottest New Weapon," *Saturday Evening Post*, 22 February 1958, 36, 76–78; Vice Admiral Daniel E. Barbey, "Let's Build This New Deterrent Force NOW," *Reader's Digest*, 72, n. 429 (January, 1958), 35–40; Admiral U.S. Grant Sharp, Oral History, USNI, I (1970), NL, 149–150; Rear Admiral Robert H. Wertheim, Oral History, USNI (1981), NL, 87–94; Rear Admiral George H. Miller, Oral History, USNI (1975), NL, 265–267; Rear Admiral Henry L. Miller, Oral History, USNI, I (1973), NL, 189–190; Rear Admiral Frederic Stanton Withington, Oral History, USNI (1972), NL, 149–150; Vice Admiral Kleber S. Masterson, Oral History, USNI (1973), NL, 304.

[2]Officer Biography, Vice Admiral William Francis Raborn, Jr., NHD; Baar and Howard, *Polaris!*, 14–36; "The Big Whoosh," *Flying*, 49, n. 5 (November, 1951), 128–129, 166; Letter, Commanding Officer, USS *Norton Sound* (AV-11) to Chief of Naval Operations (OP-57), "Summary of Technical Facilities and Shipboard Guided Missile Operations of U.S.S. NORTON SOUND for Period September 1948–June 1950," 22 June 1950, NHD; Whitmore, "The Origin of Polaris," 56; Paolucci, "The Development of Navy Strategic Offensive and Defensive Systems," 213–215; USS *Norton Sound* (AV-11), "Project Reach," 31 July 1950, NHD; Officer Biography, Admiral John Harold Sides, NHD; Withington, Oral History, 154; Masterson, Oral History, 272–273; Vice Admiral Paul D. Stroop, Oral History, USNI (1970), NL, 266–267.

[3]Rear Admiral Roy S. Benson, Oral History, USNI, II (1987), NL, 667–668; Ed Rees, *The Seas and the Subs* (New York: Duell, Sloan and Pearce, 1961), 175–186; Baar and Howard, *Polaris!*, 76–91, 242; Paul B. Ryan, *First Line of Defense: The U.S. Navy Since 1945* (Stanford, Cal.: Hoover Institution Press, 1981), 26–27; Vice Admiral William Peden Mack, Oral History, USNI, II (1980), NL, 784–790; Vice Admiral Philip A. Beshany, Oral History, USNI, I (1980), NL, 334, 382–386; George Miller, Oral History, 185–186; Admiral David Lamar McDonald, Oral History, USNI (1976), NL, 224; Wertheim, Oral History, 105–108; Henry Miller, Oral History, I, 95–97; Stroop, Oral History, 50, 61.

[4]E. B. Potter, *Admiral Arleigh Burke* (New York: Random House, 1990), 407–408; Baar and Howard, *Polaris!*, 37–51; Rees, *The Seas and the Subs*, 136–138; Paolucci, "The Development of Navy Strategic Offensive and Defensive Systems," 217; Wertheim, Oral History, 172; Vice Admiral Edwin B. Hooper, Oral History, USNI (1978), NL, 253–254; Withington, Oral History, 154–158; Officer Biography, Rear Admiral Levering Smith, NHD; Rear Admiral Francis D. Foley, Oral History, USNI, II (1988), NL, 958–959; Vice Admiral John Barr Colwell, Oral History, USNI (1974), NL, 190–192; Vice Admiral William R. Smedberg III, Oral History, USNI, II (1979), NL, 714–715; Admiral Charles K. Duncan, Oral History, USNI, II (1981), 912.

[5]Rees, *The Seas and the Subs*, 138–142; Harvey M. Sapolsky, *The Polaris System Development: Bureacratic and Programatic Success in Government* (Cambridge, Mass.: Harvard University Press, 1972), 15–34; Beshany, Oral History, I, 334–338; George Fielding Eliot, "Sea-Borne Deterrent," *USNIP*, 82, n. 11 (November, 1956), 1143–1153; *Aviation Week*, 7 January 1957, 32; Wertheim, Oral History, 102; Ramage, Oral History, 279–282; John C. Niedermair, Oral History, USNI (1978), NL, 333–334.

⁶Rees, *The Seas and the Subs*, 142; Whitmore, "The Origin of Polaris," 56–58; Sapolsky, *The Polaris System Development*, 34–58; Baar and Howard, *Polaris!*, 242, 158; Carl H. Builder, *The Masks of War: American Military Styles in Strategy and Analysis* (Baltimore: Johns Hopkins University Press, 1989), 199–200; Rear Admiral H. G. Rickover, "Another Kind of 'Satellite'—U.S. Missile-Firing Submarines," *U.S. News & World Report*, 25 October 1957, 60, 62; "New Weapon That Will Stop Russia?," *U.S. News & World Report*, 21 March 1958, 68–72, 75–76; Admiral Arleigh A. Burke, "Missiles and the Defense Organization," *Vital Speeches of the Day*, 24, n. 8 (1 February 1958), 244–247; Ramage, Oral History, 279–280; Smedberg, Oral History, II, 644–645; Masterson, Oral History, 341.

⁷Sapolsky, *The Polaris System Development*, 67–93; Rees, *The Seas and the Subs*, 215–233; Colwell, Oral History, 168–215; Withington, Oral History, 151–160.

⁸Sapolsky, *The Polaris System Development*, 160–191, 97–130; Admiral Harry D. Felt, Oral History, USNI, I (1974), NL, 304–305; Baar and Howard, *Polaris!*, 222–223, 146–160; *Missiles and Rockets*, 15 January 1962, 16; Rees, *The Seas and the Subs*, 146–155; Vice Admiral Eli T. Reich, Oral History, USNI, II (1982), NL, 742–746; Wertheim, Oral History, 173–176.

⁹Whitmore, "The Origin of Polaris," 59; *Time*, 3 March 1958, 14–15; *Life*, 1 September 1958, 42–53; Sapolsky, *The Polaris System Development*, 132–159; Baar and Howard, *Polaris!*, 52–76.

¹⁰Baar and Howard, *Polaris!*, 91–130; Rees, *The Seas and the Subs*, 158–163; Whitmore, "The Origin of Polaris," 59; Masterson, Oral History, 300–302; Wertheim, Oral History, 247–248; Mack, Oral History, II, 784–787.

¹¹Patrick Tyler, *Running Critical: The Silent War, Rickover, and General Dynamics* (New York: Harper & Row, 1986), 91–92; Rees, *The Seas and the Subs*, 163–165; Baar and Howard, *Polaris!*, 131–146; Captain Arthur C. Smith, "Sea Lords," *SM*, 50, n. 7 (September, 1987), 23–24.

¹²Captain G. M. Boyd, "Polaris Test Ship," *USNIP*, 88, n. 8 (August, 1962), 93–105; Rees, *The Seas and the Subs*, 167–174, 187–193; Baar and Howard, *Polaris!*, 227–240, 160–174, 197–207; Wertheim, Oral History, 186.

¹³J. Robert Moskin, "Polaris," *Look*, 29 August 1961, 17–28, 31; Baar and Howard, *Polaris!*, 175–196; Rees, *The Seas and the Subs*, 194–213; Benson, Oral History, II, 694–697; Admiral Arleigh Burke, Oral History, USNI (1973), NL, 136–139, 223.

¹⁴Nick Kotz, *Wild Blue Yonder: Money, Politics, and the B-1 Bomber* (New York: Pantheon Books, 1988); Strobe Talbott, *The Master of the Game: Paul Nitze and the Nuclear Peace* (New York: Vintage Books, 1989), 92; Eric J. Grove, *Vanguard to Trident: British Naval Policy Since World War Two* (Annapolis: Naval Institute Press, 1987), 233–234, 236–239, 240–241; Richard A. Stubbing, *The Defense Game: An Insider Explores the Astonishing Realities of America's Defense Establishment* (New York: Harper & Row, 1986), 270–271; Admiral I. J. Galantin, "The Resolution of Polaris," *USNIP*, 111, n. 4 (April, 1985), 80–88; Timothy E. Shea, "Project Poseidon," *USNIP*, 87, n. 2 (February, 1961), 32–41; Rear Admiral Charles E. Loughlin, Oral History, USNI (1982), NL, 287–312.

¹⁵*Aviation Week*, 24 February 1958, 28, 30; Hanson W. Baldwin, "New 'Battleship'—

the A-Submarine," *New York Times Magazine*, 16 March 1958, 13, 100–101; *U.S. News & World Report*, 22 August 1958, 52–53; Commander P. H. Backus, "Finite Deterrence, Controlled Retaliation," *USNIP*, 85, n. 3 (March, 1959), 23–29; Commander Robert D. McWethy, "Significance of the *Nautilus* Polar Cruise," *USNIP*, 84, n. 5 (May, 1958), 32–35; *U.S. News & World Report*, 15 August 1958, 40–41; *Newsweek*, 25 August 1958, 24–26, 28.

[16]Fred Kaplan, *The Wizards of Armageddon* (New York: Touchstone Books, 1984), 234–237; Baar and Howard, *Polaris!*, 207–218; Anthony E. Sokol, "Sea, Land, Air, and Missile Power," *USNIP*, 86, n. 5 (May, 1960), 27–35; Leland C. Allen, "The Role of Undersea Warfare in U.S. Strategic Doctrine," *MA*, 23, n. 3 (Fall, 1959), 153–157; Charles J. V. Murphy, "The New Mix," *Fortune*, August 1959, 76–83, 180, 182, 184, 187; David MacIsaac, "Voices from the Central Blue: The Air Power Theorists," in Peter Paret, ed., *Makers of Modern Strategy from Machiavelli to the Nuclear Age* (Princeton: Princeton University Press, 1986), 642; Lawrence Freedman, "The First Two Generations of Nuclear Strategists," in Paret, *Makers of Modern Strategy*, 757.

[17]Ronald E. Powaski, *March to Armageddon: The United States and the Nuclear Arms Race, 1939 to the Present* (New York: Oxford University Press, 1987), 64, 73; S. Nelson Drew, "Expecting the Approach of Danger: The 'Missile Gap' as a Study of Executive-Congressional Competition in Building Consensus on National Security Issues," *Presidential Studies Quarterly*, 19, n. 2 (Spring, 1989), 317–335; Paolucci, "The Development of Navy Strategic Offensive and Defensive Systems," 219–220; Walter A. McDougall, . . . *the Heavens and the Earth: A Political History of the Space Age* (New York: Basic Books, Inc., 1985), 326–328; Rear Admiral Ralph Kirk James, Oral History, USNI (1972), NL, 301–303.

[18]Arthur T. Hadley, *The Straw Giant, America's Armed Forces: Triumphs and Failures* (New York: Avon Books, 1987), 137–138; William V. Kennedy, "One Strategic Command?," *America*, 102 (6 February 1960), 545; *America*, 102 (20 February 1960), 597; Rees, *The Seas and the Subs*, 168–169; Admiral Robert Lee Dennison, Oral History, USNI (1975), NL, 474–475; Admiral Roy L. Johnson, Oral History, USNI (1982), NL, 249–255; Vice Admiral Gerald E. Miller, Oral History, USNI, I (1983), NL, 272–275, 292–295.

[19]Richard Smoke, *National Security and the Nuclear Dilemma: An Introduction to the American Experience*, 2nd ed. (New York: Random House, 1987), 110–112; Barrett Gallagher, "Sentinels Under the Sea," *USNIP*, 88, n. 9 (September, 1962), 85–99; Robert O'Connell, *Of Arms and Men: A History of War, Weapons, and Aggression* (New York: Oxford University Press, 1989), 298–299; Rear Admiral W. F. Raborn, "Polaris—Not Just Another Missile," *SM*, 23, nos. 6–7 (June–July, 1960), 4–6, 8, 10, 12–13; Harvey Sapolsky, "Technological Innovators: Admirals Raborn and Rickover," in Lieutenant Arnold R. Shapack, ed., *The Navy in an Age of Change and Crisis: Some Challenges and Responses of the Twentieth Century*, Proceedings, Naval History Symposium (Annapolis: United States Naval Academy, 1973), 23–35; Paolucci, "The Development of Navy Strategic Offensive and Defensive Systems," 216, 219; Captain Alex A. Kerr, Oral History, USNI (1984), NL, 378–380; Withington, Oral History, 129.

CHAPTER TWENTY-EIGHT

[1]Paul Kennedy, *The Rise and Fall of the Great Powers: Economic Change and Military Conflict from 1500 to 2000* (New York: Random House, 1987), 388–390; Michael A. Palmer, *On Course to Desert Storm: The United States Navy and the Persian Gulf*, Contributions to Naval History . . . No. 5 (Washington, D.C.: Naval Historical Center, 1992), 61–63; Joel J. Sakolsky, *Seapower in the Nuclear Age: The United States Navy and NATO, 1949–1980* (Annapolis: Naval Institute Press, 1991), 17, 21; Officer Biography, Admiral Lynde D. McCormick, NHD; Lieutenant Colonel Robert C. Williams, Jr., USA, "The Allied Command, Atlantic," *MR*, 32, n. 10 (January, 1953), 33–40; Rear Admiral Francis D. Foley, Oral History, USNI, II (1988), NL, 610, 615–628; Admiral Charles K. Duncan, Oral History, USNI, I (1978), NL, 55; Duncan, Oral History, III (1983), NL, 1475–1476; Lieutenant Commander D. D. Lewis, "The NATO ASW Situation," *USNIP*, 85, n. 4 (April, 1959), 55–63; Officer Biography, Admiral Jerauld Wright, NHD; Anthony E. Sokol, "Naval Aspects of European Integration," *MR*, 35, n. 3 (June, 1955), 26–36; Eileen and Robert Mason Pollock, "Mother of the Sixth Fleet," *Reader's Digest*, 75, n. 447 (July, 1959), 77–81; Admiral Alfred M. Pride, Oral History, USNI (1984), NL, 207–208; Rear Admiral Kemp Tolley, Oral History, USNI, II (1984), NL, 777–781; Admiral Alfred G. Ward, Oral History, USNI (1972), NL, 101–105; Rear Admiral Joshua W. Cooper, Oral History, USNI (1975), NL, 16; Rear Admiral William D. Irvin, Oral History, USNI (1980), NL, 503–506.

[2]Thomas G. Paterson, *Meeting the Communist Threat: Truman to Reagan* (New York: Oxford University Press, 1989), 165–166; David W. Tarr, *American Strategy in the Nuclear Age* (London: MacMillan Company, 1966), 77–79; Robin Wright, *Sacred Rage: The Wrath of Militant Islam* (New York: Touchstone Books, 1986), 252; Daniel Yergin, *The Prize: The Epic Quest for Oil, Money & Power* (New York: Touchstone Books, 1992), 210–212, 362, 371, 379, 393, 406–407, 412 [emphasis in original], 416, 425, 427–428; William H. Hessler, "By the Shores of Araby: The Persian Gulf Command," *USNIP*, 82, n. 10 (October, 1956), 1027–1041; Michael A. Palmer, "The U.S. Navy and the Persian Gulf: The Origins of the Commitment, 1945–1953," in William R. Roberts and Jack Sweetman, eds., *New Interpretations of Naval History: Selected Papers from the Ninth Naval History Symposium* (Annapolis: Naval Institute Press, 1991), 140–158; Palmer, *On Course to Desert Storm*, 3–17, 29–39, 44–46; Vice Admiral John L. Chew, Oral History, USNI (1979), NL, 179–180; Letter, Commander Middle East Force to Chief of Naval Operations (OP09B9), "History Report, 1 January 1949– 31 December 1958," 29 July 1960, NHD; Ship's History, USS *Duxbury Bay* (AVP-38) (22 October 1955–31 December 1958), 23 May 1958, NHD.

[3]Fleet Admiral William D. Leahy, *I Was There* (New York: McGraw-Hill Book Company, Inc., 1950), 375; Ed Cray, *General of the Army, George C. Marshall: Soldier and Statesman* (New York: Touchstone Books, 1991), 657; Yergin, *The Prize*, 480–485; Christopher Andrew and Oleg Gordievsky, *KGB: The Inside Story* (New York: Harper Collins, 1991), 495; Paterson, *Meeting the Communist Threat*, 168; Robert A. Divine, *Eisenhower and the Cold War* (New York: Oxford University Press, 1981), 71–73.

⁴Divine, *Eisenhower and the Cold War*, 79–83; Yergin, *The Prize*, 483; Paul A. Carter, *Another Part of the Fifties* (New York: Columbia University Press, 1983), 75–76.

⁵Sapolsky, *Seapower in the Nuclear Age*, 24–25, 29–33; Thomas A. Bryson, *Tars, Turks, and Tankers: The Role of the United States Navy in the Middle East, 1800–1979* (Metuchen, N.J.: Scarecrow Press, Inc., 1980), 105–108; Jon Winokur, ed., *The Portable Curmudgeon* (New York: New American Library, 1987), 17; Stephen E. Ambrose, *Eisenhower*, II: *The President* (New York: Simon and Schuster, 1984), 331–332; Captain John V. Noel, Oral History, USNI (1987), NL, 140–141, 151.

⁶Divine, *Eisenhower and the Cold War*, 84–85; Officer Biography, Admiral Walter F. Boone, NHD; Officer Biography, Admiral Charles R. Brown, NHD; Vice Admiral William R. Smedberg III, Oral History, USNI, II (1979), NL, 566–567; Rear Admiral Charles E. Loughlin, Oral History, USNI (1982), NL, 192–199; Rear Admiral Malcolm W. Schoeffel, Oral History, USNI (1979), NL, 135–136; Vice Admiral Charles L. Melson, Oral History, USNI (1974), NL, 230–231; Pride, Oral History, 209–210; Carter, *Another Part of the Fifties*, 77–78; Bryson, *Tars, Turks, and Tankers*, 108–122; Palmer, *On Course to Desert Storm*, 64–66; Letter, Commanding Officer, USS *Chilton* (APA-38) to Chief of Naval Information, "Evacuation of Americans and Foreign Nationals from Alexandria, Egypt, to Soudha Bay, Crete, 1–4 November 1956," 8 November 1956, NHD; Letter, Commander Sixth Fleet to Chief of Naval Operations, "A Brief History of the United States Sixth Fleet in the Mediterranean Area, 1950–1958," 5 September 1959, NHD; Lieutenant Commander William B. Garrett, "The Navy's Role in the 1956 Suez Crisis," *NWCR*, 22, n. 7 (March, 1970), 66–78; Donald Neff, *Warriors at Suez: Eisenhower Takes America into the Middle East* (New York: Simon & Schuster, 1981), 21; *Life*, 10 December 1956, 143–146, 148; *Time*, 7 January 1957, 12–14; Admiral Arleigh Burke, Oral History, USNI (1973), NL, 86–87.

⁷Captain Stephen Jurika, Jr., Oral History, USNI, II (1979), NL, 981–982; Rear Admiral Edward A. Ruckner, Oral History, USNI (1977), NL, 264–265; Eric J. Grove, *Vanguard to Trident: British Naval Policy Since World War II* (Annapolis: Naval Institute Press, 1987), 194, 196; Divine, *Eisenhower and the Cold War*, 86–88; *U.S. News & World Report*, 14 December 1956, 30–32; Yergin, *The Prize*, 492–497; Rear Admiral Henry E. Eccles, "SUEZ 1956—Some Military Lessons," *NWCR*, 21, n. 7 (March, 1969), 28–56; Andrew and Gordievsky, *KGB*, 496; Ambrose, *Eisenhower*, II, 368–369; Vice Admiral William P. Mack, Oral History, USNI, I (1980), NL, 260–262; Rear Admiral George H. Miller, Oral History, USNI (1975), NL, 204, 230–231.

⁸Divine, *Eisenhower and the Cold War*, 91–97; Paterson, *Meeting the Communist Threat*, 180–182, 184; Seyom Brown, *The Faces of Power: Constancy and Change in United States Foreign Policy from Truman to Reagan* (New York: Columbia University Press, 1983), 124–125; *Life*, 6 May 1957, 36–43; *Life*, 13 May 1957, 32–37; Ambrose, *Eisenhower*, II, 381–383, 388.

⁹*Newsweek*, 11 February 1957, 49–52; *Time*, 6 May 1957, 21; Commander Charles M. Melhorn, Oral History, USNI (1983), NL, 143–150; Harold H. Martin, "Cat Brown's Kittens Have Claws," *Saturday Evening Post*, 12 March 1957, 32–33, 81–82, 84; *U.S. News & World Report*, 10 May 1957, 50–53; *Aviation Week*,

1 July 1957, 32–33; *Business Week*, 7 September 1957, 142–144, 146, 150; Captain Slade D. Cutter, Oral History, USNI, II (1985), NL, 409–411; Pride, Oral History, 207–217; Rear Admiral Thomas H. Morton, Oral History, USNI (1979), NL, 275–282; Rear Admiral Frederic Stanton Withington, Oral History, USNI (1972), NL, 98–99; Vice Admiral Kleber S. Masterson, Oral History, USNI (1973), NL, 153–156.

[10]Divine, *Eisenhower and the Cold War*, 97–100; Paterson, *Meeting the Communist Threat*, 186–188; Palmer, *On Course to Desert Storm*, 66–70; Midshipman Second Class Christopher S. Calhoun, "Lebanon: That Was Then," *USNIP*, 111, n. 9 (September, 1985), 74–80; Lieutenant Colonel Margaret M. Bodron, USA, "US Intervention in Lebanon—1958," *MR*, 56, n. 2 (February, 1976), 66–76; Captain Elward F. Baldridge, "Lebanon and Quemoy—The Navy's Role," *USNIP*, 87, n. 2 (February 1961), 94–100; Ship's History, USS *Essex* (CVA-9), 6 February 1959, NHD; Ship's History, USS *Des Moines* (CA-134), 5 January 1959, NHD; Bryson, *Tars, Turks, and Tankers*, 123–134; Admiral Charles Donald Griffin, Oral History, USNI, I (1973), NL, 352–354; Admiral Arleigh Burke, Oral History, USNI, IV (1983), NL, 400–401.

[11]Bryson, *Tars, Turks, and Tankers*, 134–137; E. B. Potter, *Admiral Arleigh Burke: A Biography* (New York: Random House, 1990), 426–427; James Cable, *Gunboat Diplomacy, 1919–1979: Political Applications of Limited Naval Force*, 2nd ed. (London: MacMillan Press, Ltd., 1981), 74–81; H. W. Brands, Jr., "Decisions on American Armed Intervention: Lebanon, Dominican Republic, and Grenada," *Political Science Quarterly*, 102, n. 4 (Winter, 1987–1988), 607–624.

[12]Ambrose, *Eisenhower*, II, 463–475; Calhoun, "Lebanon," 77–78; Robert McClintock, "The American Landing in Lebanon," *USNIP*, 88, n. 10 (October, 1962), 65–79; Admiral Arleigh Burke, "The Lebanon Crisis," in Lieutenant Arnold R. Shapack, ed., *The Navy in an Age of Change and Crisis: Some Challenges and Responses of the Twentieth Century*, Proceedings, Naval History Symposium (Annapolis: United States Naval Academy, 1973), 70–80 [emphasis in original]; Admiral James L. Holloway, Jr., "Rapid Deployment, 1958: A Personal Memoir of the Lebanon Landings," *SM*, 45, n. 1 (January–February, 1982), 24–27; Burke, Oral History, II (1980), 247; Burke, Oral History (1973), 45–46, 109.

[13]Calhoun, "Lebanon," 79–80; Paterson, *Meeting the Communist Threat*, 188–189; Divine, *Eisenhower and the Cold War*, 101–104; Palmer, *On Course to Desert Storm*, 43–48; Bryson, *Tars, Turks, and Tankers*, 140.

[14]William H. Hessler, "Our Sixth Fleet in the Mediterranean," *Reporter*, 18, n. 4 (20 February 1958), 21–24; Paul Ginsborg, *A History of Contemporary Italy: Society and Politics, 1943–1988* (New York: Viking Penguin, 1990), 116–118; Dickey Chapelle, "Cat Brown—Master of the Med," *Reader's Digest*, 72, n. 431 (March, 1958), 76–81; William H. Hessler, "Sixth Fleet: Beefed Up for a Bigger Job," *USNIP*, 84, n. 8 (August, 1958), 23–30; Admiral I. J. Galantin, "A Seaport in Cyprus: Showing the Flag Twenty Years Ago," *SM*, 44, n. 2 (March, 1981), 17–18; Rear Admiral Roy S. Benson, Oral History, USNI, II (1987), NL, 515–536; Masterson, Oral History, 258; Ward, Oral History, 77; Martin, "Cat Brown's Kittens Have Claws," 84.

CHAPTER TWENTY-NINE

[1]"A General Says: We Need the Bluejackets," *American Mercury,* 86 (March, 1958), 136–137; Vincent Davis, *The Admirals Lobby* (Chapel Hill: University of North Carolina Press, 1967), 274–276; Rear Admiral John Livingston McCrea, "The Naval Commander and Public Relations," *NWCR,* 6, n. 3 (November, 1953), 1–23; Rear Admiral Edmund B. Taylor, "Public Relations in the Navy," *NWCR,* 9, n. 8 (April, 1957), 17–31; Vice Admiral Murrey L. Royar, SC, Oral History, USNI (1974), NL, 201–204; Rear Admiral Roy S. Benson, Oral History, USNI, I (1984), NL, 431–435, 450–458; Hanson Weightman Baldwin, Oral History, USNI, I (1976), NL, 245–247; Admiral Harry D. Felt, Oral History, USNI, I (1974), NL, 327–331.

[2]*Aviation Week,* 2 March 1953, 52–56, 59; *SNR,* in *SDR* (1 January–30 June 1953), 170–184; *SNR,* in *SDR* (1 January–30 June 1954), 153–156, 172–176; *SNR,* in *SDR* (1 January–30 June 1955), 144–163; *SNR,* in *SDR* (1 January–30 June 1956), 163–175; *SNR,* in *SDR* (1 January–30 June 1957), 173–199 [emphasis in original]; *SNR,* in *SDR* (1 January–30 June 1958), 205–221; *SNR,* in *SDR* (1 July 1958–30 June 1959), 209–225; *SNR,* in *SDR* (1 July 1959–30 June 1960), 230–250; *SNR,* in *SDR* (1 July 1960–30 June 1961), 197–212.

[3]*SNR,* in *SDR* (1 January–30 June 1957), 258–262; *SNR,* in *SDR* (1 July 1958–30 June 1959), 258–260; *SNR,* in *SDR* (1 July 1959–30 June 1960), 287–288; *SNR,* in *SDR* (1 July 1960–30 June 1961), 252–255; William V. Kennedy, "NSD, Mechanicsburg," *USNIP,* 82, n. 6 (June, 1956), 649–655; Royar, Oral History, 176; Admiral Arleigh Burke, Oral History, USNI, IV (1983), NL, 385–390, 412–415.

[4]*SNR,* in *SDR* (1 January–30 June 1953), 234–240; *SNR,* in SDR (1 January–30 June 1954), 234–241; *SNR,* in *SDR* (1 January–30 June 1956), 233–242, 247–250; *SNR,* in *SDR* (1 January–30 June 1957), 278–285; *SNR,* in *SDR* (1 January–30 June 1958), 259–262; *SNR,* in *SDR* (1 July 1958–30 June 1959), 276–282; *SNR,* in *SDR* (1 July 1959–30 June 1960), 304–310; *SNR,* in *SDR* (1 July 1960–30 June 1961), 268–275; Royar, Oral History, 261–262, 297–299; Rear Admiral R. L. Shifley, "The Role of the Chief of Naval Material in Logistics Administration," *NWCR,* 17, n. 8 (April, 1965), 1–15; Vice Admiral Kleber S. Masterson, Oral History, USNI (1973), NL, 349–350; Vice Admiral Edwin B. Hooper, Oral History, USNI (1978), NL, 280.

[5]*SNR,* in *SDR* (1 January–30 June 1956), 224–231; *SNR,* in *SDR* (1 January–30 June 1957), 263–267, 252–257; *SNR,* in *SDR* (1 January–30 June 1958), 250–252; *SNR,* in *SDR* (1 July 1958–30 June 1959), 261–264; *SNR,* in *SDR* (1 July 1959–30 June 1960), 289–292; *SNR,* in *SDR* (1 July 1960–30 June 1961), 256–259; Rear Admiral Schuyler Neilson Pyne, Oral History, USNI (1972), NL, 406–408; "Big and Urgent Navy Business in Brooklyn," *Fortune,* 66, n. 5 (November, 1962), 132–139.

[6]Ed Cray, *General of the Army, George C. Marshall: Soldier and Statesman* (New York: Touchstone Books, 1991), 343–344; Captain Arthur F. Spring, "Mobile Naval Support for Total War," *USNIP,* 81, n. 8 (August, 1955), 907–916; Captain Randolph Meade, Jr., "The Service Squadron," *NWCR,* 9, n. 10 (June, 1957), 1–21; Commander Robert C. Disher, SC, "Future Concepts of Mobile Logistic

Supply," *USNIP*, 85, n. 6 (June, 1959), 48–56; Captain Morton H. Lytle, "Replenishing the Nuclear Navy," *USNIP*, 85, n. 10 (October, 1959), 56–61; Vice Admiral George C. Dyer, "Logistical Readiness," *USNIP*, 86, n. 5 (May, 1960), 51–61; Vice Admiral John Barr Colwell, Oral History, USNI (1974), NL, 137–138, 157–164; Rear Admiral William D. Irvin, Oral History, USNI (1980), NL, 576–624.

7Rear Admiral William M. Callaghan, "Operations of the Military Sea Transport Service," *SM*, 14, n. 4 (April, 1951), 4–5, 12; Vice Admiral William M. Callaghan, "Military Sea Transportation Service," *NWCR*, 5, n. 5 (January, 1953), 31–57; Rear Admiral Arthur H. McCollum, Oral History, USNI, II (1973), NL, 814–817; Rear Admiral Roy A. Gano, "MSTS Operations," *NWCR*, 9, n. 9 (May, 1957), 25–51; Louis R. Fiore, "MSTS—The Navy's Fourth Arm," *USNIP*, 83, n. 8 (August, 1957), 868–889; Vice Admiral Roy A. Gano, "MSTS—A Fleet in Readiness," *USNIP*, 90, n. 3 (March, 1964), 56–63; Vice Admiral Lawson P. Ramage, "The Military Sea Transportation Service," *NWCR*, 21, n. 9 (May, 1969), 4–11; Benson, Oral History, II (1987), 617–655.

8Charles C. Bates and John F. Fuller, *America's Weather Warriors, 1814–1985* (College Station: Texas A&M University Press, 1986), 169–170; Captain James R. Ogden, Oral History, USNI (1982), NL, 118–119; Richard F. Dempewolff, "Under Antarctic Ice, the Seabees Build a Town," *Popular Mechanics*, 105, n. 4 (April, 1956), 89–94, 266, 268, 270, 272, 274, 276; *Popular Mechanics*, 105, n. 5 (May, 1956), 98–102, 256, 258, 260, 262, 264; Officer Biography, Rear Admiral Richard Evelyn Byrd, Jr., NHD; Officer Biography, Rear Admiral George J. Dufek, NHD; Letter, Commander Task Force 43 to Chief of Naval Operations, "Report of Operation DEEP FREEZE II," 1 May 1957, NHD; Letter, Commander Task Force 43 to Chief of Naval Operations, "DEEP FREEZE II Army-Navy Patrol Report," 10 June 1957, NHD; Lieutenant Commander James T. Strong, "The Opening of the Arctic Ocean," *USNIP*, 87, n. 10 (October, 1961), 58–65; Rear Admiral Edward K. Walker, Oral History, USNI (1985), NL, 251–253; Admiral Alfred G. Ward, Oral History, USNI (1972), NL, 118; Ambassador William J. Sebald, Oral History, USNI, III (1980), NL, 1412–1420.

9Hanson W. Baldwin, "The New Navy: A Reporter's Notebook," *New York Times Magazine*, 13 October 1957, 26–27, 85; "Ships that Have Passed into the Night," *New York Times Magazine*, 13 April 1958, 106; Admiral David L. McDonald, "Carrier Employment Since 1950," *USNIP*, 90, n. 11 (November, 1964), 26–33; *SNR*, in *SDR* (1 January–30 June 1956), 207–210; *SNR*, in *SDR* (1 January–30 June 1957), 241–247; *SNR*, in *SDR* (1 January–30 June 1958), 244–246; Norman Friedman, *The Postwar Naval Revolution* (Annapolis: Naval Institute Press, 1986), 43, 108–109; Rear Admiral Roy S. Benson, "Fleet Air Defense—Vital New Role of the Cruiser," *USNIP*, 84, n. 6 (June, 1958), 47–49; "PRISM To Be Used on Missile Ships," *Missiles and Rockets*, 25 September 1961, 42–43.

10*Newsweek*, 9 April 1956, 65–70, 72; Hanson W. Baldwin, "Is the Navy Obsolete?" *Saturday Evening Post*, 11 August 1956, 25, 59–61; *Aviation Week*, 7 March 1960, 78–81; Lou Davis, "Position Report: U.S. Navy," *Flying*, 68, n. 6 (June, 1961), 28–30, 98–100; *U.S. News & World Report*, 19 February 1962, 84–85; *Life*, 22 June 1962, 52–65, 72B.

[11]Davis, *The Admirals Lobby*, 174–175; *SNR*, in *SDR* (1 January–30 June 1956), 211–223; *SNR*, in *SDR* (1 January–30 June 1957), 268–277, 248–251; *SNR*, in *SDR* (1 January–30 June 1958), 253–258, 247–249; Ralph Lapp, *The Weapons Culture* (Baltimore: Penguin Books, Inc., 1969), 90; Stephen E. Ambrose, *Eisenhower*, II: *The President* (New York: Touchstone Books, 1984), 494, 259; Paul A. Carter, *Another Part of the Fifties* (New York: Columbia University Press, 1983), 259; Benson, Oral History, II, 601; Rear Admiral Francis D. Foley, Oral History, USNI, II (1988), NL, 674–677, 696–697, 706–709; Vice Admiral Gerald E. Miller, Oral History, USNI, I (1983), NL, 255–258.

[12]Ship's History, USS *Aggressive* (MSO-422), 31 January 1967, NHD; Tamara Moser Melia, *"Damn the Torpedoes:" A Short History of U.S. Naval Mine Countermeasures, 1777–1991*, Contributions to Naval History . . . No. 4 (Washington, D.C.: Naval Historical Center, 1991), 82–90; Commander Paolo E. Coletta, "Naval Mine Warfare," *USNIP*, 85, n. 11 (November, 1959), 82–96; Foley, Oral History, II, 565; Vice Admiral Roland N. Smoot, Oral History, USNI (1972), NL, 276–278; Vice Admiral Robert S. Salzer, Oral History, USNI (1981), NL, 535–540; Vice Admiral Eli T. Reich, Oral History, USNI, I (1982), NL, 400–401; Eugene N. Wolfe, "The Water Bugs Are Coming," *USNIP*, 85, n. 11 (November, 1959), 75–78; Jerry Hulse, "Tiny Sub Maneuvers Under Water Like a Plane," *Popular Science*, 170, n. 5 (May, 1957), 64–66, 254, 256; Patrick Tyler, *Running Critical: The Silent War, Rickover, and General Dynamics* (New York: Harper & Row, 1986), 26–29; Friedman, *The Postwar Naval Revolution*, 109; Vice Admiral Raymond E. Peet, Oral History, USNI (1984), NL, 378; Captain Stephen Jurika, Jr., Oral History, USNI, II (1979), NL, 1005.

[13]"Defense Spurs Study of Oceans' Depths," *Business Week*, 17 June 1961, 47–48, 50; Leland C. Allen, "The Role of Undersea Warfare in U.S. Strategic Doctrine," *MA*, 23, n. 3 (Fall, 1959), 153–157; Frank Harvey, "Can We Defend Our Coasts Against Russian Subs?," *Popular Science*, 171, n. 3 (September, 1957), 161–164; *Aviation Week*, 6 January 1958, 37; Ed Rees, *The Seas and the Subs* (New York: Duell, Sloan and Pearce, 1961), 25–26; Clark G. Reynolds, *Admiral John H. Towers: The Struggle for Naval Air Supremacy* (Annapolis: Naval Institute Press, 1991), 295; Foley, Oral History, I (1988), 55–57; Admiral James S. Russell, Oral History, USNI (1976), NL, 121; Admiral John S. Thach, Oral History, USNI, I (1977), NL, 146–156, 237–239; Officer Biography, Admiral John S. Thach, NHD: *Time*, 7 April 1958, 21; *Time*, 1 September 1958, 9–14; Benson, Oral History, I, 370–379; Hooper, Oral History, 264–267, 379–383; Rear Admiral Edward A. Ruckner, Oral History, USNI (1977), NL, 298–310, 481–486; Rear Admiral Charles E. Loughlin, Oral History, USNI (1982), NL, 250–256.

[14]Lieutenant A. L. Davis, "Offensive ASW: Fundamental to Defense," *USNIP*, 83, n. 6 (June, 1957), 583–589; *Aviation Week*, 14 July 1958, 32–33; Marvin Weisbord, "Nemesis of the Submarine," *Popular Mechanics*, 109, n. 3 (March, 1958), 102–105, 166; *Newsweek*, 30 June 1958, 57; Benson, Oral History, I, 405–424; Rear Admiral Thomas H. Morton, Oral History, USNI (1979), NL, 425–426; Thach, Oral History, II (1977), 686–718; Command History, Task Group ALFA / Carrier Division 16 (1 January–31 December 1959), 26 January 1960, NHD.

[15]*Time*, 1 September 1958, 9–14; *Aviation Week*, 21 July 1958, 73, 75, 77, 79; Wayne Thomis, "Can We Stop the Missile Subs?," *Science Digest*, 44, n. 5 (November, 1958), 60–66; Captain Thomas D. McGrath, "Antisubmarine Defense Group ALFA," *USNIP*, 85, n. 8 (August, 1959), 49–55; Ship's History, USS *Valley Forge* (CVS-45), 24 February 1960, NHD; Tristram Coffin, *The Armed Society: Militarism in Modern America* (Baltimore: Penguin Books, 1964), 234; Commander R. A. Weatherup, "Defense Against Nuclear-Powered Submarines," *USNIP*, 85, n. 12 (December, 1959), 71–75; Commander George P. Steele, "Killing Nuclear Submarines," *USNIP*, 86, n. 11 (November, 1960), 45–51; Benson, Oral History, II, 725–735; Vice Admiral Lawson P. Ramage, Oral History, USNI (1975), NL, 277, 284–285.

CHAPTER THIRTY

[1]Vincent Davis, *The Admirals Lobby* (Chapel Hill: University of North Carolina Press, 1967), 214–215, 312–313; Kenneth P. O'Donnell and David F. Powers, *"Johnny, We Hardly Knew Ye:" Memories of John Fitzgerald Kennedy* (Boston: Little, Brown and Company, 1972), 250–251; Thomas C. Reeves, *A Question of Character: A Life of John F. Kennedy* (Rocklin, Cal.: Prima Publishing, 1992), 38, 2, 55–67, 69–73; Neil Sheehan, *A Bright Shining Lie: John Paul Vann and America in Vietnam* (New York: Vintage Books, 1989), 297; Arthur M. Schlesinger, Jr., *A Thousand Days: John F. Kennedy in the White House* (Boston: Houghton Mifflin Company, 1965), 85–87; Letter, Captain A. G. Kirk to Captain C. W. Carr, MC, 24 March 1941 [I am indebted to Professor Robert William Love, Jr., of the department of history, United States Naval Academy, for this reference]; Lewis J. Paper, *John F. Kennedy: The Promise and the Performance* (New York: Da Capo Press, Inc., 1979), 41; Lieutenant Commander Patrick Munroe, "Luck of the Toss," *American Heritage*, 43, n. 6 (October, 1992), 32–33.

[2]O'Donnell and Powers, *"Johnny, We Hardly Knew Ye,"* 409, 265; Reeves, *A Question of Character*, 68, 91–92, 96, 119–123, 3, 260, 290 [emphasis added], 397; T. L. Bosiljevac, *SEALS: UDT/SEAL Operations in Vietnam* (New York: Ivy Books, 1991), 6; Thomas G. Paterson, *Meeting the Communist Threat: Truman to Reagan* (New York: Oxford University Press, 1989), 195, 198–199, 202–203, 207–210; *Time*, 20 April 1962, 26; Captain Slade D. Cutter, Oral History, USNI, II (1985), NL, 439–440.

[3]George Holmes, *The Florentine Enlightenment, 1400–1450* (New York: Pegasus, 1969), 157; John C. Donovan, *The Cold Warriors: A Policy-Making Elite* (Lexington, Mass.: D. C. Heath and Company, 1974), 268–269; Ron Chernow, *The House of Morgan: An American Banking Dynasty and the Rise of Modern Finance* (New York: Touchstone Books, 1991), 542–543.

[4]Donovan, *The Cold Warriors*, 152–154; Walter Isaacson and Evan Thomas, *The Wise Men: Six Friends and the World They Made* (New York: Touchstone Books, 1988), 596–597; Reeves, *A Question of Character*, 9; O'Donnell and Powers, *"Johnny, We Hardly Knew Ye,"* 236–238.

[5]Paterson, *Meeting the Communist Threat*, 202; Vasili Klyuchevsky, *Peter the Great*, trans. Liliana Archibald (New York: Vintage Books, 1961), 200; Paul B. Ryan, *First Line of Defense: The U.S. Navy Since 1945* (Stanford, Cal.: Hoover Institution

Press, 1981), 30–34; Davis, *The Admirals Lobby*, 236; Lawrence J. Korb, "Robert McNamara's Impact on the Budget Strategies of the Joint Chiefs of Staff," *ASH*, 17, n. 4 (Winter, December, 1970), 132–136; *U.S. News & World Report*, 25 November 1963, 59–60; Rear Admiral Francis D. Foley, Oral History, USNI, II (1988), NL, 825; Captain John V. Noel, Oral History, USNI (1987), NL, 196; Admiral Charles K. Duncan, Oral History, USNI, III (1983), NL, 1426.

[6]Arthur T. Hadley, *The Straw Giant, America's Armed Forces: Triumphs and Failures* (New York: Avon Books, 1987), 195; Carl H. Builder, *The Masks of War: American Military Styles in Strategy and Analysis* (Baltimore: Johns Hopkins University Press, 1989), 106–107; Vice Admiral J. Victor Smith, Oral History, USNI (1977), NL, 368–378; Admiral Alfred G. Ward, Oral History, USNI (1972), NL, 234, 242; Vice Admiral Ruthven E. Libby, Oral History, USNI (1984), NL, 165–166; Captain Charles J. Merdinger, Oral History, USNI (1974), NL, 234–235; Peter Collier and David Horowitz, *The Fords: An American Epic* (New York: Summit Books, 1987), 290; Vice Admiral Raymond E. Peet, Oral History, USNI (1984), NL, 265–270; Rear Admiral Robert H. Wertheim, Oral History, USNI (1981), NL, 228–229; Admiral Charles Donald Griffin, Oral History, USNI, II (1975), NL, 491–504; Admiral Horacio Rivero, Jr., Oral History, USNI (1978), NL, 236; Vice Admiral Lawson P. Ramage, Oral History, USNI (1975), NL, 392–394.

[7]John R. Wadleigh, "William Birrell Franke, 8 June 1959–20 January 1961," in Paolo E. Coletta, ed., *American Secretaries of the Navy*, II: *1913–1972* (Annapolis: Naval Institute Press, 1980), 895–909; Paul R. Schratz, "John B. Connally, 20 January 1961–20 December 1961," in Coletta, *American Secretaries of the Navy*, II, 911–923; O'Donnell and Powers, *"Johnny, We Hardly Knew Ye,"* 238; *Time*, 21 April 1961, 18–19; Captain Alex A. Kerr, Oral History, USNI (1984), NL, 320–321; Vice Admiral William P. Mack, Oral History, USNI, I (1980), NL, 318; Vice Admiral Paul D. Stroop, Oral History, USNI (1970), NL, 302–315.

[8]Paul R. Schratz, "Fred Korth, 4 January 1962–1 November 1963," in Coletta, *American Secretaries of the Navy*, II, 925–939; *Time*, 14 June 1963, 25; William J. Coughlin, "Navy Again Outgunned," *Missiles and Rockets*, 21 October 1963, 52; Captain Alex A. Kerr, "As I Recall . . . The Korth Resignation," *USNIP*, 111, n. 5 (May, 1985), 168–169; Kerr, Oral History, 394–396; Griffin, Oral History, II, 547–549.

[9]E. B. Potter, *Admiral Arleigh Burke: A Biography* (New York: Random House, 1990), 416–434; Rear Admiral Gerald E. Miller, Oral History, USNI, I (1983), NL, 298–311; Dean Rusk and Richard Rusk, *As I Saw It*, ed. Daniel S. Papp (New York: Penguin Books, 1991), 548–549, 554; Hanson W. Baldwin, "CNO—Past, Present, and—Future?," *USNIP*, 89, n. 8 (August, 1963), 32–43; *Aviation Week*, 25 May 1959, 34; David Alan Rosenberg, "Arleigh Albert Burke, 17 August 1955–1 August 1961," in Robert William Love, Jr., ed., *The Chiefs of Naval Operations* (Annapolis: Naval Institute Press, 1980), 317.

[10]Admiral George W. Anderson, Jr., Oral History, USNI, I (1983), NL, 1–376; Officer Biography, Admiral George W. Anderson, NHD; Admiral Roy L. Johnson, Oral History, USNI (1982), NL, 54, 56, 224; Stroop, Oral History, 77–78, 308–309; *Newsweek*, 15 May 1961, 32–34; Lawrence Korb, "George

Whalen Anderson, Jr., 1 August 1961–1 August 1963," in Love, *The Chiefs of Naval Operations*, 321–330; *Aviation Week and Space Technology*, 18 June 1962, 29; Foley, Oral History, II, 684–685; Noel, Oral History, 317–318; 168; Admiral Arleigh Burke, Oral History, USNI, II (1980), NL, 317–318: Vice Admiral Charles S. Minter, Jr., Oral History, USNI, I (1981), NL, 398–399; *WP*, 21 March 1992.

¹¹*SNR*, in *SDR* (1 July 1961–30 June 1962), 234–236, 284, 271–275, 235–240, 202–215; Paul A. Carter, *Another Part of the Fifties* (New York: Columbia University Press, 1983), 283–284.

¹²Admiral Harry D. Felt, Oral History, USNI, I (1974), NL, 1–354; Officer Biography, Admiral Henry Donald Felt, NHD; Captain Stephen Jurika, Jr., Oral History, USNI, I (1979), NL, 147–150; *Time*, 6 January 1961, 17–22; Foley, Oral History, II, 767, 818; Vice Admiral Fitzhugh Lee, Oral History, USNI (1972), NL, 18; Admiral David Lamar McDonald, Oral History, USNI (1976), NL, 219; Ramage, Oral History, 297–299; Vice Admiral Robert S. Salzer, Oral History, USNI (1981), NL, 169–170, 207; Burke, Oral History (1973), 63–65; Griffin, Oral History, I, 1–458; Officer Biography, Admiral Charles D. Griffin, NHD; A. M. Rosenthal, "On Patrol with the Seventh Fleet," *New York Times Magazine*, 1 October 1961, 27, 82–83; *U.S. News & World Report*, 23 October 1961, 66–67; William H. Hessler, "The Seventh Fleet Is Ready," *Reporter*, 8 June 1961, 30–31.

¹³O'Donnell and Powers, *"Johnny, We Hardly Knew Ye,"* 268; Trumbull Higgins, *The Perfect Failure: Kennedy, Eisenhower, and the CIA at the Bay of Pigs* (New York: W. W. Norton & Company, 1989), 151; Reeves, *A Question of Character*, 280–284; Edward J. Marolda and Oscar P. Fitzgerald, *The United States Navy and the Vietnam Conflict*, II: *From Military Assistance to Combat* (Washington, D.C.: Naval Historical Center, 1986), 30 [emphasis in original], 71–72, 40, 43–45, 24–25, 83–87; Admiral U. S. G. Sharp, *Strategy for Defeat: Vietnam in Retrospect* (Novato, Cal.: Presidio Press, 1986 [1978]), 15; Foley, Oral History, II, 761–763; Felt, Oral History, II, 504–517; Burke, Oral History, 169–173; Vice Admiral Edwin B. Hooper, Oral History, USNI (1978), NL, 342–343; Ship's History, USS *St. Paul* (CA-73) (1 January–31 December 1961), 18 January 1962, NHD; Command History, Seventh Fleet (1960), 10 February 1961, "Laos Supplement," NHD; Command History, Seventh Fleet (1961), 17 February 1962, 3, NHD.

CHAPTER THIRTY-ONE

¹Bruce Catton, *Waiting for the Morning Train: An American Boyhood* (Detroit: Wayne State University Press, 1987 [1972]), 148; Robert L. Scheina, *Latin America: A Naval History, 1810–1987* (Annapolis: Naval Institute Press, 1987), 171–175; Rear Admiral Walter C. W. Ansel, Oral History, USNI (1972), NL, 220–221; Vice Admiral Charles S. Minter, Jr., Oral History, USNI, II (1981), NL, 647–649; Stephen E. Ambrose, *Eisenhower*, II: *The President* (New York: Touchstone Books, 1984), 192–197; Trumbull Higgins, *The Perfect Failure: Kennedy, Eisenhower, and the CIA at the Bay of Pigs* (New York: W. W. Norton & Company, 1989), 26–27.

²Major Donald L. Moore, USMCR, "The Bay of Pigs: An Analysis," *NWCR*, 19, n. 3 (November, 1966), 1–35; Lyman B. Kirkpatrick, Jr., "Paramilitary Case Study: The Bay of Pigs," *NWCR*, 25, n. 2 (November–December, 1972), 32–42; Barry Rubin, *Secrets of State: The State Department & the Struggle Over U.S. Foreign Policy* (New York: Oxford University Press, 1987), 92.

³Moore, "The Bay of Pigs," 10–15; Kirkpatrick, "Paramilitary Case Study," 34–37; Ambrose, *Eisenhower*, II, 584; "Memorandum for General Maxwell D. Taylor," 26 April 1961 [I am indebted to Professor Brian VanDeMark of the department of history, United States Naval Academy, for this reference].

⁴Higgins, *The Perfect Failure*, 41, 45–46, 48–49, 52–53, 82, 84, 96–97, 112–113, 62–63, 78, 84, 91, 116–117, 124–125; Rear Admiral Daniel V. Gallery, Oral History, USNI (1976), NL, 179–181; E. B. Potter, *Admiral Arleigh Burke: A Biography* (New York: Random House, 1990), 436–437; James Leutze, *A Different Kind of Victory: A Biography of Admiral Thomas C. Hart* (Annapolis: Naval Institute Press, 1981), 219; Captain Paul B. Ryan, *First Line of Defense: The U.S. Navy Since 1945* (Stanford, Cal.: Hoover Institution Press, 1981), 34–39; Captain Donald I. Thomas, "The Bay of Pigs," *SM*, 55, n. 1 (January–February, 1992), 31, 34; James G. Blight and David A. Welch, *On the Brink: Americans and Soviets Remember the Cuban Missile Crisis* (New York: Noonday Press, 1990), 30; Officer Biography, Admiral Robert Lee Dennison, NHD; Admiral Robert Lee Dennison, Oral History, USNI (1975), NL, 330–343A; Captain William C. Chapman, "A View from PriFly," *USNIP*, 118, n. 10 (October, 1992), 45–50; Rear Admiral Draper L. Kauffman, Oral History, USNI, I (1982), NL, 414–415; Vice Admiral William P. Mack, Oral History, USNI, I (1980), NL, 77–78; Rear Admiral Kemp Tolley, Oral History, USNI, I (1983), NL, 164–165; Admiral Arleigh Burke, Oral History, USNI, I (1979), NL, 13; Rear Admiral Henry L. Miller, Oral History, USNI, I (1973), NL, 186–187; Rear Admiral Charles E. Loughlin, Oral History, USNI (1982), NL, 263–264; Vice Admiral J. Victor Smith, Oral History, USNI (1977), NL, 271–272; Captain Robin L. C. Quigley, Oral History, USNI (1978), NL, 69–70; Captain Stephen Jurika, Jr., Oral History, USNI, II (1979), NL, 707–710.

⁵Chapman, "A View from PriFly," 45–50; Burke, Oral History (1973), 216–222; Officer Biography, Rear Admiral John E. Clark, NHD; Higgins, *The Perfect Failure*, 135, 138–153, 166, 168; Midshipman First Class Robert M. Beer, "The U.S. Navy and the Cuban Missile Crisis," Trident Scholar Project Report, United States Naval Academy, 22 May 1990, 5 [I am indebted to Professor Robert William Love, Jr., of the department of history, United States Naval Academy, for this reference]; Thomas C. Reeves, *A Question of Character: A Life of John F. Kennedy* (Rocklin, Cal.: Prima Publishing, 1992), 269–270; Kirkpatrick, "Paramilitary Case Study," 38–42; Moore, "The Bay of Pigs," 16–28; Kenneth P. O'Donnell and David F. Powers, *"Johnny, We Hardly Knew Ye:" Memories of John Fitzgerald Kennedy* (Boston: Little, Brown and Company, 1972), 270–278; Richard A. Stubbing, *The Defense Game: An Insider Explores the Astonishing Realities of America's Defense Establishment* (New York: Harper & Row, 1986), 267–268 [emphasis in original]; Captain Slade D. Cutter, Oral History, USNI, II (1985), NL, 424–425; Admiral Alfred G. Ward, Oral History, USNI (1972), NL, 160–165; Admiral Horacio Rivero, Jr., Oral History, USNI (1978), NL,

330–340; Admiral James S. Russell, Oral History, USNI (1976), NL, 345–347; Dennison, Oral History, 343A–369; Vice Admiral Fitzhugh Lee, Oral History, USNI (1972), NL, 291–299; Ship's History, USS *Essex* (CVS-9), 1961 (3 February 1962), NHD; Dino A. Brugioni, *Eyeball to Eyeball: The Inside Story of the Cuban Missile Crisis* (New York: Random House, 1991), 59–60; Ronald Steel, *Pax Americana* (New York: Viking Press, 1968), 249; John C. Donovan, *The Cold Warriors: A Policy-Making Elite* (Lexington, Mass.: D. C. Heath and Company, 1974), 177–179 [emphasis in original]; Thomas, "The Bay of Pigs," 31–32; Potter, *Admiral Arleigh Burke*, 437–438; Vice Admiral Lawson P. Ramage, Oral History, USNI (1975), NL, 405–407; Michael R. Beschloss, *The Crisis Years: Kennedy and Khrushchev, 1960–1963* (New York: Edward Burlingame Books, 1992), 202.

⁶Seyom Brown, *The Faces of Power: Constancy and Change in United States Foreign Policy from Truman to Reagan* (New York: Columbia University Press, 1983), 233; Brugioni, *Eyeball to Eyeball*, 245–246, 367–368, 250; Colonel Robert D. Heinl, Jr., USMC, "How We Got Guantanamo," *American Heritage*, 13, n. 2 (February, 1962), 18–21, 94–97; Jules B. Billard, "Guantanamo: Keystone in the Caribbean," *National Geographic*, 119, n. 3 (March, 1961), 17–23; Higgins, *The Perfect Failure*, 15–16; *Time*, 16 March 1962, 33–34; *Time*, 28 September 1962, 32; *U.S. News & World Report*, 8 October 1962, 46.

⁷Dean Rusk and Richard Rusk, *As I Saw It*, ed. Daniel S. Papp (New York: Penguin Books, 1991), 227; Brugioni, *Eyeball to Eyeball*, 80, 83–84, 104–105; Commander Andrew J. Valentine, "Rx: Quarantine," *USNIP*, 89, n. 5 (May, 1963), 38–50; Commander Forrest R. Johns, "United We Stood," *USNIP*, 111, n. 1 (January, 1985), 78–84; Beer, "The U.S. Navy and the Cuban Missile Crisis," 43; Strobe Talbott, *The Master of the Game: Paul Nitze and the Nuclear Peace* (New York: Vintage Books, 1989), 85–86; Rear Admiral Samuel B. Frankel, Oral History, USNI (1972), NL, 448–452; Dennison, Oral History, 394–397.

⁸Brugioni, *Eyeball to Eyeball*, 41, 107–108, 129–130, 137; Dan Caldwell, "The Cuban Missile Affair and the American Style of Crisis Management," *Parameters*, 19, n. 1 (March, 1989), 49–60; Marcus D. Pohlmann, "Constraining Presidents at the Brink: The Cuban Missile Crisis," *Presidential Studies Quarterly*, 19, n. 2 (Spring, 1989), 337–346; *WP*, 14 January 1992; Blight and Welch, *On the Brink*, 27, 250, 330; Mack, Oral History, I, 371–375; Dennison, Oral History, 397–410.

⁹Walter S. Poole, "How Well Did the JCS Work?" *NH*, 6, n. 4 (Winter, 1992), 19–21; Brugioni, *Eyeball to Eyeball*, 160–161, 221–222, 199–210, 235–237, 239–244, 258–259, 279; Captain William Ecker, "Photo Reconnaissance over Cuba," *NH*, 6, n. 4 (Winter, 1992), 54–56; O'Donnell and Powers, *"Johnny, We Hardly Knew Ye,"* 311, 313, 317–318, 326–327; Alexander L. George and Richard Smoke, *Deterrence in American Foreign Policy: Theory and Practice* (New York: Columbia University Press, 1974), 466; Reeves, *A Question of Character*, 374; Beer, "The U.S. Navy and the Cuban Missile Crisis," 111; Captain Alex A. Kerr, Oral History, USNI (1984), NL, 399; Rivero, Oral History, 340–346; Dennison, Oral History, 410–421; Admiral George W. Anderson, Jr., "This Joint Chief Took a Bolder Stance," *NH*, 6, n. 4 (Winter, 1992), 46–48.

¹⁰Brugioni, *Eyeball to Eyeball*, 279–280; Reeves, *A Question of Character*, 378; Val-

entine, "Rx: Quarantine," 38–50; Rusk and Rusk, *As I Saw It*, 233–234; Blight and Welch, *On the Brink*, 49; Walter Isaacson and Evan Thomas, *The Wise Men: Six Friends and the World They Made* (New York: Touchstone Books, 1988), 624–625; O'Donnell and Powers, *"Johnny, We Hardly Knew Ye,"* 329.

[11]Officer Biography, Admiral Alfred G. Ward, NHD; Ward, Oral History, 1–7, 187–191; Admiral Horacio Rivero, Jr., "Amphibious Commander at the Ready," *NH*, 6, n. 4 (Winter, 1992), 49–51; Rear Admiral Francis D. Foley, Oral History, USNI, I (1988), NL, 71–72; Vice Admiral Edwin B. Hooper, Oral History, USNI (1978), NL, 271; Brugioni, *Eyeball to Eyeball*, 299–300, 272–274, 289–298, 344–345, 371, 335–336; Vice Admiral Kent L. Lee, "Waiting in the Wings: The USS *Enterprise*," *NH*, 6, n. 4 (Winter, 1992), 51–53; Blight and Welch, *On the Brink*, 143; Admiral George W. Anderson, Jr., "The Cuban Crisis," in Lieutenant Arnold R. Shapack, ed., *The Navy in an Age of Change and Crisis: Some Challenges and Responses of the Twentieth Century*, Proceedings, Naval History Symposium (Annapolis: United States Naval Academy, 1973), 81–86; Vice Admiral Gerald E. Miller, Oral History, USNI, I (1983), NL, 335–340; Dennison, Oral History, 421–423.

[12]Vice Admiral William P. Mack, "Of Missiles, Blockades, and Parleys," *NH*, 6, n. 4 (Winter, 1992), 53–54; Lieutenant Commander Michael N. Pocalyko, "25 Years After the Blink," *USNIP*, 113, n. 9 (September, 1987), 41–47; Admiral Charles K. Duncan, Oral History, USNI, II (1981), NL, 721–726; Brugioni, *Eyeball to Eyeball*, 322, 338–343, 369–370, 373–375, 551–552; O'Donnell and Powers, *"Johnny, We Hardly Knew Ye,"* 322–323; Reeves, *A Question of Character*, 379; William E. Burrows, *Deep Black: The Startling Truth Behind America's Top-Secret Spy Satellites* (New York: Berkley Books, 1988), 122–123; Anderson, "The Cuban Crisis," 84; Ward, Oral History, 191–193; Dino A. Brugioni, "Chalk Up Another Chicken!" *USNIP*, 118, n. 10 (October, 1992), 96–98, 101.

[13]Brugioni, *Eyeball to Eyeball*, 308–309, 543, 346, 384–389, 381, 377–378, 469, 398–401, 413–420, 509; Beer, "The U.S. Navy and the Cuban Missile Crisis," 142, 162–165; Vice Admiral John L. Chew, Oral History, USNI (1979), NL, 308–320; Rear Admiral William D. Irvin, Oral History, USNI (1980), NL, 550–552; Center for Strategic and International Studies, *Soviet Sea Power*, Special Report Series: No. 10 (Washington, D.C.: Georgetown University, June, 1969), 82; Norman Polmar, *Soviet Naval Power: Challenge for the 1970s*, Rev. ed. (New York: Crane, Russak & Company, Inc., 1974), 40; Ship's History, USS *Charles P. Cecil* (DDR-835), "Fact Sheet on . . . Surfacing of Russian Submarine," n.d., NHD; Ward, Oral History, 193–195; Blight and Welch, *On the Brink*, 276, 61; Forrest R. Johns, "The Cuban Missile Crisis Quarantine," *NH*, 5, n. 1 (Spring, 1991), 12–18; Anderson, "This Joint Chief Took a Bolder Stance," 46–48; Admiral Charles Donald Griffin, Oral History, USNI, II (1975), NL, 550–552; Dennison, Oral History, 423; Admiral George W. Anderson, Jr., Oral History, USNI, II (1983), NL, 551–558.

[14]Brugioni, *Eyeball to Eyeball*, 434–436; O'Donnell and Powers, *"Johnny, We Hardly Knew Ye,"* 330–334; Reeves, *A Question of Character*, 76, 81; Ship's History, USS *Joseph P. Kennedy, Jr.* (DD-850), 1962 (5 January 1963), NHD; "Boarding Report," USS *John R. Pierce* (DD-753), 29 October 1962, NHD.

[15]Brugioni, *Eyeball to Eyeball*, 367–368, 457, 466–467, 472–475; Philip Nash, "Nuis-

ance of Decision: Jupiter Missiles and the Cuban Missile Crisis," *Journal of Strategic Studies*, 14, n. 1 (March, 1991), 1–26; Stubbing, *The Defense Game*, 273; Ryan, *First Line of Defense*, 39–42; Blight and Welch, *On the Brink*, 63–64, 154; Captain John V. Noel, Oral History, USNI (1987), NL, 195–196; Anderson, Oral History, II, 559–561; Ward, Oral History, NL, 195–200; Rusk and Rusk, *As I Saw It*, 243.

[16]Blight and Welch, *On the Brink*, 86–87, 148–149; Admiral George W. Anderson, "As I Recall . . . The Cuban Missile Crisis," *USNIP*, 113, n. 9 (September, 1987), 44–45; Anderson, "The Cuban Crisis," 85; Pocalyko, "25 Years After the Blink," 42, 47; Anderson, Oral History, II, 562–568; Ward, Oral History, 200–217.

[17]Brugioni, *Eyeball to Eyeball*, 494, 521–523, 536–537, 533, 560, 506; Anderson, "The Cuban Crisis," 84–85; Caldwell, "The Cuban Missile Affair," 58–59; Rusk and Rusk, *As I Saw It*, 238–247; Johns, "United We Stood," 78–84; Scheina, *Latin America*, 178–180; Blight and Welch, *On the Brink*, 31; Reeves, *A Question of Character*, 389; Dennison, Oral History, 423–443.

[18]Rusk and Rusk, *As I Saw It*, 237, 245; Beschloss, *The Crisis Years*, 548–549.

STERNWATCH V

[1]Dino A. Brugioni, *Eyeball to Eyeball: The Inside Story of the Cuban Missile Crisis* (New York: Random House, 1991), 253–254; Ronald Steel, *Pax Americana* (New York: Viking Press, 1967), 42; *U.S. News & World Report*, 26 November 1962, 42–44; Philip Ben, "A Visit to Guantanamo," *New Republic*, 8 December 1962, 10–11; Thomas G. Paterson, *Meeting the Communist Threat: Truman to Reagan* (New York: Oxford University Press, 1988), 203–206; James G. Blight and David A. Welch, *On the Brink: Americans and Soviets Reexamine the Cuban Missile Crisis* (New York: Noonday Press, 1990), 51; Michael R. Beschloss, *The Crisis Years: Kennedy and Khrushchev, 1960–1963* (New York: Edward Burlingame Books, 1992), 549, 544.

[2]Finley Peter Dunne, *The World of Mr. Dooley*, ed. Louis Filler (New York: Collier Books, 1962), 122; Robert Hendrickson, *American Talk: The Words and Ways of American Dialects* (New York: Penguin Books, 1987), 47; Richard M. Ketchum, *Will Rogers: The Man and His Times* (New York: American Heritage Publishing Company, Inc., 1973), 354; Arnold Rampersad, *The Art and Imagination of W. E. B. DuBois* (New York: Schocken Books, 1990 [1976]), 252.

[3]Fred J. Cook, *The Warfare State* (New York: Collier Books, 1964), 203; Tristram Coffin, *The Armed Society: Militarism in Modern America* (Baltimore: Penguin Books, 1964), 116; E. B. Potter, *Admiral Arleigh Burke: A Biography* (New York: Random House, 1990), 442–447.

[4]Vern L. Bullough, "How I Became a Security Risk," *Nation*, 7 February 1976, 140–142; John C. Donovan, *The Cold Warriors: A Policy-Making Elite* (Lexington, Mass.: D. C. Heath and Company, 1974), 9–10; Coffin, *The Armed Society*, 271–272; Cook, *The Warfare State*, 25.

[5]Raymond L. Garthoff, "Cuban Missile Crisis: The Soviet Story," *Foreign Policy*, 72 (Fall, 1988), 61–80; Blight and Welch, *On the Brink*, 241, 306, 334–335; Lieutenant Commander Harlan K. Ullman, "The Cuban Missile Crisis and

Soviet Naval Development: Myths and Realities," *NWCR*, 28, n. 3 (Winter, 1976), 45–56.

[6]Winston Jordan, "Flank Speed to Eternity," *NH*, 2, n. 2 (Spring, 1988), 12–17; Patricia K. Crimmin, " 'A Community of Interest and Danger:' British Naval Power in the Eastern Mediterranean and the Levant, 1783–1815," in William B. Cogar, ed., *New Interpretations in Naval History: Selected Papers from the Eighth Naval History Symposium* (Annapolis: Naval Institute Press, 1989), 70.

INDEX

Names of individuals are without rank or rate. All modern ships with hull numbers are commissioned in the United States Navy. The hull number given is appropriate for the entry in the text.

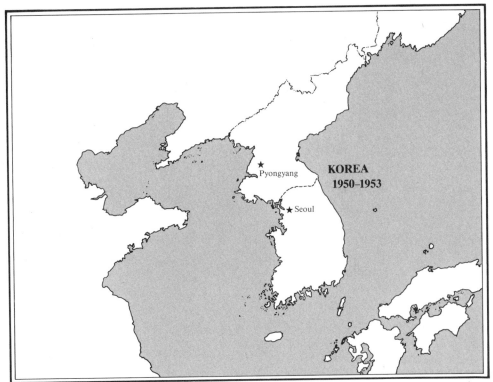

KOREA
1950–1953

Pyongyang

Seoul

MAJOR UNITED STATES

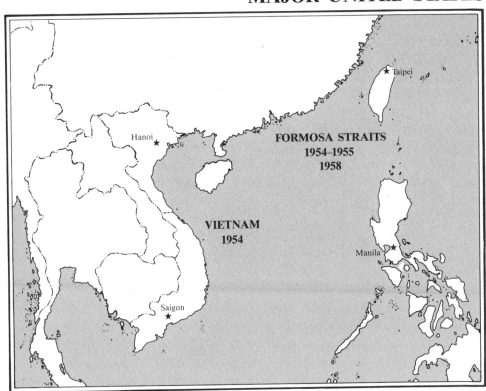

Taipei

Hanoi

FORMOSA STRAITS
1954–1955
1958

VIETNAM
1954

Manila

Saigon